D0859598

# Encyclopedia of the MIDDLE AGES

**Matthew E. Bunson**

Facts On File, Inc.

AN INFOBASE HOLDINGS COMPANY

This book is dedicated to the late
Rabbi Milton Bendiner.

There are a number of individuals whom I would like to thank for their assistance in the preparation of this work. Among them are the staff of the library at the University of California, Santa Barbara; Professor Katharina Schreiber; Professor Mark Schlenz; and Jane Freeburg of Companion Press. Special debts of gratitude are owed to Deirdre Mullane, formerly of Facts On File, and especially Jeffrey Golick, assistant editor.

—M. B.

**Encyclopedia of the Middle Ages**


Facts On File, Inc.
11 Penn Plaza
New York NY 10001

**Library of Congress Cataloging-in-Publication Data**
Bunson, Matthew.
The encyclopedia of the Middle Ages / Matthew E. Bunson.
p. cm.
Includes bibliographical references and index.
ISBN 0-8160-2456-1
1. Middle Ages—History—Encyclopedias. I. Title.
D114.B86 1995
940.1—dc20 94-33232

Facts On File books are available at special discounts when purchased in bulk quantities for businesses, associations, institutions or sales promotions. Please call our Special Sales Department in New York at 212/967-8800 or 800/322-8755.
Maps by Florence Neal
Jacket design by Catherine Rincon Hyman

VB VC 10 9 8 7 6 5 4 3 2 1

This book is printed on acid-free paper.

# CONTENTS

# INTRODUCTION

For centuries, the Middle Ages were the subject of minor interest to scholars, poets, writers and intellectuals, who considered the period to be one of little creativity, important social development or intellectual progress. The philosopher Hegel, for example, once declared that, if it were possible, he would use a pair of seven-league boots to step over the 1,000 years encompassing medieval philosophy and thus avoid everything from the sixth century until the time of René Descartes in the 17th century. This low opinion of the Middle Ages first emerged during the Renaissance, when humanists comparing the previous centuries with the rebirth of classical learning and artistic achievements of their own era found the former wanting. Petrarch coined the term "Dark Ages," a pejorative that seemed to illustrate the dimming of culture and the arts in a decayed, ruined world defined by barbarian invasions, superstition, chronic outbreaks of epidemics and stultified social and political systems.

Thanks to the work of countless scholars, however, we know today that the Middle Ages was a vibrant, interesting and progressive period, one of great significance in human history. It is accepted now that the contributions of medieval artisans, philosophers, architects, merchants and writers were significant, enduring and as worthy as those of any other age. Further, the term *Dark Ages* does not reflect the conditions found in Europe or elsewhere during the Middle Ages and does nothing to illustrate such enormous events as the construction of the Hagia Sophia by the Byzantines, the flowering of the Carolingian Renaissance under Charlemagne and the sophistication of Córdoba under the Moors.

This representative list of notable developments also suggests one of the important truths of the Middle Ages, and that is that medieval culture was not confined in some isolated fashion to Europe. We are indebted to those scholars who have recognized the many cultures present in the medieval epoch and who have examined the exchange among societies that flourished in Africa, Moorish Spain, the Near East and the Far East as well as in western Europe. Modern scholarship has encouraged understanding of the period by making available a vast treasury of historical writings and analyses documenting the affairs of peoples in Africa, Asia, the Middle East and especially the Americas. Europe was not alone.

The *Encyclopedia of the Middle Ages* has been written with this wider perspective in mind. While space limitations prevented the inclusion of every significant region that was notable in the medieval millennium, much attention has been paid to the significant non-European cultures that held a prominent role in the shaping of Western and Near Eastern civilization. The reader will find coverage not only of the West but of the Byzantine Empire; the Islamic dynasties, including those of North Africa and Spain; the Balkan empires such as those of the Bulgars and Serbs; and the Mongols.

For the individual who comes to the *Encyclopedia of the Middle Ages* with a limited familiarity with the subject, it might prove useful to follow a few guidelines in starting out, particularly as the number of entries and their complexity can at first be somewhat daunting. A study of the chronology at the beginning of the book will be helpful in establishing a framework of reference for later reading. A glance at the glossary will help familiarize the reader with many of the terms or concepts that appear in the A to Z text. From here, one might consult the broader entries (Art and Architecture, Banking, Germany, Holy Roman Empire, Universities, Warfare, etc.) for more detailed aspects of the material. For instance, those interested in the Byzantine Empire should begin with that entry and then proceed to Art and Architecture, Byzantine; Warfare; Constantinople; and the individual entries on the emperors. From these stem other entries (Iconoclasticism, Crusades) of possible interest. Throughout, the entries have been cross-referenced with related topics, and various charts, maps and genealogies have been included to enhance clarity. (Genealogies of ruling dynasties include regnal dates unless otherwise indicated.) Finally, readers should use the Suggested Reading List as the starting point of additional study, bearing in mind that it offers only a fraction of the innumerable works now available. The works listed are recommended to add a deeper understanding of the Middle Ages and to increase awareness of the events that led up to this period and that were in turn influenced by it.

**A NOTE ON ALPHABETIZATION** The first element of many Arab names, e.g., el- or al-, is left at the start of the name though the complete name is alphabetized according to the second element. For example, al-Mustansir, al-Mustasim, and al-Mutannabi are left as written but placed under M rather than A.

# CHRONOLOGY OF MEDIEVAL HISTORY 410–1492

| DATE | EVENT |
|---|---|
| 410 | Rome is sacked by the Visigoths under Alaric. |
| 418 | Visigoths settle in Aquitaine. |
| 426 | St. Augustine completes *De civitate Dei (The City of God).* |
| 429 | Vandals under Geiseric invade Africa at the invitation of the Roman general Boniface. |
| 430 | Death of St. Augustine of Hippo. |
| | Patrick is sent to Ireland as a missionary. |
| 439 | Writing of the *Codex Theodosianus.* |
| | Fall of Carthage to the Vandals. |
| 449 | Invasion of Britain by the Saxons and Angles. |
| 451 | Battle of Châlons; defeat of Attila the Hun. |
| 452 | Invasion of Italy by Attila the Hun. |
| 453 | Death of Attila the Hun. |
| 455 | Rome is sacked by the Vandals. |
| 456 | King Theodoric II establishes Visigoth kingdom in Spain. |
| 468 | Destruction of the Eastern imperial fleet by the Vandals. |
| 471 | German general Aspar is assassinated, reducing Germanic influence in the Eastern Empire. |
| 476 | Fall of the Roman Empire in the West with the deposition of Emperor Romulus Augustulus by Odoacer, a German (Herulian) leader. |
| 484 | A schism begins between the Eastern and Western Churches. |
| 488 | Italy is invaded by the Ostrogoths under Theodoric. |
| 493 | Odoacer is murdered after surrendering to Theodoric at Ravenna. |
| 496 | Defeat of the Alamanni by the Salian Franks led by Clovis. |
| 507 | Defeat of the Visigoths in southern France by Clovis. |
| 508 | Paris (Roman, Lutetia) is chosen by the Franks as their capital. |
| 519 | A reconciliation between Eastern and Western Churches is achieved. |
| 524 | Execution of the Roman consul and writer Boethius by Theodoric the Great. |
| 525 | Cosmas Indicopleustes journeys up the Nile River; he extends his travels to Ceylon. |
| 526 | Death of Theodoric the Great. |
| 527–565 | Reign of the Byzantine emperor Justinian I. |
| 529 | Foundation of Monte Cassino near Naples by Benedict of Nursia, bringing monasticism to the West. |
| | Justinian closes the academy at Athens, founded in 347 B.C. by Plato. |
| 532 | Justinian, urged by his wife Theodora, brutally represses the Nika Revolt. |
| 533 | Byzantine general Belisarius invades Africa and defeats the Vandals. |
| 534 | Justinian issues the *Codex Justinianus.* |
| 536 | Belisarius captures Rome, bringing to an end the Ostrogothic kingdom in Italy. |
| 537 | Completion of the new church of Hagia Sophia at Constantinople. |
| 540 | The Byzantines occupy Ravenna. |
| 542 | Outbreak of bubonic plague in Europe. |
| 543 | Conquest of North Africa by Byzantines and end of the Vandal kingdom. |
| 546 | Rome is recaptured by the Ostrogoths under Totila. |
| 547 | Completion of the Church of San Vitale in Ravenna. |
| 548 | Death of Empress Theodora at Constantinople. |
| 549 | Completion of the Church of St. Apollinaire near Ravenna. |
| 552 | Silk industries are begun by Justinian. |
| 554 | Resistance by the Ostrogoths ends in Italy. |
| 558 | The Frankish kingdom is united by Clotaire I, king of Soissons. |
| 559 | General Belisarius comes out of retirement and defends Constantinople against marauding Huns and Slavs. |
| 563 | The monastery at Iona is founded by the Irish missionary Columba. |
| 565 | Death of Emperor Justinian. |
| 568 | Foundation of the Lombard kingdom of Italy; it will endure until 774. |
| 572–591 | War between the Byzantines and Persians. |
| 575 | Alexander of Tralles compiles *De re medica.* |
| 584 | Foundation of the British kingdom of Mercia. |
| 587 | Conversion of the Visigoths to Christianity. |
| 589 | Conversion of the Lombards to orthodox Christianity. |
| 597 | Augustine of Canterbury begins conversion of Kent. |
| 602 | Creation of the archepiscopal see at Canterbury. |
| 608 | Persian forces capture Syria during a phase of their war with the Byzantine Empire. |
| 613 | Muhammad begins to preach publicly. |
| 615 | The Persians sack Jerusalem, taking the "True Cross." |
| 616 | The Persians capture Egypt. |

| DATE | EVENT |
|---|---|
| 622 | Muhammad embarks on the Hegira from Mecca to Medina. |
| 625 | Constantinople, under Emperor Heraclius, repulses both the Avars and Persians. |
| 632 | Death of the prophet Muhammad (June 7). |
| | Ahu Bakr becomes the first caliph. |
| 633 | Beginning of Islamic conquests as war is launched against the Persian empire. |
| 636 | An imperial Byzantine army is defeated by a Muslim force at the Battle of Yarmuk. |
| 639 | Egypt is invaded by Muslim armies; it will be subjugated by 642. |
| 642 | The Sassanid Persian empire is destroyed by Islamic armies. |
| 651–652 | The Koran has its text officially established under the caliph Uthman. |
| 656 | Civil war erupts within the Islamic empire. |
| 661 | The Umayyad caliphate is founded; it will last until 750. |
| 664 | The Synod of Whitby brings Britain into the Roman church. |
| 669 | Theodore of Tarsus becomes archbishop of Canterbury. |
| | Constantinople is besieged by Islamic forces. |
| 670 | North Africa is conquered by Islam. |
| 677 | A Bulgar khanate is established. |
| 677 | A crushing defeat of the Islamic fleet is accomplished by the Byzantine navy. |
| 686 | Conversion of Sussex to Christianity. |
| 687 | Pepin the Younger wins the Battle of Tertry, thereby uniting the Frankish kingdom and marking Carolingian ascendancy in France. |
| 697 | Islamic troops capture Carthage, ending Byzantine control of Africa. |
| 711 | Islamic forces invade the Iberian Peninsula from North Africa. |
| 712 | Islamic conquests begin in India. |
| 717–718 | Arabs are repulsed from Constantinople. |
| 727 | Election of the first doge of Venice. |
| 730–840 | The Iconoclast Controversy. |
| 731 | Bede completes his *Ecclesiastical History*. |
| 732 | The Battle of Tours; the Frankish chief Charles Martel defeats a Moorish army, thereby checking the Islamic advance into Europe. |
| 735 | Charles Martel captures Burgundy. |
| 746 | A plague strikes Constantinople. |
| 750 | Overthrow of the Umayyad caliphate by the Abbasids; they will rule over Islam until 1258. |
| 751 | Pepin the Short is crowned king of the Franks. |
| 756 | Donation of Pepin spurs the establishment of the Papal States. |
| | Córdoba becomes the major city in Moorish Spain. |
| 762 | Baghdad becomes the seat of the Abbasid caliphate; construction is finished in 766. |
| 768–814 | Reign of Charlemagne. |
| 771 | Charlemagne becomes king of the Franks. |
| 772–804 | Charlemagne wages war against the Saxons. |
| 774 | Charlemagne defeats the Lombard kingdom of Italy. |
| 778 | The Battle of Roncesvalles in the Pyrenees; the rear guard of Charlemagne's army is defeated by the Basques. |
| 779 | Offa, king of Mercia, becomes ruler of England. |
| 782 | Offa builds Offa's Dyke. |
| 786–809 | Reign of Harun al-Rashid as Abbasid caliph; he establishes Baghdad as a cultural, political and intellectual city. |
| 787 | End of the Iconoclast Controversy in the Byzantine Empire. |
| 790 | Iceland is reached by Irish monks. |
| 793 | First Viking raids on England; the monastery of Lindisfarne is sacked. |
| 800 | On Christmas Day in Rome, Charlemagne is crowned emperor of the Roman Empire in the West. |
| 804 | Alcuin dies. |
| 811 | Byzantine emperor Nicephorus I is defeated by the Bulgars. |
| 814 | Death of Charlemagne and spread of the Carolingian empire. |
| 817 | Partitioning of the Carolingian empire. |
| 827 | Sicily is invaded by Muslim forces. |
| 836 | Danes become established in Ireland. |
| 843 | The Treaty of Verdun ends the civil strife within the Carolingian empire, formally terminating the imperial unity created by Charlemagne. |
| 846 | Arab pirates sack the Vatican. |
| 850 | The Varangian (Viking) chieftain Rurik becomes ruler of Kiev, founding the Rurik dynasty. |
| 860 | Vikings from Kiev (Varangians) attack Constantinople. |
| 861 | Norse raiders attack Paris, Cologne and other cities. |
| 863–879 | Schism between the Eastern and Western Churches. |

(continued)

| DATE | EVENT |
|---|---|
| 863 | Cyril and Methodius invent the Cyrillic alphabet. |
| 864 | The Bulgarians led by their ruler Boris I are converted to Christianity. |
| 865 | Norse raiders attack Constantinople. |
| 867 | Another schism erupts between the Eastern and Western Churches. |
| 874 | Iceland is discovered by Norse explorers. |
| 876 | Byzantines reconquer much of southern Italy. |
| 878 | Alfred the Great, king of Wessex, defeats the Danes at the Battle of Eddington, ending Danish ascendancy in England. |
| 886 | Siege of Paris by the Vikings. They are bribed by Emperor Charles III (the Fat) who is subsequently deposed (887). |
| 899 | Death of Alfred the Great; he has centralized the monarchy and promoted learning. |
| 900 | Greenland is discovered by Norse explorers. |
| 906 | Magyar invasion of Moravia. |
| 909 | Edward the Elder defeats a force of invading Danes. |
| | Foundation of the Fatimid caliphate of Egypt. |
| 910 | The Benedictine abbey of Cluny is founded. |
| 911 | The dukedom of Normandy is established with the signing of the Treaty of St. Clair-sur-Epte between Rollo the Viking and Charles III of France. |
| 927 | Famine strikes the Byzantine Empire. |
| 929 | Foundation of the caliphate of Córdoba. |
| 938 | The oldest form of parliament, the Althing, is established in Iceland. |
| 948 | Missionaries are sent by Otto the Great to Brandenburg, Aarhus, Schleswig, Havelburg and other regions. |
| 955 | The Battle of Lechfeld results in the defeat of the Magyars at the hands of Otto the Great. |
| 960 | Mieszko I becomes the first ruler of Poland. |
| 962 | Otto I is crowned the first Holy Roman Emperor at Rome. |
| 981 | Norse settlers from Iceland led by Eric the Red establish colonies in Greenland. |
| 986 | Subuktigan, sultan of Ghazni, founder of the Ghaznavid dynasty, invades India. |
| 989 | Truce of God is declared at Charroux. |
| 997 | Stephen I (St. Stephen) becomes king of Hungary. |
| 1000 | Lief Ericsson discovers the lands of the New World in the West. |
| | King Olaf introduces Christianity to the Swedes. |
| 1002 | King Aethelred II orders the massacre of Danish settlers in England on St. Brice's Day. |
| 1008 | Mahmud of Ghazni campaigns in the region of modern Pakistan. |
| 1013 | The Danes invade and conquer England. |
| 1014 | The Irish led by Brian Boru defeat the Norse at the Battle of Clontarf, ending Viking domination of Ireland. |
| | Byzantine emperor Basil II defeats the Bulgars and blinds many in the vanquished army. |
| 1016 | Canute the Great is recognized as king of England. |
| 1028 | Sancho III Garcés, el Mayor, of Navarre, conquers Castile. |
| 1031 | The Umayyad rulers of Córdoba fall. |
| 1040 | To protest the high taxes inflicted on the citizens of Coventry by her husband, Lady Godiva rides unclothed through the streets. Her husband, Leofric, earl of Mercia, had said he would remit the taxes if she did so. |
| 1046 | The Synod of Sutri launches the reform of the Western Church. |
| 1053 | The Normans establish an empire in southern Italy led by Robert Guiscard after his capture of Benevento. |
| 1054 | On July 5, a star in the constellation Taurus becomes a supernova and is visible for 633 nights. |
| | Major schism between the Eastern and Western Churches. |
| 1055 | Seljuk Turks capture Baghdad. |
| 1057–1185 | The reign of the Comnenus dynasts in the Byzantine Empire. Rulers will include Isaac I, Romanus IV and Alexius I. |
| 1059 | Pope Nicolas II decrees papal election solely by the College of Cardinals. |
| 1060 | Arabs conquer West Africa from the kingdom of Ghana. |
| 1066 | Duke William of Normandy invades England and defeats the Saxons under Harold II Godwinson at the Battle of Hastings on October 14. He is crowned King William I on Christmas Day in London. |
| | What would later be called Halley's Comet appears in the sky. |
| 1071 | The Battle of Manzikert between the Byzantines led by Romanus IV Diogenes and the Seljuk Turks results in the crushing defeat of the Byzantine army and the loss of Anatolia. The Byzantine Empire loses possession of Italy to Robert Guiscard. |
| 1075 | The Investiture Controversy between the Holy Roman Empire and the papacy commences. |
| 1076 | The Synod of Worms is convened by Emperor Henry IV to depose Pope Gregory VII. |
| | The Almoravids attack and plunder Kumbi, capital of Ghana. |

| DATE | EVENT |
|---|---|
| 1077 | Emperor Henry IV, defeated in his conflict with Pope Gregory VII, humbles himself in the snow at Canossa. |
| 1084 | Gregory VII is declared deposed by the Synod of Rome in favor of the antipope Clement; Clement crowns Henry IV emperor. |
| 1085 | The Moorish city of Toledo falls to Christian armies. |
| 1086 | The Oath of Salisbury decrees that all English vassals owe fealty to the Crown. |
| 1095 | In the wake of Seljuk advances in Anatolia and the Holy Land, the difficulties encountered by pilgrims there, and appeals from Byzantine emperor Alexius I Comnenus, Pope Urban II calls for a Crusade to free the holy places at the Council of Clermont. |
| 1095–1099 | The First Crusade. Following the capture of Jerusalem on 15 July 1099, the Crusaders pillage the city, burn mosques and synagogues and massacre some 40,000 Muslims and Jews. |
| 1104 | Crusaders under Baldwin I capture Acre. |
| 1105 | Emperor Henry IV is captured by his son Henry and compelled to abdicate; he will die the following year. |
| 1106 | The Battle of Tinchebrai (September 28) results in the triumph of Henry I of England over Robert Curthose, bringing Henry to the throne. |
| 1112 | Emperor Henry V is excommunicated during the Synod of Vienna. |
| 1115 | Clairvaux, the influential Cistercian abbey, is founded. |
| 1120 | The order of the Knights of the Temple is established near Jerusalem by Hugh of Pajens. The Knights Templars will become one of the most powerful military orders until destroyed in 1314. |
| 1121 | Peter Abelard's teachings are condemned by the Concordat of Worms. |
| 1122 | Emperor Henry V renounces the right of investiture, effectively surrendering to the papacy. |
| 1123 | Omar Khayyam dies. |
| 1128 | The Knights Templars are recognized by Pope Honorius II. |
| 1130 | Roger II is crowned king of Sicily. |
| 1136 | The construction of the Church of St. Denis is completed under the aegis of the abbot Suger, a work that is to exemplify Gothic architecture. |
| 1142 | Peter Abelard dies. |
| 1147–1149 | The Second Crusade is launched. It is preached by Bernard of Clairvaux but is a failure. |
| 1150 | The University of Paris is established. |
| 1154 | Nicholas Breakspear is elected Pope Adrian IV; he is the sole English pope. |
| | Henry II becomes king of England. |
| 1155 | Pope Adrian IV gives Ireland to King Henry II of England. |
| | Frederick Barbarossa becomes emperor. |
| 1157 | Frederick Barbarossa invades Poland, while his other troops near Rome are stricken by typhus. |
| 1158 | Lübeck is founded on the Baltic. It will emerge as a major trading depot and chief city of the Hanseatic League. |
| 1162 | Thomas à Becket becomes archbishop of Canterbury. |
| 1164 | King Henry II decrees the Constitutions of Clarendon, causing a major conflict with Thomas à Becket, archbishop of Canterbury. |
| 1167 | Oxford University is established. |
| | Foundation of the Lombard League in Italy. |
| 1170 | Thomas à Becket is murdered in Canterbury Cathedral on December 29 by a group of knights in the service of King Henry II. |
| 1171 | Saladin conquers Egypt and brings to an end the Fatimid caliphate. |
| 1174 | King Henry II does penance for complicity in the murder of Thomas à Becket in 1170. |
| 1176 | Frederick Barbarossa is defeated by the troops of the Lombard League at the Battle of Legnano in Italy. |
| | Saladin conquers Syria; continuing his jihad (holy war) against the Crusader States; his ultimate aim is the capture of Jerusalem. |
| | The Byzantines are defeated at the Battle of Myriocephalon. |
| 1178 | A meteorite strikes the moon and is observed by monks at Canterbury. |
| 1182 | King Philip II Augustus of France expels the Jews there. |
| | In an eruption of hostility, Latins are massacred at Constantinople. |
| 1184 | The architect William of Sens completes construction of the new cathedral at Canterbury. |
| 1187 | Saladin captures Jerusalem and destroys a Crusader army at Hattin. The disasters for the Christians bring about the Third Crusade. |
| 1189–1192 | The Third Crusade is led by Richard the Lion-Hearted of England, Philip II Augustus of France and Frederick Barbarossa of the Holy Roman Empire. It is a failure with the exception of an agreement between Richard and Saladin that includes permission for pilgrims to enter Jerusalem and the Holy Sepulchre. |
| 1190 | Chrétien de Troyes dies. |
| 1193 | Richard the Lion-Hearted is captured and eventually handed over to Emperor Henry VI, who ransoms him for 150,000 marks. The ransom is paid and Richard returns home to England (1194). |

**(continued)**

| DATE | EVENT |
|---|---|
| 1194 | Emperor Henry VI captures Sicily, ending Norman supremacy over southern Italy. |
| 1198 | The Teutonic Knights are established at Acre, which is to serve as their headquarters until 1291. |
| 1202–1204 | The Fourth Crusade is called by Pope Innocent III. The Crusaders request the Venetians to transport them to the Holy Land. Unable to raise funds for the endeavor, the Crusaders agree to pay Doge Enrico Dandolo and the Venetians by capturing the Hungarian town of Zara. They are soon diverted from their original cause by the doge and are convinced to assist in the overthrow of the Byzantine Empire. |
| 1203 | Crusaders reaching Constantinople effect the restoration of Emperor Isaac II Angelus (he had been deposed by Alexius III). |
| 1204 | Isaac II is deposed once again, and the Crusaders take Constantinople, sacking and pillaging the city. A Latin Empire is established under Baldwin of Flanders, while the Byzantines form small splinter states. |
| 1208 | Students from Bologna establish a medical school at Montpellier. |
| 1209 | King John of England is excommunicated by the pope for opposing the election of Stephen Langton as archbishop of Canterbury. |
| 1210 | The Franciscan order receives approval from the pope. |
| 1212 | The Battle of Las Navas de Tolosa results in the crushing defeat of the Moors by King Alfonso VIII; most of the Iberian Peninsula is now lost by the Moors. |
| | The Children's Crusade is led by Peter the Hermit. It will end with the death of thousands of children and slavery for others. |
| 1213 | The Council of St. Albans is convened, establishing the origin of Parliament in England. |
| 1214 | The Battle of Bouvines ends with King Philip II Augustus triumphant over an allied force led by John of England, Emperor Otto IV and the count of Flanders. |
| 1215 | King John of England is compelled by his barons to sign Magna Carta in June at Runnymede. |
| | The influential Dominican order Fratres Praedictores (Preaching Friars) is founded by the Spanish priest Dominic. |
| | The University of Paris receives its first statutes. |
| 1217–1221 | The Fifth Crusade is launched at the behest of Pope Innocent III. The Crusader military efforts in Egypt are failures. |
| | Cambridge University is founded. |
| 1221 | As Mongol armies led by Genghis Khan continue to sweep across the Near East, Samarkand is burned and sacked. |
| 1222 | King Andrew II of Hungary issues a Golden Bull. |
| | Mongol armies reach Russia. |
| 1226 | Francis of Assisi dies on October 3. |
| 1227 | Genghis Khan dies having established the largest empire in history. |
| 1228–1229 | The Sixth Crusade is launched by Emperor Frederick II. His effort, a peaceful one, results in a truce that gives the holy places to the Christians. Frederick's achievements are unrecognized by the Crusader States and Pope Gregory IX, the latter having excommunicated him in 1227. |
| 1231 | Emperor Frederick II establishes a medical school at Salerno. |
| 1232 | The Nasrid kingdom of Granada is founded in the Iberian Peninsula. It will endure until 1492. |
| 1236 | Christian forces capture Córdoba. |
| 1237 | Mongol armies invade Russia, bringing massive destruction. |
| 1240 | Kiev falls and is burned by the Mongols. |
| | Prince Alexandr of Novgorod wins the name Nevsky for his triumph over a Swedish army at the Neva River. |
| 1241 | The Mongols of the Golden Horde annihilate a Christian force at the Battle of Liegnitz; included among the vanquished are many from the Knights Templars, elements of the Teutonic Knights, and the flower of eastern European chivalry. The battle is the highwater mark of the Mongol advance into western Europe. |
| 1242 | Alexandr Nevsky defeats a small contingent of Teutonic Knights at the Battle of Lake Peipus. |
| 1244 | Elements of the destroyed Khwarizmian kingdom recapture Jerusalem, spurring the Seventh Crusade. |
| 1245 | The struggle between Pope Innocent IV and Emperor Frederick II escalates as the pope declares Frederick deposed. |
| 1248–1254 | The Seventh Crusade is led by King Louis IX of France. The effort, aimed again at Egypt, is a failure. |
| 1250 | Emperor Frederick II dies at Fiorentino. |
| | The Ayyubids, who have ruled Egypt since 1169, are overthrown by their own troops, the Mamluks. The Mamluks will rule Egypt until 1517 and will bring about the final destruction of the Crusader States in the Middle East. |
| 1252 | King Louis IX expels the Jews from France. |
| | The first gold florins are struck in Florence. |

| DATE | EVENT |
|---|---|
| 1253 | Franciscan friar and traveler William of Rubruquis journeys to Karakorum and visits the Mongols. |
| 1258 | A Mongol host invades the Near East and sacks Baghdad. The troops of Hulagu Khan massacre the inhabitants and bring to an end the Abbasid caliphate that had ruled Islam since 750. |
| 1260 | Kublai Khan establishes the Yuan dynasty in China. |
| | The Mongols are finally defeated at the Battle of Ain Jalut as a Mamluk army defeats a small force of Mongols, thereby destroying the image of Mongol invincibility. |
| 1261 | The Latin Empire of Constantinople is overthrown by the resurgent Palaeologus dynasty. Michael VIII Palaeologus becomes Byzantine emperor. |
| 1268 | The dynasty of the Hohenstaufen rulers of the Holy Roman Empire is ended at the Battle of Tagliacozzo. The 16-year-old imperial claimant Conradin is captured and beheaded at Naples by Charles of Anjou. |
| 1270 | The Eighth Crusade is launched by King Louis IX. He dies at Damietta in Egypt, cutting short the renewed Christian effort. |
| 1271 – 1272 | The Ninth Crusade is led by Prince Edward (later King Edward I) of England. It is unsuccessful and is the last major effort of the crusading movement. The last of the Christian strongholds in the Near East will fall during the next years. |
| 1274 | Thomas Aquinas dies. |
| | Kublai Khan attempts a disastrous invasion of Japan. |
| 1277 | The Visconti family gains political control of Milan. |
| 1281 | Another failed attempt is made by the Mongols to invade Japan. |
| 1282 | The war of the Sicilian Vespers erupts in Sicily as the French overlords are massacred by opponents of their rule and the taxation by Charles of Anjou. |
| 1290 | Having stringently taxed and financially oppressed the Jews there, King Edward I of England expels them. |
| 1291 | The League of the Three Cantons is established by Uri, Schwyz and Unterwalden, thereby laying the foundation for the formation of Switzerland. |
| | The Mamluks capture Acre, thus bringing an end to the Crusader States in the Middle East. |
| 1294 | Kublai Khan dies. |
| 1295 | The Model Parliament convenes at London. |
| | Marco Polo returns to Venice after years in the East. |
| 1302 | The Battle of Courtrai (or the Spurs) ends in a terrible defeat for the French led by King Philip IV. The Flemish troops of the burghers of Flanders annihilate the French and end Philip's ambitions toward the region. |
| 1309 | The Babylonian Captivity begins as Clement V moves the papal court to Avignon. It will remain there until 1377. |
| 1310 | The notorious Council of Ten is established in Venice to oversee security in the city. |
| 1312 | Piers Gaveston, his favored courtier, is kidnapped and murdered by the English barons, demonstrating the weakness of King Edward II. |
| 1314 | The Battle of Bannockburn (June 24) results in the defeat of King Edward II of England by Robert the Bruce of Scotland, thereby assuring the independence of Scotland. |
| | The Knights Templars are crushed through the machinations of King Philip IV of France. Their lands are seized, and the Grand Master of the order, Jacques de Molay, is arrested, convicted of heresy and burned at the stake. |
| 1321 | Dante Alighieri dies in Ravenna. |
| 1326 | The Ottoman Turks capture Bursa. |
| 1327 | King Edward II is effectively removed from power by his wife Isabelle and her lover, Mortimer. He is soon forced to abdicate and is replaced by his son Edward (III). |
| 1334 | Islamic traveler Ibn Batuta journeys to the Far East. |
| 1337 | The Hundred Years' War commences between England and France. It will continue sporadically until 1453. |
| 1345 | The cathedral of Notre Dame in Paris is completed after 182 years of construction. |
| 1346 | English troops led by King Edward III crush a French army led by King Philip VI at Crecy (August 26). The mounted French knights are massacred by the English bowmen. |
| 1348 | The Black Death decimates the city of Florence and begins its march across Europe. |
| 1351 | The Statutes of Labourers are established to fix wages for English workers at the level in place in 1346 (before the Black Death). |
| 1352 | Italian despot and reformer Cola di Rienzo, who had seized power in Rome in 1347, is arrested and sentenced to death. He escapes execution after receiving a pardon from Pope Innocent VI. |
| 1354 | Cola di Rienzo falls from favor with the Romans and is savagely brutalized by a mob. |
| 1356 | The Battle of Poitiers (September 19) ends in another triumph for the English. This time, England's Black Prince (Edward, Prince of Wales) routs a French army led by King John II. The French king is captured, and France is reduced to political chaos. |
| | Emperor Charles IV issues a Golden Bull establishing the form to be used for imperial elections. |

(continued)

| DATE | EVENT |
|---|---|
| 1358 | The Jacquerie (a violent uprising of French peasants) occurs in May, opposing the nobility and oppressive taxation, and results in pillaging companies of soldiers in the countryside. The revolt is suppressed by Charles II of Navarre, with thousands put to death in retaliation. |
| 1360 | The Peace of Brétigny is signed at Calais, bringing a brief pause in Anglo-French hostilities. |
| 1365 | The Ottoman Turks, who have steadily advanced into Europe, capture Adrianople in Thrace. The city subsequently becomes their capital. |
| 1368 | The Mongol Yuan dynasty founded in 1271 by Kublai Khan is replaced by the Ming dynasty of China. |
| 1370 | The powerful Hanseatic League forces King Waldemar IV of Denmark to accept the Treaty of Stralsund, granting the league a monopoly on trade throughout the Baltic. |
| 1374 | The city of Aachen (Aix-la-Chapelle) is afflicted with a strange dancing mania as the inhabitants pour into the streets and inexplicably and uncontrollably dance for hours. |
| 1375 | The Truce of Bruges effects another brief halt in the Hundred Years' War. |
| 1377 | The Avignon papacy ends with the return of the papacy to Rome under Pope Gregory XI. |
| 1378 | Attempted reforms by newly elected Pope Urban VI cause the Great Schism within the church that will last until 1417. |
| 1381 | Wat Tyler leads a rebellion in England that is the result of social instability caused by the ravages of the Black Death and the Statutes of Labourers (1351). Briefly successful, the uprising is ultimately crushed and Tyler treacherously cut down by William Walworth, lord mayor of London. |
| 1382 | The reforms granted to Wat Tyler during the uprising of the previous year are rescinded. |
| 1384 | John Wycliffe dies. |
| 1389 | The Battle of Kosovo (June 15) brings the irreparable defeat of the Serbian empire as the Serbs are crushed by the Ottoman Turks. Serbia becomes a vassal state to the Turks. |
| 1393 | Mongol armies led by Tamerlane (Timur the Lame) capture Baghdad. |
| 1396 | The Crusade of Nicopolis, led by King Sigismund of Hungary, is routed by an Ottoman army (September 25). |
| 1397 | The Kalmar Union is established. Denmark, Sweden and Norway are united under one monarchy. |
| 1399 | King Richard II of England is imprisoned in the Tower of London and abdicates. He is succeeded by Henry IV Bolingbroke. Richard dies the following year. |
| 1400 | Geoffrey Chaucer dies (October 25). |
| 1402 | The Battle of Ankyra is fought between the armies of Tamerlane and the Ottoman Turks of Sultan Bayazid I. The Turks are destroyed, Bayazid captured and the Ottoman Empire thrown into political chaos. The battle also spares Constantinople from capture by the Turks for half a century. |
| 1405 | Tamerlane dies suddenly, leaving a massive empire ungoverned. |
| 1409 | The Council of Pisa is convened in an unsuccessful effort to end the Great Schism. |
| 1410 | The Battle of Tannenberg (July 15) results in the crushing defeat of the Teutonic Knights by a coalition of Lithuanians and Poles. |
| 1414 | The Council of Constance is reconvened and attempts to end the Great Schism. At the council, heresy is also discussed. Controversial Bohemian reformer Jan Hus is seized and executed. |
| 1415 | The Battle of Agincourt (October 25) results in the complete triumph of King Henry V of England over the French. |
| 1417 | The Great Schism is ended through the work of the Council of Constance. |
| 1419 | The Hussite Wars begin in Bohemia and Moravia. They will continue until 1436. |
| 1422 | King Henry V dies, having been England's most able and aggressive general. |
| 1424 | Lorenzo Ghiberti wins the competition to design the baptistery doors of the Church of San Giovanni in Florence. The event is generally considered the starting point of the Renaissance. |
| 1429 | Joan of Arc liberates Orléans and convinces the dauphin to be crowned at Reims as Charles VII. |
| 1430 | Joan of Arc is captured at Compiègne. |
| 1431 | Handed over to the English, Joan of Arc is condemned by an ecclesiastical court headed by Pierre Cauchon, bishop of Beauvais. She is burned at the stake on May 30. |
| 1434 | The duomo (Cathedral of Santa Maria del Fiore) of Florence is completed after 140 years of construction. |
| 1437 | The death of Emperor Sigismund brings to an end the house of Luxembourg. |
| 1446 | Filippo Brunelleschi dies. |
| 1448 | King Charles VII captures Maine from the English. |
| 1450 | In England, Cade's Rebellion erupts in protest against taxation and government corruption. |
| 1453 | The Ottoman Turks under Sultan Mehmet (Muhammad) II capture Constantinople, ending the Byzantine Empire. |
| | The Hundred Years' War draws to a close as the English lose all their Continental possessions with the exception of Calais. |
| 1455 | The Wars of the Roses begin in England with the House of Lancaster and the House of York in conflict for the throne. |
| | Fra Angelico and Lorenzo Ghiberti die. |

| DATE | EVENT |
|---|---|
| 1456 | The first printed Bible is published at Mainz by Johann Gutenberg. |
| 1458 | Matthias Corvinus becomes king of Hungary. |
| 1464 | Cosimo de' Medici dies. |
| | Rogier van der Weyden dies in Brussels. |
| 1465 | King Henry VI is imprisoned in the Tower of London as the Wars of the Roses continue. |
| 1469 | Ferdinand of Aragon and Isabella of Castile marry. |
| | Francesco Petrarch dies. |
| 1476 | Galeazzo Sforza, despotic ruler of the duchy of Milan, is assassinated. |
| | William Caxton establishes the first printing press in England. |
| 1477 | The ambitious duke of Burgundy, Charles the Bold, is killed and his troops defeated by the Swiss at the Battle of Nancy (January 5). |
| 1479 | The grand duchy of Moscow, ruled by Ivan III, annexes the city of Novgorod. |
| 1483 | Tomás de Torquemada is placed in charge of the Inquisition of Spain. |
| 1485 | The Battle of Bosworth Field (August 22) ends the Wars of the Roses as the army of Henry Tudor defeats that of King Richard III. Richard is killed in battle, his crown found hanging in some bushes. Henry is crowned king at Westminster on October 30, bringing the House of Tudor to the English throne. |
| 1487 | Torquemada is named Grand Inquisitor by Pope Innocent VIII. |
| 1489 | The *Malleus maleficarum* is published. It will serve as the manual for witch hunters for centuries to come. |
| 1492 | Christopher Columbus reaches the island he calls San Salvador in the Western Hemisphere (the "New World"). |
| | Ferdinand and Isabella complete the Christianizing of Spain by conquering Granada, the last Moorish holdings in the peninsula. |

## Europe in 800

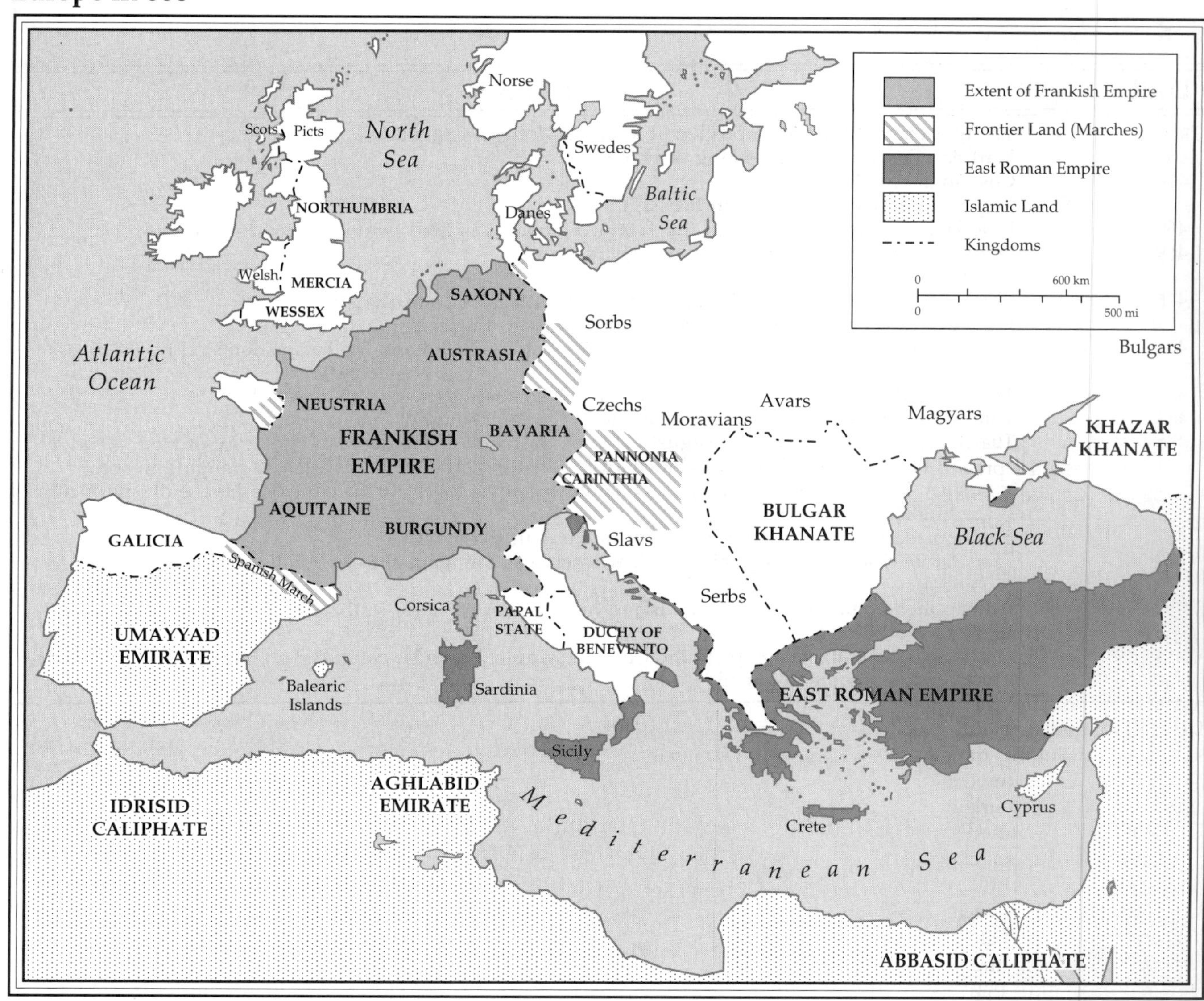

# A

**AACHEN** Also known as Aix-la-Chappelle, this was one of the most important sites of the Middle Ages in Europe. Aachen is situated on the North Rhine in present-day WESTPHALIA. Its preeminence was based on the favor shown to it by the Carolingian dynasts and later by the heads of the Holy Roman Empire. The city began as a small Celtic community, attracting the Romans in the 1st century A.D. because of its mineral springs. Seemingly forgotten after that, Aachen was chosen in the eighth century as the headquarters for Charlemagne's campaign against the Saxons.

Pleased with the location, Charlemagne transformed Aachen to become the heart of his Frankish empire. Throughout the late eighth century extensive building was conducted, including mineral baths, palaces and a celebrated chapel, considered an architectural achievement and which still houses Charlemagne's throne. From 814 (when Charlemagne was buried there) until 936, the city endured a decline in status paralleling that of the Carolingian empire itself. Then, in 936, Otto I succeeded Henry I as the German king and, aligning himself with the Carolingians, ordered his coronation to be held at Aachen. Henceforth almost all of his successors, the Holy Roman Emperors, were crowned there until 1531. Using their city's status to great advantage, the people of Aachen ensured their financial and economic prosperity throughout the medieval era. The city received municipal rights in 1166 and became a free imperial city around 1250. See also ALCUIN; CAROLINGIAN RENAISSANCE; HOLY ROMAN EMPIRE.

**AARON BEN ELIJAH OF NICOMEDIA** (c. 1328–1369) Jewish theologian, born in Nicomedia but spending much of his life in Constantinople. He was an important spokesman for the views of Karaism, the Jewish religious movement challenging Talmudic authority. Aaron ben Elijah wrote several books on the cause: *Etz Hayyim (Tree of Life)*, *Gan Eden (Garden of Eden)* and *Keter Torah (Crown of Law)*. See also JEWS AND JUDAISM.

**ABARBANEL, ISAAC** See ABRAVANAL, ISAAC.

**ABBADIDS** See SEVILLE, KINGDOM OF.

**ABBAS** (c. 567–c. 653) Paternal uncle of the prophet Muhammad and the ancestral founder of the ABBASID CALIPHATE, named after him. Al-Abbas ibn al-Muttalib ibn Hashim was by profession a trader of the Kuraysh tribe of Mecca and apparently was not counted among the earliest adherents of Muhammad's faith, joining, albeit reluctantly, Mecca in its struggle with Muhammad in 624. By 628, however, he had probably been converted to the Muslim faith. In 630 he participated in the conquest of Mecca and retained a respected position within the Islamic world following the death of the Prophet in 632. Much of the information relating to Abbas has been questioned, as it originated from the early years of the Abbasid caliphate, a time of propaganda to ensure legitimacy and security for the future of the line.

**ABBASID CALIPHATE** The second great Islamic dynasty, after the Umayyad caliphate, that ruled from 749 until destroyed by the Mongols in 1258. The caliphs took their name from al-Abbas ibn al-Muttalib, the uncle of Muhammad and the head of a branch of the Banu Hashim clan. Claims to the important line of ABBAS were not pressed by the early Abbasids, who played a minor role in the first caliphate and voiced little opposition to the rise and dominance of the Umayyad caliphate. All of that changed, however, when Muhammad ibn Ali ibn Abd Allah ibn al-Abbas became chief of the Abbasids circa 716. Henceforth a secret revolution was organized with great care. Only after years of establishing clandestine support and decades of waiting for a propitious moment did the Abbasids strike.

In 747 the time was right. The Umayyads, weakened by deteriorating internal conditions and civil strife in the provinces, were attacked in Khorasan by the Abbasids, who, led by the generals Abu Muslim and Abu Salama, took the war into Syria and killed the last Umayyad caliph, Marwan II, in 750 at the Battle of Zab. Abn 'l-Abbas, known as al-Saffah, came out of hiding and was proclaimed caliph at Kufah in 749. He recognized, however, that he owed his success to a combination of military might from the generals and the religious fervor of both moderates and extremists of ISLAM. These extremists were the Shiites, with whom the Abbasids would never be reconciled and who would work to overthrow the government and the caliphate.

Al-Saffah died in 754, and it was left to his successor, Abu Ja'far al-Mansur, his brother, to consolidate Abbasid power. He removed all potentially troublesome elements in the state, including Abu Muslim, and then moved the administrative center to Baghdad. Islam was to be universal, the religion of all peoples governed not only by an elite Arab aristocracy but effective agents of the dynasty who owed their advancement to the caliphs rather than to noble lineage.

Weakness in the Abbasid system was seen in the military, which was not directly answerable to the caliphs, and in the succession characterized by conflicts between heirs, deficiencies repaired only partially by Harun al-Rashid. This legendary ruler (786–809), his son al-Amin (809–813), and his grandson al-Mamun (813–833) headed the golden age of the Abbasids, when caliphs exercised unquestioned theological influence as being accepted as the living embodiment of Islam. They promoted the arts, trade and commerce and brought about prosperity throughout the empire. By the end of al-Mamun's reign, however, the Abbasids were in decline, owing in large measure to the rise of mercenary armies, most notably the Turks, who replaced the unreliable armed forces of the caliphate. Inevitably the Turkish generals assumed mastery in Baghdad as a process of decentralization occurred in the provinces. Smaller but respectfully autonomous states appeared, paying lip service to Baghdad while administering their own affairs. There were the Tahirids in Persia; their successors, the Samanids; Idrisids, Rustamids, and Aghlabids in Africa; and the Egyptian Tulunids. Other parties were opposed to the Abbasid caliphate and sought to destroy it. Two such groups were the Saffarids from eastern Iran, who were defeated only 50 miles from Baghdad, and the Fatimid caliphate, the champion of the Ismaili sect, which conquered Africa and Egypt in 969 and was even recognized for a time in Baghdad.

The Abbasid caliphs were political prisoners of their own protectors, whether Turks or the Buyids who exercised control over Baghdad from about 945 to 1055, when the Seljuk Turks arrived in Persia. Bearing the title of sultan, the chiefs of the Seljuks, beginning with Toghril Beg and his nephew Alp Arslan, were the pillars supporting the declining Abbasids. The Seljuks proceeded to carve for themselves a vast empire. Upon its collapse in the late 12th century, the caliph al-Nasir (1180–1225) reestablished caliphal independence. His policy was short lived and only recognized in the regions around Baghdad. Finally, in 1256, the Mongols marched into the west, and in February 1258 the Mongol horde arrived at Baghdad. Al-Mutasim, the last caliph of Baghdad, was executed and the dynasty ended, with the exception of the line of Egyptian Abbasids, who had the patronage of the Mamluk sultans. The Egyptian Abbasids remained caliphs, in name only, until 1517 and the conquest of Egypt by the Ottomans.

Abbasid importance was complex. The caliphs ended the supremacy of the Arabs in Muslim government by favoring the Oriental or the Persian model. They brought Islam to the entire Near East, while encouraging the flowering of artistic and intellectual expression. The eighth to the 13th centuries saw the emergence of some of the greatest writers and poets and the preservation of the Greek heritage, a cultural treasure that would enrich the West in succeeding generations.

**ABBO** (c. 945–1004) Also called Abbo of Fleury, he was the abbot of Fleury and a notable scholar of the 10th century. Born near Orléans, Abbo joined the Benedictine order, and was responsible for the instruction of English monks at Ramsay from 985 to 987. A leader of MONASTICISM in England, he was elected abbot of Fleury in 988 and was a supporter of both the papacy and Cluniac reform. His writings on numerous subjects (e.g., canon law, astronomy, mathematics) include *Epitome of Popes' Lives*. His most celebrated work was *Quaestiones grammaticalae*. See also CLUNY.

**ABBO OF SAINT GERMAIN-DES-PRÉS** (d. c. 923) Also known as Adbo of Saint Germain, an author of the historical poem *Bella parisiacae urbis* (Battle of the City of Paris), in three books, describing the siege of PARIS by the Vikings in 885. Abbo also discussed other notable events in this work.

**ABD ALLAH** Emir of Córdoba from 888 to 912. The reign of Abd Allah reflected the continuing decline of the emirate in Spain. The son of Muhammad I, he succeeded to the throne on the death of his brother, al-Mundhir (886–888) in 888, a death some Arab historians attribute to Abd Allah. From the start he was beset with problems throughout the country, as rebellions in the provinces resulted in a loss in revenues. The most notable opponent that Abd Allah faced was Ibn Hasfun, who occupied strategic positions along the Guadalquivir River. Despite victories in the field, the emir could not quell the rebellions and died with the conflicts unresolved. Abd Allah's notably enduring achievement was to name as his heir Abd al-Rhaman III (912–961). See also CÓRDOBA, EMIRATE OF; MOORS.

**ABD ALLAH IBN AL-ZUBAYR** (624–692) A rival for the Umayyad caliphate from 683 until 692 and a nephew of Aisha, the favorite wife of MUHAMMAD. The son of the early Muslim convert al-Zubayr and Asma, Abd Allah ibn al-Zubayr used his affiliations, both familial and political, to cement a powerful position within the Islamic world. He fought in Syria, Egypt and Iran and unsuccessfully attempted to defend the caliph OSMAN in 656. Unable to prevent Osman's assassination, Abd Allah joined the Meccan party (with Aisha) against Ali ibn Abi Talib in his attempt to gain the caliphate. An officer at the Battle of the Camel in 656, he withdrew to MEDINA after the victory of Ali. He soon after supported the Umayyad pretender Muawiyah ibu Abi Sufyan for caliph.

Muawiyah named as his successor his son Yazid (as YAZID I) in 680, who was opposed by Abd Allah. Yazid attempted to seize his opponent, but Abd Allah evaded capture. A civil war ensued, and the final siege of Abd Allah at Mecca was cut short in 683 by Yazid's death. While elements of the Muslims hailed Abd Allah as caliph, his rival Marwan ibn al-Hakam reunited the Umayyad line and recaptured Egypt and Syria, leaving Abd Allah only Iraq. Even this grip was shaken with the rebellion of al-Mukhtar ibn Abi Ubayd. Al-Mukhtar was crushed, but when Marwan's heir, Abd al-Malik, launched his final campaign, about 691, Abd Allah's defeat was assured. Abd Allah died in battle in 692. The historian Jalaludin wrote of him that he was an observer of the faith, given to long hours of prayer. See also UMAYYAD CALIPHATE.

**ABD AL-MALIK** See AL-MALIK, ABD.

**ABD AL-RAHMAN I** (c. 731–788) Emir of Córdoba (756–788), the founder of the Umayyad dynasty of SPAIN and the architect of the long Islamic domination of the peninsula. Abd al-Rahman was a member of the Umayyad family of caliphs, surviving the Battle of Zab in 750 and the elimination of the Umayyads of North Africa following the fall of the caliphate at the hands of the Abbasids. Abd al-Rahman eventually reached Spain, where he found a country already occupied by the forces of Islam but lacking cohesion. He began amassing a large army while manipulating the leading political factions, the Yaman and Qais. In 756 he judged his opponents sufficiently weakened and defeated the governor of ANDALUSIA, thus establishing the emirate of CÓRDOBA, making that city the heart of his administration and the center of Arab life in Spain.

The emirate attracted many former members of the Umayyad caliphate and all those who opposed the Abbasids. Abd al-Rahman thus faced attacks from both the Christians led by Charlemagne in the north and the Abbasid armies in the south. Further troubles were caused by the Berber tribes and by rebellious clans in Spain. Each threat was met successfully, and the dynasty he established lasted for centuries. See also ABBASID CALIPHATE; CÓRDOBA, EMIRATE OF.

**ABD AL-RAHMAN II** Emir of CÓRDOBA from 822 to 852 and the grandson of ABD AL-RAHMAN I. During the reign of Abd al-Rahman II, the emirate reached heights of prosperity and stability not to be attained again until the caliphate of ABD AL-RAHMAN III in the 10th century. Relations with the Abbasid caliphate in Baghdad were markedly improved, while Abd al-Rahman used the opportunity to make Córdoba an even greater city by erecting extensive public works. The arts, including poetry and music, were encouraged, especially by patrons in the opulent court of the caliph. Abd al-Rahman died in 852 of suspicious causes. See also CÓRDOBA, EMIRATE OF.

**ABD AL-RAHMAN III** (891–961) Emir of CÓRDOBA from 912 to 929, caliph from 929 to 961 and the most distinguished of all the Umayyad rulers of SPAIN. Abd al-Rahman III an-Nasir was born in January 891 and was named in 912 to be successor to his grandfather, Abd Allah, as the emir of Córdoba. Chosen because of his intelligence and energy, the young emir faced massive problems, for civil war was raging throughout Islamic Spain. Turning immediately to the task of subduing the insurgents, he beheaded a number of rebel chiefs before embarking upon a campaign against the guerrilla leader, Umar ibn Hasfun, who had plagued his grandfather. Ibn-Hasfun died in 917, and Abd al-Rahman recaptured the strongholds of SEVILLE and Algeciras before 917, while Bobastro fell in 928 and Toledo in 933.

The Christian kingdoms in Spain were preparing to seize parts of the emirate in the early years of Abd al-Rahman's reign, but his retaliations against them in 920 and 924 produced peace for some years. The highlights of his war were the smashing victory at Valdejunquera in 920 over the armies of Navarre and León and the sack of Pamplona in 924. In 939 King Ramiro II of León (930–951) routed Abd al-Rahman's army and nearly captured the ruler, but the Christian advantage was short lived.

Muslim Spain enjoyed prestige of nearly legendary status during the reign of Abd al-Rahman, for he encouraged religious tolerance, promoted the cultivation of the arts and advancement in the sciences and added extensively to the already remarkable city of Córdoba. His consolidation of power came at a price, however, for he was constantly on the watch for ambitious governors and had to execute his own son in 949. By far his most radical decision came in 929, when, to counter the growing influence of the Fatimid Shiite opponents, he himself became a caliph. His war with the Fatimids proved unresolved. Abd al-Rahman died in 961, known and respected throughout the entire medieval world. See also ABBASID CALIPHATE; CÓRDOBA, EMIRATE OF.

**ABD AL-RAHMAN IV** Umayyad caliph of CÓRDOBA who reigned only one year, 1018. He came to the throne at a time of severe instability in ANDALUSIA. HISHAM III (1027–1031), the last caliph of Córdoba, was his brother. See also CÓRDOBA, EMIRATE OF; MOORS.

**ABD AL-RAHMAN V** Umayyad caliph of CÓRDOBA from 1023 to 1024. Abd al-Rahman was one of the last caliphs in ANDALUSIA. His successor was Muhammad III (1024–1025). See also CÓRDOBA, EMIRATE OF; MOORS.

**ABD AL-RAHMAN AL-GHAFIQI** (d. 732) A leading general of the Umayyad caliphate, who took part in the expansion of ISLAM into Europe. Abd Al-Rahman was sent into Afghanistan in the early eighth century, where he reduced opposition to the caliphate by the king of Kabul. Under the caliph Hisham, he was named governor of Muslim-occupied lands in Europe, advancing deep into FRANCE and, in 732, fighting the Battle of Tours against Charles Martel. Abd al-Rahman was killed during the encounter, and his troops were forced to withdraw.

**ABEL** King of Denmark from 1250 to 1252. Abel was one of three sons of WALDEMAR II (1202–1241), receiving from him the dukedom of South Jutland. Not content with this, and jealous of his brother, Eric, who had been crowned in 1232 as ERIC IV PLOVPENNIG (1241–1250), Abel waited until his father's death in 1241 to launch an attack upon his brother. The civil war ended only in 1250 with the capture and murder of Eric. Abel was now king but reigned only two years, as his death came during a battle against the Frisians in 1252.

**ABELARD, PETER** (1079–1142 or 1144) Theologian, teacher, philosopher and one of the foremost thinkers of the Middle Ages. Peter Abelard was unquestionably an intellectual of the first order, but his views earned him repeated condemnation by the church. His life was in many ways shaped by the title of his own work: *Historia calamitatum (History of My Calamities)*. He was born in 1079 at Le Pallet in Brittany and was educated under Roscelin of Compiègne, by William of Champeaux and later by Anselm of Laon at Loches (Anjou), PARIS and Laon respectively. Of an independent mind, he argued with his teachers, especially William, whose concept of realism he refuted with such eloquence that his career as a teacher was assured.

He lectured at Paris on philosophy and theology to such acclaim that the canon Fulbert of the Cathedral of NOTRE DAME DE PARIS asked him to act as a tutor to his niece, Héloise. This association ended in disaster about 1118–1119. Abelard and Héloise had an affair and were secretly married after the birth of their son Astralabe; Abelard was then castrated at the instigation of the canon. Héloise fled to the convent of Argenteuil near Paris with her child, and Abelard joined the monastery of SAINT-DENIS. There he continued his theological studies, writing two important works, *Sic et non (Yes and No)* and a version of *Theologia Christiana,* the latter condemned and burned at the Council of SOISSONS in 1121. After a brief period of incarceration at the Abbey of Saint-Médard, Abelard returned to Saint-Denis but had to flee after insulting the name of the abbey's patron saint. He went to the county of CHAMPAGNE, continuing his teaching from about 1122 until 1125.

In 1125 Abelard was elected abbot of Saint Gildas de Rhuys in Brittany. Despite encountering hostility from the community, forcing his eventual departure, he assisted Héloise in starting a new community of nuns at Quincey, called Le Paraclet, where he served as abbot. By 1136 he had returned to Paris as a teacher. Among his pupils were John of Salisbury and Arnold of Brescia, and his works included another attempt at *Theologia, Scito te ipsum (Know Thyself* or *Ethica),* and *Dialogus inter philosophum, Judaeum et Christianum (Dialogue between a Philosopher, a Jew and a Christian).* The popularity of his ideas made a confrontation with the church inevitable. It came in 1140, during the Council of Sens, at which the powerful Bernard of CLAIRVAUX led the assault. Condemnation by the council was upheld by Pope INNOCENT II. Abelard retired to the abbey of CLUNY and was welcomed by PETER THE VENERABLE and assisted by him in making proper reconciliations with the authorities. He died at Cluny but was eventually buried beside Héloise at Père Lachaise in Paris.

Abelard's genius and the extent of his philosophical and theological vision made classification of his writings and teachings difficult. In addition to Bernard of Clairvaux, he was opposed by such contemporary giants as Hugh of Saint Victor and William of Saint-Thierry, while winning their acceptance of his place in history. He increased his era's understanding of Aristotle through his glosses on Aristotelian philosophy and advanced the currents of ideas concerning universals by striking a middle ground between the realism of William of Champeaux and the nominalism of Roscelin. Ethically, Abelard viewed the motives or intentions of a person, especially in relation to God, as far more important than the actions springing from them. Abelard and Héloise were immortalized by the compilations of their love letters and other, religious communications, published sometime during the 13th century.

**ABRAHAM BEN DAVID** (c. 1110–1180) Also known as Abraham ibn Daud or Rabad I, a respected Jewish philosopher and historian. Although he fled from the Muslim invasion of Spain by the ALMOHADS, he was actually martyred in TOLEDO by the Christians. His principal work was *The Book of Tradition.* See also JEWS AND JUDAISM.

**ABRAVANEL, ISAAC** (1437–1508) Jewish theologian, philosopher and statesman. Originally from LISBON, Abravanel (also Abarbanel and Abrabanel) entered the service of ALFONSO V of Portugal (1438–1481), assuming control of the treasury in 1471, a post held by his father. With the death of the king in 1481, Abravanel was suspected of complicity in a rebellion to topple the monarchy. Fleeing to Spain about 1483, he became a member of the government of Ferdinand the Catholic and Isabella (1474–1516). There he also assumed a post in the treasury while working to end the persecution of the country's Jewish population. He reportedly attempted to bribe Ferdinand and Isabella but in vain. Exiled with his fellow Jews in 1492, he moved to NAPLES, Corfu, Monopoli and finally VENICE in 1504. In Venice he wrote many of his works and acted in some official capacities for the Venetian government. Philosophically, Abravanel was opposed to the rational precepts of Moses MAIMONIDES. He was the author of numerous biblical commentaries. See also JEWS AND JUDAISM.

**ABSALON** (c. 1128–1201) Also called Axel, the archbishop of Lund, a statesman and a powerful political and ecclesiastical figure in 12th-century DENMARK. Half brother to King WALDEMAR I (1157–1182), Absalon was instrumental in securing his succession. In 1196 he defeated the Wends (Slavs) and added parts of northern Germany to the Danish kingdom. As archbishop in 1177, he continued to influence kings, advising King Canute VI (1182–1202), most notably in his dealings with the HOLY ROMAN EMPIRE, of which Absalon was an opponent. Further campaigns were led by the prelate in 1184, giving Denmark control of Pomerania and Mecklenburg. He was also the patron of the Danish historian SAXO GRAMMATICUS.

**ABU AL-ATAHIYA** (748–828) Poet of the golden age of the ABBASID CALIPHATE whose name meant "Father of Insanity." Born to a poor family, he began composing love poetry while still a young man in al-Kufah, works that attracted the attention of HARUN AL-RASHID. His major work was the *Zuhdiyat,* or poetry on life. Atahiya's poetry was characterized by extreme introspection. Although moralistic in tone, the poems were nevertheless considered unorthodox.

**ABU BAKR** (c. 572–634) The first caliph, father-in-law of MUHAMMAD and the most valued of his companions. Abu Bakr's influence had a profound effect on the early history of ISLAM, especially in his direction of the Arabs upon a course of expansion. He was a member of a merchant clan of the Kuraysh in Mecca and thus was present in the first days of the preaching of Muhammad. One of the first converts to Islam, he earned a place as friend and adviser to Muhammad that he was never to relinquish. Aisha, his daughter, married Muhammad, and Abu Bakr was at Muhammad's side during the Hegira, the flight from Mecca to MEDINA in 622.

Over the next years Abu Bakr served also as general, although his role in the wars of consolidation and growth against Mecca was no doubt limited by his age. He probably proved of help in dealing with the Meccans who surrendered in 630. A sign of continued favor was shown in 632, for he led the *umma,* or community of believers, in prayer during Muhammad's illness. When the Prophet died in 632, Islam was torn by internal strife. To provide steady leadership, it was decided that Abu Bakr should be elected as *khalifah* (caliph), or successor. He was precisely the right leader, suppressing the *ridda* (apostates), who had opposed the political situation, quelling numerous religious and civil uprisings, thereby proving that a military and theocratic state was capable of conquering and governing. Abu Bakr died in 634, naming as his successor his close associate Umar ibn 'Abd al-Khattab.

**ABU HANIFA** (c. 699–767) One of the great minds in Islamic jurisprudence and for whom the Hanifa school of law is named. Born in the city of Al-Kufa in Iraq, Abu Hanifa (full name Abu Hanifa al-Numan ibn Thabit ibn Zuta) was the grandson of a freed slave. He studied in Kufa under some of the foremost teachers of the time, including the scholar Amir ibn Sharakil al-Shabi and the lawyer Hammad ibn Abi Sulayman. Eventually Abu Hanifa succeeded Sulayman as chief legal expert in Kufa, although he neither held the important post of judge *(qadi)* nor left any major writings other than a short commentary on dogma. His apparent refusal to accept the office of judge from the Abassid caliph al-Mansur may have led to his imprisonment and death while in custody in 767. Despite the scarcity of actual, verified treatises, Abu Hanifa had a major hand in the evolution of Islamic religious laws. He argued that legal opinions must be the result of individual reasoning, not a joint opinion. Many of his students wrote works attributed to him or included his ideas in their own efforts.

**ABU'L-ABBAS AL-SAFFAH** (d. 754) The first Abbasid caliph, who ruled from 749 to 754. When, in 716, the Abassid leader Abu Hashim died, Abu'l-Abbas was named as his heir and given the task of organizing resistance to the Umayyad caliphate. This he did with considerable skill, fostering the clandestine machinations of revolution in Iraq and elsewhere. With the help of such generals as Abu Muslim and Abu Salama, he launched his war in 747, destroying the weakened Umayyads. As the first caliph, Abu'l Abbas came out of hiding in 749 to seize his new throne, taking steps immediately to liquidate all potential threats to the line, including both Abu Muslim and Abu Salama. Having placed relatives and trusted advisers in key positions, he died on June 9, 754, of smallpox. Most historians view him favorably, although civil strife followed his death. See also ABBASID CALIPHATE.

**ABULAFIA, ABRAHAM BEN SAMUEL** (1240–1292) Important Jewish mystic and scholar. Born in Zaragoza Spain, he spent many years traveling throughout the Mediterranean world promulgating the ecstatic cabala, his own brand of mysticism, a belief so powerful that he sought a meeting with the pope in order to convert him. The conference never took place, and Abulafia was sentenced to death because of his continued teaching among Jews and Christians. His liberation was subsequently secured. His writings contributed to the development of the Cabala, his works having been translated into Italian and Latin.

**ABU'L-'ALA AL-MA'ARRI** (973–1057) Well-known poet during the Abbasid caliphate, who lost his sight while still a young man but nonetheless produced highly praised poetry. He lived in Spain, where he lectured on history, philosophy and poetry until journeying to Baghdad about 1009. There he studied at the college founded by the vizier Sabur ibn Ardashir and was later honored by having an academy established in his name. A number of years passed before he returned home to Ma'arri and to a quieter, simpler existence. He disdained classicism, and his poetry reflected his personal doubts about divine revelation and life after death.

**ABUL ATAHIYA** See ABU AL-ATAHIYA.

**ABULCASIS** See ABU'L-QASIM.

**ABU'L-FARAJ** See BAR-HEBRAEUS, GREGORIUS.

**ABUL FARAJ ALI OF ISFAHAN** (897–967) Arab scholar and musicologist who wrote the *Book of Songs,* a collection of annotated poems in Arabic set to music.

**ABU'L-HASAN ALI** Nasrid king of Granada from 1464 to 1485, whose reign was marked by the beginning of the war with Ferdinand and Isabella (1474–1516) of Spain that ended with the final triumph of the RECONQUISTA. When, in 1481, the truce that had been negotiated between the monarchs in 1478 was broken by the Muslim seizure of Zahara, Abu'l-Hasan was in immediate difficulty when his son, Abu Abd Allah, known to the Christians as Boabdil, attempted to usurp the throne, taking the title Muhammad XII (1482–1492). Sensing the need for support within the Granadan kingdom, Abu'l-Hasan inflicted a defeat on the army of Castile at Malaga in 1483 and then secured his position in Granada by exploiting the rout of his son's forces by the Christians. Ironically, Abu'l-Hasan survived another attempt at a coup by his son in 1484 but was deposed by his own brother, Muhammad ibn Sad, known as el Zagal. He died in exile in 1485. See also NASRID KINGDOM OF GRANADA.

**ABUL KASIM** See ABU'L-QASIM.

**ABU'L-QASIM** (c. 936–c. 1013) Also known as Abulcasis, the greatest of the Islamic physicians of the Middle Ages. Born in Córdoba, Abu'l-Qasim studied medicine and was eventually appointed court physician to Abd al-Rahman III (912–961). His work, especially preserved in his writings, was to have lasting influence on medical treatment in the West. Abu'l-Qasim wrote an encyclopedia on surgical practices, the *at-Tasrif liman 'ajaz' an al-Ta'alif (The Method),* which explains his views. Although utilizing many details from earlier sources, *The Method* also presented surgical techniques, drawings of essential instruments and diagnoses. Translated by GERARD OF CREMONA in the 12th century, *The Method* was more important to European medical practitioners than to their Arab counterparts, who favored the teachings of Avicenna and Rhazes. See also MEDICINE.

**ABU MUHAMMAD AL-QASIM AL-HARIRI** See AL-HARIRI.

**ABU MUSLIM** (d. c. 754) A Persian general and rebel leader who was important in securing the supremacy of the Abbasid caliphate and the ultimate fall of the Umayyad caliphate in 750. Of obscure origins, Abu Muslim emerged around 747 as the leader of a major revolt against the Umayyads in Persia. This was the principal impetus for the eventual Abbasid campaign against the caliphate that ended in 750 with the defeat of the Umayyads and the capture of Syria at the Battle of Zab. Abu Muslim was instrumental in solidifying the political and military position of the Abbasids. A perceived threat to the power of the Abbasid caliphs, however, he was assassinated about 754 by the caliph Abu Jafar al-Mansur.

**ABU NUWAS** (c. 747/762–813/815) Viewed as one of the most distinguished Arab lyric poets of the Middle Ages. Born in Iran sometime around the middle of the eighth century, he was destined from childhood to be a poet, studying with a number of teachers in both Al-Kufa and Basra, two important centers of learning. By 786 he had earned a place of note in the capital of the Abbasid caliphate, Baghdad, and had attracted the attention of the caliph Harun al-Rashid. Throughout Harun's reign, Abu Nuwas increased his reputation both for the excellence of his poetry and the wildness of his personal life. His excesses probably prevented him from receiving the title of court poet and led to his imprisonment on several occasions.

A more congenial atmosphere was found in the court of Harun's successor Amin in 809, who revelled in life's pleasures to the same degree as Abu Nuwas. For four years the poet and the caliph Amin were close friends, but in 813 Amin was assassinated, and his brother, al-Mamun, came to power. Nuwas died a short time later with various stories circulating as to the reason for his death.

**ABU SAID IBN ABI KHAIR** (967–1049) Persian poet of the Sufi dervish sect. Abu Said won fame for composing the first Sufi version of *Rubaiyat.*

**ABU TAMMAM** (804–c. 845) Islamic poet, born near Damascus. Originally trained as a weaver, Abu Tammam traveled to Egypt, where he studied poetry. A poet of growing repute, he earned a place at the court of the caliph al-Mutasim, becoming the foremost panegyricist of the time. His most important work was the *Hamasah,* a collection of poems on events of the day that was heralded as a brilliant example of Arabic verse.

**ACCIAIUOLI, HOUSE OF** Prominent family in Florence in the 14th and 15th centuries. Originating in Bergamo, the Acciaiuoli owned a major Florentine bank, using this financial position to acquire political power. Although the bank was bankrupt by 1345, members of the house continued to wield influence. See also FLORENCE.

**ACRE** Called also Akko, an important fortress and seaport on the Bay of Haifa on the Palestinian coast. Considered a valuable possession by most of the conquerors in the ancient world, it fell in 638 to the Arabs. A major objective in the Holy Land for King Baldwin I of Jerusalem, Acre was captured in 1104, only to be retaken by SALADIN for Islam in 1187. There followed the bloodiest siege in the long history of the Crusades, as an army of French, English, Germans, Danes, Frisians, Pisans, Venetians and Genoese laid siege to the city from August 1189 until July 12, 1191, when it finally succumbed under the leadership of Richard the Lion-Hearted of England. During the siege, however, plagues, starvation, incompetence and the SARACENS caused appalling losses, some chroniclers putting the figure as high as 100,000 dead. The loss of Acre was a cruel blow to the *jihad* of Saladin. Acre was given to the Knights Hospitalers, who controlled it until 1291, when the Muslims reclaimed it, an event that signaled the demise of the CRUSADER STATES. See also CRUSADES.

**ACROPOLITES, GEORGE** (1217–1282) Byzantine historian and statesman. Acropolites was a tutor of the

In Acre, a Hospitalers building

Byzantine emperor THEODORE II LASCARIS (1154–1158) and also held several government posts as well as leading the delegation sent from Constantinople to the Council of Lyons in 1274. His most important written contributions were a chronicle and funeral oration. The chronicle was an invaluable account of the years 1203 to 1261, thus including the fall of Constantinople to the Crusaders, the creation of the Latin Empire and the victory of the Byzantines in recovering their city in 1261. The oration was delivered on the passing of the emperor JOHN III DUCAS VATATZES in 1254. See also BYZANTINE EMPIRE; LYONS, COUNCILS OF.

**ADALBERT, KING OF ITALY** See BERENGAR II.

**ADALBERT OF BREMEN** (c. 1000–1072) Archbishop of Hamburg-Bremen and an ardent proponent of missionary work in Scandinavia. A Saxon by descent, he was named a archbishop in 1043 and was appointed papal legate to the north in 1053. As prelate, Adalbert concentrated on bringing Christianity to the Scandinavian countries and to the Slavs, meeting with only limited success. His personal power and prestige in Germany were heightened by the approval given him by the emperor HENRY III (including an offer of the papacy in 1046) and his service as tutor and counselor to Henry IV between 1063 and 1066. Ambition and the favor of the emperors brought him into conflict with the Saxon dukes and jealous nobles who secured his banishment from the court, an exile that ended three years later when he was forgiven by Henry IV. He remained at court for the rest of his life, but his death was probably hastened by the destruction of Hamburg by the Wends in 1071–1072.

**ADALBERT OF PRAGUE, SAINT** (956–997) Bishop of Prague from 982 to 988 and from 992 to 994. Adalbert was the first native of the region to hold the post of prelate in Prague. A supporter of BOLESLAV II, prince of Bohemia, he hoped to use the ruler's favor to advance the cause of Christianity in the region. He had faced such opposition from nobles that he stepped down in 988 but was sent back in 992 by the pope. Again bitterly opposed, he became a missionary to Prussia, in 994, where he was martyred in 997. Saint Bruno of Querfurt wrote his biography. See also BOHEMIA.

**ADALBOLD OF UTRECHT** (c. 970–1026) Bishop of Utrecht from 1010 until 1026. Adalbold was also a writer, dedicating a scientific treatise to Pope Sylvester II (999–1003). He also wrote a biography of Emperor Henry II (1002–1024) and a commentary on the philosophy of the sixth-century philosopher and statesman BOETHIUS.

**ADALOALD** King of the Lombards from 615 to 625, the son of Agilulf, who convinced the Lombard warriors to accept him. Only 14 years old at his accession, Adaloald was in the care of his mother, THEODELINDA, who acted as regent. By 625, however, the young king had become mentally ill and was deposed to be replaced by Arioald, the duke of Turin. His reign was marked by the struggle between the Arian heretics and orthodox Christians. See also ARIANISM; LOMBARDS.

**ADAM DE LA BASSÉE** (d. 1286) A 13th-century priest and writer who composed a version of Alan of Lille's epic poem *Anticlaudianus.* Written about 1280, his own poem, *Ludus super Anticlaudianum,* contained monophonic and polyphonic music and songs.

**ADAM DE LA HALLE** (c. 1237–c. 1285) French composer and an important figure in the development of medieval music. Called the Hunchback of Arras, he is thought to have lived and studied for a time in Paris, entering into the service of Robert II, Count of Artois. Adam composed a number of influential works, including *Le jeu de pèlerin (Play of the Pilgrim), Le roi de Sicile* (*The King of Sicily,* for Charles of Anjou), the witty and informative *Le jeu de feuillée (Play of the Greenswords)* and *Le jeu de Robin et de Marion (Play of Robin and Marion),* thought to be one of the earliest comic operas. Adam's music followed a variety of forms, with some of his finest efforts in the field of polyphonics.

**ADAMNAN, SAINT** (c. 624–704) The abbot of Iona. Adamnan was one of the foremost monastic leaders to be produced by the monastery at Iona and won respect in Britain, Ireland and Scotland as a crusader for Roman ecclesiastical supremacy. The "Canon of Adamnon" (also called *Lex innocentium*) was adopted in Ireland and Britain in 697, making the seizure of women and children in war illegal. He also produced numerous commentaries, the most important of which was the *Life of St. Columba* (c. 688–692), a valuable account of early Celtic monasticism. Also attributed to him was *De locia sanctis,* a compendium of holy places. See IONA.

**ADAM OF BREMEN** (c. 1040–c. 1081) German canon, originally from Franconia, who was the author of the important chronicle, *Gesta Hammaburgensis ecclesiae pontificum* (c. 1073–1076, *History of the Bishops of Hamburg*). A teacher in the cathedral school of Bremen, Adam also traveled to Denmark. His history of the Hamburg bishops, dated at about 1075, was extremely useful as a chronicle of the events in parts of Northern Europe (Germany and Scandinavia) during the 10th century and the first half of the 11th. Composed of four volumes, the history recounts the evangelizing efforts of missionaries and provided useful information on Adalbert of Bremen, as well as much secular material including information on geography, ethnography plus religious history. His writing reflected a gift for organization and accuracy as well as literary flair. See also BREMEN; HAMBURG.

**ADAM OF MARSH** (fl. early 13th century) Prominent Franciscan theologian in England and France. Adam received his education at Oxford, joining the Franciscan order sometime around 1230. His reputation as the teacher of the young Franciscans at Oxford brought him such acclaim that he was offered a chair in theology at the University of Paris, an offer that he declined. He had been the student and the friend of the reknowned teacher and prelate Robert Grosseteste and was later consulted for his political advice by HENRY III, the English king, and by the reformer Simon de Montfort. Also called Adam de Marisco, he died about 1258. See also MONTFORT (2), SIMON DE.

**ADAM OF SAINT VICTOR** (c. 1110–c. 1180) Canon at the Abbey of Saint Victor and a composer of hymns or sequences (hymns sung after the Alleluia in the Mass during the liturgy during special feasts of the Church). Born a Breton, he entered the monastic life about 1130 at Saint Victor, composing sequences of great complexity. He was one of the most highly regarded sequence writers, and his compositions are noted for outstanding philosophical or theological depth. A dictionary of biblical terms has also been attributed to him. See also HUGH OF SAINT VICTOR.

**ADELAIDE** (931–999) Empress of Germany, wife of the emperor OTTO I. Originally married to Lothair, king of Italy, she was imprisoned by BERENGAR II of Ivrea in 950, upon the death of her husband. Appealing to Otto I, she was rescued and wed the monarch in December 951; they were crowned emperor and empress in 962. A supporter of Cluniac reform, she was also viceroy to Italy, adviser to Otto II, her son, and regent for Otto III from 991 to 994.

**ADELA OF CHAMPAGNE** (d. 1206) Queen of France and the third wife of Louis VII of France (1137–1180). Also called Alix of Champagne, she gave to Louis a much needed heir, Philip II Augustus (1180–1223), while helping to ensure improved relations between the king and the counts of Champagne.

**ADELARD OF BATH** (c. 1070–c. 1142–1146) An early 12th-century English scholar and philosopher. Adelard was one of the great travelers of his age, journeying throughout Europe, North Africa, Greece and Asia Minor. His writings reflect the extent of the knowledge he had accumulated on his travels and the degree to which he respected Islamic scientists. From 1105 to 1110 he was occupied in writing *De eodem et diverso* (*On the Identical and the Diverse*), a dialogue examining the liberal arts and the philosophies of Plato and Aristotle. *Quaestiones naturales* (*Natural Questions*) (1111–1116) comprised Aristotelian views of the world. Adelard also made translations of Arabic scientific studies, manuals and treatises. See also ASTRONOMY.

**ADEODATUS II** (d. 676) Pope from 672 to 676, also known as Deusdedit II. His reign was largely uneventful, although he was responsible for the restoration of many churches.

**ADHEMAR OF MONTEIL** (d. 1098) Also called Adhemar de le Puy, the bishop of Puy, a papal legate and one of the organizers of the First Crusade. Nobly born, perhaps related to the counts of Valentinois, he was named bishop by 1180. Having made a pilgrimage to the Holy Land in 1086–1087, he was the first Christian to pledge to go on crusade after Pope Urban II's call for an attempt to free the holy places of Palestine from Muslim occupation. On November 28, 1095, Adhemar was appointed papal legate and as such spiritual leader of the crusading armies. He traveled with Raymond IV of Saint-Gilles, count of Toulouse, to Constantinople, where he established excellent relations with the leaders of the Eastern Empire and the Eastern Church. During the Crusade he was instrumental in subduing quarrels among the princes, worked to aid the poor, helped establish a Christian ecclesiastical presence in the Holy Land and maintained communications with the Byzantines. His death from plague at Antioch on August 1, 1098, was a terrible blow to the unified Christian effort. See also CRUSADES.

**AL-'ADID** (r. 1160–1171) The 14th and last of the Fatimid caliphs of Egypt. On his death in 1171, while still a youth, the Fatimid caliphate, long moribund politically, was replaced by Saladin (Salah al-Din, 1169–1193), founder of the Ayyubid dynasty. See also AYYUBIDS; FATIMID CALIPHATE.

**ADOLF OF NASSAU** (c. 1250–1298) German king from 1292 to 1298 and a member of the Habsburg dynasty. Originally the count of Nassau and a successful mercenary general, he was chosen by the German electors rather than Albert of Habsburg to succeed Rudolf I (1273–1291), Albert's father. Adolf proved himself adroit at strengthening his position against the demanding electors. Because of this he was deposed by Albert in 1298. Attempting to fight this action, he was killed in battle, and Albert I (1298–1308) succeeded him. See also HOLY ROMAN EMPIRE.

**ADOPTIONISM** A heresy originating in Spain during the eight century that promulgated the belief that Christ was the Son of God in the sense of having been adopted by God. The controversy probably began as a result of the writings of the otherwise unrenowned Migetius, who opposed the concepts of the Incarnation of Christ and the Second Person of the Holy Trinity. In response, ELIPANDUS, the archbishop of Toledo, stated that there was a clear distinction between the human and the divine within Christ, with Christ becoming divine by adoption at his baptism. Support was given to Elipandus's cause by Felix, bishop of Urgel, despite the obvious similarities in adoptionism to NESTORIANISM.

Felix attempted to defend adoptionism before Charlemagne at Ratisbon (modern REGENSBURG) in 792 but was compelled to recant. Spanish bishops succeeded in having the Council of Frankfurt convened in 794 by Charlemagne, but failed once more to receive the blessing of Christian orthodoxy. Felix returned to Urgel and wrote Alcuin, who replied with his seven-volume attack *Contra Felicem* (*Against Felix*) in 799. Felix was anathematized that same year and recanted again. Upon the death of Elipandus, however, the heresy was easily stamped out. In the 12th century it reappeared in a modified form, in the concepts of Peter Abelard and even later in the theories of Duns Scotus. See also DUNS SCOTUS, JOHN; HERESIES.

**ADRET, SOLOMON BEN** See SOLOMON BEN ADRET.

**ADRIAN I** (d. 795) Pope from 772 until his death in 795; he was an effective pontiff, both politically and administratively. By continuing the papal policy of amity with Charlemagne, he was able to convince the emperor to invade Lombardy and depose its king Desiderius in 774. Thus Rome was freed from the Lombard threat, the papal lands were enlarged significantly, and Charlemagne gained significant advantages from his conquest. Adrian maintained communications with Charlemagne, seeking his imperial assistance against the heresy of ADOPTIONISM. A difference of opinion between and Adrian and Charlemagne was caused by the Iconoclastic Controversy. See also ICONOCLASTICISM.

**ADRIAN II** (d. 872) Pope from 867 to 872 and related to two previous pontiffs, Stephen IV and Sergius II. Coming to the papacy after Nicholas I, he inherited a papal throne of considerable power but was unable to maintain his advantages because of his advanced age and a conciliatory nature. Thus papal authority was rebuffed in dealings with the Carolingian dynasty, the Byzantine emperors and patriarchs of Constantinople, and Roman jurisdiction in the Balkans was broken when Boris I, king of the Bulgars, invited the patriarch of Constantinople, Ignatius, to send missionaries from the Eastern Christian church to Bulgaria. Adrian permitted the use of the Slavonic language in the liturgy to advance acceptance of Christianity among the Slavs. He also sponsored the mission of CYRIL AND METHODIUS.

**ADRIAN III** (d. 885) Pope from 884 to 885, whose most notable achievement was his aid to the Romans during a famine. He died en route to Worms to meet with French king Charles III the Fat. He was going to Worms to settle the succession dispute; his death may have been the result of foul play.

**ADRIAN IV** (c. 1100–1159) Pope from 1154 to 1159 and the only prelate of English origin elected to the Holy See. Born Nicholas Breakspear, he was the son of a minor royal clerk. Studying in France, he entered the Augustinian monastery of Saint Rufus at Avignon and was named abbot in 1137. Disagreements with his monks brought him to the attention of the papal court and led to his appointment by Eugenius III to the rank of cardinal bishop of Aldano (c. 1149). Soon he was named papal legate and given the task of reorganizing the Christian church in the Scandinavian countries. His work was so successful, most notably in Norway and Sweden, that in 1154 he was unanimously chosen by the cardinals to succeed Anastasius IV as pope.

As Adrian IV (also called Hadrian IV), he placed the city of Rome under papal interdiction after riots and bloodshed had erupted in the streets at the instigation of the popular leader Arnold of Brescia. On June 18, 1155, Frederick I Barbarossa was crowned Holy Roman Emperor by Adrian, but relations between them were never cordial. His insistence that the imperial crown was held as a *beneficium* (gift) from the papacy precipitated a conflict that would rage long after Adrian's pontificacy. Adrian also quarreled with William I of Sicily but had to reforge the papacy's relations with the Normans after a military campaign ended in total defeat. Other notable events were his granting of the overlordship of Ireland to Henry II of England, reportedly at the urging of JOHN OF SALISBURY, although the authenticity of the bull (*Laudabiliter*) has long been questioned, and the execution of Arnold in 1155. A gifted administrator and strong-willed pontiff, Adrian died suddenly in 1159.

**ADRIAN V** (b. 1205) Pope for only weeks in 1276 and never ordained, crowned or consecrated. The nephew of Pope Innocent IV, he was elevated to the rank of cardinal by him. As a legate to England from 1265 to 1268, he helped reconcile King Henry III and his barons. Dante mentioned Adrian V in his *Purgatory*—and called him avaricious.

**ADRIANOPLE** A commercial center in Thrace. Adrianople was founded by the Roman emperor Hadrian in 125 and is still notable because of the defeat of Emperor Valens there by the Goths in 378, a disaster considered by some scholars to be the starting point of the medieval era. The city was historically part of the Byzantine Empire, but because of its strategic location, it fell prey to many conquerors: the Bulgars in the ninth, 10th and 13th centuries, Venetians in the early 13th century during the Fourth Crusade and finally the Ottoman Turks in 1362. From then on, until 1453 and the capture of Constantinople, Adrianople was the residence of the Ottoman sultans. See also BYZANTINE EMPIRE; OTTOMAN EMPIRE.

**AED** (d. 878) King of Scotland from 877 to 878, the son of King Kenneth I and the brother of Constantine I. He was killed in Strathallan by his cousin Giric after reigning only one year. Giric then shared the throne with Eochaid from 878 to 889.

**AELFRIC** (c. 955–c. 1010–1015) Abbot of Eynsham, near Oxford, a leader of the English monastic movement and one of the greatest prose writers of Anglo-Saxon England. Educated under the tutelage of Ethelwold, bishop of Winchester, he emerged as a brilliant monk and scholar. About 987 he was sent to Cerne Abbas in Dorset to act as the abbot of that monastic foundation. In 1005, having composed most of his writings at Cerne, he was named abbot for another newly founded monastery, this one at Eynsham. Aelfric's writing reflected brilliance and diversity. He wrote a biography of Ethelwold, an abridgement of Ethelwold's autobiography, and a *Lives of the Saints.* He also wrote for students a Latin grammar in English and a glossary with a reader, and he translated parts of the Old Testament and a collection of homilies. Aelfric was rediscovered in the 16th century, his work becoming very popular during the Reformation.

**AELRED OF RIEVAULX, SAINT** (c. 1109–1167) Cistercian abbot, historian and a major figure in medieval monasticism. Born to a noble family in Hexham, Northumberland, Aelred grew up at the court of King David I of Scotland. Joining the Cistercian order about 1134, by 1143 he had become abbot of Revesby. In 1147 came the appointment as abbot of Rievaulx and in this capacity he won admiration for his personal spirituality, which in turn was reflected in his monastery. Later traveling to Scotland, France and throughout England, he helped to shape the development of the medieval monastic life, with such distinction that he was called as the "Bernard of the North," a reference to Bernard of CLAIRVAUX. Aelred was a prolific writer and historian; his works include *De Jesu puero duodenui (On Jesus at Twelve Years Old); De spirituali amicitia (On Spiritual Friendship); Genealogia regum Anglorum (Genealogy of the English Kings); Speculum caritatis (Mirror of Charity);* and *Vita S. Eduardi Confessoris (Life of Edward the Confessor).*

**AENEAS OF GAZA** Sixth-century philosopher and Neoplatonist who was Hierocles' student at Alexandria, later writing on various aspects of Platonism. With Zacharias Scholasticus and Procopius of Gaza he was a member of the Gaza Triad.

**AESCWINE** King of the West Saxons from 674 to 676, who was succeeded by Centwine (676–c. 685).

**AETHELBALD, KING OF MERCIA** (d. 757) Ruler of the Mercians from 716 to 757, a grandson of Eowa, the brother of Penda. Aethelbald was exiled by King Ceolred, who died in 716, possibly of insanity, and succeeded to the throne of Mercia. He inherited a kingdom largely dominated by two southern kings, Wihtred of Kent and Ine of Wessex. Wihtred died in 725 and Ine in 726, and, using political opportunism and campaigning, Aethelbald was able to assert his ascendancy over the lands south of the Humber River by 731. In a charter dating from 736, he claimed the title of king of Britain *(rex Britanniae).* At the height of his reign, he was the leader of a confederation of Anglo-Saxon domains between the Humber and the Channel. Generally considered a patron of the church, he was criticized in 746 or 747 by Boniface by letter for his abuses of ecclesiastical privilege and for his immorality with women. Called a royal tyrant by contemporary sources, Aethelbald was killed in 757 by his own men, ending one of the longest and most successful reigns in early English history. A civil war ensued. See also ENGLAND; MERCIA, KINGDOM OF; OFFA.

**AETHELBALD, KING OF WESSEX** King of the West Saxons from 855 to 860 and an unconventional monarch. The second of the five sons of King Aethelwulf and the older brother of Alfred the Great, Aethelbald became the leading heir to the Saxon throne on the death of his father in 853. A sign of his ambition was given in 856 while his father was away in Rome. Aethelbald, in his absence, refused to acknowledge his father's power. Aethelwulf returned and avoided civil war, giving Aethelbald control of Wessex, retaining Kent, Essex, Sussex and Surrey. Upon Aethelwulf's death in 858, Aethelbald became king, appalling his courtiers by marrying his stepmother, Aethelwulf's widow, Judith. His death in 860, after a reign of only two years, was greeted with joy by many in the kingdom. See also WESSEX.

**AETHELBERT, KING OF KENT** (d. 616) Ruler of Kent from 560 to 616, a powerful figure in southern England, considered by Bede to be the master of the region south of the Humber River. Aethelbert was the first Anglo-Saxon king to be converted to Christianity. He welcomed Saint Augustine to England in 597, influenced probably by his wife, Bertha, daughter of Charibert, king of Paris. His legal codes, the earliest surviving of their kind, established a system of punishments for crimes against the clergy and the Crown. See also ENGLAND; KENT.

**AETHELBERT, KING OF WESSEX** (d. 865) Ruler of the West Saxons from 860 to 865, a brother and predecessor of Alfred the Great (ruled 871–899). Aethelbert was the successor of the unpopular King Aethelbald (ruled 855–860), whose death allowed him to reunite the kingdom. His reign was threatened by the Vikings, who launched a major raid between 860 and 864. They were defeated, but Winchester was sacked. As he had no heir, Aethelbert was succeeded by his brother, Aethelred I (865–871). See also ENGLAND.

**AETHELFLAED** (d. 918) Daughter of Alfred the Great; her mother was called Lady of the Mercians. Aethelflaed married Aethelred of Mercia, an ealdorman, or nobleman, and prior to his death in 911 she was made the Anglo-Saxon ruler of the Mercians. She was closely associated with her brother, Edward the Elder (ruled 899–924), in preparing the army and defenses of the kingdom for a combined Mercian and Saxon war against the Danes in England. In 917 they were ready, and a joint assault was launched. Aethelflaed was very successful, capturing Derby and Leicester, but she died in 918 leaving her throne vacant. Edward claimed the crown of Mercia, adding vast territories in central England, Northumbria and Wales to the already large domain of Wessex. Aethelflaed and her husband were also responsible for raising Athelstan, her nephew, in Mercia, at the insistence of her father. See also ENGLAND.

**AETHELFRITH, KING OF NORTHUMBRIA** (d. 617) Ruler of Northumbria from 592 to 617, originally the king only of Bernicia but extending his titles to all of Northumbria by taking the throne of Deira as well. The grandson of Ida of Bernicia, he led wars both into the north and, more vital, to the southwest, where he defeated an army of Britons and reached the Irish Sea. In 617, however, he was killed in battle against the forces of Edwin, the refugee claimant to the crown of Deira. Bede's *Historia ecclesiastica* has been the chief source on this era. See also NORTHUMBRIA.

**AETHELFRITH, KING OF BERNICIA** See AETHELFRITH, KING OF NORTHUMBRIA.

**AETHELHEARD** King of the West Saxons from 726 to 740, following King Ine to the throne, although there is little evidence to suggest he was of the family of Ine. His reign was an indication of the growing power of Mercia, as around 733 he lost parts of Wessex to Aethelbald, the king of Mercia. See also ENGLAND.

**AETHELRED I, KING OF WESSEX** (d. 871) Ruler from 865 to 871, one of the sons of Aethelwulf and the immediate predecessor of Alfred the Great (ruled 871–899). The reign of Aethelred I was the time of the largest and most dangerous invasion of England by the Danes, the so-called Great Army. The Norsemen marched out of East Anglia, ravaged Northumbria in 867 and then struck Mercia. Aethelred and Alfred, his brother, set out with the Saxon army, but a united effort against the invader was not achieved. By 870 the Danes had smashed East Anglia and turned on Wessex. There, however, Aethelred, aided by Alfred, put up fierce resistance, defeating the Danes repeatedly, even though they proved too resilient to be destroyed. In the midst of his campaign, just after Easter, Aethelred died, leaving his young son, Aethelwald, in the care of Alfred, the choice of the Saxons as king. See also ENGLAND.

**AETHELRED II, KING OF ENGLAND** (c. 968–1016) Ruler from 978 to 1016, he earned the reputation as one of the most disastrous rulers in English history because of his incompetence and his inability to repulse the invasion of the Danes. His title, "the Unready," was actually derived from the word *unred* (or *unrald*), meaning evil counsel, and was probably a pun on the name Aethelred, which meant "noble counsel." The reign of such a weak king was exacerbated by its longevity and the seeming unwillingness of the royal council (the Witan) to depose him.

The son of King Edgar (ruled 957–975) and the half brother of King Edward the Martyr, who was murdered in 978 after ruling for three years, Aethelred was thought to be involved in the death, as Edward was slain in his presence. He was lauded, however, in the *Anglo-Saxon Chronicle* as being illustrious and beautiful in manner and in appearance, and his coronation was reportedly hailed with great rejoicing. Two years later, however, the Vikings arrived once again in England, finding the country's defenses wholly deficient. They ravaged with complete impunity, and the young monarch was advised to appease them with offerings from the treasury, which had increased during times of peace and prosperity. Such tactics only drew more raids, as word spread of England's inability to mount serious opposition. After local resistance was stamped out, Aethelred accepted Archbishop Sigeric's opinion that the Crown should negotiate. In 991, a humiliating treaty was signed in which Aethelred paid a huge ransom of 22,000 pounds in gold and silver (see DANEGELD).

The *Anglo-Saxon Chronicle* contained a great many details about the succeeding years, providing lamentable reading. Through Aethelred's personal reluctance to mount a campaign and the continued dominance by traitorous nobles, England's hardships continued. Aethelred did resort to a massacre of the Danes called the Saint Brice's Day Massacre, on November 13, 1002, as a punishment against their raids. Under Sven Forkbeard (985–1014) and his son, Canute the Great (1018–1035), the Danes turned from raids to actual conquest of the nation. In 1013 Sven was accepted as the king, and Aethelred fled the country. When Sven died in February 1014, the Witan refused to acknowledge Canute, writing instead to Aethelred of his popularity. Aethelred returned to England, but his rule was overshadowed by the power wielded by his son, Edmund II Ironside (1016). On his death at London in 1016, England was again involved in war. Canute returned to press his claim to the throne, a right made possible by Aethelred's failures. See also EDWARD THE CONFESSOR, SAINT; ENGLAND.

**AETHELWULF** (d. 858) King of the West Saxons from 839 to 858 and the father of four succeeding kings: Aethelbald, Aethelbert, Aethelred, and Alfred the Great. Aethelwulf inherited a kingdom that was both stable and powerful, thanks to the astuteness of his father, Egbert (802–839). Although Aethelwulf did not add to the possessions of the West Saxons, he did not lose any of the conquered territories of Kent, Sussex, Essex and Surrey. Although a humble and deeply religious man, he nevertheless earned the position of preeminent monarch in England through his victory over the Danes at Ockley in 851. His reign was troubled by his sons: Athelstan, his eldest, to whom he gave the eastern portions of his kingdom, died sometime before 855, and Aethelbald, next in line, waited for a chance to seize power. In 855, Aethelwulf went on a pilgrimage to Rome, learning in 856 that Aethelbald had questioned his right to rule. He agreed to give that son Wessex and took for himself the eastern regions once governed by his son Athelstan. Aethelwulf's marriage was arranged in 856 to Judith of France, daughter of Charles the Bold, and in 858 he died. See also ENGLAND; WESSEX.

**AFONSO I–V, KINGS OF PORTUGAL** See ALFONSO I–V, KINGS OF PORTUGAL.

**AFRICA** See ABBASID CALIPHATE; AGHLABIDS; ALGIERS; ALMOHADS; ALMORAVIDS; AYYUBIDS; BARBARY STATES; BELISARIUS; BYZANTINE EMPIRE; CAIRO; CÓRDOBA, EMIRATE OF; CRUSADES; EGYPT; FATIMID CALIPHATE; FEZ; IDRISIDS; ISLAM; JEWS AND JUDAISM; MAGHRIB; MAMLUKS; MARRAKESH; MOORS; OTTOMAN EMPIRE; TAHIRIDS; TRADE AND COMMERCE; TULUNIDS; VANDALS; ZIRIDS.

**AGAPETUS** See AGAPITUS.

**AGAPITUS I** (d. 536) Pope from 535 to 536, known for his orthodox views concerning the Arian and Monophysite heresies. He founded a library of ecclesiastical authors with Cassiodorus at Rome.

**AGAPITUS II** (d. 955) Pope from 946 to 955, whose reign was rendered largely ineffective because of the temporal powers exercised in Rome by Alberic II of Spoleto, the nobleman who secured Agapitus's elevation. Agapitus surrendered to the German emperor Otto I administrative control over the German bishops and placed all of Christianized Denmark under the jurisdiction of the metropolitan see of Hamburg, through a bull of 948. In Rome, Alberic II controlled the papacy and even made certain that his bastard son Octavian would succeed Agapitus as pope, which he did as John XII.

**AGATHIAS** (c. 531–c. 580) Called Agathias Scholasticus, a Byzantine historian and poet. His *Histories* was the chief source for information on the reign of Justinian from 552 to 559. He was the author of erotic tales as well as a collector of epigrams. His love poems were entitled *Daphni-*

*aca,* and 100 epigrams were preserved in the *Greek Anthology*.

**AGATHO, SAINT** (d. 681) Pope from 678 to 681, who was instrumental in encouraging the use of the Roman liturgy in England. His intervention in the dispute between Theodore of Tarsus, archbishop of Canterbury, and Wilfrid, bishop of York, over the division of the latter's see in 678 was advantageous for Wilfrid. Agatho also worked to end the quarrel with heretical Monothelitism, supporting the Council of Constantinople of 680–681 and reestablishing amicable relations with Constantinople.

**AGHLABIDS** Islamic dynasty that ruled much of North Africa from 800 to 909 and was notable for being the first quasi-independent state during the Abbasid caliphate and for acquiring territorial possessions in Sicily and Italy. The Aghlabids were founded by the Arab soldier Ibrahim ibn al-Aghlab, who in 800 received the rank of emir and the rights of ruler of Afrikiya (Muslim Africa) from the caliph Harun al-Rashid in return for his acceptance of Abbasid suzerainty. To centralize his power in Africa and as a gesture to the Abbasid caliphate, in 800 the ruler established his capital, al-Abbasiyya, or the City of the Abbasids. Aghlabid activity in the Mediterranean increased from 827 with the invasion of Sicily, then under Byzantine control. The next decades were spent extending Muslim domination over the island and raising expeditions against Italy. Bases were established in Apulia and Calabria, and sorties were launched up the Tiber River against Rome in 846. Internal decline, coupled with constant unrest among the African Berber tribes, made the Aghlabids susceptible to conquest. In 909, Rakhada, the capital since 878, fell to the troops of Ubayd Allah, founder of the Fatimid caliphate.

**AGILULF** (d. 651) King of the Lombards from 590 to 615; his rule was one of the longest of the Lombard kings. He was successor to Authari (r. 583–590) but, unlike him, was never forced to deal with the Franks, who were involved in civil strife for much of this era. Agilulf's reign is noted for two major events: the settlement and development of Lombardy and a protracted war against the Byzantines on the Italian peninsula. The struggle with the Byzantine exarchs raged for years and was ended, albeit temporarily, by the intervention of Pope Gregory I in 598. The following year fighting was renewed when Agilulf's daughter was kidnapped. This time peace was secured only by the payment of tribute by the Byzantine emperors. Although the conquest of all of Italy was possible, the king chose to solidify the Lombard position in Lombardy alone. Permanent settlements were encouraged, and Christianity was accepted by virtually everyone in the state. Agilulf died in 615 but only after naming his son, Adaloald, as his colleague. See also LOMBARDS.

**AGINCOURT, BATTLE OF** See HUNDRED YEARS' WAR.

**AGIUS OF CORVEY** Ninth-century priest and poet who about 876 wrote a biography and a poem on Hathumoda, abbess of Gandersheim, presumably as a gift for the nuns of the convent. The poem was thought to be derived from Virgil because of its classical quality.

**AGNELLUS OF PISA** (c. 1194–1236) One of the leading Franciscans of the 13th century. Agnellus was responsible for the establishment and early acceptance of the Franciscan order in England. Brought into the order by Saint Francis himself c. 1211, Agnellus was first sent to Paris in 1217 to establish a monastery there and, in 1224, received instructions to go to England. With a group of friars, several of them English, he founded Franciscan houses at Oxford, London, Cambridge, York and Canterbury. See also ADAM OF MARSH; GROSSETESTE, ROBERT.

**AGNELLUS OF RAVENNA** (805–c. 850) Historian and cleric, the author of an account of the See of Ravenna from the fourth to the eighth century. Andreas Agnellus used the term Roman Empire in his writings when referring to the realm of Charlemagne. He was an opponent of marriage within the clergy. See also RAVENNA.

**AGOBARD** (769–840) Archbishop of Lyons and a theologian. Entering the priesthood in 804, by 813 Agobard was made co-adjutor to the See of Lyons in 816, a position he held until his death in 840, with the exception of a brief period of exile (c. 834–838) because of his opposition to Empress Judith. During that time, in Italy, he was under the protection of Lothair I. A diverse and notable scholar, Agobard was an enemy of adoptionism but nevertheless had his books placed on the list of prohibited works because of some of his controversial theological views. He attacked folklore, paganism, the veneration of images, trial by ordeal and the Jews. See also LYONS.

**AGRICULTURE** See FEUDALISM; JACQUERIE; MANORIAL SYSTEM; PEASANT REVOLT; PLAGUES; TRADE AND COMMERCE.

**AIDAN, SAINT** (d. 651) Seventh-century English monk at Iona and the founder of the important monastic institution of Lindisfarne in 635. Little is known of his early life but about 635 he was consecrated a bishop and given the task of reviving missionary work in Northumbria. He left Iona and settled on the island of Lindisfarne, making it his base for many travels. Aidan was friend to both Oswald, who had asked him to undertake the conversion of Northumbria, and Oswy, the kings of Northumbria. Upon Oswy's death in 670, Aidan supposedly had a hut constructed against the west wall of the church in Bamborough, capital of the kingdom. There he died of a broken heart. See also CELTIC CHURCH.

**AILRED** See AELRED OF RIEVAULX, SAINT.

**AIMOIN DE FLEURY** (c. 960–c. 1010) A monk of Fleury and a prolific historian. Aimoin was a member of the French nobility but entered the monastic life. Few other details have survived about him, although his works were of some importance. He was the author of two collections, both histories of abbots; one, entitled the *Vital abbonis* (c. 1005–1008), focused exclusively on the abbots of Fleury. Another work, the *Miracula sancti Benedicti* (*Miracles of Saint*

*Benedict*, c. 1000), was a continuation of the book begun by Adrevald of Fleury in the mid-ninth century. Aimoin's most influential effort was the *Gesta Francorum* or *Historia Francorum*, a chronicle of the Franks, dedicated to Abbo, abbot of Fleury (d. 1004) which comprised the history of the Franks from their earliest days until the reign of Pepin the Short. Well written and informative, it gave legitimacy to the Capetian dynasty while laying the groundwork for other French chroniclers of that era. See also FRANKS.

**AIN-JALUT, BATTLE OF** A battle fought on September 3, 1260, between the Mongols and the Mamluks of Egypt that had far-reaching consequences for Islam. The Mongol armies, sent out by Mongke Khan (1251–1254), seemed unconquerable; annihilating the Assassins in 1256, bringing the Abbasid caliphate to ruin and besieging Baghdad in 1258, as well as waging bloody war in Aleppo and Damascus. Egypt was on the verge of invasion when the Il-Khan Hulagu, leading the Mongol campaign, received word that the Khan had died. With civil war erupting among the Mongol claimants, Hulagu ordered a withdrawal. Egypt was not only spared, but the Mamluks then launched a counterattack, trapping a small Mongol detachment of 10,000 men near Nazareth at Ain-Jalut (Goliath's Spring). The Mongols, outnumbered by more than 100,000 men, were overwhelmed, the first time such an event had occurred. Although writers have overexaggerated this event as a battle, Ain-Jalut nevertheless marked the end of the steady Mongol advance into the Islamic world and gave much prestige to Egypt's Mamluks. See also ASSASSINS, ORDER OF; MONGOLS.

**AISHA** (d. 678) The third and favorite wife of the prophet Muhammad, the daughter of the first caliph, the venerable Abu Bakr. It was said that after Muhammad's death in 632 he was buried beside the courtyard of the mosque at Medina, beneath Aisha's chamber. The fact that Abu Bakr was Aisha's father and related by marriage to the Prophet was of help in securing his election as caliph, and Aisha was to play other roles in the shaping of early Islamic history. Following the assassination of the caliph Osman in 656, she accused Muhammad's cousin, Ali ibn Abi Talib, of complicity. In the ensuing struggle for power between Ali and the Meccan aristocrats, Aisha supported the latter. The Battle of the Camel was fought in Iraq in 656, thus called because Aisha sat on a camel while the combat raged about her. Ali triumphed, and Aisha was sent into retirement at Medina. She is honored with the title "Mother of the Believers." See also ISLAM.

**AISTULF** King of the Lombards from 749 to 756 and an ardent proponent of Lombard expansion in Italy. Aistulf attacked and conquered (751) the Byzantine Exarchate of Ravenna, which he followed by reducing the duchy of Benevento to vassal status. Although he had already added considerable territory to the Lombard kingdom, he wanted more. In 752–753, he marched into the Tiber Valley demanding the submission of the pope, Stephen II (752–757). The pope turned to Pepin the Short (751–768), king of the Franks, who gathered an army and, in the summer of 754, routed Aistulf. The Lombards accepted Pepin's terms but only briefly, for in 755 Aistulf laid siege to Rome, now ignoring the terms of the treaty. Pepin returned once again to crush the Lombard army and inflicted even harsher terms: the loss of Ravenna and other cities, one-third of the Lombard treasury and an annual tribute. Aistulf died in 756 after a fall from his horse. See also PAPAL STATES; PEPIN THE SHORT.

**AIX-LA-CHAPELLE** See AACHEN.

**AKINDYNOS, GREGORY** (c. 1300–1394) Byzantine theologian, writer and monk who played a prominent role in the controversy surrounding the heretical movement of Hesychasm, a mystical system of belief that claimed to lead to a spiritual union with God. Probably born in Bulgaria, Akindynos was a student of Gregory Palamas, learning from him the important doctrines of Hesychasm. Knowledgeable in Latin philosophy, he came to oppose Palamas's views, emerging as the chief spokesman for the anti-Hesychast party and writing a history of the heresy (c. 1343) and seven theological treatises in opposition to Palamas and his movement. Akindynos was condemned as a heretic in 1347 by a synod then influenced by Emperor John VI Kantakouzenos (1347–1354), a supporter of Palamas. He was condemned once again in 1351, this time posthumously. See also HESYCHASM.

**ALAIN OF LILLE** (c. 1120–1202) French theologian, mystic and leading intellectual of the 12th century. Also called Alain de L'isle and given the title *doctor universalis*, he was born in Lille, a student of the great Gilbert de la Porrée at Paris or Chartres. Eventually teaching in Paris, he joined the Cistercian order only in his final years, having already achieved a formidable reputation.

In 1160–1175 Alain composed the complex *De planctu naturae (On the Lamentation of Nature)*; influenced by the work of Boethius, it presented the role of nature in relation to God and humanity. *De planctu naturae* was followed (c. 1182) by his epic poem *Anticlaudianus*, thought by many scholars to be a continuation of the first work. In *Anticlaudianus* Alain further developed his ideas on nature, using the liberal arts as a metaphor in his advice on how humanity might attain perfection. A masterful theologian, he wrote numerous treatises, among them *Theologicae regulae*, establishing guidelines for theological studies; an untitled *summa theologica;* and *Distinctiones, Ars praedicandi.* As a mystic he was an adherent of the combined theories of Pythagoras and those of Neoplatonism.

**ALAMANNI** The name given to a group of Germanic peoples who threatened the Roman Empire for centuries before taking large stretches of territory in Gaul (France), southern Germany and Switzerland. The term *Alamanni*, "All Men," came from the gathering of many German tribes, which included the Juthungi, Suevi, Quadi and Bucinabantes. They battled Roman legions from 213 until the fifth century when they poured across the Rhine frontier, in 406, and began competing for land with other migratory groups such as the Alans, Burgundians, Frank, and Vandals.

By the end of the fifth century the Alamanni had moved westward into Roman Gaul, where they encountered the Franks. Clovis, king of the Franks, defeated the Alamanni in 495, placing them under Frankish control. Over the next two centuries the tribes settled in southern Germany and Switzerland, where Christianity took foot, thanks largely to the missionary efforts of Saint Columban. During the reign of King Theodoric II of the Merovingians, they probably acquired a set of legal codes, early in the seventh century. The Alamanni struggled for their own independence from the Franks, with a brief success in the eighth century. Their hopes for autonomy were crushed by Pepin III. See also FRANKS.

**ALAMUT** A large castle, situated in Persia, south of the Caspian Sea in the Elburz Mountains, that endured in history as the headquarters of the Order of the Assassins. It was known as Alamut or the Eagle's Nest. It was occupied by Shiite supporters in the ninth century, and in 1090 Hasan ibn-al-Sabah, founder of the Assassins, claimed it as the base for the extremist Nizari-Ismaili sect. Its strength lay in a combination of brilliant defenses and the terrorist tactics wielded by the order. Both allowed the Assassins to survive attempts by the orthodox Muslims to destroy them, but in 1256 the Mongols were given entry by the grand master Rukn al-Din Khurshah. Alamut's defenses were stripped and, like the Assassins, subject to further attack. Alamut was described by Marco Polo, who visited Persia in 1273 and had supposedly seen the interior of the fortress firsthand.

**ALANS** A migratory Indo-Iranian people who were of importance toward the end of the Roman Empire and the subsequent development of Europe. The Alans, or Alani, were originally of Sarmatian extraction, forging a sizable domain along the Black Sea. Under pressure from advancing tribes of the east (the Huns), they headed west. For some centuries the Alans had little contact with the Roman Empire, but in 406, allied with the Vandals, they crossed the Rhine frontier. Many Alans settled in Gaul (see FRANCE), while others came into the pay of the Eastern Empire or allied themselves with the Vandals and established kingdoms in the Iberian peninsula. By the sixth century, Alani influence was broken in Constantinople by Emperor Leo I (457–474), and their territories in the peninsula were destroyed by the Visigoths. The Alans were subsequently absorbed by the Vandals and followed the Vandal kings. See also VANDALS; VISIGOTHS.

**ALARIC I** (c. 370–410) King of the Visigoths from 395 to 410, Alaric earned a place in the history of the early Middle Ages for his major achievement, the sack of Rome in 410 and the conquest of virtually all of the Italian peninsula. This act, such a blow to contemporaries such as Saint Ambrose, reflected the state of decline in the western Roman Empire. Rome was plundered of its gold, treasures and, according to legend, every ounce of pepper. Unable to move his people from the Italian peninsula to Africa, Alaric died in 410 with the Visigoths still a migratory people in the West. See also VISIGOTHS.

**ALARIC II** King of the Visigoths from 484 to 507; the successor to King Euric, who inherited a Visigoth kingdom stretching from the Iberian peninsula across the Pyrenees, into Gaul (see FRANCE). After a decade of continuous fighting on several fronts, Alaric had the misfortune of entering into war against Clovis, king of the Franks. In 507 the Visigoths, outnumbered and lacking in allies to assist, and the Franks met at the Battle of Vouille. Alaric was routed and killed. Clovis then drove his army south, capturing Toulouse, the Visigoth stronghold, thus putting to an end Visigoth ambitions north of the Pyrenees. Alaric was also remembered for promulgating the so-called *Breviary of Alaric* (506), the codification of laws for his Roman subjects in Gaul and his Iberian territories. See also CLOVIS I; VISIGOTHS.

**ALBA** A popular medieval song that found its greatest expression in Provence. The name *alba* was derived from dawn song and was the song of lament by lovers who must part from each other's arms with the coming of sunrise. Written and sung by troubadours of southern France, the *alba* gained wide fame; examples were found in other cultures, most notably Spain.

**ALBALAQ, ISAAC IBN** Thirteenth-century Jewish philosopher in Spain or southern France. His most important work was a Hebrew translation of al-Ghazali's *Maqasid al-falasifah (Aims of the Philosophers)*. See also AL-GHAZALI.

**ALBERIC I** (d. c. 928) Duke of Spoleto and margrave of Camerino who was a major figure in the history of the Italian peninsula during the 10th century. He was largely responsible for political affairs there and had a major role, with the aristocrat Theophylactus, in the restoration of Pope Sergius III (904–911) to the Holy See. An adventurer and general, Alberic took part in the defeat of the Saracens at the Battle of Garigliano in 915. His wife was Marozia, the mother of Alberic II (932–954). Alberic was thought to have been murdered sometime before June 928. See also ROME.

**ALBERIC II** (d. 954) Duke of Spoleto, the son of Alberic I (d. c. 928) and Marozia and virtual king of Rome from 932 to 954. Alberic used his family position and the vacuum of power in Rome to forge for himself near absolute political suzerainty in the Eternal City. His influence dominated the papacy, especially the reign of Agapitus II (946–955), whom he would not allow to crown Otto I (936–973) as Holy Roman Emperor in 952. Alberic died in 954 after ensuring that his son would succeed Agapitus as pope, taking the name John XII (955–964). See also ROME.

**ALBERIC OF MONTE CASSINO** (d. 1105) A monk of the major monastery at Monte Cassino in Italy, who was an important figure in the revival of classical culture and the author of a wide variety of works, including treatises on grammar and rhetoric. Alberic also composed hymns and wrote on music and astronomy. He corresponded with contemporaries such as Peter Damian. See also MONTE CASSINO.

**ALBERT I** (c. 1165–1229) Bishop of Livonia from 1199 to 1229, also called Albert von Buxhoevden. He was responsible for the foundation of the city of Riga in 1201 and the powerful military organization the Order of the Brothers of the Sword, the body of knights who came to occupy much of Estonia. See also MILITARY ORDERS.

**ALBERT III, DUKE OF SAXONY** (1443–1500) Son of Frederick II, Elector of Saxony, and the founder of the Albertine line of the House of Wettin. He shared his responsibility for Saxony with his brother from 1485 and had been an unsuccessful claimant to the throne of Bohemia. His abduction while still a youth became a legend as the *Prinzenraub* in German literature. See also SAXONY.

**ALBERT III OF BRANDENBURG** (1414–1486) An Elector of Brandenburg and one of the most gifted statesmen of his day. Nicknamed Achilles, Albert spent most of his life at war, fighting opponents of the German emperors or those political elements in Germany seeking autonomy, most notably in Nuremberg. An ardent advocate of the ideal of the German imperial system, he repeatedly supported the emperors while working for reforms within the empire. In 1473, he handed down a major decree as Elector of Brandenburg, the *Dispositio Achillia (Disposition of Achilles)*, by which he ensured the dynastic succession to the electorship by designating that the oldest son receive the title while the younger sons were granted rich and prestigious holdings in FRANCONIA. See also BRANDENBURG (1).

**ALBERT I OF HABSBURG** (1225–1308) German king from 1298 to 1308, the eldest son of King Rudolf I and a member of the Habsburg dynasty. Already thought to be too powerful, the Habsburgs were feared by the German Electors, and so, in 1291, when Rudolf died, it was their decision to ignore the hereditary claims of Albert and to elevate Adolf of Nassau to the throne. Albert was given the duchies of Austria and Styria. By 1298, however, Adolf had proved too ambitions, and Albert formed an alliance with the Electors, deposing Adolf on June 23, killing him in battle on July 2.

Crowned at Aachen on August 24, Albert soon allied himself (in 1299) with Philip IV of France (1285–1314) against Pope Boniface VIII (1294–1303), a policy opposed by the Electors of the towns along the Rhine, who feared the loss of prestige from Albert's efforts to claim control of the land at the mouth of the Rhine. The Electors were defeated in 1300–1302, after which a peace was made with Rome. In 1306, Albert placed his son Rudolf on the Bohemian throne, only to have him ousted by the Bohemians, a failure followed by a defeat at Lucka in 1307, ending the king's hopes of expansion. Albert won the admiration of many subjects by encouraging the development of the Rhine cities and by his protection of the Jews. See also HOLY ROMAN EMPIRE.

**ALBERT II OF HABSBURG** (1397–1439) Originally called Albert V of Austria, a German king and ruler (1438–1439) of Bohemia and Hungary. On the death in 1437 of Sigismund, the Holy Roman Emperor, Albert was chosen as heir to the Hungarian throne, having married Sigismund's daughter. He was accepted by the Hungarians as their king in January 1438 only on condition that he not become Holy Roman Emperor and that he remain in the country. Nevertheless, in March of that year he was also elected German monarch, and in June, despite the opposition of the Hussites, he was also crowned king of Bohemia. Albert demonstrated a capacity for governing, ending the civil strife within the empire, improving the administration of Germany and strengthening the defenses of Hungary. Unfortunately, he died in 1439 while fighting the Turks. Significantly, Albert was the first of the continuous Habsburg rulers of the Holy Roman Empire. See also HOLY ROMAN EMPIRE.

**ALBERTI, LEON BATTISTA** (1404–1472) Italian architect and humanist. Alberti was born in Genoa, the illegitimate son of an exiled merchant-banker from Florence. Raised in Venice and educated at Bologna and Padua, he eventually became a secretary in the papal chancery in Rome. In 1432 he visited Florence and was there in 1434 with Pope Eugenius IV. There he met and became an associate of Donatello, Brunelleschi, Bracciolini and Ghiberti. Henceforth he maintained ties with leading artists and intellectuals of Florence, although the majority of his years were spent in Rome in the service of the popes.

Having long been an adviser on the building and restoration of churches, Alberti wrote several treatises, reflecting not only his study of classical art and architects, such as Vitruvius, but also a high degree of humanism. His most important humanist work was *Della famiglia (On the Family)*; another was *De iciarchia (On the Head of His Family)*. In addition to poetry he wrote *De pictura* and *De statua*, on painting and sculpture, and was hailed for his masterwork, *De re aedificatoria* on architecture, dedicated to Pope Nicholas V in 1452 but only published in 1485. Alberti died in Rome.

**ALBERT OF AIX** Twelfth-century historian, author of the most detailed account of the First Crusade (written c. 1130). The *Liber Christianae expeditionis* (in full, *Liber Christianae expeditionis pro ereptione, emundatione et restitutione sanctae hierosolymitanae ecclesiae*) relied no doubt to a large degree upon eyewitness accounts but was organized in a haphazard manner. Though considered reliable, Albert's work gradually fell out of favor with many scholars; parts of the material are still regarded as accurate. See also CRUSADES.

**ALBERT OF MECKLENBURG** King of Sweden from 1364 to 1389, the son of King Magnus II Ericsson's sister. Albert was elected ruler of Sweden in 1364 when both Magnus (1319–1369) and Haakon Magnusson were considered no longer fit to rule. Albert remained on the throne until 1389, but his reign grew increasingly unacceptable to the Swedish nobles because of his policies. Thus, in 1388 they hailed Margaret of Norway as regent and embarked on a war against the king. Although he held out for nearly a year, in 1389 Albert lost Stockholm, falling from power. See also SWEDEN.

**ALBERT OF SAXONY** (c. 1316–1390) Also called Albert of Riggensdorf or Albert of Rickmersdorf, he was a mathematician, philosopher and teacher. From Saxony, Albert was both a student and instructor at the University of Paris before traveling to Vienna, where he was instrumental in establishing a university in 1365. He was consecrated bishop of Halberstadt in 1366. Also a scientist and logician, he was a supporter of William of Ockham and the popular ideas of the Oxford-based intellectuals. In his own work, *Quaestiones,* Albert discussed extensive theories on physics, mathematics and logic.

**ALBERT THE BEAR** (c. 1100–1170) The nickname given to the first margrave of Brandenburg, Albert I. This shrewd nobleman and soldier inherited extensive holdings in central Germany and from there launched his long career in the East. In 1131 Albert received from Emperor Lothair II (1075–1137) the eastern regions of the Elbe as his own mark, or territory. For the next years he was engaged in the Drang nach Osten, the Drive to the East, warring upon the Wends (Slavs). His conquests opened the region to Saxon colonists, towns and missionaries. For his accomplishments he was probably made archchamberlain of the Holy Roman Empire by Frederick I Barbarossa (1152–1190), a position that helped to establish the margraves of Brandenburg as Electors because of the powers they inherited. See also BRANDENBURG.

**ALBERTUS MAGNUS, SAINT** (c. 1200–1280) Known as Albert the Great and Albert of Cologne, one of the foremost intellectual figures of the Middle Ages and an important Aristotelian philosopher. Albertus was born in Lauingen, studying at the University of Padua before joining the Dominican order in 1223. Years of study followed in Padua, Bologna and Germany.

In 1241 he was sent to Paris to study theology and began his crucial introduction to the works of Aristotle. A lecturer on theology, he probably met during this time his future friend and learned ally Thomas Aquinas, influencing Thomas's own exceptional development. Albertus returned to Germany in 1248, organizing a Dominican center for learning in Cologne and serving as its master until 1254. In that year he was made head (provincial) of the Dominicans in Germany, a post that he resigned in 1257 in order to teach again. As provincial of the Dominicans, Albertus successfully defended them from attacks by theologians from Paris. Unable to resist the wishes of Pope Alexander IV, and despite the protest of his Dominican superiors, Albertus served as bishop of Regensburg from 1260 to 1261. Pope Urban IV then required him from 1263 to 1264 to preach another crusade throughout German lands.

Finally, free of responsibilities, Albertus was asked by the head of the Dominicans to retire to Cologne as lector emeritus. He made only two more trips away from Cologne, one in 1274 and another in 1277, when he went to Paris to defend two of his most beloved causes: Thomas Aquinas and Aristotle, both of whose theories were under attack by theologians. Albertus left a massive treasury of writings, including commentaries on Aristotle, Lombard's *Sentences* and the Bible and works on theology, metaphysics, logic, philosophy and ethics. He was called "the Great" long before his death, earning as well the titles "Universal Doctor" and "Doctor of the Church." He was also credited with making Aristotle intelligible to Europeans and earned the praise of such scholars as Siger of Brabant, Ulrich of Strasbourg and Roger Bacon, who wrote that Albertus was held in equal esteem with Avicenna, Averroës and Aristotle himself. Bacon also lauded Albertus as the best known of the Christian scholars.

**ALBI** City in southern France in the department of Tarn in the region of Languedoc. Albi was recognized from the late 12th century as the center of the Albigensian movement. The city was also the site of the impressive Gothic cathedral Saint-Cecile (dated 1277–1512), the archbishop's palace, the Palais de la Berbie (13th century) and the Old Bridge (ninth century). See also ALBIGENSIAN MOVEMENT.

**ALBIGENSIAN MOVEMENT** A heretical sect of the 12th–13th centuries that originated in southern France, in the city of Albi. The heresy spread to other parts of Europe and acquired several names and variations, such as CATHARI (see also WALDENSES). Essentially, the Albigensians believed in a Manichaean-based dualism between God and evil; the spirit was created by goodness and the body or matter by evil. Believers used aspects of the New Testament and elements of the Old Testament to show that Christ was merely an angel whose death and resurrection were solely allegorical. In their view the world of matter was the work of the devil, and the Christian church, by adhering to its view of the Incarnation of Christ and its role in Christendom, had been corrupted and was disseminating the devil's ways.

Strict Albigensians, called the "perfects," practiced the most severe forms of austerity, including starvation; regular practitioners, leading less stringent lives, were known as "believers." They promised to accept the baptism into the "perfects" upon death. With gifted preachers gathering support from the masses, the movement acquired such protectors as Pedro II of Aragon and Raymond VI of Toulouse, who seized the chance to oppose the papacy.

The church's response to the Albigensians was condemnation at various councils and, failing that, attempted conversions. Innocent III appointed Cistercian missionaries and later Saint Dominic, all to little avail. The fanatical hatred of the Albigensians for the church led inevitably to bloodshed. Thus in 1208, Peter of Castelnau, the papal legate, was murdered. What followed was the Albigensian Crusade, a bloody, merciless and often politically motivated extirpation of the heresy. Command of the crusade was given to Simon de Montfort, who routed the forces of Peter of Aragon at Muret in 1213. In 1209 the city of Béziers, an Albigensian stronghold, was captured, and the inhabitants were massacred. Arnaud Amaury, the papal legate, was erroneously credited with this comment: "Kill them all, let God sort out the good ones," but the statement accurately reflected contemporary policy. By 1219 the French kingdom used the crusade as a pretext for seizing Toulouse and Languedoc. In 1233, Pope Gregory IX gave the Dominicans the task of using the Inquisition to repress the heresy, thereby eradicating all trace of the Albigensians by the end of the 1300s. See also HERESIES.

**ALBIZZI, RINALDO** (1370–1442) The most distinguished member of the House of Albizzi, a major family in Florence about 1380 to 1434. Rinaldo came to power in 1417 on the death of his father and directed the political future of the city until 1434. In that year the long conflict with Cosimo de 'Medici ended in a Medici triumph. Rinaldo was exiled, and the Albizzi hold on Florence was shattered.

**ALBO, JOSEPH** (c. 1380–c. 1444) Spanish philosopher of Jewish descent. He was the author of the *Sefer ha-Ikkarim,* a book of Jewish dogma. See also JEWS AND JUDAISM.

**ALBOIN** (d. 573) King of the Lombards from 565 until his assassination in 573. Alboin was responsible for the migration of his people into the Italian peninsula (c. 568). The son of King Audoin, Alboin inherited the throne while the Lombards still inhabited Pannonia. He ended the war with the Gothic Gepidae, reportedly beheading their king, Cunimund. Later he gilded the skull for use as a drinking cup, from which he forced the vanquished Cunimund's daughter, now his wife, Rosamund, to drink.

Deciding that the Italian peninsula offered fertile land, Alboin ordered an advance over the Carinthian Alps in the summer of 568. The Lombards moved through the Po Valley, seizing Milan and Aquileia but finding opposition at Padua, Verona and Pavia. Alboin found support among the Saxons, Suebi and Bulgars and one by one the cities fell, the final victory over Pavia in 571, where he made his capital. The following year he was assassinated in a conspiracy led by his wife. Alboin's decision, however, to move into the peninsula had far-reaching consequences for its development and its history. See also LOMBARDS.

**ALBORNOZ, GIL ÁLVAREZ CARILLO DE** (c. 1302–1367) Cardinal, general and statesman who championed the cause of the Avignon papacy. Albornoz came from Spain, where he fought the Moors and entered into the service of King Alfonso XI of León and Castile. Appointed archbishop of Toledo in 1338, he was exiled by Alfonso's successor, Pedro I in 1350 and went to the papal court at Avignon. By 1353, he was sent by the pope to the Papal States as legate. Years of war followed as Albornoz struggled with the Guelph forces, including Florence. Entering Rome with Cola de Rienzo, he made numerous administrative changes in the papal machinery of government, reforms that made possible the return and survival of papal authority in the Papal States in 1377. See also AVIGNON; BABYLONIAN CAPTIVITY.

**ALCANTARA, ORDER OF** See MILITARY ORDERS.

**ALCHEMY** An ancient art and mystical tradition that came, from the 12th century onward, to have a profound influence among some medieval thinkers. In its strictest sense, alchemy has been defined by scholars as the art of transmuting base metals into gold. To this definition can be added the metaphysical concept, put forth by other writers, that the practice of the art transformed the alchemist himself from base imperfection to high spiritual grace.

Alchemy, like its counterpart, astrology, was universally known and had practitioners among the Egyptians, Chinese, Indians and Greeks long before it was pursued by the Byzantines, Arabs and Europeans. Called the "Art" or the "Great Work," it sought, through a seemingly endless number of compounds or materials, including gold, silver, lead, iron, copper, sulfur, tin, mercury, salts, alums, chlorides, ammonium, arsenic and acids, to confer immortality. Eternal life was said to be a useful by-product of the most complex formula, the *elixir vitae,* called the philosophers' stone, which was supposed to turn base metals into gold.

In terms of the Western tradition, the practice of alchemy began probably around the third century B.C. in the Hellenic world, although the Arabs had their own currents of thought. Greek alchemists of note were Bolos of Mendes, Synesius and Zosimos. Their efforts were especially important in preserving alchemical theories or doctrines such as those of Hermes Trismegistos (the Greek version of the Egyptian god Thoth)—the *Corpus hermeticum* and the *Emerald Tablet*—and Appolonius of Tyana's *Book of the Secret Tradition.* Hellenic alchemy, influenced by the Chinese and Indians, passed to the Byzantines and thence to the Arabs.

Arabic alchemy owed its evolution not only to the Greeks but to its Eastern practitioners, particularly those in the Syrian city of Harran. Al-Razi, the early 10th-century alchemist and physician, left a major mark on his craft and was influenced by his predecessor Jabir ibn Hayyan, or Geber, and the Jabirians. Their writings, including their contributions to medicine, penetrated to the West in the 12th century.

Thanks to the Crusades and increased contact between the East and the West, Arabic works began appearing in Europe. In the 12th century, Gerard of Cremona translated al-Razi and Robert of Chester, in the *Book of Morienus,* taking initial steps toward the wider dissemination of alchemical learning. Further understanding, examinations and collections of lore and precepts were published in the 13th century by Vincent of Beauvais, Arnold of Villanova, Roger Bacon and Albertus Magnus.

The more widely accepted alchemy became, the greater the opportunity for deceit and fraud among its dishonest practitioners. With the aim of creating gold from base metals the activity of spurious alchemists, false treatises were sold to the unwary. A work like the *Sum of Perfection* (c. 1300), attributed to Geber, was most likely of European origin. In response to the decline of genuine alchemy, the legitimate alchemists hid their formulas and books behind a purposely complicated amalgam of symbols, messages and arcane imagery. Many professed to having made a fortune through the "Great Work." Despite the condemnation of the church and a lingering air of disrepute, alchemy was a vital transition to the study of Paracelsus and to making advances in pharmacology, medicine and the new science of chemistry. See also WITCHCRAFT.

**ALCUIN** (c. 730–804) Called Alcuin of York, Flaccus and Albinus, the key figure in the Carolingian renaissance and one of the most remarkable intellects of the eighth century. Born in Northumbria, he was educated at the Cathedral School of York, where he became a teacher in 768 and was headmaster by 778. On a visit to the Continent, Alcuin met Charlemagne in 781 and the following year held the position of adviser to the king and head of instruction in the palace school of Aachen. This institution was soon attracting the finest minds of the time, including Paul the Deacon and Peter of Pisa, and Alcuin claimed as his students Rabanus Maurus and Amalarius of Metz.

The course of study applied by Alcuin included the use of dialogue, the trivium and elements of the quadrivium. Boethius and Augustine had their places, as did the writings of Alcuin himself—manuals on education. He was also a poet and theologian on whom Charlemagne relied during the Adoptionist Controversy, during which he presented the decision of the Crown at the Council of Frankfurt in 794. His letters tell much about contemporary society. Alcuin left Aachen in 796 to assume the position of spiritual adviser to the monks of Saint Martin in Tours. There he died in 804, a vital influence on a generation of scholars. See also CAROLINGIAN RENAISSANCE.

**ALDFRITH,** King of Northumbria from 686 to 705, inheriting a realm that under his father Oswy (655–670) and brother Ecgfirth (670–685) had been weakened by wars with the Picts. Ecgfirth was killed and the Northumbrian army destroyed in 885 at the Battle of Nechtanesmere, and Aldfrith was left with the task of rebuilding the country. Bede wrote in the *Historia ecclesiastica* that the king reorganized and strengthened Northumbria but it was smaller than before.

Aldfrith's greatest achievement was the preservation of the Northumbrian churches and thus the scholarly environment that was beginning to blossom there. An intellectual and poet, he was a friend or patron of such writers as Aldhelm and Adamnan; Alcuin called him king and master. Aldfrith had an important influence English education and was nearly the equal in kingly qualities to Alfred the Great, although he enjoyed none of Alfred's fame. See also NORTHUMBRIA;SCHOLASTICISM.

**ALDHELM, SAINT** (c. 640–709) A Saxon by descent, the bishop of Sherborne, a leader of the English ecclesiastical reform movement and an important figure in preconquest Anglo-Latin literature. In 675 he was made abbot of Malmesbury but spent time at Canterbury, studying under the tutelage of the scholars attracted there by the teaching of Theodore of Tarsus. It is said that Aldhelm had great trouble with mathematics, especially fractions. Appointed bishop of Sherborne in 705, a new diocese, he joined the reform movement in England, writing against the Celtic church and calling on a unified Christian community, based on the precepts of the Roman church. The founder of churches and monasteries, Aldhelm was also a poet whose songs were appreciated by King Alfred the Great. His poems are extant, but most of what survives are prose works. Two sources for the study of his life are Faricius of Abingdon and William of Malmesbury.

**ALDUS MANUTIUS** See MANUTIUS, ALDUS.

**ALEPPO** An ancient city in northern Syria that was a valuable pawn in the struggle between Islam and the Byzantine Empire and vital to the trade between East and West. Aleppo (Arabic, Halab; Turkish, Halep) was founded sometime in the second millennium before Christ and was subsequently occupied by the Hittites, Macedonians (who named it Beroia) and Romans. During Roman imperial times and under the first Byzantines, the city enjoyed the prosperity of Syria. The largely Christian city fell to the Muslims in 636 but was allowed to remain in religious freedom in return for payment of tribute.

By the 10th century Aleppo had become part of a Syrian Islamic kingdom. Its capture by Nicephorus II Phocas and the Byzantines (c. 969) marked a time of repeated conquests during the 11th century by the Arabs, the Fatimid Empire of Egypt and the Seljuk Turks. Under the Seljuk rulers Nur al-Din and Saladin, the city was favored, serving as an economic center for Syria and as a place of intellectual freedom in the Islamic world. Crusaders unsuccessfully besieged it in 1124, but in 1260 the Mongols sacked the city so ruthlessly that recovery was not possible until the late 1400s, under Mamluk domination. The Black Death struck the city in 1348, and in 1401 Tamerlane briefly claimed it. In 1517 the Ottoman Turks seized Aleppo, and it became a leading commercial city of Levant. See also TRADE AND COMMERCE.

**ALEXANDER** Byzantine emperor from 912 to 913, although he was ranked as a co-emperor, either with Leo VI or Basil I for most of his life. Born in 870, the third son of Basil I, Alexander was viewed by historians as a pleasure-seeking monarch, uninterested in affairs of state but eager to rule alone. This he did in 912 on the death of Leo, leaving Alexander with a six-year-old nephew, Constantine. The new emperor immediately sent Empress Zoë to a convent and replaced Leo's advisers. More important, he refused to pay the annual tribute to the Bulgars and so began a war with Simeon, czar of the Bulgars, a conflict that Byzantium could ill afford and the end of which was not seen by Alexander, who died in 913. See also BULGARS, EMPIRES OF; BYZANTINE EMPIRE.

**ALEXANDER II** (c. 1010–1073) Pope from 1061 to 1073, whose reign was characterized by attempts at reform and strengthening of the papacy. Born Anselm, he was always a supporter of reform and was sent in 1039 by the archbishop of Milan to Emperor Henry III. Bishop of Lucca in 1057, he was elected Pope Alexander II in 1061, although Emperor Henry IV, who opposed him, had secured the election of an antipope, Honorius II (who died in 1072). Most of Alexander's reign was spent in efforts at church reform. Celibacy was encouraged, simony forbidden and the power of legates used to enforce papal will. Significantly, Alexander excommunicated the courtiers of Henry IV but gave his blessing to William of Normandy for the invasion of England in 1066.

**ALEXANDER III** (c. 1105–1181) Pope from 1159 to 1181 and the successor to Adrian IV. Born Orlando Bandinelli, he was one of the foremost canonical legalists of his day, having taught at the University of Bologna and acting as an adviser to Pope Adrian. Elected to the papacy in 1159, he was the first of the lawyer popes who were to dominate the succeeding pontificacius. As part of the continuing struggle with Emperor FREDERICK I, Alexander confronted an antipope in Victor IV, a schism ended only in 1177. During this time he lived in France and there became involved in the dispute between Thomas à Becket and King Henry II of England. Although not an admirer of Becket, he did inflict a penance upon Henry II for Becket's murder in 1170. Alexander's most lasting contribution to the papacy was his determination to have the election of a pope dependent on the vote of two-thirds of the College of Cardinals, a tradition adopted at the Third Lateran Council in 1179.

**ALEXANDER IV** (d. 1261) Pope from 1254 to 1261, whose reign was marked by a continuation of the Inquisition in France against the Albigensians, problems with the Franciscans and attempts at a reunification of the Eastern and Roman churches.

**ALEXANDER V** (c. 1340–1410) Pope from 1409 to 1410, although his pontifical reign has long been debated by scholars as eligible for inclusion in the papal lists. Born Peter of Candia, he was a member of the Franciscan order and was a brilliant theologian. Elected in 1409 as pope at the Council of Pisa, he lived for only 10 months. His election was an attempt to resolve the Great Schism, which had created two popes—one in Avignon, one in Rome. Neither of these two recognized Alexander V. In the 1370s he taught at the Franciscan convent of Saint Mary Magdalene; his lectures there on Lombard's *Sentences* (see PETER LOMBARD) revealed depth of understanding. These lectures, as well as his other theological writings, have been praised by medievalists.

**ALEXANDER VI** (1431–1503) Pope from 1492 to 1503, infamous in large measure owing to his family, the Borgias. Rodrigo Borgia was the nephew of Pope Calixtus III. Born in Spain, he was appointed head of the papal administration by his uncle, serving from 1457 to 1492, a powerful and influential figure in the Vatican. Having secured the election of a predecessor, Sixtus IV, he used bribery to have himself named pope in 1492, spending much of his reign encouraging the ambitions of his children, Cesare and Lucrezia Borgia. He staged a jubilee in 1500, diverting most of the money to his son to pay for the campaigns of the Borgias in their quest for supremacy in Italy. During his pontificacy, Alexander divided acquisitions in the New World between Portugal and Spain in 1493–1494 (Treaty of Tordesillas) and ensured the prosecution and the death of the reformer Girolamo SAVONAROLA in 1498. Alexander's papacy was a dark period in the history of the popes, open to excessive political machination and corruption.

**ALEXANDER I, KING OF SCOTLAND** (c. 1077–1124) Ruler of Scotland from 1107 to 1124, although the southern regions of the kingdom were administered by his brother and eventual heir, David. The son of King Malcolm III Canmore (1058–1093), Alexander succeeded his other brother, Edgar, who died in 1107. His reign was characterized by his ability to balance the nationalistic tendencies of his subjects with a recognition of the supremacy of the English. He married Sibylla, the illegitimate daughter of Henry I, and served as a lieutenant in the English campaigns in Wales. Despite his allegiance, he was steadfast in refusing to make the Scottish church subordinate to that of England. Under his patronage abbeys were established at Scone and Inchcolm. See also SCOTLAND.

**ALEXANDER II, KING OF SCOTLAND** (c. 1198–1249) Ruler of Scotland from 1214 to 1249, the son of William I the Lion (1165–1214). Alexander succeeded his father in 1214 and spent most of his reign consolidating the power of the Scottish monarchy while maintaining generally peaceful relations with England, despite a violent beginning. In 1215 he joined the rebellion of the English barons against King John (1199–1216) but had to acknowledge the overlordship of Henry III (1216–1272) in 1217 when the uprising proved unsuccessful. Ties to the English crown were furthered by two arrangements: marriage to Joan, sister of Henry III, in 1221, and the signing of the Peace of York (1237), by which Scotland was given parcels of English land in return for the withdrawal of its claim over Northumbria. Alexander died while traveling to join troops in Norway who hoped to conquer the Western Isles. His patronage resulted in the establishment of religious houses and the flourishing of ecclesiastical architecture. See also SCOTLAND.

**ALEXANDER III, KING OF SCOTLAND** (1241–1286) The last of the kings from the Dunkeld family, the successor to Alexander II (1214–1249), ruling from 1249 to 1286, a reign considered the last great era in Scotland before the long struggles with England. While still a boy in 1251, he married the 11-year-old daughter of the English King Henry III, Margaret, and for a time fell under the influence of the pro-English faction at the Scottish court. In 1257, however, Scottish nationalists regained the upper hand, and the remainder of Alexander's reign was one of solid Scottish independence.

Alexander waged a campaign to regain Norwegian holdings in the Hebrides, and a counterattack was repulsed in 1263 in which the forces of King HAAKON IV (1217–1263) were badly beaten both on land and on sea. He died on the return to Norway. His son, Magnus VI (1263–1280), signed a peace treaty at Perth in 1266, ceding to Scotland both the Hebrides and the Isle of Man. Even more amicable relations came in 1283, with the marriage of Margaret, Alexander's daughter, to King Eric II Priesthater. Scotland itself was both economically healthy and politically stable and seemed poised for dynastic greatness when, in 1286, Alexander was killed in a fall from his horse. Every possible successor was dead, and his second wife, Yolette, had given him no sons. Only Margaret, the "Maid of Norway," daughter of Eric II and Alexander's granddaughter, was eligible for the throne, a situation that doomed the country to civil strife and opened it to English intervention. See also SCOTLAND.

**ALEXANDER NEVSKY** See NEVSKY, ALEXANDER.

**ALEXANDER OF HALES** (c. 1185–1245) Theologian, teacher and the holder of the title Doctor Irrefragabilis ("Irrefutable Teacher"). Alexander was born at Halesowen, or Hales, in Worcestershire, England. Having studied at Paris, he remained there to teach and served as master of theology from 1220 until his death. In 1236 he surrendered all of his possessions and became a Franciscan monk. However, he retained his chair at the University of Paris. A theologian relying on biblical and sacred writings, Alexander was influential in making Peter Lombard's *Sentences* a cornerstone of theological training. He wrote glosses on the *Sentences* as well as *Quaestiones* (*Questions*, on theology) and, with the contributions of other Franciscan theologians of Paris (John de la Rochelle, William of Melitona and others), a *Summa Theologiae*, first published in 1475. See also FRANCISCANS.

**ALEXANDRIA** (Arabic Al-Iskandariyah.) For many centuries the most important city in Egypt and one of the great trading ports in the Mediterranean world. Alexandria was unable to retain its prominence during the Middle Ages. The capital of the Roman province of Egypt, the city developed into a Christian city and one of the patriarchates of the East, a position it held even under the Byzantines. On September 17, 642, it fell to the conquering tide of Islam, although the Christians were permitted to keep their churches. Despite widely circulated stories, the Arabs did not burn the last books of the Library of Alexandria, as it was later thought that Christian fanatics of the fifth century were perhaps responsible.

Under Arab domination Alexandria lost its place as the heart of the Egyptian administration. Al-Fustat (near Cairo) fulfilled this requirement after 641, although Alexandria was given its own administration and later an emir (governor) and a qadi (judge). Centuries of reduced prestige changed in the 12th century with the increase of contact between the Muslim states and those of the Crusaders. The city was besieged by Christian Crusaders in 1167 and partly destroyed by Christians in 1365. The Mamluks used Egypt's monopoly of the spice trade to conduct extensive business with European trading centers. Unfortunately, such profit could not last, and Alexandria's fate was sealed in 1498 with the Portuguese discovery of the southern route by sea to India. Ottoman conquest in 1517 brought further decline. Venetian travelers in the early 16th century wrote of the city's decay. See also EGYPT.

**ALEXIUS I COMNENUS** (c. 1048–1118) Byzantine emperor from 1081 to 1118, the founder of the Comnenus dynasty and the ruler of the Byzantines at the time of the early Crusades. The nephew of Isaac I, Alexius served as a very successful general from 1068 to 1081, amassing political support from the army and the prestigious Ducas family, of which his wife, Irene, was a member. Thus Alexius was supported in seizing power from Nicephorus III. He was crowned on April 4, 1081, and from the start he implemented those policies considered essential to the survival of the Byzantine Empire: the strengthening of the empire and the reclamation of its political viability. With the help of foreign troops, such as Germans and Cumans, and with the backing of Venice, triumphs were achieved over the Normans in Greece, led by Robert Guiscard (the Wily) (1081–1082), the Petchenegs (1091) and the Seljuk Turks, with whom he made agreements.

Alexius's call for help from the West brought unwanted results, however, for from 1097 the armies of the Crusades descended upon Constantinople, marched east and disrupted the entire framework of peace negotiated with the Muslims as well as the return of Byzantine influence in Anatolia. The reign of Alexius I was noted for its temporary efforts to save the empire from total collapse. Unfortunately it was not so effective as to render any transformation permanent. Alexius's biographer was his daughter, the historian Anna Comnena. See also BYZANTINE EMPIRE; CRUSADES; NORMANS.

**ALEXIUS II COMNENUS** (1169–1183) Byzantine emperor from 1180 to 1183, coming to the throne at the age of 12, on the death of his father, Manuel I Comnenus. His mother, Mary of Antioch, acted as regent, but her position was broken by the governor of Pontus and cousin of Manuel, Andronicus Comnenus (1120–1185), who entered Constantinople in 1182 amid riots against Latins living in the city and upheaval in the palace. Andronicus executed most of the court, including Mary, all in the name or signature of Alexius. In September 1183, Andronicus was crowned co-emperor (1183–1185). Having no further use for Alexius, the young ruler was murdered and buried at sea. See also BYZANTINE EMPIRE.

**ALEXIUS III ANGELUS** (d 1211) Byzantine emperor from 1195 to 1203, the brother of Isaac II Angelus. Alexius had ambitions for the throne and, on April 8, 1195, blinded his sibling, threw him in a dungeon and usurped power. Alexius was weak, easily manipulated and unequal to his role as emperor, given the severe circumstances that were about to confront the Byzantine Empire. Another war with Bulgaria began, and sections of the empire were destroyed, as well as a Byzantine army. Failed attempts at the assassination of Bulgar rulers assured the rise of Kalojan (1197–1207) as king of the Bulgars, a brilliant ruler and an implacable enemy of Constantinople.

At this crucial moment Alexius's inability to restore any order in Byzantine affairs made possible the landing of troops, bound for the Fourth Crusade, at Constantinople in July 1203, led by Alexius IV, the son of the blinded Isaac. Facing a Crusader attack that he knew he could not repeal, Alexius III fled the city on July 17. Now an exile, the emperor at last found an ally in the sultan of Iconium, who, in Alexius's name, waged war against the Greek empire of THEODORE I LASCARIS, who ruled in Nicaea. Unfortunately, Theodore proved triumphant in 1211, and Alexius spent the rest of his life in a monastery in Nicaea. See also BYZANTINE EMPIRE; CRUSADES.

**ALEXIUS IV ANGELUS** (d. 1204) Byzantine emperor from 1203 to 1204, sharing power with his father, Isaac II Angelus. Alexius IV shared as well in the fall of his father from power in 1195, joining the blinded former emperor in the prisons of Constantinople, sent there by his uncle, Alexius III Angelus. The young prince managed to escape, however, journeying to the courts of Europe in search of allies. He found support among the Venetians and the organizers of the Fourth Crusade. Promising financial contribution, Alexius gained the help of the Crusaders, who stormed Constantinople on July 17, 1203, forcing Alexius III to flee and installing Alexius IV with his father, Isaac II, on the Byzantine throne. Alexius was unable to make good his pledge to the Crusaders, thus angering his besieged subjects. In January 1204, an uprising of the citizens ended with the death of Alexius and the imprisonment of his father. See also BYZANTINE EMPIRE; CRUSADES.

**ALEXIUS V MOURTZOUPHLOS** (d. 1204) Byzantine emperor for a brief time in 1204, replacing the murdered Alexius IV and the imprisoned Isaac II. The son-in-law of the deposed Alexius III, he was the leader of the anti-Latin forces in Constantinople and openly hostile to the Crusaders camped outside the city. His antagonism finally led to his execution and allowed the rise of the Latin empire of Constantinople. See also BYZANTINE EMPIRE.

**ALFASI, ISAAC BEN JACOB** (1013–1103) Jewish Talmudic scholar born in Fez, Morocco; he moved to Lucena, Spain, about 1088 after being denounced by his enemies to the local Islamic government. Known by the name Rif from the title Rabbi Isaac Fasi's initials, Alfasi was remembered for his important work *Sefer-ha-Halakhot* (*Book of Laws*), a major codification of the Talmud. See also JEWS AND JUDAISM.

**ALFONSINE TABLES** Astronomical tables, based on the Ptolemaic formulas for the heavens, completed in Toledo about 1272. The name was derived from King Alfonso X of León and Castile, who commissioned them, and they were composed with the guidance of Isaac ben Sid and Yehuda ben Moses Cohen, two Jewish astronomers. Alfonso supposedly said of them that had he been present at the creation, he would have suggested a number of changes to God, no doubt to simplify the entire system. The tables were first published in 1482 in Venice. See also ASTRONOMY.

**ALFONSO I, KING OF ARAGON AND NAVARRE** (c. 1073–1134) Ruler from 1104 to 1134, his main achievement was the securement of his marriage to Urraca, daughter of Alfonso VI of León and Castile (c. 1109). Alfonso and Urraca were first cousins, and thus there were many opponents to the marriage. The marriage gave him a claim to that kingdom, but he eventually gave up his struggle to rule both kingdoms in 1114, in favor of his stepson as the couple had no heir. In 1118 he won Zaragoza from the Moors.

**ALFONSO II, KING OF ARAGON** (1157–1196) Count of Barcelona from 1162 to 1196 and king of Aragon from 1164 to 1196. The union of Barcelona and Aragon gave Alfonso a formidable political position, to which he added Valencia and Provence (the latter he received as an inheritance). In 1179 Alfonso signed the Pact of Cazola with Alfonso VIII of Castile, dividing the lands won by Aragon and Castile from the Moors, which he soon abandoned. He wrote Provençal poetry. See also BARCELONA.

**ALFONSO III, KING OF ARAGON** (1265–1291) Ruler of Aragon from 1285 until 1291, he was forced by his

Troops of King Alfonso I of Aragon

nobles to surrender much of his powers in the Privilegio de la Unión, signed in 1287. He also completed the conquest of the Balearic Islands in 1287.

**ALFONSO IV, KING OF ARAGON** (1299–1336) Ruler of Aragon from 1327 to 1336, known by his contemporaries as "the Benign." During his reign the Aragonese holding of Sardinia was challenged by a revolt of the local inhabitants, encouraged by the Genoese, who opposed the expansion of Aragon. The subsequent war with Genoa lasted for years. See also GENOA.

**ALFONSO V, KING OF ARAGON, NAPLES AND SICILY** (1396–1458) Ruler of Aragon and Sicily from 1416 to 1458 and king of Naples from 1443 to 1458. Called "the Magnanimous," Alfonso V did much to further the power of Aragon in the Mediterranean. However, he consequently earned a lukewarm verdict from Spanish chroniclers who saw his foreign conquests coming at the expense of the Aragonese kingdom. The son of Ferdinand I Antequera of Aragon, he succeeded to the throne in 1416 and by 1420 was involved in overseas entanglements. Following attacks on Sicily, Sardinia and Genoese-controlled Corsica, he made an arrangement with Joanna II, queen of Naples, for her adoption in return for his army in 1421. Joanna's subsequent dealings with Louis III of Anjou and RENÉ OF ANJOU precipitated a civil war from which Alfonso emerged triumphant in 1442 after years of struggle, including his capture and brief imprisonment at Milan.

Pleased with his new possession, Alfonso moved his entire court from Barcelona to Naples, making it a leading center for the arts and letters. His original holdings in

Aragon, meanwhile, deteriorated both financially and politically, with uprisings and wars with Castile and Navarre and a peasant revolt in Catalonia. Alfonso, however, was focused on Italian acquisitions, besieging recently French-acquired Genoa. He died in Naples on June 27, 1458. See also ARAGON.

**ALFONSO I, KING OF ASTURIAS** (c. 693–757) Ruler of Asturias from 739 to 757. Alfonso defeated a Berber force in 741 and was able to seize control of Galicia, as well as parts of Santander and León.

**ALFONSO II, KING OF ASTURIAS** (c. 759–842) Ruler of Asturias from 791 to 842. Alfonso II was responsible for the restoration of Visigothic tradition in Asturias, thus helping to foster a sense of national identity.

**ALFONSO III, KING OF ASTURIAS** (c. 838–910) Called the Great, the ruler of Asturias from 866 to 910. He did much to consolidate the position of Asturias in the Iberian Peninsula while working to add to its territorial possessions. He continued the process of restoring the Visigothic style of life and rule, thereby giving the royal line a claim to legitimacy, based on the old dynasty of Toledo, and won an important battle against Muslims at Polvoraria. The city of Burgos was founded during his reign, during part of a wider campaign against the Moors.

**ALFONSO IV, KING OF LEÓN** (d. 933) Ruler from 925 to 930, who presided over a country confronting considerable internal disorder. He abdicated in 930 in favor of his brother, Ramiro II, and retired to a monastery at Sahagún. He came to regret this decision, attempted to regain power, but was defeated and blinded with his sons by Ramiro.

**ALFONSO V, KING OF LEÓN** (994–1028) Ruler of León from 999 to 1028, called "the Noble." He helped to extricate León from its subordinate position to the caliphate of Córdoba. He also introduced the *fuero,* or Code of Municipal Law, to the principal towns of the kingdom.

**ALFONSO VI, KING OF LEÓN AND CASTILE** (1040–1109) Ruler of León from 1065 to 1109 and of Castile from 1072, a monarch during the era of El Cid, Rodrigo Díaz de Vivar. The second son of King Ferdinand I, he inherited León in 1065, arousing the envy of his elder brother, Sancho II, king of Castile. War erupted, and after suffering two defeats at his brother's hands, Alfonso was captured and exiled. Meanwhile, his sister, Urraca, with whom he had a close relationship, attempted a rebellion at Zamora. Sancho laid siege to the city but was assassinated in 1072, possibly at her order. Alfonso thus reclaimed León but also acquired Castile, although he had to swear an oath at the church in Burgos that he was innocent of Sancho's death.

With two powerful kingdoms at his command, Alfonso added even more territory, Basque lands and Rioja, while acknowledging the vassalship of Navarre. In 1077 he took the title emperor of Spain and then launched a war against the Moors. Toledo fell in 1085, one of most important dates in Spanish history, and the Muslim subjects were so oppressed and heavily taxed that they sent pleas for help to the Almoravids of North Africa. Yusuf ibn Tashufin landed in Spain in 1086, crushing Alfonso at Zallaqa. The Almoravids were repeatedly successful over the next years, forcing Alfonso to recall the Cid, whom he had long disliked and mistrusted. Obsessed with his war against the Muslims, Alfonso watched his son, Sancho, die in battle in 1108 and then negotiated a marriage between his daughter, Urraca, and Alfonso I of Aragon and Navarre. He died in Toledo in 1109, the war still unresolved. His reign was also marked by the end of the Visigothic traditionalism in the court of León and the introduction of Carolingian and northern European culture, as intellectuals and artists came to his kingdom. The reign of Alfonso is considered one of the high points of medieval Castile.

**ALFONSO VII, KING OF LEÓN AND CASTILE** (c. 1104–1157) Known as "the Emperor" (crowned emperor in 1135), he ruled from 1126 to 1157, during a time of considerable upheaval in Castile, owing in large measure to the arrival (c. 1147) of the Almohads from North Africa, who worked to bring down the Almoravid dynasty. Alfonso was considered the last of the Spanish emperors, for in 1128 Portugal, included in the peninsula, was established as an independent kingdom.

**ALFONSO VIII, KING OF CASTILE** (1155–1214) Known as "the Noble" and reigning from 1158 to 1214. He was responsible for breaking the power of the Almohads in Spain in 1212 at the battle of Las Navas de Tolosa, an important turning point in reconquest of Muslim-held lands. The son of Sancho III of Castile, Alfonso spent many years struggling to maintain Castilian independence from the kingdoms of Navarre and León. To this end he established excellent relations with Aragon, receiving aid from Peter II of Aragon in 1185 to halt an invasion by León and Navarre following Alfonso's defeat in that year by the Almohads. In 1212 the king enjoyed his revenge by destroying the Almohads at Las Navas de Tolosa. See also ALMOHADS; SPAIN.

**ALFONSO IX, KING OF LEÓN** (1171–1230) Ruler of León from 1188 until 1230, he was noted for his defeat of the Moors in 1225 near Jaén and Granada, which led to the eventual capture of Seville in 1248. See also SEVILLE.

**ALFONSO X, KING OF LEÓN AND CASTILE** (1221–1284) Long-reigning king (1252–1284), called "the Wise" because of his patronage of the arts and his major contributions to Spanish legal history. The grandson of Emperor Philip of Swabia, Alfonso spent many years working toward his acceptance and coronation as the German king and the Holy Roman Emperor. He was only partially successful, for while a German faction actually elected him king in 1256, the pope refused to give his blessing. More time was wasted fighting the papal decision, but Alfonso finally surrendered his claim in 1275. His wars against the Muslims were more fortunate, and he succeeded in capturing Cartagena and Cádiz in 1262. Alfonso's principal achievement came in the areas of literature and government. He made his court a center of learning and promulgated the Siete Partidas, the massive collection of civil, criminal and constitutional laws. The Alfonsine Tables were also assembled during his reign (c. 1252). There was considerable unrest late in his reign: Nobles protested the Siete Partidas, and his sons plotted among themselves against their father and the French king got involved; Alfonso's reign ended in disarray and humiliation.

**ALFONSO XI, KING OF LEÓN AND CASTILE** (1311–1350) King from 1312 until 1350, Alfonso was the monarch greatly responsible for the strengthening of the monarchies of León and Castile in the 14th century. Only a year old on the death of his father in 1311, he came to his majority in 1325, determined to correct the internal dissension and administrative shortcomings of the kingdom. The powers of the nobles were curtailed in favor of bureaucratic beholders to the crown. By 1348 he made his reforms official, with the *Ordinance of Alcala de Henares.* Most of his reign was spent fighting the Moors, specially the Marinid kings of Morocco. He defeated them at Salado in 1340 and regained the city of Algeciras in 1344. He died at the siege of Gibraltar in 1350, from the plague.

**ALFONSO I, KING OF PORTUGAL** (c. 1109–1185) Also Afonso and Alfonso I Henriques, the first king of Portugal, reigning from 1128 to 1185. He was the son of Henry of Burgundy, count of Portugal, and Teresa, the illegitimate daughter of Alfonso VI of Castile. The relationship of Teresa to Castile allowed her to remain in power even after the death of Henry in 1112, and she became virtual regent until 1128, when Alfonso demanded the right to succeed to his father's titles. A brief war followed, won by Alfonso, who was considered by many to be the king. Allegiance was given to Alfonso VII of León and Castile, but by 1139, after his defeat of the Muslims at Ourique, he was calling himself monarch. Brief struggles erupted with the Castilians over the next years, ending in 1143 with Alfonso VII's recognition of Portuguese independence. See also PORTUGAL.

**ALFONSO II, KING OF PORTUGAL** (c. 1183–1223) Ruler of Portugal from 1211 to 1223, known as "the Fat." He suffered most of his life from a variety of diseases, including leprosy. Nevertheless, his era was marked by his military triumphs in war against the Moors, including a share in the Castilian victory at Las Navas de Tolosa in 1212. He was excommunicated in 1219 over a dispute with the church and the nobles, an excommunication upheld by the pope and in effect at his death from leprosy in 1223. See also PORTUGAL.

**ALFONSO III, KING OF PORTUGAL** (1210–1279) Ruler from 1248 until 1279, whose reign marked the final expulsion of the Moors from Portugal, thus retaking for Portugal the rest of the Algarve. While he fostered economic prosperity and summoned the first *cortes,* or national assembly, in 1254, he came into disfavor with the church by seizing lands alienated to it. He also married a second wife while his first, Matilde, countess of Boulogne, was still alive. At her death this conflict with the church was ended. See also PORTUGAL.

**ALFONSO IV, KING OF PORTUGAL** (1291–1357) Ruler from 1325 to 1357, who joined with Alfonso XI of Castile, his son-in-law, in the victory over the Moors at the Battle of Salado in 1340. His order to assassinate Inés de Castro, mistress of his son Peter, set off a brief civil war in 1355. See also PEDRO I, KING OF PORTUGAL; PORTUGAL.

**ALFONSO V, KING OF PORTUGAL** (1432–1481) Ruler of Portugal from 1438 until 1481; distinguished for his campaigns against the Muslims. He was, however, defeated in his attempts at political expansion in the peninsula. After attaining his majority, Alfonso embarked upon a campaign against the Muslim states of North Africa, capturing Tangiers in 1471, thus earning the nickname "the African." Further ambitions led him to seek to wed Juana la Beltraneja, daughter of Henry IV of Castile, giving himself the pretext that he needed to invade that kingdom and to ascend its throne. Alfonso and Juana were betrothed but never married. His plans nevertheless contributed to the start of his war of succession with Ferdinand and Isabella. Isabella and Ferdinand defeated him in 1476 at the Battle of Toro. Unable to secure French assistance, he threatened to abdicate in 1477 but remained on the throne until his death in 1481. See also PORTUGAL.

**ALFRED THE GREAT** (849–899) King of Wessex from 871 to 899; considered one of the most enlightened rulers of the Middle Ages. He was the fifth son of Aethelwulf of Wessex and seemingly the least likely to succeed to the Anglo-Saxon throne. In 853 he journeyed to Rome and was accepted as godson by Pope Leo IV, perhaps an indication that his father, with whom he had traveled, desired him to enter the clergy. Two years later he visited the Carolingian court of Charles the Bald. Always interested in learning, he was nevertheless unable to learn the rudiments of Latin until around the age of 10; he loved English poetry, owing in part to his mother, who gave him a book of poems.

Following the death of Aethelwulf in 858, his surviving sons succeeded him. Alfred did not actively serve the Crown until 868, when he and his brother Aethelred I marched against a Danish army that was threatening the Mercian king Burgred. In 871 the Danes returned, and the two brothers once more set out to defeat them. Aethelred died that year, and Alfred was made king despite the fact that Aethelred had sons. The virtually unthinkable had happened, but Alfred assumed command of the Saxon domain. Years of hard, bitter fighting ensued against the Danish armies of conquest. The year 871 was particularly difficult, as the Saxons were reduced to guerrilla warfare, a situation that continued for seven years. Finally, in 878, to his fort in Somerset marshes, Alfred gathered a large army and attacked, defeating the Danes at the Battle of Edington. One result of the Saxon victory was the baptism of the Danish king Guthrum. Saxon troops occupied London in 886, marking the recognition of Alfred as monarch of all England not under Danish domination, the end of years of war and the formal signing of the treaty with the

Danes that established the DANELAW. The few years of peace were broken in 895 with an invasion of Kent by another Danish host, supported by Danes who had settled in East Anglia. By 896 these Norsemen had been beaten back on land and sea.

The success of Alfred's victories was found in the policies that he established in the kingdom. He created an organized, levied army with naval support, erected forts throughout southern England and maintained secure relations with his neighbors, such as Mercia, although ties were guaranteed through his marriage to the Mercian Ealhswith and the marriage of his daughter, Aethelflaed, to Aethelred of Mercia. Alfred thus established the elements that would be used by his heirs to conquer the Danelaw and to unify all of England.

Of equal importance to his martial achievements were Alfred's artistic, intellectual and legal triumphs. Having mastered Latin, he, with ASSER, translated or had translated Latin books into English while encouraging European scholars to come to his court. Among the more significant translations were the works of Bede, Augustine, Gregory I, Boethius and Orosius. The ANGLO-SAXON CHRONICLE was begun during his reign, and interest in art and architecture increased, due to the influence of foreign artisans. Alfred utilized the legal codes established by Offa of Mercia, Aethelbert of Kent and Ine of Wessex, applying them to his own people's needs. Alfred died in 699, but he had created a state thoroughly altered from the one he had inherited. He earned the title "the Great" because of his success in war and in peace. He attained legendary, even mythic, stature and had a biography written by his friend and adviser Asser. In his own translation of Boethius's *Consolation of Philosophy*, Alfred paraphrased what might have been his own epitaph: "I may say that it has always been my wish to live honourably, and after my death to leave to those who come after me my memory in good works." See also ENGLAND; WESSEX.

**ALGIERS** An ancient city in Algeria, Africa, founded originally by the Phoenicians. During the Carthaginian and Roman eras it was called Icosium. A period of decline was ended in the 10th century by the Berbers of North Africa, who made Algiers a leading port of trade in the Mediterranean. It achieved greatness in the 17th century under Turkish domination. See also TRADE AND COMMERCE.

**ALHAMBRA** A series of magnificent palaces and gardens created on a plateau just below Granada by the Nasrid rulers of that city. The Alhambra has long been considered the most impressive artistic and architectural achievement of the Moors in the Iberian Peninsula. The palaces were built between 1238 and the late 14th century during the reigns of several rulers of Granada. Muhammad I initiated the expansion of the original ninth-century Alcazba, or citadel, in 1238, work carried on by his son Muhammad II (c. 1273–1303). Yusuf I did much to beautify and strengthen the Alhambra from 1333 to 1354, and Muhammad V, from 1362 to 1391, was responsible for such architectural embellishments as the Court of the Lions.

Typical of Spanish conquest, much of the Alhambra was effaced or marred, some parts being destroyed to erect palaces more European in style, such as those by Pedro de Machuca in 1526 for Charles V. Renovation began in 1828, in an attempt to restore the Alhambra to its former greatness. The most important or beautiful sections of the complex include the Court of the Lions, Hall of the Two Sisters, Hall of the Ambassadors and Court of the Myrtles. The Gardens of the Generalife warranted the admiration of landscape artists. See also ART AND ARCHITECTURE, ISLAMIC; GRANADA; MOORS.

**'ALI** (c. 600–660/661) The fourth caliph and the first imam of the Shiites in Islamic history, the cousin and son-in-law of Muhammad and the figure considered by the Shiite element in Islam to be the only legitimate heir to the Prophet. 'Ali ibn Abi Talib was born at Mecca around 600, the son of the chief Abu Talib. Growing up in the house of Muhammad, 'Ali was thought to be one of the earliest converts to the teachings of the Prophet, remaining one of his most faithful companions. According to tradition, he slept in Muhammad's bed in order to impersonate him when Muhammad fled to Medina in 622, thus duping the Meccan plotters who planned to murder him. 'Ali then joined Muhammad in Medina, married the Prophet's daughter Fatima and had two sons: Hasan and Husayn. 'Ali served over the next years in a variety of capacities, including secretary, but his most important role was that of general. He proved himself both gifted and fearless.

Muhammad's death in 632 precipitated the crisis of the succession that was to have great historical and religious significance. A temporary solution was found in the election of ABU BAKR as the first caliph. 'Ali did not press his claims, nor did he recognize the caliphate of Abu Bakr for six months. Instead, he retreated to private life and under the caliph Umar, who was chosen over him, became noted as an authority on Islamic law. Relations with the third caliph, Osman, were poor, but 'Ali refused to accept the leadership of the faction that was rebelling against Osman. He also did not take part in Osman's assassination in 656. 'Ali was subsequently elected at Medina, although not necessarily by a unanimous vote.

From the start there was opposition to ʿAli's caliphate, from the Prophet's old companions, the party of Osman and numerous factions in Egypt and in Syria. Mu'awiya, governor of Syria, rebelled, and 'Ali was preparing to set out with a force against him when a Meccan faction, supported by Aisha, wife of the Prophet, rose up against 'Ali. There followed the Battle of the Camel in 656, where 'Ali triumphed. In 657, however, his continued struggle with Mu'awiya remained unresolved, and it was agreed that arbitration was to be used. This displeased many of his own supporters, who denounced his conciliatory measures. Called the Kharijites, they were routed at Nahrawan in 658 with such losses that many from 'Ali's own army began to defect. His situation worsened in 659 when during arbitration it was decided that Osman had acted according to the law of God and thus had not deserved death. Mu'awiya seized Egypt and was now a rival caliph. How events might have turned out is a mystery, for in 660 or 661, 'Ali was stabbed by a Kharijite, Abd al-Rahman ibn Muljam al-Muradi, dying two days later. He was buried at Kufah.

Many of the sources on 'Ali were understandably biased one way or another, writings made more controversial by the importance given him by the Shiites. All could agree that he was a genuinely spiritual man who adhered strictly to the Koran and to the Sunnah (sayings of Muhammad). His own writings were compiled in the 11th century by Al-Sharif al-Radi in the *Nahj al-balagha (Road of Eloquence).* 'Ali was also called "the Haydara" (the Lion). See also ISLAM.

**'ALI AD-HADI** (d. 868) Tenth imam of the Shiite cause.

**'ALI AL-RIDA** (d. 818) Eighth imam of the Shiite cause.

**ALIDS** See ISLAM.

**ALIGHIERI, DANTE** See DANTE ALIGHIERI.

**'ALI ZAYN AL-ABIDIN** Fourth imam of the Shiite cause in Islam.

**ALMOHADS** The successors to the Almoravids as the ruling Islamic power in North Africa and the Iberian Peninsula from about 1147 to 1269. Originally a Berber tribe, the Almohads (Arabic for *al-Muwahhidun,* or "Those Who Acclaim the Oneness of God") were organized as resistance against the Almoravids in Africa. Their base was Tinmel in the Atlas Mountains, and their founder was the conservative Muslim Muhammad ibn Tumart, who not only preached fundamentalism but was hailed by the Berbers as the Mahdi, or the prophesied savior, claiming to be a direct descendant of Muhammad, the prophet. He purged the Almohad army of any lukewarm followers before embarking on a war against the Almoravids, a struggle finished successfully by his successor, Abd al-Mu'min, with the capture of Marrakesh in 1147. Almohad consolidation focused almost exclusively on Northern Africa (the Maghrib) from about 1147 to 1171, leaving Andalusia virtually untouched. In 1171 Abd-al-Mu'min's son, Abu Yaqub Yusuf (who reigned from 1163 to 1184), arrived in the peninsula, captured Seville and made it his capital in a rapidly subjugated Moorish dominion. Abu Yusuf Yaqub (1184–1199) succeeded his father as ruler over an empire beset by rebellions in Africa and attacks by the Christians of the Iberian Peninsula. He defeated the rebels and routed Castile in 1195, taking the title al-Mansur ("the Victorious") after his victory at Alarcos.

His son, Muhammad al-Nasir (1199–1214), continued the conflict with the Christian kingdoms of the peninsula, a mistake culminating with the catastrophic Battle of Las Navas de Tolosa (1212) that shook the Almohad regime and was to cause permanent weakness. Years passed before the opposing parties in Africa would be strong enough to dispense with Almohad mastery, but in 1236 the appointed viceroy of the Hafsids, in Tunis, proclaimed himself independent. The Banu Marin, called the Marinids, founded a new state at Fez, capturing Marrakesh in 1269, ending the Almohad dynasty. The Almohad administration was overly centralized and plagued with doctrinal and political crises to the extent that it proved disastrous, especially in the face of a defeat of the magnitude of Las Navas de Tolosa. See also ISLAM.

**ALMORAVIDS** The name given to a strictly austere religious movement and a Berber dynasty that extended its rule over northwestern Africa and Moorish Spain from the middle of the 11th century into the 12th. Almoravid was a derivation of the Arabic *al-murabit* and *murabitin,* the former a Muslim living in a sanctuary or hermitage and the latter a title for the faithful Islamic soldier who fought against unbelievers.

By the 11th century, the Umayyad caliphate in Spain had declined to such a state that by 1031 its holdings in Africa, especially in the Maghrib, or the Berber lands of the Sahara, were virtually autonomous and were governed by two tribal groups, the Zanata and the Sanhaja. Islamic teaching was not perfect among the tribes, however, and in 1036 the Sanhaja head, Yahya ibn Ibrahim al-Judali, sought a teacher to improve the knowledge of his people. Abd Allah ibn Yasin al-Jazuli was that person. Later, with the aid of Yahya ibn Umar, chief of the Lamtuna, in the Sanhaja confederacy, ibn Yasin created a powerful force of *murabitin,* with whom he fought the Berbers in order to bring them under his strict code of Islam, the cause being taken up by ibn Umar's brother, Abu Bakr ibn Umar, and by Abu Bakr's cousin, Yusuf ibn Tashfin.

Yusuf proved a brilliant general and statesman, establishing Almoravid administration at Marrakesh around 1070. He acknowledged the ascendancy of the Abbasid caliph of Baghdad, receiving from him the rank of *amir al-muslimin* (commander of the Muslims) in 1073. By 1084 virtually all of North Africa was under Almoravid domination, from Tangier to Marrakesh to Algiers. Further opportunity for expansion presented itself in 1085 when Yusuf finally accepted the appeals of the smaller kingdoms of the Moors in the peninsula (the so-called *taifas* of Andalusia) for help against Alfonso VI, King of Léon and Castile, who was partitioning Islamic territory in the Iberian Peninsula. In 1086 Yusuf landed in Spain, and on October 23, he defeated Alfonso at Zallaqa. By 1088 he was back in Andalusia, this time subjugating the Moors and placing them under direct Almoravid rule. The concept of a North African and Iberian empire found full expression with the accession of Yusuf's son 'Ali ibn Yusuf, who ruled from 1106 to 1147. As his father had learned in 1099 from his defeat at the hands of Rodrigo Díaz de Vivar (El Cid) at Valencia, the Christians proved formidable opponents; subsequent wars with them were inconclusive.

'Ali ibn Yusuf's reign demonstrated both the strengths and the growing weaknesses of the Almoravids. Although the dynasty still controlled extensive territories and was noted for its influence in the spread of Islam in Africa and as a bulwark against Christian advance, it was handicapped and eventually destroyed by its own diversity. The Almoravids were a minority in the peninsula, and the Christian kings were better prepared for Muslim armies. In Africa the rebel Almohads gained victories and supporters against a government reduced to using Christian mercenaries, and in Andalusia the depleted treasury could not pay for war with the Christian realms. Abd al-Mu'min, caliph of the

Almohads, triumphed in 1146 over the Almoravid army at Ishaq and Marrakesh. Surviving members of the family maintained control from the Balearic Islands until 1203, when they were crushed. The Almohads were their vanquishers and heirs.

Almoravid art was generally far more austere than that of both its Umayyad predecessor and Almohad successor, a reflection of the strict religiosity of the Saharan Berbers and the nomadic lives they led. Of particular artistic interest was the Great Mosque of Hemcen in Algeria, completed in 1097. Scholarly appraisal of the Almoravids has been changed significantly because of the recent discovery of new sources, including Abd al-Wahid al-Marrakushi, al-Bakri and Ibn Khaldun. See also ISLAM.

**ALP ARSLAN (1)** (d. 1072) Sultan of the great Seljuk Empire from 1063 to 1072 and a faithful successor to the Seljuk throne who did much to expand the possessions and political power of the Turks in medieval Islam. The son of the chieftain Chaghri Beg and nephew of the sultan Toghril-Beg, Alp Arslan assumed his father's position as governor of the eastern provinces in 1058, aided in his task by the vizier Nizam al-Mulk. In 1063, however, when Toghril-Beg died without an heir, Alp marched from his eastern capital of Marw to Rayy, the Seljuk capital in Iran, seized control of the state and proclaimed Nizam al-Mulk his vizier, or chief minister.

Already an accomplished general, the new sultan crushed all possible rivals, giving the empire a unified government and sense of grandeur and embarking on a massive campaign of conquest. Using the nomadic and hard-fighting Turkish levies, Alp captured Ani, the Armenian fortress, in 1064 and swept into Georgia in 1068. Returning to the east, he seized large portions of Turkhistan before naming his son, Malik-Shah, heir apparent in 1066. Next came Anatolia, where Turkish advances were making inevitable a collision between the Seljuks and the Byzantine Empire. The Byzantine emperor and general Romanus IV Diogenes launched a counterattack in 1068 and another one in 1071. This second operation forced Alp to abandon his planned invasion of the Fatimid caliphate in Egypt. On August 16, 1071, the Byzantine army was destroyed at the Battle of Manzikert, and the Turks controlled virtually all of Anatolia. Alp was assassinated in November 1072, however, his throne inherited by his son Malik-shah. The Turks were now to play a major role in the course of events over the next centuries. See also SELJUK TURKS.

**ALP ARSLAN (2)** Seljuk sultan of Syria from 1113 to 1114. He was the successor to the long-reigning Duqaq. See also SELJUK TURKS.

**ALPERT OF METZ** An early-11th-century monk of Saint Symphorian of Metz and the author of two works: a history of the bishops of Metz and *De diversitate temporum.* The history, preserved only in fragments, was actually a continuation of the work of Paul the Deacon up to the year 984; *De diversitate temporum (On the Changing Times,* c. 1024–1025) consisted of observations on contemporary life.

**ALPHANUS OF SALERNO** (c. 1015–1085) Archbishop of Salerno (1058), translator of classical works and author of medieval treatises and poetry. Alphanus was born in Salerno, taught there and, after becoming a member of the Benedictine order at Monte Cassino, returned to serve as abbot and later as archbishop. An ardent classicist, he was influential in the revival of interest in classical civilization in the Italian Peninsula. He also translated medical texts from Greek into Latin. A pilgrim to the Holy Land, Alphanus was one of the earliest humanists. See also GREGORY VII.

**ALPHONSE DE POITIERS** (1220–1271) Count of Poitiers and Toulouse, son of Louis VIII of France and brother of Louis IX. Alphonse accompanied Louis IX on the Seventh Crusade, acting as a hostage following Louis's capture by the Muslims in 1250. Returning to France, he served as regent of the country with Charles of Anjou until 1254. He embarked on the Eighth Crusade in 1270 but died on the way home. As he was without children, his appanage, the county of Toulouse, was seized by the crown. See also LANGUEDOC; TOULOUSE.

**ALSACE** A region of western Europe situated in the present French departments of Haut-Rhin and Bas-Rhin. Part of the Roman holdings during the imperial era, Alsace fell in the early fifth century to the Alamanni, who settled there around 450–470. Subsequently given to Carloman, the son of Pepin the Short, it became a Frankish duchy before incorporation into Charlemagne's German kingdom (East Frankish kingdom) in the ninth century and the Holy Roman Empire in the 10th.

**ALTHING** The name given to the parliament of Iceland. Convened first in 930, it was the earliest of its kind in Europe. See also ICELAND.

**ALTICHIERI** (c. 1320–1395) Italian painter of Verona, called Altichieri da Zevio. He was most active in Verona but also painted in Padua. He was heavily influenced by Giotto, and in turn his work had an impact upon Titian, Masaccio and Donatello. Altichieri's major works were the frescoes for sacral buildings in both Verona and Padua; the most well known were in the Basilica Santo Antonio in Padua (in the Chapel of Santo Felice and the Oratorio of Santo Giorgio) and the Church of Santo Stefano and Sant'Anastasia in Verona. See also VERONA.

**ALVAREZ DE VILLASANDINO, ALFONSO** (d. 1425) A court poet in Castile who was considered one of the finest and most influential lyric poets in Spain. His departure from the use of Galician to Castilian language marked an important development in Spanish poetry.

**AMADEUS VI, COUNT OF SAVOY** (1334–1383) Called the "Green Count," he held his title from 1343 to 1383, using every opportunity to extend, with cunning and ruthlessness, the power and prestige of Savoy. Receiving his title in 1343, Amadeus immediately formed alliances with noble families who could support him and then embarked on military campaigns to extend Savoy's hold throughout the Alps, gaining control of Lake Geneva, Lake Neuchâtel and the Piedmont. He fought in the Crusade at Nicopolis against the Turks, capturing Gallipoli in 1365. In 1382 he died of plague in southern Italy, while fighting for Queen Joanna of Naples. His epithet came from his green velvet tournament costume. See also SAVOY.

**AMADEUS VII, COUNT OF SAVOY** (1360–1391) The son of and successor to Amadeus VI, called the "Red Count" after wearing that color at his marriage to the niece of the king of France in 1377. He succeeded his father as count of Savoy in 1383 but died in 1391, after a pharmacist gave his doctor the wrong medicine for the treatment of an ailment. See also SAVOY.

**AMADEUS VIII, DUKE OF SAVOY** (1383–1451) Ruler of Savoy from 1391 to 1451, succeeding his father, Amadeus VII, as count after his sudden demise in 1391. Only eight years old at the time, Amadeus was placed in the care of his grandmother, Bonne of Bourbon, who forced his mother, Bonne of Berry, to leave Savoy. His reign was characterized by the continuation of Savoy expansion, aided by his elevation to duke by Emperor Sigismund (1410–1437) in 1416. Geneva, Bresse and other parts of Liguria were acquired, but two attempts to seize Genoa and Naples failed. He abdicated in 1434, in name only, in favor of his son, Louis. In 1440 he was elected antipope by various prelates who were in dispute with Pope Eugene IV (1431–1447). Taking the name Felix V, he retained his title of pope until 1449, when, having lost his political allies, he surrendered to Nicholas V (1447–1455). He remained a cardinal of the church for two years until his death. See also ANTIPOPE; SAVOY.

***AMADIS OF GAUL*** Known also as *Amadís de Gaula,* an Arthurian prose romance of chivalry, composed in the late 13th century or early 14th by a Spanish (probably from León) writer, thought originally to have been Juan Lobeira (a view no longer widely accepted). Based on an earlier French verse, *Amadis of Gaul* has survived only in part and was most likely changed, rewritten or was the basis of modified versions by several subsequent authors. The chief instrument of change in the work was Garcí Rodríguez de Montalvo during the late 1400s. *Amadis of Gaul* was extremely popular throughout Europe, especially in the 16th century, given its motif of valor and antiquated chivalry.

**AMALARIC** (d. 531) King of the Visigoths from 503 to 531, the son of Alaric II, grandson of Theodoric the Great (ruled 511–526), king of the Ostrogoths by his daughter Amalaric. Still an infant on Alaric's death in 507, Amalaric faced opposition to his kingship from a Visigoth party supporting Gesalec, a bastard son of Alaric. Theodoric then marched into the Iberian Peninsula (c. 507) to defend his grandson, spending the next years fighting until Gesalec was finally killed in 511. For the next 11 years Theodoric shared the throne with Amalaric until, in 526, Amalaric assumed sole power. He married Chrotichildis, sister of the Frankish king Childebert, but being an Arian, Amalaric refused her right to practice orthodox Christianity. This insult was used as a pretext for Childebert to make war on Amalaric. After losing a battle, Amalaric was killed near Barcelona, possibly by his own outraged retinue. See also VISIGOTHS.

**AMALARIUS OF METZ** (c. 775–c. 850) Bishop of Trier, a liturgist and an influence in the Carolingian renaissance. Amalarius was a student of Alcuin, earning his appointment to the See of Trier in 811. Trusted by the Carolingian kings, he was sent in 813 to Constantinople by Charlemagne as his ambassador, and in 935 Louis the Pious named him as the replacement for the exiled archbishop of Lyons, Agobard. On Agobard's return, Amalarius faced a formidable opponent. Amalarius wrote a four-volume treatise, *De ecclesiasticus officus,* widely known as *Liber officialis,* in which he presented a union of the liturgies used in the Roman and Gallican rites. Considered extremely important in preserving elements of the medieval liturgy, his work had broad appeal but was attacked at the Synod of Quiercy in 838 by orthodox clerics, led by Agobard, as being, in part, heretical. See also GALLICAN RITES.

**AMALASUNTHA** (d. 535) Daughter of King Theodoric, married to the Visigoth Amal Eutharic, regent over the Ostrogoths from 526 to 535 and queen with Theodahad in 535. On the death of Theodoric in 526, his 10-year-old grandson Athalaric (526–534) was named successor. Amalasuntha was appointed regent. From the start she had difficulty holding the loyalty of her people, who were unaccustomed to being governed by a woman. Her attempts at a classical education for Athalaric failed in 531, when a Gothic upbringing was imposed on him. The young ruler died in 534, and Amalasuntha, very unpopular, married Theodahad to retain power. He turned on her and imprisoned her before allowing her murder by her enemies in May 535. See also OSTROGOTHS.

**AMALFI** City in southern Italy, southeast of Naples, in Campania, on the Gulf of Salerno. Amalfi was not important to Italian trade until the sixth century, when the Byzantines made the city one of their acquisitions in Italy. By the early ninth century Amalfi had become one of the earliest maritime republics in the peninsula and one of the wealthiest, competing with Genoa, Venice and Pisa as a trading power in the Mediterranean. In 1131 the city was seized by King Roger II of Sicily and later sacked by the forces of Pisa (c. 1135). These were blows that Amalfi could not sustain, and its decline thereafter was swift. See also TRADE AND COMMERCE.

**AMALRIC** (d. 1206) Scholar and philosopher known also as Amalric of Bène after his town near Chartres. A student and teacher in Paris, he was the author of highly controversial ideas concerning the nature of God. His ideas were furthered by his students and adherents who called themselves the Amalricians. Essentially, Amalric believed that God was the universe and that all things took their form from God. Furthermore, pure love of God meant an inability to sin, a concept seized on by the Amalricians as grounds for the rejection of the concept of transubstantiation and the belief in the opposition of good and evil. Amalric and the Amalricians were condemned in 1210 at the Council of Paris and in 1215 at the Fourth Lateran Council. See also DAVID OF DINANT.

**AMALRIC I** (1137–1174) King of Jerusalem from 1162 to 1174, the successor to his brother, Baldwin III. His reign was marked by the long struggle with Nur ed-Din of Syria for control of Egypt. Amalric came to the throne at the age of 25, remarkably intelligent and a fine statesman. Around 1163 he set out to conquer Egypt and destroy the Fatimid caliphate. Nur ed-Din, however, launched a counterattack from Syria, delaying Amalric's advance until 1167. That year he captured Alexandria, exacting tribute from the Fatimids. The following year he reentered Egypt with the aim of dominating the entire country. In 1169 he was met and defeated by Shirkuh, lieutenant of Nur ed-Din, and the kingdom of Jerusalem was thus threatened by Syria and Egypt. Although he was compelled to annul his marriage to his cousin Agnes of Courtenay, his children were given full legitimacy. Thus his son, Baldwin IV the Leper, succeeded him in 1174. Amalric was considered very honorable by Muslim writers, Ibn al-Athir and others, who noted that he had no equal among the Frankish kings. See also JERUSALEM, KINGDOM OF; SALADIN.

**AMALRIC II** (c. 1155–1205) King of Jerusalem from 1198 to 1205 and the king of Cyprus from 1194 to 1205. An ambitious nobleman, Amalric, also known as Amalric of Lusignan, was given the position of constable of Jerusalem before receiving word in 1194 that his brother, Guy of Lusignan, had died, leaving the throne of Cyprus vacant. Chosen to succeed to the Frankish realm, he immediately made plans to improve his political position by betrothing his sons to the daughters of Henry of Champagne, husband of Isabella, queen of Jerusalem. When Henry died in 1197, negotiations soon began for Isabella to wed Amalric, and in 1198 Jerusalem and Cyprus were united. Amalric proved a competent king in Cyprus and regent in Jerusalem. He made peace with the Muslims, renewing it in another treaty in 1204, just before he died. On his death, Cyprus was given to his son Hugh, and Jerusalem reverted to his widow, Isabella. See also CYPRUS; JERUSALEM, KINGDOM OF.

**AMALRIC OF LUSIGNAN** See AMALRIC II.

**AMANDUS, SAINT** (d. c. 675) Called the Apostle of Flanders, an ascetic and missionary who helped to spread Christian doctrine in the regions of Flanders and Carinthia. Taught by Saint Austregisilus in Bourges, he received his appointment as a bishop through the influence of the Merovingian king Clotaire in 628, working over the next years to establish monasteries. Much of the information about him, as well as those writings attributed to him, is dubious.

**AMBROISE** A later-12th-century chronicler also called Ambrose d'Evereux and Ambrose. A Norman poet and minstrel, probably from Evereux, Ambroise accompanied Richard I the Lion-Hearted on the Third Crusade, recording the event in an epic poem of 12,000 lines, the *Estoire de la guerre sainte (History of the Holy War)*. The only surviving copy was a Norman manuscript, actually a version of the original. Ambroise's work was the source for Richard the Canon's *Itinerarium Regis Ricarde (On the Expedition of King Richard)*.

**AMIENS** A city in northern France, in the department of Somme. Amiens was the historical capital of Picardy on the river Somme. The city accepted Christianity in the fourth century when, according to tradition, it was introduced by Saint Firmin. During the Middle Ages it was known as a center for textile manufacture and for one of the finest cathedrals in Europe. Amiens's cathedral was begun about 1220 by Robert du Luzarches and completed about 1280. It is a brilliant example of French Gothic architecture. See also CATHEDRAL; GOTHIC ART AND ARCHITECTURE.

**AL-AMIN** (d. 813) Abbasid caliph from 809 to 813, the son of Harun al-Rashid (786–809) and brother of al-Mamun and al-Khazim. Attempting to ensure the continuation of the Abbasid line, Harun, before his death, made arrangements for the succession: al-Amin was to be caliph, and al-Mamun was to govern the eastern half of the empire, under al-Amin and as al-Amin's appointed heir. Al-Khazim was to be the governor of Mesopotamia. This arrangement was set in motion immediately after Harun's death in 809, but al-Amin soon attempted to gain total control of the caliphate. He dismissed al-Khazim and, in 810, named his son, Musa, as his heir. Civil war erupted between al-Amin and al-Mamun, lasting three years. Al-Mamun's generals, Tahir ibn Husain and Harthamah, routed al-Amin's armies, besieged and captured Baghdad and put the caliph to death. The historian Jalaludin described al-Amin as handsome but wholly unsuited to govern. See also ABBASID CALIPHATE.

**AL-AMIR** the tenth Fatimid caliph of Egypt. See FATIMID CALIPHATE.

**AMR IBN AL-'AS** (d. 663) Prominent companion of the prophet Muhammad and an early Islamic general who was one of the most successful figures in the first years of Arab conquest. Originally a member of the Kuraysh tribe in Arabia, he converted to Islam about 630 and was sent to the southeastern regions of the country by Muhammad to convert the local inhabitants. Later serving as one of the officers under Abu Bakr's caliphate, Amr helped subjugate Palestine. In 641, however, he undertook his most memorable campaign, the invasion of Egypt. He crushed the Byzantine garrison there, entering Alexandria in 642. His administration of Egypt was imaginative and sound, including the creation of al-Fustat, a Muslim fort town at the Nile delta. In 657 he aligned himself with Mu'awiya against 'Ali in the struggle to decide the succession to the caliphate.

**AMSTERDAM** The present-day capital of the Netherlands, founded early in the 13th century as a small fishing village. It expanded quickly, using its position on the coast to become a major link between the traders of the north and the merchants of Flanders. The right to charge tolls came in 1275, and by the late 15th century the city was given imperial recognition by Emperor Maximilian I. The name Amsterdam derived from the dam constructed in 1270 between the city's dikes, built to prevent flooding, the so-called Amstel-dam. See also TRADE AND COMMERCE.

**ANACLETUS II** See INNOCENT II.

**ANASTASIUS II** (d. 498) Pope from 496 to 498. Anastasius provoked dissension in Rome immediately following his election by attempting to improve relations with the Eastern Church through a conciliatory gesture to Acacius, patriarch of Constantinople, who had been deposed and excommunicated by Pope Felix III in 484 as a heretic, despite the fact that Anastasius had been elected to make peace with the Eastern Church. Dante, in the *Inferno*, placed Anastasius in hell.

**ANASTASIUS III** (d. 913) Pope from 911 to 913, during the height of the powerful Roman official Theophylact's influence in Rome.

**ANASTASIUS IV** (d. 1154) Pope from 1153 to 1154, originally known as Corrado di Subura. He helped to repair fragile diplomatic relations between Frederick I Barbarossa and the city of Magdeburg.

**ANASTASIUS I, BYZANTINE EMPEROR** (430–518) Ruler from 491 to 518 and the successor to Zeno, he inherited an already stable imperial system and made increasing improvements to it. Holding posts in the imperial treasury and in the bodyguard, Anastasius was chosen as emperor in 491, mainly through the influence of the imperial widow, Ariadne, whom he had married, and because he was orthodox and not a foreigner. He immediately initiated many reforms in administration, including taxation, land grants, advances in the government and steps to reduce corruption. His reign was also noted for its civil wars and internal revolts.

Anastasius recognized the position of Theodoric the Great, king of the Ostrogoths in Italy, but eventually sent a fleet to attack the Italian coast (c. 508). This was not the only military involvement of his reign, for in 502 he began with Persia another war that ended in 505 with the signing of a peace treaty. Incursions by the Bulgars and Slavs prompted him to construct a wall from the Black Sea to the Sea of Marmara in 512. Anastasius also adhered to the belief of Monophysitism, thus causing unrest in parts of the empire and creating a severe breach with the Roman church. He died in 518 and was followed not by his appointed heirs but by Justinian I, chief of the palace guard. See also BYZANTINE EMPIRE.

**ANASTASIUS II, BYZANTINE EMPEROR** (d. 721) Ruler from 713 to 715, originally known by the name Artemis. An imperial secretary before being chosen as emperor in 713 after the removal of Emperor Philippicus, he tried to implement both military and political reforms but was deposed in 715 in favor of the rebellious tax collector Theodosius III; a six-month civil war followed. Retiring to a monastery, Anastasius was executed by Leo III after attempting to reclaim the throne. Among his reforms were the strengthening of Constantinople's defenses and the selection of Rhodes as a naval base. See also BYZANTINE EMPIRE.

**ANASTASIUS BIBLIOTHECARIUS** (c. 815–c. 879) Called "the Librarian" (Bibliothecarius), a theologian, influential religious figure and the foremost Greek scholar of the ninth century. Named antipope in 855 by opponents to Benedict III, he lost political support because of lack of discipline and was later reconciled to the church. Henceforth from 862 he was a librarian to the Roman church throughout the pontificates of Nicholas I (858–867) and Adrian II (867–872). He was also a writer on the early popes.

**ANATOLIA** See ALP ARSLAN; BYZANTINE EMPIRE; CONSTANTINOPLE; CONSTANTINOPLE, LATIN EMPIRE OF; CRUSADER STATES; CRUSADES; MANZIKERT, BATTLE OF; MONGOLS; NICAEA, EMPIRE OF; OTTOMAN EMPIRE; SELJUK TURKS; TRADE AND COMMERCE; TREBIZOND, EMPIRE OF.

**ANDALUSIA** The southern region of Spain and the territory occupied for centuries by the Moors. Although the name Andalusia (Arabic, al-Andalus) was used by the Moors to represent all of the Iberian Peninsula, it came to define only those territories actually possessed by the Muslims in the south of the country. Andalusia was to retain forever the flavor of Islamic life and culture.

The southern Iberian peninsula was the Roman province of Hispania Baetica but was occupied by the fifth century by the Vandals, who probably gave it the etymological root for al-Andalus, the land of the Vandals. The Muslims invaded in the eighth century, establishing a presence that would remain until the late 15th century. During that time a number of Islamic dynasties rose and fell, including the emirate and later caliphate of Córdoba (755–1031), the Reys de Taifa (1031–1086), the Almoravids (1086–1147), the Almohads (1150–1250) and numerous other small kingdoms, including that of the Nasrid kings of Granada. Traditional ties between North Africa and Andalusia were broken in the 14th century, and the last of the Moorish domains, that of Granada, fell in 1492 to the Reconquista. Henceforth the entire country was Christian.

**ANDREA DEL CASTAGNO** See CASTAGNO, ANDREA DEL.

**ANDREW I** (d. 1061) King of Hungary from 1046 to 1060, killed in 1060 while fleeing from his brother, Bela I (1060–1063), during civil strife. See also HUNGARY.

**ANDREW II** (1175–1235) King of Hungary; one of the most significant of the Hungarian monarchs, who reigned from 1205 to 1235, succeeding his brother, Ladislas III (1204–1205). From the start he ruled with abandon, granting important tracts of land to his closest supporters in the nobility and spending vast amounts of revenues and the treasury on wasteful and expensive projects or extravagances. With the economy on the verge of ruin, he then embarked on a crusade to Palestine in 1217. Affairs were in such a state by 1222 that he found himself facing hostile barons who forced on him the GOLDEN BULL. This document placed limits on royal power and was called the "Magna Carta of Hungary." See also HUNGARY.

**ANDREW III** (d. 1301) The last of the Arpad kings of Hungary, ruling from 1290 to 1301. While many in Hungary disputed his affiliation with the Arpad dynasty, Andrew was nevertheless crowned in 1290, after being brought back from Italy. He proved an excellent king but died without heir, and thus the Arpad dynasty, which had ruled from 907, was ended. See also HUNGARY.

**ANDREW BOGOLYUBSKY** See BOGOLIYUBSKI, ANDREI.

**ANDREW OF CRETE, SAINT** (c. 660–740) Archbishop of Gortyna, Crete, poet and an important writer of hymns in the Eastern Church. A deacon at Constantinople serving in the Church of Santa Sophia, he was made archbishop of Gortyna about 692. At the Synod of Constantinople in 712, he professed belief in Monothelitism but recanted in 713. A composer of hymns, he was credited with inventing a new kind of canon or type of hymnography. Among his works was the Great Canon, used still by the Greek church.

**ANDREW OF WYNTOUN** See WYNTOUN, ANDREW OF.

**ANDRONICUS I COMNENUS** (c. 1120–1185) Byzantine emperor from 1183 to 1185, and the last member of the Comnenus dynasty. The cousin of Emperor Manuel I Comnenus (1143–1180), he was thus related to Manuel's successor, Alexius II Comnenus (1180–1183) and was bitterly opposed to the regency of Alexius's mother, Mary of Antioch. In 1182, supported by an army, Andronicus marched to Constantinople. In the name of Alexius he liquidated all political opponents and ensured the death of Mary. Having assumed power, he had Alexius strangled, marrying his 13-year-old widow and embarking on a violent reign. The focus of his imperial policy was reform of government and an abandonment of Manuel's Western approach to government. This brought a sharp response from the West: William II of Sicily attacked Greece in 1185, and the riots caused in Constantinople by the fall of Thessalonica led to Andronicus's murder by a mob; he was literally torn to pieces. See also BYZANTINE EMPIRE.

**ANDRONICUS II PALAEOLOGUS** (1260–1332) Byzantine co-emperor from 1272 and emperor from 1282 to 1328, the son of Michael VIII Palaeologus, who inherited little of that ruler's drive or belief in a renewed Byzantine Empire. Andronicus preferred scholastic pursuits and theology to war and thus allowed the state of Byzantine affairs to decline very seriously. The army was reduced in size, the defenses weakened and the navy replaced altogether with Genoese mercenary forces that were worthless and earned the enmity of a far greater Venetian naval presence. However, he also strengthened the Byzantine church and fostered monasticism. A revival in art and culture could

Fra Angelico angel, monastery of San Marco, Florence

do nothing to preserve the state against the gains of the Serbian empire in the Balkans and the Ottoman Turks in Anatolia. Andronicus, who disliked his grandson Andronicus III, was forced in 1325 to name him co-emperor and then, in 1328, to abdicate entirely, when he entered a monastery. See also BYZANTINE EMPIRE.

**ANDRONICUS III PALAEOLOGUS** (1296–1341) Byzantine co-emperor from 1316 and emperor from 1328 to 1341. Andronicus III was not the first choice as successor to his grandfather, Andronicus II, because of his frivolous and violent nature, but in 1316, joined by several Byzantine nobles, including John VI Cantacuzenus, he forced the aged emperor to make him co-ruler. In 1328 he deposed Andronicus II and ruled alone. As emperor, Andronicus III proved acceptably competent; he rebuilt as best he could the deteriorating Byzantine war machine, making progress in the improvement of the navy. See also BYZANTINE EMPIRE.

**ANDRONICUS IV PALAEOLOGUS** Byzantine emperor from 1376 to 1379. See also BYZANTINE EMPIRE.

**ANGELICO, FRA** (c. 1395/1400–1455) One of the greatest painters of the Middle Ages, also viewed as a leading artist of the Renaissance. His date of birth has recently been judged to have been about a decade earlier than previously believed (from c. 1387 to c. 1395), an important change, placing him in the era of the quattrocento and forcing a reappraisal of the chronology of his many works. He was born Guido di Pietro near Florence, probably studying under Battista di Bagio Sanguigni. Sometime between 1418 and 1421 he joined the Dominican order at the house of Santo Domenico of Fiesole, taking the religious name of Fra Giovanni da Fiesole but earning the title Fra Angelico for the sacred subject of his paintings.

Fra Angelico did not cease painting as a Dominican, leaving a large body of masterpieces, especially the frescoes at Santo Marco in Florence and in the Chapel of Sacraments in the Vatican. Pope Nicholas V summoned him back to Rome in 1445 to paint a private chapel with frescoes from the lives of Saints Lawrence and Stephen. Serving as the prior of Fiesole from 1449 to 1452, he died in 1455 with his prestige ever increasing. It was written of him that he was without equal.

**ANGELI DYNASTY** The ruling dynasty of the Byzantine Empire from 1185 to 1204.

**ANGEVIN DYNASTY** The name of two dynastic branches, one English and the other French. Both lines of the Angevins were descended from French nobility and claimed control of England through William the Conqueror (d. 1087), who led the Norman Conquest in 1066. Specifically, the English, or Plantaganet, Angevins ruled England from 1154 to 1216. The dynasty was founded by Geoffrey, count of Anjou, whose son reigned from 1154 to 1189 as King Henry II. His sons both succeeded to the throne, Richard I the Lion-Hearted (ruled 1189–1199) and John Lackland (1199–1216). The Angevins controlled vast parts of France, including Brittany, Normandy, Maine, Anjou, Touraine, the duchy of Aquitaine, Gascony and Toulouse, called by scholars the Angevin Empire. The French Angevins came to control parts of Naples and Sicily through

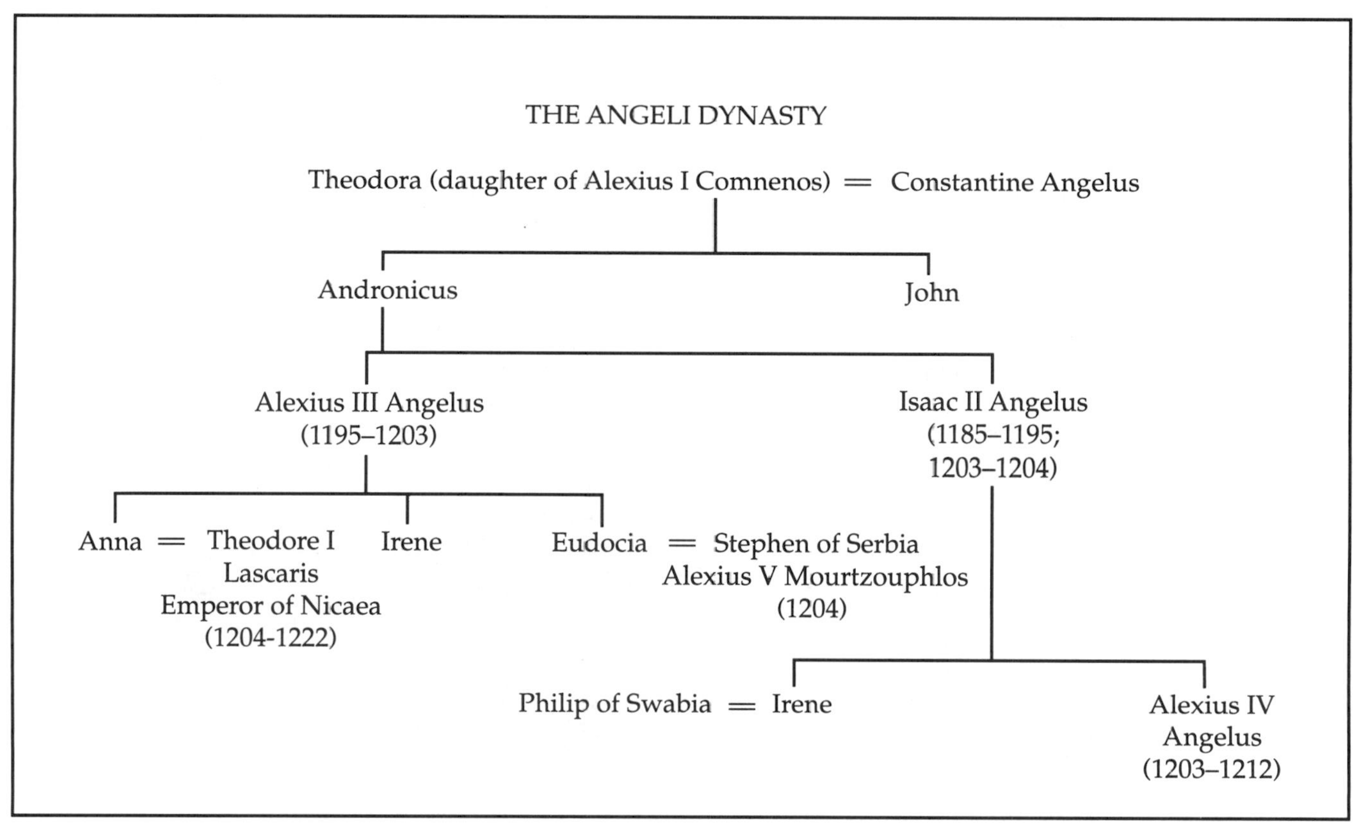

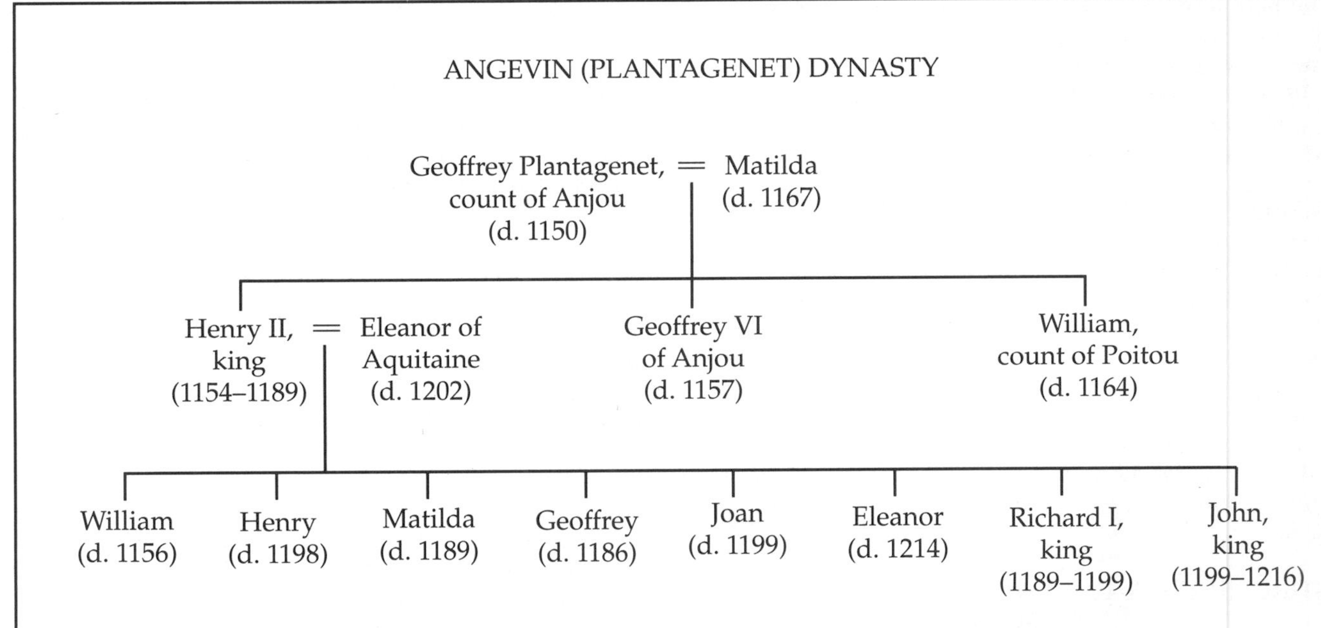


acquisitions of Charles of Anjou (c. 1240s–1280s), René I (1430s–1440s) and John (d. 1470). See also ANJOU and the Genealogical Table.

**ANGILBERT** (c. 750–814) Court official and a noted Carolingian poet. Angilbert was educated at Aachen in the palace school headed by Alcuin, who later called him "Homer" for his poetry. Abbot of Saint Riquier from 781, Angilbert wrote poems on various subjects, from monastic life, to the family of Charlemagne, to events in his own time. He fathered two illegitimate children by Charlemagne's daughter Bertha.

**ANGLES** An important Germanic tribe, originally from the area of Schleswig, the Angles took part in the invasion of the British Isles in the fifth and sixth centuries. They settled in regions throughout the north and east of Britain, laying the foundations for the kingdoms of Northumbria, East Anglia and Mercia and giving their name to England. See also ANGLO-SAXONS; ENGLAND; SAXONS.

**ANGLO-FRENCH WAR** See HUNDRED YEARS' WAR.

***ANGLO-SAXON CHRONICLE*** Annals covering the history of England throughout the Anglo-Saxon era and the time of the Normans, ending with the year 1154. A major historical source for events in the island, the chronicle was begun (c. 892) by monks at Winchester during the reign of Alfred the Great. See also ANGLO-SAXONS.

**ANGLO-SAXON CHURCH** The name used by church historians to denote the Christian church in England from the sixth century until the Norman Conquest in 1066. The early history of the Anglo-Saxon church was characterized by evangelization from both the Continent and Ireland, creating disputes over a number of issues including the date for observing Easter. A union of Roman and Celtic observances was achieved through the Synod of Whitby in 663 and through the labors of Theodore of Tarsus, archbishop of Canterbury. Noted figures in the Anglo-Saxon period include Bede, author of *A History of the English Church and People,* and King Alfred the Great. The Viking invasions of the eighth and ninth centuries threatened but did not destroy the Christian church in the British Isles. Further ties to the European mainland were made in the 10th century through Saint Dunstan, until the Norman invasion in 1066 ended the Anglo-Saxon tradition, bringing about the removal of virtually every Anglo-Saxon prelate, except for Wulfstan of Worcester, replacing them with Norman-French prelates. See also ANGLO-SAXONS; CELTIC CHURCH; NORMANS.

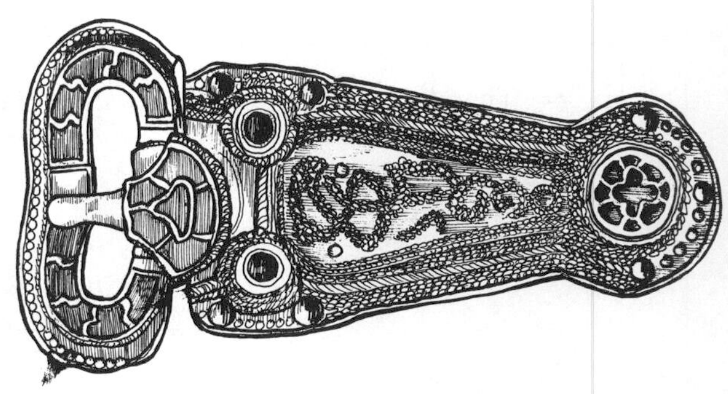
Anglo-Saxon belt buckle

**ANGLO-SAXONS** The term used to describe the Germanic tribes who settled in ENGLAND in the fifth century, dominating and developing until the conquest by the Normans in 1066. Traditionally, little evidence has been available to trace the migrations of the Germans into the British Isles, but general agreement has been reached that from the fifth to the sixth century extensive settlement took place in the eastern and northern sections of Britain, at the expense of the Celtic inhabitants. According to Bede and *Ecclesiastical History,* these Germans were, in the main, of three tribes: the Saxons, Jutes and Angles. The name Anglo-Saxon thus originated in the eighth century and was used by writers to mean not only these three tribes but also the other Germanic strains, who had migrated to Britain and had settled along the coast.

The term Anglo-Saxon found importance because, from the eighth century, it enabled German descendants to distinguish themselves from those from the Continent, the people whom Bede called Antiqui Saxones. The Anglo-Saxons laid the foundations for the language, culture and life of the English. Kings, from the time of Alfred the Great, used the title *rex Angul-saxonum,* and, after the Norman Conquest, Anglo-Saxon meant the native people of England, to distinguish them from the newcomers. See also ANGLES; JUTES; SAXONS.

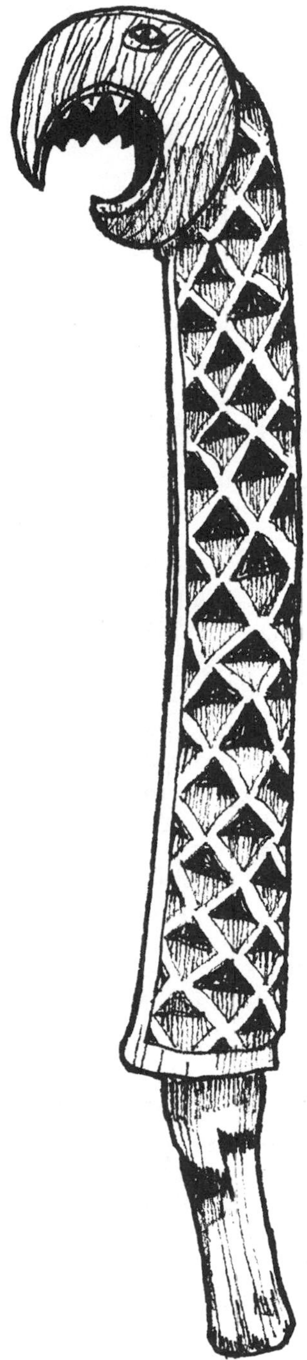
Anglo-Saxon ship's prow

**ANJOU** A territory in France now occupying the department of Maine et Loire and, in the Middle Ages, the possession of the powerful House of Anjou (the Angevin dynasty). Originally the home of a Celtic people called the Andes, Anjou fell under Roman occupation and was later occupied by the Franks. Under the Carolingians it became a county, and by the 10th century it was a prominent feudal holding. In 1129 Geoffrey Plantagenet inherited the county from his father, Fulk V, King of Jerusalem. The father of Henry II, king of England (1154–1189), Geoffrey died in 1151, and Anjou thus became part of the vast English holdings in France. Henry II and Eleanor of Aquitaine were both buried there. Philip II Augustus, king of France (1180–1223), regained Anjou in 1204. Charles, brother of Louis IX (1226–1270), was count of Anjou from 1246 to 1285, founding the dynasty that would see members on the thrones of Poland, Hungary and Naples. Anjou became a duchy in 1360, and the Angevin dynasty died out in 1481; the duchy became part of the royal domain in 1486. See also FRANCE.

**ANNA COMNENA** See COMNENA, ANNA.

**ANNE DE BEAUJEU** (c. 1460–1522) Daughter of Louis XI, sister of Charles VIII, king of France, and regent of the country for the first years of Charles's reign. The wife of Pierre de Bourbon, lord of Beaujeu, Anne was entrusted with the regency by her father, as Charles was considered too young at 13 and intellectually immature to assume power. In 1483 Louis died, and Anne, despite the protests of the duke of Orléans, took the reins of government. Her most important act was the arrangement of the marriage between Charles and Anne of Brittany in 1491. See also FRANCE.

**ANNE OF BRITTANY** (1477–1514) Twice queen of France, duchess of Brittany and one of the most powerful women of the age. Anne became duchess on the death of her father, Francis I of Brittany, in 1488, and despite her reportedly plain appearance, she was pursued by the French nobles and foreign kings eager to lay claim to Brittany, a rich prize. Charles VIII of France (1483–1498), urged by his sister, Anne de Beaujeu, compelled her to marry him in 1491, despite the previous arrangement made between Anne and Emperor Maximilian I. Charles died in 1498 without heirs, so another union was negotiated with Louis XII, Charles's successor. Anne was a rare figure in

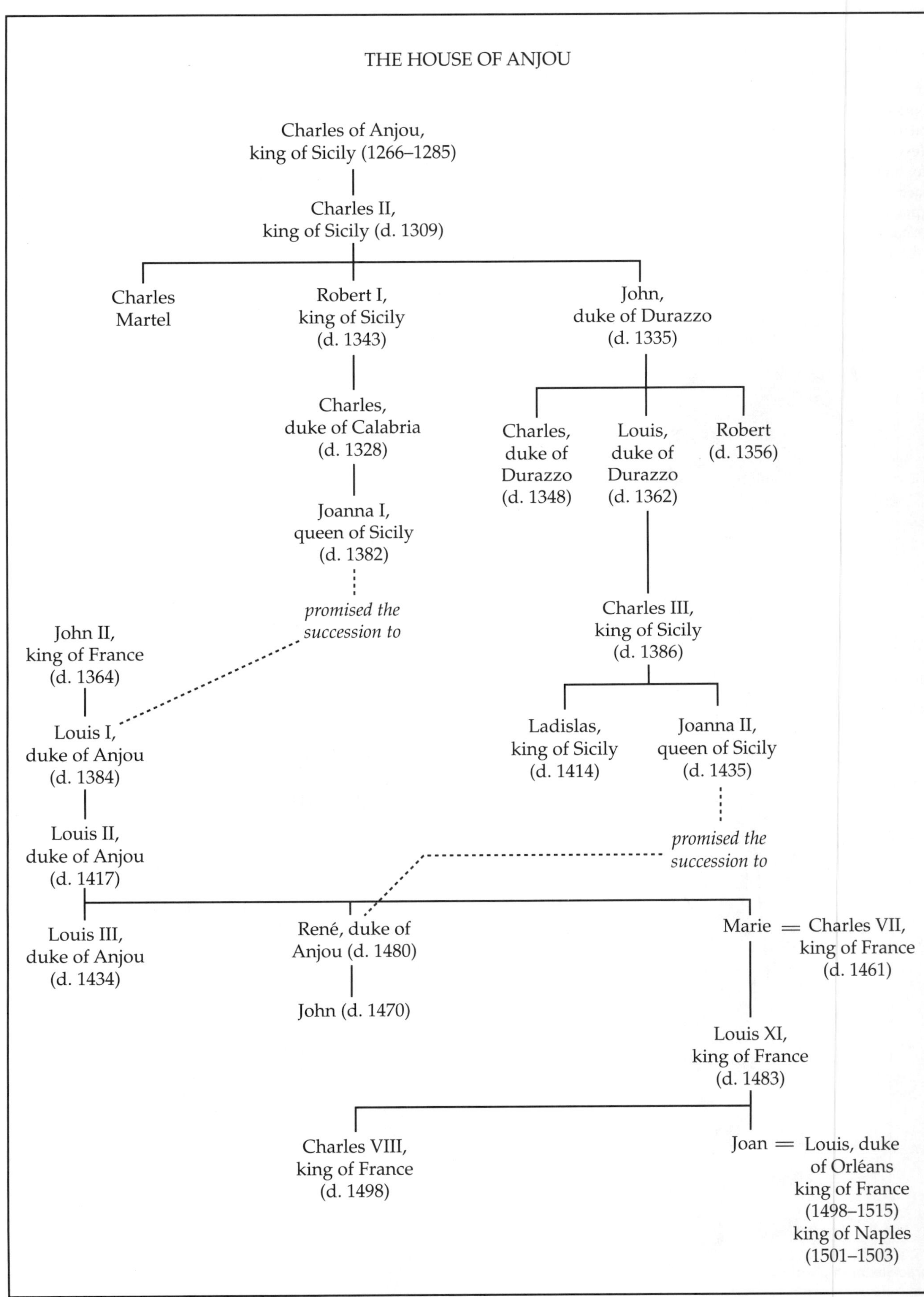
THE HOUSE OF ANJOU
Charles of Anjou, king of Sicily (1266–1285)
Charles II, king of Sicily (d. 1309)
Charles Martel
Robert I, king of Sicily (d. 1343)
John, duke of Durazzo (d. 1335)
Charles, duke of Calabria (d. 1328)
Charles, duke of Durazzo (d. 1348)
Louis, duke of Durazzo (d. 1362)
Robert (d. 1356)
Joanna I, queen of Sicily (d. 1382)
promised the succession to
John II, king of France (d. 1364)
Charles III, king of Sicily (d. 1386)
Louis I, duke of Anjou (d. 1384)
Ladislas, king of Sicily (d. 1414)
Joanna II, queen of Sicily (d. 1435)
Louis II, duke of Anjou (d. 1417)
promised the succession to
Louis III, duke of Anjou (d. 1434)
René, duke of Anjou (d. 1480)
Marie = Charles VII, king of France (d. 1461)
John (d. 1470)
Louis XI, king of France (d. 1483)
Charles VIII, king of France (d. 1498)
Joan = Louis, duke of Orléans king of France (1498–1515) king of Naples (1501–1503)

the era, for she cared for both of her husbands and was loved by them but never ceased in her attempts to preserve the integrity and independence of Brittany. In this she failed ultimately, for her daughter married the future Francis I of France, linking forever Brittany to the throne of France. See also BRITTANY.

**ANSELM OF CANTERBURY, SAINT** (c. 1033–1109) Archbishop of Canterbury and an important figure in the Scholastic movement. The son of a noble Lombard family in Aosta, Anselm became a monk at Bec in Normandy in 1059. Having studied theology, in 1063 he was named prior and in 1078 abbot of Bec, succeeding Abbot Herluin. It was the desire of the English clergy that he become archbishop of Canterbury in 1089, but disputes with king William Rufus delayed his assumption of the see until 1093, when the king fell ill. As archbishop, Anselm struggled bitterly with William Rufus and Henry I over the rights of the church, especially investiture. He faced exile twice, in 1097 and in 1103. A compromise was made in 1107 at the Synod of Westminster with Henry's renunciation of the right to invest bishops with religious ceremony if the bishops agreed to pay homage to the king.

Anselm was long held in high regard not only as the most able archbishop of Canterbury but also as one of the leading minds of the Middle Ages. He applied intellectual reasoning to defend his faith, was a leader of the Scholastic school and conceived the ontological argument for God, whereby the simple notion "that than which no greater can be conceived" for the existence of God proves His being. His *credo ut intelligam* ("faith leads to understanding") marked him as a philosophical innovator, a realist and an influence on the thought of Thomas Aquinas and the later philosophers René Descartes and Karl Barth. Anselm left a large body of works, including the *Monologion* (*Monologue*), *Proslogion* (*Addition*) and his masterpiece, *Cur Deus Homo?* (*Why Did God Become Man?*).

Saint Anselm of Canterbury

**ANSELM OF LAON** (c. 1050–1117) French theologian, early member of the Scholastic movement and an important teacher. Anselm was educated at Bec by Anselm of Canterbury before teaching in Paris and establishing a school at Laon (c. 1100) with his brother Rudolf. This theological institution grew in stature, claiming as students Peter Abelard and William of Champeaux. Anselm wrote an influential commentary on the Bible. See also ANSELM OF CANTERBURY, SAINT.

**ANSELM OF LUCCA** See ALEXANDER II.

**ANSGAR, SAINT** (801–865) First archbishop of Bremen and the missionary known as the "Apostle of the North." Also called Anskar, he worked tirelessly to evangelize Scandinavia, becoming its patron saint. Originally from Picardy, Anskar entered the monastery at Corbie, where he was educated. He then went to Corvey in Westphalia and established a school at Schleswig. Confronted by opposition from the local pagans, he was forced to leave but had been successful in visiting Denmark. In 828 he returned to the Frankish territories, only to be asked by the Swedes to go to their country as a missionary. He thus became the first Christian preacher in Sweden. He was made bishop of Hamburg in 832 and archbishop of Hamburg-Bremen in 848. Ansgar's last years were spent continuing missionary work in Denmark and Sweden and opposing the practice of slavery. Scandinavia reverted to PAGANISM after his death in 865.

**ANSPRAND** (d. 712) King of the Lombards in 712, having acted as regent for the young king Liutbert in opposition to the usurper Aribert II. A civil war erupted, and when Liutbert was murdered in 701, Ansprand fled the country. In 711 he returned with an army and defeated Aribert, becoming king for only a few months. His successor was his son, Liutprand. See also LOMBARDS.

**ANTHEMIUS OF TRALLES** A sixth-century Byzantine architect and mathematician who was one of the principal architects, with Isidorus of Miletus, in the construction of the Hagia Sophia in Constantinople from 532 to 537. See also HAGIA SOPHIA.

**ANTHONY OF KIEV, SAINT** (d. 1073) An ascetic and monk generally considered the founder of Russian monasticism. Anthony entered the Greek Orthodox monastery of Mount Athos in Greece about 1028, where he was trained in the monastic life and encouraged to go to Russia. Returning to his homeland, he settled in a cave on Mount Berestov as a hermit. He soon attracted followers in such numbers that Izyaslav, prince of Kiev, gave Anthony the mountain, on which to establish his monastery. It was the basis for all subsequent Russian monastic institutions and exerted a deep influence on the Russian Orthodox Church. Anthony was included in the *Russian Primary Chronicle.* See also RUSSIA.

**ANTHONY OF NOVGOROD** Thirteenth-century Russian monk, archbishop of Novgorod and a writer. He was consecrated to the see of Novgorod in 1211, spending the next years promoting the city's evolution as an economic power and acting as domestic and foreign mediator. After a visit to Constantinople around 1200, he wrote the *Pilgrim's Book,* in which he recorded life in the city of Constantinople in such exceptional detail that it is considered one of the most important sources on 12th-century Byzantium. See also BYZANTINE EMPIRE.

**ANTHONY OF PADUA, SAINT** (c. 1195–1231) A doctor of the church, a Franciscan friar and the best known of the early Franciscans. Born Ferdinand to a noble family of Lisbon, he joined the Augustinian canons in 1210 but reportedly saw the relics of several martyred Franciscans from Morocco and was filled with a desire to follow in their footsteps. He became a Franciscan in 1220, setting out for Morocco, only to fall ill. Returning to Europe, the Franciscan discovered by chance his gift for preaching. His skills were put to work in the schools of Bologna, Montpellier and Toulouse, and he was acclaimed for his sermons in France and Italy. He died in 1231 on his return to Padua, where he was buried. See also FRANCISCANS.

**ANTIOCH** A city in present-day southeastern Turkey (Antakya), in ancient times the foremost metropolis of Syria. Situated on the main trade route from the East to the West, it enjoyed great prosperity during the Seleucid dynasty and the Roman Empire, and became one of the five patriarchates of the Christian church. It was still wealthy and influential at the start of the sixth century but then suffered a series of calamities: a fire in 526, earthquakes in 526 and 528, and a plague later in the century; the city was also sacked in 540 by the Persians, who occupied it until 628. Byzantine control of Antioch was broken in 638 with the Muslim invasion of Syria. From 638 to 969, Antioch declined steadily with the movement of trade routes to the East, and it could retain only military importance.

The Byzantines reclaimed and rebuilt the city in 969 but were unable to sustain lasting restoration, as the Seljuk Turks conquered Antioch in 1084. Fourteen years later Crusaders besieged and captured it, making it the center of a feudal principality. Wealth and economic growth marked the Crusader era, a final period of good fortune that ended in 1268, when the Mamluks marched in and destroyed Antioch. See also CRUSADER STATES.

**ANTIPOPE** The term for a rival claimant for the papacy, who was elected, appointed or assumed the title of pope illegally or in opposition to the legitimate holder of the title. Antipopes emerged in the early centuries of Christian history, but they were especially common during the Middle Ages, for a number of reasons. Doctrinal disagreements, secular interference, double or confused elections, the struggle between the popes and the Holy Roman Empire in the 11th and 12th centuries and the Great Schism of 1378–1415 were among these causes.

A list of antipopes traditionally has presented scholars with some difficulty because of disagreements concerning papal legitimacy from one century to another, the reason for the election of an antipope and the obscurities resulting from inadequate information or records. A possible compilation of antipopes would include the following:

Hippolytus (217–235)
Novatian (251–258)
Felix II (355–365)
Ursinus (366–367)
Eulalius (418–419)
Lawrence (498–505 and 501–506)
Dioscorus (530)
Theodore (687)
Paschal (687)
Constantine II (767–768)
Philip (768)
John (844)
Anastasius Bibliothecarius (855)
Christopher (903–904)
Boniface VII (974, 984–985)
John XVI (997–998)
Gregory VI (1012)
Benedict X (1058–1059)
Honorius II (1061–1064)
Clement III (1080, 1084–1100)
Theodoric (1100–1101)
Albert (1101)
Sylvester IV (1105–1111)
Gregory VIII (1118–1121)
Celestine II (1124)
Anacletus II (1130–1138)
Victor IV (1138)
Victor IV (1159–1164)
Paschal III (1164–1168)
Calixtus III (1168–1178)
Innocent III (1179–1180)
Nicholas V (1328–1330)
Clement VII (1378–1394)
Benedict XIII (1394–1417)
Alexander V (1409–1410)
John XXIII (1410–1415)
Clement VIII (1423–1429)
Benedict XIV (1425)
Felix V (1439–1449)

**ANTI-SEMITISM** See JEWS AND JUDAISM.

**ANTONELLO DA MESSINA** (c. 1430–1479) Influential Italian painter who was credited with the introduction of oil painting in the Flemish style to Italian artists of his own time. Probably trained in Naples, he returned to Messina in 1457 and there continued to develop his work in oils, creating form with the use of color instead of shade. His *Portrait of a Condottiere* (1475) made his reputation, and the next years were spent in Venice (and perhaps Milan), gaining further acclaim for such works as *St. Sebastian* and *The Virgin Annunciate.*

**ANTONINUS, SAINT** (c. 1389–1459) Archbishop of Florence, reformer and one of the founders of the notions of moral theology. He joined the Dominican order in 1405 and eventually became the head of monasteries in Rome, Naples, Siena, Fiesole and elsewhere. In 1436 he laid the foundations of the Florentine monastery of San Marco and constructed a church with the support of Cosimo de Medici. An archbishop in 1446, he was also the author of *Summa moralis* (also known as the *Summa theologica*) and a world history. His charity and reported miracles were legendary.

**ANTWERP** A port city situated in modern Belgium, on the Schelde River near the North Sea. Because of its location on the coast, Antwerp was inhabited in the early second century. Occupied by German tribes, by the ninth century it was held by the Holy Roman Empire, eventually passing to the dukes of Brabant, who encouraged its economic development. Throughout the later Middle Ages the city was a member of the Hanseatic League. See also TRADE AND COMMERCE.

**ANUND JAKOB** King of Sweden from about 1022 to 1050. Anund adhered to his father's policy of supporting Christianity in SWEDEN.

**ANUND AND BJORN** Rulers of SWEDEN during the early ninth century.

***APPOLONIUS OF TYRE*** A medieval romance of unknown authorship that enjoyed great popularity throughout Europe. It was based on a lost Greek original, dating perhaps from the third century A.D., and the first Latin version of the story was written by Venantius Fortunatus in the sixth century. Other versions appeared from the 9th to the 11th century, often in other compilations, such as the *Gesta Romanorum* and the *Pantheon* by Geoffrey of Viterbo.

**APULIA** The southeastern region of Italy, originally comprising only ancient Apulia but eventually including parts of Calabria as well. Its capital was Bari, but there were other notable cities, such as Taranto, Lecce and Brindisi. After the collapse of Roman imperial power in the sixth century, Apulia was occupied by the Goths, Lombards and Byzantines. The latter were driven out in the 11th century by the Normans, who established the duchy of Apulia. Among its rulers were Robert Guiscard, William of Sicily and Roger II, who made it part, with Calabria and Sicily, of the Kingdom of Sicily in the mid-12th century. It fell under the domination of the Holy Roman Emperor Frederick II (1215–1250), who was responsible for its lavish beautification program. He died there in 1250, and Apulia declined in importance as a province.

**APULIA, DUCHY OF** See APULIA; SICILY.

**AQUILEIA** A city near the Adriatic coast in northeastern Italy. Throughout Roman imperial eras Aquileia was one of the most important trading centers in the Roman Empire because of its position along the trade routes between Italy and the Danubian provinces. Sacked in 452 by the Huns, it sustained damage so severe that not only was its social and economic strength ruined, but the devastation resulted in the eventual commercial dominance of Venice. The Lombards captured Aquileia in 568, making the site a portion of the duchy of Friuli. Aquileia fell to the Venetians in 1419–1420, making official a subjugation long a reality. The patriarch of Aquileia held a powerful position in the Christian world for many centuries. See also VENICE.

**AQUINAS, THOMAS** See THOMAS AQUINAS, SAINT.

**AQUITAINE** A region in southwestern France that was for centuries part of the Roman province of Gaul and was considered a great prize when captured by the Visigoths under Euric in the fifth century. In 507, possession passed to the Merovingian Franks when they defeated the Visigoths at the Battle of Vouille. Under the Franks, Aquitaine became an important kingdom in their empire; two of its kings were Charlemagne's son Charles (d. 811) and Pepin I (d. 838), Charlemagne's great-grandson. The kingdom reverted to a duchy in 877, falling under the influence of the counts of Poitiers in the 10th century. William X was the last duke of Aquitaine. His daughter, Eleanor of Aquitaine, first married Louis VII of France (1137–1180) and then Henry II of England (1154–1189). Aquitaine was thus disputed between England and France from the 12th to the 15th century, ending with French domination at the termination of the Hundred Years' War in 1453. The duchy was reduced over the years both in size and in importance, losing areas such as Gascony. In 1422, Aquitaine was formally annexed to the royal domain. See also FRANCE; GASCONY; HUNDRED YEARS' WAR.

**ARABIA** The arid desert region situated in the Arabian Peninsula between the Red Sea, Arabian Sea and the Persian Gulf and bordering many modern Middle Eastern states such as Yemen, Oman, Jordan and Iraq. Arabia's place in both medieval and world history was assured if for no other reason than its having been the cradle of Islam. The Islamic history of Arabia began in 622, year one of the Muslim calendar with Muhammad's flight to Medina from Mecca. Years of growth and expansion came next as Muhammad and his faithful disseminated their new creed throughout the region and beyond. After the Prophet's death in 632, Abu Bakr, the first caliph, crushed the attempts of Arabian tribes to repudiate their allegiance to Islam.

Abu Bakr pointed the way toward the establishment of the Islamic empire, expansion that became reality under Umar, the second caliph. Many Muslims left the Arabian Peninsula during these years to settle in occupied lands, while new converts began making pilgrimages to Mecca, diversifying the population. Wealth, meanwhile, poured into the holy cities of Mecca and Medina, but the fabric of Islamic unity was torn by the rise of the Shiites, who supported the claims of 'Ali. Coinciding with the formation of the Umayyad caliphate in Spain was the seizure of parts of the Arabian Peninsula by the Shiites, who for a time controlled Mecca and Medina. However, most Muslims belonged to the Sunni majority of Islam, and the Umayyads derived their administration and prestige from the Arab aristocracy who had joined Muhammad.

All of this changed with the fall of the Umayyads in 750 and the victory of the Abbasids, who set up their own caliphate. Already the trend had been visible during the Umayyad era, namely that the Arabian Peninsula was no longer the heart of the Islamic empire. The Abbasids confirmed this by moving the capital of the caliphate to Baghdad in present-day Iraq. Hegemony was shattered in the peninsula as Mecca and Medina retained importance only in the religious sense. Strife between the Shiites and the Sunnis would rage for centuries. In the ninth century the powerful faction of the Ismailis produced two dynasties that would dominate the peninsula, the Qaramitians and the Fatimids. The Qaramitians actually plundered Mecca of the revered and holy Black Stone of the Kaaba, and only their Fatimid counterparts could induce them to return it. Another party, the Hasanids, created a sharifate around Mecca, officially subject to the greater powers outside Arabia (the Abbasids or the Fatimids) but actually independent. Other Arab dynasties were the Sulayhids of Yemen, the Ibadites of Oman, the Nabhani of Oman, the Zaydis of Yemen and the Rasulids of Yemen, who succeeded the Ayyubids.

Ayyubid supremacy over Fatimid Egypt in 1171 led Saladin to dispatch an army to the Arabian Peninsula. Yemen was seized, and Sunni doctrine was given permanency throughout the peninsula. The Mamluks replaced the Ayyubids but continued the prudent policy of caring for the places of pilgrimage. They were removed by the Ottomans in 1517, who would develop the Holy Cities even further, most notably under Sultan Suleyman the Magnificent in the 16th century. See also ISLAM.

***ARABIAN NIGHTS*** See THOUSAND AND ONE NIGHTS, THE.

**ARABIC ART AND ARCHITECTURE** See ART AND ARCHITECTURE, ISLAMIC.

**ARAGON** A powerful kingdom and one of the leading states in the Iberian Peninsula during the Middle Ages. Aragon (or Aragón) played a major role not only in the reconquest of the peninsula but in Mediterranean affairs as well. Aragon proper referred specifically to a region in northeastern Spain in the Pyrenees and on the Ebro plain, including Zaragozza, Huesca and Teruel. In time it claimed ascendancy over Catalonia and Valencia.

The Kingdom of Aragon was established in 1035 when Sancho III of Navarre bequeathed to his third son, Ramiro I, the county of Aragon. This area was transformed into a royal domain, and Ramiro reigned from 1035 to 1063. Succeeding kings added new possessions inhabited by the Moors to the south (to the Ebro River) and the Pyrenee districts to the north. More acquisitions followed, such as Navarre in 1076. In 1137 Aragon was without a ruler, and Ramon Berenguer IV of Catalonia wed the Aragonese heiress Petronila, ensuring stability dynastically and also expanding the Iberian and maritime opportunities for the kingdom, henceforth called the Crown of Aragon. Navarre regained its independence in 1134, a loss that did not prevent Aragon from signing the Treaty of Cazola in 1179, effectively dividing the Iberian peninsula power between Aragon and Castile.

From 1229 to 1235 James I captured the Balearic Islands, a first but significant overseas addition to the fledgling Aragonese empire and a victory that balanced the setback of Pedro II's support of the Albigensians in France and defeat at Muret in 1213. Valenica fell in 1238 to James, and under Pedro III in the war of the Sicilian Vespers in 1282 Aragon claimed Sicily. Continued growth in the Mediterranean dominated Aragonese policy: an Aragon-based family ruled Sicily, Sardinia was taken in 1326 after struggles with Genoa and Pisa and the imperial might of Aragon reached its height under Alfonso V the Magnanimous. He attacked Genoan Corsica and then made an arrangement with Joanna II, the queen of Naples, to succeed to the throne of Naples. A war ensued over the rights to the Neapolitan crown, a conflict won by Alfonso in 1442. Alfonso moved the Aragonese court to Naples and remained there until 1458, when he died.

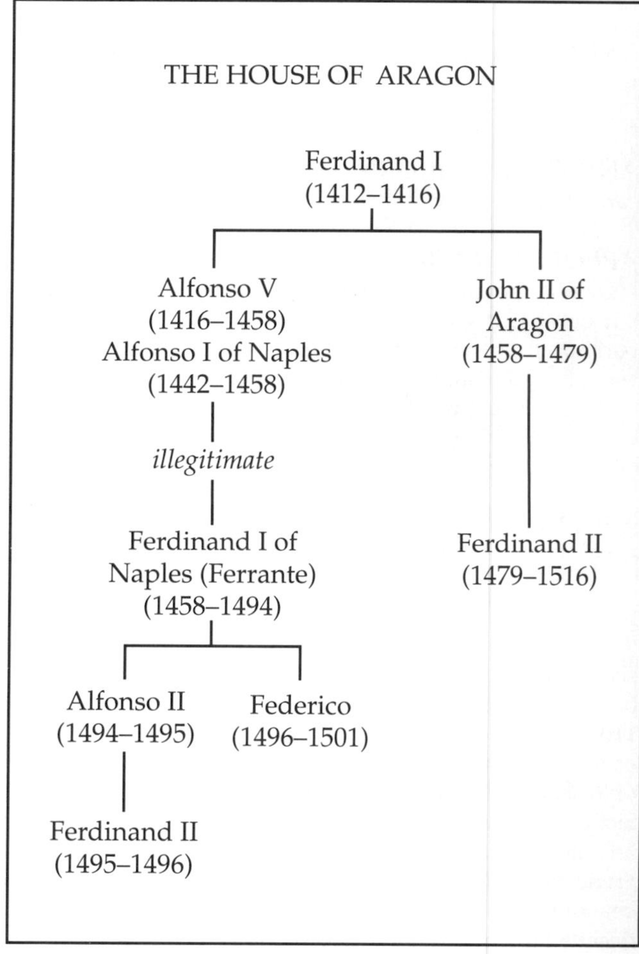

Ferdinand I became king of the Crown of Aragon in 1479. Ten years earlier he had married Isabella of Castile, and thus the two kingdoms of Aragon and Castile were united. Aragon retained its own internal administration. See the Appendix for individual rulers; see also BARCELONA; CASTILE; CATALONIA; CORSICA; GENOA; MOORS; NAPLES, KINGDOM OF; NAVARRE, KINGDOM OF; PISA; RECONQUISTA; SARDINIA; SICILIAN VESPERS; SICILY; VALENCIA; ZARAGOZA.

**ARCHITECTURE, BYZANTINE** See ART AND ARCHITECTURE, BYZANTINE.

**ARCHITECTURE, ISLAMIC** See ART AND ARCHITECTURE, ISLAMIC.

**ARGYROPOULOS, JOHN** (c. 1415–1487) Byzantine scholar, humanist and teacher, who was known both in Constantinople and in Italy. He visited Italy for the first time sometime before 1434 and returned in 1439 with the Byzantine emperor John VIII Palaeologus (1425–1448) to attend the Council of Florence. In 1442 he was teaching at the University of Padua, Piero and Lorenzo di Medici among his pupils. When Constantinople fell in 1453, he fled to the Peloponnesus; he then went to France before taking up a professorship in Florence and finally settling in Rome in 1471. Little of his writing was ever published, although his translations of Aristotle were important. Argyropoulos was remembered especially for his influence in the revival of classical learning in Italy.

**ARIANISM** A major heresy in the Christian church from the fourth century to the late 5th that divided Christianity in the Roman Empire and had a lasting influence on converted Germanic tribes. Advanced by the priest Arius (c. 250–336), the doctrine taught that Christ was not divine but a demigod. Arianism was opposed by practitioners of orthodox Christianity, and a struggle raged for years on both spiritual and temporal battlefields. Condemned by the Council of Nicaea in 325 and virtually dead after the Council of Constantinople in 381, the heresy prospered among the numerous tribes beyond the Roman Empire, thanks to the evangelization efforts of Ulfilas, an Arian missionary. Thus, when the Goths and Vandals burst upon the weakened Western Empire, they were not only pillagers but religious persecutors of the vanquished. This was especially true in Africa under the yoke of Vandal domination. The conversion of the Franks, under the insistence of the Frankish king Clovis, to orthodox christianity in 496 was a major blow to Arianism, for the Franks smashed the Arian Goths and the Byzantine Christians destroyed the Vandals in 534–535. See also HERESIES; LOMBARDS.

**ARIBERT I** King of the Lombards from 653 to 662, the nephew of the beloved Queen Theodelina. Aribert was elected king because of his relationship to the revered queen. His reign was uneventful; he established churches and continued to lead the Lombard people away from the Arian heresy. See also LOMBARDS.

**ARIBERT II** (d. 711) King of the Lombards from 701 to 711, the grandson of King Godebert. Aribert and his father, Reginbert, the duke of Turin, opposed the election of the child Liutbert as king in 700. They embarked on a civil war with the support of the Lombards of Neustria. Reginbert died (c. 700) and Aribert ended the war, driving out the regent, Ansprand, and having Liutbert strangled. He reigned as Aribert II for 10 years, fighting incessantly against rebellious dukes and expansionist Slavs. Finally, in 711, Ansprand returned, and Aribert, failing to defeat him in battle, tried to flee but drowned in the Ticino, weighted down by the treasure with which he was attempting to escape. See also LOMBARDS.

**ARIOALD** King of the Lombards from 625 to 636, the duke of Turin chosen to succeed the deposed King Adaloald in 625. His claim was based on holding a duchy and his union with Gundiberga (c. 626), the sister of Adaloald. An Arian, Arioald ruled for more than a decade, but little record of his era has survived. See also LOMBARDS.

**ARI THORGILSSON** (1068–1148) Called "the Learned," the author of the earliest history of Iceland, the *Íslendingabík*. Covering the first years of settlement in Iceland, from about 870 to 1120, the book was of importance in preserving details of early Icelandic events, including the formation of the ALTHING. See also ICELANDIC LITERATURE.

**ARLES, KINGDOM OF** See BURGUNDY, KINGDOM OF.

**ARMAGH** A county and administrative seat in the province of Ulster, in northern Ireland, that was of great importance in early Irish history and in Ireland's subsequent ecclesiastical development. The county was the heart of the Kingdom of Ulster, with the defenses of Emhain Macha providing a stronghold until the fourth century. A period of decline was ended in the fifth century with the arrival of Saint Patrick.

Known as Ard-Macha, or Heights of Macha, after a legendary queen, Armagh emerged as the county seat in the fourth century when the hill fort Ard-Macha increased in importance as the fortress of Emhain Macha collapsed. According to Irish tradition, in 445 Saint Patrick established the site as the religious heart of Ireland, an ecclesiastical see and an influential school visited by many scholars from Anglo-Saxon England. Ravaged during the invasions by the Vikings, the see fell under English domination from 1215, and its bishops lost much of their influence. See also IRELAND.

***ARMAGH, BOOK OF*** Known to some scholars as the *Codex Dublinensis*, an important collection of documents dating from the eighth or ninth century that includes various aspects of Irish history. In the *Book of Armagh* were contained two lives of Saint Patrick, a life of Martin of Tours and several other religious works, including the Gospels.

**ARMAGNAC** A county in southwestern France that rose to prominence in the Middle Ages owing to its ruling noble family. Armagnac was originally part of Gascony but became independent in the 10th century. The counts of Armagnac derived their prestige and independence from their strategic location between English and French possessions in the region, Guyenne and Toulouse respectively. Traditionally allied with France, the counts did give aid to England when it was expedient, and in 1360 the Treaty of Calais handed the county to the English. This arrangement ended in 1368 with the resumption of hostilities during the Hundred Years' War, a conflict that served to expedite the increase in Armagnac holdings.

By the 15th century the counts of Armagnac, specifically Bernard VIII, were in a position to challenge the powerful House of Burgundy. The Armagnac Party, or Armagnacs, came to the forefront of French politics after the murder of Louis, duke of Orléans, in 1407 by John the Fearless, duke of Burgundy. Bernard, brother-in-law of Louis, thus a distant relative of King Charles VI of France (1380–1422), took control of the monarchy and ran its affairs from 1413 to 1418. The swift decline in his political supremacy was brought about by the disastrous Battle of Agincourt in 1415 and his inability to perpetuate the notion that only the Armagnacs could lead the national movement of France. Bernard was constable of France, but John of Burgundy gathered together allies and in 1418, under the pretext of negotiations, recaptured Paris. A bloodbath ensued in which Bernard and every other member of the Armagnac faction who could be found were murdered.

The dauphin, the future Charles VII (1422–1461), however, became leader of the Argmagnac faction, and a meeting with Duke John on September 10, 1419, on the Montereau Bridge ended with the ax murder of the duke of Burgundy. There followed one of the darkest hours of French history as the Burgundians allied themselves with the English and the Armagnacs supported a royal claimant who was ruler of a rapidly declining state. Ironically, the future of France was assured in 1435 when Charles VII was reconciled with Charles the Bold of Burgundy. The Armagnacs soon lost influence, and their lands were invaded by King Louis XI (1461–1483) late in the 15th century and confiscated by the crown. See also BURGUNDY, DUCHY OF; FRANCE.

**ARMAGNAC PARTY** See ARMAGNAC.

**ARMENIA** An ancient and consistently contested land situated just below the Caucusus Mountains and the Black Sea, Anatolia lying to the west, Syria to the south and Azerbaijan to the east. It included part of the Euphrates River, its strategic position placing it at the crossroads between East and West and hence a vital possession to any power in the region. For centuries Armenia (divided at times between Greater and Little or Lesser Armenia) was vied for by the Roman Empire and the Parthians and their successors, the Sassanid Persians. During those eras the region was influenced by a mixture of cultures, but the acceptance of Christianity took firm root in Armenia thanks to the works of Gregory the Illuminator in the late third century and to the translation of the Bible into Armenian in the fifth century.

The Byzantine Empire continued to war with the Persians, effectively dividing Armenia between them. The feudal Armenian aristocracy was more closely identified with its Persian counterpart, while the Armenian Christians, who adhered to the heretical view of Monophysitism condemned in 451 by the Council of Chalcedon, were more acceptable to the Sassanids than the Byzantines. A new kind of conflict began in 640 with the conquest of the Persians by the Arabs. Many Armenians accepted Arab suzerainty in return for limited autonomy, a decision that brought brief prosperity. Economic recovery ended with the attacks of the Khazars in the mid 860s and the violent reconquest of Armenia by the Byzantine emperor Justinian II in the late seventh century. The subsequent decline of the Abbasid caliphate, its center in Baghdad, allowed the Armenians to take control of their own dynastic affairs.

In 884 Asot I was crowned king. From then until 1040 Armenia prospered under the rule of the Bagratid line of monarchs. Unfortunately both inherent weaknesses in Armenian political life and the wave of Islamic and Turkish expansionism threatened them. The Byzantine emperor Michael IV seized the Armenian capital of Ani in 1040 or 1041, and the principalities of Armenia fell one by one to the Seljuk Turks, who sold Ani to the Shaddadid emirs in 1072. As the domination of Seljuk Turks was survived, around the 13th century another influence gained prominence. The Georgians, who defeated the Shaddadids, allowed the last notable Armenian principality outside Little Armenia to emerge: the Zaka'rids.

In turn they were obliterated by the Khwarazmians around 1230, and the entire area was further devastated by the invasion of the Mongol horde and then by Tamerlane.

Little Armenia was established as a result of the migrations of the Armenians to the Anatolian territory of Cilicia during the Seljuk onslaught. A small kingdom had already

Armenian prince, c. 13th century

been in existence from 1080 until 1375, tied to the fortunes of the Crusader States of the East and dependent on them for political order. The realm fell in 1375 to the Mamluks, and later all of Armenia came under the sway of the Ottoman Turks.

**ARMIES, BYZANTINE** See BYZANTINE EMPIRE; CRUSADES; WARFARE.

**ARMIES, CHRISTIAN** See CRUSADES; MILITARY ORDERS; WARFARE.

**ARMIES, ISLAMIC** See CRUSADES; WARFARE.

**ARMOR, BYZANTINE** See WARFARE.

**ARMOR, CHRISTIAN** See CHIVALRY; MILITARY ORDERS; TOURNAMENTS; WARFARE.

**ARMOR, ISLAMIC** See WARFARE.

**ARNARSON, INGÓLFUR** The 9th century Norse founder of ICELAND.

**ARNAULT, DANIEL** (fl. 1180–1210) Provençal poet who made many contributions to the genre.

**ARNOLD OF BRESCIA** (c. 1100–1155) Ecclesiastical reformer and a theological ally of Peter Abelard. Originally from Brescia, he studied in Paris, perhaps under Abelard. On his return to Brescia he was a member of the monastery there and by 1137 its prior. He attracted much attention by calling for a radical reform of the church, decrying its temporal wealth and the corruption of its clergy. Condemned as a schismatic in 1139 and involved in local political disputes, he went to France. There he was an avid supporter of Abelard, opposing both his own and Abelard's condemnations by Bernard of Clairvaux and the Council of Sens in 1141. Expelled from France, in 1145 Arnold was in Rome, supporting the Roman party opposed to papal power in secular affairs. Excommunicated in 1148, by Eugene III (1145–1153), he nevertheless called the pope a "man of blood." Arnold became a leader of a popular movement against papal temporal power, forcing Pope Adrian IV (1154–1159) to use papal interdiction to bring the insurgents to their knees; Arnold was handed over to Frederick I Barbarossa (1152–1190), who was in Rome in 1155 for his coronation. Condemned to death by an ecclesiastical court, Arnold was hung and burned, and his ashes were thrown into the Tiber. Ironically, even Bernard of Clairvaux could not dispute the uprightness of Arnold's life.

**ARNOLFO DI CAMBIO** (c. 1245–1310) Italian architect and sculptor who influenced the art of Florence. His most significant achievement was his design for the Cathedral of Florence in the late 13th century.

**ARNULF** (c. 850–899) King of the East Franks from 887 to 891, the duke of Carinthia and, for a time, holder of the title of emperor. He was the son of Carloman, hence the illegitimate nephew to Emperor Charles III the Fat (884–887). As a descendant of Charlemagne, Arnulf was chosen as the replacement for Charles, whom the Frankish nobles deposed in 887 for failing to repulse the Vikings. True to his purpose, Arnulf warred upon the Slavs in Moravia (c. 889) and then routed the Vikings in 891 at the Dyle River.

A summons for help arrived in 893 from Pope Formosus (891–896), who was opposed to the ambitions of Guy of Spoleto and his son, Lambert, whom he had been forced to crown king of Italy with his father. Arnulf's campaign ended in disaster. He returned in 894, following Guy's death, meeting this time with success. Formosus crowned him emperor in 896. Ironically, his last three years were spent attempting to stave off repeated Germanic incursions. See also GERMANY.

**ARPAD** (c. 840–907) A powerful Magyar chieftain and the founder of the Arpad dynasty, the ruling house of Hungary from 907 to 1301. Arpad was elected leader of the Magyars and given the task of moving them from their home on the Don River to a new site. He chose Pannonia, near modern-day Hungary, and there the Magyars settled. See also HUNGARY; MAGYARS.

**ARRAS, TREATY OF** An important agreement in the history of France, signed in 1435 between Charles VII of France and Philip the Good, duke of Burgundy. The treaty secured the alliance between the two parties and, though at great expense to the French crown, made Charles's position far stronger with respect to the English king Henry VI and hastened the end of the Hundred Years' War. In addition to the English at odds with Burgundy, the other political faction in France to lose power as a result of the treaty was Armagnac, thus strengthening the French monarchy at home.

**ARSLAN SHAH** Seljuk ruler of Iraq from 1161 to 1177. See also SELJUK TURKS.

**ARSUF, BATTLE OF** A battle fought between the armies of Saladin and Richard the Lion-Hearted (1189–1199) on September 7, 1191. During the Third Crusade, Richard captured the city of Acre in July 1191 and was marching toward Jaffa, with Jerusalem his ultimate goal. On the way, however, near the town of Arsuf, he encountered heavy resistance from the more mobile forces of Saladin, who hoped to defeat his rear guard composed of the Knights Hospitalers. Waiting for the most opportune moment to strike, Richard's troops held back until evening and then attacked, his knights smashing the forces of Saladin. Unfortunately for Richard, his victory was incomplete, and the Saracens regrouped by the 9th, making the Christian advance on Jerusalem impossible. See also CRUSADES.

**ART AND ARCHITECTURE, BYZANTINE** The style of the art and edifices common throughout the lands influenced by the Byzantine Empire, including Russia. The Byzantine style of art and architecture has been called the first truly Christian form of artistic expression, with its origins springing from Christianity and its purpose in large

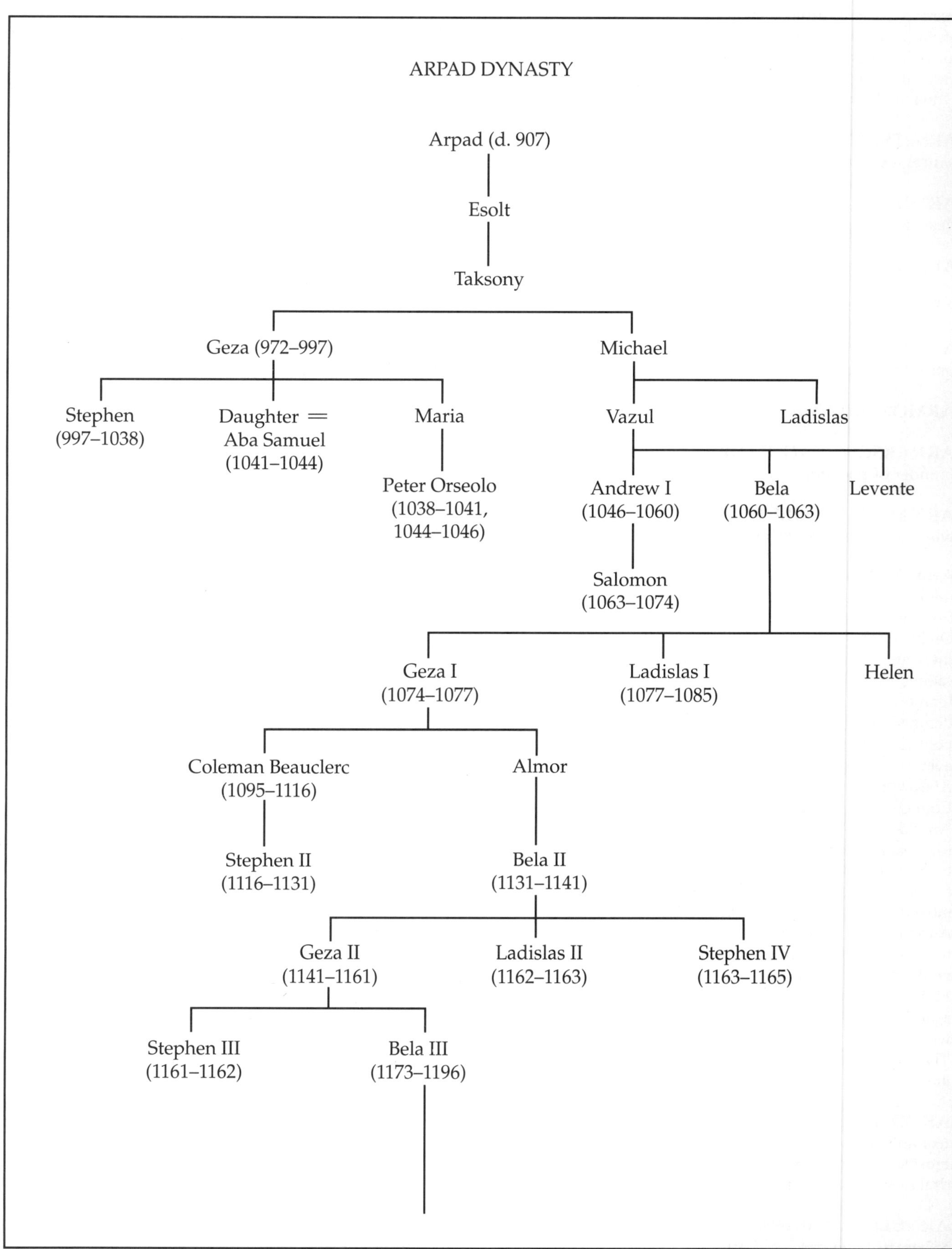
ARPAD DYNASTY
Arpad (d. 907)
Esolt
Taksony
Geza (972–997)
Michael
Stephen (997–1038)
Daughter = Aba Samuel (1041–1044)
Maria
Vazul
Ladislas
Peter Orseolo (1038–1041, 1044–1046)
Andrew I (1046–1060)
Bela (1060–1063)
Levente
Salomon (1063–1074)
Geza I (1074–1077)
Ladislas I (1077–1085)
Helen
Coleman Beauclerc (1095–1116)
Almor
Stephen II (1116–1131)
Bela II (1131–1141)
Geza II (1141–1161)
Ladislas II (1162–1163)
Stephen IV (1163–1165)
Stephen III (1161–1162)
Bela III (1173–1196)

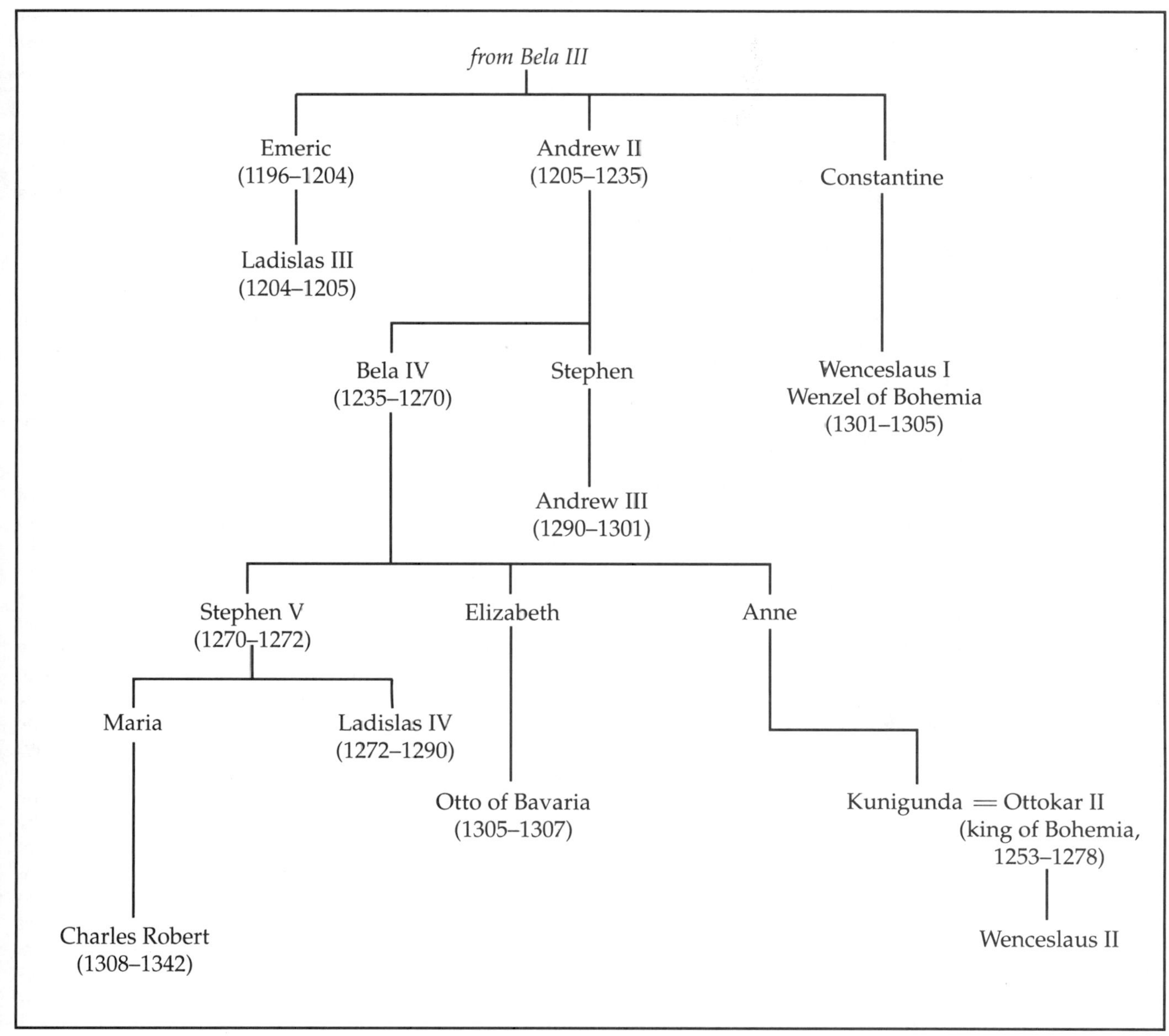


measure to express spiritual aspirations. It may be divided into four main eras: the First Golden Age from 330 to 726, the Iconoclast Period from 726 to 843, the Second Golden Age from 843 to 1204 and the Late Byzantine from 1204 to 1453.

### *Art*

In the strictest sense, Byzantine art began with the establishment of Constantinople, by order of Constantine the Great in the early fourth century. From 330 until the irreversible break with the Western Roman Empire in the fifth century, its art reflected the nature of its Roman founders. The classical style was in use everywhere in statuary, mosaics, ivory and especially in architecture. Inevitably, the distancing of relations between East and West, the division in the Christian church and the Greek majority inhabiting the most important regions of the empire made adoption of new Byzantine styles possible. Henceforth Byzantium was on its own evolutionary path in art.

The First Golden Age seemingly found its most evocative expression in the architectural jewel of Justinian I (527–565), the palace church, the Hagia Sophia, and in mosaics, ivories and sculpture the vitality of the era was quite evident. Mosaics in the Hagia Sophia must have been exceptional, given the enthusiasm of contemporary accounts and the few remains of this early period left in the cross vaults. Hagia Sofia's mosaics are of two periods—this early era and later in the 14th century. For excellent examples of early mosaic art, the sixth century church architecture of Ravenna had no rivals. With four great displays, at the Mausoleum of Galla Placidia, Sant'Apollinare Nuovo, Sant'Apollinare at Classe and at San Vitale, the Byzantine technique of orientalizing Hellenistic style is clear. Sculpture was used to decorate or to preserve the visage of the emperors, but the tendency was to turn away

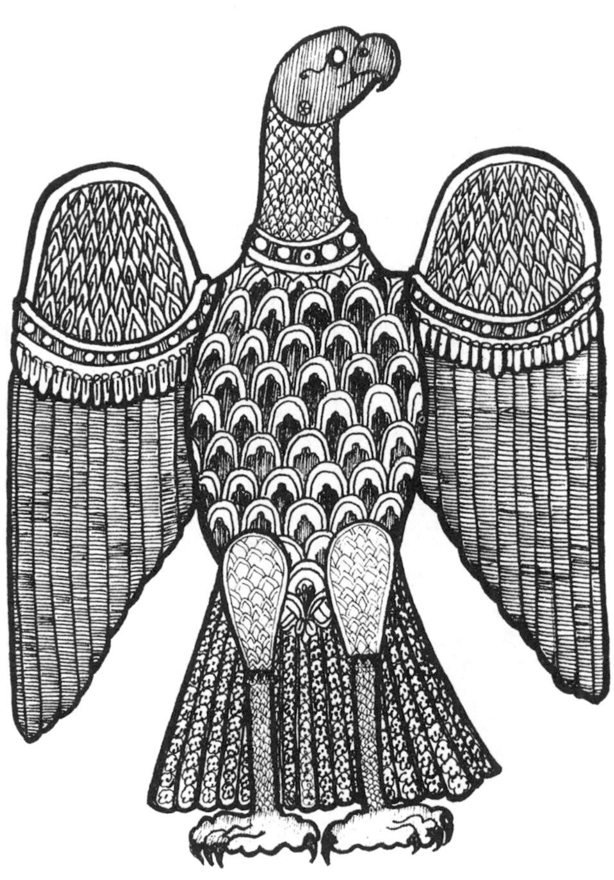

Byzantine eagle

from classicism toward greater abstraction in presentation. Ivory sculpture, too, helped to standardize the features of Byzantine art, especially the diptychs, or two-paneled ivory carvings, used in a variety of ways, including as book covers.

Art throughout the age, however, became increasingly centered on religious display, the use of icons or holy images to depict saints. The fear that works of art had become the objects of excessive veneration led to the decision of the authorities to issue the ban on the representational works of saints or divine persons, lasting from about 726 to 843, a period called the Iconoclastic Age (see ICONOCLASTICISM). Not all art ceased, of course, during the years, and a few contributions were made, but with the end of the ban and the final victory of the opponents of iconoclasm there erupted a flowering of art that matched the political stability and prestige of the Byzantine Empire.

According to many scholars, the artistic achievements of the Second Golden Age outlasted and remained free of the Byzantine decline after the era of Basil II (976–1025). Basil I (867–886) erected churches and then used the paintings within them to represent the mode of thought that would be in place for hundreds of years—namely, the idea of artistic representations of Byzantine hierarchical order. God reigned supreme in heaven, and the dome of the church (the obvious implication being that the emperor ruled by divine assent), the saints and Virgin were arranged in dignity in the area of wall space just below, and the floor of the church was the earth. This style, using the best elements of classicism, formalism and certain freedom of emotional expression, was universal in the Byzantine context by the 11th century.

Painting was divided into two types: wall painting and the production of icons. Few exceptional examples of Byzantine wall painting have survived, but two are the works at Nerezi in Macedonia and the Church of Saint Sophia at Ohrid, Macedonia. Icons were by far the most widely accepted art form of the time, as they fulfilled not only artistic expression but religious needs. In Russia, icon painting was extremely popular. Ivories, work in metal and the delicate enamelware called cloissonné flourished.

The true legacy of the Second Gold Age was its influence on eastern Europe, Russia and the Mediterranean. Byzantine art came to dominate the work of artisans of the Balkans and Russia to such a degree that, in Russia especially, Byzantine tastes endured long after the demise of the Byzantine Empire in 1453. Further, the Normans in Sicily and the Venetians used the Byzantine model to decorate their churches. The Normans' most extraordinary creation was the *Pantocrator,* a mosaic depicting Christ as ruler of the world in the apse of the royal church at Monreale, Sicily; in Venice the testament to the ascendancy of Byzantine art was the interior and exterior of the duomo Saint Mark's. Subtle infusions of the Byzantine artistic philosophy could be found also in the medieval West. The Ottonian rulers owed much to their Byzantine counterparts.

In 1204 the Second Golden Age ended abruptly with the Latin conquest of Constantinople by the armies of the Fourth Crusade. Many of the most beautiful aspects of Byzantine art were lost after the occupation, such as enameling, but painting, mosaics and ceramics survived and continued to evolve. Further, many works of art were stolen from Constantinople and taken to the West, especially Venice. A brilliant feat was the preservation of frescoes in the Mosque of Ka'riye in Istanbul, dating from the early 14th century. That mosaics were still abundant was seen in their wide use in the churches of Constantinople and in the variety of miniatures. Miniature mosaics were produced especially in monasteries, the best of them from Mount Athos. Paintings and mosaics were still available, but icons remained the most important export of late Byzantine art. Schools for the study of making icons were established in Russia, with mastery attained by the artisans of Moscow and Novgorod. Inevitably the Russians came to equal and then surpass their Byzantine teachers, a fitting inheritance, for after 1453 and the fall of Constantinople, Russia was the primary repository of Byzantine artistic endeavor.

### *Architecture*

As was the case with early Byzantine art, the architecture of the Byzantine Empire was, at the start, wholly based on the Roman model that was used in the creation of Constantinople. Thus palaces, forums and churches of the basilica style, as well as square versions, were more reminiscent of Rome than of Byzantium. By the mid-fifth century changes were visible. The basilicas were more centrally constructed, vertical instead of horizontal in the Roman tradition, and the use of domes is one of the most striking features of Byzantine architecture. This use of domes reached its pinnacle in the reign of Justinian I (527–565). His churches in Constantinople, including that dedicated to Saint Irene, paled in comparison with what can be called one of the greatest architectural structures of all time, the Church of Hagia Sophia. No Byzantine emperor or architect ever tried to match the work of Justinian and his designers, Anthemius of Tralles and Isidorus of Miletius. Around the Hagia Sophia, however, sprang up many new buildings, walls and palaces, making the rest of the city a fitting setting for Justinian's masterpiece.

The Iconoclastic Age did little to impede the continuing development of Byzantine architecture, and many churches were constructed. Those outside Constantinople often had mosaics despite the ban on images as decoration. By the Second Golden Age, architects, especially from the reign of Basil I (867–886), had mastered the desired form for churches. They used what has been called the cross-in-square. Essentially this meant that the entire church was square because its length equalled its width; there were three aisles, ending in a chapel on the east and a nave on the west; four vaulted columns supported the central dome making the entire roof cruciform; the chapel and the sanctuary were then divided from the rest of the church by the use of a screen, later called the iconostasis. This model, with some variation, was used everywhere that the Byzantine influence was felt.

Santa Costanza, Rome

Change to some degree came during the Late Byzantine Age as the dome of the church became higher but thinner. In Constantinople architects continued to work on the palaces of the emperors. Clearly, however, two realities characterized the architecture of the time. First, grandeur in Constantinople, with a few exceptions, ceased, and second, the most vital and imaginative forms of the Byzantine style were found outside the empire. Ravenna, Venice and to a degree much of western Europe itself all borrowed either subtly or consciously from the Byzantines. It was in Russia, from the time of the Second Golden Age until the 18th century, that Byzantine architecture flourished most.

See the Art and Architecture section in the Bibliography for suggested works on this subject; see also CONSTANTINOPLE; HAGIA SOPHIA; KIEV; KREMLIN; MANUSCRIPT ILLUMINATION; MOSCOW; NOVGOROD; RAVENNA; RUSSIA.

**ART AND ARCHITECTURE, ISLAMIC** The multifaceted expressions of artistic inspirations from India to Persia, into Spain, Egypt, North Africa, Syria and even Sicily. The study of Islamic art and architecture is the examination not of one cultural entity or style but a vast composite of interrelated influences and subjects, just as the Islamic world was composed of many nations and a multitude of peoples. It would thus be impossible to detail within the scope of his work what would take many volumes to accomplish—the examination of every aspect of the arts of Islam. What follows, however, is a broad overview of the most important types and subjects.

### *Art*

Islamic art was aided at its inception by being able to draw on the rich heritage of the lands that were conquered and converted by the Muslims. There was little discussion in early Islamic history of the nature or rules to govern artistic expression, and the Islamic masters of the newly acquired lands were forced to reconcile their faith with the art they found throughout the Islamic empire. Ultimately, a compromise was found. Muslim iconoclastic doctrine prohibited the display of representations of living persons or the prophet Muhammad, but the visual arts of ceramics, pottery, silks, woodworking, ivory and glassworks all flourished. Local art forms continued, and the individual dynasties, the Umayyads and Abbasids, both allowed the creation of nonfigural decorations to match their grand palaces and mosques.

The decline of the central authority of the Islamic empire permitted the rise of both independent and semi-independent states throughout the Islamic region. This change in government had marked effect on Islamic art. Traditional, far-flung provinces, such as Afghanistan, Spain and North Africa, had retained a certain amount of artistic freedom. Now, under the control of local dynasties, or Shiite factions, art flourished, both from individual inspiration and by state sponsorship.

Fatimid period luster dish (11th century)

One of the best examples of this new era was found in Egypt, in the Fatimid caliphate (909–1171). Both architecture and ceramics seemed to integrate Islamic custom with the influences of European or Mediterranean styles. Pottery was decorated with the human figure, a bold innovation that would be seen in other eras and in other Muslim lands. The Ayyubids (1171–1250) allowed representations of images, and the Mamluks of Egypt (1250–1517) were noted for both their glassware and their carvings. The Seljuk Turkish dynasties fostered ceramics and metalworks of often stunning complexity. Images were used, especially in terms of decorations, but again, Seljuk art was highly regional in development and thus subject to debate and difficult classification. The Ottoman Turks enjoyed a vibrance and vitality of artistic expression in the 14 to 16th century that was reflected by their architecture and, to a lesser degree, their art. Pottery, ivory, silks and especially Ottoman miniatures were prized for their detailing. Ornamental objects, such as rugs, also displayed a high level of artistic achievement.

Two other art forms must be mentioned in terms of Islamic art: book illustration and architectural decoration. Much importance was attached to the illustration of religious texts and the art of calligraphy, which made them objects to delight the senses. Under the Seljuks the illumination of manuscripts included textbooks on history, medicine or science, and literature, such as the Persian epics. Architectural decorations, meanwhile, found almost universal application in mosques and palaces, and much progress was made toward the perfection of mosaic art, reliefs, work in tile and interwoven calligraphy. Some of the beautiful examples of Islamic architecture were enhanced by their wall decorations, among them the former church of Hagia Sophia, the Alhambra, Mshatta Palace in Jordan, the Rabat Gate of Marrakesh, the Great Mosque of Córdoba and the Rüstem Pasa Mosque of Istanbul.

### *Architecture*

It was in architecture that Islam found some of its most profound expressions of faith and artistry, both because of its innovations in construction and because of its genuinely unique creation, the mosque. Derived from the arab term *masjid,* the mosque was simply a religious center, a meeting place for the community where many matters were discussed and where all could come to pray as a unified people. None of the earlier models of the mosques are extant, but the details of their appearance were preserved in texts describing the structures at Kufah, Basra and al-Fustat. Early definition of construction techniques was probably offset by the lack of a specific tradition and the infrequent habit of converting local temples into mosques. The house of the Prophet, for example, had served as the original *masjid,* with its courtyard and two *zullahs,* or shaded areas, on the northern and southern perimeters.

In time the mosque assumed very specific characteristics, including the *mihrab* and the minarets. The *mihrab* was a specially decorated niche in the wall of the mosque called the *qiblah,* or the east wall, toward Mecca, to which prayers were directed. Debate has long been conducted as to the meaning of the *mihrab,* with some believing that it represents the place where Muhammad stood while leading prayers at Medina. The minaret was a tower used by the *muezzin* to summon the faithful to prayer. Its origin is perhaps in Iran. Early minarets were square and more reminiscent of Christian churches; the slim, higher versions known today, most notably around the Hagia Sophia, did not come into fashion until the 11th century.

The tendency among Muslim leaders was to build mosques of great size and grandeur in a city or area once Islam had been established there. Their purpose was to make a place of prayer large enough to accommodate everyone and to impress the local populations who might not have accepted Islam. As a result, over the centuries some remarkable architectural achievements were created. A few notable early mosques were in Córdoba (begun in 784), the Great Mosque of Damascus (705–715) and the Great Mosque of al-Qayrawan, Tunisia (836–866). Innova-

Great Mosque of Samarra, Iraq

Mosque of Selimiye

tions in building techniques and interior decorations continued throughout all of Islamic medieval history. Some of the finest edifices were built by the Ottomans, either as single mosques or as part of a complex, comprising a mosque and a *tekke,* or house for a community of ascetics, such as the Dervishes, in which case it was known as a *külliye.* The *külliye* was a distinctive Ottoman architectural innovation, and both this and the mosque came to command much of the skyline of Istanbul after the conquest of Constantinople in 1453.

The mosque, though essential to Muslim life, was not the only architectural project for Islamic artisans. Palaces, including urban ones, country versions and entire palace cities, displayed the opulence of the Muslim princes, the degrees to which artistic imagination could be taken and the manner in which the royal household members and their subjects lived. Of particular interest to art historians and archaeologists are the cities of Muslim foundation, such as al-Fustat in Egypt and Baghdad, capital of the Abbasid caliphate from the eighth century until 1258. Thanks in large part to the Seljuk Turks and their architecturally influential mosque of Isfahan, the dome or cupola became nearly standard in construction of Turkish buildings. The Mamluks made advances in the use of stone, and the wide attainment of technical perfection allowed them to leave behind thousands of buildings and monuments. Special note must be made of Moorish architecture in Spain. The architects of the Almohad and Almoravid dynasties that controlled the Iberian Peninsula and North Africa from the 11th to the 13th century were known for work that reflected the austerity of their masters, but the Moorish contribution to Islamic and world art was to be everlasting, through the labors of the Nasrid kings of Granada and their masterwork, the Alhambra. For a legacy of beauty and importance in preserving the skill of Muslim artistry, it has few equals.

Several other forms of architecture existed. The mausoleum grew out of the Shiite tradition of reverence for Muhammad and his descendants and the desire of dynastic rulers to be remembered after their death. Thus the use of mausoleums, decorated and impressive, became popular among Fatimids, Seljuks and Ottoman emperors and emphasized their powerful status. Finally, there was the *madrasah,* or combined school and mosque. Its origins, heavily debated, probably were to be found in Iran, and it was brought into other regions by the Seljuks around the 11th century. It was typically smaller in construction, deemphasizing columns, in favor of denser brick and stone. There were rooms for teaching and for living quarters. A mosque and a mausoleum for the founder of the school was not unusual. It was another demonstration of the deep relationship that existed between the faith of Islam and architectural pursuits.

See the Art and Architecture section in the Bibliography for a list of suggested works; see also ALEPPO; ALEXANDRIA; CAIRO; CONSTANTINOPLE; CÓRDOBA; CÓRDOBA, EMIRATE OF; DAMASCUS; EGYPT; GRANADA; ISLAM; SEVILLE; SYRIA.

**ART AND ARCHITECTURE, WESTERN** One of the great humanistic achievements during the medieval epoch was the incorporation of art and architecture into daily life. The subject of Western medieval art (including architecture) is studied widely. It would be impossible to examine the artistic evolution of the Middle Ages to its full extent here, for the subject lends itself to many interpretations based on a variety of perspectives. The reader is asked to see the topic as it is covered under individual entries: see BAYEUX TAPESTRY; CAMBRIDGE; CANTERBURY; CAROLINE BOOKS; CAROLINGIAN ART AND ARCHITECTURE; CASTLE; CATHEDRAL; CLAIRVAUX; CLUNY; COLOGNE; CONSTANTINOPLE; CRUSADER STATES; CRUSADES; FLORENCE; GOTHIC ART AND ARCHITECTURE; GUILDS; HAGIA SOPHIA; HERALDRY; JERUSALEM; KELLS, BOOK OF; LONDON; MANUSCRIPT ILLUMINATION; MEROVINGIAN ART AND ARCHITECTURE; NOTRE DAME DE PARIS; PARIS; PISA; RAVENNA; ROME; TOWER OF LONDON; UNIVERSITIES; VENICE; WESTMINSTER ABBEY; YORK; and individual artists.

**ARTEVELDE, JACOB VAN** (c. 1290–1345) Flemish businessman and political figure who was a power in the city of Ghent from 1336 to 1345. A member of a patrician family of merchants in Ghent, van Artevelde was made head of the city government. He secured the trust of the Flemish people, who feared that the imminent outbreak of hostilities between England and France would mean an end to their profitable and essential textile trade. Van Artevelde negotiated the city's neutrality in 1338 at the start of the Hundred Years' War and, two years later, joined the English cause to acquire further concessions from England's Edward III (1327–1377). His position in Ghent was unchallenged until 1343, when Jan van Steenbeke attempted a coup. Van Artevelde could not maintain his position as city magistrate in 1345 and was killed in a riot that same year. Philip van Artevelde, his son, eventually led a revolt against the count of Flanders but was slain by the French in 1382. See also FLANDERS; GHENT.

***ARTHUR*** See ARTHURIAN LEGEND.

**ARTHUR I** (1187–1203?) Duke of Brittany; the posthumous son of Geoffrey (son of Henry II, 1154–1189), duke of Brittany, and claimant to the throne of England. Arthur was originally (c. 1190) the designated heir to the childless Richard the Lion-Hearted (1189–1199) but lost his position after 1196 because of his affiliations with King Philip II Augustus of France (1180–1223). Thus in 1199 he was passed over, and his uncle John (1199–1216) was invested with the royal title, succeeding Richard. Having claimed the duchy of Brittany in 1196, on the death of his mother, Constance, Arthur also took possession of Aquitaine, Anjou and Marne at the instigation of Philip. In the ensuing struggle with John, Arthur was captured in 1201, imprisoned at Rouen and, according to tradition, perhaps murdered in 1203.

**ARTHUR III, DUKE OF BRITTANY** See RICHEMONT, ARTHUR, COMTE DE.

**ARTHURIAN LEGEND** A body of stories and romances, called the Matter of Britain or the British Matter, that was one of the most widely disseminated of medieval literature. The Arthurian Legend developed around the figure of the British hero Arthur, but it also drew on material from the legends of many lands, becoming associated with other tales and motifs, including those of Arthur's knights, Lancelot, Galahad, Gawain and Parsifal, and mythical people or ventures such as the Green Knight or the search for the HOLY GRAIL.

Scholars have long attempted to trace Arthur's life and activities, but despite the vast amounts of literary material on the subject, he has escaped thus far efforts to prove his existence conclusively. The sources for the period of early British history have been of only limited assistance. The earliest mention of the events connected to Arthur's supposed achievements (his war with the Saxons or the Battle of Badon Hill) was made by the chronicler Gildas in the sixth century, who put the date of the Battle of Badon Hill at 516 but did not name Arthur specifically. These details were generally supported by the *Anglo-Saxon Chronicle* and Bede. It is the opinion of many scholars that what happened over the succeeding years was that Arthur's name was somehow mysteriously connected to the Roman rulers of the islands and became attached to the growing stories of the warrior mentioned in the early annals. The Old Welsh poem the *Gododdin* (c. 600) mentions an Arthur who was noted for his bravery in battle. Once he was established as the possible hero of Badon Hill, national pride, indigenous folktales and traditional cultural motifs embellished the myth. Henceforth, Arthur was the victor of Badon Hill, brilliant captain in war and, within a few centuries, the shining king whose reign would capture the European imagination.

Thus the *Annales Cambriae* of the 9th–10th centuries named Arthur at Badon Hill in 516 and made mention of his death in 537 in battle with Mordred at Camlann. More important than the *Annales Cambriae* was the ninth-century miscellany of Nennius, compiling the *Historia Brittonum* and *Mirabilia*. Here influential details on Arthur were written, perhaps based on a combination of tales within the early chronicles. Welsh stories increased Arthur's reputation, and in the 12th century, Geoffrey of Monmouth's *Historia regum Britanniae* (c. 1136) celebrated the glorious achievements of the king until his mortal wounding by his nephew Mordred. The *Historia* was certainly derived in part from Celtic tales, altered to meet Geoffrey's needs. His work was, in turn, used as a model by two slightly later authors, Wace of Jersey (*Roman de Brut,* 1155) and Layamon (*Brut,* c. 1200). Doubts concerning Arthur's identity inevitably appeared in William of Malmesbury's *Gesta regum Anglorum* (1125) and William of Newburgh's *Historia rerum Anglicarum* (c. 1198), but Geoffrey remained the main source throughout the Middle Ages for Arthur's era. It was not until John Major's *Historia majoris Britanniae* (1521) that historians dismissed Arthurian events as fiction.

By the time of the Renaissance, however, Celtic and Welsh literary traditions had been used by the writers of Europe to fashion a vast collection of works. Much of the basis for the literary Arthurian productions was in Celtic and especially Welsh literature, preserved in such compilations as the *Black Book of Camarthen,* the *Book of Taliesin* and the *Red Book of Hergest* (dating from around 1200, 1275 and 1400 respectively). Prominent in 12th-century Welsh prose was the romance *Culhwch and Olwen,* in which Arthur and his knights figured and which helped to give substance to the notion of Arthur and the Knights of the Round Table.

Cultural diffusion, either encouraged by the Normans or through the ties of Brittany with the English, made the spreading of the British Matter inevitable. So complete was the distribution of ideas that toward the end of the 12th century Chrétien de Troyes wrote what are considered to be the most important of the Arthurian romances. His five romantic adventures *(Erec et Enide, Cligès, Launcelot ou le chevalier de la charette, Perceval ou le conte du Graal* and *Yvain ou le chevalier au lion)* were composed between 1160 and 1180 and made Arthur a more suitable subject while introducing the search for the Grail as part of the theme. These romances became extremely popular in France, using the story lines of Arthur while focusing on two facets of the tale, the Holy Grail and the characters of Lancelot and Guinevere.

The Grail added crucial spiritual dimension to the Arthurian Legend, intertwining the fabled cup used at the Last Supper with Parsifal (Percival), Joseph of Arimathea and the theme of Christian redemption. Meanwhile, the Grail and Lancelot were united in the Prose Lancelot, known commonly as the Vulgate Cycle. This collection of five romances (c. 1225) covered territory familiar to the modern reader, a testament to its impact on subsequent writings. The five stories were *Estoire del Saint Graal,* about Joseph of Arimathea; *Merlin,* a prose version of Robert de Boron's poem, telling of Arthur's childhood and rise to the throne, adding an account of his campaigns; *Lancelot,* on the life of the knight, especially his siring Sir Galahad; *Queste del Saint Graal,* the search for the Grail in which Galahad was the fullest beatific vision attainable by mortals; and *Mort Artu,* the sad recounting of how Lancelot's guilt led to the end of the kingdom and the departure of Arthur.

The Arthurian Legend also found rich expression in the hands of other poets and writers. Hartmann von Aue (c.

1202), Gottfried von Strassburg (late 13th century), Heinrich von Freiburg and Ulrich von Türheim (co-authors of a continuation of Gottfried's work), as well as romances by Scandinavians, Spanish and Portuguese, all drew on some aspect of the tales or attempted to complete others. The best known of the German writers was Wolfram von Eschenbach and his *Parzival* (early 13th century), which was considered not only a superb romance but a compendium on how to reach spiritual fulfillment. It illustrated the Christian virtues but made literary innovations as well. Another romance, referred to as the Post-Vulgate Grail Romance, and dating from the mid-13th century, used elements of the Tristan romances.

All of the threads of the British Matter were united with imagination and vigorous prose by Thomas Malory in *Le Morte Darthur* in the 15th century. This long work utilized both the Vulgate and Post-Vulgate Cycles as well as the numerous prose and poetic efforts of other writers. Due to Malory and Geoffrey of Monmouth, Arthur and the Arthurian Legend became part of the mythological heritage of England, a place of honor that the fabled king has not lost over the centuries.

**ARTOIS** A region of France situated in the modern department of Pas de Calais. Originally the land of the tribe of Atribates, Artois belonged to the counts of Flanders from the 9th the to 12th century until annexed around 1180 by Philip II Augustus of France (1180–1223). Possession of the region changed hands several times over the ensuing years: in 1329 it was given to Burgundy, and in 1493 the Habsburgs claimed it, holding Artois until the 17th century. See also FRANCE.

**ARUNDEL** A borough in the county of West Sussex, England, and the traditional home of the earls of Arundel. It was a small community from the 8th to the 11th century but was recorded in the Domesday Book (1086) as a prosperous town. Arundel Castle was erected about 1066 to protect the region. A line of earls was established by William d'Aubigny in the 12th century, although the first actual earl was Richard Fitzalan. In the late 16th century the earlship passed to the dukes of Norfolk. See also ARUNDEL, THOMAS.

**ARUNDEL, THOMAS** (1353–1414) Chancellor of England and archbishop of Canterbury, the son of Richard Fitzalan, earl of Arundel. He was consecrated the bishop of Ely in 1374, allying himself with nobles against King Richard II (1377–1399), becoming chancellor of England in 1386 and archbishop of York in 1388. Removed in 1389 as chancellor, he was reappointed in 1391 but stepped down to become archbishop of Canterbury in 1396. Impeached in Parliament in 1397, Arundel was banished, returning in 1399 with Henry Bolingbroke, who became Henry IV (1399–1413) with the deposition of Richard II. Arundel served twice more as chancellor (1407–1409 and 1412–1413) and took up his duties as archbishop of Canterbury. He was noted for his opposition to the Lollard heresy. See also LOLLARDY.

**ASAPH, SAINT** (fl. mid-sixth century) Sixth-century Welsh saint, little known, except that he was a disciple of Saint Kentigern. Asaph was one of the first bishops in Wales.

**ASCALON** Also called Askalon and Askelon, a city in Palestine, situated on the Mediterranean Sea between Jaffa and Gaza. An ancient site, it was captured by the Arabs in 636 and remained an Islamic possession until the 12th century and the Crusades. In 1150 it was besieged by a Crusader army but resisted Christian attempts to take it for half a century. It was not until 1153 that it fell, becoming an important port for Crusader activities, although its acquisition was more of a political triumph than a military one. Saladin reclaimed it in 1191, destroying its walls to the extent that Ascalon was a ruin for centuries. It was called the Bride of Syria. See also CRUSADES.

**ASEN DYNASTY** The ruling line of the Second Bulgarian Empire from 1185 to 1257. See also BULGARIA; BULGARS, EMPIRES OF THE.

**ASGRIMSSON, EYSTEIN** (c. 1310–1361) Icelandic monk who was the author of *Lilja (Lily)*, generally considered to be the greatest of all religious poems in Icelandic history. There has been much debate as to Asgrimsson's identity, for he held positions of power in the bishopric of Skalaholt but was excommunicated in 1360. *Lilja* covered the history of Christianity from the Creation to the Last Judgment. See also ICELANDIC LITERATURE.

**AL-ASH'ARI** (c. 873–935) One of the most famous Islamic theologians. Abu'l-Hasan 'Ali ibn Ismail al-Ash'ari worked to counter the doctrine of the Mu'tazilites in favor of a more traditional study of orthodox theology through the Koran and the collection of customs based on the deeds of Muhammad, the Sunnah. Born in Basra, he was a student of the famed Abu Ali al-Jubba'i, leader of the Mu'tazilites in Basra. Having long examined Mu'talizilism with its rational views on the nature of God, al-Ash'ari renounced the doctrine in 912, establishing himself (c. 915) in Baghdad. Followers were attracted to his school, and Ash'arism found support among those who did not agree with Mu'talizilism. Nizam al-Mulk, the great Islamic vizier, was an Ash'arist. Al-Ash'ari wrote a number of influential works: *Maqālāt al-Islāmīyyīn (Theological Views of the Muslims), Risālah ilā ahl ath-thagh (Treatise for the Men of the Frontier), Ibāna'an usūl ad-diyānah (Statement on the Principles of Religion)* and *Kitāb al-Luma (The Luminous Book).*

**ASHER BEN JECHIEL** (c. 1250–1327) Acknowledged leader of European Jewry after the death of Solomon ben Adretin 1310 and one of Judaism's greatest experts on the Talmud. Asher fled from Germany at the outset of the German persecution of the Jews and, with the help of Adret, was made rabbi of Toledo. He codified Talmudic law, placing the codes in his *Piske Halachot*, or *Decisions on the Laws* (dated at the early 14th century), a work used as the basis of subsequent codifications. See also JEWS AND JUDAISM.

**ASPARUKH** (c. 650–701) King of the Bulgars and the traditional founder of the First Bulgarian Empire. Known on some lists of Bulgarian kings as Isperukh or Isperich, he led his people from the Black Sea region and the threat of the Khazars to what had been Roman Moesia (present-day Bulgaria) around 670. The arrival of a formidable host of Bulgars aroused the Byzantine Empire, and in 680 Constantine IV (668–685) led a large army against them. He was thoroughly defeated by Asparukh. By the terms of the treaty signed by Constantine, not only was the Bulgarian Empire recognized but annual tribute was paid as well. Asparukh was succeeded by Tervel in 701. See also BULGARIA; BULGARS, EMPIRES OF THE.

**ASSASSINS, ORDER OF** A powerful religio-political organization in the Islamic world from the 11th to the 13th century that furthered the cause of the Islamic Shiite sect of the Nizari-Ismailis. The Assassins, so-called in the West, used murder and intimidation as a policy weapon; in so doing they earned the enmity of orthodox Islam and captured the imagination of European writers and travelers.

Their origins date from the eight century and to the split in the Shiite movement, which resulted in the Ismailis (see ISMAILI SECT). The catalyst that created the actual Assassins group was a dispute over the succession of the Fatimid caliphate following the death of al-Mustansir in 1094. One group supported the old order and the new caliph; another desired Mustansir's son, Nizar. The latter formed the Nizari Ismailis, a radical sect that disappeared from Egypt but elsewhere found a champion in the mystical genius Hasan ibn Sabbah. He seized the fortress of Alamut in Persia in 1090, transformed it into an impregnable citadel and training ground and then set out to spin a web of agents, murders and terrorism throughout the Muslim domain. All who opposed the Assassins or those who stood in their way were killed in outrageously imaginative ways, the membership of the Assassin Order earning a reputation for stealth, efficiency and ruthlessness. By the 12th century the Assassins were to be found in Syria, establishing castles from which more deaths were ordered.

The training of the order was intense and complex. Hashish was smoked in some aspects of indoctrination, and hence its name was applied to the Nizari Ismailis. They were called the *hashishiyyun*, a term that was taken by the European chroniclers and from which "Assassins" is derived. The order had a definite hierarchy. It was headed by the Grand Master of Assassins, aided by the Grand Priors, or the *Dailkebir*. They were served by the *Dais*, who were gifted in doctrine and above the *Refiks*, the students advancing through the grades of initiation in Ismaili tenets. Most numerous were the *Fedai*, the agents of death who killed without remorse, hoping to attain the paradise that had been shown them, no doubt while under the influence of hashish. Their lives were spent carrying out the Master's orders, and it was said that a *Fedai* who returned from a mission alive caused his mother to weep in sorrow.

Assuming covers; learning Greek, French, Latin and other languages; wearing disguises; and dying willingly were all expected. Such efficiency allowed the order to survive severe persecution by the Abbasid caliphate, the Seljuk Turks and even Saladin while exacting severe retributions. They eliminated high government officials, including the vizier Nizam al-Mulk in 1092, and brought Saladin to his knees in 1176. Although most victims were Muslims, they were not all. The order dealt with the Crusaders, including the Templars, plying their trade throughout the Holy Lands against their Sunni opponents when expedient. In 1192 they stabbed Conrad of Montferrat in the streets of Tyre, to avenge the execution of a fellow member, and they were soon credited with deaths in Europe itself.

The chronicler Ambroise described Conrad's murder as coming at the instruction of the Old Man of the Mountain, the title used to describe the Grand Master of the Assassins but which also was applied to the virtually autonomous chief of Assassins in Syria. The most notable Syrian head was Sinan ibn Salman ibn Muhammad, called Rashid ad-Din. An alchemist, he held sway over the castle of Masyaf, negotiating with any potentate, Christian or Muslim, if it was in the best interest of the order. It was Rashid ad-Din who tried repeatedly, without success, to be rid of SALADIN by assassination.

Murder tactics were useless, even disastrous, in dealing with the Mongols. In 1256, Hulagu, ilkhan of the Mongol armies, sweeping into the Middle East, captured Alamut and exacted punishment for the murder of Jagatai, second son of Genghis Khan, by the Assassins. Ruknud-Din, the last Grand Master, was kicked to death, and his wives, children and 12,000 supporters were massacred. The joy of orthodox Muslims was even greater when the Mamluks ended the Assassin reign of terror with their liquidation of surviving Assassin elements. Nizari Ismailism lingered for many years and even prospered in India, but the Assassins were gone forever.

The influence of the order was displayed in the number of references made to them by Arab historians and often unreliable or romantic European writers. Juvaini, Ibn al-Athir and Ibn al-Qalanisi made mention of them, as did Ambroise, Marco Polo, William of Tyre, Arnold of Lübeck, Joinville, Matthew Paris, William of Rubruquis and Jacques de Vitry. See also CRUSADER STATES; CRUSADES; ISLAM.

**ASSER** (d. c. 909) Welsh monk and bishop and the friend, tutor and biographer of King ALFRED THE GREAT. Asser became a monk in Pembrokeshire, acquiring a reputation for being a learned scholar and teacher. Thus in 886 Alfred summoned him to court and asked to be taught Latin. Over the next years Asser was more than an instructor. He was a valued counselor and a friend of the king. Abbot of several monasteries in England, he was made bishop of Sherborne in Dorset just before his death, about 909. His *Life of King Alfred*, though questioned by a few scholars as genuinely his, covered all of the events in Alfred's early days and his reign until 887. Based partly on the *Anglo-Saxon Chronicle* and at times poorly constructed and written, the biography was nevertheless an important source of knowledge on Alfred and ninth-century England. He helped Alfred translate the *Cura pastoralis (Pastoral Care)* and perhaps Boethius's *Consolatio philsophiae (The consolation of Philosophy)*.

**ASSISI** Town in the Italian region of Umbria and the birthplace of Saint Francis in 1182. Originally part of the duchy of Spoleto, Assisi became independent in the 12th century but was later absorbed by the Papal States. The town had many churches, the most popular of which was that of Saint Francis, the double church built between 1228 and 1253 over the tomb of the saint. See also FRANCIS OF ASSISI, SAINT.

**ASSIZES OF JERUSALEM** The term used for the compilation of legal codes and procedures applied in the Latin Kingdom of Jerusalem and in other Crusader States of the East. It was probably Geoffrey de Bouillon in the late 11th century who first organized the legal codes of the Kingdom of Jerusalem by collecting the customs and practices of the European kingdoms and then applying them to the Latin domains of the region. Called the *Lettres du Sepulchre* because it was kept in the Holy Sepulchre in Jerusalem, the original body of laws was lost in 1187 with the fall of the city. The idea, however, persisted, and legal treatises were placed together into the Assizes of Jerusalem with emphasis on feudal jurisdiction of the kings and nobility and that of the burgess courts or the non-noble courts of justice.

Written in French, the Assizes of Jerusalem were the product of a group of legalists living in the Latin domains of the East, including Cyprus. The four major contributors, writing in the 13th century, were Philippe de Navara, Geoffrey le Tor, James d'Ibelin and his father, Jean. Generally the most important of these writers was Jean d'Ibelin, who preserved important details of law and jurisprudence. Cyprus was a leading center for the continuation of the practice of Latin law after the loss of Palestinian strongholds. See also CRUSADES; JERUSALEM, KINGDOM OF;

**ASTROLOGY** A major form of divinatory science (or to many a pseudoscience) based on the idea that human affairs are influenced by the stars and the moon. Astrology was very old before the Greeks applied it, originating in Mesopotamia but also practiced in Egypt, India and China. Hellenistic astrology, which was linked with astronomy, became an essential element in Greek observation of the heavens and its science.

Although the Romans had their own types of divination, astrology was eventually accepted and practiced throughout the Roman Empire. Considered part of the pagan establishment, it was condemned by the Christians and ultimately suppressed in the West in large measure because of the writings of Saint Augustine (in *The City of God*). Such official condemnation coupled with the decline of Greek knowledge virtually extinguished the practice of astrology. Only a few astrological texts were in Latin: Manilius's poem *Astronomicon*, Firmicus Maternus's *Matheseos libri VIII* and the *Liber Hermeticus*, by an anonymous astrologer.

After several centuries of decline, the astrologers in the Byzantine Empire flourished, starting around the ninth century, and they translated many Arabic texts. Islamic astrologers were heavily influenced by Indian, Persian and Hellenic traditions, compiling but rarely expanding on the ideas of the originals. They, too, faced severe repression at the hands of Islamic conservative theologians but were nevertheless able to impart to Europe by the 13th century the vast body of astrological texts via the Crusades, Spain and the ports of Sicily and Italy.

Translations of astrological texts were increasingly common after the 13th century, and astrology found broad acceptance in medieval thinking, even among intellectuals such as Roger Bacon and Albertus Magnus. The use of astrology, according to mainstream thinking, to predict the future or to aid in finding the most suitable hours or days for embarking on an enterprise captured the popular imagination. Court astrologers were hired, and writers used astrological concepts in their literature (Chaucer, for example, in the *Knight's Tale*). Inevitably, theologians and the church resurrected the views of Saint Augustine. Thomas Aquinas fired the first salvo; attacks were furthered by Pico della Mirandola. Papal bans on astrology, occult practices and sorcery were instituted, but it was not until the Renaissance and after, and the works of such astronomers as Copernicus, Galileo and Kepler, that astrology gradually lost its reason for being, having been proved to lack a basis in fact. See also ASTRONOMY; WITCHCRAFT.

**ASTRONOMY** The scientific study of the heavens that has been one of humanity's most vital pursuits because of its direct relationship to the designation of time intervals and its use in navigation and agriculture. Historians of astronomy refer to the Middle Ages as the period between the *Almagest* of Ptolemy and the Copernican revolution, during which only improvements in observations and mathematics were made. This was especially true in the early Middle Ages in the West, until the study of Arab works that had preserved vital elements of classical learning and included the achievements of Islamic astronomers became known in the 12th century.

Western astronomy was almost dormant in the early medieval period, although essential astronomical skills necessary for the compilation of calendars were retained. There was a brief revival during the Carolingian Renaissance, but it was small compared with the extensive work conducted by the Muslims. The reign of the Abbasid caliph al-Mansur (754–775) was noted for its patronage of science. Syrian Christians were the translators of Greek texts, first in medicine and later in astronomy. It was during the rule of Harun al-Rashid (786–809) that the *Almagest* of Ptolemy was translated and observatories established at Baghdad. Al-Mamun (c. 829) founded a new observatory, initiating advances in Greek methodology. In Spain, Moorish astronomers drew up the Toledan Tables (c. 1080), predecessors to the Alfonsine Tables. Notable astronomers were at Battani, testing Ptolemaic principles and making observations from 878 to 918. Abul Wafa of the 10th century, the author of his own *Almagest*, and Ibn Yunos of Cairo, during the Fatimid caliphate, the author of the Hakeniite Tables, which were revived by the Persian astronomers at Meraga, were among the pioneers in astronomy. Although the Arabs invented nothing new, they nevertheless preserved and built on older concepts in astronomy, mathematics and observation and made a useful contribution in the naming of stars.

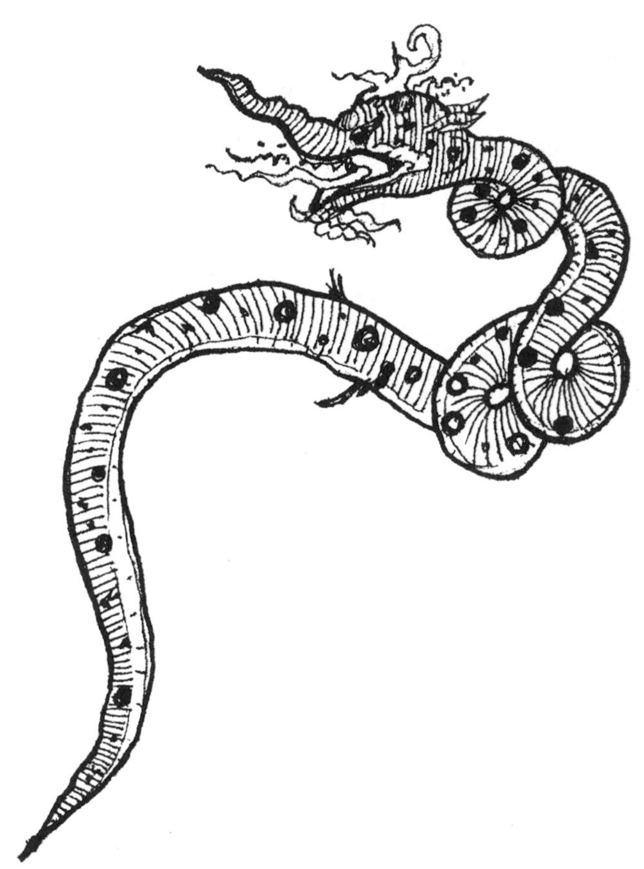

Draco symbol (Islamic)

Arab translations of Greek texts began trickling into Europe, starting in the 10th century during Moorish influence in largely Christian Spain. By the 12th century major steps were being taken toward the dissemination of astronomical concepts. Adelard of Bath and Gerard of Cremona translated Arabic texts; Gerard was responsible for 70 scientific translations, including the *Almagest* and the Toledan Tables. In the 13th century King Alfonso X of León and Castile (reigned 1252–1284) summoned all available Christian and Jewish scholars to Toledo, where two important compilations were made: the Alfonsine Tables and the *Libros del Saber de astronomia,* an encyclopedia of astronomical knowledge and lore. Roger Bacon included astronomy among his many fields of learning but sometimes presented inaccuracies, such as giving Julius Caesar possession of a telescope with which he supposedly viewed Britain before sailing across the Channel to conquer it. John of Sacrobosco (d. 1256), a mathematician of Paris, wrote *Tractatus de sphaera,* a treatise on the sky.

Beginning with the 15th-century German astronomers, Europe took its first steps toward the use of scientific methods and independent research, pointing to the age of Copernicus and the shedding of the old stigma of astrological superstition. Georg del Peuerbach, professor at Vienna University, made a Latin version of Ptolemy's planetary theory and, based on the *Almagest,* began an *Epitome of Astronomy.* His work was finished by his friend and student Johannes Regiomontanus. He settled in Nuremburg, where he conducted his observations, traveling to Rome in 1475 to assist the pope in the revision of the calendar. He died that year, but his astronomical research was continued by the scientists of the Renaissance, especially by Copernicus. See also ASTROLOGY.

**ASTURIAS, KINGDOM OF** See LEÓN for the history of Asturias from 718 to 910.

**ATHALARIC** (d. 534) King of the Ostrogoths from 526 to 534, the grandson of Theodoric the Great and inheritor of the Ostrogothic kingdom in 526, while only 10 years old. His troubled reign was marked by the struggle of his mother, Amalasuntha, against the Ostrogothic leaders opposed to her regency. Originally educated along Roman lines, in 532 Athalaric was taken from the strict control of his mother and given to the Ostrogoths to train as king. His death left the realm in a state of deep division. See also OSTROGOTHS.

**ATHANAGILD** (d. 568) King of the Visigoths from 555 to 568, not one of the most influential kings of his people, in large measure because he came to the throne with the aid of a Byzantine army sent by Justinian I (527–565) to help him win a civil war with King Agila. Once established as a monarch, Athanagild found it impossible to dislodge the Byzantines from Córdoba, Cádiz, Cartegena and other parts of Andalusia. He died in 568 and was remembered more for his daughters, Brunhilde and Galswintha, the "Pearls of Spain." See also VISIGOTHS.

**ATHANASIUS THE ATHONITE** (c. 925–1001) Byzantine monk who founded the monastery at Mount Athos, called the Lavra, and thus was a major influence on Byzantine monasticism. Athanasius came originally from Trebizond, entering a monastery in Bithynia before journeying to Mount Athos, where he established his monastic system. Although opposed by the ascetics already living on the mountain and later by several political and ecclesiastical parties in Constantinople, from 963 the Lavra enjoyed imperial patronage from Nicephorus II Phocas (963–969) and John I Tzimisces (969–976). The latter gave to Athanasius a charter in 971–972. Abbot eventually of 58 monasteries on the mountain, Athanasius died in 1001 when a building that he was dedicating collapsed

**ATHELSTAN** (d. 939) King of Wessex and Mercia and the first Saxon monarch to be hailed as the ruler of all England. Athelstan, called "the Glorious," was one of the most successful but little-known kings in English history. The son of Edward the Elder (899–924), he grew up among the Mercians with his aunt, Aethelflaed, Lady of Mercia. Despite being known as Alfred the Great's favorite grandson, Athelstan was apparently not Edward's first choice as heir on the old king's death in 924; that was the obscure other son, Aelfweard, who reigned for only a few weeks before dying. The Mercians chose Athelstan as their ruler, and the Saxons did the same, and he was crowned on September 4, 925, at Kingston.

War soon followed as Athelstan extended the influence of the Saxons over all of Northumbria and into Scotland

Athelstan and Cuthbert

before turning to Wales and Cornwall. Years of fighting ended in 928 with the court of Exeter, where he was acknowledged as undisputed master of all the English. Athelstan thus put into effect a broad program of reforms or efforts aimed not only at consolidation but at earning him as well the respect of the rest of Christendom. Foreign states established relations with him, and permanent ties were made through the marriages of relatives to Continental princelings or kings. The law codes were rewritten or adjusted to make them virtually universal. Their intent was to punish wrongdoing, protect the weak and dispense justice with an even hand. A competent system of clerks and bureaucracies established an embryonic civil service. The currency was more standardized, and the realm was divided into the shire system that lasted for many centuries.

An invasion of Scotland to subdue the rebellious spirit of Constantine II in 934 produced short-term pacification. It also created a fierce determination on the part of several shires to seek revenge. So, in 937, Constantine, allied with Olaf Guthfrithson of the Norse domain of York and with Owain of Strathclyde, launched an onslaught against Athelstan. The king made his preparations and on a fall day in 937 won the famed battle of Brunanburgh. He died two years later at the height of his power and prestige at home and in Europe. His reign was summed up by William of Malmesbury, who wrote that "no one more just or wise administered the state." See also ENGLAND.

**ATHENS** See GREECE.

**AL-ATHIR, IBN** See IBN AL-ATHIR.

**ATTALEIATES, MICHAEL** Also called Michael Attaliates, an 11th-century historian and Byzantine courtier. In addition to a collection of laws, he was the author of a valuable account of the Byzantine Empire for the period 1034–1079, dedicated to Nicephorus III Botaneiates.

**AUGSBURG** A city in present-day Bavaria positioned at the confluence of the Werbach and Lech Rivers. Augsburg was the site of a Roman colony in the late first century B.C. and was Christianized by the middle of the eighth century. Its position was strengthened in the Middle Ages with the famed Battle of the Lechfeld, fought just to the south between Otto I (936–973) and the Magyars in 955. Part of the Holy Roman Empire, it was made a free imperial city in 1276 and was later a member of the Swabian League, working for reforms within the imperial system. Through the leadership of several influential families, most notably Weleser and Fugger, Augsburg flourished as a leading commercial center. See also HOLY ROMAN EMPIRE; TRADE AND COMMERCE.

**AUGUSTINE OF CANTERBURY, SAINT** (d. 604 or 605) First archbishop of Canterbury and the missionary most responsible for the evangelization of southern England in the sixth century. A Roman by birth, Augustine was prior of the monastery of Saint Andrew's in Rome when, in 596, Pope Gregory the Great chose him to reintroduce Christianity to England after it had suffered a decline in the previous years during the Anglo-Saxon invasions. He set out with a group of monks, but losing his nerve, he turned back in Gaul. Encouraged by Gregory, however, he continued his journey, arriving in England in 597.

Of great assistance to his cause was the support given by King Aethelbert of Kent, whose wife was a Christian. Enjoying royal patronage, Augustine was extremely successful in finding converts and was consecrated bishop of the English by Saint Virgilius at Arles. Corresponding with the pope on virtually every detail of his work, Augustine was granted the full powers of a metropolitan in 601, with the task of consecrating other bishops and blessing churches. His efforts made Canterbury the ecclesiastical heart of England. In 603 he attempted without success to unite the Celtic church with Rome, but the traditions he established, namely the Roman rite and calendar, did eventually find acceptance in all of England. He was called the "Apostle of England."

**AUGUSTINE OF KENT** See AUGUSTINE OF CANTERBURY.

**AUGUSTINIAN CANONS** Also called the "Black Canons," the first religious order in the Christian church to adhere to a common life for canons.

This meant that the canons of a diocese (priests belonging to the staff of the cathedral) adhered to the Rule of Augustine (the strict observance of monastic ways, poverty, celibacy and obedience) and encouraged scholarship and evangelical spirituality. The Augustinian canons probably originated in Italy and parts of France in the 11th century, although the idea had existed for centuries. Receiving sanction from the church at the Lateran Councils of 1059 and 1063, the order became very popular. By the 12th century most canons were members of the Augustinians, called "Regular Canons." The ideal of the Augustinian rule was diluted by the end of the Middle Ages through the disorders of the age, and the Augustinian Canons were neglected during the Reformation.

**AUGUSTINIAN HERMITS** Officially called the Order of the Hermit Friars of Saint Augustine, or commonly the Augustinian Friars, and closely related to the less austere Augustinian canons; in England they were called the Austin friars. The Augustinian Hermits were one of the leading mendicant, or begging, orders of the medieval church. They began as widely separated communities of hermits, adhering to the rule of Saint Augustine (monastic life), but for reasons of organization and leadership, they were united in 1256 by Pope Alexander IV, who used as their model the Dominican order. The duties of the Augustinian Hermits were thus changed from a secluded religious life to active participation in the life of towns and cities, and they became well known throughout western Europe. Less austere congregations eventually appeared, to which Martin Luther would belong in the 16th century.

**AURELIUS** King of Asturias from 768 to 774.

**AURISPA, GIOVANNI** (1370–1459) Sicilian-born scholar who translated Greek texts and helped to preserve classical works. He traveled to the East twice, in 1405–1413 and 1421–1423, returning with a large number of Greek manuscripts, including the Greek anthology, Aeschylus, Sophocles and Apollonius of Rhodes. His value to the Renaissance revival of classicism was thus considerable.

**AUSGAR** See ANSGAR, SAINT.

**AUSTRASIA** The name given to the Eastern Kingdom of the Franks from the sixth to eighth century, separate from Neustria or the Western Kingdom of the Franks. Originally the domain of the Ripuarian Franks, Austrasia covered the present regions of western to central Germany and northeastern sections of France. Its peoples influenced not only German history but, more important, directly shaped the dynastic evolution of France. From Austrasia's capital of Metz (chosen about 629) the Merovingian kings of the realm, supported by the mayors of the palace, exercised considerable autonomy, culminating in the Battle of Tertry in 687, when the mayor Pepin II of Heristal (687–714) defeated THIERRY III and the Neustrians. Austrasia now dominated the Merovingian empire, the line of the Austrasian Pepinids retaining the politically impotent Merovingian kings until 751. In that year Pepin III (741–768) deposed King CHILDERIC III (737–751), ending the Merovingian dynasty. See also FRANCE.

**AUSTRIA** See AUSTRIA, DUCHY OF; AVARS; BABENBERG, HOUSE OF; BAVARIA; BOHEMIA; BULGARS, EMPIRES OF THE; CARINTHIA; CHARLEMAGNE; FRANKS; GERMANY; GRAZ; HABSBURG DYNASTY; HOHENSTAUFEN; HOLY ROMAN EMPIRE; HUNGARY; LEOPOLD III; LOMBARDS; MAGYARS; MONGOLS; MORAVIA; OTTO I; OTTOMAN EMPIRE; RUDOLF I; SALZBURG; SAXONS; SLAVS; STYRIA; TEUTONIC KNIGHTS; WELF, HOUSE OF; WITTELSBACH.

**AUSTRIA, DUCHY OF** The territory that during the Middle Ages was composed of Upper and Lower Austria, including Vienna, and was held by several noble houses. Austria was first given to the House of Babenburg in 976 as a margravate by the German emperors, the date usually described as the birth of Austria. A duchy by 1156, Austria passed into the control of Ottokar II of Bohemia in 1251. In 1276, however, he surrendered Austria, Carinthia and Styria to Rudolf I of Hungary (1273–1291), and the region remained a vital Habsburg possession for the next 642 years.

**AUTHARI** King of the Lombards from 583 to 590, whose reign was marked by incessant warfare with the Franks, Burgundians and the Byzantines in Italy, the Exarchate of Ravenna. He married Theodelinda, daughter of Garibald, Duke of Bavaria (c. 590), who became one of the most beloved queens of the Lombards. See also LOMBARDS.

**AUVERGNE** A region of east-central France occupying the present-day departments of Cantal, Puy-de-Dome and a part of Haute-Loire. A rich area in terms of agriculture, livestock and spas, it was placed under the control of the viscounts of Clermont in 913, who became the counts of Auvergne. For a time in the 12th century Auvergne was attached to Aquitaine and held by the English. By the 13th century the area was divided into several great counties, those of the Dauphiné d'Auvergne, the episcopal countship of Auvergne and the Terre d'Auvergne. These were eventually annexed by Francis I during his reign (1515–1547). See also FRANCE.

**AVARS** A tribal people, probably of Altaic descent, who settled in the region of present-day Hungary during the sixth century, playing a role in eastern Europe until the ninth century. Known to the Byzantines as the Abaroi, the Avars perhaps originated in the region of Turkestan, although some scholars have given them a more eastern homeland. By the middle of the sixth century they had migrated to the Caucasus and from there began searching for a permanent home at the expense of other confederations. They attacked Thuringia in 565 and in 567, allied with the Lombards, and then crushed the Gepidae, Byzantine allies, and encouraging the Lombards to move on into the Italian peninsula.

The Avars now possessed old Roman Pannonia. The Hungarian plain near the Danube and Tisza Rivers became their home and the center of their empire. Under their Khagan Bayan they occupied or dominated much of the

Balkans, encouraging Slavic migration into the Balkan territories. Avar ambitions led to wars against the Byzantines, including a combined Avar-Persian assault on Constantinople in 626. Lacking the strength to capture Constantinople and unable to maintain subject populations, the Avars began to decline in the second half of the seventh century with the rise of the independent Slavs and Bulgarian states. In the late eighth century, Charlemagne inflicted severe defeats on them. Eventually the Avars were absorbed by the Hungarians. See also HUNGARY.

**AVENPACE** See IBN BAJJAH.

**AVENZOAR** See IBN ZUHR.

**AVERROËS OF CÓRDOBA (IBN RUSHD AVERROËS)** (1126–1198) A major figure in the history of Islamic religious philosophy, whose full name was Abu al-Walid Muhammad ibn Ahmad ibn Muhammad ibn Rus, although he was called by the Westerners who adhered to his teachings "the Commentator." A member of a respected family of Islamic jurists at Córdoba, he was educated in law, theology, medicine, mathematics and philosophy. A chief judge (*qadi*) of Córdoba, Averroës was appointed personal physician to two caliphs, Abu Yusuf in 1182 and his son, Abu Yaqub, in 1184. Out of favor and exiled in 1195, he returned to Córdoba just before his death.

Averroës left a lasting influence on the history of philosophy through his many works, the most important of which are his commentaries on Aristotle (from 1162 to 1195) and on Plato's *Republic*. He was a careful student of Aristotle, holding him to be the foremost mind of all time. Averroës sought to reconcile philosophy with religion, holding faith to be symbolic in the expression of philosophical truth, and believing that truth was derived from reason not from faith. Influenced by Neoplatonism, he stressed the monopsychism of the human intellect, that there was but one intellect and that immortality of a personal nature did not exist. His views were the bases for the philosophy called Averroism, practiced by many Western philosophers from the 13th century until the Renaissance. Averroës's other writings were *Kulliyat (General Medicine), Fasl (Decisive Treatise on the Agreement between Religious Law and Philosophy), Tahafut al-Tahafut (Incoherence of the Incoherence)* and *Manahij (Examination of the Methods of Proof Concerning the Doctrines of Religion)*. See also AVERROISM; AVICENNA.

**AVERROISM** The name given to a philosophical movement based on the teachings of the Islamic writer Averroës. Averroism was derived from Averroës's interpretations and commentaries on Aristotle when they became known to Christian Europe's intellectual centers in the 13th century. Essentially, the philosophy argued for the rational harmonizing of reason and faith and for the existence of one intellect for all humanity, thus rendering the ideas of immortality or personal potentiality unacceptable. A major step in Averroism's acceptance came in 1255 when it was supported by the arts faculty of the University of Paris and found articulation in the words of Siger of Brabant. Other Averroists were John of Jandun and Taddeo of Parma. The doctrine was attacked strongly by Thomas Aquinas and was condemned by the church in 1270 and 1277. Nevertheless, it persisted until the Renaissance.

**AVICEBRON** See IBN GABIROL.

**AVICENNA (IBN SINA)** (980–1037) Muslim philosopher and doctor who was one of the most influential figures in Islamic and Western philosophical and medical history. Abu Al al-Husayn ibn Abd Allah ibn Sina, called by Westerners Avicenna, was a brilliant Aristotelian and a gifted physician, mathematician, astronomer and scientist. He was born in Bukhara in Persia, the son of a follower of Ismaili doctrine. Although he never adopted his father's beliefs, as a child he profited from the visits to his home by the finest minds of his day. He accumulated knowledge at an astonishing rate on a multitude of subjects, so that by the time he was 20, Avicenna had earned a reputation for genius. Court physician to the Persian dynasts, the Samanids, especially Nuh ibn Mansur, he had a bright future.

Catastrophe struck doubly when Avicenna's father died and the Samanids were liquidated by Mahmud of Ghazna. He spent years wandering across Persia, but his work continued, especially during those periods at court, such as when he was appointed vizier by the Buyids in Hamadan. Trouble for him continued, including imprisonment, and he found peace only in his last years at Isfahan. While on a military expedition with his patron, the ruler of Isfahan, Ala ad-Dawlah, he died in 1037, most likely from acute exhaustion.

The works of Avicenna were vast and ambitious. At Hamadan he compiled two of his most important efforts, the *Book of Healing* and the *Canon of Medicine*. The *Book of Healing* was a huge compendium of knowledge encompassing mathematics, metaphysics, music and philosophy. The *Canon of Medicine* was a synthesis of the medical traditions of the Greeks, Romans and Arabs and included his own extensive experience. It served as the most widely used medical text from the 12th century until as late as the 16th century and has long been viewed as one of the finest medical books ever composed. Avicenna also left an important body of philosophy. He was an Aristotelian, but his complex philosophical views were influenced by Neoplatonism. The Scholastics were indebted to him, and Islamic thought reflected for many years the ideas to which he had given substance.

**AVIGNON** A city in southeastern France, the present-day capital of the department of Vaucluse and, during the Middle Ages, the site of the so-called Babylonian Captivity of the popes, who resided there from 1309 to 1377. Avignon was originally the home of a Gallic tribe before falling to Rome and being renamed Avennio. According to tradition, the bishop of Avignon was Saint Rufus. The city was unimportant until the 12th century when the Albigensians prevailed, precipitating the destruction of most of the city walls in 1226.

Avignon was vassal to the papacy in 1309 when the popes first took up residence but became actual papal property in 1348, when Clement VI (1342–1352) purchased it outright from Joanna I, queen of Naples, who was also countess of Provence. There the popes remained in residence until 1377, and even later; during the Great Schism, two antipopes lived there, Clement VII (1378–1394) and Benedict XIII (1394–1417). The city itself was dominated by the double fortress of the Palais Vieux and the Palais Nouveau, built between 1334 and 1352. A gathering place for some of the worst elements of medieval society seeking asylum, subject to outbreaks of disease and infamous for debaucheries and houses of prostitution, Avignon was reviled by many, including Petrarch, who called it a sewer. See also BABYLONIAN CAPTIVITY; SCHISM, GREAT.

**AVIGNON PAPACY** See BABYLONIAN CAPTIVITY; SCHISM, GREAT.

**AVILA** The present-day capital of the Avila province in central Spain in what was Old Castile. Avila still enjoys popularity because of its splendidly preserved medieval structures, not least the city's celebrated wall, surrounding the Old City. Known as Abula during the early Middle Ages, Avila fell to the Muslim invasion of Spain around 715 but was recaptured in 1088 by ALFONSO VI (1065–1109) of León and Castile. The remains of the building projects of the Middle Ages include the walls, built in the 12th century, the gothic cathedral (late 11th century) and the Convento de Santo Tomas, which houses the tomb of Torquemada (late 15th century). See also RECONQUISTA.

**AVIS, HOUSE OF** See AVIZ, HOUSE OF.

**AVITUS** (d. 518) Bishop of Vienne and an ecclesiastical figure of prominence among the nations occupying old Roman Gaul in the late fifth century. Avitus was born to a Roman senatorial family but became a cleric and a bishop about 490. It was through his efforts that Sigismund, king of the Burgundians, was converted from Arianism to Christian orthodoxy. Avitus was the author of poems and epistles. See also ARIANISM.

**AVIZ, ORDER OF** See MILITARY ORDERS.

**AVIZ, HOUSE OF** The ruling dynasty of Portugal from 1383 to 1580, established by John I, who emerged (c. 1383) as the leader of Portuguese nationalism against the expansionist policies of Henry II, king of León and Castile. Members of the Aviz family ruled for the next centuries and counted in its line HENRY THE NAVIGATOR (1394–1460), prince of Portugal and explorer. See also PORTUGAL.

**AYYUBIDS** An Islamic dynasty that controlled Egypt, Syria, Iraq and Yemen for much of the 12th and 13th centuries. The dynasty was named after the Kurd Ayyub ibn Shadhi (d. 1173) but was founded by his son, the gifted general and statesman SALADIN (c. 1137–1193). Saladin rose to power as a brilliant soldier of the Zangid rulers, especially Nur al-Din, working with his brother Shirkuh to extend Zangid influence over the Shiite Fatimid caliphate of Egypt. In 1169 he became vizier to the Fatimids and, in 1171, took the vital initiative of abolishing the Fatimid caliphs, stepping into the vacuum of power. A Sunni Muslim, Saladin labored to convert the Shiite faction, consolidating his own power by sending expeditions to Tripoli, Tunis and Yemen. By 1186 he controlled Egypt, Yemen, Syria and Iraq, deciding the time was right to wage his jihad, or holy war, against the Crusaders.

Saladin died in 1193, clearly having intended to make his political position dynastic but failing in this regard. His empire broke apart on his demise into principalities, including Yemen, Homs, Edessa, Aleppo, Hama, Diyarbakir, Bosra, Banyas, Baalbek, Transjordan, Damascus and, of course, Egypt. His sons lost the leadership of the Ayyubid cause to another brother, al-Adil. Further, internal rivalries and strife weakened both the Ayyubids and the resolve of Islam to continue the holy war. Thus, twice the Crusaders were able to recover Jerusalem, in 1229 and in 1244. In 1250 the Ayyubid soldiers, the Mamluks, overthrew their masters, extirpating the Ayyubid principalities and becoming leaders in the Islamic world. Ironically, the Mamluks accomplished the goal that Saladin had set for his own dynasty—the final defeat of the Crusader States. See also EGYPT; ISLAM; SYRIA.

**AL-AZHAR** The famed center of teaching in the Islamic world, the University of al-Azhar was founded in Cairo, Egypt, and built around a mosque of the same name. It came into being as a result of Fatimid patronage in 970, and its teachings covered such fields as theology and Islamic law. It is still operating today.

**AL-AZIZ** (955–996) Fifth Fatimid caliph and the first to rule entirely from Egypt. Al-Aziz Bi'llah Nizar Abu Mansur ruled from 975 to 996 over a Fatimid domain larger and more vital than that of its Sunni counterpart in the East, the Abbasid caliphate. He succeeded his father, al-Mu'izz, in 975 and embarked on long campaigns against both the Byzantine Empire and the Abbasids. His wars in Syria, however, proved inconclusive, as were his attempts against the Umayyads in Spain. Al-Aziz is noteworthy as a very tolerant caliph; his wife was a Christian, and those not of Islam were not persecuted. A patron of the arts who also built mosques, gardens, public works and palaces in Cairo, al-Aziz was considered one of the great Fatimids, reigning at the time of full Fatimid glory. See also FATIMID CALIPHATE.

**AZNAR I GALINDO** Ruler of early Aragon, from about 809 to 839. See also ARAGON.

**AZNAR II GALINDO** Ruler of Aragon from 867 to 893. See also ARAGON.

# B

**BABENBERG, HOUSE OF** The ruling house of Austria from 976 to 1246, coming to prominence in 976 when Emperor Otto II (973–983) installed Leopold I of Babenberg (976–994) as margrave of the East Mark, or Austria. He made territorial acquisitions around Vienna, extended by his son, Henry I, but the political position of the family was not yet at its height. That changed during the time of Leopold III (1095–1136), who joined Henry V (1106–1125) in his efforts against his father, Emperor Henry IV (1056–1106), in 1106. Leopold received not only Henry's sister in marriage but also a high position in German politics. Leopold V (reigned 1177–1194) took part in the Third Crusade (1189–1192) and was responsible for the imprisonment of the English king Richard the Lion-Hearted, using part of the ransom paid by England to Emperor Henry VI to build in the duchy and to issue a new coin, the Wiener Pfennig (Vienna Penny). In 1192 Styria was added to the ducal holdings, and Leopold VI the Glorious (1198–1230) and Frederick II the Warlike (1230–1246) extended Babenberg control into Carniola. When Frederick II was killed while fighting the Hungarians in 1246, the Babenberg line was ended. Austria soon passed to Ottokar II of Bohemia (1253–1278), who had married Frederick's niece, Margaret. See also HENRY JASOMIRGOT.

**BABYLONIAN CAPTIVITY** The name given to the period from 1309 to 1377, when all the French popes were in residence at Avignon, France, and were subject to the dominance of the French state. The move was made by Pope Clement V (1305–1314) to the city that subsequently acquired a foul reputation because of the abuses of power and greed of many popes, prompting such writers as Petrarch to liken the exile of the popes to the captivity of the Jews by the Babylonians. Although some effective and positive developments took place during the Avignon papacy (such as some reforms of papal administration and the clergy), the prestige of the popes was severely damaged. On the return of the papacy to Rome in 1378, the church was immediately beset by the Great Schism. See also SCHISM, GREAT.

**BACON, ROGER** (c. 1213–1291) English Franciscan philosopher, teacher and one of the foremost figures of medieval science. Bacon was born probably at Ilchester in Somerset and went on to study at Oxford. He then went to Paris, where he lectured on Aristotle, but from about 1247 he turned his attention to experiments in science, later resigning his chair and returning to Oxford in 1250 or 1251. Under the influence of his friend, the learned Robert Grosseteste, Bacon was drawn by an interest in classical learning and languages while also exploring scientific research in astronomy, alchemy, mathematics and optics. A return to France in 1256 resulted in ill health and other problems that forced him to make a radical analysis of his life.

Bacon had joined the Franciscans by 1257. Although his views are considered by many modern scholars to be subject to exaggeration and lacking genuine originality, Bacon's studies nevertheless were complex enough to raise questions from his superiors concerning his orthodoxy. Difficulties with the order and a decline in his academic reputation probably led to his writing to the pope for intervention. Pope Clement IV (1265–1268) asked to see his writings, and Bacon eventually sent him (c. 1268), in secret, along with a work on alchemy, the *Opus maius (Great Work)*, the *Opus minus (Lesser Work)* and the *Opus tertium (Third Work)*, massive compendiums of philosophy, mathematics, experimental science and theology. Bacon sought papal approval for his labors and a recognition of science as a legitimate aspect of education. His hopes came to naught, however, for Clement died in 1268, and further troubles with the Franciscans (mentioned in the *Opus tertium*) led to his condemnation, and possibly his imprisonment, sometime between 1277 and 1279.

Among Bacon's other writings were the fragmentary *Communia naturalium* (*General Principles of Natural Philosophy*, 1268), *Communia mathematica* (*General Principles of Mathematics*, 1268), *Compendium studii philosophiae* (*Compendium of Philosophy*, 1272, in which he attacked contemporary education and the clergy), the unfinished *Compendium studii theologiae* (*Compendium of Theology*, 1292) and a Greek and Hebrew grammar (c. 1268).

Bacon was certainly far ahead of his time in his studies on science, reportedly inventing an early telescope, spectacles (working with optics) and the first gunpowder used in the West and drawing plans for a copper balloon and a flying machine. His experiments and refusal to adhere to convention, as well as his dabbling in the occult, alchemy and astrology, led to the notion that he was a sorcerer, although more correctly he was known as Doctor Mirabilis ("Amazing Doctor"). See also ASTROLOGY.

**BACONTHORPE, JOHN** (c. 1290–1346) Theologian, philosopher and a leading Carmelite monk. Also known as John Bacon and Johannes de Baconthorpe, he studied at Oxford and Paris before assuming a teaching position at

Cambridge and possibly Oxford. From 1329 to 1333 he was provincial of the English Carmelites, retiring, however, to pursue his studies and writing. Baconthorpe's importance was based on his work in examining the philosopher Averroës. Although he did not adhere to Averroës's doctrines, his analysis earned him a place of honor for Renaissance Averroists. Among his writings were commentaries on the *Sentences* of Peter Abelard and *The City of God* by Augustine. Baconthorpe held the title "Doctor Resolutus" (the "Resolute Doctor").

**BADAJOZ** A strategically important city in southwestern Spain, near the border of modern Portugal. Originally a small Roman site, Badajoz fell to the Moors, who made it a local center with the title Batalyans. In 1229 King Alfonso IX of León (1188–1230) captured it from the Moors. Henceforth the city was a major trading depot between Spain and Portugal and was the capital of what became the Badajoz province. See also RECONQUISTA.

**BADEN** City in northern Switzerland, founded in 1291 by the Habsburgs. It was conquered in 1415 by the forces of the Swiss Confederation, serving as the meeting place of the Diet of the Swiss Confederation from 1424 to 1712. See also SWITZERLAND.

**BADI AZ-ZAMAN AL-HAMADANI** See AL-HAMADANI.

**BAGHDAD** Capital of the Abbasid caliphate from 762 to 1258 (in modern Iraq), and one of the most important social, economic and religious centers in the Islamic world. Baghdad was an ancient site even before the arrival of the Arabs, having been a city for the Babylonians, Seleucids and Sassanid Persians. Its central location and history thus convinced the Abbasid caliph, al-Mansur, to place the residence and the heart of administration there in 762. Reportedly, at the cost of millions of dirhams and after four years of labor, Baghdad was completely rebuilt by the artists, architects, landscapers and craftsmen of Islam. Built in a circular pattern, the center of the city was the famous "Round City"; called the "City of Peace," it had three surrounding walls and four gates symbolically leading to the four directions of the empire. Also in the center of the city was the golden palace of the caliph, with the dome of the Diwan Amm, or audience hall, reaching some 100 feet high. Merchants were not allowed into Baghdad, so there developed another whole urban complex around the city proper. Considered a magnificent architectural achievement, Baghdad also developed into the trading heart of the Islamic empire, serving as a major depot for the abundant trade of East and West.

The golden age of Baghdad arose during the reign of Harun al-Rashid (785–809), when it came the closest to the description of the legendary metropolis of *The Thousand and One Nights*. Its gardens, palaces and riches were known throughout Islam. Harun's wife, Zubaida, supposedly would not allow any vessels at her table that were not solid gold or silver and encrusted with jewels. Equally, however, Baghdad enjoyed enormous wealth in learning, especially science, philosophy and medicine. This time of undisputed greatness ended with the civil war between Harun's son, al-Amin (809–813) and his brother al-Mamun (c. 813–883), in which the central city was badly damaged. Baghdad would never recover, and from 936 the caliphs spent much of their time away at Samarra, a new capital, or at Mukharrim. The caliphate fell under the control of the Buyids in 945 and the Seljuk Turks in 1055, but its political deterioration was offset by the continued riches of the trading routes. Total obliteration came in 1258 with the arrival of the Mongols, who extirpated the caliphate, wrecked Baghdad and massacred most of its inhabitants (supposedly 800,000 people). The subsequent history of Baghdad was one of decline and repeated conquest by Mongols (under Tamerlane in 1401) and Turks (the Black Sheep Turks and White Sheep Turks), the city finally falling to the Ottoman Empire in the 16th century. See also ABBASID CALIPHATE.

**BAJEZID I** (c. 1360–1403) Sultan of the Ottoman Empire from 1389 to 1402, who did much to extend Ottoman influence throughout the Balkans and Anatolia. Bajezid responded to the ambitious policies of Venice in Greece and Byzantium with attacks on Istanbul (1391–1399), Bulgaria (1393) and Salonika (1394) and an invasion of Hungary in 1395. As a result of the latter operation, a joint Hungarian-Venetian crusade was organized against the Turks at Nicopolis in 1396. Bajezid virtually annihilated the Christians in this campaign. Realizing, however, the need to strengthen the Islamic nature of his empire, the sultan subjugated large parts of Anatolia hitherto under independent emirates. Such a decision precipitated a war with Tamerlane in 1402, a conflict that Bajezid lost. He was captured, paraded in an iron carriage and died in captivity in 1403. His nickname, Yildirim, meant "Lightning." See also OTTOMAN EMPIRE.

**BAJEZID II** (c. 1447–1512) Sultan of the Ottoman Empire from 1481 to 1502, called Adli, or "the Just," and

Sultan Bajezid II

one of the most enlightened and successful of the Ottoman rulers. The son of Muhammad II the Conqueror, Bajezid had to face a challenge on his succession in 1481, from his brother Djem (or Cem). He eventually triumphed, driving his brother into exile in Europe. Bajezid immediately terminated the pro-Western leanings of the court that had been initiated by his father, returning Ottoman policy to a more Islamic orthodoxy. The majority of his reign was spent at war.

Bajezid continued the Ottoman expansion in the Balkans and Anatolia as well as in Asia Minor. Having built a mighty fleet, from 1499 to 1503, he fought numerous campaigns against the Venetians, winning territory along the Adriatic and making Balkan possessions more secure. Other conflicts were less successful, such as those against the Mamluks in Asia Minor and the Safavids of Persia. In 1512, he abdicated in favor of one of his sons, Selim, in the hope of preventing civil strife over the succession. Bajezid II was considered an intellectual and was a patron of Islamic arts. See also OTTOMAN EMPIRE.

**BALDOVINETTI, ALISSO** (c. 1425–1499) Italian painter and mosaicist whose work was influenced by Domenico Veneziano and Andrea del Castagno. Baldovinetti worked almost exclusively in Florence, as was recorded in his diary. His work was considered lacking in innovation and sophistication but was notable for his use of lighting, form and early introduction of the landscape. Most remarkable among his paintings were the *Madonna and Child* (in the Louvre) and the fresco of the Nativity in the Church of Santa Anunziata, in Florence, both depicting the landscape of the Arno Valley.

**BALDWIN I, COUNT OF EDESSA** See BALDWIN II, KING OF JERUSALEM.

**BALDWIN I, KING OF JERUSALEM** (c. 1058–1118) Ruler of the Kingdom of Jerusalem from 1100 to 1118, called Baldwin of Flanders, the brother of Godfrey de Bouillon, with whom he joined the First Crusade (1096–1099). During the Crusade he entered into an agreement with the Christian prince of Edessa to give him aid in return for being named heir to the land. In 1098, however, he forced the prince to abdicate, founding the Crusader State of Edessa. Two years later, his brother, the "Defender of the Holy Sepulchre" in Jerusalem, died, and Baldwin was elected as his successor. A campaign against the Fatimids of Egypt gave him enough political strength to be crowned king of Jerusalem.

Baldwin proved himself a more than able monarch, establishing a unified administration, promoting commerce and cementing the position of the kingdom by his marriage to Adelaide of Saona, countess of Sicily, having forced his Armenian wife, Arda, into a convent. Territorial expansion increased throughout his reign. He captured Arsuf, Caesarea, Acre and Sidon and, in 1115, built the castle Krak de Montréal. Baldwin died in 1118 without an heir but was nevertheless called the founder of the Kingdom of Jerusalem. See also CRUSADER STATES.

**BALDWIN II, KING OF JERUSALEM** (d. 1131) Ruler of the Kingdom of Jerusalem from 1118 to 1131, called Baldwin de Bourg, the cousin of Baldwin I of Jerusalem and Godfrey de Bouillon, with whom he embarked on the First Crusade (1096–1099). On the election of Baldwin I (1100–1118) as ruler of Jerusalem, Baldwin was named prince of Edessa. Wars with the Seljuk Turks ensued, and Baldwin was captured in 1104; he was released in 1108, only to have to fight Tancred to regain Edessa. In 1118 Baldwin I died, and Baldwin II was again chosen his successor, this time as monarch of the Kingdom of Jerusalem. More war followed, including Baldwin's capture and holding as hostage from 1123 to 1124. His policy was to promote the Crusader States, especially military orders such as the Templars and Knights Hospitalers. With the help of the orders and both Genoa and Venice, the king strengthened the power of his realm. See also CRUSADER STATES.

**BALDWIN III, KING OF JERUSALEM** (1131–1162) Ruler of the Kingdom of Jerusalem from 1143 to 1162, the son of King Fulk of Jerusalem and Melisend; he became king in 1143 but shared power with his mother until 1151, especially during the Second Crusade (1147–1149). His taking, in 1151, sole control of the kingdom precipitated a civil war between his supporters and those of his mother, but once he had consolidated his position, he became known as a gifted—even ideal—monarch. An active Crusader, he engaged in numerous campaigns, capturing Ascalon in 1153 but proving incapable of repulsing the growing strength of Nur al-Din, who took northern Syria and Damascus. Baldwin married the Byzantine princess Theodora, thus linking the Crusader States and the Byzantine Empire. See also CRUSADER STATES.

**BALDWIN IV, KING OF JERUSALEM** (1161–1185) Ruler of the Kingdom of Jerusalem from 1174 to 1185, called "the Leper" because of the disease from which he suffered. The son of King Amalric I and Agnes of Courtenay, he was educated by William of Tyre. Extremely intelligent and, as would be seen, gifted militarily, he succeeded his father but had as a regent until 1177 Count Raymond III of Tripoli. Three problems dominated his reign: the challenge of the Saracen Saladin, his illness and the deterioration of unity within the kingdom.

Saladin launched his attack on the Crusader States in 1177, besieging Ascalon. Baldwin succeeded in defeating Saladin at Montgisard and negotiated a truce that lasted until 1180. At its termination the Muslim prince continued his war, aided by the struggle for power among the nobles of Jerusalem. Baldwin's leprosy not only caused increasing difficulty for the ruler but made questions of succession inevitable. Chief among the claimants were Raymond and Guy of Lusignan, who married Baldwin's sister, Sybil. Ailing, Baldwin named his nephew, Baldwin V (1185–1186) as his heir and died in 1185 leaving the kingdom in turmoil. See also CRUSADER STATES.

**BALDWIN V, KING OF JERUSALEM** (1177–1186) Ruler of the Kingdom of Jerusalem from March 1185 until August 1186. He was the nephew of Baldwin IV, the son of Baldwin's sister Sybil and William of Montferrat. He became king on Baldwin's death, with Count Raymond III of Tripoli acting as regent. While his early actions pointed to a potentially bright future (a truce with Saladin and increased trade), he died in 1186 at Acre, succeeded by Guy of Lusignan. See also CRUSADER STATES.

**BALDWIN I, LATIN EMPEROR** (1172–c. 1205) Count of Flanders and Hainault and the first Latin emperor of Constantinople, from 1204 to 1205. The son of Baldwin V of Hainault and Margaret of Flanders, he fought for the cause of the English king Richard I the Lion-Hearted against Philip II Augustus of France before answering the plea of Pope Innocent II in 1195 to begin another Crusade. Baldwin left for Jerusalem in 1202 and thus became one of the leaders of the infamous Fourth Crusade. He and his fellow Crusaders, in alliance with the Venetians, toppled the Byzantine emperor Alexius III Angelus, installed Alexius IV Angelus and his father, Isaac II Angelus, and after their deposition, seized control of Constantinople. With the support of the Venetian doge Enrico Dandolo, Baldwin was crowned the first Latin emperor on May 16, 1204, in the church of the Hagia Sophia at Constantinople.

As emperor, Baldwin introduced Western feudalism to the Byzantines, sweeping away the centuries-old traditions of the Eastern Empire. Supported by his own knights, now the nobility of the new order, Baldwin secured recognition of the pope, who saw opportunities for a united Christendom. Baldwin's reign was brief, however, for the Bulgars under Kalojan invaded the empire in 1205, defeating and capturing Baldwin at Adrianople. Executed by the Bulgars, he was succeeded by his brother, Henry of Flanders. See also CONSTANTINOPLE, LATIN EMPIRE OF.

**BALDWIN II, LATIN EMPEROR** (1217–1273) Ruler of the Latin Empire of Constantinople. His reign (1228–1261) marked the decline and end of the Latin Empire. He was the son of Emperor Peter of Courtenay and Yolanda, coming to the throne in 1228 after the death of his brother, Robert. John of Brienne, titular king of Jerusalem, acted as regent until Baldwin reached his majority. During this time, however, two invasions, one by John III Ducas Vatatzes (1222–1254) of Nicaea and a second by Ivan Asen II, king of the Bulgars (1218–1241), were launched. On reaching an age when he could assume royal duties, Baldwin found his realm in a state of financial, military and political bankruptcy. Journeys to the courts of Europe were made in order to seek support and funds, but these proved insufficient. In 1261 Michael VIII Palaeologus (1259–1282) recaptured Constantinople for the Byzantines. Baldwin fled to the West and died in 1273, still attempting to plan a recovery. See CONSTANTINOPLE, LATIN EMPIRE OF.

**BALEARIC ISLANDS** Islands just off the coast of Spain, comprising two major groups, the first including Majorca and Minorca, and the more westerly group, called the Pine Islands, composed of Formentera, Ibiza and smaller islets. Roman occupation of the Balearic Islands ended in the fifth century with their conquest by the Vandals, who in turn lost the islands to the Byzantines. Moorish raids commenced with the fall of Africa to the Muslims, but direct seizure did not come until 903, under the Emirate of Córdoba. Moorish ownership changed several times over the next centuries as the last of the Almoravids used the islands as their base for seagoing activities until their destruction by the Almohads in 1203. King James I of Aragon claimed the islands about 1229, taking Majorca and Ibiza. Minorca was taken by Alfonso III of Aragon in 1286.

**BALIOL** For entries under this name, see BALLIOL.

**BALKANS** See AVARS; BOHEMIA; BULGARIA; BULGARS, EMPIRES OF THE; BYZANTINE EMPIRE; CUMANS; EPIRUS; EPIRUS, DESPOTATE OF; GREECE; HUNGARY; MOLDAVIA; MONGOLS; SERBIA; SLAVS; VENICE.

**BALL, JOHN** (d. 1381) Former English priest who became one of the leaders of the Peasant Revolt in England in 1381. Ball was excommunicated in 1366 for his antiestablishment sermons and calls for a destruction of the mobility and upper clergy. Although stripped of his priestly title, he nevertheless continued to preach wherever a crowd would listen. Frequently imprisoned, he was rescued in 1381 by participants in the Peasant Revolt and went to London, where he called for a revolution. He was captured, condemned and hung at Saint Alban's. Contemporary accounts of his activities were naturally biased, such as that of Jean Froissart, who called him the mad priest. See also TYLER, WAT.

**BALLIOL, EDWARD DE, KING OF SCOTLAND** (c. 1283–1364) Ruler of Scotland from 1332 until 1356, but as monarch he was never able to control all of Scotland and was opposed by the national party of King David II (1329–1371). Edward, the son of John de Balliol, king of Scotland from 1292 to 1296, was wholly dependent on the English king Edward III (1327–1377) for his political position. He inherited his father's claims to the throne and in 1324 was supported by Edward III and a group of English nobles who had been exiled from Scotland by Robert I the Bruce (1306–1329). Edward invaded Scotland from France in 1332, defeating the eight-year-old King David II and his regent, Donald, earl of Mar, at the Battle of Dupplin in August. Crowned in September, he soon acknowledged the supremacy of England and was thus embroiled in a war with his own subjects. Archibald Douglas inflicted a defeat on him in December, a loss avenged by Edward III the following July. Edward, however, maintained power only aided by England, and his position deteriorating steadily after David's return from France in 1341. He abdicated in favor of Edward III in 1356 and died in 1364, in England. See also SCOTLAND.

**BALLIOL, JOHN DE** (d. c. 1269) English baron and the father of John de Balliol, king of Scotland. A powerful noble, he was named regent to the Scottish king Alexander III, holding office from 1251 to 1255, when he was reportedly driven from the post because of treasonous acts. He sided with Henry III of England (1216–1272) during the Baron's War (1264–1267) and was imprisoned briefly after the Battle of Lewes in 1264. He is also important for his contribution in founding Balliol College at Oxford, which through his wife's continued endowments was given its charter in 1282. See also OXFORD.

**BALLIOL, JOHN DE, KING OF SCOTLAND** (c. 1250–c. 1313) Ruler of Scotland from 1292 to 1296, the son of John de Balliol, regent to Alexander III of Scotland from 1251 to 1255. Already linked to the royal house of Scotland by family connections, Balliol claimed the throne in 1292 following the death of Margaret, the "Maid of Norway," despite 12 other claimants to the title. Known to the Scots as Toom Tabard ("the empty cloak," because he was stripped of his royal regalia), he acknowledged England's suzerainty over Scotland in return for King Edward I's support of his right to rule. This act of homage was renounced in 1296, and he was soon defeated by Edward at the Battle of Dunbar and compelled to abdicate. John de Balliol died in Normandy around 1314, his son, Edward de Balliol, taking up his claim to the Scottish throne. See also SCOTLAND.

**BALSAMON, THEODORE** (b. c. 1130; d. after 1195) Byzantine patriarch of Antioch and an important Byzantine scholar of the 12th century. Originally from Constantinople, he was made patriarch about 1185–1190 but was prevented from fulfilling his duties because of the installation of a Latin patriarch at Antioch by the Crusaders, and he was forced to reside at Constantinople. During his years in the Byzantine capital he acted as chancellor of law to the patriarch of Constantinople, making valuable contributions to the preservation of Byzantine theological, canonical and political history. His major work was a commentary on the *Nomocanon*, a collection of the decrees and laws of the Eastern Church.

**BALTIC SEA** See DENMARK; HANSEATIC LEAGUE; HOLY ROMAN EMPIRE; LIVONIA; MILITARY ORDERS; POLAND; RUSSIA; SWEDEN; TEUTONIC KNIGHTS; TRADE AND COMMERCE.

**BANKING** A profession responsible for the activities of saving, safeguarding, issuing and loaning money. Banking during the Middle Ages underwent extensive development, playing a major role in the socioeconomic life of Europe and beyond, with many facets of modern banking emerging during this period. With the fall of the Roman Empire in the West, there was an inevitable deterioration in economic life, as trade and industry were shattered by Germanic invasions and political destabilization. Roman banking and finance were equally susceptible, and while commercial ventures and investment capital continued to be used to sustain the economic life of various areas, most opportunities were local or fulfilled a limited need. Overseas trade was in the hands of Jews and Syrians, who supplied goods from the East to very small groups of aristocratic clientele. This remained the case from the 6th to the 10th century, unlike the Islamic world, including Byzantine Empire, where the issue of currency, trade and commerce were promoted on a larger scale.

Change came in the 10th century in the West, thanks in large measure to the economic recovery propelled by the growth of population. With increases in the numbers of people in a region came new opportunities for commercial expansion. The Italians, especially the maritime powers such as Venice, Genoa, Pisa and Amalfi, were the first to recognize the changing economic climate, and thus the earliest examples of medieval banking were found there. Henceforth the Italians were to enjoy a position of prominence in banking over the next centuries. The first evidence of bankers came from the 12th century notarial records of Genoa. The Genoese term for changer was *cambitor,* who conducted his business behind a benchlike table, the *banchus;* in time the term *bancherius* (banker) became synonymous with *cambitor.* The early days, however, were far from sophisticated, for the *bancherius* did not involve himself in credit, deposits or transfers but was still only a *cambitor,* or money changer. By 1200 the bankers were accepting deposits and paying interest while allowing two kinds of deposits: time and demand. Time deposits were made for a specific period with penalties for early withdrawal; demand deposits were self-explanatory. Money was transferred from one account to another, and overdrafts were permitted at times. An important innovation was the use of investment funds to pay for commercial ventures, a practice later widely accepted that had considerable impact on long-term trade.

With the 14th century came the influx of more active and diverse bankers to the commercial centers of Europe. Many were Jews because of the prohibitions by canon law concerning usury (the charging of excessive interest on a loan), but generally the church was willing to make allowances to banks about interest so long as the interest rates did not exceed tolerable limits and thus become usurous. Far more dangerous, in many ways, was the real possibility of a bank facing insolvency through incompetence or poor choices in terms of foreign investments. There was a high mortality rate in banking, and very often a more reliable institution was the mercantile bank (or merchant bank). Most of the great merchant banks were Italian, such as those of the powerful Medici, Bardi and Acciaiuoli families. As commerce was increasingly concentrated in cities, banks ceased relying on the set fairs (such as the Champagne fairs), turning instead to the creation of networks of agents, partnerships, branches and correspondents in the trading centers of Europe, including London, Paris, Barcelona, Bruges and Frankfurt am Main. Foreign governments were clients, as were nobles and the church. As the House of Bardi discovered in dealing with King Edward III (1327–1377), and as others learned with various princely recipients of loans, such transactions could be disastrous if the king defaulted, as did Edward, as a result of the costs he incurred during the Hundred Years' War, causing Bardi's ruin. Long-distance trade and investments could be profitable, however, and the means of accomplishing them were made simpler by the use of foreign exchange, the process by which a letter of credit entitled the bearer to receive currency equal to the value of his own money, but at the current rates of exchange. Once again a potentially hazardous transaction because of often wild fluctuations in exchange rates, foreign exchange was still a leading method of fostering extensive foreign expansion and a safer means of transferring funds than carrying actual money on wartorn roads in many territories. The failure of many Italian banks in the 14th century culminated in the demise of the fortunes of the Medici toward the end of the 15th century. Into the gap left by the Italians (who, by 1500 had lost their primary position) stepped the banks of northern countries, marking a new era in finance, that of modern banking. See also ACCIAIUOLI, HOUSE OF; BARDI, HOUSE OF; FLORENCE; MEDICI, HOUSE OF; PERUZZI, HOUSE OF; TRADE AND COMMERCE.

**BANNOCKBURN, BATTLE OF** A major battle fought on June 23, 1314, between the Scots led by Robert I the Bruce (1306–1329) and the English led by King Edward II (1307–1327). It marked the crushing defeat of an English army and the establishment of an independent Scotland. Attempting to regain England's dominance over Scottish affairs, as had been the case in the time of his father, Edward I, Edward II launched another invasion of the country but was challenged by Robert the Bruce. The forces confronted each other at Bannockburn near Stirling Castle.

Robert deployed his troops of about 40,000 infantry and 1,500 cavalry on a slope near Bannockburn with a forest to the right and a marsh to the left. Before his position was marshy land and a stream, fordable only by one road. Despite the tactical superiority of the Scots, Edward launched his 60,000 infantry, 20,000 archers and nearly 15,000 mixed cavalry. Governed by the restraints of the terrain, the superior English army was unable to deploy properly and faced growing confusion. Losses mounted as their clumsy assaults were repulsed, and panic set in when a charge by Robert's camp followers, waving banners and blowing trumpets, was heard in the woods. Edward took flight, joined by his troops, who were massacred by the thousands. One of the worst defeats ever inflicted on England, the battle allowed the Scots to force the English to recognize Scotland's freedom and accept Robert as its king. See also SCOTLAND.

**BAPHOMET** An idol of varying shape and symbolism, supposedly worshiped by the Knights Templars during the Middle Ages, prior to their extirpation in the early 14th century. It had the aspects of a bull, ass, goat or dog and was cited by the opponents of the Templars as proof of their practice of sorcery and black magic. See also TEMPLARS.

**BARBAROSSA, FREDERICK** See FREDERICK I, EMPEROR.

**BARBARY STATES** A group of independent states in the region of North Africa extending from the western fringes of Egypt to the Atlantic, including the territories of Libya, Tunisia, Morocco, Algeria and the desert sections of the northern Sahara. The Barbary States came into being with the decline of centralized Islamic control over Africa, the title deriving from their principal inhabitants, the Berbers. Moorish piratic activities had been an element of life along the Mediterranean coast of Africa, Spain and Italy for centuries (see AGHLABIDS; MOORS). The Barbary States were the inheritors of that tradition, achieving their greatest prominence in the 17th century.

**BARBOUR, JOHN** (c. 1320–1395) Influential Scottish poet and writer, best remembered for his epic *The Bruce* (in Scottish, *The Brus*). Archdeacon of Aberdeen, Barbour studied at Oxford and in France and was known to King Edward III of England (1327–1377), who gave him permission to study there. A favorite of Scottish royalty, he was allotted a pension. *The Bruce*, or as it was fully known, *The Actes and Life of the Most Victorious Conqueror, Robert Bruce King of Scotland*, was written during the 1360s, detailing with a high degree of accuracy, style and realism the life and battles of Robert the Bruce. Barbour's account of the Battle of Bannockburn was the centerpiece of the romance, and other descriptions of events from the demise of Alexander III in 1286 to the burial of Robert's heart in 1332 are included. Barbour was credited with having been the author of the first major work in Scottish literature, as well as the authorship of other, lost works, including the *Stewartis Oryginalle*, a genealogy of Scottish kings. See also SCOTLAND.

**BARCELONA** City in northeastern Spain, on the Mediterranean Sea, during the the Middle Ages the capital of Catalonia and, for a time, the political heart of the Crown of Aragon. Originally founded by the Romans, it was captured by the Muslims in 717 but fell to a Carolingian army in 801. Frankish dominance and ability to hold back the Moors allowed Barcelona to prosper and encouraged the rise of the counts of Barcelona, who in the 10th century declared their independence. The region of Catalonia soon was subjugated by the city, as were parts of southern France. The union of Aragon and Catalonia was sealed on the marriage of Berenguer IV of Catalonia with the Aragonese heiress Petronila in 1137.

With the royal residence of Aragon established at Barcelona, and with Aragonese expansionism acquiring new territories in the Mediterranean from the 13th century, the political oligarchy led by merchants of the city, headed by the Consell de Cent, or Council of One Hundred, took steps to transform it into a maritime economic power. Barcelona thus competed with Genoa and Venice until a plague in the 14th century and Alfonso V's decision in 1442 to move the Aragonese capital to Naples contributed to the decline of the city. The University of Barcelona was founded in 1450. See also ARAGON; CATALONIA.

**BARDI, HOUSE OF** A powerful and influential Florentine family that was one of Europe's greatest merchant banking establishments during the first half of the 14th century. The Bardi used political alliances, shrewd business dealings and careful cultivation of finances to become by 1250 a major participant in the commerce of Florence. By 1310 it was the city's most prominent banking house. In 1338, however, they began making massive loans to King Edward III of England (1327–1377), in order to fund his war with France. The king defaulted on his payments in 1341, and with that the Bardi hope of entering the English wool trade failed. The Bardi also found themselves irretrievably overextended because of their financing of Florentine attacks on the city of Lucca. The Bardi were economically and politically bankrupt by 1345–1346. See also FLORENCE; TRADE AND COMMERCE.

**BAR-HEBRAEUS, GREGORIUS** (1226–1286) Syrian bishop, philosopher and scholar. One of the greatest historians of the Middle Ages, Bar-Hebraeus was the common name given to Abu'l-Faraj, the son of a Jewish physician who had been converted to Christianity. Having studied medicine in Antioch and Tripoli, he was made bishop at the age of 20, archbishop at 26 and by 1264 the primate of the East for the Eastern Jacobite Church, with his residence at Mar Mattai near Mosul (see JACOBITES). As a result of his extensive travels in Armenia and Syria, Bar-Hebraeus visited libraries and acquired vast amounts of information on a wide variety of subjects. His subsequent writings included treatises on classical learning, astronomy and speculative theology. Some of his most important works were *Chronography*, a compendium of Middle Eastern history from the dawn of creation; *Granary of Mysteries (Horreum mysteriorum)* a biblical analysis; and the *Butter of Science*, a massive encyclopedia on many branches of knowledge, which reflected his familiarity with Aristotelian philosophy as transmitted through the teachings of Avicenna. Bar-Hebraeus was a notable figure during the time of increased communication between the Christian West and the Islamic East; although most of his works were written in Syriac, they were translated into Arabic.

**BARI** Adriatic seaport and the capital of the Apulia region in southern Italy. Bari was founded probably around 1500 B.C. and subsequently developed as a leading port. It fell to the Muslims in 841 but 24 years later it was captured by the Byzantines. In 885 it was made the center of Byzantine administration in the region. In 1071 Robert Guiscard seized the city for the Normans of Italy. Over the next years Bari was involved in the Crusades as elements of the First Crusade embarked for the Holy Land from there, and Peter the Hermit preached there. After being severely damaged by William the Bad in 1156, the city was rebuilt by Emperor Frederick II (1215–1250) in the mid-15th century. Many medieval buildings have been preserved, including its 12th-century Romanesque cathedral, the Basilica of Saint Nicholas, and a Norman castle. See also APULIA.

***BARLAAM AND JOSAPHAT*** A popular anonymous collection of hagiography (Saints' lives) found in various languages in the countries of medieval Europe. The earliest versions, dating from around the seventh century, were written in Greek, and by the 12th century in Latin. Essentially the story of Barlaam and Josephat was a Christianized retelling of the Buddha story. In one variation, written by Euthymius, a monk of Georgia in the 10th century, Barlaam, an Indian prince, was converted to Christianity by Josaphat, a hermit.

**BARNET, BATTLE OF** See WARS OF THE ROSES.

**BARONS' WAR** The name given to a civil war fought from 1263 to 1266 between Henry III, king of England (1216–1272), and his nobles. It was part of the continuing struggle between the English monarchy and the barons for political control of the kingdom. The direct cause of the conflict was the baronial opposition to the incompetent rule of Henry III, especially the loss of Aquitaine and Poitou to the French, and unpopular fiscal policies. Under the leadership of Earl Simon de Montfort, a rebel army defeated and captured Henry at the Battle of Lewes on May 14, 1264. Prince Edward (the future Edward I, 1272–1307) escaped to raise an army in the western part of England, but Simon was in truth in control of the country, using the opportunity to make administrative reforms in the government. His power was broken by the brilliant campaigning of Edward, who defeated the barons at Newport in July 1265 and then annihilated them at Evesham on August 4, 1265. With Simon de Montfort killed in the fray, final opposition to the king was destroyed at Chesterfield in 1266. Peace was signed with the Dictum of Kenilworth in 1266 and the Statute of Marlborough in 1267. Edward I, the real victor of the Barons' War, would make concessions to the nobility and would institute constitutional changes. See also ENGLAND.

**BARTHOLOMAEUS ANGLICUS** Early-13th-century Franciscan writer, also called Bartholomew the Englishman. He taught at Paris but was well known in England and in Germany. Bartholomaeus gained lasting fame because of his 19-volume encyclopedia *De proprietatibus rerum (On the Properties of Things)*, a massive compendium of the knowledge of the time. It was translated into English by John of Trevisa in 1495 and was extremely popular in the centuries to follow.

**BARTOLO OF SASSOFERRATO** (1314–1357) Also known as Bartolo of Saxoferrato, a lawyer, influential writer and leader of the group of Italian jurists who concentrated their studies on the *Corpus juris civilis* of Roman law, specifically established by Justinian I. A teacher at Perugia, he worked to advance the understanding both of classical law and of legal procedures.

**BASEL** City in northern Switzerland and capital of the Swiss canton of Basel-Stadt. Originally a Roman colony, Basel became a bishopric in the seventh century and derived its subsequent prosperity from the power of its prelate. In the 11th century it was made a free imperial city, with its own university (founded in 1460). A member of the Swiss Confederation from 1501, Basel was best known for the council held there from 1431 to 1449. See also BASEL, COUNCIL OF.

**BASEL, COUNCIL OF** A general council of the church, sitting from 1431 to 1449 in Basel, Switzerland, to settle several pressing problems facing Christianity and the papacy. Summoned by Pope Martin V (1417–1431) and confirmed by his successor, Eugene IV (1431–1447), the council attempted to settle the Hussite heresy and the question of papal supremacy. From the start the meeting was plagued by poor attendance and the pope's refusal to dissolve it because of a lack of delegates. Eventually the council began its deliberations. Questions concerning the Hussites were solved with the creation of the Compactata of Prague, signed about 1436 and responsible for the return of most of the heretics to communion with Rome.

The principal crisis remained unresolved, however, namely the conflict between the pope and the council over the conciliar theory, advanced by the Council of Constance (1414–1418), which held that ultimate authority rested with the council and not with the Holy See. Antipapal measures were taken, and in 1437 Eugene denounced the council in the bull *Doctoris gentium*, ordering that it be moved to Ferrara, Italy. After many delegates departed, the remaining rump council was excommunicated. That group then deposed the pope, electing Amadeus VIII, duke of Savoy, as his replacement, who took the name Felix V (1439–1449). Ten years of bickering followed until, in 1449, Felix abdicated in favor of Eugene's successor, Nicholas V (1447–1455). The council was finally dissolved, and the conciliar theory died with it. The activities and the legitimacy of the council have been debated by theologians and scholars of church history.

**BASIL I, BYZANTINE EMPEROR** (d. 886) Ruler from 867 to 886, called "the Macedonian," the founder of the Macedonian dynasty that ruled the empire until 1056. Originally of a peasant family in Macedonia, Basil rose through the ranks of the imperial government in Constantinople, eventually serving as chamberlain and then as co-emperor with Michael III (842–867). Once in a favorable political position, Basil rid himself of all possible opponents and finally assassinated his patron, Michael, in 867.

As emperor, Basil continued the long war with the Muslims in Asia Minor, recaptured Cyprus and extended Byzantine influence, political and religious, into the Balkans. Such advances threatened the already strained relations between the Eastern and Western Churches. Basil, however, dealt adroitly with Rome by excommunicating the patriarch PHOTIUS and replacing him with Ignatius. Although Photius was reinstated by the Eastern Church in 877, on Ignatius's death, he was accepted nevertheless by the Western Church. In Italy, Byzantine acquisitions were made more secure by the work of the governor there, Nicephorus Phocas. Basil's lasting achievement was a necessary legal reform that led, under his son Leo VI (866–912), to the Byzantine code of law, which was called the *Basilics*. He died in 886 while hunting and was succeeded by Leo. See also BYZANTINE EMPIRE.

**BASIL II, BYZANTINE EMPEROR** (958–1025) Ruler from 976 to 1025 who earned the nickname Bulgaroctonus, or the "Killer of the Bulgars." The son of Emperor Romanus II (959–963), Basil was crowned co-emperor with his brother, Constantine, in 960, but on Romanus's death in 963, imperial power was usurped by two powerful generals, Nicephorus II Phocas (963–969) and John I Tzimisces (969–976). Finally, with the help of the powerful eunuch chamberlain Basil, Basil II came to the throne, defeating two rival claimants with the help of the Russians under Vladimir of Kiev and then removing all political opposition, including that of Basil the chamberlain.

Basil's policy of expansion and consolidation was an outgrowth of his having inherited an empire both strong and stable. He maintained Byzantine authority in Asia Minor and annexed parts of Georgia and Armenia. The most obvious demonstration of his imperial ambitions came in Bulgaria, where, from 986 until 1014, he waged a merciless war against the Bulgar king Samuel. His final victory in 1014 at Kleidon was notorious for his having blinded thousands of prisoners (he spared only each 100th man), before returning them to Samuel, who died a broken man shortly thereafter. Other plans for expansion included a proposed marriage between his niece, Zoë, with the emperor Otto III (r. 996–1002). At home he had a reputation for severity and austerity, repressing the aristocracy and confiscating so much land and treasure that during his reign there was never a need for additional funds. Driven and extremely able, Basil died in 1025 leaving an empire unable to find a replacement worthy of him. His brother Constantine VIII (1025–1028) was not such a man. See also BYZANTINE EMPIRE.

**BASIL I OF MOSCOW** See VASILY I.

**BASIL II OF MOSCOW** See VASILY II.

**BASQUES** Inhabitants of northern Spain, specifically in the provinces of Alava, Vizcaya and Quipuzcoa. A fierce and independent people, the Basques were separate from the Iberian races, possessing from the earliest time their own traditions and language. They were opposed to the Roman occupation of Spain, especially their own territories, and later fought the Visigoths, Moors and Franks. Their repeated attempts to repulse Frankish domination led to the Battle of Roncesvalles in 778, preserved for history in the romance *The Song of Roland*. A Basque kingdom was founded at Navarre in 824, eventually uniting all Basques during the reign of Sancho III Garcés, el Mayor (1000–1035). The region was later absorbed by the Kingdom of Castile, while the Basques themselves retained a certain degree of autonomy.

**BASRA** City in southeastern Iraq, called al-Basrah, a leading Islamic center for art and literature and a financial power from the 7th to the 10th century. It was founded as a military camp by the caliph Umar in 636 (or 638) as a duplicate of Kufah (al-Kufah) in Iraq and soon developed both political importance and wealth. The Battle of the Camel was fought there in 656, an appropriate event given the subsequent years in which the city was rent by intense Islamic religious factionalism between Sunni and Shiite supporters.

Because of its reputation for welcoming intellectuals, Basra attracted many nationalities that increased its population and created social volatility at the same time. Arabic was not spoken by everyone: Abu al-Aswad al-Duali wrote an early Arabic grammar and Al-Khalil ibn Ahmad the first dictionary. These efforts failed to help unite the numerous social groups, and Basra was faced with constant upheaval and rebellion during the Umayyad and Abbasid caliphates. The city's irreversible decline began after the invasion of the Qarmatians in 923, a situation that had already slowly begun with the concurrent rise of Baghdad in the eighth century. See also UMAYYAD CALIPHATE.

**AL-BATTANI** (c. 858–929) The most renowned Arab astronomer known to medieval Europe. Abu Abd Allah Muhammad Ibn Jabir Ibn Sinan al-Battani was known to the West as Albatemius and made important observations from 878 to 918, testing the astronomical principles of Ptolemy. His work on astronomy, a series of tables, was translated into Latin in the early 12th century. See also ASTRONOMY.

**BAVARIA** Known in German as Bayern, the region of southern Germany consisting of a group of territories, including Bavaria proper (Upper and Lower), Franconia, Swabia and the Palatine, and which included a number of important cities, such as Munich, its capital, Landshut, Nuremberg, Augsburg and Regensburg. Much of the cultural flavor of Bavaria was determined by the Celtic and then Roman occupiers, especially the Roman colonists who founded both Augsburg and Regensburg. By the fifth century, however, Roman control had been broken and the area overrun by Germanic tribes. One tribe, the Baivarii or Bavarians, settling there in the sixth century, gave their name to the region and battled with nearby peoples, the Alamanni, Franks and Thuringians, for supremacy. In the mid-sixth century a duchy was established under the Agilolfing family. Christianity was introduced by the missionary saints Rupert, Emmeram, Boniface and Corbinian in the seventh and eighth centuries.

The Duchy of Bavaria was first absorbed into the Carolingian empire and later annexed to the Kingdom of the East Franks (817). Christian dominance prevailed over the next centuries as Bavaria, from about 1070–1180, served in varying degrees as a repository for GUELPH (imperial) power. In 1180, Frederick I Barbarossa (1152–1190) gave part of the region to Count Otto of Wittelsbach. The Wittelsbachs would receive new portions and lose others, depending on prevailing circumstances, until Duke Albert IV (1467–1508) brought all of Bavaria under his control. Decentralization of authority and fragmentation continued to plague the family and indeed all of Bavaria for some time. Bavaria was nevertheless important politically and economically to Germany and the Holy Roman Empire, and the Wittelsbach dynasty was to rule for a thousand years. See also GERMANY; WITTELSBACH; individual cities or territories.

**BAYBARS** (c. 1223–1277) Sultan of the Mamluks from 1260 to 1277 and the ruler considered by many historians to be the true founder of the Mamluk state. Baybars al-Bunduqdari (or Al-Malik az-Zahir Rukn ad-Din Baybars) was born in the Kipchak steppes region of southern Russia. Captured during the Mongol invasion around 1240, he was sold as a slave to Syrian merchants in 1242 and purchased by an officer of the Ayyubids of Egypt. Baybars next came into the possession of the Ayyubid sultan al-Malik al-Salih Ayyub (1240–1249), who entered him in the elite Turkish slave regiments who were then the core of the Ayyubid armies.

Trained in warfare and exhibiting ability in this field, Baybars took a prominent role in smashing the Crusader army of Louis IX of France (r. 1226–1270) at al-Mansura in 1250, in which the king was captured (and later ransomed). Al-Malik died a short time later, but his son and heir, Turan Shah, was assassinated by his own troops, guided by Baybars and the Mamluk officers. The Ayyubid dynasty was extinguished, and an internal struggle followed among the Mamluks. Baybars fled to Syria in 1254, remaining there until 1260, when Sultan Qutuz invited him to return. It was Baybars who led the Mamluks in the victory over the Mongols at Ain Jalut in 1260, using this triumph as a springboard to the sultanate by assassinating Qutuz and taking power. Once in place he took the title al-Malik al-Zahir (Triumphant King), consolidated his rule and proved to be as able a sultan as he was a general.

Baybars strengthened the Syrian castles, stockpiled arsenals, improved intelligence networks and created a postal service for swifter communications. Once ready, he embarked on a long series of campaigns. From 1265 to his final success in 1271, he dealt mortal blows to the Crusader States in the Holy Land. Arsuf, Caesarea, Safad, Jaffa, Antioch and the fortress of Krak des Chevaliers all fell, and Crusader hopes of a lasting presence in the region were subdued forever. The Mongols were attacked and contained east of the Euphrates River. Armenia was sacked, the last vestiges of the Assassins destroyed from 1271 to 1273, the Turks defeated in 1276 and sorties sent against Nubia.

While capable of great cruelty, Baybars was also responsible for many positive achievements. Embassies were sent to Constantinople, Sicily and Italy and treaties of trade were made with Spain. Public works were initiated, such as canals, and education, especially in law, was promoted. Finally, Baybars took the shrewd step of inviting a descendant of the toppled Abbasid caliphate to come to Cairo and assume a symbolic role as leader of the Muslims. Baybars died in 1277 in Damascus, after accidentally drinking poison. The popular acclaim in which Baybars was held was to last a long time. The *Sirat Baybars,* an epic on his life, is still known in Egypt. See also MAMLUKS.

**BAYEUX** Town in the French region of Normandy to the northwest of Caen. Bayeux became, in 880, a major foothold for the Normans in France, when it fell to the Norse king Rollo. Subsequently a Norman possession, it was the bishopric of Odo, half brother of William the Conqueror. The Bayeux Tapestry, a tableau depicting the Battle of Hastings and commissioned in the late 11th century, hangs there still. See also BAYEUX TAPESTRY.

**BAYEUX TAPESTRY** An important embroidered tapestry, dating from the late 11th century (probably between 1066 and 1083), that depicted the Norman conquest of England in 1066 by William the Conqueror, of Normandy. The tapestry was commissioned probably by Odo, bishop of Bayeux, half brother of William, and earl of Kent, to commemorate the triumph of the Normans over the Saxons, although tradition has erroneously attributed it to William's wife, Matilda. It is more than 231 feet long and 21 inches wide. The eight colors of wool thread were embroidered onto linen depicting scenes of the entire campaign from the troubled King Edward sitting on an heirless throne to the flight of the Saxons from the field of Hastings. Several lost panels have been thought to depict images of William on the English throne. Latin commentaries accompanied the figures, and the borders on the top and bottom were enhanced by many handsome designs. Further speculation has argued that, although it is a Norman work, the

Bayeux Tapestry

style and stitching were of Saxon origin. The tapestry was consecrated about 1177 and displayed in the Bayeux Cathedral and was largely forgotten until mentioned in a cathedral inventory dating from 1476. The importance of the tapestry was manifold. It was a major work of art and was of incalculable value in preserving details about the conquest, the political climate of the period, style and military customs. The detailing is extremely impressive, especially the battle scenes and in the events less heralded, such as Halley's comet, which blazed across the sky just before the invasion.

**BEATRICE PORTINARI** (1266–1290) The woman to whom the poet Dante dedicated his work, and his love. Beatrice was the daughter of a Florentine noble and first met Dante when he was nine years old. She left such an impression on him that on her death in 1290, at the age of 24, he was devastated and wrote of his love for her and of their profound friendship in his *La vita nuova (The New Life,* c. 1293). Beatrice reappears in her full glory in the *Divine Comedy,* as Dante's guide to Paradise. He wrote that she was "so gentle and so pure." See also DANTE ALIGHIERI.

**BEAUFORT, EDMUND** See SOMERSET, EDMUND BEAUFORT.

**BEAUFORT, HENRY** (c.1375–1447) Cardinal and bishop of Lincoln and Winchester and the chancellor of England who was a major figure in the English government in the first half of the 15th century. He was the son of John of Gaunt and Catherine Swynford, receiving legitimacy after their marriage in 1396. Educated at Cambridge, Oxford and Aachen, he was made chancellor of Oxford University in 1397. A year later he was named bishop of Lincoln. The half brother of King Henry IV (1399–1413), he became chancellor of England in 1403, resigning his post to serve as bishop of Winchester in 1404, the successor of William of Wykeham.

Beaufort did not relinquish politics, however, for he led the opposition on the royal council against Archbishop Arundel of Canterbury in favor of the Prince of Wales, his nephew, the eventual Henry V (1413–1422). Henry came to the throne in 1413, and Beaufort again acted as chancellor until 1417. He then entered papal service, helping Martin V become pope in 1417 in return for a cardinalate and the rank of papal legate. Henry forced him to decline these gifts. A guardian of Henry VI (1422–1461), Beaufort sat as chancellor from 1424 until 1426, virtually administering the entire kingdom. Attacks by Humphrey, duke of Gloucester, probably added to the decision to accept the rank of cardinal and to lead an unsuccessful campaign against the Hussites. Returning to English politics, he survived the assaults of Gloucester (who fell in 1441) and, from about 1435–1443, was again the foremost royal adviser. Negotiations with France over the Hundred Years' War led to nothing in 1435 and 1439. Beaufort retired in 1443, dying at Wolvesey Palace on Palm Sunday, 1447. See also ENGLAND.

**BEAUFORT, LADY MARGARET** (1443–1509) Known as Lady Margaret, the countess of Richmond and Derby and the mother of Henry VII of England (1485–1509). The daughter of John Beaufort, the first duke of Somerset, Margaret married Edmund Tudor, half brother of Henry VI (1422–1461) in 1455, and their son, Henry, was born in 1457, a short time after Edmund's death in 1456. A second marriage to Henry Stafford was childless and unhappy. Stafford died sometime before 1482, and Margaret wed Lord Stanley, the first earl of Derby, who would be instrumental in winning the Battle of Bosworth Field in 1485 for Henry. Lady Margaret help end the dynastic Wars of the Roses by arranging Henry's union with Elizabeth of York. A patron of learning, Margaret established Lady Margaret Hall at Oxford and professorships at Oxford and Cambridge (1502–1503), founded Christ's College, Cambridge (1505), and left provision in her will for the endowment of Saint John's College, Cambridge, completed in 1511.

**BEAUVAIS** Town in northern France, the capital of the department of Oise, noted for its Cathedral of Saint-Pierre, the largest of its kind and considered the most architecturally ambitious of its time. The cathedral was begun in the 13th century. Its Gothic choir vault (157 feet high) collapsed in 1284 but was restored and reinforced. The nave was never completed, the Romanesque church of the Basse Oeuvre standing in its place. See also CATHEDRAL; GOTHIC ART AND ARCHITECTURE; ROMANESQUE ART AND ARCHITECTURE.

**BEC** A famous Benedictine abbey near Rouen in Normandy that was founded in 1041 by Herluin; it was rebuilt and enlarged in 1061. Notable monks serving there included Lanfranc, Anselm and the future Pope Alexander II (1061–1073). Destroyed by a fire in 1263, the abbey was reconstructed and stood until the French Revolution. See also BENEDICTINES.

**BECCUS, JOHN** See JOHN XI BECCHUS.

**BECKET, THOMAS À** See THOMAS À BECKET, SAINT.

**BEDE, SAINT** (c. 673–735) Called "the Venerable," a biblical scholar, historian and one of the foremost medieval chroniclers. Details concerning Bede's life dates from his being sent into the care of Saint Benedict Biscop, abbot of Wearmouth, at the age of seven. He was later (c. 681) transferred to the Monastery of Saint Paul at Jarrow. Ordained a deacon at 19 and a priest at 30, he very rarely left Northumbria, with the exception of a journey to Lindisfarne and one to York. He was buried at Jarrow, but his remains were transferred to Durham Cathedral in the 11th century.

Bede's writings were both prolific and influential, with works on grammar, Scripture and history. Aside from his grammars, he produced two treatises on chronology, *De temporibus (On time)* and *De temporibus ratione (On the Reckoning of Time)*; commentaries on Scripture, including the Gospels, Acts of the Apostles and elements of the Old and New Testaments; and a scientific study based on the writings of Suetonius and Pliny the Younger. His biographies and histories were especially important. A *Life of St. Cuthbert* was composed in verse and prose, and better known was the *Historia abbotum (Lives of the Abbots of Wearmouth and Jarrow)*. By far Bede's most ambitious history was the *Historia ecclesiastica*, covering English events from 55 B.C. to A.D. 597 and compiled with the utmost care for source material. The *Historia* also a major record of early Christianity in Kent and Anglo-Saxon England. See also ENGLAND.

**BEDFORD, JOHN, DUKE OF** (1389–1435) Also called John of Lancaster, John Plantagenet and John Beaufort, the brother of King Henry V of England and one of the leading English generals in years 1415–1435 during the Hundred Years' War (1337–1453). The son of Henry IV, John received the title of duke of Bedford from his brother in 1414 and was given the rank of lieutenant of the kingdom. He led campaigns against the French until Henry's death in France in 1422. A regent for Henry VI, he continued to conduct the war, winning the Battle of Verneuil in 1424 and working to maintain the alliance with the Burgundians. His efforts were thwarted by the antagonism of his brother Humphrey, duke of Gloucester, toward Philip of Burgundy, and the dangerous Henry Beaufort. After forging a reconciliation between the parties, Bedford returned to France in 1427 but two years later was forced by Joan of Arc to end his siege of Orléans. He soon found an English triumph virtually impossible because of the kingdom's finances and the return of the Burgundians to the French cause. Bedford died in 1435, having failed in his ultimate goal, the capture of France. See also HUNDRED YEARS' WAR.

**BEGHARDS** A religious organization founded in the Netherlands and traditionally first appearing at Louvain in 1220. The Beghards took their name from the preacher Lambert le Begue (d. 1177) and were the male equivalent of the Beguines. The Beghards found supporters in the Low Countries, Italy, France and Germany and followed certain rules of austerity but were under no lasting obligation to the group and could leave and marry. The general aim of the Beghards was to lead lives of contemplation while aiding the sick and the poor. The Council of Vienne condemned them in 1311 as heretics; Pope John XXII allowed a reformed version of the Beghards to continue its work after 1321. See also BEGUINES; HERESIES.

**BEGUINES** The female equivalent of the BEGHARDS, a religiously inclined sisterhood established in the late 12th century in the Netherlands. The Beguines did charitable work, caring for the sick and the poor, and had no set of rules. They did not live in cloistered communities but shared common expenses and income. They were often engaged in the textile industries, an important source of income. Any member could marry and leave the Beguines, but some sense of community was maintained through austerity and prayer. Members were found in the Low Countries but also in France and in western Germany. Condemned as heretical, the communities (or *beguinages*) declined in popularity and began disappearing by the 13th and 14th centuries. See also HERESIES.

**BEIRUT** A major port city on the Mediterranean in modern Lebanon, during the Middle Ages subjected to numerous invasions. An ancient site with legendary divine origins, it enjoyed a brief period of prosperity under the Romans and was known for its schools, especially law, and for its architecture. Earthquakes and a tidal wave in 551 destroyed most of the buildings, and the city never truly recovered for many centuries. The Muslim occupation of Beirut was ended in 1110 when Baldwin I of Flanders (1100–1118) captured the city for the Crusader cause. War raged in and around Beirut until 1187 when Saladin (1137–1193) finally wrested it from the Latin Kingdom of Jerusalem. The Mamluks did nothing to aid the economic revival that would come, only partially, under the Ottomans and their Druze emirs in the 16th century. See also CRUSADES.

**BEK, ANTONY** (1240–c. 1310) Bishop of Durham and one of the leading advisers of King Edward I of England (1272–1307). Bek served as chancellor in Edward's government, using his considerable political gifts not only to advance the power of the king but also to establish his own episcopal jurisdiction over much of northern England. He also served as the royal representative to Scotland, France, Germany, Italy and the Kingdom of Aragon. See also ENGLAND.

**BÉLA I** (d. 1063) King of Hungary from 1061 to 1063, driving his brother Andrew from the country (c. 1060). Following his death, the country was beset by troubles between his sons Géza and Ladislas and his nephew, Salamon. See also HUNGARY.

**BÉLA II** (d. 1141) King of Hungary from 1131 to 1141, whose reign was generally considered peaceful despite the tragic nature of his youth. To prevent any possible rivals to the successon of his son, Stephen II, King Colman I blinded his own brother, Almos, and his son, Béla. Béla was raised by Hungarian nobles and came to the throne after the reign of Stephen (1116–1131). He was succeeded by his eldest son, Géza II (1141–c. 1162). See also HUNGARY.

**BÉLA III** (d. 1196) King of Hungary from 1173 to 1196, noted for his attempts at improving the status of Hungary within medieval Europe and for promoting education among his courtiers, especially Byzantine learning. He was the successor of Stephen III and came to the throne with the help of the Byzantines under Manuel I Comnenus (1237–1263). Domestic control was aided by the lack of rivals for power that seemed a chronic element of Hungarian dynastic politics. Improved relations with the church aided Hungary's dealings with France, and Béla wed the sister of Philip II Augustus of France, Margaret, following the death of his first wife, Anne of Chatillon. Efforts to extend Hungarian influence into Dalmatia and Galicia were only partially successful and precipitated two wars with Venice in Dalmatia from 1181 to 1188 and 1190 to 1191. See also HUNGARY.

**BÉLA IV** (1206–1270) King of Hungary from 1235 to 1270, during one of the blackest periods in Hungarian history, the Mongol invasion of 1241. The son and successor of Andrew II, he began his reign by taking steps to improve the political position of the royal house, but his efforts were terminated in spring 1241 with the arrival of the Mongols under Batu Khan. The army of Hungary did what it could to oppose the invaders, but at the Battle of Mohi, on April 9, Béla's entire force was annihilated. Hungary was subjected to nearly total destruction with entire regions of the country depopulated. Béla fled to Dalmatia and returned (c. 1242) to his kingdom in ruins.

Béla spent the remainder of his reign working to rebuild Hungary and defend its territorial integrity from ambitious neighbors. Known to the Hungarians as the nation's second founder, he reconstructed towns and cities, encouraged colonists to repopulate certain areas, pieced together a new army and fostered renewal of national pride. He fought with Frederick of Austria in 1246, the nearby Serbs, Bohemia and then the Mongols in 1261. While some measures were not successful, Béla's long-term program made Hungary once more a viable state. He died in 1270 and was followed by his son, Stephen V, whom he had arranged to marry a Cuman princess, a gesture designed to pacify the Cuman settlers brought into Hungary after the Mongol invasion. See also HUNGARY.

**BELISARIUS** (c. 505–565) One of the greatest generals of the Byzantine Empire and the foremost military figure in the reign of Justinian I (527–565). Belisarius was born in the Balkans and by 530 was a trusted officer in Justinian's imperial guard. That same year he was given a command to lead an army against the Sassanid Persians, winning a battle at Dara. Two years later he ruthlessly suppressed the Nika Revolt at Constantinople and was thus chosen in 533 as supreme general in the Byzantine effort to regain territories in the West.

The next years saw him engaged in brilliant campaigns against the Vandals and Ostrogoths, restoring Byzantine control over most of what had been the Western Roman Empire. From 533 to 534 he destroyed the Vandal Kingdom of Africa and then arrived in Sicily in 534 to begin the recapture of Italy. He took Naples and Rome, fought off a siege by the Ostrogoths, seized Milan and Ravenna and, by 540, had broken the Goths' hold in the peninsula. Although Belisarius had refused the request of the Ostrogoths to become their king, Justinian viewed him with suspicion. Recalled to Constantinople in semidisgrace, he was given the task of defeating the Persians again and in 544 was dispatched to Italy to salvage imperial control. His operations against the Goths were hampered by Justinian's refusal to give him enough men and support. A replacement, the eunuch Narses, was named in 548, and Belisarius was summoned to the capital. His patron, Empress Theodora, had died, and Justinian was now unrestrained. Despite being used in 559 against the Huns, Belisarius was forced into retirement and later had his possessions confiscated. He was briefly imprisoned and died in March 565, a short time before Justinian's death. The general had a gifted military mind, and his career was aided by Theodora, a friend of his beloved wife, Antonia. The historian Procopius was the best source on Belisarius. See also BYZANTINE EMPIRE; WARFARE.

**BELLINI, GENTILE** (c. 1429–1507) One of the leading Venetian painters of the early Renaissance, the son of Jacopo Bellini, brother of Giovanni Bellini and brother-in-law of Andrea Mantegna. Gentile's work was influenced by his father and by Mantegna. After achieving early recognition among the Venetians, he was sent in 1479 by the doge to Constantinople to paint for the Ottoman sultan Muhammad II. He was especially noted for his paintings, which reflected aspects of Venetian life in the 15th century. Among his greatest works were the *Portrait of Muhammad II*, *Procession in St. Mark's Square* and *Recovery of the Holy Cross*. See also BELLINI, GIOVANNI; BELLINI, JACOPO; VENICE.

**BELLINI, GIOVANNI** (c. 1430–1516) Italian painter who had an important impact on the early Renaissance by helping to establish Venice as city where art flourished. He was the son of Jacopo Bellini, brother of Gentile Bellini, and brother-in-law of Andrea Mantegna, studying under Jacopo but also being influenced by Mantegna. In 1483 he was given the honor of being named state painter for Venice, a post he held until his death in 1516. From this position he elevated Venice's status as a patron of Italian arts, raising it to a position equal to that of Rome and even Florence. Bellini's students included Titian, Giorgione and Palma Vecchio. Some of his major works are *Agony in the Garden*, *Feast of the Gods*, *Toilet of Venus*, the *Doge Leonardo Loredan* and a number of fine altar pieces.

**BELLINI, JACOPO** (c. 1400–1470) Italian painter who was influential in Venetian art. Born in Venice, he worked with Gentile de Fabriano, with whom he journeyed to Florence around 1423. While there he was much influenced by such Florentine masters as Donatello and Masaccio. By 1429 he returned to Venice and there earned a reputation as a major artist at that time. Although he was a gifted painter, Jacopo's historical importance is based on his two extant sketchbooks, preserved today in the Louvre and in the British Museum. In these he experimented with a variety of compositional forms, and the drawings were used by later artists as the basis for other works. Jacopo's experimentations were continued by his sons, Gentile and Giovanni, and he was a major figure in the introduction of Florentine style into Venetian art. Among his most important works are *Virgin and Child*, *Madonna* and *Christ on the Cross*.

**BENEDETTO DA MAIANO** (1442–1497) Italian sculptor noted for his extraordinary technical achievement and decorative realism in his work. Having trained as a stone carver, Benedetto was influenced by the earlier sculptors Antonio Rosellino and Desiderio da Settignano. His earliest surviving work is the shrine of Santo Savino in Faenza Cathedral, dating from 1427. Other notable works were marble reliefs in Santa Croce, Florence, the altar of Santa Fina and the altar of San Bartolo, both at San Gimignano.

**BENEDICT, RULE OF SAINT** The monastic regulations established by Benedict of Nursia in the sixth century for use in his monastic institutions at Monte Cassino. Based in large measure on the rules of John Cassian and other earlier monastic innovators, it was less a strict set of codes and rather a guide for leading a religious life of moderation while adhering to vows of community, chastity and obedience. The rule of Benedict was adopted as the basis for Western monasticism in the early Middle Ages. See also BENEDICTINES.

**BENEDICT I** (d. 579) Pope from 575 to 579, the successor to John III, who died in July 574; Benedict did not actually come to the Holy See until June 575 because of sporadic warfare in the Eastern Empire. He reigned during a time of trouble, the invasion of the Goths and Lombards, and he died during a Lombard siege of Rome.

**BENEDICT II, SAINT** (d. 685) Pope from 684 to 685. Very little is known of his reign; he was seriously ill for most of the year.

**BENEDICT III** (d. 858) Pope from 855 to 858, imprisoned by the Holy Roman Emperor Louis II and replaced by the antipope Anastasius Bibliothecarius because of the contested election. The matter of the antipope was ended in October 855 when Benedict finally was allowed to assume the Holy See. Little else is known of his brief reign.

**BENEDICT IV** (d. 903) Pope from 900 to 903, a little-known pontiff who excommunicated Baldwin II, count of Flanders, for the murder of Fulk, archbishop of Reims, in 900.

**BENEDICT V** (d. 966) Pope in 964 and, according to some lists, an antipope. He was elected on May 22, 964, during a time of bitter factional rivalry, to succeed John XII, an act of defiance against Emperor Otto I, who had already deposed John and named Leo VIII pope. The emperor marched on Rome, removed Benedict (on June 23) and exiled him to Hamburg. He died in 966, still considered by many to be the legitimate pope.

**BENEDICT VI** (d. 974) Pope from January 973 to July 974. Strangled by order of the powerful Roman Crescentii family, Benedict was a victim of the virulent rivalry between the emperor and the Crescentii, who had him replaced with the antipope Boniface VII.

**BENEDICT VII** (d. 983) Pope from 974 to 983, named as successor to Benedict VI through the patronage of Emperor Otto II, who worked to remove the antipope Boniface VII, who was elected by the powerful Crescentii family of Rome. Benedict's most important papal activity was to resolve the jurisdictional confusion of the German church, so he abolished the post of the bishop of Merseburg about 981. Although this was done to appease Emperor Otto II, it deprived the region of northern Europe of a vital outpost of Christianity. See also SLAVS.

**BENEDICT VIII** (d. 1024) Pope from 1012 to 1024, his pontificate marked by a resurgence of papal power in Italian political affairs. He routed the Muslims in their attack on northern Italy in 1016–1017 and allied himself with the Normans, at the expense of the Byzantines, making the papacy supreme in Campagna. Benedict was also a member of the influential Tusculani family, who replaced the Crescentii family of Rome as the true masters of the Holy See.

**BENEDICT IX** (d.1055) Pope from 1032 to 1044, again in 1045, and finally from 1047 to 1048. He was noted for his greed and scandalous behavior but was able to survive repeated attempts at deposing him by using the power of his own family, the Tusculani. Elected at the instigation of his family, he so outraged Romans that they tried to remove him by electing John of Sabina as Sylvester III in 1045. Benedict, who had never been formally deposed, ejected Sylvester a short time later and sold the throne to his godfather, the priest Giovanni Graziano, who called himself Gregory VI. Regretting his decision, Benedict returned to Rome and found himself facing Sylvester. The Council of Sutri (1046) rejected all three popes and named Suidger of Bamberg to be Clement II. When Clement died after an eight-month reign, Benedict claimed the See again, only to be deposed in 1048 by order of Emperor Henry III. He died in a monastery.

**BENEDICT X** Antipope from 1058 to 1059; his contested election and later deposition prompted reforms in papal elections that led to the creation of the Sacred College of Cardinals, which was to elect future popes.

**BENEDICT XI** (d. 1304) Pope from 1303 to 1304, whose brief reign was marked by the continuation of the struggle between the papacy and Philip IV the Fair (1285–1314), King of France, specifically over the monarch's demand to levy taxes from the French church.

**BENEDICT XII** (b. c. 1280) Pope from 1334 to 1342, born Jacques Fournier and the third of the Avignon popes. A noted Cistercian theologian, he was named abbot of Fontfroide in 1311 and bishop of Pamiers in 1317. A cardinal by 1327, he succeeded John XXII in 1334 as pope. Benedict XII initiated a series of ecclesiastical reforms, among both the diocesan clergy and the religious orders, noted in that era for numerous excesses and corruption. While many measures remained in force until the Council of Trent (1545–1563), others were to be rescinded by his successors. He settled the theological dispute over the question of the deposition of the Beatific Vision, issuing the bull *Benedictus Deus* in 1336, in which he stated that the deserving perceived the Vision upon death instead of after the Day of Judgment, as had previously been taught.

In temporal affairs he had far less success, as his hope of returning to Rome and his efforts to end the Hundred Years' War were failures. So too were his efforts to launch another Crusade. Because of the interference and the influence of Philip IV, papal overtures of reconciliation with the Holy Roman Empire were destroyed. Benedict did construct a lavish palace at Avignon, which ensured that the papacy would continue to reside away from Rome.

**BENEDICT XIII** (d. 1423) Antipope at Avignon from 1394 to 1417, born Pedro de Luna and originally a professor of canon law. Made a cardinal in 1375 by Gregory XI, he was originally a supporter of Gregory's successor, Urban VI, but then became an adherent of the antipope, Clement VII. On Clement's death in 1394, he was chosen as pope at Avignon with his promise to end the Great Schism even if it meant his abdication. He subsequently refused to step down, precipitating a siege of the papal castle at Avignon and his loss of political support, especially among the cardinals. Negotiations with the Roman popes Boniface IX, Innocent VII and Gregory XII all came to nothing, and the Council of Pisa deposed him in 1409. Still possessing some allies, most notably Scotland and states in Spain, Benedict held out until 1417 when the Council of Constance upheld his deposition. He refused to accept his fall, taking up residence in a castle in Peniscola, still declaring his legitimacy on his death.

**BENEDICT BISCOP, SAINT** (c. 628–690) Originally called Biscop Baducing, a monk, abbot and an important figure in the development of Benedictine monasticism in England. A Northumbrian noble by birth, he spent his early years at the court of King Oswy of Northumbria. In 653 he renounced all interest in worldly matters, journeying to Rome with Saint Wilfrid. Another trip to Rome was made in 666, and he became a monk at Lerins soon afterward, taking the name Benedict. A companion of Theodore of Tarsus, archbishop of Canterbury, Benedict came to England and was named abbot of the monastery of Saints Peter and Paul (later Saint Augustine's), Canterbury, in 669. In 674 he founded the monastery of Saint Peter at Wearmouth and that of Saint Paul in Jarrow in 682. Because of his trips to Rome and his promotion of learning, Benedict acquired a vast collection of manuscripts, relics and paintings, setting the Benedictines on the intellectual path that was to be the hallmark of the order for centuries. His life was recorded by Bede in the *Historia abbatum (History of the Abbots of Wearmouth and Jarrow).* See also BENEDICTINES.

**BENEDICTINES** Monks who belong to the Order of Saint Benedict, the important religious institution established in the sixth century in an attempt to continue the example of Benedict of Nursia (c. 480–c. 547). Benedict of Nursia left a major impression on early monasticism with his monastery at Monte Cassino and especially with his rule. Pope Gregory I (590–604) applied it to his own monastery, and Augustine of Canterbury brought it to Britain. Henceforth the Benedictines assumed the leading role in the establishment of monasticism in Europe. In England the rule replaced the more stringent counterpart of Saint Columbanus and spread to the Continent via Saint Boniface, archbishop of Mainz, and Benedict of Aniane. The Benedictines became associated with the preservation and advancement of learning, receiving royal approval and patronage.

Beginning with Emperor Louis at the Synod of Aachen in 817, an effort was made to bring the Benedictine order to greater uniformity, as from its inception each monastery had retained nearly total autonomy. Independence made reform difficult, and the first successful version of collective reformation came in the 10th century with the foundation of the Abbey of Cluny by William of Aquitaine. Cluniac monasteries, answerable to Cluny, represented the highest spiritual ideal of the Christian life in the Middle Ages and led to the rise of other new orders in the 11th century, including the Camaldolese, the Carthusians and the Cistercians, each adhering to a more austere rule. Papal programs, such as the Fourth Lateran Council of 1215, could do little to bring the Benedictines under one command, and the order faced decline and decay, repairing itself from the 15th century through the use of congregations, a slightly larger form of organization that allowed a high degree of self-determination while making the monasteries more accountable for their religious activities. The leading congregations were the Maurists in France, the Bursfeld in Germany and the San Justina in Italy. Such changes, of course, could do little to prevent the general decline of monasticism in the late Middle Ages because of plagues, the Hundred Years' War, the deterioration of papal prestige during the Great Schism and the rise of urban lay religious communities such as the Beguines and the Augustinians and the mendicant orders, the Franciscans, and Dominicans. Nevertheless, the Benedictines from the 6th to the 12th century had led the way in learning and intellectual development as well as in religious service and devotion. See also BENEDICT, RULE OF SAINT.

**BENEDICT OF ANIANE, SAINT** (b. c. 750; d. 821) Abbot of Aniane and an important monastic reformer. In 779 Benedict used his own property at Aniane in Languedoc to create his own monastic institution, aimed at reforming contemporary French monasticism. An adviser to Louis the Pious, he made recommendations for the systemization of the Benedictine order, which were made official royal policy in 817. At the Synod of Aachen a modified Rule of Saint Benedict was introduced for all monasteries.

**BENEDICT OF NURSIA, SAINT** (c. 480–c. 547) Founder of the monastery of Monte Cassino and the patriarch of Western monasticism. Born about 480 at Nursia, he was sent to Rome to be educated, eventually leaving the city because of its corruption and vice. He settled in a cave at Subiaco about 500, rejecting the world. There he lived a rigorously ascetic life, attracting followers. This small community developed into a dozen monastic institutions, headed by abbots appointed by Benedict himself.

Local difficulties prompted his departure from Subiaco (c. 525) with a small band, leaving behind his established monasteries. He went to Monte Cassino, situated between Rome and Naples, converting the local inhabitants and spending the rest of his days there, composing his rule.

Benedict had a profound effect on Western Christianity. Although never ordained and probably not intending to create an order of religious, he shaped monasticism for centuries to come with his quiet sanctity and his rule. The rule of Benedict formed the basis of the Benedictine order, but it also became the guiding principle behind the monastic movement in the West. Virtually the only source on Benedict was the *Dialogues* of Saint Gregory the Great, specifically book 2. See also BENEDICTINES.

**BENEVENTO, DUCHY OF** The name given to an important duchy in southern Italy dating from the 6th to the 11th century. Benevento was virtually ruined by Totila, king of the Ostrogoths, in 452 but was captured by the Lombards in the sixth century and, about 571, was converted into a Lombard duchy. Its first duke was Zotto (d. 591), and subsequent rulers exercised considerable autonomy and even usurped the Lombard throne, as in the case of Grimoald in 663. From the mid-eighth century Benevento came under the influence of the Carolingians, who eventually made the duchy a principality, moving its capital to Salerno. Divided into two and later into three territories, it was occupied by the Moors, Byzantines and, in 1081, the Normans under Robert Guiscard. The Norman ruler gave the region to the papacy, which held it for the next 100 years.

**BENJAMIN OF TUDELA** (d. c. 1173) Jewish traveler and rabbi who was probably the first Westerner to Journey into China, in the 1160s and 1170s. His exploits were recorded in the *Sefer Massa'ot (Itinerary of Benjamin of Tudela)*, an often inaccurate account but a useful source for the conditions of the Jews in the 12th century. See also JEWS AND JUDAISM.

**BENNO** (c. 1010–c. 1106) A largely legendary figure, Benno had been a canon at Goslar but was named bishop of Meissen in 1066. In the dispute between the papacy and Emperor Henry IV, he allied himself with the pope, thus facing imprisonment and deportation. He was eventually restored to his bishopric through the intercession of the antipope Clement III (1187–1191).

**BENTIVOGLIO, HOUSE OF** One of the most powerful families in Bologna during the 15th century, who were leaders of the Guelph (pro-papal) forces in the 14th century. Giovanni I made himself master of Bologna in 1401 but was overthrown by the Visconti family of Milan in 1402. His son, Anton Galeazzo, took power in 1420 only to be removed by Pope Martin V. It was in 1443 that the Bentivoglio resurgence came, as Anibale, son of Anton Galeazzo, ousted papal troops and reigned as *signore* until his assassination in 1445. Sante, his cousin, was then elected by the family, ruling from 1445 to 1463. Under Sante and his successor, Giovanni II, Bologna was transformed into a major artistic, intellectual and military city. Bentivoglio preeminence endured until the early 16th century. See also BOLOGNA.

***BEOWULF*** An anonymous epic poem considered the highest attainment of Anglo-Saxon literature. *Beowulf* is the tale of a great Scandinavian hero and was constructed in two parts, based on Beowulf's three great battles against the fen-dwelling monster Grendel, Grendel's mother and, in the second part, a dragon. It was probably composed by a Northumbrian bard during the first half of the eighth century and survived in only one manuscript dated at around 1000, now in the British Library (Cotton Vitellius A XV, Cottonian Collection). Although some scholars argue that it was written in the 10th century or later, there is general agreement that the poet was Christian and that many of the places and characters mentioned in the 3,182 lines actually existed. The figure of Beowulf was almost certainly fictitious.

The complex narrative pattern of *Beowulf* relied metrically on the strict Germanic literary traditions, although there was injected into it combined pagan and Christian elements that altered the story thematically. Many critics have seen this transformation as allegorical, suggesting a battle between good and evil. In addition, *Beowulf* revealed insights into the Anglo-Saxon culture (events take place in Denmark and Sweden), including the ideals of service, loyalty and the honors paid to triumphant warriors.

**BERCEO, GONZALO DE** (c. 1196–c. 1264) Spanish poet and a Benedictine monk. Berceo was the earliest known Castilian poet.

**BERENGAR I** (d. 924) Known also as Berengar of Friuli, ruler of Italy from 888 as king and from 915 as emperor until 924. Grandson of Louis the Pious (814–840), Berengar was elected king of Italy in 888, although his actual powers were limited because of the presence of Arnulf, king of the East Franks, and the supremacy in Italian politics of Guy of Spoleto (d. 894) and his son, Lambert (d. 898). Finally undisputed monarch of Italy, he faced numerous setbacks, a defeat by the Magyars in 899 and the machinations of Italian nobles who called in Louis of Provence (later Louis III the Blind) as his replacement. A struggle ensued, ending in 905 with Louis's blinding and ejection from Italy. Crowned emperor in 915 by the pope, Berengar was nevertheless unable to quell his rebellious nobles, who called upon Rudolf II of Burgundy to aid them. Vanquished in 923 at the Battle of Fiorenzuola, Berengar lost his army and was assassinated the following year in April.

**BERENGAR II** (c. 900–966) The so-called king of Italy from 950 to 963. The holder of the title of marquis of Ivrea, Berengar seized power in Italy in 950 and made designs on the Italian heiress Adelaide, who called for aid from the German king Otto I (936–973). In 952, Otto intervened in Italy, forcing Berengar to acknowledge his suzerainty. Berengar continued, however, to refuse to recognize Otto's authority and launched an attack on Pope John XII (955–

964). Another intervention ended in Otto's crowning as emperor in 962 and Berengar's imprisonment in Bavaria in 963. He died still a prisoner in 966.

**BERENGAR OF FRIULI** See BERENGAR I.

**BERENGAR OF TOURS** (c. 1000–1088) Theologian and participant in the Eucharist Controversy of the 11th century. A student of Fulbert of Chartres, Berengar became a canon of the cathedral school of Saint Martin at Tours and was made an archdeacon of Angers in 1040. An intellectual of stubborn ideals, he began, after 1040, to teach ideas in disagreement with church views on the nature of the Eucharist. He opposed the model of transubstantiation of Paschasius Radbertus, that the bread and wine became Christ, preferring that of Ratramnus of Corbie, who argued a symbolic presence of Christ rather than literal incarnation. A letter he had written to Lanfranc in defense of this theory was read at the Council of Rome in 1050, and he was excommunicated. Through the influence of Cardinal Hildebrand, Berengar recanted in 1054 (and again in 1059) but apparently returned to his position, for more synods, councils and trials took place from 1076 to 1080. Thereafter he pursued the life of a hermit.

**BERGEN** One of the largest cities in Norway, a major seaport and, during the Middle Ages, the capital and royal residence of the Norwegian kings.

According to the chronicler Snorri Sturlason, it was founded by King Olaf III about 1070 and was called Bjorgvin. It soon developed into the most important and cosmopolitan city in the country. In 1170 the old center of the episcopal see, Selje, lost its importance when the relics of Saint Sunniva were moved to Bergen. The city was a leading economic center for the north, maintaining relations with most of the states of northern Europe. Eager to extend its influence even further, the Hanseatic League sought and won virtual control of the League of Bergen around 1350. Its monopoly on trade would last for centuries. See also NORWAY.

**BERK YARUQ** Seljuk sultan of Persia from 1093 to 1104. The son of Malik Shah, he ruled during the period of the First Crusade. See also SELJUK TURKS.

**BERLIN** Originally a small community of Slavs (Wends), it emerged by the end of the Middle Ages as the capital of the Electors of Brandenburg and an important German political center. The Slavs in the region were eventually subdued by the 12th century by Albert I the Bear (d. 1170), first margrave of Brandenburg. His successors, the Ascanians, built a fortress on the site of the old village on the Spree, and in 1232 it was officially declared a town by the margrave John I. The town developed rapidly because of its location for trade and thus gained membership in the Hanseatic League in the 14th century. Brandenburg passed to the Hohenzollerns in 1411, and, with Berlin's promience already established, they chose to make the city their capital and the seat of the Electors there around 1470. See also GERMANY.

**BERN** Capital of present-day Switzerland and once the major city of the Swiss Confederation. Bern was founded sometime in the late 12th century as a military outpost by Berthold V, duke of Zähringen. Because of its location in central Switzerland, the town prospered and by the early 13th century was independent (traditionally in 1218), holding the rank of imperial city. In 1353 it joined the Swiss Confederation and has maintained its prominence. Bern has retained its medieval appearance and architecture, including the celebrated Cathedral of Munster (1421–1598), the City Hall (c. 1406) and the Nydegg Church (1494). See also SWITZERLAND.

**BERNARD, KING OF ITALY** (d. 818) The illegitimate son of Pepin, king of Italy, who was placed on the throne of the Italian kingdom after his father's death about 810. Although a vassal to Louis I the Pious (814–840), Bernard refused to accept the Partition of Aachen in 817 and rebelled against his uncle, who had planned to grant Italy to his own son, Pepin. Louis summoned him to Chalon-sur-Saône and there deposed him, transferring him to Aachen, where he was condemned. Louis in addition chose to punish Bernard by blinding him. The punishment was incorrectly carried out, and the prince died from the wounds in 818. It was said that Louis regretted his cruel act for the rest of his life.

**BERNARD VII, COUNT OF ARMAGNAC** (d. 1418) Constable of France and leader of the Armagnac Party that vied with the Burgundians for political control of France from 1407 to 1435. Bernard used the increased power of the Armagnacs and his position as brother-in-law of Louis, duke of Orléans (killed in 1407), to embark on a bitter fight with Duke John the Fearless of Burgundy. He proved triumphant and, from 1413 to 1418, ran virtually every aspect of French government, dominating King Charles VI (1380–1422). The loss of the Battle of Agincourt against the English in 1415 dealt a blow to his supremacy, and in 1418 he was lured to his death by the Burgundians under the pretense of negotiations. His assassination marked the beginning of Armagnac decline. See also ARMAGNAC.

**BERNARDINO OF SIENA** (1380–1444) Called "Apostle of the Holy Name," a Franciscan theologian and a leading reformer of the early 15th century. Bernardino was of noble descent, born and orphaned at Massa Marittima. He joined the Franciscans at the age of 22, becoming a member of the Observants, or those Franciscans who adhered strictly to the rule of Saint Francis. Horrified by the decline of morality in Italy during the Great Schism, he began preaching about 1417 and soon became a powerful religious figure. Pope Pius II (1458–1464) described his oratorical skill as equal to Saint Paul's. Bernardino was also a powerful proponent of reform. He attended the Council of Florence in 1439, its decisions instrumental in the short-lived union of the Roman and Greek churches. See also FRANCISCANS.

**BERNARDO DEL CARPIO** The name of a hero in the Spanish chanson de geste (epic poem) *Cantares de gesta,* from the 12th–13th centuries. Bernardo has been considered a Spanish equivalent of the Frankish warrior extolled in the *Song of Roland*.

**BERNARD OF CHARTRES** (d. c. 1130) French humanist and Scholastic philosopher, the leader of the school of Chartres, older brother of Thierry of Chartres and the leading Platonist of the Middle Ages. A teacher at Chartres from 1114, he became chancellor there in 1119 and about 1124 taught at Paris with John of Salisbury, his most famous student. Through his writings, study of Plato and Aristotle and treatises on the fourth-century Neoplatonist Porphyry, he played a crucial role in the rise of the Platonic tradition at Chartres. John of Salisbury wrote of him in the *Metalogicon*, calling him "the perfect Platonist."

**BERNARD OF CLAIRVAUX** (1090–1153) Abbot of Clairvaux, mystic and one of the most influential figures of the Middle Ages, who dominated the political and religious issues of the time. Born to a noble family at Fontaines near Dijon, Bernard grew up in a large family and was pursuaded by his mother, Aloth, to devote his life to the church. Her death, around his 17th year, had a profound effect on him, for soon after, he left the school of Chatillon-sur-Seine, joining the monastery at Citeaux in 1113. Abbot Stephen Harding was his mentor for the next two years, and he led an austere life, saying that he was "conscious of the need of my weak nature for strong medicine." Such austerity, however, weakened an already poor constitution, and he was plagued by ill health.

By 1115 Stephen Harding had enough faith in him to name him the founder of the new monastery at Clairvaux in Champagne. Granted a charter in 1119 by Pope Calixtus II, Clairvaux emerged as one of the foremost Cistercian institutions, and Bernard, although increasingly a mystic, became its powerful leader in religious affairs, to whom much of the Christian church looked for guidance. In 1118 he was secretary to the Synod of Troyes, composing the rules for the Knights Templars, securing the victory of Pope Innocent II over the antipope Anacletus in 1130, preaching the Second Crusade and fighting for the practice of Christian orthodoxy. His firm stand against all heresy led him to attack Henry of Lausanne, but, more zealously, he led the campaign against Peter Abelard, ensuring his condemnation by the Council of Sens in 1140. He was deeply disappointed by the failure of the Crusade. In his later years (1148) he condemned Gilbert de la Porrée.

Although Bernard exercised considerable political authority, the basis of his power was his saintliness and spirituality. An ascetic, criticized for being too much so by William of Champeaux, he adhered to strict moral beliefs, assailing the persecution of the Jews, and, in more than 300 letters and sermons, stressing the importance of prayer. His mystical treatises, most notably *De diligendo Deo (On the Diligence of God)*, revealed the depth of his contemplative understanding. For these attributes he was canonized in 1174, and in 1830 he made a doctor of the church. See also CISTERCIANS.

**BERNARD OF CLUNY** Twelfth-century Benedictine monk, also called Bernard of Morval or Morlass, a member of the monastery at Cluny during the time of Peter the Venerable. A moralist and poet, he was acclaimed for his sermons but won lasting recognition for his 3,000-line poem *De contemptu mundi*, in which he attacked the material world and the appalling immorality of the times and argued that only by accepting the transitory nature of this life and the reality of the next world would one find happiness. He also composed a devotional poem to the Blessed Virgin Mary. See also BENEDICTINES; CLUNY.

**BERNARD OF MENTHON** (d. 1081) Famous Savoyard cleric who served in the diocese of Aosta, in Italy, becoming so concerned for the safety of travelers over the Alps that he founded two hospices in the passes between Switzerland and Italy. These places of refuge were so successful that the Great and Little Saint Bernard Passes were named for him. Bernard also initiated the use of rescue dogs and was chosen as the patron saint of mountain climbers.

**BERNERS, JULIANA** Fifteenth-century author whose treatise on hunting was included in the *Book of St. Albans*, a compilation of works on heraldry and hunting, originally published at Saint Albans. Berners was known under several names, such as Julyan Barnes and Julyans Bernes. Little has survived concerning her life. Tradition held that she was a prioress. Her writings on hunting were probably based on the *Art de venerie (Art of Hunting)*, the Anglo-Norman treatise written by Guillaume Twiti in the early 14th century.

**BERNICIA, KINGDOM OF** An early Anglo-Saxon kingdom in England, established in 547, of which Ida was its first recorded ruler. The realm was situated in England, north of the Tyne River, with its capital at Bamburgh and royal residences there and at Yeavering. From the time of King Aethelfrith (ruled 593–616), Bernicia was closely tied to its neighboring land Deira, the two kingdoms becoming united under the name Northumbria in 670. See also NORTHUMBRIA.

**BERRY, JEAN DE FRANCE, DUC DE** (1340–1416) The third son of King John II the Good (1350–1364), who became an important leader of the French cause during a period of the Hundred Years' War. Berry was originally the count of Poitiers, but in the absence of his father (a captive in England) he assumed greater political power at the expense of the dauphin Charles, who became Charles V. As lieutenant of France, he controlled the regions of Languedoc, Perigord, Poitou, Auvergne and Berry. His repressive methods of taxation forced a revolt by the peasants from 1381 to 1384, but such unrest did not prevent his acquiring a seat on the regency council for Charles VI, who came to the throne in 1380. Berry played a role on the Council of Twelve that administered French affairs and was noted for effecting the end of the devisiveness between the Armagnacs and Burgundians and the Hundred Years' War between France and England. A great patron of the arts, he reportedly spent so much money on collecting art treasures that there were no funds to pay for his burial in 1316. The *Très Riches Heures du duc de Berry*, done for him by the Limbourg brothers, is an exquisite illuminated manuscript. See also HUNDRED YEARS' WAR.

**BERTHA THE BIGFOOT** (d. 783) The wife of Pepin the Short (751–768), queen of the Franks and the mother of Charlemagne. She was a descendant of the Merovingian dynasty and was crowned with Pepin and her children Charlemagne and Carloman by Pope Stephen II (752–757) in January 754. Bertha proved instrumental in keeping the peace between her sons. See also CHARLEMAGNE.

**BERTHARI** (d. 688) King of the Lombards from 672 to 688, a son of King Aribert I. Berthari succeeded to the throne in 662, with his brother Godebert, but civil war erupted and Godebert was slain by the duke of Benevento, Grimoald, who seized power. Grimoald reigned as a usurper from 662 to 671 while Berthari wandered, an exile, until he was recalled by the Lombards after Grimoald's death. Returning in 672 to serve as king, he spent 17 peaceful years, aiding the church, acquiring a reputation for devoutness and refusing to embark on wars against Rome or the Byzantines in Italy. See also LOMBARDS.

**BERWICK** Also Berwickshire, a region of southwestern Scotland, separated from England by the Tweed River and the scene of considerable Roman activity. Berwick passed into the hands of the Saxons in the sixth century, was Christianized from the 6th to 7th century and eventually was attached to the Kingdom of Northumbria. Danish invasions caused considerable damage in the ninth century, but after 1016 it was annexed to Scotland. Because of its location, Berwick became a bitterly contested territory between England and the Scots, culminating in a final English victory in 1482. See also BORDER, THE.

**BESSARION, JOHN CARDINAL** (c. 1399–1472) Cardinal, statesman and scholar of Greek, who was one of the great intellectual leaders in the Renaissance. Born at Trebizond, he was educated at Constantinople and became a Basilian monk in 1423. He studied under the noted philosopher Gemistus Pletho (c. 1431–1436), working to bring together the two systems of Aristotelian and Platonic thought. Emperor John VIII Palaeologus (1425–1448) made him archbishop of Nicaea in 1437, and he joined the emperor on a journey to Italy, where he participated in the Councils of Ferrara and Florence in 1439, aimed at uniting the Eastern and Western Churches.

Having acquired the attention and favor of Pope Eugene IV (1431–1447), Bessarion was elevated to the rank of cardinal (1439), almost elected pope and settled in Italy, where he labored to revive Greek and Latin classical learning. A patron of Byzantine scholars who flocked to his palace, Bessarion was responsible for numerous translations, including Aristotle's *Metaphysica,* Xenophon's *Memorabilia* and treatises on Platonism, *In calumniatorem Platonis, (Against the Calumniator of Plato),* in which he attacked George of Trebizond.

His collection of 800 manuscripts, most in Greek, was given to the Senate of Venice in 1468 and was the basis of the Bibliotheca Marciana. He also served as governor of Bologna (1450–1455) and was sent to several courts, such as France in 1471, as papal ambassador.

**BÉZIERS** City in southern France in the department of Herault that gained lasting notoriety as the scene of the bloodiest massacre of the Albigensian Crusade. A former Roman colony, Béziers became a holding of the viscounts of Carcassonne and later a stronghold of the Albigensians. Thus, in 1209 as victim of the ruthless destruction of the heretical movement, it was besieged and captured by Simon de Montfort. The population was exterminated with such ferocity that the papal legate, Arnaud Amaury, was spuriously credited with the phrase "kill them all, let God sort out the good ones." The most notable medieval building remaining is the fortified Cathedral of Saint-Nazaire. See also ALBIGENSIAN MOVEMENT; HERESIES.

**BIEL, GABRIEL** (c. 1412–1495) Scholar, philosopher, preacher and theologian, known as Ultimus Scholasticorum (the "Last of the Scholars") because of his role as one of the great intellectuals of the late medieval period. Educated at Heidelberg and Erfurt, he became a vicar at Mainz about 1460. Eight years later he joined the Brethren of the Common Life at Butzbäch, subsequently serving as prior there (1470) and at Urach (1479). Biel was next instrumental in establishing the University of Tübingen with Count Eberhard of Württemberg and served as professor of philosophy and theology. A gifted philosopher, he espoused the teachings of William of Ockham and was so respected by the Ockhamists at Erfurt and Wittemberg that they were called Gabrielistae. Among his writings were the *Collectorum circa IV libros sententiarum,* a commentary on *The Sentences of Peter Lombard.*

**BINCHOIS, GILLES DE** (c. 1400–1460) Flemish composer of church music, one of the most important musicians of the 15th century, ranking with Dufay and Dunstable. He was an organist at Mons from 1419 to 1423 and served as composer (c. 1424) to William de la Pole, earl of Suffolk. From 1431 until his death he played and composed in the court chapel of the dukes of Burgundy. In addition to his extensive liturgical compositions (including six *Magnificats* and 28 Mass sections), Binchois also wrote secular music.

**BIONDO, FLAVIO** (1392–1463) Influential Italian historian and archaeologist who was the first historian to assign the period of the Middle Ages as separating the classical and Renaissance eras. Born at Forlì, he was superbly educated at Cremona but spent years in exile at Imola, Ferrara and Venice. In 1434 he received appointment to the papal Curia as a secretary, later serving as a diplomat to Venice and to Francesco Sforza at Milan. Biondo wrote two important works. The first was *Italia illustrata* (1453), covering Italian history and geography through the years of classical Rome, the early medieval period and its subsequent development under the emperors, with details on contemporary social and political life. This work introduced topographical studies and specific interest in local Italian history. His second work, still unfinished at his death, was the massive 42-volume *Historiarum,* an examination of

European history from the Sack of Rome in 410 to the early years of the Renaissance, around 1442. Titled *Historiarum ab inclinatione Romane imperii decades (1439–1463; Decades of History from the Fall of the Roman Empire)*, the work was instrumental in conceptualizing the Middle Ages as a historical entity, thus acknowledging Biondo as one of the founders of modern historiography.

**BIRGER JARL** (d. 1266) The name given to a Swedish nobleman of the Folking family who was virtual ruler of Sweden from 1248 to 1266. Having married Ingeborg, sister of King Eric Ericsson (1234–1249), sometime before 1238, he was named by the monarch to be the jarl, or chief earl of the country, in 1248. On the death of Eric in 1250, Birger had his son Valdemar elected king, while he acted as regent. Birger Jarl defeated the Swedish magnates (nobles) with the help of the church, began the construction of Stockholm, improved relations with Denmark and Norway through intermarriage, launched an attack (in 1249) on Finland that brought the territory into Swedish domination and encouraged trade between Sweden and the Baltic states. Most important, Birger helped create the laws that improved rights of inheritance for women and made possible the King's Peace. See also SWEDEN.

**BIRGER MAGNUSSON** (1280–1321) King of Sweden from 1290 to 1318, who succeeded his father, Magnus I Birgersson (1275–1290), but because of his youth was controlled by the powerful regent Torgils Knutsson until the latter's murder in 1306. Birger's reign was frought with internal political struggles with his brothers, Eric and Valdemar. The brothers were driven into exile in 1304, reconciled with Birger in 1305 and later imprisoned the king. Only direct intervention from Denmark and Norway restored Birger to power. He waited several years and in 1317 captured his brothers and executed them. Swedish nobles overthrew Birger in 1318, executed his son and forced him into exile in Denmark, where he died in 1321. See also SWEDEN.

**AL-BIRUNI** (c. 973–1050) Famed Muslim scholar whose studies encompassed a variety of subjects, including medicine, philosophy, astronomy and languages. His full name was Abu'l-Rayhan Muhammad al-Biruni, also written by some Arab scholars as Muhammad Ibn Ahmad Abu'l-Rayan al-Biruni. A traveler of considerable achievement, he visited India sometime after 1017 and was fluent or familiar with Turkish, Hebrew, Syriac, Sanskrit, Persian and Arabic. His writings were well known: *Tahqiq ma li'l-Hind (History of India), Kitab as-Saydalah* (a compendium on medicine commonly known as the *Saidanah), al-Athar al-baqiyah (Chronology of Ancient Nations)* and on astronomy, *at-Tafhim (Elements of Astronomy)* and *al-Qanun al-Mas'udi (Masudi Canon)*, dedicated to Sultan Masud of Ghazna, where he had settled.

**BLACK ARMY** A powerful military force named after its commanding general, "Black" John Haugwitz, that was formed by King Matthias Corvinus of Hungary in the second half of the 15th century. Instead of relying on the levies from the Hungarian nobles, Corvinus chose to levy taxes on the entire country and thus pay for a permanent mercenary force of some 30,000 men that was answerable to the crown. The support of the Black Army gave the Hungarian king far more strength and enabled him to inflict defeats on the Turks in 1463 and 1476. It was disbanded by King Vladislav Jagiello sometime before 1514. See also HUNGARY; WARFARE.

**BLACK DEATH** See PLAGUES.

**BLACK PRINCE** See EDWARD THE BLACK PRINCE.

**BLANCHE OF CASTILE** (1188–1252) Twice regent of France, wife of Louis VIII (1223–1226), mother of Louis IX (1226–1270) and one of the major political figures of the 13th century. The daughter of Alfonso VIII of Castile (1158–1214) and Eleanor, daughter of Henry II of England (1154–1189), she was the granddaughter of Eleanor of Aquitaine. In 1199 her grandmother accompanied Blanche to France, where she wed Louis, son of King Philip II Augustus (1180–1223) in a union that brought a brief period of peace between England and France. As queen and regent she was strict and morally uncompromising, ever diligent in her concern for the well-being of the French kingdom. On the death of Louis VIII in 1226, she became regent for her son, serving from 1226 to 1236. During that time she suppressed a revolt of the nobles, defeated Henry III of England (1216–1272) and made a temporary truce with the English and secured the internal stability of the country. Louis came of age in 1236, but she remained his most important adviser and again served as regent (from 1248 to 1252) while he was away on crusade. She died in 1252, causing severe distress to Louis, who was aware of the debt that he owed her. Blanche symbolically wore the color white. Jean de Joinville wrote of her in his *Histoire de Saint Louis*. See also FRANCE.

**BLOIS** A county in France that was the seat of the powerful counts of Blois, a considerable influence in French politics from the 10th to 13th century. Robert the Strong in the 10th century claimed an extensive dukedom that included Blois, but the first actual count was Thibaut I the Cheat, who acquired Chartres and Touraine around 940. His successors held the countship and expanded their holdings, often at the expense of the Capetian kings of France, who held only nominal suzerainty over them. Such was the case under Count Eudes II, who seized Champagne about 1023. Brie also fell under the influence of Blois.

Capetian dominance was established in the second half of the 11th century, but under Thibaut IV in the early 12th century, Blois regained Champagne. An influence on England, Stephen of Blois and Henry of Blois (the brothers of Thibaut) became king of England (1135–1154) and bishop of Winchester (d. 1171) respectively. Further, the counts acted as a counterbalance to the power of the French kings until the mid 1200s, when Blois passed to a cadet branch of the line, that of Chatillon. In 1397 the county was sold to Louis de France, duke of Orléans, and in 1498, when Louis XII became king, it was a royal possession. See also FRANCE.

**BLOIS, COUNTS OF** See BLOIS.

**BLONDEL** Twelfth-century troubadour minstrel and lyric poet who according to tradition rescued Richard the Lion-Hearted during the king's imprisonment in Austria and later wrote of him. A favorite of Richard, Blondel (also called Blondel de Nesle) supposedly found his master by singing a song known only to the two of them and to which Richard responded when sung below his prison window by Blondel. See also RICHARD I; TROUBADOURS.

**BLUES AND GREENS** See NIKA REVOLT.

**BOCCACCIO, GIOVANNI** (1313–1375) Italian poet, writer and scholar, a major figure in European literary history. He was born in Tuscany, the illegitmate son of a Florentine merchant. His youth was spent in Florence, and about 1328 he was sent to Naples to learn business from the Bardi family. During his stay there he came under the influence of humanists and intellectuals, finding a patron in Robert of Anjou and falling in love with Fiammetta (the name, meaning "beloved flame," given to his unidentified lover), who would dominate his early writings, much as Beatrice would dominate Dante's. Attempts at identifying Fiammetta (perhaps as the natural daughter of Robert) have remained purely speculative. In 1340 Boccaccio was summoned back to Florence, and during the next 10 years he developed into a brilliant writer, culminating with the *Decameron* (see DECAMERON).

The *Decameron* was written from 1348 to 1353 and was soon not only immensely popular but also the basis for other Renaissance writing, such as Chaucer's (see CHAUCER, GEOFFREY). Meanwhile, Boccaccio was appointed a councillor by the Florentines and an ambassador to Romagna, Milan, Naples, Bavaria and to the court of Pope Innocent VI in 1354. While writing the *Decameron* he met PETRARCH (1350). Their resulting friendship had a profound influence on medieval scholarship, for Boccaccio took up classical studies, with Petrarch's support. At his death he was compiling an encyclopedia of ancient mythology, *De genealogia deorum (The Genealogy of the Gods)*. He wrote a biography of Dante, lectured on the *Divine Comedy* and wrote biographies of important men and women. Retiring to Certaldo in 1374, he died in 1375, only months after Petrarch. Boccaccio helped introduce classicism as a model for common experience, made lasting contributions to scholarly development and was, with Petrarch, one of the luminaries of the Renaissance. Following are the works of Boccaccio.

### *Early Period*

*La caccia di Diana (Diana's Hunt;* c. 1333–1335), his earliest work; *Il filocolo* (c. 1336–1338), a love story in five books; *Il filostrato* (c. 1335), on Troilus and Cressida; and *Teseida* (1339–1341), written in ottava rima, or verse meter, on the love of two men, Arcita and Palemone, for the same woman, Emilia.

### *Florentine Period*

*Comedìa delle ninfe fiorentine* (c.1341–1342), Ameto's story of nymphs; *Amorosa visione* (1342; *Amorous Vision*); *Eligia di Madonna Fiammetta* (1343–1345); *Ninfale fiesolano* (c. 1345), on the nymph Mensola; and *Decameron* (1348–1353).

### *Later Period*

*De vita et moribus domini Francisci Petrarcchi* (1350), a biography of Petrarch; *Corbaccio* (1355), on a widow; *De genealogiis deorum; Bucolicu, carmen* (1351–1366), pastoral poems; *De mulieribus claris* (1360–1374), biography of famous women; *De casibus virorum illustrum* (1355–1360), on the fates of famous men; *De montibus, silvis, fontibus, lacubus, fluminibus, stagnis seu paludibus, et de nominibus maris* (1355–1374; *On Mountains, Forests, Springs, Lakes, Rivers, Swamps, and on the Names of the Seas*); and *Vita di Dante Alighieri*, a biography of Dante.

**BOCCANEGRA, HOUSE OF** A prominent Genoese family that produced several important figures in the city's history. The first was Guglielmo, who, in 1257–1262, was captain of the people and despot of the city. His brother, Marino, admiral of the Genoese fleet, contributed to the Byzantine defeat of the Venetians, thus ending the Latin Empire of Constantinople in 1261. The following year the Genoese overthrew Guglielmo, exiled him and stripped Marino of his position. Boccanegra resurgence came in 1339, when Simone, a descendant of Guglielmo's other brother, Lanfranco, used the Guelph-Ghibelline crisis to have himself named doge of Genoa. He failed to end the fighting and was removed in 1344 because of his greed and harsh taxation. Exiled to Pisa, he returned to Genoa in 1355 to assist in the city's revolt against the Visconti of Milan. The next year he became doge once more, holding the post until his sudden death in 1363. According to tradition, he was poisoned at a banquet. Verdi's opera *Simon Boccanegra* was an idealized account of his life. See also GENOA.

**BODEL, JEHAN** (c. 1167–1210) French poet and jongleur who wrote the popular and historically important miracle play *Jeu de Saint Nicholas (The Play of Saint Nicholas)*. Bodel was a member of the literary community at Arras and had planned to join the Fourth Crusade. He contracted leprosy, however, dying in 1210. Among his works were *Chanson des Saxons (Song of the Saxons), Les Congés (Goodbyes)* and both *fabliaux* and *pastourelles*. *Jeu de Saint Nicholas* was certainly the best known of his works. It was highly stylized for its time, using comedy, satire and reverence to tell the story of a miracle by Saint Nicholas and the resultant conversion of the Saracen to Christianity.

**BOETHIUS** (c. 480–c. 524) Roman philosopher, theologian and statesman who made important contributions to the preservation of classical learning during the early Middle Ages. Anicius Manlius Torquatus Severinus Boethius was born to the ancient Roman house of the Anicii. Educated at Athens and Alexandria, he was named, in 510, consul under the Ostrogoth king Theodoric. By 522 he was also *magister officiorum* (master of offices) for Theodoric but fell out of favor, probably because of his orthodox views on Christianity, which were in opposition to Theodoric's Arianism. His defense in 523 of the former consul

Albinus, who was charged with treason, led to Boethius's condemnation, imprisonment and execution for the same crime.

While in prison, Boethius wrote his major work, *De consolatione philsophiae (The Consolation of Philosophy).* In this he argued that knowledge of the good, virtue, and of God are attainable through the study of philosophy. The work, which attempted to reconcile divine providence with human freedom, became one of the most popular medieval books and was translated into Anglo-Saxon by Alfred the Great. Among his other works were translations of Aristotle's works and Porphyry's *Isagoge* and a commentary on the *Topica* of Cicero. The question of Boethius's Christian beliefs, was answered finally by the discovery of a biography by Cassiodorus and Boethius's own theological treatises on the Trinity *(De Sancta Trinitate)* affirming his orthodoxy. He was thus of considerable influence in the subsequent development of medieval philosophy and education, particularly the movement of Scholasticism.

**BOGOLIUBSKII, ANDREI** (c. 1109–1174) The son of Yuri Dolgoruky, grandson of Vladimir Monomakh and ruler of northeastern Russia from 1157 to 1174. On the death of his father in 1157, Andrei was elected prince of (Rostov-) Suzdal, a principality in northern Russia. His reign was harsh, but the principality increased its power and influence over neighboring territories. Andrei moved the capital to Vladimir, built fortifications and churches and then launched a campaign against Kiev, sacking it in 1169, a victory for which he was awarded the title grand prince of Vladimir. Although murdered by a group of boyars (nobles) in 1174, he was admittedly responsible for the principality's strength and political stability. See also RUSSIA.

**BOGOMIL** A heretical sect that first appeared in Bulgaria during the 10th century, surviving in the Balkans until the 15th century. The Bogomils were a dualistic religious group, named after their founder, Pop Bogomil, probably a Bulgarian translation of Theophilus, a preacher who lived in the first half of the 10th century. Essentially, Bogomil doctrines espoused a kind of neo-Manichaeanism, arguing that the material world was created by the devil and the spiritual world by God. They thus rejected all forms of mundane activity, as well as doctrines pertaining to the Incarnation; they also condemned the sacraments of Baptism, the Eucharist, marriage, churches and the clergy.

The sect attracted many members and by 1100 had attained such popularity, even in Constantinople, that Alexius I Comnenus (1081–1118), the Byzantine emperor, took steps to suppress them, imprisoning the sect's adherents, burning their books and executing by fire their leader, Basil. Its practice condemned in the Byzantine Empire, Bogomilism became a national movement in Bosnia and Serbia from the 12th to the 15th century, ending only with the royal decree of the Bosnian ruler in 1450 that all of his subjects should accept orthodox Christianity. Elsewhere in the Balkans the Bogomils were converted not to the orthodox Christian belief but to Islam, introduced into the region by the Ottoman Turks. The Bogomils, however, were one of the most pervasive heretical sects of the Middle Ages, having varying influence on such dualist heretical movements as the Cathari and the Albigenses of Southern France. See also HERESIES.

**BOHEMIA** A region in central Europe, now the western part of the Czech Republic. During the Middle Ages the region was important because of its position relative to Poland, Hungary, Moravia and the Holy Roman Empire. Bohemia took its name from the Celtic tribe of the Boii, who had been superseded by the Germanic Marcomanni. They, in turn, were replaced by the Slavs by the sixth century. Chief among the Slavic people were the Czechs, who dominated Bohemia after about 800 and were converted to Christianity by Saints Cyril and Methodius. According to legend, the Czech ruling house was founded by a plowman who lent his name to the dynasty that would reign in Bohemia from the mid-ninth century until 1306, the Premysl (or Przemysl).

A major change in the political life of Bohemia came during the reign of Wenceslas (921–929), when the country came under the sway of the Holy Roman Empire. With the imperial coronation of Otto I in 962 (936–973) as emperor, Bohemia became a duchy of the empire, the Premysls bearing the title of prince. Boleslav II (967–999) brought Bohemia to a position of prestige and good relations with the emperor and pope. His grandson, Bretislav I (reigned 1035–1055), seized Moravia, attaching it to Bohemian possessions. A son of Bretislav, Vratislav II (ruled 1061–1092), was made king of Bohemia in 1085, and Vladislav I earned the place of Elector. It was the great Ottokar I (1197–1230) who as king made it an inherited title. In the reign of Ottokar II (1253–1278), Bohemia reached the pinnacle of greatness under the Premysls, marking as well the rise of the Germans as a political entity within the kingdom. The success of Ottokar II would not last, however, and when Wenceslaus III was assassinated in 1306, the dynasty came to an end.

Four years of strife were ended in 1310, with the election of John of Luxembourg as king of Bohemia and his marriage to Wenceslas's daughter, Elizabeth. John was the son of Emperor Henry VII (1308–1313) and thus bequeathed to his own heir Charles VI (1346–1378) the opportunity to rule Bohemia well. Charles did not fail. In 1346 he was crowned king of the Romans and in 1355 Holy Roman Emperor. Bohemia had reached its zenith, for Charles IV moved the imperial administration to Prague, established the University of Prague in 1348 and issued the Golden Bull of 1356, making better provision for the terms of imperial election, including the monarchs of Bohemia as Electors.

The golden age of Charles was in sharp contrast to the increasing chaos that gripped the nation after his death in 1378. His son, Wenceslas IV, was deposed in 1400 and died in 1419; his successors, most notably Sigismund (1436–1437), were incapable of reconciling the nationalistic tendencies of the Czechs in response to German immigration. Czech feeling found embodiment in the Bohemian reformer Jan Hus (see HUS, JAN), whose execution at the stake in 1415 precipitated years of bloody warfare (1420–1434). Jan Zizka, the brilliant Hussite general, defeated Emperor Sigismund and was virtually the head of Bohemia until his demise in 1424 (see ZIZKA, JAN). Sigismund finally took control with the aid of the Utraquiste (moderate Hussites) in 1436 but died in 1437. The Compactata (Compacts) of Prague of 1436 were signed but again did little to unite the country, and the division between the German Catholics and the Utraquist Czechs lasted into the 15th century. The last Bohemian king, George of Podiebrad (1458–1471), tried to bring peace to the country but failed and died in 1471. From 1471 until 1526 Bohemia was ruled by the Jagiello dynasty of Poland, with the crown's powers very much reduced. Finally, in 1526, Ferdinand I of Habsburg (emperor, 1556–1564) was chosen as king of Bohemia, inaugurating Habsburg control that would endure for nearly 400 years.

See the Appendix for individual rulers; see also HERESIES; HOLY ROMAN EMPIRE; MORAVIA; PRAGUE; SILESIA.

**BOHEMOND I OF ANTIOCH** (c. 1050/8–1111) Prince of Antioch and one of the most celebrated Normans in the First Crusade. The son of Robert Guiscard, Norman duke of Apulia and Calabria, and his first wife, Alberada, Bohemond (whose Christian name was Marc) was born sometime around 1050 and was given the nickname Bohemond after the legendary giant. He joined his father in his campaigns against the Byzantines from 1081 to 1085, often victorious but unable to defeat the resilient Emperor Alexius I Comnenus (1081–1118). On Robert's death in 1085, Bohemond was deprived of his inheritance by the naming of his half brother, Roger Borsa, as the successor to Robert.

Tomb of Bohemond I of Antioch at Canosa

Several years passed during which Bohemond attempted to improve his own political position, but it was not until 1095 that an opportunity presented itself. With the call for a Crusade against the Muslims in 1095, by Pope Urban II (1088–1099), he gathered together a group of Norman knights and set out for the Holy Land. After signing an agreement with Alexius at Constantinople, Bohemond emerged as one of the leaders of the First Crusade, instrumental in the capture of Antioch in June 1098. He remained there for the remainder of the Crusader effort, nominal ruler of the city until his capture in 1100 by a neighboring Turkish emir. He was released in 1103, and by 1107 his relations with the Byzantines had deteriorated to the extent that he renewed his quarrel with Alexius by invading the Byzantine Empire. Negotiations resulted in an agreement of 1108, granting Bohemond control of Antioch in return for recognition of imperial suzerainty. As prince of Antioch, he took steps to ensure the succession by marrying (1106) Constance, daughter of Philip I of France (1060–1108), by whom he had two sons. He was the architect of the major Crusader State of Antioch but seriously harmed the relationship between the Western Crusaders and the Byzantines. Contemporary writers, especially Anna Comnena, related that he was a physically impressive man but impatient, ambitious, cunning and even cruel. See also CRUSADER STATES; CRUSADES.

**BOHEMOND II OF ANTIOCH** (c. 1108–1130) Prince of Antioch from 1126 to 1130, the son of Bohemond I of Taranto and Constance of France. He inherited the principality of Antioch only after years of fighting, aided in his cause by Baldwin II, king of Jerusalem (1118–1131). Bohemond arrived in 1126 from Sicily to take up the duties for which he was wholly unprepared. A quarrel erupted with Joscelin of Courtenay, count of Edessa, ended only by the intervention of Baldwin II and the patriarch of Antioch. Eager to engage the Muslims, the young prince launched an attack on the castle of Kafarta and, in 1130, with designs on Armenian territories, marched on Cilicia. There he was defeated and decapitated by the Turks, probably by accident, and his head was sent to the caliph of Baghdad. Most historians of the Crusades mentioned him; Matthew of Edessa, Michael the Syrian and William of Tyre wrote of his impetuosity, conceit and immaturity. See also CRUSADER STATES.

**BOHEMOND III OF ANTIOCH** Prince of Antioch from 1163 to 1201, the brother-in-law of the Byzantine emperor Manuel I Comnenus (1143–1180), who married his sister, Maria. In 1164 he campaigned against Nur al-Din, emir of Aleppo, and was captured along with Raymond of Tripoli and Hugh of Lusignan. Nur al-Din ransomed him, forcing Bohemond to seek additional funds from Manuel at Constantinople. He returned with a Greek patriarch for Antioch, marking the Greek ascendancy in that city. Bohemond survived the onslaught of Saladin's forces from 1187 to 1193 and passed his title to his son, Bohemond IV. See also CRUSADER STATES.

**BOHEMOND IV OF ANTIOCH** Prince of Antioch from 1201 to 1216 and again from 1216 to 1233 and also count of Tripoli. Noted as an able and learned ruler, especially in law, he was unpopular with rulers of other Crusader States because of his policy of tolerance toward the Muslims, with the exception of the Assassins. See also CRUSADER STATES.

**BOHEMOND V OF ANTIOCH** Prince of Antioch from 1233 to 1252 and count of Tripoli. He was a more active Crusader than his father, sending troops to aid in other expeditions against the Muslims, especially the disastrous Battle of Gaza in 1244. He married Alice of Jerusalem-Champagne, queen of Cyprus, but divorced her and wed Lucienne of Segni, a relative of the pope. Bohemond's rule was troubled by the dominance of Greek influence in Antiochene life, religion and politics. He resided at Tripoli. See also CRUSADER STATES.

**BOHEMOND VI OF ANTIOCH** Prince of Antioch from 1252 to 1268 and count of Tripoli. The last actual prince of Antioch, he lost the city to the Mamluks in 1268 while away at Tripoli. His reign had long been controlled by his father-in-law, Hethoum I, king of Armenia, and he was an ally and vassal of Hulagu, ilkhan of the Mongols, aiding in the Mongol destruction of Damascus in 1260. Through a truce with Baybars, sultan of the Mamluks, he retained Tripoli. See also CRUSADER STATES.

**BOHEMOND VII OF ANTIOCH** Titular prince of Antioch and count of Tripoli from 1275 to 1287. As the ruler of a weakened domain, Bohemond tried to exercise political power but was noted mainly for his bloody feud with the Knights Templars in 1277. Tripoli fell to Sultan Qalawun of the Mamluks 10 years later. Bohemond did not live long after this. He had no children. See also CRUSADER STATES.

**BOHEMOND OF TARANTO** See BOHEMOND I OF ANTIOCH.

**BOLESLAV I, KING OF POLAND** (c. 966–1025) Called Boleslav the Brave; ruler of the Poles from 992 to 1025, crowned king of Poland in 1000 and developer of the strong medieval Polish state begun by his father, Mieszko I (c. 962–992). Inheritor of the principality of Great Poland in 992, on his father's death, Boleslav (also Boleslaus) continued to further political consolidation and then launched a campaign to enlarge the domains of his Piast dynasty, uniting large elements of the Slavs at the expense of his neighbors. In 996 he seized Pomerania and later Cracow, using his positive relationship with Emperor OTTO III (983–1002) to be crowned king in 1000. Following Otto's death in 1002, Boleslav's unabated program of expansion caused a break with Emperor Henry II (1002–1024) and a series of wars lasting from 1001 to 1018. Boleslav conquered the province of Lusatia and for a time broke Henry's grip on Bohemia. The conflict was ended in 1018 with the Treaty of Bautzen, but that same year Boleslav marched east, defeating Prince Yaroslav I of Kiev at the Battle of the Bug, temporarily occupying Kiev and replacing Yaroslav with his brother and Boleslav's son-in-law, Svyatopolk.

Boleslav was a great patron of the church, winning papal and imperial approval to establish the Archdiocese of Poland at Guiezno. He later enabled the Polish church to be answerable only to Rome, thus removing it from the jurisdiction of the Germans. Boleslav was crowned again in 1024. On his death, Polish territory stretched from the Elbe to the Bug and from the Baltic to the Danube. See also POLAND.

**BOLESLAV II, KING OF POLAND** (1039–1081) Called Boleslav the Bold, Boleslaw and Boleslau the Generous, the ruler of Poland from 1058 to 1079. Vigorous and ambitious, Boleslav II pursued a policy similar to that of Boleslav I (992–1025), manipulating contemporary politics to regain Poland's strong position in central Europe. He twice failed to recapture Bohemia and launched successful campaigns elsewhere: Upper Slovakia (1061–1063), Hungary (1060–1077) and Kiev (1068 and 1077). Further, he helped Béla I (1060–1063) gain the throne of Hungary in 1060 and used the struggle between the papacy and the emperors to have Pope Gregory VII (1073–1085) accept his coronation as king of Poland in 1076. The resurgence of the German king Henry IV (1056–1106) led to a rebellion of Boleslav's nobles, including the bishop of Cracow, Stanislaus, who was executed by royal decree on April 11, 1078. This murder brought about a palace revolt, and Boleslav was ousted from the throne and excommunicated by Pope Gregory VII, dying in exile. See also POLAND.

**BOLESLAV III, KING OF POLAND** (1086–1138) Known also as Boleslav the Wry-Mouthed and Boleslaus III, the ruler of Poland from 1102 to 1138. A strong prince, he decided to split the country into territorial principalities, which eventually led to chaos and to a weakened nation. The son of Wladyslaw I Herman (1077–1095) and Judith of Bohemia, he succeeded his father as prince (the kingly title no longer being in use) and spent from 1102 to 1106 fighting his illegitimate brother for power. There soon followed an invasion of Silesia (1109) by Emperor Henry V (1106–1125), repulsed at the Battle of Glogau near Breslau. Most of his remaining years were spent at war, attempting to recapture and Christianize Pomerania, defeating the Pomeranians in 1109 at Naklo. He campaigned from 1113 to 1122, finally incorporating the region of Eastern Pomerania and Gdansk (Danzig) into Poland. Missionaries were sent into Western Pomerania, but its Christianization and absorption into the Polish realm did not come until 1135, when he gave his fealty to Emperor Lothair III (1125–1137). In an attempt to solidify the ambitions of his sons, Boleslav divided Poland into provincial principalities, with the eldest son, the prince of Silesia, serving as senior prince, with a seat at Cracow. Theoretically efficient, Boleslav's system would be unable to sustain internal disputes. See also POLAND.

**BOLESLAV IV, KING OF POLAND** Duke of Mazovia and effective ruler from 1146 to 1173. Called Boleslav the Curly, he was the brother of Wladyslaw II (1138–1146), the first of the so-called senior princes who were to rule a divided Poland. In 1146 he exiled Wladyslaw, administering most of the country until 1173, when he was overthrown by Frederick I Barbarossa (1152–1190), in favor of

Wladyslaw's sons, who established the dynasty of the Silesian Piasts. See also POLAND.

**BOLESLAV I, KING OF THE SLAVS** See BOLESLAV I OF BOHEMIA.

**BOLESLAV II, KING OF THE SLAVS** See BOLESLAV II OF BOHEMIA.

**BOLESLAV I OF BOHEMIA** (d. 967) Prince of Bohemia from 929 to 967 and one of the founders of the Bohemian state. A member of the Premysl dynasty, Boleslav, called "the Cruel," had his brother Wenceslas (or Vaclav) murdered and took power in 929. Consolidating his political gains, he moved the Bohemian capital to Prague and expanded control to include Silesia, Moravia and Slovakia. He was eventually forced to recognize the suzerainty of Emperor Otto I (936–973) and participated in the Battle of Lechfeld in 955. Boleslav II succeeded him in 967. Boleslav I also supported Christianity. See also BOHEMIA.

**BOLESLAV II OF BOHEMIA** (d. 999) Prince of Bohemia from 967 to 999, the son and successor of Boleslav I (929–967), who made further attempts to increase the territorial possessions of his realm, adding to it portions of Upper Silesia. Although maintaining amicable relations with the emperors and the church (including the sponsorship of an episcopal see in Prague in 973), Boleslav was willing to exercise strict authority for the furtherance of political consolidation. Thus he joined in a revolt against Otto II (973–983) and, more important, extirpated the Slavnik family in 995, removing serious dynastic rivals. See also BOHEMIA.

**BOLOGNA** A city in northern Italy at the foot of the Apennine Mountains and the modern capital of the Emilia-Romagna region. Bologna was originally the Etruscan town of Felsina and later a Roman colony. A Byzantine possession in the sixth century under the Exarchate of Ravenna, it later came under papal domination in the eighth century. By the 12th century it was a free commune but torn by the strife caused by the struggle between the Guelphs and the Ghibellines. Claimed by the papacy in 1278, Bologna was dominated by a series of lords, including the Visconti and the Bentivoglio in the 15th century. Finally, in 1506, Pope Julius II (1503–1513) reestablished his authority there.

Medieval Bologna prospered because of its excellent location in Italy, as it was on the trade route to Florence. The University of Bologna, founded in the 12th century, flourished in the 12th and 13th centuries when it was one of Europe's leading places of learning, especially in law. Granted special privileges under Frederick I Barbarossa (1152–1190), it added to its curriculum other branches of study, such as medicine (c. 1200). The first meeting of the chapter of the Dominicans, a teaching order, was held at Bologna in 1220. See also UNIVERSITIES.

**BONAVENTURE, SAINT** (c. 1217–1274) Franciscan theologian, cardinal, doctor of the church and the so-called Second Founder of the Franciscan order. Born Giovanni di Fidanza near Viterbo, Italy, he joined the Franciscans in 1238 or 1243. Attending the University of Paris, he studied under Alexander of Hales and in 1248 began to teach in Paris. He held this post until 1255, when two years of struggle with the secular teachers of the universities ensued, after which he was named a doctor of theology. That same year he was elected minister general of the order, working tirelessly and brilliantly to restore the unity of the Franciscans, torn internally by calls for leniency by some members and by declarations of the need for greater austerity by others. His revival of the order's rule, based on that of Saint Francis himself, was codified in 1260, and a new *Life of St. Francis* was written in 1263. It was approved as the official biography of the founder, replacing in 1266 all previous versions of Francis's life.

After aiding in the election of Gregory X to the papacy in 1271, he was made cardinal of Albano in 1273. He died during the Council of Lyons in 1274. A complex theologian, Bonaventure worked to reconcile Augustinian Christianity with Aristotelian philosophy, later focusing on mysticism. His writings included *Journey of the Soul to God,* on Christian mysticism, and a comprehensive *Commentary on the Sentences* of Peter Lombard. For his sublime wisdom, he was given the title Doctor Seraphicus (the "Seraphic Doctor") and declared a doctor of the church in 1588. See also FRANCISCANS.

**BONIFACE, ARCHBISHOP OF MAINZ** (675–754) English missionary whose work at evangelization in northern Europe earned him the title "Apostle of Germany." Originally called Wynfrith, he was born in Devon, England. Leaving England in 716, he journeyed to Frisia but was unable to convert the local inhabitants, returning in 719 after a trip to Rome, supported by papal authority. Thus conversions were made in Hesse, Bavaria and Thuringia, and he was subsequently summoned to Rome in 722 by Pope Gregory II, who made him a missionary bishop and gave him a collection of legal canons. Once again in Germany, Boniface won a victory over paganism by cutting down the Sacred Oak of the god Thor at Geismar. Henceforth he established Germany within the ecclesiastical organization of the church, establishing churches and monastic institutions, with the help of the Benedictines, that would flourish over the next centuries. His labors also aided in bringing portions of Germany—most notably Bavaria—into the Carolingian empire. After the death of Charles Martel in 741, and with the aid of Martel's sons, Carloman and Pepin the Short, Boniface initiated the reform of Frankish clergy, calling five synods to achieve his ends. Made archbishop of Mainz about 732, he was later killed by the pagans, according to tradition, on Pentecost Sunday in 754. He was buried in the abbey at Fulda, the monastery that he had established about 743. See also PAGANISM.

**BONIFACE II** (d. 532) Pope from 530 to 532, the first German pontiff, named by Felix IV to be his successor. Because of his Gothic origins, the Romans elected the deacon Dioscorus of Alexandria, creating a schism that lasted until Dioscorus's death in October 530.

**BONIFACE III** (d. 607) Pope in 607, having been sent to Constantinople as a legate for Gregory I the Great. His pontificate was noted for the amicable relations between the Eastern and Western Churches.

**BONIFACE IV** (d. 615) Pope from 608 to 615, his reign troubled by the heresies of the times, most notably Monophysitism. He was successful in converting the Roman Pantheon into a church, called Our Lady of the Rotunda, in 609, the first pagan structure to be transformed into a place of Christian worship. He was also particularly active in the English church and monasteries.

**BONIFACE V** (d. 625) Pope from 619 to 625, best known for his considerable support given to Christian evangelists in England.

**BONIFACE VI** (d. 896) Pope for little more than 15 days in 896 after a bitterly divisive election. He was probably murdered by the supporters of Stephen VI, who was subsequently elected as his successor.

**BONIFACE VII** (d. 985) Considered an antipope, he reigned from June to July 974 and again from 984 to 985. In 974, while serving as a cardinal deacon, he had his predecessor, Benedict VI, strangled and, with the help of the Roman family the Crescentii, was made pope. Emperor Otto II had him exiled, and he fled to Constantinople. Benedict VII was elected to replace Boniface, but the Crescentii brought Boniface back to Rome, where he murdered Pope John XIV but was soon executed by the Romans, unable to sustain his corrupt practices.

**BONIFACE VIII** (c. 1235–1303) Pope from 1294 to 1303 and one of the strongest advocates of papal supremacy. He was born Benedict Gaetani at Anagni and studied at Todi, Spoleto and law at Bologna. In 1276 he was named consistorial advocate and notary apostolic, advancing during the next years in the hierarchy of the church. He was made cardinal deacon in 1281, cardinal priest in 1291 and papal legate and was an important legal authority who advised the abdication of Celestine V in 1294. Named his successor at Naples, he returned to Rome and tried unsuccessfully to mount another Crusade. He soon became embroiled in the affair that would dominate his pontificate, the struggle with King Philip IV the Fair, of France.

The affair involved Philip's heavy taxation of the clergy, but the real issue was the question of the right of suzerainty of the pope over Christian rulers. Boniface was a difficult and strong-willed man who believed that the wars between England and France would end if the monarchs could not tax their subjects in order to pay for them. He promulgated the bull *Clericis laicos* (1296), which banned royal taxation of ecclesiastical revenues; Philip retaliated by prohibiting the export of currency, which threatened papal income. He amended his position because of Philip's pressures, but in 1301 the king tried the papal legate Bernard de Saisset, a clear threat to papal authority, prompting Boniface to issue the famous bull *Unam sanctam* (1302), declaring the temporal rights of the papacy. Philip remained adamant, and Boniface, planning to excommunicate the French monarch, was taken captive by Guillaume de Nogaret, Philip's adviser. Held at Anagni for several days, and probably mistreated, Boniface was sent home to die in Rome a few weeks later; he had been unable to restore the papacy to previous heights.

In addition to *Unam sanctam,* Boniface's bulls included *Clericis laicos* (1296) and *Ausculta fili* (1301). He also established the first Jubilee Holy Year in 1300 and organized the *Corpus juris canonici,* or Canon Law, into the *Liber sextus,* called the *Sext.*

**BONIFACE IX** (c. 1350–1404) Pope from 1398 to 1404, the successor of Urban VI to the Roman line of popes during the Great Schism (1378–1417). He made no serious attempts to resolve the schism and further degraded the papacy by selling indulgences and benefices to raise money for a lavish papal court.

**BOOK OF KELLS** See KELLS, BOOK OF.

**BORDEAUX** City in southwestern France on the Garonne River and capital of the medieval province of Guyenne, known to the Romans as Burdigala, an important center for commerce and chief city of the province of Aquitania. Once a proud walled city, lauded by the poet Ausonius, it faced irreversible decay with the collapse of Roman control in Gaul, and despite the presence of the archepiscopal see, from the fourth century, it fell to the Visigoths in 413. Part of the Visigoth kingdom until the early eighth century, Bordeaux was of little importance until the 10th century, when it became the seat of the dukes of Aquitaine. Henceforth a power in the struggle between France and England, Bordeaux passed into the possession of the English kings in 1154 as a portion of the dowry of Eleanor of Aquitaine. Its status as an English holding was reconfirmed with the Treaty of Paris in 1259, and it remained so until the end of the Hundred Years' War in 1453, enjoying considerable municipal freedom and participation in the flourishing trade with England. Following the Battle of Castillon (1453), Bordeaux returned to French territory. See also FRANCE.

**BORDER, THE** The name given to the heavily disputed and chronically violent region between England and Scotland, for centuries considered a virtual no-man's-land, and subject to neither Scottish nor English law. Attacks, feuds and atrocities committed by both sides were common. The so-called border songs or border ballads were written to commemorate the unsung deeds of the heroes and villains who rose along the dividing line. See also ENGLAND; SCOTLAND.

**BORGIA, HOUSE OF** The famed family that shaped the complex events of early Renaissance Italy. Although considered a house that belonged to the Renaissance period, the Borgias became prominent during the late medieval era. Of Spanish-Italian descent (the name originally was spelled Borja), the first great Borgia was Alfonso (1378–1458), who became the pontiff Calixtus III (1455–1458). Through his patronage his nephew, Rodrigo, was elevated to the rank of cardinal while still in his twenties. He became Alexander VI (1492–1503), one of the most infamous pontiffs and the father of Cesare and Lucrezia Borgia. Ironically, a family noted for its ruthless ambition, cruel despotism and total corruption produced Saint Francis Borgia (1510–1572.)

**BORIL** King of the Bulgars during the Second Bulgar Empire, from 1207 to 1218. See also BULGARS, EMPIRES OF THE.

**BORIS I** (c. 830–907) King of the Bulgars from 852 to 889, considered by many to be the greatest of the so-called czars or khans of the First Bulgarian Empire. The successor to a large and powerful Bulgarian state, he spent the early years of his reign consolidating the position of the Bulgars by attempting to expand into Serbia and Croatia. Convinced that the varieties of language and cultures within the empire were far too diverse to be held together politically (there were Slavs, Bulgars and Turkic peoples), Boris decided that a universal religion was essential. Defeats by the Byzantine Empire, however, forced him not only to check territorial ambitions but to accept Eastern Orthodox Christianity at Constantinople in 964 as well, despite his personal preference for Western Christianity.

Baptized Michael, Boris compelled his subjects to be baptized as well, massacring the members of the inevitable pagan counterreaction. Unhappy with the demands of the Byzantines for ecclesiastical control over the new Bulgarian church, he negotiated unsuccessfully with Rome. By the terms of the Fourth Council of Constantinople (869–870), Boris secured the virtual autonomy of the local church with an independent archbishop, under the nominal authority of Constantinople. Boris's remaining years were speent promoting the Christian faith and serving as patron of the development of Slavic culture and learning. He retired in 889 to a monastery but had to return in 893. His son, Vladimir, had reinstated paganism, and Boris removed him from the throne, replacing him with Symeon, another son, called "the Great." Boris returned to his retreat and died in 907. See also BULGARIA; BULGARS, EMPIRES OF THE.

**BORIS II** King of the Bulgars from 969 to 971, the last king of the First Bulgarian Empire, who was captured in battle with the Russians, allied to the Byzantines, about 969. His reign officially ended in 971 with the annexation of Bulgaria by the Byzantine Empire. See also BULGARIA; BULGARS, EMPIRES OF THE.

**BOSNIA** Territory in the Balkans on the Dalmatian coast, situated to the north of Montenegro, west of Serbia and to the south of Hungary and Croatia. Originally divided between the Roman provinces of Pannonia and Illyricum, Bosnia was settled in the seventh century by the Slavs and had direct links to Serbia until the late 10th century, when it gained a certain degree of independence. From the 12th century the country was largely under the domination of the Hungarians and was from time to time called a *banate,* or district, answerable to Hungary. Because of its location, Bosnia was subjected to invasion by the Ottoman Turks, beginning in 1386. After surviving the initial Turkish onslaught, the Bosnians recovered enough to annex neighboring Hercegovina but fell, finally, to the Ottomans in 1463 to became part of the Ottoman Empire.

**BOSWORTH FIELD, BATTLE OF** See WARS OF THE ROSES.

**BOTTICELLI, ALESSANDRO** (1444–1510) Florentine painter, born Alessandro (or Sandro) di Mariano Filipepi, the son of a leather tanner. He began his career as an apprentice to a goldsmith and from about 1458 to 1467, he was a student of the painter Filippo Lippi, whose influence, with that of Verocchio and the Pollaiuolo brothers, was evident in his work. The important patronage of Botticelli's career came after 1470 when Lorenzo de' Medici took an interest in him. Henceforth he was a member of the bright circle surrounding the Medici, and the elements of the Renaissance found expression in his paintings: family portraits, *La primavera* and the *Birth of Venus.*

While most of his work was commissioned by the Medici, he traveled to Rome in 1481–1482, where he painted frescoes for the Sistine Chapel at the request of Pope Sixtus IV (1471–1484). From 1493 he was in close association with the religious Savonarola and after 1498 concentrated on ecstatic and mystical religious motifs in his painting. Stylistically he was one of the most serene and gentle painters. The true worth of his paintings was overlooked for centuries, a situation reversed by his rediscovery in the 19th century, when appreciation was accorded his genuine contribution the history of art.

**BOUCICAUT** (c. 1366–1421) Marshal of France and one of medieval Europe's last chivalrous Crusaders. Born Jean le Meingre, the son of a marshal, Boucicaut served ably as a soldier in the army of France and became marshal in 1391. He subsequently took part in the Crusade at Nicopolis (1396) but was captured and ransomed by the Ottoman Turks. Three years later he assisted Constantinople in its defense against the Turkish siege of Bajezid I. Through Boucicaut's efforts, leading a small volunteer force, the Turks were repulsed on land and at sea. He was next governor of Genoa from 1401 to 1407 and later served in the French army at Agincourt in 1415. Captured by the English, he died in England in 1421. A writer of poems and ballads, he also founded the "Order of the White Lady of the Green Shield," an organization dedicated to the protection of ladies whose knights were absent. See also CHIVALRY.

**BOURBON, HOUSE OF** The noble family that, during the 17th and 18th centuries, became one of the greatest in all Europe, whose members ruled France, Spain, the Kingdom of the Two Sicilies and Parma. Although the Bourbons were preeminent from the 16th century, their origins were rooted in medieval history. The Bourbon line was a cadet branch of the Capetians, deriving its name from the castle found in Bourbonnais (now the department of Allier). Its first lord was Adhemar in the ninth century. The figure generally considered instrumental in the rise of the Bourbons was Robert, count of Clermont (1256–1318), sixth son of King Louis IX of France (1226– 1270). He married Beatrix of Bourbon and thus was the founder of the Bourbon line as well as eventually those of Vendôme and Montpensier. His son Louis (1279–1342) was made first duc de Bourbon in 1327, establishing the line of descendants who would occupy a multitude of thrones.

**BOURCHIER, THOMAS** (c. 1404–1486) Archbishop of Canterbury, an English cardinal and the leading ecclesiastical figure in the WARS OF THE ROSES (1455–1485). Educated at Oxford, he became chancellor there, later receiving an appointment to the post of bishop of Worcester (1434) and Ely (1443). On the agreement of both the Yorkist and the Lancastrian factions, Bourchier was made the archbishop of Canterbury in 1454. Chancellor from 1455 to 1456, he negotiated to end the war, unsuccessfully. Edward IV (r. 1461–1483) had him elevated to cardinal in 1467, and he lived long enough to crown Henry VII (r. 1485–1509) king of England in 1485. Bourchier participated in the heresy trial of Bishop Reginald Pecock of Chichester in 1457 and played a part in the events leading to the usurpation of Richard III (r. 1483–1485) in 1483. See also ENGLAND.

**BOURGES** Historical capital of the province of Berry in central France, the political stronghold for Charles VII (1422–1461) from 1422 until 1437, during the period of the Hundred Years' War. The city was also the site of the issuance of the Pragmatic Sanction in 1438. Architecturally Bourges was notable for the Gothic Cathedral of Saint Étienne and the house of JACQUES COEUR. See also UNIVERSITIES.

**BOUTS, DIRK** (c. 1420–1475) Netherlandish painter (also called Dirck or Dierick) who was born at Haarlem but eventually (1445–1448) visited and settled in Louvain, marrying a merchant's daughter and named city painter in 1468. From that point on, he spent virtually the remainder of his life in that city. Influenced by Roger van der Weyden, the leading painter in Brussels, Bouts drew considerable acclaim. His most important works were the *Last Supper* (1464–1467), a triptych for the Brotherhood of the Holy Sacrament at Louvain, and *Portrait of a Man* (1462), possibly a self-portrait. His style was widely initiated but his work was overshadowed, however, by his contemporaries, Roger van der Weyden and Jan van Eyck.

**BRABANT** Region in Belgium occupied by modern Antwerp and Brabant, called during the Middle Ages the duchy of Brabant. It was established originally in the duchy of Lower Lorraine during the 12th century having its capital at Louvain until the 15th century, when Brussels became preeminent. Governed by generally enlightened dukes who gave considerable autonomy to the cities, Brabant flourished as a trading and commercial center, with extensive wealth a result of the textile industry there. In 1430 the duchy passed to the control of the dukes of Burgundy. See also TRADE AND COMMERCE.

**BRACTON, HENRY DE** (d. 1268) English priest and one of the foremost medieval legalists of England. Also called Henry de Bretton or Bratton, he served as a justice to King Henry III (1216–1272) and, from 1247 to 1257 he was a judge at the King's Court (the early form of the King's or Queen's Bench). Bracton's importance was due to his systematic and comprehensive corpus on English law, *De legibus et consuetudinibus Angeliae (On the Laws and Customs of England),* the first of its kind in common law.

**BRAGI BODDASON THE OLD** Early-ninth-century Norwegian skald, one of the first practitioners of skaldic poetry. He led the movement away from the traditional Eddic prose. Bragi has been identified by some scholars with the Norse god Bragi, patron of poetry.

**BRANDENBURG (1)** Former province of Prussia occupying much of northern Germany, including Magdeburg, Frankfurt, Potsdam and Cottbus. During the early Middle Ages, Brandenburg was occupied by the Slavs (Wends) called the Havelli, with their capital at Brennaburg, or Brandenburg (see next entry). Germanic invasions of the region commenced in the reign of Henry I the Fowler (919–936), who captured Brennaburg. The Slavs reclaimed the region, necessitating further wars during the leadership of Lothair, duke of Saxony, and Albert the Bear, culminating in the decision of King Pribislav in 1150 to name Albert as his heir (d. 1170). Albert thus chose to rename his margravate (originally of Nordmark) Brandenburg.

Christianity and the rise of the margraves of Brandenburg to political prominence, especially as Electors of the Holy Roman Empire, brought both prosperity and development. Albert's descendants, called the Ascamians, ruled over the margravate until 1319. There followed a period of internal decline, halted briefly by Wenceslas of Luxembourg (c. 1373–1378). In 1417 Frederick of Hohenzollern was made Elector (d. 1440), marking a return to strong, centralized rule, most notably under the succeeding margraves. The Hohenzollerns thus established for themselves the powerful state that would enable them to dominate German politics from the 17th century. See also GERMANY.

**BRANDENBURG (2)** City in northern Germany on the Havel River that served as the seat of the margravate of Brandenburg. Originally known as Brennaburg, it was founded in the early sixth century by the Slavic tribe of the Havelli, falling to Henry I the Fowler (919–936) around 928 but retaken in 983. It was the object of the struggle between the Germans and the Slavs, its fate finally settled in 1150 when King Pribislav of the Havelli chose Albert the Bear (d. 1170) as his successor. Albert adopted the name Brandenburg for his margravate and made Brandenburg his capital. As the region of Brandenburg prospered under the margraves and later Electors, so too did the city.

**BRANKOVIC** See GEORGE BRANKOVIC; LAZAR BRANKOVIC.

**BREAKSPEAR, NICHOLAS** See ADRIAN IV.

**BREMEN** A major port on the North Sea in Germany that was one of the most important trading cities of northern Europe during the Middle Ages. Bremen was originally a small settlement called Breme, but its inevitable development was due to its position on the Weser River, which permitted connections from the North Sea to central Germany. Over the succeeding years it became a vital hub in the trade routes of Germany and Europe, outgrowing its dependence on the episcopal see of Bremen. In 1358 the city joined the Hanseatic League, adding to its prestige; the affiliation of the city with the league has survived, so that Bremen's title is *Freie Hansestadt Bremen (Free Hanseatic City State of Bremen).*

The presence of its archbishopric was major importance to Bremen. Charlemagne established a diocese there in 787, but its real influence came in 845 with the establishment of the archdiocese. This see became essential for the direction of all missionary activities into Scandinavia and thus for a time had ecclesiastical jurisdiction over Norway, Sweden, Denmark, Iceland and Greenland. See also GERMANY; TRADE AND COMMERCE.

**BRENDAN, SAINT** (c. 486–578 or 583) Known also as Brenainn or Brendan of Clonfert, the legendary abbot and traveler, the hero of the *Voyages of Brendan* and one of the great figures in Irish lore. Traditionally raised by an abbess, he entered a monastery in Ireland and later was named abbot of Ardfert. He established the monastery of Cluain Ferta (Clonfert in County Galway) about 561. A voyager, Brendan, called "the Navigator," is the hero of the eighth-century irish epic the *Voyages of Brendan,* translated in the 10th century into Latin. Relying on remarkably accurate geography, the tale recounts his sailing to islands the north and west of Ireland, probably the Orkneys and Hebrides, perhaps even as far as Iceland. The story of Saint Brendan was immensely popular in the Middle Ages.

**BRESLAU** Site of modern Wrocław, Breslau was the capital of the region of Silesia. Positioned on the Oder River, it was of commercial importance to eastern Europe and was an episcopal see as early as 1000. The capital of the duchy of Silesia under the Piast dynasty of Poland, it was sacked by the Mongols in 1241. Rebuilt, it was claimed by Bohemia in 1335 and eventually by the Habsburgs in the 16th century. See also SILESIA.

**BRETHREN OF THE COMMON LIFE** See COMMON LIFE, BRETHREN OF THE.

**BRETISLAV I** (d. 1055) King of Bohemia from 1034 to 1055, the grandson of Boleslav II and thus a prince of the Premysl dynasty of Bohemia. His reign was noted for the successful acquisition of Moravia, which became a permanent acquisition of Bohema. An unsuccessful invasion of Poland in 1039 necessitated his recognition of the German king Henry III in 1041. See also BOHEMIA.

**BREVIARY OF ALARIC** The title given to the compilation of laws by King Alaric II of the Visigoths in 506. Called the *Breviarium Alaricianum* or the *Lex Romana Visigothorum,* the codification derived largely from the Roman legal tradition and was applied for his Roman subjects in Gaul and in Spain. By 654 the people of Roman and Gothic origins had become so geographically dispersed that it was nearly impossible to unite them under one law code, so the breviary was repealed.

**BRIAN BORU** (941–1014) High king of Ireland from 1002 to 1014 and one of the great rulers in Irish history. Also known as Brian Bóruma mac Cennétig he was of the royal house of Munster. In 976 he succeeded his murdered brother as king of the small domain of Thomond (Dal Cais) and in 978 was crowned king of Munster as well. Over the next years he subdued the surrounding clans, routed the Norse invaders in county Dublin and then proceeded to lay claim to land further south in 983. Using diplomacy and military might, he removed High King Mail Sechnaill II (Malachy II) in 987 and was crowned in his stead in 1002. Virtually all Ireland acknowledged his claim as high king, but deteriorating relations with the Norse colonists precipitated a final war in 1013–1014. The Battle of Clontarf on April 23, 1014, resulted in the defeat of the Viking invaders, for Brian's son, Murchad, annihilated the enemy, including contingents that had sailed further north from Ireland and the Hebrides. Too old to fight himself, Brian awaited news of the victory in his tent but was murdered by a band of fleeing Vikings. See also IRELAND.

**BRIDE** See BRIDGET OF IRELAND, SAINT.

**BRIDGET** See BRIDGET OF IRELAND, SAINT.

**BRIDGET (BRIGID) OF IRELAND, SAINT** (c. 450–c. 523) Abbess of Kildare, called "Mary of the Gael" and, like Saint Patrick, one of the saints of Ireland. Her life has been largely obscured by legend and Christian lore, but her achievements and legacy have never been questioned. According to tradition she was born in county Louth, the daughter of a nobleman and a slave mother, both baptized by Saint Patrick. Early recognized for her saintliness, she so impressed the king of Leinster that he gave her a parcel of land in Kildare, where she established the first convent in Ireland, which eventually included a monastery as well. Through prayer and the establishment of religious communities, she gave aid and supported the early Irish church. Bridget was mentioned in many works of Irish literature and collections of Irish legends. See also IRELAND.

**BRIDGET (BIRGITTA) OF SWEDEN, SAINT** (c. 1303–1373) Patron saint of Sweden, founder of the Brigittine order and a noted mystic. The daughter of Birger Persson, a chief judge of Uppland, she married Ulf Gudmarsson and bore eight children, including Saint Catherine of Vadstena, or of Sweden. About 1343 she and her husband made a pilgrimage to Santiago de Campostela, but Ulf died later that year. Bridget chose to join the religious life near the Cistercian monastery of Alvastra and there dictated her visions and divine messages. One of the commands she received was to establish a new religious order, the Order of the Holy Savior, or the Brigittines, which she did in 1346, securing papal confirmation in 1370. In 1350 she went to Rome to urge the pope to accept the order and there remained for most of her life, with the exception of a series of pilgrimages, including one to the Holy Land. Bridget labored tirelessly for the poor and also worked to restore the papacy to its Roman residency from its French captivity at Avignon. Her visions were celebrated and were the subjects of extensive study; accounts of them were published for the first time in 1492. See also BRIGITTINE ORDER.

**BRIGITTINE ORDER** Also the Brigittines, an order of religious founded by Saint Bridget of Sweden in 1346 and approved by Pope Urban V in 1370. Known officially as the Order of the Holy Savior (Ord. Sanctissimi Salvatoris), the Brigittines were born of Saint Bridget's belief that Christ had told her to establish a new community. She journeyed to Rome in 1350 to gain papal acceptance of the order, and the mother house was constructed in 1371 at Vadstena, two years before Bridget's death. According to the initial organization, the order was to be a double community, with a convent and monastery under the overall control of an abbess. The Brigittines became very popular throughout northern Europe. A separation of the houses was made in the 16th century, and the order survived into the 20th century.

**BRIHTRIC** King of Wessex from 786 to 802, placed on the West Saxon throne by King Offa of Mercia, who sought to ensure the division of Wessex and Kent by preventing the heir, Egbert, from receiving the Saxon crown. Brihtric subsequently married Offa's daughter, Eadburh. See also ENGLAND.

**BRITAIN** See ENGLAND.

**BRITTANY** The northwestern peninsula of France, now a department and a culturally unique region in France. Known throughout the Roman imperial era as Armorica, Brittany was invaded by the Celts from England who were seeking to escape the wars caused by the arrival of the Anglo-Saxons. The Celts of Brittany remained in close contact with their English, Irish, Welsh, Cornish and Manx counterparts, spoke a Celtic language and preserved their ancient customs for centuries. Their conversion to Christianity was at the hands of missionaries from England. Fiercely independent, the Bretons fought Frankish domination from the sixth to the eight century, with Carolingian supremacy lasting until around 870. A high degree of independence was won by Nomenoë, who defeated Charles the Bald in 845, a policy extended by his successors, who made war on the Norsemen and declared themselves the dukes of Brittany.

Breton affiliation with England came in the 1100s when Geoffrey, son of King Henry II (1154–1189), married Constance, heiress to the duchy of Brittany. Geoffrey's son held the duchy until his murder in 1203, when it passed to his brother-in-law, Peter I of Drenx, and thus came under the influence of the Capetians of France. In 1341 the line of dukes became extinct, causing the War of the Breton Succession from 1341 to 1364, ending with the victory of John de Montfort, the English claimant who pursued a neutral policy during that period of the Hundred Years' War. Anne of Brittany, heiress to the duchy, married Charles VIII (r. 1483–1498) of France in 1491 and later Louis XII (r. 1498–1515) in 1499, leading to the formal absorption of Brittany into France in 1532. See also FRANCE.

**BRUCE** One of the illustrious families in medieval Scotland producing two kings of the Scots, Robert I the Bruce (1306–1329) and David II (1329–1371), as well as one of Ireland, Edward Bruce (1317–1318). The House of Bruce originated with Robert de Brus, a Norman duke who joined in the Norman Conquest of 1066. Robert received land in England, and his son, also Robert (d. 1141), was made lord of Annandale in Scotland; a descendant, Robert (d. 1295), made a claim to the Scottish throne from 1290 to 1292, after the death of Margaret, Maid of Norway. His grandson was the celebrated Robert I the Bruce, victor at Bannockburn and ruler of Scotland from 1306 to 1329. His brother, Edward, was monarch in Ireland from 1317 to 1318, and his son, David II, was king of Scotland from 1329 to 1371. See also SCOTLAND.

**BRUCE, DAVID** See DAVID II.

**BRUCE, ROBERT THE** See ROBERT I, KING OF SCOTLAND.

**BRUGES** City in West Flanders and one of the most important commercial centers in medieval Europe. Known in Dutch as Brugge, Bruges was first mentioned in the seventh century as the Municipium Brugense, becoming by the ninth century the military base for the counts of Flanders and their capital by the 1100s. The wealth of Bruges was due to its development as the center of the wool industry of northern Europe. By the 13th century it had a monopoly on the English wool trade and was a major depot for the Hanseatic League. A golden age was achieved in the late 14th century under the dukes of Burgundy, when Bruges was known as the "Venice of the North." Trade, however, began to decline in the early 15th century because the Zwijn Estuary became silted. Within years its economic prominence had been reduced, but its prestige remained, thanks to the continued political support of the dukes of Burgundy and city wellspring of Flemish art. See also FLANDERS.

**BRUNELLESCHI, FILIPPO** (1377–1446) Outstanding Florentine architect of the Renaissance. Trained originally as a goldsmith, about 1401 he entered a competition to design the bronze doors of the Baptistery in Florence. He was second, losing only to Lorenzo Ghiberti, and henceforth applied himself to architecture, becoming responsible for some of Florence's greatest architectural monuments: the Basilica of Santo Spirito (1434–1482), the sacristy of the Basilica of San Lorenzo (1421–1428), the Foundling Hospital (1421–1440), the Pazzi Chapel (1429–1469), Santa Maria degli Angeli (1434–1437) and the Duomo (1430), the dome of the Cathedral of Florence, his most celebrated achievement. He also established laws of perspective, devised by Alberti, using them to resolve questions of engineering. Antonio Manetti (1423–1497), his biographer and student, maintained that Brunelleschi deserved the title of first architect of the Renaissance. See also FLORENCE.

**BRUNHILDE** (c. 534–613) Queen of the Franks, wife of Sigebert I of Austrasia and daughter of King Athanagild of Spain. Brunhilde played a major role in the bitter war fought between Austrasia and Neustria from 567 to 613, because she sought revenge against Fredegunde, mistress of King Chilperic, who had conspired to have her sister, Galswintha, Chilperic's wife, murdered. The most powerful figure in the kingdom, she administered Austrasian affairs as regent until 613, when Clotaire II of Neustria had her cruelly executed. See also FRANCE.

**BRUNI, LEONARDO** (c. 1370–1444) Humanist, scholar and prominent figure in Florentine history. Bruni was also called Aretino because of his birthplace at Arezzo, Italy. A gifted historian, he made extensive translations of classical works, including those of Aristotle, Plato, Plutarch, Xenophon, Demosthenes and even Homer. He spent many years as a papal secretary but became chancellor of Florence, serving from 1427 to 1444. His outstanding work was *Historia del florentini populi libri XII*, a 12-volume history of Florence, which he began perhaps as early as 1404. It was translated into Tuscan in 1476 at Venice. Bruni was one of the important intellects of the early Renaissance, promoting as he did the revival of classical learning.

**BRUNO, SAINT** (c. 1033–1101) Founder of the Carthusian order. Educated at Cologne (Köln) and Reims, Bruno became a canon at Cologne and later received an appointment (c. 1057) as head of the cathedral school at Reims. Among his students was the future Pope Urban II. In 1075 he was made chancellor for the diocese of Reims by Archbishop Manasses de Gournai, with whom he soon began to quarrel because of the prelate's corruption. Bruno was forced to flee in 1076, returning in 1080 with Manasses's dismissal. Refusing a promotion to archbishop, Bruno rejected the world and set out to lead an ascetic life. Briefly under the care of one Robert of Citeaux, he eventually journeyed to a mountain retreat named the Grande Chartreuse, near Grenoble, where, with the support of Saint Hugh of Grenoble, the bishop and six companions, he established the Carthusian order in 1084. The order emphasized the joining of both the solitary and communal elements distinct in other orders. Pope Urban II called him to Italy and offered him the archbishopric of Reggio in 1090, but Bruno refused again, retiring to a desolate region in Calabria to live a monastic life at La Torre, where he died.

**BRUSSELS** Now the capital of Belgium, a major trading city during the Middle Ages and from the 15th to 16th century the capital of the duchy of Brabant. Brussels was originally a small community of traders who had settled on the banks of the Senne River, receiving the patronage of the dukes of Brabant. By the 11th century the city flourished as a vital market town, its subsequent wealth due to its manufacture of luxury goods, most important, lace. A group of merchant families had, by the 13th century, acquired virtual control of the city, and their abuses of power caused the workers to revolt in 1280, 1303 and 1421. As a result of the last uprising, a fairer distribution of local power was made, with rights allocated to the guilds of artisans and workers. Subject to local wars, Brussels was captured and occupied in 1357 by the army of the duke of Flanders. Its liberation was followed by the construction of large city walls. A period of great prosperity came under the aegis of the dukes of Burgundy, who assumed mastery over Brabant in 1430. The city was henceforth a leading artistic and intellectual center, home of Roger van der Weyden, the official artist of the city. See also NETHERLANDS.

**BRYENNIUS, NICEPHORUS** (1062–1137) Byzantine historian and courtier, who was married to Anna Comnena and was thus related to Emperor Alexius I Comnenus (1081–1118). He served as a trusted adviser to the ruler, bearing the rank of caesar. He was especially important during the difficult period of 1096–1097, when skirmishes erupted between the Byzantines and the newly arrived armies of the First Crusade. He defended Constantinople from an attack by Godfrey de Bouillon in 1097. Although not the equal of his wife as a historical writer, Bryennius wrote a history of the Comneni dynasty from the reign of Romanus IV Diogenes (1068–1071) to around the middle of Nicephorus III Botaneiates' time (1078–1081). The book, called *Material for a History*, was influenced by other writers, such as John Scylitzes and Michael Psellus but contained many details of the imperial family, which could have been known only to such an intimate member of the Comneni household. See also COMNENI DYNASTY.

**BUBONIC PLAGUE** See PLAGUES.

**BULGARIA** Country in the southeastern corner of the Balkan Peninsula situated along the Black Sea, north of Thrace, south of the Danube River and east of modern Yugoslavia. Bulgaria was the site of two important empires that rose to be major states in medieval Europe. Originally part of the Roman and then the Eastern Roman Empire, the region comprised part of the provinces of Moesia and Thrace and was invaded in the fifth century by the Slavs. Slavic domination was ended in the seventh century with the arrival of the Turkic people, the Bulgars. Under the famed founder of the First Bulgarian Empire, Asparukh, the Bulgars subjugated the Slavs and in 681 defeated the armies of the Byzantine Empire, forcing the Byzantines to recognize Bulgar autonomy.

The Bulgars established their capital at Pliska and by the reign of Khan Tervel (c. 701–718) were able to help Justinian II (685–695; 705–711) reclaim his imperial throne and send aid to Constantinople in 717–718 against the Arabs. A period of civil strife ensued with the death of Sevar in 739, ending in 803 with the securing of power by Krum, a Bulgar boyar (noble) who led a war against the Byzantines, crushing Emperor Nicephorus I (802–811) in 811; Krum died in 814 while marching against Constantinople. His son, Omurtag (814–831), made peace with the Byzantines but was also noted for his persecution of Christians. A major change in Bulgarian history took place in 852, when Boris I (d. 889) succeeded Presiam as king. Boris made Christianity the state religion and promoted Slavic culture, unifying the numerous peoples within the Bulgarian borders. Henceforth the Bulgars were Slavic in their ethnic disposition, while the practice of Christianity furthered a Byzantine societal and artistic homogeneity. Boris also liquidated dissident elements of the boyars, Bulgaria's traditional aristocracy.

Boris's son, Symeon (893–927), was crowned "Emperor of the Bulgars" by the patriarch of Constantinople but then waged war against the Byzantines from 913 to 927, which culminated in the annexation of Serbia in 924. His heir, Peter (927–969), made a new peace with Constantinople, in a reign generally seen as a weak one. Boris II (969–979), son of Peter, thus fell victim to a rejuvenated Byzantine Empire in 972 when Emperor John I Tzimisces conquered the country and ended the First Bulgar Empire. From 972 to 1187,

Bulgaria was under Byzantine rule, annexed officially in 1018 by Basil II (958–1025), who ruthlessly suppressed the attempt of the Bulgar claimant, Samuel, to gain independence. During this time Bulgaria was stamped by its Byzantine culture, retaining enough nationalism to support local efforts at rejecting foreign mastery. This came in 1187 when a Byzantine army was defeated by Bulgarian rebels. Recognized as independent, the Bulgars formed the Second Bulgarian Empire at Trnovo, under King Ivan Asen I (1187–1196).

The Second Empire began its decline in the reign of Koloman Asen (b. 1214, ruled 1241–1246). A Mongol invasion in 1242 and the bitter feuding of the boyars destroyed all hopes of restoration to its previous prominence in the Balkans. Throughout the 13th century the country was rent by civil war and political chaos, including the division of Bulgaria into two smaller states: Trnovo and Vidin, and the installation of puppet rulers such as Ivan Asen III (1279–1280) and Smiletz (1292–1298). The Sisman dynasty that came to the throne from 1323 to the late 14th century saw the collapse of Bulgarian influence in 1330 at the hands of the Serbs, when King Michael Sisman was killed at the Battle of Velbuzd on July 28. Serbian supremacy was replaced in 1372 or 1373 by the Ottoman Empire. By stages Bulgarian vassalage deteriorated into increased servitude and finally, in 1396, direct annexation. The latter move was taken in response to Ivan Stracimir's support of the Crusade of Nicopolis in 1396, which ended in total Ottoman triumph. The Ottomans so firmly controlled Bulgaria that it remained part of their empire until 1878. See also BYZANTINE EMPIRE; CONSTANTINOPLE; HUNGARY; OTTOMAN EMPIRE; PAGANISM; SERBIA; SLAVS; and individual Bulgarian and Byzantine rulers.

**BULGARS, EMPIRES OF THE** Two empires created by the Bulgar people that helped shape the history of the Balkans. The First Bulgarian Empire lasted from 681 to 972, founded by Asparukh and falling during the reign of Boris II to the Byzantines. The Second Bulgarian Empire was established by Ivan Asen I in 1187. It was destroyed by the Ottoman Empire after the disastrous battles of Kossovo (1389) and Nicopolis (1396). See also BULGARIA.

**BURGOS** City in northern Spain, in Old Castile, founded in 884 as an eastern outpost in Asturias to guard against the Moors. Established by Count Diego Rodríguez Porcelos of Castile, Burgos was, by 1000, the capital of the Kingdom of Castile. Much prestige was lost in 1087 with the move of the royal residence to Toledo, although the city still claimed the tomb of El Cid (see RODRIGO DÍAZ DE VIVAR) and the Gothic Cathedral of Burgos, begun about 1220. See also CASTILE.

**BURGUNDY, COUNTY OF** See FRANCHE-COMTÉ.

**BURGUNDY, DUCHY OF** Political unit in the Kingdom of France formed out of the division of the Carolingian empire in the ninth century. Also known as the Franche-Comté, the duchy emerged as the most prestigious and powerful of the feudal holdings in France, stretching across the region to the west of the Saône River and including such important cities as Dijon, Autun, Chalon and Châtillon. Originally part of the Kingdom of Burgundy (Regnum Burgundiae), Burgundy belonged for a time to Boso, ruler of Viennois and brother-in-law to Charles the Bald (843–877). His brother, Richard the Justiciar (d. 921), was a supporter of Charles and so received the right to administer Burgundy in return for taking part in his war against the Normans. After a series of successions, King Robert II the Pious (996–1031) seized the duchy (c. 1002), establishing his son Henry (the future Henry II; 1031–1060) as its master. Henry was crowned in 1032, and the new duke of Burgundy was Robert I (d. 1075), the first of the Capetian dukes who would hold the duchy until 1361.

During the period of the Capetian dukes, Burgundy expanded and gained in influence. The dukes, allied to the royal house, exercised their authority as the most powerful nobles of the country. Their towns developed economically through trade and the monasteries of Cîteaux and Cluny, which helped further the cause of ecclesiastical reform and attracted many pilgrims, drawn there because of the reputation of these institutions as bastions of faith and spirituality in the 11th and 12th centuries. In 1335 Duke Eudes IV married the daughter of Otto IV of the county of Burgundy and thus united the duchy and the county. This arrangement added extensive holdings east of the Saône, but this expansion was ended in 1361 with the death of Philip of Rouvre and the duchy taken by the crown. King John II severed the county from the duchy, giving it to his son-in-law, the count of Flanders.

A new era was initiated in 1363 when King John granted to his son, Philip the Bold (1363–1404), the title of duke of Burgundy. The first duke of Valois, Philip married Margaret of Flanders, heiress to the county of Flanders through the arrangement of Charles V (1364–1380). In 1384, Philip inherited Flanders, adding to his ducal possessions Flanders, Artois, Nevers, Rothel and Franche-Comté (the county of Burgundy). Further acquisitions were made under John the Fearless (1404–1419)—Hainaut and Holland; under Philip the Good (1419–1467)—Brabant, Limburg, Luxembourg and the Somme region; and under Charles the Bold (1467–1477)—Upper Alsace, Lorraine, Bar and Guelderland.

The Valois differed greatly from the Capetian line in that they commanded a strong army and possessed vast wealth and thus were far less obedient to the French royal house. Throughout the 15th century they attempted to control virtually the entire country while maintaining their own autonomy. Burgundy's golden age evolved from 1404 to 1477, under the aegis of the dukes Philip the Bold, John the Fearless, Philip the Good and Charles the Bold. John waged a political war with the Armagnacs, who were allied to the French crown, and after his murder in 1419, his son, Philip, supported England in the Hundred Years' War, reconciling himself to King Charles VII (1422–1461) in the Treaty of Arras in 1435. Charles the Bold tried for years to claim the position of king of Burgundy but failed because of the gifted statecraft of King Louis XI (1461–1483). While Burgundy suffered during the Hundred Years' War, it remained one of the great states of Europe on Charles's death in 1477, to such degree that the shrewd Louis XI lay claim to it, ending decades of intrigue and dispute. See also BURGUNDY, KINGDOM OF; FRANCE; FRANCHE-COMTÉ.

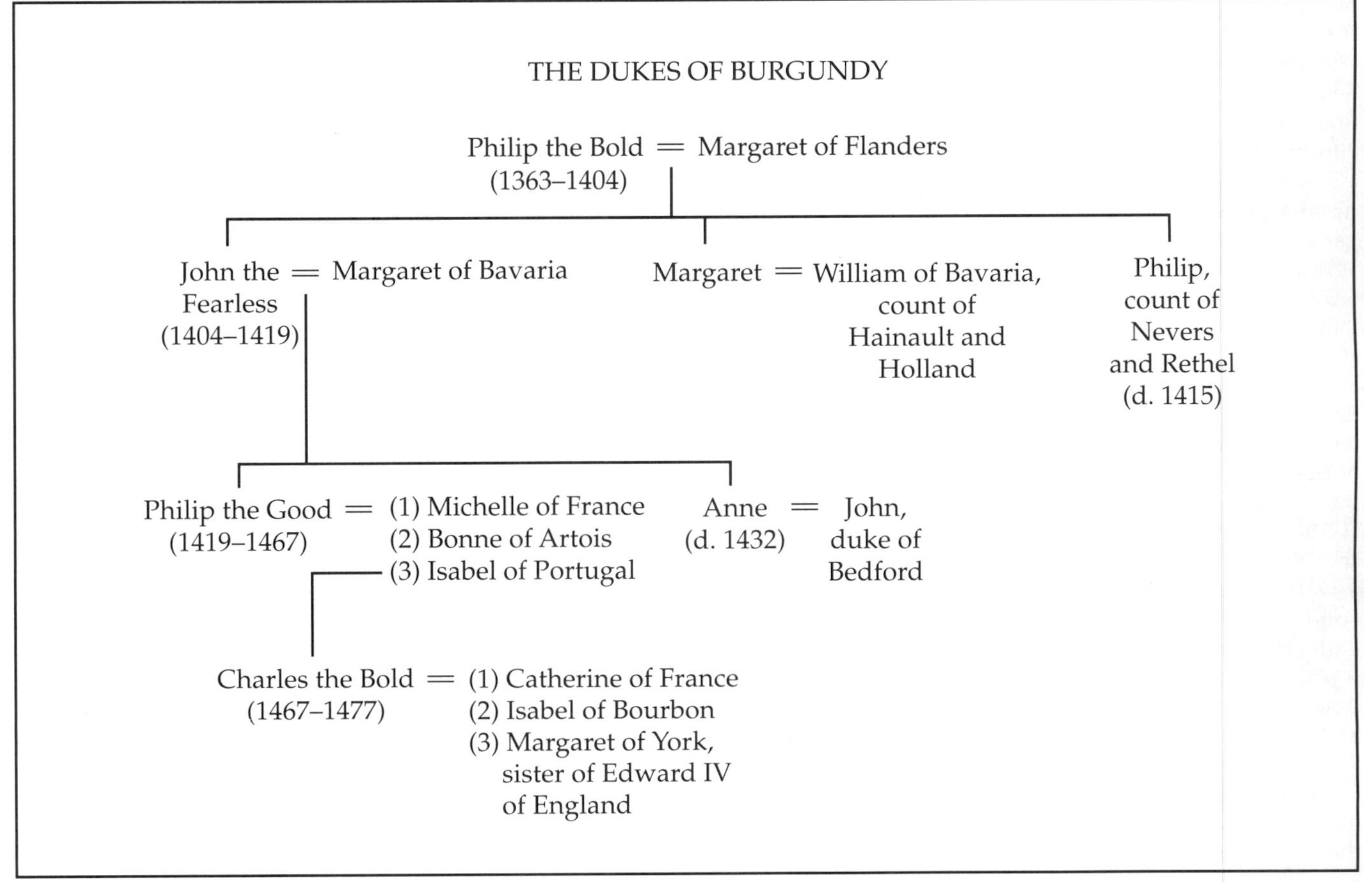


**BURGUNDY, KINGDOM OF** Kingdom composed of two Carolingian states, stretching from the Rhine River to the Mediterranean along the Rhone Valley and thus occupying the regions of southern Switzerland, Savoy and southeastern France. The Kingdom of Burgundy (called after the 13th century the Kingdom of Arles) was actually composed of two major territories: Provence (Lower Burgundy) and Jurane (Upper Burgundy). Its origins were in the old Kingdom of Burgundy, the Regnum Burgundiae, claimed by Clovis in 524 and finally occupied by the Franks in 534. After withstanding partitions under the Carolingians, Boso, ruler of Viennois, secured his claim over the entire region in 879 and thus ruled from Autun to the Mediterranean. Portions of the kingdom were lost to the Carolingians, most notably Upper Burgundy, and eventually Boso and his heirs could claim only Provence. Meanwhile, the heir to the Welf family of Germany, Rudolf I (888–912), was named king of Jurane in 888, and his son, Rudolf II (d. 937), secured by treaty in 933 the union of Upper and Lower Burgundy into the Second Kingdom of Burgundy, later called the Kingdom of Arles. When Rudolf II died without heir, he had named Emperor Henry II (1002–1024) his successor. Henry's son, Conrad II (1024–1039), was opposed by the Burgundians as their king, but from 1033, with the subjugation of his opposition, Burgundy became a territory of the Holy Roman Empire. The kings of Burgundy were politically weak, especially when opposed by independent nobles, such as those in Upper Burgundy and the Franche-Comté. From 1295, therefore, Burgundy was taken, region by region, by France, culminating in the appointment of the dauphin Charles VI (1380–1422) as imperial vicar in 1378, an act that presaged French domination over Burgundy. The realm then existed only in theory, its last holdings, Nice and Savoy, surviving until 1860. See also BURGUNDY, DUCHY OF; FRANCE; FRANCHE-COMTÉ; GERMANY; HOLY ROMAN EMPIRE; LYONS; MARSEILLES; SAVOY; SWITZERLAND.

**BURIDAN, JEAN** (c. 1295–c. 1358) French Scholastic philosopher and an important Aristotelian, who studied at the University of Paris as a student of William of Ockham. In 1328 he became rector at Paris and was still teaching there in 1358. A nominalist and an adherent of causality, he proposed a version of determinism, arguing that humanity had the will to choose good but also possessed the free will to delay such a decision. The famous but falsely attributed case Buridan's Ass examined the action of suspending moral deliberation. An ass, positioned between two equal piles of hay, had no motive to choose one and thus starved to death. Buridan's works were condemned by the supporters of Ockham, but his translations of Aristotle's writings on logic, metaphysics and science were of great value to medieval scholars.

**BUYIDS** Also known as Buwayhids, an Islamic military dynasty of Shiite belief dominating Baghdad from 945 to 1055. The Buyids originated in the Daylam region of northern Iran and were called Daylami or Daylamites, claiming descent from Parthians or Sassanians. The founder of the line was a common soldier, Buyih (or Buyeh), whose three sons, Ali, Hasan and Ahmed, carved out the Buyid state, taking the names Imad ad-Dawla, Rukn ad-Dawla and Mu'izz ad-Dawla respectively. Imad conquered the Persian territory of Fars, and Rukn subdued central Persia. Mu'izz, however, took the dramatic step of subjugating Iraq and, in December 945, captured Baghdad. Henceforth the Sunni Abbasid caliphs were to be controlled by the Shiite Buyids, most notably after Mu'izz deposed Caliph al-Mustakfi (944–946) and replaced him with al-Muti, a more pliant and obedient Abbasid claimant.

Buyid power rested on the close agreement of the dynasty's members, but all cooperation ended in 977 when Rukn, the last of the three brothers, died. A struggle ensued among the Buyid princes, with Adud ad-Dawla (949–983) the victor. His reign (977–983) as head of the Buyid dynasty was notable for its wealth, stability and tendency to aggression. Territorial acquisitions were made in Oman, Tabaristan and Gorgan. Further, the Buyids were noted builders and patrons of the arts and recognized by other major Islamic powers as well as by the Byzantine Empire. Adud could not establish a lasting system of order, and on his death in 983 the bitter feuds and the decline began. Economic decay made the Buyids susceptible to attack, first by the Ghaznavids in 1029 and culminating with the Seljuk Turks, who crushed the Buyid political dominance in the Abbasid caliphate and, in 1095, deposed the last of the Buyid rulers. See also ABBASID CALIPHATE; ISLAM.

***BYLINI*** The Russian narrative and heroic poetry recounted orally for centuries and collected at the start of the 18th century. The *bylini* probably originated with the legendary minstrel bards of Russia, the *skomorokhi*, and were present from early periods of Russian history, flowering during the golden age of Kiev, from the 10th to the 12th century. *Bylini* dealt with a variety of subjects, the longest cycle telling of Prince Vladimir of Kiev and the knight Ilya of Muron. The city of Novgorod was the theme of another major cycle.

**BYZANTINE EMPIRE** The name given to the Eastern Roman Empire, a major political and cultural entity in medieval Europe and one of the enduring empires in history. The Byzantine Empire, its heart the celebrated city of Constantinople, derived its name from the ancient town of Byzantium and encompassed at various times regions as diverse as Asia Minor and the Balkans. Founded in the antiquity of the Roman Empire, falling at last in 1453 to the Turks, the Byzantine realm was a remarkable bridge between the old world and the modern and a unique constant in an era of change and development. The fall of Constantinople on May 29, 1453, with the entry of the Ottoman Turks and the death of Emperor Constantine XI has been called by many scholars the end of the Middle Ages and a prologue to the modern era.

In 330, Constantine the Great established his city, Constantinople, as the vital center of the Roman Empire. By 395 the political division of the old Roman world into the East and West was made permanent. The Eastern Roman Empire, however, survived the Germanic migrations and the seemingly irreversible decay that brought down the West, and from 476, after the last Roman emperor was deposed by the Germanic king Odoacer, the emperors of Constantinople claimed their rights as rulers of all of the Western Roman Empire, although their actual power was confined to the East. Further, what had begun as a copy of Roman culture in Constantinople evolved from an inherited Hellenic tradition—permeated by what came to be called the Byzantine style—into a more Eastern orientation, heavily influenced by the Christian church, specifically the Orthodox or Eastern Christian church, as compared with the later Roman or Western model.

### *Early Byzantine Period* (476–867)

The Byzantine emperor who reigned during the demise of the West was the Isaurian general Tarasicodissa, called Zeno (ruling from 474 to 491). By dealing adroitly with invading peoples, he prevented their assault in the East by diverting their attention elsewhere and even gained nominal suzerainty over the Ostrogothic Kingdom of Italy, of Theodoric the Great. The empire was spared debilitating warfare, and its economy actually prospered under Anastasius I (who reigned from 491 to 518). His successor was Justin I (518–527), who made certain that his nephew succeeded him. This was to be Justinian I.

Considered by many to be the greatest of the Byzantine emperors, Justinian, reigning from 527 to 565, inaugurated the first great resurgence of the Eastern Roman Empire. He codified Roman law, encouraged Hellenic art and culture and brought the sixth century into the golden age of Byzantine art and architecture. Moreover, he believed in restoring the political prominence of his empire and, aided by his brilliant generals, Belisarius and Narses, inflicted defeats on the Persians, destroyed the Vandals in Africa and reclaimed Italy. Justinian's achievements were offset by a cruel and jealous nature. He slaughtered 30,000 rioters in the Nika Revolt of 532, and the crushing cost of his pogroms, combined with depopulation caused by the plague of 541–543, left a legacy of problems for his heirs. That Byzantium survived the ensuing decades at all was a testament to the vitality of the society, the durability of the institutions and the capacity of the emperors, such as Justin II (ruled 565–578) and Maurice (ruled 582–602), to make the right decisions at the necessary hour.

The seventh century would bring new and even more pressing crises, specifically the conquering tide of Islam and the arrival of the Slavs in the Balkans. Emperor Heraclius (610–641) defeated the Persians and divided the provinces into the "themes," or semimilitary zones, under the civil and martial control of the governors. His triumph over Persia and the easing of political tensions made the Islamic advance even easier. Starting with the Battle of Yarmuk in 636, the Arabs took most of the Eastern possessions of the empire, including Palestine, Syria, Egypt, Africa and much of Asia Minor, and finally besieged, unsuccessfully, Constantinople in 674–678 and 717–718. By the reign of Leo III (717–741), only Sicily remained as a Byzantine holding, other regions being lost to the Arabs or the Bulgars.

Although the years from 711 to 843 were noted for the Iconoclastic Controversy, the Byzantine Empire also enjoyed a recovery, owing mainly to the struggles within Islam between the Umayyad and the Abbasid caliphates.

Charlemagne's coronation in 800 as emperor of the West precipitated the religio-political disagreements that cut the Christian world in half, having the most far reaching and ominous implications for the Byzantines. The cultural imprint of Byzantium, however, was more enduring among the converts to Orthodox (Eastern) Christianity, the Bulgars, Slavs and especially the Russians, adopting the art, architecture and ideals of their religious converters. Such evangelization was extremely successful under Michael III (842–867), who was assassinated by Basil I, the founder of the Macedonian dynasty of emperors.

### *Middle Byzantine Period* (867–1261)

The Macedonian dynasty, lasting from 867 to 1025, was the second golden age of imperial history. From Basil I (867–886) to the death of Basil II in 1025 (ruled 976–1025), the empire saw a rebirth of the arts, continued acceptance of Orthodox (Eastern) Christianity, further centralization of imperial authority at Constantinople and a rejuvenation of Byzantine might, including campaign victories against the Muslims, the capture of Aleppo in 962, the recapture of Antioch and the termination of the First Bulgarian Empire in 972. When Basil II became emperor in 976, the Byzantines controlled most of Syria and Palestine, while Christianization forged strong links with the Slavs, Russians and Bulgars. Basil II added Armenia and ruthlessly suppressed a Bulgar revolt in 1014, dying without an heir in 1025. The key to the prosperity of the Macedonian dynasty was in the gifted emperors who occupied the throne, among them Nicephorus II Phocas (963–969) and John I Tzimisces (969–976). Macedonian claimants held the imperial title until 1055–1056, a date of interesting coincidence, for at about the same time the Seljuk Turks moved into Baghdad, announcing their domination of the Abbasid caliphate and their intent to become a major state.

The Byzantine Empire was once more beset with problems. Its armies were now too weak to resist the onslaught of enemies from virtually all directions, the Petchenegs, Turks and even the Normans. The Norman knights in Sicily seized Bari in 1071, ending Byzantine presence in the West. Far worse, in August 1071, Romanus IV Diogenes (1068–1071) was captured by the Turks in the disastrous Battle of Manzikert, after which the Seljuks poured across Asia Minor and reduced the Byzantine provinces one by one. Meanwhile, all hopes of a reconciliation with the

## Byzantine Empire, 1270

Roman church were dashed by the declaration in 1054 of a schism between East and West. Some hope rose with the elevation of Alexius I Comnenus in 1081. His policies were aimed at consolidating Byzantine strength and then reclaiming lost territories. Thus, while he routed the Petchenegs in 1091, he signed agreements with Venice in 1082, granting trade rights in return for aid against the troublesome Normans, who were working to extend their influence into Greece. A plea for aid in defending Constantinople was answered by Pope Urban II in 1095, who called for a Crusade against Islam. Thus was launched the First Crusade in defense of Constantinople. Some progress was made toward strengthening the empire, but the Crusaders, in the name of Christ, fought their way into Antioch, Edessa and Jerusalem and failed to adhere to their agreements with Alexius, keeping the cities for themselves and establishing the Crusader States. Throughout the 12th century, the Second and Third Crusades (1147–1148 and 1189–1193 respectively) would bring more Latins to the East, thus increasing Western interference in the affairs of the empire and threatening Byzantium's order and stability.

The conditions were set by the Fourth Crusade of 1201–1204 to topple the Byzantine Empire entirely. Venice, eager to exploit the decline of the Byzantines, encouraged the leaders of the Fourth Crusade to sack the city of Constantinople in April 1204, removing the claimants to the imperial title and, finally, creating thereby the Latin Empire of Constantinople. Despite the rule of the Latins from 1204 to 1261, an unbroken chain of Byzantine emperors was maintained by three small but vital splinter states, those of Nicaea, Trebizond and Epirus. The heir of the Empire of Nicaea, Michael VIII Palaeologus (1259–1282), defeated the Epirians in 1259 and terminated the Latin empire in 1261, with his coronation in Constantinople. The years 1204–1261, although ending with Byzantine independence, had unfortunately drained the empire beyond its capacity to recover. Michael VIII Palaeologus (1259–1282) was the first of the Palaeologi dynasty, the last in Byzantium, for its economy and armies were shattered. Nearly two centuries were to pass before the Ottomans captured Constantinople, but the death blow to the empire came in 1204.

### *Late Byzantine Period* (1261–1453)

Michael VIII actually faced greater danger from the West than he did from the Turks. Charles of Anjou attempted to mount a repetition of the Fourth Crusade and was eventually defeated in 1282 only by the war of the Sicilian Vespers and the pro-Byzantine intervention of Peter III of Aragon. Thus, pleas from Constantinople to the Western kingdoms went unanswered, and from the papacy came only the demand for acknowledgment of the Roman church's ecclesiastical supremacy. What was left of former economic prosperity went to levy troops to fight the Christian armies in Albania and the Turks in Anatolia.

Andronicus II Palaeologus (ruled 1282–1328) attempted to recoup the economic health of the empire by slashing the military expenditures, relying on the Genoese for naval intervention and the Catalan Company, not completely reliable mercenaries from the Crown of Aragon, for protection on land. Subsequent Byzantine history was marked by internal feuding and civil war between the heirs to the throne, the rise of the Serbians under Stefan Dushan and the continued victories of the Ottoman Turks. John VI Cantacuzenus labored to revive the economy and the military force during his reign from 1347 to 1354, but he was brought down by the ruler he had deposed, John V (first reign was 1341–1347), who ruled again from 1354 to 1391. This unfortunate reign saw the Ottomans gain a foothold in Europe, defeating the Serbs in 1371 and compelling the Serbians, Bulgarians and the desperate Byzantines to accept vassal status in 1373. A final respite came during the years 1413–1421, the dynasty aided largely by the crushing of the Ottoman sultan Bayazid II (1389–1402) by Tamerlane in 1402. Muhammad I (reigned 1413—1421) became sole ruler with the aid of Manuel II Palaeologus (1391–1425) and so granted privileges to the Byzantines. Manuel utilized the time to prepare for the inevitable.

The last centuries of the moribund empire did, however, produce artistic, intellectual and spiritual renascences. Greek classical learning was promoted, and the Eastern Church regained its former vitality. The Byzantines remained loyal to their creed as Emperor John VIII Palaeologus (1425–1448) was to learn. He made a final appeal to the West in 1439 at the Council of Florence, agreeing to accept the domination of the Roman church. This agreement came to naught, for the citizens of Constantinople rebelled against their ruler, whom they declared a traitor. The army organized by Hungary, Serbia and Poland to repel the Turks was annihilated at Varna in 1444, joining the similarly massacred forces at Kossovo in 1389 and Nicopolis in 1396.

In 1447 and 1448, the Black Death struck Constantinople's population. John died in 1448, and his brother, Constantine XI Palaeologus, was made emperor in 1449. More protests were hurled at the official union of the churches in 1452, but attention was soon directed elsewhere. Muhammad II (1451–1481), "the Conqueror," had arrived at Constantinople, and the final siege of the city began in April 1453. With artillery having destroyed its walls, the city was breached on May 29, and Constantine died in battle. Three days of looting followed, and then the sultan rode into Constantinople to lay claim to it. The Byzantine Empire was totally obliterated by 1461, leaving its legacy of religion, art, architecture and literature to the West, which had once forsaken it, and the Balkan countries and the Russians, who had embraced it. See also ALEXANDRIA; ARMENIA; ART AND ARCHITECTURE, BYZANTINE; ASTROLOGY; ASTRONOMY; BESSARION, JOHN CARDINAL; BYZANTIUM; CHRYSOLORAS, MANUEL; COMNENA, ANNA; COMNENI DYNASTY; DALMATIA; EXARCHATE; GEORGE OF TREBIZOND; GREECE; HERESIES; HOLY ROMAN EMPIRE; ISLAM; JEWS AND JUDAISM; KIEV; MACEDONIAN DYNASTY; MANIACES, GEORGE; MEDICINE; MONOPHYSITISM; PALAEOLOGI DYNASTY; PALAMAS, GREGORY; PLAGUES; TRADE AND COMMERCE; TRUE CROSS; VIKING.

**BYZANTIUM** An ancient city positioned at the geographical crossroads between East and West, chosen by Constantine the Great as the site for the new city to become Constantinople. The name Byzantium, however, never lost its symbolic influence and was applied to the culture of the Byzantine Empire.

# C

**CABOCHE, SIMONE** Early-15th-century leader of the Parisian merchant guilds, called the Cabochiens after him. Also known as Simon le Coustellier, he led the guilds, whose members were discontented with heavy taxation and lack of political reform, and in 1413 was instrumental in the riots that led to the seizing of the Bastille. With the encouragement of John the Fearless (1404–1419), duke of Burgundy, and the Burgundian party, whom the Cabochiens supported, Caboche forced King Charles VI (1380–1422) to issue the Ordonnance Cabochienne to bring about changes in the government. Not satisfied, the tradesmen maintained pressure, giving Charles, duke of Orléans, and the Armagnacs the pretext they needed to suppress the movement. The Ordonnance was withdrawn, and Caboche lost his position of influence. See also PARIS.

**CADE, JACK** (d. 1450) English rebel, instrumental in a major uprising against King Henry VI (1422–1471) of England in 1450. Also called John Cade, according to tradition he was born in Ireland, fought in the Hundred Years' War and, in 1449, while living in Sussex, was charged with murder. He fled to France but returned in 1450, using the pseudonym John Mortimer, and emerged as a leader of a group of Kentish rebels opposed to government corruption and crushing taxes. His troops defeated the king's army at Sevenoaks, in Kent, on June 18, and London was captured on July 3. Among the executions that took place was that of James Fiennes, Lord Saye and Sele. Londoners grew outraged at the activities of the insurgents, however, and from July 5 to 6, Cade lost control of the city. A peace was arranged, including pardons for Cade and his men. Despite losing most of his supporters, Cade refused to end his war with the Crown, and on July 12 he was captured, dying before he could be brought to London. The rebellion of Jack Cade brought attention to the corruption of the royal administration and was to be one factor in the start of the Wars of the Roses. See also ENGLAND.

**CAEDMON** (d. c. 675) The first English Christian poet. Virtually all knowledge of Caedmon was preserved by Bede in his *Ecclestiastical History*. According to this source, he was an illiterate laborer at the monastery of Whitby. He was so ashamed of being unable to sing and to compose verse that at the time of musical performances he would hide. One night, however, he received the gift from God to transform the Scriptures into verse and so armed with this recognition, became a monk with the permission of the abbess Hilda. Trained in the knowledge of the Scriptures, he was the earliest Anglo-Saxon composer of popular vernacular poetry. A fragment of a poem he was given in a dream was recorded by Bede; other poems were also attributed to him.

**CAEDWALLA** (d. 689) King of Wessex from 686 to 688, mentioned in the Anglo-Saxon Chronicle as being eager to have the kingdom for himself. His life and most of his reign were spent at war. He invaded Kent, Sussex and the Isle of Wight, losing all but the last. His brother Mul was burned in 687 by the people of Kent. Caedwalla was not a baptized Christian, waiting until 689 to receive the sacrament, when he journied to Rome. There he was baptized on Easter, dying a few days later from wounds he had received in battle. See also WESSEX.

**CAIRO** City of medieval and modern Egypt, an important cultural and religious center in the Islamic world and the largest metropolis in Africa. Cairo was founded on the banks of the Nile River on the site that had been the ceremonial center of Heliopolis in ancient Egypt during the centuries of Roman occupation. Its importance in the Middle Ages began with the conquest of the country by the Arabs in 641, when the great Muslim general Amr ibn al-As founded the community of al-Fustat to the north of a captured Byzantine fortress. Around al-Fustat, various ruling regimes were to establish new garrisons or districts, building palaces, forts and mosques and then encouraging urbanization. The Abbasids established al-Askar in 750, to the north of al-Fustat. Ahmad ibn Tulun developed al-Qata'i to the northeast, and the returning Abbasids in 905 favored al-Askar, while relying on al-Fustat for economic prosperity.

In 969 the Islamic sect of the Fatimids invaded and subdued Egypt. They erected another garrison and city to the north of al-Fustat and al-Qata'i, called al-Mansuriya (al-Mansuriyah), renamed al-Qahira, the City of Victory, around 973. Al-Qahira lent its name to the entire complex of districts surrounding it, especially after the burning of al-Fustat in 1168 to protect Cairo from the Crusaders. This destruction caused a period of decay for the city, ending in 1171 with the rise of Saladin as master of Egypt and the founder of the Ayyubid dynasty. Under the aegis of the Ayyubids, especially Saladin, a program of development was initiated, in which Cairo was expanded, with new walls erected; its renovation became a force in reinvigorating the trade of al-Fustat. Cairo was the capital of an extensive Islamic empire, a haven for Sunni religious life

Aqsunqor mosque, Cairo

and a center for learning and commerce. The Mamluks, successors to the Ayyubids and dominating a vast imperial domain, not only kept Cairo as their chief city but also added to its prosperity, encouraging religious learning and trade. It was during the Mamluk era (1250–1517) that Cairo reached its zenith, the number of inhabitants estimated at around 500,000 in the mid-11th century.

Crises and disasters soon struck, however. In 1348 the Black Death caused terrible depopulation, and there were subsequent and severe outbreaks of plague. The Mamluks were beset by internal disorder and civil strife and in 1400 were defeated by Tamerlane, creating an irreparable economic depression. Any hope of a lasting recovery was dashed by the loss of the spice trade in the late 15th century. The Ottoman Turks captured Egypt in 1517, reducing Cairo to a mere provincial capital. See also EGYPT.

**CAKA** King of the Bulgars, the son-in-law of King George I Terter, who attempted to become ruler of the Second Bulgarian Empire in 1300. He was replaced by George's son, Theodore Svetoslav, that same year.

**CALABRIA** See NAPLES, KINGDOM OF.

**CALAIS** An important port in northern France, situated on the Strait of Dover. Calais evolved from a small fishing community, emerging in the 10th century as a strategically crucial port of entry vital in the struggle between France and England. The city was captured in 1347 after a year-long siege. According to tradition, King Edward III of England (1327–1377) promised to spare Calais if six citizens would give up their lives. The mayor and five burghers volunteered but were spared by the king. The 19th-century sculptor Auguste Rodin commemorated the event in *The Burghers of Calais.* See also FRANCE; HUNDRED YEARS' WAR; TRADE AND COMMERCE.

**CALATRAVA ORDER** See MILITARY ORDERS.

**CALIPHATE** From the Arabic *khilafa,* the title "caliph" was given to the theocratic leader of the Muslim community. In essence, the caliph was the ruler or the agent of God, the successor of the Messenger of God. The caliphate as a governmental entity came into being after the death of Muhammad in 632. Abu Bakr is named as the first caliph, and although Islamic factions were created after the death of Ali in 661, the title of caliph was applied to heads of various Islamic dynasties. See also ABBASID CALIPHATE; ASSASSINS, ORDER OF; FATIMID CALIPHATE; ISLAM; ISMAILI SECT, OTTOMAN EMPIRE; UMAYYAD CALIPHATE.

**CALIXTUS II** (c. 1050–1124) Also Callistus, pope from 1119 to 1124, born Guido of Burgundy, the son of Count William of Burgundy. Named archbishop of Vienne by Pope Urban II in 1088, he became a leader of the opposition to Emperor Henry V on the question of investiture, presiding over the Council of Vienne in 1112, which declared lay investiture to be a heresy. On the death of Gelasius II at Cluny in 1119, he was elected Pope Calixtus II, embarking immediately on a struggle with Henry. The emperor was excommunicated in 1119, but the German princes were able to complete negotiations, and the controversy of investitute was finally ended with the Concordat of Worms in 1122.

**CALIXTUS III** (1378–1458) Pope from 1455 to 1458, also called Callistus III. Born Alfonso de Borja at Valencia, he was a member of the powerful Borgia (Spanish spelling, Borja) family. A jurist of some repute and private secretary to Alfonso V of Aragon, he gained prominence in the church by convincing Clement VIII, the antipope from 1423 to 1429, to submit to and abdicate in favor of Pope Martin V (1417–1431). He was made a bishop of Valencia in 1429 and a cardinal in 1444, and his election as pope was a compromise between the claims of the leading families of Italy at the time. He was concerned mainly with launching a Crusade in 1453 against the Turks to recapture Constantinople. Despite victory at Belgrade in 1456, the campaign was ultimately a failure. In 1456 the trial of Joan of Arc was reexamined and declared null and void, her innocence receiving papal confirmation. Although relatively uncorrupt by reputation, Calixtus did, nonetheless, elevate members of the Borgia family to positions of prominence, most notably his nephew Rodrigo Borgia, the future Pope Alexander VI, whom he named cardinal.

**CAMBRIDGE** The county seat of Cambridgeshire in England and the site of Cambridge University. Originally a group of settlements, Cambridge came into being around the fifth century as part of local attempts at resistance to invaders, most notably the Danes (until the ninth century). It gained prominence for the presence of astute local government officials, and its university was founded in 1209. Universities were at first comprised of itinerant teachers whose lectures drew the interest of students who came to learn. Cambridge University at first possessed no permanent colleges or residences as such, and these were not installed until 1284, with the establishment of Saint Peter's (or Peterhouse). Other colleges soon followed: Clare (1326),

Pembroke (1347), Gonville and Caius (1348), Trinity Hall (1350), Corpus Christi (1352), King's College (1441), Queen's College (1448), Saint Catherine's (1473) and Jesus (1496); more houses were established over the centuries. See also UNIVERSITIES.

**CAMPANIA** Region in southern Italy, bordering the Tyrrhenian Sea and the locale of cities including Benevento, Salerno and the capital, Naples. Campania was occupied by a succession of invaders, beginning with the Goths in the fifth century. The Byzantines, Lombards and Normans followed. From 1282, however, it was attached to the Kingdom of Naples. See also SICILIAN VESPERS; SICILY.

**CAMPIN, ROBERT** (c. 1379–1444) Early Flemish painter called the "Master of Flémalle." Born at Valenciennes, he was a resident by 1406 of Tournai and claimed as his pupil the great Roger van der Weyden. A gifted artistic innovator, he utilized the decorative style found in manuscript illumination but infused it with the perspective and sophistication of a heightened realism. Among his most acclaimed works were the Mérode altarpiece (a triptych depicting the Annuniciation, c. 1428); *St. Veronica and the Virgin* (c. 1440), believed to have come from Flémalle; *Nativity* (c. 1415–1420); the Werl altarpiece (c. 1438); and *Virgin in Glory* (c. 1430).

**CANDIA** The largest port and city on the island of Crete, now called Iráklion. Candia derived its name from the Italian corruption of the Arabic *khandak* (moat), used to describe the ditch that surrounded its walls. Taken by the Muslims in the ninth century, Candia was sold to the Venetians (c. 1210), who built massive fortifications and defenses and transformed the port into such a vital trading center that the appellation Candia was eventually applied to all of Crete. Most of the Venetian fortifications have survived. See also CRETE; VENICE.

**CANOSSA** A castle in the area of Reggio, in northern Italy, that was the site in late January 1077 of the flagellation of Emperor Henry IV (1056–1106) before Pope Gregory VII (1073–1085). Originally constructed by Azzo Adalbert and the possession of the subsequent counts of Canossa, the fortress was, in 1077, a holding of Countess Matilda of Tuscany, who invited the pope to stay there on his journey to Germany, in his fight with the emperor concerning the Investitute Controversy. Henry arrived around January 25 to seek absolution and thereby to reclaim the loyalty of his princes; according to tradition, he stood as a humble penitent in the snow for three days until receiving absolution from the pope on January 28. Canossa was destroyed in 1255 and now lies in ruin.

***CANTAR DE MIO CID*** One of the great Spanish epics, dating from the 12th century, concerning the exploits of the Spanish hero Rodrigo Díaz de Vivar, called El Cid. Treating the decline in his prestige from the king's standpoint and his eventual reinstatement to his former nobility, *Cantar de Mio Cid* was probably composed in the Castilian vernacular around 1140, but the original manuscript was lost. The earliest copy, called *Poema del Cid*, dates from 1207.

**CANTERBURY** A cathedral city in Kent, England, the site of a major episcopal see and traditionally the spiritual center of the nation, dominating religious and political movements throughout the Middle Ages. Canterbury's earliest importance was due to its position on the road from the English Channel to London and beyond. Legends claimed that it was founded by the British king Lud-Hudibras, around 900 B.C., but archaeological remains indicate that there was already a community along the Stour River sometime before 200 B.C. It was established as a Roman site after the invasion of A.D. 43, developing into a Roman walled town by 200, with the name Durovernum. The Saxons were present in the fifth century, and in the late sixth century it was the capital of Aethelbert, king of Kent (d. 616), called Canterbury, derived from Cantii, the original inhabitants (*Cantwaraburh*, or town of the Kents).

Aethelbert wed the Frankish Christian princess Bertha, who introduced Bishop Luithard, who took up residence at Saint Martin at Canterbury. This preceded the arrival in 597 of Saint Augustine, to Christianize the Anglo-Saxons, converting Aethelbert, founding a Benedictine monastery and, as bishop of the English, building the cathedral of Christ Church at Canterbury. Thus was established the city as the primary see of England. Subsequent bishops, most notably Theodore of Tarsus (668–690), brought most of the country under Canterbury's ecclesiastical control. Surviving Viking raids, and their murder of Archbishop Alphege in 1012, Canterbury became a place of learning and culture.

William the Conqueror (1066–1087) subdued England in 1066, naming as archbishop in 1070 Lanfranc, the first Norman prelate of the English. He was succeeded by a monk of Bec, Anselm (1093–1109), one of the leaders in the argument against lay investiture. The struggles between the archbishops and the English crown reached serious and dramatic heights in the quarrel between Thomas à Becket and King Henry II (1154–1189). Becket was murdered on December 29, 1170, in Canterbury Cathedral, and his miracles that were soon reported made Canterbury the site of pilgrimages, which were the inspiration for *The Canterbury Tales* of Geoffrey Chaucer. Becket's remains were placed in a special shrine behind the altar. The Cathedral of Christ Church has been rebuilt several times after damaging conflagrations. See also ENGLAND.

### *Archbishops of Canterbury,* 597–1500

Augustine 597–604
Laurence 604–619
Mellitus 619–624
Justus 624–627
Honorius 627–653
Deusdedit 655–664
Theodore of Tarsus 668–690
Berhtwald 692–731
Tatwine 731–734
Nothhelm 736–739

Cuthbert 741–759
Breguivine 759–763
Lambert 763–790
Aethelard 790–803
Wulfred 803–832
Feologild 832
Ceolnoth 833–870
Aethelred 870–889
Plegmund 890–914
Aethelm 914–923
Wulfhelm 923–942
Odo 942–958
Aelfsige 959
Dunstan 960–988
Aethelgar 988–990
Sigeric Serio 990–994
Aelfric 995–1005
Alphege 1006–1012
Lyfing 1013–1020
Aethelnoth 1020–1038
Eadsige 1038–1050
Robert of Jumièges 1051–1052
Stigand 1052–1070
Lanfranc 1070–1089
Anselm 1093–1109
Ralph d'Escures 1114–1122
William of Corbeil 1123–1136
Theobald 1139–1161
Thomas à Becket 1162–1170
Richard of Dover 1174–1184
Baldwin 1185–1190
Reginald Fitzjoscelin 1191
Hubert Walter 1193–1205
Stephen Langton 1207–1228
Richard le Grand 1229–1231
Edmund Rich of Abingdon 1234–1240
Boniface of Savoy 1245–1270
Robert Kilwardby 1273–1278
John Peckham 1279–1292
Robert del Winchelsey 1294–1313
Walter Reynolds 1313–1327
Simon Mepeham 1328–1333
John del Stratford 1333–1348
Thomas Bradwardine 1349
Simon Islip 1349–1366
Simon Langham 1366–1368
William Whittlesey 1368–1374
Simon del Sudbury 1375–1381
William Courtenay 1381–1396
Thomas Arundel 1397–1397 (1)
Roger Walden 1398
Thomas Arundel 1399–1414 (2)
Henry Chichele 1414–1443
John Stafford 1443–1452
John Kempe 1452–1454
Thomas Bourchier 1454–1486
John Morton (Cardinal) 1486–1500

**CANTILUPE, THOMAS DE, SAINT** (c. 1218–1282) Known also as Thomas of Hereford and Thomas de Cantelupe, the bishop of Hereford, chancellor of England and an important English prelate of the 13th century. A member of a noble family, he was educated at Oxford, Paris and Orléans before teaching at Paris and Oxford and serving as chancellor of the latter in 1262. In his position as chancellor he supported the cause of the barons against Henry III (1216–1272) during the Barons' War (1263–1267) and was an advocate of Simon de Montfort. After the Battle of Lewes in 1264, and the triumph of the barons, Cantilupe became chancellor of England on February 22, 1265. His term ended with the death of Simon and the collapse of baronial power later in the year. He retired to Paris to lecture from 1265 to 1272. Returning to Oxford (in 1272), he was named bishop of Hereford in 1275, working to reform the diocese while an adviser to King Edward I (1272–1307). In 1279, however, John Peckham was named archbishop of Canterbury, and bitter disagreements led to Cantilupe's excommunication in 1282. He died while making an appeal to the pope. Buried at Hereford, reported miracles led to his canonization in 1320. His uncle was Walter de Cantilupe.

**CANTILUPE, WALTER DE** (d. 1266) Bishop of Worcester and the uncle of Thomas de Cantilupe, a supporter of the baronial cause during the Barons' War (1263–1267) against Henry III (1216–1272), espousing the cause of Simon de Montfort. A friend of Robert Grosseteste, bishop of Lincoln, he also maintained amicable relations with the papacy.

**CANUTE II, KING OF DENMARK, ENGLAND AND NORWAY** (c. 995–1035) King of England from 1014 to 1035 as well as ruler of Denmark from (1018) and Norway (from 1027), called "the Great" because of his considerable achievements but also for his remarkable enlightenment and piety. He was the son of King Sven I Forkbeard of Denmark (985–1014), accompanying him on his campaign to England in 1013. His father secured the English throne that same year, while Canute met Aegilfu, the mother of two of his sons, Sven and Harold Harefoot. After Sven Forkbeard's death in early 1014, Canute embarked on a long and ruthless war to secure the kingship of England. The deaths of Aethelred II the Unready (986–1016) and Edmund Ironside in 1016 gave him access to the throne.

While his early years as king were marked by murder and the promotion of Danes to prominent royal posts, by 1018 Canute had taken a second wife, Emma, widow of Aethelred, learned to rely on the English nobles, encouraged the church and promoted a set of laws, promulgated at Oxford, based on those of King Edgar. In 1019, English troops helped him assume the vacant Danish throne. England enjoyed peace, but Canute spent much time in Scandinavia, fending off attacks by Norway and Sweden. King Olaf II of Norway (1015–1028) lost his realm to Canute in 1028 and died two years later while trying to reclaim it. Canute also improved trade between his countries and other states, making a pilgrimage to Rome (1026–1027) to attend the coronation of Emperor Conrad II (1024–1039) and to make economic agreements with the Holy Roman Empire and other states. His empire did not survive long after his death. See also DENMARK; ENGLAND.

**CANUTE III, KING OF DENMARK** See HARDECANUTE.

**CANUTE IV, KING OF DENMARK** (c. 1043–1086) Ruler of Denmark from 1080 to 1086, also its patron saint. The illegitimate son of King Sven II Estridson (1047–1074), he succeeded his brother, Harald III Hen (1074–1080) and was known as a patron and ardent supporter of Christianity in Denmark. His policies toward the Christians, coupled with his attempts at a reform of government, outraged his nobles. In 1085 he ignored his domestic troubles, however, and in an alliance with King Olaf III of Norway (1067–1093) and the count of Flanders, he planned to invade England. Shortly before the start of the campaign, the conspiratorial nobles struck. Canute took refuge at Saint Albans Church, Odense, but was murdered with most of his family and entourage. He was canonized in 1101, his biography written by Saxo Grammaticus and Aelnoth. See also DENMARK.

**CANUTE LAVARD** (d. 1131) Duke of Schleswig also called Prince of the Wends. He was the son of King Eric I Ejegod (1095–1103) and was named by King Niels (1104–1134) as duke and protector of South Jutland, specifically to guard against the Wends (Slavs). His campaigns against them were so successful that Niel's son, Magnus the Strong, became so jealous that he had him murdered. His death set off a civil war that lasted until 1157 and resulted in the rise of Canute's son, Waldemar I (1157–1182), as king. So popular was Canute in southern Denmark that his advocates there murdered King Niels in 1134. Canute was declared the patron saint of guilds; he is often confused with Canute IV. See also DENMARK.

**CANUTE VI, KING OF DENMARK** (1163–1202) Ruler from 1182 to 1202, the son of Waldemar I (1157–1182), made co-regent in 1170 and succeeding to the throne in 1182. The vital political power in the early years of his reign, however, was Absalon, the archbishop of Lund. It was this prelate who guided Canute's policy of separation from the influence of the Holy Roman Empire, specifically Frederick I Barbarossa (1152–1190). Through Absalon's campaigns, Mecklenburg, Holstein and Pomerania, as well as other German holdings, fell to the control of the Danish crown. Canute's sister was given in marriage to Philip II Augustus of France (1180–1223), indicating Denmark's newly developed international position. He died without an heir and was followed by his brother, Waldemar II Sejr (1202–1240). See also DENMARK.

**CANUTE I ERICSSON, KING OF SWEDEN** Ruler of Sweden from 1167 to 1196. He murdered the son of King Sverker in 1167 and was crowned king. His reign was noted for its reform of Swedish finances and for his close association with and support of the church. See also SWEDEN.

**CANUTE II, KING OF SWEDEN** Ruler of Sweden from 1229 to 1234, a member of the Eric dynasty; called Canute the Tall. See also SWEDEN.

**CAPETIAN DYNASTY** The ruling house of France from 987 to 1328, founded by Hugh Capet (reigned 967–996), ending with the death of Charles IV the Fair (r. 1322–1328) in 1328 without an heir. Philip VI, count of Valois (r. 1328–1350), Charles's cousin, succeeded to the throne and established the Valois dynasty. See Genealogical Table; see also FRANCE and individual rulers.

**CAPREOLUS, JOHN** (c. 1380–1444) Dominican theologian and philosopher who earned the title *Thomistratum princeps* ("Prince of the Thomists") for his teachings in defense of the opinions of Saint Thomas Aquinas. Capreolus was from Languedoc, joining the Dominican order and eventually teaching at the University of Paris where he began his master work, the *Defensiones*. Written from 1410 to 1433 in four books, it was a defense of Thomistic theological theory against the attacks of such philosophers as Duns Scotus, Henry of Ghent and William of Ockham. The *Defensiones* was an important element of the rediscovery of Thomas Aquinas in the 15th century.

**CARCASSONNE** City in southern France and the capital of the department of Aude, west of Narbonne. An ancient site, Carcassonne was a Roman city and fell under the influence of the Visigoths in the late fifth century, resisting the attempts of Clovis (481–511) and the Franks to capture it in 508. In 728, however, the Muslims took it, eventually losing control to Pepin II the Short (741–768) in 752. Subsequently, ruled by counts and viscounts until 1209, the city was seized by Simon de Montfort during the Albigensian Crusade, and the crown claimed it in 1247. Carcassonne was of architectural importance because of the preservation of its walled city, restored by the 19th-century architect Viollet-le-Duc. See also FRANCE.

**CARDIFF** Town in Wales on the Bristol Channel, established as a Roman fort around A.D. 75 but becoming strategically important in 1090, with the construction of a Norman castle mound by Robert FitzHamon on the site once occupied by the Romans. Subsequently, an actual castle was erected and the town developed around it, receiving a charter from the Normans in the 12th century from Hugh le Despenser in 1340 or from the king at a later date. A Dominican friary and a house for Franciscans were founded there in the 13th century, which were dissolved in 1538. Owen Glendower caused extensive damage to the town in 1404. See also WALES.

**CARINTHIA** The mountainous region of southern Austria, known in German as Karnten, with its capital at

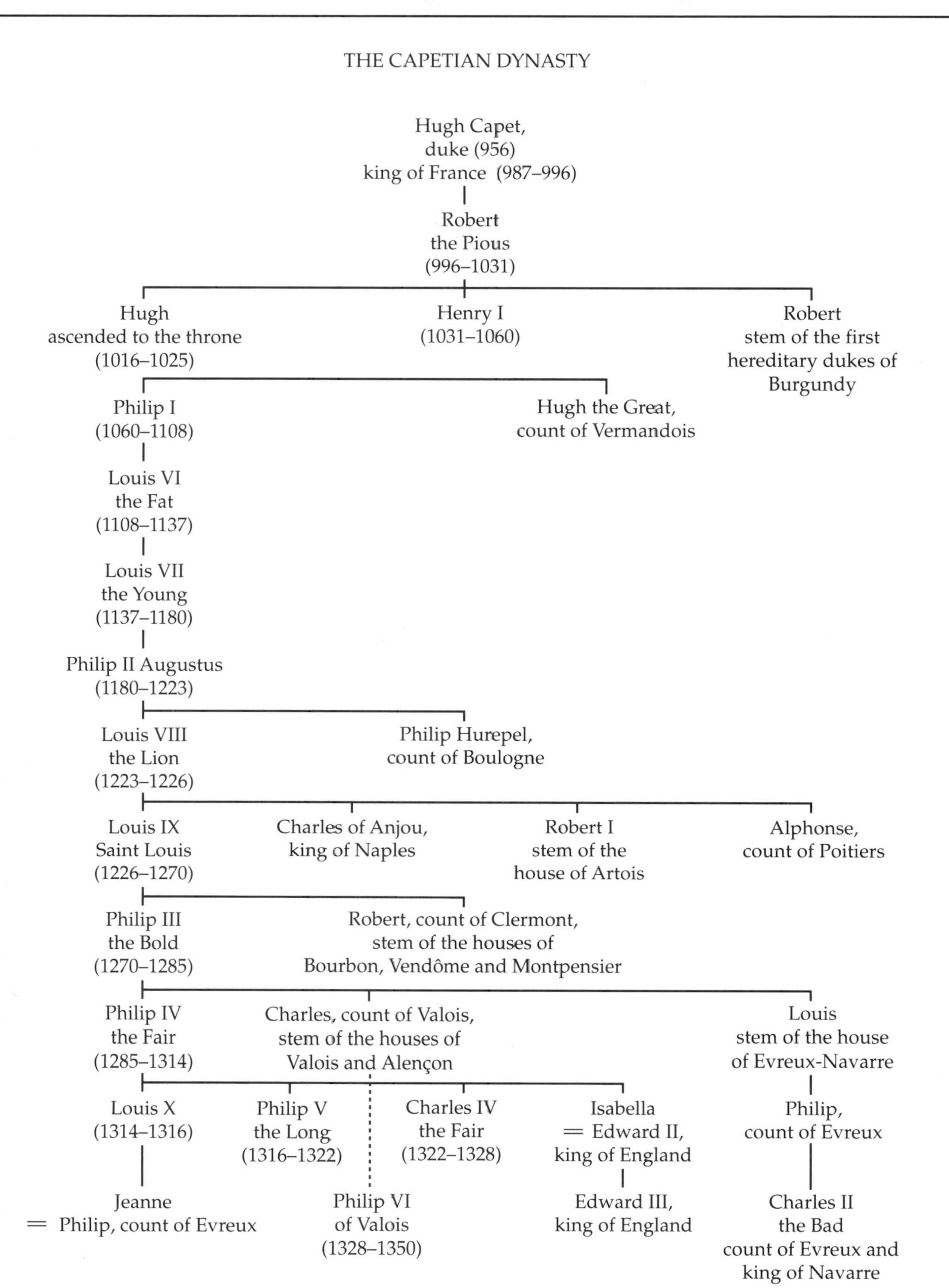
THE CAPETIAN DYNASTY
Hugh Capet,
duke (956)
king of France (987–996)
Robert
the Pious
(996–1031)
Hugh
ascended to the throne
(1016–1025)
Henry I
(1031–1060)
Robert
stem of the first
hereditary dukes of
Burgundy
Philip I
(1060–1108)
Hugh the Great,
count of Vermandois
Louis VI
the Fat
(1108–1137)
Louis VII
the Young
(1137–1180)
Philip II Augustus
(1180–1223)
Louis VIII
the Lion
(1223–1226)
Philip Hurepel,
count of Boulogne
Louis IX
Saint Louis
(1226–1270)
Charles of Anjou,
king of Naples
Robert I
stem of the
house of Artois
Alphonse,
count of Poitiers
Philip III
the Bold
(1270–1285)
Robert, count of Clermont,
stem of the houses of
Bourbon, Vendôme and Montpensier
Philip IV
the Fair
(1285–1314)
Charles, count of Valois,
stem of the houses of
Valois and Alençon
Louis
stem of the house
of Evreux-Navarre
Louis X
(1314–1316)
Philip V
the Long
(1316–1322)
Charles IV
the Fair
(1322–1328)
Isabella
= Edward II,
king of England
Philip,
count of Evreux
Jeanne
= Philip, count of Evreux
Philip VI
of Valois
(1328–1350)
Edward III,
king of England
Charles II
the Bad
count of Evreux and
king of Navarre

Klagenfurt. Originally part of the Celtic territory of Noricum, Carinthia fell to the Romans in 16 B.C. and remained in the province of Noricum until the fifth century, when the Slavs, Avars and Bavarians invaded. In 976 it was separated from Bavaria and made an independent duchy, containing the neighboring areas of Istria, Carniola and Styria and ruled by the dukes of the Carinthian line. When they died out in 1269, Ottokar II of Bohemia claimed the duchy, but in 1276 it passed to Emperor Rudolf I of Habsburg (1273–1291). Briefly given to the counts of Tyrol, it was reclaimed to the Habsburgs in 1335 and was made an Austrian crownland.

**CARLISLE** City in northern England (Cumberland) near the Scottish border. It was established during the Roman era as Luguvalium, a civilian community and fort along Hadrian's Wall. In 685 the town, eventually called Carlisle, was attached to the See of Lindisfarne and was destroyed by the Danes around 875. In the 10th century it was given by King Edmund I to Malcolm I of Scotland, being reclaimed by England during the reign of William II Rufus (1087–1100), who began construction of a castle there in 1092. Struggles with Scotland marked much of its subsequent history. The city walls offered protection for the clergy and merchants, and thus Carlisle developed into a religious and economic center. Henry II granted the city its charter in 1158, making it an undisputed English possession. See also ENGLAND.

**CARLOMAN (1)** (d. 754) Prince of the Franks, son of Charles Martel (714–741) and brother of Pepin II the Short (741–768). Carloman effectively divided rule of the Franks with his brother, reigning over Alemannia, Austrasia, Bavaria and Thuringia after the death of Charles in 741. From that year until 745 he and Pepin campaigned repeatedly to subdue vassals and to retain Frankish suzerainty. Haunted by his violent life, Carloman abdicated in 745, retiring as a monk (c. 747) to a monastery at Monte Soratte and later to Monte Cassino. He tried unsuccessfully to prevent a war against Pepin and the Lombards. See also FRANKS.

**CARLOMAN (2)** (d. 771) The younger brother of Charlemagne (768–814), the son of Pepin III (741–768) the Short, who divided power with his brother, ruling eastern Aquitaine, Burgundy, Provence, Paris, Soissons, Reims, Metz, Strasbourg and Trier, roughly eastern France. Crowned on October 9, 768, at Soissons, he soon came to a disagreement with Charlemagne, most notably over his support of the Lombard king Desiderius. Carloman was an ally of the Lombards, whereas Charlemagne supported Pope Stephen III (768–772). Eventually the hostility of Desiderius against Rome compelled Carloman to join his brother in a campaign against the Lombards. He died suddenly on December 4, 771, and Charlemagne immediately exacted the allegiance of his subjects.

**CARLOMAN (3)** (d. 880) The son of Louis II the German (843–876), who inherited his father's title as king of the Germans in 876, ruling over Bavaria, Moravia and Pannonia from 876 to 879. Despite papal refusal to acknowledge his rank as emperor, he was king of Italy from 877 to 879. The first German king to rule Italy, he abdicated in 879 because of ill health, in favor of his brother, Louis the Younger. His son, Arnulf, became emperor in 896. See also HOLY ROMAN EMPIRE.

**CARLOMAN, KING OF FRANCE** (d. 884) Ruler from 879 to 884, the son of Louis II the Stammerer of France. In 879 he and his brother, Louis III, were crowned as joint rulers of the country. Louis died in 882 and Carloman two years later. His most notable achievement was a defeat inflicted on the Normans on the Aisne River. See also FRANCE.

**CARLOS II** (1332–1387) King of Navarre from 1349 to 1387, called "the Bad" because of his treacherous nature. He was an enemy of King John II of France, using France's difficulties in the Hundred Years' War to seize parts of Normandy (c. 1354) that he alleged had been seized unjustly by the Valois kings. In 1358 he betrayed Étienne Marcel, provost of Paris, and helped suppress the Jacquerie, losing most of his French holdings, despite this, in 1366 to Charles V the Wise. An alliance with Pedro the Cruel of Castile did nothing to enhance the position of Navarre. See also NAVARRE.

**CARLOS III** (1361–1425) Ruler of Navarre from 1387 to 1425, Carlos III was called "the Noble," a title in marked contrast to his predecessor, Carlos II the Bad (1349–1387). Carlos III pursued a policy of careful relations with France and especially Castile. He married the sister of John I of Castile (1379–1390) and followed his example of supporting Clement VII (1378–1394), the pope at Avignon during the Great Schism. See also NAVARRE.

**CARMELITES** One of the four mendicant orders established during the Middle Ages, known officially as the Order of Our Lady of Mount Carmel. The Carmelites were founded by Saint Berthold about 1154, when, according to tradition, he organized the pilgrims, former Crusaders and hermits living on Mount Carmel in the Holy Land. According to legend, they claimed descent from the prophet Elijah and the eremites who had historically resided on the mountain. A rule was laid down (c. 1209) by Albert de Vercelli, Latin patriarch of Jerusalem, and the community was approved by Pope Honorius III in 1226. Their rule demanded asceticism, poverty, abstinence and self-mortification. The order was forced to leave Mount Carmel after 1238 because of the deterioration of the Crusader States, and in 1247 the first general chapter or meeting was held in England under the leadership of Saint Simon Stock, who redirected the thrust of the order from asceticism to mendicants. They were soon to be found in all parts of Christendom. In the late 16th century, under the auspices of Saint Teresa of Avila and Saint John of the Cross, asceticism again became the hallmark of a group of Carmelites, and the order was divided into separate units, called Calced and Discalced. See also MENDICANT ORDERS.

***CARMINA BURANA*** The name given to a collection of secular Latin songs and poems and six religious plays that were produced in the Middle Ages. Also called the Benediktbeuren ("the songs of Beuren"), *Carmina Burana* was a manuscript dating from the 13th century, found in 1803 at the Benedictine monastery of Benediktbeuren in Bavaria. The roughly 300 songs were written mainly in Latin, but some were in Middle High German. They were probably composed by goliards—itinerant scholars and students who wandered around Europe from the 10th to the 13th century—and thus were principally drinking songs, songs of love and satire. The plays were religious in subject: Christmas, Easter and two important extant Passion Plays. Although part of the same manuscript, the poems and songs were separate from the plays. See also GOLIARDS.

**CAROLINE BOOKS** See LIBRI CAROLINI.

**CAROLINGIAN ART AND ARCHITECTURE** A period in the development of medieval Western art extending from the late eighth to the ninth century. It was characterized by a return or revival of classicism, influenced by the Byzantine or Greek model and local Frankish custom or culture. The patron of the Carolingian era in art was Charlemagne (768–814), who, when establishing an extensive Frankish empire, sought to elevate learning and the arts (see CAROLINGIAN RENAISSANCE). He invited to his court at Aachen the finest minds, artists and architects of the time, and their projects fused Christian motifs and subject matter with imperial classicism. Inevitably influenced by contemporary Byzantine style, a distinctive Carolingian art form was created. While the form would not outlast the chaos of the ninth century, its influence was evident in the later Romanesque period.

The Carolingians were especially successful in painting, manuscript illumination and craftwork. Few pieces of monumental sculpture have survived, and it was in manuscript illumination that artists of the period left superb examples. Chief among these were the *Coronation Gospels* (or the *Gospel Book of Charlemagne*) and the *St. Matthew*, illuminated for the *Gospel Book* of Archbishop Ebbo of Reims. Illumination, copying the motifs of the Byzantines and early Christians, was to be found in the greatest manuscript of the age, the *Utrecht Psalter*. Using the illustrations and illuminations as prototypes, Carolingian artisans created highly complex and intricate reliefs in ivory or metal. Mosaics and murals, chalices and patens and exquisite clerical vestments remain as testament to the Carolingian renaissance.

For his building programs, Charlemagne looked to two enduring architectural examples for inspiration, Rome and Ravenna—Rome because of its traditional role as heart of the Roman Empire, and Ravenna because of the Byzantine influence. Priests were sent to Rome to make drafts of old Saint Peter's, and the abbey church at Fulda (built between 744 and 751) followed the basic design of the original. There has been discussion of the relation between San Vitale at Ravenna and the Palatine Chapel at Aachen. Stylistically distinct, there was probably no direct connection between the two structures, but Byzantine architectural techniques were certainly adopted and were important to the formation of the Romanesque style. See also MEROVINGIAN ART AND ARCHITECTURE; OTTONIAN ART AND ARCHITECTURE.

**CAROLINGIAN DYNASTY** See Genealogical Table and individual rulers; see also AACHEN; AQUITAINE; AUSTRASIA; CAROLINGIAN ART AND ARCHITECTURE; CAROLINGIAN RENAISSANCE; FRANCE; FRANKS; GERMANY; HOLY ROMAN EMPIRE; LOTHARINGIA; MEROVINGIAN DYNASTY; NEUSTRIA; PARIS; PROVENCE; VERDUN, TREATY OF.

**CAROLINGIAN RENAISSANCE** The name given to the revival of art and learning in the late eighth and ninth centuries that took place in western Europe under the patronage of the Carolingians. The Carolingian renaissance began with Charlemagne, who sponsored schools, supported scholars and was a powerful patron of the movement's leaders, such as Alcuin and Theodulf of Orléans. While the intensity of learning and intellectualism could not last because of the decline of the Carolingian dynasty, it did lay the foundations for an interest in scholarship that would endure throughout the Middle Ages. See also UNIVERSITIES.

**CARPINI, GIOVANNI DE PIANO** (c. 1180–1252) Franciscan monk and one of the noted travelers of the Middle Ages. Born in Umbria, he was a disciple of Francis of Assisi, joining the Franciscans about 1220 and becoming a leading teacher of the order, most notably at Cologne. In 1245 he was chosen by Pope Innocent IV (1243–1254) to take part in a special mission to the Mongol empire, setting out on Easter, 1245, with Stephen of Bohemia. Later accompanied by Benedict the Pole, Carpini and Stephen reached the camp of Batu Orkhan in spring 1246. The leader of the Mongol horde in the West gave the friars permission to continue their journey and in August of that year they came to the Sira Ordu, the camp of the Great Khan, having traveled thousands of miles. There they witnessed the coronation of Güyük, leaving in November 1246 bearing a letter from the khan to the pope. On June 9, 1247, they arrived in Kiev and then went on to Lyons to meet the pope. Carpini was made archbishop of Antivari.

Writing an account of his adventures, he produced the *Historia Mongalorum* and *Liber Tartararum* (*History of the Mongols* and the *Book of Tartars*). He carefully and very accurately preserved the nature of the Mongols' life, their customs, history and political organization. Although some details, especially geography, were incorrect, Carpini's works were notable scholarly efforts. Despite the lack of attention the works received from Carpini's contemporaries, being known mainly in an abstract version in the writings of Vincent of Beauvais, they are important documents. See also MONGOLS; POLO, MARCO; WILLIAM OF RUBRUQUIS.

***CARROCCIO*** A war wagon or chariot used mainly in Lombardy, in northern Italy, from the 9th to the 14th century but which appeared in France and England as well. According to tradition, the *carroccio* was invented either by Archbishop Angilbert of Milan in the ninth century or, less likely, by Aribert, archbishop of Milan, in the 11th century. It was a four-wheeled vehicle, drawn by three or four oxen. In the center stood a pole with a cross or golden orb at the top, from which was flown the flag of the city. An altar was usually placed at the base of the pole to allow a priest to celebrate services, and trumpeteers

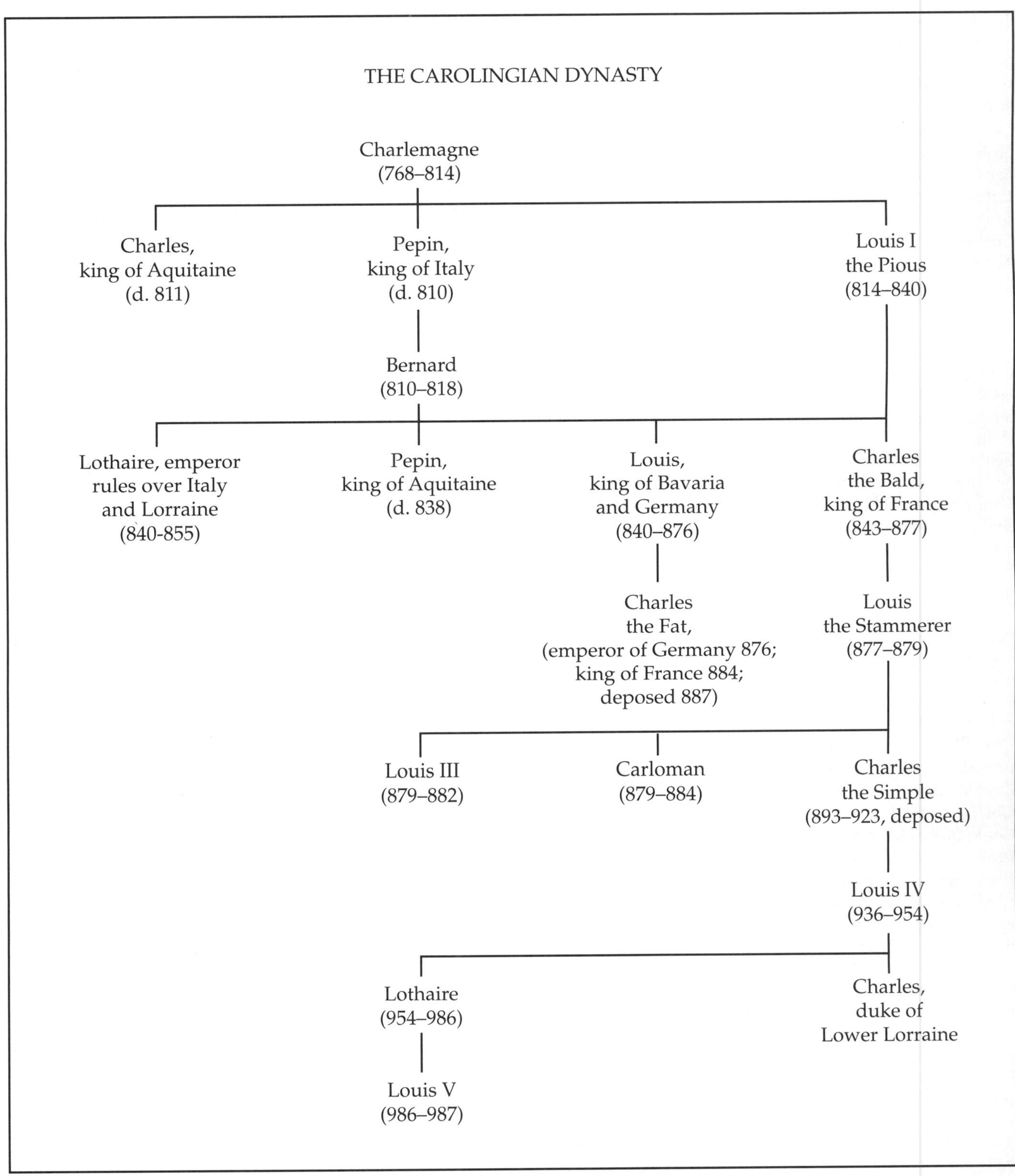


stood on the wagon to announce the city's triumphs. The *carroccio* was thus an important symbol of the freedom of a particular community, and starting with Milan, it was widely used across Italy. To allow capture of the *carroccio* or to surrender it was an act of abject humiliation. A guard was posted to protect it, the most famous of these groups being the Milanese "Company of Death" that led the decisive charge against Frederick I Barbarossa (1152–1190) at the Battle of Legnano in 1176. The wagon did not survive with the development of professional armies in the 14th century. See also LOMBARD LEAGUE.

**CARTHAGE** An ancient and famous city in North Africa on the Bay of Tunis, traditionally said to have been founded by the Phoenician queen Dido in the ninth century B.C. Destroyed by the Romans in 146 B.C., it later became the center of a Roman African province. In 439 Carthage fell to the Vandal army of Geiseric; it was sacked but then became the capital of the Vandal kingdom until 533, when the Byzantine general Belisarius defeated the last Vandal ruler, Gelimer, at the Battle of Decimum. Belisarius captured Carthage easily, and during the reign of Emperor Maurice the city was made the headquarters of the Exarchate of Carthage, the Byzantine province of Africa. This semi-independent territory was headed by an exarch who was given wide latitude in the administration of its affairs. Carthage resisted the wave of Islam until 698, when it was virtually destroyed. King Louis IX of France died near Carthage during the Seventh Crusade in 1270. See also EXARCHATE.

**CARTHUSIANS** A contemplative monastic order founded in 1084 by Saint Bruno, deriving its name from its location at the Grand Chartreuse, a valley near Grenoble, France. As established by Bruno, the order had no specific rule, but certain strict, austere regulations were followed, including silence, hours of prayer and isolation, in which each monk lived in a cell and worked, ate, prayed and studied alone. Community life involved meeting for the morning Mass, afternoon vespers and evening office. Meals were taken together only on feast days. Gigues de Chatel, prior of the Grand Chartreuse, wrote the order's rule in 1127, and it was approved in 1133 by Pope Innocent II. Subsequent additions or amendments were made in 1368, 1508 and 1581. Of virtually all of the medieval religious orders the Carthusians were least affected by the crises and upheavals of the era. Because they were isolated from the world, most events never touched them, the most serious of which was the Great Schism (1378–1417), which was ended in the order by compromise.

**CASIMIR I** (1016–1058) Grand duke of Poland from 1034 to 1058, called "the Restorer" because of his role in reestablishing order in the Polish government and for reclaiming lost Polish territory. The son of Miezsko II (1025–1034), he was the only surviving heir and, having taken monastic orders, had to receive papal dispensation to rule Poland in 1034. In 1037, however, he was deposed in a palace coup and forced to flee to Germany. With the support of Emperors Conrad II (1024–1039) and Henry III (1039–1056), he regained his throne, marrying the Russian princess Dobronega, sister of his political ally, Grand Prince Yaroslav of Kiev. Although the price of his return was heavy (the nobles and clergy were given concessions and German suzerainty was affirmed), Casimir succeeded in reclaiming Mazovia, Pomerania and Silesia during the years 1047 to 1050. See also POLAND.

**CASIMIR II** (1138–1194) King of Poland, called "the Just," a Piast ruler of Poland, the son of Boleslav III (1102–1138). In 1177 he defeated and exiled his brother, Mieszko III (1173–1177), from the duchy of Silesia and its important city of Cracow. In 1186 he added Mazovia to his holdings and thus founded the line of Mazovian Piasts. See also POLAND.

**CASIMIR III** (1310–1370) King of Poland from 1333 to 1370, called "the Great" for his enlightened government and his fostering of a unified Polish state. He was the son of Wladyslaw I (1306–1333) and thus heir to a reunited kingdom. An adroit statesman, he used diplomacy as a means of policy instead of military might, surrendering East Pomerania to the Teutonic Knights and claims to Silesia, thus securing peace with Bohemia. Casimir, however, added Mazovia to Polish territory and later took control of Red Ruthenia. By naming as his heir Louis of Hungary (1370–1382), he cemented ties with that country and through intermarriage became one of the most respected and popular monarchs of the time. He acted as mediator between Emperor Charles IV of Bohemia and Louis of Hungary. At home he encouraged economic growth and was a patron of the arts and learning. The University of Cracow was founded in 1364, and the law was codified in the system of the *Liber juris Teutonici (Book of Teutonic Law)*. The last of the Piast kings of Poland, Casimir left his government in such stable condition that on his death in 1370 from a hunting accident, it remained strong and centralized. See also POLAND.

**CASIMIR IV JAGIELLONCZYK** (1427–1492) King of Poland from 1447 to 1492 and grand duke of Lithuania, who brought Poland to a position of preeminence in eastern Europe. His dynasty, the Jagiello, came to rule many states. He was the son of Wladyslaw II Jagiello (1386–1434) and brother of Wladislaw III (1434–1444), who became king in 1434. Never formally educated, Casimir was made grand duke of Lithuania in 1440, and in 1444, on his brother's death at the Battle of Varna, he succeeded to the throne as the only heir. Despite his role as king of Poland, he considered Lithuania a prized possession but mounted no major campaigns against the growing grand duchy of Moscow and actually lost control of a number of Lithuanian vassal states. He lost two important ports on the Lithuanian coast to the Turks.

His great success, however, was at the expense of the Order of Teutonic Knights. A revolt of the Prussians against the knights gave Casimir the opportunity in early 1454 to seize all of Prussia. A Polish defeat at Konitz was avenged, and in 1466 the Treaty of Torun (Thorn) granted Poland western Prussia and forced the knights to hold the rest in fiefdom to the Polish crown. Casimir was married to Elizabeth of Habsburg in 1454, and by this union and the strategic marriages of his sons and daughters, the Jagiello dynasty was connected to a number of European royal houses. The dynasty would include kings in Hungary, Bohemia, Lithuania and Poland. Casimir was considered a hard but simple man and was happier on the hunt than at court. Nevertheless, he was able to secure considerable benefits for his kingdom and is, historically, one of the great Polish kings. See also POLAND.

**CASLAV KLONIMIROVIC** Ruler of the Serbs from about 927 until sometime after 950, a prince of Serbia until the subjugation of his country by Symeon and the Bulgars in 924. When Symeon died, Caslav escaped from Bulgar control and reestablished an independent Serbian state recognizing the political suzerainty of the Byzantine Empire as an added protection against a Bulgar threat. See also SERBIA.

**CASSINO** See MONTE CASSINO.

**CASSIODORUS** (c. 490–583) Roman senator and monk and important to the preservation of Roman literature and culture in the sixth century. Born Flavius Magnus Aurelius Cassiodorus, he was a member of a noble Roman family but served in the government of the Ostrogoth kings of Italy. He was a *quaestor* (507–511), consul (514) and *magister officiorum* (master of the offices, 526) at the death of Theodoric the Great. Subsequently he served as praetorian prefect (533), retiring in 540.

An influential adviser to Theodoric, Cassiodorus convinced the ruler to forsake his Arian Christianity and embrace the Roman church, while working to save what he could of Roman life under the Goths. Having resigned public service, he became a monk, founding two monasteries on the Benedictine model at Vivarium. His effort to preserve learning of both pagan and Christian origin was crucial to the role of monasteries as repositories of classical knowledge in the early medieval period and as centers of intellectualism in the Middle Ages.

Cassiodorus was a prolific writer whose works were extremely popular and influential. His best known was *Variae,* a compilation of letters and edicts in 12 books. Other works included *Historica ecclesiastica tripartita,* a church history derived from Socrates, Theodoret and Sozomen; a *Chronicle* from Adam to 519; *De anima,* on the nature of the soul; *De artibus ad disciplinis liberalium litterarum; De orthographia,* a compilation of classical grammar; the lost *Historia Gothica* in 12 books, abridged by Jordanes; and *Institutiones divinarum et seculaerium litterarum,* a much used study of religious and secular thought in two parts—the first written for monks, focusing on Scripture and shaped by the thought of Saint Augustine and the church fathers; the second part a manual on the seven liberal arts.

**CASTAGNO, ANDREA DEL** (c. 1419–1457) Italian painter and a leader of the early Renaissance in Florence. Castagno was a gifted innovator in painting, introducing to the Florentine artistic community a heightened realism in art and, in his later years, a marked degree of emotion in his subjects. Similar in style to those of Tomasso Masaccio, his works reflect much expression and movement. Castagno's best-known panels were in the Sant'Appollonia in Florence, the *Last Supper with Scenes of the Passion,* dated about 1445. Other works were *Assumption of the Virgin* (1449–1450), *Famous Men and Women* of Florence (c. 1450), *Victorious David* (c. 1450) and *Trinity Adored by St. Jerome and Two Female Saints* (c. 1454).

**CASTILE** A region in central Spain, home of the Kingdom of Castile, traditionally divided into Old Castile in the north and New Castile in the south. The Castilian kingdom played a vital role in Spain, and its culture was to have great influence in the Iberian Peninsula and beyond. The name Castile (probably originating from castle) was first used in the ninth century to designate the fragmented district in the Cantabrian Mountains north of Burgos dotted by castles built in defense against the Moors. Under the leadership of Fernán González, count of Castile (d. 970), political autonomy was finally achieved for the county within the Kingdom of León. A capital was established at Burgos under Ordoño IV (958–960). Castile eventually expanded southward, reaching the Douro River.

A major change came in 1029 when King Sancho III (1000–1035) of Navarre took control, made Castile a kingdom and passed it on to his son, Ferdinand I of León (1035–1065), who combined León and Castile. The kingdoms twice united (from 1037 to 1065 and 1072 to 1157) and then separated; by 1188 Alfonso VIII of Castile was able to exact the homage of León. Castile subsequently led the movement of reconquest against the Moors (see RECONQUISTA), surpassing León and, through Ferdinand III in 1230, finally bringing the two kingdoms together. Castilian domination in most of Spain soon followed, including its conquest of Andalusia. Only Aragon and Portugal, and the Moorish city of Granada, remained outside the Castilian sphere of influence. Portugal resisted annexation in 1383–1385, but Aragon was compelled to accept the Castilian Ferdinand of Trastamara in 1412, although the Crown of Aragon remained independent until 1469, when Castile and Aragon were united by the marriage of Ferdinand of Aragon to Isabella of Castile. The foundations of modern Spain were thus laid by the political will and the generally superior arms of Castile.

**CASTLE** A fortified residence that served the dual purpose of housing a lord or king and providing architectural strength to withstand attack in times of war. As was true with the cathedrals of Europe, the castle (*château* in French or *burg* in German) was a characteristic and pervasive entity in medieval construction, a powerful and popular symbol of feudalism and the social structure of life in the Middle Ages.

Castle, as a word, was derived from the Latin *castellum* or *castrum* (fortress), an appropriate etymological foundation, for the castle construction that developed in the Middle Ages was influenced by the remains of the fortifica-

Marksburg Castle

tions that had been erected in the Roman era. Early versions of defensive constructions were earthen mounds surrounded by a ditch. Eventually known as the *motte* (mound), it was eventually surrounded on its upper wall by a rampart. This kind of defensive structure was widespread until the 12th century. Wood was a common construction material, as it offered the least expensive and simplest means of construction. This was especially true in heavily wooded regions, but by the end of the 11th century siege warfare, advances in metallurgy and masonry and a shortage of wood in many parts of France and Germany made finding alternatives to wooden castles vital. Thus the trend of building in stone was begun. City walls as well as castles came to be erected in this material.

Over the next centuries, however, architects and builders had to keep up with and even anticipate innovations in warfare. The Crusades brought technical and tactical improvements in siege warfare, for the Crusaders learned to undermine enemy forts by digging trenches and tunnels along the outer walls. When the supporting wood was set on fire, the tunnel collapsed, bringing down the entire wall above it. As a result of the examples of failures to withstand siege in the Holy Land, most notably the Third Crusade (1189–1192), castles were built on the summit of a large hill, often with surrounding cliffs used to defend the flanks. With advances narrowed to the front, extra lines of defense could be designed. Where the castle was solitary, moats were dug around the outer walls and filled with water.

From the 10th century, careful attention was paid to the interior of the castle. While some structures were solitary towers, many others were built with increasingly complex interior defenses. There were outer walls surrounded by protective moats, passable only by a drawbridge that could be retracted from within. The entrance to the castle (an outerwork in front of the gate) was protected by a portcullis, which was raised mechanically. In time the gates were themselves flanked by two towers, out of recognition of the fact that the gateway was the weakest point in the wall. Above the outer walls were parapets on which the defenders stood to fend off attacks from below. On the parapet were crenels and merlons, the former being depressions in the rock that were alternated with the latter, vertical blocks that afforded protection from missile fire.

Such outer defenses were aimed at safeguarding the very heart of the castle, the keep and *donjon* (dungeon), the actual residence of the lord. Not only was this area the place where food and arms were stored, it was normally the most stoutly constructed part of the entire complex, into which the defenders could retreat in the event that the outer walls were breached. The walls of the keep were thicker, but some connection with the outer walls was maintained by tunnel, very often with access to an adjoining field to allow escape if necessary. With increased concern given to the devastating siege weaponry such as catapults or mangonels and ballista, the keeps were later moved against the outer walls, so that the resulting courtyard would be clear for the mustering of troops for a counterattack.

Two of the key factors in the demise of the castle as a fortification were the cost of such structures and the use of gunpowder. Advances in weaponry and construction and the price of maintaining the necessary armies made castle building an expenditure that could be undertaken only by towns or kings. At the same time, the use of early artillery in the 15th and 16th centuries made even the strongest walls indefensible. Bombardments, starting in the Hundred Years' War, proved more and more deadly. Thicker walls were useless, and new construction techniques had to be adopted: new forts were lower, wider and surrounded by pointed, irregular walls, supported by artillery mounted the length of the perimeter on bastions and redans. The increasingly sophisticated warfare that ensued ended the role of the castle as a feudal residence, signaling the permanent division of architecture into civilian and military uses. Armed forces utilized the fortresses, and monarchs and their nobles constructed mansions, palaces and mock castles for residential purposes. See also ACRE; CHÂTEAU GAILLARD; CRUSADES; FEUDALISM; HUNDRED YEARS' WAR; KNIGHTS AND KNIGHTHOOD; KRAK DES CHEVALIERS; MILITARY ORDERS; TEMPLARS; TEUTONIC KNIGHTS; WARFARE.

**CASTRACANI, CASTRUCCIO** (1281–1328) Italian military and political leader who was prominent in the quarrel between the Guelphs and the Ghibellines in the early 14th century. Castracani was a member of the Antelminelli family, which was exiled from Lucca in 1300 when the pro-papal Guelph party rose to power there. He then became a condottiere, or Italian mercenary captain, in the pay of the Ghibellines, who supported the Holy Roman Emperors. In 1314, allied with Uguccione della Faggiuola of Pisa, he captured Lucca and the next year was instrumental in defeating the Guelphs of Florence at Montecatini. A rivalry between the two leaders led to Faggiuola's removal as ruler of Lucca and his replacement by Castracani. During the next two years he consolidated his political position while supporting the emperors. He received the title of duke of Lucca from Louis IV, with extensive powers in Rome, in 1324, and in 1325 he was at the height of his power after defeating the Florentines at Altopascio. He was twice excommunicated by the pope for his Ghibelline and antipapal activities. Castracani died suddenly in 1328, and his holdings were soon claimed by the city of Florence.

**CASTRO, INÉS DE** (d. 1355) Noblewoman from Galicia who was the mistress of Pedro of Portugal, later King Pedro I, whom she is thought to have married in secret. Because of her influence on Pedro, his father, Alfonso IV, had her murdered in 1355, an act that set off a brief civil war. When Pedro became king in 1357, he ordered the deaths of two of her assassins. According to an apochryphal story, Pedro disinterred his beloved, seated her corpse upon a throne and had her crowned. He did, however, exhume her body and have it reinterred in a splendid tomb in the Church of Alcobaça. See also PORTUGAL.

**CATALAN COMPANY** A force of Spanish mercenaries, known as *almògavers,* in the 14th century who fought in Sicily under the command of the German captain Roger de Flor in 1303, when hired by Emperor Andronicus II Palaeologus to defend the Byzantine Empire against the Turks. Their success against cavalry gave new importance to infantry forces. Unpredictable and violent light-armed footsoldiers, the company mutinied repeatedly, especially after the murder of Roger in 1306. They soon regrouped near Gallipoli, plundering Thrace. In 1311 they overthrew Walter of Brienne and the duchy of Athens, sacked the city and established themselves as masters of the region until 1388. See also CATALONIA.

**CATALONIA** Region in northeastern Spain, extending from the Pyrenees southward along the coast of the Mediterranean. Its historical capital was Barcelona. A possession of the Roman Empire, Catalonia was overrun by the Visigoths in the fifth century and later captured by the Muslims in 712. In the eighth century, however, Charlemagne attached the region to his empire, declaring it the Spanish march. Local rule was administered by the counts of Barcelona, who at first acknowledged the domination of the Franks but in the 10th century declared their independence. Barcelona and Catalonia were the heart of the political entity known as the Crown of Aragon, commencing in 1137 with the marriage of Ramon Berenguer IV of Barcelona to Petronilla of Aragon. Jointly the Catalan merchants and soldiers (see CATALAN COMPANY) continued to effect the rise of the Crown of Aragon as leading economic power in the Mediterranean during the 13th to 15th centuries. The line of Catalan counts of Barcelona was extinct by 1410, and its replacement, the Trastámara dynasty of Aragon, was eventually unacceptable to the independent Catalan people. An unsuccessful revolt against King John II (1458–1479) took place from about 1462 to 1472, and as a result, Catalonia declined in importance after the union of the kingdoms of Castile and Aragon under Ferdinand and Isabella in 1469.

**CATHARI** A heretical sect practicing in Europe during the 12th to 13th centuries. Cathari, or Cathars, were adherents of Manichaean dualism, which taught that the spirit was intrinsically good and matter was inherently evil. They were also practitioners of asceticism and fierce opponents of the orthodox Christian church and the clergy. Influenced by the Bogomils, the Cathari developed fully in Germany and Italy; members of the sect in France came to be known as the Albigensians. By the 14th century, after the Albigensian Crusade in France and other, less severe persecutions in Italy, the Cathari sect lost its impetus. See also HERESIES.

**CATHEDRAL** The name for the principal church of a diocese, derived from the ecclesiastical term *cathedra,* or chair of the bishop or archbishop. Although the episcopal see was indeed headed by a bishop, whose authority was paramount in the see (ex cathedra), the cathedral itself was not his alone. Rather, according to canon law, the cathedral was the responsibility of a chapter (or *capitulum*), a community of clerics called canons, who elected their own deans and aided in the bishops' diocesan administration. Eventually allowed to own property, the canons came into possession of the cathedrals, responsible for their upkeep and their repair. This situation led to a corporate sense between the canons and the bishops, especially when a new cathedral was to be constructed, for cathedrals could take a century to complete in the Middle Ages.

During the early years of the church, the seat of bishops, called correctly a cathedral church, were not necessarily large. As the church in general and the prelates in particular acquired extensive social and political power, the cathedrals began to reflect change. Edifices of increasing grandeur were built, varying greatly because there was no set rule as to the style of their construction. From country to country the cathedrals reflected local tastes and customs or the styles of architecture in vogue at the time, usually Romanesque and Gothic. Elaborate churches were often mistakenly called cathedrals, and many cathedrals without episcopal authority remained such in name or reputation. Nevertheless, cathedrals represented the temporal position of Christianity in contemporary society and were the greatest challenges to medieval architects, who pushed the limits of their craft to the furthest degree and beyond. Entire communities labored on their monuments to faith, sometimes for generations. The results were remarkable architectural achievements, such as Notre Dame, Chartres, Canterbury, Amiens and Santiago de Campostela. See also GOTHIC ART AND ARCHITECTURE; PILGRIMAGES; RELICS; ROMANESQUE ART AND ARCHITECTURE.

**CATHERINE OF SIENA, SAINT** (c. 1347–1380) One of the great medieval mystics, a Dominican tertiary and a patron saint of Italy. Born Caterina Benincasa, she reportedly saw visions and had mystical experiences in her youth and about 1367 joined the Sisters of Penitence of Saint Dominic in Siena, or the Third Order of the Dominicans, open to lay persons. Working to care for the sick and the poor, she acquired a reputation for holiness that drew many followers to her. In 1376 she journeyed to Avignon to plead with Pope Gregory IX on behalf of the city of Florence, then under interdict by the pope. Unsuccessful in being granted an audience, she returned to Siena. A supporter of Pope Urban VI against rival papal claimants, she assisted him in obtaining the obedience of the cardinals and clergy during the Great Schism; Catherine died in 1380 of exhaustion. Never having learned to write, Catherine dictated hundreds of letters still extant and the important *Dialogo,* her expression of mystical life. Her works were first published around 1475.

**CATHERINE OF VALOIS** (1401–1437) Queen consort of Henry V (1413–1422) of England, mother of Henry VI (1422–1461) of England and grandmother of Henry VII (1485–1509), the founder of the Tudor dynasty. The daughter of Charles VI (1380–1422) the Mad or Well-Beloved, king of France, and Isabella of Bavaria, she wed Henry V in 1420, giving birth to a son, Henry VI, in 1421. Widowed in 1422, in 1425 she became the mistress of the Welsh Owen Tudor, whom she later married. She bore three sons by Owen, the eldest the future father of Henry VII. Catherine eventually retired to a convent and died there. See also TUDOR DYNASTY.

**CAUCHON, PIERRE** (1371–1442) Bishop of Beauvais memorable for having presided at the trial of Joan of Arc in 1431. Rector at the University of Paris from 1403, supporter of the Burgundian cause and a client of the English during the Hundred Years' War, he was appointed bishop of Beauvais in 1420. He was adviser to Henry VI of England (1422–1461) and then led the trial of inquisition of Joan of Arc. He later held the See of Lisieux. The trial of Joan was declared invalid during the reign of Pope Calixtus III (1455–1458).

**CAVALCANTI, GUIDO** (c. 1250–1300) Florentine poet and true founder of the *dolce stil nuovo* ("sweet new style"). Cavalcanti was born to an important Guelph family in Florence and married the daughter of a prominent Ghibelline house in 1267 in an attempt to end the long struggle between the parties. Affiliations with the Guelphs led to his exile in 1300 by city officials, among them Dante Alighieri, who had been counted a friend to Cavalcanti. He died in August of that year. Cavalcanti was considered the finest of the poets in the *dolce stil nuovo,* second only to Dante himself. He composed sonnets and ballads of which 52 are extant, including two *canzoni,* a lyric derived from Provençal poetry. Dante had dedicated his *Vita nuova* to Cavalcanti but later turned against him.

**CAVALLINI, PIETRO** (c. 1250–1330) Roman painter and mosaicist and an important figure in medieval art, whose work represented the first major break with Byzantine styles of representation. Cavallini developed a use of sculptural techniques and greater naturalism in paintings. Among his important works were frescoes of the Last Judgment, the Old Testament and the Annunciation and the early frescoes in the nave of Santo Paolo Fuori le Mura in Rome, painted between 1277 and 1290. Cavellini was an influence on artists including Giotto and Cimabue.

**CAXTON, WILLIAM** (c. 1422–1492) English merchant and the first printer in England. Born in Kent, he apprenticed to the London merchant Robert Large in 1438, traveling to Bruges (c. 1441). Over the next years he acquired considerable wealth and was chosen head of the English traders in the Low Countries in 1463, with the title Governor of Merchant Adventurer. Around 1470 he entered the service of Margaret, duchess of Burgundy. Having developed an interest in literature, he translated into English the *Recuyell of the Historyes of Troye,* beginning in 1469 and completing the work in 1471. Having learned printing, probably at Cologne, he published the *Recuyell* in 1474 at Bruges, the first book printed in English. Late in 1476, Caxton returned to England to set up the first printing press there, at Westminster, where some 100 books were published, 73 of which were in English, many his own translations. Among the notable works were *Dictes and Sayings of the Philosophers* (1477), Boethius's *Consolatio Philosophiae* (c. 1479), the *Golden Legend* (c. 1483) and Chaucer's *Canterbury Tales* (1484).

**CEAWLIN** (d. 593) King of Wessex from 560 to 592 and one of the most successful warriors of the time. He was the son of King Cynric, succeeding to the throne in 560 but probably sharing power with at least two brothers, Cutha and Cuthwulf, from 568 to 584. In 568 he won a major triumph over Aethelbert of Kent at what the Anglo-Saxon Chronicle called Wibbandun. His victory added much of southern England to his kingdom, including Gloucester and Bath. Ceawlin was driven into exile in 592 after a mighty battle, dying a year later with Crida and Civichelm (probably his sons). See also CEOLA; ENGLAND.

**CELESTINE II** (d. 1144) Pope from 1143 to 1144. Born Guido di Citta di Castello, he was a close friend and pupil of Peter Abelard. Elected on September 26, 1143, Celestine ended Innocent II's interdict on King Louis VII of France (1137–1179).

**CELESTINE III** (d. 1105–1198) Pope from 1191 to 1198, a member of the House of Orsini, born Giacinto Bobo. Ordained a priest the night before his consecration, he was 85 years old when elected pope. He was known for his conciliatory position toward Emperor Henry VI (1190–1197). He defended Peter Abelard at the Council of Sens in 1140–1141 and was a friend of Thomas à Becket's (1118–1170). Crowning Henry VI a day after becoming pontiff, Celestine did nothing in the face of Henry's aggressive policy in Italy, most notably toward Sicily, or Henry's imprisonment of Richard the Lion-Hearted. Henry prevented eventual papal retribution by promising to support Celestine's call for a Crusade that never occurred. Celestine approved the military orders of the Templars, Knights Hospitalers and the Teutonic Knights.

**CELESTINE IV** (d. 1241) Pope from October 25 to November 10, 1241. A compromise candidate, he was already old and ill when elected and died after only a few days without performing any official act.

**CELESTINE V** (d. 1296) Pope in 1294 and the first pontiff to abdicate. Born Pietro da Morrone, he joined the Benedictines at 17 but chose to live a hermit's existence at Monte Morrone at Abruzzi. There, with a group of supporters, he established the Celestine order, becoming known for his stringent asceticism. Although nearly 80 years old, he was elected pope on July 5, 1294, ending the pontifical interregnum that had lasted for two years because of disagreement in the papal conclave. He was deeply pious but completely lacking in diplomacy or administrative skill and soon fell under the influence of Charles II of Sicily and Naples, alienating the cardinalate. Realizing his increasingly precarious position, Celestine abdicated on December 13. His successor, Boniface VIII (1294–1303), had difficulty in obtaining universal recognition, and thus Celestine was eventually imprisoned at Fumone Castle, where he died. Celestine's views were attacked by Dante.

**CELTIC CHURCH** The name applied to the Christian church in England, Ireland and Scotland from around the second century to the arrival of Saint Augustine in the late sixth century. The insularity of the Celts kept them isolated from the Continent in the fifth century. Such isolation prevented the Celtic church from the influence of the orthodox Roman church, and thus, in 603, when Saint Augustine called on the Celts to accept the jurisdiction of Rome, he faced considerable opposition. The Synod of Whitby in 664 theoretically ended the independence of the

Celtic church, but pockets of Celtic Christianity lasted for a long time.

**CENNINI, CENNINO** (c. 1370–c. 1440) Italian painter, one of the last of the Florentine Gothic painters. He was also the author of *Il libro dell'arte (The Artist's Handbook,* c. 1390), a highly useful source on the training, life and techniques of contemporary artists. None of his paintings survived.

**CENTWINE** King of Wessex from 676 to about 686, the successor of Aescwine. According to Aldhelm of Malmesbury, Centwine was a gifted ruler and a patron of the church. He continued the Saxon policy of expansion into southern England. See also ENGLAND.

**CENWEALH** King of Wessex from 642 to 672, the son of King Cynegils, whom he succeeded. Considered one of the more important of the minor kings of the seventh century, he was driven out of Wessex in 645 by Penda, king of Mercia, and lived for three years in East Anglia under the protection of Queen Anna. It was during this time that he was converted to Christianity. On his death in 672, according to the *Anglo-Saxon Chronicle,* his wife, Queen Seoxburh, assumed his throne and ruled for a year. See also ENGLAND.

**CEOLA** King of Wessex from 592 to 597, probably the son of Cutha, son of Cynric, and thus nephew of King Ceawlin. He apparently overthrew Ceawlin about 592 amid great slaughter and reigned until 597. His brother, Ceolwulf, succeeded him. See also ENGLAND.

**CEOLWULF, KING OF NORTHUMBRIA** Ruler from 729 to 737, reigning in Northumbria at the time Bede completed his *Ecclestiastical History.* He reportedly read the work in 731, gave it his critique and was mentioned in Bede's dedication. See also ENGLAND.

**CEOLWULF, KING OF WESSEX** Ruler from 597 to 611, the son of Cutha and the brother of King Ceola, whom he succeeded. His nephew, Cynegils, followed him to the throne. See also ENGLAND.

**CERDIC** (d. 534) King of Wessex, a Saxon adventurer, generally considered to be the founder of Wessex. The main source for Cerdic's life and activities was the *Anglo-Saxon Chronicle.* According to this, he landed in Britain with his son, Cynric, about 494 or 495, launching an invasion of Hampshire and Wiltshire. By 500 their conquests had carved out the Kingdom of Wessex, over which Cerdic ruled until his death in 534. See also ENGLAND; WESSEX.

**CHAMPAGNE** Region in northeastern France, a medieval province and one of the most powerful counties in the country, both economically and politically. With its capital at Troyes, it occupied the modern departments of Marne, Haute-Marne, Aube, Ardennes and Yonne. The county of Champagne was founded in the 10th century by the House of Vermandois, with the union of the counties of Troyes and Meaux. A century later the counts of Blois controlled the region, dividing the territory until 1125, when Thibaut II the Great (1102–1152) reassembled each district into one county. Because of their financial wealth and their proximity to royal lands, the counts exercised considerable influence, adding to the line even greater prestige by ruling Navarre from 1234. Jeanne of Navarre, heir to both Navarre and Champagne, wed Philip IV the Fair (1285–1314) in 1284, and thus on the coronation of their son, Louis X (1314–1316), in 1314, the county became the possession of the king. See also CHAMPAGNE, FAIRS OF.

**CHAMPAGNE, FAIRS OF** The important commercial events held in the Champagne province of France, chosen because it was the crossroads of mercantile routes from Germany, Italy, Flanders and France. The fairs were of great value in the 12th and 13th centuries in creating an international market system. English wool, German furs, Spanish leather and Mediterranean dyes, as well as precious goods and spices, were traded there. From casual assemblies, a fixed system of fairs was established, each one lasting 49 days. The first week was spent bringing the goods to the stalls, the next four weeks selling them and the last one settling various accounts. There were six fairs: at Lagny, Bar-sur-Aube, two at Provins and two at Troyes. Supported by the counts, the fairs were sources of much revenue and were vital to the rise of medieval trade, commerce and finance. Decline in the fairs' popularity began in the final years of the 13th century, and they were no longer essential by the end of the 14th, owing mainly to the improvements made in trade routes, the rise of cities as commercial entrepôts and the disruptions caused by the Hundred Years' War (1337–1453).

**CHANSON DE GESTE** The so-called Song of Deeds, the name given to Old French epic poems, numbering about 80, and dating from the 12th to the 15th century. Usually anonymous in origin and often thousands of lines long, the epics dealt with the time and the deeds of Charlemagne and his knights. Two basic poetic themes characterized the chanson de geste: the first was the struggle between Christianity (with the ideal warrior Charlemagne at its head) and Islam; the other was the activities of the lords and knights in service to the kings, figures such as Doon de Mayence, Ogier the Dane, Girart de Rousillon and Raoul de Cambrai. By far the most famous of any Old French epic was the *Chanson de Roland,* the "Song of Roland," which, with other chansons, had a major influence on medieval epic poetry, especially in Spain, Germany and Italy. See also CHIVALRY; LOVE, COURTLY; ROLAND.

**CHARIBERT** (d. 567) King of Paris, the son of King Clotaire I, called king of Paris from 561 to 567, inheriting the region of western France that had belonged to his uncle, Childebert I, including the Seine, most of Brittany, the Somme and Paris. On his death his brothers Guntram, Sigebert I and Chilperic I divided his kingdom among themselves. See also FRANKS.

**CHARLEMAGNE** (724–814) King of the Franks from 768 to 814. Charlemagne, or Charles the Great, was one of the most influential figures in history, whose reign re-

## Carolingian Europe, 814

flected the ideal of kingly rule, commemorated in song and epic (the chansons de geste) and preserved and glorified in legend. He was given the title of emperor and *rex pater Europa* (king father of Europe), for through him the diverse nations of western Europe were brought under one crown, with established ecclesiastical, cultural and political institutions.

The son of Pepin III the Short (741–768), he grew up (with his brother Carloman) as his father rose in prominence from mayor of the palace *(major domus)* to king after the deposing of the last Merovingian ruler in 751. The papal blessing of this dynastic change, culminating with the arrival of Pope Stephen II (752–757) in the Frankish kingdom in 753–754, and his anointing of the entire royal family, had a profound effect on the young Charlemagne, who henceforth maintained close relations with the church and its pontiffs. Having served with his father in numerous campaigns, Charlemagne was prepared for the wars that would dominate during his reign, but, on Pepin's death in 768, he was forced to share power with his brother because of the Frankish custom of dividing possessions among the surviving children of a warrior. The competition between the brothers was intense, nearly erupting into civil war on several occasions, especially over the Lombards and their king, Desiderius, whose daughter, Desideria, Charlemagne married. This union was repudiated in 771 after Desiderius marched on Rome. A moderating influence between the brothers was their mother Bertha, whose intervention was not needed after 771, with the sudden death of Carloman. Charlemagne ignored the claims of his two nephews, now demanding recognition by all of his subjects. His nephews and Carloman's widow fled to Lombardy, to live in obscurity. Having claimed sole control of the Franks, Charlemagne united a vast domain and embarked on campaigns not only to ensure his political position but to carve out a Christian empire.

In 773 he marched into Italy to make war on his former father-in-law, besieging and capturing Pavia. He took for himself the crown of Lombardy in 774, suppressing a revolt there the following year. Perhaps as early as 772 his eyes had turned toward the pagan Saxons, but in 775 he brought the full might of the Franks to bear on the task of subduing and Christianizing them. Fighting raged for two years, and by 777, at Paderborn, the Saxons acknowledged his suzerainty. After this he launched an expedition into Spain, with only limited success. The retreat, however, was disastrous after an attack in the Pyrenees by the Basques, who massacred Charlemagne's rear guard in which Roland fought and in commemoration of which the *Chanson de Roland* was written. As was true with the Saxons, there would be more bloodshed in Spain, but the Saxon rebellion remained a more pressing problem. Another revolt erupted, suppressed with absolute ruthlessness in 782, including the execution of 4,500 Saxon warriors. More sorties followed in 783, 784 and 785, ending finally with the surrender of Witikund, the Saxon king, and the permanent absorption of the Saxon people into the Carolingian empire, an integration of the utmost importance for the subsequent evolution of the frankish state.

Aside from a successful siege of Barcelona in 800–801 and raids into southern Italy, Charlemagne continued to concentrate on German territory and to expand Frankish influence in the Danube Valley. In 788 he deposed Duke Tassilo III of Bavaria, his cousin, making the territory part of his empire. There followed an occupation of Istria in 789 and then a series of campaigns from 791 to 796 against the Avars and the Slavs. Ultimately, his domain stretched from the Spanish march along the Pyrenees, through France, Italy and Switzerland, into Germany and the Balkans. Europe had not been so unified since the days of the Roman Empire and the Pax Romana.

This reality was not lost on Charlemagne or the papacy. He had long been a patron of the church, promising to grant the pope territorial acquisitions in Italy and reaffirming the Donation of Pepin, but he was mindful of his place as ruler of an empire and thus his considerable authority over the church, which recognized its own dependence on him. Such a reliance was seen clearly in 799, when Pope Leo III (795–816) fled Rome for the safety of the imperial court against political enemies. The pope was restored, the opposition crushed, and in November 800, Charlemagne came to Rome. On Christmas Day in Saint Peter's Basilica, Leo took the decisive step of crowning Charlemagne Emperor of the West. This momentous act, probably displeasing to Charlemagne (if the historian Einhard can be believed) was nevertheless the means for the papacy to free itself of Byzantine influence. Charlemagne had to have the overt support of the church to rule with authority and for the Western Empire to legitimize its claims, which negated the Byzantines' adherence to the tradition that theirs was a universal empire. In 812, Emperor Michael I Rangabe (811–813) accepted Charlemagne as an emperor but did not recognize his authority in the Eastern Empire, only in the West. The connection had been made between Frankish imperial power and the long-dead glory of Rome. The Carolingian Empire was taking shape, and Charlemagne was its architect. He chose, however, to make himself independent of the popes, achieving this by having his son, Louis the Pious, crowned as his successor in 813, not at Rome but at his capital, Aachen. See also HOLY ROMAN EMPIRE.

Charlemagne resided at Aachen from 794 because of its curative thermal springs, making it the heart of his administration and of his cultural and political endeavors. His court became the gathering place for theologians, church leaders, writers and intellectuals, men such as Peter of Pisa, Alcuin, Einhard and Theodulf, who were the lights of the Carolingian renaissance. Although Charlemagne was illiterate, he was certainly the driving force behind the encouragement of learning and the faith. He spoke several languages, including Latin, and was versed in theological debate, showing himself also current in the study of mathematics and astronomy. An ardent defender of Christian ideals, he was also famously lenient, especially toward illegitimate children, refusing to punish his family for sins he had himself committed.

The feudal government revolved around Charlemagne and the court at Aachen, but the overall machinery of rule was at times inefficient. Charlemagne relied heavily on his counts and bishops, kept informed and alert by his *missi dominici*, or imperial commissioners. Further guidance was given through annual assemblies held at Aachen. Laws took the form of decrees (capitularies) promulgated through an increasingly organized system, interweaving religious and ethical idealism with the social and political realities.

It was perhaps a tribute to the overwhelming character of Charlemagne that his vast empire disintegrated so quickly after his death. There were countless stories pertaining to or associated with his reign, and he was described invariably in glowing terms, a view of history only made more elaborate with the passage of time. Einhard wrote that he was tall and strong, very impressive even in advanced age, when his hair was silver and he had grown corpulent. He died on January 28, 814, at Aachen, the court mourning this emperor whom the scribes called King David.

**CHARLES, COUNT OF VALOIS** (1270–1325) French prince and count of Valois and Anjou, the son of Philip III of France, brother of Philip IV and father of Philip VI. He became the count of Valois in 1285, on the death of his father, and acquired the title count of Anjou through his marriage. Throughout his long career at the French court and in the service of the papacy, he tried repeatedly to ascend to the throne in Sicily, France, the Byzantine Empire and the Holy Roman Empire. In each case he was unsuccessful. In 1301 he captured Florence for Pope Boniface VIII and was instrumental in Dante's exile. He was condemned to Purgatory in Dante's *Divine Comedy*. See also VALOIS DYNASTY.

**CHARLES, DUC D'ORLÉANS** (1394–1465) The son of Louis, duc d'Orléans, and nephew of Charles VI of France (1380–1422), one of the finest and the last of the court poets. Following the murder of his father in 1407 by the Burgundians, Charles assumed his title and worked with the help of Bernard VII, count d'Armagnac, to topple the Burgundian party, then in control of Charles VI. He succeeded in 1414 and the following year was one of the generals leading the French army at the disastrous Battle of Agincourt (1415). Captured by the English, he spent the next 25 years as an honorably treated prisoner. While in England, he mastered the art of poetic verse, composing ballads and poems. His release was brought about in 1440 when he used a dowry he received from Mary of Cleves to pay his ransom. He subsequently married Mary and became the father of King Louis XII.

**CHARLES III, EMPEROR** (839–888) Called Charles the Fat; also Charles II of France, he was emperor from 884 to 887 and the last ruler of a unified Carolingian empire. The son of Louis the German (843–876), Charles was made king of Swabia in 876 and became king of Italy in 879. Two years later Pope John VIII (872–882) crowned him emperor, and in 882 and 884 he succeeded to the thrones of the East and West Franks, respectively. By 886, with the exception of Burgundy, he had brought the entire Carolingian empire under his domination. Unfortunately, his abilities and health did not match his diplomatic skills in being able to acquire the territories of his deceased relatives. Suffering possibly from epilepsy, he proved a disappointment to his nobles, failing to rescue Italy from the Saracens and choosing financial means to appease the Norsemen besieging Paris (c. 886). In 887, the disaffected nobility, led by Arnulf, Charles's nephew, deposed him in favor of Arnulf. Charles died the following year. See also FRANCE.

**CHARLES IV, EMPEROR** (1316–1378) King of Bohemia, a German king and Holy Roman Emperor from 1355 to 1378, who was considered one of the foremost rulers of his time. He was the son of John of Luxembourg, king of Bohemia, spending the years 1323–1330 at the French court and marrying Blanche, sister of Philip VI (1328–1350). In 1346, after spending years administering the lands of Moravia and as acting monarch of Bohemia for his father, Charles was elected German king, replacing Emperor Louis IV of Bavaria, who had been excommunicated in 1324 by the pope. After fighting at Crécy in 1346 against the English, Charles succeeded his father as king of Bohemia and the following year followed Louis IV as German king, obtaining the support of the German towns and using diplomatic means to end the opposition by other rivals. Leading an army into Italy in 1354, he was crowned emperor at Rome on Easter, 1355.

Charles was best known for the issuance of the Golden Bull (1356), a decree establishing the procedure for electing the German king. He made Bohemia a hereditary monarchy, elevating the prestige of the kingdom and making Prague his capital, and establishing a university, founded in 1348. A patron of the arts and learning, he was also highly responsive to the wishes of the church, earning the title Rex Clericorum ("King of the Clergy") from William of Ockham. See also HOLY ROMAN EMPIRE.

**CHARLES II, KING OF FRANCE** (823–877) Called Charles the Bald, king of France (West Franks) from 843 to 877 and emperor from 875 to 877. Charles was the son of Louis I the Pious (814–840) and Judith, acquiring the western regions of the Carolingian empire in 843 with the Treaty of Verdun. The agreement ended years of civil war between Charles and his brothers. Although he promoted a brief revival of the Carolingian renaissance and worked closely with the church, most of Charles's reign was spent at war. The Normans were a constant menace, a Breton army defeating him in 845, and he narrowly avoided being deposed by his brother, Louis the German, in 858. The Treaty of Mersen, in 870, divided Lotharingia between Charles and Louis, and, on the death of Louis II in 875, Charles was crowned emperor in Italy by Pope John VIII (872–882).

**CHARLES III, KING OF FRANCE** (879–929) Called Charles the Simple, ruler of France (the West Franks) from 893 to 923, actually succeeding to the throne in 884 but not crowned because of his youth. The government was administered by Emperor Charles III the Fat (884–887) and then by Eudes, count of Paris. In 983 Eudes was superseded by Charles, and a civil war raged until 989, when Eudes died. Although Charles acquired Lorraine, he proved unable to hold the loyalty of his nobles. They rebelled in 923, capturing and imprisoning him. He died in 929. Of note, Charles tried to end the Norman raids on France by signing in 911 the Treaty of Saint-Clair-Sur-Epte, granting Rollo, the Norman chief, a region northern France that was to become the duchy of Normandy. See also FRANCE.

**CHARLES IV, KING OF FRANCE** (1294–1328) Called Charles the Fair, the ruler from 1322 to 1328 and the last monarch of the Capetian dynasty. The third son of Philip IV the Fair (1285–1314), Charles became king on the death of his brother, Philip V (1316–1322), by ignoring the claims of Philip's daughter. His reign was marked by hostilities and intrigues against England, especially those involving his sister, Isabella, wife of King Edward II of England (1307–1327). He sent his brother, Charles of Valois, into Aquitaine with an army, which was one cause of the Hundred Years' War in 1337. Charles died without a male heir and was succeeded by his nephew, Philip VI of Valois (1328–1350). See also FRANCE.

**CHARLES V, KING OF FRANCE** (1338–1380) Called Charles the Wise, ruler from 1364 to 1380, during the Hundred Years' War, who proved himself a gifted monarch. The son of King John II the Good (1350–1364), he became acting ruler in 1356, when his father was captured at the Battle of Poitiers. He was troubled by the military success of England, the ambitions of the provost of Paris, Étienne Marcel, and the Jacquerie (Peasant Revolt), led by Marcel in 1358. Forced to sign a decree of reform in 1357, Charles was able to suppress the Jacquerie in 1358, culminated with Marcel's assassination on July 31. In 1360 he agreed to the humiliating terms of the Treaties of Bretigny and Calais, losing most of southwestern France and paying a ransom of 3 million gold crowns for his father's return.

Charles became king in his own right in 1364 and immediately took steps to reverse France's declining fortunes. With the aid of his gifted generals, especially Bertrand du Guesclin, he inflicted defeats on his enemies: Navarre in 1364 and England from 1369 to 1375. At the time of his death, France was once more a major state in Europe, with England having lost many of its possessions on the Continent. France was also allied to its neighbors by marriage and alliance. A patron of the arts and culture, Charles was also instrumental in the Great Schism in the church, having supported the Avignon pope Clement VII (1378–1394). See also FRANCE; MARMOUSETS.

**CHARLES VI, KING OF FRANCE** (1368–1422) Ruler from 1380 to 1422, whose reign was marked by often violent political struggles within the government, over which he exercised little control. Charles was called "the Well-Beloved" because of his popularity, but he also became known as "the Mad" because of his frequent bouts of insanity. Crowned in 1380, he was too young to rule alone until 1388, taking up his duties on November 2 of that year and giving extensive powers to the former ministers of his father, Charles V (1364–1380), the Marmousets. From 1392, however, he suffered from periodic attacks of mental instability, partially causing the conflict between his brothers, the dukes of Burgundy and Orléans, the parties of the Burgundians and the Armagnacs. The Burgundians were subsequently allied to England, which won the Battle of Agincourt in 1415. Despite the claim in 1418 of his son Charles (VII, 1422–1461) to be regent, in 1420 Charles and his wife, Isabella of Bavaria, gave their daughter Catherine of Valois in marriage to Henry V of England (1413–1422), naming Henry regent and heir to the French throne as part of the Treaty of Troyes. France was thus divided, the north belonging to England and King Henry and the south remaining loyal to Charles VII. See also FRANCE.

**CHARLES VII, KING OF FRANCE** (1403–1461) Ruler from 1422 to 1461 and the king called "the Well-Served," who drove the English out of France and ended the Hundred Years' War. The son of Charles VI (1380–1422) and Isabella of Bavaria, he became dauphin (royal heir) in 1417 and general of the kingdom. Because of the frequent bouts of insanity suffered by his father, the court and government broke into rival political parties and his mother allied with the Burgundians, headed by Duke John the Fearless of Burgundy (1404–1419). After the Burgundian occupation of Paris, Charles fled to Bourges, where, as the leader of the Armagnacs, he declared himself regent. Negotiations with the Burgundians were ended abruptly on September 10, 1419, when John was murdered in Charles's presence at Montereau. The next duke of Burgundy, Philip the Good (1419–1467), allied with England against France, and the Treaty of Troyes (1420) made King Henry V of England (1413–1422) heir to the French throne.

From his headquarters at Bourges, Charles organized his own royal government, ruling over much of the area south of the Loire, claiming the crown on his father's death. By 1428 and the English siege of Orléans, his cause seemed doomed. Joan of Arc then took up his cause, and his fortunes were dramatically reversed. Orléans was freed, he was crowned at Reims on July 17, 1429, and in 1435 he signed the Treaty of Arras with Philip of Burgundy, thus ending the Burgundian support of England and causing the turning point in the war. With the help of Jacques Coeur, the influential merchant, and the Estates General, Charles levied taxes, reorganized the armies and finally took personal command of his troops. More years of war remained, but Paris was captured in 1436, Normandy fell in 1450 and in 1453 the French won the Battle of Castillon, leaving only Calais in English hands. The Hundred Year's War was over.

The task of reunifying the country remained. His nobles were restive and dangerous, requiring adriot negotiations to suppress intrigue and rebellions. The towns were hesitant to accept royal control, especially taxation, but Charles's conciliatory nature won them over—he pardoned many cities that had been English sympathizers. By using his great popularity to instill a heart in French nationalism and relying on his advisers (his wife Yolande and his mistress, Agnes Sorel, most notably), he overcame his own passive nature and strengthened the French monarchy. Relations with the papacy were strained by his refusal to organize a Crusade, and the Pragmatic Sanction of Bourges, issued in 1438, favored Gallicanism and reduced papal authority in France.

Charles was born into a weakened kingdom, beset by war and political strife, exacerbated by his father's mental condition. By his death in 1461, the state had been reinvigorated and France made a virtual single political entity. Still recovering from near economic ruin, repairing social upheaval and suffering caused by ambitious noblemen, France nevertheless had undergone a remarkable transformation and was victorious in war. Although possessing many faults, Charles had proved himself an able king and one of the most influential monarchs in French history. See also FRANCE.

**CHARLES VIII, KING OF FRANCE** (1470–1498) Ruler from 1483 to 1498, the son of Louis XI (1461–1483), becoming king in 1483 with the real power and government administration in the hands of his sister, Anne, and her husband, Pierre de Bourbon, sire de Beaujeu. Anne arranged Charles's marriage to Anne of Brittany in 1491, thus, at last, bringing the region of Brittany under French control. About 1492, with the help of Étienne de Vesc, his adviser, Charles broke the grip of his regents and subsequently became obsessed with the ascendancy of France in Italy. He used his claim to the throne of Naples to launch an invasion of Italy in 1494. Crowned at Naples in 1495, he was soon unable to hold his conquests in the face of widespread opposition. Following the Battle of Fornovo, he retreated to France, dying there while preparing for another invasion. Generally considered mentally weak, Charles began an interest in Italian affairs that would plague French policy for many years to come. See also FRANCE.

**CHARLES I, KING OF HUNGARY** (1288–1342) Ruler from 1308 to 1342, also called Charles Robert of Anjou, the grandson of Charles II of Naples. About 1301 he claimed the throne of Hungary when it had fallen vacant following the death of Andrew III (1290–1301), the last of the Arpad dynasty. A struggle over the crown ensued between Charles, Wenceslaus of Bohemia and Otto, duke of Lower Bavaria. Charles won his claim in 1308 and was crowned in 1310. His reign, the first of the Angevin kings of Hungary, was noted for the restoration of Hungarian unity and cultural achievement. He reorganized the army, aided the middle and lower social classes and was a great patron of the arts. Through alliances, most notably with Poland, he defeated the Holy Roman Emperor Louis IV (1314–1347) and, failing to secure the kingship of Naples for his son Louis I (1342–1382), gained instead his son's succession to the throne of Poland. See also HUNGARY.

**CHARLES II, KING OF HUNGARY** See CHARLES III, KING OF NAPLES.

**CHARLES I, KING OF NAPLES AND SICILY** (1226–1285) Known also as Charles of Anjou, the ruler of Naples and Sicily from 1268 to 1285. Originally the count of Anjou, the brother of Louis IX of France (1226–1270), accompanying him on the Seventh Crusade (1248–1250), Charles was a champion of the papal cause against the Hohenstaufens, Manfred and Conradin, in Italy. Charles conquered Naples and Sicily in 1266 and defeated his German opponents at the Battle of Benevento in the same year and was crowned king by Pope Clement IV (1265–1268). In 1268 he had Conradin executed. Extending his reach into the Balkans, he seized Albania from the Byzantines but lost Sicily in the war of the Sicilian Vespers of 1282 to Pedro III of Aragon. Charles's navy was subsequently defeated by the Sicilians, and the war with Aragon continued after his death. See also NAPLES.

Charles I, King of Naples and Sicily

**CHARLES II, KING OF NAPLES** (c. 1250–1309) Ruler of Naples from 1285 to 1309, count of Provence and holder of numerous other titles. The son of Charles I of Naples and Sicily, Charles II commanded his father's fleet in 1284, attempting to regain Sicily following the war of the Sicilian Vespers of 1282. In the battle he was captured and was still imprisoned when Charles I died in 1285. Eventually released, he received a papal blessing to continue the war, which ended in 1302 with the Peace of Caltabellotta. Charles chose a more peaceful method of securing territory, entering into many alliances and marriages, thus gaining control over such regions as Athens and Piedmont. See also NAPLES.

**CHARLES III, KING OF NAPLES** (1345–1386) Ruler of Naples from 1381 to 1386 and king of Hungary (as Charles II) from 1385 to 1386. Known also as Charles of Durazzo, he became heir to the throne of Naples through marriage to his cousin Margaret, daughter of Mary of Naples and Charles of Durazzo in 1369. Named heir by Joanna I, queen of Naples (1343–1382), Charles used the blessing of Pope Urban VI (1378–1389) to reject the claims of Louis of Anjou (who died in 1384) and to imprison Joanna, whom he later strangled. Meanwhile, Louis of Hungary died in 1382, and Charles, tied to the Hungarian royal family by Angevin blood, was crowned monarch in Hungary in 1385 by suspending the claims of Louis's daughter, Maria. Charles was assassinated in 1386, perhaps at the instigation of Elizabeth, Louis's widow. See also HUNGARY; NAPLES.

**CHARLES II, KING OF NAVARRE** See CARLOS II, KING OF NAVARRE.

**CHARLES III, KING OF NAVARRE** See CARLOS III, KING OF NAVARRE.

**CHARLES VII SVERKERSSON, KING OF SWEDEN** (d. 1167) The son of Sverker the Elder, reigning from 1161 to 1167, until his murder by Canute Ericsson. Charles's son, Sverker II, ruled Sweden from 1196 to 1208. See also SWEDEN.

**CHARLES VIII KNUTSSON, KING OF SWEDEN** (c. 1408–1470) Ruler of Sweden from 1448 to 1457, from 1464 to 1465 and from 1467 to 1470. A powerful nobleman, Charles (or Karl) was opposed to the union of Sweden and Denmark and thus supported the revolt against Eric of Pomerania, king of Sweden, Denmark and Norway. Elected regent in 1436 (or 1438), he compelled Eric to abdicate in 1439, exercising considerable power in the reign of Christopher of Bavaria and succeeding him in 1448. As king he fought with Christian I of Denmark, remaining adamant that Sweden not be part of a united Scandinavia. In 1457 he was overthrown and exiled by a group of

Swedish nobles, returning supported by other nobles in 1464. Deposed again, he was reinstated in 1467; his last years were marked by his political decline in the face of increased aristocratic prominence. See also SWEDEN.

**CHARLES MARTEL** (c. 688–741) Frankish mayor of the palace from 714 to 741, victor of the Battle of Tours in 732 and the virtual ruler of the Franks. Charles, called the Hammer (Martel), was the illegitimate son of Pepin of Héristal and thus was deprived of any share in the inheritance when Pepin died in 714. He revolted, however, against Pepin's Austrasian widow Plectrude but first defeated King Chilperic II of Neustria and his mayor of the palace, Ragenfrid. Austrasia soon submitted, and Charles extended his control over all of the Franks, eventually receiving the recognition of his suzerainty by Burgundy and Aquitaine.

He did lay claim to the funds of the church to help finance his army but also granted ecclesiastical offices, was a patron of the clergy and made donations to abbeys. Campaigns were launched against the Frisians, Saxons and Bavarians, and his greatest victory came in 732 at Tours. In this near legendary engagement he repulsed a Moorish invasion of Gaul and thus claimed the honor of having saved Christendom. His son, Pepin the Short (741–768), would be the first Carolingian king of the Franks. See also FRANCE; FRANKS.

**CHARLES OF ANJOU** See CHARLES I, KING OF NAPLES AND SICILY.

**CHARLES OF BLOIS** (c. 1319–1364) A nephew of King Philip IV (1285–1314) and a claimant to the throne in Brittany during the war of the Breton Succession. His claim was based on his marriage to Joan the Lame, niece of Duke John III of Brittany, and he was opposed by John of Montfort and his son, Duke John IV of Brittany. The war was seemingly ended in 1363 with a treaty dividing Brittany between Charles and John IV, but at Joan's urging, Charles resumed hostilities. He was killed at the Battle of Auray on September 29, 1364. A deeply religious man, he was considered saintly by his contemporaries.

Charles Martel

**CHARLES OF VALOIS** See CHARLES, COUNT OF VALOIS.

**CHARLES THE BOLD, DUKE OF BURGUNDY** (1433–1477) Duke from 1467 to 1477 and an ambitious noble who nearly established Burgundy as an independent kingdom. Also called "the Rash," he was the son of Duke Philip the Good (1419–1467) and Isabella of Portugal. During his father's final illness he assumed the duties of duke and succeeded Philip in 1467. Even before his father's death Charles had engaged in a struggle with King Louis XI of France (1461–1483) for control of the territories along the Somme. He entered into an alliance with Edward IV of England (1461–1483) but was continually frustrated by the statecraft of Louis. Eager to extend his domain to the Rhine, he reformed his army and government, while putting pressure on Cologne and the Swiss. It seemed he would be crowned king of Burgundy by Emperor Frederick III (1440–1493) in September 1473, only to have the Holy Roman Emperor depart hurriedly, no doubt concerned about Charles's ultimate ambitions. Charles would come no closer to his goal, for Louis negotiated a treaty with Edward in 1474, and, to repulse his Rhineland incursions, a coalition was formed by the Swiss, the leading cities on the Rhine and Sigismund of Austria. After defeats by the Swiss in 1476, Charles was killed in battle near Nancy on January 5, 1477. Burgundian hegemony died with him, and his daughter, Marie, married Maximilian of Habsburg, the future Holy Roman Emperor (1493–1519), bringing Burgundy under Habsburg influence. See also BURGUNDY entries.

**CHARLES THE GREAT** See CHARLEMAGNE.

**CHARLES THE RASH, DUKE OF BURGUNDY** See CHARLES THE BOLD, DUKE OF BURGUNDY.

**CHARTIER, ALAIN** (c. 1385–1433) Poet and political, moral and historical writer. Born in Bayeux, he was educated at the University of Paris, serving then as secretary to King Charles VI of France and his son, Charles VII. Chartier's writings covered a wide variety of topics, for he was an orator, historian and pamphleteer, able to compose in both Latin and French. Among his most important prose works were the Latin *De vita curiali,* on life at the court of Charles VII; *Quadrilogue invectif,* a discussion on the state of France among the Three Estates, the clergy, nobility and commoners; and *Livre des quatre dames (Book of the Four Ladies).* His poetry was largely allegorical; his most celebrated poem was *La belle dame sans merci.*

**CHARTRES** City in northern France and capital of the department of Eure-et-Loire, southwest of Paris. Site of a Celtic community, Chartres was a Druidic gathering place until Roman occupation. Subsequently it was attacked by the Burgundians in the early seventh century and then by the Vikings in 858 (when it was burned), and again, unsuccessfully, in 911. From the 10th century until 1216, it was ruled by counts who controlled Blois and Champagne until the crown purchased it. Chartres was most known for its magnificent 13th-century Cathedral of Notre-Dame. An example of the High Gothic architecture, the cathedral was completed about 1260 and contains exquisite stained-glass windows and sculpture. See also CATHEDRAL.

**CHARTRES, SCHOOL OF** A seat of learning founded in the 11th century by Fulbert at Chartres in France. The school was dedicated to a humanistic program of studies, most notably the classics, and at its height in the 12th century it drew brilliant instructors such as Gilbert de la Porrée.

**CHASTELLAIN, GEORGES** (d. 1475) Chronicler and court poet known for his patronage by the House of Burgundy. Originally a soldier in the army of Philip the Good, duke of Burgundy, Chastellain joined the court of the duke in 1446. In 1455 he became the official chronicler of the Burgundian dukes and was the author of a history, the *Chronique des ducs de Bourgogne,* a record of the period from 1419 to 1474. See also BURGUNDY.

**CHÂTEAU GAILLARD** An impregnable castle built by Richard the Lion-Hearted (1189–1199) in 1196–1198 on the Andelys cliffs along the Seine, protecting the strategic approach to English-held Normandy. Meaning "Saucy Castle," Château Gaillard was carefully constructed with triple moating, formidable towers and a plan that made nearly any approach impossible. It was said that during its construction Richard exclaimed: "How beautiful she is, my one-year-old daughter." The château was besieged by Philip II Augustus of France for eight months, finally falling in 1204. The castle was captured not by assault but by devious entry through an unsuspected place. The enemy entered through the latrines. The siege was described by William le Breton. See also CASTLE; WARFARE.

**CHAUCER, GEOFFREY** (c. 1340–1400) English poet and one of the most important writers of the Middle Ages. Chaucer was the son of a London merchant, raised in the house of the earl of Ulster, where he served as page from 1357 to 1358. Joining the army of Edward III (1327–1377) in France, he was captured during the siege of Reims in 1359 but was ransomed by the king a year later. Chaucer possibly spent the next years studying law, and in 1366 he was on a diplomatic mission to Spain. Around that year he married Philippa, a well-born lady in the service of Philippa of Hainault, consort of Edward III. Chaucer was thus admitted into the royal household in 1367, and his career was soon assured: diplomatic missions to the Continent (Italy in 1372–1373 and in 1378); comptroller of the London ports (1374–1386); head of petty customs (1382–1386); justice of the peace for Kent (1385); knight of the shire in Kent with parliamentary duties (1386); and clerk of the king's works (1389–1391). Appointed a forester in the king's park at Somerset, he was also shown royal favor with gifts, pensions and a continuation of the long friendship and patronage of John of Gaunt, duke of Lancaster. Chaucer received pensions from Edward III, Richard II (1377–1399) and Henry IV (1399–1413), a major achievement in changing political times. Taking a lease on a house in the garden of Westminster Abbey in 1399, he died in 1400 and was buried in the abbey.

Geoffrey Chaucer

Chaucer was a brilliant and prolific writer and translator. He translated Boethius's *De consolatione philosophiae* and wrote several prose works but was especially known for his poetry. Based on French sources, his first important poems, both written in the 1360s, were the *Book of the Duchess* and a partial translation of *Roman de la Rose.* His time in Italy brought him into contact with the writings of Dante, Petrarch and Boccaccio, works that had a profound effect on him and his craft. Dante's influence and that of other Italian writers are reflected in the *House of Fame* and *Parliament of Fowls.* In Chaucer's *Troilus and Criseyde* (c. 1385–1386), based on Boccaccio's *Filostrato,* he displayed his talents in full maturity and power. About two years later he began his best-known and influential effort, the *Canterbury Tales.* Known throughout the world, the *Tales* were a collection of stories told by a group of pilgrims lodging at the Tabard Inn during a journey from London to Canterbury to the shrine of Thomas à Becket. The delightful General Prologue introduced each of the pilgrims, with the stories linked together by brief scenes of a dramatic nature. Among the tales were those of a knight, miller, reeve, cook, lawyer, friar, clerk, merchant, squire, physician, prioress and a woman of Bath.

Chaucer's contributions to English literature were remarkable. He has been called the most important writer in the English language before Shakespeare, establishing

English as a language of literature and using the meter iambic pentameter as a device of his verse. His compositions were of lasting value to those interested in the development of verse as well as a vital key to understanding the social aspects of the 14th century.

**CHESTER** Port city in Cheshire, England, near the Welsh border. Chester was an important strategic site during both the Roman and the medieval eras. A camp for the Roman legion, it became a fort for the Mercians and was, in 1070, the last city in England to surrender to William the Conqueror. William made it the local capital of an earldom, and from 1071 until 1237, Chester Castle was the residence of prominent earls. Henry III (1216–1272) claimed the earldom (c. 1241), giving it to his son, the future Edward I (1272–1307). He chose Chester as his center of operations against the Welsh from 1275 to 1284, when Wales was conquered. Chester enjoyed great prosperity from the 13th to the 14th century, conducting trade, mainly with Ireland. Many medieval buildings remain. See also WALES.

**CHESTER PLAYS** A cycle of 25 religious plays dating from the 14th century and traditionally performed in the city of Chester in England by members of the city's craft guilds. Presented during the summer feast day of Corpus Christi, the cycle took three days to complete and covered the Old Testament and the life of Christ, including his return at the Last Judgment.

**CHILDEBERT I** (d. 558) King of Paris from 511 to 558 and the son of Clovis I. Childebert received, on his father's death in 511, the northwestern region of the Merovingian kingdom, specifically Paris, the Seine and Somme Valleys and Brittany. His reign was marked by constant intrigue and conquest, aimed at acquiring other territories. Thus he killed his nephews by his brother Clodomir, annexed Chartres and Orléans (c. 524), seized Burgundy in 534 and eventually took Arles (c. 537.) From 541 to 542 he campaigned with his brother, Clotaire I, against the Visigoths in Spain. See also FRANKS.

**CHILDEBERT II** (d. c. 595) King of Austrasia from 575 to 595 and ruler of Burgundy and Orléans from 592 to 595. Childebert was the son of Sigibert I and Brunhilde. With his mother acting as regent and chief adviser, he was able to secure his adoption by his uncle Guntram and thus inherited Burgundy on Guntram's death in 592. Childebert died while trying to bring the rest of the Frankish lands under his control. See also FRANCE; FRANKS.

**CHILDEBERT III** (c. 683–711) Merovingian king of France from 695 to 711. Childebert II was one of the "lazy kings" of the late Merovingian dynasty. He was puppet to the Carolingian mayor of the palace, Pepin of Héristal. See also FRANCE; FRANKS.

**CHILDERIC I** (d. 481) Father of Clovis I and an early Merovingian king of the Salian Franks. An ally of the Roman Empire in the West, Childeric fought the Visigoths at Orléans for the Roman general Aegidius in 463 and later (469) campaigned against the Goths for Count Paulus. Childeric ruled and was buried at Tournai. His tomb was discovered in 1653, with his body clothed in full armor, his signet engraved with the title Childerici Regis. See also FRANCE; FRANKS.

Childeric I

**CHILDERIC II** (649–675) Merovingian king of Austrasia from 662 to 675 and king of Merovingian France from 673 to 675. Childeric II was the son of Clovis II and was made ruler of Austrasia in 662 in the place of Dagobert (II), the rightful heir to the throne. In 673 his brother Clotaire III, king of Neustria and Burgundy, died, and Childeric replaced his successor Thierry III (his own younger brother) with himself, thus uniting all of the Merovingian Franks under his rule. Unable to control the Neustrian nobles who resented him, Childeric was assassinated in 675. See also FRANCE; FRANKS.

**CHILDERIC III** King of France from 743 to 751 and the last of the Merovingian dynasty. Childeric was one of the "lazy kings" of the powerless Merovingians, who were under the complete control of the Carolingian mayors of the palace. In 743 he was taken from a cloister and placed on the throne to end an interregnum that had lasted since 737 with the death of Thierry IV. By 751, however, Pepin the Short resolved to end Childeric's rule and had him deposed and sent to a monastery at Sithiu. With the pope's blessings, Pepin became king of France. See also FRANCE; FRANKS.

**CHILDREN'S CRUSADE** See CRUSADES.

**CHILPERIC I** (539–584) Merovingian king of Soissons (Neustria) from 561 to 584, the son of King Clotaire I by his mistress Aregund, sister-in-law of his queen, Ingund. Inheriting Soissons in 561, Chilperic tried to acquire more territory at the expense of his half brother, Sigibert, king of Austrasia (East Franks), but was defeated. In 567, however, another half brother, Charibert, died, and Chilperic received extensive parts of the Seine, Normandy and Maine. The following year he wed Galswintha, sister of Brunhilde, wife of Sigibert. Galswintha was soon murdered by or at the behest of Fredegunde, Chilperic's mistress, whom he married. This act precipitated a bitter feud between Austrasia and Neustria that raged for years. Sigibert had crushed Chilperic by 575 but was assassinated, probably at the instigation of Fredegunde. Chilperic thus survived and prospered. A poet and amateur grammarian, he taxed his subjects ruthlessly and was long an opponent of the church. Finally killed in 584, he was called the Nero and the Herod of his time by Gregory of Tours but had nonetheless left his son, Clotaire II, a vast realm. See also AUSTRASIA; FRANCE; NEUSTRIA.

**CHILPERIC II** (d. 721) King of Neustria from 715 to 721, one of the last, weak Merovingians, who became king because of the desire of the Neustrians (West Franks) to free themselves of Austrasian domination. Controlled by the mayor of the palace, Ragenfrid, Chilperic was defeated by Charles Martel in 717 and 719 and was forced to flee to Aquitaine. On the death of Clotaire IV in 720, Charles Martel installed him on the French throne to reign briefly. See also FRANCE.

**CHINDASWINTH** (d. 652) King of the Visigoths from 641 to 652, chosen originally by the Goth nobles because of his advanced years (he was 79) and because of his supposedly docile nature. Instead, Chindaswinth proved to be a gifted, active and utterly ruthless monarch. He crushed without mercy those Visigoths who had previously dominated the kings, reportedly massacring 200 nobles and 500 warriors. The church bishops who had come to exercise equal power were broken and compelled to condemn all who would oppose Chindaswinth and his decrees. The result was a stable government, affording the king time to raise his son, Recceswinth, to be co-ruler in 649. Chindaswinth also reformed Goth law, ending the prohibition of marriage between Visigoths and other citizens. See also VISIGOTHS.

**CHINTHILA** King of the Visigoths from about 636 to 640. He was the successor of Sisinand and was dominated by the Visigoth nobles and the church in Spain. His son, Tulga, was crowned his successor before his death. See also VISIGOTHS.

**CHIOGGIA, WAR OF** A long war between Genoa and Venice, fought from 1378 to 1381. Chioggia was a city situated in the Venezia province in northern Italy, positioned on several islands and the territory disputed for many years by two great maritime powers, Genoa and Venice. Their struggle erupted into military conflict in 1378. A Genoese fleet captured Chioggia but was blockaded by the Venetians and compelled to surrender after being reduced by starvation. The fleet and thousands of troops were captured, and the war was ended in 1381 by the Treaty of Turin. Genoa was unable to recover from this defeat.

**CHIVALRY** An element in the society of the Middle Ages that by the 12th century had evolved into a knightly code of social behavior demanding courage, skill in battle, virtue, service to God and loyalty to a liege lord. Chivalry flourished from the 12th to the 16th century, taking various forms through the years, and was an influence on and influenced in turn by literature and Christianity. Chivalry probably originated during the rise of the chevalier, or knight, in 10th-century France, when a military aristocracy was also a political power in the feudal order. An elite circle, the knights were separated from the rest of society by their warrior existence, military prowess and their association with the ruling houses of the time, eventually adhering to strict rules regarding their behavior with one another and with other levels of society.

On this way of life, however, were imprinted powerful and pervasive ideas and ideals from contemporary institutions. In literature, the chansons de geste, poets, troubadours and the concepts of courtly love all contributed to glorifying chivalry, distinguished by its code of honor and valor on the battlefield, in the tournament or in daily life. Models of chivalry included the paladins of Charlemagne, the knights of the Arthurian Legend and the warriors of German songs, exemplars of the maxim *durch mitleid wissen*, "compassion to self-knowledge," and extolled in the *Parzival* of Wolfram von Eschenbach and in the writings of Chrétien de Troyes. In tournaments, despite the disapproval of the church, knights fought one another (often to the death) while at the same time honoring their ladies, as their champions, and demonstrated their aptitude for combat (see TOURNAMENTS).

One of the great gentling influences was, of course, the church. Christianity helped introduce to the hard-bitten soldiers of the Middle Ages the nature of respect, mercy and culture, making them more civilized in the process and hence a more valuable and productive segment of society. Highly useful tools in this regard were the Peace and the Truce of God (cease-fires observed during religious holidays), bans on knights by attacks made on church members, the weak and the defenseless. The value of human life was declared important, even the life of a mortal enemy. Liturgies were written for the blessings of banners, swords and armor, and saints such as George and Michael found wide appeal among knights seeking to emulate their holy patrons. At the same time, the church made chivalry a device of policy, introducing the holy war—conflicts waged for a cause or in defense of the faith. The cry *Deus volt!* (God wills it) was shouted by the armies of the Crusaders as they set out for the Holy Land. The Albigensians were massacred ostensibly to protect Christianity from heresy. The Crusaders remained a significant chivalric inducement even into the 15th century, and from these arose the Orders of Chivalry, the semireligious knightly orders that often began humbly but acquired enormous political or military prestige (e.g., the Teutonic Knights, Knights Templars, Knights of Malta and Knights Hospitalers). There were also decorative orders originating in the late Middle Ages, such as the Order of the Golden Fleece of Burgundy and the Order of the White Elephant of Denmark.

Chivalry, in turn, had an effect on other medieval customs. Heralds became important figures during tournaments, and the families of celebrated knights, wishing to prove their ancestry, took up the study of heraldry and genealogy. This was especially true toward the end of the medieval age, for with the end of the Crusades, the loss of the Holy Land and the centralization of authority in the royal houses, chivalry as it had been practiced became a more romantic, less bellicose and ultimately anachronistic concept.

**CHLOTHAR** See CLOTAIRE.

**CHRÉTIEN DE TROYES** (c. 1135–1183) Noted French poet known principally for his great epics, from which arose much of the romance literature of the Middle Ages. Very little information has survived on his life beyond a few details derived from the dedications in his works. He was a member of several aristocratic courts—in the service of Marie, countess of Champagne, and Philip, count of Flanders—and he was trained in Latin. His five major poems were *Érec et Enide, Cligés, Yvain ou le Chevalier au Lion, Lancelot ou le Chevalier de la charrette* and *Perceval ou le Conte du Graal.* These were influenced by the Arthurian Legend and other chivalric and heroic legends, dealing with chivalry, contemporary morality and the ideal of religious virtue, especially as exemplified by the quest for the Holy Grail.

Chrétien had a major influence on the literature of the era, intertwining the concepts of love, marriage, knighthood and spiritual redemption, as well as elements of the Tristan legend, into highly imaginative popular tales. He gave body to an already extensive cycle and shaped the later writings of such authors as Wolfram von Eschenbach and Hartmann von Aue. See also ARTHURIAN LEGEND.

**CHRISTIAN I OLDENBURG** (1426–1481) King of Denmark from 1448–1481 and Norway from 1450 to 1481 and King of Sweden from 1457 to 1464, the founder of the Oldenburg dynasty, the ruling house of Denmark until the 19th century. He was the son of Count Dietrich the Happy of Oldenburg and Hedvig of Holstein and was chosen in 1448 to fill the throne left vacant by Christopher III of Denmark and Norway (1440–1448). This decision was certified in 1449 by his marriage to Christopher's widow, Dorothea of Brandenburg, but the attempt to make him the successor to the Swedish king Charles VIII (1448–1457; 1464–1465; 1467–1470) was the cause of a war, lasting from 1451 to 1457. In 1457 Christian replaced Charles and ruled Scandinavia until 1464, when Swedish nobles rebelled against him. Attempts to regain Sweden's throne ended finally in 1471, with his defeat at Brunkeberg. In 1460, however, he acquired Schleswig-Holstein and later as a dependent of the Hanseatic League fought a war with them against England from 1469 to 1474 over trading rights. See also KALMAR UNION.

**CHRISTIAN CHURCH** For the history of Christianity during this period, the reader is referred to the chronology of church history and the following entries:

### *Western Church*

See ABELARD, PETER; ALBERTUS MAGNUS, SAINT; ALCUIN; ALFRED THE GREAT; ANSELM OF CANTERBURY, SAINT; ANTHONY OF PADUA, SAINT; ARTHURIAN LEGEND; ARAGON; AUGUSTINE OF CANTERBURY, SAINT; AVERROËS OF CÓRDOBA; AVERROISM; AVIGNON; BABYLONIAN CAPTIVITY; BACON, ROGER; BASEL, COUNCIL OF; BEC; BERNARD OF CLAIRVAUX; BERNARD OF MENTHON; BESSARION, JOHN CARDINAL; BOHEMIA; BYZANTINE EMPIRE; CANOSSA; CANTERBURY; CAROLINGIAN ART AND ARCHITECTURE; CAROLINGIAN RENAISSANCE; CASTILE; CATHEDRAL; CELTIC CHURCH; CHARLEMAGNE; CHARTRES; CHIVALRY; CLARENDON, CONSTITUTIONS OF; CLERMONT, COUNCIL OF; COLUMBA; COLUMBANUS, SAINT; COMMON LIFE, BRETHREN OF THE; CONCILIAR MOVEMENT; CONSTANCE, COUNCIL OF; CRACOW; CRUSADER STATES; CRUSADES; CYRIL AND METHODIUS; DANTE ALIGHIERI; DENMARK; DONATION OF PEPIN; JOHN DUNS SCOTUS; DURROW, BOOK OF; ECKHART, MEISTER; ENGLAND; FEUDALISM; FLAGELLANTS; FLORENCE; FRANCE; FRANKS; GALLICANISM; GEORGE, PATRON OF ENGLAND, SAINT; GERMANY; GOTHIC ART AND ARCHITECTURE; GREECE; HERESIES; HOLY GRAIL; HOLY ROMAN EMPIRE; HUS, JAN; JOHN SCOTUS ERIGENA; ICELAND; INQUISITION; INVESTITURE CONTROVERSY; IRELAND; ISLAM; JERUSALEM; JEWS AND JUDAISM; JOAN OF ARC; KELLS, BOOK OF; KNIGHTS AND KNIGHTHOOD; LATERAN COUNCILS; LINDISFARNE; LISBON; LITHUANIA; LIVONIA; LONDON; LYONS, COUNCILS OF; MANUSCRIPT ILLUMINATION; MENDICANT ORDERS; MEROVINGIAN ART AND ARCHITECTURE; MILITARY ORDERS; MYSTICIAM; NAPLES, KINGDOM OF; NAVARRE, KINGDOM OF; NORWAY; NOTRE DAME DE PARIS; OTTOMAN EMPIRE; OTTONIAN ART AND ARCHITECTURE; PADUA; PAGANISM; PAPAL STATES; PARIS; PEACE OF GOD; PETRARCH; POLAND; PORTUGAL; PROVENCE; PRUSSIA; RAVENNA; RECONQUISTA; ROMANESQUE ART AND ARCHITECTURE; ROME; SAINT GERMAIN-DES-PRÉS; SALISBURY; SALZBURG; SANTIAGO DE COMPOSTELA; SCHISM, GREAT; SCHISMS; SCHOLASTICISM; SCOTLAND; SERBIA; SICILY; SIENA; SOISSONS; SWEDEN; SWTIZERLAND; TEUTONIC KNIGHTS; THOMAS À BECKET, SAINT; THOMAS À KEMPIS; THOMAS AQUINAS, SAINT; TORQUEMADA, TOMÁS DE; TRIER; TRUCE OF GOD; TRUE CROSS; UNIVERSITIES; VALOIS DY-

NASTY; VANDALS; VENICE; VERONA; VISIGOTHS; WALES; WESTMINSTER ABBEY; WHITBY, SYNOD OF; WILLIAM OF OCKHAM; WITCHCRAFT; YORK; and individual popes and rulers.

### *Monasticism*

See ABBO; AUGUSTINIAN CANONS; BENEDICT OF NURSIA, SAINT; BENEDICT, RULE OF SAINT; BENEDICTINES; BERNARD OF CLAIRVAUX; BERNARD OF CLUNY; BRIDGET OF IRELAND, SAINT; BRIDGET OF SWEDEN, SAINT; BRIGITTINE ORDER; CARMELITES; CARTHUSIANS; CISTERCIANS; CLAIRVAUX; CLUNY; DOMINICANS; FRANCIS OF ASSISI, SAINT; FRANCISCANS; MENDICANT ORDERS; MONTE CASSINO; MYSTICISM.

### *Heresies*

See ADOPTIONISM; ALBI; ALBIGENSIAN MOVEMENT; ARIANISM; CATHARI; HERESIES; HUS, JAN; HUSSITE WARS; LOLLARDY; NESTORIANISM; and individual philosophers.

### *Eastern Church*

See ART AND ARCHITECTURE, BYZANTINE; BULGARIA; BYZANTINE EMPIRE; CONSTANTINOPLE; CONSTANTINOPLE, LATIN EMPIRE OF; COPTIC CHURCH; CROATIA; CRUSADER STATES; CRUSADES; CUMANS; EGYPT; HAGIA SOPHIA; HUNGARY; ICONOCLASTICISM; MAGYARS; MONOPHYSITISM; MONOTHELITISM; MYSTICISM; NESTORIANISM; NICAEA, EMPIRE OF; OTTOMAN EMPIRE; PAGANISM; PILGRIMAGES; POLAND; RAVENNA; ROME; RUSSIA; SCHISMS.

**CHRISTINE DE PISAN** See PISAN, CHRISTINE DE.

**CHRISTOPHER I** (d. 1259) King of Denmark from 1252 to 1259, the son of King Waldemar II Sejr (1202–1241) and brother of King Eric IV Plovpennig (1241–1250) and Abel. After Eric was named as successor to Waldemar in 1232, Christopher and Abel received duchies, the former being given Lolland-Falster. Waldemar died in 1241, and Abel embarked on a civil war with Eric, killing him in 1250. Abel was dead two years later, from battle wounds, and Christopher became king. His relations with the church were strained (he was excommunicated in 1259), and he died while fighting the dukes of South Jutland, who had attacked him as a result of his having imprisoned an archbishop, Jacob Erlandsen. See also DENMARK.

**CHRISTOPHER II** (d. 1332) King of Denmark from 1319 to 1326 and 1330 to 1332, the successor to Eric VI Menved (1286–1319), who died in 1319 without an heir. The reign of Christopher was one of social and political strife, as the balance of power was disputed between the king and the Danish nobles and the counts of Holstein. From 1326 to 1330, Christopher was removed from the throne, with Duke Waldemar of Schleswig, known as Waldemar III, ruling in his place. After he returned, Christopher's last years were spent trying to remove the Holstein party that had come to dominate virtually every aspect of the Danish government. See also DENMARK.

**CHRISTOPHER OF BAVARIA** (1418–1448) Ruler of Denmark from 1440 to 1448 and Sweden from 1441 to 1448 and King of Norway from 1442 to 1448. He was the son of John, count of the Upper Palatinate, and the nephew of the Scandinavian ruler Eric of Pomerania. Eric had been deposed by all three countries, and Christopher's election as his successor marked not only the return to peace in the region but also the reunification of Scandinavia. Christopher reversed Eric's policy of hostility toward the Hanseatic League, while his acceptance of increased powers for the state councils of Sweden and Denmark markedly reduced the political position of the monarch. As he was childless, Christopher's death in 1448 resulted in deunification of the three countries again. See also KALMAR UNION.

**CHRISTUS, PETRUS** (c. 1410–1472/73) Netherlandish painter who was born in Baerle in Brabant but became a citizen of Bruges in 1444. Probably a student of Jan van Eyck, his work was clearly influenced by him, especially in paintings such as the *Exeter Madonna* (1450). His single-point perspective reflected his masterful definition of space. Other important works were *Portrait of a Carthusian* (1446) and *St. Eligius* (1449).

**CHRONICLES** Historical accounts describing events, political or religious, that were recorded chronologically, without comment or interpretation of fact. Chronicles differed from annals or histories in that regard but nevertheless often demonstrated ingenuity, imagination and independence of thought and made valuable contributions to historians. The early chronicles of the Middle Ages followed the pattern set by such influential works as those of Eusebius of Caesarea, Orosius and Sulperius Severus. These were universal chronicles, covering events from the creation of the world to the present day and remained popular until the 11th century.

There developed, however, a tendency for the chronicles to concentrate more on local history, and thus many were written about a specific monastery, town or people. The *Anglo-Saxon Chronicle,* Thietmar's *History* and the *Gesta Danorum* of Saxo Grammaticus were all examples of works concerning kingdoms. Monastic chronicles were widely known and were considered an important but not exclusive type. Monks usually compiled the chronicles in the early medieval period because of their learning (especially the Benedictines), their proximity to monastic events (but not secular ones, creating problems in the accuracy of their sources) and their access to the libraries of the times. The great writers in the monasteries were anonymous for the most part until the 12th century, when names began to appear. Among the notable authors were Matthew Paris of Saint Albans, Ordericus Vitalis of France and Ranulf Higden of Chester.

Thanks in part to the Crusades and the increase in trade with the East, and the broadening of intellectual horizons as well, new types of chronicles emerged. There were biographical chronicles of the lives of important personages, chronicles of noble families and, of particular interest, the city histories or urban chronicles. Composed to celebrate the prestige of an important city, urban chronicles were known in England but also in Italy and Germany. It was in Italy, however, that what is termed *modern history* began, for early Renaissance writers, immersed in the

# CHRONOLOGY OF MEDIEVAL CHURCH HISTORY

| DATE | EVENT |
|---|---|
| 313 | Emperors Constantine and Licinius issue the Edict of Milan granting tolerance to all Christians in the Roman Empire. |
| 325 | Council of Nicaea is convened. It condemns the theological concepts of Arianism. |
| 381 | First Council of Constantinople is convened. It grants to the See of Constantinople the right of "seniority of honor" second only to Rome. |
| 410 | Rome is sacked by the Goths. |
| 430 | Death of Augustine of Hippo. |
| 431 | Council of Ephesus. It condemns Nestorianism and upholds the decrees of the Council of Nicaea. |
| 451 | Council of Chalcedon. It declares Christ to have two natures in one person, laying the groundwork of the separation of Christians in Egypt and Syria who reject this tenet. |
| 455 | Rome is sacked by the Vandals. |
| 476 | Deposition of Emperor Romulus Augustulus by the German general Odoacer, signaling the final demise of the Western Roman Empire. |
| 484 | A schism begins between the churches of the East and West. |
| 496 | Clovis, king of the Franks, is baptized a Christian. |
| 519 | A reconciliation of the churches is accomplished. |
| 527–565 | Reign of Justinian as Byzantine emperor; he will reassert Byzantine supremacy in Italy, Africa and throughout the Mediterranean. |
| 529 | Foundation of Monte Cassino by Benedict of Nursia. |
| 537 | Completion of the Hagia Sophia (Church of the Holy Wisdom) at Constantinople. |
| 553 | Second Council of Constantinople. |
| 563 | The monastery at Iona is founded by the Irish missionary Columba. |
| 573 | Gregory becomes bishop of Tours. |
| 587 | Conversion of the Visigoths. |
| 589 | Conversion of the Lombards. |
| 590–604 | Reign of Pope Gregory I. |
| 638 | Jerusalem falls to the Muslims. |
| 664 | The Synod of Whitby brings the English church into the Roman ecclesiastical fold. |
| 681 | The Third Council of Constantinople. |
| 726 | Beginning of the Iconoclastic Controversy as icons are banned within the Byzantine Empire. |
| 735 | Death of the venerable Bede, author of the *Ecclesiastical History of the English People.* |
| 754 | Boniface is martyred while converting the Frisians. |
| 756 | The Donation of Pepin establishes the formation of the basis of the Papal States. |
| 800 | Charlemagne is crowned Emperor of the West by Pope Leo III on Christmas Day. |
| 843 | The Iconoclastic Controversy is ended and icons are restored to the churches of the Byzantine Empire. |
| 863 | The Photian Schism erupts between Pope Nicholas I and Photius, patriarch of Constantinople. It will last until 867. |
| 909 | The monastery at Cluny is founded; it will become a center of church reform. |
| 988 | Vladimir, prince of Kiev, is converted to Christianity by missionaries from Byzantium. |
| 996–1021 | The Copts of Egypt are persecuted by order of Caliph al-Hakim. Persecutions in other eras will prove ineffective because of the role played by the Copts in the Egyptian government. |
| 1046 | The Council of Sutri begins church reform. |
| 1049–1054 | Reign of Pope Leo IX; he will bring extensive reforms. |
| 1054 | Continuing deterioration of relations between the Eastern and Western Churches as Cardinal Humbert and Patriarch Michael Cerularius exchange enmity and anathemas. |
| 1059 | Pope Nicholas II decrees that all papal elections must be made by the cardinals. |
| 1073–1086 | Reign of Pope Gregory VII. His reign will be marked by his struggle with Emperor Henry IV. |
| 1075 | The Investiture Controversy begins between the Holy Roman Empire and the papacy. |
| 1076 | Gregory is declared deposed by the Council of Worms; the pope, however, deposes the emperor. |
| 1077 | Emperor Henry IV does penance at Canossa. (He will be excommunicated again in 1080, and his struggle with the papacy will continue for years.) |
| 1084 | The Carthusian order is founded by Bruno. |
| 1095 | Pope Urban II calls for the First Crusade at the Council of Clermont. |
| 1098 | The Abbey of Cîteaux is established, marking the beginnings of the Cistercian order. |
| 1099 | The First Crusade ends with the capture of Jerusalem. Bernard (of Clairvaux) enters the Abbey of Cîteaux. |
| 1112 | The Cistercian Abbey of Clairvaux is established. |
| 1122 | The Concordat of Worms brings to an end the Investiture struggle between the popes and Holy Roman Emperors. |
| 1123 | The First Lateran Council formally certifies the Concordat of Worms. |

| DATE | EVENT |
|---|---|
| 1139 | The Second Lateran Council ends the schism that had occurred after the disputed elections of Popes Innocent II and Anacletus II. |
| 1142 | Death of Peter Abelard. |
| 1146 | Bernard of Clairvaux calls the Second Crusade. |
| 1154 | Nicholas Breakspear is elected Pope Adrian IV; he is the only English pontiff. |
| 1159 | The election of Alexander IV is contested by the support of the antipope Victor IV by the Holy Roman Emperor Frederick Barbarossa. The result is a schism that will last for 17 years, ended only by Frederick's surrender at Venice in 1177. |
| 1164 | King Henry II of England issues the Constitutions of Clarendon, opening a major conflict with Thomas à Becket, archbishop of Canterbury. |
| 1170 | Thomas à Becket, archbishop of Canterbury, is murdered at Canterbury Cathedral by knights in the service of King Henry II. |
| 1177 | The schism in the church is ended with the final victory of Alexander III. The subsequent Third Lateran Council removes all vestige of Victor IV and establishes papal elections by the College of Cardinals (with the added requirement of a two-thirds vote). |
| 1187 | Jerusalem falls once more, this time to Saladin, who is leading a jihad against the Crusader States. |
| 1198–1216 | Reign of Pope Innocent III, one of the most outstanding pontiffs in church history and a major historical figure of the medieval era. |
| 1204 | The Fourth Crusade is diverted to Constantinople, where the Byzantine Empire is overthrown. The Latin Empire is established, marking a reunion of the Eastern and Western Churches. |
| 1209 | Francis of Assisi provides the first rule to his followers and receives approval from the pope. |
| | A crusade is launched against the Albigensians. There will be much fighting and bloodshed as the heresy is ruthlessly extirpated. |
| 1212 | The Children's Crusade ends with the deaths of thousands of children and enslavement for many others. |
| 1215 | The Fourth Lateran Council is convened by Innocent III. Through it a definition of the Eucharist is decreed (including the word *transubstantiate*), annual confession is prescribed and ecclesiastical countenance is removed from ordeals. |
| 1216 | The Dominican order is established. |
| 1220 | The Dominican order receives its final organization by Dominic at the General Chapter at Bologna. |
| 1223 | Pope Honorius III approves the Franciscan rule. |
| 1226 | Death of Francis of Assisi. |
| 1232 | The papal inquisition is established by Pope Gregory IX. |
| 1239 | Pope Gregory IX excommunicates Emperor Frederick II. |
| 1245 | The First Council of Lyons deposes Emperor Frederick II. |
| 1261 | The Latin Empire falls and is replaced by a reconstituted Byzantine Empire under Michael VIII Palaeologus. |
| 1274 | Death of Thomas Aquinas. |
| | The Second Council of Lyon effects the union of the Eastern and Western Churches, but the union is opposed by the Greeks and Slavs. |
| 1291 | The fall of Acre signals the final expulsion of the Crusaders from the Holy Land. |
| 1302 | Pope Boniface VIII issues the bull *Unam Sanctam,* which declares the supremacy of the spiritual authority over the secular. |
| 1309 | Beginning of the so-called Babylonian Captivity, in which the papacy resided at Avignon. |
| 1314 | The Military Order of the Knights Templars is destroyed by order of Pope Clement V, who is under pressure from the ambitious King Philip IV of France. |
| 1324 | Marsilius of Padua completes *Defensor pacis,* a treatise that declares that the church should be ruled by councils and adhere to the supremacy of the state. |
| 1327 | Death of Meister Eckhart. |
| 1377 | The Avignon Papacy ends with the return of the papacy to Rome. |
| 1378 | The Great Schism begins with the election of Pope Urban VI and his attempted reforms of the church. The schism will last until 1417. |
| 1384 | Death of reformer John Wycliffe. |
| 1414–1418 | The Council of Constance ends the Great Schism through the election of Pope Martin V; it also seizes the Bohemian reformer Jan Hus and has him burned at the stake. |
| 1419–1436 | The Hussite Wars rage in Bohemia and Moravia. |
| 1431 | The Council of Basel is convoked by Pope Martin V. It will continue until 1449 (moving to Ferrara and Florence from 1438 to 1439) and will examine a number of issues including the Hussite question and conciliarism. The Council of Ferrara-Florence attempts a union of the churches, but it is not accepted by the Byzantines, marking the final break between the faiths. |
| 1438 | The Pragmatic Sanction of Bourges is issued by the French clergy, declaring the independence of the French church from the papacy. |
| 1453 | The city of Constantinople falls to the Ottoman Turks. |

(continued)

| DATE | EVENT |
|---|---|
| 1479 | The Spanish Inquisition is established. |
| 1492 | The Reconquista is accomplished by Ferdinand and Isabella of Spain, bringing an end to the Muslim presence in the peninsula. |
| 1493–1494 | Pope Alexander VI divides the newly discovered regions of the world between Spain and Portugal. The partition is certified by the Treaty of Tordesillas (1494). |

classics and in humanism, revived the styles of the Latin historians, such as Livy.

**CHRYSOLORAS, MANUEL** (c. 1350–1415) Byzantine humanist, diplomat and founder of Greek studies in Italy. He was one of the most important figures of the early Renaissance. Born in Constantinople, Chrysoloras was the student of the philosopher Gemisthus Pletho. His first journey to Italy was about 1393, when Emperor Manuel II Palaeologus (1391–1425) sent him to plead for aid to the Byzantines against the Ottoman Turks. Having returned to Constantinople, he was invited (c. 1395) to teach at Florence. His students there included Francesco Bracciolini, Guarino of Verona and Leonardo Bruni. After 1400 he resided in Europe permanently, living in Milan, Paris, Venice and Rome. Interested in ending the schism between the Eastern and Western Churches, he helped organize the Council of Constance, dying while en route there as the representative of the Greeks. Chrysoloras made Latin translations of Homer and Plato and wrote *Erotemata,* the earliest Greek grammar in the West.

**CID, EL** See RODRIGO DÍAZ DE VIVAR.

**CIMABUE** (c. 1240–1302) Italian painter from Cenni di Peppi, called Cimabue, meaning "Bullheaded." He was an artist of the Florentine school and was important to medieval art because of his injection of naturalism into traditional Byzantine forms, thus marking the departure in the West from the formalism of the Byzantine style. Two surviving works attributed to him were the *Christ in Glory,* known as the Maestà (c. 1302) in the apse of the cathedral in Pisa, and the decayed but still dramatic frescoes in the upper basilica of the church of San Francesco of Assisi. He certainly influenced Giotto, perhaps by teaching, but was surpassed by him in technique. He earned, however, from the 16th-century biographer Vasari, praise as the first painter of the Renaissance.

**CINO DA PISTOIA** (c. 1270–1336/37) Known originally as Cino Sinibuldi, a lawyer and a poet. Studying law at the University of Bologna, Cino was a supporter of Italian unification and thus supported Henry VII (1308–1313) in 1310 when he was crowned emperor. Following Henry's death, he returned to his studies (c. 1313), later teaching in Siena, Bologna, Florence, Perugia and Naples. His legal writings included a commentary on the first nine books of the Justinian Code, the *Codex Constitutionum (Lectura in codicem),* as well as a number of legal treatises. Cino was also a poet of the *dolce stil nuovo* ("sweet new style"), earning the praise of Dante, who called him a master of love poetry. He was a close friend of Guido Cavalcanti and was admired by Petrarch, but his style was less acclaimed than that of his more celebrated contemporaries.

**CIOMPI, REVOLT OF** See FLORENCE.

**CISTERCIANS** A monastic order founded in 1098 by Robert of Molesme and named after its motherhouse at Cîteaux, in Burgundy. Unhappy with the relaxed attitude toward monasticism displayed in their own abbey at Molesme, Robert and a group of fellow Benedictines established themselves at Cîteaux, adhering to a far stricter and more traditional rule. Robert was succeeded by Saint Alberic and then by Saint Stephen Harding. Abbot from 1109 to 1133, Harding was called the second founder of the Cistercians, for in 1119 he wrote the "Charter of Love," the constitution for the order. It insisted on asceticism, manual labor for all monks and a simplified liturgy.

The Cistercians were relatively obscure until joined by their illustrious member Saint Bernard of Clairvaux, who entered the order in 1113. By 1115 he founded the Abbey at Clairvaux, and henceforth, through the driving spiritual will of Bernard and the appeal of the Cistercian rule, the order spread throughout Europe. By the start of the 13th century, there were more than 500 Cistercian abbeys, including Rievaulx and monasteries in Scandinavia and Scotland. The golden age of the order was the 12th century, for

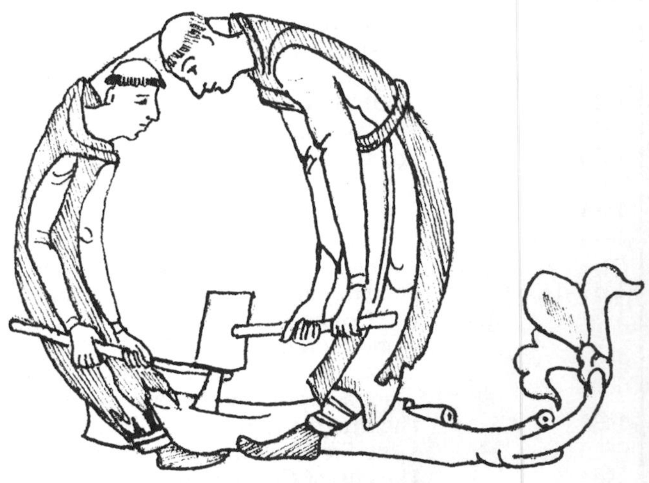

Cistercians, from an 11th-century manuscript

after that time uniformity and adherence to the constitution increasingly lapsed. Nevertheless, the Cistercians, or White Monks, had a profound effect on medieval monasticism with their deeply ascetic observances, adherence to annual chapters (or general meetings) and the fame of Bernard. They also made advances in agriculture and stock breeding. The order is in existence today. See MONASTICISM.

**CLAIRVAUX** A small village in northeastern France and the home of the fourth house of the Cistercian order. Clairvaux Abbey was founded in 1115 by Saint Bernard of Clairvaux and emerged as the virtual heart of the Cistercian order. In 1143, Alfonso I Henriques of Portugal (1128–1185) declared the vassal position of his kingdom to the abbey, paying an annual tribute. The monastery of Clairvaux was the model for hundreds of other monastic institutions.

**CLARE** See MUNSTER.

**CLARE, RICHARD DE** See PEMBROKE, RICHARD DE CLARE, EARL OF.

**CLARENCE, DUKES OF** A title reserved for the younger sons of the English royal house, first bestowed in 1362 on Lionel, third son of Edward III (1327–1377). The name was derived from the lineage of Lionel's wife, Elizabeth, a member of the family of Clare. Lionel served as governor of Ireland from 1361 to 1366 and presided over the assembly that adopted the infamous Statute of Kilkenny, prohibiting all relations between the indigenous Irish population and English living in Ireland. Two other notable dukes of Clarence were Thomas and George. Thomas (d. 1421) was the second son of Henry IV (1399–1413) and brother of Henry V (1413–1422). He was killed, leaving no heir, at Bauje in France during the Hundred Years' War. George (d. 1478) was the son of Richard, the duke of York, made duke of Clarence in 1461 by Edward IV (1461–1483) and in 1462 the lieutenant of Ireland. By 1468, however, George was an ally of Richard Neville, earl of Warwick, and supported him in the rebellion against Edward from 1469 to 1470. He turned against Neville in 1471, was reconciled with his brother Edward and was given the further titles of earl of Warwick and Salisbury in 1472. Another rupture between them led to George's imprisonment and execution in 1471. See also WARS OF THE ROSES.

**CLARENCE, GEORGE, DUKE OF** See CLARENCE, DUKES OF.

**CLARENCE, LIONEL, DUKE OF** See CLARENCE, DUKES OF.

**CLARENDON, CONSTITUTIONS OF** Sixteen articles issued by King Henry II of England in January 1164 to define the relations between church and state in the kingdom. Presented at the Council of Clarendon, the constitutions were originally accepted by Thomas à Becket, archbishop of Canterbury, but within a year he had withdrawn his approval, beginning the long struggle between Thomas and Henry. The articles were important in English ecclesiastical history because of the king's attempt to place the church courts in a subordinate position to the secular legal system.

The constitutions were ostensibly to restore a balance in English law that had been upset during the reign of King Stephen (1135–1154) when the church had superseded many of its rights, but they went far beyond a reinstatement of precedent. Henry's reforms included restrictions on excommunications, royal permission for clergy to travel from England or to make appeals to Rome, the placing of secular courts in a generally superior position to their ecclesiastical counterparts and the most harsh, Article Three, making clerics charged with a felonious crime answerable to a lay court and punishment. The last clause was opposed especially by Becket, whose murder in 1170 forced Henry to ease his pressure on the English church, although the constitutions were never revoked.

**CLARE OF ASSISI, SAINT** (1194–1253) Abbess, saint and founder of the Poor Clares. Clare was greatly influenced by Francis of Assisi, refusing to accept a marriage that was desired by her family and, in 1212, giving up all worldly interests to join Francis at Portiuncula, near Assisi. Originally housed in a Benedictine establishment, Clare, joined by many women, including her own mother and sister, moved to the church and convent of San Damiano at Assisi, where from about 1215 she acted as abbess. Her desire to have a rule far stricter and more austere than that of the Benedictines was approved by Pope Innocent III in 1215. The order of Poor Clares spread to Italy, France and Germany, and although the original rule for several of the new houses was eased, the austerity of the life was maintained at San Damiano and was revived elsewhere by later reforms. Clare was canonized in 1255.

**CLEMENT II** (d. 1047) Pope from 1046 to 1047 and known as Suidger. He was a Saxon of noble birth, serving as imperial chaplain and from 1040 to 1046 bishop of Bamburg. In 1046 he joined the German king Henry III on his trip to Italy. Henry deposed the three rival popes, Sylvester III (1045), Gregory VI (1045–1046) and Benedict IX (1032–1044; 1045; 1047–1048), naming Suidger to the Holy See under the name Clement II. As pope he crowned Henry emperor and attempted church reform at the Council of Rome in 1047. He died suddenly in 1047; Benedict IX returned soon after to Rome.

**CLEMENT III** (d. 1191) Pope from 1187 to 1191, born Paolo Scolari, a cardinal bishop of Palestrina when elected. Clement was known for his work in organizing the Third Crusade (1189–1193), the ultimately disappointing effort to recapture Jerusalem. He was also involved in preventing Henry VI of Germany from claiming southern Italy for the German crown, granting Tancred of Lecce suzerainty over Sicily. During Clement's pontificate, Scotland was removed from English jurisdiction of the archbishop of York and made answerable to Rome.

**CLEMENT III** (d. 1100) Antipope from 1080 to 1100. Named archbishop of Ravenna in 1072 by Henry IV of Germany, he opposed the Gregorian Reforms of Gregory VII and was excommunicated. Henry, however, had him elected an antipope in 1080. Clement did not exercise any papal authority until Henry captured Rome in 1084. In 1085, Clement and Henry were driven from Rome by Robert Guiscard, and Clement spent the remainder of his pontificate in Ravenna.

**CLEMENT IV** (c. 1195–1268) Pope from 1265 to 1268, born Guy Foulques at Saint-Gilles-sur-Rhoñe, an eminent lawyer in the service of King Louis IX of France (1226–1270). He was ordained in 1256, on the death of his wife, and the following year was made bishop of Le Puy and subsequently the archbishop of Narbonne (1259). Made a cardinal in 1261, he was elected pope in 1265. Clement was largely responsible for the immense political achievement of driving from Italy the Hohenstaufen rulers, thus ending many years of struggle between the papacy and the German dynasty. His threat was the person of Charles of Anjou, whom he crowned king of Naples and Sicily in 1266. Charles defeated the two Hohenstaufens, Manfred and Conradin of Swabia, the latter being killed in 1268. Clement, however, died realizing that Charles and his Angevin successors now themselves threatened the papacy.

**CLEMENT V** (c. 1260–1314) Pope from 1305 to 1314 and the first pontiff to reside at Avignon. Born Bertrand de Got, he was a French lawyer, becoming bishop of Comminges in 1295 and archbishop of Bordeaux in 1299. His election as pope was a compromise and came through the influence of King Philip IV the Fair of France, who had recently quarreled bitterly with Clement's predecessor, Boniface VIII, over the right to tax clergy, and he chose to remain in France, appointing numerous French cardinals to assure French monopoly of the papacy. From 1309 he lived at Avignon, under the influence of Philip. For him Clement ordered the extirpation of the Knights Templars in 1312 and allowed France to confiscate the wealth of the order, absolving the king of any wrongdoing in his conflict with Clement's predecessor, Boniface VIII. While accused of financial misconduct, simony and nepotism, he did establish the Universities of Orléans (1306) and Perugia (1308) and promoted the study of medicine and Oriental languages. See also BABYLONIAN CAPTIVITY.

**CLEMENT VI** (1291–1352) Pope from 1342 to 1352, born Pierre Roger, and a Benedictine monk at the age of 10. He was abbot of Fécamp (1326), the bishop of Arras (1328), archbishop of Sens (1329), archbishop of Rouen (1330) and a cardinal by 1338. He was the fourth of the Avignon popes, a period marked by its French sympathies and continued development of the papal administration at Avignon. He was an opponent of Emperor Louis IV of Bavaria (1314–1347) and, after his death in 1347, was instrumental in removing the imperial patronage of William of Ockham and the extreme Franciscans who, about 1347, were reconciled with the papacy. Originally a supporter of Cola di Rienzo, he later attacked him. Clement was an ardent believer in the need for mounting a crusade against the Turks and, in 1344, helped organized a naval campaign against them. In addition to appointing many French cardinals, he was responsible for the purchase of Avignon from Joanna I, queen of Naples, in 1348. The opulence of his court at Avignon rivaled that of secular princes and aroused animosity toward Avignon popes, generating the name "Babylonian Captivity." See also BABYLONIAN CAPTIVITY.

**CLEMENT VII** (1342–1394) Antipope from 1378 to 1394, known as Robert of Geneva, a cardinal by 1371 and as papal legate responsible for the slaughter of 4,000 rebels at Cesena in 1377. A leader of the cardinals opposed to Pope Urban VI (1378–1389), he was chosen antipope at Fondi. His election launched the Great Western Schism that divided the church for many years. His pontificate was recognized by France (against England's support of Urban) and a number of other countries. See SCHISM, GREAT.

**CLEPHO** King of the Lombards from 572 to 573, the successor of Alboin. Clepho was not of royal blood but had served as a duke. His reign marked the conquest of northern Italy, as far as Ravenna, but was ended abruptly with his murder in 573 by a slave. Ten years of strife followed. See also LOMBARDS.

**CLERMONT, COUNCIL OF** A council summoned in November 1095 by Pope Urban II (1088–1099) that was instrumental in launching the first of the Crusades to the Holy Land. Clermont began as a council of reform, attended by more than 200 bishops and many members of the European feudal nobility. It confirmed the Truce of God and issued 32 canons on secular and ecclesiastical behavior. In response to the pleas of Alexius I Comnenus, (1081–1118), Byzantine emperor, Urban called for a holy crusade to wrest Palestine from Islam. The council thus had a profound effect on medieval history; there originated the powerful rallying cry to crusade: *"Deus Volt!"* (God Wills!). See also CRUSADES.

**CLISSON, OLIVIER DE** (c. 1336–1407) French military commander who fought for England, France and Brittany. During the War of the Breton Succession, he served with the army of John IV, duke of Brittany, against Charles of Blois, winning the Battle of Auray in 1364. The following year, however, he joined the French and in 1369 was made lieutenant of Guienne by King Charles V (1364–1380). He succeeded Bertrand de Guesclin as constable of France in 1380, defeating the Flemish in 1382 at the Battle of Roosebeke. By 1395 he was once again in the service of John IV, maintaining close relations between Brittany and France. Clisson also amassed a huge fortune.

**CLODOMIR** (d. 524) King of Orléans from 511 to 521, the eldest son of Clovis I. On the death of his father in 511, the kingdom of the Franks was divided between Clodomir and his brothers, Theodoric, Childebert and Clotaire, Clodomir receiving the Kingdom of Orléans, roughly the region from Orléans to Tours, and Sens, Auxerre and Chartres. On his death in 524 his siblings, Clotaire and Childebert, murdered his children in order to seize his territory. The only son to escape was Clodald, who according to tradition founded a monastery and was canonized at Saint Cloud. See also FRANCE; FRANKS.

**CLOTAIRE I** (d. 561) King of Soissons (roughly the region of Neustria) from 511 to 558 and king of the Franks from 558 to 561. One of the sons of Clovis I (481–511), he received Soissons on the division of the kingdom of the Franks after the death of his father, sharing land with Theodoric, Clodomir and Childebert. While Burgundy and Thuringia fell to an alliance between Clotaire, Theodoric and Childebert, the peace between them was never sound. Through premature death and murder, one by one Clotaire's siblings and relatives died until he remained sole king (c. 558). His position did not last long, for he was dead by 561, leaving four sons who divided the realm. One son, Chram, tried to overthrow him in his final years but was defeated by him, and he had Chram and his family burned to death. Clotaire II was his grandson. See also FRANCE;FRANKS.

**CLOTAIRE II** (d. 629) Merovingian king of the Franks from 613 to 629, the son of Chilperic I. He succeeded to the throne in 584, while still an infant, but was secure in his position thanks to his mother, Fredegunde (d. 597). Around 600, however, much of the kingdom was lost to his cousins, Theudebert II and Thierry II, but reclaimed in 613 after both were dead. At that time he cruelly executed Brunhilde, ending the struggle of many years between Austrasia and Neustria. His reign was also notable for the foundation of the position of mayor of the palace for Austrasia, Neustria and Burgundy. See also FRANCE; FRANKS.

**CLOTAIRE III** (d. 673) Merovingian king of Neustria from 637 to 673. He succeeded his father, Clovis II, in 657 but was dominated throughout his reign by the mayor of the palace, Ebroin. See also FRANCE; FRANKS.

**CLOTAIRE IV** (d. 719) Merovingian King of Austrasia, who owed his throne to the support of Charles Martel, in opposition to Chilperic II, king of Neustria. Clotaire died in 719, however, and Chilperic was placed on the Frankish throne. See FRANCE; FRANKS.

**CLOTILDA** (c. 470–545) Queen of the Franks and wife of Clovis I (481–511). A Burgundian princess, the daughter of King Chilperic, she was forced to flee to her uncle Gundobad after the murder of her parents. In 492 or 493, Clovis, king of the Franks, received Gundobad's permission to marry Clotilda. An ardent Christian, she encouraged the conversion to Clovis, finally succeeding in 495 after Clovis made a vow to accept Christianity if he won his war against the Alamanni. The following year the king and thousands of his warriors were baptized by Remigius, bishop of Reims (known as Saint Remy). Her years after Clovis's death were very unhappy, for her sons divided the Frankish kingdom and then feuded and attempted to murder one another. Crushed by the bloody events, she

Clotilda, from Notre Dame de Corbeil

retired to the Monastery of Saint Martin at Tours. There her good works earned her a reputation for saintliness. Her surviving sons buried her next to Clovis. She was mentioned by Gregory of Tours. See also FRANKS.

**CLOVIS I** (c. 465–511) King of the Franks from 481 to 511 and the traditional founder of the French monarchy. The son of Childeric I, he succeeded to the throne of the Salian Franks in 481 but was in a weak position both politically and militarily, with Frankish opponents around him, an independent Roman governor, Syagrius at Soissons, and other rivals to the south and west. He turned first on his own rivals in the Frankish lines, eliminating them by ruthless force and, when necessary, deceit. A major triumph came in 486 at Soissons when he crushed Syagrius in battle, thereby extending his control through northern Gaul (France) and as far south as Paris by 494. A strategic marriage took place about 493 when he wed the Burgundian princess Clotilda, who was an orthodox Christian and not an Arian, as were her family and compatriots.

According to legend, Clotilda's Christianity was of great importance, for Clovis campaigned against the Alamanni

Clovis I, from Notre Dame de Corbeil

(c. 496) and, after praying to God, was granted victory over the enemy at Tolbiac (Zülpich). Two years later he and thousands of his troops were baptized at Reims by Archbishop Remigius. Being an orthodox Christian, he not only represented the cause of the Franks but was the champion of Catholicism against Arianism, adding significance to his campaigns against the Burgundians and especially the Visigoths, whom he routed at Vouillé in 507. He received an honorary consulate from the Byzantine emperor Anastasius I (491–518) and moved his capital from Tournai to Paris. There he was a patron of the church, supporting monastic development and granting lands. He summoned a council of the church at Orléans in 511 and, like other Christian monarchs, promulgated a legal code, the law of the Salian Franks (Lex Salica). Clovis died in 511. As was the custom, his extensive holdings were divided among his four sons, Theodoric, Clodomir, Childebert and Clotaire. A major source for information on Clovis has long been Gregory of Tours's *History of the Franks.* See also FRANCE; FRANKS.

**CLOVIS II** (c. 634–657) King of Neustria and Burgundy from 639 to 657, the son of Dagobert I and a member of the Merovingian dynasty. He died virtually insane, his reign dominated by the mayor of the palace, Erchinoald. See also FRANCE; FRANKS.

**CLOVIS III** (682–695) King of Neustria and Burgundy from 691 to 695, one of the last of the Merovingian kings, dominated by Pepin II of Héristal, his mayor of the palace. See also FRANCE; FRANKS.

**CLUNIAC ORDER** See CLUNY.

**CLUNY** A monastic organization based at Cluny, France, and under the authority and leadership of the abbot there. Cluny was founded in 910 by William the Pious, duke of Aquitaine, who then granted it complete freedom. Its first abbot was Berno of Baume (909–926), and it was this monk who helped create the atmosphere that would be emulated by so many other monastic institutions. The Cluniac model called for strict adherence to Benedictine rule, reductions in manual labor in order to allow for increases in worship, especially the liturgy and choir office, with much of the day spent in prayer. Also important was the independence exercised by the house, both from temporal affairs and lay political or financial jurisdiction.

From the time of the second abbot, Saint Odo (from 926 to 944), Cluny began to be affiliated directly with old and new monasteries from France to Italy, as these houses adopted their reforms. With papal approval (John XI in 931) the order of Cluny spread throughout Europe, with monasteries in Spain and especially in England. Influential and respected, members of the Cluniac order held the confidence of popes and kings, while promoting Cluniac Reform, a movement that sought to eliminate the practice of simony, lay investiture, and to strengthen the vow of celibacy. By the later Middle Ages, the control of Cluny over its many houses was severely reduced.

**CNUT** See CANUTE.

**COBLENZ** Also Koblenz, a city in the Rhineland, at the confluence of the Rhine and Moselle Rivers, founded in 9 B.C. by the Roman general Drusus and known as Confluentes. During Frankish domination the city was a royal possession, given in 1018 by Emperor Henry II to the archbishop of Trier as his palace. Many medieval structures remain, including Saint Castor's Church (ninth century) and Liebfrauenkirche and Saint Florins, both 12th-century churches. See also GERMANY.

**COEUR, JACQUES** (c. 1395–1456) An influential merchant prince, one of the wealthiest men of his age and an adviser to King Charles VII of France (1422–1461). He was the son of a furrier from Bourges, Pierre Coeur, teaching himself the practice of commerce and developing many valuable contacts in Europe and in the Middle East. Having acquired the reputation of an adroit financier, he gained admission to the court of Charles VII, becoming the king's *argentier,* or financial steward, his collector of taxes and, by 1439, master of the mint. A trusted counselor, Coeur was elevated to the nobility, using his government posts to add to his fortune, which included mansions, manors and a palace in Bourges so remarkable that it was considered a superb example of Gothic architecture.

The basis for accumulating vast wealth was his indomitable entrepreneurial spirit. From his early travels to Beirut

(c. 1432) he formed a commercial empire with more than 300 agents, opening the Levant to French trade. Established in the Mediterranean at Montpellier, and with the support of Aragon and the pope, Coeur conducted trade throughout Europe, selling wool, cloth, furs, salt, wheat, lead, copper, armor and the entire spectrum of trade goods from the Islamic world and beyond. Loyal to the crown, he made loans to Charles and was instrumental in financing the French triumph in the Hundred Years' War. Having made many enemies at court, and even incurring the envy of the king, he was falsely accused of complicity in the poisoning of the royal mistress, Agnes Sorel, and of embezzlement. Imprisoned until a fine might be paid, he escaped to Italy, entering the service of the pope as a naval commander. In 1456 he was killed leading an expedition against the Turks. See also TRADE AND COMMERCE.

**COIMBRA** City in central Portugal, the historical capital of the Beira province. Coimbra was an important Roman site, captured in the eighth century by the Moors but taken in 878 by King Alfonso III of Asturias and León (866–910). Subsequently, the city was one of the most prestigious in Portugal, serving from 1139 to 1260 as capital of the kingdom, until replaced by Lisbon. The University of Lisbon, founded in 1290, was moved to Coimbra in 1308, and after another move to Lisbon in 1338, it finally settled in Coimbra in 1355. A Romanesque cathedral, dating from 1170, has survived. See also PORTUGAL.

**COLA DI RIENZO** (1313–1354) Tribune of the Romans, popular leader and humanist, the son of a Roman shopkeeper. He lived in Anagni until 1333, returning to Rome, where he became a papal notary and was sent to Pope Clement VI (1342–1352) in Avignon to seek the pope's return to Rome. Three years later, in Rome, he assumed with wide public support dictatorial powers, styling himself the Tribune of the Sacred Roman Republic. His dream was to create unified Italian state having Rome as its capital, but his pretensions brought opposition from the Roman nobles, whom he ruthlessly suppressed. Pope Clement denounced him, and he was forced to resign in December 1347. In 1354, however, he made a remarkable political recovery, receiving the favor of the new pope, Innocent VI (1352–1362). A triumphant return to Rome took place on August 1, with Rienzo holding the additional title of senator. His rule in the city proved harsh, and he was murdered by a mob in October of that same year. See also ROME.

**COLLEONI, BARTOLOMEO** (1400–1475) Italian condottiere who served both Milan and Venice, deserting from one to the other with amazing regularity. He was a brilliant innovator in the use of field artillery, and his skills at war were highly prized. Venice retained him after 1454 as its general for life in charge of the republic. A bronze statue of Colleoni made in Venice (1483–1488) by Andrea del Verrocchio is considered one of the finest equestrian monuments of the Renaissance. See also WARFARE.

**COLMAN OF LINDISFARNE, SAINT** (c. 605–c. 664) Spiritual leader of the Celtic church in England and one of the founders of monasticism in Ireland. Colman was a native of Ireland, joining the monastery at Iona and, in 661, succeeding Finan as bishop of Lindisfarne. An avowed supporter of the Celtic church, he opposed adoption of Roman church custom. Thus, in 664, at the Synod of Whitby, summoned by King Oswy of Northumbria (642–670), he called for maintaining Celtic ecclesiastical practice, losing his argument with Wilfrid, bishop of York. Colman rejected the decision of the synod, resigned his see and, with a large group of followers, sailed to Ireland about 668. There, at Inishbofin, he founded a monastery, later building a second one at Mayo and acting as abbot for both. The best source for his life is Bede's *Ecclesiastical History*.

**COLOMAN** (c. 1070–1116) King of Hungary from 1095 to 1116, also known as Kalman, the son of King Geza I (1074–1077). His uncle, King Laszlo (1077–1095) attempted to place him in a monastery, but he fled Hungary to Poland, returning in 1095 to claim the throne. Coloman proved himself an able monarch and was king during the First Crusade, allowing the Crusader army of Godfrey de Bouillon to cross the Hungarian lands to reach the Byzantine Empire. He supported legal reform, encouraged the development of feudalism in a Hungarian model and, in 1097 and 1102, conquered Croatia and Dalmatia respectively. To ensure the succession of his son, Stephen II, he had his own brother Almos and Almos's young son imprisoned and blinded. See also HUNGARY.

**COLOGNE** In German Köln, a city on the Rhine River in Rhine-Westphalia, founded by the Romans in A.D. 50 and called Colonia (Colonia Agrippinensis). It was the site of an episcopal see from the fourth century. About 456 it fell to the Franks and became the residence of the Frankish kings of Austrasia, starting about 561. Charlemagne elevated the post of bishop to that of archbishop, marking the rise of the archdiocese that dominated the spiritual and political life of the city. The prelate received extensive financial contributions from Cologne merchants, coming into conflict with them in time over ultimate authority. The struggle ended in 1288 with the archbishop's support at the Battle of Worringen when secular leaders secured a charter of self-government. The prelate, however, retained considerable prestige within the Holy Roman Empire, for he was one of the imperial Electors from 1356, owning a strip of land along the west bank of the Rhine.

Cologne was one of the most prosperous cities in Europe, its economic growth dating from the 10th century. Textiles, leather goods, articles of gold and artistic works gave Cologne's merchants the means of conducting a diverse and extensive trade. Having claimed political power from the church, the wealthy merchants maintained control until 1396, when a popular but peaceful uprising divided municipal authority among the major guilds. A leading member of the Hanseatic League, Cologne was finally recognized as a free imperial city in 1475. Its magnificent cathedral was begun in 1248 but not completed until 1880, with restoration continuing today. It was said that the earth would stop spinning when the Cathedral of Cologne was completed. The city's university, established by papal charter in 1388, profited from the Great Schism of the late 14th century, for German students ceased attending the schools of France. Teachers at Cologne included Duns Scotus, Albertus Magnus and Thomas Aquinas. See also GERMANY.

**COLUMBA, SAINT** (c. 521–c. 597) Abbot and one of the foremost missionaries of his time. Born to a noble Irish family, he joined a monastery and was taught by Finian of Clonard and others; he was ordained about 551. Responsible for founding numerous churches in Ireland, he decided (c. 563) to leave his country for missionary work. With a group of followers he settled on the island of Iona, establishing a monastery and a church there to launch evangelical efforts in Scotland and the surrounding islands. Over the next 34 years he worked tirelessly to convert Scotland, transforming Iona into the ecclesiastical center of the region. While only a priest, Columba was recognized both as an important spiritual leader and as a saintly man. His biography was written by Adamnan.

**COLUMBANUS, SAINT** (c. 550–615) Also Columban, a great abbot and missionary. Born in Ireland and educated at the monastery of Bangor in County Down, Columbanus left Ireland about 590 joined by his followers, journeying via England to the Continent. In Gaul (France) he established highly austere monasteries at Luxeuil and Annegray in the mountains of Vosges. He found much opposition from the local ecclesiastical authorities because of his adherence to Celtic customs and had to defend himself at a synod in 603. In 610, however, he was forced to leave Burgundy after being expelled for hurling condemnations on the immorality of the Burgundian court. Going to Switzerland, Columbanus preached to the Alamanni but again fled in 612 when Burgundian influence reached the region. He went to Lombardy and founded the monastery of Bobbio (c. 612), which became known as an estimable seat of learning. Columbanus was both influential and revered as a miracle worker, and his sermons, poems and letters demonstrated his familiarity with classical literature.

**COMMERCE** See TRADE AND COMMERCE.

**COMMON LIFE, BRETHREN OF THE** An extremely influential religious association begun in the 14th century by Gerhard Groote. The Brethren (and Sisters) of the Common Life (Latin: Fratres Communis Vitae) were dedicated to furthering the Christian life, increasing the devotion of the people and accomplishing good works. Groote, a canon in Utrecht, established the Brethren during his wanderings through the Netherlands, calling for others to repent. The appeal of the association was in its promotion of spirituality while allowing the continuance of a regular vocation, as either a lay person or as a cleric. After Groote's death in 1384, Florentius Radwijns was instrumental in its organization. Great importance was placed on education, and the Brethren founded many schools. It was during the late 15th century that they exercised the greatest influence, claiming such members as Thomas à Kempis, Pope Adrian VI (1522–1523) and Nicholas of Cusa and playing a role in the education of Erasmus and Martin Luther.

**COMNENA, ANNA** (1083–c. 1155) Byzantine historian and a daughter of Emperor Alexius I Comnenus. Born in Constantinople, she was the presumed heir to the throne, being betrothed to Constantine Ducas, the descendant of two emperors. The birth of her brother, John II (c. 1087), signaled the end of her position as successor. Constantine died in 1097, and a short time later she married Nicephorus Bryennius, on whom she counted for support in a plan to take the throne with the help of her mother, Irene, on the death of Alexius. Nicephorus, however, refused when the emperor died in 1118. John became emperor, sending Anna to a convent on the Golden Horn, where she died sometime around 1153, no earlier than 1148.

Anna Comnena was superbly educated, having acquired an extensive knowledge of Greek literature and history, as well as philosophy, theology and medicine. After taking up residence at the convent, she began writing the *Alexiad*, a history of the life and career of Alexius I. Using family archives, eyewitness accounts and the chronicles written by monks, she provided an important glimpse into the life of the Byzantine emperor and the era. Biased toward her father, the *Alexiad* was nevertheless of great value in detailing the arrival of the armies of the Crusaders. She was still working on it in 1148. See also BYZANTINE EMPIRE.

**COMNENI DYNASTY** The ruling house of the Byzantine Empire from 1086 to 1185 and one of the most influential families in Byzantine history. Its founder was General Manuel Eroticus Comnenus, whose son, Isaac, reigned as emperor from 1057 to 1059. His nephew, Alexius, ruled from 1081 to 1118, inaugurating a line of emperors who would reign until 1185 at the death of Andronicus I. See individual rulers.

**COMNENUS** For Byzantine emperors under this name, see individual rulers.

**COMO** City in Como province in northern Italy, in the region of Lombardy. Long a Roman site, Como fought for many years to secure its independence as a free commune from both the Lombards and the Franks, finally succeeding in the 11th century. Its period of autonomy ended in 1127, however, for the city joined Emperor Frederick I Barbarossa (1152–1190) in his war against the Lombard League and was virtually destroyed by Milan. Milanese influence would continue to be felt until 1353, when Como came under the authority of the Viscontis and Sforzas of Milan after a long struggle. Numerous medieval structures remain.

**COMPOSTELA** See SANTIAGO DE COMPOSTELA.

**COMYN, JOHN, THE ELDER** (d. c. 1300) Scottish noble, lord of Badenoch, known as Black Comyn, one of the six Guardians of Scotland, who signed the agreement that Margaret, Maid of Norway, would marry Edward I's (1272–1307) eldest son. On Margaret's death he was claimant to the Scottish throne but later supported John de Balliol, who was crowned in 1291. See also SCOTLAND.

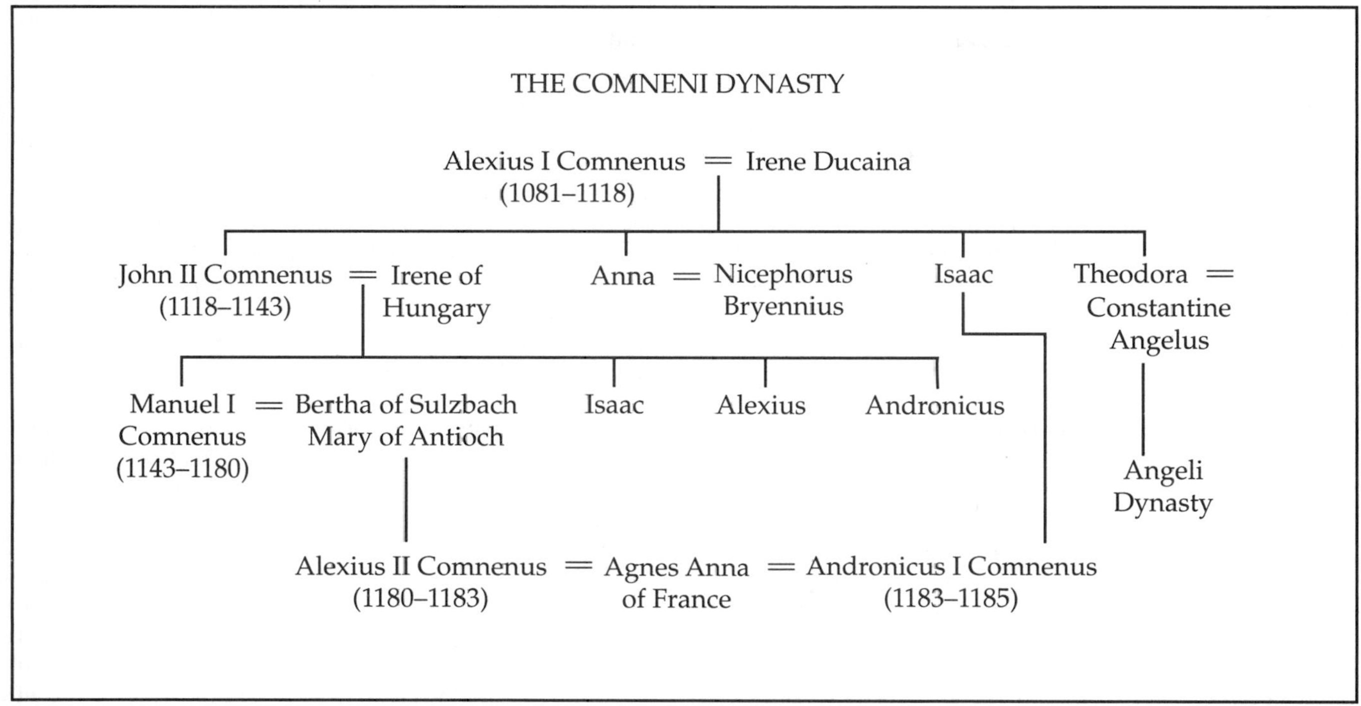


**COMYN, JOHN, THE YOUNGER** (d. 1306) Son of John Comyn, the Elder (the Black Comyn), called "the Red" to distinguish him from his father. A supporter and ally of John de Balliol against King Edward I of England (1272–1307), he succeeded William Wallace as a Guardian of Scotland but was murdered by the party of Robert the Bruce to remove him as a claimant to the Scottish throne. See also SCOTLAND.

**CONCILIAR MOVEMENT** Also called conciliarism, the concept originating from within the Roman Catholic Church of the Middle Ages that a general council of the church wielded higher authority than the pope and thus could depose him. The movement had its origins in the 12th and 13th centuries among academicians and theologians who were trying to systematize the powers of the papacy and gained respect in the 14th century among such notable thinkers as Marsilius of Padua and William of Ockham. The argument, supported by church groups, including the Spiritual Franciscans, stated that only the entire Christian community could prevent errors of faith, not one person, not even the pope. Such thinking gained wide acceptance in the early 15th century (councils of Pisa, 1409; Constance, 1414–1418; Pavia-Siena, 1423–1424; Basel-Ferrara-Florence, 1431–1449), when the Great Schism was left unresolved by the Avignon, Roman and Pisan popes. See also CONRAD OF GELNHAUSEN.

The Council of Constance (1414–1418) was the moment of greatest success for the conciliar movement, for it deposed two popes (a third resigned) and chose Martin V (1417–1431) as successor to the Holy See, thereby ending the Great Schism. Its legitimacy to act, however, and its pronouncement making conciliarism an accepted element of the church's order (*Haec Sancta,* or the *Sancrosancta*) were never totally approved. While the conciliarists could compel the pope to convene the councils of Pisa in 1423 and Basel in 1431, the latter was strife ridden, and the movement lost much support after its adherents deposed Eugene IV (1431–1447). Basel signaled the decline of conciliarism, and in 1460 Pope Pius II (1458–1464) issued the bull *Exacrabilis,* and in 1870 the First Vatican Council condemned the conciliar movement.

**CONCORDAT OF WORMS** See WORMS, CONCORDAT OF.

**CONDOTTIERE** See Glossary.

**CONNAUGHT** Also Connacht, one of the four old kingdoms of early Ireland, situated in the western region of the island and comprising the modern counties of Mayo, Leitrim, Sligo, Roscommon and Galway. Connaught was in the fourth century under the influence of the high kings of Tara of the midlands. Tairdelbach O'Connor (d. 1156) and his son Rory (Ruadrí, d. 1198) became kings of Ireland, but it was during their time that the influence of the Anglo-Normans began to encroach. English domination was such by the 13th century that King Henry III (1216–1272), in 1227, gave Connaught to Richard de Burgh. His son, Walter, was made earl of Ulster, as well as lord of Connaught. Walter's death without a male heir left his daughter to wed Edward III's (1327–1377) third son, and through their union the title passed to the English crown in 1461. See also IRELAND.

**CONON** (d. 687) Pope from 686 to 687, the son of a Thracian soldier, who was elected as a compromise. He was already very old and in poor health.

**CONRAD, KING OF JERUSALEM** See CONRAD OF MONTFERRAT.

**CONRAD I, KING OF GERMANY** (d. 918) Duke of Franconia and German king from 911 to 918. A member of the Conradines of the Franconian dynasty, Conrad I was elected to succeed Louis the Child, the last of the Carolingians in the East. His reign was one of constant and generally unsuccessful wars, especially against the Magyars and his own dukes, including those of Savoy, Swabia and Bavaria. Unable to impose his will on the duchies, he also failed to provide a lasting ruling family and was forced to choose a successor on his deathbed. His decision to pick a bitter foe, Henry the Fowler, duke of Saxony (emperor, 919–936), was a wise one. See also HOLY ROMAN EMPIRE.

**CONRAD II, KING OF GERMANY** (c. 990–1039) King of Germany from 1024 to 1039 and emperor from 1027, an active ruler and the founder of the Salian dynasty in Germany. He was the son of Count Henry of Speyer but was raised by the bishop of Worms, marrying in 1016 Gisela, duchess of Swabia. In 1024, on the death of Emperor Henry II (1002–1024), Conrad was elected the German king, suppressing local rebellions before marching into Italy in 1026. On Easter Day, 1027, he was crowned emperor by Pope John XIX (1024–1032) in Rome. His efforts were bent on strengthening the German monarchy, promoting nobles of lesser rank and lower-class government officials in order to impose his control over much of the country. To ensure the survival of the dynasty, he had his son, Henry (III, 1039–1056), crowned at Aachen in 1028, but relations between the two were strained at times. Conrad campaigned vigorously in the East, reclaiming land from Poland and conquering local tribes. He also returned to Italy in 1036, working for two years to subdue the princes of the peninsula, replacing many with his own supporters. See also HOLY ROMAN EMPIRE.

**CONRAD III, KING OF GERMANY** (1093–1152) Ruler from 1137 to 1152 and the first ruler of the Hohenstaufen dynasty. Conrad was the son of Frederick I, duke of Swabia, receiving appointment as the duke of Franconia in 1115 from his uncle, Emperor Henry V (1106–1125). On Henry's death in 1125, Conrad was not considered by the Electors, who chose Lothair, duke of Savoy (1125–1137). With his brother, Frederick II of Swabia, he embarked on a civil war in 1127, was elected anti-king in Nuremburg and crowned king of Italy in 1128. From 1132 to 1135, he waged an unsuccessful campaign against Lothair, finally submitting and given a pardon by him. Lothair died in 1137, and Conrad was finally made the German king.

War soon erupted again, however, as Henry the Proud, son-in-law of Lothair, refused to accept Conrad. Henry died in 1137, and peace came in 1142 between the Hohenstaufens and their enemies, the Welfs. In 1147, he set out for the Second Crusade (1147–1149), joining Louis VII of France (1137–1180). His crusading ended with his return to Germany to prevent any attempts to seize power by Welf of Bavaria, brother of Henry the Proud. Conrad died in 1152, having named as his heir his nephew, Frederick III of Swabia, who became Frederick I Barbarossa (1152–1190). See also HOLY ROMAN EMPIRE.

**CONRAD IV, KING OF GERMANY** (1228–1254) German king from 1237 to 1254, king of Sicily from 1251 to 1254, duke of Swabia and, through his mother Isabella of Brienne, heir to the Kingdom of Jerusalem. The son of Emperor Frederick II (1215–1250), he was crowned king of Rome in 1237 but spent many years in conflict with the papal supporters in Germany, which were led by Archbishop Siegried of Mainz and Conrad of Cologne and encouraged by Frederick's bitter enemy, Pope Innocent IV (1243–1254). The pope deposed both Conrad and his father in 1245, and he was defeated by the anti-king Henry Raspe in 1246, surviving only with the support of Otto II of Bavaria. Frederick died in 1250. Continued conflict, especially with the papal party, led by Henry Raspe's successor, William of Holland, compelled Conrad to leave Germany for Sicily, where he became king in 1251. He died while trying to restore amicable relations with the pope and to improve his political position. See also HOLY ROMAN EMPIRE.

**CONRADIN** (1252–1268) Also Conrad V, duke of Swabia, and nominal king of Germany and Sicily from 1254 to 1268. The son of Conrad IV (1250–1254) and grandson of Frederick II (1215–1250), he was heir to the Kingdom of Sicily, losing it to his uncle, Manfred, illegitimate son of Frederick, in 1258. Conradin thus held the title of duke of Swabia until 1266, when Manfred died at the Battle of Benevento at the hands of Charles of Anjou, recently named king of Sicily by Pope Clement IV (1265–1268). The following year Conradin became the champion of the Ghibelline cause, marching into Italy with the hope of defeating Charles. Rome fell in July 1268, but on August 23 he was crushed by Charles at Tagliacozza. Captured and sent to Charles, Conradin was beheaded at Naples, thereby bringing to an end the Hohenstaufen dynasty. See also HOLY ROMAN EMPIRE.

**CONRAD OF GELNHAUSEN** (d. 1390) German theologian and one of the leading advocates of the conciliar movement. Conrad taught at Paris, was chancellor of the University of Heidelberg and was also provost of Worms. He believed that the Great Schism then dividing the church should be resolved by a general council, empowered with the authority to choose a legitimate pope. Such views were developed in his *Epistola Concordiae* (1380) and were based in large measure on the ideas of William of Ockham and Marsilius of Padua.

**CONRAD OF MARBURG** (1180–1233) Papal inquisitor. Conrad probably came from Marburg and studied either at Paris or Bologna. A preacher of the Crusade of Innocent III (the infamous Fourth Crusade), he received numerous ecclesiastical appointments and was made confessor to Elizabeth of Hungary. In 1231 Pope Gregory IX made him the first papal inquisitor in Germany, with total power to annihilate heresies. His campaign against heretics, including the Cathari and Waldenses, was absolutely merciless with many executions based on insufficient evidence. After Conrad charged, Henry II, count of Sayn, with heresy in 1233, a court of bishops and nobles denounced him at Mainz, and he was murdered while traveling to Marburg. See also INQUISITION.

**CONRAD OF MONTFERRAT** (1146–1192) Marquis of Montferrat and king of Jerusalem in 1192. One of the leaders of the Third Crusade (1189–1192), he was able to defend Tyre from the Saracens in 1187 and became its lord. Ambitious, Conrad proved himself one of the best of the Frankish rulers in the Holy Land, rivaling both Richard the Lion-Hearted and his political enemy, Guy of Lusignan. He hoped to displace the latter by marrying Isabella, daughter of King Amalric I, and thus secured the title of king of Jerusalem in 1192. His reign was very brief, for he was murdered by the Assassins in the streets of Tyre, an act of vengeance for the execution of one of their own, at the behest of Saladin or, probably unlikely, at the paid request of Richard. The death of Conrad was nevertheless greeted with joy by both Saladin and Richard. See also CRUSADES.

**CONRAD THE RED** (d. 955) Duke of Lotharingia and a member of the Franconian line of counts. He was originally a close ally of Emperor Otto I, helping him from 937 to 939 to crush rebellious dukes and receiving Lotharingia (Lorraine) as a result in 944, as well as the hand of Otto's daughter, Liudgard. In 953, however, Conrad joined a rebellion against Otto, headed by Luidolf, Otto's son. Defeated, he lost his duchy but was later reconciled with Otto. Indispensable at the Battle of Lechfeld, he was killed in that conflict, in which the Magyars were annihilated. Conrad was the ancestor of the Salian kings of Germany. See also HOLY ROMAN EMPIRE.

**CONSTABLE** See Glossary.

**CONSTANCE** (1152–1198) Wife of Emperor Henry VI, empress of the Holy Roman Empire from 1191 to 1197 and queen of Sicily from 1194 to 1198. The daughter of King Roger II of Sicily, she married the future emperor, Henry, in 1186 and was crowned empress in Rome in 1191. She was the mother of Frederick II and aunt of William II of Sicily, whom she succeeded in 1189. Support among the Sicilians could not be found, and another nephew, Tancred, ruled in Sicily until his death in 1194. With the help of Pope Innocent III, Constance had Frederick crowned in 1198, acting as his regent until she died. Through her the Hohenstaufens claimed the Sicilian throne.

**CONSTANCE, COUNCIL OF** Sixteenth Ecumenical Council, held from 1414 to 1418, with the aim of ending the Great Schism and convened by the antipope John XXIII (1410–1415) in 1413 at the urging of Emperor Sigismund (1410–1437). The council was seen as the zenith of the conciliar movement and helped to terminate the division of the church into three papal camps, represented by John (in Pisa), Gregory XII (1406–1415) (in Rome) and Benedict XIII (1394–1417) (in Avignon). The council assembled at Constance, but political disputes forced a compromise among the cardinals. A unique system of voting was adopted in which the major delegations from Italy, France, Germany and England each received one vote, and one vote was given to cardinals acting as a group; Spain was eventually granted one vote as well.

Finally able to deliberate, the council took the dramatic step of continuing to function even after Pope John fled from Constance in the hope of forcing a legal end to the proceedings. Urged by Emperor Sigismund, the delegates issued the decree *Sancrosancta*, asserting the authority of the general councils over the papacy, and the decree *Frequens*, which made frequent meetings possible by declaring that they were essential for the good of the church. John was deposed in May 1415, Gregory resigned in July and finally, in July 1417, Benedict XIII was removed. In November of that year Oddone Colonna was elected Martin V (1417–1431) and the Great Schism was resolved. The council went on to condemn John Wycliffe, and Jan Hus was tried as a heretic, found guilty and burned at the stake. Other attempts at reform were made, but their effects were limited and concentrated mainly on curbing papal powers. Ending in 1418, the council was the subject of intense theological debate as to its enactments and legality.

**CONSTANS II POGONATUS** (630–668) Byzantine emperor from 641 to 668, whose reign was marked by the rise of the Islamic empire. The son of Emperor Constantine III (641), he had ruled for only one year when the armies of Islam swept into Egypt, ending Byzantine control there and later capturing most of the empire's Eastern holdings. Constans attempted to defeat the Muslims at sea but was routed and lost naval supremacy in the Mediterranean as well. Only the murder of Caliph Osman spared Constantinople from attack, allowing Constans to sign a peace with the Arab governor of Syria in 659. He imprisoned and exiled Pope Martin I (649–653) in 653 after the pontiff disagreed with the *Typos*, Constans's decree to curb speculation on the nature of Christ. About 663 he left Constantinople and entered Italy with an army, probably hoping to improve Western defenses by ordering the transformation of Syracuse in Sicily into a strategic base. His plans were cut short by his assassination. See also BYZANTINE EMPIRE.

**CONSTANTINE I** (d. 715) Pope from 708 to 715, a Syrian who succeeded in asserting papal authority over the See of Ravenna. In 711 he journeyed to Constantinople, where he was received by Emperor Justinian II, who wished to normalize relations with Rome.

**CONSTANTINE II** Antipope from 767 to 768, a soldier who used the influence of his brother, Duke Toto, to have himself elected the successor to Paul I (757–767). His opponents, aided by the Lombards, drove him from Rome, installing Stephen III (IV) in his place.

**CONSTANTINE IV, BYZANTINE EMPEROR** (d. 685) Ruler from 668 to 685, the son of Constans II (641–668), made co-emperor in 664 and succeeding his father in 668. Constantine faced many crises during his reign. From 674 to 678 the Islamic armies laid siege to Constantinople and were repulsed only with the aid of Greek fire, an invention that was used in warfare. The Slavs were driven out of Thessalonica, and the Bulgars crossed the Danube River and established themselves in the Balkans. The latter he could not defeat, and he was forced to pay tribute. Constantine also convened the Council of Constantinople (680–681) to purge the Monothelitist heresy. See also BYZANTINE EMPIRE.

**CONSTANTINE V, BYZANTINE EMPEROR** (718–775) Ruler from 741 to 775 and an ardent iconoclast, maintaining the policy of his father, Leo III (717–741). He persecuted monks who opposed his views and was unable to keep control over northern Italy, as the Lombards captured the Exarchate of Ravenna in 751, thus driving the papacy into a relationship with the Franks. These events overshadowed the military achievements of his reign, primarily his wars against the Bulgars and the Arabs. See also BYZANTINE EMPIRE; ICONOCLASTICISM.

**CONSTANTINE VI, BYZANTINE EMPEROR** (d. c. 803) Ruler from 780 to 797, the son of Emperor Leo IV (775–780) and the powerful Empress Irene. He came to the throne at the age of 10 with his mother acting as regent. Irene subsequently extended her authority over the entire government, and a protracted conflict arose in 790 when Constantine asserted his right to rule. He proved to be a weak and surprisingly unpopular emperor in his mother's place, displaying cowardice in war against the Bulgars, murdering opponents and divorcing his wife to wed his mistress, Theodote. Irene instigated a palace coup, deposing him in 797. He was blinded, and she assumed control of the Byzantine Empire.

**CONSTANTINE VII PORPHYROGENITUS, BYZANTINE EMPEROR** (905–959) Ruler from 908 to 959 but a greater scholar than a monarch. The illegitimate son of Emperor Leo VI, he succeeded to the throne in 908, but owing to the strength of the regency council, he did not rule until 945. Power in the capital was usurped by his father-in-law, Romanus I Lecapenus, who administered the government from 920 to 944, when he was exiled. In the interim, Constantine had developed scholarly skills and was a gifted writer. As emperor he proved himself able, continuing the policies of Romanus. A cultural revival was initiated, and the court was a haven for intellectuals and classicists. His own writings included a treatise on the imperial provinces (*De thematibus*); a biography of Basil I, *De administrando imperio;* a discourse on foreigners, especially useful information on the Slavs and Turks; and *De ceremoniis aulae Byzantinae,* a study of Byzantine ceremonies. See also BYZANTINE EMPIRE.

**CONSTANTINE VIII, BYZANTINE EMPEROR** (c. 960–1028) Ruler from 1025 to 1028, the brother of the powerful Basil II, who acted as his co-emperor from 976 to 1025. He played little part in the affairs of state in that era, and his own reign was spent in a similar fashion because he was elderly when crowned and used to a life of great ease. See also BYZANTINE EMPIRE.

**CONSTANTINE IX MONOMACHUS, BYZANTINE EMPEROR** (c. 1000–1055) Ruler from 1042 to 1055; a senator at Constantinople, Constantine wed Empress Zoë and became emperor with his wife and her sister, Theodora. Brought into the government in an attempt to salvage it, Constantine proved ineffective as the sisters squandered the imperial treasury, while two threatening events took place. The Petchenegs from Russia crossed the Danube River in 1048, and the Byzantines failed to defeat them, with the result that the empire had to pay them tribute. Second, the final schism between the Eastern and Western Churches commenced in 1054. See also BYZANTINE EMPIRE; SCHISMS.

**CONSTANTINE X DUCAS, BYZANTINE EMPEROR** (c. 1006–1067) Ruler from 1059 to 1067 and the disappointing successor to Isaac I Comnenus (1057–1059). Constantine proved unequal to the disasters that beset the empire during his reign. The Normans in Italy were ending any hope for Byzantine restoration of influence in the West. The Hungarians captured Belgrade in 1064, and the Petchenegs, Uzes and Cumans remained major threats in the Danube region. The Seljuk Turks also emerged as the dominant force in the East. Under Alp Arslan (sultan, 1063–1073), the Seljuks swept into Armenia and then marched across Asia Minor. See also BYZANTINE EMPIRE.

**CONSTANTINE XI PALAEOLOGUS, BYZANTINE EMPEROR** (1405–1453) The last Byzantine ruler, reigning from 1449 to 1453, the son of Emperor Manuel II (1391–1425) and the ruler of Morea from 1428 to 1449. He was summoned to Constantinople to succeed the childless John VIII Palaeologus (1425–1448) and proved himself an able emperor. It was his misfortune that he came to the

Constantine IX Monomachus

throne in the last years of Byzantine power. He tried unsuccessfully to gain support from the West to fight the Turks, including a very unpopular union of the Eastern and Western Churches in 1452. His defense of the city in the face of hopelessly superior Turkish numbers was courageous, but he died in the attempt, on May 29, 1453, near the city gates. See also BYZANTINE EMPIRE.

**CONSTANTINE I, KING OF SCOTLAND** (d. 877) Ruler from 863 to 877 and the son of Kenneth I McAlpin. Most of his reign was spent at war with the Norsemen, most notably Olaf the White, the Norwegian king of Dublin, and his son, Thorstein the Red. He was killed in a battle against this enemy. See also SCOTLAND.

**CONSTANTINE II, KING OF SCOTLAND** (d. 953) Ruler from 900 to 943. Succeeding King Donald II (889–900), he inflicted a crushing defeat on the Irish Norse in 904, thus freeing the country from continued harassment. A strong monarch, Constantine was nevertheless forced to submit to King Athelstan of Wessex in 934. Three years later he probably joined the confederation of Britons and Danes that marched against Athelstan and was defeated at the Battle of Brunanburh in 937. He abdicated in 942, in favor of Malcolm I (943–954), the son of Donald II, and spent his last years in a monastery. The "Song of the Fight of Brunanburh" described him as a "hoary warman." See also SCOTLAND.

**CONSTANTINE III, KING OF SCOTLAND** Ruler from 995 to 997. He died in battle and was succeeded by Kenneth III (997–1005). See also SCOTLAND.

**CONSTANTINE BODIN** (d. 1101) Serbian king of Zeta from about 1081 until his death. He led a rebellion against the Byzantine Empire in 1072 that failed, and he subsequently commanded a Serbian force that deserted from the Byzantine army at Dyrrachium in 1081, thus ensuring the fall of the city to the Norman Robert Guiscard. He became king over the principality of Zeta a short time later. See also SERBIA.

**CONSTANTINE OF SCOTLAND** (789–820) Ruler of the Picts in Scotland from 789 to 820, the son of King Fergus. Constantine was king at the time of the arrival of the Norsemen in the region (c. 793). Their destruction of Iona convinced him to move the ecclesiastical center from that site to Dunheld. See also SCOTLAND.

**CONSTANTINE THE AFRICAN** (c. 1020–1087) Physician, scholar and an important translator of Arabic medical texts. Born in North Africa, Constantine traveled extensively in the Middle East as well as in India and Ethiopia and thus spoke Greek, Latin, Arabic and other languages. He came into the service of Robert Guiscard, later studying at the University of Salerno before entering the monastery of Monte Cassino. The remaining years of his life were devoted to translating into Latin numerous Arabic works, especially Arabic texts on Greek medicine. The West thus received the body of Greek medical learning, including that of Galen and Hippocrates, as well as the writings of the learned Islamic physicians. See also MEDICINE.

**CONSTANTINE TICH** (d. 1277) King of the Bulgars from 1257 to 1277, the ruler during the recapture of Constantinople by the Nicenes and the return of the Byzantine Empire. Urged by his wife to attack Byzantine Thrace, he was defeated in 1263 during a counteroffensive. In the ensuing political struggles, Bulgaria was effectively divided, with Constantine ruling at Trnovo and the Hungarian-supported Jakov Svetoslav reigning at Vidin until his murder in 1275. Constantine was killed in battle against the usurper Ivajlo. See also BULGARIA.

**CONSTANTINOPLE** Capital of the Byzantine Empire until its capture by the Ottoman Turks in 1453. Now called Istanbul, the city amassed incalculable wealth and led the cities in Christendom in commerce, art and culture. Constantinople shared in the glories and tragedies of the Eastern Roman Empire while preserving for the West the vast heritage of its Greco-Roman heritage. It was called the New Rome, or Queen of the Cities, accurate titles distinguishing Constantinople as a metropolis superior to all others in the Middle Ages.

It was the desire of Constantine the Great (c. 288–337) to build a new capital for the Roman Empire. He chose the ancient city of Byzantium because of its position on the Bosporus, separating Europe and the East. According to legend, he allowed God to lead him from the shore of the Bosporus inland, not stopping until he had marked out the boundaries of the city that was to bear his name, Constantinopolis (City of Constantine). Inaugurated in 330, it was completed probably about 336, an astonishingly short time. From the start, life in the city was different from anywhere else. Roman law and government were influenced by Oriental custom and art, and a population that spoke Greek lived there. The result was an increasingly synthesized culture that became interwoven with the great heart of Byzantium, the church. An ecclesiastical center of tremendous importance, Constantinople emerged as a city of churches and the bulwark of Christianity in the East, a position that it would not lose even in the face of the schisms dividing it from the Western Church after the 11th century.

In 395 Constantinople was the capital of the Eastern Empire and in 476 (after the fall of Rome to the Goths) the center of the Roman Empire's declining authority. The transformation of the Roman to the Byzantine Empire was part of the acceptance of Greek and Oriental cultural stamped on all facets of government and society. Stable and wealthy, the city came into its golden age under Emperor Justinian I, whose reign (527–565) not only marked the zenith of Byzantine glory but also to its ultimate weakness. Whole portions of the city were rebuilt on grandiose lines after the Nika Revolt (532), reflecting the empire's resurgent power. Starting in 542, however, disasters and crises beset the empire and its capital. A plague in 542 depopulated many of the quarters, and sieges followed: Avars (626), Arabs (674–678, 717–718), Bulgars (813, 913), Russians (860, 941, 1043) and Petchenegs (1090–1091). Even the trade that had for centuries provided capital and riches fell to the hands of foreign states, the maritime empires of Venice, Pisa and Genoa.

Foreign pressure only mounted in the 11th century, culminating with the arrival of the armies of the Crusades. The overthrow of the Byzantine government by the stronger Latins came in 1204 with the Fourth Crusade. On April 13, 1204, the Crusaders burst into the city, bringing their own regime, the Latin Empire of Constantinople. The churches, palaces, shops and residences were looted, burned or confiscated by the Westerners, whose insatiable greed was matched only in the eyes of the Byzantines by their propensity for cruel massacres. By the time that Michael VIII Palaeologus (1259–1282) had restored the Byzantine Empire in 1261, Constantinople was only a shadow of its former self. Art and culture made a recovery, but the capital of the imperial lands of the East was, like the nation it represented, weakened and doomed.

For two centuries Constantinople lingered, with parts of the city falling into ruin, while the Ottoman Turks crossed from Asia Minor to Europe in the mid-14th century, seizing most of the empire, except for Constantinople itself. Appeals from the emperors to the West went unanswered, and the proud people, devoted to their Eastern creed, rejected a union with the Roman church that might have brought aid. In April 1453 the Ottomans began the last siege, using cannons to reduce the centuries-old walls. On May 29 the Turks breached the defenses, and Constantine XI (1448–1453) died while defending a city gate. Three days of plunder followed until Sultan Mehmet II (1451–1481), the Conqueror, entered. In 1457 he moved his capital from Adrianople to Constantinople, inaugurating a new age of Islamic rule. See also ART AND ARCHITECTURE, BYZANTINE; BYZANTINE EMPIRE; CONSTANTINOPLE, LATIN EMPIRE OF; CRUSADES; ICONOCLASTICISM; OTTOMAN EMPIRE; and individual emperors.

**CONSTANTINOPLE, LATIN EMPIRE OF** A feudal empire lasting from 1204 to 1261 and founded by the leaders of the Fourth Crusade with their Venetian allies as a replacement for the Byzantine Empire. The Byzantines, by 1200, had already been weakened by the arrival of the first Crusaders and by the resulting creation of the Crusader States in the East; thus the circumstances were set for the overthrow of the imperial government at Constantinople by the Latins. This came in 1203, when the chiefs of the Fourth Crusade, influenced by the Venetian doge Enrico Dandolo, were deflected by a set of circumstances away from a mission in the Holy Land to Constantinople. On April 13, 1204, they captured the city, sacked it and named one of their knights, Baldwin I (1204–1205), as the first ruler of the Latin Empire.

The empire's core was still in Constantinople, with feudal holdings in Thrace, Athens, Morea and Thessalonica. The Venetians claimed control of part of the capital, the harbor, islands and the churches, enforcing a Latin creed on the appalled Eastern Christian subjects. In place of the old Byzantine institutions, Baldwin named his fellow knights as aristocrats of the new feudal state that had the blessings of Pope Innocent III (1198–1216), who saw this as an opportunity to unite all of Christendom. Notorious for its corruption and tendencies toward pillage and greed, the Latin Empire was beset by troubles from the start. Baldwin was defeated and killed by the Bulgars in 1205, and three key splinter kingdoms kept alive the claim of Byzantine Emperors, those of Epirus, Trebizond and especially Nicaea. Latin mastery over the region was thus rendered tenuous, and after the death of Emperor Henry of Flanders in 1216, the empire was increasingly weak.

By the 1250s, it held jurisdiction only over Constantinople, having lost Thessalonica to Theodore Ducas of Epirus, Morea to the French, who gave nominal fealty to the Latin Emperor, and other territories to the Nicaeans. The empire of Nicaea proved far more stable and enduring, but the demise of its enemy, the Latin Empire, was delayed by Byzantine inability to unite. Under the Nicaean monarch John III Ducas Vatatzes (d. 1254) and Michael VIII Palaeologus (1259–1282), Epirus was defeated and subjugated in 1259. Two years later Michael entered Constantinople, toppling the Latin government and receiving the crown of the Byzantine emperor. The years 1204–1261, however, maimed the Byzantine Empire beyond the point of restoration. The city had been looted repeatedly and the economy ruined. See also BYZANTINE EMPIRE; CRUSADES.

**CONTARINI, ANDREA** (d. 1382) Doge of Venice from 1368 to 1382 and a brilliant statesman who initiated Venetian naval supremacy. A member of the Contarini family of Venice, in the War of Chioggia (1378–1381) he brought his city control of the seas, surpassing the Genoese, with the signing of the Peace of Turin (1381). See also VENICE; WARFARE.

**COPENHAGEN** Capital city of Denmark, situated on the eastern coast of the island of Zealand and the northern coast of the island of Amager. Copenhagen was originally a fishing village called Havn in existence from the early 10th century but first mentioned in 1032. A very important development came in 1167, when Bishop Absalon of Roskilde built a castle near the town and then built a wall around Havn for protection from raiders. Economic growth followed, and the city was a leading trading center for the region, eventually coming under the authority of the crown (c. 1417). About 1443 it was made the royal capital and was given a university in 1479 by Christian I (1448–1481). See also DENMARK.

**COPTIC CHURCH** The name given to the Egyptian Christian church, according to tradition founded by Saint Mark the Evangelist; the name derives from the Egyptian Christians' original name for themselves—from the Greek *Aigyptos* (Arabic *Qibt* and hence "Copt" in the West). They were staunch Alexandrian Christians, led by the patriarch there. Orthodox in their views, they headed the opposition to Arianism but supported such a precise view on the singularly divine nature of Christ that the patriarch Dioscorus was condemned by the Council of Chalcedon in 451. This caused the Coptic community to accept the doctrines of Monophysitism and thus to become increasingly separated from the rest of the Christian world. The Copts argued with their fellow Egyptians, who accepted the findings of Chalcedon and were called Melkites (or emperor's men). Attempts at uniting the Copts with the church failed and were made virtually impossible by the fall of Egypt to the Persians in 616 and then to the Arabs in 642. Under Muslim rule, the Coptic Church was permitted to practice its doctrine, generally unharassed. Aside from infrequent purges, the Copts were viewed more favorably than other Christians because of their disputes with the Byzantine Christian theologians. The Coptic language, a Hamito-Semitic tongue and a Bohairic dialect of Alexandria, was banned by the Islamic masters of Egypt in 997 but survived through its use in the liturgy, which also came to utilize extensive elements of Arabic. The Copts were aided by their ability to act as public servants in the government, being literate and generally possessing a superior education. Under the Mamluks (1250–1517) they became the backbone of the administration but were purged from all offices by the Ottoman sultans, an act leading to such chaos that they were quickly reinstated. See also EGYPT.

**CÓRDOBA** City in the region of Andalusia, Spain, situated on the Guadalquivir River. During its period of glory, from the 9th to the 10th century, Córdoba was the largest, wealthiest, most cultivated and prosperous city in the world, a bastion for art, literature and learning. It was probably founded by the Carthaginians, prospering as Roman Corduba, a major colony in the Roman province of Hispania Baetica. The birthplace of Seneca and Lucan, it was also the home of the influential bishop Hosius and an episcopal see from the fourth century. Under the Visigoths, who resided in Spain from the sixth to the eighth century, it was of reduced importance, the site of a religious struggle around 570 between Orthodox Christians and their Arian counterparts. In 711 it fell and was virtually destroyed by the Moors, who struggled for control over it among themselves until 756. In that year Abd-al-Rahman I (756–788) became the first Umayyad ruler of Córdoba.

As capital of the Emirate of Córdoba, the city grew quickly, reaching its zenith after 929, when Abd al-Rahman III (912–961) proclaimed himself a caliph. Córdoba soon became renowned in Europe and throughout Islam for its riches, both material and intellectual. Its artisans worked in leather and metal and its buildings were unmatched in architectural detail. The palace city of Madinat al-Zahra supposedly had fountains of quicksilver and roofs of gold. According to Muslim writers there were one million inhabitants, more than 250,000 buildings and a library of 400,000 volumes. While such figures were probably exaggerated, the last numbers were believed correct, for the Umayyads were great patrons of learning. The city was a center for the study of medicine, music (the Andalusian school), Islamic law and linguistics, attracting students and scholars from the East and West. Christians were allowed to worship until the days of the Reconquista, and there was a large Jewish population.

Starting in the 11th century, Córdoba was subject to the deterioration of Moorish unity in Spain and was sacked in 1013, during which the palace of Madinat al-Zahra was ruined. There followed a period of occupation by the Abbasids of Seville, the Almoravids and the Almohads, in which the political significance of Córdoba declined, but it lost none of its cultural greatness. This was the era of the development of such philosophers as Averroës and Maimonides. The collapse of the Almohads in 1223, however, made victory inevitable for the Christians, and in 1226 King Ferdinand III (1217–1252) took possession of Córdoba, marking the end of centuries-long Moorish occupation. Its economic position was retained for a time, mainly because of its strategic position for the Christian campaigns against Granada, but the fall of that city in 1492 extinguished any hope of a return to commercial prominence. The Great Mosque of Córdoba, finished in 476 and considered one of the finest examples of Islamic architecture, was converted to a cathedral in 1238. See also CÓRDOBA, EMIRATE OF; MOORS; and individual rulers.

**CÓRDOBA, EMIRATE OF** An Umayyad state ruling over much of the Iberian Peninsula from 756 to 1031, more precisely divided into two periods: an emirate from 756 to 929, and a caliphate from 929 to 1031. During this time the culture and power of the Moors were at their height in Spain and beyond, and the capital, Córdoba, attained its full glory. The dynasty was founded in 756 by Abd al-Rahman I (756–788), a member of the Umayyad dynasty who had survived the Battle of Zab in 750, in which the Abbasids defeated and subsequently massacred most of the reigning Umayyads. He fled to Spain, built an army and in 756 defeated the Islamic governor of Andalusia. Elements of the old Umayyad government soon joined him, helping in the successful repulse of Christian armies and Abbasid attempts at overthrowing him. He died in 788, and his immediate successors, Hisham I (788–796) and al-Hakam I (796–822), worked to consolidate the Umayyad position, mainly with the strength of Berber and Slavic mercenaries.

Abd al-Rahman II (reigned 822–852) was considered the most successful of the emirs, for his reign proved stable and prosperous. Relations with the Abbasid caliphs were improved, and diplomatic ties were made with the Byzantine Empire and the Franks. Problems occurred in the following years as Muhammad I (852–886), al-Mundhir (886–888) and Abd Allah (888–912) struggled with rebellions by Muslim freedmen in the provinces, the *muwallads*, most notably Ibn Hasfun, who occupied the region of Guadalquivir. Abd Allah failed to suppress the revolts but took the significant step of naming his heir, Abd al-Rahman III, in 912.

Abd al-Rahman III was the greatest of the Spanish Umayyads, by virtue of his long reign (912–961) and his immense political and religious achievements. He ended his grandfather's wars and won major triumphs over the armies of León and Navarre in 920, although he was routed in 939 by King Ramiro II of León. More important, he was a bitter enemy of the Shiite Fatimid caliphate of Africa, choosing in 929 to counter their influence by naming himself caliph of Córdoba. The city, under his patronage, acquired an even wider reputation for its religious tolerance and beauty. Rahman's war with the Fatimids was unresolved, however, despite the expansion of Umayyad influence in Morocco. The caliphs al-Hakam II (also called al-Mustansir, 961–976) and Hisham II (976–1009, 1010–1013) confirmed their ascendancy over Morocco, an acquisition made possible by the general and statesman al-Mansur (d. 1002), who eventually dominated the government. His sons, al-

Muzaffar and Abd al-Rahman Sanchuelo, failed to maintain control over the state and the caliphs. Sanchuelo's death (c. 1009) brought the decline of the dynastically exhausted caliphate.

Deterioration of central authority at Córdoba led to the rise of independent Muslim kingdoms throughout the fragmented caliphate, the Kings of the *taifas,* which were of Berber and Arab extraction. Civil wars ensued, compounded by the intervention of the Spanish kingdoms, such as Castile and Catalonia. Córdoba was sacked in 1013, and the caliphs were deposed or assassinated with appalling frequency. Further disorder resulted from the usurpation of the caliphate by the governor of Ceuta, Ali ibn Hammud (ruled 1016–1018). His family fought with the Umayyads from 1018 to 1027 for the throne until Hisham III finally claimed it for the Umayyads. His lackluster reign (1027–1031) ended with his deposition by the Córdoban nobles and the abolition of the caliphate. With that event, not only was the Córdoban administration eliminated, but so too was any semblance of order in Andalusia. See also ALMOHADS; ALMORAVIDS; MOORS; RECONQUISTA; individual rulers.

**CORK** Port and city in southern Ireland, which derived its name from the Irish *corcaigh* ("swamp"). A monastery was erected there in the sixth century, and the local community suffered repeatedly from the attacks of the Norse, especially in 821, 846 and 1012. The present city was founded by the Norse invaders, who made it a trading center and major cultural link with Scandinavia, ruling it with considerable autonomy until 1172. In that year Cork accepted a charter from King Henry II of England (1154–1189) and came subsequently under English influence. See also IRELAND.

**CORNWALL** See DUMNONIA, KINGDOM OF.

***CORPUS JURIS CIVILIS*** See JUSTINIAN, CODE OF.

**CORSICA** Island in the Mediterranean Sea to the southeast of France and bounded also by the Tyrrhenian Sea, the Ligurian Sea and the Strait of Bonifacio. It was conquered by Rome in 259 B.C. and lost in the mid-fifth century to the Vandals, who obliterated all vestiges of Roman civilization. The Vandals were driven out in 552 by the Byzantines, who in turn lost Corsica to the Lombards in 725. From the ninth century, and lasting until around 1050, Saracen raiders pillaged the coast, finally defeated by the navies of Genoa and Pisa. These two maritime powers then embarked on a long struggle. Pope Gregory VII, in 1077, used the Donation of Pepin to give jurisdiction to the bishop of Pisa, but even this prelate could not end the fighting. The question of supremacy was settled with the Battle of Meloria in 1284, a Genoese triumph. Genoa, however, faced a new rival, starting in 1296, when Pope Boniface VIII granted James II, king of Aragon, the right to rule over both Corsica and Sardinia. The ensuing war lasted until 1434, and Genoese colonies, conquered briefly by King Henry II (1553–1559), remained until the 18th century. Genoese rule was generally harsh but permitted a high degree of autonomy in local affairs. Corsican nobles were often at odds with one another and with certain other elements of island society, such as the Giovannali, a radical group of Franciscans who seized part of Corsica in 1358 and then required the help of Genoa to administer island affairs and to watch the nobles. Corsica was thus one of the numerous islands or cities that were wholly subject to the changing fortunes of medieval maritime politics or trade and commerce.

***CORTES*** The parliaments of the medieval Spanish kingdoms, first formed in the 11th century. They evolved out of the need of the various kingdoms to discuss matters such as warfare and to raise more money than would be naturally forthcoming from regular taxation. The municipalities, however, were required to give their consent, and thus elected representatives were permitted to attend and deliberate on certain matters as members of the Curia Regis (King's Council). The *cortes* of León and Castile held joint sessions after the union of the two crowns in 1230 and comprised the nobility, clergy and elected officials *(procuradores)* who represented their respective municipalities *(concejos).* In León-Castile the will of the king was highly influential, but other *cortes,* such as those of Aragon (there a *cort*), Catalonia and Valencia, were much more independent. Generally, throughout the 14th century the parliaments were ruled by the *procuradores* because they possessed the sole right to declare extra forms of taxation.

**COSSA, FRANCESCO** (1436–1478) Italian painter of the early Renaissance, probably born at Ferrara. A pupil of Cosima Tura, Cossa was later influenced by Florentine painters and Andrea Mantegna. The seven years that he spent at Bologna had a decisive effect on the development of Bolognese art. His most famous works were the polyptych for the altar of Santo Petronio in Bologna (c. 1474) and his frescoes the *Months* (c. 1470) in the Palazzo de Schifonoia in Ferrara, based on similar frescoes by Piero della Francesca and portraying the daily life of the court of Borso d'Este of Ferrara, also comprising astrological themes.

**COUNCIL OF SEVENTEEN** Venetian government council comprising the doge, his advisers and the Council of Ten. See also VENICE.

**COUNCIL OF TEN** Secret committee in Venice, established in 1310 to oversee the security of the city. It became a dreaded organ of state authority and a court from which there was no appeal. Founded to investigate the conspiracy of Baiamonte Tiepolo, the council was composed of the doge, his advisers and a varying number of members, 10 of whom were elected. Service was for one year only, and consecutive terms were not permitted. Aided by police, spies, assassins, and, after 1539, three state inquisitors, the council concerned itself with all matters vital to Venetian politics or economics. See also VENICE.

**COURTLY LOVE** See LOVE, COURTLY.

**COURTRAI, BATTLE OF** See SPURS, BATTLE OF THE.

**COVENTRY** City in Warwickshire, central England, evolving around a Benedictine monastery originally built by Earl Leofric of Mercia and his celebrated wife Godiva (Godgifu) in 1043. Ravaged by the Norse invasions, Coventry was reestablished in 1182 by royal charter. Its economy was based on wool and later cloth, and it emerged by the start of the 15th century as a center of textile-weaving and one of the largest English cities after London. Coventry was also the location of the Coventry plays, miracle pageants dating from the 1400s. See also TRADE AND COMMERCE.

**CRACOW** An important city in southern Poland, situated on the Vistula River. During the Middle Ages it was a leading economic and political center both for the Polish kingdom and for eastern Europe. Also called Krakow, according to legend it was founded around 700 by Prince Krak. The settlement of the local tribe of Wislanie, the community was subdued by Mieszko I in the late 10th century, developing into a trading depot for the region and named a bishopric in 1000. By 1138 it was the capital of the Piast dynasty of Little Poland. Destroyed by the Mongols in 1241, Cracow embarked in restoration, received the Magdeburg rights of a municipal constitution and, in 1320, was declared the capital of Poland's kings by Wladyslaw I the Short. Henceforth the monarchs were crowned and buried in the Cathedral of Saint Stanislas. The city prospered with extensive trade and a university (established in 1364) and was known until well into the Renaissance as an artistic, intellectual and cultural haven. See also POLAND.

**CRÉCY, BATTLE OF** See HUNDRED YEARS' WAR.

**CREMONA** City in the Lombardy region of Italy, situated on the Po River. Originally an ancient Roman town, Cremona was sacked repeatedly by the Goths and Huns and rebuilt in the seventh century by the Lombards. A commune in 1098, it gave its support to Frederick I Barbarossa (1152–1190) in his struggle with Lombardia but finally joined the Lombard League in 1167; its never denied its Ghibelline sympathies, however. Milanese influence was strong from 1334, when the city was first dominated by the Sforzas, and Milan's control there lasted until the 16th century.

**CRESCAS, HASDAI** (c. 1340–1412) Spanish Jewish philosopher and scholar. He was a merchant who became the leader of the Jewish community of Barcelona before gaining Aragonese royal favor. King John I (1379–1390) gave him the title "Crown Rabbi" with authority over the Jews of the kingdom, according to Jewish law. His position and wealth were lost, however, in 1391, during a persecution that led to a Jewish massacre at Barcelona, which included his own son. He wrote of these events in a letter to the Jews of Avignon. Crescas also composed "Refutation of the Principles of the Christians" (1397–1398) and *Or Adonais* (*Light of the Lord,* 1410), in which he attacked the Jewish Aristotelian philosophical tradition as represented by Maimonides. See also JEWS AND JUDAISM.

**CRESCENTII** Also Cressenzi, a powerful patrician family of Rome that dominated the papacy from the 10th to the 11th century and feuded with the Holy Roman Emperor for papal control. Crescentius de Theodora (d. 984) was responsible for the removal and strangulation of Pope Benedict VI (973–974) in 974, whom he replaced with Boniface VII (974; 984–985). He could not oppose the deposition of Boniface by agents of the emperor and died in a monastery. His son, John Crescentius (d. 991), probably was pivotal in having John XIV (983–984) deposed and murdered in 984, passing his patrician title to his younger brother, John Crescentius II (or Crescentius II). This Crescenti overthrew Pope John XV (985–986) in 995 and then drove Gregory V (996–999) the candidate of Emperor Otto III (982–1002), from Rome. In Gregory's place, Crescentius had the antipope John XVI (997–998) elected, but when Otto captured Rome in 998, Crescentius was decapitated. His own son, John II, duke of Spoleto, controlled Rome from 1002 to 1012, dying in 1012 just before the arrival of Henry II to be crowned Holy Roman Emperor. See also ROME.

**CRETE** A Greek island in the Mediterranean Sea at the southern limit of the Aegean Sea. Cretan history was ancient when the island came under Roman control about 67 B.C., and on the division of the Roman Empire in 395, Crete became part of the Eastern Empire (see BYZANTINE EMPIRE). It remained under Byzantine domination until 826, when the Arabs occupied it. In 961 Emperor Nicephorus II Phocas (963–969) reclaimed the island. In 1204, the Venetians purchased Crete during the Fourth Crusade, which brought the sack of Constantinople. Venice added it to its Mediterranean empire, maintaining Candia as a commercial outpost until 1669 and a successful Ottoman conquest. See also CANDIA.

**CRIVELLI, CARLO** (c. 1435–1495) Italian painter, born in Venice, who probably studied under the Paduan brothers Antonio and Bartolomeo Vivarini. He was also influenced by painters from Padua such as Andrea Mantegna and Schiavone. Originally a resident of Venice, he left the city (c. 1468) after being imprisoned for adultery, settling in the region south of Venice, the Provincia di Ancona. His works were religious in theme and reflected complexity and extreme attention to detail, with figures highly compressed and displayed in a formal hieratic style. Among his major paintings were *Madonna della Passione* (c. 1457), a *Pieta* (1485), the *Annunciation* (1486) and *Madonna della Candellata* (c. 1490).

**CROATIA** Region in the Balkans to the south of Hungary and northwest of Serbia, comprising the approximate extent of the old Roman provinces of Pannonia and Dalmatia. The named was derived from the Croats, a Slavic people who settled in the area around the seventh century and who were converted to Christianity probably a short time later. Croatia as an independent state came into being in the mid-ninth century; its first king was Tomislav, crowned in 925 by Pope John X (914–928). During the reign of Basil II (976–1025) the country fell under the control of the Byzantine Empire, but independence was reasserted under the leadership of Peter Kresimir (1058–1074). After Kresimir's death, Croatia was torn apart by civil war and annexed by Hungary. From about 1091 it was a part of the Hungarian kingdom, the king there ruling as monarch of Croatia as well, although a high degree of independence was retained in Croatia's internal affairs. The Croats were Christianized abiding by the rites of the Roman church and thus differed historically from their neighbors, who adhered to the Eastern or Byzantine rites.

**CROSSBOW** See WARFARE.

**CRUSADER STATES** The governments established by the Crusaders in the Middle East as part of the division of their conquests into feudal holdings. These states endured variously from 1098 to 1289, even longer in titular form. They evolved principally as a result of the First Crusade (1096–1099) and were officially under the control of the government at Jerusalem, although they exercised virtual autonomy. Of varying strength and stability, the Crusader States reflected the precarious position of the Crusaders in the Holy Land, and their demise marked the decline of Christian influence in the region. The Crusader States were:

**County of Edessa** (1098–1144), a territory founded by Baldwin I (1204–1205), its power in the city of Edessa. Baldwin became king of Jerusalem in 1100, successor to Godfrey de Bouillon. Edessa fell in 1144 to the forces of Imad ed-Din Zengi, atabeg of Mosul, a disaster that set off the Second Crusade. Its last count was Joscelin II.

**County of Tripoli** (1109–1289), the feudal county created by the capture of Tripoli by Raymond of Toulouse in 1109. He had claimed the title from about 1101, while still besieging the city, largely in response to the assumption of titles by his fellow nobles Baldwin and Bohemond. Tripoli lay between the Kingdom of Jerusalem and the Principality of Antioch, and was the site of castles such as Krak des Chevaliers. Ruled by the line founded by Raymond, it enjoyed considerable prosperity, and its fortunes were enhanced by the presence of a Latin episcopal see. The county was captured by the Mamluks in 1289, only two years before the fall of Acre and the loss of Palestine by the Crusaders.

**Kingdom of Armenia** See ARMENIA.

**Kingdom of Jerusalem** (1099–1187) See JERUSALEM, KINGDOM OF.

**Kingdom of Jerusalem-Acre-Cyprus** See JERUSALEM, KINGDOM OF.

**Principality of Antioch** (1098–1268), a state established by Bohemond I of Taranto (1098–1111) and one of the leading Frankish powers in the Holy Land as well as a major regional economic center. Antioch itself was a beautiful, cultivated city with fountains, running water, paved streets and sumptuous palaces. The ideal of Frankish colonial life was probably achieved there, although from the reign of Bohemond III (1163–1201) there was a Greek cultural ascendancy. Its last prince was Bohemond VI (1201–1233), who lost Antioch while away at Tripoli in 1268. The principality fell to the Mamluks, one of the most severe losses endured by the Christians in the Holy Land (see ANTIOCH; BOHEMOND I–VII).

**CRUSADES** Nine military undertakings during the Middle Ages, the Christian holy wars aimed at defeating the "enemies of Christ", such as Muslims or heretical sects, protecting the holy sites of Christianity and defending Christendom from attack, both from within and without. The Crusades, especially those launched in the Holy Land from 1095 to 1271, captured the historical imagination and reflected the pervasive force of religion within medieval society. Although often initiated for deeply spiritual reasons and executed by many out of faith, the Crusades also gave kings, popes, and knights who embarked on them opportunity for material gain, titles and thrones and the means to conduct political and military adventurism. For the maritime powers, such as Venice and Genoa, the wars meant the chance for trade and commerce of vast dimensions, principally at the expense of the Byzantine economy in the Levant. The campaigns of the Latins in the East not only resulted in the demise of the Byzantine Empire but also made possible the rise of the Crusader States and the evolution of military orders, organizations such as the Teutonic Knights and the Knights of Saint John, who carried on their own wars of religion long after the final loss of the Crusader holdings in the Holy Land.

There were crusades in other lands and for reasons that went beyond the goal of defeating Islam. The church led the Albigensian Crusade against the heresy of the Cathars in France, and the Teutonic Knights embarked on a conflict with the pagan peoples of the Baltic and in eastern Europe. The social and political atmosphere of the major endeavors to reclaim Palestine for Christendom, however, was established by the centuries-old hostility between Christianity

Crusader knight

and Islam. In Spain during the 11th century the Christian kingdoms launched offensives against the Moors, including the capture of Toledo by Castile in 1085. The idea of the "just war" to save Christendom was thus present in the minds of its leaders and the various populations in the West by the end of the century, requiring only circumstance to bring it to life. The first of these events was the triumph of the Seljuk Turks over the Byzantines in 1071 at the Battle of Manzikert. Asia Minor and the Holy Land were conquered, dealing a blow to the Byzantine Empire and the Fatimid caliphate, long tolerant of Christian pilgrimages to Jerusalem. The Seljuk Turks, devout Muslims, not only threatened Constantinople but were oppressive toward all pilgrims to the Holy Land. Emperor Alexius I Comnenus appealed for assistance from the West, and in 1095 Pope Urban II took up his cause. At the Council of Clermont he called on all Christians to join a Crusade, promising the blessing of God and with the cry: *"Deus volt!"* (God wills it!), the banner of the Crusades. See also CRUSADER STATES.

**The First Crusade** (1096–1099), generally considered the most successful of the Crusades, capturing Jerusalem and marking the foundation of the Crusader States, the Latin states in the East. A truly international army, its leaders were Bohemond I of Taranto, Tancred (Prince of Galilee), Count Raymond of Toulouse, Godfrey de Bouillon, Stephen of Blois and other nobles. After taking various routes, the Crusader armies arrived at Constantinople, alarming the local citizens. An agreement was signed with Alexius I, however, in which the Byzantines promised support in return for the loyalty of the Latins and the return to the empire of any previously held territory. Nicaea fell on June 19, 1097, and on July 1, the Crusaders won the Battle of Dorylaeum against Kilij Arslan, sultan of Rum. From October 1097 until June 1098, Antioch was besieged and finally fell on June 3. The city was then attacked by a relief army under Kerbogha, emir of Mosul, but he was defeated at the Battle of the Lance, so called because of the discovery of the Holy Lance in the city, which served as a rallying point for the troops. Jerusalem was reached in June 1099 and captured on July 18, followed by a massacre of the Islamic and Jewish populations, adding to Jewish massacres throughout the advance of the Crusaders. The Crusade ended with the triumph of Godfrey, now Guardian of Jerusalem, at Ascalon over an Egyptian army trying to regain Jerusalem. Many soldiers returned home, but a large number chose to stay in the Holy City or in one of the four Crusader States that had been formed: the kingdom of Jerusalem, Baldwin's County of Edessa, Bohemond's Principality of Antioch and Raymond's County of Tripoli. Godfrey died in 1100 and Baldwin succeeded him, becoming king of Jerusalem. Christian domination of the Holy Land seemed permanent.

**The People's Crusade** (1096), a famous mass effort organized by Peter the Hermit and Walter the Penniless, composed of many poorly disciplined and unruly groups who were fired by the crusading spirit and journeyed to the East. After causing chaos and conflict in parts of the Balkans, they arrived at Constantinople, only to be told by Emperor Alexius that it would be better to wait for the armies from the West. The mobs proved so unmanageable that the Byzantines allowed their departure, transporting them across the Bosporus. Many died of starvation, and Peter was forced to return to Constantinople for aid. Help never arrived, and most of the unarmed travelers were cut to pieces by the Turks near Civelot or were killed throughout Anatolia.

**The Second Crusade** (1147–1149), a crusade mounted in response to the shocking loss of Edessa in 1144 to Imad ed-Din Zengi, atabeg of Mosul. Emperor Conrad III of Germany (1137–1152) and King Louis VII of France (1137–1180), with his wife, Eleanor of Aquitaine, were the principal leaders, inspired by the preaching of Saint Bernard of Clairvaux. The Germans arrived first at Constantinople, moving not along the well-supplied coastal route but inland, following the path of the First Crusade. Near Dorylaeum, Conrad was assaulted by the Turks and nearly overrun. Louis learned of Conrad's defeat in November 1147 at Nicaea, moving on to Antioch with Eleanor. An assemblage of Frankish and German nobles decided to launch a massive sortie against Damascus, neglecting the fact that the real threat was Nur ed-Din Zengi, Imad's son. In July 1148, the ill-conceived siege of Damascus was begun by a very large Crusader army, but Nur ed-Din approached swiftly, necessitating the retreat of the increasingly factionalized Crusader military. A total disaster, the Second Crusade was a serious blow to the hope for Latin expansion in Palestine. Great European leaders had been routed, and much of the blame was hurled at Emperor Manuel I Comnenus, whom king Louis deeply resented. As for the Muslims, their cause was encouraged, and the reputation of the Zengids was assured.

**The Third Crusade** (1189–1192), legendary and probably the most knightly and gallant of the Crusades, led by nobles of great fame. The christian cause was represented by Richard the Lion-Hearted of England (1189–1199), King Philip II Augustus of France (1180–1223) and Emperor Frederick I Barbarossa of Germany (1152–1190), opposing Saladin. It was, in fact, the remarkable political and military success of Saladin that brought about the Third Crusade. The founder of the Ayyubid dynasty, Saladin became master of Egypt and then carved out his own empire, taking the territories of the Zengids and reigning from 1169 to 1172. His jihad, or holy war, against the Crusader States was brilliant, culminating in the capture of Jerusalem on October 2, 1187. Previously having completely destroyed the military power of the Latin Kingdom of Jerusalem and having taken prisoner Guy of Lusignan at Hattin (July 4, 1187), Saladin released him in late 1188. Guy gathered his few surviving followers and laid siege to Acre, a bold move that proved crucial for morale, even at the cost of thousands of lives. Saladin tried to break the siege but failed, and by 1191 help had arrived.

Frederick's march was the least successful and fatal to him, for he drowned in 1190 in Asia Minor (Cilicia) either while bathing or, more probably, while crossing a river, his armor being too heavy to carry. His sudden death was a crucial blow to the large German army, and only Frederick's son, and the infamous Leopold of Austria, with 1,000 hungry men, continued on to Acre. Richard conquered Cyprus while Philip sailed directly to Acre, joined after a time by the English. With Richard at their head from June 8, 1191, the Crusaders pressed foward, winning Acre on July 12, after two years of slaughter and disease. The victory was tempered by Philip's departure for France, a result of his bickering with Richard. The English warrior continued on and won the Battle of Arsuf on September 7, inflicting a heavy defeat on Saladin. Despite his best efforts, however, Richard knew that Jerusalem was beyond his reach. A treaty was signed with Saladin, allowing pilgrims to visit Jerusalem. More important, Cyprus was claimed by the Crusaders, and Saladin, the most able warrior that the West would encounter, died in 1193.

**The Fourth Crusade** (1202–1204), initiated by Pope Innocent III (1198–1216) but a Crusade that was fraught with crimes and that brought about the usurpation of the Byzantine Empire by the Latins. In response to appeals from Innocent, Baldwin of Flanders, his brother Henry, Boniface of Montferrat and Godfrey de Villehardouin all agreed to take up the Crusade. Transport was to be provided by the Venetians, headed by the doge Enrico Dandolo. Originally destined for Egypt, the Crusaders were convinced instead to sail to Constantinople, a plan aided by Henry VI (1190–1197), the German emperor, who opposed the Byzantines and was supported by the Venetians and Alexius, son of the deposed Byzantine emperor Isaac II Angelus.

When the Crusaders, fewer in number than expected, assembled at Venice in 1202, the doge suggested that because they could not pay the sum agreed on for the journey, they might earn their transport by aiding Venice in its conquest of the Hungarian dependency of Zara. The Christian city fell despite the pope's objections, and while at Zara, the expeditionary force was offered considerable financial inducement by Alexius to overthrow the government of Alexius III Angelus at Constantinople and to replace him with Alexius (IV) and his father. Dandolo was in favor, and the Crusader Boniface was swayed by Henry VI's representative, his friend Philip of Swabia, who, like the Venetians, was eager to see the decline of the Byzantines. On June 23, 1203, the fleet came to Constantinople, and in July Alexius III was deposed. Alexius IV and Isaac proved unable to hold the loyalty of the Byzantine people or to pay their promised sums to the Crusaders. Thus, on April 13, 1204, Constantinople fell to the Latins; it was pillaged and looted, and a new state was established: the Latin Empire of Constantinople, a disastrous regime lasting from 1204 to 1261, noted for its corruption and its damage to relations between the Eastern and Western cultures of Europe.

**The Children's Crusade** (1212), a Crusade that damaged severely the cause and the ideals of crusading. Elements of society still supported the ideal of freeing the Holy Land. This devotion led to a march of deluded children from all over Europe that originated in France but had no official royal patron. They were captured, murdered, shipwrecked, starved and sold into slavery, shaming the leaders of Christendom, who had greeted calls for another Crusade with cynicism and apathy.

**The Fifth Crusade** (1218–1221), a Crusade called by Pope Innocent III (1198–1216) in 1215. Once more Egypt was the strategic target, and Emperor Frederick II (1215–1250) and knights from Holland, Scandinavia, Austria and elsewhere joined. John of Brienne, king of Jerusalem, promised his support. An initial army, headed by John, landed at Damietta, beginning a siege that would last for more than a year. In September 1218, a papal force was added to the Crusader army, but its leader, the papal legate Cardinal Pelagius, insisted on assuming overall command as the representative of the supreme authority of the church. Frederick never arrived, despite Pelagius's optimism that he would. He rejected offers of peace by the Muslims, including the surrender of Jerusalem because of this conviction. Only Hermann von Salza and his Teutonic Knights arrived, joined by Louis of Bavaria, in 1221. Meanwhile, Damietta fell in November 1219, and after waiting for months, Pelagius (July 1221) ordered an advance on Cairo, in the heat and in the face of Nile floods. Not surprisingly, the Crusaders were forced to retreat and, after negotiations, surrendered Damietta in return for an eight-year truce and some holy relics.

**The Sixth Crusade** (1228–1229), a Crusade undertaken by Frederick II to lift the onus borne by him as a result of his actions in the Fifth Crusade. Eager to extricate himself from papal disapproval, he embarked on his mission in 1227, having already secured his position in the Holy Land by marrying Yolande, heiress to the Kingdom of Jerusalem. Fever broke out in the fleet, however, and the emperor returned to Sicily. Believing this act to be further proof of Frederick's insincerity, Pope Gregory IX (1227–1241) excommunicated him. Neglecting to resolve the problems the ban placed on him, Frederick sailed for the island of Cyprus in 1228, and the pope, thinking Frederick was countermanding his papal supremacy, renewed the excommunication, calling for a crusade against the emperor. Frederick consequently found no assistance in Palestine, other than the Teutonic Knights', but nevertheless opened negotiations with Sultan Malik al-Kamil of Egypt. The result was a treaty in 1229 in which Jerusalem, Bethlehem and Nazareth were ceded to Frederick as well as a strip of land to the coast. In return, peace would last for years and Islamic religious rights were kept for the Dome of the Rock and other sacred sites. No fighting had occurred, and the objectives of Christendom had been achieved. The pope, however, refused to accept the treaty, and Frederick had to crown himself king of Jerusalem on February 18, 1229. After Frederick's departure from the East and the salvaging of relations with the papacy, Jerusalem disintegrated into a city of bickering factions. The local barons fought with Frederick for independence, and their division made the final capture of Jerusalem by the Khwarizmian Turks much easier in 1244.

**The Seventh Crusade** (1248–1254). This and the Eighth Crusade were the last two great crusading endeavors, and both were commanded by King Louis IX (Saint) of France (1226–1270). His decision to go to war was in response to the appeals of Pope Innocent IV (1243–1254), who was horrified by the loss of Jerusalem to the Khwarizmian Turks and their Egyptian allies in 1244. Louis set sail in

1248 and in June 1249 took control of Damietta in Egypt. Waiting until the autumn to advance on Cairo, his army marched on November 20 but was halted by Muslims along the Ashmo Canal near Mansura. On February 8, 1250, the Battle of Mansura was fought, and initially victorious, Louis was nearly captured after the reckless and disastrous charge of his brother, Robert of Artois. Egyptian counterattacks compelled Louis to retreat, and on April 6 he was captured at Fariskur. The payment of a ransom of 400,000 *livres tournois* and the surrender of rights to Damietta secured his release in May, but he spent four years negotiating unsuccessfully for the help of the Mongols.

**The Eighth Crusade** (1270), brought about by the titanic campaigns of the Mongols in the Holy Land in 1258, as well as by the Mamluks. Mongol domination in the region was ended with the Battle of Ain-Jalut in 1260, marking the ascendancy of the Mamluks, especially under their sultan Baybars. City by city, he reduced the Crusader States, claiming Antioch in 1268. These losses convinced Louis IX (1226–1270) to make another attempt, largely because of the false promises tendered by the bey of Tunis to the king. Induced to land at Tunis instead of Egypt, Louis was joined by Charles of Anjou and found that the Tunisians were not eager to accept Christianity. A siege ensued during which an epidemic broke out. Louis and his son, John Tristan, both died in 1270. Charles took command, extricated the reduced army and, with the prince of England, Edward, at his side, sailed away.

**The Ninth Crusade** (1271 to 1291), the last strongholds and states of Christendom in the East were stamped out by Islam. In 1291 the city of Acre fell, the last holding of the Crusaders in Palestine. See also ALBIGENSIAN MOVEMENT; CASTLE; CHIVALRY; HERESIES; INQUISITION; LITHUANIA; LIVONIA; MILITARY ORDERS; NICOPOLIS, BATTLE OF; OTTOMAN EMPIRE; PAGANISM; POLAND; RECONQUISTA; RUSSIA; SLAVS; TRADE AND COMMERCE; WARFARE; and individual leaders or rulers.

**CULEN** (d. 971) King of Scotland from 967 to 971, who defeated King Dubh for the throne but died in battle with the Britons. His successor was Kenneth II (971–995). See also SCOTLAND.

**CUMANS** A nomadic people of Turkish origin, known as Kipchaks or in Russia as Polovtsy. The Cumans migrated during the 11th century to the Ukraine, where they became auxiliary troops of the Russian princes. They fought with the Hungarians and, threatening Byzantine interests, were eventually allied to Constantinople, annihilating the dangerous Petchenegs. By the 13th century, they had moved into the area near Hungary and were able to conduct raids into Russia and Transylvania. Christianized under Prince Barc about 1227, they came under the influence of the Kingdom of Hungary, from which they sought asylum in 1239, following their crushing defeat at the hands of the Mongols. Cuman power was broken by the Mongol invasion (1239–1241), and the remaining population was settled in Hungary by Béla IV in 1245. See also MONGOLS.

**CUNIBERT** King of the Lombards from 688 to 700, the son of King Berthari. He was troubled for most of his reign by uprisings among his dukes, especially Duke Alahis, who very nearly won the kingdom. See also LOMBARDS.

**CUSA, NICHOLAS OF** See NICHOLAS OF CUSA.

**CUTHBERT, SAINT** (c. 634–687) Bishop of Lindisfarne and one of the most popular and revered saints of medieval England. Originally a shepherd, Cuthbert had a vision and joined the monastery of Melrose in Northumbria in 651. He succeeded the prior of the monastery in 661 after an outbreak of plague, reportedly working miracles in his care of the sick. With the abbot of Melrose, Eata, he attended the Synod of Whitby in 664 and, despite his own Celtic background, supported the adoption of the Roman form. A short time later he and Eata were transferred to Lindisfarne, but in 676 Cuthbert retired to a life of strict asceticism. King Ecgfrith of Northumbria made him bishop of Hexham in 684, and the following year he became the bishop of Lindisfarne. Considered one of the holiest men of his time, Cuthbert was eventually entombed at Durham, a place visited throughout the Middle Ages by pilgrims. He also worked to protect the birds on the Farne Islands and thus was an early patron of animal conservation. Bede was the author of his biography. See also LINDISFARNE.

**CUTHRED, KING OF THE WEST SAXONS** Little-known king of the West Saxons from 740 to 756. He was able to assert his independence from the king of Mercia in 752, maintaining it until his death in 756. See also ENGLAND.

**CYDONES, DEMETRIUS** (c. 1324–1398) Byzantine statesman, humanist and scholar whose work in translating Greek knowledge for the West made him a forerunner of other Renaissance humanists. A supporter of the usurper

Saint Cuthbert's cross

Emperor John VI Cantacuzenus (1347–1354), he was compelled to leave for Italy after the ruler's fall in 1354. While there, he began translations of the leading Western writers, including Thomas Aquinas, and was converted to the Latin (Western) church in 1365. Having gained a scholarly reputation, Cydones returned home, taking a post in the government of Emperor John V Palaeologus (1341–1391), aiding him in his efforts to secure support against the rising threat of the Turks. Retiring about 1383, Cydones journeyed to Venice in 1390 with Manuel Chrysoloras. There he continued to introduce classical knowledge to the West, encouraging a reunion of the Western and Eastern Churches, and was a leading influence in the intellectual life of the city. Recalled briefly by Manuel II Palaeologus (1391–1425), he retired again (c. 1396) to Crete. A brilliant writer, in addition to his many translations, he composed an apologia for his conversion to the Latin church, a call for the union of the churches in order to prevent the demise of the Byzantine Empire, and many letters. With his brother, Prochorus, he attacked Hesychasm, the mystical philosophy developed by the monks at Mount Athos.

**CYNEGILS** (d. 642) King of the West Saxons from 611 to 642, who spent many years at war, most notably with the Britons and the Mercians. According to the *Anglo-Saxon Chronicle,* he defeated the Britons in 614 with such success that 2,000 of the enemy were left on the field. His campaigns against Penda of Mercia (621) and the Northumbrians were not as triumphant. In 635 he became the first Saxon to be baptized, at Dorchester. See also ENGLAND.

**CYNEWULF** English monk of the eighth or ninth century who was the author of four poems in Old English that were preserved in two 10th-century manuscripts, the Vercelli Book (the poems *Eleni* and *The Fates of the Apostles*) and the Exeter Book (*The Ascension* and *Juliana*). Although he is little known, his name is derived from epilogues for the poems containing runes that spelled out Cynewulf or Cynwulf. There is no evidence to connect him with Cynewulf, the bishop of Lindisfarne in the eighth century.

His poems reflect deep religious devotion, knowledge of Latin rhetoric and a style derived from Old English and Germanic epic traditions. *Eleni,* composed of 1,321 lines, recounts the finding of the true cross by Saint Helena. *The Fates of the Apostles,* 122 lines, concerns the legends arising from the deaths of the 12 apostles of Christ. *Juliana,* composed of 731 lines, deals with the martyrdom of Juliana by a Roman prefect and the cruel end he suffered. Finally, *The Ascension* was a lyrical rendition of the homily by Gregory the Great and was part of a trilogy, *The Christ,* on the Incarnation, Ascension and Last Judgment.

**CYNEWULF, KING OF THE WEST SAXONS** (d. 786) Ruler for an unusually long period, 757 to 786, the successor to Sigibert, who was overthrown in 757. Cynewulf had dealings with both Aethelbald and Offa of Mercia. In 786 Cyneheard, Sigibert's brother, attempted to depose Cynewulf, and both died in the struggle. See also ENGLAND.

**CYNRIC** (d. 560) King of the West Saxons from 534 to 560 and with his father, Cerdic, one of the founders of the West Saxon kingdom in England. He succeded Cerdic in 534 and was long engaged in war with the surrounding Britons, whom he defeated with the aid of his son and heir Ceawlin. Important battles took place at Searobyrg (Old Sarum, Salisbury) in 552 and Beranbyrg (Barbury) in 556. See also ENGLAND.

**CYPRUS** Island in the eastern Mediterranean Sea. Cyprus was part of the Byzantine Empire (or Eastern Roman Empire) for centuries but fell to the Muslims in 649. It was not recaptured until the campaign of Emperor Nicephorus II Phocas (963–969) in 965. It remained under Byzantine control until 1191, when Richard the Lion-Hearted (1189–1199) seized the island during the Third Crusade. The following year Guy of Lusignan purchased it, establishing the Kingdom of Cyprus under the Lusignan dynasty. That line ended in 1489 with Venetian annexation of Cyprus, control lasting until the late 16th century. See also TRADE AND COMMERCE.

**CYRIL** See CYRIL AND METHODIUS.

**CYRIL** (c. 827–869) **AND METHODIUS** (c. 815–885), **SAINTS** The "Apostles of the Slavs," two brothers who were scholars, linguists and important missionaries. Born to a noble family of Thessalonica and working together in 860 to convert the Khazars along the Black Sea, they were sent two years later by Emperor Michael III (842–867) to Moravia, where they evangelized the Slavs. They taught in the vernacular, using Slavonic even in the liturgy and making translations of the Scriptures in Slavonic. Cyril, however, invented an alphabet (Glagolithic) based on Greek letters, which became known as Cyrillic. He thus was instrumental in establishing the Slavic literature and language spoken in Russia and throughout the Slavic world. In 869 Cyril and Methodius were in Rome, where they secured papal permission to use the Slavic language in their liturgies. Cyril (known originally as Constantine) died there, and Methodius returned to Moravia as a bishop but faced constant conflict with German rulers and clergy, including a three-year imprisonment, ended only through the intervention of Pope John VIII (872–882). He died in 885, his supporters later exiled as the Slavic tongue in the liturgy was forbidden. See also SLAVS.

**CZECHOSLOVAKIA** See BOHEMIA.

# D

**DADDI, BERNARDO** (c. 1290–c. 1348) One of the important painters in Florence during his time, a pupil of Giotto, mastering his instructor's style of monumentalism but modifying it to apply his own sense of grace and simplicity, a style popular among contemporary painters in Siena. Among his works were a *Madonna* triptych (1328), *Madonna and Child with Saints* (1334), *Enthroned Madonna* (c. 1340), frescoes on the martyrdom of Saint Lawrence and Saint Stephen and *Madonna and Child* (1347).

**DAFYDD AP GWILYM** (c. 1320–c. 1380) The greatest of the medieval poets of Wales, a master poetic innovator, integrating the bardic form traditional in Welsh poetry with the styles of the French troubadours. He was born in Cardiganshire, the son of a Welsh noble. Considered superior to such contemporaries as Iolo Goch and Madog Benfras, Dafydd composed elegies, but his foremost contributions were in poems on love and nature, presented with humor, wit and sensitivity. He was buried in the Cistercian abbey of Strata Florida.

**DAGOBERT I** (c. 639) King of Austrasia from 623 to 629 and ruler of the Franks from 629 to 639, the last of the Merovingian kings to exercise actual political power, for after him the dynasty fell under the influence of the mayors of the palace and the monarchs became known as the "Lazy Kings." Aided by his competent minister, Saint Eloy, he was able to resist the plottings of his younger brother, Charibert, and his uncle Brodulf, putting the latter to death and forcing the former to renounce all claims to the throne. His reign was generally peaceful and prosperous, although there were some conflicts. In 631 he intervened in Visigothic Spain, suppressed a Gascon revolt in 637 and was faced with a constant threat from the Slavs to the east of Austrasia.

Dagobert visited Burgundy and Austrasia (630–631) to establish his supremacy but also to ensure local justice. He probably first met Pepin of Landen, the future mayor of the palace, around this time. Paris, he decided, would be his new residence, a move that required the appeasement of the Austrasian nobles. They were given his three-year-old son, Sigebert, as their king in 634, with the promise that Neustria and Burgundy would be secured for another son, Clotaire III. Considered a great king, Dagobert was also a patron of the church and learning. Monasteries were founded, including Saint-Denis, and his years saw a cultural revival. See also FRANCE; FRANKS.

**DAGOBERT II, SAINT** (d. 679) King of Austrasia from 676 to 679, the son of Sigebert III, succeeding to the throne in 656 but being deposed about 660 by the mayor of the palace, Grimoald, who established his own son, Childebert, on the throne. Sent to Ireland, Dagobert was not returned to the kingship until 676. Three years later he was assassinated while hunting; subsequently he was canonized. See also FRANCE; FRANKS.

**DAGOBERT III** (d. c. 715) King of Neustria and Burgundy from 711 to 715 or 716, the son of Childebert III. One of the weak Merovingian kings, he was dominated by the mayor of the palace, Pepin of Héristal. See also FRANCE; FRANKS.

**DALMATIA** Region in the Balkans along the eastern Adriatic coast, corresponding to the former Roman province of the same name. In the fifth century, Odoacer overran the territory, followed by the Ostrogoths under Theodoric. Years of fighting ended in 538 when the Byzantine Empire reclaimed Dalmatia, instituting a generally prosperous rule that was interrupted in the early seventh century by the Slavs. A theme (administrative division) by the end of the ninth century, it was successful economically as a link in Byzantine trade and thus became the object of foreign acquisition. From 1000, with the short-lived Venetian conquest, Dalmatia was under assault from Venice, Croatia and Hungary. By the start of the 12th century (the union of Hungary and Croatia in 1102), the country was essentially divided among the Byzantines, Venetians and Hungarians. The two latter powers struggled for centuries over Dalmatia. Venice controlled it from about 1204 to 1358, Hungary from 1358 to 1409, and finally Venice purchased it from Hungary in 1409, ruling from about 1420 to 1797. See also TRADE AND COMMERCE.

**DÁL RIATA, KINGDOM OF** A kingdom established in Ireland eventually incorporating Scotland, forming the basis of the Scottish kingdom. The origins of Dál Riata were lost in legend, but the rulers, situated in northern Ireland, were strong enough by around the fifth century to extend their influence beyond Ireland. Members of the Dál Riata dynasty crossed the Northern Channel, arriving in Scotland. There (in Argyll) they carved out a new domain, warring for many years with the Picts, Angles and Britons. One line of kings, that of Cenél Gabráin, outlived the others and was aided by the friendship and support of the monks of Iona. Scottish Dál Riata prospered despite the struggle during the seventh century between the line of Cenél Gabráin and that of Cenél Loairn, but the most serious development was the rise of the Picts. By the eighth century the Scottish Dál Riata kings and their Pict neighbors were bound inexorably together, culminating with the reign of Kenneth MacAlpin (843–858) and the union of the Picts and Scots under one crown. In Ireland, Dál Riata could not survive the invasions of the Vikings in the ninth century, and already declining, it inevitably vanished from history. Dál Riata was remembered in lore and often unreliable genealogies. More trustworthy sources included Adamnan's *Life of Columba* and the *Irish Annals.* See also IRELAND; SCOTLAND.

**DAMASCUS** The major city in Syria, one of the most ancient sites in the Near East, and, during the Middle Ages, a metropolis in the Islamic world. Damascus (Arabic: Dimashq) was an extremely old city by the fourth century, when it belonged to the Eastern Roman Empire. A Byzantine stronghold, it nevertheless fell in 635 to the armies of Islam. The Umayyad caliphs, beginning with Mu'awiya in 661, made it their capital. From there they launched their continued campaigns of expansion, maintained in close contact with the provinces. Damascus came to reflect the new position of the Umayyads, who erected palaces, public buildings and a large mosque, the former Christian cathedral that had been purchased by the caliphs. The Umayyads fell in 750, however, to the Abbasids, and the city was virtually destroyed by the armies of rebellion, eager to eradicate the Umayyad presence. With the new capital at Baghdad, Damascus declined seriously in population and in wealth.

In Damascus, a marble window from the Great Mosque

The Seljuk Turks occupied it in 1079, making it the headquarters for an emirate stretching to the Euphrates River. A strategic target for an advance on all of Syria, Damascus was besieged unsuccessfully by King Louis VII of France (1137–1180), Conrad IV of Germany (1250–1254) and nearly 50,000 troops. The powerful atabeg Nur al-Din claimed it in 1154, marking the beginning of a period lasting until 1516, during which the Damascenes were ruled by the masters of Egypt. The Ayyubids (1171–1250) initiated construction in the city, while the Mamluks (1250–1517) made Damascus part of their extensive empire, starting in 1260. Trade and culture were promoted, and the economic position of the estimable and proud Damascenes was greatly enhanced. Two Mongol invasions, in 1260 and 1401, caused considerable damage and loss of life, especially the latter attack by Tamerlane. Artists, scholars and artisans were all taken prisoner and sent to the Mongol capital in Samarkand. Rebuilding began immediately, but in 1516 the Ottoman Turks added Damascus to their territorial acquisitions, remaining in control for 400 years. See also SYRIA.

**DAMASUS II** (d. 1048) Pope in 1048, originally known as Poppo. He reigned for only 23 days, dying from malaria on August 9. See also BENEDICT IX.

**DAMIANI, PETER** See PETER DAMIEN, SAINT.

**DAMIEN, PETER** See PETER DAMIEN, SAINT.

**DAMIETTA** Also Dimyat, a town in Egypt at the Nile Delta, once very near the Mediterranean Sea and east of Alexandria. It was originally known as Tamiati, a Coptic name, falling to the Arabs in 638. A city with a lucrative textile trade, Damietta also commanded access to the Nile River, thus being strategically placed for launching advances on Alexandria and then Cairo. The armies of the Fifth Crusade (1218–1221) used the site in an attempt on Cairo, as did Louis IX (1226–1270) in the Seventh Crusade (1248–1254). Both campaigns failed, and Damietta was only briefly in the control of the Christians. Under the Mamluks the original community was moved further inland, thus becoming a favored site for banishment of exiles. See also EGYPT.

**DANCE OF DEATH** A common motif of the later Middle Ages that presented, allegorically, the idea of death as an inescapable and ultimately equalizing force. Known as the *danse macabre,* or the *totentanz,* the concept was expressed in art, literature, music, poetry and especially dance; it originated in the 13th or 14th century as a response to contemporary obsession with sin and penance or to the seemingly universal presence of war and death, as exemplified by the Hundred Years' War and the Black Death. Probably the earliest artistic work on the dance was the painting series found in the Cimetière des Innocents, in Paris, dating from 1424–1425. The image of Death, dancing while dragging away another victim, soon spread across Europe, serving as a powerful reminder that no one, neither pope nor king, knight nor lowly serf, could hope to be spared. See also PLAGUES.

**DANDOLO, ENRICO** (c. 1107–1205) Doge of Venice from 1192 to 1205, whose strong and vigorous term of office was made especially notable by his leading role in the capture of Constantinople during the Fourth Crusade (1202–1204). A member of the powerful Dandolo family of Venice, he spent years traveling on behalf of the Venetian cause, repeatedly to Constantinople, and was elected doge on June 1, 1192, at the age of 85, despite his nearly total blindness. His first act was to swear the "ducal promise" delineating his authority. He then revised the penal code, issued the earliest collection of civil codes, reformed the currency, promoted even greater trade and signed agreements with Verona, Aquileia, Armenia and the Byzantine Empire.

A war against Pisa in 1199 was successful, displaying Dandolo's willingness to go to extreme lengths to further the influence of the city. Nowhere was this clearer than in the Fourth Crusade. An arrangement was made with the Crusaders to transport them to Egypt in return for 85,000 gold *livres.* When the Christian army could not pay that amount, he gave them free transport in return for their agreement to attack the Hungarian (Christian) city of Zara. He also had a decisive influence in the Crusaders' decision to support the Byzantine claimant to the throne, Alexius IV Angelus (1203–1204). The fleet sailed to Constantinople, where the Byzantine emperor was overthrown and a Latin government installed (see CONSTANTINOPLE, LATIN EMPIRE OF). Having shown courage in the attack, the doge, nearly 100, took his large share in the division of the Byzantine Empire. A close ally of Baldwin of Flanders, the first Latin emperor (1204–1205), Dandolo was included in their defeat at the hands of the Bulgars in 1205. He returned to Constantinople and died there, having enormously increased Venice's prestige and wealth. He was called the "Blind Doge" because of his poor eyesight, the result, according to legend, of being blinded by the Byzantines about 1172. This story was denied by the chronicler of the Fourth Crusade, Geoffrey de Villehardouin. See also DANDOLO, HOUSE OF; VENICE.

**DANDOLO, HOUSE OF** One of the most important families in Venetian history, providing the city with four doges. The House of Dandolo rose to prominence in the 10th century, claiming increasingly powerful positions in the government of Venice until Enrico Dandolo (c. 1107–1205) became doge in 1192. His term of office saw the aggrandizement of Venetian power, including the overthrow of the Byzantine Empire and the sack of Constantinople in 1204 during the Fourth Crusade (1202–1204). The next Dandolo to become doge was Giovanni (d. 1289), who ruled from 1280 to 1289. He strengthened the republic and prepared it for its eventual conflict with Genoa. Francesco (d. 1339) was doge from 1329 to 1331 and promoted Venetian Continental expansion in addition to purely maritime acquisitions. Andrea (d. 1354) served as doge from 1343 to 1354 and was responsible for conducting the long war against Genoa. See also VENICE.

**DANEGELD** A tax levied by a number of Christian kingdoms in Europe to pay off the Vikings, especially the Danes, so they would to cease their raids. Though used from the ninth century on the Continent and in England, the danegeld developed into a systematized form of taxation during the reign of King Aethelred II (978–1016). According to tradition, it was Sigeric Serio, archbishop of Canterbury (990–994), who first advised Aethelred to buy peace with the Danes, following the English defeat at the Battle of Maldon in 991. Danegeld (or "Dane tax gold") was paid by the collection of levies, normally through already utilized forms of English taxation. As recorded in the *Anglo-Saxon Chronicle,* the sums were quite high, but not all of the money went to satisfy the Danes; some was applied to improve defenses and to pay for the fleets. The tax was collected irregularly until 1162. See also VIKINGS.

**DANELAW** A territorial division of Anglo-Saxon England, created as the result of a treaty signed about 886 by Alfred the Great and Guthrum, king of the Danes of East Anglia. Its name was derived from the Old English *Den lager* (Law of the Danes), the region being given to the Danes as their own, occupying much of northern, central and eastern England. One of the most important differences between the Danelaw and the rest of England was its legal system. Although the laws of Wessex and Mercia were quite similar, those of the Danelaw adhered to Danish custom, including uniformity of punishments for lesser crimes and the use of rank to determine the degree of a penalty. Socially, the stamp of Danish culture was irregular, with those areas directly colonized more Scandinavian. Over the entire Danelaw, however, the peasantry was generally freer, often responsible to a lord rather than bound to the land. Danish names also endured. East Anglia was the first part of the Danelaw to be reclaimed, followed by the rest toward the end of the 10th century. Subsequent Norman legal experts viewed the Danelaw as one of the three regions of England, with Wessex and Mercia.

**DANES** See VIKINGS.

**DANIEL OF GALICIA** (1202–1264) Also called Danilo Romanovich, prince of Galicia (Poland) and Volhynia (in Russia) from 1221 until his death, securing actual control of Galicia in 1238. He was the son of Prince Roman Mstislavich, a formidable man of wealth in eastern Europe. From 1221 to 1238 he suppressed all rivals in Volhynia and Galicia and then used his powers to increase the size and wealth of his territories. The cities of Lvov and Chelm were founded, and traders were invited to conduct business in the country. His political situation changed in 1240–1241, with the Mongol invasions. He crushed the Poles and the Hungarians at the Battle of Yaroslav in 1245, but he was never able to free himself entirely from Mongol supremacy, dying as their unhappy vassal. See also GALICIA (1).

**DANIEL OF KIEV** (d. 1122) Also Daniel Palomnik or Daniel the Pilgrim, a Russian monk, abbot and traveler. Daniel was best known for an extant account of a journey to the Holy Land in 1106–1107. An excellent source information on Palestine in his era, the narrative begins at Constantinople and continues with an account of his travels through Asia Minor, Cyprus and Jerusalem. He spent a year in Jerusalem and wrote a detailed description of the liturgical services conducted there on Easter.

**DANTE ALIGHIERI** (1265–1321) The father of Italian poetry and one of the greatest writers of Western literature. Dante was the son of Alighiero d'Alighiero, a Florentine noble and a supporter of the Guelphs, the family deriving its position from moneylending. He was educated in Florence, and his development was influenced heavily by Brunetto Latini and Guido Cavalcanti. The latter was especially helpful in fostering Dante's talent for poetry; an example of his regard for Cavalcanti can be found in a sonnet eventually used in *La vita nuova (The New Life)*, dedicated to his former friend. Another source of inspiration was Beatrice Portinari, who died in 1290 but would be extolled in Dante's *Vita* and again in the *Divine Comedy*.

In 1283 his father died, and Dante wed Gemma di Manetto Donati two years later. Subsequently he was involved in the political life of Florence. An ardent Guelph supporter, he was a member of the Guild of Doctors and Pharmacists, the Council of the the Hundred (1296) and one of the six priors of the guilds of Florence, elected in the summer of 1300. One of his acts was to exile Cavalcanti in an effort to show impartiality in the priorate, regarding the split that had occurred in the Guelph party, the group dividing into two main factions, the Blacks and the Whites. As a White, in 1301, he joined a delegation to Pope Boniface VIII (1294–1303) in an effort to reach a settlement with the Blacks, but in his absence Florence fell to the control of the Blacks. Dante was one of the first names that appeared on the Black's list of Whites to be condemned and exiled. He would never return to his native city, refusing to take up arms against Florence. He wandered through Italy until 1301, when he was accepted at the University of Bologna. Eventually forced to leave there as well in 1306, his hopes for a return to Florence were rekindled in 1308, with the election of Henry VII of Luxembourg as emperor of Germany (1308–1313). Dante begged him to march on Florence in 1310, when Henry arrived in Italy. The campaign was a failure, and Henry died in 1313. Dante then stayed in Tuscany, Verona and finally in Ravenna, where he lived as the guest of Guido da Polenta. In 1321, after returning to Ravenna from Venice, he suffered a bout of malaria and died.

Dante left a massive treasury of writings, the greatest of which is the *Divine Comedy*. About 1283 and 1291 he composed 31 lyric poems, comprising the *Vita nuova*, largely inspired by his love for Beatrice. Two other works were unfinished, *Convivio* (*Banquet*, 1304–1308) and *De vulgari eloquentia* (*On the Vernacular Language*, c. 1304). Another interesting minor effort was *Monarchia*, in which he put forth his arguments for a world government established in Rome, a destiny that he considered divinely ordained. There were also epistles in Latin and various poems, including *Canzoniere*, influenced by Beatrice.

His foremost contribution to Western literature was the *Divine Comedy* (or *Comedia*), an epic allegorical poem on the journey taken to salvation. Modeled on Virgil's *Aeneid* and drawing inspiration from the Holy Scriptures, the *Divine Comedy* was begun in 1306 or 1308 and was divided into three parts *(cantiche)*, *Inferno*, *Purgatorio* and *Paradiso*. The *Inferno* was completed by 1312. *Purgatorio* was completed by 1315 and *Paradiso* sometime after 1316 but before 1321. The story begins on Good Friday, 1300, with Dante discovering himself lost in the woods. Unable to find his way and prevented from ascending a hill by three beasts, he is forced back into the forest, where he discovers Virgil, the representative of Reason. Virgil has been sent to him by Beatrice, the Virgin Mary and Saint Lucy, to guide him through hell in the hope that he will acquire humility and the means of ascending into Paradise. His trip through the netherworld is penitential and imaginative, ending at the pit where Lucifer dwells. Purgatory is visited next, and Dante reaches the summit and begins his ascent into heaven, this time led by Beatrice, who takes him through the various spheres until he beholds the Beatific Vision, the supreme vision of divine love.

**DANZIG** Now called Gdansk, a seaport on the southern Baltic Sea at the mouth of the Vistula River. Originally a Slavic community, Danzig was first mentioned as a Polish town in 997. Swift development came through German immigration and German merchants, who made it a prosperous commercial center with eventual membership in the Hanseatic League in the 13th century. From 1308 to 1466 the Teutonic Knights were masters of the city, their rule ending as a result of a war launched by King Casimir IV of Poland. Autonomy was granted to the inhabitants, and by the end of the 15th century Danzig was the foremost Baltic port. See also HANSEATIC LEAGUE; POLAND.

**DARK AGES** A term formerly used to describe the era of medieval history from roughly the fall of the Roman Empire in the West to around 800. The precise eras involved, especially the dates of the beginning and the end of the Dark Ages, vary according to popular understanding and opinion. It was probably first adopted during the time of Petrarch (d. 1374) to distinguish European history from the collapse of Rome (c. 476) and the birth of the Renaissance. Intended to belittle intellectually the centuries that were covered by that era, the name Dark Ages was eventually narrowed in the 18th century to mean the years from either 476 to 800 or 476 to 1000, a time viewed as having been one of chaos, incessant warfare and formative government, virtually devoid of cultural vitality or practical advances. Recent scholarship has rejected the terminology because it is now widely accepted that the Dark Ages were far more complex and significant than previously believed.

**DA'UD** Ruler of the Seljuk Turks in Iraq from 1131 to 1132. He was succeeded by Toghril I. See also SELJUK TURKS.

**DAUPHIN** See Glossary and DAUPHINÉ.

**DAUPHINÉ** Region and province in southeastern France, corresponding to the modern departments of Haute-Alpes, Isère and Drôme. The territory was originally part of the Kingdom of Arles, nominally a fief of the Holy Roman Empire and controlled by the counts of Viennois. From about 1030 to 1162, it was ruled by the House of Albon, from 1162 to 1282 that of Burgundy, and from 1282 to 1349 that of La Tour du Pin. During the time of one of the Albon counts (c. 1133–1142), the name Dauphin became attached to the counts of Viennois and was used so often that it was ultimately synonymous with the countship. Their holdings became known as Dauphiné, and the word Dauphin was meant as a title. In 1349, however, the future Charles V of France (1364–1380) purchased Dauphiné from Humbert II (1333–1355). Once king, Charles established the practice of ceding Dauphiné to the royal heir (hence the term *Dauphin* for the successor). The area was annexed by the crown in 1457. See also FRANCE.

**DAVID I** (1084–1153) King of Scotland from 1124 to 1153, one of that nation's greatest monarchs, most remembered for his introduction of the Anglo-Norman nobility into the country, an act that had lasting importance in the history of the Scots. He was the son of King Malcolm III (1058–1093) and Margaret of Scotland, the brother of King Alexander I (1107–1124). David acquired Cumbria, Lothian and Strathclyde in 1107, lands that he held until the death of Alexander in 1124, when he succeeded to the throne. As king he continued to favor the Anglo-Norman aristocrats, whom he had come to know while staying in England (his sister Edith wed King Henry I) and during his reign over Cumbria and elsewhere. With their help a strong feudal government was established, for he granted them territory, built castles in such places as Edinburgh, Berwick and Stirling and issued a royal currency. Among the noble houses that migrated to Scotland were Bruce, Stewart, de Balliol, Comyn and Oliphant. David also supported the church in Scotland by founding numerous abbeys (Melrose especially) and forcing Scottish Christians to adhere to the Roman model. His ultimate aim was the independence of the Scottish church from the See of York. In his dealings with England he supported his niece, Matilda, against King Stephen (1135–1154). He lost the Battle of the Standard in 1138 and was thus compelled to negotiate a peace. His reign was considered one of success and prosperity. See also SCOTLAND.

**DAVID II** (1324–1371) King of Scotland from 1329 to 1371, whose reign was marked by political instability and the decline of monarchical power. The son of Robert I the Bruce (1306–1329), he was married in 1328 to Joanna, the sister of King Edward III of England (1327–1377), a union that did not prevent the outbreak of war between the two kingdoms. In 1333 Edward defeated David's regent, Archibald Douglas, at Halidon Hill, paving the way for Edward de Balliol to become the virtual king of Scotland. David fled to France, fought for Philip VI against Edward and returned home in 1341. A campaign to regain the throne was a failure and ended with his defeat and capture at Neville's Cross in 1346. It was not until the Treaty of Berwick in 1357 that he could secure his release with a promise to pay a huge ransom. He remained king until his death, but his authority had been reduced severely by the Scottish parliament, the nobles and his own unpopular tendency toward financial excesses. See also SCOTLAND.

**DE BURGH, HUBERT** See HUBERT DE BURGH.

***DECAMERON*** The famous work of Giovanni Boccaccio, written from 1348 to 1353, a collection of 100 tales told over a period of 10 days by 10 young people (seven women and three men), hence the title. The *Decameron's* genesis was the flight of the young people from Florence in 1348 in order to escape the plague (Black Death). Gathered together, each of the 10 agrees to tell a tale, every day, until the plague passes. These stories, ranging from the ribald to the humorous to the sublime, reveal depth, sensibility and, not least, Boccaccio's literary greatness. The book was the first masterpiece in Italian prose, inspiring the writers and, scholars of the Renaissance and the centuries thereafter. The songs (*canzone*) closing each day were some of Boccaccio's greatest lyric poems. See also BOCCACCIO, GIOVANNI.

**DEIRA, KINGDOM OF** Kingdom in northern England lasting, according to tradition, from 560 until its union with Bernicia in 670 to form the Kingdom of Northumbria. Deira stretched from the Humber to the Tyne River, its first king, according to legend, being Aelle (d. c. 590). From the time of Aethelfrith (ruled 593–616) it was linked with Bernicia. See also NORTHUMBRIA.

**DELLA ROBBIA, LUCA** See ROBBIA, LUCA DELLA.

**DELLA SCALA** See SCALA, DELLA.

**DENMARK** Country in northern Europe and the southernmost of the Scandinavian nations, with which it was closely tied culturally and politically. The history of early Denmark, which included the Viking age, has long been viewed romantically, but the often bloody social and political conflicts that characterized much of Danish development had a profound effect on other regions, most notably England, Germany and the Baltic. The Danes first enter medieval events in the fifth century, when the Jutes and Angles of the region invaded the weakened Roman province of Britain, bringing massive cultural upheavals to the island. Christianity was brought to Denmark during the eighth century, through the work of Willibrord, who established churches and monasteries; paganism, of course, still flourished.

Throughout the 800s, the Danes participated in the extensive migrations and Viking raids that brought the Norse to England, Ireland, France, Spain and even Africa. The Danish foothold in England was strong, including the establishment of the Danelaw, the region in England under Danish domination, and the danegeld, payments to them by the English ruler to prevent further bloodshed. According to tradition and his own personal claims, the first king to unify all of Denmark was Harald Bluetooth, who

(c. 960) accepted Christianity. His son, Sven Forkbeard, and formidable grandson, Canute, not only reigned in Denmark but also established and expanded an empire that came to encompass England, lasting until their separation following the death of Canute in 1042. Peace and relative stability allowed a number of kings to improve political organization and to encourage an acceptance of Christianity by the people of Denmark.

The 12th century brought frequent civil wars between royal claimants and between the king and the people or the church. Denmark was also troubled by the Wends (Slavs), who interfered with Baltic trade. Waldemar I the Great (1157–1182) undertook several campaigns against the Wends. His son, Canute VI (1182–1202), annexed Pomerania and Mecklenburg, while Waldemar II Sejr (1202–1241), added Holstein and made attempts to acquire Estonia. In 1227, however, he was routed at Borkved, captured by Henry of Schwerin and lost most of his imperial possessions. Waldemar was also the creator of the royal council, or *hof*, composed of nobles and church officials. Representing the dual powers of the aristocracy and the church, the *hof* compelled Eric Glipping, Waldermar's grandson, to sign in 1282 the first Danish constitution, by which he agreed to adhere to certain laws. King Christopher II (ruled 1319–1326; 1330–1332) made the *hof* permanent, but on his death the chaos of succession and social unrest were such that the counts of Holstein, already in control of vast stretches of Danish land, ruled the country with a harsh hand from 1332 to 1340.

A major change came during the reign of Waldemar IV Atterdag (d. 1375) in 1340. Considered one of the greatest Scandinavian monarchs, he reestablished the unity of Denmark, reclaimed Danish holdings abroad, seized the Ore Sound to demand dues on vessels entering the Baltic and defeated the Hanseatic League in 1362. An alliance of the Hanse, rebellious Danes of great wealth, and the Holstein and Mecklenburg nobles drove him out in 1367, and three years later the Treaty of Stralsund was signed, granting concessions to the Hanseatic League. After Waldemar's death in 1375, without a male heir, his daughter Margaret, wife of King Haakon VI of Norway (1355–1380), ruled as regent for her son, Olaf II (1375–1387). In 1387 Olaf died, and she was accepted as queen of Denmark and Norway. Unhappy with their king, Albert of Mecklenburg, the Swedish nobles accepted her as queen of Sweden as well in 1389, although she was not able to govern the kingdom until 1398. This arrangement, known as the Kalmar Union, was probably never signed in 1397, but Eric of Pomerania, Margaret's sister's grandson, was chosen as successor. He reigned from 1396 to 1439, when he was deposed, followed by Sweden's independence in 1439 and Norway's cessation in 1442. In 1440, his nephew, Christopher of Bavaria, was made king by the Danish royal council, adopted later by Sweden (1440) and Norway (1442). His childless demise in 1448 brought a complete change of dynasties as Count Christian of Oldenburg was chosen to succeed, ruling from 1448 to 1481 as Christian I and receiving acknowledgment by the Norwegians in 1450 but holding the crown in Sweden only from 1451 to 1454. John I (ruling 1481–1513) continued the Oldenburg line, following his father as king of Denmark and Norway. See also VIKINGS and individual rulers.

**DERMOT MACMURROUGH** (d. 1171) Also Diarmuid mac Murchada, Irish king of Leinster and the man largely responsible for the arrival of the English in Ireland. He became king in 1126, spending the next years fighting and removing rivals or usurpers of the throne, finally establishing his control by 1141. In 1153 he abducted the wife of Tiernan O'Ruark, king of Breifne (a minor Irish realm), setting off a bitter struggle that ended only in 1166 with Dermot's deposition and exile into England. Traveling to King Henry II (1154–1189), he received permission to mount an expedition to Ireland and recruited several Norman lords to his cause, including Robert Strongbow (Robert de Clare, second earl of Pembroke). The force, headed by Dermot, landed at Leinster in 1167, later supported by Pembroke, who arrived with his troops in 1170. Dublin fell in 1170, and Dermot reclaimed his crown. When he died in 1171, the throne was claimed by Pembroke, who had married his daughter. See also IRELAND.

**DESCHAMPS, EUSTACE** (c. 1346–c. 1406) French poet, born at Vertus and student of the poet Guillaume de Machaut before taking up law at Orléans. Under Charles V (1364–1380) and Charles VI (1380–1422), he held a variety of government and diplomatic offices, returning home in 1380 to write poetry. Active as a writer, he composed rondeaux, ballades, dramatic and comic plays and a satire on women, *Le miroir de mariage*. Of particular note were his ballad for Geoffrey Chaucer and his 1392 treatise on verse, *L'Art de dictier*. A moralist, political observer and gifted satirist, his work changed toward the end of his life dwelling on more serious themes, largely because of the effect of the Hundred Years' War on his views.

**DESIDERATA** The daughter of the Lombard king Desiderius, who married Charlemagne in 770. Because of her father's march on Rome, however, Charlemagne repudiated the union and declared war on the Lombards. See also CHARLEMAGNE.

**DESIDERIO DA SETTIGNANO** (1430–1464) One of the acclaimed Florentine sculptors of his time and a brilliant technical artist. Few facts about his life are known, except that he came from Settignano and probably studied with Antonio Rossellino. His work reflected the influence of Donatello, especially in his use of low-relief carving (the *rilievo stiacciato* or *schiacciato*), choosing, however, to pursue themes that were more delicate and subtle. Thus his finest carvings were church decorations or busts of women and children. Among his notable works were the monument to Carlo Marsuppini in Santa Croce, Florence (1453), and the altar of San Lorenzo in Florence (1461).

**DESIDERIUS** (d. after 774) King of the Lombards and the last ruler of the Lombard kingdom, whose reign (757–774) was ended by his defeat at the hands of Charlemagne (768–814). Desiderius was the duke of Tuscany, becoming king on the death of Aistulf in 756. His relations with the papacy were poor, an agreement with Pope Stephen II (752–757) made by Desiderius was broken and later he would march on Rome. With the powerful Franks, however, he adopted a conciliatory attitude, establishing links with both Charlemagne and his brother, Carloman. In 770 Charlemagne married Desiderata, his daughter, repudiating the union the following year, officially because she was barren and ill but probably because he was aware that in the event of civil war between the Frankish monarchs, Desiderius was prepared to ally himself with Carloman. On Carloman's death (771) Charlemagne seized his brother's lands. The royal widow and her sons fled to Lombardy, taking refuge with Desiderius. The Lombards then took the provocative step of attacking Rome. Pope Adrian I (772–795) appealed to Charlemagne, who in late 772 invaded Italy, besieging and capturing Pavia in 773, at which time he deposed Desiderius and took the iron crown of the Lombards for himself. Desiderius and his wife were sent to France, dying after a number of years in a monastery, probably Corbie. See also LOMBARDS.

**DESPENSER, HUGH LE** The name of two influential English nobles, father and son, called Hugh le Despenser the Elder and the Younger. Hugh the Elder (1262–1326) became an important adviser to Edward II (1307–1327) after the execution of Piers Gaveston in 1312. He was soon joined by his son, but both were exiled by the barons in 1321. Returning to England in 1322, the Elder received the title of earl of Winchester and his son the position of chamberlain to the king. Together they ruled the country in Edward's name until 1326, when Queen Isabella and her political ally and paramour, Roger Mortimer, returned to England. The Despensers were overthrown, fleeing with the king. Hugh the Elder was captured in October 1326 at Bristol, and his son was taken a month later. Both died immediately. See also ENGLAND.

**DEUSDEDIT (1)** (d. 618) Pope from 615 to 618, also called Adeodatus I or Deusdedit I. His reign was distinguished largely by his support of the war fought by the armies of the Byzantine Empire against the Lombards for control of Italy.

**DEUSDEDIT (2)** (d. 664) Archbishop of Canterbury, the ranking prelate of England from 655 to 664, the first Anglo-Saxon made archbishop of Canterbury. He was mentioned by Bede in the *Ecclesiastical History*. See also CANTERBURY.

**DEVENTER** Town in the east-central Netherlands, situated on the Ijssel (Yssel) River. Founded in the eighth century, it developed into a regional economic center, joining the Hanseatic League in the 13th century. Its two major financial strengths were its ownership of most of the trade in dried cod and its five annual fairs. Deventer was also a noted site of learning, claiming such students as Thomas à Kempis and Gerhard Groote, founder of the Brotherhood of the Common Life.

***DICTATUS PAPAE*** A collection of 27 statements defining papal power, issued probably during the papacy of Gregory VII (1073–1085). The proclamations were an attempt to support the position of the popes as the spiritual leaders of Christendom, essential because of the papacy's struggle with the emperors. From broad general claims to detailed assertions, the statements ultimately declare the pope to be superior to all other members of the clergy, his authority exceeding that of kings and even emperors. Further, while the pontiff could depose or remove any monarch, kings and emperors did not have that power over him.

**DIETRICH OF NIEHEIM** (d. 1418) Papal official and writer, a member of the papal Curia, holding several posts but eventually an ardent supporter of the conciliar movement. Hoping to end the Great Schism, he attended the Council of Constance (1414–1418), leading the attack on the antipope John XXIII. His writings favored conciliarism, reform and the reduction of papal power. They included *De schismate* (1410) and two treatises on curial administration. See also CONCILIAR MOVEMENT.

**DIETRICH VON BERN** Legendary Germanic heroic figure whose deeds were preserved in many epics, including *Thidricks Saga* (Iceland, 13th century) and the *Niebelungenlied*. Dietrich has been identified with Theodoric the Great, king of the Ostrogoths from 493 to 526.

**DIGENES AKRITAS** The most famous Byzantine hero, whose life and deeds were preserved in folktales and in the epic of the same name. Digenes Akritas was probably an actual figure of the eighth century, whose reputation as the supreme Byzantine warrior became the basis for tales and, in the 11th or 12th century, for an epic. He was the son of a Saracen convert and a Byzantine mother, spending most of his life engaged in defending the empire from foreign threats. The epic, appearing in versions until the 17th century, relied on a number of motifs, including Greek and Oriental. It also contained valuable information on the conflict between the Byzantine Empire and Islam.

**DIMITRY DONSKOI** (1350–1389) Grand prince of Moscow from 1359 to 1389, who was responsible for the rise of Moscow as the primary seat of power in central Russia. The son of Ivan II the Meek of Moscow, he succeeded his father at the age of nine but within three years also possessed the title of grand prince of Vladimir, thanks to the acquiescence of the khan of the Golden Horde, then politically and militarily supreme in Russia. Years of war, followed however, as Dimitry struggled with his main rival, Michael, prince of Tver, who was allied with Lithuania. By 1375, Dimitry was able to secure the surrender of Michael and his acceptance of Moscow's suzerainty. Having solidified his position, Dimitry next turned on his Mongol overlords, defeating them in 1378 and again at the Battle of Kulikovo on the Don River in 1380. This triumph over the Golden Horde not only dealt a major blow to Mongol invincibility but also prevented the alliance of the Mongols, the Lithuanians and the Principality of Ryazan.

Dimitry claimed the title Donskoi ("of the Don") in celebration of the victory. His status as the hero of Russia was short lived, for in 1381–1382, a new Mongol army poured into the country, sacking Moscow and establishing control. Dimitry is also listed as Dimitry III Donskoi. See also MOSCOW, GRAND PRINCES OF; RUSSIA.

**DINIS** (1261–1325) King of Portugal from 1279 to 1325, whose reign was particularly successful for the economy and the monarchy of Portugal. Trade was encouraged, and he so encouraged agricultural advances that he earned the name "the Farmer." The church and aristocracy were reduced in power and authority, thereby strengthening the crown, and further territory was added by its seizure of the Templars' holdings. Dinis also supported the arts and founded the University of Lisbon in 1290. His wife was Isabel of Portugal, later canonized by the church. See also PORTUGAL.

**DIONYSIUS EXIGUUS** (d. c. 560) Noted Scythian monk, mathematician, canonist, astronomer and the creator of the Christian calendar. According to the sixth-century historian Cassiodorus, he was extremely humble hence his name Dionysius Exiguus (Denis the Little). In the service of the popes from about 496, including the organization of the papal archives, he began in 525 to organize a Christian chronology. Using the Roman calendar as the basis for his work, he calculated the birth of Christ to be 754 years after the founding of Rome. On the Roman model, Christ was born in 753. This system was accepted by the Synod of Whitby in 664 and was adopted throughout Christian lands. Dionysius was also a leading canonist, responsible for the *Collectio Dionysiana*, a compilation of the canons of the councils of Sardinia, Nicaea, Constantinople and Chalcedon, the Apostolic Canons and papal decretals from the late fourth to the late fifth century. He made translations of the Greek patristic writings into Latin, including a life of Saint Pachomius.

**DIONYSIUS THE AREOPAGITE** See PSEUDO-DIONYSIUS.

**DIONYSIUS THE CARTHUSIAN** (1402–1471) Flemish theologian and mystic as well as an important spiritual writer. Dionysius (Denys van Leeuwen, Denys Rychel) was educated at Cologne, joining the Carthusian order in 1423 or 1425 at Roermund in the Netherlands. He later journeyed to Germany (1451–1452) with Nicholas of Cusa to preach reforms in the church and to call for a Crusade against the Turks. A popular spiritual author, he wrote commentaries on the Old and New Testaments, works on theology, moral discipline and mysticism (the widely read *De contemplatione*) and further commentaries on Boethius, Peter Lombard and Dionysius the Areopagite (Pseudo-Dionysius). His intense mysticism earned him the title "Doctor Ecstaticus." See also MYSTICISM.

***DIVINE COMEDY*** See DANTE ALIGHIERI.

**DOGE** The highest governmental position in the republic of Venice from 697 to 1805, an office later adopted by Genoa in 1339. It originated in Venice during the era of Byzantine control, the name deriving from the Latin *dux* ("leader"); the first doge is traditionally considered to have been Paulutius (Paolo) Anafestus, elected and confirmed by the Byzantines in 697. Throughout the first years of doge rule, Venice remained under Byzantine influence, and the doges exercised restricted power. It was not until the ninth century and the securing of Venetian independence that the doges assumed greater political significance. Elected for life, they guided the Venetian state, but efforts to make the post hereditary, or to extend their powers, were rebuffed by Venice's aristocracy. From the 11th century the office was increasingly limited to command of the navies of the republic and the conduct of wars or operations for state security. Crucial in this decline of the doge's power was the development of councils, such as the Maggior Consiglio (Great Council) and the Council of Ten. In time, the doge's role became largely ceremonial in Venice, while the doges in Genoa had difficult and frequently short terms of office, having been elected to end the chronic conflicts between the city's political factions. See also GENOA; VENICE; and individual doges.

***DOLCE STIL NUOVO*** The "sweet new style" of writing adopted by a group of Italian (Florentine) poets during the years 1250–1300, originally employed by Dante in his *Purgatorio* and characterized by delicacy, by an idealization of courtly love and womanhood and by a musicality finding rich expression in ballads, sonnets and *canzoni*. According to Dante, the greatest practitioners of his time were Guido Guinizelli, Guido Cavalcanti and Dante himself. Others were Cino da Pistoia, Dino Frescobaldi and Lapo Gianni. Petrarch was also influenced by the style. The origins of *dolce stil nuovo* were probably the troubadour poetry of Provence.

**DOMENICO VENEZIANO** (d. 1461) Italian painter of the early Renaissance, probably from Venice but studying in Florence and remaining there throughout his life from 1439, except for brief intervals of travel. He was a master of the use of color and light. Only two of his signed works have survived: the Carnesecchi Tabernacle, dating from about 1440, and the altarpiece painted for the church of Santa Lucia dei Magnoli (c. 1445), depict a Madonna and four saints. The now separated predellas (altarpiece bases) included the very remarkable *Annunciation*. Paintings attributed to him include the *Adoration of the Magi* and portraits of Matteo and Michele Oliviere and Saints John and Francis.

**DOME OF THE ROCK** See JERUSALEM.

**DOMESDAY BOOK** The two-volume manuscript containing the survey of the geography, people and landholdings conducted throughout England at the order of William I the Conqueror in 1087. Originally termed the "description of England," the book became known as the Domesday, for from its directives there was no appeal. The means by which Norman feudal institutions were absorbed by the English, the book represents one of the most impressive feats of government administration in medieval history.

The survey and subsequent compilations were undertaken by order of William in 1086 and completed in 1087, just prior to his death, but in great haste and in the face of widespread resentment. Not only were the royal commissioners ruthless and swift, the assessment was conducted with the aim of institutionalizing Norman feudal organization, in the belief that all land was held by the king or by those who had been given such land for service to the Crown. The king was thus aware of his total holdings, and for the subsequent distribution of feudal titles to the Norman landholders there was a highly detailed record of tenure and taxation.

The process used by the royal commissioners in the execution of their duties was preserved in the *Inquisitio Comitatus Cantabrigiensis (Inquisition of the County of Cambridge)*, the original material used for Domesday in the region of Cambridgeshire. A Norman inquest was applied, with jurors summoned to swear to the accuracy of the data compiled on each piece of land, even the smallest village. This information, reorganized to make clear that ownership rested with the king, was then sent to Winchester for abbreviation and summation by the scribes of the treasury. The basic manner of organization was by county, with a list made of all landholders, starting with the king and including all ranks to the very lowest tenant. Details included the size of an estate, a topographical description, its number of workers and other pertinent figures and an assessment of its total value in pounds. Unfortunately, the reports were not consistent, with omissions obvious, the most notable of which was London. All of the descriptions were entered into a massive compendium. Domesday (although that name was not applied until the 12th century) included two volumes: Volume 1, Great Domesday, contained the survey for most of the country; Volume 2, called Little Domesday, contained the survey for Essex, Suffolk and Norfolk. For some reason these counties were not summarized, possibly because of William's death, and are preserved in the unabbreviated text. Of interest as well was the Exon Domesday, an original draft for the returns from Devon, Cornwall, Somerset, Dorset and Wiltshire. Domesday, in all of its forms and volumes, was a vital source for historical detail in Norman England and provided information on life in the 11th century.

**DOMINIC, SAINT** (c. 1170–1221) Founder of the Order of Friars Preachers (the Dominicans) and a major spokesman for the medieval mendicant friars. He was born Domingo de Guzmán at Calaruega, Castile, the son of a noble. Educated at Palencia, he joined (c. 1196) the Canons of Osma, his native diocese, becoming subprior in 1201. In 1203 he journeyed to the Languedoc, encountering the Albigensian heretics in southern France, and by 1206 had embarked on a preaching tour with Diego, bishop of Osma, against Albigensianism, founding a house for women who had been converted from that heresy. One year later, the papal legate Peter of Castelnau was murdered, thereby igniting the spark for the Albigensian Crusade. Dominic spent the years 1208–1215 attempting to convert the Albigensians but with little success. His work, aided by other friars, led to the formation of an order that was welcomed by Bishop Fulk of Toulouse in 1215 and recognized with a charter from the prelate. Papal approval was sought, but the pope suggested that the order adhere to a more conventional style of monasticism in an attempt to alleviate opposition by the Cistercians.

In 1216, however, Dominic and Bishop Fulk traveled to Rome, in the hope of having the order formally accepted. He brought with him the results of the *capitulum fundationis* (chapter foundation), held in Toulouse earlier in the year, in which it was agreed by the friars to adopt the Augustinian rule along with other regulations to govern the order. Satisfied, the pope, Honorius III, gave sanction to the monks. Dominic spent the rest of his life working ceaselessly to promulgate the order in Italy, Spain and France. Houses were established at Bologna and Paris, near the universities there, and thus the bond was created between the Dominicans and the dissemination of learning. Dominic attended the first general chapter in 1220, held in Bologna, and in 1221, he set out for Hungary to preach to the pagans there. He fell ill and returned to Bologna; he died on August 6. Dominic was a major influence on the education of his era and was an inspiration, both spiritually and as an opponent of heresy. A friend of Saint Francis of Assisi, he was not as famous as his contemporary, but his order claimed such intellectual giants as Thomas Aquinas and Albertus Magnus. See also DOMINICANS; MONASTICISM.

**DOMINICANS** One of the four great mendicant orders of the Middle Ages, officially the Order of Friars Preachers (Ordo Praedicatorum, O.P.), founded in 1215 by Saint Dominic (see DOMINIC, SAINT). Born out of Dominic's attempts to convert the Albigensians in southern France, the Dominican order was originally composed of Dominic and his band of wandering preachers. In 1215 Bishop Fulk of Toulouse gave Dominic initial approval, which was confirmed by Pope Innocent III at the Fourth Lateran Council. The following year at Toulouse a chapter foundation (*capitulum fundationis*) provided for the acceptance of the basic Augustinian rule and other monastic guides in order to provide the Dominicans with the basis for their institutions. Pope Honorius III gave his sanction in 1216. Henceforth Dominic traveled and sent his priests throughout Spain, Italy and France, establishing houses in Paris and in Bologna, near the universities. Two general chapters held at Bologna in 1220 and 1221 laid down the formal government of the order.

The Dominicans differed from their contemporaries in that they placed primary importance on the intellect, encouraging study, preaching and learning, whereas other groups emphasized manual labor. There was an adherence to monastic life, with poverty extending to the entire membership, as well as devotion to prayer and to the liturgy. A democratic administration was established by its constitution, with elected chapters and superiors. All houses, however, belonged to the order as the whole and were not independent. Of vital importance to development was the focus on education. From the start the Dominicans were affiliated with universities, concentrating at first only on theological studies, but through the teaching of such intellects as Albertus Magnus and Thomas Aquinas the curriculum encompassed philosophy. Throughout Europe's universities there were Dominican institutions, themselves noted place of learning. The breadth of the Dominicans' learning and their capacity for preaching made them ideal instruments to combat heresy. They spoke against the Albigensians, called for Crusades and were in the forefront of the Inquisition, earning the title Domini Canes ("Watch-dogs of Orthodoxy"), a position maintained during the expansion of Spain in the New World. As with the Franciscans, the Dominicans were supported by the Second and Third Orders, with women composing the Second Order in convents and lay men and women constituting the Third. Because of their habit, a white tunic covered by a black mantle, they were known in England as the Black Friars. In France they were called the Jacobins, after their first house in Paris, Saint James (Saint Jacobus).

**DONALD I** (d. 862) King of Scotland from c. 859 to c. 862, the brother of Kenneth I MacAlpin (c. 841–c. 859). Few details of his reign have survived. His successor was his nephew, Constantine I (863–c. 877). See also SCOTLAND.

**DONALD II** (d. 900) King of Scotland from 889 to 900, about whose brief rule little is known. His successor was Constantine II (900–943). See also SCOTLAND.

**DONALD III** (d. c. 1097) King of Scotland, brother of King Malcolm III (1058–1093), who laid claim to the Scottish throne on Malcolm's death. His reign was divided into two periods: 1093–1094 and 1094–1097. The first period was distinguished by a stern anti-English policy, ending in early 1094 with the arrival of Duncan, the son of Malcolm, supported by the English. With the aid of William Rufus of England (1087–1100), Duncan deposed his uncle. Later in the year, however, Donald found an ally in another of his nephews, Edmund, and they slew Duncan in battle. Donald and Edmund then divided the kingdom, Donald receiving the north. In 1097, however, another claimant, Edgar the Atheling, with one more army supported by the English, embarked on a campaign to win the throne. Donald and Edmund were defeated; the latter was executed immediately, and Donald died a few days later. See also SCOTLAND.

**DONATELLO** (1386–1466) Florentine sculptor, one of the greatest artists of the Italian Renaissance. Born Donato di Betto Bardi, he was raised in Florence and apprenticed to Lorenzo Ghiberti. He worked with him on the famed bronze doors of the baptistery of the cathedral of Florence, from 1404 to 1407, a project considered by many art historians to have been the starting point of the Renaissance. Feeling he now rivaled Ghiberti, Donatello joined Filippo Brunelleschi, the loser of the competition to determine the creator of the doors, and worked for various guilds and societies in Florence, such as the board of works for the cathedral. His marble statuary, most notably the early pieces for the exterior of San Michele, the church of the Florentine guilds, *St. George* and *St. Mark*, were revolutionary. These were not Gothic but celebrated instead classical Roman sculpture, at the same time brilliantly expressive and sensitive.

In these works Donatello employed his new form of relief, the *schiacciato* (or *rilievo schiacciato*). A kind of shallow carving that had the effect of creating deep space through manipulation of shadows and angles, *schiacciato* provided the sculpture with modulation, movement and emotion. Although imitated by Desiderio da Settignano, Donatello's reliefs were matchless, finding rich expression in *St. George and the Dragon* (c. 1415) and *Assumption of the Virgin* (1428–1430). His major works include *David* (1408–1409); *St. John the Evangelist* (1408–1415); *Pazzi Madonna* (1422), a marble relief; *Lo Zuccone* (1423–1425), a celebrated work; *Annunciation Tabernacle* (1428–1433), of limestone; the *Gattamelata* (1447–1453), a well-known bronze equestrian statue of Erasmo da Narni in the Piazza del Santo, Padua; *Mary Magdalen* (1454–1455), a wooden figure in the Florentine baptistery; *Judith and Holofernes* (1456–1457), a bronze designed for the palace of the Medicis; *Lamentation* (1458–1459), a bronze relief; and a bronze pulpit (c. 1460–1470) in the Church of San Lorenzo in Florence. See also FLORENCE.

**DONATION OF CONSTANTINE** A document supposedly issued by Constantine the Great (306–337) to Pope Sylvester I (314–335) in the fourth century, granting to the popes spiritual supremacy over all of Christendom and temporal authority over Rome and the Western Empire. Accepted now as a fabrication written sometime in the fifth century, the Donation of Constantine was used by the papacy during the Middle Ages as a powerful political weapon because of its general acceptance by the allies and even the enemies of the popes as an authentic decree. Probably forged originally to allow the popes to repulse Byzantine influence in Rome, it was later applied against the powers of the Eastern Church and during the conflicts between the papacy and the emperors. It was not until the 15th century that the document was considered seriously to be a fraud. In 1440 Lorenzo Valla declared it a forgery. Scholarly debate subsequently raged for centuries about it.

**DONATION OF PEPIN** A grant of territory in Italy that formed the nucleus of the Papal States, made in 756 by Pepin III the Short (741–768), founder of the Carolingian dynasty, to Pope Stephen II (752–757). The donation originated with a promise made to the pope by Pepin in 754, probably in return for papal approval of the dynastic changes that were made in the Kingdom of the Franks, specifically the deposition of the last Merovingian king and the election of Pepin as the ruler of the Franks. Following his conquest of extensive portions of Lombard territory in Italy, Rome and the former holdings of the Byzantines were given to the Papal States and increased by Charlemagne, although militarily the papacy was dependent on the Franks for protection.

**DONUS** (d. 678) Pope from 676 to 678. He was elected as successor to Adeodatus II and was responsible for the rebuilding of churches.

**DOUGLAS** Scottish noble family famed for its fierce independence and its bitter feuds with the crowns of Scotland and England. Its founder was William de Douglas, lord of Douglas, who joined in the 1297 revolt of William Wallace, dying as a prisoner in the Tower of London in 1298. His son, probably the most famous of the Douglas clan, was Sir James (d. 1330), called "the Black" or "the Good." A supporter of Robert the Bruce (1306–1329), he was deprived of his castle by the English, so he attacked it and tore it apart. His subsequent raids along the Border (see BORDER, THE) were so ferocious that he was dubbed "the Black." He fought at Bannockburn with such bravery that he was granted an exemption from all feudal duties, except military service. After Robert died (1329), he set out with his king's heart to bury it in the Holy Land, but he died in Spain while fighting the Moors.

Archibald Douglas, third earl of Douglas (d. c. 1400), labored to acquire extensive holdings in the Scottish kingdom, and on his death the Douglases were the most powerful house in Scotland. His son, Archibald, was killed at the Battle of Verneuil in 1424, fighting for the French against England. James Douglas, 9th earl of Douglas (1426–1488), was a noted rebel against King James II of Scotland (1437–1460). He was twice unsuccessful (1452–1455) and died in prison. Another line was founded for the Douglas family through the illegitimate son of William Douglas, first earl of Douglas and Margaret Stuart, countess of Angus. This "Red" line was brought to prominence by Archibald Douglas, the 5th earl of Angus (d. 1514). He was chancellor of Scotland from 1493 to 1498 and had been a leader in the revolt of Scots nobles against James III (1460–1488) from 1487 to 1488. During the struggle he captured Robert Cochrane, a feared and hated royal favorite, thus earning the nickname "Bell-the-Cat." The Douglases remained influential throughout the 15th century. See also SCOTLAND.

**DOUGLAS, JAMES** See DOUGLAS.

**DOUKAS** See DUCAS.

***DRANG NACH OSTEN*** German phrase, meaning the "Drive to the East," that was used to describe the Germanic cultural and physical invasion of the Slavic East during the 12th and 13th centuries. The *Drang nach Osten* was spearheaded at various times by the German noble families, most notably the Welf and Ascanian dynasties, who saw the advance into eastern Europe as an opportunity to expand their political powers. Christianization and immigration were encouraged, furthered from the 13th to the 15th century by the often ruthless Teutonic Knights. The entire idea of a drive to the East became interwoven with the ideals of Teutonic legend. See also GERMANY; PAGANISM; SLAVS; TEUTONIC KNIGHTS.

**DRESDEN** City in Saxony, situated on the Elbe River, that became politically prominent in the late Middle Ages. It was first inhabited by a community of Slavs, joined about 1216 by German colonists under Margrave Dietrich of Meissen. Through his patronage the town expanded and, in 1270, was made the capital of Henry the Illustrious, margrave of Meissen. Briefly held by Bohemia and the margravate of Brandenburg, it was returned to Meissen in 1319. By 1485 Dresden was the home of the Wettins, eventually kings and Electors of Saxony. See also SAXONY.

**DRIVE TO THE EAST** See DRANG NACH OSTEN.

**DROGHEDA** City in county Louth, in eastern Ireland, situated on the Boyne River and known in Irish as Droichead Atha (Crossing of the Ford). It was established as a trading site by the Vikings in Ireland, coming under the control of the Anglo-Normans in the 12th century. The English subsequently made it an important commercial stronghold, Edward III (1327–1377) declaring it a staple town (a royal trading post), with the right to issue currency and to hold parliaments. In 1494, at Drogheda, the lord deputy of Ireland, Edward Poynings, issued his law (Poyning's Law) stipulating that the English privy council had authority over the calling and subsequent legislation of the Irish parliament. See also IRELAND.

**DRUZES** A small Islamic Shiite sect spread out during the Middle Ages in Lebanon and Syria. They adhered to the belief that al-Hakim, the sixth caliph of the Fatimids of Egypt (996–1021), was actually the incarnation of God. Although he disappeared in 1021, the Druzes claimed that he was not murdered, as was supposed, but had gone into hiding to return after a thousand years. The name of the sect was derived from the Shiite missionary al-Darazi, one of the earliest missionaries, who was killed in 1019 while preaching al-Hakim's divinity to the Lebanese Shiites. Subsequent development of doctrine was made by the first disciple of al-Hakim, Hamzah, and his closest followers.

**DUARTE** (1391–1438) King of Portugal from 1433 to 1438, a greater intellectual than a warrior, earning the nickname the "Philosopher King." The son of John (João) I of Aviz (reigned 1385–1433), he came to the throne having received a superb education and displaying a particular aptitude for law. He subsequently instituted a land reform, reclaiming for the crown certain land grants and thus strengthening the Portuguese monarchy. Support was also given to the projects of his brother, Henry the Navigator. Among these were continued maritime explorations and an attempt to seize Tangier in 1437, an event ending in disaster. Duarte died soon after, a victim of the plague. See also PORTUGAL.

**DUBH** (d. 966) King of Scotland from 962 to 967. Most of his reign was plagued by civil war against Cuilean (also, Culen), a rival. He was finally defeated and slain, and Cuilean became king (c. 967–971). See also SCOTLAND.

**DUBLIN** City in eastern Ireland, situated on Dublin Bay at the mouth of the Liffey River and called in Irish Baile Átha Cliath. Dublin was founded in ancient times, its bay attracting settlements, and a town was present by the third century, taken in 841 by the Viking invaders of Ireland, who made it the capital of their Irish colonial kingdom. Defeated in 1014 by Brian Boru, first of the O'Brien dynasty, at the Battle of Clontarf, the Vikings were nevertheless able to hold the city, but their power was greatly reduced. The Viking nobles took part in the revolt against Dermot MacMurrough, king of Leinster, in 1166 but then lost Dublin in 1170, when Dermot returned with an Anglo-Norman army. There followed futile attempts by the Norse to regain the city, and in 1172 King Henry II of England (1154–1189) arrived with a force, established his court, granted a charter and made it clear that English presence was to be permanent. For the remainder of the Middle Ages Dublin was the foremost city of the English Pale, the portion of territory occupied directly by England on the eastern Irish coast. See also IRELAND.

**DUBOIS, PIERRE** (c. 1250–c. 1320) French lawyer and political writer, a royal legal advocate by 1300, gaining admission into the royal administration through his association with a courtier favored by King Philip IV (1285–1314). He subsequently aided the king in his struggle with Pope Boniface VIII (1294–1303). A polemicist, he called for stern monarchical reform, while in his most famous work, *On the Recovery of the Holy Land* (1306), he declared that the only hope for Christendom against Islam was to acknowledge the suzerainty of France as leader of the West, including authority over the Holy Roman Empire.

**DUBROVNIK** See RAGUSA.

**DUCAS** Also Doukas, a noble Byzantine family that rose to prominence in the ninth century and claimed the imperial throne in the 11th century. Constantine X Ducas ruled from 1059 to 1067, and his son, Michael VII Ducas, ruled from 1071 to 1078. Michael's son, Constantine, was associated with the royal family of Alexius I Comnenus by his betrothal to Anna Comnena but died before the wedding. The family remained active in Byzantine political life. In 1204 Alexius V (Ducas) Mourtzouphlos overthrew Isaac II and Alexius IV Angelus, but could not prevent the capture of Constantinople by the army of the Fourth Crusade. In the 15th century a member of the family became famous for writing a history of the Byzantines from 1341 to 1462. In it, the writer (named Ducas) called for the union of the Eastern and Western Churches in the hope that it would bring support from the West. See also BYZANTINE EMPIRE.

**DUCCIO DI BUONINSEGNA** (c. 1260–c. 1318) Italian painter and the founder of the Sienese school. He was born in Siena and considered a gifted painter by 1278; however, few details of his life have survived beyond the fact that he was repeatedly in conflict with the Sienese commune. He was fined for various reasons, accumulated some wealth, owned a vineyard by 1304 and died quite poor about 1318. Duccio was a master of Byzantine formalism but injected it with the rich expressions of his age and with subtlety and the spiritual vitality of the Gothic style. He influenced the Sienese school in much the same way that Giotto affected Florence, although Duccio was overshadowed by Giotto.

His first known commission was the *Madonna* of Santa Maria Novella, a church in Florence, dating from 1285, now called the *Rucellai Madonna*. By far his greatest project was the *Maestà* (Majesty), the main altarpiece for the cathedral in Siena, painted from 1308 to 1311. Carried in a lavish procession through the streets, the *Maestà* depicted the Madonna and Child and included panels on the life and Passion of Christ and the saints. In all there were roughly 60 panels, which were separated in 1771. Other works included *Madonna with Child and Angels* (c. 1300), *Madonna Enthroned with Angels* (n.d.), *Madonna of the Franciscans* (c. 1280) and *The Marriage at Cana* (n.d.).

**DUFAY, GUILLAUME** (c. 1400–1474) French composer, considered one of the finest musical masters of his time. Born at Cambrai, he sang in the cathedral there (1409) and was writing musical compositions by the 1420s, some of them for the Malatesta family of Pesaro. In 1128 he joined the papal choir, already having served as a canon at Laon and Cambrai. He was next associated with the houses of Este and Savoy, leaving the service of the latter about 1440 to settle in Cambrai. There he remained, with the exception of periods of service for the duke of Savoy, until his death.

Dufay was a brilliant composer of both religious and secular music. Although he was not an innovator of note, his complete mastery of established styles made him renowned throughout Europe. He composed secular works, including chansons, rondeaux, virelays and ballades; his religious music was devoted to Masses, Mass sections, hymns and remarkably complex motets. His most acclaimed motets were composed for the election of Pope Eugene IV (1431); the dedication of the dome of Santa Maria del Fiore in Florence, Brunelleschi's masterpiece (1436); and the Treaty of Viterbo (1433). Influenced certainly by John Dunstable and a leader of the Burgundian school of music, he achieved lasting recognition for the intricacy, grace and richness of his music, combining elements of the Gothic, Italian and French traditions.

**DU GUESCLIN, BERTRAND** (d. 1380) Brilliant French general and, after 1370, constable of France in the service of King Charles V of France (1364–1380) during the Hundred Years' War. He was originally from Brittany, first gaining notoriety in 1357 for his duel with Sir Thomas Canterbury during the siege of Rennes by the English. Henceforth he was involved in numerous campaigns against the English in France, captured and ransomed three separate times. In 1364 he defeated the army of Charles II the Bad, king of Navarre, at Cacheral but was unsuccessful later in the year at Auray, once more becoming a prisoner. Of great value to Charles V, he led the French to several triumphs against the English (1370–1374), using tactical skill to overcome general English superiority in the field.

His military skills were also directed against the Free Companies (*compagnies*), mercenary groups who were marauding through the countryside. He was killed in battle in 1380, becoming a hero to his compatriots, especially in Brittany. See also HUNDRED YEARS' WAR.

**DUKUM AND DICEVQ** Two successive rulers of the Bulgars, who reigned briefly in 814, following the death of Krum. Virtually nothing is known of their years as rulers, and this period of Bulgarian political disorder was ended in the same year with the rise of Krum's son, Omurtag, to the throne. See also BULGARIA.

**DUMNONIA, KINGDOM OF** A realm that included Cornwall, Devon and Somerset in England during the early Middle Ages. Dumnonia was established probably as a result of the migration of the Celts into the southwest of

England during the Anglo-Saxon invasions and had taken shape sometime in the early sixth century. It was distinguished by the extent of Celtic influence on the region. Celtic culture outlasted the kingdom and became permanent there, especially in Cornwall. The advance of the Saxons in the south of the isle came at the expense of the kingdom of Dumnonia, which lost Devon and Somerset and eventually was confined to Cornwall proper (c. 730). Weakened, Dumnonia fell in the ninth century, but the Celts refused to submit until the reign of Edward the Confessor (1042–1066). See also ENGLAND.

**DUNCAN I** (1001–1040) King of Scotland from 1034 to 1040, the grandson of King Malcolm II (1005–1034), receiving from him (c. 1034) the Kingdom of Strathclyde on the death of its last independent king. He became king of Scotland despite tradition, which dictated that there be alternate succession between the two branches of the royal house, and thus he made an enemy of Macbeth, *mormaer* (earl, or subking) of Moray, who had a slight claim to the throne. Duncan's reign was a troubled one, for he faced the rivalry of Aldred, earl of Northumbria, the rebellious activities of the little-known relative of the king named Thorfinn and the continual conflict with Macbeth. An attempt to capture Durham in 1039 was a total disaster, including the loss of most of his infantry. The following year, at Bothgouanan, Macbeth used Duncan's weakened position to murder him, claiming the crown that he would wear for 17 years. Duncan's son, Malcolm III (1058–1093), would avenge his father in 1057. See also SCOTLAND.

**DUNCAN II** (1064–1094) King of Scotland, the son of King Malcolm III (1058–1093), reigning for six months in 1094. He had been sent to England as a hostage in 1072, to William the Conqueror, and had thus acquired the customs of the Normans. Following the death of his father in 1093, his uncle, Donald Ban, claimed the throne. With the blessing of William II Rufus (1087–1100), Duncan marched north, deposing Donald in early 1094. Only his grant of land to the churches of Durham and Dunfermline distinguished his time on the throne, for an alliance between Donald, another claimant, Edward, and the *mormaer* (earl, or subking) of Mearns, Malpei MacLoen, was formed against him. He died in battle at Mondynes, a stone marking where he fell. See also SCOTLAND.

**DUNFERMLINE** City in the county of Fife, Scotland, and site of a famous Benedictine abbey. The monastery was founded about 1072 by Queen Margaret of Scotland and became an important religious institution for the country. It was also the resting place of numerous Scottish kings, the entombment of every monarch from Malcolm III to Robert I the Bruce (1093–1329). See also SCOTLAND.

**DUNOIS, JEAN, COMTE DE** (1403–1468) The "Bastard of Orléans," a French general and diplomat during the final period of the Hundred Years' War with England. The natural son of Louis, duke of Orléans, Jean joined the Armagnacs, winning the trust of his cousin, the future Charles VII (1422–1461). He earned fame for his defense of Orléans from 1428 to 1429, when Joan of Arc marched to the city's relief. Subsequently, he was active against the English, achieving a major triumph by recapturing Paris in 1436. Three years later he received the county of Dunois, followed by that of Longueville in 1443. More campaigning followed in Normandy (1449–1450) and Guienne (1451). A loyal member of the aristocracy, he wavered in his allegiance to the crown in his later years, participating in the League of Public Weal against Louis XI (1461–1483), only to rejoin his cause. See also FRANCE.

**DUNS SCOTUS, JOHN** See JOHN DUNS SCOTUS.

**DUNSTABLE, JOHN** (d. 1453) English composer, as well as a gifted mathematician and astronomer, considered one of the greatest composers of his time. Few details of his life or career have survived, except that he was in the service of John, duke of Bedford. With him he presumably journeyed to France while the duke was campaigning during the Hundred Years' War. Dunstable was buried in Saint Stephen's Walbrook, in London. His music, while not technically innovative, was influential. It was the culmination of the English musical tradition and was noted for its exquisite harmonies. Composing some 60 works, he wrote both sacred and secular music, including motets, songs and Mass sections. Many of his compositions were preserved in German and Italian manuscripts.

**DUNSTAN, SAINT** (c. 909–988) Abbot of Glastonbury, archbishop of Canterbury and the principal figure in the revival of monasticism in England. Born about 909 to a noble family near Glastonbury, he was educated at the monastery there before entering into the service of his uncle, Athelm, archbishop of Canterbury. His position with the court of King Athelstan was degraded by enemies, who caused his removal on charges of black magic, and he fled to Aelfheah, bishop of Winchester, becoming a monk. Having retired from the world to live as a hermit at Glastonbury, he was suddenly recalled (c. 939) by Edmund I. Surviving another attack by jealous courtiers in 943, Dunstan was made abbot of Glastonbury, instituting strict adherence to the Benedictine rule. Under Edmund's successor and brother, Edred, he acted as counselor and treasurer. In 955, Edwy the Fair became king of the Saxons, and Dunstan was soon expelled after a quarrel, journeying to Flanders. At the Abbey of Blandinium, he was an observer of monasticism on the Continent and returned in 957 at the behest of Edgar the Peaceful, eager to apply his experiences to English monasticism.

Edgar named him bishop of Worcester and soon thereafter bishop of London. In 959 Edwy died, and Edgar appointed him archbishop of Canterbury in 960. The monarch and his prelate labored together to reform the church in England. Dunstan used Benedictine monasticism as his model, restored the churches after the Danish invasions, attempted to eradicate paganism and supported bishops throughout the country who instituted reforms, bringing such efforts together in the *Regularis concordia,* a compendium of monastic rules. He remained influential throughout Edgar's reign and then ensured the succession (in 975) of Edward the Martyr (killed in 978). Aethelred II (978–1016) was less dependent on him. He soon retired to

Canterbury to teach at the cathedral school, having transformed the nature of England's monastic life. See also MONASTICISM.

**DURAND OF SAINT-POURÇAIN** (c. 1275–1334) Scholastic philosopher, theologian and the primary intellectual opponent of Thomas Aquinas. He joined the Dominicans and studied in Paris, eventually receiving his doctorate in 1311 before lecturing on the *Sentences* of Peter Lombard. In 1313 he was summoned to Avignon by Pope Clement V (1305–1314) to teach theology, subsequently receiving an appointment as the bishop of Limoux (1317), Le Puy en Velay (1318) and Meaux (1326). Philosophically, Durand was an adherent of nominalism (the denial of universal concepts in favor of individuality), and theologically he believed in a division between religion and faith. These views brought him into debate with Thomas Aquinas and earned him censure from the church as well. Among his writings were a *Commentary on the Sentences* and *De origine potestatum et jurisdictionum* (*On the Origins of Powers and Jurisdictions;* 1329). Durand was given the titles "Doctor Modernus" and "Doctor Resolutissimus."

**DURAZZO** Port (Albanian: Durres) on the Adriatic Sea, situated in modern Albania. Founded in the seventh century B.C. as Epidamnus, the town eventually came into the possession of Rome about 229 B.C. Renamed Dyrrhachium, it developed into one of the key ports of the Roman Empire. In 481, however, it was attacked by the Ostrogoths. Subsequent invaders included the Bulgars (10th and 11th centuries), the Norman Robert Guiscard (1082), the Byzantines (12th century) and King William II of Sicily (1185). As a result of the Fourth Crusade (1202–1204), Venice laid claim to the city, only to lose it to the Sicilians. Additional rulers included Charles I of Anjou, king of Naples and Sicily, the Serbs under Stephan Dushan (until 1355), the Albanians (until 1392) and finally the Venetians. Venice maintained control from 1392 until 1501, when it fell under the authority of the Ottoman Turks. See also TRADE AND COMMERCE.

**DURHAM** City in Durham County, in northeastern England, dating from Anglo-Saxon times and of military importance from the time of William I the Conqueror (1066–1087), when it was chosen as a strategic defensive site along the Border (between England and Scotland; see BORDER, THE). A castle was built there in 1072, and the crown relied on the bishops of Durham to provide leadership in secular as well as spiritual matters. They thus exercised broad powers, including the right to issue currency and to appoint justices. Durham was already a leading ecclesiastical site, having achieved fame in 995 when the bones of Saint Cuthbert were moved to the cathedral. A Benedictine monastery was constructed in 1083 to replace the original Saxon structure, and the Romanesque cathedral (constructed between 1093 and 1133) was an important example of Norman architecture. See also ENGLAND.

**DURROW, BOOK OF** The earliest of the illuminated Gospel books, dating from 675–680. It displayed the exquisite Hiberno-Saxon style. Its title was derived from the Columban monastery of Durrow, Ireland, and it was kept there until 1661, when it was moved to Trinity College Library in Dublin (MS. 57). See also KELLS, BOOK OF; MANUSCRIPT ILLUMINATION; SUTTON HOO.

**DUSHAN, STEPHEN** See STEPHEN DUSAN.

# E

**EAST ANGLIA** Region in eastern England that comprised the counties of Norfolk and Suffolk, with portions of Essex and Cambridgeshire. From about the fifth to the ninth century it was one of the kingdoms of Anglo-Saxon England. First settled by the Angles in the fifth century, East Anglia became an extremely wealthy domain, its riches evidenced by Sutton Hoo, the ship burial site (c. 400–800). Beginning in the mid-seventh century, however, it fell under the influence of the kings of Mercia, rebelling around 825 and controlled instead by Wessex. The Danish invaders of the country marched through East Anglia and took the region from 865 to 866 as their base, before subduing it entirely in 869. As part of the agreement between the Danes and Alfred the Great in 886, it became part of the Danelaw, remaining in Danish hands until 917, when the Saxons reclaimed it. Throughout the Middle Ages East Anglia was noted for its wool trade. See also DANELAW; ENGLAND.

**EASTERN CHURCH** See ORTHODOX EASTERN CHURCH; see also ART AND ARCHITECTURE, BYZANTINE; BYZANTINE EMPIRE.

**EASTERN EMPIRE** See BYZANTINE EMPIRE.

**EASTERN ROMAN EMPIRE** See BYZANTINE EMPIRE.

**EBROIN** (d. c. 680) Mayor of the palace during the period of weak rule by the Merovingian "Lazy Kings." He was the last Neustrian figure to exercise power over the Austrasians. The successor of Erchinoald as administrator of Neustria, he took advantage of the death of Clotaire III (c. 673) to place the retarded Theuderic on the Frankish throne. Nobles, recognizing this as an attempt to secure the crown for himself, allied with Childeric II of Austrasia and deposed him, sending him to a monastery in Luxeuil. Ebroin escaped, however, defeating and killing the new mayor, Leudesius, restoring Theuderic and ordering the cruel mutilation and execution of his long-time rival Bishop Leger of Autun in 679. He defeated the Austrasians in battle, becoming even more oppressive. Unable to withstand his rule any longer, Frankish men of influence, led by Ermenfred, assassinated him. See also FRANCE; FRANKS.

**ECGFRITH** (d. 685) King of Northumbria from 670 to 685, his reign torn by conflicts, principally with Mercia to the south and the Picts to the north. He was killed in battle against the Picts at Nechtanesmere (modern Forfar, in Scotland). See also NORTHUMBRIA.

**ECKHART, MEISTER** (c. 1260–c. 1328) Medieval German mystic and one of the foremost Dominican theologians of the 13th and 14th centuries. Eckhart (also known as Eckhart von Hochheim) was born in Hochheim, Thuringia, to a noble family, joining the Dominicans about 1280 at Cologne, completing his studies in Paris. By 1293 he was lecturing in Paris, becoming prior of the Dominicans at Erfurt in 1294 and a short time later the head of the Dominican vicarate in Thuringia. Considered one of the order's most gifted thinkers, he twice received the professor's chair at Paris for foreigners and was granted the title *magister sacrae theologiae,* master of sacred theology, hence his name, Meister. Subsequently he was provincial for Saxony (1303), vicar-general of Bohemia (1307) and leader of the order's *studium generale* (1322).

Eckhart was a theologian of immense skill and influence, yet his speculative theology caused him to be the first member of the Dominicans to be accused of heresy. He was tried in 1326 before the archbishop of Cologne, and despite his appeal to the pope, a papal bull condemned 28 sentences of his writings as heretical or dangerous, which Eckhart recanted before his death. Eckhart was the author of 59 known sermons, preserved chiefly by having been memorized and written down. A brilliant writer in the vernacular (German), he wrote *Buch der göttlichen Tröstung (Book of Divine Consolation), Von Gescheidenheit (On Emptiness)* and *Reden der Unterscheidung (Talks of Instruction).* Only part of his Latin works survive, an ambitious compendium of his theological premises of which the *Opus expositionum* is largely complete. He also composed a commentary on the *Sentences* of Peter Lombard and a defense of his works, *Rechtfertigungschrift (Letter of Justification).*

His censure by the papacy darkened his reputation after his death and created considerable difficulties in interpreting his theological outlook. Considered a pantheist by his detractors, he advocated personal prayer and the *Gottesgeburt in der Seele* (or "Birth of God in the Soul"), with its elements of overcoming temporal concerns and reflecting the divine light of God. His was an enduring influence on philosophy and philosophers, most notably Johann Tauler, Henry Susa, Nicholas of Cusa, Martin Luther, Jakob Boehme and later figures such as Hegel and Alfred Rosenberg.

**EDDA** See ICELANDIC LITERATURE; SNORRI STURLUSON.

**EDESSA** City in eastern Turkey situated on the Euphrates River. An ancient site, it was a Roman and later a Byzantine possession and from the third century a Christian city. Occupied briefly by the Persians, it was captured in 638 by the Arabs. Achieving a goal of the First Crusade (1096–1099), Baldwin I, brother of Godfrey de Bouillon, took Edessa in 1097. He proclaimed himself count of Edessa and thus established one of the first Crusader States. The county of Edessa was conquered in 1144 by the Muslims, precipitating the Second Crusade, which failed to reclaim the city. See also CRUSADES.

**EDGAR, KING OF SCOTLAND** (c. 1074–1107) Ruler of the Scots from 1097 to 1107, the son of Malcolm III (1058–1093) and Margaret of Scotland, on amicable terms with William II Rufus of England (1087–1100), receiving his help in 1097 and that of his uncle, Edgar the Aetheling, in overthrowing King Donald III Ban. His reign was noted for the favor shown to the church in Scotland. See also SCOTLAND.

**EDGAR I, KING OF ENGLAND** (943–975) Ruler from 957 to 975, a highly successful monarch who earned the title "the Peaceful" because of his quiet reign and his close association with the church. The son of King Edmund I (939–946), he was chosen ruler of Mercia and Northumbria in 957, in place of his brother Edwy, by the dissatisfied men influential in that kingdom and was then crowned king of Wessex in 959, his power making him effective head of England. Edgar was blessed by a period of reduced tension for the Norse invasions had eased, allowing the continued development of English culture. A contribution of his reign was legal reform. His laws were accepted by Canute the Great in the 11th century. Of special importance was his work with the church. Aided by Saint Dunstan, whom he had recalled from exile and promoted to archbishop of Canterbury, along with Oswald of York and others, he helped bring reforms in English monasticism while strengthening Christianity in England. His coronation was notable for his anointing by Saint Dunstan, which set ceremonial precedent. See also ENGLAND.

**EDGAR THE AETHELING** (d. c. 1125) Anglo-Saxon prince, the grandson of Edmund II Ironside and the designated heir to King Harold after the Battle of Hastings in 1066. Despite the support of much of Saxon England, Edgar submitted to William the Conqueror (1066–1087), finding refuge with his father-in-law, Malcolm III of Scotland, from 1069 to 1072. Briefly exiled, he surrendered to William and subsequently joined a number of the missions for the country in the service of William I and William II Rufus (1087–1100). In 1097 he helped overthrow Donald III Ban of Scotland (1093–1097), installing Malcolm's son Edgar on the throne. He then went on crusade in 1102 and next supported Robert of Normandy in his conflict with Henry I (1100–1135) for the English crown. Captured at the Battle of Tinchebrai in 1106, he was later released and died virtually alone.

**EDINBURGH** City in southeastern Scotland, situated on the Midlothian River near the Firth of Forth and known in Gaelic as Duneideann (Din Eidyn). Edinburgh was established around the Castle Rock dominating the region and had fortifications built on it from around the sixth century. During the time of Anglian occupation, the Church of Saint Cuthbert was constructed near the western portion of the rock and was, like the small trading community nearby, under the control of the Scottish kings in the 10th century. Edinburgh's known history dates from the time of King Malcolm III Canmore (ruled 1058–1093), the son of Duncan, who was murdered by Macbeth. Malcolm's wife, Margaret, reportedly constructed a small chapel in the castle at Edinburgh, dying there according to tradition. Her son, David I (ruled 1124–1153), established the Augustinian abbey of Holyrood, which was to be the final resting place for many kings.

The virtual symbol of Scottish nationalism, the royal castle at Edinburgh was the target of English attacks in the long and bitter war between those two countries. In 1296, Edward I of England (1272–1307) bombarded it for three days before it fell, but the Scots reclaimed it in 1314. It was taken again in 1333 by the English, only to be rewon in 1341. Other sieges were made about 1385 and in 1400 and 1482. The status of burgh was granted in 1130, a charter was granted by Robert I the Bruce (1306–1329) in 1329 and the city's status as capital received impetus and development from David II (ruled 1329–1371). James II (ruled 1437–1460) and James III (ruled 1460–1488) made Edinburgh the seat of government, the latter ruler leaving its confines only rarely. See also SCOTLAND.

**EDMUND** See EDMUND OF ABINGDON, SAINT.

**EDMUND, KING OF SWEDEN** Ruler from 1056 to 1060. He was a supporter of Christianity in the kingdom. See also SWEDEN.

**EDMUND I, KING OF ENGLAND** (921–946) Ruler of England from 939 to 946, profiting from the unification of the country accomplished by his father, Edward the Elder (ruled 899–924) and his brother, Athelstan (ruled 924–939). The successor of Athelstan (he had been a member of the English army at Brunanburh in 937), in 939 Edmund faced an immediate invasion of Northumbria by Olaf Guthfrithson, the Viking king of Dublin. Olaf proved a dangerous foe, but his death in 942 allowed Edmund to seize the initiative and recapture all of the territory that had been lost. To ensure the continuation of the peace after his campaigns, he granted Strathclyde to Malcolm I of Scotland (943–954) in 945, a brilliant diplomatic effort. Edmund also issued legal codes. In 946 he was murdered by an exiled robber and was succeeded by his brother, Edred (946–955). See also ENGLAND.

**EDMUND II IRONSIDE, KING OF ENGLAND** (c. 993–1016) Son of Aethelred II the Unready, who ruled from 978 to 1016, Edmund reigned as king of the English for a brief time in 1016 while bearing the full weight of the English cause against the Norse. Despite his marriage to a Danish princess, he proved proudly nationalistic on the invasion of the country by Canute the Great in 1015. With his father ailing, he raised an army and strove to defeat the Norse. Aethelred died in April 1016, and some of the English nobles elected Edmund king; others chose to support Canute's claims. His subsequent campaign against Canute was successful in the early stages, but Edmund was nearly destroyed at the Battle of Ashingdon on October 18. For his stubborn will in continuing the conflict, he earned the title "Ironside." Negotiations ended the fighting later in the year, with Edmund retaining Wessex. He died soon after, however, and Canute became king. See also ENGLAND.

**EDMUND OF ABINGDON, SAINT** (d. 1240) Also Edmund Rich, a gifted scholar, preacher and an influential archbishop of Canterbury. Educated at Oxford and Paris, he taught at both universities and acquired a reputation for holiness and austerity. About 1222 he was made canon of Salisbury Cathedral, preaching the Sixth Crusade in England in 1227, and in 1233 became archbishop of Canterbury. Most of his reign was spent in disagreement with King Henry III (1216–1272) over the monarch's favoritism toward foreign advisers and for his involvement in Sicilian affairs. As a counter to Edmund's influence with the barons, Henry convinced the pope to appoint a papal legate, Cardinal Otto (or Otho), whose very presence was a threat to the ecclesiastical supremacy of Canterbury. Failing to resist the the changes because of his own purity and natural moderation, he crossed the Channel to take up residence at the Cistercian monastery of Pontigny, dying in that same year, 1240. He was canonized belatedly in 1247. Edmund's fame as a holy prelate outlasted his administrative shortcomings, and his treatise on spiritual devotion was considered important in shaping subsequent theological literature. See also CANTERBURY.

**EDMUND THE MARTYR, SAINT** (d. 869) King of East Anglia from about 855 to 869 and a famed martyr for his ardent Christian beliefs. Late in his reign the kingdom was attacked by invading Norsemen. Edmund resisted but was defeated and captured by the Danish leader, Ingwar (or Inguar), in 869. He refused to forsake his faith or to share his throne with a Dane. As punishment he was tied to a tree, shot with arrows and beheaded. His remains were eventually placed in a shrine at Bury Saint Edmund's in Suffolk, becoming a popular place of pilgrimage. See also ENGLAND.

**EDRED** (d. 955) King of Wessex from 946 to 955, also called Eadred, the brother of his predecessor, Edmund I (ruled 939–946), and the son of Edward the Elder (ruled 899–924). The major events of Edred's reign took place in Northumbria, where he was forced to reestablish Saxon domination again and again. The Northumbrians acknowledged as their king (c. 940) Eirik Bloodaxe of Norway, bringing the vengeance of Edred in 948, when much of Northumbria was destroyed. See also ENGLAND.

**EDWARD I** (1239–1307) King of England from 1272 to 1307, one of the most formidable and successful monarchs of England, whose accomplishments in war and especially in law earned him the epithet the "English Justinian." He was born at Westminster in June 1239, son of King Henry III (1216–1272) and Eleanor of Provence, receiving lands in Ireland, Gascony and Wales as his own, as well as the earldom of Chester in 1254, the year he wed his beloved Eleanor of Castile. In November 1255, he invaded Wales to crush the leader of Welsh nationalism, Llewelyn ap Gruffydd, but was routed in a humiliating fashion. Nevertheless, considered dangerous and intelligent by the barons who were then in conflict with Henry III, Edward was forced to sign the Provisions of Oxford in 1258, and by the outbreak of hostilities the following year he had come under the influence of Simon de Montfort (the younger), his uncle by marriage and the leader of the baronial party. Edward thus refused to choose sides in the early part of the Barons' War, but after the Battle of Lewes in 1264 and the capture of his father, his allegiance was given to Henry. Through Edmund's skill as a general and as prince, the barons were defeated, Simon being killed at the decisive Battle of Evesham in 1265. Peace was made with the Dictum of Kenilworth in 1266. Having secured the first place in the kingdom, Edward took the cross, embarking on a Crusade to support his revered uncle, Louis IX of France (1226–1270), in 1268. He arrived too late to save Louis, who died at Tunis in 1270, but remained in Syria until 1272. Journeying home, he heard of Henry's death while in Sicily, arriving at Dover on August 2, 1274, and celebrating his coronation on August 19.

Edward's reign was divided between his wars and his legislation. His conflicts began in 1277 with another campaign against Wales. Llewelyn ap Gruffydd had refused to pay homage to the king in 1274, and Edward was determined to reduce Welsh independence. Rebellions were suppressed ruthlessly, so much so that by 1284 Llewelyn was dead, as was his brother David. The Statute of Wales (1284) incorporated large parts of that country into an English principality, and castles throughout Gwynedd (the heart of opposition to England) solidified English control. He was strained to pay for his expeditions to Wales, however, and soon after was embroiled in struggles with Scotland and France that virtually bankrupted the treasury. The cause of his involvement was the vacancy of the Scottish throne following the deaths of King Alexander III (1286) and Margaret, Maid of Norway (1290), and the resulting strife in trying to find a successor. John de Balliol was made king through Edward's influence, but interference in Scottish affairs drove de Balliol in 1295 to form an alliance with France (see BALLIOL, JOHN DE). Edward invaded Scotland in 1296, smashed resistance and returned with the Scottish coronation stone, of Scone, placing it in Westminster. Uprisings drew him back in 1298. At Falkirk on July 22, 1298, Edward annihilated a Scottish army led by William Wallace, but years of fighting still loomed ahead. Peace was made with France in 1303, and William Wallace was executed in 1305. Robert I the Bruce then emerged as leader of the Scots in 1306, fomenting further unrest that Edward was still attempting to eradicate on his death (see ROBERT I, KING OF SCOTLAND). For his merciless retaliations against them, Edward was declared the "Hammer of the Scots" and even on his deathbed was calling on his son, Edward II (1307–1327), to carry on the war.

Often overlooked because of his martial enterprises were Edward's efforts in reorganizing the feudal government in

England. While he used the enactments of his court to strengthen royal power, he also instituted reforms in law and procedure, issuing important statutes from 1275 to 1290. Of equal influence was Edward's adherence to the precedents set by Simon de Montfort, namely the summoning of representatives of local communities to a central meeting or parliament. Used as a form of his royal council, the parliament could, with the king's consent, make amendments to law or levy taxes. The Parliament of 1295, with representatives of shires, the clergy, boroughs, nobility and knights, came to be called the Model Parliament, and by 1307 the body was seen as a generally accepted part of English political life.

Edward's ambitions came at a terrible cost. His relations with the barons were poor, at times even hostile, and his need for money caused a rupture with Pope Boniface VIII (1294–1303) over taxation of the clergy. Taxes were harsh, particularly against the Jews, who were so reduced to poverty that in 1290, unable to press them any further, Edward expelled them entirely. Debts weakened the royal position, and he left to his son, Edward II, an unfortunate legacy that the feeble king would never be able to overcome. Edward himself was called the maker of laws and defender of the weak, but his manner and dealings could be harsh, cunning and even merciless. His tendencies toward cruelty or absolutism were tempered by his wife, Eleanor. After her death in 1290 and that of his trusted chancellor, Burnell, in 1292, no advisers were their equal. See also ENGLAND; PARLIAMENT; SCOTLAND.

**EDWARD II** (1284–1327) King of England, a weak and generally incompetent monarch, ruling from 1307 to 1327, when he was deposed. The son of Edward I (1272–1307) and Eleanor of Castile, he was born at Caernarvon, succeeding his father in 1307 and marrying Isabella of France in 1308. Having come to the throne after the strong and successful reign of Edward I, he was an immediate disappointment; he proved wholly unsuited to be king, rewarding his favorite courtier, Piers Gaveston, with position and prominence, including the earlship of Cornwall. The outraged barons forced Edward to exile Gaveston and to accept the Ordinances of 1311, placing limitations on royal power. Gaveston returned, however, prompting his murder by baronial assassins in 1312.

Soon after, in 1314, a new war erupted with Scotland; Edward marched against Robert I the Bruce (1306–1329) and was defeated at Bannockburn on June 24. This catastrophe reduced his power further and marked the ascendancy of his royal cousin, Thomas of Lancaster. He fell from favor in 1319, to be replaced by Hugh le Despenser and his son, and their influence survived their exile in 1321, allowing Edward to revoke the Ordinances of 1311. By 1326 Queen Isabella and her lover, Roger MORTIMER, arrived from France, executed the Despensers and imprisoned her husband. Deposed, Edward was kept a prisoner until September 1327, when he died at Berkeley Castle. It was generally believed that he was murdered by a red hot poker piercing his bowels. Recent theories have presented a possibility that he managed to escape. Regardless of his ultimate end, his time on the throne was a disaster for England, noted for the sharp decline of the Crown's authority and prestige and the considerable political chaos in the land. See also ENGLAND.

**EDWARD III** (1312–1377) King of England from 1327 to 1377, succeeding the deposed Edward II (1307–1327) and restoring the power of the monarchy while launching England into a massive and prolonged war with France. Crowned while still a youth, after his mother, Isabella, and her lover, Roger MORTIMER, had deposed Edward II, he lived for three years with the pair, who served as regents. In 1330, however, Edward and a group of supporters surprised Mortimer at Nottingham and slew him. Isabella no longer held power and was compelled to enter a convent.

Free to reign alone, Edward was eager to avenge the Battle of Bannockburn, where Robert I the Bruce (1306–1329) had humiliated his father. On the death of Robert, Edward supported the baron Edward de Balliol, in his attempt to defeat the claim of David II (1329–1371) for the Scottish throne. By 1356, however, Balliol was forced to abdicate, but Edward was concerned with France, as relations between the two countries had been deteriorating over the years. In 1337, Edward laid claim to the French throne, and the Hundred Years' War began. English victories came at Sluys (1340) and Crécy (1346), and Calais fell in 1347. Fame was won by his son Edward, the Black Prince, in 1356, at Poitiers, but the campaigns proved both costly to the treasury and ultimately ephemeral. King John II the Good of France (1350–1364) was captured at Poitiers, and with the Treaty of London (1359) England won so many concessions that France repudiated the agreement. In an attempt to secure its acceptance, an unsuccessful military campaign was launched in 1360. Negotiations led to the Treaty of Calais (1360), giving England the region of Aquitaine. Under Charles V (1364–1380) a French recovery was launched, prompted by Edward's growing exhaustion and the declining health of the Black Prince. A truce was signed in 1375, and by 1377 only Calais, Bordeaux and the coastal sections of the France remained in English hands.

The war had forced Edward to find new sources of income, a need that awakened the political awareness of Parliament. That body, as exemplified by the Good Parliament of 1376, attempted to remove royal ministers but was defeated easily when its champion, the Black Prince, died at a crucial moment. Economic hardships from the conflict with the French were also worsened by the arrival of the Black Death in 1348. Further plague outbreaks occurred in 1361 and 1369, combining with the fighting to depopulate much of the country, reducing the government's capacity to recover economically. Over increasingly desperate subjects ruled an aging Edward who, after the death of his wife Philippa in 1369, saw his court torn apart by the quarrels of his sons, Edward and John of Gaunt, while he was captivated by a mistress, Alice Perrers (see PERRERS, ALICE). He died alone on June 21, 1377, at Sheen.

Despite his military failures, Edward III was considered a worthy successor to his grandfather, Edward I, and a vast improvement over Edward II. His court was one of the brightest in Europe, and he was seen as a figure of chivalric glory. He promoted the cause of knighthood, founding the Knights of the Garter. Furthermore, his government, for much of his reign, was sound and generally accessible as well as lenient, issuing innovative laws such as the Statute of Laborers (1391) and other practical ordinances. Public opinion changed toward the end of Edward's life as taxes became crushing, and Edward, in his dotage, took less part in royal affairs. An excellent source on his era was Jean Froissart's *Chronicles*. See also ENGLAND.

**EDWARD IV** (1442–1483) King of England from 1461 to 1469 and from 1471 to 1483. He came to the throne through war and strategic political alliances but proved himself a canny monarch and a gifted administrator. The son of Richard, duke of York, he became a participant in the struggle between his father and Henry VI (1422–1461; 1470–1471), both descendants of Edward III (1327–1377). In 1460, Richard, who had been declared the heir of Henry VI as a compromise, was surprised at the Battle of Wakefield and slain with his son, Edmund, in December. Edward, now the duke of York, gathered an army and defeated a Lancastrian foe at Mortimer's Cross in February 1461, slaughtering captive nobles. On March 29 he fought the Battle of Towton in a blizzard, eventually the victor but taking part in one of the bloodiest battles in English history. With the help of Richard Neville, earl of Warwick, he was able to secure his own coronation on June 28, 1461.

The early part of his reign left doubts as to his fitness to rule, as he relied on Richard while spending hours as a womanizer. The woman who particularly attracted him was Elizabeth Woodville, and so ardent was his desire for her that he wed her in 1464, despite having entered into a marriage contract with Lady Eleanor Butler. Warwick, having labored long to eradicate the Lancastrian opposition, and who planned to wed the king to a French princess, was horrified. Edward's private dealings with Burgundy against France also nettled his adviser. Warwick negotiated secretly with France's Louis XI (1461–1483) and in 1460 entered into open rebellion, capturing Edward in July. The king, however, displayed some of his hidden qualities. He used his new allies in London and the nobility (thanks to his favor of the Londoners and the family of the Woodvilles) to force a reconciliation with Warwick. Peace could not last, and by 1470 Warwick was in revolt again, this time forced to flee to France. With Louis and the exiled Lancastrians as allies, Warwick returned in September, driving Edward into exile. The king gathered his own support in Charles, duke of Burgundy, and his brother, Richard, duke of Gloucester, invading England in March 1471. On April 14 he met and crushed Warwick at Barnet, killing him. A final battle was fought on May 4, when he destroyed the Lancastrians at Tewkesbury, murdering Henry VI a short time later.

Edward thus embarked on the second period of his reign, less eventful but more successful. He decided on a new course of hostilities with France, launching a campaign in 1475. Charles of Burgundy failed to come to his aid, however, and Edward was forced to make the Treaty of Picquigny, retreating in return for a large ransom. In England he began a reform of the royal finances by improving the organization of the crown lands, establishing controls on expenditures and devising methods of increasing revenues. He was thus free of the task of asking Parliament for money, a fact that made the monarchy more centralized and foreshadowed the autocratic methods of the coming Tudors. He lost his trusting nature in personal dealings and grew more suspicious in his later years. Edward died on April 9, 1483, having ruled England in a period of liberal patronage of the arts and learning (including printing) and leaving his son, Edward V, as his heir. See also ENGLAND.

**EDWARD V** (1470–1483?) King of England from April until June 1483, deposed by Richard, duke of Gloucester (ruled as Richard III, 1483–1485). Edward and his brother, Richard, became the subject of considerable mystery as to their untimely end. He was the son of Edward IV (1461–1483) and Elizabeth Woodville, receiving the title of Prince of Wales in 1471. His father then sent him to Wales in 1473, where he remained until Edward's death 10 years later. Richard of Gloucester was named Protector of the Realm, however, breaking the power of the Woodvilles, taking possession of the young king and his brother. In late June he secured the deposition of Edward from the Lords and Commons, moving the brothers into the Tower of London. The boys disappeared there and were never seen again. Richard III's foul reputation made him the prime suspect in what was assumed to be their murder, but recent scholarship points to other individuals as bearing the guilt for the crime, including King Henry VII (1485–1509). Their deaths remain one of the darkest mysteries of the Middle Ages, stirred by the modern discovery of two small skeletons in the Tower of London. See also ENGLAND; WARS OF THE ROSES.

**EDWARD THE BLACK PRINCE** (1330–1376) The elder son of King Edward III (1327–1377) and Philippa of Hainaut, a famous chivalric figure of his age. Born at Woodstock, he held various titles in succession and became the Prince of Wales in 1343. Two years after assuming that title he embarked on his first campaign against France, in the Hundred Years' War, ravaging the Cotentin. Subsequently he fought at Crécy (1346) and earned lasting fame at Poitiers (1356) when he routed a French army, capturing King John II the Good (1350–1364). His father made him prince of Aquitaine (1367–1372). He established his court at Bordeaux (1363), a sumptuous gathering but one ruled with little statecraft. Aid was given to Pedro I the Cruel, of Castile and León (1350–1369), in 1367, to regain Castilian lands, but the venture was so expensive that Edward's taxation became harsh, causing both a revolt and a war with Charles V of France (1364–1380). Ill from his expeditions in Spain, he returned home in 1371, resigned his princely holdings in 1372 and never regained his health. He opposed his brother, John of Gaunt, and the Lancastrian party but died a year before his father. His son, Richard II (1377–1399) succeeded to the throne. Accounts of his activities were written by Jean Froissart and the herald of Sir John Chandos. He was called the Black Prince because he reportedly wore black armor at Crécy. See also HUNDRED YEARS' WAR.

**EDWARD THE CONFESSOR, SAINT** (c. 1005–1066) King of England from 1042 to 1066, a politically weak ruler dominated by the Saxon and Norman factions in the kingdom. His reputation for saintliness made him legendary in the Middle Ages as an ideal king. He was the son of King Aethelred II the Unready (ruled 978–1016) and Emma of Normandy, who later married Canute the Great. During the period of Danish supremacy in England, he lived in Normandy at the court of Emma's brother, Duke Richard the Good. There he was educated with his brother, Alfred (d. 1037). After a failed attempt to press his claim to the throne in 1035, against Hardecanute, he went back to Normandy, returning to England only in 1041, when Hardecanute, ill and without an heir, probably named him as successor. Edward was taken to Canterbury and crowned.

He had a difficult reign from the start, as Emma's fortune was seized in 1043, out of fear that she had worked against Edward's accession. Real power, however, rested with the earls, particularly with Godwin of Wessex. In 1045 Godwin arranged a marriage between Edward and his daughter Edith, but his ambitions and those of his family were so unacceptable to Edward that by 1050 he was actively seeking a counterinfluence. He relied on the Normans, whom he favored with government positions, much to the resentment of the Anglo-Saxons. Godwin and his family were exiled around 1051. Their fall was short lived, for they mustered an army, compelling Edward to reinstate them. Godwin died in 1053, his son, Harold II Godwinson (1066), emerging as the most formidable figure in England. Edward, overshadowed in matters of state, spent his last years continuing the construction of Westminster Abbey. He supposedly named Harold as his successor in 1066, while on his deathbed, although Duke William of Normandy declared that he had been chosen much earlier (probably about 1051). Edward's lack of a direct heir and the claims of Harold and William made war inevitable, an issue settled at the Battle of Hastings (1066). Edward was canonized in 1161. See also NORMANDY.

**EDWARD THE ELDER** (d. 924) King of the West Saxons from 899 to 924, the successor to Alfred the Great (871–899) and one of the finest soldier kings in England, who continued Saxon conquest throughout the country. Coming to the throne on the death of his father in 899, Edward defeated a rival claimant, Aethelwald, in 902 and spent the next years consolidating his political position. In 912 he was ready to deal with the Danes, launching a campaign against Danish-held East Anglia. From 917 to 920 he waged constant war, first with his sister Aethelflaed, queen of Mercia, and then, on her death, as ruler of Mercia as well. Before his death, all of the territory south of the Humber was in Saxon hands, the result of his labors. He laid the groundwork for the unification of England under his son, Athelstan (924–939). See also ENGLAND.

**EDWARD THE MARTYR, SAINT** (d. 978) King of England from 975 to 978, the son of King Edgar I (ruled 959–975) and brother of King Aethelred II the Unready (978–1016). Elected in 975, he was assassinated in 978, probably as part of the antimonastic movement that had developed in parts of England. Because he died while visiting his brother and successor, there has been some question as to Aethelred's complicity. His body was transferred to Shaftesbury, where miracles were soon reported. Edward was considered a martyr and a saint. See also ENGLAND.

**EDWIN** (d. 632) King of Northumbria from 616 to 632, the first Christian monarch of Northumbria. He was the son of King Aelle of Deira (560–c. 590) but was forced into exile by a usurper, returning in 616 with the help of the ruler of East Anglia. He was converted with a large number of subjects in 627, owing mainly to his wife, Aethelburga, daughter of Aethelbert of Kent, who brought with her Paulinus, the Roman missionary. Through conquest and reputation, Edwin became the most powerful monarch in England at the time, receiving the allegiance of every other ruler on the isle except for Kent. In 632, however, an alliance of the Mercian ruler Penda (c. 626–655) and the people of Gwynedd declared war on Northumbria and killed Edwin in battle, ravaging much of his defeated realm. See also ENGLAND.

**EDWY** (d. 959) King of the Saxons from 955 to 957 and king of Kent and Wessex from 957 to 959. Edwy (or Eadwig), called "the Fair," the son of Edmund I (ruled 939–946), nephew of Edred (ruled 946–955) and brother of Edgar the Peaceful (957–975), had a poor reputation as a monarch, probably because of his enmity for Saint Dunstan. This was caused by an episode during his coronation feast. He slipped away to visit a woman, hoping for a royal marriage, and was found on a couch with her, his crown on the floor. Dunstan dragged him back to the feasting hall. Edwy subsequently exiled Dunstan and was thus disapproved of by the church. His alienation of the clergy, compounded by a fondness for kingly pleasures and a general inability to rule, resulted in a revolt by his nobles in Mercia and Northumberland in 957. Edwy died two years later, and Edgar was made king of the Saxons. See also SAXONS.

**EGBERT** (d. 839) King of Wessex from 802 to 839, the instigator of English resistance to the Danish invasion and, for a time, the most powerful king in the isles. He was the son of a magnate of Kent but was driven into exile, spending time at the court of Charlemagne. In 802 he was able to succeed to the throne of Wessex, immediately asserting the independence of the kingdom from the Mercian confederation. Starting in 815, he advanced against Cornwall, probably in response to raids from there, and soon came to dominate the region. Mercian attempts at reestablishing dominance over Wessex were rebuffed by Egbert in 825, at the Battle of Ellendun, a victory that allowed Egbert to proclaim himself king of Kent, Sussex, Surrey and Essex. Briefly he was made master of Mercia (829) as well. In 838 he won his greatest triumph at Hingston Down (in Cornwall) over a Danish and Cornish army. See also ENGLAND.

**EGICA** (d. 701) King of the Visigoths, one of the last Visigothic rulers of Spain, reigning from 687 to 701. He became notorious for his persecution of the Spanish Jews, promulgating a law at the 16th Council of Toledo (695) that ordered all Jewish males to be sold into slavery and the children given to Christians to be raised in the Catholic faith. Many Jews converted by force, and others fled to Africa. See also VISIGOTHS.

**EGILL SKALLAGRÍMSSON** (c. 910–990) One of the great Icelandic skaldic poets and a renowned adventurer. An account of his life comprises the 13th-century *Egils saga*, attributed traditionally to SNORRI STURLUSON, and his surviving poetry is thought to be some of the finest ever written. He was the author of three extant poems: *Sonatorrek*, *Arinbjarnarkvioa* and *Hofuolausn*. See also ICELANDIC LITERATURE.

**EGYPT** Country situated in the northeastern corner of Africa, nurtured and irrigated by the Nile River. Egypt's medieval history was one of foreign domination, inclusion in the vast Islamic world and gradual transformation to a largely Muslim country. It has been the view of scholars that medieval Egypt's origins arose with the invasion of General Amr ibn al-As in 639. During the preceding centuries it had been controlled by native rulers, then by the Ptolemies and then by the Romans (from 30 B.C.), whose agricultural practices and policies did much to cause economic and social distress. During the time of the Byzantines (395–639) the region was a bastion of Christianity, for monasticism and Coptic culture were both important and influential. The Byzantines, however, were in some difficulty trying to maintain their authority in the wake of Persian advances in the early seventh century, reestablishing themselves only in 628 with the treaty signed by Emperor Heraclius. Such was the scenario of events prior to to the Arab conquest.

Amir ibn al-As routed the garrison troops of the Byzantine Empire with remarkable skill and ease. By 642 the Christian army had been expelled, and an attempt to reclaim Egypt in 645 was defeated. No major changes were made in the fabric of Egyptian life, despite the remarkable military victory. Arabic did not replace Greek as the language of government, there was no serious attempt at mass conversion and life generally went on as before. A mosque was constructed in the new city of al-Fustat, but Alexandria still held prominence as a leading Mediterranean port. For two centuries, then, Egypt was treated merely as one of the provinces of the Umayyad and later Abbasid caliphates, with a premium placed on the collection of taxes. Toward this end an enlightened policy of toleration was pursued, and conversions were of secondary importance to sound fiscal administration. Equally important, Egypt was considered a strategically vital base from which to launch the expansion of Islam into Africa and beyond. Gradually strife developed as Arab settlements increased and the Islamic Empire shifted its attentions to Ifriqiyah (modern Tunisia). Political and social discontent erupted with the revolts of the Kharijites (a dissident Islamic sect) in the eighth century and the Copts in the ninth. Governors were replaced with alarming frequency, especially during the reign of Harun al-Rashid (786–809), and inevitably deterioration of the central authority of the Abbasids made possible the seizure of Egypt in the ninth century by a dynast of independent bent, Ibn Tulun.

In Egypt, lamp of Mamluk sultan al-Nasir

The Tulunid dynasty of Egypt (868–905) was founded by Ahmad ibn Tulun, the stepson of a Turkish general, Babak, who had been made governor but sent Tulun in his stead. He created an army and by 877 acted independently from the Abbasids. Egypt became self-sufficient and prosperous under Tulun, albeit temporarily, for his son, Khumarawayh, was far less conscientious in matters of treasury. On his murder in 896, the Tulunids were bankrupt, and anarchy was rampant on the Nile. In 905 the Abbasids reestablished their hold, only to lose it in 935, when the governor, Muhammad ibn Tughj, from Sogdiana claimed the treasury for himself. His brief dynasty, called the Ikshidid, from the princely title *ikshidid*, fell under the influence of a slave tutor, Kafur, and outlived Muhammad ibn Tughj by only one year. In 968 the Fatimids entered Egypt.

The Fatimid caliphate (969–1171), a Shiite dynasty with ambitions to replace the orthodox Abbasids, made Egypt the heart of a broad imperial state that encompassed territory from Africa to Sicily, Yemen, Arabia and parts of Syria. Unpopular with the Sunni majority of Muslims, the Fatimids nevertheless distinguished themselves for their tolerance toward nonbelievers, most notably the Copts, who held powerful state posts. One terrible exception was Caliph al-Hakim (ruled 996–1021), who was widely held to be mad and who instigated a purge of Christians and Jews. Throughout the Fatimid era, however, continued Arabization of the country, as well as the return of Egypt to economic prosperity, was the major policy.

Encouraged by decentralization of the political centers of Iraq and Syria during the period, Egypt was able to extend its commercial activities to Europe, finding its monopoly of the Red Sea to be a formidable boon. Prosperity survived, despite the decline of the Fatimid dynasty in the second half of the 12th century, when the armies of the Sunni Muslim regimes of Syria were needed to restore order. Intervention culminated in 1171 with the final overthrow of the Fatimid line by the great statesman and general Saladin, father of the Ayyubid dynasty.

Through Saladin (d. 1193) Egypt was reinstated as a Sunni territory and served as the core of his jihad (holy war) against the Crusader States, which were established across the Holy Land. While he waged intense war against the Crusaders, at home he pursued a fair and even-handed government, treating the Copts well, working to gain and keep the popular support of his subjects and maintaining commercial ties to Europe, Italy in particular. His campaigns not only brought him Jerusalem and dealt crippling blows to the survival of the Crusaders in Palestine but also served to carve out an empire, an Egyptian empire, ruled from the city of Cairo. Saladin, however, allowed the custom of fiefdoms to develop, parceling provinces to family members. Governors thus became autonomous under Saladin's successors, and Egypt was spared for a time only by the presence of the crack regiments of slave troops, the Mamluks. These Turkish slaves grew restless, and in 1250 they elevated one of their own, Aybak, as a replacement for their defunct predecessors.

The period of the Mamluks (1250–1517) brought Egypt to its height as a medieval nation but was also responsible for sending it spiraling into irretrievable social and economic decay. As the Mamluk capital, Egypt attained a preeminence unmatched by the Fatimid or Ayyubid regimes. Mamluk armies conquered the remaining Crusader States, reinstituted the caliphs (with no real power) in Cairo—after they had been abolished by the Mongol sack of Baghdad in 1258—and brought Egypt to the forefront of Islamic culture. The processes of Arabization and Islamization, centuries in the making, found completion and rich expression under the Mamluks. More than a receptacle of Islamic political and military authority, Egypt became a country for the flowering of Muslim religious thought, scholasticism and art. Architectural projects, including mosques, universities and hospitals, abounded, reflecting both the Mamluk encouragement of artistic expression and Islam.

Religious policies changed the status of Christians and non-Muslims. Christians endured markedly curtailed rights under the Mamluks, with the result that the Copts were reduced in number and in favor, and conversions increased. A response to some degree to the repeated attempts of Christian leaders to ally themselves with the Mongols, the persecutions seemed to have no effect on the trade of the 13th and 14th centuries, which provided Egypt with an economic explosion paralleling the cultural one. Commerce was conducted throughout the Mediterranean and Black Seas and as far away as India. A series of disasters, however, befell Mamluk Egypt, beginning with the death of Sultan Al-Nasir in 1340. Plague struck in 1348, and then in 1381, bringing severe depopulation. The Burji Mamluks, ruling from 1382 until 1517, could do little to prevent the slow collapse of the empire, despite rigorous activity to delay it. The final blow came in the late 15th century, when the Portuguese seized control of Egypt's crucial trade with India. In 1517, Egypt fell to the Ottoman Turks, regressing to provincial status.

**EIGHT SAINTS, WAR OF THE** A conflict from 1375 to 1378 between a Florentine coalition and Pope Gregory XI (1370–1378). It originated with the opposition of Florence to the power exercised by the papal legates in Italy, on behalf of the papacy, then residing at Avignon. The pope excommunicated the Florentines and sent Cardinal Robert of Geneva to Italy. Although the war was ended with the Peace of Tivoli in 1378, the danger of losing Rome convinced Pope Gregory to return to the city, thus ending the 70-year residence at Avignon. The name Eight Saints was derived from the war council of Florence (the Otto della Guerra—Eight of War), euphemistically called the Saints. See also FLORENCE.

**EILHART VON OBERGE** Twelfth-century German poet, the author of a literarily influential version of Tristan and Isolde. This tale was a major theme in Romantic literature. See also TRISTAN AND ISOLDE.

**EINHARD** (c. 770–840) Frankish scholar and historian, best known for his important biography (*Vita Caroli Magni*, c. 830–833) on Charlemagne (768–814). Einhard (also called Einhartus or Eginhard) was probably from Franconia, educated at the monastery of Fulda and then (c. 791) recommended by the abbot there to the royal court at Aachen. Known for his intellectual skills, he became an adviser to Charlemagne, as well as a teacher, poet, artistic counselor and an architect. He helped design the palace and basilica of Aachen. His reputation outlived Charlemagne (who died in 814), for he was trusted completely by Louis the Pious (814–840), who recognized Einhard's assistance in gaining the throne. As a reward, the king gave him several abbeys and later a land grant at Mühlheim. Einhard retired in 830, going with his wife Imma to the monastery he had constructed at Mühlheim. He died there as a monk. He wrote several Latin religious works, but, influenced by classical historians such as Livy, Suetonius and Tacitus, he was best remembered for the *Vita Caroli Magni*. Despite errors in fact, it was a vital source for information on Charlemagne and the early years of the Carolingian empire. It was also the first secular biography of the Middle Ages. See also CAROLINGIAN RENAISSANCE.

**EINSIEDELN, ABBEY OF** A Benedictine abbey situated in central Switzerland and founded in 934. According to tradition, the monastery was built on the site of Meinrad's cell, the residence of the famed hermit who was murdered in 861. Favored by the Ottonian kings of Germany, Einsiedeln was made a principality of the Holy Roman Empire in 1274 and granted protection first by the counts of Rapperswil and then the Laufenberg Habsburgs. In 1386 it was transferred to Schwyz, a Swiss canton. A popular place of pilgrimage, the abbey was the resting place of the *Black Madonna*, the smoke-discolored statue of the Virgin Mary brought to the site by Meinrad. See also SWITZERLAND.

**EIRIK I BLOODAXE, KING OF NORWAY** See ERIC I BLOODAXE, KING OF NORWAY.

**EIRIK II PRIESTHATER, KING OF NORWAY** See ERIC II PRIESTHATER, KING OF NORWAY.

**EISTEDDFOD** The Welsh name for assembly, used to signify the gathering of bards and musicians came to be a Welsh national festival. Although such gatherings took place earlier in the Middle Ages, the term Eisteddfod was not known as such until the mid-15th century, when one took place at Carmarthen, under the sponsorship of Gruffud ap Nicolas. Early conferences were probably competitions between the minstrels and the poets, but they were also crucial in the formulation of complex Welsh bardic poetic principles. An important 12th-century gathering was the one held at Christmas in 1176, described in the *Brut,* historical chronicles.

**EKKEHARD** Also Ekkehart, two monks at the Abbey of Saint Gall (Sankt Gallen), a Benedictine monastery and center of learning in Switzerland. Ekkehard I, called the Elder (c. 910–973), was a hymnist and poet. He was of noble birth and was elected dean of Saint Gall, later retiring to the abbey, declining the office of abbot. A composer of hymns, he may have been responsible for the Latin poem *Waltherius,* on King Walter of Aquitaine.

The second Ekkehard of note, Ekkehard IV (d. c. 1060/1069), was educated at Saint Gall, teaching for a time at the cathedral school of Mainz before returning to Switzerland. He was one of the major authors of the *Casus Sancti Galli (Events of St. Gall),* a record of the monastery, an invaluable source for contemporary history. He was also responsible for a revision of the poem *Waltherius.* It was a statement about Ekkehard I by Ekkehard IV in the *Casus* that established the former as the attributed author of *Waltherius.* See also GALL, SAINT.

**EL CID** See RODRIGO DÍAZ DE VIVAR.

**ELEANOR OF AQUITAINE** (c. 1122–1204) Queen consort of King Louis VII of France (1137–1180) and King Henry II of England (1154–1189), mother of Richard the Lion-Hearted and John Lackland and one of the most influential and powerful women in medieval history. Eleanor was the daughter of William X, duke of Aquitaine and count of Poitiers, whose holdings matched those of the French crown. Thus, when William died in 1137, Eleanor's inheritance made her a wealthy and important figure, so much so that she wed Louis VII in July 1137, and became queen of France a month later, when he succeeded his father, Louis VI (1108–1137). She proved a brilliant adviser to Louis, guiding his policy and accompanying him on the Second Crusade (1147–1149). This journey, however, led to the couple's estrangement, and in 1152, despite having produced two daughters, the marriage was annulled by Louis. Eleanor received her feudal possessions in Aquitaine, marrying a few months later Henry Plantagenet, the son of Henry I of England (1100–1135) and heir to the throne.

Her husband was crowned Henry II in 1154, and, with English possessions united with her own, she was queen consort of England, Normandy and much of France. She gave birth to eight children, five sons and three daughters: William (died at three years of age), Henry (d. 1183), Richard (king, 1189–1199), John (king, 1199–1216) and Geoffrey, duke of Brittany; Matilda (wife of Henry the Lion, duke of Saxony and Bavaria), Eleanor (wife of Alfonso VIII, king of Castile) and Joan (wife of William II of Sicily and then of Raymond VI, count of Toulouse). Relations between Eleanor and Henry deteriorated in time, mainly because of his adultery. She probably had a hand in the revolt of her sons against Henry in 1173, lending them political and military assistance. Captured by Henry, she was imprisoned from 1174 to 1189 and released only on the king's death. Her position was considerable in the royal government of Richard, whom she had supported in securing the crown. While he was on Crusade (1189–1192), she served as chief administrator and was vitally active in gathering the ransom that brought Richard freedom from his captor the duke of Austria. When Richard died in 1199 without an heir, Eleanor was instrumental in assuring the coronation of John. In an attempt to improve the situation between France and England, she negotiated the marriage of her granddaughter Blanche to Louis VIII (1223–1226), son of Philip Augustus of France.

Eleanor was a patron of troubadours and court poetry, especially verse extolling courtly love. Her court at Poitiers

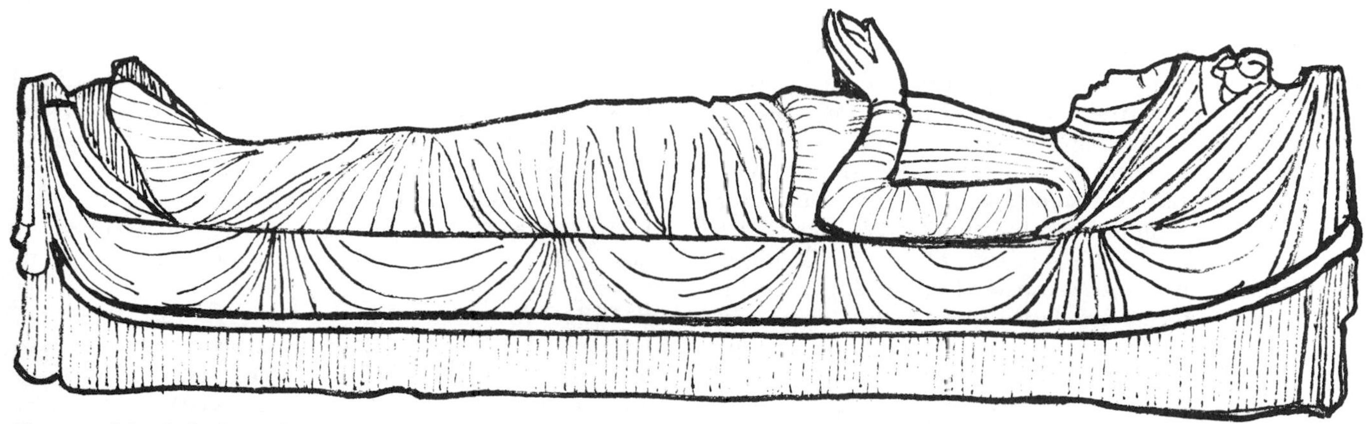

Eleanor of Aquitaine's tomb

was a brilliant literary circle. She died on April 1, 1204, having guided the destinies of France and England, elevated two kings and proved herself a gifted administrator, a brilliant political strategist and a truly regal figure of the age. See also ENGLAND; FRANCE.

**ELEANOR OF CASTILE** (1246–1290) Daughter of King Ferdinand III of Castile (1217–1252) and Joan of Ponthieu and queen consort of King Edward I of England (ruled 1272–1307). Eleanor wed Edward in 1254 while he was still a prince, bringing him the control of Gascony. During the Barons' War (1263–1267) she fled to France for safety, returning in 1265 after Edward's triumph. At his side until her death in 1290, she was reportedly extremely loyal, exercising a positive influence over his moody nature. After her death, Edward had crosses erected along the route of her funeral procession. Called Eleanor Crosses, they were reportedly placed at Grantham, Lincoln, Stamford, Saint Albans, Gaddington, Northampton, Stony Stratford, Woburn, Dunstable, Waltham, Westcheap and Charing. Some still stand. See also EDWARD I.

**ELEANOR OF PROVENCE** (1223–1291) Queen consort of King Henry III of England (ruled 1216–1272). Daughter of Raymond Berengar IV, count of Provence, she wed Henry in 1236, quickly outraging the English barons with her favors shown to Provençal and Savoyard relatives and vassals, who appeared in England asking for and receiving offices. This caused dissatisfaction with Henry III, erupting into the Barons' War (1263–1267). Following the capture of Henry at the Battle of Lewes in 1264, Eleanor fled to France but was instrumental in raising troops for the royal cause. She returned to England in 1265 after Edward (the future Edward I, 1272–1307) won the Battle of Evesham. Her final days were spent in a convent at Amesbury. See also HENRY III, KING OF ENGLAND.

**ELECTORS** Princes of the Holy Roman Empire who were responsible for the election of the German kings. According to the stipulations of the Golden Bull issued by Emperor Charles IV in 1356, there were seven Electors: the king of Bohemia, the margrave of Brandenburg, the duke of Saxony, the count Palatine of the Rhine and the archbishops of Cologne, Mainz and Trier. Changes were subsequently made in the 17th and 18th centuries. See also HOLY ROMAN EMPIRE.

**ELIAS OF CORTONA** (d. 1253) A companion of Francis of Assisi and twice vicar-general of the Franciscan order. A native of Assisi, he rose through the ranks of the Franciscans, traveling to the Holy Land in 1217 and becoming the provincial of Syria in 1219. Returning to Italy with Francis in 1220, the following year he was made vicar of the order, retaining his office until 1227, when John Parenti was elected as his replacement. In 1232 Elias was reelected, but his term was marked by dissent and difficulty. Many members called for a return to the strict austerity that characterized the early years of the order and thus opposed Elias's indulgent way of life and his dictatorial rule. Pope Gregory IX (1227–1241) deposed him in 1239, recognizing Elias's lack of support from the Franciscans. He soon joined Emperor Frederick II (1215–1250) in the ruler's policy against the papacy, for which Elias was expelled from the order and excommunicated. A small group of friars went with him to Cortona, where a monastery was established in honor of Saint Francis. Before his death he was reportedly reconciled with the pope. Elias was the guiding force behind the construction of the basilica of Assisi, raised in memory of the saintly founder of the Franciscans. See also FRANCISCANS.

**ELIPANDUS** (c. 718–802) Archbishop of Toledo and the leading figure in the adoptionist heresy in Spain, which taught that Christ, since he was man, was the adopted son of God. His views were condemned as heretical at a number of synods between 792 and 800, but he could not be removed from his see because of the occupation of the region by the Moors. See also ADOPTIONISM; FELIX, BISHOP OF URGEL; HERESIES.

**ELIZABETH OF HUNGARY, SAINT** (1207–1231) Also called Elizabeth of Thuringia, a legendary figure of charity and spirituality. The daughter of King Andrew II of Hungary (d. 1235), she was betrothed at the age of four to the future Louis IV of Thuringia (1200–1227) and married in 1221 on his succession as landgrave of Thuringia. Upon Louis's death in 1227, she became the victim of Henry Raspe, her brother-in-law, who exiled her on the charge that he could not afford her obsession with charitable work. She found refuge with her uncle, the bishop of Bamberg, rejecting all worldly interests. Having become a member of the Third Order of Saint Francis, she settled at Marburg and fell under the influence of Conrad of Marburg (c. 1228), who dominated her life, forcing her to live under extreme ascetic conditions. His treatment of her was eventually deemed too harsh, and she was removed from his care. Her works for the poor included the building of a hospital at Marburg. Always portrayed with roses, Elizabeth supposedly found those flowers miraculously transformed into loaves of bread for the poor. This miracle convinced her husband that she should be allowed to continue her work. See also MYSTICISM.

**ELY** Cathedral town to the north of Cambridge, called the Isle of Ely because of its origins on an island of rock surrounded by marshes or bogs. Its medieval history began in 673 when Saint Etheldreda, the daughter of the king of East Anglia, founded a twin monastery for both monks and nuns there. Ely became a popular place of pilgrimage after her death in 679, but the monastery was destroyed in 870 by the Danes; it was rebuilt in 970. Abbot Simeon of Ely (1082–1093) began construction of a cathedral. Subsequently completed in the Norman style, it had additions made in contemporary architectural style. In 1109 King Henry I (1100–1135) and Archbishop Anselm of Canterbury made Ely a separate diocese from that of Lincoln.

**EMERIC** (d. 1204) King of Hungary from 1196–1204. He succeeded his father, Béla III (d. 1196), but spent most of his reign feuding with his brother, Andrew, who succeeded him in 1204, ignoring the claims of Emeric's young son. See also HUNGARY.

**EMPIRE, HOLY ROMAN** See HOLY ROMAN EMPIRE.

**EMUND ERICSSON** An early king of Sweden, who reigned from 1050 to 1060. See also SWEDEN.

**ENGLAND** Nation whose medieval history began in the early fifth century and terminated with the introduction of the Tudor absolutism of Henry VII (ruled 1485–1509). During that period the country withstood invasions and periods of political upheaval, empires being won and lost and religious or political figures emerging who were to have a major influence on English and European affairs. The medieval history of England presents a very complex process of social, political and economic evolution. What follows is an overview of the period, and references are provided to offer detailed accounts of other aspects of the country.

The transformation of Britain to England began in the year 407 when the usurper, Constantine III, was declared emperor of the West by the army occupying the country. He embarked on what would be an unsuccessful bid for the imperial throne, but in so doing he stripped the Roman territory of Britain of badly needed troops. Within a few years the inhabitants were suffering from severe and largely unopposed invasions by the Picts, Saxons and other raiders from the Continent. An appeal was sent to Emperor Honorius in 410, but his only response was to suggest that the Britons provide for their own defense. Thus, according to scholars, ended the Roman era in Britain, for the island was partitioned into small territories or domains and fell, ultimately, to domination by Germanic peoples.

During the next two centuries (the fifth to the seventh), England endured one of its darkest eras. The unsettled political conditions of the fifth to seventh centuries left few written records. Little is known, therefore, of this period. The sixth-century writer Gildas claimed that the first Saxons were invited into Britain (c. 430, perhaps later) by the British king Vortigern, who hoped for their support against the Picts and the Scots. They were soon followed by tribes described by Bede as Jutes and Angles. Despite a temporary repulse (c. 500) at Mons Badonicus (Badon Hill) involving the legendary Arthur, the waves of newcomers continued into the sixth century, pushing the Britons to the west and north. Inevitably, the Celts in the island were split; one group survived in the north and the other in the west, present-day Scotland and Wales, respectively, as the Anglo-Saxon presence dominated the lingering Roman of cultural influence and Christianity. The Anglo-Saxons retained their own language and civilization, changing rather than being changed, altering even the name of the country to the land of the Angles, England.

Archaeological remains suggest a wide mixing of the tribes mentioned so distinctly by Bede, a distinction between Jutes, Angles and Saxons serving as a reflection of the origins of their chiefs, or the noble lines, rather than the ethnic definition of their subjects. By the late sixth century, however, separate kingdoms had emerged in the land controlled by the tribes. By the seventh century there were seven major nations, called the Heptarchy: East Anglia, Northumbria, Mercia, Essex, Wessex, Sussex and Kent. The three most powerful were Mercia, Wessex and Northumbria, each achieving prominence and temporary regional superiority. Far more influential and ultimately pervasive was Christianity, which revived in England after being brought from the Continent in 597.

Pope Gregory I (590–604) sent a group of missionaries to England under Augustine, who landed in Kent in 597. His evangelization of the countryside was swift, encouraged by the conversion of King Aethelbert of Kent, who was married to a Frankish Christian woman. Augustine became the first archbishop of Canterbury, and the faith was carried to much of southern and eastern England, its progress halted only by the political realities of several of the Anglo-Saxon kingdoms, where paganism was still practiced. Another factor, and an important one, was the presence of flourishing Christianity in the northern and central parts of the island. Here conversion had been accomplished by the Celtic church in the sixth century, the Christian community that had existed in Ireland and had carried its teachings to England and Scotland (see IONA). Celtic missionaries brought Christianity to the kingdoms of Northumbria, Mercia and Essex, but a crisis soon developed in the Celtic church, as it differed with the Roman church on certain aspects of liturgical usage. At the Synod of Whitby in 664, presided over by King Oswy of Northumbria (655–670) and attended by representatives of both the Celtic and Roman churches, it was decided that the Roman rite should be officially adopted by the church in England. Theodore of Tarsus, archbishop of Canterbury from 668 to 690, helped organize the Christian clergy, and by the late seventh century massive strides had been made in scholarship and culture. The foremost writer of the time was Bede (d. 735). English missionaries sailed to the Continent, including evangelists such as Boniface, Wilibrord and Wilfrid.

Toward the final years of the eighth century, the ascendancy of Mercia was replaced by that of Wessex, a development profoundly affecting English history, for around the same time the Norse invasions began. Danes, or Vikings, these raiders from Scandinavia embarked on expeditions to invade, plunder and pillage, eventually arriving in such numbers that camps were established and plans made for the total conquest of the island. The severity of their attacks brought Mercia and Wessex into an alliance, which ultimately brought to the fore the renowned Saxon king Alfred the Great (871–899). Surviving defeat and hardships, Alfred revived Saxon fortunes and routed the Danes at Edington in 878, eventually signing a peace treaty with the Danish leader, Gunthrum (884), granting the Norse extensive English holdings, the Danelaw. Through Alfred's influence, however, the Danes became Christians.

A gifted ruler, Alfred left a sound administration, having encouraged justice, learning and good government. His son, Edward the Elder (ruled 899–924), crushed the Danelaw, winning all of the lands south of the Humber, and his son, Athelstan, called "the Glorious," annexed Northumbria, claiming the title "king of all Britain" as the crowning achievement of his active reign (924–939). Civil strife strained English unity during the succeeding years. Edgar the Peaceful (ruled 957–975) restored the kingdom; Sven I Forkbeard (d. 1014) of Denmark drove Aethelred II the Unready (978–1016) from the throne. Sven's son, Canute the Great, then reigned over England from 1016 to 1035. Wessex was unable to regain royal power until 1042, when Edward the Confessor, son of Aethelred II, was crowned king. Edward ruled until 1066, but real political authority rested in the hands of the earl of Wessex, Godwin, and after his death in 1053, in those of his son, Harold II Godwinson. In January 1066 Edward himself died. Harold took the crown only to have two other claimants declare themselves, Harald Sigurdsson of Norway and William, duke of Normandy. Harald invaded England in September and was defeated and killed at the Battle of Stamford Bridge. William and the Normans met Harald at Hastings, on October 14. In a fierce battle depicted in the extraordinary Bayeux Tapestry, William conquered England, putting on the crown on Christmas Day 1066.

Called "the Conqueror," William subdued all of England quickly, bringing about extensive social changes by the introduction of Norman feudalism and thereby associating Britain with France for centuries to come. He was also responsible for the Domesday Book. His successor, WILLIAM II (ruled 1087–1100), was harsh and maintained the feudal system. Henry I (ruled 1100–1135), his brother, married into the Saxon royal line, wedding MATILDA, a descendant of Ethelred II. Matilda was named as heir, but the barons chose instead Stephen of Blois, Henry's nephew. Stephen assumed the throne, but in 1153 Matilda returned with her formidable son, Henry Plantagenet, heir to the house of Anjou. Henry was named Stephen's heir, and the Plantagenet dynasty achieved supremacy in 1154.

HENRY II, founder of the Plantagenets, or ANGEVIN DYNASTY, ruled from 1154 to 1189, long remembered as one of the greatest English kings, whose achievements extended the nation's government and law, stretching from the isle into France. Through his marriage to Eleanor of Aquitaine, he acquired vast holdings in France that were to be more profitable and influential than those of the French kings. This Angevin Empire required spirited defense, and Henry employed both war and diplomacy to achieve his ends. In England he introduced the most enlightened legal system to be found in Europe, advancing the judicial policies of juries, writs and processes. In the cause of his legal reforms he issued the Constitutions of Clarendon (1164), which brought him into a bitter dispute with his former friend and confidant Thomas à Becket, the man he had chosen to be archbishop of Canterbury. Becket was murdered by Henry's order in Canterbury Cathedral in 1170, and Henry faced his own rebellious wife and four sons. He died in 1189, convinced that he had failed, although he left a strong feudal state and empire.

Richard I the Lion-Hearted, his son and heir (ruled 1189–1199), known primarily for his war with King Philip II Augustus (1180–1223) and his exploits in the Third Crusade, was followed by John, called Lackland, one of the most infamous of the medieval monarchs (ruled 1199–1216). His three major conflicts, with Philip II Augustus of France, with the papacy and with his own barons, held some victories, but he died in 1216 never having achieved greatness. He lost Normandy to the French, was humiliated by the pope and, on June 15, 1215, was forced by his barons to sign Magna Carta, a document drawn up to extend and protect the rights of the nobility, becoming a landmark in the history of law and democracy. It guaranteed that the king would not abuse feudal privileges, would respect the laws of the land and would consult with the nobility in matters of importance, especially royal revenues. John attempted to nullify the document, but it was reissued after his death.

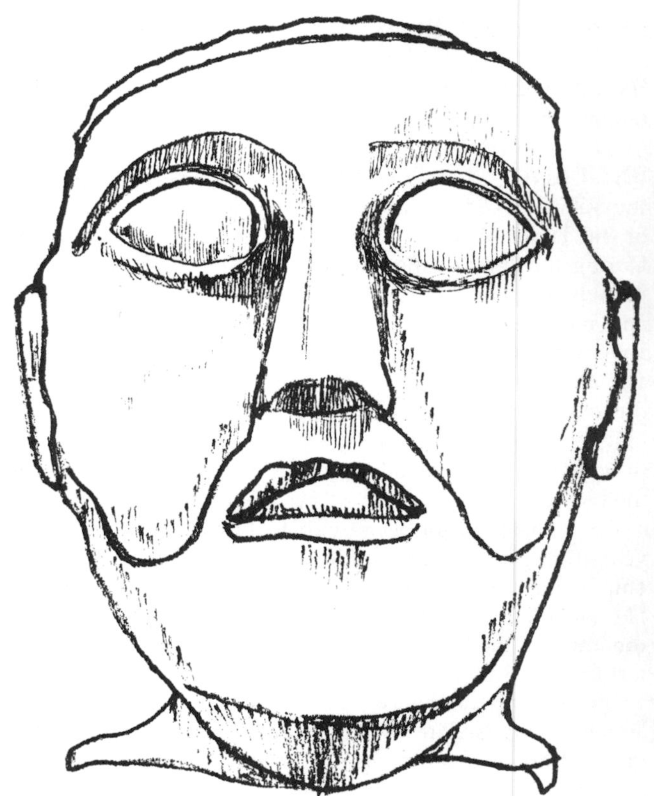

Celtic head, ninth century

In 1216, his heir, Henry III, embarked on a 56-year reign (1216–1272) that was torn by factionalism, disputes with the barons and more internal war. Henry was compelled to issue the Provisions of Oxford in 1258, surrendering many of his principal powers to the nobility. He later revoked the provisions, and a civil war ensued, the royal forces being routed by Simon de Montfort at Lewes in May 1264 (see MONTFORT, SIMON DE [2]). Prince Edward, the future Edward I (1272–1307), rallied the forces loyal to Henry, slew de Montfort at the Battle of Evesham on August 4 and became master of England on his father's death in 1272. A competent and energetic monarch, he pursued policies of administrative reform and foreign political aggressiveness. He issued a number of statutes to amend or clarify common law, while cementing an alliance with the merchant groups to ensure trade and revenues. A notable factor in his reign was the use of Parliament. The 1295 assembly eventually was known as the Model Parliament because of its similarity to later ones, the attendance of both nobles and commoners and the application of writs to summon the representatives. Wales was subdued, but Edward met fierce resistance in Scotland, conquering it in 1295–1296 but unable to curb the influence of William Wallace and Robert the Bruce (1306–1329). Called the Hammer of the Scots, Edward died in 1307, ordering his son, Edward II, to carry his bones before the English army until every Scot had surrendered.

Edward II (ruled 1307–1327) faced rebellious Scots, a huge debt and restless barons and was inhibited by a certain innate incompetence and inability to chose wise advisers. His favoritism in court and the presence of the le Despensers, as well as a foiled Scottish campaign in 1314, culminating in the Battle of Bannockburn, and the triumph of Robert the Bruce, led to conflict. In 1311 the barons had again restricted monarchical rights, provisions repealed by Parliament in 1322, followed by Edward's collapse in 1327, when Queen Isabella returned from France with her lover and ally, Roger Mortimer, earl of March. Edward was deposed, imprisoned and cruelly murdered.

Celtic buckle

Regents administered the affairs of Edward III (ruled 1327–1377) until 1330, when he took control. He reigned during the Black Death (1348–1350) and the start of the Hundred Years' War in 1337. The war was a result of disputes over English possessions in France, French support of Scottish independence, economic differences, control of Flanders and Brittany, and Edward's claim to the French throne. The positive effect of initial English victories could not be maintained, despite that at Crécy in 1346. Then in 1356 the English, led by the Black Prince, Edward, defeated the French at Poitiers. Peace was maintained for a time, as England was beset by internal problems. The Black Prince died in 1376, and Richard, his son, became king in 1377, ruling until 1399. His reign inaugurated a century of strife and instability, set the stage for another civil war and brought an end to the Plantagenet dynasty. His methods of taxation sparked the Peasant Revolt in 1381. He was then confronted by the "Lords Appellant," who had brought about the condemnation of his friends in 1388. Among the lords was Henry Bolingbroke, son of John of Gaunt, who was exiled. On John's death, Richard confiscated his estates, an act that brought Henry home to launch a revolt. Richard abdicated on September 30, 1399, in favor of Henry (IV), dying at Pontefract Castle in 1400.

Henry IV (ruled 1399–1413) relied heavily on the support of Parliament, summoning 10 such assemblies in his reign. He bartered concessions and power for money and became more and more unpopular, hated at the time of his death for his cruelty, bitterness and a suspicious nature. His son, Henry V, was removed from government for a time for suspected disloyalty, returning, however, before the old king's demise. As ruler (1413–1422) Henry V was one of the finest generals of the age, leading England to the brink of total victory in the Hundred Years' War, only to die of dysentery. He adopted a scheme of annexation, consolidation and careful strategy in his war against France, intending to make the conquered territories governed regions rather than occupied foreign soil. At Agincourt in 1415 he annihilated a French army, and his next campaigns and his alliance with the Burgundians brought France to its knees. Under the terms of the Treaty of Troyes (1420), Henry married Catherine of Valois, daughter of Charles VI of France (1380–1422) and was named heir to the French throne. Henry's eight-year-old son was his heir, ruling from 1422 to 1461 and from 1470 to 1471.

The deterioration of the English position was not at first evident, as Henry's uncle, John, duke of Bedford, assumed command of the war, pressing on against the French and their leader, the dauphin Charles VII (1422–1461). At Orléans, however, in 1429, Joan of Arc led the French to a stunning victory from which the English did not recover. Joan was captured and burned as a witch and heretic in 1431, and Henry was crowned king of France in Paris. Charles VII's generals, however, waged relentless campaigns against the English. As the result of lack of will on the part of Henry VI, the death of Bedford in 1435, the desertion of the Burgundians by 1453 and the end of the Hundred Years' War, all that remained of English possessions in France was Calais.

A council of nobles administered English affairs in this period, unable to rely on Henry and not trusting Parliament, which was having difficulty finding money. Cade's Rebellion, led by Jack Cade, broke out in the southeast of England in 1450; it was a protest against the abusive and corrupt regime, and thus the participants' demands were political, not social. Although crushed, Cade's Rebellion signaled the start of the Wars of the Roses, which would rage off and on during the next 35 years. At the Battle of Wakefield, in 1460, Richard, duke of York, leader of the Yorkists, died, his army soundly beaten. The next year his son, Edward of York, rallied the Yorkist cause, winning the battles of Mortimer's Cross and Towton. The latter drove the Lancastrians into Scotland. Edward was crowned (as Edward IV) on June 28, but his reign commenced when he was officially accepted by the city of London on March 4. He ruled from 1461 to 1470 and from 1471 to 1483.

Edward was a good but profligate king, reducing Lancastrian opposition and alienating his one-time ally, Richard Neville, earl of Warwick. Warwick joined forces with the Lancastrians, represented by Henry VI and Margaret of Anjou, and set out to depose Edward, who reclaimed his crown after a brief period of Henry's rule. Henry was put to death in the Tower of London. Edward died in 1483 after years of peace, with the treasury sound and the nation generally content. The reign of his son, Edward V (1483), unfortunately lacked political stability because of questions concerning his birth. Richard, duke of Gloucester, the royal protector of Edward and his brother, Richard, imprisoned them in the Tower of London. He was crowned king of England (as Richard III) in July 1483, possibly having murdered the princes. His many enemies, both Yorkists and Lancastrians, flocked to the banner of Henry Tudor, earl of Richmond, who landed in England from France in August 1485. The battle at Bosworth Field decided English history, ending the Wars of the Roses and England's medieval era. The Age of the Tudors had begun.

See also ANGLES; ANGLO-SAXON CHRONICLE; ANGLO-SAXON CHURCH; ANGLO-SAXONS; AQUITAINE; ARTHURIAN LEGEND; ARUNDEL; ARUNDEL, THOMAS; AUGUSTINE OF CANTERBURY, SAINT; BALL, JOHN; BANKING; BARONS' WAR; BAYEUX TAPESTRY; BEAUFORT, HENRY; BEAUFORT, LADY MARGARET; BEDE, SAINT; BEOWULF; BERNICIA, KINGDOM OF; BERWICK; BORDER, THE; BOURCHIER, THOMAS; BRITTANY; CADE, JACK; CALAIS; CAMBRIDGE; CANTERBURY; CANTILUPE, THOMAS DE, SAINT; CANTILUPE, WALTER DE; CARDIFF; CARLISLE; CASTLE; CATHEDRAL; CATHERINE OF VALOIS; CAXTON, WILLIAM; CELTIC CHURCH; CHAUCER, GEOFFREY; CHIVALRY; CLARENCE, DUKES OF; CLARENDON, CONSTITUTIONS OF; CRUSADES; CYNEWULF; DÁL RIATA, KINGDOM OF; DANEGELD; DANELAW; DOMESDAY BOOK; DUNSTABLE, JOHN; DUNSTAN, SAINT; DURHAM; DURROW, BOOK OF; EAST ANGLIA; EDGAR THE AETHELING; ELEANOR OF AQUITAINE; ELY; ESSEX; EXCHEQUER; FALKIRK, BATTLE OF; FALSTOF, SIR JOHN; FEUDALISM; FITZNEALE, RICHARD; FLAMBARD, RANULPH; FLANDERS; FOLIOT, GILBERT; FORTESCUE, SIR JOHN; FRANCE; GASCONY; GAVESTON, PIERS; GAWAIN; GEOFFREY OF MONMOUTH; GEORGE, PATRON OF ENGLAND, SAINT; GIRALDUS CAMBRENSIS; GLASTONBURY; GLOUCESTER; GLOUCESTER, GILBERT DE CLARE, EARL OF; GLOUCESTER, HUMPHREY, DUKE OF; GLOUCESTER, RICHARD DE CLARE, EARL OF; GODIVA; GODWIN; GOTHIC ART AND ARCHITECTURE; GRIMOIRES; GROSSETESTE, ROBERT; GUILDS; HANSEATIC LEAGUE; HAWKWOOD, JOHN; HENGIST AND HORSA; HERALDRY; HEREWARD THE WAKE; HOLY GRAIL; HOWEL THE GOOD; HUBERT DE BURGH; HUGH OF LINCOLN, SAINT; HUNDRED YEARS' WAR; IPSWICH; IRELAND; JEWS AND JUDAISM; JOAN OF ARC; JOHN OF GAUNT; JOHN OF SALISBURY; JOSEPH OF ARIMATHEA, SAINT; KELLS, BOOK OF; KENILWORTH; KENT; KENT, KINGDOM OF; LANCASTER, HENRY, DUKE OF; LANCASTER, HOUSE OF; LANFRANC; LANGTON, STEPHEN; LINCOLN; LINDISFARNE; LLEWELYN AP GRUFFYDD; LOLLARDY; LONDON; MAGNA CARTA; MALMESBURY; MALORY, SIR THOMAS; MANORIAL SYSTEM; MERCIA, KINGDOM OF; MYSTICISM; NORFOLK; NORMANDY; NORMANS; NORTHAMPTON, ASSIZE OF; NORTHUMBRIA; NORWICH; NOTTINGHAM; OFFA'S DYKE; OWEN GLENDOWER; OXFORD; OXFORD, PROVISIONS OF; PAGANISM; PALE, THE; PEASANT REVOLT; PERCY; PICTS; PILGRIMAGES; PLANTAGENET; ROBIN HOOD; ROLLO; ROMANESQUE ART AND ARCHITECTURE; SAINT ALBANS; SALISBURY; SAXONS; SCHOLASTICISM; SCOTLAND; SOMERSET; STAINED GLASS; SURREY; SUSSEX, KINGDOM OF; SUTTON HOO; THOMAS À BECKET, SAINT; TOWER OF LONDON; TRADE AND COMMERCE; TUDOR DYNASTY; TYLER, WAT; UNIVERSITIES; VIKINGS; WALES; WARS OF THE ROSES; WESSEX; WESTMINSTER ABBEY; WESTMINSTER, STATUTES OF; WHITBY; WHITBY, SYNOD OF; WILLIAM OF MALMESBURY; WITCHCRAFT; WYCLIFFE, JOHN; YORK; YORK, HOUSE OF; and individual rulers.

**ENNODIUS, MAGNUS FELIX** (c. 473–521) Bishop of Pavia, poet, rhetorician and Christian writer. He was born to a noble Roman family (the Anicii), becoming a deacon about 483 under Saint Epiphanius, bishop of Pavia. After teaching for a number of years, probably at Milan, he was made bishop of Pavia in 513, traveling twice to Constantinople on behalf of Pope Hormisdas (514–523) to attempt a reconciliation with the Eastern Church. He was also traditionally considered a friend of the Ostrogothic king Theodoric (471–526). Gifted, Ennodius was one of the last literary figures to combine Roman tradition with Christian beliefs. Among his works were a useful biography of Epiphanius, a panegyric on Theodoric, a collection of hymns, *Dictiones,* discourses on rhetoric, poems and *Eucharisticum de vita sua,* an account of his religious experiences.

**ENZIO** (c. 1220–1272) King of Sardinia, the illegitimate son of Emperor Frederick II (1215–1250), who, after marrying a Sardinian heiress, was installed by his father on the island as ruler. In 1249 he was captured by the Guelphs and imprisoned for the rest of his life at Bologna.

**EPIRUS** Region in western Greece situated on the Ionian Sea. Epirus was conquered by the Roman Empire in 167 B.C., inaugurating centuries of Roman and then Byzantine rule. It became important only after 1204, with the sack of Constantinople during the Fourth Crusade and the subsequent appearance of small Byzantine states. One of these was the Despotate of Epirus, lasting from 1204 to 1340. Epirus was overrun in 1318, however, by the Serbs and Albanians, annexed again to the Byzantine Empire in

1337 and lost once more in 1348 to the Serbian revival, led by Stephen Dusan. Finally, Epirus was seized by the Ottoman Turks in 1430. See also EPIRUS, DESPOTATE OF.

**EPIRUS, DESPOTATE OF** A Byzantine principality from 1204 to 1340, situated on the southern Adriatic Sea on the western coast of Albania and Greece. It was established following the sack of Constantinople by the Fourth Crusade and the creation of the Latin Empire of Constantinople (ruling from 1204 to 1261) as a means of organizing resistance to the Latins. The first despot was Michael I Angelus Ducas (1204–c. 1215), related to the Byzantine imperial family. His brother and successor, Theodore (c. 1215–1224), captured Thessalonica in 1224 and henceforth reigned as an emperor until 1230, when he was captured by Ivan Asen II of Bulgaria. This loss was a blow to Epirus, and its domain was subsequently reduced. By 1264, Michael II "the Despot" recognized the suzerainty of the Byzantine Empire ruled by Michael VIII Palaeologus. The murder of John Orsini (ruled from 1323) by his wife, Anna Despina, gave Emperor Andronicus III Palaeologus the excuse he needed to annex the despotate entirely, placing it under a local governor. See also EPIRUS.

**ERARIC** King of the Ostrogoths for a brief time in 541. The successor to the murdered Hildibad, Eraric was replaced by the great king Totila. See also OSTROGOTHS.

**ERIC I EJEGOD, KING OF DENMARK** (c. 1056–1103) Ruler from 1095 to 1103; the son of Sven II Estridson, he succeeded his brother Olaf (d. 1095) to the throne. Under Eric's aegis Lund was made an archbishopric of Scandinavia (1103). See also DENMARK.

**ERIC II EMUNE, KING OF DENMARK** (1090–1137) Ruler from 1134 to 1137, the son of Eric I Ejegod and brother of Canute V Lavard. Eric avenged Canute's murder by Magnus, son of Niels, by defeating and killing Magnus in battle. When Niels was murdered soon after, the throne fell vacant and Eric became king. His three-year reign was marred by civil wars. See also DENMARK.

**ERIC III, KING OF DENMARK** (1110–1146) A participant in the civil war for the throne between Eric II Emune, Magnus the Strong and Canute Lavard. See also DENMARK.

**ERIC IV PLOVPENNIG, KING OF DENMARK** (1241–1250) Ruler from 1241 to 1250, crowned during the reign of his father, Waldemar II Sejr (c. 1232), succeeding to the throne on Waldemar's death in 1241. Civil war erupted, however, between Eric and his brother Abel for the monarchy. In 1250 Eric was captured and put to death by supporters of Abel. See also DENMARK.

**ERIC V KLIPPING, KING OF DENMARK** (c. 1249–1286) Ruler from 1259 to 1286; he was never politically strong, actual power resting in the hands of his nobles. In 1259 his father, Christopher I (1252–1259), was murdered, probably by the archbishop, Jacob Erlandsen, and after the defeat of the royalist forces in 1261, Eric and his mother were held prisoners for three years. Finally allowed to rule alone in 1270, he was dominated by his nobles, who in 1282 forced on him the *haandfaestnig,* Denmark's first royal charter or constitution. It provided additional authority to the nobility, reduced the role of the provincial *things* (assemblies) and the crown and called for an annual meeting of the *hof,* the council of nobles and prelates of Denmark. In 1286, for an unknown reason, he was murdered, and his son, Eric VI Menved (1286–1319), was chosen as his successor.

**ERIC VI MENVED, KING OF DENMARK** (1274–1319) Ruler from 1286 to 1319, the successor to his father, Eric V Klipping, inheriting reduced powers for the monarchy and a conflict between the crown and the Danish church. He was elected king following the murder of his father, facing a revolt of a group of nobles who had been convicted and expelled for involvement in Eric V's death. They were aided by Duke Waldemar of Schleswig and Archbishop Jens Grand. Eric was supported by a majority of the nobles, defeating Waldemar in battle, convincing Norway's king not to interfere and then imprisoning Jens Grand. A papal interdict was placed on Denmark for this; it was lifted in 1303 when Eric agreed to pay a fine for Grand's transfer by Pope Boniface VIII (1294–1303). Ambitions toward the German states in the north led to extreme military involvement, including the purchase of mercenaries. Despite early success, his venture became so expensive that the treasury was strained, the kingdom's finances sinking into disorder. By his death in 1319, most of his gains had been lost, and the kingdom was without an heir. See also DENMARK.

**ERIC VII OF POMERANIA, KING OF DENMARK, NORWAY AND SWEDEN** See ERIC OF POMERANIA, KING OF SCANDINAVIA.

**ERIC I BLOODAXE, KING OF NORWAY** (d. 954) Ruler of Norway from 940 to 945 but also king of Northumbria twice before his death. He was the son of Harald Fairhair (ruled 872–930), succeeding to the throne while earning the name Bloodaxe for the murder of most of his brothers. Unable to withstand him any longer, the Norwegian nobles expelled him from the throne about 934. Recovering from this political blow, he went to Northumbria and was chosen as ruler there with the prospect of his support of their independence from the Saxons. In 948, Edred, king of Wessex, invaded Northumbria, deposing Eric. The Northumbrians soon elected Olaf Sihtricson, but he was removed by Eric, who returned in 952. Eric reigned at York for two years before being murdered by a rival. See also NORTHUMBRIA; NORWAY.

**ERIC II PRIESTHATER, KING OF NORWAY** (d. 1299) Ruler from 1280 to 1299, the son of Magnus VI Lawmender (ruled 1263–1280). Eric earned the name Priesthater for his policies aimed at limiting the power of the church, which had grown considerably during his father's time, largely at the expense of the secular government. He also attempted to curtail the influence of the

Hanseatic League, but the resulting pressures from the Hanse forced him to end his campaigns. See also NORWAY.

**ERIC OF SWEDEN** An early ruler of the Swedes. He reigned sometime around 800. See also SWEDEN.

**ERIC THE VICTORIOUS, KING OF SWEDEN** (d. 995) An early ruler of the Swedes, reigning from about 980 to 995. His successor was Olaf.

**ERIC IX, KING OF SWEDEN, SAINT** (d. 1160) Ruler from about 1156 to 1160, a symbol of Swedish nationalism. Successor to Sverker the Elder (c. 1135–1156), he was an ardent supporter of Christianity and became the patron saint of Sweden. His reign was viewed during the later Middle Ages as a kind of golden age. He may have led a crusade into Finland and suffered a martyr's death. The line of Eric dynasts of Sweden was descended from him, vying until 1250 with the Sverker dynasty for control of the throne. Eric was always depicted as a young knight, holding a sword and the banner of Sweden. See also SWEDEN.

**ERIC X CANUTESSON, KING OF SWEDEN** (d. 1216) Son of Canute Ericsson (d. 1196), he deposed Sverker II Charlesson in 1208, claiming the throne for himself. He is generally considered to be the first ruler of Sweden crowned by the archbishop of the nation, dying in 1216 of natural causes. See also SWEDEN.

**ERIC XI ERICSSON, KING OF SWEDEN** (d. 1250) Ruler from 1222 to 1229 and again from 1234 to 1250. He was the last king of the country to be descended from Saint Eric (Eric IX). Originally the successor to John I Sverkersson in 1222, he was replaced in 1229 by Canute II the Tall, returning to power in 1234. During his second reign Birger Jarl came to prominence, and on Eric's death, Valdemar, Jarl's son, was elected king (1250–1275). See also SWEDEN.

**ERIC XII MAGNUSSON, KING OF SWEDEN** (d. 1359) Ruler from 1357 to 1359, actually sharing power with his father, Magnus II Ericsson (ruled 1319–1364). Named an heir in 1344, he used excellent relations with the Swedish nobility to compel Magnus to split the kingship in 1357. He died, however, two years later. See also SWEDEN.

**ERIC XIII OF POMERANIA** See ERIC OF POMERANIA, KING OF SCANDINAVIA.

**ERIC OF POMERANIA, KING OF SCANDINAVIA** (c. 1382–1459) Ruler of Scandinavia (Denmark, Norway and Sweden) from 1396 until his deposition in 1438. Eric was the son of Duke Vratislav II of Pomerania and great-nephew of Margaret of Scotland, queen of a united Scandinavia (Denmark, Norway and Sweden). He was adopted by her in 1387, and she secured recognition of him as her heir, had him crowned in 1396 but continued to exercise actual political control until her death in 1417. His major aim as king after 1412 was the expansion of Scandinavian interests along the Baltic Sea, specifically Schleswig. Toward this end he waged two wars against the counts of Holstein, from 1416 to 1422 and 1426 to 1432. The conflicts soon involved the Hanseatic League, which looked upon his ambitions suspiciously. In the ensuing economic and military struggle, Eric proved initially successful, but the loss of trade with the Hanse, high taxes and a royal tendency to favor Danish merchant leaders caused resentment in the three kingdoms and finally rebellion. By 1438 the merchants of Norway and Sweden, with elements of Danish nobility, were in a position to demand extensive constitutional changes. When Eric refused, he was deposed, replaced by Christopher III of Bavaria (1439–1448). His attempts to recover the throne were unsuccessful, and departing his exile at Gotland, he returned to Pomerania. See also KALMAR UNION.

**ERICSSON, LEIF** See LEIF ERICSSON.

**ERIC THE RED** Famed 10th-century Norse explorer who established the first colony on Greenland and was the father of Leif Ericsson. The son of Thorvald, Eric moved from Norway to Iceland with his exiled father and became known there as Eric the Red. Around 980 he was himself exiled, sailing to explore the western regions beyond Iceland. His journeys brought him and his family to Greenland about 982. There he brought fellow Norsemen, having returned to Iceland in 986 to find others who would help him establish a permanent presence in Greenland. This colony proved successful for several years but eventually declined (c. 1002) because of hardship and disease. There were to be other settlements, however, over the next centuries. See also GREENLAND.

**ERIGENA, JOHN SCOTUS** See JOHN SCOTUS ERIGENA.

**ERWIG** (d. after 687) King of the Visigoths from 680 to 687, one of the last Visigothic kings of Spain. His reign was marked by the ascendancy of the church in state affairs, most notably the influence of Julian, bishop of Toledo, who guided royal policy. He was a great-nephew of King Chindaswinth and a former loyal courtier of King Wamba. In 680, however, he had seized the royal treasury, declared himself king and possibly through deceit forced Wamba to become a monk. Ironically, in 687, he chose Egica as his successor, and he, too, entered a monastery. See also VISIGOTHS.

**ESCHENBACH, WOLFRAM VON** See WOLFRAM VON ESCHENBACH.

**ESSEX** One of the Anglo-Saxon kingdoms of England, composed of the East Saxons and comprising Essex, Middlesex and parts of Hertfordshire; its chief city was London. Essex probably was settled in the sixth century, accepting Christianity only slowly, with pagan revivals occurring until the Northumbrian missionary Cedd (d. 664) was successful in permanently converting the Saxons. The kings of Essex were never the strongest in the isle and from 664 to 825 were under the domination of Mercia. In 825 King Egbert of Wessex made Essex one of his territorial acquisitions, ruled by the princes of Wessex. As part of the agreement between Alfred the Great and the Danish king Guthrum (r. 878–884), Essex was included in the Danelaw, being won back by Edward the Elder in 917. It was eventually made an earldom. See also ENGLAND.

**ESTATES GENERAL** See STATES GENERAL.

**ESTE, HOUSE OF** Italian noble family that occupied a prominent place in Italian politics and culture from the 13th to the 16th century and was a leader of the Guelph, or papal, party. The Este, or Estensi, were originally of Lombard descent, eventually establishing estates at Este (from which they took their name), Rovigo, Friuli and Moselice. The acknowledged founder of the house was Alberto Azzo II (d. 1097), a margrave. His son, Welf, his mother the sister of Welf III, duke of Carinthia, became Welf IV, duke of Bavaria and father of a line of politically powerful men who included the Electors of Hanover. Prestige in Italy was increased by the membership of the Este head, Azzo VII, in the Guelph league, allowing Obizzo II to become the lord of Ferrara (1288) and Modena (1289). Subsequent Este princes utilized strategic marriages, alliances and their wealth to further their position in Italy and to make Ferrara a vital cultural and intellectual city. The Estes were noted patrons of the arts in the Renaissance.

**ESTONIA** See LIVONIA.

**ETHELBALD, KING OF MERCIA** See AETHELBALD, KING OF MERCIA.

**ETHELBERT, KING OF KENT** See AETHELBERT, KING OF KENT.

**ETHELDREDA, SAINT** (d. 679) Daughter of the king of East Anglia, the founder of the monastery for monks and nuns at Ely. Having led a life of prayer and spiritual dedication, she was convinced by her relatives to marry Egfrid, who would become king of Northumbria (670–685). Her marriage was never consummated, however, and after 12 years she received Egfrid's permission to become a nun. About 672 she retired to the convent and soon after laid the foundation for Ely. Traditionally she was also called Saint Audrey. (The word *tawdry* was derived from the cheap finery sold at the Saint Audrey's fair.) See also ELY.

**ETHELRED I, KING OF WESSEX** See AETHELRED I, KING OF WESSEX.

**ETHELRED II, KING OF ENGLAND** See AETHELRED II, KING OF ENGLAND.

**ETHELWULF, KING OF WESSEX** See AETHELWULF.

**ETON COLLEGE** School in England in Berkshire, near London, founded in 1440 by King Henry VI. It was closely associated with King's College, Cambridge, which received many graduates of Eton into its halls.

**EUGENE I** (d. 657) Pope from 654 to 657, the successor of Martin I, who had been deposed by the Byzantine emperor Constans II, receiving from the exiled pontiff a recognition of his legitimacy. The heresy of Monothelitism dominated his pontificate.

**EUGENE II** (d.827) Pope from 824 to 827, who was forced shortly after his election to greet Emperor Lothair I and to acknowledge that ruler's domination of Rome. In return, however, the emperor accepted the right of the nobles and clergy of Rome to choose the popes, subject to imperial approval. Eugene also fought against the doctrine of iconoclasticism in the Byzantine Empire.

**EUGENE III** (d.1153) Pope from 1145 to 1153, born Bernardo Pignatelli. He was a Cistercian after 1135, under Bernard at Clairvaux, becoming the abbot of Saints Vincent and Anastasius in Rome and then pope. Shortly after he was elected, he was forced to flee Rome because of the conflicts with the secular leadership of the city, the Roman Senate. He eventually journeyed to France (1147), promoting the Second Crusade in response to the fall of Edessa in 1144. Bernard was named as the preacher of the cause, and King Louis VII of France (1137–1179) was called on to lend his support. Eugene was an ardent advocate of reform of both the episcopal clergy and the religious orders. In 1148, Eugene excommunicated the rebellious Roman leader Arnold of Brescia, holding numerous councils from 1147 to 1148 to combat heresy and to strengthen doctrine. A treaty was concluded in 1153 (the Treaty of Constance) with Emperor Frederick I Barbarossa (1152–1190) concerning the rights of the church. Returning to Rome, Eugene died in July 1153; deep spirituality and the advice of Bernard had been his guiding principles.

**EUGENE IV** (c. 1360–1447) Pope from 1431 to 1447, whose reign witnessed the decline of conciliarism within the church and the brief reunion of Christianity in the East and West. Born Gabriel Condulmaro at Venice, he joined the Augustinian Canons while still young and in 1408 became the cardinal of San Clemente. Elected the successor to Pope Martin V, he was confronted immediately by the Council of Basel (1431–1449), assembled to discuss reforms in the church but which soon advanced the conciliar view so dominant at the Council of Constance (1413–1417). A struggle ensued between the council and the pope, including an unsuccessful attempt by Eugene to dissolve it in 1433. By 1439 relations were poor, largely because of the Council of Ferrara-Florence (1438–1439), and the council tried to depose him, electing an antipope, Felix V (1439–1449, Amadeus VIII, duke of Savoy), in response to his excommunication of its founding members.

Despite his trouble with the Council of Basel, he proved ultimately successful in the argument against conciliarism, because of his triumph at Ferrara-Florence in uniting the Eastern and Western Churches. Given additional ecclesiastical authority, he was ably to defy the Council of Basel and break its will. He did face other setbacks, however, such as the preaching of an ill-fated Crusade against the Turks (1444) that was ended in catastrophe at Varna. In 1438, Charles VII of France issued the Pragmatic Sanction of Bourges, curtailing the powers of the papacy in France and straining his dealings with Eugene.

**EUGENIKOS, MARK** (d. 1445) Fifteenth-century Byzantine theologian and poet, the author of an ode on the fall of Constantinople to the Ottoman Turks in 1453. An accomplished archivist, teacher and deacon, as metropolitan of Ephesus John was a member of the delegation accompanying Emperor John VIII Palaeologus (1425–1448) to the Council of Ferrara-Florence in 1437, signing in 1439 the decree uniting the Eastern and Western Churches. He later repudiated his assent to that agreement. His ode was the "Oratorio for the Great City," which compared the fall of Constantinople to the destruction of Jerusalem and the Crucifixion of Christ. See also CONSTANTINOPLE.

**EULENSPIEGEL, TILL** Also Tyl Ulenspiegel, a German clown who was said to have died in 1350. Eulenspiegel was infamous for his cruel, farcical and broadly humorous practical jokes against clergy and townspeople. Stories appeared about him in the 14th century, and by the late 15th century they were being compiled into several Low German versions. He was eventually known in England as well and was always the symbol of social revenge on the upper classes, the victims of his many pranks.

**EURIC** (d. 484) King of the Visigoths in Gaul and in Spain from 466 to 484, having a major role in the demise of the Roman Empire in the West. The brother of the Visigothic king Theodoric II (453–466), in 466 he murdered him, claiming the throne. He immediately launched campaigns against the weakened Roman province of Gaul, taking Aquitaine and Arles and pillaging the Rhône Valley. By 476 Marseilles and Provence were in his control, as his power extended from Gaul into Spain, surrounding states such as those of the Goths, Franks and Burgundians acknowledging his position. He was also a champion of Arianism and promulgated the *Codex Euricianus* (475), a series of laws, also called the Code of Euric. See also VISIGOTHS.

**EVESHAM, BATTLE OF** See BARONS' WAR.

**EXARCHATE** The term applied to the two provinces controlled by the Byzantine Empire in Italy and Africa, following the resurgence of Byzantine power under Justinian I (ruled 527–565). They were the Exarchates of Ravenna and Africa, so termed because they were headed by an exarch, or governor.

The Exarchate of Ravenna was formed as a result of Belisarius's conquest of the Italian peninsula and the Ostrogoths in 540. Byzantine rule was soon contested (c. 568) by the Lombards, who launched a conflict that lasted for nearly two centuries. Sometime before 584, administration was entrusted to an exarch, who had supreme authority in Italy and was answerable to the emperor in Constantinople. Ravenna thus reflected the exarch's power, and the entire exarchate was prosperous and strong for many years. Declining Byzantine strength in the seventh century extended to overseas possessions, and the exarchate was forced to curtail its expansion to concentrate on the protection of Ravenna itself from the increasing Lombard menace. Deteriorating conditions culminated in 751, with the fall of the exarchate to the Lombard king Aistulf, ending the Byzantine presence in northern Italy.

Also called the Exarchate of Carthage, the Exarchate of Africa was established in 533 by Belisarius following his defeat of the Vandals. The exarch had considerable autonomy, but the great collapse of Byzantine strength in the seventh century doomed the empire's possessions abroad. In 698 Carthage fell to the Muslims.

See also CARTHAGE; RAVENNA.

**EXCHEQUER** The department of the English government responsible for financial administration. Finances during the Saxon regime were, for their time, generally advanced, but following the occupation of England by William the Conqueror and the Normans (1066), centralization of authority and improvements were made in the financial system to make it more efficient and responsive to the Crown. One of the results of these changes came during the reign of Henry I (1100–1135) when the royal household chamber, with its treasury at Winchester, was enlarged to assume a supervisory position over royal finances. From this governmental body emerged the Exchequer. Its name was derived from the Latin *scaccarium* (chessboard), or the checkerboard counting table used to make calculations. The Exchequer resembled the treasury at first but assumed a different character in time, acquiring authority as a court and carrying out duties as a counting agency.

Aside from the pipe rolls (Rolls of the Exchequer), which, with the receipt rolls, were excellent records, the best source for information on the procedures used by the Exchequer was *The Dialogue of the Exchequer* (1180) by Richard Fitzneale (Richard Fitz Nigel), a former treasurer of the Exchequer. Its offices permanently at Westminster, the department was divided into two bodies, Lower and Upper. The Lower Exchequer compiled financial records, and twice a year, at Easter and at Michaelmas (September 29), it received from the sheriffs or accountable officials all money due to the king. As a receipt, a type of wooden tally was used, a shaft of wood approximately nine inches long on which various notches were made to show the amounts paid. The tally, which was kept in a long scroll-like roll, thus the name, was then cut in half, lengthwise, one half for the official, the other kept by the Exchequer. Members of the Upper Exchequer were called Barons of the Exchequer and were actually included in the King's Council, or Curia Regis. They audited the accounts of the sheriffs, checking that the correct amounts of money were paid and that all financial responsibilities were met. Their table of accounting was quite large (5 feet by 10 feet), covered with a cloth marking off, in vertical lines, columns for certain amounts. The table was thus a form of abacus.

England's Exchequer was considered the model for the rest of Europe during the Middle Ages, although the financial agency for the Normans in Sicily was highly regarded. A number of reforms were made in the department, including the introduction of new accounting procedures and simplification of the collections.

For a time the Exchequer was under the influence of the royal wardrobe, especially during the reigns of Edward I (1272–1307) and Edward III (1327–1377). The rise of Parliament also brought changes, for it compelled the king to have the Exchequer collect parliamentary taxes and then audit the department to avoid any abuses. See also PARLIAMENT.

**EYCK, HUBERT VAN** (d. 1426) Dutch painter and brother of the better-known Jan van Eyck. Together they established the Flemish school of painting. Little else has survived about Hubert. He left no authenticated works but did make important contributions to the beautiful Ghent altarpiece, possibly having been responsible for creating the general form of the work and painting most of the interior before his death, leaving the completion of the work to his brother.

**EYCK, JAN VAN** (c. 1390–1441) An illustrious Dutch painter, brilliant technical artist and with his older brother, Hubert, the founder of the Flemish school of painting. Born at Maeseyck (c. 1390), he came to prominence in the service of the count of Holland (1422). Three years later he was established as court painter to Duke Philip the Good of Burgundy, for whom he journeyed to Spain and Portugal on diplomatic missions. Credited incorrectly by the 16th-century art historian Vasari with the introduction of oil painting, Jan van Eyck was certainly one of the earliest painters to use oil as a medium in order to capture the effects of spatial depth, perspective and naturalism, as well as richness of color. He incorporated many religious themes and disguised religious symbolism in his works, especially that of the Annunciation.

Generally considered his master project was the Ghent altarpiece (the Adoration of the Lamb), possibly begun by his brother but its work left to him after Hubert's death in 1426. Completed about 1432, the altarpiece was soon acclaimed as the foremost example of this workmanship in northern Europe, although scholarly effort has continued in an attempt to determine the role played by each brother in the achievement. A master of weaving diverse elements into a simple but visually extraordinary whole, he influenced but was never surpassed in this style by the great painters of the Netherlands, including Petrus Christus (see also WEYDEN, ROGER VAN DER). Among his other works were the *Portrait of a Young Man* (1432); *Man in a Turban* (c. 1433); *Annunciation* (1434); *Marriage of Arnolfini* (1434); *Lucca Madonna* (1435–1436); *Madonna with Chancellor Robin* (c. 1436); *St. Barbara* (1437); *Triptych* (1437); *Margaret van Eyck* (1439); *Madonna at the Fountain* (1439); and *Annunciation* (n.d.).

**EYSTEIN I** (d. 1125) King of Norway, one of the sons of Magnus III Bareleg (1093–1103), dividing the kingship of Norway with his brothers Olaf IV (ruled 1103–1115) and Sigurd I (ruled 1103–1130). Eystein ruled from 1103 until his death. He and his brothers encouraged the promotion of the church in the nation, including the establishment of monasteries and churches. Olaf died in 1115, and the two brothers who remained were never amicable. Civil war was averted by Sigurd's departure for the Holy Land on crusade, leaving Eystein as nominal king. See also NORWAY.

**EYSTEIN II** (d. 1157) King of Norway from 1142 to 1157, sharing power with his three brothers, Sigurd II (1136–1139), Ingi Hunchback (1136–1161) and Sigurd III (1136–1155). The son of Harald IV Gilchrist (1130–1136), he had lived in Scotland for some time when, in 1142, he returned home to claim his place in the kingship. He was, however, always politically weak because of a lack of supporters among the Norwegian thanes (nobles). Ingi became the strongest of the brothers, and in 1155 Eystein joined with Sigurd in a plot to depose him. Having learned of the plot, Ingi journeyed to Bergen, where he confronted Sigurd. Denying complicity, Sigurd was nevertheless killed, and two years followed in preparation for the inevitable civil war between Ingi and Eystein. In 1157, however, Eystein was murdered in a wood. See also NORWAY.

**EZZELINO III DA ROMANO** (1194–1259) Italian nobleman who became the podesta, or mayor, of Verona, Vicenza and Padua and who was considered one of the most tyrannical Ghibelline soldiers of the day. A gifted but notoriously cruel military man, Ezzelino secured control of Verona in 1226, using his position to oppose Emperor Frederick II. By 1230, however, he was forced to resign his office and allied himself with the Holy Roman Emperor, recapturing Verona in 1232, and supported by imperial troops and favor, he extended his power. A useful and merciless lieutenant of the Guelphs, Ezzelino was rewarded with the mastery of Vicenza (1236–1259) and later Padua (1237–1259). For his support at the Battle of Cortenuova in 1237, he was given Frederick's illegitimate daughter, Selvaggia, in marriage. His political position was secure enough to survive the death of Frederick in 1250, and he was not only excommunicated by Pope Innocent IV in 1254 but was the object of a Guelph crusade. During the subsequent wars he was captured and wounded in battle at Cassano in September 1259. Refusing food or medical aid, he died a few days later, never having been reconciled with the church. Dante placed him in Hell in the *Inferno*. See also GUELPHS AND GHIBELLINES.

# F

**FABRIANO, GENTILE DA** See GENTILE DA FABRIANO.

**FÁFILA** (d. 739) King of Asturias from 737 to 739, who was succeeded by his brother-in-law, Alfonso I (739–757). See also LEÓN.

**FAIRS** Gatherings of merchants, traders, bankers and artisans at set locations for the purpose of buying and selling a variety of goods. Medieval fairs were of great importance until the 14th century, for they served as the means of bringing together the business representatives of Europe while providing the means for the distribution of services and trade items from the West and the East, including commodities generally unavailable anywhere else. Fairs originated through the assembly of merchants on church holidays or festivals *(feriae),* normally at a site such as a bridge, crossroad or well-traveled region, where they could be certain that large numbers of customers would be available. Proven successful economic ventures, the fairs became regularly held events, often retaining the names of the saints with whom they were originally associated. Because of the increased revenue brought into the region, local governments allowed special privileges to the fairs, which lasted for days or even weeks.

Fairs were extremely successful during the 13th and 14th centuries, but their decline was inevitable. The causes of decline varied, such as in France, where the famous Champagne Fair was hampered by the Hundred Years' War (1337–1453) and the improvements made in trade routes. The mortal blow to the fairs of Europe was the rise of the large, permanent trading centers in the urban areas. Unable to withstand the competition, most fairs ceased, but others, the Leipzig, Dresden and Nuremburg fairs, managed to survive into modern times. Fairs, however, provided a vital service, bringing together members of widely separated nations, making possible the modernization of business practices, the organization of commercial law and the standardization of weights and measures. See also CHAMPAGNE, FAIRS OF; TRADE AND COMMERCE.

**AL-FAIZ** The next to the last Fatimid caliph of Egypt, who succeeded to the caliphate in 1154, while still a child, following the murdered caliph al-Zafir. Under the control of the vizier, Talai ben Ruzzik, for a number of years, Faiz had him assassinated in 1161 and his sons in 1163. This resulted in a power struggle in the court and made possible the intervention of Nur-al-Din, who sent an army under Shirkuk and his nephew, Saladin. See also FATIMID CALIPHATE.

**FALIERO, MARINO** (1274–1355) Doge of Venice from 1354 to 1355 and a member of a Venetian noble family, becoming a leading figure in the republic's government. In 1348 he led the defeat of a Hungarian army at Zara; he was a commander of the defeated Venetian forces against Genoa (1352) and a negotiator for the city in its peace negotiations with Genoa. Elected doge in 1354, he was routed by the Genoese at the naval battle of Porto Longe a short time later and was forced to sign a humiliating truce, thereby receiving a major political setback. This loss also strengthened the noble faction in Venice then in conflict with the doge. In 1355 Faliero decided to liquidate his enemies entirely but was discovered in his scheme. He was tried by the nobility, along with his plebeian co-conspirators, and was executed. See also VENICE.

**FALKIRK, BATTLE OF** A conflict fought on July 22, 1298, between Edward I of England (1272–1307) and a rebel Scottish army led by Sir William Wallace. Edward had launched an invasion into Scotland in response to a Scottish uprising, bringing with him some 15,000 infantry and 10,000 cavalry. Despite Wallace's attempts at avoiding a pitched engagement, Edward cornered him and his 25,000 infantry and 3,500 cavalry at Falkirk. The Scots stood firm in the center where Wallace had placed his infantry (pikemen), but their position deteriorated as the Scottish horse was routed and Edward brought his longbowmen into play. Reduced severely, the infantry broke under an English charge and the losses mounted. Wallace fled only to be captured and executed in 1305. See also SCOTLAND.

**FALSTOF, SIR JOHN** Fifteenth-century English soldier. His character was the basis for the comic role Falstaff in the plays of William Shakespeare. Unlike the lying coward in the play *Henry IV,* the true Falstof was a gifted commander who had amassed a fortune as a result of the Hundred Years' War.

**AL-FARABI** (c. 870–950) Islamic philosopher, scholar and musician, called the "Second Teacher," the first being Aristotle. Al-Farabi was born in Transoxiana, of Turkish descent, and was raised and educated in Baghdad. There he was introduced to the study of philosophy, especially that of Aristotle, and ultimately attempted to combine Aristotelian thought with Platonic ideals, while adding elements of

Muslim mysticism. He wrote many works, including metaphysical and philosophical treatises and studies on mathematics, medicine, logic and music. A brilliant lute player, he composed chants still used today by the Dervishes. Of additional interest was his version of the ideal state, based on Plato's *Republic*, the *al-Madina al-fadila*.

**FARAJ, ABUL** See BAR-HEBRAEUS, GREGORIUS.

**FARMING** See BALL, JOHN; FEUDALISM; JACQUERIE; MANORIAL SYSTEM; PEASANT REVOLT; PLAGUES; TYLER, WAT; TRADE AND COMMERCE.

**FATIMA** (d. 633) Daughter of the prophet Muhammad, who was called the Shining One and has been revered by the Muslims, especially by the Shiites because of her marriage to Ali, accepted by the Shiites as the legitimate heir to the Prophet. She journeyed with her father to Medina in 622 and married Ali soon afterward. During Muhammad's final days she cared for him, but after his death her dealings with Abu Bakr were strained, especially in a dispute over property, which she believed she had received from her father. See also ISLAM.

**FATIMID CALIPHATE** Islamic Ismaili Shiite dynasty that ruled in Egypt and North Africa from 909 to 1171 and, for a time, exercised extensive power in the Islamic world, controlling Sicily, the African coast of the Red Sea, Yemen, the Hejaz, Palestine and parts of Syria. It accomplished as well the expansion of Egyptian commercial enterprises, despite being in a Shiite minority ruling subjects who were in the Sunni majority. Although the Fatimids would never succeed in their ultimate goal, the overthrow of the Abbasids, they brought prosperity to Egypt.

The Fatimids were leaders of the religious sect of the Ismaili branch of the Shia that was opposed to the Sunni establishment and plotted its demise. They traced their lineage to the house of the Prophet through his daughter, Fatima (hence the name), and her kinsman, Ali, and were thus recognized by their supporters as the legitimate caliphs. For many years they prepared secretly for the day when they could declare themselves openly against the Abbasids, but the leader of the movement, the imam, and his successors remained secretive to avoid persecution and death. In time, and after repeated unsuccessful uprisings, a foothold was secured in Africa. The Fatimid leader, Ubayd Allah, arrived there, established himself and, in 920, founded the new capital of Mahdiyah (al-Mahdiyya). For many years Ubayd and his immediate successors, al-Qa'im (ruled 934–946) and al-Mansur (ruled 946–953), pursued a policy of political consolidation while launching numerous but unsuccessful expeditions against Egypt. In Africa they met resistance from their Sunni citizenry while dealing with hostile elements, such as the Kharijites and the Byzantines, who threatened their hold over Sicily.

In 953, al-Mu'izz succeeded al-Mansur, bringing a new age to Fatimid history. Under his general, Jawhar, Egypt was finally captured, giving the Ismaili Shiites their long-hoped-for strategic position from which to launch their war against the Abbasids. Near al-Fustat, the Fatimids established a new city, Cairo, to serve as their capital while the country's wealth and stability, virtually in ruins left by

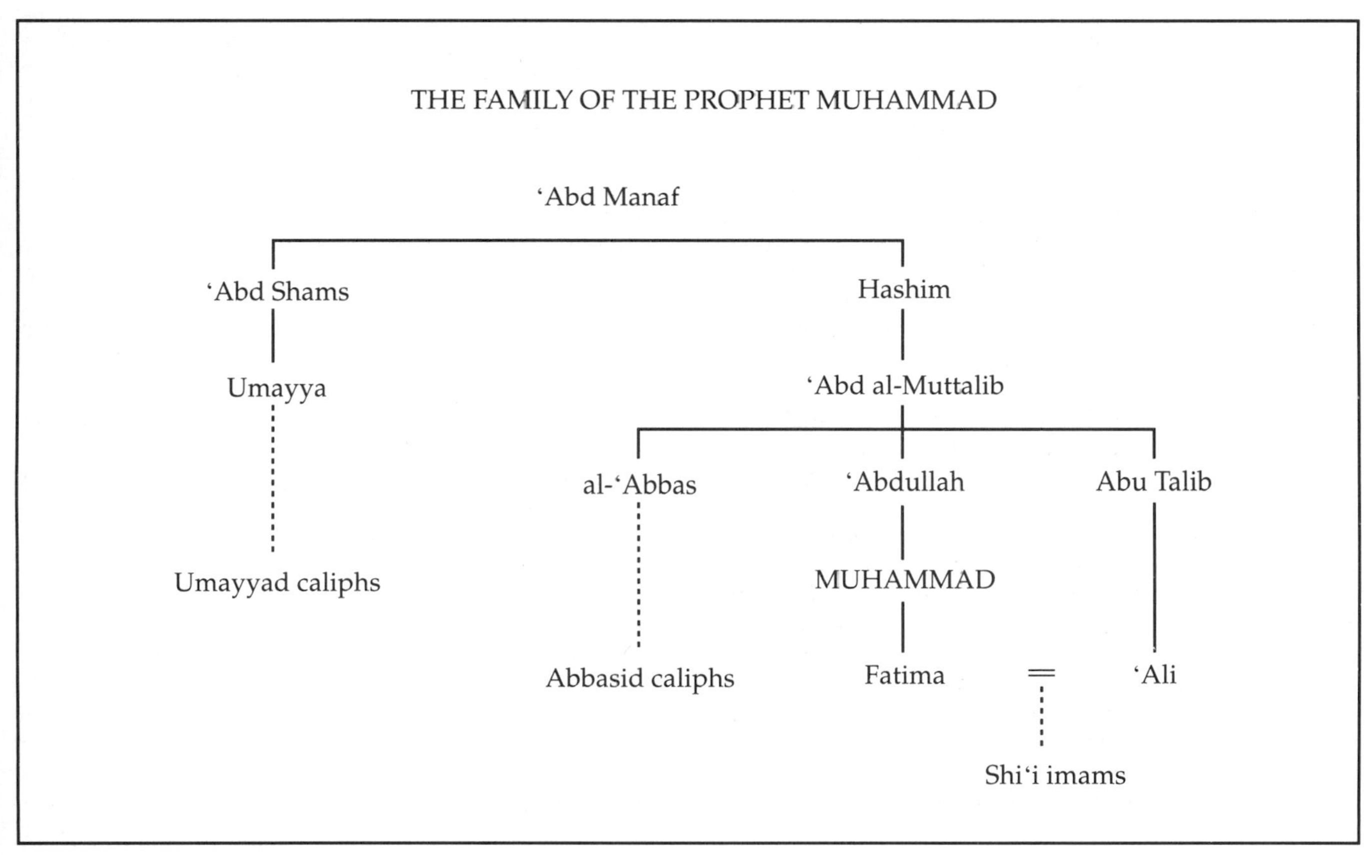

previous regimes, was revived. The figure largely responsible for this was Yaqub ibn Killis, a Jewish convert to Islam who, for his many achievements, was given the title of vizier (*wazir*).

Domestic economic revitalization was furthered by Fatimid concentration on commercial growth. Trade was promoted along the Red Sea and in the East, allowing at the same time the continued pursuit of still another Fatimid aim, religious and political advancement in the Islamic world. Through propaganda and gold they were able to win recognition in Mecca and Medina in 970–971, and Fatimid (Ismaili) missionaries carried the Shiite word across Islam. The use of missionaries was an imaginative policy that was proven by a defection (1057–1059) of a general, al-Basasiri, in Mosul, to the Fatimids. As was the case throughout the Fatimid caliphate's political existence, however, the resources were lacking to exploit the gains won in Syria or elsewhere. The Seljuk Turks crushed the general and drove him out of Baghdad, where he had entrenched himself. These setbacks, combined with the inability of Fatimid generals to triumph in the field against the Abbasids, contributed to the eventual Fatimid defeat.

Conflict within Egypt itself began during the reign of al-Aziz (975–996), who followed al-Mu'izz. The army for a long time had been Berber, but eventually Mamluk, Turkish and even Sudanese soldiery was introduced, bringing conflicts that threatened to tear apart the unity of the state and the armed forces. To this disunity was added a marked deterioration of the prestige of the office of caliph, due mainly to the bizarre actions of al-Hakim (ruled 992–1021), considered a religious eccentric. Under al-Mustansir (ruled 1036–1094) the decline in the caliphate became so pronounced that he sent an appeal to the governor of Acre, an Armenian and former slave named Badr al-Jamali, to come to Egypt. He did so in 1074, massacring all possibly troublesome officials and assuming the multiple titles of *amir-al-juyush* (general of the armies), *hadi al-du at* (guide of the missionaries) and *wazir*, although he was generally known by the first title. His role, like that of Yaqub ibn Killis, had a major impact on the final century of Fatimid rule, for henceforth the viziers exercised virtual control of the dwindling empire and Egypt. Badr al-Jamali and his son, followed by other autocratic viziers, filled the vacuum of degenerated authority on the part of the caliphs, but they could not reverse the fortunes of the Fatimids, only delay their final collapse.

Al-Mustansir died in 1094, and Badr's son, al-Afdal, now vizier, took upon himself the decision of appointing a successor. He chose not Nizar, al-Mustansir's elder son and designated heir, but the younger son, Ahmad, whom he could control with greater ease. Al-Afdal wed his sister to Ahmad and named him Caliph al-Mustali. The rule of al-Mustali (1094–1101) forever divided the caliphate, with many Ismaili members proclaiming their steadfast devotion to Nizar and his descendants. Chief among these was HASAN IBN SABBAH, the founder of the Order of the Assassins (see ASSASSINS, ORDER OF). Dynastic chaos began with the murder of al-Mustali's son, al-Amir, in 1130, for there was no immediate heir. A cousin, al-Hafiz (ruling 1130–1149), claimed the throne. Viziers kept the caliphate functioning during the rule of the last three caliphs, al-Zafir, al-Faiz and al-Adid. In 1169 the vizierate was claimed after a battle by Shirkuh, a lieutenant of the Syrian dynast Nur-al-din. Shirkuh was succeeded by his nephew, Saladin, who in 1171—while the last caliph lay dying in the palace at Cairo—ordered a prayer to be read in the name of the Abbasid caliph of Baghdad. The Fatimid caliphate was abolished a few days later. See also ABBASID CALIPHATE; AYYUBIDS; EGYPT; ISLAM; ISMAILI SECT; and individual rulers.

**FEAST OF FOOLS** Also called the Feast of Asses, a celebration held around the first of January (the Feast of the Circumcision), consisting of wild behavior, buffoonery and drinking on the part of the lower clergy in the churches throughout France and in parts of England and Germany. The Feast of Fools probably developed in the 12th century when clerics of lower rank (subdeacons and others) were permitted to elect their own bishops, archbishops and even a "Pope of Fools" for several days of merrymaking. The behavior of the celebrants eventually went beyond the proscribed limits set by church officials. By the 13th century it was deemed scandalous behavior and was criticized. Actual condemnation of the tradition came in 1435 by the Council of Basel. See also HERESIES.

**FELIX, BISHOP OF URGEL** (d. 818) Christian prelate in Spain and, with Elipandus, the bishop of Toledo, a leader of the heretical movement of adoptionism, which taught that because Christ was human, he was the adopted son of God. At the Council of Regensburg in 792, he was compelled by reason to accept that his adoptionist views were heretical, eventually formally recanting before Pope Adrian I (772–795). A short time later, however, he reverted to his former stance and was accused again at the Council of Frankfurt (794) and at Aachen (798). Convinced by Alcuin of his errors, Felix finally repented but was watched closely by church authorities for the duration of his life. See also HERESIES.

**FELIX III, SAINT** (d. 492) Pope from 483 to 492, who excommunicated Acacius, patriarch of Constantinople, in 484 for espousing the cause of Monophysitism, the doctrine concerning the nature of Christ, declared heretical by the Western Church. His act led to the Acacian Schism, which lasted for 35 years.

**FELIX IV, SAINT** (d. 530) Pope from 526 to 530, elected chiefly through the influence of Theodoric, the king of the Ostrogoths, to replace John I (513–516). Felix was responsible for ending the controversy within the church concerning the doctrines on grace and will by convening the Second Council of Orange (529). There he condemned Pelagianism and accepted the teachings of the church fathers, especially those of Saint Augustine, concerning the nature of original sin and the need for God's grace. Before his death he hoped to ensure a steady succession and thus named as his successor the archdeacon Boniface (Boniface II).

**FELIX V** See AMADEUS VIII, DUKE OF SAVOY.

**FERDINAND I, KING OF ARAGON** (c. 1379–1416) Ruler of Aragon from 1412 to 1416, the co-regent of Castile (after 1406) during the minority of his nephew, John II of Castile. As regent he proved himself loyal to Castile, refusing to remove John even were he to have gained by so doing. On the death of King Martin I in 1410 without an heir and without naming a successor, however, Ferdinand made a claim to the throne of Aragon and was eventually accepted, as a result of the Compromise of Caspe (1412). A member of the Castilian family the Trastámaras, he ended the influence of Catalonia in Aragon's political affairs and was also instrumental in terminating the Great Schism by withdrawing his support of Benedict XIII, the Avignonese pope. Ferdinand was remembered for capturing the fortress of Antequera from the Moors in 1410. See also ARAGON.

**FERDINAND II, KING OF ARAGON** (1452–1516) Also called Ferdinand of Castile and Ferdinand the Catholic, ruler of Aragon from 1479 to 1516. His marriage to Isabella of Castile in 1469 and their subsequent efforts to complete the Reconquista forged Spain into a unified kingdom. Ferdinand saw the rise of Spain as a European power with his acquisitions of Naples and Navarre. The son of John II of Aragon and Juana Enriquez, he became heir to the throne in 1461 and king of Sicily in 1468. A year later he married Isabella at Valladolid and in 1474, on the death of King Henry IV of Castile (1454–1469), journeyed to Segovia to support his wife in her claim to the Castilian throne. Years of conflict followed as Ferdinand attempted to win the allegiance of the Castilian nobles, finally succeeding in 1479, the same year that John II died. Castile and Aragon were thus allied, thereby establishing a single state.

King Ferdinand II

Ferdinand and Isabella pursued an aggressive policy in the application of statecraft, forging a universal and stable joint rule. The last of the Moors in the peninsula were conquered in 1492, with the fall of the Kingdom of Granada. Religious toleration was ended, and the Jews refusing to convert to Catholicism were expelled. Doctrinal orthodoxy was enforced after 1478 by the infamous Spanish Inquisition, and for his defense of the church, especially of the papacy, Ferdinand was called "the Catholic" in 1496. Greater monarchical power allowed him to support Christopher Columbus in 1492, laying the groundwork for Spanish imperial expansion in the New World. In Europe, Spain's holdings were increased by the conquest of Naples in 1503 and the seizure of Navarre in 1512, adding maritime possessions in the Mediterranean Sea. Isabella died in 1504, one of many personal losses suffered by the king in his later years. In 1516, while on a journey to Granada, he fell ill and died. Ferdinand left behind a revitalized peninsula, a sound government and a flourishing empire. Whereas many contemporaries viewed him as the ideal Christian ruler, others, such as Machiavelli, saw him as cunning, ruthless and coolly ambitious. He was the last medieval king of the Spanish kingdoms and one of the first Renaissance princes.

**FERDINAND I, KING OF CASTILE AND LEÓN** (c. 1016–1065) Ruler from 1035 to 1065, called "the Great" for his political and military achievements in bringing much of Christian and Moorish Spain under his control. The son of Sancho III Garcés of Navarre (1000–1035), he married Sancha, sister of Vermudo III (1028–1037), and thus inherited Castile in 1035 on his father's death and León in 1037 when Vermudo was killed in battle. His next years were spent extending his territorial possessions, reclaiming Castilian lands given to Navarre in 1054, winning the recognition of his position over Navarre and then turning his attention to the Moors. Portions of Portugal were seized, and he forced the rulers of Toledo, Seville and Zaragoza to acknowledge his dominion. His empire did not last, however, for with his death in 1065 the domains were divided among his sons, Sancho II (Castile) (1065–1072), Alfonso VI (León) (1065–1109) and García (Galicia) (1065–1072). See also CASTILE.

**FERDINAND II, KING OF LEÓN** (c. 1145–1188) Ruler from 1157 to 1188. Also called Fernando, he was the son of Alfonso VII of León and Castile (1157–1188) and a brother of Sancho III of Castile (ruled 1157–1158), inheriting his throne on his father's death. His long reign was noted mainly for his triumphs over the Almohad dynasty, including the capture of Badajoz. For the defense of the borders he relied on the Christian military orders. It was said of him that although never defeated in battle he was always "conquered by the appeals of the downtrodden."

**FERDINAND III, KING OF CASTILE AND LEÓN** (c. 1201–1252) Ruler of Castile from 1217 to 1252, called "the Saint" for his religious devotion. Ferdinand III was an active king and an ardent crusader against the Moors in Spain. The son of Alfonso IX of León (1188–1230) and

Berenguela, daughter of Alfonso VIII of Castile (1158–1214), he was forced to use arms against his father to secure his throne and was thus removed as heir to the crown of León by Alfonso IX's will. Nevertheless he succeeded in negotiating the Pact of Benavente in 1230, making him king of León as well, a union of the kingdoms that was never again broken. The main achievement of his reign, however, was his long war to reduce Moorish Andalusia. Years of fighting led to the capture of Córdoba in 1236 and Seville in 1248. The Kingdom of Granada survived the Christian onslaught only by accepting vassal status to Castile. His victories were crucial to the reconquest of Spain by Christians, but they had a devastating effect on the once-flourishing Andalusian economy. A daughter by his second marriage, to Joan of Ponthieu, was Eleanor of Castile, who became the beloved wife of Edward I of England. See also RECONQUISTA.

**FERDINAND IV, KING OF CASTILE** (1289–1312) Ruler from 1295 to 1312 and the son of King Sancho IV (1284–1295). His minority was spent under the protection of his mother, Maria de Molina, who defended her son and the crown from ambitious nobles of Castile, especially Ferdinand's uncle, Juan. His relations with his mother after 1301 were strained, as the young king struggled to establish himself in the face of continuing conspiracies. The greatest victory of his reign was the capture of Gibraltar in August 1309. He died while preparing to go to war in Andalusia. An interesting source on his era was the *Cronica de Fernando IV (Chronicle of Ferdinand IV)*. See also CASTILE.

**FERDINAND V, KING OF CASTILE** See FERDINAND II, KING OF ARAGON.

**FERDINAND I, KING OF NAPLES** (1423–1494) Illegitimate son of the Aragonese king Alfonso V (1416–1458) and king of Naples from 1458 to 1494. He was named by Alfonso to the throne of Naples but throughout his reign faced rebellions by his barons and the threat of defeat and deposition by other Mediterranean states. The first crisis struck shortly after his succession, when nobles tried to replace him with René of Anjou. This was suppressed, but new uprisings took place from 1485 to 1487, ended only by the extirpation of baronial resistance by harsh means. Ferdinand was forced to campaign against the Turks after they captured the port of Otranto in 1480. His ally in this war and in his conflict with Venice, from 1482 to 1484, was Florence. Ferdinand's court was noted for attracting men of learning, especially in the field of humanism. In Italy he was known as Don Ferrante. See also NAPLES, KINGDOM OF.

**FERDINAND II, KING OF NAPLES** (1467–1496) Ruler from 1495 to 1496, holding also the titles of prince of Capua and duke of Calabria. The son of Alfonso II of Naples (ruled 1494–1495), he assumed command of the Neapolitan forces that resisted the invasion of Italy in 1494 by Charles VIII of France. Crowned in 1495 after his father's abdication, Ferdinand fled to Sicily when Naples fell to the French, regaining his lands the following year supported by Venice and Spain. Very popular and a respected humanist, he died unexpectedly on October 5, a short time after his triumphant return to Naples. See also NAPLES, KINGDOM OF.

**FERDINAND I, KING OF PORTUGAL** (1345–1383) Ruler from 1367 to 1383, who spent much of his time at war with Castile, often in unsuccessful attempts to claim the Castilian throne. Toward this end in 1380 he negotiated an alliance with John of Gaunt against Castile, but this resulted in John I's (1379–1390) invasion of Portugal in 1381. The Portuguese navy was defeated, and Ferdinand, unable to brook the atrocities committed by the English troops, made peace. The 1382 agreement provided for the marriage of John I and the Portuguese heiress Beatriz; their son would become the king of Portugal.

**FERID EL-DIN ATTAR** (d. c. 1229) Also called Faridun, one of the great mystic poets of Islam. A Persian, he was converted to Sufism and became one of its best-known exponents, composing a series of epic poems. The most celebrated of these was *Mantiq al-tayr (Language of the Birds)*, derived from an allegory by Abu Hamid al-Ghazali, presenting the doctrines of the Sufis. He had met Jalaii'd-Din Rumi and had a considerable influence on him. See also SUFISM.

**FERNANDO, KING OF PORTUGAL** See FERDINAND I, KING OF PORTUGAL.

**FERRANTE I, KING OF NAPLES** See FERDINAND I, KING OF NAPLES.

**FERRARA** City in northern Italy, at the Po Delta, in the Emilia-Romagna region. Its earliest known existence was in 753, when the Lombards captured it, separating it from the Exarchate of Ravenna. In 774, following the defeat of the Lombards by Charlemagne, Ferrara was granted to the papacy, eventually receiving commune status in the 10th century. Subsequently occupied by the margraves of Tuscany, it was a member of the Lombard League against Frederick I Barbarossa (1125–1190), who conquered it in 1158. Final political domination came in 1288, when the House of Este, headed by Obizzo II, claimed lordship. Under the aegis of that house, Ferrara became a cultural and intellectual force, establishing a university in 1391. This period of prestige ended with the incorporation of the city into the Papal States in 1598. See also ESTE, HOUSE OF; FERRARA-FLORENCE, COUNCIL OF.

**FERRARA-FLORENCE, COUNCIL OF** A general council of the church held at Ferrara and later at Florence, from 1438 to 1445. The purpose of this council was to discuss important doctrinal matters and to unite the Eastern and Western Churches, but it ultimately strengthened the position of the papacy against the conciliarist movement. The Council of Ferrara-Florence was actually a continuation of the Council of Basel, in session from 1431. Pope Eugene IV (1431–1447) ordered the members of that assembly to move to Ferrara, Italy, to meet with the huge delegation from the Byzantine Empire, headed by Emperor John VIII Palaeologus (1425–1448), with the patriarch of

Constantinople and 700 other officials. Only those supporters of the pope agreed to journey to Ferrara, and the council opened on January 8, 1438. After an outbreak of plague in Ferrara, it was agreed to move the proceedings to Florence on January 10, 1439.

After protracted negotiations, influenced by the political needs of the Byzantines, an agreement was reached in July 1439. In it the Eastern Church accepted the tenets of Western doctrine that had once separated the churches and had been the source of serious disagreement, namely the questions concerning Purgatory, the Eucharist, the *Filioque* (the phrase meaning "and from the Son" in the Nicene Creed to proclaim that the Holy Spirit came from both God the Father and the Son) and, especially important for Pope Eugene, papal primacy. The pope issued the bull *Laetentur Caeli*, proclaiming the union of the churches, and was thus able to oppose the conciliarists from a stronger position. Additional years were spent advancing the return of the numerous Eastern churches to the Holy See, and from 1443 the council met in Rome. Many of the delegates repudiated their acceptance of reunification once they had returned home, and the union was quite unpopular in Constantinople. See also BESSARION, JOHN CARDINAL.

**FEUDALISM** One of the most complex and controversial aspects of medieval life, an institution peculiar to the Middle Ages but which also had an effect on other social and political developments in Europe. Feudalism defined a system of landholding in which a lord agreed to provide protection in return for military service, taxes or personal service. As terms, *feudal* and *feudalism* did not come into usage until the 17th and late 18th centuries respectively. This understanding of feudalism, linking to possession of land the concept of the fief (Latin, *feodum*), was a derogatory one. In practice, a fief was the unit of land worked by a tenant for an overlord. The term *feudalism* was used by these scholars to describe the decaying social system of the time that seemed archaic or no longer germane to current political thinking and so was the object of considerable debate by subsequent scholars as to its evolution and value. Of particular interest were the variations manifested by feudalism in European countries and the degree to which it was adopted.

Twentieth-century scholars generally agree that the institutions of feudalism gained accelerated organization in the ninth century with the decline of the Carolingian empire. Its origins, however, were traced to the break up of centralization of the Roman Empire in the West during the fourth and fifth centuries and the Germanization of much of its former imperial territories. Throughout the fifth century, Germanic kingdoms (the Visigoths, Ostrogoths, Burgundians and Franks) were established in the West. In the chaos that preceded the final collapse of Roman order, there was a trend toward clientage as small land holders proved unable to compete economically with the larger estates, also proving incapable of defending themselves. They decided therefore to commend themselves to landlords, surrendering their lands to a lord in return for safety and the right to farm the properties. These processes, formative vassalage, were not halted by the German states, for they tended as well to disintegrate into smaller, autonomous holdings, divisions hastened by the German custom of distributing a man's property among his sons.

In the Frankish lands the military fiefs were established to strengthen the warrior class, making the vassal or retainer one of the keys to the emerging social system. Since they owned land (held for the king), they could therefore support themselves in war with a horse, armor and weapons. The position of the vassals was improved greatly by the decline of the Carolingians, especially in the face of attacks by Vikings, Magyars and Muslims. Unable to find protection from the king, the populace turned to the local vassals, handing to them their lands and receiving them back as part of the transaction known as subinfeudation. The kings remained, but justice and peace in the region and the administration of government were left to men of power. Monarchs, unable to pay troops or compel the loyalty of the nobility, gave fiefs in the hope of binding those men to them by homage. Decentralization was therefore inevitable as the crown became weaker compared with the vassals, who exercised virtual independence, ruling their districts in a private manner.

The resultant feudal system was a complicated interweaving of vassalage and fief (see MANORIAL SYSTEM), culminating in the dual system of service: on a local level the vassals gave their homage to a lord, including service, thus guaranteeing his protection, while the lord gave the king his own, albeit symbolic, oath of fealty. Vassalage usually entailed providing a lord with loyalty, court service, obedience, monetary contributions, military assistance and, at times, marriage or even ransom. These duties were called feudal aids, a powerful means of binding a vassal to his lord. Meanwhile, the vassal was granted as stable an existence as possible, either a place in the castle or a piece of property, a fief. Because castles during the early feudal period were notoriously small, a fief was preferable, rarely enough to provide anything other than a subsistence and ensuring that the vassal was incapable of plotting the destruction of the most visible sign of his lord's supremacy, the symbol of the feudal order, the castle. By the 12th century the fiefs were much grander estates, worked by large numbers of peasants who were vassals given to the lord by order of his ban (command). Peasants provided him with an income by paying rent and certain dues and by working the land. The fief, of course, was held only for the duration of the vassal's life, and while the fief could be inherited, the acts of homage and investiture and the oaths of loyalty had to be renewed. A new vassal was required to pay relief, a large sum of money to provide compensation and as a recognition of the lord's superior position. Should the only heir be a daughter, the lord decided whom she should marry, while a young male could be taken as a ward of the lord or presented as a ward to another vassal who would be entitled to the income of the fief. Forfeiture was made when a vassal failed to uphold his obligations. Finally, when a vassal died without an heir, the fief reverted to the lord, who could keep it or distribute it again.

During the 12th and 13th centuries, commensurate with the growing size of the fiefs, there was the process of subinfeudation, in which a vassal gave part of his own fief to other vassals, who gave their homage and oaths immediately to him, rather than his lord. Officially, the permission of the original lord was required, but the act of subinfeudation was extremely difficult to stop. A chain of landed dependencies was thus formed as a consequence, and conflicting loyalties arose. Vassals maintaining lands in different regions met conflicting loyalties when two lords were involved.

As for the lords and their kings, another level of feudalism was in existence. Under the feudal order a ruler wielded prestige but little actual power. He relied on his magnates, who gave him their oaths of fidelity. A question has long been debated as to the nature of this relationship, for the nobles were conscious of their political positions, their high degrees of independence and their authority to extend their personal privileges downward into the masses. An equilibrium was probably in place, in which they agreed to serve as nominal vassals, but the kings never exacted too much from these men. These lords served the king when it suited them and ran their own affairs as they saw fit.

Another feudal participant was the church, which was a very formidable landholder, possessing estates in Europe or wielding broad political powers, as was especially true of the archbishops of Cologne, Mainz and Trier, who were princely Electors of the Holy Roman Empire. Secular rights were one thing, but they were often inadequate to provide suitable protection. A neighboring lord might agree to provide defense for the local church, but his assistance would come at a heavy price, such as the domination of ecclesiastical activities. Far more advantageous and cunning was an appeal to the king or an overlord (an influential duke or count), such as the duke of Normandy or the counts of Flanders or Anjou. By aiding the church they acquired wide reputations for their generosity and concern for the well-being of the faith. Further, their military operations were often conducted against a grasping or recalcitrant vassal who could thereby be brought under direct control.

Feudalism on a national scale made its first appearance in France, where the royal domains were only a fraction of the total political area of the country. It soon spread to Germany, northern Spain, Italy and England, with variations notable in each instance. Feudalism in north Italy was never a major system of government, for the trading cities prevented the establishment of such an order; to the south, the well-organized Norman holdings in Sicily and Naples offered Italy's most successful version of feudalism, but the collapse of the Normans in the region ended the experiment. Because Spain was in constant warfare with the Moors, feudal structures could not be fully realized.

Germany and England were to offer the two most interesting examples of feudal systems. German duchies and tribal characteristics survived well into the Middle Ages, causing alteration of feudal hierarchies: the dukes and German kings were ultimately equal to the noblity, extending control over wide expanses east of the Rhine River in wars against the Slavs, reigning over allodial estates, those held in absolute ownership, unmatched even in France. At the same time, as in Spain, conflict on the borders with the Slavs and the peoples of the Baltic left the frontiers in a state of chronic tension, weakening the capacity of the kings to bring any long-lasting reform. Emperor Henry IV (d. 1106) tried to reduce the strength of the duchies during his reign. Other emperors, most notably Frederick II (d. 1250), sacrificed any progress in Germany to extend imperial ambitions in Italy. German feudalism lingered as a result for many centuries, while other lands fell to the mastery of increasingly absolute monarchs.

England was unique in that it presented feudalism in its most highly developed form. The introduction of the efficient Norman model came in 1066, immediately after the conquest of the island by William the Conqueror. The entire kingdom was the property of the king, who then distributed his land to his vassals or tenants, who were responsible to their master for fulfilling feudal obligations. Government was centralized in the royal court, which acted on the will of the king, and was composed of vassals, officials owing everything they possessed to the ruler. This political reality was made clear in Domesday Book, a meticulous and imposing assessment of the entire country, a compilation describing the royal possessions down to the smallest tenancy. The decentralization so evident in France and Germany was largely avoided here, as it was difficult for a single baron to resist the demands of the Crown for long. In response to monarchical threats the barons united to form a political faction strong enough to make certain demands of their own. Magna Carta, signed under duress by King John in 1215, was the result of baronial desire to bring royalty to heel and to compel it to uphold its own feudal obligations.

Feudalism was brought into decline by a combination of factors, including governmental centralization, the advent of the modern money economy and the rise of large trading towns. Another conduit of change was warfare in the later Middle Ages. The Hundred Years' War (1337–1453) decimated the French nobility in such disastrous battles as Crécy and Agincourt, a similar process taking place in England during the Wars of the Roses (1455–1485). Advances in gunpowder and tactics rendered the mounted, heavily armored knights obsolete. Kings in France and England allied themselves with the middle classes and with the merchants to obtain new sources of revenue, removing traditional dependency on the lords to supply money and arms. By bringing the cities under royal administration the kings gave themselves greater opportunity for consolidation against the nobles. By 1500 most of Europe was moving away from feudal monarchies to nation-states, ending the medieval era and ushering in the modern one.

See also BANKING; BARONS' WAR; CASTLE; CHIVALRY; CRUSADER STATES; CRUSADES; ENGLAND; FRANCE; GERMANY; HOLY ROMAN EMPIRE; HUNDRED YEARS' WAR; INVESTITURE CONTROVERSY; JERUSALEM, KINGDOM OF; MAGNA CARTA; TRADE AND COMMERCE; WARFARE; WARS OF THE ROSES; and individual rulers.

**FEZ** Also Fes or, in the Arabic, Fas, a city in Morocco, situated on the Wadi Fez on the major route to Tangier, Rabat and Marrakesh. Fez was established by the Idrisids from the late eighth and ninth centuries in two divisions. The right bank was founded in 790 by Idris I, the city of the left bank by Idris II in 809. Both cities grew and were finally combined into a large metropolis by the Almoravids in 1075. Although it was already a major Islamic city in North Africa, its population increased with the arrival of refugees from Spain, as a result of the Reconquista. By the 14th century Fez was at its height with nearly 200,000 residents, with a university (opened 858) and with strong religious significance owing to its many mosques. It also played an extensive trade role in the region.

**FIBONACCI, LEONARDO** See LEONARDO OF PISA.

**FICINO, MARSILIO** (1433–1499) Italian humanist, scholar and Platonist who was one of the important intellectual figures of the early Renaissance. Born in Figline, near Florence, he was educated at Florence with the patronage of Cosimo de Medici, studying medicine and philosophy and developing a familiarity with Platonic and Neoplatonic traditions, as well as the writings of Thomas Aquinas and Augustine of Hippo. A master of Greek, he strove to combine Platonic concepts of philosophy with Christian theology. In 1462 Ficino was named the head of the Platonic Academy of Florence, established by Cosimo de Medici at his villa in nearby Careggi. By attracting brilliant scholars and philosophers and serving as the repository for Greek manuscripts, the Academy became one of the most celebrated institutions of learning in western Europe.

Ficino translated the writings of Plato into Latin from Greek, his translations serving as the standard work for many years. He led the revival of Platonic thought in the Renaissance, considering it harmonious with Christian doctrine and a necessary response to the Aristotelian view of the times. In addition to his translations of Plato, he translated philosophers including Plotinus, Iamblichus and Dionysius the Areopagite, and was the author of *De Christiana religione* (1476) and *Theologica Platonica* (1482), defending his Platonic and Christian philosophy and works on mysticism, astrology and medicine.

**FIESOLE, FRA GIOVANNI** See ANGELICO, FRA.

**FILARETE** (c. 1400–c. 1470) Italian architect and sculptor, a Florentine, whose given name was Antonio di Pietro Averlino and whose nickname meant "Lover of Virtue." One of the innovators of the Renaissance style in Lombardy, he earned acclaim for his masterwork, the bronze doors of Saint Peter's in Rome, commissioned by Pope Eugene IV and completed about 1445. Returning to Florence in 1448, he earned the patronage of Francesco Sforza, duke of Milan, honoring the family with his *Treatise on Architecture* (c. 1465) by naming the ideal city in the world Sforzinda. In the treatise Filarete proposed ambitious architectural projects, including palaces and towers. He also produced a smaller copy of the Roman statue of Marcus Aurelius in bronze, presenting it to Piero de Medici in 1465, to whom he had dedicated his treatise.

**FILELFO, FRANCESCO** (1398–1481) Italian scholar and humanist, who studied at Padua before journeying to Constantinople in 1420, where he learned Greek, collected manuscripts and married Theodora, daughter of John Chrysoloras, his teacher. On his return to Italy he traveled extensively as an instructor in classical languages and literature. Among the cities were Venice, Bologna, Florence and Milan. He remained in the service of the dukes of Milan from 1440 to 1471. A prolific writer, he was responsible for works on poetry, philosophy and classical literature in Italian, Greek and Latin. Although of a difficult nature, he was nevertheless well respected, earning a reputation as one of the foremost men of letters in his time. His correspondence was of great value in its reflection of life in the 15th century.

**FINANCE** See ACCIAIUOLI, HOUSE OF; ARAGON; BANKING; BARDI, HOUSE OF; BOLOGNA; CHAMPAGNE, FAIRS OF; COEUR, JACQUES; DANEGELD; DOMESDAY BOOK; EXCHEQUER; FAIRS; FEUDALISM; FLANDERS; FLORENCE; GENOA; HAMBURG; HANSEATIC LEAGUE; JEWS AND JUDAISM; MANORIAL SYSTEM; MILAN; PARLIAMENT; PISA; TRADE AND COMMERCE; VENICE.

**FINLAND** Called Suomi by its inhabitants, a region occupied by tribes of Finno-Ugrian descent from the fifth to eighth centuries, who replaced the Lapps, droving them into northern regions. By the eighth century, the Finns were settled, but part of the southwestern coastal regions were soon occupied by the Swedes. Trade routes were established through Finland to Russia, and, inevitably, the protracted attempts at Christian conversion began. According to the claims of the monastery at Valmo, missionaries were in Finland as early as 992, the date of the monastery's founding, but major conversions did not take place until the 12th century. About 1157, King Eric IX of Sweden (c. 1156–1160) launched a crusade into Finland, supported by an English missionary, Henry, who became bishop and patron saint (he was martyred about 1160).

Finland was considered a major strategic possession in the north and was thus the object of conflicts between Sweden and Russia, both utilizing Christian conversions as a useful political weapon. Eastern Finland came under Russian spiritual control, and the western parts of the region remained under Western Christian jurisdiction. In 1249 the Swedish magnate BIRGER JARL launched a major effort to bring Finland into the Swedish sphere, setting off a war with the Russians that ended only in 1323, with the Treaty of Noteborg, recognizing Swedish suzerainty. By 1362 the Finns were permitted the right to participate in the election of the king. Bo Jonsson Grip was crowned ruler of Finland in 1374, but on his death in 1386, the terms of the Kalmar Union were extended to the kingdom. Throughout the Middle Ages, however, the Finns maintained their own cultural identity as well as their own language. The Church of Finland was well respected. Olaus Magni, bishop of Aho (1450–1460), was twice rector of the Sorbonne.

***FIORETTI DI SAN FRANCESCO*** See LITTLE FLOWERS OF ST. FRANCIS.

**FIRDAWSI** (c. 940–c. 1020) Also Firdausi, a celebrated poet and the composer of the Persian national epic, *Shah-Nama* (*Book of Kings*). According to the traditional accounts of his life, Firdawsi was actually named Abu'l Qasim Mansur, born in a small Persian village, Tus. He wrote his epic poem supposedly to provide his daughter with a suitable dowry. *The Book of Kings* contained 60,000 verses and was derived from a prose translation of a history (Pahlavi–Middle Persian) of the kings of Persia from mythological times to the reign of Khosrow (Chosroes) II (590–628). He presented the work to Sultan Mahmud of Ghazna, who gave Firdawsi such a meager reward, only 20,000 dirhams, that Firdawsi bathed and then gave the money to the attendant and to a beer seller. Forced to flee the country because of this outrage to the sultan, he died and was being carried out of Tus the day he was sent a more just reward by the sultan.

**FIREARMS** See WARFARE.

**FITZGERALD** An Irish noble family, arising through the marriage of the nobleman Gerald with Nesta, daughter of a Welsh prince in 1169. The establishment of the family in Ireland took place with Maurice Fitzgerald (d. 1176), who was one of the Anglo-Norman lords who invaded Ireland about 1170. Two branches of the Fitzgeralds were founded through his sons—the earls of Kildare and dukes of Leinster, and the earls of Desmond. See also IRELAND.

**FITZNEALE, RICHARD** (c. 1130–1198) Bishop of London from 1189 to 1198 and treasurer of England from about 1169 to 1198, thus serving Henry II (1154–1189) and Richard I (1189–1199). His family was already familiar with the finances of the Crown, his father, Nigel, bishop of Ely, and his uncle, Roger, bishop of Salisbury, being largely responsible for the development of the Exchequer. Richard was responsible for the *Dialogue of the Exchequer,* a description of the procedures of the Exchequer during his lifetime. See also EXCHEQUER.

**FLAGELLANTS** Groups of religious extremists who attempted to do penance for the sins of the world by beating themselves. Self-flagellation was practiced in the 13th century and was common throughout the 14th century until condemned by the church. The origin of this behavior could be traced to the prophecies announcing the apocalypse by Joachim of Fiore, the famine, and the chaos created by the wars of the time, especially in Italy and the Hundred Years' War, and by the Black Death. These events were said to be evidence of God's displeasure and the imminent end of the world. Unable to find solace in organized religion, bands of flagellants took to wandering the countryside, scourging themselves and one another, the men in public ceremonies often accompanied by spiritual readings, and the women privately. Church authorities first censured the flagellants in 1261, and in 1349 Pope Clement VI (1342–1352) officially condemned the practice. Flagellation continued in parts of Europe, such as Germany, where an organized sect arose, also condemned as heretical and eradicated by the Inquisition.

**FLAMBARD, RANULF** (d. 1128) Bishop of Durham (1099) and chief minister of state to King William II Rufus (1087–1100). A Norman by descent, Flambard won royal favor with William the Conqueror (d. 1087), becoming keeper of the seal. At first chaplain to William II, he was appointed an adviser and chief justician. Placed in charge of royal finances, he was successful but notorious in his manner of raising funds, which included extortion and exorbitant taxation. When Henry I (1100–1135) succeeded to the throne in 1100, Flambard was imprisoned for his part in the tyrannical administration of William II. Escaping to Normandy, he supported the unsuccessful attempt of Robert II, duke of Normandy, to overthrow Henry, but he was subsequently restored to royal favor. The cathedral of Durham was built largely through his efforts. See also DURHAM.

**FLANDERS** County located in the Low Countries, extending along the North Sea, west of the Schelde River, established in 862 when Charles the Bald, the Carolingian king, gave it to his son-in-law, Baldwin I (d. 879). Through his successors, especially Baldwin II (879–918), Baldwin IV (988–1035) and Baldwin V (1036–1067), the county was expanded eastward and, in part, westward. Supporting in the political rise of the counts was a process of centralization that allowed Count Robert Le Frison (1071–1093) to promote both the creation of towns and the establishment of the woolen industry that was to make Flanders an economically powerful region. Further development came under Count Thierry of Alsace (1128–1168) and his son Philip (1168–1191).

The wealth of Flanders attracted the ambitions of France in the 12th century, marking the beginning of the long conflict between the counts and the French kings. A major reason for this conflict was the independence of towns such as Ghent, Bruges, Ypres and Courtrai. Within the cities industry and wealth from the wool trade caused social strife, including a class war. This spilled over into the disputes between the counts and kings, in which the working class lent its support to the Clanwaerts, adherents of the counts, while the upper class gave its support to the Leliaerts, or royalists. France gained the upper hand around 1300, only to be defeated badly at Courtrai in 1302, in the Battle of the Spurs. A treaty, signed in 1305 at Athis-sur-Orge, recognized the freedom of Flanders in return for territorial concessions. The social upheaval remained, however, and the growing concern that Ghent, with other towns, would claim independence forced the counts to side with the French kings during the Hundred Years' War (1337–1453) against the Flemish traders, who joined the English fearing the loss of crucial financial markets in England. Despite the efforts of Jacob and Philip van Artevelde, the French party was victorious in 1382.

In 1369 Philip the Bold, Duke of Burgundy (1384–1404), married the heiress of Flanders, bringing the country under Burgundian control and once more involving the Flemish in war between England and France (see BURGUNDY, DUCHY OF). Charles the Bold of Burgundy (1467–1477) tried to forge a Burgundian kingdom with Flanders playing an important part in his schemes, but with his death in 1477 the county came under the aegis of his daughter, Mary of Burgundy. She subsequently married Maxmilian of Habsburg, and Flanders was henceforth ruled by the Habsburg dynasty. The Burgundian dukes encouraged artistic and commercial enterprise in Flanders, but its industries declined, and the freedom of its cities was substantially reduced. See also NETHERLANDS; TRADE AND COMMERCE.

**FLORENCE** City in north-central Italy, in Tuscany, situated on the Arno River. Florence first attained importance during the Middle Ages around 1200 and came to be known as the cradle of the Renaissance. By the 15th century it was a magnet for the study of humanism, art and culture in Europe. It was founded in the first century B.C. as a military colony, called Florentia, subsequently thriving economically. Although it resisted an Ostrogothic siege in 405, the subsequent deterioration of Roman imperial organization made the community susceptible to attack. It suffered at the hands of the Goths, Byzantines and Lombards, and only after the destruction of the Lombard kingdom in 774, bringing Carolingian rule, were the city's fortunes reversed. Frankish officials governed the city for a time, but in the mid-ninth century a powerful family of margraves had established themselves in Tuscany. This margravate eventually extended from the Po River to the Roman state, thriving under Margrave Boniface (d. 1052) and his daughter, Countess Matilda (1051–1115).

An ardent defender of the papacy, Matilda invested her influence heavily in the conflict between the popes and the emperors, with the result that the towns of northern Italy were able to free themselves of the control of the margraves. Guild organizations were founded, extending their influence to the entire city, and although evidence of the evolution of the Florentine commune has remained elusive, 1138 was the year noted for the earliest references to the consuls. Government rested in the hands of the consuls, who were elected by a communal *parlamentum*, composed of members of the prominent noble families of Florence. The commune, once released from the restraints of the margravate, began expanding, seizing land and important possessions, such as castles. Driven by economic, political and military considerations, the Florentines found themselves in conflict with other towns (Siena, Bologna and Pisa), receiving a charter from Emperor Henry VI (1165–1197) in 1187 that granted certain communal rights but restricted advances beyond a five-mile radius surrounding the city walls *(contado)*. After Henry's death in 1197, new struggles developed with Siena and Pistoia, wars that would become a common place over the succeeding years.

While engaging other states for regional supremacy, Florence was undergoing continued civil unrest as political factions vied for internal power and authority. To end this, it was hoped, a new office replaced that of the consulate, the podesta (magistrate). The podesta was a foreigner, chosen from Lombardy, whose term of office was normally one year. His duties included the leadership of the magistracy, judiciary, police and, in time of war, the army. Subject to the checks and balances of the city councils, his authority was not absolute, and thus, during the next century, he was unable to prevent or end the long, bitter conflict between the Guelphs and the Ghibellines, reflected in the blood spilled in the streets of Florence. Ghibelline advantage was secured in 1237 with the victory of Emperor Frederick II (1194–1250) over the Guelph forces at Cortenuova, and in 1246 Frederick's natural son, Frederick of Antioch, became podesta. Two years later the first mass expulsion in Florentine history took place as the Guelphs were driven into exile. In 1250 they returned, overthrowing the Ghibellines and embarking on wars with Siena and Pisa, with their Ghibelline allies, exiled from Florence. At the Battle of Montaperti (1260), the Guelphs were routed by the Sienese, heralding a return of the Ghibellines. Their period of dominance lasted only seven years, for in 1267 the Guelphs and French troops compelled the pro-imperial party to withdraw. Purges against the Ghibellines were instigated as the influence of Charles of Anjou became clear. He held the office of podesta from 1267 to 1282, although vicars actually administered in his name, a situation that remained until 1282, when the war of the Sicilian Vespers so weakened the Angevin grasp of Florence that Charles's agents were expelled, bringing still another political upheaval.

In 1250, there coincided with the Guelph triumph the birth of a new regime, the *popolo*, granting a monopoly of communal authority to the guilds that virtually excluded the nobility from government. The podesta was retained, but the interests of the people and the guilds were protected by the *capitano* (chief) and the new council of the *popolo*. It was this fledgling body that issued the florin in 1252, which soon became the standard gold coin in Italy and in Europe as well. With the removal of the Angevin representative in 1282, further reforms were instituted, completing the transformation of the republic into an oligarchy composed of the Florentine merchant and craft guilds. Members of the aristocracy were allowed no place in the regime unless they joined a guild, for only guild members were eligible for civic posts. The initial 12 guilds were ultimately increased to 21, 7 major and 14 lesser. After steps were taken to reduce the presence of the magnates in the city, more stringent measures were enacted in 1293 to ensure their perpetual subservience. The Ordinances of Justice made necessary the performance of a profession for the right to join a guild, issued strict penalties for disturbing the peace and demanded payment of large sums to the city as a promise from the nobles that they would not engage in violence.

The Guelph party, however, still remained in the city, dominated by the magnates. The Guelphs were divided by the rivalry of the extremists, called the Blacks, led by Corso Donati, and the moderates, the Whites, their leader Vieri Cerchi. In 1301 the Whites gained the upper hand only to lose it because of the intervention of Pope Boniface VIII (1294–1303) and Charles of Valois. The Whites (including Dante) were exiled, driving many of their supporters into the pro-imperial camp of Emperor Henry VII (1308–1313), who attempted to restore imperial rights in Italy but failed in his cause. Years of war followed with Pisa's leaders, Uguccione della Faggiuola and Castruccio Castracani. To support them, the Guelphs summoned Duke Charles of Calabria to be the city's leader, but the dangerous Castracani died in 1328, followed by Charles that same year.

During the period between the death of Castracani and the outbreak of plague, beginning in 1340, Florence attained what was called its golden age. The city was at the height of its prestige and wealth, with a population estimated at 90,000 and building programs that made the city an architectural wonder. It would not last, for a severe epidemic in 1340, a plague killing thousands, was a preface to the Black Death, which struck in 1348, followed by a famine causing the death of half the city's population. Economic and military strength declined rapidly. Added to these terrors were the financial crises, as the two largest banks in Florence, the Bardi and the Peruzzi, went bankrupt in 1343 and 1346. The city was already on the verge of financial ruin after a long war with Lucca (in the 1330s). The brief reign of Walter of Brienne, duke of Athens, who had been asked to restore order, ended with his removal in 1343 and the eruption of civil war between the magnates and the *popolo.* The resulting government was organized around the victorious *popolo,* who shared their rule with the "new men" of the rising classes of lawyers and industrialists and the crafts guilds. Lesser guilds were alienated from civic administration, while the plight of the poor and lower-income workers was made more acute by the collection of taxes to finance Florentine wars against Pisa and Milan.

By 1370 the Guelphs were causing new conflicts in their efforts to dominate the city and their insistence that the lesser guilds be suppressed further. From 1375 to 1378, the enemies of the Guelphs launched a war with the papacy, suggesting that the popes were attempting to interfere with Florentine autonomy by the appointment of papal legates in Italy. This War of the Eight Saints, as it was called, worsened fiscal and social strains. An uprising in July 1378 by the cloth workers of the city struck. The revolt deposed the communal regime, called the Ciompi composed of representatives of the three cloth workers guilds. They prevailed for a mere six weeks before falling to the old establishment, which was in turn destroyed by a more conservative but tenuous union between the Guelphs and the guilds. Guelph superiority was achieved within a number of years.

The late 14th and early 15th centuries saw a renewal of external conflicts and rivalries as Florence opposed the ambitions of Italian leaders while pursuing its own territorial aggrandizement. Allied with Milan and its lord, Giangaleazzo Visconti, Florence fought three separate wars. Visconti died in 1402. Florence fought two wars with Naples (1408–1410 and 1413–1414) and finally another bitter conflict with Milan's Filippo Maria Visconti (1423–1428). Real gains were made when Pisa was conquered in 1406, and Florentine preeminence in Tuscany was inaugurated in 1421 with the acquisition of Livorno, to the south of Pisa, allowing Florence access to the sea. The last war with Milan proved far too costly, so that even tax reform, the *catasto,* was unable to ease the financial crisis or prevent further factionalism. Using an unsuccessful campaign against Lucca (1429–1433) as an excuse, Rinaldo degli Albizzi exiled his bitter foe, Cosimo de Medici, in 1433. A year later, Cosimo returned, driving out the Albizzi. From that time until 1494, the House of Medici became the core of Florentine political life, while serving as great patrons of humanism, learning and the arts. Under their aegis the city of Florence would become the crowning achievement of the Renaissance.

See also ALBERTI, LEON BATTISTA; ANGELICO, FRA; BOCCACCIO, GIOVANNI; BOTTICELLI, ALESSANDRO; BRUNELLESCHI, FILIPPO; CASTAGNO, ANDREA DEL; CHRYSOLORAS, MANUEL; CIMABUE; DANTE ALIGHIERI; DESIDERIO DA SETTIGNANO, DOMENICO VENEZIANO; DONATELLO; FICINO, MARSILIO; FILARETE; GHIBERTI, LORENZO; GHIRLANDAIO, DOMENICO; GIOTTO; LIPPI, FRA FILIPPO; MASACCIO, TOMMASO; MICHELOZZO DI BARTOLOMMEO; NANNI DI BANCO; PETRARCH; PIERO DELLA FRANCESCA; POLLAIUOLO, ANTONIO DEL; ROBBIA, LUCA DELLA; UCCELLO, PAOLO; VERROCCHIO, ANDREA DEL; VILLANI, GIOVANNI.

**FLORENCE, COUNCIL OF** See FERRARA-FLORENCE, COUNCIL OF.

**FLORENTIUS RADWIJNS** (1350–1400) Successor to Gerhard Groote in 1384 as leader of the Brethren of the Common Life in the Low Countries. Florentius was one of the earliest members of the community, and after Groote's death (1384) he was responsible for the founding of the first house at Deventer, Holland. See also COMMON LIFE, BRETHREN OF THE.

**FLORIN** See FLORENCE.

**FOIX, COUNTY OF** Region in southwestern France corresponding to the department of Ariege that was home to the powerful House of Foix. The counts of Foix first rose to prominence in the 11th century, when Count Roger was granted his own feudal possession. From their capital at Foix, the counts wielded considerable autonomy until the 15th century, allied with the counts of Toulouse during the Albigensian Crusade and enduring the siege of their castle at Foix by Simon de Montfort (1212–1217). By the end of the 13th century they had recovered enough from the defeats of the Albigensian Crusade to acquire the viscounty of Bearn and in 1479 inherited the Kingdom of Navarre. The best known of the Foix was Gaston III (d. 1391), who fought for France in the early period of the Hundred Years' War, later served with the Teutonic Knights, held the post of lieutenant general of Languedoc and was called Phoebus because of his handsome demeanor. Foix was incorporated into the French royal domain in 1607.

**FOLIOT, GILBERT** (d. 1188) Bishop of London, a noted ecclesiastic and an opponent of the primacy of Canterbury in England. Norman by birth, Foliot served as a Cluniac monk and then, by virtue of his austerity and intellect, received appointment as the abbot of Abbeville, abbot of Gloucester, bishop of Hereford and, finally, bishop of London in 1163. Already a respected although unpopular religious figure, he opposed the election of Thomas à Becket in 1162 as archbishop of Canterbury on the grounds that he was not deserving of the post and that he had persecuted the church while in service to Henry II (1154–1189). His disagreement with the primacy of Canterbury surfaced the following year when he was transferred to London, refusing to take the vow of obedience to Canterbury, declaring that he had already done so while bishop of Hereford. Differing with Becket in his conflict with Henry over the Constitutions of Clarendon, Foliot served as envoy for the king to Pope Alexander III and in 1169 was excommunicated. An appeal was upheld by the pope, but he was again excommunicated by Becket in 1170. Foliot was widely regarded as being guilty of complicity in Becket's murder in 1170, although he was absolved of any involvement in 1172. His letters were a source of information on prominent men of the time, and he was the attributed author of the treatise "Song of Songs." See also CANTERBURY.

**FONTEVRAULT, ORDER OF** An order or twin order of monks and nuns established at the Abbey of Fontevrault in western France near the Vienne and Loire Rivers by Robert d'Arbissel (d. 1117) in 1099. The monastery, with separate houses for the nuns and monks, was governed by an abbess and adhered to the Benedictine rule with some minor but marked additions. Throughout France and in parts of Spain and England, the order was able to establish dependent houses, although the communities were quite poor until the 14th century. Reforms were instituted between 1475 and 1502. The monastery of Fontevrault was famous throughout France and was the final resting place of King Henry II of England, as well as Eleanor of Aquitaine and Richard the Lion-Hearted.

**FOOLS, FEAST OF** See FEAST OF FOOLS.

**FOPPA, VINCENZO** (c. 1427–1515) Italian painter and one of the innovators of the Lombard school of painting. He was a celebrated painter in Lombardy and Milan during the late 15th century. Probably trained at Padua, Foppa was influenced by Jacopo Bellini and Andrea Mantegna, as well as by the Flemish style of art. His earliest work was a *Crucifixion* (1456); other notable paintings included *Boy Reading Cicero, Epiphany* and a fresco depicting the martyrdom of Saint Sebastian.

**FORMIGNY, BATTLE OF** See HUNDRED YEARS' WAR.

**FORMOSUS** (c. 815–896) Pope from 891 to 896, made cardinal of Porto in 864 and sent by Pope Nicholas I (858–867) and Adrian I (867–872) on various missions to aid in the conversion of Bulgaria. Pope John VIII (872–882) feared him, drove him into exile and had him excommunicated. Returning in 883 during the reign of Marinus I (882–884), he was elected successor to Pope Stephen V (VI) in 891. As pontiff he was active in promoting the Church in England and Germany and dealt harshly with the Eastern Church, and in an attempt to break the power of Guy of Spoleto, he crowned King Arnulf emperor in 896, dying a short time later. Lambert, duke of Spoleto, supported by Formosus's enemies, proceeded to launch a posthumous attack on the pope, instigating the Cadaver Synod. Stephen VI (VII) (896–897) presided over a trial of Formosus, in which the body was exhumed, propped up in a chair and required to defend itself through a deacon, its spokesman. Formosus was thus convicted, his corpse violated, and his pontificate declared illegal. Succeeding popes reinstated him in the papal records and repudiated the bizarre synod.

**FORTESCUE, SIR JOHN** (c. 1390–c. 1478) Legalist, chief justice of the King's Bench and an adviser to King Henry VI of England (1422–1461; 1470–1471). Named chief justice in 1442, he served Henry until the defeat of the Lancastrians at the Battle of Towton in 1461, at the hands of the Yorkists, fleeing with the king to Scotland and then journeying to France. He remained there from 1463 to 1471, in the service of Henry's wife, Margaret of Anjou, serving as tutor to Prince Edward (Edward IV, 1461–1483). In an attempt to restore the House of Lancaster to the throne, he fought at the Battle of Tewkesbury in 1471 but was captured. Edward IV released him. Fortescue was the author of the legal treatise *De laudibus legum Angliae (In Praise of the Laws of England,* c. 1470), intended to instruct Prince Edward. He was also responsible for the legal phrase "better the guilty should escape than the innocent be punished." See also WARS OF THE ROSES.

**FORTUNATUS, VENANTIUS** See VENANTIUS FORTUNATUS.

**FORTÚN GARCÉS** An early ruler of Navarre, reigning from 870 to 905. He was the predecessor of King Sancho I Garcés (ruled 905–926), the founder of the Jimena dynasty of Navarre.

**FOSCARI, FRANCESCO** (c. 1373–1457) Doge of Venice from 1423 to 1457, who was largely responsible for guiding the city's imperial expansion in Italy and its long war with Milan. Having already served on the Council of Ten (1405–1413), the nobleman was elected doge and was soon negotiating an alliance with Florence against Milan. War erupted in 1424 against the Milanese, lasting for 30 years with only brief interruptions brought by largely useless treaties such as the Peace of Ferrara in 1433. The conflict proved bloody and costly, so much so that despite acquiring Brescia, Bergamo and Cremona, the republic was weakened and unable to defeat its enemies, finally acquiescing in the Peace of Lodi, in 1454. Foscari's obsession with Italian expansion had the most unfortunate consequences for Venetian interests in the eastern Mediterranean. Constantinople fell in 1453 to the Ottoman Empire and the loss of Venice's territorial possessions produced discontent at home, especially with the concomitant decline in trade and trading rights. After the death of his son in 1457, at Cardia, Foscari was unable to continue as doge. The Council of Ten demanded his resignation on October 23, 1457, and he died a few days later. His life later was the basis for a tragedy by Byron and an opera by Verdi. See also VENICE.

**FOUQUET, JEAN** (d. c. 1481) The most important French painter and illuminator of the 15th century, the founder of the French school of painting, the works of which reflected not only the influence of the Flemish school but that of the Italians as well, most notably Fra Angelico, Piero della Francesca, Donatello, and Andrea del Castagno.

Fouquet subsequently influenced French illuminators. Details of his early years remain elusive, but he probably studied in Paris under the Bedford Master, spent some time in the Netherlands and, about 1447, was in Italy, where he executed a portrait of Pope Eugene IV and absorbed the styles of Italian painting of the time. Returning to his native Tours, he embarked on a long career of works for the French royalty, becoming court painter in 1475.

Fouquet's most celebrated work was his illuminations for the *Book of Hours* of Étienne Chevalier, dating from about 1452 and 1462, now preserved in Chantilly. Around the same time he painted a portrait of Chevalier on a diptych in Notre Dame at Mélun with Chevalier on one panel and a Madonna, bearing a striking resemblance to the royal mistress, Agnes Sorel, on the other. Dating from 1458 or 1459 were two major illustrations: the *Munich Boccaccio,* his illustrations for the French translation of Boccaccio's *De casibus virorum illustrium* and *De claris mulieribus (On the Lives of Famous Men* and *On Famous Women),* and the *Grandes chroniques des rois de France,* in Paris for King Charles VII. Other notable works were the single miniature for the *Book of Hours* of Charles, brother of Louis XI (1465), an illumination for the frontispiece for the statues of the Order of Saint Michael (1469–1470) and the illustration of two volumes of Josephus's *Antiquities Judaiques* (c. 1476) for the duc de Nemours.

**FRANCE** A major country in medieval Europe, emerging from the feudal disunity and monarchical weakness of the 9th and 10th centuries to become one of the most governmentally powerful states in the West from the 13th century. France was remarkable in its geographical, economic and cultural diversity, with wide ethnic variety found in its many territories, from Brittany and Normandy in the north to Guienne and Poitou in central France, to Gascony and Languedoc in the south. In its position it was inevitable as well that the country should become associated with the histories of England, Germany, Flanders, Spain and other European and Mediterranean regions.

The lands of Roman Gaul (Gallia Lugdenensis, Gallia Aquitania, Gallia Narbonensis and Gallia Belgica) were some of the most prosperous provinces in the Roman Empire, conquered by Julius Caesar in 59–51 B.C. and subjected to intense Romanization. The region maintained relative peace until the third century A.D. when the empire in the West declined. The fourth and fifth centuries brought the disintegration of the Western Roman Empire, the overthrow of the old social and political order and the creation of several Germanic kingdoms, including those of the Visigoths, Ostrogoths, Burgundians, Alemanni and Franks. Of these the most indomitable and resilient proved to be the Franks, who settled in northeastern Gaul. Under the brilliant leadership of Clovis (d. 511), all the Franks were united and led on a prolonged series of conquests that brought most of old Gaul under Frankish supremacy. By accepting Christianity, Clovis won the support of the church, seizing the Gallic possessions of the Visigoths, who were Arians, and building a kingdom that was to be ruled by his descendants. The succeeding Merovingians (reigning over the Franks from 481 to 711) were said t[illegible] descended from the warrior Merovius; they extended [illegible] borders of Frankish control but became susceptible to i[illegible]nal weakness and political instability, owing in large [illegible]sure to the Germanic custom of partitioning the royal lands among a dead king's sons, producing civil wars and political unrest. Later Frankish rulers became known as the "Lazy Kings," monarchs who in the seventh century surrendered effective political power to their chief ministers, the mayors of the palace.

The growing anarchy of the time was evidenced by the bitter conflict erupting between the Neustrian and Austrasian branches of the Merovingian house, conflict that was not ended until 687, when the formidable Pepin II of Héristal (d. 714) crushed the Neustrians for Austrasia, dominating both as mayor of the palace. His son, Charles Martel (714–741), brought the Franks into prominence in Christendom by his victory at the Battle of Tours in 732, over the advancing Muslims, while his son, Pepin III the Short (751–768), toppled the declining Merovingian line. He won the blessing of the pope, was crowned king of the Franks and marched into Italy to defeat the Lombards. By granting to the papacy certain claims to Italian territory, which formed the basis of the Papal States, Pepin made the Donation of Pepin, receiving in return papal anointing as king. Dying in 768, he was succeeded by his two sons, Carloman and Charlemagne. Carloman died in 711, and Charlemagne soon embarked on one of the most celebrated reigns in European history.

The West Franks became absorbed into a vast imperial domain, the Carolingian empire, that survived the death of Charlemagne (d. 814) by only a few years. His son, Louis the Pious (d. 840), was unable to sustain Carolingian vitality, and thus on his death war erupted among his sons, Charles the Bald, Louis the German and Lothair. After forming an alliance against Lothair and defeating him at Fontenay in 842, Louis and Charles took the Strasbourg Oath, pledging mutual assistance but marking the linguistic division of the empire. A year later the three brothers signed the Treaty of Verdun (see VERDUN, TREATY OF), partitioning the empire politically, an event seen by many scholars as setting the borders of the kingdom and thus as the forerunner of French unity.

The Carolingians were doomed to dynastic decline because of the emergence of feudalism—the parceling out of extensive holdings to feudatory lords who only rarely upheld their duties as vassals and strengthened themselves through subinfeudation. By the 10th century France was one of the clearest example of feudalism to be found in the West. Despite positive contributions to culture and education, the Carolingian dynasts became wholly incapable of resisting the predatory challenges around them, such as those posed by the Muslims and the Vikings. In 887 Charles the Fat was deposed in favor of Count Odo (Eudes), and the next century witnessed bloodshed and strife as the Carolingians fought extinction at the hands of the magnates of the country. That finally came in 987, when Hugh Capet became king (987–796), founding the Capetian dynasty, which endured until 1328. The early Capetians were relatively weak, controlling only a meager feudal area, one of the smallest in France, while other members of the nobility, the counts of Champagne, Flanders and Anjou and the dukes of Aquitaine, Normandy and Burgundy, were stronger and more forceful.

Change came during the reign of Louis VI the Fat (1108–1137), who strengthened his position in the Île de France, appointed competent administrators *(prevôts)* and was ultimately able to command the allegiance of several lords beyond his own region. Louis also granted charters to numerous towns, thereby assuring their loyalty. His son, Louis VII (ruled 1137–1180), was not as shrewd, committing the blunder of divorcing Eleanor of Aquitaine in 1152. She married the future Henry II of England, giving him vast possessions in France. At his succession in 1153, Henry had Normandy, Anjou, Maine, Tours and Aquitaine, an Angevin empire that virtually surrounded the Île de France. French history might have been different had Louis not been succeeded by his son, Philip II Augustus. His reign (1180–1223) was a brilliant one as he employed the skillful combination of diplomacy and war against Henry II and his sons Richard the Lion-Hearted and John. He was particularly successful against John, taking his French holdings, except for Gascony, and inflicting a severe defeat on him and Otto IV, the German emperor (1208–1215), and a coalition of German and Flemish forces at Bouvines in 1214. Other acquisitions were made during the Albigensian Crusade in southern France, reducing the strength of Philip's rivals, most notably the counts of Toulouse. Philip then continued governmental reform, improved the legal system and fostered trade and the growth of towns.

Philip's son, Louis VIII (ruled 1223–1226), brought Toulouse under direct royal authority, but his greatest achievement was to produce his heir, Louis IX (Saint Louis). Revered as a saint and Christian soldier, Louis IX (ruled 1226–1270) was known for his preference for diplomacy over war, and his reign was considered the brightest hour for France in the Middle Ages. Despite fighting on two Crusades, he fostered the consolidation of monarchical power but not by conquest. The Treaty of Paris (1259) guaranteed English mastery over Gascony but brought the surrender of English claims to Normandy as well as Maine and other French territories. Another treaty with James I of Aragon ensured widespread peace. Spared from wars as a result, Louis concentrated on sound government, strengthening the judicial system, demanding the fulfillment of feudal obligations from his lords and creating large feudal estates (appanages) to satisfy the ambitions of his brothers.

Philip III (ruled 1270–1285) strove to add further luster to the crown. Acquiring the county of Champagne, he failed in his most audacious scheme, a war with Aragon in 1285 that ended in total disaster. His failure, however, was forgotten because of the achievements of Philip IV the Fair (1285–1314). He has been credited with having been the architect of French absolutism. He laid hold of his vassals' lands by applying feudal privilege, reduced the influence of the magnates and appointed the *enqueteurs,* the agents of the crown administered royal concerns in France. The church in France was brought under control, curtailing papal involvement in secular matters and humiliating Pope Boniface VIII (1294–1303). Philip's agents captured the pontiff in 1303, brutalized him and, when the broken pope died a short time later, made certain that his successor was French. The papacy was then pursuaded to move to Avignon, where it came under the watchful eye of the French kings of the 14th century. Jealous of the Knights Templars, Philip arranged their condemnation by the church on various charges, massacring them and bringing their large estates and treasury into his keeping. He called the first States General (Estates General) in 1302 to fund his wars and to give evidence of his cause in the public arena. An assembly including representatives of the first (clergy), second (aristocracy) and third (middle class) estates was convened. It met again in 1308 but did not become a great political force, having little influence on Philip.

The king left behind a stable government when he died in 1314. Capable officials such as Pierre Dubois and Guillaume de Nogaret served the crown. Trade flourished and the economy was sound. Philip had not fared as well militarily, as his army was routed at Courtrai in 1302 by a multitude of Flemish townsmen, ending his hopes for annexing Flanders. Problems of inheritance arose when Louis X (1314–1316) died without a male heir. It was decided that his brother should be crowned as Philip V. He died as well without a male heir in 1322, and the throne was claimed by his brother, who ruled as Charles IV from 1322 to 1328. With his demise, once more without a son, a complete dynastic change took place, as his cousin, Philip of Valois, became king, establishing the Valois line that would rule France during the terrible Hundred Years' War and into the Renaissance (until 1515).

Philip VI of Valois (ruled 1328–1350) was too weak to oppose Edward III of England (1327–1377), who launched the Hundred Years' War in 1337 because he claimed that he, not Philip of Valois, was the legitimate heir to the throne of France. The French were annihilated by the English at Crécy in 1346, and years of military defeats followed as Philip's successor, John the Good (ruled 1350–1364), faced another terrible defeat at Poitiers in 1356, this time at the hands of the English led by Edward the Black Prince. John was captured, and it was necessary for the French to ransom him. The war devasted the land, which was roamed by brigands, and the Black Death (1348–1350) left hundreds of thousands dead.

Charles V (ruled 1364–1380) was next of the line, renewing the war, reclaiming most of the territory lost to England and surviving the Jacquerie, the peasant uprising of 1358. Charles crushed the rebellion ruthlessly. His successor, Charles VI (ruled 1380–1422), did not pursue the same course, not having the financial resources available. He also faced severe political factionalism that divided France into two camps, the Burgundians and the group of Orléanais, called the Armagnacs.

King Henry V of England (1413–1422), invaded France in 1415, defeating the French at Agincourt, ruling France through the duke of Bedford and conquering the northern regions. Duke John the Fearless of Burgundy had been assassinated in 1419, driving his group into the English camp. In the following year Henry concluded the Treaty of Troyes, by which terms he was to marry Catherine, daughter of Charles VI, thus inheriting the French throne when Charles died. Henry died in 1422, and his young son Henry was proclaimed ruler of France, but he was unable to press his claims. Charles VI died in that same year, and the young and inexperienced Charles VII (1422–1461) came to the throne. The English suffered a defeat by the French at Orléans led by Joan of Arc, and after more victories the dauphin was crowned at Reims in 1429. Joan of Arc was captured by the British in 1430 and burned in Rouen as a witch in 1431, but she stood as a symbol for the French. By 1453 Charles's forces had captured Bordeaux, driving the English from the Continent, leaving only their holding at Calais. After a century of conflict, the Hundred Years' War was at an end. Charles set about uniting the kingdom and the crown. Following the pattern set by his predecessors, he won the right to levy taxes, was able to rely on a standing army and set aggressive policies. The heir to the throne, Louis XI (ruled 1461–1483), followed the same course, forming a crucial alliance with the French middle class, thus reducing the power of the nobility. The Burgundians were rendered harmless by the death of Charles the Rash (or the Bold) in 1477 at the Battle of Nancy. With Burgundy effectively diminished, France bordered Germany from the North Sea to the Alps. Louis concentrated as well on trade and economic recovery, achieving such gains that the modern French state of the 16th century was provided with essential financial strength and a sound foundation in commerce.

See also ALBI; ALBIGENSIAN MOVEMENT; AMIENS; ANGEVIN DYNASTY; ANGILBERT; ANJOU; AQUITAINE; ARMAGNAC; ARTOIS; AUSTRASIA; AVIGNON; BABYLONIAN CAPTIVITY; BANKING; BAYEAUX; BEAUVAIS; BEC; BENEDICTINES; BERNARD OF CLAIRVAUX; BERRY, JEAN DE FRANCE, DUC DE; BLANCH OF CASTILE; BLOIS; BOURBON, HOUSE OF; BURGUNDY, KINGDOM OF; BURIDAN, JEAN; CABOCH, SIMONE; CALAIS; CAPETIAN DYNASTY; CARMELITES; CAROLINGIAN ART AND ARCHITECTURE; CARTHUSIANS; CASTLE; CATHERINE OF VALOIS; CHAMPAGNE; CHARLES, COUNT OF VALOIS; CHARLES OF BLOIS; CHARTIER, ALAIN; CHARTRES; CHASTELLAIN, GEORGE; CHÂTEAU GAILLARD; CHIVALRY; CISTERCIANS; CLAIRVAUX; CLERMONT, COUNCIL OF; CLUNY; COEUR, JACQUES; CONCILIAR MOVEMENT; DOMINICANS; DUBOIS, PIERRE; DUFAY, GUILLAUME; DU GUESCLIN, BERTRAND; DUNOIS, JEAN, COMTE DE; ELEANOR OF AQUITAINE; FAIRS; FEUDALISM; FLANDERS; FOIX, COUNTY OF; FOUQUET, JEAN; FRANCHE-COMTÉ; FRANKS; FROISSART, JEAN; FULCHER OF CHARTRES; FULK, KING OF JERUSALEM; FULK III NARRA; GALLICANISM; GASCONY; GEOFFREY, COUNT OF ANJOU; GERMANY; GODFREY DE BOUILLON; GODFREY OF FONTAINES; GODFREY OF SAINT VICTOR; GOTHIC ART AND ARCHITECTURE; GREGORY OF TOURS, SAINT; GUILDS; GUILLAUME DE LORRIS; HAUTEVILLE, DROGO DE; HAUTEVILLE, HUMPHREY DE; HAUTEVILLE, WILLIAM DE; HERALDRY; HINCMAR OF REIMS; HOLY ROMAN EMPIRE; HUGH THE GREAT; HUNDRED YEARS' WAR; ÎLE-DE-FRANCE; INVESTITURE CONTROVERSY; JACQUERIE; JACQUES DE VITRY; JEWS AND JUDAISM; JOAN OF ARC; JOINVILLE, JEAN; JONGLEURS; LANQUEDOC; LYONS; MAINE; MANORIAL SYSTEM; MARSEILLES; MEROVINGIAN ART AND ARCHITECTURE; MEROVINGIAN DYNASTY; MILITARY ORDERS; MOLAY, JACQUES DE; MONTPELLIER; MONT-SAINT-MICHEL; NANCY; NARBONNE; NEUSTRIA; NORMANDY; NORMANS; NOTRE DAME DE PARIS; ODO OF PARIS; ODO OF CLUNY; ORLÉANS; PARIS; PLAGUES; POITIERS; POITOU; REIMS; ROMANESQUE ART AND ARCHITECTURE; ROUEN; SAINT GERMAIN-DES-PRÉS; SALIC LAW; SCHISM, GREAT; SOISSONS; STATES GENERAL; STRASBOURG; STRASBOURG OATH; SUGER; TEMPLARS; TOULOUSE; TRADE AND COMMERCE; TROUBADOURS; UNIVERSITIES; VALOIS DYNASTY; VIKINGS; VISIGOTHS; WARFARE; WILLIAM OF AUVERGNE; WILLIAM OF AUXERRE; WILLIAM OF SAINT THIERRY; and individual rulers.

**FRANCHE-COMTÉ** Called the Free County of Burgundy, a region in eastern France, including the departments of Jura, Haute-Saone and Doubs. It was established in the ninth century and ruled for a time by the kings of Burgundy, until 1032 or 1034, when it came into the possession of the Holy Roman Empire. Because of the location of the Franche-Comté, with its proximity to France, French influence ultimately proved stronger than the German, and in the 14th century King Philip V of France (1316–1322) acquired the region. Philip the Bold, duke of Burgundy, laid claim to the territory in 1384 through his marriage to the heiress of Franche-Comté, but after the death of Charles the Bold in 1477, his daughter, Mary of Burgundy, married Maxmilian I of the Habsburg dynasty, establishing the era of Habsburg rule. Under Habsburg domination the county retained considerable autonomy. See also BURGUNDY, DUCHY OF; BURGUNDY, KINGDOM OF.

**FRANCISCANS** The religious order also called the Friars Minor, established by Saint Francis of Assisi in 1209. His order was created as a result of Francis's spiritual, ascetic and religious motivations, and its rule deliberately embraced a life of poverty in imitation of those recounted in the Gospels. In 1209 the order received a rule, now lost, that was approved by Pope Innocent III. The early Franciscans established themselves in Umbria but then preached and journeyed throughout Italy, adhering strictly to the rule of poverty. Within a few years, however, it became clear that the growing number of Franciscans made impossible the loose structure proposed originally by Saint Francis. Despite his original objections, he was forced to correct the increasing irregularities within the order by composing a rule approved by Pope Honorius III in 1223, the *regula bullata*.

Poverty and the need for the order to survive in the secular world proved the most chronic and divisive problem facing the Franciscans. Even before Francis's death in 1226, conflict had erupted concerning the degree to which poverty should be practiced. Some called for easing the restrictions, whereas others favored a return to the original ideals set by Francis himself. A third group hoped to find a middle ground. The difficulties were made evident in the deposition of Elias of Cortona in 1239. About 1245 the conflict threatened to divide the order, although a temporary settlement was found through the labors of Saint Bonaventure, general of the Franciscans from 1257 to 1274. He became known as the second founder of the order, for he brought a temporary truce, sent friars throughout Europe, into Syria and Africa, and directed the Franciscans into the realm of instruction. They thus became teachers of theology, and their houses in the university cities were renowned as places of learning.

After Bonaventure's death, the issue of poverty reappeared, manifesting itself in two main factions. The Spirituals demanded absolute poverty, and the Conventuals called for moderation. The matter was debated before the pope from 1310 to 1312 and from 1317 to 1318. Pope John XXII decided to support the Conventuals. A large number of the Spirituals fled the order as a result, creating their own heretical organization called the Fraticelli. Persecutions reduced their effectiveness, and within a few years they had all but disappeared. The Franciscans were subject to the decline of the orders in the church in the 14th century, resulting from the Black Death, the Great Schism and the deterioration of the rule in the wake of greater financial strength.

Attempts at reform were made, led by a group of friars adhering to the original spirit of Francis, called the Observants. Their austerity, in sharp contrast to the Conventuals, made continued union with the more moderate members impossible. Ecclesiastical recognition came in 1415 at the Council of Constance. Complete separation was authorized in 1517, when the Observants, joined by all of the reform bodies within the Franciscan order, were renamed Friars Minor of the Observance.

Two other orders were attached to the Franciscans, the Second and Third Order of Saint Francis. The Second Order was a religious body of women, founded in 1212 by Saint Clare of Assisi at San Damiano. It was originally known as the Poor Ladies but then took the name Poor Clares. The Third Order was established by Francis in 1221 as a semireligious secular organization for men and women. See also MENDICANT ORDERS.

**FRANCIS OF ASSISI, SAINT** (c. 1181–1226) Founder of the Franciscan order and one of the most admired and revered saints of the Middle Ages. Born Giovanni di Bernardone, he was the son of Pietro Bernardone, a cloth merchant of Assisi, and his wife, Pica. He worked for his father until the age of 20, reportedly acquiring the name Francesco because of his father's journeys through France. Known for his spirit, generosity and carefree attitude, he was a popular figure in Assisi. In 1202, after joining a force of soldiers on campaign against the city Perugia, he was captured. Held prisoner for some months, he was released but was no longer content with his life, especially after experiencing a lengthy illness. Increasingly given to prayer, he underwent what was called his "conversion." He had visions of Christ sharing in the poverty of beggars in Saint Peter's in Rome and of Him kissing a leper. Returning home, Francis was disowned by his father because he sold a bale of cloth from his father's warehouse to pay for the restoration of the church of San Damiano, which was in a state of ruin, taking literally a command he had received from Christ to "repair my house, which is virtually ruined."

In 1210 Francis worshiped at a Mass in the town of Portiuncula, below Assisi. He heard the Gospel account of Christ telling his disciples to go forth on their missions. As a result of this he set out himself, preaching throughout the region and attracting followers. For them he composed a simple rule of life, the *regula primitiva,* receiving the reluctant approval of Pope Innocent III in 1210 to establish his small group of friars. The early Franciscans practiced extreme poverty, wandering across Italy to preach while gathering more and more numbers. In 1212, a second order of Franciscans was begun by Clare of Assisi. The women gathering to her came to be known as the Poor Clares. About 1221 a third order, allowing men and women of the laity to practice semireligious lives, was begun.

Saint Francis of Assisi

About 1214, Francis, having established his friars in Italy, felt it was now time to carry his message to other countries, even to the Holy Land and to the Muslim world. He attempted to reach Palestine but was shipwrecked and became ill. A missionary attempt in Egypt was made in 1219. Francis witnessed the siege of Damietta in November of that year before journeying into the camp of the sultan. The Muslim leader was so impressed with him that he supposedly gave Francis permission to visit the Holy Land's religious sites. Francis, however, was needed at home to stem the tide of irregularities within the Franciscan order and to deal with the increasing needs of its membership. Support was given him by Peter Catanii (Petrus Cataneo) and, after his death in 1221, by Elias of Cortona.

Reluctantly Francis asked Pope Honorius III to approve a revised version of his rule and received papal authorization on December 29, 1223. This was called the *regula bullata.* From that date Francis left the direction of the order's affairs to others, retreating from the world. In 1224, while at Mount Alvernia in the Apennines, he received the stigmata, body scars corresponding to the five wounds of the crucified Christ. He died in the chapel at Portiuncula on October 3, 1226. His canonization by Pope Gregory IX came in 1228. See also FRANCISCANS; MENDICANT ORDERS; MYSTICISM.

**FRANCIS OF MEYRONNES** (d. after 1328) Franciscan theologian and philosopher who was one of the founders of the Scholastic school and an ardent advocate of the philosophical premises of John Duns Scotus. Born in Meyronnes, in France, he was a student of Duns Scotus at the University of Paris, and his subsequent works on theology earned him the title "Prince of the Scotists." He also founded the Maronitae school of philosophy (Meyronist), an offshoot of the Scotus school. Among his many works were commentaries on Aristotle's *On Interpretation, Physics* and *Universal and Categories;* commentaries on the *Sentences* of Peter Lombard; and his own treatises *De formalitatibus* (*On Formalities*) and *De univocatione entis* (*On the University of Being*).

**FRANCIS OF PAOLA, SAINT** (1416–1507) Founder of the Minim Friars (Ordo Fratrum Minimorum) and a revered ascetic. Born in Paola, Italy, of a poor family, he spent a year with the Franciscans at San Marco before becoming a hermit in 1430, living in a cave near the sea at Paola. He was joined (c. 1435) by two followers, establishing themselves as the Hermits of Saint Francis of Assisi, later called the Fratres Minimi, the "Least Brothers" in 1492. The congregation grew throughout Italy, France, Spain, Germany and even Bohemia, while Francis's reputation as a holy figure included reports of miraculous cures. In 1483, King Louis XI of France summoned him to his deathbed in an attempt to obtain a cure. His son, Charles VIII, asked Francis to remain in France as a spiritual adviser, building monasteries for him. Canonized in 1519, Francis was also named a patron saint of the sailors of Italy in 1943, honoring his many miracles worked for those at sea. See also MYSTICISM.

**FRANCONIA** Called Franken in German, one of the five major duchies of medieval Germany, including Saxony, Bavaria, Lotharingia and Swabia. The region was settled by the Franks in the sixth century and during Merovingian rule was annexed to the territorial possessions of the crown. As part of the Treaty of Verdun in 843, Franconia was included in the formation of the Kingdom of the East Franks (or the German Kingdom). Conrad of Franconia ruled as a German king from 911 to 918, but in 919, with the rise of the Saxon kings, the duchy lost a powerful ducal line. Under Otto I (912–973) Franconia was divided into two nominal duchies, West or Rhenish Franconia and East Franconia. Rhenish Franconia was dominated by the Palatinate, the free cities of Frankfurt and Worms and the influential archbishoprics of Mainz and Speyer. East Franconia included Nuremberg, the margravates of Ansbach and Bayreuth and the bishoprics of Bamberg and Würzberg. The decentralization of West Franconia was generally applied to the East Franconian region. In the 15th century the bishops of Würzburg att[...] revive the ducal title long in disuse. See also GER[...]

**FRANKFURT AM MAIN** City in the Hesse [...] Germany on the Main River. Frankfurt am Main, [...] furt, was probably originally a Celtic settlement [...] in the first century A.D. by the Romans. Its na[...] derived from Frankfurt (crossing of the Franks), [...] first written mention of the site was by the chronicle[...] Einhard in 793. In 856 Lothair II was elected king of Lotharingia, beginning the tradition that the German kings were to be elected there, formally stipulated in the Golden Bull of 1356. The city did not reach its full potential until the time of the Hohenstaufens, and from 1240 it prospered thanks to the rise of its trade fairs. In 1372, Frankfurt was made a free imperial city. See also GERMANY; TRADE AND COMMERCE.



**FRANKS** A group of Germanic tribes that was important in the settlement of western Europe, especially France, whence its name is derived. Frankish tribes first made their appearance on the Lower Rhine River in the middle of the third century A.D., crossing into Roman imperial territory but, facing defeat, withdrawing across the Rhine. By the fifth century they had separated into two major branches, the Salian and Ripuarian Franks. Participating in the massive tribal migrations of the time, the Salian Franks seized much of northern Gaul beyond the Loire River; the Ripuarian Franks chose to settle around Cologne, in northeastern Gaul. Federates of the moribund Roman Empire in the West, the Salian Franks ultimately became independent, establishing their mastery over virtually all of Gaul under their celebrated ruler Clovis (d. 511). Converted to Christianity, the Franks, united by Clovis, emerged as defenders of Christian orthodoxy against the Arian Visigoths, whom they defeated in 507 at the Battle of Vouille. Having assured themselves of church support in Gaul, the Frankish ruling house, the Merovingians, consolidated its political position, making it the forerunner of the Kingdom of France. See also FRANCE; GERMANY; HOLY ROMAN EMPIRE; MEROVINGIAN DYNASTY; PAGANISM.

**FRAUENLOB** See HEINRICH VON MEISSEN.

**FREDEGUNDE** (d. 597) Frankish queen, mistress and then the wife of King Chilperic I of Nuestria (ruled 561–584). Once a servant, Fredegunde charmed Chilperic to become his lover and finally his adviser. She convinced him to end his first marriage and then, according to Saint Gregory of Tours (see GREGORY OF TOURS, SAINT), was instrumental in planning the murder of his second wife,

Galswintha, about 567. The queen, however, was the sister of Brunhilde, wife of Sigebert I of Austrasia, Chilperic's half brother, and her murder with Fredegunde's complicity plunged Nuestria and Austrasia into a feud that lasted for decades. Having married Chilperic, Fredegunde advanced the claim of her son, Clotaire II, who came to the throne in 584. Fredegunde died in 597; her son later executed Brunhilde, in 613. See also NEUSTRIA.

**FREDERICK I, ELECTOR OF BRANDENBURG** (1372–1440) First of the House of Hohenzollern and politically important as Elector of Brandenburg from 1417 to 1440. The son of the burgrave of Nuremberg, he inherited the possession of Ansbach from his father (1398) and the principality of Beyreuth from his brother (1420). A friend and trusted ally of King Sigismund of Hungary (emperor, 1410–1437), he was named in 1410 his representative for Brandenburg during the election of the German king, proving himself useful in establishing the claim of Sigismund as king. Sigismund appointed him the first governor of Brandenburg (1411) and then Elector and margrave in 1417. Frederick left Brandenburg in 1425, handing its administration to his son, John the Alchemist. Subsequently he was an imperial agent, serving most notably in the negotiations with the Hussites. See also HOLY ROMAN EMPIRE.

**FREDERICK I, ELECTOR OF SAXONY** (1369–1428) Called "the Warlike," the Elector of Saxony from 1423 to 1428. His position within the Holy Roman Empire was assured by his support of Emperor Sigismund (1410–1437) against Jan Hus, the heretical religious spokesman, and the Hussites in Bohemia. For his loyalty and constancy in reviling the Hussite heresy, he was granted the duchy of Saxony, becoming an Elector in 1423, succeeding Albert III. A scion of the House of Wettin, Frederick gave his line political prominence. See also HOLY ROMAN EMPIRE.

**FREDERICK II, ELECTOR OF SAXONY** (1411–1464) The successor to, and son of, Frederick I the Warlike, as Saxon Elector, ruling from 1428 to 1464. He was called "the Mild," in contrast to his father, and his dealings with the Hussites were markedly different as well. He made peace with them in 1432, and in 1464 his daughter married George of Podiebrad, ruler of Bohemia. Much of his time as Elector was spent attempting to acquire territory or in quarreling with other dynasties over land claims. From 1446 to 1451 he fought the *Bruderkrieg* (Brother's War) with his brother William over certain rights. See also SAXONY.

**FREDERICK I, EMPEROR** (c. 1122–1190) King of Germany from 1152 to 1190 and emperor from 1155, known as Barbarossa (Red Beard) and one of the most formidable Holy Roman Emperors, as well as a leader of the Third Crusade and an opponent of the papacy. His reign witnessed the zenith of German unity in the Middle Ages, and he emerged as a legendary figure in German history. The son of Frederick II, duke of Swabia, and Judith, daughter of Henry IX, duke of Bavaria, he was a member of both dynasties, the Hohenstaufen and Welf, which were vying for power. For this reason, and in the hope that he would end the dynastic conflict, he was elected German king, successor to his uncle, Emperor Conrad III (1138–1152). In 1154 he embarked on the first of six campaigns in Italy, refusing to enter into an alliance with the Byzantines and hanging the contentious Roman leader Arnold of Brescia. As a reward, Pope Adrian IV crowned him emperor on June 18, 1155.

Emperor Frederick I Barbarossa

In Germany he attempted to bring peace while curbing the powers of the princes, and a major dispute was settled when he bestowed Bavaria on Henry the Lion of Saxony. He also elevated the margrave Henry Jasomirgott of Austria to the rank of duke. Intending to maintain the dukes of Poland as vassals, Frederick gave the archbishop of Bremen more influence and in 1158 granted certain rights to King Waldemar I the Great of Denmark (1157–1182) in return for his recognition of imperial supremacy. Of importance was his major effort in bringing parts of Germany under his direct political control as counterbalance to the princes. Imperial territories were positioned between the princely holdings, governed by his own agents, the *ministeriales* (imperial ministers), who reported to him alone. Peace laws were decreed and steps were taken to resist the princes, most notably by the archbishops of Cologne and Magdeburg and by Louis of Thuringia, and his decision to crush Henry the Lion was successful. This prominent former ally of Frederick refused to send support in 1176 when it was urgently needed in Italy, and he often disturbed the peace. Frederick was able to strip Henry of his titles, but he did not fare as well against the other princes.

He turned his attention instead to Italy again. In 1158 he planned to promote imperial rights in that region. At the Diet of Roncaglia (1158) he proclaimed these rights and strove to absorb Italy into the empire. Castles were constructed, ministers appointed and taxes collected and used to appease the German princes and to fund military campaigns. Quite naturally, the papacy and the Italian cities opposed him. In 1160, the disputed Pope Alexander III (1159–1181) excommunicated Frederick. He moved to France in 1161 and established France and England as allies, as well as Spain and the Lombards. Frederick supported, the antipopes Victor IV (1159–1164) and Paschal III (1164–1168), launching another attack on Italy in 1166. He wanted to crush the Lombard League and seized Sicily, attempting to break the will of the pope, who had returned to Italy. The advance was a disaster, and in 1174 a fifth campaign was initiated. Although a military triumph was not achieved, Frederick did compel the Lombards to sign the Armistice of Montebello. His plans were thwarted, however, in 1176 when he was defeated at the Battle of Legnano. He reached an agreement with the pope at Anagni and a year later (1177) acknowledged Alexander III as the true pontiff. Peace was made in 1183 with the Lombards, and a lasting claim on Italy was achieved through marriage. Frederick's son, Henry (VI), married Constance, heiress of Sicily, in 1186.

Deciding to join Richard the Lion-Hearted of England (1189–1199) and Philip II Augustus (1180–1223) of France on the Third Crusade, Frederick set out in the spring of 1189. While crossing the Saleph River in Cilicia, he drowned, a strange end to so remarkable a life. According to legend, he lives still, inhabiting a cave in the Kyffhauser, a forested mountain in Thuringen, awaiting the day that he will return to Germany to restore it to greatness. See also GERMANY; HOLY ROMAN EMPIRE.

**FREDERICK II, EMPEROR** (1194–1250) German king, ruling from 1212 to 1250, and emperor from 1220, also king of Sicily and one of the most gifted and politically astute rulers of the Middle Ages, whose reign was marked by his long conflict with the papacy. The son of Emperor Henry VI (1190–1197) and Constance of Sicily, he was the grandson of Frederick I Barbarossa (1152–1190). After Henry's death in 1197, Frederick traveled to Sicily, where he was crowned in May 1198, placed under the guardianship of Pope Innocent III (1198–1216) by his mother, who died that same year. In 1208 he married Constance of Aragon (d. 1222), receiving in 1211 support from the German princes in his claim to the German crown. The rival king, Otto (IV) of Brunswick, was deposed, and in 1212 the princes elected Frederick king. Two years later Otto was defeated at the Battle of Bouvines by Frederick's French allies.

In 1220, Pope Honorius III (1216–1227), with some reluctance, crowned him emperor, but only after exacting an oath that he would embark on crusade to the Holy Land, a vow similar to one he had made in 1212 at his election. He spent several years consolidating his position, marrying Isabella of Brienne in 1225, the heiress of the titular king of Jerusalem, but he did not set sail, preferring to issue the Diet of Cremona in 1226, a reinforcement of imperial rights in Italy. In 1227 he began his crusade, but an epidemic broke out among his transport ships, forcing a return to Brindisi. Pope Gregory IX (1227–1241), unconvinced by Frederick's protestations concerning the disease, excommunicated him in 1228. Undeterred, he set out once more. Employing skillful diplomatic ingenuity, he won from the sultan of Egypt the control of Jerusalam, Nazareth and Bethlehem. This remarkable bloodless triumph allowed him to enter Jerusalem on March 18, 1229, where he was crowned king. Unfortunately, his supporters were few in number because of the papal interdict and were composed mainly of Teutonic Knights. His kingship, recognized only by the Muslims of Egypt, was spurned by the Christian princes, who resented his German origins and his successes.

Pope Gregory called for a holy war against him, forcing Frederick to return to Italy, where he reclaimed his lost Italian possessions. He then negotiated with the pope and in 1230 signed the Treaty of San Germano, revoking his excommunication. A year later he issued a new constitution for Sicily at Malfi, only to have his imperial plans ruined by his son, Henry, whom he had made king of Germany in 1220. Henry had entered into an alliance with the Lombard League and was removed in 1234, dying in prison in 1245. Another son, Conrad IV, was made German king in 1237 (emperor, 1250–1254), the same year that Frederick crushed the Lombards at the Battle of Cortenuova. Confident that all of Italy could be brought under his domination, he rejected peace overtures from Milan and pressed the rights of an illegitimate son, Enzio, as king of Sardinia, contesting papal claims. The break with the Holy See, long in coming, erupted in 1239, when Gregory excommunicated him for a second time.

Frederick responded with a campaign against the pope, marching on the Papal States in 1240. He captured a fleet bound for a council in Rome, taking as hostage more than 100 prelates, an act that brought him condemnation as an oppressor of the church. Pushing on to Rome, he was just outside the walls of the city when he discovered that Gregory IX was dead (1241). Withdrawing from Italy, Frederick negotiated for a time with Pope Innocent IV (1243–1254). The collapse of these negotiations led to bitter hostilities. Frederick suffered defeats from 1247 to 1250, and Enzio fell into the hands of the Bolognese, but he made a recovery both in Italy and Germany and then died suddenly of severe dysentery on December 13, 1250, in Apulia.

Frederick's sudden demise caught the Christian world unawares. It was left to his son, Conrad IV, and to his grandson, Conradin (emperor, 1254–1268), to end the war. They were not only vanquished but so disgraced that the entire Hohenstaufen dynasty collapsed as well. Frederick's military activities put him at risk, especially when he trusted his sons, but he was known as a creative monarch, promoting enlightened reforms in law and finance in Sicily and expanding commercial enterprise. His court drew brilliant men of letters and he was celebrated by his contemporaries as a poet, scientist, linguist and the author of a book on falconry, as well as a student of mathematics, astronomy and medicine. See also HOLY ROMAN EMPIRE.

**FREDERICK III, EMPEROR** (1415–1493) German king from 1440 and Holy Roman Emperor from 1452 to 1493. His reign saw the rise of the Habsburgs in Europe, although he was viewed as a weak and ineffectual ruler, especially regarding the regional problems in Germany and Austria. The son of Ernest, duke of Austria, Frederick became the senior member of the Habsburg dynasty in 1439, and the following year he was elected king of Germany. He showed a surprising lack of interest in German affairs, perhaps prompted by the alienation of the German princes, who in turn became incensed by his idleness. Rival claimants emerged but were unsuccessful, mainly because Frederick outlived them and withstood the revolts by the nobles of Austria. His political position was not enhanced by the temporary losses of the Habsburgs in Bohemia and Hungary.

Frederick supported Pope Eugene IV (1431–1447) in the pontiff's conflict with the conciliar movement at the Council of Basel and for his views was crowned emperor in 1452 by Pope Nicholas V (1447–1455). His later years witnessed the ascendancy of his son, Maxmilian, who reclaimed Austria in in 1490–1491 after the Hungarian king, Matthias, had seized it in 1485. It was through Maxmilian that Frederick achieved his greatest success, the marriage of his son to Mary of Burgundy in 1477, uniting the Burgundian and Habsburg possessions. This event laid the groundwork for the extensive power of the Habsburgs in the 16th century and later, fulfilling, at least in part, Frederick's personal motto: *Austriae est imperare orbi universo* ("It is Austria's destiny to rule the whole world"). Frederick lived in virtual retirement at Linz in his last years, pursuing his personal interests: botany, alchemy and astronomy. See also HOLY ROMAN EMPIRE.

**FREDERICK III, KING OF SICILY** (1272–1337) Ruler of Sicily from 1296 to 1337, actually Frederick II but taking that title to reflect his Ghibelline sympathies as a successor to the antipapist Holy Roman Emperor Frederick II (1215–1250). He served from 1291 to 1296 as regent for his brother, James II of Aragon (1291–1327) and Sicily, but in order to prevent the return of the Angevins under Charles II of Anjou, he was named by the Sicilians as king. He waged war for many years with the papacy and with Naples, proving ultimately successful in acquiring the possession of Sicily for the Aragonese. His son Peter was named his heir. See also SICILY.

**FREDERICK THE FAIR, DUKE OF AUSTRIA** (1286–1330) Also called Frederick III the Handsome, the duke of Austria from 1308 and German king from 1314. A son of Albert I, king of Germany, Frederick was a claimant to the throne following the death of Emperor Henry VII (1309–1313) in 1313. In October 1314, he received four votes from Electors but was defeated by Louis (IV) of Bavaria, who received five the next day. Declared an antiking, Frederick fought an eight-year war, finally being captured in 1322 by Louis. Three years later, Louis, facing a crisis with the papacy, offered to abdicate in Frederick's favor, a proposal that was never carried out. Frederick was released, however, and returned to Austria in 1426. There he remained, having renounced his imperial claims. See also HOLY ROMAN EMPIRE.

**FREIBURG IM BREISGAU** City in southern Germany in the region of Baden-Wurtemberg, situated on the edge of the Black Forest, established in 1120 by a duke of Zahringen to serve as a major place of commerce for the region. The city was situated in the Rhine Valley, with proximity to both Switzerland and Italy. In 1218 it was in the possession of the counts of Urach, who thereafter held the title counts of Freiburg, although Habsburg rule was instituted in 1368. The university at Freiburg, the Albert Ludwig University, was founded in 1457 by Archduke Albert VI of Austria. Fine medieval buildings remain there, including the 13th-century church of Saint Martin.

**FRIARS MINOR** See FRANCISCANS.

**FRIARS PREACHERS** See DOMINICANS.

**FRIENDS OF GOD** See GOTTESFREUNDE.

**FRISIA** Also Friesland, a region in the Netherlands on the North Sea, including several western Frisian islands. The Frisians were an old Germanic people, long accustomed to sea travel and major sea traders at the start of the Middle Ages. Although they may have participated to a lesser degree in the invasions of England, they were most powerful during the seventh century. After that they came into conflict with the Franks, suffering defeat in the eighth century and coming under Frankish domination. Attempts at Christianization among the Frisians were largely successful as Anglo-Saxon missionaries strove to convert them. Sporadic outbursts of paganism did occur, however, the most notorious taking place in 754, when Boniface (680–754) was murdered. Eventually under the aegis of the counts of Holland, the Frisians continued to assert their independence, retaining their language and, after 1433, resisting control by the dukes of Burgundy, Duke Albert of Saxony and the Habsburgs. Complete pacification came only in 1523 during the reign of Emperor Charles V. Their primacy on the sea was supplanted by the Vikings after the acceptance of Christianity by the Frisians.

**FRIULI** Region in northeastern Italy, bordering on Yugoslavia, the eastern Alps and the Adriatic Sea. Friuli was conquered by the Lombards in the sixth century and made a duchy. When the Lombards were defeated by the Carolingians in the eighth century, the duchy was supplanted, and Friuli was made a strategic mark, or march, from which to guard the troublesome Italian frontier. About 1077 it was in the possession of the patriarch of Aquileia, who purchased both Friuli and Istria. Using his ecclesiastical authority, the patriarch retained control until 1419–1420, when the power of Venice compelled him to surrender it. See also VENETIA; VENICE.

**FROISSART, JEAN** (c. 1337–c. 1404) French chronicler, poet and traveler whose work, *Chroniques,* was a major source for the study of medieval history from 1325 to 1400 and a vital repository of information concerning the Hundred Years' War. Born in Valenciennes in Hainault, a county in Flanders, he studied for the priesthood but renounced that pursuit at the age of 20 in order to compose a chronicle of recent events in France for Robert of Namur. By 1361 he was in England and, having won the favor of Queen Philippa, earned the patronage of Edward III (1327–1377) and Edward the Black Prince. From 1367 to 1373 he journeyed through France and Italy, visiting royal courts and the papal residence at Avignon. In 1373 he returned to Hainault and then in 1382 entered the service of the duke of Brabant, Wenceslaus. When the duke died in 1383, Froissart became chaplain to Guy de Chatillon, count of Blois. William of Ostrevant, the governor of Hainault, then became his patron, and he remained there after a final trip to England, until his death about 1404.

Chivalry and pageantry fascinated Froissart. His *Chroniques,* organized into four books, described the figures, events and nations of the Middle Ages. Patronage was obvious, as his works favored those whom he currently served, and chivalry was exalted over the horrors of war. Froissart's works rank as some of the best in medieval times. He also composed ballads, rondeaux and an epic romance of some 30,000 lines, called *Meliador* or *The Knight of the Golden Sun.*

**FRUELA I** (d. 768) King of Asturias from 757 to 768. His major accomplishment was the defeat of the Muslim forces at the Battle of Pontuvium in Galicia. He was succeeded by Aurelius (768–774). See also LEÓN.

**FRUELA II** (d. 925) King of Asturias and Ovielo from 910 to 925. The son of King Alfonso III of Asturias (866–910), Fruela was a recipient of the partitioning of the kingdom at his father's death in 910, with his brothers García I (910–914) and Ordoño II (910–925). After Fruela died in 925, his sons were blinded by his nephew, Ramiro II (930–951). See also LEÓN.

**FULBERT OF CHARTRES** (c. 970–1028) Bishop of Chartres, educated at Reims and Chartres under Gerbert of Aurillac (the future Pope Sylvester II). In 990 Fulbert was appointed chancellor of the cathedral school of Chartres by Bishop Odo (968–1004), where he transformed the institution into one of the foremost institutions of learning in Europe. Named bishop of Chartres in 1007, he served as a representative of King Robert II of France and Duke William V of Aquitaine. He wrote many sermons, poems and hymns, including *Chorus Novae Jerusalem (Choirs of the New Jerusalem).* He also began the restoration of the cathedral of Chartres in 1020, after a fire, but he died before it could be completed. See also CHARTRES.

**FULCHER OF CHARTRES** (c. 1059–c. 1127) French chronicler and chaplain who wrote an account of the First Crusade. He attended the Council of Clermont in 1095 and accompanied Stephen of Blois on crusade in 1096, journeying with him to Constantinople. In 1097 he became chaplain to Baldwin I of Flanders, remaining thereafter a member of his entourage. His chronicle, the *Gesta Francorum et aliorum Hierosolymitanorum,* was composed in three installments, in 1101, 1106 and 1124–1127. This work is thought to be the most reliable available on the events of the Crusade and has long been referred to by scholars of the period. See also CRUSADES.

**FULDA** Celebrated Benedictine monastery founded in Hesse in 744 by Saint Sturmi, a disciple of Boniface. Boniface used the monastery as his headquarters for Missionary labors among the Saxons and was buried there. During the office of abbot Rabanus Maurus (822–842) the prestige of Fulda grew, as the monastery became acclaimed for its encouragement of culture and learning. Fulda possessed land all over Germany, and its abbots held certain rights not given other German Benedictine houses. Abbots from Fulda also wielded considerable secular influence within the Holy Roman Empire.

**FULK, KING OF JERUSALEM** (1092–1143) Count of Anjou (as Fulk V) from 1109 to 1131 and the ruler of the Kingdom of Jerusalem from 1131 to 1143. The son of Fulk IV Rechin and Bertrada de Montfort, he proved himself a gifted soldier and an astute political figure, ending the traditional hostility of the Angevin counts toward the Normans by negotiating the marriage of his son, Geoffrey Plantagenet, with Matilde, daughter of Henry I of England (1100–1135), thus giving rise to the Angevin dynasty of English kings. Fulk visited the Holy Land for the first time in 1120, deciding to return in 1129 to marry Melisende, the daughter of King Baldwin II of Jerusalem. Abdicating in favor of his son, Fulk became the successor to Baldwin, receiving the throne of Jerusalem in 1131. His early rule was beset with difficulties, especially with the nobles of the other Crusader States, Tripoli, Antioch and Edessa, and with his wife's lover, Hugh le Puiset. Establishing himself, however, he ruled effectively, encouraging trade and erecting castles in order to strengthen the defenses of the kingdom. He was described as short, fat and red haired. See also JERUSALEM, KINGDOM OF.

**FULK III NARRA** (d. 1040) Count of Anjou from about 987 until his death and one of the most feared nobles of the Middle Ages. The son of Geoffrey Greymantle, he killed Conan of Rennes at Conquereuil, was a bitter opponent of the counts of Blois and attempted for years the capture of Tours. His reputation for violence was borne out by his burning and looting of monasteries and by the murder of his first wife, Elizabeth (c. 1000). He also set fire to his own city of Angers. Engaged in a civil war against his son, Geoffrey Martel, Fulk was victorious and forced his son to do penance by crawling for miles along a road with an ass's saddle strapped to his back. A tale records that he once brought his second wife a cup that he had made himself. When he told her that it was from the man she loved most, she denied knowing anyone else and threw herself out a window, nearly drowning in the river below. Fulk undertook three pilgrimages, perhaps as penance, and visited the Holy Land and established monasteries there. Other accomplishments were also significant. He constructed castles, strengthened his line and firmly established the House of Anjou in France. See also ANJOU.

**FUST, JOHANN** (d. 1466) Early German printer, goldsmith and financial supporter of Johann Gutenberg. In 1450 he made Gutenberg a loan for the projected casting of a movable-type printing press, but additional loans were also necessary. As Gutenberg neared completion of his invention, Fust sued for return of his money (1455), winning the case and claiming Gutenberg's work. He established a printing firm with a friend, Peter Schöffer, publishing several important books, including the Bible in 1456, the Psalter in 1457 and Cicero's *De officiis* in 1465. See also GUTENBERG, JOHANN.

**AL-FUSTAT** Also Fostat, a city situated on the Nile River, predating Cairo and the capital of Islamic Egypt until 969. Al-Fustat originated as an Arab military camp, founded in 641 by the Arab general Amr ibn al-As as strategic to the capture of the Byzantine fortress called Babylon. It was the first Muslim community in Egypt and grew sporadically and chaotically over the succeeding years, dominated by Egypt's various Islamic masters—the Umayyads, Abbasids and Tulunids—who constructed new buildings outside the city and quarters within it. In 969 Egypt fell to the Fatimid caliphate, and Cairo was established as its new capital. Al-Fustat was destroyed in 1168 to ensure that it did not fall into the hands of the Crusaders. On its rebuilding by Saladin, it was joined with Cairo, eventually to become another quarter of the capital. The most important source of al-Fustat's prosperity was its ceramics industry, producing excellent work called Fustat ware. See also CAIRO.

# G

**GADDI, AGNOLO** (c. 1350–1396) Italian painter, the son of Taddeo Gaddi and the pupil of Giotto, who was a major influence. He worked for a time as an assistant to his brother, Giovanni, in Rome and then became a painter of extraordinary frescoes, executing a series of them in Santa Croce in Florence. These included the illustration the *Legend of the True Cross* (1388–1393). His frescoes reflected his concern for overall design, which overshadowed expressiveness in the work. He also designed medallions and painted scenes for the cathedral at Prato. At his death he was working on an altar in San Miniato al Monte, near Florence.

**GADDI, TADDEO** (c. 1300–1366) Italian painter, student of Giotto and a major Florentine artist. The son of Gaddo Gaddi, he was Giotto's assistant. His earliest authenticated work was a triptych of the Virgin and Child (1334). In 1332 he received an independent commission to paint a cycle of frescoes on the life of the Virgin in the Baroncelli chapel in Santa Croce, Florence. Completed in 1338, it was called his finest work, reflecting Giotto's influence but his own creative use of light to dramatize the work as well. Other important contributions include sacristy panels depicting the life of Christ and the life of Saint Francis in Santa Croce (c. 1338), a Tree of Life in the refectory of Santa Croce in the 1440s, a polytych for San Giovanni Fuorcivitas at Pistoia (1347–1353) and a Madonna for San Lucchere at Poggibonsi (1355). His son was Agnolo Gaddi.

**GAETANI, BENEDETTO** See BONIFACE VIII.

**GAISERIC, KING OF THE VANDALS** See GEISERIC.

**GALEOTTI, MARTIUS** (1442–1494) Italian astrologer who found service at the court of Hungary and achieved recognition as personal astrologer to King Louis XI of France (1461–1483). He was mentioned by Sir Walter Scott as being a counselor to the French king. See also ASTROLOGY.

**GALICIA (1)** Region in Poland called also Red Ruthenia or Red Rus, for a time one of the major states in eastern Europe. First conquered in 981 by Grand Prince Vladimir of Kiev, Galicia regained virtual independence in 1087, emerging as a stable principality. In 1200, however, Prince Roman of Volhynia annexed it, transforming Galicia into an impressive principality, chiefly during the reign of his son, Daniel Romanovich, who in 1253 was crowned king of Galicia. Devastated by the ambitions of its nobles, or boyars, and compelled to become a vassal state to the Mongols throughout the 13th century, the dynasty of Roman was extinct by 1323. A polish claimant, Boleslaw of Mazovia, became king, but after his death Casimir III of Poland annexed Galicia to Poland, in 1349. See also POLAND.

**GALICIA (2)** Region in the northwestern corner of Spain, bordering on the Atlantic Ocean and Portugal, which was originally the home of the Celtic tribe of Gallaeci, who were conquered by Rome about 137 B.C. The Suevi (c. 410) established an independent kingdom there, only to be destroyed by the Visigoths in 585. The invasion of Spain by the Muslims in the eighth century forced large numbers of Visigoths to seek refuge in Galicia, although Moorish incursions were common. Asturias repulsed the Moors in the ninth century, claiming the territory, but ultimately León came to possess it. Eventually Galicia became one of the minor vassal states of Castile. Galicia was celebrated during the Middle Ages for pilgrimages at the shrine of Santiago de Compostela, and the language and style of its lyric poetry was emulated by the Castilian lyric writers.

**GALL, SAINT** (c. 550–c. 645) Christian missionary and a disciple of Saint Columban. A native of Ireland, Saint Gall was educated at the monastery of Bangor in County Down, becoming one of the 12 companions of Saint Columban on his journey to France (Gaul), around 590. He helped to establish the monasteries at Luxeuil in the Vosges Mountains and in 610 traveled with Columban to Switzerland, where they preached to the pagan Alamanni tribe. When Columban departed for Italy in 612, Gall remained in Switzerland, embracing the life of a hermit, rejecting ecclesiastical rank and the post of abbot for Luxeuil. The celebrated monastery of Saint Gall was founded about 720 on the site of one of his hermitages. This monastery maintained close ties with Ireland, and its architectural design was a superb example of Benedictine monastic institutions. The monastery's symbol was a bear.

**GALLICANISM** A religious and political theory supporting a body of doctrine that asserted independence from the papacy for the church in France. The theory was rooted in the intense ideological nationalism in France during the eighth and ninth centuries, which was defined in the writings of noted French theologians at the University of Paris in the 14th century, especially those influenced by Peter d'Ailly and Jean Gerson. They argued that the French or Gallican church was entitled to special status because of its history. The conciliar movement supported this concept, and Gallicanism was encouraged by the French monarchy. In 1398 King Charles VI (1380–1422) refused his obedience to the Avignonese antipope Benedict XIII. He declared the French church autonomous. Of even greater importance was the Pragmatic Sanction of Bourges, issued in 1438 by King Charles VII, reaffirming that in France papal authority was conditional upon conciliarism and by the king's will. Gallicanism remained in dispute until the 19th century.

**GALLICAN RITES** Liturgies used in Gaul before the late eighth century, when Charlemagne ordered adherence to the Roman Rite. The Gallican Rites were practiced in regions of Gaul, Spain and northern Italy, possibly the result of the inability of the Merovingian rulers to effect any long-lasting ecclesiastical unity. It is possible that these rites, much debated, date from the formative period of Christianity in the West. Reflecting elements of the Celtic church and the Rite of Saint Ambrose, they still influenced aspects of the Roman Rite even after their official eradication. See also GALLICANISM.

**GALLUS ANONYMOUS** Twelfth-century writer, thought to have compiled the earliest list of events of Polish history. He was probably a Benedictine monk who lived in Cracow, composing his chronicle in Latin, which listed events to the year 1113. See also POLAND.

**GARCÍA I SANCHEZ** (d. 970) King of Navarre from 926 to 970 and ruler of Aragon after his marriage to Andregoto, the Aragonese heiress. He inherited a weak domain, his father, Sancho I Garcés, having been defeated by Abd al-Rahman III, the Umayyad caliph of Córdoba. Its capital, Pamplona, was sacked in 924. García allied himself with Sancho I of León against the Moors, but the union proved unequal to the army of Caliph al-Hakam II (961–976). In revenge, the Moors ravaged León, Castile and Navarre. See also NAVARRE, KINGDOM OF.

**GARCÍA II SANCHEZ** (d. 1000) King of Navarre from 994 to 1000, the son of Sancho II Garcés (970–994). He ruled for only a brief period and died during the conflict with the Moors. See also NAVARRE, KINGDOM OF.

**GARCÍA III SANCHEZ** (d. 1054) King of Navarre from 1035 to 1054 and the eldest son of Sancho III Garcés el Mayor, who, on his father's death in 1035, inherited Navarre. His brothers, Ferdinand I and Ramiro I, were each allotted separate territories, Castile and Aragon respectively. García and Ferdinand remained hostile to each other, especially as Ferdinand proved an able monarch, claiming the throne of León in 1037. Their rivalry erupted into warfare in 1054, but García was defeated and killed at the Battle of Atapuerca. Ferdinand thus acquired Navarre after the succession of García's son, Sancho IV Garcés (1054–1076). See also NAVARRE, KINGDOM OF.

**GARCÍA IV RAMIREZ** (d. 1150) King of Navarre from 1134 to 1150, elected king by the magnates of Navarre in 1134 principally because of his claims of descent from the great Sancho III Garcés el Mayor. His reign was spent as vassal to Alfonso VII of León and Castille (ruled 1126–1157). See also NAVARRE, KINGDOM OF.

**GARGOYLES** Originally the name given in architecture to the spout projecting from a parapet gutter, designed to drain rainwater from buildings. In classical design, the gargoyle was given the form of a lion, with the water carried through the mouth. During the Middle Ages, however, the gargoyle took the form of a fanciful or grotesque creature, often birdlike, which leaned forward to ensure that the water drained at a proper distance. Gargoyles were especially common on Gothic buildings; some of the best examples are found on the Cathedral of Notre Dame in Paris. See also GOTHIC ART AND ARCHITECTURE.

**GASCONY** In French, Gascogne, a province in southwestern France, including the modern departments of Gers, Landes, Haute-Pyrenees, Basses-Pyrenees, Lof-et-Garonne, Haute-Garrone and Tarn-et-Garonne. Part of the Roman possession of Aquitania, Gascony was overrun and occupied in the fifth century by the Visigoths, who were defeated at the Battle of Vouille in 506 by the Franks. The control of the Franks was ended by a Basque invasion in 561, which established the duchy of Vasconia, or Gascony,

Gargoyle on Cathedral of Notre Dame de Paris

imbuing the region with Basque culture from the seventh century. The fiery reputation of the Gascons was to become a theme in French literature.

By the 10th century the Gascon dukes had extended their control over Bordeaux, Bozadais and Agenais, but their line died out in 1032. The war of succession that ensued was ended in 1052, with the victory of the future William VIII of Aquitaine. From 1058 Gascony was annexed to Aquitaine and thus became a major territorial holding of England until its reconquest by the French at the end of the Hundred Years' War. It was then divided into small fiefs, held by the counts of Armagnac and Foix and by the lords of Albret. See also FRANCE.

**GASTON III, COUNT OF FOIX** See FOIX, COUNTY OF.

**GAUTIER DE METZ** Thirteenth-century French poet, who wrote a treatise on the universe, *L'image du monde* (*Image of the World,* c. 1245). Extremely popular during the Middle Ages, the treatise dealt with such topics as geography, astronomy, the Creation, monsters and treasures and suggested that ultimately destiny rested in the hands of God.

**GAVESTON, PIERS** (d. 1312) Earl of Cornwall and the favorite courtier of King Edward II of England (1307–1327). Gaveston was the son of a Gascon knight, raised in the household of Edward, then Prince of Wales. He was called "brother Perrot" by the prince, leading to Gaveston's banishment by King Edward I on two occasions. When Edward II succeeded to the throne in 1307, Gaveston returned and became the earl of Cornwall. He also married Edward's niece, Margaret de Clare, and was made regent in 1308, while the king was on the Continent to meet his bride, Isabella of France. The English barons were so outraged by this display of royal favor that in June 1308 Edward was forced to banish Gaveston once more, allowing him to return a year later. In 1311 another baronial commission demanded his exile. Gaveston fled to Flanders, returning by Christmas of that same year. Deciding that a more permanent solution was required, the barons seized him and on Blacklow Hill near Warwick murdered Gaveston. The first of many such deaths over the succeeding years, this execution caused permanent divisions between the barons and the king. See also ENGLAND.

**GAWAIN** Arthurian knight and hero, possibly the nephew of Arthur. Gawain was probably associated with the Celtic sun god Gwalchmei and was thus granted additional powers according to the position of the sun, as it waxed and waned during the day. In medieval literature the figure of Gawain was considerably transformed, most notably in the 13th-century Vulgate cycle, being presented as a warrior unable or unwilling to call on the grace of God in order to seek the Holy Grail (this was recounted in the *Queste du Saint Graal*). He was mentioned in Geoffrey of Monmouth's *Historia regum Britanniae* and in the works of Chretien de Troyes, *Tristan* and *Morte d'Arthur.* Of particular significance was the anonymous alliterative Middle English romance *Sir Gawain and the Green Knight* (preserved in the British Library, MS Cotton Nero A.X.). Dating from the late 14th century, the manuscript recounts the tale of a challenge made to Arthur's companions by the Green Knight. Gawain accepts, decapitates his foe but then watches him restore his own head while reminding Gawain that in time he must forfeit his own head in the Green Chapel, one year hence. Gawain spends the year adventuring, surviving through the trickery of wearing a magic girdle. He relates his dishonor to the knights of Arthur, who promise to wear green in remembrance of the dead knight. See also ARTHURIAN LEGEND; HOLY GRAIL.

**GDANSK** See DANZIG.

**GEDIMIN** (d. 1341) Grand duke of Lithuania from 1316 to 1341, a pagan who conducted diplomatic negotiations with the church and neighboring territories to protect his lands. Gedimin (also Gedymin or Gediminas) succeeded his brother, Vytennis, as grand duke in 1316, of the region including Lithuania, Volhynia, parts of the Ukraine and Belorussia and, for a time, the principalities of Novgorod, Kiev and Pskov. He faced threats from the Teutonic Knights and the Livonian Knights of the Sword as well as tensions among his Christian and pagan subjects. His diplomatic conduct with Poland, Riga and the church proved successful. He secured a treaty of peace, negotiating with the papacy and the Hanseatic League, the Dominicans, Franciscans and other regional powers, including the Teutonic Knights. When the Teutonic Knights became hostile, he revoked his pledge of 1323 to be baptized by the papal legates. By postponing this baptism indefinitely and by marrying his daughter, Aldona, to the son of King Wladyslaw I the Short of Poland, he allied himself with the church and with Poland against the Teutonic Knights, who spent the next years at war with Lithuania. Gedimin protected the clergy in his domain, appreciating their civilizing influence. Economic development was encouraged, and the frontier defenses were improved with fortresses and powerful towns. See also LITHUANIA.

**GEILER VON KAISERBERG, JOHANNES** (1445–1510) German preacher, called the "German Savanarola," who attacked the faults and abuses of the church of that era. Born in Schaffhausen on the Rhine River and educated at Ammerswerker in Alsace, he lectured on Aristotle there from 1465 to 1471 and then went to Basel to lecture on theology in 1476. Going to Freiburg, he became the rector of the university and in 1478 took up the position of preacher in the cathedral of Strasbourg. He called for reform but never considered leaving the university. His illustrative sermons provide a useful glimpse into the social conditions of his period.

**GEISERIC** (d. 477) Celebrated Vandal King, ruling from 428 to 477, whose strategy during his long reign hastened the demise of the Roman Empire in the West. The successor to Gunderic, king of the Vandals and Alans, Geiseric was the son of a slave woman, half brother to Gunderic and his heir, despite being partially lame after falling from a horse. The cornerstone of his success was laid after his coronation (c. 428) when the Roman *magister* *militum*, or general, Boniface, then vying for control of the West, invited Geiseric and the Vandals to enter Africa to rule there rather than the Goths, whom he considered more dangerous. Boniface regretted his decision instantly, as the Vandals conquered Africa, signing an agreement with the emperor in 435 granting Geiseric large parts of Africa. He broke the treaty in 439, by seizing Hippo and Carthage, thereby commencing 30 years of war.

By 455 all of Africa was under Geiseric's control, and he marched into Rome later that year, pillaging the city and taking as hostage Empress Licinia Eudoxia, with her daughters. After Geiseric attempted to interfere in the imperial succession, Emperor Leo I (457–474), at Constantinople, ordered in 468 a massive expedition against the Vandals. The campaign ended in a Byzantine disaster, leaving Geiseric in a stronger military and political position. On his death the Vandals were firmly entrenched in Africa. See also VANDALS.

**GELAMIR** Last king of the Vandals in Africa, ruling from 530 to 533, when he was defeated by forces of the Byzantine Empire. A cousin of King Hilderic (ruled 523–530), he was thus related to King Hunneric (ruled 477–384), who accepted the orthodox Catholic faith rather than Arianism, practiced by the Vandals. While this led to amity with Justinian I (527–565), the Byzantine emperor, it caused a Vandal revolt, led by a noble named Gelamir, who took the throne when the revolt succeeded. After fruitless negotiations, Justinian launched an invasion of Africa in 533, under the command of his general Belisarius. The Vandals were vanquished, and Gelamir and the city of Carthage fell, Gelamir surrendering to Belisarius. See also VANDALS.

**GELASIUS I, SAINT** (d. 496) Pope from 492 to 496, probably from Africa, elected as the successor to Pope Felix III in March 492. He was considered one of the architects of papal ecclesiastical supremacy, opposing Constantinople during the Acacian Schism (caused by the attempts to reconcile the heretical Monophysites in the East). The Gelasian Doctrine (494), addressed to Emperor Anastasius I, demonstrated his views on the relations between church and state, and he insisted that both institutions must cooperate for the good of all as ordained by God, both institutions being divinely created. He was also the author of many letters and treatises, including one on the two natures of Christ (*Adversus Eutychen et Nestorium*). See also MONOPHYSITISM.

**GELASIUS II** (d. 1119) Pope from 1118 to 1119, born John of Gaeta; an Italian monk at Monte Cassino when Pope Urban II (1088–1099) made him a cardinal in 1088 and then papal chancellor in the following year. He succeeded Pope Paschal II in 1118. His brief pontificate came during the Investiture Controversy, which had caused Emperor Henry V to imprison Paschal. Gelasius was also captured by supporters of the emperor, the powerful Frangipani family, and he was twice driven from Rome by the imperial faction. Cruelly treated, he died in 1119, to be succeeded by Calixtus II.

**GEMISTUS PLETHO, GEORGIUS** See PLETHO, GEORGIUS GEMISTUS.

**GENEVA** Known also as Genf (German), Gênêve (French) and Ginevra (Italian), an important Swiss city and canton in the Rhône Valley, bordering part of Lake Geneva. Traditionally an ancient Celtic site, the city was conquered by the Romans. Christianity was firmly entrenched there by the late fourth century, having a bishopric and, from 443 to 534, serving as capital for the kings of Burgundy. For a time part of Lotharingia, Geneva returned to Burgundian control from the 9th to the 11th century. About 1034, the counts of Geneva began to exert political authority, but they were challenged ultimately by the bishops who became, after the 12th century, princes of the Holy Roman Empire. The House of Savoy, however, had ambitions concerning Geneva, taking advantage of the discontent of the populace with the bishops to assume control of the episcopal see. Savoyard hopes were dashed by the widespread acceptance of the Reformation by the inhabitants of Geneva in the 16th century.

**GENGHIS KHAN** (d. 1277) Leader of the Mongols, who united the many divided clans of his people into one of the most formidable and feared armies in the world. He established the Mongol empire that would under successive khans reach from the steppes of Russia to the Pacific Ocean and would become a devastating and destabilizing social and political force in the Middle East and beyond.

Born Temüjin, named for a rival chieftain slain by his father, Yesukai, a ruler of the respected Bourchikoun clan of the Yakka Mongols, he was forced to flee when he was nine after the murder of his father. His family, led by his mother, Houlun, faced considerable hardship because the clan refused his claim to his father's rank. He survived, however, and began to gather allies, including To'oril Khan of the Kereyid (the character in the tales about Prester John) and the tribal leader Chamuka (Jamuqa). With their help he vanquished the Merkids, a powerful people in northern Mongolia, who had long been blood enemies of his clan. His mother had been stolen from them, and his wife, Bourtai, had been kidnapped and raped by them. Genghis Khan then conquered the Taidjuts, under Targoutai, at the Battle of the Carts. He boiled 70 of the enemy chieftains in retribution. Genghis then systematically eliminated all rivals as he built his military and political strength, allied with To'oril and Chamuka, routing the Kereyids, Tatars and Maimans. The survivors, especially the women and children, he brought into his own ranks to unify the nation. This confederation was achieved by 1206, an event thought to have been an impossibility, and he was declared the Genghis Khan, the Khan of Khans or Ruler of the Universe.

From 1206 and the gathering of his armies on the Onon River, the Khan embarked on a colossal campaign of imperial expansion. With his sons and brilliant military advisers, men such as Chepe Niyon, Muhuli, Subotai Bahadur and others, he drove his well-trained horsemen into battle. He began with the neighboring states, most notably the Hsi-Hsia, reducing their capacity to cause dissension while he concentrated on his primary objective, China. The Chin empire of northern China that had once given To'oril Khan the title of *wang*, or prince, had also given Genghis Khan a lesser award for his support against the Tatars. From 1211 to 1214, the Mongols waged ruthless war, accepted monetary appeasement in 1214 and then captured Peking. The Mongol empire subjugated the Chin territories and opened trade with the Khwarezmian empire to the west. Dealings were cool, but trade continued until a caravan of Muslim merchants, under Mongol protection, was slaughtered by the governor of Otrar. Not satisfied with the response from the shah of Khwarezm concerning this event, Genghis Khan was provoked. In a campaign virtually unmatched in bloodshed and destruction, the Mongols ravaged Khwarezm, slaughtering everyone and annihilating the Khwarezm army at the Battle of the Indus (c. 1222). Except for his demolition of the Hsi-Hsia in 1226–1227, Genghis Khan ceased his active involvement in the Mongol wars, creating the fabric of the empire that would survive his death, traditional thought to have been on August 18, 1227.

The name Genghis Khan epitomizes the qualities of terror and horror as a historical figure, earning acclaim as well for his military tactics and his political skills. Judged harshly by the chroniclers of his own era, who witnessed the cruel savagery of the Mongols, he was the product of the world of the Mongol clans, believing that it was his destiny to unite them and to bring them to greatness. His legacy was to be the largest empire in the history of the world, a domain so vast that Fra Carpini, a Western visitor to the region, wrote: "No kingdom or land can resist the Tatars [as the Mongols were commonly known]." Religious toleration made the visit of this Christian friar possible, and the laws that Genghis Khan laid down provided many regions with peace after his initial onslaught. See also MONGOLS.

**GENNADIUS** (c. 1400–c. 1473) Patriarch of Constantinople from 1454 to 1464, the first under the Turks, and a Greek scholar and theologian. Known as Gennadius Scholarius (or Gennadius II Scholarios), he was a teacher of Aristotle and Neoplatonism and was considered the great exponent of orthodox Christianity in his time. Serving as secretary to Emperor John VIII Palaeologus (1425–1448), Gennadius accompanied the emperor to the Council of Ferrara-Florence in 1438, supporting the union of the Churches of East and West, a stand he repudiated when he led those opposing the union in Constantinople.

He lost the favor of Emperor Constantine XI Palaeologus (1449–1453), the last Byzantine emperor, and retired to a monastery. When Constantinople fell in 1453, Gennadius was asked by the Ottoman sultan Muhammad II the Conqueror to serve as patriarch of the city. Gennadius helped stabilize the relations between the Muslims and the Christians and influenced the sultan toward a liberal policy. He resigned in 1464, returning to monastic life. There he wrote theological and philosophical works, prayers, commentaries and tracts on Aristotelian ideals. See also BYZANTINE EMPIRE;

**GENOA** Important port city and republic situated in northwestern Italy on the Mediterranean Sea, one of the major maritime powers of the Middle Ages. Genoa ultimately competed with Pisa and Venice for the lucrative trade in the Mediterranean and elsewhere. The city was originally a Ligurian site in the fifth century B.C., becoming a Roman possession in the third century B.C. When the empire declined, Genoa, geographically vulnerable, was sacked by invading tribes, including the Ostrogoths, and recaptured by the Byzantine general Belisarius in the sixth century, only to be destroyed by the Lombards. It was reduced to a minor trading city and then sacked by the Saracens before taking steps to restore its luster. Genoa attacked Saracen strongholds on Corsica, Sardinia and Sicily in the 10th century, recognized as a result by the Holy Roman Empire as a commune, with a podesta, or chief magistrate, appointed. From 1339 the city was governed by doges (as in Venice), the first of whom was Simone Boccanegra. The doges ruled for life but proved themselves generally unable to effect great social or political changes. Genoa was occupied variously by Milan, France and Savoy.

Following a victory over the Saracens, Genoa embarked on a program of expansion, becoming adept at banking, trade, shipbuilding and navigation. With the support of Pisa the Genoese cleared the Mediterranean of Muslim ships while establishing themselves in Naples, Spain and Sicily. The Crusades, starting in 1095, opened new opportunities for trade, as Genoa made loans, provided transportation and established economic bases in the Holy Land or in the Byzantine Empire. Venice was soon alarmed by Genoa's progress, and when the Venetians became involved in the Fourth Crusade and shared responsibility for the fall of Constantinople to the Latins, Genoa supported the emperor in exile, Michael Palaeologus, when he reclaimed the empire in 1261.

Genoa held superior trading privileges as a result, colonizing Corsica and Sardinia and establishing an economic empire that reached from Spain to the Crimea and as far away as England and India. The Genoese destroyed Pisa at the Battle of Meloria in 1284, fighting long and bitter wars with Venice and Aragon as well. In the 14th century the wars continued, but Genoa confronted too the loss of markets owing to the Black Death from 1348. Internal disorders also caused dissension in the city, bringing foreign occupation after 1396, and the Genoese were saved from financial ruin only by the foundation of the Banco di San Giorgio, an alliance of bankers who took upon themselves the national debt. Venice was still a formidable power in the 15th century, and the Aragonese were intent on adding Genoa to their domains. Genoese activities in the Black Sea and Anatolia were forced to undergo change by the Ottoman Empire, and the city itself was forced to adapt. The people diversified, pursuing markets in the West and working with a unified Spain. By the 16th century, with the emergence of Genoa's great admiral, Andrea Doria, the city was once again a superior maritime power. See also TRADE AND COMMERCE.

**GENTILE DA FABRIANO** (c. 1370–1427) Italian painter, considered the foremost master of the international Gothic style. Born Niccolo di Giovanni de Massio, he may have studied with the Lombard school, becoming known at first for his works in northern Italy. Few have survived, but it is known that in 1409 he was commissioned to execute frescoes (later destroyed) in the palace of the doge in Venice, a project eventually completed by Pisanello. He worked in Brescia from 1414 to 1419 and later in Siena, Florence, Orvieto and Rome, where he painted a cycle of frescoes for the church of Saint John Lateran, works again completed by Pisanello. An important extant work is the Quaratesi Polyptych (1425), an altarpiece made for the Aquaratesi family, depicting a Madonna. His masterpiece was the *Adoration of the Magi,* a painting long called the primary example of International Gothic style, having decorative motifs, graceful figures and rich detail. Gentile thus was a strong influence on Florentine artists of the time and presented a powerful counterbalance to the artistic views of Tommaso Masaccio.

**GEOFFREY, COUNT OF ANJOU** (1006–1060) Count of Anjou from 1040 to 1060, called Martel and a man of drive and ambition. The son of Count Fulk and his second wife, Hildegarde of Lorraine, Geoffrey married Agnes, the widow of William V the Great, duke of Aquitaine. Ignoring the claims of her children, he seized the duchy, making war on William the Fat, who asked for and received support from Fulk, who was concerned about his son's designs. Geoffrey attempted to overthrow his father as a result in 1039. Losing the conflict, he was forced to crawl several miles with an ass's saddle strapped to his back as penance. Once count of Anjou, he embarked on a long series of campaigns to expand Angevin territory, adding Touraine and part of the Maine, while incurring the enmity of such contemporaries as William I of Normandy (king of England, 1066–1087) and King Henry I of France (1031–1060). He was succeeded by his nephew, Geoffrey the Bearded. See also ANJOU.

**GEOFFREY OF MONMOUTH** (c. 1100–1155) Bishop of Saint Asaph and a chronicler whose *Historia regum Britanniae* had a major influence on medieval literature. Probably a Breton, he joined a Benedictine monastery at an early age, although he may have been an Augustinian canon at one time. He witnessed the Orseney Charter of 1129, becoming archdeacon of Saint Teilo's around 1140 and the bishop of Saint Asaph in 1152, dying before he could assume his duties. In addition to the *Historia,* he wrote *Prophetiae* (c. 1130–1135), a compilation of the prophecies of the legendary wizard Myrddin (Merlin), probably his own writings proposed as Merlin's words. The work was dictated to Alexander, bishop of Lincoln, and Goeffrey claimed that they were translations from the Welsh. This work was eventually included in the *Historia.* Later (c. 1148–1151) he composed a poem of more than 1,500 hexameters, the *Vita Merlini.* Dedicated to Robert de Chesnery, bishop of Lincoln, in 1149, the work presented the prophetic genious of Merlin and appears to have been based on Celtic tales.

The *Historia regum Britanniae (The History of the Kings of Britain)* was completed sometime after the death of King Henry I (1135) and was dedicated to Robert, earl of Gloucester. The work chronicles the lives of the kings from Brutus, great-grandson of Aeneas the Trojan, to Cadwallader, who left Britain for the Continent, surrendering his kingdom to the Saxons in the seventh century. It was purportedly a Latin translation of an older Celtic book given to Geoffrey by Walter, the archdeacon of Oxford. Although it was organized using legitimate sources, such as the *Annales Cambriae* or *Culhwch and Olwen,* the work was largely the result of Geoffrey's own considerable imagination. The *Historia* was attacked as a worthless historical account but became very popular and survived even the harshest denunciations by scholars. The 12 volumes of the *Historia* expressed the concept of a common origin for the Saxons, Britons and Normans, introducing to the European literary consciousness the elaborate tales of Arthur and the Knights of the Round Table. Chrétien de Troyes and others developed the same theme as a result. It was also the inspiration for such writers as Geoffrey Gaimar, Wace, Ranulf Higden, Raphael Holinshed, Michael Drayton and Shakespeare. See also ARTHURIAN LEGEND; GRAIL, HOLY.

**GEOFFREY PLANTAGENET** See PLANTAGENET; PLANTAGENET, GEOFFREY.

**GEORGE, PATRON OF ENGLAND, SAINT** Saint and martyr whose actual death is undocumented but whose legend was subject to intense religious and literary significance from the sixth century. He may have been martyred in the fourth century near Lydda, and although he had not been associated with the Arian bishop of the same era, George of Cappadocia, he was possibly mentioned (not by name) by Eusebius. The first evidence of his cult was in the sixth century, and his home was known throughout England by the eighth. Elaborations on his deeds by the 12th century included the account of his having slain a dragon. The 13th-century work the *Golden Legend* described Saint George's rescue of a maiden from an evil dragon. It was probably King Edward III who, about 1347, named him the protector of the Order of the Garter, elevating him to the role of patron saint of the kingdom. During the Crusades Saint George was widely revered by the soldiers in the Holy Land and was reportedly seen in 1098 encouraging the Franks at the Battle of Antioch.

**GEORGE I TERTER, KING OF THE BULGARS** Ruler from 1280 to 1292, elected by the Bulgarian boyars as successor to Ivan Asen III (1279–1280), who lost his throne. Of Cuman descent, George was never particularly powerful politically and lost parts of Bulgaria to rebellious boyars. By 1292 his situation had become so desperate that he fled to Byzantium. His son, Theodore Svetoslav, reclaimed the throne in 1300 (ruled until 1322). See also BULGARIA.

**GEORGE II TERTER, KING OF THE BULGARS** Ruler from 1322 to 1323, the son of Theodore Svetoslav (1300–1322) and grandson of George I Terter (1280–1292). He barely outlived his father, dying in 1323 and succeeded by Michael Sisman (1323–1330). See also BULGARIA.

**GEORGE BRANKOVIC** Ruler of Serbia from 1427 to 1456. See also SERBIA.

**GEORGE HAMARTOLOS** Also called George the Monk, a ninth-century Byzantine chronicler who flourished during the reign of Emperor Michael III (ruled 942–867). George Hamartolos, "George the Sinner," was the author of a world chronicle, the history of humanity from the Creation to the year 842. Completed about 866 or 867, the work is a valuable source on events taking place in the Byzantine Empire during his era, especially concerning the Iconoclastic Controversy (see ICONOCLASTICISM) and the years 813–842. Religiously oriented, his chronicle relies on numerous texts and sources to authenticate its account. The work was extremely popular, influencing later Byzantine chroniclers; this resulted in many translations and versions, including an anonymous continuation to 948, called the *Georgius continuatus,* a far more politicized edition.

**GEORGE MANIACES** See MANIACES, GEORGE.

**GEORGE OF PISIDIA** (d. c. 631) Also called George the Pisidian, a seventh-century Byzantine epic poet, later compared by the Byzantines to the Greek tragic playwright Euripides. Born in Antioch in Pisidia, he served as deacon of Hagia Sophia in Constantinople and was also an archivist. He demonstrated skill in classically structured verse and was learned in classicism. The author of several important epic poems, he wrote theological works after 630. His account of the reign of Emperor Heraclius (610–641), with whom he traveled as an eyewitness on his military campaigns, is of major importance to scholars. He also wrote of Byzantine successes in his *In Heraclium ex Africa redeunteum, Expeditio Persica, In bonum patricium, Bellum avaricum* and *Heraclias* or the *Heracliad,* celebrating the final triumph of Heraclius over the Persians and the return of the True Cross, which had been lost in the fall of Jerusalem. Other important works included *Hexaemeron* (Greek, *Of Six Days*), on the creation of the world; *De vanitate vitae (On the Vanity of Life),* and a hymn honoring the Resurrection. He also composed minor poems, a prose work on Saint Anastasius the Persian and epigrams.

**GEORGE OF TREBIZOND (TRAPEZOUNTIOS)** (1395–c. 1472) Greek humanist, scholar and teacher. From Trebizond stock, he was born on Crete and well educated before traveling to Venice. A professor of Greek there in 1420, he remained for the rest of his life in Italy, teaching in the major cities and translating Greek works to further the study of humanism. Pope Eugene IV (1431–1447) enlisted his skills as an interpreter and adviser at the Council of Ferrara-Florence in 1439.

Teaching in Rome, he won the favor of Pope Nicholas V (1447–1455) and translated Aristotle's *Rhetoric,* Ptolemy's *Almagest* and Plato's *Law.* His position and quarrelsome nature, however, alienated him from the Roman humanists, and he disputed with Cardinal Bessarion and Lorenzo Valla, causing his inevitable banishment from Rome. He taught in Venice and Naples but returned to Rome and was imprisoned by Pope Paul II (1464–1471). He was penniless at his death.

**GEORGE SCHOLARIUS** See GENNADIUS.

**GERALD THE WELSHMAN** See GIRALDUS C[illegible]BRENSIS.

**GERARD OF CREMONA** (c. 1114–1187) Italian scholar and translator, born in Cremona and later studying at Toledo in order to master Arabic. He remained there, making translations of important Greek philosophical and scientifics works from the Arabic. He translated the works of Aristotle, Euclid, Galen and Ptolemy, although his name does not appear on early editions and the authenticity has been questioned. Scholars believe that more than 70 or 80 works attributed to him were the actual products of a school of translators over which he presided. He also made translations of original Arab texts on medicine, alchemy and astronomy.

**GERBERT OF AURILLAC** See SYLVESTER II.

**GERMANUS, SAINT** (c. 495–576) Abbot, bishop of Paris and mediator who attempted to end the civil strife that plagued the Merovingian Frankish kings of the sixth century. A native of Autun, he became an abbot and was noted for his kindness to the poor. He was appointed the bishop of Paris in 555, chosen by King Childebert (ruled 511–558), on whom he had considerable influence. When Childebert died, Germanus tried to stem the brutal conflicts for power that ensued, excommunicating Charibert I for his behavior and prophesying that Sigebert, king of Austrasia, would die if his rousing of the German tribes against his brother, Chilperic, did not cease. Sigebert was murdered in 575. The church of Saint Germain-des-Prés was constructed with his blessing, named in his honor and the site of his tomb. Two of his letters were of great value in reconstructing the Gallican Rites of his time. His biography was written by Venantius Fortunatus. See also PARIS.

**GERMANUS, PATRIARCH OF CONSTANTINOPLE** (c. 634–730) Byzantine patriarch, theologian and an ardent opponent of iconoclasticism. A noble and well educated, he protested the execution of his father in 668 and was made a eunuch by Emperor Constantine IV (668–685) and forced to enter the clergy of Hagia Sophia. He became the head of clerics there and, about 705–706, the bishop of Cyzicus. In 712, Emperor Philippicus Bardanes forced him to sign a decree restoring Monothelitism. Once more embracing orthodoxy, Germanus was elected in 715 the patriarch of Constantinople, immediately condemning Monothelitism. He then had to deal with the Iconoclastic Controversy in 725, resigning in 730 because of his convictions. He retired to his Greek estates at Platonum, where he wrote such works as *De haeresibus et synodis* (*On Heresies and Synods*). See also ICONOCLASTICISM.

**GERMANY** A nation characterized by long, complex and bitter conflicts during the Middle Ages. Feudalism, monarchical power, Christianity, lingering paganism and demands for independence collided there. The region was probably nationalized during the Carolingian empire in 843, although some scholars place the date at 911, when Conrad I became the German king. Throughout the fourth

Germanic warrior

and fifth centuries the Germanic peoples had participated in the Western migrations, bringing about the destruction of the Roman Empire in the West. The Germanization of Roman provinces began in the second century, reaching its natural conclusion in the sixth and seventh centuries, as Germanic kingdoms were forged. The greatest of these was the Frankish kingdom, led by the dynasties of the Merovingians and the Carolingians. The Franks carved out an empire in Gaul and beyond the Rhine River, with the most historically significant campaign launched by Charlemagne (d. 814). Frankish authority was carried to the Elbe River, and the Saxons, fiercely independent, were subdued only after years of conflict.

With the death of Charlemagne's son Louis the Pious in 840, civil war erupted between the heirs. The empire was divided among three heirs, and their quarrels resulted in the STRASBOURG OATH in 843, which also provided for a linguistic separation of the Frankish empire, employing French and Rhenish German. After 876, the Carolingians lost power as a result of internal feuds and tribal incursions made by the Magyars, Danes and even Saracens. By the 10th century feudalism was weakening the central authority of the emperors, as the autonomous duchies of Saxony, Swabia, Bavaria, Lorraine and Franconia started wielding power. These duchies rejected the claims of the Carolingian ruler Charles III the Simple and elected Conrad, duke of Franconia, as Conrad I in 911. The nobles, however, did not relinquish their powers, uniting under the king only to oppose invaders. The rulers also did not have a centralized administrative authority for governing, and hereditary succession was not always the norm. Conrad, for example, on his deathbed in 918, named as his heir his former foe Henry I, duke of Saxony.

Henry I was the first of the Saxons who were to rule until 1024. Ruling from 919 to 936, he was known chiefly for his campaigns against the Magyars and was followed by his son, Otto I the Great (ruled 936–973). Otto was able to centralize his government and collected revenues from the secular lands held by the bishops. Seizing the crown of the Lombards in 951, he became the first Holy Roman Emperor in 962. His immediate heirs, Otto II and Otto III (ruled 973–983 and 983–1002 respectively), failed to maintain or expand his gains, and Otto III had interests in Italy. Henry II (ruled 1002–1024) was the last Saxon king. Conrad II, the first of the Salian kings (ruled 1024–1039) from a Rhine-Frankish line, became involved with the Investiture Controversy and in quarrels with the popes. Henry III (ruled 1039–1056) supported the church but then deposed three rival popes in 1046, at the synods of Suti and Rome, installing his own man. Gregory VII (pope from 1073 to 1085) challenged Henry, incurring problems for the throne, which was dealing with opposing nobles again. Henry V (1106–1125), his son, rebelled in 1104 and succeeded him in 1106. He was unable to consolidate monarchical power, and the Concordat of Worms was signed in 1122, ending the dispute with the popes but weakening the power of the crown.

When Henry died in 1125, divisiveness caused dissension among the Germanic people. Archbishop Adelbert of Mainz led the nobles in ignoring the claims of Henry's relatives. Lothair of Supplinburg was elected, ruling from 1125 to 1137 and as emperor from 1133. To combat the Hohenstaufens, the nobles of the Salian line, the Welfs (or Guelphs) were organized. Conrad III, a Hohenstaufen, who ruled from 1138 to 1152, was elected. His short reign accomplished little, and his heir was a member of both the Hohenstaufens and the Welfs, Frederick I Barbarossa (see FREDERICK I, EMPEROR).

Ruling from 1152 to 1190 and emperor from 1155, he was to become the foremost figure of his age, and his powers were legendary. He wanted Germany to become a feudal state stretching from the North Sea to the Mediterranean, including the Lombard cities of Italy. Imperial agents *(ministeriales)* were appointed, and the princes were encouraged to extend their authority while keeping the peace. The Germans advanced on the East, and a program of colonization called *Drang nach Osten*, the "Drive to the East," begun in the ninth century, was conducted. Brandenburg, Pomerania, Lusatia and Silesia were acquired. The revolt of the Slavs and Italians forced Frederick to insist that they subsidize the Holy Roman Empire. In the face of other problems the emphasis was on consolidation. Frederick elevated a select group of nobles, discouraging smaller holdings and destroying his rivals, such as the duke of Saxony, Henry the Lion. He also failed in his attempt to subdue the Lombard League, having lost the Battle of Legnano in 1176. The resulting peace brought about a cultural renaissance and also allowed the smooth election of his son, Henry VI (ruled 1190–1197), who attached southern Italy to the empire by his marriage to Constance, the Sicilian heiress, in 1186.

When Henry died in 1197, factions arose again, opposing his son Frederick II and supporting Henry's brother, Philip of Swabia. Richard the Lion-Hearted of England (1189–1199) even became involved by supporting the activities of the archbishop of Cologne, who advocated Otto IV of Brunswick, son of Henry the Lion. Otto received papal blessing, as the pope hoped to free Sicily from the empire. Philip of Swabia died in 1208, and Otto stated his intention of holding Sicily. The pope thus supported Frederick II on campaign, and he crushed Otto at Bouvines in 1214, two years after being crowned king.

Frederick II (ruled 1212–1250 and emperor from 1220) was another remarkable medieval monarch, cultured, militarily capable and astute politically. He abandoned the imperial cause in Germany, however, in favor of Sicily, the place of his birth. He surrendered to the princes' confirmation of their territorial possessions in 1232 and to the ecclesiastical princes in 1220. He then installed his son Henry as German king and concentrated on Italian affairs. Henry tried to reverse the policy and was deposed in 1235, with the rebels supported by Frederick. Another son, Conrad IV, was installed but faced two anti-kings, Henry Raspe and Count William of Holland. Frederick died in 1250, and the Hohenstaufen dynasty was doomed. When Conrad died in 1254, Manfred, a natural son of Frederick, was defeated and slain by Charles of Anjou in 1266. A grandson, Conradin, was similarly routed at Tagliacozzo in 1268, tried for treason and beheaded. The Great Interregnum had begun in Germany.

From 1250 to 1273 this period of rivalry continued, with claimants to the throne in bitter conflict. The election of Rudolf of Habsburg in 1273 put an end to the quarrels, which had involved such men as William of Holland; Richard, earl of Cornwall; and Alfonso X of Castile. Rudolf proved ineffectual and could not ensure his son's succession. When he died, the nobles chose Adolf of Nassau, deposing him in 1298 and then electing Rudolf's son, Albert. He was murdered in 1308, replaced by Henry VII of the Luxembourg dynasty. He managed to give his son the Kingdom of Bohemia and died in 1312, just a year after being crowned in Rome, while fighting in Italy. The resulting election brought another series of disputes, involving Frederick the Fair, a Habsburg contender, and the duke of Bavaria, a Wittelsbach who became Louis IV. His reign, from 1314 to 1346, and that of his successor, Charles IV (1346–1378), were decisive in the history of the Holy Roman Empire. Louis made the Declaration of Rhens in 1338, decreeing that the election of a German king was valid and did not necessitate papal sanction. At the Diet of Frankfurt (1338) he made the declaration into law. Pope John XXII supported a rival, Charles of Luxembourg, in 1346, and Louis died soon after. Charles, crowned in Rome as his heir, returned to Germany to reconstruct the electoral system, issuing the Golden Bull of 1356. This put into place seven Electors who had autonomy of office. Elections were to be held in Frankfurt and the coronation at Aachen (see ELECTORS; GOLDEN BULL).

Charles's son, Wenceslas, was acceptable to the Electors in 1378 but was deposed in 1400 because he appeared to be plotting the destruction of the princes. Rupert of the Palatinate was elected but died in 1410, and then Sigismund, from Luxembourg (ruled 1410–1437), claimed the throne. He involved himself in church affairs, including the Council of Constance, and the Hussite conflict in Bohemia. He also started a process of reform in government. He named Albert II of Habsburg (ruled 1438–1439) as his heir, thus starting the Habsburg line. In 1440, Albert's second cousin, Duke Frederick of Styria, became Frederick III, reigning until 1493 as king and as emperor from 1452. Austria was lost in 1485 to Matthias Corvinus of Hungary, and reforms took shape in the empire. In time Frederick faced reformists such as Berthold von Henneberg, archbishop of Mainz, and retired from the throne. His son Maximilian was elected in 1486 and administered the state until Frederick died in 1493. He was thus in control of Germany at the start of the 16th century. The traditions remained, as the Habsburgs found ways to maintain their hold on the land. Germany progressed, inexorably, into the Reformation.

See also AUSTRIA, DUCHY OF; BAVARIA; BERLIN; BOHEMIA; BRABANT; BRANDENBURG; BREMEN; BURGUNDY, KINGDOM OF; CARINTHIA; COLOGNE; ENGLAND; FEUDALISM; FLANDERS; FRANCE; FRANCONIA; FRANKFURT AM MAIN; FRANKS; FRISIA; HAMBURG; HANSEATIC LEAGUE; HESSE; HOLY ROMAN EMPIRE; HUNGARY; LITHUANIA; LUXEMBOURG; MAGDEBURG; MAINZ; MECKLENBURG; MEISSEN; MILITARY ORDERS; MORAVIA; NASSAU; NETHERLANDS; NORDGAU; NUREMBERG; PAGANISM; PALATINATE; POLAND; POMERANIA; SALZBURG; SAXONY; SILESIA; STYRIA; SWABIA; TEUTONIC KNIGHTS; THURINGIA; TRIER; WESTPHALIA.

**GERSHOM BEN JUDAH** (c. 960–1028) Noted Jewish theologian and rabbi who had a profound influence on the Jewish world in the Middle Ages. Originally from Metz, Gershom became the rector of the rabbinical school at Mainz; introducing into western Europe the study of the Talmud as practiced in Palestine. Esteemed for his learning and wisdom, he was called *Rabbenu Gershom,* or "Our Teacher," and the "Light of the Exile." Of great significance were his decisions (*tagganot*) that shaped Jewish society, including laws against polygamy and prohibitions against the cruel treatment of Jews who had recanted their faith but had then returned. His *Response,* which addressed questions on Jewish law, helped preserve details of Jewish life in France at the time. See also JEWS AND JUDAISM.

**GERSON, JEAN** (1363–1429) French theologian, chancellor of the University of Paris, church reformer and spiritual writer who earned the title "Doctor Christianissimus." Also called Jean le Charlier de Gerson, he was educated at the College of Navarre in Paris, studying with Pierre d'Ailly and earning his doctorate about 1394 and succeeding d'Ailly as chancellor. The Great Schism, which had begun in 1378, still raged, and he strove to end the division and to sponsor reform. While in Bruges (1397–1401), to which he fled from Paris, he wrote two treatises calling for unity and loyalty to the antipope Benedict XIII (1394–1417).

His moderate views on the conciliar movement ended when he returned to Paris, and he emerged as one of the leaders of the conciliarists, attending the Council of Constance (1414–1418) as the leader of the French delegation. He promoted the concept of the superiority of a general council, helped shape the Four Articles of Constance (the basis of Gallicanism) and condemned Jan Hus, an act that culminated in Hus's execution at the stake on July 6, 1415. The schism was ended with the election of Martin V (1417–1431) as pope. Also at the council, Gerson defeated the proposals of Jean Petit to defend John the Fearless, duke of Burgundy (1404–1419), who had ordered the assassination in 1407 of Louis, duc d'Orléans. This endangered Gerson, keeping him out of France until 1419, when John the Fearless died. He then settled in Lyons, remaining there until his death. Gerson played a critical role in Gallicanism and in the conciliar movement. He was a mystic and poet as well as a statesman, respected by such contemporaries as Nicholas of Cusa and Ignatius Loyola. The authorship of the *Imitation of Christ* was, for a time, incorrectly credited to Gerson. See also CONCILIAR MOVEMENT; CONSTANCE, COUNCIL OF; GALLICANISM; SCHISM, GREAT.

**GERSONIDES** See LEVI BEN GERSHOM.

**GERTRUDE THE GREAT, SAINT** (d. c. 1302) German mystic and nun at the Benedictine convent of Helfta in Thuringia. Called "the Great" because of her spirituality and her superb mystical writings, she had entered the convent at the age of five, working for a time as a copyist. She led a contemplative life from the age of 25, undergoing numerous mystical experiences, including visions of the Sacred Heart, to which she was subsequently devoted. She was the author of a collection of prayers and also wrote the highly respected *Legatus divinae pietatis*. See also MYSTICISM.

**GESTA DANORUM** See SAXO GRAMMATICUS.

**GESTA FRANCORUM** An anonymous 11th-century account of the First Crusade, titled in full the *Gesta Francorum et Aliorum Hierosolimitantorum*, or *Hierasolymitanorum*. It was probably the diary of a Norman soldier in the service of Bohemond of Tarante, offering an honest but biased account of the events up to the Battle of Ascalon in 1099, including the march of Tancred to Jerusalem. Bohemond cited the work to further his own prestige. The *Gesta* was first published in 1100 or 1101 and was soon revised and rewritten. Several authors, including Guibert of Nogent, Baudri of Bourgueil and Robert of Reims, made it their source of reference. See also CRUSADES.

**GESTA HAMMABURGENSIS** See ADAM OF BREMEN.

**GESTA ROMANORUM** Also called the *Deeds of the Romans*, a 14th-century collection of short stories or tales, probably assembled in England but of unknown authorship. The anecdotes included in the *Gesta* were concerned with magic, monsters and other popular themes, each with a moral explanation, leading scholars to believe that they were homiletic in nature. Widely read throughout the era, the tales were drawn on by writers and poets, including Chaucer and Shakespeare.

**GESTE, CHANSON DE** See CHANSON DE GESTE.

**GEZA** (d. c. 997) Ruler of the Magyars from 972 to 997, succeeding to the chieftainship of the Magyar tribes. By 973 he was able to improve negotiations with the Holy Roman Empire, sending an embassy to Otto II and often royal protection to the Christian missionaries who journeyed into Hungary. In 975, Geza and his family were baptized into the Western Church. His son, Stephen I (ruled 997–1038), became a renowned Christian king. See also HUNGARY; MAGYARS.

**GEZA I, KING OF HUNGARY** (d. 1077) Ruler from 1074 to 1077, coming to the throne after years of bitter conflict with his brother, Ladislas (I), and his cousin and predecessor, Solomon (ruled 1063–1074). Ladislas took the crown after his death. See also HUNGARY.

**GEZA II, KING OF HUNGARY** (d. 1161) Ruler from 1141 to 1161, in a reign that was a continuation of the peaceful administration achieved by his father, Béla II (ruled 1131–1141). He was succeeded by his son, Stephen III. See also HUNGARY.

**AL-GHAZALI** (1058–1111) One of the greatest Islamic theologians and mystics, considered the founder of Sufism, called by the Muslims a *mujaddid*, or a "renewer of the faith." Abu Hamid al-Ghazali was born at Tus in Khorasan and was educated by al-Juwayni. He was invited in 1085 to the court of the Seljuk vizier Nizam al-Mulk, receiving an appointment in 1091 as the chief professor in the Nizamiyya university of Baghdad. There he lectured on philosophy and Islamic law. In 1095 he underwent a mystical experience and took up the life of a Sufi, or a mystic, after visiting Mecca in 1096. Settling at Tus, he attracted followers before returning in 1106 to teach again at the Nizamiyya college in Nishapur. He returned to Tus in 1110, dying there.

Al-Ghazali rejected the intellectual and speculative means of attaining true knowledge or final reality. A prolific writer, he produced treatises on philosophy, religion, theology and law. His *Tahafut (Inconsistency)* was a defense of Islam, opposing the ideas of Avicenna. His *al-Mustasfa (Essence or Essentials)* presented general principles of law. His most important work was *The Revival of the Religious Sciences*, assembled in 40 books, presenting Islamic doctrine and the path to mysticism (Sufism). See also ISLAM.

**GHAZNAVIDS** Afghanistan dynasty of Turkish origin, with its capital at Ghazna (Ghazni), ruling Afghanistan and later parts of India and Khorasan, from 977 to 1186. The Ghaznavids followed the patterns of most Islamic kingdoms, in that it was established by a regional governor or general who broke away from a central authority. The founder of this line was a Turkish slave in the service of the Samanids, named Alptigin. Becoming the governor of Khorasan, he then went to eastern Afghanistan, his political ascendancy taking place at Ghazna. His former slave, also his son-in-law and heir, Sebüktigin, was actually responsible for organizing the Ghaznavid state, reigning from 977 to 997. He consolidated his holdings and went further, into India, as far as Peshawar, conquering as well Khorasan, dominating the Samanids.

The period of dynastic greatness came for the Ghaznavids during the era of Sebüktigin's son, Mahmud of Ghazna (998–1030). He partitioned the Samanid holdings, seized a large empire through campaigns and amassed lands from Persia to the Indus Valley. A devout Muslim, he converted his subjects into adherents of Islam, earning the title "Champion of Islam" for introducing the faith into India. His son, Masud I, served well as his heir from 1030 to 1041 but was unable to prevent the defeat of the dynastic troops at the Battle of Dandanqan in 1040, at the hands of the

Seljuk Turks. The Ghaznavids lost control of much of Persia as a result, and the empire disintegrated until all that was left was a small realm in the Punjab. The last of the line fell in 1186, removed by the Ghurids.

During Ghaznavid dynastic supremacy, however, the city (modern Ghazne) had a cultural influence that affected even the enemies of the dynasty. The most important architectural contribution during this dynasty was the *eyvan*, a vaulted hall with an opening onto a court on the fourth side. See also ART AND ARCHITECTURE, ISLAMIC; FIRDAWSI.

**GHENT** The traditional capital of Flanders (in modern Belgium), situated on the Schelde and Lys Rivers, and one of northern Europe's important cities economically and a leader in the field of textiles. Gent in Flemish, the city began to prosper in the late ninth century, when Viking raids were eased by the construction of a castle to protect the region. A town developed around it, allowing the establishment of a cloth industry, and by the 11th century the city was reaching commercial prominence, forming economic ties with England, which supplied the Ghent workers with high-quality wool.

While officially under the rule of the counts of Flanders, Ghent, like the other Flanders city, Bruges, enjoyed considerable autonomy. Its real power rested in the hands of the patricians, who controlled trade through the group called the Thirty-nine Aldermen. Social upheaval erupted in the 13th century as the guilds opposed the attempts of the counts to impose their will, being countered in turn by social organizations. The Battle of the Spurs (or Courtrai) took place in 1302, in which the French, who had wanted control of the region, were defeated by a Flemish army. French animosity toward the city of Ghent continued through the 14th century, and from 1338 to 1345 the city, under Jacob van Artevelde, remained neutral in the Hundred Years' War. Two years later, however, Ghent allied with the English. Jacob's son, Philip, was routed at the Battle of Roosebeke, ending another revolt, and in 1384 Philip the Bold, duke of Burgundy, inherited Ghent as part of his holdings. Ghent resisted unsuccessfully and signed a peace treaty at Tournai (1385). The financial position of the city deteriorated because of the decline in markets, and social and economic difficulties led to uprisings and resistance. Philip the Good curtailed many liberties in 1453, and in time the city came under the rule of Maxmilian I, who had married Mary of Burgundy, thus including Ghent in the Habsburg domain. See also FLANDERS; TRADE AND COMMERCE.

**GHIBELLINES** See GUELPHS AND GHIBELLINES.

**GHIBERTI, LORENZO** (c. 1378–1455) Florentine sculptor, goldsmith and architect, considered one of the masters of Renaissance sculpture. Born in Pelago, he moved with his mother to Florence, to live with her second husband, a goldsmith, Bartolo di Michele, his father having died in 1405. Ghiberti studied his stepfather's trade and painting. For a time he studied with Sigismondo Malatesta, the Florentine master in Pisaro, and then entered the competition to design and execute the bronze doors for the baptistery of the cathedral of Florence. Ghiberti, who had submitted sample panels in relief depicting the scene of Abraham's sacrifice of Isaac, won the competition, defeating Brunelleschi.

The doors, placed on the north side of the baptistery, took from 1403 to 1424 to complete, and the east doors, called the "Gates of Paradise" by Michelangelo, were begun in 1425. Ghiberti's doors demonstrated the International Gothic style but were seen to integrate as well a high degree of classical sculpture, reflecting his interest in the design of antiquity. He also wrote a series of commentaries in three books, including a self-assured autobiography. Other works included *St. John the Baptist* (1412–1416) in the Or San Michele; *St. Matthew* (1419–1422) in the Or San Michele; the Tomb of Leonardi Dati (1423–1427) in Santa Maria Novella; *St. Stephen* (1425–1428) in the Or San Michele; and the shrine of Saint Zenobius (c. 1430) the cathedral of Florence. The competition for the baptistery doors has been viewed by many scholars as the commencement of the artistic Renaissance, and thus Ghiberti and Brunelleschi both played a role in its beginnings.

**GHIRLANDAIO, DOMENICO** (1449–1494) Florentine painter of the early Renaissance, so called because of the garlands made by his father, a goldsmith. He was born Domenico di Tommaso Bigordi and was the celebrated fresco painter of his time. Little information has survived about his early life, but he was certainly apprenticed to his father, and his earliest works (dating from the 1470s) were influenced by Andrea del Castagno. Technically, his frescoes were masterful, with his emphasis on detail, but his work was often overshadowed by that of Botticelli and others. He never received a major commission from the Medicis but won a certain fame within Florence for his habit of including portraits of friends or prominent Florentines in his work, especially in his *Christ Calling the First Apostles* (1481–1482) in the Sistine Chapel in Rome. Among his other works were frescoes for the Vespucci altar (c. 1472–1473) in the Florentine chapel of Ognissanti; *Madonna and Child Enthroned* (c. 1480); a *Last Supper* in Ognissanti; *Adoration of the Magi* (1488); and two interesting fresco cycles, the first (c. 1485) on the life of Saint Francis in the Sassetti chapel Santa Trinita and the other (c. 1490) from the lives of the Virgin and Saint John the Baptist in the choir of Santa Maria Novella. One of Ghirlandaio's later apprentices was Michelangelo. See also MASACCIO, TOMMASO.

**GIKATILLA, JOSEPH BEN ABRAHAM** (1248–1305) Jewish mystic and an important Spanish Cabalist. His writings reconciled philosophy with the Jewish mysticism of the Cabala. A student of the esteemed Cabalist Abraham Abulafia, Gikatilla was influenced by him, specifically in the *Ginna'egoz (Nut Orchard)*. In turn, he influenced Moses de León, the attributed author of the *Zohar*, the *Book of Splendor*. See also JEWS AND JUDAISM.

**GILBERT DE LA PORRÉE** (1076–1154) Scholastic theologian and philosopher who studied at Poitiers and became one of the respected students at the theological school of Chartres, under Bernard of Clairvaux. Gilbert served as a teacher in Paris and as chancellor of the cathedral school of Chartres and, in 1142, was made bishop of Poitiers. His teachings, which reflected an extreme form of universalist thought, and his writings on the Trinity brought charges of heresy by Bernard of Clairvaux at the Synod of Reims in 1148. In an effort to appease Bernard, he altered his views. Other works included commentaries on Boethius, the Psalms and the Epistles of Paul; the *Liber sex principiorum,* a metaphysical treatise on Aristotle, was attributed to him.

**GILDAS, SAINT** (c. 500–c. 570) British saint, monk and historian. Few certain details of his life have survived, although an 11th-century source (from the Abbey of Saint Gildas-de-Ruys in Brittany) claimed that he was born in Strathclyde, fled to Wales, spent time in Ireland and Rome and then founded a religious community in Brittany, Saint Gildas-de-Ruys. He was noted as the author of *De excidio et conquestu Britanniae,* a history of Britain from the Roman conquest to his own time. (The *De excidio* was probably written in part by Gildas and finished by an anonymous monk just after Gildas's death.) Its value was derived from its being one of the few sources on the isles after the departure of the Romans in 410, especially in its commentary on the Celts. Although it provides a generally creditable historical outline, Gildas' work was hampered by its emphasis on the deteriorated moral condition of the time and its often heavy-handed style. Also attributed to Gildas were several penitential canons. See also ENGLAND.

**GILES, SAINT** Saint of the seventh or eighth century, also called Aegidius, considered one of the Fourteen Holy Assistants, or Auxiliary Saints, and the patron of beggars, cripples and blacksmiths. He was included in several legends and was reported to have lived near the mouth of the Rhône River. According to tradition, a monastery was built in his honor by Wamba, king of the Visigoths (ruled 672–680), the future Saint-Gilles, around which a town grew to become a pilgrimage site. The man was much revered, and in England there were as many as 160 churches dedicated in his honor. See also ENGLAND.

**GILES OF ROME** (d. 1316) Also called Aegidius Romanus, a Scholastic theologian, philosopher and intellectual. He joined the Hermits of Saint Augustine about 1257 and studied in Paris under Thomas Aquinas from 1269 to 1271, becoming an ardent Thomist philosopher. In 1292 he was made father general of the Augustinian Hermits, serving until 1295, when Pope Boniface VIII (1294–1303) appointed him archbishop of Bourges. During the conflict between Boniface and King Philip IV the Fair of France (1285–1314), Giles wrote (in 1301) that the pope was deserving of direct political power over humankind. Giles had served Philip as a tutor and had written for him (c. 1285) the *De regimine principum,* an extremely popular work.

A voluminous writer and philosopher, Giles supported Thomas Aquinas in his view on the unity of substantial form and the distinction between essence and existence in beings. He was the author of a vast number of works: commentaries on Aristotle and the *Sentences* of Peter Abelard, among others, and treatises on angels, Averroism and *De summi pontificis potestate,* probably the foundation for Boniface's bull *Unam sanctam* (1302). His genius was so respected that he was given the title "Doctor Fundatissimus," the "Well-Grounded Teacher."

**GILLES DE LAVAL** See RAIS, GILLES DE.

**GILLES LE MUISIT** (1272–1352) French chronicler and poet, born in Tournai, also called Le Muiset. A monk at the monastery of Saint-Martin, Gilles was appointed prior in 1329 and abbot in 1331. Under his leadership the monastery was restored to a position of local prominence. He was most noted for his two Latin chronicles: the *Chronicon majus* and the *Chronicon minus,* eyewitness accounts of the history of France during this period. He also composed rustic poetry.

**GIOTTO** (c. 1267–1337) Italian painter from Florence who had a decisive influence on the course of European art. Giotto di Bondone was credited with the transformation of painting from the static formality of Byzantine art to the humanistic and expressive naturalism that followed. Despite his importance artistically, few details of his life have survived. According to tradition he was the pupil of Cimabue; his work displayed the influence of such sculptors as Pisano, who adopted three-dimensional realism in their work. He also was affected by the Franciscan movement in religious circles.

Like the facts concerning Giotto's life, his works have presented problems of documentation, with many paintings attributable to him. A precise chronology of his development thus proves difficult. He made frescoes and panels in tempera to decorate chapels in Florence, Padua, Naples, Rome and Assisi and in 1334 was responsible for designing the campanile of Santa Maria del Fiore in Florence, succeeding Arnolf di Cambio as chief architect. Among his greatest attributed works are frescoes in the Church of Saint Francis of Assisi; biblical frescoes in the Arena Chapel, Padua; frescoes in the Church of Santa Croce, Florence; *Madonna Enthroned,* Ognissanti Florence; and the mosaic *Navicella,* Saint Peter's, Rome.

**GIOVANNI CAPISTRANO** See JOHN CAPISTRAN, SAINT.

**GIOVANNI DI PAOLO** (c. 1403–1482) One of the last of the painters in the Gothic style, from Siena. He never left his native city and thus remained free of the influences of the progressive artists of Italy. Gentile da Fabriano had some influence on his work, and with Stefano di Giovanni Sassetla (1392–c. 1450) he championed the cause of conservative mystical traditions in the Gothic style, as exemplified by the Sienese school. But, as he had little influence on subsequent artistic development, his paintings were largely overlooked until their rediscovery in the 20th century. Among his works were *Madonna and Child with Angels* (1426), *Madonna* (1427), *Presentation of Christ in the Temple* (1447–1449), the *Madonna* altarpiece (1463) in the Piacenza Cathedral and *St. John in the Wilderness* (n.d.).

**GIRALDA** A tower constructed in Seville, Spain, from 1163 to 1184 (or 1184 to 1198), which originally served as a minaret for an adjoining mosque. The tower stood 197 feet high and in 1568 was converted into a bell tower for the cathedral of Seville, the Renaissance superstructure 123 feet in height. See also SEVILLE.

**GIRALDUS CAMBRENSIS** (c. 1146–c. 1223) Also known as Gerald de Barri, Gerald of Wales and Gerald the Welshman, a historian and major churchman in Wales. Born in Pembrokeshire to a noble family, he studied in Paris and in 1175 received an appointment as archdeacon of Brecon (or Brecknock), holding the post until 1204. He was twice elected bishop of Saint David's (in 1176 and in 1198) but was never consecrated because of the fears of the Anglo-Normans that he would attempt to remove his see from the jurisdiction of Canterbury and establish himself over the church in southern Wales. Despite championing the Welsh church, he worked for Henry II of England (1154–1189) from 1184, holding several posts and preaching the Third Crusade. He had to be persuaded by King Henry not to go on the Crusade himself. A historian of note, Giraldus wrote *Topographia Hibernica* and *Expugnatio Hibernica* on Ireland, *Itinerarium Cambriae,* and *Descriptio* on Wales. He also wrote *De rebus a se gestis* (an autobiography), as well as poems and letters. See also WALES.

**GLANVILLE, RANULF DE** (d. 1190) Judicial official and an important adviser to King Henry II of England (1154–1189), serving from 1180 to 1189. During his term he was virtual ruler of England while Henry was away in France, and through his influence several changes took place in English legal practices, such as making of an inquest in cases involving land. His greatest contribution was the attributed authorship of the *Tractatus de legibus et consuetudinibus regni Angliae (Treatise Concerning the Laws and Customs of the Kingdom of England),* c. 1189, a work that helped broaden the scope of common law, applying it in cases that had been tried under canon and feudal law. Removed from his post by Richard the Lion-Hearted (1189–1199), he accompanied the new king on the Third Crusade and died at Acre.

**GLASTONBURY** A famous and influential Benedictine monastery in Somerset, England, one of the oldest Christian sites in the isles and to which numerous legends have been attributed. Joseph of Arimathea is traditionally credited with the founding of Glastonbury Church, where his staff took root and blossomed into the Glastonbury thorn. In actual fact, Glastonbury was probably a Celtic foundation, dating from the seventh century, becoming Anglo-Saxon and a monastery (c. 708) under the patronage of King Ine of Wessex. Destroyed by the Danes in the ninth century, the monastery entered a brief period of decline but was revived by Saint Dunstan, appointed abbot in 943 by King Edmund I. Under Dunstan's administration (943–955), the monastery underwent extensive reform. The Benedictine rule was adopted, and Glastonbury became a cultural and intellectual institution, a key to Benedictine revival in England, monastic unity and, eventually, wealth. Pilgrims flocked to the site, reported in tradition as the burial place for King Arthur and Queen Guinevere. The site was also associated with the Holy Grail and with Saint Patrick. Oliver Cromwell ordered it destroyed in the 17th century. The Glastonbury thorn, a species of hawthorn found normally in the Levant, bloomed at Christmas and in May. A history of Glastonbury, *De antiquitate Glastoniensis ecclesiae,* was written by William of Malmesbury about 1135.

**GLENDOWER, OWEN** See OWEN GLENDOWER.

**GLOSSATORS** Medieval scholars who made interpretations and commentaries on civil and canon law (usually Roman legal texts) or on religious or rabbinical writings. These scholarly analyses were called "glosses." Legal glosses began in the late 11th century at Bologna, where legalists initiated a vigorous reconstruction of Justinian's *Digest;* the work of Irnerius during this early period is considered the finest. In the 13th century the last of these glossators, Accursius (of Bologna), made a vast series of glosses that had the authenticity of Roman law, their value derived from their origins in actual Roman legal codes, supplemented by the annotations and views of previous legalists. While their labors were generally of an academic nature, the glossators nevertheless proved highly influential in the formation of subsequent medieval law, providing a link between classical legalism and formative laws in the courts of Europe. Religious glosses were concerned with canon law (see GRATIAN) but also with biblical texts, so that by the end of the 12th century the entire Bible was available in the form of glosses.

**GLOUCESTER** Town and county seat of Gloucestershire, England, on the Severn River near the Bristol Channel. Originally a Roman colony, the city was called Glevum and was founded about A.D. 96. An abbey was built there by King Osric of Northumbria in 681, the Abbey of Saint Peter, and the site was chosen as the capital of the Kingdom of Mercia. A first charter was granted under King Henry II (ruled 1154–1189), and the position of borough was created in 1483.

**GLOUCESTER, GILBERT DE CLARE, EARL OF** (1243–1295) Son of Richard de Clare, earl of Gloucester, and one of the leaders of the barons under Simon de Montfort during the Barons' War (1263–1267). After the Battle of Lewes (1264) Henry III (1216–1272) surrendered to him, but then Gilbert renounced his allegiance to de Monfort, joining Edward I (1272–1307) in the triumph of Evesham in 1265. Edward succeeded to the throne with his help in 1272, giving Gilbert the hand of his daughter in 1290. Gilbert's son, Gilbert de Clare, was also earl from 1291 to 1314, serving as regent of England for a time. He died at the Battle of Bannockburn.

**GLOUCESTER, HUMPHREY, DUKE OF** (1391–1447) English nobleman and son of Henry IV (1399–1413), appointed duke of Gloucester in 1414 by his brother, Henry V (1413–1422). He campaigned in France from 1415 to 1420, served as regent of England from 1420 to 1421, during Henry's absence, and was chosen as regent for the infant Henry VI (1422–1461) in 1422. The duke of Bedford,

John, the official regent, was on campaign at the time in France. Wielding considerable influence, Humphrey was soon embroiled in a struggle with his uncle, the chancellor Henry Beaufort, and in 1447 was arrested on charges of conspiracy to seize the throne, dying in prison. A patron of Oxford University, Humphrey made donations to the institution that formed the origins of the Bodleian Library. Called "good Duke Humphrey," he promoted classical learning and was one of the first humanists in England. See also HENRY V, KING OF ENGLAND; HUNDRED YEARS' WAR; OXFORD.

**GLOUCESTER, RICHARD, DUKE OF** See RICHARD III.

**GLOUCESTER, RICHARD DE CLARE, EARL OF** (1222–1262) English nobleman and a participant in the Barons' War (1263–1267). While wielding both power and influence second only to Simon de Montfort, Richard wavered between the cause of King Henry III (1216–1272) and that of the barons. His son was Gilbert de Clare, earl of Gloucester.

**GLOUCESTER, ROBERT, EARL OF** (d. 1147) English nobleman, the illegitimate son of Henry I (1100–1135), who made him earl of Gloucester in 1122. After the death of his father in 1135, he refused to press a claim to the throne, supporting initially King Stephen (1135–1154). A quarrel between them, however, led Robert to ally himself with his half sister, Matilda, the heir designate. As one of her chief adherents he accompanied her to England in 1339, winning much of the country in her name and capturing Stephen in 1141 at Lincoln. That same year he was taken captive at Winchester and traded for Stephen. His remaining years were spent championing Matilda's cause. Robert was the first of the powerful Gloucester line. See also ENGLAND.

**GLOUCESTER, THOMAS OF WOODSTOCK, DUKE OF** (1355–1397) English nobleman and the seventh son of Edward III (1327–1377). He was the major opponent to the rule of Richard II (ruled 1377–1399). Becoming the duke of Gloucester in 1385, he led baronial opposition to Richard, taking virtual control of the kingdom with his noble allies, the "Lords Appellant." After murdering several of his nephew's supporters, Thomas made peace with the king in 1389, receiving appointment as lieutenant of Ireland in 1342. In 1397 he was arrested on charges of treason. Taken to Calais, he was probably murdered by his jailer, Thomas Mowbray, earl of Nottingham, perhaps suffocated under a feather mattress. See also RICHARD II.

**GODEBERT** (d. 662) King of the Lombards for less than a year (662) and the son of King Aribert I (ruled 653–662) and brother of Berthari. On Aribert's death, Godebert and Berthari were named by the Lombard witan to be joint successors. A civil war erupted, but Godebert was murdered by Grimvald, the duke of Benevento, his chief retainer, who then claimed the Lombard crown and married Godebert's sister. See also LOMBARDS.

**GODFREY DE BOUILLON** (c. 1060–1100) First Crusader ruler of Jerusalem, the duke of Lower Lorraine and a dauntless Christian warrior. Godfrey was the son of Count Eustace II of Boulogne and nephew of Duke Godfrey II of Lower Lorraine (Lotharingia). Named heir in 1076, he received the duchy from Emperor Henry IV (1056–1106) in 1082 as a reward for his support in the war against the Saxons. Godfrey answered the call to the First Crusade (1095–1099) and went to the Holy Land, taking his brothers Eustace and Baldwin (his eventual successor) with him. He became the undeclared leader of the Crusade, playing a major role in the capture of Jerusalem in 1099. Raymond of Toulouse declining the crown of Jerusalem, Godfrey assumed the title "Advocate (Defender) of the Holy Sepulchre." He defeated a Muslim attack from Egypt but was unable to prevent the establishment of other Christian independent states, which weakened the Christian cause in the region. When Godfrey died in 1100, Baldwin became king of Jerusalem. Godfrey was honored as an ideal Christian knight and Crusader. See also CRUSADES.

**GODFREY OF FONTAINES** (d. after 1306) French philosopher and theologian, espousing Aristotelian doctrine as a professor and dean of the University of Paris. Godfrey differed with Thomas Aquinas on the concept of identifying essence with existence. He thus disputed Thomist philosophy and that of John Duns Scotus. He also opposed the appointment of mendicant friars to teaching posts at the university. His works include the *Quodlibeta* and the *Scholia* and annotations on the *Summa theologica* of Thomas Aquinas.

**GODFREY OF SAINT VICTOR** (d. 1194) Philosopher, theologian and monk of Saint Victor, the Augustinian abbey, who held humanistic beliefs and debated Walter of Saint Victor, another major philosopher. Persecuted, Godfrey left the monastery and remained away until Walter's death in 1190. He was the author of many works, including *Microcosmus (Microcosm)* his most famous text, presenting man as essentially good but injured by sin. He also wrote *Fons philosophiae (Fount of Philosophy)* and a treatise on the theological anatomy of the Body of Christ. See also SCHOLASTICISM.

**GODIVA** Eleventh-century Anglo-Saxon lady, the wife of Earl Leofric of Mercia, lord of Coventry, who was the subject of a famous historical anecdote. To secure the reduction of taxes in the region, imposed by her husband, she rode naked through the town of Coventry. The reported incident, presumed legendary, appeared for the first time in the *Chronicle* of Roger of Wendower (d. 1236) under the year 1057 but was not mentioned by Florence of Worcester (d. 1118) in his references to Leofric and Godiva. The account included a "Peeping Tom," a villager who spied on the lady as she rode by and was blinded or fell dead as a result. Lady Godiva and her husband founded the monastery at Coventry. See also COVENTRY.

**GODWIN** (d. 1053) Also known as Godwine, an Anglo-Saxon noble, the earl of Wessex and one of the most powerful figures in England during the reign of Edward the Confessor (1042–1066). He was a favorite of King Canute the Great (ruled 1017–1035), becoming earl of Wessex in 1018. Supporting Edward in his quest for the throne, he arranged to make his daughter, Edith, Edward's wife. Edward, seeking to be rid of Godwin, turned to the Normans and by 1051 was able to exile the noble. Godwin returned in 1051 with his son, Harold Godwinson, invading and forcing Edward to reinstate him. Harold, on his death, tried to gain the throne but was defeated by William at the Battle of Hastings in 1066.

**GOLDEN BULL** The name given to important decrees or enactments because of the use of gold on the seals. The following medieval documents bore this name:

*Golden Bull of Sicily*, issued in 1212 by Emperor Frederick II (1215–1250), granting autonomy to Bohemia.

*Golden Bull of Rimini*, issued in 1226 by Frederick II (1215–1250), establishing the rights of jurisdiction for the Teutonic Knights over Prussia, including the territories of the pagan Slavs and Prussians (see TEUTONIC KNIGHTS).

*Golden Bull of 1222*, the celebrated bull decreed in Hungary, issued by King Andrew II, guaranteeing the rights of his aristocracy and clergy. Containing 31 articles, the decree was forced on Andrew by the nobles and compelled him to hold sessions of the Diet. He was also restrained from imprisoning any members of the nobility without trial and from collecting taxes from the aristocracy or the church. From 1222 every ruler of Hungary had to swear to uphold the rights set forth in this document (see HUNGARY).

*Golden Bull of 1356*, issued by Emperor Charles IV (1355–1378), establishing the process by which future kings of Germany were to be elected. According to the terms of the constitution, there were to be seven Electors (see ELECTORS) who would decide the royal succession (see HOLY ROMAN EMPIRE).

**GOLDEN FLEECE, ORDER OF THE** A chivalric order established in 1430 by Philip the Good, duke of Burgundy (1419–1467), to promote chivalry and the ideals of knighthood. The symbol was the legendary Golden Fleece of Greek legend sought by Jason. Called in French the Ordre de la Toison d'Or, the order was headed by the dukes of Burgundy until 1477, when the grand mastership passed to Maxmilian I of Habsburg. It became the highest attainable position in chivalry throughout Spain and Austria. According to its chapters, any member knight charged with treason or heresy had the right to trial by his peers. See also CHIVALRY; MILITARY ORDERS.

**GOLDEN HORDE** The name given to the army of the Mongols but also the name used to describe the Mongol empire in the West, the Kipchak Khanate, including nearly all of Russia and large parts of western Asia. The Golden Horde was derived from the Russian name of the Golden Tent (Zolotaya Orda) of the first khan of the Horde, Batu (d. 1256), grandson of Genghis Khan (d. 1227), whose magnificent camp was pitched at Sarai (Serai) on the Volga River. It was established during the massive invasion of Russia and eastern Europe by the Mongols and consolidated from 1236 to 1241, lasting until the 14th century. During the leadership of Batu's brother and successor, Berke (1257–1267), the Golden Horde came under the influence of Islam and was gradually converted. Prince Dimitri Donskoi of Moscow dealt the Horde its earliest defeat in 1380 at the Battle of Kulikovo. The empire reclaimed its hold on Russia but collapsed in 1395 in the time of Tamerlane. The Golden Horde eventually disintegrated into the smaller khanates of Jazan, Crimea and Astrakhan. See also MONGOLS.

**GOLEM** A large image or clay statue that in Hebrew legend was given life by a powerful charm or Shem ha-Meforash (or Shem), one of the names of God or a sacred word composed by using letters of spiritual power. The clay would animate when the Shem was placed in its mouth or attached to its head. Its purpose was to act as a servant or as a guardian of the Jewish community in the 16th century. Many such images were said to have existed, but the most celebrated was the Golem of Prague, constructed by Rabbi Judah Low (or Judah Loew, d. 1609) to defend the Jews of the city. See also JEWS AND JUDAISM.

**GOLIARDS** Wandering scholars and clerics in England, France and Germany during the 12th and 13th centuries, who composed satirical secular poems in Latin on drinking, debauchery, women and the church. They were purportedly the followers of Bishop Golias, who abandoned the religious life to journey. Goliardic poets also claimed that their name derived from the Old Testament Goliath/Golias, whose name was often used in medieval literature to signify the devil. The Goliards gambled, rioted and, when sober, composed poetry. The church censured their attacks on the clergy and the papacy at the Council of Trier (1227) when restrictions were placed on their clerical rights, and by 1300 they were forbidden to serve as members of the clergy at all. Throughout the 14th century the Goliards lost all ecclesiastical association, becoming known as minstrels, their lives recounted in the writings of Geoffrey Chaucer among others. Celebrated Goliards included Pierre de Blois, Gautier de Chatillon and the Archpoet. The major collection of Goliardic verse was the *Carmina Burana*.

**GONZAGA, HOUSE OF** Italian princely family, dominating the city of Mantua from 1328 until the 18th century. Luigi Gonzaga (c. 1268–1360) established the family in Mantua, driving the Bonacolsis from the city and receiving the title of imperial vicar from Emperor Louis III (1314–1347). Gonzaga fortunes and power were furthered by Gianfresco Gonzaga (d. 1444), who was given the rank of marquis by Emperor Sigismund (1410–1437) in 1433, a title held until 1530, when the heirs were granted the title of duke. See also MANTUA.

**GORM** (d. c. 950) Danish king of Jutland from about 935 until his death, controlling Denmark from his native Jutland, largely with the support of fellow pagan chieftains. The balance of Danish power shifted to his capital, Jelling. His son was Harald Bluetooth, who became the Christian unifier of Denmark and the conqueror of Norway. Gorm raised a memorial stone to the memory of his wife, Thyri. See also DENMARK.

**GOTHIC ART AND ARCHITECTURE** The style of art in Europe from the mid-12th century until the end of the 15th century. The name Gothic was a term of derision when used by the connoisseurs of the Renaissance, who saw it as the destroyer of the Romanesque and referred to the "barbarian" invaders of the empire, the Goths, centuries before. People living in the 12th to the 15th century, however, called their style the *opus modernum*, according it esteem and believing it to be a reflection of deep Christian faith.

### *Early Gothic*

This style evolved from the Romanesque in France. The writings of Suger, the abbot of Saint-Denis, and Bernard of Clairvaux influenced artists and architects, who began to use open skeletons of stone to support vaulting and introduced diagonal ribs to give strength to the traditional groined vaults, producing the characteristic pointed arch while attaining great height. To ensure stability, flying buttresses (arches leaning on sections of the outer walls to absorb pressures from the vaults) were applied to add height. The effect of space was achieved by the unique lighting of the interior through stained glass. These two elements, pointed arches and flying buttresses, became synonymous with Gothic architecture.

Many view the project of Suger, restoring the abbey church of Saint Denis (c. 1140), as the origin of Gothic architectural endeavors. With its vaulting and careful integration of windows, the abbey church was a worthy first effort, followed by the initiation of two of the most remarkable examples of Gothic achievement: Notre Dame de Paris (begun in 1163) and Lâon Cathedral (c. 1165–1205). At Chartres begun in 1145, the cathedral was built along slightly different lines during the late 12th century, with buttresses adding height to the clerestory, making possible more light, a feature that would be evident in the cathedrals of Reims and Amiens in the 13th century, in the High Gothic tradition.

As in the Romanesque, most sculpture was carved in conjunction with architectural projects. Beginning with Saint Denis, magnificent examples of Gothic art were to be found adorning the facades of churches, the supporting columns and interior tomb sculpture. Throughout the Early Gothic period, sculpture underwent a number of style changes, including tendencies toward realism and restrained realism and the adoption of drapery surrounding the figures.

### *High Gothic*

This style evolved in France, where the Rayonnant (radiating) form emerged. Chartres, which burned down in 1194 and was rebuilt during the 13th century, was the model for many other cathedrals. The emphasis on flying buttresses creating more light was stressed. The square design was replaced by the rectangular bay system, with a change in vault design to allow organic flow throughout. Other remarkable works from the period included the Bourges cathedral begun in 1195 (with its great height and continuous side aisles) and Amiens cathedral begun in 1218.

Around 1230, however, architects came to the realization that they had pushed their designs to vertical heights that went beyond their technical capacity for safety. The most severe example of such a hazard was Beauvais cathedral, the most ambitious example of the period, the vaults of which collapsed, making its completion impossible. Unable to achieve greater height, the architects decided to concentrate on interior decorations, originating the Rayonnant style. Intense experimentation was the hallmark of the Rayonnant architects, whose work flourished in the second half of the 13th century encouraged by the patronage of Louis IX (ruled 1226–1270). Of particular note was the palace chapel of Sainte Chapelle in Paris (c. 1248). Intended to resemble an intricately fashioned reliquary to house Crusader relics, the chapel was supported by markedly reduced stone elements, allowing space for an enormous amount of stained glass. Rayonnant monuments found elsewhere were at Aachen, Troyes and in the transepts of Notre Dame. The enthusiasm for the style had an effect on sculpture in this period, and patterning was stressed. Statues of Saint Martin and Saint Jerome, on the Porch of the Confessors at the Chartres cathedral, the west facade of Reims and the west portals of Brouges give evidence of the period's accomplishments. Tomb carvings and monuments became popular as well, with excellent examples surviving throughout Europe, especially in England.

### *Late Gothic*

This period in France was characterized by a moving away from the Rayonnant toward the Flamboyant, so called because of the extravagent flamelike designs used in the tracery. Elaborate facades were produced, as well as improvements in window tracery. In the 14th and 15th centuries, however, France underwent considerable hardship from the Hundred Years' War, and the Flamboyant style was used only in such cities as Rouen and Alençon. Vaulting was still experimental in Germany and Austria, and the curvilinear patterns became the hallmark of the late 15th century in eastern Europe. In England, around 1350, the Perpendicular style, a more restrained and formal architectural design, came into fashion. It was adopted in the chapel of King Henry VII in Westminster Abbey (c. 1500–1512).

One of the most influential figures in Late Gothic period sculpture was the Netherlandish Sculptor Claus Sluter (d. 1406), who carved the tomb of Philip the Bold (completed by his nephew Claus de Werue in 1411) and the monumental figures at the Carthusian monastery of Champmol. His direct, forceful, realistic and decorative style was imitated throughout Europe and found further expression with the sculptor Jacques de Baerze. In Germany during this period there was enthusiastic experimentation with detail and decoration, but the flowering of naturalism in the European mainstream of art was prevented by a retreat in the 15th century to idealization, albeit temporary. The transformation of art and architecture from the Gothic to the Renaissance was gradual, the result both of the rebirth of humanism and classical culture in Italy and the decline in use of Gothic forms. Artists and architects, seeking new sources of inspiration, turned to the long-forgotten period of classical antiquity. See also MANUSCRIPT ILLUMINATION; ROMANESQUE ART AND ARCHITECTURE; STAINED GLASS.

**GOTHS** See OSTROGOTHS; VISIGOTHS.

**GOTTESFREUNDE** The "Friends of God," groups of men and women in Switzerland, the Rhineland, and Bavaria who attempted to live a Christ-like existence. They cared for the poor, expecting transformation of their spirituality in adhering to a life of prayer and ascetism. Unlike other religious movements, the *Gottesfreunde* remained largely free of extremism, retaining their allegiance to the church. Important figures in the movement included Henry Suso, Meister Eckhart and Johann Tauler. See also MYSTICISM.

**GOTTFRIED VON STRASSBURG** Early-13th-century poet ranked as one of the greatest writers in Middle High German. Well educated, although little is known of his early years, he was familiar with the French Arthurian legends and earned lasting recognition for his romance *Tristan und Isolde,* written sometime around 1210. This courtly romance was based on the Celtic legend of Tristan and Iseult (Isolde), which reached Germany in the 12th century. Other versions, including that of Eilhart von Oberg, are not as highly thought of as Gottfried's work. See also HARTMAN VON AUE; TRISTAN AND ISOLDE; WALTHER VON DER VOGELWEIDE; WOLFRAM VON ESCHENBACH.

**GOTTHARD, SAINT** (d. 1038) Bishop of Hildesheim, abbot and leader of monastic reform in Upper Germany. He was ordained in 990, entering the Benedictine order, and was named abbot in 996 or 997. He so impressed Henry, duke of Bavaria (the future Emperor Henry II, ruled 1002–1024), that he was commissioned to institute reforms in the monasteries of the region. In 1022 he became bishop of Hildesheim, establishing schools and churches and improving education. The Saint Gotthard Pass in the Alps probably derives its name from the chapel of Saint Gotthard at its summit, constructed in his honor by the dukes of Bavaria.

**GOTTSCHALK OF FULDA** (d. 868) Also known as Gottschalk of Orbais, a monk, theologian, poet and controversial figure for his ideas on predestination. He was forced by his parents to become an oblate, a youth surrendered to a monastery, in the Benedictine monastery at Fulda. In 829, however, he was freed from the monastic life by the Synod of Mainz, only to be returned to the Benedictines by Rabanus Maurus. He was sent to Orbais, where he was ordained about 838, and continued his study of theology, developing his theories. His views were opposed by Walafrid Strabo, but Prudentius of Troyes supported them. Attacked by Maurus and Hincmar of Reims for his heretical ideas and for denying free will and the saving grace of God, he was condemned at the Synod of Mainz in 848. Gottschalk was defrocked and imprisoned for the rest of his life at the monastery of Hautvilliers, where although cruelly mistreated, he never recanted. He died physically broken and probably insane. See also HERESIES.

**GOVERNMENT** See AACHEN; ABBASID CALIPHATE; AGHLABIDS; ALMOHADS; ALTHING; ARAGON; ARPAD; ASSIZES OF JERUSALEM; AYYUBIDS; BAGHDAD; BARONS' WAR; BOHEMIA; BOURBON, HOUSE OF; BULGARIA; BURGUNDY, DUCHY OF; BURGUNDY, KINGDOM OF; BUYIDS; BYZANTINE EMPIRE; CAIRO; CALIPHATE; CAPETIAN DYNASTY; CASTILE; CATALONIA; CHAMPAGNE; CHIVALRY; COEUR, JACQUES; COMNENI DYNASTY; CONSTANTINOPLE; CONSTANTINOPLE, LATIN EMPIRE OF; CORDOBA; CORDOBA, EMIRATE OF; COUNCIL OF SEVENTEEN; COUNCIL OF TEN; CRUSADER STATES; CRUSADES; DANEGELD; DANELAW; DENMARK; DOGE; DOMESDAY BOOK; DONATION OF PEPIN; EGYPT; ELEANOR OF AQUITAINE; ELECTORS; ENGLAND; EXARCHATE; EXCHEQUER; FAIRS; FATIMID CALIPHATE; FEUDALISM; FLANDERS; FLORENCE; FRANCE; GALLICANISM; GERMANY; GHAZNAVIDS; GHENT; GOLDEN BULL; GUELPHS AND GHIBELLINES; GUILDS; HABSBURG DYNASTY; HANSEATIC LEAGUE; HOHENSTAUFEN; HOHENZOLLERN; HOLY ROMAN EMPIRE; HUNDRED YEARS' WAR; HUNGARY; ICELAND; IDRISIDS; IKSHIDIDS; INVESTITURE CONTROVERSY; IRELAND; JAGIELLO DYNASTY; JERUSALEM, KINGDOM OF; JEWS AND JUDAISM; KALMAR UNION; KIEV; LANCASTER, HOUSE OF; LOMBARD LEAGUE; LOMBARDS; LONDON; MACEDONIAN DYNASTY; MAGGIOR CONSIGLIO; MAMLUKS; MANORIAL SYSTEM; MARCHES, THE; MEROVINGIAN DYNASTY; MOORS; MOSCOW, GRAND PRINCES OF; NAPLES, KINGDOM OF; NASRID KINGDOM OF GRANADA; NAVARRE, KINGDOM OF; OTTOMAN EMPIRE; PALAEOLOGI DYNASTY; PAPAL STATES; PARIS; PEASANT REVOLT; PIAST DYNASTY; PLAGUES; POLAND; PORTUGAL; PRAGMATIC SANCTION OF BOURGES; PRAGUE; RECONQUISTA; ROLLS, PIPE; ROME; RUSSIA; SALIAN DYNASTY; SAXON DYNASTY; SCHISM, GREAT; SCOTLAND; SELJUK TURKS; SERBIA; SEVILLE, KINGDOM OF; SICILY; STATES GENERAL; STRASBOURG OATH; SWITZERLAND; TEUTONIC KNIGHTS; TRADE AND COMMERCE; TREBIZOND, EMPIRE OF; TRUCE OF GOD; TULUNIDS; VALOIS DYNASTY; VENICE; WALES; WESTMINSTER, STATUTES OF; YORK, HOUSE OF.

**GOWER, JOHN** (d. 1408) English poet and friend of Geoffrey Chaucer and King Richard II (ruled 1377–1399), who also won the favor of Henry IV (ruled 1399–1413). Henry IV awarded Gower two casks of wine every year for life, as an honorarium for extremely favorable comments made on the ruler in one of Gower's poems. He wrote in French, English and Latin on a number of themes. Gower's works include *Confessio Amantis,* a collection of love tales in English; *Speculum meditantis,* on the seven deadly sins and the seven virtues (in French); and the *Vox clamantis* (in Latin), a view of society in his era. He also wrote ballades in French and an examination of war that made a plea for peace in the wake of the Peasant Revolt (1381).

**GRAIL, HOLY** See HOLY GRAIL.

**GRANADA** A remarkably beautiful city in Andalusia, Spain, situated near the Sierra Nevada and for centuries the major Muslim city in the Iberian Peninsula. Originally occupied by the Iberii and then the Romans, Granada was refounded in the seventh century, falling to Muslim hands in 711. Its name was perhaps derived from the Spanish *granada,* or pomegranate, a regional fruit, or from the Arabic *Gharnatah,* meaning a hill of strangers. The city became prominent for its Moorish culture, learning and trade in 1238, when it served as the capital of the Nasrid Kingdom of Granada (1232–1492), the last Moorish foothold in Spain. Although forced to pay tribute to Castile from 1246, the Nasrids strove to foster art, architecture and beauty, attaining their finest achievement in the fortress of the Alhambra. The Nasrids, divided by feuds among the city's nobles, fell in 1492 to the Christian armies of Ferdinand and Isabella (1474–1516), who drove out the Moors, ending the Reconquista. The cultural life of the city declined quickly, its deterioration hastened by the expulsion of the Jews (1492) and the Moors (1502) themselves. See also NASRID KINGDOM OF GRANADA.

**GRANADA, KINGDOM OF** See NASRID KINGDOM OF GRANADA.

**GRANDE CHARTREUSE** See CARTHUSIANS.

**GRANDMONT, ORDER OF** French religious community for men established about 1077 by Saint Stephen of Muret (c. 1054–1124), also called Grandmontines. The order was devoted to strict poverty and severe discipline, including silence and occupancy of individual cells. Headquartered at Grandmont, Normandy, the order eventually spread to England, where three houses were founded.

**GRATIAN** (d. before 1159 or around 1179) Canonist and monk, considered by many the father of canon law. He won lasting recognition and influence with his work the *Decretum* or *Concordia discordantium canonum*. He was probably a Camaldolese monk and lecturer at the monastery of Saints Felix and Nabor in Bologna, completing the *Decretum* around 1140, a date chosen by scholars as the earliest possible because of his inclusion of material from the Lateran Council of 1139. The work was a massive collection of some 3,800 texts, conciliar decrees, papal declarations, patristic writings and apostolic constructions, supplemented by Gratian's own analysis and commentary to rectify the contradictions and combine the many sources into a complete, harmonious text. The *Decretum* became a standard work in the study of canon law, especially in the training of lawyers at Bologna and then at Oxford, Paris and elsewhere. Later papal decrees made much of it obsolete, but it remains a valued work.

**GRAZ** City in southeastern Austria and the capital of the region of Styria, established probably in the ninth century. At Graz (or Gratz) a castle was erected on the Schlossburg, a hill overlooking the land below as an effort to protect the Carinthian march from inroads by the Slavs. The name was Slavic for "little fort." The town grew around the castle, receiving rights in the 13th century. A branch of the Habsburgs took up residence there in the late 14th century. The fortress was destroyed by the French in 1809, but a Gothic cathedral and several churches remain. See also STYRIA.

**GREAT BRITAIN** See ENGLAND; IRELAND; SCOTLAND, WALES.

**GREAT SCHISM** See SCHISM, GREAT; SCHISMS.

**GREECE** An important land of the ancient world, declining in political significance during the Roman era but having strong cultural influence on the Romans and on the Europeans of the Middle Ages. On the division of the Roman Empire in 395, Greece was included in the East, and its culture was the origin for that of the Byzantine Empire, overshadowing the Roman model in the construction of the social and governmental systems of the Eastern Roman Empire. During the centuries immediately following, Greece endured invasions by the Goths, Huns, Slavs, Avars and Bulgars. A brief respite was allowed from the 9th to early 11th century, when Byzantine rule was established, but the Normans from Sicily were a powerful and destabilizing force. Turkish influences were felt as well.

In 1204, with the fall of Constantinople to a Latin army, Greece became the object of territorial ambitions of a number of Western groups, including the Angevins, French, Burgundians and Italians, especially Venice. Although the Byzantines were able to regain Constantinople in 1261 and reestablish control over parts of Greece, much of the country remained in the control of Venetian or Italian trading powers or was ruled by feudal nobles or other organizations, including the Catalan Company which had begun as a mercenary unit in the service of the Byzantine emperors. Throughout the 15th century Greece, like the Byzantine Empire and the Balkans, observed the advance of the Ottoman Turks, culminating with the capture of Constantinople in 1453 and with the seizure of Greece in 1456. See also BYZANTINE EMPIRE; OTTOMAN EMPIRE.

**GREEK FIRE** See WARFARE.

**GREENLAND** Danish island, Grønland, within the Arctic Circle, midway between Canada and Iceland. It was possibly discovered by the Norwegian Guunbjorn Ulfsson in the 10th century, but generally credit for its discovery in 982 was given to Eric the Red. Under his leadership a colony of Scandinavians, mostly Icelanders, founded camps on the eastern and western coasts, flourishing probably into the 15th century. Explorers made Greenland a base from which to launch explorations to the West, to North America, or Vinland, as it was called by the Norsemen. Notable voyagers were Bjarni Herjulfsson and Leif Ericsson. Christianity was introduced in Greenland around the start of the 11th century. A cathedral, an Augustinian monastery, a Benedictine convent and a number of parishes were founded. Ties were maintained with Scandinavia, so that in 1261 the island was incorporated into the Norwegian empire. Problems with the weather and with indigenous peoples and breakdowns of communication with Iceland weakened the colony, and by the late 14th century permanent decline had set in. By the final years of the 15th century the settlements were largely depopulated, ended by the Eskimos and by the harsh weather conditions. See also VINLAND.

**GREGORIAN REFORM** An attempted church reform, named for its leader, Pope Gregory VII (reigned 1073–1085), although the program was undertaken by his predecessors throughout the 11th century. The popes intended to end lay investiture and reclaim direct control of episcopal appointments. Gregorian Reform also entailed instituting ecclesiastical changes and adjustments in canon law. Gregory's reforms were opposed by Emperor Henry IV (1056–1106), causing a bitter conflict between them. See also GREGORY VII; HENRY IV; HOLY ROMAN EMPIRE; INVESTITURE CONTROVERSY.

**GREGORY AKINDYNOS** See AKINDYNOS, GREGORY.

**GREGORY I, SAINT** (c. 550–604) Pope from 590 to 604, called Gregory the Great, one of the last of the four Latin fathers of the church, who strengthened the papacy in the Middle Ages, and one of the great patrons of monasticism and missionary activity. A member of a patrician family, he was entering a successful political career when he was appointed prefect of the city *(praefectus urbi)* of Rome (572–574), then renouncing secular honors for a spiritual life. He established seven monasteries with his own inheritance, six in Sicily and one in Rome on his family estate. By 574 he was one of the important deacons of the city and was sent to Constantinople in 578 or 579 as ambassador, asking for the support of the Eastern Empire in dealing with the Lombards. Returning to Rome (c. 585), he became deacon once more and the abbot of San Andrea, his Roman monastery. His attempts to avoid his elevation to the papacy failed in 590, and he was unanimously chosen successor to Pelagius II, as Gregory I.

At the start of his papal reign, the Lombards threatened Rome, the Byzantines were unreliable Christian allies and Italy was in a state of near ruin. Despite chronic illness, brought on by his stringent asceticism, he undertook intense activities. He began by making available a series of charitable services to alleviate hunger in Rome, protecting Rome from the Lombards and laying the foundations of the Papal States. In 592–593 he concluded a peace with the Lombards, ignoring the presence of the Byzantine representative, the Exarchate of Ravenna. By naming his own governors in various cities he further curtailed Byzantine influence and began to accumulate temporal power for the papacy. With relations strained in dealing with Constantinople, Gregory recognized the political status of the Byzantine emperor, while condemning the ambitions of the patriarchs of Constantinople, who claimed their ecclesiastical rights in the West, the rights upheld by Gregory for Rome.

Saint Gregory the Great, from a 10th-century ivory

Within the church he strove for many reforms, redesigning the process of administering church estates, believing that the holdings should be made available to the poor. In his *Liber regulae pastoralis (Book of Pastoral Rules)* he set the guidelines of religious practice that would be followed for the next centuries. He also encouraged monasticism and sent a mission to the British Isles in 596 to bring the monasteries there under Roman church control. His chief agent for this purpose was Saint Augustine of Canterbury. In addition to his well-regarded guide for bishops, the *Regulae pastoralis,* Gregory wrote *Dialogues* (c. 593), an account of the lives and miracles of early Latin saints, especially Benedict of Nursia, and the *Magna moralis* (595), an exegesis on the Book of Job. There were also homilies on the Gospels and 854 letters. He was canonized after his death in 604, and by virtue of his achievements and the esteem in which he was held, he was named a doctor of the church and steward of the property of the poor. See also PAPAL STATES.

**GREGORY II, SAINT** (669–731) Pope from 715 to 731, originally a priest and treasurer of the church in Rome, elected as successor to Constantine (708/9–715). He encouraged the missionary work of Boniface and others in Germany, consecrating Boniface in 722. His pontificate, however, had to come to terms with the Iconoclastic Controversy in the Byzantine Empire, which began with the issuing of imperial decrees by Emperor Leo III the Isaurian (717–741), ordering the destruction of religious images. Gregory, who had supported Leo, condemned him, precipitating a deterioration in relations between Rome and Constantinople. Gregory generally maintained amicable dealings with the Romans and the Lombards. See also ICONOCLASTICISM.

**GREGORY III, SAINT** (d. 741) Pope from 731 to 741, a Syrian by birth. He followed Gregory II and was thus faced with the Iconoclastic Controversy with the Byzantine emperor Leo III the Isaurian (717–741), whom he condemned for decreeing the destruction of religious images. The iconoclasts were also attacked in 731 at a council in Rome, and excommunications were used as a weapon in the doctrinal conflict. Gregory then faced the sudden threat of the Lombards, who destroyed the Exarchate of Ravenna and imperiled Rome. Gregory called on Charles Martel (716–741) and the Franks, and while support was not immediately forthcoming, the precedent had been set, allying the Franks with the papacy. See also ICONOCLASTICISM.

**GREGORY IV** (d. 844) Pope from 827 to 844, esteemed for his mediation between Lothair, king of the Franks (840–855), and Louis I the Pious (814–840). Gregory supported Lothair in his territorial claims. Pope Gregory also promulgated the observance of the Feast of All Saints.

**GREGORY V** (d. 999) Pope from 996 to 999, born Brunone di Carinzia and the first pope to come from an ecclesiastical post in Germany. The cousin of the emperor Otto III (996–1002), he was his chaplain and was installed by him in 996 as pontiff, in gratitude for crowning Otto emperor on May 21 of that year. He soon had a confrontation with Crescentius II, however, and was driven from Rome when the antipope John XVI was placed on the papal throne, in 997. Otto returned in 998, removing John, imprisoning and blinding him, while reinstating Gregory.

**GREGORY VI** (d. 1047) Pope from 1045 to 1046, born Giovanni Graziano, the successor to Benedict IX (1032–1044; 1045; 1047–1048), who abdicated because of reports of scandal. At the Council of Sutri Gregory was accused of simony, and under pressure he abdicated and retired to Germany with his private secretary, Hildebrand, the future Gregory VII (1073–1085).

**GREGORY VII, SAINT** (c. 1020–1085) Pope from 1073 to 1085, originally called Hildebrand, and the most important ecclesiastical reformer of the Middle Ages. He also engaged in a bitter conflict with Emperor Henry IV (1056–1106). A native of Tuscany, Hildebrand served the papacy all his life, accompanying Pope Gregory VI into exile and then entering a monastery when the abdicated pope died in 1047. Two years later Pope Leo IX (1049–1055) made him the administrator of the Patrimonium Petri (Papal States), inaugurating a long period of increasing influence with successive pontiffs, who sent him as emissary to France and Germany. Finally, under Alexander II (1061–1073), he was chancellor of the Holy See. In 1073 he was elected successor to Alexander.

From the start Gregory was concerned with reform and with moral renewal within the church. The charges for which he was responsible came to be called the Gregorian Reform and were carried on through decrees and the convening of the Lenten Synods (a synod held every Lent in Rome). He attacked simony (the selling of ecclesiastical offices and benefits) and nicolaitism (clerical marriages), especially during the Lenten Synod of 1074. Bishops and monarchs were enlisted in this cause, and Gregory appointed papal legates to administer regions and to coerce the reluctant bishops. At the Synod of Rome in 1075, Gregory turned his attention to the problem of lay investiture, condemning the practice.

His declarations proved only mildly effective and started a great conflict in the West. In France and in England some advances were made, but Germany was the focus of Gregory's attention, as well as the young king Henry IV. Henry took steps to depose him and was excommunicated by Gregory in return, freeing his subjects from obedience (as well as from paying feudal dues and taxes). With his adherents dwindling and the Saxons in revolt, Henry submitted, arriving at Canossa asking for forgiveness in 1077. He was excommunicated again three years later, and Henry plotted to have an antipope, Clement III (1080), the former archbishop of Ravenna, replace Gregory. Rome fell to Henry's army in 1084, and Clement III became pontiff. Robert Guiscard and the Normans arrived to rescue Gregory but enraged the Romans by putting parts of the city to the torch. Gregory fled, dying in exile at Salerno. Reportedly his dying words were "I have loved justice and therefore die in exile." See also DICTATUS PAPAE; GREGORIAN REFORM; INVESTITURE CONTROVERSY.

**GREGORY VIII** (c. 1110–1187) Pope in 1187, born Alberto de Morra and a member of the Cistercian order. He was named cardinal in 1155 or 1156 and was successor to Urban III (1185–1187). Gregory preached for a crusade, reconciled King Henry II of England (1154–1189) to the church after the murder of Thomas à Becket and initiated reforms in the curia.

**GREGORY VIII** (d.c. 1140) Antipope from 1118 to 1121, a Benedictine monk, bishop of Coimbra and archbishop of Braga (1103). In 1117 he was an envoy of Pope Paschal II (1099–1118) to Emperor Henry V (1106–1125) during the conflict between the two leaders; Gregory joined the emperor's camp and was excommunicated. On Paschal's death, Henry had Gregory elected pope in opposition to Gelasius II (1118–1119) and then Calixtus II (1119–1124). Calixtus was responsible for Gregory's arrest and exile in 1121. He died in prison. See also ANTIPOPE.

**GREGORY IX** (1155–1241) Pope from 1227 to 1241, noted for his long conflict with Emperor Frederick II (1220–1250). Originally Count Ugolino of Segni, Gregory was a nephew of Pope Innocent III (1198–1216); he was made a cardinal in 1198 and received other ecclesiastical appointments as well. In 1220, Gregory accepted the vow of Emperor Frederick II to crusade in the Holy Land. When he became pope in 1227, he demanded that the vow be kept, finally excommunicating Frederick in order to force him to set sail in 1228. Frederick's considerable diplomatic efforts in the Holy Land were wasted because of Gregory's war against him.

A reconciliation took place in 1230, with the Treaty of San Ceprano, but Frederick was excommunicated again in 1239, precipitating years of conflict over the church in Sicily. Gregory summoned a general council in 1241, but the vessels carrying the papal entourage were seized by imperial troops. Gregory himself was besieged in Rome and died on August 22, 1241. He is also notable for having established the Court of Inquisition in 1232 and for his friendship with Francis of Assisi. About 1230, Gregory also ordered the organization of papal decretals, called the *Decretals of Gregory IX,* including papal decrees from Gratian and the *Decretion* or *Concordia discordantium canonum* (1140). The *Decretals* were published in 1234.

**GREGORY X** (1210–1276) Pope from 1271 to 1276, born Teobaldo Visconti, and chosen as a compromise can-

Pope Gregory X

didate to end the three-year papal vacancy following the death of Clement IV (1265–1268). Not even an ordained priest, Gregory was, at the time of his election, in the service of the future Edward I of England, during his trip to the Holy Land. He received word of his election at Acre. Despite his lack of experience, Gregory proved capable, and one of his first acts was to repair the disunity between the papacy and the Holy Roman Empire. He was responsible for naming Rudolf of Habsburg as emperor and for inducing other claimants to withdraw. An attempt at union with the Eastern Church was made with the Council of Lyons (1274–1275), but it did not come to fruition, as did his plan to mount another Crusade to Jerusalem. His lasting achievement was the ecclesiastical innovation of introducing the conclave-style election of popes. The decree, *Ubi periculum* (1274), ordered that an assembly of cardinals be convened to elect each new pontiff, a reform that remedied the chaotic proceedings surrounding papal succession in the past.

**GREGORY XI** (1329–1378) Pope from 1370 to 1378, the last French pontiff and the last pope to reside at Avignon, returning to Rome in 1377. Born Pierre Roger de Beaufort, he was a nephew of Pope Clement VI (1342–1352), receiving the cardinalate in 1348, although never ordained a priest. A skilled canon lawyer, he was elected successor to Urban V (1362–1370) at Avignon, where he mediated a war with Florence over the Papal States, the War of the Eight Saints (1375–1377). This war ended with the Peace of Tivoli. Gregory then, at the urging of Saint Catherine of Siena, reentered Rome on January 17, 1377, despite opposition from King Charles V of France and others. Unrest in Rome brought problems until his death. This pope also condemned of the teachings of John Wycliffe.

**GREGORY XII** (d. 1417) Pope from 1406 to 1415, the pontiff who brought an end to the Great Schism. Born Angelo Correr, he served as a bishop and as a cardinal (1405) before being elected the successor to Innocent VII (1404–1406). He abdicated on July 4, 1415, after agreeing to summon the Council of Constance, which was already in session. This act caused the removal of the Avignonese antipope Benedict XIII (1394–1417), thus terminating the schism and permitting the subsequent election of Martin V (1417–1431). As a gift the council made Gregory the cardinal of Porto, where he died in 1417. See also SCHISM, GREAT.

**GREGORY OF RIMINI** (d. 1358) Italian philosopher and theologian who influenced late medieval thinking and the Reformation, especially Martin Luther, who studied his doctrines at the University of Wittenberg. Gregory was a member of the Augustinian Hermits, becoming general of the order in 1357. He taught as well in Bologna, Padua, Perugia and Paris and was an ardent adherent of Saint Augustine of Hippo (fourth century). His views on nominalism were Augustinian but without the severity of others. An adherent of the concept that salvation was entirely dependent on the grace of God, he earned the epithet *tortor infantium* (infant torturer) for preaching that all unbaptized infants were damned. His works included a commentary on the *Sentences* of Peter Lombard and a treatise on usury.

**GREGORY OF TOURS, SAINT** (c. 538–594) Renowned Frankish bishop and author of the *Historia Francorum* (*History of the Franks*). He was named bishop of Tours in 573 and was remarkable for his dealings with the Frankish rulers of France, especially during the fratricidal wars that erupted there. Gregory dealt with King Chilperic (ruled 561–584) and his infamous wife, Fredegunde, holding firm against threats and attacks. After Chilperic's murder in 584, Gregory dealt with the Merovingian king of Burgundy, Guntran, and found him more amicable. Under King Childebert II of Austrasia, he secured the political protection of the church and had both spiritual and temporal influence on it.

A writer of energetic but unsophisticated Latin, Gregory was considered one of the most important historians of the Middle Ages. Most of his works were hagiographic in nature, such as his *De vita partum (Lives of the Fathers)* and *In gloriam martyrum*, an examination of the miracles of Christ and the Apostles. Of far greater value was the *Historia Francorum*, compiled using both documents and eyewitness accounts. This work became the primary source for information on France in the sixth century. While it was intended to cover the period from the Creation to 591, it was concerned chiefly with the period after 397, the era dealing with the rise of the Franks and the rule of their kings, especially Gregory's contemporaries. See also FRANCE; FRANKS.

**GREGORY PALAMAS** See PALAMAS, GREGORY, SAINT.

**GRENDEL** See BEOWULF.

**GRIMOALD** (d. 671) King of the Lombards from 662 to 671. Grimoald was the Lombard duke of Benevento and retainer to the young king Godebert when, in 662, he rebelled against the king, who was engaged in a civil war with his own brother, Berthari. Murdering Godebert at Pavia, Grimoald claimed the Lombard crown and married his victim's sister. Berthari fled the country, seeking refuge with the Avars. Through strength of will, Grimoald held the Lombard throne for nine years, despite unrest and a Byzantine invasion in 663, led by Emperor Constans II (641–668). His son, Romuald, held Benevento, which was attacked by the Byzantines, and Grimoald compelled Constans to withdraw. Rome was sacked, and Grimoald's daughter, Gisa, a Byzantine hostage, was killed. The Byzantines, however, were forced to retreat to Sicily. Grimoald also defeated an Avar force in Venetia and repulsed the Franks sent by Ebroin, mayor of the palace to King Clotaire III. On Grimoald's death, probably by assassination, his son was dismissed to be replaced by Berthari. See also LOMBARDS.

**GRIMOIRES** The name given to various books of magic, generally believed to have been written by celebrated practitioners of the art, such as Solomon, Albertus Magnus or even Pope Honorius III (1216–1227). *Grimoires* were widely read during the Middle Ages, particularly by occultists and sorcerers. Most were rare and expensive, copied in secret and by hand. The most important *grimoire* was the *Key of Solomon* (*Clavicule de Solomon*), supposedly written by the legendary ruler and containing spells, including those to summon demons and devils. The work probably entered Europe through Spain or was brought back by the Crusaders. It was associated with the Knights Templars. The work attributed to Pope Honorius was considered the product of a dangerous sorcerer. Other *grimoires* included *Liber spirituum, Grimorium verum* and the *Lesser Key of Solomon*. See also ALCHEMY; BACON, ROGER; MAGIC; WITCHCRAFT.

**GRINTRAM, KING OF BURGUNDY AND ORLEANS** See GUNTRAM.

**GROOTE, GERHARD** (1340–1384) Also called Geert de Groote or Gerardus Magnus, a mystic and founder of the Brethren of the Common Life. Born to a rich family in Deventer, Netherlands, he was educated in various cities but in 1374 abandoned the academic life for the spiritual. He entered the Carthusian monastery at Munnikhuizen (Munnikhausen, near Arnhem), leaving there about 1377 to become a deacon. His sermons on poverty and abuses in the church drew much animosity, and in 1383 his license was withdrawn in an attempt to silence him. He died the following year, probably of the plague. Through his example, however, followers established themselves at Deventer, founding the Brethren of the Common Life, and Groote was personally responsible for founding the Sisters of the Common Life. His influence as a preacher and mystic helped support Devotio Moderna (Modern Devotion), a popular ascetic movement. See also MYSTICISM.

**GROSSETESTE, ROBERT** (c. 1168–1253) Bishop of Lincoln, ecclesiastical reformer and a respected intellectual of his era. Educated at Oxford and probably Paris, he served as chancellor of Oxford from 1215 to 1221. He also became the archdeacon of Leicester and then, in 1235, the bishop of Lincoln. Church reform was his primary concern, and he removed recalcitrant abbots and monks, opposed ecclesiastical benefices and demonstrated an ardent belief in the supremacy of the church over the state. In 1245 he attended the Council of Lyon and in 1250 spoke before the pope on the custom of granting English church offices to Italians. He was also the author of a series of *Statutes* (1240–1243), guidelines for clerical behavior and the administration of dioceses. A friend to the Franciscans, he taught in the Franciscan house at Oxford from 1224 to 1235.

Grosseteste was also noted as an astronomer and was well versed in optics, mathematics and science, anticipating his pupil, Roger Bacon, in experimentation and the scientific method. A Hebraicist and Greek scholar, he espoused the study of Arabic and Greek to advance learning while making translations of Aristotle, Pseudo-Dionysius and Saint John of Damascus.

**GRUFFYDD AP LLEWELYN** See LLEWELYN AP GRUFFYDD.

**GUARINO DE VERONA** (1370–1460) Italian scholar and humanist who studied in Constantinople with Manuel Chrysoloras from 1403 to 1408, returning to Italy with a large collection of Greek manuscripts. He became one of Italy's foremost Greek instructors, teaching in Florence (1410–1414), Venice (1414–1418) and Verona. In 1429 he became the tutor of Leonello d'Este, son of Nicolo d'Este, lord of Ferrara, continuing to further Greek studies. Among his works were translations of Strabo and Plutarch and *Regulae grammaticae*, a guide to the rules of grammar.

**GUELPHS AND GHIBELLINES** Two Italian political factions during the 13th and 14th centuries. These factions divided Italy by supporting the claims of the Hohenstaufen emperors in Italy (the Ghibellines) or by opposing them to support the papacy (the Guelphs). The Guelphs derived their name from the German Welf family, Bavarian aristocrats who had competed for the German throne in the 12th and 13th centuries. The term Ghibelline was derived from a castle belonging to the Hohenstaufens, Waiblingen, a stronghold opposing Welf ambitions. Both names came into use during the time of Frederick II's conflict with the papacy (c. 1227–1250).

During the reign of Frederick I Barbarossa (1155–1190), the Italians were confronted by his ambitions, and in Florence the political rivalry began. Citizens associated themselves with one party or the other for certain advantages, and wars ensued. Florence and the Guelphs campaigned against Pisa and Siena, the Ghibelline adherents. Losers in the conflicts faced death or exile, and the survivors plotted revenge. Changes in the nature of the Guelph and Ghibelline factions took place after 1268, with the death of Conradin (1254–1268), the last of the Hohenstaufens. Ghibelline lands were seized and many were exiled, their adherents reflecting a nostalgic wish to restore the declining powers of the Holy Roman Empire in Italy. The Guelphs, meanwhile, took on the label of conservative supporters of the papacy and French-Avignonese expansion in southern Italy. A brief revival of Ghibelline power took place during the time of Louis of Bavaria (ruled 1324–1347) when another conflict arose against the papacy, but after this episode the effectiveness of both parties declined, reduced to local political divisions. See also HOLY ROMAN EMPIRE.

**GUIBERT OF RAVENNA** See CLEMENT III.

**GUIDO DA SIENA** Mid-13th-century Italian painter, generally considered the founder of the Sienese school. Virtually nothing is known about his life, and one work, a Madonna and Child in the Siena town square (Palazzo Publico), has been accepted by a majority of scholars, principally because his name appears on the painting. The date, however, has been subject to debate. Guido was important because of his conscious rejection of the formal style of the Byzantines and the use of natural elements in his work.

**GUIDO DI BERGOGNE** See CALIXTUS II.

**GUIDO DI PIETRO** See ANGELICO, FRA.

**GUIDO OF SPOLETO** (d. 894) Emperor of Italy from 888 to 894 and a participant in the politics of the Holy Roman Empire. Also called Guy of Spoleto, he used the deposition of Charles the Fat in 887 to advance his own claim to the French throne. Marching north in 888, he learned that Odo of Paris had become king and that in his absence Berengar of Friuli had usurped power in Italy. He defeated Berengar in 889 and was elected king of Italy. Two years later he compelled Pope Stephen V (VI) to crown him emperor. Stephen's successor, Formosus, was forced in 893 to anoint Guido's son, Lambert, as co-emperor. Arnulf, duke of Carinthia, responded to the pleas of Formosus in 894, but his campaign ended in disaster. Guido died that year, still in power. His son, however, was soon forced from the throne. See also SPOLETO.

**GUIENNE** Also Guyenne, a region in southwestern France, long identified with Aquitaine but becoming synonymous with the territorial holdings of the English in France. Guienne first became an English possession in 1152, with the marriage of Eleanor of Aquitaine to Henry II of England (1154–1189). This right of ownership was confirmed in the Treaty of Paris in 1259, between Henry III of England (1216–1272) and Louis IX of France (1226–1270) and despite the brief conquest of the region in the early stages of the Hundred Years' War, the Treaty of Bretigny (1360) reestablished it as an English domain. Guienne fell, finally, to France, in 1453, at the end of the Hundred Years' War. Granted as a duchy to Charles de France, duc de Berry, it was attached to the crown in 1472, after his death. See also FRANCE.

**GUILDS** Economic and social associations of merchants and artisans arising in western Europe, flourishing during the 12th and 13th centuries. They were established with multiple aims: self-protection, economic gain and the promotion of special interests for those who were members. Though declining in the 14th century, they had fulfilled an essential role in advancing trade and commerce, while encouraging the growth of cities.

Guilds have been traced to ancient Egypt and Mesopotamia and evolved during Roman control as *collegia*, organized essentially as voluntary associations. Constantinople strictly controlled its guilds, and those established in the West confronted tribal invasions and the devastation of economies. It is possible that none of these *collegia* of former eras survived into the Middle Ages, except in some regions of Italy, France and Sicily. The German tribes encouraged a social group called the *gilda*, but it was not economic in purpose, and the *collegia* of the Byzantines, so clearly described in the 10th-century work the *Book of the Prefect*, had little impact on the West, even in Byzantine-controlled Ravenna, where a professional group of merchants came into being, although emphasizing other matters.

Prior to the 11th century the society was primarily agrarian, and there was little urban commerce; therefore it was exceedingly difficult for a guild to exist, let alone flourish. Only the growth of cities and a revival of trade and commerce allowed merchant and craft organizations to multiply. These groups banded together, and in time there was an important division between the merchant and the craft guilds.

### *Merchant Guilds*

These guilds first appeared in the 11th century, preceding the craft guilds, and were established to maintain financial soundness when severe competition arose. The guilds also regulated local markets and safeguarded the passage of goods during dangerous times. In time the guilds found wider acceptance, most notably in Germany, England and the Low Countries, and even dominated some city administrations. Because of the political turmoil on aristocratic and imperial levels, these same guilds provided a stable organization in dealing with other countries. The Hanseatic League, which controlled trade among the cities of northern Europe, was established in the 13th century, which in turn gave impetus to the establishment of English guilds, who regarded the Germans as clever rivals.

From the 12th century, as business dealings became more complex, the merchants found it wise to institute various departments, including transportation, supply and security. Continued specialization brought renown to some communities as commercial centers for manufacturing. Flanders, for example, became noted for its wool cloth. Monopolies within a city, the control of prices and tariffs, not only added to the influence of the merchant guilds but provided great political leverage—hence the prominence of such groups in Ghent, Bruges and Florence.

### *Craft Guilds*

The craft guilds were developed sometime during the 12th century, as a result of increased markets for goods, and were entirely separate from the merchant guilds, establishing their own traditions, regulations and leadership. In essence, the craft guilds were divided into three levels of participation: masters, journeyers and apprentices. The masters were skilled artisans who guided their organizations, handling crises and operations. Workshops were controlled by this group. The other members normally began as apprentices, at age 10 or older, and learned their chosen craft over a period of two to seven years. A minimal education was provided, with emphasis on the intended profession. Food, clothing and shelter were made available to apprentices, but a supplementary payment might be given to a master to obtain an apprenticeship in a particularly prestigious craft.

Once apprentices had fulfilled their obligations and term of service, they had to pass rigid tests before receiving the rank of journeyer. They were then able to work for a master for wages or could seek employment elsewhere. The artisan saved as much capital as possible and attempted to produce a masterpiece. In times of economic stability, most journeymen could become masters, acquiring their own businesses and apprentices. If economic conditions worsened, or if the guild decided that there were too many masters, the journeyers were faced with high fees and restrictions. By the 14th century most of them were reduced to the status of employees without hope of progressing further.

Just as the craft guilds were exclusive, so too were the merchant guilds, which became increasingly autocratic in the 13th century, viewing artisans as common. Tensions developed between the guilds in certain regions, as in Italy and Flanders, and the artisans demanded greater political power. Furthermore the guilds faced political opposition in some countries (England, France and Spain), for they were viewed as disruptive elements. The recognition of the legal rights of guilds was slow in coming and depended in many instances on royal favor.

The guilds declined because of economic recession, foreign competition and the lack of expansion. The Black Death of 1348, which annihilated half of Europe's population, decreased their numbers. Higher wages and lower prices became the economic norm and there was a rush to the cities, which made the guilds hesitant to accept members. Merchant guilds, meanwhile, suffered from the rupture of long-distance trade, and some regions were averse to them altogether. Masters were reduced to the role of supervisors over production, and labor-saving devices were accepted reluctantly to prevent the loss of work. Rural industry also endangered the guilds, as people took up weaving and metalworking to increase their incomes. The Ciompi uprising in Florence (1378) and the Peasant Revolt in England (1381) further complicated the situation, reducing the guilds in England and forcing the ones on the Continent to assume lesser status.

Medieval guilds reflected in many ways the contemporary need for social order, differing in their internal composition, effectiveness and scope. Each, however, contributed to the economic and cultural enrichment of their own region. Merchant guilds encouraged the growth of cities, building fortifications, churches, roads and schools, and the craft guilds enhanced them. Debated by scholars as to their actual value, their place in the medieval world and their role in technology, they nevertheless shaped the practices of commerce and industry in the West. See also FEUDALISM; TRADE AND COMMERCE.

**GUILLAUME DE LORRIS** (d. 1278?) French poet and author of the first part of the verse allegory *Roman de la rose,* written sometime between 1225 and 1240. The second section was written by Jean de Meun. See also ROMAN DE LA ROSE.

**GUISCARD, ROBERT** See ROBERT GUISCARD.

**GUNDIMAR** (d. 612) King of the Visigoths only briefly, from 610 to 612. He was elected the successor to Witterich and was acclaimed for his piety as well as for being a defender of Christian orthodoxy. His plans to enter into the civil war gripping the Franks were cut short by his death. See also VISIGOTHS.

**GUNDOBAD** (d. 516) King of Burgundy from 474 to 516. The son of King Gundioc and nephew of the later Roman general *(magister militum)* Ricimer, he served his uncle during his father's reign, achieving mastery over the moribund Western Roman Empire, participating in the siege of Rome, where he personally beheaded the emperor Anthemius. When Ricimer was murdered in 472, Gundobad succeeded him as *magister militum,* taking control of the West and naming Glycerius emperor in 473. Gundioc died in 474, and Gundobad ruled during the final years of the Roman Empire in the West. He was subsequently defeated by Clovis and the Franks, paying them tribute and supporting them in the Battle of Vouille in 507 against the Visigoths. Around 500, he promulgated his notable code of law, the *Lex Gundobada.*

**GUNPOWDER** See WARFARE.

**GUNTHAMUND** (d. 496) King of the Vandals in Africa from 484 to 496, successor and nephew of Hunneric (d. 484). He inherited a kingdom increasingly troubled by the inroads made by the Moors in North Africa. To improve Vandal unity, he ceased persecution of Catholics, relaxing the harsh policies of the traditionally Arian regime, allowing churches to open and bishops to return from exile. These decrees were reversed by Thrasamund, his successor. See also VANDALS.

**GUNTRAM** (d. 592) King of Burgundy and Orléans from 561 to 592, who spent much of his reign opposing the ambitions of his brothers while maintaining power in the divided lands of the Franks. The son of Clotaire I, he inherited Burgundy and Orléans, while his brothers, Charibert, Sigebert I and Chilperic I, divided the rest of the kingdom. In 567 Charibert died, and a conflict over his Paris domain ensued. Guntram seized Saintorge, Perigord, Nantais, Agenais and Augoumois. He then supported one brother against the other, thereby preventing each from achieving success, especially in the dispute between Neustria and Austrasia.

Sigebert was assassinated in 575 or 576, and Guntram was regent for his surviving child, Childebert II, whom he ultimately adopted in order to thwart Chilperic. Both the nephew and brother, however, wanted Guntram's throne and about 583 attempted to claim it. Surviving the plots, Guntram saw Chilperic murdered in 584. Fredegunde, the infamous Neustrian queen, attempted to assassinate Guntram and Childebert, who signed the Treaty of Andelot in 583, ending the conflict. Guntram died in 592, his amicable terms with the church and his attempts to maintain peace earning him the praise of Gregory of Tours and a reputation for being a Christian prince and miracle worker. See also FRANCE; FRANKS.

**GUTENBERG, JOHANN** (c. 1399–1468) German printer, the inventor of the technique of printing from movable type. Born in Mainz, he was called Johannes Gensfleisch zur Laden zu Gutenburg and originally trained as a goldsmith and gem cutter. He left Mainz in 1430, probably escaping the civil strife there caused by the guilds. Moving to Strasbourg, he probably developed there the first models for his printing press, but his work was kept secret. By 1448 he had returned to Mainz, borrowing a large amount of money from a financier, Johann Fust, to complete his experiments and another loan for presses and assistants. The result of his efforts was the extraordinary 42-line (or Mazarine) Bible, completed sometime between 1450 and 1455. He was probably responsible for the second masterwork of early printing, the Mainz Psalter, dated at 1457. None of these bore his name because Fust foreclosed on the loan and sued Gutenberg, and the two men divided the assets, equipment and profits from the partnership. Fust put his name, and that of his son-in-law, Peter Schoeffer, on the books. Gutenberg eventually went blind, receiving from the Elector Adolf of Nassau a small appointment and an allowance.

**GUTHRUM** (d. 890) Ruler of the Danes who led an invasion of England in 865. Arriving with a large Danish army, he launched an attack on the north coast, encountering King Alfred the Great in 868, when the Saxons sent a force to Mercia. Beginning about 871, the Saxon domain of Wessex was also under siege, but Guthrum was unable to prevail. In 878, at the Battle of Edington, the Danes were defeated (but not completely) by the Saxons. Negotiating a peace with Alfred, Guthrum received a Christian baptism, Alfred serving as his godfather. Diplomatic ties with Wessex after 880 were at times strained, especially in 885, but the seizure of London in 886 by Alfred led to a formal treaty and establishment of the Danelaw. Guthrum settled in East Anglia, reigning there from 880. See also DANELAW.

**GUY OF LUSIGNAN** See LUSIGNAN.

**GWYNEDD** Region in northwestern Wales, comprising the counties of Anglesey, Caernarvon and Merioneth. While Gwynedd remained for many years a bastion of Welsh nationalism against the Anglo-Normans, it also produced, from Anglesey, the Tudor dynasty, which ruled England from 1485 to 1603. See also ENGLAND; HENRY VII, KING OF ENGLAND; LLEWELYN AP GRUFFYD; LLEWELYN THE GREAT; OWEN GLENDOWER; WALES.

# H

**HAAKON I HARALDSSON** (c. 920–960) King of Norway from 946 to 960, called "the Good." The son of Harald I Fairhair (c. 860–c. 930), he was sent as a youth to England and was raised at the court of King Athelstan. Following the death of his father, Haakon, then aged 15, sailed home to Norway and with the support of the English deposed his half brother Eric Bloodaxe, who had reigned from about 940 to 945. King Haakon strove to increase his military might, to improve administration and to establish new codes of law. His chief effort, however, was the introduction of Christianity into Norway. Encountering strong opposition from local magnates, he ultimately failed in his attempt. The sons of Eric Bloodaxe, including Harald II Graycloak (c. 960–c. 970), returned to Norway with a Danish force, defeating and slaying Haakon in battle. See also NORWAY.

**HAAKON II SIGURDSSORN** (c. 1147–1162) King of Norway, a usurper who claimed the throne in 1157 but actually ruled only from 1161 to 1162. The illegitimate son of Sigurd III Mouth (ruled 1136–1161), he was elected king in 1157 by opponents of King Ingi Haraldsson, the Hunchback (1136–1161). Described as cheerful and well loved by the poet and historian Snorri Sturluson, Haakon waged war against Ingi until 1161, when Ingi fell in battle. After less than a year, however, Magnus V Erlingsson's father, Erling Wrunech, led a revolt in his name, killing Haakon with the support of the Danes. See also NORWAY.

**HAAKON III** (d. 1204) King of Norway from 1202 to 1204, the son of King Sverre (1184–1202), chosen to be sole ruler. He adopted a conciliatory policy toward the church and his magnates. After his sudden death, his successor was Ingi II Bardsson (1204–1217).

**HAAKON IV** (1204–1263) King of Norway from 1217 to 1263 and called Haakonsson the Old. He is celebrated as one of the great kings of Norway, ruling in Norway's golden age. The illegitimate son of Haakon III (d. 1204), he was raised at the court of Ingi Bardsson (ruled 1204–1217) and on his death came to the throne. His mother is reported to have endured an ordeal of hot irons to prove his legitimacy.

Much of his reign was spent suppressing revolts, including an attempt by a usurper, his half brother Skuli Baardsson, to overthrow him. He took a decisive step in 1247 when he had a papal legate crown him king. Through his negotiations Greenland and Iceland became part of the Norwegian empire (1261–1264), and trade was promoted with England and Lūbeck. Legal reforms were enacted to curb unrest, to restore civil order and to define the position of the church in Norway. His enlightened court was the meeting place of poets and artists, including the acclaimed poet and historian Snorri Sturluson (1178–1241), who wrote Haakon's biography. The king's last act was to press his claim to the Hebrides against the Scots, dying in the Orkneys after fighting several inconclusive campaigns. See also NORWAY.

**HAAKON V** (1270–1319) King of Norway from 1299 to 1319, succeeding his brother, Eric II Priesthater (d. 1299), and reversing the royal policy of favoritism toward the powerful Norwegian magnates. Haakon reduced the influence of the nobles, and in 1308 he abolished the rank of baron altogether. His determination to formulate a policy against England led to curtailment of trade with that country, abandonment of Norway's western colonies and encouragement of German merchants of the Hanseatic League. He was succeeded by his grandson, Magnus VII (1319–1355). See also NORWAY.

**HAAKON VI** (1340–1380) King of Norway from 1355 to 1380, who laid the groundwork for the Kalmar Union of 1397 through political alliances and marriages. The union brought together Norway, Denmark and Sweden. The son of Magnus VII (1319–1355) and great-grandson of Haakon V (1299–1319), he joined his father in suppressing an uprising of Swedish nobles, led by his brother, Eric, receiving as a reward the joint rule of Sweden in 1362. Prior to that he had been named the heir only in Norway. Two years later both he and his father were defeated and captured by the Swedes, and Haakon was unable to rescue him until 1371. In 1363, however, he had married Margaret, the daughter of King Waldemar IV Atterdag of Denmark (1340–1375), and in 1375 his son Olaf became king of the Danes. Haakon also concluded a treaty of trade with the Hanseatic League in 1376. On his death Olaf also became king of Norway. See also KALMAR UNION; NORWAY.

**HABSBURG** Also Hapsburg, the ruling house of Austria that emerged as one of the most powerful dynasties in Europe. The line was established in Switzerland in the 10th century, its name derived from the castle of Habichtsburg (Habsburg), now in ruins at Aargau. By the 13th century the dynasty held most of Upper Alsace, Switzerland and Baden, true political ascendancy coming in 1273 when

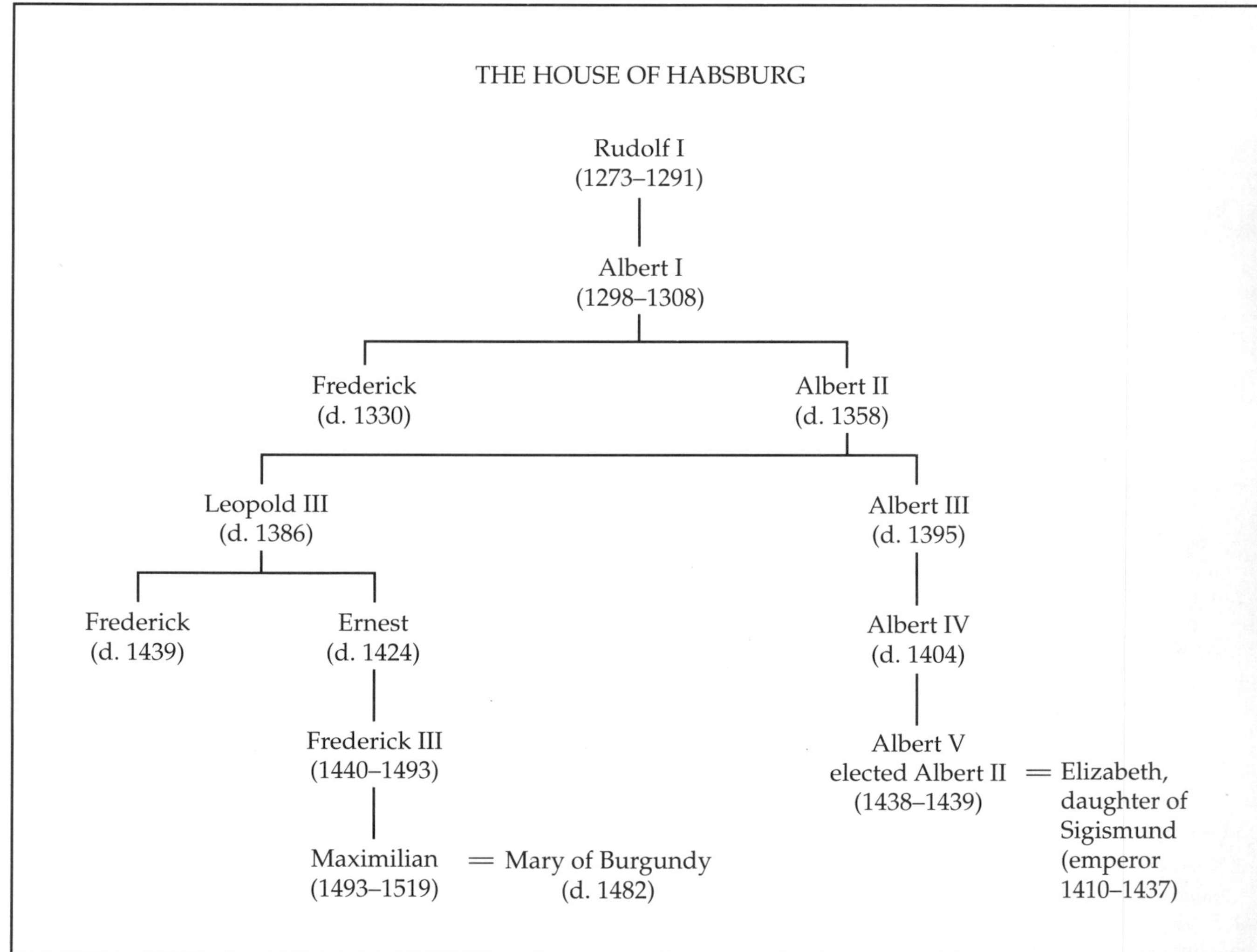


Count Rudolf IV was elected German king as Rudolf I (1273–1291), thereby bringing an end to the interregnum. He seized Styria, Carinthia and Carniola, declaring in 1282 these possessions to be hereditary. Switzerland was lost, but Tyrol was acquired in 1363. Rudolf's son, Albert I of Habsburg (1298–1308), ruled until his murder in 1378, initiating a period of Habsburg absence from the throne of the Holy Roman Empire. The year 1438, however, saw the election of Albert II of Habsburg and the vesting of the imperial office in the family. Maximilian I (ruled 1453–1519) was largely responsible for the establishment of the Habsburgs as a world power. See also HOLY ROMAN EMPIRE.

**AL-HADI** Fourth caliph of the Abbasids, reigning from 785 to 786. During his reign a Meccan revolt against his persecution of the Shiite sect of the Alids took place. His successor was not his son, as he wished, but Harun al-Rashid (786–809). See also ABBASID CALIPHATE.

**HADRIAN THE AFRICAN** (d. 709) Monk, abbot and teaching missionary in England. A member of a monastery in Naples, having been born in Africa but educated in Europe, he was offered the See of Canterbury but refused it. In 668, however, he set out for England, becoming abbot of the monastery of Saints Peter and Paul. He spent the rest of his life establishing schools and Romanizing the English church. See also CANTERBURY.

**HAFIZ** (c. 1325–c. 1390) One of the celebrated Persian lyric poets, whose full name was Shams al-Din Muhammad, Hafiz being a surname taken by one who had memorized the Koran. A dedicated Sufi who lectured on the Koran, he spent his entire life in Shiraz. His poetry reflects his own era, its constant wars, the occupation of his city and the rise and fall of its leaders. Throughout his life he sought God, and this gave a certain mystical dimension to his verse. According to tradition, he met Tamerlane in 1387.

**HAGIA SOPHIA** The extraordinary domed basilica in Constantinople, considered the supreme example of Byzantine architecture. The Hagia Sophia (or Sancta Sophia) was first constructed by Emperor Constantius II in 360. After it was destroyed by fire, a new church was erected in 415 by Theodosius II, but it too fell to ruin during the Nika Revolt of 532. Emperor Justinian I (527–565) thus decided to erect a fireproof edifice. The result was a masterpiece of design, following plans by the imperial architects, Anthemius of Tralles and Isidorus of Miletus. Work continued from 532 to 537. The dome in the nave, when completed, was 184 feet high and 102 feet in diameter, the interior decorated in magnificent polychrome marble and gold mosaic. After the fall of the city in 1453, the Ottoman Turks transformed Hagia Sophia into a mosque, placing four slender minarets at its corners. See also ART AND ARCHITECTURE, BYZANTINE; CONSTANTINOPLE.

**HAGON MAGNUSSON, KING OF SWEDEN** See HAAKON VI.

**HAGUE, THE** Known in the Dutch as 'S Gravenhage or Den Haag, a city in southern Holland near the North Sea. The Hague (derived from a woodland region, the *Haghe*, or hedge) was established originally as a hunting lodge for the counts of Holland. In 1248, Count William II constructed a castle there, later the Binnenhof. Around the castle and palace emerged a small community serving the count, growing considerably over the next years and acquiring set boundaries in 1370. A prosperous wool trade developed, controlled by the dukes of Burgundy from 1436.

**HAI BEN SHERIRA** (939–1038) *Gaon*, or overseer, of the celebrated Talmudic academy the Pumbedita (Babylonia), in Baghdad. The son of Sherira ben Hanina, Hai was an assistant to his father until 998, when he was appointed *gaon*. A moderate in rational and fundamental Jewish thought, he was the author of nearly 1,000 *responsa*, receiving questions from all over the Jewish world and replying in a variety of languages. His own *responsa* equalled those written by all other *gaonim*. The academy reached the zenith of its fame and influence under his aegis. See also JEWS AND JUDAISM.

**HAINAUT** Region in southwestern Belgium, also called Hainault or Henegouwen. It was first established (c. 843) as a countship under Reginar I, who held it in fief to Lotharingia. It was united with, and then separated from, Flanders throughout the 11th and 12th centuries. In 1191 the counts of Hainaut acquired Flanders through marriage. Baldwin VI (as Baldwin IX, count of Flanders) became the ruler of the Latin Empire of Constantinople in 1204. His great-grandsons, Guy of Dampierre and John of Hainaut (or Avesnes), separated Flanders from Hainaut respectively, John becoming count of Holland in 1299. In 1433 Hainaut was acquired by the House of Burgundy and in 1482 by the House of Habsburg.

**AL-HAKAM I** (d. 822) Umayyad emir of Córdoba who survived a turbulent reign from 796 to 822. The son of Hisham I (788–796), al-Hakam was beset from the start by revolts and conspiracies, suppressing them with brutal force and, at times, excessive cruelty. An uprising in Toledo in 792 in opposition to crushing taxes resulted in the massacre of hundreds, perhaps thousands. In Córdoba itself a cabal formed to depose him but was crushed, with more than 70 members crucified. In response, a large section of the populace of the city rioted in 818. Al-Hakam died in 822, succeeded by Abd al-Rahman II (822–852). He was noted for having been the first emir to recruit a force of mercenaries, composed of Sudanese, Berbers and Christians from Galicia and France. See also CORDOBA, EMIRATE OF.

**AL-HAKAM II** (d. 976) Spanish Umayyad and caliph of Córdoba, the son of and worthy successor to the great Abd al-Rahman III (912–961), reigning from 961 to 976. Also called Mustansir Hakam II, he inherited the caliphate at the height of its glory, proving himself a gifted diplomat, especially regarding Christian Spain. When King Sancho I of León repudiated his alliance with Córdoba, an army was sent north, ravaging León, Castile and Navarre. Al-Hakam also extended Córdoban influence into Morocco. An extremely learned man and patron of the arts, he was succeeded by his son Hisham II (976–1009; 1010–1013), but the golden age of the Umayyads in Spain died with Hakam. See also CORDOBA, EMIRATE OF.

**AL-HAKIM** (985–1021) Sixth Fatimid caliph, whose reign (996–1021) was erratic and ended strangely. Abu Ali al-Mansur al-Hakim was the successor of al-Aziz in 996 and was able to enforce his will, despite his youth, through the Berber troops at his disposal. Erratic and given to harsh purges and persecutions against Jews and Christians as well as against the Sunni Muslims, he also allowed periods of tolerance. A peace was signed with the Byzantine Empire in 1001 but was nullified by his attack on the Church of the Holy Sepulchre in 1009. He relieved famines with food distributions but then sacked the city of al-Fustat near Cairo. Dogs were also eliminated because of his personal dislike of them. Around 1017, he gave his blessing to a number of Ismaili (Shiite) missionaries, instructing them to proclaim him a divine incarnation, an demand that brought charges of insanity by the Sunni Muslims. Hakim disappeared on the night of February 13, 1021, and was presumed murdered. According to the Druses, he went into hiding to await his triumphant return in 1,000 years. See also DRUZES; FATIMID CALIPHATE.

**HALEVI, JUDAH** See JUDAH HALEVI.

**HALLE** City in east-central Germany, situated on the right bank of the Saale River to the northwest of Leipzig. Halle was first mentioned in 806, when it was referred to as a fortress. It was important because of the local salt mines. In 968 both Halle and its salt were given by Emperor Otto I (961–973) to the recently established archbishopric of Magdeburg, receiving a charter from Otto II (973–983) in 981. Chronic social strife was caused in the city by the legal separation of the German settlers from the Halloren, but both sides were united in their opposition to the archbishops. From 1281 until 1478, Halle was a member of the Hanseatic League, ending that affiliation in 1478 when the archbishop's army seized it. See also MAGDEBURG.

**HALSTEN** King of Sweden with his brother Inge, from about 1066 to 1080. He was the son of King Stenkil (1060–1066) and thus of the Stenkil dynasty (c. 1060–c. 1122). See also SWEDEN.

**AL-HAMADANI** (968–1008) Arabic poet of Persia and later Afghanistan, his full name Abu al-Fadl Ahmad ibn al-Husayn al-Hamadani, called also Badi a-Zaman, "Wonder of the Age." Considered the originator of the *maqama (maqamah),* a compositional form uniting prose and poetry in the presentation of a short story or tale, he wrote some 400 of these, of which 52 are extant.

**HAMBURG** A major city situated on the Elbe River near the entrance to the North Sea. The Free and Hanseatic City (Freie und Hansestadt) of Hamburg was founded around 825 with the construction of Hammaburg, a castle designed to protect the region from attacks by the Slavs. A church was erected there in 811, and in 834 Emperor Louis the Pious established an archdiocese, with the celebrated missionary Ansgar making the city the place from which to plan the conversion of Scandinavia. The Vikings attacked nine times in three centuries, but Hamburg emerged from this period as a stable and prosperous trading site. The strategic placement of Lübeck, situated on the Baltic Sea, encouraged its development. In 1189 Frederick Barbarossa granted Hamburg a special charter with trading privileges, alleviation of tolls and other rights. The profitable alliance with Lübeck led to Hamburg's major role in the establishment of the Hanse, or the Hanseatic League. As league members, the traders of Hamburg supplied goods from northern and eastern Europe, acquiring enough power to survive the decline of the league in the 15th century and surpassing Lübeck in stature in the mid-16th century. See also HANSEATIC LEAGUE; TRADE AND COMMERCE.

**HAMDANIDS** Arab dynasty of Muslims ruling much of Iraq and Syria from 905 to 1004. The first Hamdanid was a local potentate of al-Jazirah, Hamdan ibn Hamdum, whose sons established the line as an important political element during Abbasid rule. The dynasty, having a powerful position at Mosul, declared its independence from the Abbasids and governed as far as Syria. One of the great Hamdanids was Sayf ad-Dawla (ruled c. 943–967), who captured Aleppo and Homs and made war against the Byzantines. The dynasty, however, could not maintain its position against the threat of the Byzantine Empire and the Fatimids of Egypt. It was reduced to vassal status during Fatimid suzerainty.

**HANS I, KING OF DENMARK, NORWAY AND SWEDEN** See JOHN I, KING OF DENMARK, NORWAY AND SWEDEN.

**HANSEATIC LEAGUE** A mercantile union of German and northern European towns and merchants established to defend mutual trading rights, to advance commerce and to protect against piracy. The league (*Hanse* or *Hansa,* a group or association) reached its zenith during the 14th century, but from the 12th to the 16th century it held considerable prestige in northern Europe, encouraging the development of the major German cities. Originally a *hanse* was a group of traders who traveled to other countries, and the rise of these groups was made possible by the resurgence of the German river trade (chiefly in Cologne, Munster and Dortmund) along the Rhine and by Germanic expansion into the east, especially the Baltic region. Trading posts were established at Wisby (Gotland), Novgorod, Bergen and London. The chartering of Lübeck (founded 1143) in 1226 further strengthened the league, as did the grant of a charter to Hamburg in 1266–1267.

The most important of the league's alliances was between Lübeck and Hamburg, signed in 1241. In 1256 the Wendish towns of Lübeck, Stralsund, Rostock and Wiemer held the first recorded meeting, and out of it Lübeck emerged as the league's principal city, with most of the other towns acknowledging the Code of Lübeck. The league functioned as a safeguard against conditions caused by the absence of a stabilized government in Germany, but the name was not used until 1344, and the league remained a loose confederation. The meetings, the *Hansetage,* usually summoned by Lübeck, were never regular, and there was no treasury, no established naval support and no flag. Economic growth was the primary goal, although navigational techniques were also improved and pirates were ruthlessly pursued.

Beginning in 1340, King Waldemar IV of Denmark (1340–1375) embarked to break the league's position in his kingdom, taking Wisby in 1361 and defeating the German fleets at Helsinborg in 1362. Forced to sign the Treaty of Wordingborg in 1365, the league lost its monopoly on Danish trade and vowed revenge. Gathering allies within Germany and Scandinavia, it launched a war against Waldemar and triumphed in 1370, compelling the Danish king to sign the Treaty of Stralsund, which granted the Germans virtual mastery over Danish affairs and vast trading rights. As a result there were soon more than 100 members, and through boycotts, embargoes, tariffs or wars the waters of northern Europe were in their control. In foreign lands, such as England, Flanders and Russia, the league firms *(kontors)* found their way into the economies, holding privileges in England that would endure well into the 16th century.

Decline came about in the 15th century because of the league's internal problems and competition. Resentment flared in other countries, new trade routes were discovered and nations such as Lithuania, Russia (the Grand Duchy of Moscow), Poland and the Kalmar Union threatened the league. Town members also became independent, and rivalries and jealousies raged the German princes also began to take control of their regions. By the 17th century the Hanseatic League was barely in existence; the last meeting was held in 1669. See also TRADE AND COMMERCE and individual cities.

**HAPSBURG** See HABSBURG DYNASTY

**HARALD I, KING OF NORWAY** (d. c. 940?) Ruler from about 900 to about 940, called "the Fairhair" (in Norwegian, *Haarfager*). His rule is thought to have been the first to extend throughout Norway, although realistically he probably did not actually control it all. The successor to Halvdan the Black, Harald became chief of the powerful Ynglinga dynasty while still a youth. Sometime around 872 he won the decisive Battle of the Hafrsfjord, defeating rivals to become master of western Norway. He established a vast administrative system, which included heavy taxation, ruling for many years and extending Norwegian influence into Orkney and Shetland. Among his sons were Haakon I the Good (945–c. 960) and Eric Bloodaxe (c. 940–945). An major result of his reign was the departure of large elements of the population from the region, many of whom settled in Iceland or sailed to other countries to escape his government. These migrations profoundly affected the history of Europe. Harald I's life was recorded by Icelandic and Norwegian chroniclers. See also NORWAY; VIKINGS.

**HARALD II, KING OF NORWAY** (d. c. 970) Ruler from about 960 to 970, called Harald Graycloak or Graypelt, the son of Eric Bloodaxe (c. 940–945). Eric Bloodaxe (d. 954) was deposed by his half brother Haakon I (945–960), and Harald and his brothers fled the country. With the support of his uncle, Harald Bluetooth of Denmark (c. 935–985), he launched expeditions against Haakon, eventually killing him in 961. Although an ardent Christian, Harald ruled oppressively, murdering any nobles who opposed him and banning paganism. He was killed in a battle against Haakon Sigurdsson of Lade (c. 970–995), his successor, who was supported by the Danish. See also NORWAY.

**HARALD III SIGURDSSON, KING OF NORWAY** (c. 1015–1066) Ruler from 1046 to 1066 and one of the most feared warriors of the age. Called Hardraade, or "Hard-counsel," he was the last of the Viking adventurers. The son of Sigurd, a minor king of eastern Norway and Estrid, and half brother of King Olaf II (Saint Olaf), with whom he fought against the Danes at the Battle of Stiklestad in 1030, he was injured in that campaign, which cost Olaf his life. Harald escaped to Russia, entering the service of Yaroslav I the Wise, grand prince of Kiev, marrying his daughter Elizabeth. He then joined the Varangian Guard of the Byzantines in Constantinople and fought in Sicily and in Bulgaria.

In 1045 he returned home, at first sharing the throne with his nephew, Magnus I the Good (1035–1047), but reigning alone after Magnus's death in 1047. He alienated his nobles and drove his armies into wars of expansion against Denmark, Orkney, Shetland and the Hebrides. Finally he attacked England in 1066. This last campaign was organized with the support of Tostig, an English earl, and was initially successful. At the Battle of Stamford Bridge against Harold II Godwinson and his Saxon army, on September 25, he was killed, and his troops were routed from the field. See also NORMAN CONQUEST; NORWAY.

**HARALD IV MAGNUSSON (GILCHRIST), KING OF NORWAY** (d. 1136) Ruler from 1130 to 1136, whose claims to the throne precipitated a civil war. Born in Ireland, he sailed to Norway about 1128, claiming to be the son of King Magnus III Bareleg (ruled 1093–1103), walking over hot irons to prove himself. King Sigurd I Magnusson Jerusalemfarer (ruled 1103–1130) accepted him, giving his oath not to demand the throne while Sigurd or his son, Magnus (IV), lived. When Sigurd died in 1130, Harald repudiated his oath, and by 1134 the land was rent by civil war. Defeated, Harald returned from exile in Denmark in 1135, captured Magnus and blinded him, ruling alone for less than a year before being murdered. See also NORWAY.

**HARALD BLUETOOTH, KING OF DENMARK** (d. c. 987) Ruler of the Danes from about 935 to 985, uniting the country and conquering parts of Germany and Norway. The son of Gorm the Old (d. c. 940), Harald was in turn defeated by Emperor Otto II (973–983) and compelled to recognize the suzerainty of Otto in accepting Christianity. As a result Christianity was introduced into Denmark. Harald's son, Sven I Forkbeard (985–1014), and his grandson, Canute the Great (1018–1035), continued his policy of Norwegian involvement. See also DENMARK.

**HARALD III HEN, KING OF DENMARK** (d. 1080) Ruler from 1074 to 1080, one of the five sons of Sven II Estridson (d. 1074) who were to follow their father to the Danish throne. Harald had difficulty in accepting the role of the church in Denmark and in governing his people. See also DENMARK.

**HARDECANUTE** (1018–1042) King of Denmark from 1035 to 1042 and king of England from 1040 to 1042. Hardecanute was the son of Canute the Great (1018–1035) and Emma, daughter of the duke of Normandy. Named by his father as the ruler of Denmark, he was the immediate claimant to the English throne, following the death of his father in 1035, but his mother and the earl of Wessex, Godwin, failed to arrange his appointment. Canute's illegitimate son, Harald Harefoot, was made regent. Hardecanute assumed the throne on Harald's death, but his two years of rule were violent, with sporadic episodes of murder and massacres. See also ENGLAND.

**HARDING, STEPHEN** See STEPHEN HARDING.

**AL-HARIRI** (1054–1122) Arabic prose writer and scholar, called Abu Muhammad al-Qasim ibn ali al-Hariri. A native of Basra, he won literary acclaim for his collection of tales, the *Maqamat,* written in the *maqama (maqamah)* style developed by al-Hamadani. The *Maqamat* related the tale of Abu Zaid, a wily, charming thief, and the quality of its prose was virtually unequaled in Arabic literature. Al-Hariri also wrote poems and a treatise on grammar.

**HARLECH CASTLE** A fortification on Cardigan Bay in the region of Gwynedd, in northern Wales, constructed after 1283 by King Edward I, following his victory over the Welsh leader Llewelyn ap Gruffydd. Harlech was the goal of a Welsh attack by Owen Glendower (c. 1404), who held the independent Welsh parliament there. During the Wars of the Roses (1455–1485), it was the last Lancastrian castle to surrender to the Yorkists in 1468, and its stout defenses were commemorated in the battle song "Men of Harlech." See also WALES.

**HAROLD I HAREFOOT, KING OF ENGLAND** (d. 1040) Anglo-Saxon ruler from 1035 to 1040, the illegitimate son of Canute the Great (king of England, 1014–1035) and regent of England on his father's death. He was supported by Earl Leofric of Mercia and the city of London, and his success was also due to his half brother, Hardecanute, being unable to come from Denmark to press his own claim. After murdering the son of King Aethelred II the Unready (ruled 979–1016), Alfred Aetheling, in 1036, Harold seized the throne and banished Hardecanute's mother, Emma. When he died, Hardecanute became king (1040–1042). See also ENGLAND.

**HAROLD II GODWINSON, KING OF ENGLAND** (1020–1066) The last Anglo-Saxon ruler of England, dying at the Battle of Hastings after reigning less than a year. The son of Godwin, earl of Wessex and Kent, he was made earl of Anglia in 1044 and then was banished with his family by King Edward the Confessor (ruled 1042–1066). In 1052 Harold led a return to England, and Godwin compelled the king to restore the family to its former prominence. When Godwin died in 1053, Harold inherited his titles and his former prestige. He elevated his relatives and strove to suppress a revolt in Mercia, giving to the Mercians the holdings of his brother, Tostig.

Edward died on January 5, 1066, and Harold took the crown. William, duke of Normany, however, proclaimed himself the true heir, and Harald III Sigurdsson (1046–1066), in a plot with Tostig, invaded with his Norse armies. Harold was able to defeat the Norwegians at Stamford Bridge but then confronted William's army. On October 14 he engaged William at Hastings, losing the battle and his life. The vitality of Saxon England died with him. Depictions of events during his reign were woven into the Bayeux Tapestry. See also NORMAN CONQUEST.

**HARTHACANUTE** See HARDECANUTE.

**HARTMANN VON AUE** (c. 1170–c. 1220) Epic poet in Middle High German noted for his contributions to the Arthurian romances. From Swabia, he wrote the chivalric epics *Erek* and *Yvain;* a religious work, *Gregorius,* and the poem *Der arme Heinrich,* which appears in Longfellow's *Golden Legend.*

**HARUN AL-RASHID** (c. 766–809) Fifth Abbasid caliph, whose reign (786–809) was immortalized in *The Thousand and One Nights* and is thought to be the zenith of Islamic wealth and brilliance. Harun was a son of the caliph al-Mahdi (ruled 775–785) and a former slave girl, al-Khayzwan. Well educated, he was tutored by Yahya ibn Khalid of the Barmakid family.

In 779–780, and again in 781–782, he was nominal commander of the forces against the Byzantine Empire, reaching the Bosporus and exacting favorable terms from the Byzantines. Henceforth known also as al-Rashid, the "Follower of the Right Path," he was appointed governor over a number of Syrian and Egyptian provinces. When his father died, his brother, Musa al-Hadi, came to the throne (785). He survived only a year, dying under mysterious circumstances. Harun was now caliph of the vast Abbasid state that reached from Africa to India. In order to maintain control, he appointed a governor of Ifriqiyah (Islamic Africa) in 800, Ibrahim ibn al-Aghlab, who paid tribute but was allowed virtual independence. This was followed by further decentralization, but at his death the Abbasids were strong enough again to attack the Byzantines. In 806 he captured Heraclea and Tyana and in 805 and 807 Cyprus and Rhodes. Peace was made with Emperor Nicephorus, and the caliph was awarded additional power.

The opulent lifestyle at Baghdad was maintained in palaces and courts of vast wealth, and *The Thousand and One Nights* and other tales describe the lavish presents, entertainments and grandeur enjoyed by Harun and his attendants. A patron of the arts, Harun encouraged philosophers, artists and scientists who advanced Islamic learning. Harun himself was a complex blend of majesty and political cunning. He allowed Yahya and the Barmakids to maintain their influence but then executed Yahya's son, Ja'far, in 803, confiscating the family's holdings.

Harun drank heavily, had many wives and allowed graven images in his palace, all of which outraged the Muslim hierarchy of his time. He undertook 10 pilgrimages, however, and practiced the Islamic codes on charity. Jalaludin described him as eloquent, fair, tall, handsome and captivating in appearance. Harun al-Rashid fell ill while suppressing a rebellion in Khorasan, dying at Tus on March 24, 809. He condemned the caliphate to civil war and ruin by dividing the holdings among his sons. See also ABBASID CALIPHATE.

**HASAN IBN SABBAH** (d. 1124) The feared founder of the Order of Assassins and the leader of the Islamic sect the Nizari Ismaili. His life was veiled in mystery, with most available information detailed in a work called *Barguzasht-i-sayyidna (Adventures of Our Master),* found in the vast collection of books at Alamut, the Assassin capital, by the conquering Mongols of Hulagu and referred to by the writer Ata-Malik Juvaini. According to tradition he was born in the city of Ray, a descendant of the Himyar tribe. His education was very sound; he was reportedly a fellow student of Omar Khayyam and the grand vizier Nizam al-Mulk. The spokesman for the Nizari Ismailite adherents in Ray, he was sent to Cairo (c. 1078–1079) to establish contact with their imam. There he involved himself in intrigue and was arrested by the *amir* Badr al-Jamali and sent aboard a slave ship. When the vessel sought safety from a storm by entering a Christian port, he escaped, wandering into Syria and Iran, attracting converts to his cause.

In 1090, with the support of his followers, Hasan captured the impregnable fortress of Alamut in Daylam, making it the headquarters for his Order of Assassins. Sending his servants, the *dais,* throughout much of Islam, he seized castles, amassed armies of assassins and then launched a war of terror. Among the political figures murdered at his command were Nizam al-Mulk; Maudud, prince of Mosul; Ab el Muzafar Ali, vizier of Sanjar, son of Malik-Shah; Kasim Aksonkar, prince of Mosul; and Ahmed and Fahkr al-Mulk, sons of Nizam. The retribution of the Seljuk Turks was terrible—they slaughtered Ismailis throughout the empire. In 1118 Muhammad, ruler of Syria and Persia, sought a program against the order, and Alamut was saved from destruction only by Muhammad's death. After 1118 Alamut and Hasan were left in peace, and he spent his days in retreat. He executed both his sons and was forced to choose his trusted lieutenant, Kiya Buzurg-Ummid, chief of the Assassin stronghold of Lamassar, as his heir. He died on May 23, 1124. See also ASSASSINS, ORDER OF.

**HASTINGS, BATTLE OF** A decisive engagement fought on October 14, 1066, resulting in the defeat of King Harold II of England (1066) and its conquest by William (I) the Conqueror and the Normans. William, the duke of Normandy, claimed the English throne by asserting that he had been named heir by the childless King Edward the Confessor (1042–1066). On the king's deathbed, however, Harold had been appointed heir. He was crowned the day after Edward's death (January 5, 1066). Harold confronted Harald Sigurdsson of Norway, who landed in England on September 20. At the Battle of Stamford Bridge he defeated Sigurdsson, only to learn that the Normans, with some 5,000 men, had arrived. Harold had 7,000 men and went on to meet him at Hastings.

Without cavalry or archers, Harold took up defensive positions on Senlac Hill, surrounding his banner with his best troops and using the less-experienced units on his flank. The battle, one of the hardest fought during the Middle Ages, saw William's archers and cavalry taking their toll, incurring casualties as well because of the English shield wall and the heavy battle axes used with skill. The turning point, however, came when the English were lured from their wall of shields by a feigned Norman retreat and were cut down. William repeated this maneuver and it succeeded again. The English were then reduced by attrition and exhaustion, and two of Harold's brothers died in the fray. The English king was slain by an arrow in the late afternoon. Refusing to yield, the English fought on but were broken by the relentless Norman pressure, finally fleeing the field. Victorious, William marched north to London, where he was crowned king on Christmas Day. See also BAYEUX TAPESTRY; ENGLAND; NORMANS; ODO OF BAYEUX.

**HATTIN, BATTLE OF** A decisive engagement fought on July 4, 1187, between the Crusaders under Guy of Lusignan, king of Jerusalem, and a Muslim army led by Saladin that resulted in the nearly total destruction of the Christian army. In June 1187, Saladin launched a jihad, or holy war, against the Crusader States in the Holy Land, besieging the city of Tiberias with an army of between 18,000 and 20,000 men. Guy responded by raising an army of comparable size but chose to ignore the advice of the far more competent Count Raymond of Tripoli and went in haste to do battle. Drawn into an arid plain near the town of Hattin, the Crusaders found themselves without water and surrounded by the advantageously placed Muslims. Saladin waited until the thirsty enemy made an attempt to reach water, prevented them from approaching the nearby lake and then counterattacked, annihilating most of Guy's troops. The king was captured, later released after pledging to make no more war on Islam. Saladin was thus able to initiate his campaign to recapture Jerusalem, taking the Crusader States of Jerusalem, Antioch and Tripoli and causing Europe to mount the Third Crusade. See also CRUSADES.

**HATTO I** (d. 913) Archbishop of Mainz, abbot of Reichenau and a politically powerful figure in the affairs of the eastern territory of the Frankish Carolingian empire. He was an adviser to King Arnulf and tutor to the heir, Louis the Child (d. 911), serving also as guardian and regent with Adelbero of Augsburg. He later arranged the election of Conrad, duke of Franconia, as king of the East Franks. Attacked by chroniclers as harsh and cruel, he was reportedly killed by lightning. See also MAINZ.

**HATTO II** (d. c. 970) Archbishop of Mainz, reportedly eaten alive by mice as a punishment for slaughtering starving peasants who had stolen grain. His name is associated with the Mauseturm, or Mouse Tower, on an island in the Rhine River. See also MAINZ.

**HAUTEVILLE, DROGO DE** (d. 1051) Count of Apulia, a leader of the Normans in southern Italy and a member of the renowned family that produced Robert Guiscard and Bohemond, prince of Antioch. Brother of William de Hauteville, called Iron Arm, he accompanied another brother, Humphrey, to Italy in 1035. He fought the Saracens in Sicily and for the Lombards against the Byzantines and then (in 1046) succeeded William as count of Apulia. Emperor Henry III (1039–1056) confirmed his title. Drogo was assassinated by a group of conspirators against the Normans in 1051 while attending Mass. See also NORMANS.

**HAUTEVILLE, HUMPHREY DE** (d. 1057) Count of Apulia, a Norman leader in southern Italy and brother of William and Drogo. He traveled to Italy with Drogo about 1035 and became count of Lavello in 1045 and count of Apulia in 1051. Marrying the sister of the Lombard prince, Gaimar V of Salerno, he aided his wife's family against a faction supporting the Byzantines and achieved a Norman victory over Pope Leo IX at the Battle of Civitate in 1053. His successor was the formidable Robert Guiscard. See also NORMANS.

**HAUTEVILLE, WILLIAM DE** (d. 1046) Called Iron Arm, the count of Apulia, and one of the architects of Norman power in southern Italy. Arriving in Italy about 1035 with his brothers, Humphrey and Drogo, he distinguished himself at the siege of Syracuse in Sicily against the Saracens, earning his nickname after leading a charge against the city's emir and killing him. In 1042 he became the count of Apulia, having commanded the Norman forces that joined in the conquest of the region with the Lombards. Drogo succeeded him. See also NORMANS.

**HAWKWOOD, JOHN** (c. 1320–1394) One of the notable mercenary captains (condottiere) in Italy, who spent some 30 years fighting for Italian cities. Born in Essex in England, he served in the armies of Edward the Black Prince and King Edward III of England (1327–1377) during the Hundred Years' War, possibly receiving a knighthood. About 1363 he joined a group of English mercenaries known as the White Company, and as a servant of Pisa he was named captain general of the city in 1364, subsequently serving the pope and the cities of Milan and Florence. He was made Florentine captain general in 1378. In 1382 he bought land near Florence and was awarded honorary citizenship for life. Dying in preparation for a return to England, he was honored with a magnificent funeral by the Florentines and then buried in Essex. He was one of the most brilliant military tacticians of his age. See also WARFARE.

**HAYMO OF FAVERSHAM** (d. 1244) English Franciscan friar and theologian, a native of Kent. He entered the Franciscan order in 1224 and taught for a time at Oxford. He was a participant in the general chapter of the order in Rome in 1237 when Elias of Cortina was deposed. He was then named provincial of England and the following year elected general. At the request of Pope Innocent IV (1243–1244) he helped revise the ordinals of the Missal, the Breviary and prayers. He had also been sent to Constantinople in 1233 to effect a union of the Eastern and Western Churches. See also FRANCISCANS.

**HEGIRA** In the Arabic *Hijrah* (meaning "immigration"), the flight of Muhammad from Mecca to Medina to escape persecution. The date of this event has been placed at 622, and it is the start of the Islamic calendar, as decreed by the second caliph, Omar, in 639. The system of dating is currently represented by the initials AH, Anno Hegirae in Latin.

**HEINRICH** For rulers of this name, see HENRY.

**HEINRICH VON MEISSEN** (c. 1260–1318) Poet in late Middle High German, a troubadour and a founder of the first Meistersinger school. Called popularly Frauenlob ("In praise of Ladies"), he came originally from Meissen. He demonstrated considerable talent at an early age and began to travel as a minstrel. After spending time in Prague he settled in Mainz and (c. 1311) established a guild for singers, the origin of the Meistersingers in the 15th century. A brilliant composer of moral and didactic verse, he was the author of "Marienleich" ("Mary's Song") a sophisticated poem in praise of the Virgin. See also MEISTERSINGER.

**HEJIRA** See HEGIRA.

**HELIAND** Ninth-century Old Saxon epic poem in alliterative verse, written by an unknown Saxon of the period. It was probably an attempt to make the figure of Christ more appealing to the Saxons, providing Christ with Germanic origins and his Apostles described as warriors who were rewarded by their king. Some 6,000 lines long, the poem was, with a fragmentary *Genesis,* the only surviving example of Old Saxon poetry. See also SAXONS.

**HÉLOISE** (d. 1164) Wife of Peter Abelard, abbess and, like her husband, one of the tragic romantic figures in the Middle Ages. The niece of Fulbert, canon of Notre Dame, she was entrusted to Abelard for her education, commencing a romantic involvement and eventually marrying him in secret and bearing a son. Abelard was castrated by her outraged uncle and retired to the monastery of Saint-Denis. Héloise became a nun at Argenteuil and later abbess of the Paraclete (Le Paraclet) near Troyes, a convent established by Abelard. The two were buried beside each other at the Paraclete but were moved in the 1800s to Père-Lachaise cemetery in Paris. See also ABELARD, PETER.

**HELVETIA** See SWITZERLAND.

**HENGIST AND HORSA** Two legendary brothers of the mid-fifth century who were the leaders of the first successful Anglo-Saxon settlers in England. According to tradition they were invited to the isles by the British king Vortigern, to support him in his war against the Picts, sometime around 450. Hengist and Horsa established their people in Kent and within a few years were at war with Vortigern. In 455 they battled with the Britons at Agaelesthrep (perhaps Aylesford). Horsa was killed there, but two years later Hengist and his son, Aesc, defeated their enemy and claimed Kent as their own. Wars continued, the last occurring in 473. Hengist presumably died in 488, for Aesc was mentioned in the *Anglo-Saxon Chronicle* as becoming king and ruling for 24 years. The kings of Kent traced their ancestry to Hengist, although the royal house derived its name from Oisc (or Oiscingas, from Aesc). Bede, in his *Ecclesiastical History,* mentions the two. See also ANGLO-SAXONS; SAXONS.

**HENRY, DUKE OF LANCASTER** See LANCASTER, HENRY, DUKE OF.

**HENRY, KING OF NAVARRE** (c. 1210–1274) Ruler from 1270 to 1274, the younger son of King Thibaut I (of Champagne, ruled 1234–1250) and brother of his predecessor, Thibaut II, whom he succeeded in 1270. He was also considered the count of Champagne. His daughter Jeanne followed him, but the lack of a male heir led to the union of Navarre with France for many years, through Jeanne's marriage with the future Philip IV (1285–1314). See also NAVARRE, KINGDOM OF.

**HENRY X, DUKE OF SAXONY AND BAVARIA** See HENRY THE PROUD.

**HENRY I, KING OF CASTILE** (1203–1217) Ruler of Castile from 1214 to 1217, the son of Alfonso VIII (1158–1214) and Leonora. Henry (or Enrique) succeeded to the throne after the death of his father, and as his mother died shortly afterward, he was entrusted to the care of his sister, Berenguela. She in turn was compelled by the Castilian nobles to entrust the boy to Count Alvaro Nuñez de Lara, who used his position to further his own ambitions until Henry died in an accident. See also CASTILE; FERDINAND III, KING OF CASTILE AND LEON.

**HENRY II, KING OF CASTILE AND LÉON** (1333–1379) Ruler from 1369 to 1379, called Henry (Enrique) of Trastámara, the illegitimate son of Alfonso XI of Castile (ruled 1312–1350) and half brother of Pedro the Cruel (ruled 1350–1369). Long an enemy of Pedro's, Henry used his half brother's political difficulties and amity with England as a means of destroying him. Forming an alliance with Pedro IV of Aragon (1336–1387) and France, Henry invaded Castile in 1366 with the support of Bertrand de Guesclin, deposing Pedro, who called on Edward the Black Prince of England for support. On April 13, 1367, an English army arrived, meeting Henry and Bertrand at Najera and defeating them. They fled to France to gather troops and returned in 1369, luring Pedro into an ambush, where he was murdered at Henry's hands on March 23, 1369.

Henry was involved in the Hundred Years' War during his reign, on the side of the French. He sent a fleet in 1372 to assist in the siege of La Rochelle, annihilating an English fleet in 1375 and launching raids with the French on the English coast in 1377. In response, John of Gaunt attempted to stir up opposition, but Henry maintained his throne and forced Portugal, Navarre and Aragon to sign peace treaties. On his deathbed he advised his heir, John I (1379–1390), to maintain amity with France. See CASTILE.

**HENRY III, KING OF CASTILE** (1379–1406) Ruler from 1390 to 1406, called "the Sufferer," the son of King John I (1379–1390), who died suddenly. Because Henry (Enrique) was a boy of 12 at his father's death, power rested in the hands of a council of nobles and churchmen, who quarreled over ultimate authority. Castile was damaged severely during the 1391 massacre of thousands of Jews and the enforced conversion of others. In 1393 Henry seized control of the state, proving himself capable despite ill health. He curbed the rights of the nobles and established monarchical supremacy while his marriage to Catherine of Lancaster provided dynastic stability. Henry supported the Norman captains Jean de Bethencourt and Gadifer de la Salle in their conquest and colonization of the Canary Islands in 1402. He had strained relations with England for a time because of English piracy, and eager to find an enemy of the Ottoman Turks, he sent a diplomatic mission to Tamerlane (c. 1404). He died while planning a campaign against the Nasrid dynasty at Granada, and his son, John II (1406–1454) succeeded him. See CASTILE.

**HENRY IV, KING OF CASTILE AND LÉON** (1425–1474) Ruler from 1454 to 1474, giving way in time to his sister, Isabella of Castile (1474–1506). The son of King John II (ruled 1406–1454), he allowed his chief adviser, Juan Pacheco, marques of Villena, to enrich himself at the expense of the state. Henry (Enrique) appointed Beltran de la Cueva as a counterbalance, which compounded the problem. Demands were then made by Villena's camp that Alfonso, Henry's younger brother, be named heir because his royal daughter was reportedly the child of Beltran. This was a slur on Henry's ability to sire children. His marriage to Blanche of Navarre had been annulled for that reason, and he was married to Juana of Portugal for six years before she bore a child. Henry was deposed in 1465, and civil war ensured. Young Alfonso died of plague in 1468, permitting the ascendancy of Isabella, who made an agreement in 1468 with Henry at Los Toros de Guisando that she would be heir in return for Henry's right to involve himself in her choice of a husband. Henry died in 1474, after Isabella, without his consent, had wed Ferdinand of Aragon in 1469. See also CASTILE.

**HENRY I, KING OF ENGLAND** (1069–1135) Ruler from 1100 to 1135, the youngest son of William the Conqueror. He became king on the death of his brother, William Rufus (1087–1100), and issued the Charter of Liberties, curbing the government of William Rufus, which had appropriated church lands and demanded harsh taxes. Anselm of Canterbury was also brought back from exile under his aegis. In 1101, Henry's brother, Robert Curthose, duke of Normandy, arrived in England, returning from the First Crusade. Robert, anxious to press his own claims to the throne, agreed to surrender them in return for Henry's holdings in Normandy. The peace lasted only until 1106, however, when Henry declared Robert incompetent and seized Normandy and Robert, holding him a prisoner for life. Anselm of Canterbury, meanwhile, opposing lay investiture and feudal homage by bishops, was exiled a second time. The Compromise of Bec (1106) resolved the problem. Most of Henry's remaining years were concentrated on governmental reform and the search for an heir. His son, William, died in a shipwreck in 1120, forcing him to recall his daughter, Matilda, from Germany. On his death, however, the barons refused to swear allegiance to Matilda, electing Stephen of Blois instead. See also ENGLAND.

**HENRY II, KING OF ENGLAND** (1133–1189) One of the celebrated monarchs of the Middle Ages, a Plantagenet (ruling from 1154) responsible for the creation of the Angevin ruling dynasty in England and many reforms. He was the son of Geoffrey Plantagenet, count of Anjou, and Matilda, daughter of Henry I of England, becoming the duke of Normandy in 1150 and count of Anjou a year later on the death of his father. Already a formidable landholder in France, he married Eleanor of Aquitaine, the former wife of King Louis VII of France. This brought him the extensive lands of Aquitaine in southwestern France. As Stephen of Blois had been chosen in Matilda's place as the heir to Henry I, he was forced as well to accept Henry II as his heir. Stephen's own son, Eustace, had died in 1153.

Receiving the throne, Henry set about restoring peace in England and centralized royal administration. His main achievements, however, were in the realm of law. Henry instituted the Assizes of Clarendon (1166), which created a jury of presentment of 12 lawful men of every hundred and four of every village to determine the guilt of the accused. The actual trial was in the hands of the king's justices. There were also visits by justices on circuits, called "on eyre." There were three categories of justices: on tour, on the bench at Westminster and one with the king when the court was away from London. Private pleas from the circuit justices were heard at Westminster. Henry also created the possessory writ, which was an order from the Exchequer to instruct a sheriff to convene a jury to investigate dispossession, with the sheriff reinstating the defendant prior to the trial to determine the specifics of the case with the writ of *novel disseisin*. He also brought about financial reforms and made the Exchequer a department of the government.

From 1154 to 1162, Henry was advised by his chancellor, Thomas à Becket, whom he had elected archbishop of Canterbury in 1162. Henry had hoped to control the En-

King Henry II of England

glish church through him, but a bitter conflict ensued as Becket defended the church, a stance that ended with Becket's murder in 1170 in Canterbury Cathedral (see THOMAS À BECKET, SAINT) Equally difficult was Henry's relationship with his own family. Eleanor had borne him eight children during the years from 1153 to 1167, four of whom survived infancy: Henry, Richard (1189–1199), Geoffrey and John (1199–1216). They took part in a rebellion against Henry but were defeated and pardoned in 1174. Further quarrels ensued between his sons, eased to some extent by the deaths of Henry (1183) and Geoffrey (1186), leaving John as Henry's favorite. Henry's efforts to provide John with an inheritance led Richard and King Philip I Augustus of France (1180–1223) to plot against Henry, eventually joined by John as well. This rebellion probably hastened Henry's death. Eleanor was imprisoned for 11 years as the result of the first rebellion, and Henry engaged in liaisons with others (see ROSAMOND).

He was respected, however, by three saints, Aelred of Rievaulx, Gilbert of Sempringham and Hugh of Lincoln. He also wielded considerable power on the Continent, owing in part to his considerable territorial holdings in France (Aquitaine, Normandy, Anjon, Maine) and especially in Germany, Sicily and Castile, through the marriage of three daughters. He ensured the homage of King Malcolm III of Scotland and invaded Wales in 1157. His major political acquisition in the isles was the result of an Anglo-Norman expedition to Ireland, commanded by William Marshal, earl of Pembroke, extending English supremacy there in 1171. See also ANGEVIN DYNASTY; ENGLAND.

**HENRY III, KING OF ENGLAND** (1207–1272) Ruler from 1216 to 1272, generally thought to have been weak and incompetent. The son of King John (1199–1216), he came to the throne during a time of trouble, confronted by angry barons and an invasion by Prince Louis (the future King Louis VIII, 1223–1226) of France. William Marshal, earl of Pembroke, and a council of regents suppressed the nobles, and Louis was forced to leave England. Pembroke, who died in 1219, was replaced by Hubert de Burgh, who controlled the state, to be replaced in turn by Peter de Roches in 1232 and by Peter of Ruiseaux until 1234, when the barons had these men removed.

Henry, left to his own devices as a result, embarked on an extravagant foreign policy that included military adventurism in France and Italy. The Provisions of Oxford, signed by Henry in 1258, put an end to his campaigns, as it provided England with a privy council. Henry revoked the provisions in 1261, causing a civil war, called the Barons' War. Led by Simon de Montfort, the rebels captured Henry at the Battle of Lewes in 1264 and administered the state in his name until 1265, when Henry's son, Edward (later Edward I, 1272–1307), defeat the baronial faction at Evesham. Edward henceforth was the true king in England, as Henry, increasingly senile, surrendered his powers to indulge his interests in artistic and architectural pursuits. The story is told that a jester once compared Henry to Christ, explaining to his flattered king that Christ was as wise at the moment of His conception as he was at the age of 30, just as Henry was as wise in his dotage as he had been as a child. See also ENGLAND.

**HENRY IV, KING OF ENGLAND** (1366–1413) The first Lancastrian ruler, reigning from 1399 to 1413 after usurping the crown. His reign was one of difficulty and conflict. The sole surviving son of John of Gaunt and Blanche of Lancaster, his first wife, Henry was called Bolingbroke, receiving the titles earl of Derby in 1377 and duke of Hereford in 1397. John of Gaunt was powerful in the government of Richard II (ruled 1377–1399). In 1387 he joined the Lords Appellant, forcing Richard to grant them virtual domination of the kingdom. John of Gaunt was abroad in Spain, so he could not block the coup, returning in 1389 to find Richard with the upper hand. A reconcilation was achieved, and in 1390 Henry embarked on a crusade to Lithuania, where he joined the Teutonic Knights at the siege of Vilna. In 1392 he went to Jerusalem, visiting other European courts as well.

Richard, still smarting over the coup, used a dispute between Thomas Mowbray, duke of Norfolk, and John of Gaunt to banish both from England. Furthermore, on John's death, he seized Henry's inheritance. Henry responded by invading England and deposing Richard in September 1399. He claimed royal rights as a descendant of Henry III (1216–1272) but was beset by rebellious barons and the formidable Welsh leader Owen Glendower. Richard's supporters were crushed in 1400, which led to the old king's murder, an act that haunted Henry's remaining years.

He campaigned unsuccessfully against Owen in Wales, confronting an alliance between the rebel and the house of Percy. Henry Percy and his son, Henry, called Hotspur, were earls of Northumberland. Victory was finally achieved in 1403 when Prince Henry (the future Henry V) defeated Hotspur in the field near Shrewsbury. Two years later, on charges of conspiracy, Henry executed Mowbray and Richard Scrope, archbishop of York. The death of Percy in 1408 strengthened Henry's political security, but his health was deteriorating and he died in 1413. See also ENGLAND.

**HENRY V, KING OF ENGLAND** (1387–1422) The victor of Agincourt and king of England from 1413 to 1422, whose achievements in the Hundred Years' War were legendary.

The eldest son of Henry Bolingbroke (Henry IV) and Mary de Bohun, he was shown favor by Richard II (1377–1399), who cared for him during his father's exile in 1398. His education, encouraged by his uncle, Henry Beaufort, bishop of Winchester, was excellent, and when his father became king in 1399, he was both literate and musically inclined, possessing too a reckless nature, which was to be immortalized by Shakespeare. As Shakespeare called him, Prince Hal took command of the armies in Wales, fighting against Owen Glendower and proving triumphant against Sir Henry, called Hotspur, at Shrewsbury in 1403. By 1406 he was a vital member of the government, actively involved from 1408, opposing the influence of the chancellor, Thomas Arundel, archbishop of Canterbury. His support of the Burgundians in France caused tension with Henry IV just before he died. Prince Hal became Henry V on March 21, 1413.

King Henry V of England

Confronted by an immediate conspiracy led by Richard of York, the earl of Cambridge, and Henry, Lord Scrope, of Masham, as well as an uprising of Lollards, the king was merciless. He then collected taxes, amassed an army, stirred up rabid nationalism and set out for war with France. In 1415 he captured Harfleur and on October 25, 1415, won the Battle of Agincourt, which brought him fame and demoralized France. An alliance was made with Emperor Sigismund that ended Genoa's support in France and brought about the election of Pope Martin V in 1417. With the conquest of Normandy (1419) and an arrangement with the Burgundians, Henry negotiated the Treaty of Troyes in 1420. He was recognized as the heir to the French throne and married Catherine, the daughter of King Charles VI (1380–1422). At the zenith of his power, Henry contracted a fever and died in August 1422. His death condemned England to a long and troubled minority reign. See also ENGLAND; HUNDRED YEARS' WAR.

**HENRY VI, KING OF ENGLAND** (1421–1471) The last Lancastrian, ruling from 1422 to 1461 and from 1470 to 1471. His mental weakness and the defeat of England in the Hundred Years' War brought about the conflict called the Wars of the Roses (1455–1485). Henry VI was named king of England and France when his father died in 1422 at the age of 35. His youth (he was an infant at the time of his father's death) rendered him unfit for the throne, and his ministers assumed the burden of government. Normandy was lost in 1449–1450, and a dispute arose between the Lancastrian nobleman Edmund Beaufort, duke of Somerset, and Richard, duke of York. These crises were deepened in 1453 by Henry's deteriorating sanity, and hostilities between the Lancastrians and Yorkists erupted in 1455. Henry was captured in 1460 at Northampton but was allowed to remain on the throne with Richard as his designated heir. Edward of York, son of Richard, made an alliance with Richard Neville, earl of Warwick, defeating the Lancastrians and taking the throne in 1461 as Edward IV (1461–1483). Henry fled to Scotland after the Yorkist victory at Towton on March 29, 1461. He returned years later to foment an uprising, was captured and imprisoned in the Tower of London in 1465, released in time by Warwick and restored briefly to the throne. His second reign ended in 1471, with Edward's political recovery. He was murdered in the tower as a result on May 21. His wife, Margaret of Anjou, and his ministers are credited with maintaining order in England throughout Henry's reign. See also ENGLAND; WARS OF THE ROSES.

**HENRY VII, KING OF ENGLAND** (1457–1509) Ruler from 1485 to 1509, first of the Tudor dynasts, bringing an end to the Wars of the Roses. Henry Tudor was the son of Edmund Tudor, earl of Richmond, and Margaret Beaufort. On the death of King Henry VI, he became head of the House of Lancaster (1471) but could not press his claims. Exiled to Brittany, he invaded England in 1485, defeating Richard III (1483–1485) at the Battle of Bosworth Field, which ended the Wars of the Roses and secured his throne. His marriage to Elizabeth, daughter of King Edward IV, united the houses of York and Lancaster.

Henry's reign was noted for his avoidance of foreign entanglements and wars. He promoted trade and attempted to bring order to England's political scene. The Star Chamber (a court of civil and criminal jurisdiction introduced in 1487) allowed him to establish Tudor absolutism and to control the country effectively. Political consolidation included the suppression of several Yorkist conspiracies, the sending of Edward Poynings to Ireland (1494), peace with Scotland (1498) and the marriage of his daughter, Margaret, to King James IV of Scotland. Many scholars view him as the first monarch in modern English history. His son was Henry VIII. See also ENGLAND.

**HENRY I, KING OF FRANCE** (d. 1060) Ruler from 1031 to 1060, considered an ineffectual monarch whose reign was marked by constant struggles with rebellious members of his family and with his nobles. The son of Robert II the Pious (996–1031) and the grandson of Hugh Capet, he was designated heir at the death of his older brother, Hugh, in 1026. Another brother, however, Robert, instigated a civil war with the support of their mother, Constance. This was settled in 1032 by giving Burgundy to Robert, but he continued to plague Henry. He was succeeded by Philip I (1060–1108). See also FRANCE.

**HENRY I, KING OF GERMANY** (c. 876–936) Known as Henry the Fowler, duke of Saxony, German king (919–936) and first of the Saxon dynasty. Succeeding his father, Otto the Illustrious, as duke of Saxony in 912, Henry spent three years at war with Conrad I, German king from 903 to 918, over the domain of Thuringia. He was, however, designated by Conrad to be his heir and was elected king despite the opposition of the dukes of Swabia and Bavaria. In 925 Giselbert of Lotharingia was defeated, and his kingdom, independent of Germany since 910, was reclaimed. After negotiating a truce with the Magyars in 924, Henry reinforced the defenses of the eastern border towns and increased his army. He defeated the Slavs in several campaigns and by 933 felt ready to oppose the Magyars. He routed the Magyars but failed to bring Bavaria and Swabia under his authority despite his victory over Arnulf, duke of Bavaria, in 921. Henry's son, Otto I (936–973), became emperor. His wife, Matilda (d. 968), established many monasteries. See also GERMANY.

**HENRY II, KING OF GERMANY** (973–1024) German king from 1001 to 1024 and emperor from 1014, consolidating Germany. The son of the exiled duke of Bavaria, Henry the Quarrelsome, he was supported in his election by Willigis, archbishop of Mainz, succeeding Otto II (973–983). He actually seized the royal insignia, despite opposition. The first years of his reign were thus spent in warfare, campaigning against the Poles until 1018, marching into

King Henry II of Germany

Italy on several occasions, subduing the Italian usurper, Arduin of Ivrea, and then fighting the Lombards and the Byzantines. In 1014, while on an expedition to Rome, he was crowned Holy Roman Emperor by Pope Benedict VIII (1012–1024).

His policy included the strengthening of imperial administration, using the Ottonian system of Otto I (936–973), and strengthening the church. He interfered frequently in church affairs but maintained the support of Rome. As well as a number of land grants and the enforcement of episcopal celibacy, Henry was responsible for the establishment of the influential See of Bamberg in 1012. A devout Christian, given to biblical quotations, Henry was canonized in 1146 and was thought to have been a model of monarchical piety. See also GERMANY; HOLY ROMAN EMPIRE.

**HENRY III, KING OF GERMANY** (1017–1056) German king from 1039 to 1056 and emperor from 1046. He is viewed by some as the most notable medieval ruler, bringing the Holy Roman Empire to its political zenith, dominating the papacy and encouraging ecclesiastical reform. A scion of the Salian dynasty, he was the son of Emperor Conrad II (1024–1039) and Gisela of Swabia. Succeeding to the throne after the death of his father, he embarked on policies of eastern expansion, bringing Bohemia and Moravia into his domain, as well as the duchies of Swabia, Carinthia, Bavaria and Franconia.

In 1043 he announced to the Synod of Constance his intention to reform the Western Church, marching into Rome in 1046 to depose three rival papal claimants at the Synod of Sutri. He placed Clement II (1046–1047) on the throne and was crowned emperor by him in gratitude. He also named Clement's three successors. His leniency and just hand, however, brought about rebellions in Germany, Italy and Hungary, and his reforms alienated the clergy. As he confronted growing opposition, he fell ill and died at Bodfeld. His son, Henry (IV), inherited the throne and its attendant problems. See also GERMANY; HOLY ROMAN EMPIRE.

**HENRY IV, KING OF GERMANY** (1050–1106) German king from 1056 to 1106, whose reign was marred by his long and bitter conflict with the papacy over the question of investiture (see INVESTITURE CONTROVERSY). The surviving son of Emperor Henry III (1039–1056) and Agnes of Poitou, he was only six when he inherited the throne. Archbishops Adelbert of Bremen and Anno of Cologne, as well as his mother, were his regents and guardians. Agnes surrendered Carinthia, Swabia and Bavaria in his name, and when Henry came into his majority at 1065, he was unable to reduce the power of the local dukes and brought about their enmity.

Henry acquiesced to the authority of the pope (1073) in the question of investiture but reversed himself in 1075 and appointed bishops, thus incurring condemnation by Pope Gregory VII (1073–1085). He deposed the pontiff at Worms in 1076. Gregory retaliated by excommunicating Henry, forcing him to recant in 1077. Henry traveled to Canossa to endure a humiliating penance. The German nobles, however, infuriated, elected another king, Rudolf of Swabia, starting a civil war in 1080. Gregory excommunicated Henry once more, but this time Henry invaded Italy and deposed the pope (1084). He put Guibert of Ravenna on the papal throne, as antipope Clement III (1080; 1084–1100). Gregory died in exile, but the true popes, Urban II (1088–1099) and Paschal II (1099–1118), continued to oppose Henry, as did the German nobles and his own sons, Conrad and Henry (V). After Henry's abdication in 1105, he died suddenly at Liège in August 1106. See also HOLY ROMAN EMPIRE.

**HENRY V, KING OF GERMANY** (1086–1125) German king from 1106 to 1125 and emperor from 1111, the last of the Salian dynasty, whose reign was concurrent with the end to the Investiture Controversy. The second son of Emperor Henry IV (1056–1106), he ascended the throne after the unsuccessful rebellion of his brother, Conrad, the former heir. He immediately abandoned his father, allying himself with the papacy, Saxons and Bavarians, and in 1105 captured his father, deposing him and claiming the throne on his death. Aside from the reassertion of German domination of Bavaria, and his marriage to Matilda, daughter of King Henry I of England, he concentrated on the Investiture Controversy. In 1111 he seized Pope Paschal II (1099–1118), releasing him only after affirming the right of investiture and his coronation as emperor.

At home, however, his efforts at administrative consolidation met with enormous opposition, and Rome excommunicated him, declaring his treaty with Paschal invalid. Henry attempted to elect another pope but failed, and the German princes were forced to formulate a compromise concerning investiture at the Concordat of Worms in 1122. Henry was in conflict with his nobles for the remainder of his reign, dying at Utrecht. His widow, Matilda, married Geoffrey Plantagenet, duke of Anjou. See also GERMANY; HOLY ROMAN EMPIRE.

**HENRY VI, KING OF GERMANY** (1165–1197) German king from 1190 to 1197 and emperor from 1191, whose major achievement was the acquisition of Sicily and southern Italy. A member of the Hohenstaufen dynasty, he was the son of Emperor Frederick I Barbarossa (1152–1190), crowned as heir in 1169 and marrying Constance, heiress of Sicily, in 1186. He administered the government while Frederick was on crusade and then succeeded to the throne in 1190. He was crowned emperor by Pope Celestine III in 1191. Henry faced constant opposition from the duke of Saxony and Bavaria, Henry the Lion, but peace was made in 1194. This allowed him to pursue his interests in the Kingdom of Sicily, since on his death in 1189 King William II had left Sicily to his heiress, Constance. Sicilian nationalists fought against a German ruler, electing Constance's cousin, Tancred, in his place. Henry launched a campaign against Sicily and killed Tancred in February 1194 and was crowned on December 25 of that year. He made plans to

King Henry VI of Germany

go on crusade but died of malaria at Messina. It is interesting that Henry imprisoned Richard the Lion-Hearted (1189–1199) from 1192 to 1194, having bought him for a price from Duke Leopold of Austria. Henry held him until the English paid his ransom, and Richard accepted vassal status. See also GERMANY; HOLY ROMAN EMPIRE.

**HENRY VII, KING OF GERMANY** (c. 1275–1313) Count of Luxembourg (as Henry IV), German king from 1308 to 1313 and emperor from 1312. The successor to his father, Henry III, as count in 1288, he was elected king following the murder of Albert I in 1308. His greatest political achievement was the acquisition of Bohemia, by the marriage of the Bohemian princess, Elizabeth, to his son, John of Luxembourg. John was crowned king of Bohemia in 1310. The following year Henry vainly attempted to restore imperial dominion over the region and to end the strife between the Guelphs and Ghibellines. His efforts came to naught, and in May 1312 he entered Rome, where he was crowned emperor, despite the opposition of Robert, king of Naples. Henry then set out to subdue Tuscany but failed to capture Florence and died of fever at Buonconvento. His death disappointed the Ghibellines and Dante, who had hoped to return to Florence. See also HOLY ROMAN EMPIRE.

**HENRY BOLINGBROKE** See HENRY IV, KING OF ENGLAND.

**HENRY GOETHALS OF GHENT** See HENRY OF GHENT.

**HENRY JASOMIRGOT** (d. 1177) First duke of Austria from 1156, responsible for the aggrandizement of the House of Kahenberg. The half brother of the German king Conrad III (1093–1152), Henry was given the margravate of Austria in 1140, following the death of his brother, Leopold IV. Through his marriage, in 1142, to Gertrude, widow of Henry the Proud, he laid claim as well to the duchy of Bavaria. A crisis occurred, however, after Gertrude's death in 1143, for Henry the Proud's son, Henry the Lion, demanded Bavaria. Frederick I Barbarossa, the new German king, as of 1152, granted Henry the Lion's request. Henry Jasomirgot protested in 1156, receiving the title duke of Austria as a result.

**HENRY OF BLOIS** (d. 1171) Bishop of Winchester, papal legate and a participant in the contest for the English throne following the death of King Henry I in 1135. A grandson of William the Conqueror (1066–1087) and the brother of King Stephen of Blois (1135–1154), he became influential in ecclesiastical and political circles and crowned Stephen in 1135. Attempting to gain the See of Canterbury, he was opposed by Bernard of Clairvaux and was made a papal legate instead. He deserted Stephen's cause in 1141, joining Matilda, but then returned to his brother, swearing loyalty at the Council in London in 1141. During the reign of Henry II (1154–1189) he supported the king against Thomas à Becket. Noted for his interest in buildings, he established the monastery of Saint Cross at Winchester and was known for the construction of the castles of Wolvesey and Farnham. See also ENGLAND.

**HENRY OF BURGUNDY** (d. 1112–1114) Brother of Eudes, duke of Burgundy, father of Alfonso I, king of Portugal (1128–1185) and count of Coimbra (Portugal), who established the foundations for an independent Portuguese kingdom. Henry went to Spain in 1086, in response to a call from King Alfonso VI of León-Castile (1072–1109), after the crushing defeat of Zallaqahin, standing against the Moors. There he married Teresa, illegitimate daughter of Alfonso, receiving as well a portion of Portugal, from the Minho River to Coimbra. He died before he could accomplish his ambitions, but his son, Alfonso, secured the throne. See also PORTUGAL.

**HENRY OF FLANDERS** (c. 1174–1216) Ruler of the Latin Empire of Constantinople from 1206 to 1216. The son of Baldwin V, count of Flanders, and the brother of Baldwin I of Flanders (the future first Latin Emperor of Constantinople, 1204–1205) Henry distinguished himself in the vanquishing of the Byzantine Empire during the Fourth Crusade in 1204. He marched into Asia Minor and, in his brother's name, began the conquest of the region, with the aim of crushing the Byzantine loyalist Theodore I Lascaris (1204–1222).

His campaigns were cut short by the capture and death of his brother at the hands of the Bulgars, who had invaded Thrace. Named first as regent in 1205, he was crowned emperor the following year. Through hard campaigning he recaptured Thrace and secured the borders along the Nicaean front by compelling Theodore to come to terms. Having made the Latin Empire reasonably safe from attack, he tried to improve relations with his Greek subjects. His attempts were only partially successful, and he died, probably by poison, at Thessalonica. See also CONSTANTINOPLE, LATIN EMPIRE OF.

**HENRY OF GHENT** (1217–1293) Eminent philosopher and theologian noted for his advocacy of the teachings of Augustine and his opposition to the teachings of John Duns Scotus. Henry studied at Tournai, becoming a canon and an archdeacon at Bruges (1276) and Tournai (1278). Although few details of his life survive, it is known that he condemned Averroism in 1277 and received a censure for his opposition to the privileges of the mendicant orders about 1290 from Cardinal Caetani, the future Pope Boniface VIII. His two major works were *Quodlibeta* and an unfinished *Summa Theologica*. Henry was known as "Doctor Solemnis."

**HENRY OF LANGENSTEIN** (d. c. 1397) Theologian and philosopher in Paris who had a role in establishing the conciliar movement to end the Great Schism in the Western Church. He wrote the *Epistola Concilii Pacis* (1381), presenting the argument that a general church council was superior in authority to the pope. He was also a founder of the University of Vienna (1384). See also CONCILIAR MOVEMENT; SCHISM, GREAT.

**HENRY RASPE** (c. 1202–1247) Landgrave of Thuringia from 1227 to 1247 and a German anti-king to Emperor Frederick II (1215–1250) and his son Conrad (IV, 1250–1254) from 1246 to 1247. Henry inherited Thuringia from his brother, Louis IV, ignoring the claims of his nephew,

Hermann II, and allying himself with Frederick II, supporting him in the suppression of the rebellion instigated by the duke of Austria in 1236. When the emperor was excommunicated by Pope Gregory IX (1227–1241), Henry remained loyal. In 1242 he was made vice-regent of Germany, but his relations with the emperor deteriorated, especially after his own excommunication in 1240 and his earlier marriage to the sister of Frederick of Austria. By 1244 he had deserted the imperial cause and, in 1246, through the influence of Pope Innocent IV (1243–1254), was elected anti-king. Initially successful against Conrad, he died suddenly at Wartburg Castle in Thuringia. See also FREDERICK II, EMPEROR; HOLY ROMAN EMPIRE.

**HENRY SUSA** See SUSA, HENRY.

**HENRY THE LION** (c. 1129–1195) Welf duke of Saxony from 1142 to 1180 and of Bavaria from 1156 to 1180, the son of Henry the Proud who emerged as one of the most powerful princes in Germany and the Holy Roman Empire. He spent his early years reclaiming the duchies of Saxony and Bavaria, winning Saxony in 1142 and Bavaria in 1156. Supporting Frederick I Barbarossa (1152–1190) and consolidating his own lands, he fought in Italy (1154–1155 and 1160–1161) and against the Poles (1157). He established Lübeck and other cities, enlarged existing towns and strengthened dioceses, especially Oldenburg and Mecklenburg, Mecklenburg having been conquered, colonized and Christianized in a series of campaigns against the Slavic Obodrites (Obotrites, c. 1158). In 1168 he married Matilda, daughter of King Henry II of England (1154–1189), winning prestige in England, France and Constantinople, where he was received warmly in 1172 by Emperor Manuel I Comnenus (1143–1180).

Eventually alliances were formed against Henry, the most notable being that of Albert the Bear, the margrave of Brandenburg and archbishop of Cologne. In 1176, Henry refused to send troops to Frederick for the emperor's war against the Lombard League, and Frederick was defeated at Lugano, blaming Henry for the outcome. In 1180, as a result, Henry was stripped of his holdings and forced to submit the following year. He was allotted only Brunswick and Luneburg when he did surrender. Driven into exile, he spent his remaining years in England at the court of King Henry II. Subsequent efforts to regain his lands failed, even after a reconciliation with Emperor Henry VI (1190–1197) in 1190 at Fulda and again in 1194. Emperor Otto IV (1208–1215) was his son. See also BAVARIA; HOLY ROMAN EMPIRE;SAXONY.

**HENRY THE NAVIGATOR** (1394–1460) Prince of Portugal and patron of explorers (also known as Henrique), the third son of King John I of Portugal and Philippa of Lancaster, daughter of John of Gaunt. He won distinction in 1415 at the capture of the Moroccan city of Ceuta and was appointed governor there, a position he held in 1418, when he was summoned to the city to support its defense against a Moorish attack, although the troops at hand repulsed the sortie. Henry had been sponsoring voyages of discovery even before the event, seeking a way to outflank the Islamic world, making inroads into Muslim trade and establishing contact with other parts of Africa and the Far East. His patronage was encouraged from 1419 when he retired to the governorship of the Algarve in southwestern Portugal. There, at Sagres, he founded a school that drew navigators, shipbuilders, cartographers and sailing men. Funds were made available because of Henry's rank as grand master of the Order of Christ, the chivalric equivalent of and replacement for the Templars in Portugal. His ships bore red crosses on their sails.

Starting in 1420, Henry's ships began moving down the Atlantic coast of Morocco, but progress was slow at first. The voyagers then proved that distant lands could be reached and that expeditions could finance themselves by returning with gold and slaves. A list of the discoveries made by Henry's captains, such men as Zarco, Tristão Vaz Teixeira, Dinis Dias and Nuno Tristão, included the Madeira Islands (1416), Cape Bojador (1434), the mouth of the Senegal (1445), the mouth of the Gambia (1446) and the Cape Verde Islands (1456). So lucrative was the slave trade that by 1448 a fort and warehouse were built on Arguin Island just below Cape Blanco, the first European trading center overseas.

Despite his worldly successes, Henry led a troubled personal life. The question of royal succession plagued his family, and he was often a mediator between his brother, Pedro, and King Alfonso V, his nephew. When civil war erupted in 1449, Henry agreed reluctantly with the king, attempting to retire from public life when Pedro was slain at Alfarrobeira (1445). He died at Sagres after fighting two years earlier against the Moroccan city of Alcácer Seguir. Ironically, he was severely in debt by that time. Although Henry never made any actual sea voyages of discovery, his role in encouraging exploration was instrumental in bringing the Age of Discovery to Europe.

**HENRY THE PROUD** (c. 1108–1139) Duke of Bavaria from 1126 to 1139 and duke of Saxony from 1137 to 1139, one of the leaders of the powerful Welf family. Becoming duke in 1126, as Henry X, he married Gertrude, the daughter of the German king (and future emperor) Lothair II (1125–1137). As an important ally of Lothair, he joined the king's war against the Hohenstaufens, receiving as a reward land in Italy and standing as candidate for election as German king on Lothair's death in 1137. Conrad III (1138–1152), a Hohenstaufen, won the imperial succession, however, and hostilities ensued when he refused to invest Henry with the duchy of Saxony, which he had inherited from Lothair. Henry was deprived of both Saxony and Bavaria in the summer of 1138 but managed to reclaim the latter territory from Albert the Bear. While mounting an expedition to Bavaria in 1139, he died. See also HENRY THE LION.

**HERACLIUS** Byzantine emperor from 610 to 641, responsible for restoring the military fortunes of the Byzantines, but whose reign was also witness to the titanic rise of Islam. Born around 575, Heraclius was the son of Heraclius, exarch of Carthage, who in 610 rebelled against the hated emperor Phocas, sending his son with a fleet to Constantinople. Heraclius arrived there on October 3, 610, deposed the regime of Phocas and amid wild celebration was crowned by the patriarch. He confronted many problems, including the declining state of the army, a drained treasury and government administration in a condition nearing chaos.

He made peace with the Avars to facilitate a campaign against his most pressing adversary, the Persians, and waged war from 622 to 628 in Anatolia, in Armenia and finally in Persia itself. He reclaimed the lost Byzantine lands and forced peace on the enemy, returning the "True Cross" to the Church of the Holy Sepulchre in Jerusalem in 631. The Persians, unable to rally after Heraclius's campaigns, became an easy target for the Arabs. Heraclius forged an alliance with the Khazars and entered Constantinople in triumph.

At home he reorganized the entire structure of government and was probably the one to introduce the system of themes, military smallholdings in Asia Minor, replacing the inefficient zones. The themes provided him with recruits and ended the reliance of the empire on mercenary armies. He raised troops solely to ensure the survival of the state (see THEMES). Having reformed provincial government, Heraclius concentrated on the central administration, reducing the all-powerful Praetorian Prefecture and putting finances into the hands of independent and efficient departments. These changes brought about a significant change in the Byzantine Empire, replacing the Roman structure with Greek culture and outlook. Greek was adopted as the language of the empire, and Hellenic culture was absorbed by it.

The years of conquest and struggle, however, came at a cost to Heraclius, and he was unable to muster the strength to oppose the armies of Islam that were sweeping into Syria and Palestine in 634. In 636, a Byzantine army was annihilated by the Arabs at Yarmuk as Syria and later Egypt were lost. Heraclius died in 634, described by his contemporaries as blond, gray-eyed and vitally energetic monarch who provided Constantinople with the reforms necessary to survive in a time of crisis. See also BYZANTINE EMPIRE.

**HERACLONAS** Byzantine emperor in 641 (also Heracleonas), the son of Emperor Heraclius and his second wife, Martina. In 641 he was made co-emperor with his half brother Constantine III. This arrangement was brief, as Constantine died in May 641, probably of natural causes. Heraclonas and Martina, however, were charged with Constantine's murder, deposed in a revolt and exiled to Rhodes in September. Constans II (641–668) came to the throne as a result. See also BYZANTINE EMPIRE.

**HERALDRY** The art and science of armorial bearings that began as the simple placing of a distinguishing figure or mark on a helmet or shield, evolving into a complex and sophisticated field of practice. Although heraldic systems varied from country to country in Europe, they were the same in the sense that the symbols of heraldry represented hereditary or family lines and thus became another means of emphasizing feudal life with its concepts of rights, privileges, authority and control of land. Heraldic devices became trademarks, and to use them falsely was thus to commit more than a social error.

Coats of arms, probably the most obvious displays of armorial bearings, began as a means of presenting one's markings on the two most easily identifiable pieces of battle equipment, the shield and the helmet. In time, thanks to the desert conditions of warfare during the Crusades, an additional space was found on the surcoats, the cloth coverings worn by the knights over their armor. Such devices were, of necessity, simple, distinct and clearly visible, having sharp colors. During the early period of heraldry variety was allowed, but this changed by the 14th century, by which time heralds had become more than scouts. They presided over tournaments, decided who was qualified for knighthood and eventually organized into heraldic bodies such as the Herald's College in England, serving as masters of genealogy and diplomacy.

The language of heraldry was, and would remain, French, the specific terminology the result of a need to make the composition of a shield absolutely clear. Elaborate vocabulary came into use, with terms for colors (tinctures), divisions (ordinaires) and charges (animals, symbols or even plants). Virtually any figure was acceptable as a charge. Animals (lions, leopards, boars) were popular, but there were also trees, celestial bodies and often symbols that came to represent a pun on the name of the bearer. See also CHIVALRY; MILITARY ORDERS.

**HEREFORD, NICHOLAS** See NICHOLAS OF HEREFORD.

**HERESIES** Beliefs held to be contrary to the orthodox views or doctrines of the church. There were many heretical movements in the Middle Ages, and many individuals were condemned as heretics. See also ABELARD, PETER; ADOPTIONISM; ALBIGENSIAN MOVEMENT; ARIANISM; AVERROISM; AVICENNA; BACON, ROGER; BEGHARDS; BEGUINES; BERNARD OF CLAIRVAUX; BOGOMILS; CATHARI; DOMINICANS; FLAGELLANTS; FRANCISCANS; HUS, JAN; INQUISITION; LOLLARDY; MONOPHYSITISM; MONOTHELITISM; MYSTICISM; NESTORIANISM; PATARINES; SCHISM, GREAT; SCHISMS; WALDENSES.

**HEREWARD THE WAKE** Anglo-Saxon hero and a rebel of the second half of the 11th century. An ardent foe of William the Conqueror (1066–1087) and the Normans following their conquest of England in 1066, he joined a small force of Danes, expecting a Danish invasion of the country in 1070 by King Sven II (1047–1074). Sailing to Ely, Hereward participated in the sack of Peterborough Abbey to prevent its treasures from falling into the hands of the new Norman abbot. Sven made peace with William the Conqueror, however, and Hereward continued his outlaw activities from Ely from about 1071. William captured Ely eventually, but Hereward escaped, conducting his rebellious activities for some time. Hereward earned legendary stature as a threat to the Normans. See also ENGLAND; NORMAN CONQUEST.

***HERMANDAD*** Spanish word for brotherhood, used to refer to a league of towns founded in Castile during the 12th century. *Hermandades* provided the cities with protection and were extreme, effective in counteracting the lawlessness of the aristocracy. While they supported the king, especially against the nobles, the *hermandades* eventually proved unnecessary as the process of royal centralization was completed. (see also Inquisition.)

**HERMANN I** (d. 1217) Landgrave of Thuringia and count palatine of Saxony. Hermann played a role in the dynastic conflicts of the Holy Roman Empire of the time. He became landgrave in 1190, elected by the German princes, despite the opposition of Emperor Henry VI (1190–1197). Thuringia had been the fief of his brother, Louis III (d. 1190), who had granted him the rank of count palatine in 1180. Hermann won concessions from both Emperors Otto IV (1208–1215) and Philip of Swabia (1197–1208) during their conflict, but in 1204, Philip invaded Thuringia and forced him to swear fealty. Wavering in his loyalties, he finally joined the Hohenstaufen cause to support Frederick II (1215–1250) in 1212. Hermann was a patron of Walther von der Vogelweide. See also THURINGIA.

**HERMANNUS VON REICHENAU** (1013–1054) Also known as Herimannus Contractus and Herman the Lame, a Christian poet, chronicler, musician and astronomer. Educated at the Benedictine abbey at Reichenau, he was one of the learned men of his age, the author of many works, including *De utilitatibus astrolabii (On the Uses of the Astrolabe), De mense lunari (On Lunar Cycles), De divisione (On Division,* a mathematical work) and *De figura quadrilatera (On the Quadrilateral Figure);* he also wrote poetry, treatises on music, hymns and a martyrology. His major effort was a world chronicle from the time of Christ until 1054, an important source for contemporary events. See also ASTRONOMY.

**HERMANN VON SALZA** See TEUTONIC KNIGHTS.

**HERRINGS, BATTLE OF** Engagement fought in 1429, during the English siege of Orléans, when the supply wagons under the command of Sir John Falstolf bringing supplies to the English was attacked at Rouvray by the French. Forming a barricade with his wagons, he repulsed the enemy. The name of the battle derived from the barrels of herring used as part of the defense. See also HUNDRED YEARS' WAR; ORLÉANS.

**HERRING TRADE** See HANSEATIC LEAGUE.

**HESSE** Region in central Germany situated roughly between Thuringia and the Rhine River. The people of Hesse, called Hessians, were probably Germanic in origin, possibly the Chatti tribe described by Tacitus. Christianized by Saint Boniface (d. 754), Hesse became a county sometime in the early 10th century and was attached to the landgravate of Thuringia. Henry I the Child (d. 1308), son of Henry II of Brabant, was the first landgrave of Hesse, bearers of this title also holding the rank of princes of the Holy Roman Empire from 1242. See also HOLY ROMAN EMPIRE.

**HESYCHASM** A form of mysticism in the Eastern Church, propagated especially by the monks of Mount Athos, having as its goals the attainment of inner quietude (from Greek *hesychia*) and a vision of the Divine Light. Very popular in the Byzantine Empire in the 13th and 14th centuries, the mysticism was also the source of controversy. According to Hesychast teachings, as presented most notably by Saint Nicephorus the Hesychast, it was possible to achieve *hesychia* through the application of rigorous exercises, fixing the eye on a certain spot or reciting a prayer, called the Jesus Prayer, in time with one's breathing.

Hesychasm was defended by Gregory Palamas, but his writings were condemned in 1342 by two synods. The movement was given new life with the accession of John VI Cantacuzenus (reigned 1347–1354), who appointed Hesychasts to high positions. Opponents were excommunicated in 1351 at the Blackerna Synod, but the group's doctrines gained ground in the Eastern Church in the late 1400s. The sect spread to Russia but never became popular in the West. See also MYSTICISM.

**HIGDEN, RANULF** (d. 1364) Chronicler and Benedictine monk whose greatest work was the *Polychronicon,* a universal history from the Creation to sometime during the reign of King Edward III of England (1327–1377). Organized into seven books, the work was completed around 1350. Additions were made to the *Polychronicon,* the years including the reign of Richard II (1377–1399), and it was translated into English in 1385 or 1387 by John of Trevisa.

**HILARIUS** Early-12th-century poet and wandering scholar, also called Hilary the Englishman, although there is little to suggest that he was of English origin. Several poems were dedicated to English patrons. He composed light verse and three religious plays in Latin and was a student of Peter Abelard.

**HILARY THE ENGLISHMAN** See HILARIUS.

**HILDA OF WHITBY, SAINT** (614–680) Abbess of Whitby and one of the most influential religious figures in Anglo-Saxon England of her era. A member of the Northumbrian royal family, she was baptized with her great uncle, King Edwin of Northumberland, in 627, by Paulinus, archbishop of York. In 649 she was made abbess of Harttepool by Saint Aidan and was tutor to Aelfflaed, daughter of King Oswin of Northumbria. King Oswin granted her land about 657 or 659 on which she founded the dual monastery of Streaneshalch, called eventually Whitby. She encouraged the poet Caedmon, counseled bishops and supported the Celtic church, standing with Colman of Lindisfarne in opposition to Saint Wilfrid and his calls for adoption of the Roman Rite at the Synod of Whitby in 664. When Oswin accepted the Roman Rite, Hilda acquiesced and abandoned Celtic custom. See also CELTIC CHURCH.

**HILDEBERT OF LAVARDIN** (1056–1133) Archbishop of Tours and an eminent literary figure. Born at Lavardin and educated at Le Mans, he was appointed archdeacon in 1091 and bishop of Le Mans in 1096. Hildebert was opposed by William II Rufus of England (1087–1100), who captured him in 1099, holding him prisoner until his own death in 1100. Released, Hildebert returned to Le Mans to establish his cathedral. A staunch defender of doctrine, he ousted Henry of Lausanne, an itinerant preacher of the diocese, and became known as a powerful preacher in his own right. Hildebert was made archbishop in 1125.

**HILDEBRAND** See GREGORY VII, SAINT.

**HILDEBRAND, KING OF THE LOMBARDS** Ruler for some months in 744. The successor to and nephew of King Linprand (d. 744), he proved incompetent and cruel and was deposed by the Lombard royal council. His replacement was Rachis, duke of Friuli (744–749). See also LOMBARDS.

***HILDEBRANDSLIED*** A fragmentary Old High German alliterative epic poem composed sometime around 800. Translated as the *Song of Hildebrand,* it recounted the tale of a German warrior by that name who was also an adviser of Dietrich von Bern. He fought with Hadubrand, who was unaware that Hildebrand was his father. The poem's conclusion is not extant, but the contents that remain make it clear that Hildebrand was forced to slay his son.

**HILDEGARD, SIBYL OF THE RHINE** See HILDGARD OF BINGEN, SAINT.

**HILDEGARD OF BINGEN, SAINT** (1098–1179) German mystic and abbess of Rupertsberg, near Bingen, who was called "Sibyl of the Rhine" because of her many visions. A member of a German noble family, she experienced visions at an early age and was entrusted to the care of a reputed recluse. In 1136 she became prioress of a local Benedictine community and traveled throughout Germany, conducting correspondence with major figures of her age, including Bernard of Clairvaux and Frederick I Barbarossa (1152–1190). She wrote the *Scivias* (1141–1150), an account of her visions, and a number of hymns, scientific treatises and theological works.

**HILDERIC** (d. 533) King of the Vandals, next to the last ruler of the Vandals, reigning from 523 to 530, the son of King Hunneric (ruled 477–484) and a Roman, Eudocia, daughter of Emperor Valentinian III. He was chosen to succeed King Thrasamund but soon alienated the Vandals because of his ignorance of affairs of state, his adherence to orthodox Christianity and his execution of Amalafrida, the widow of Thrasamund and the sister of Theodoric, king of the Ostrogoths. He also failed to prevent the defeat of his troops by the Moors. In 530 he was overthrown by his cousin, Gelamir, who imprisoned him. This act provided Justinian with justification to send BELISARIUS and a Byzantine army to Africa in 533. Gelamir put Hilderic to death to prevent his rescue by the Byzantines. See also VANDALS.

**HILDIBAD** (d. 541) King of the Ostrogoths from 540 to 541, a nephew of the Visigothic king Theudis. He was elected by the remaining Goths in Italy, who had just been routed by the Byzantine general Belisarius. His sole achievement was a victorious engagement near Treviso against one of the minor Byzantine commanders in the region. In 541 he was murdered by a personal enemy. See also OSTROGOTHS.

**HILTON, WALTER** (d. 1396) English mystic and devotional writer who studied at Cambridge before becoming a hermit. Eventually he joined the Augustinian Canons at Thurgarton Priory and was the author of spiritual writings, the greatest of which was the *Scala perfectionis (Ladder of Perfection),* a two-volume guide on spiritual attainment. The first book of its kind to appear in England, the *Scala perfectionis* remained popular through the 15th and 16th centuries. Hilton was also credited with the first three books of the *Imitation of Christ,* attributed to Thomas à Kempis.

**HINCMAR OF REIMS** (c. 806–882) Archbishop of Reims, theologian and influential figure in the Frankish church. Educated at Saint-Denis in Paris, he was introduced into the royal court in 822 by Abbot Hildisia, his teacher, entering the service of King Louis the Pious (814–840) and serving as well Charles the Bald (840–877). In 840, when Charles succeeded to the Carolingian throne, Hincmar was retained as counselor, incurring the hostility of Charles's rival, emperor Lothair I (840–843). Elected archbishop of Reims in 845, Hincmar reorganized the archdiocese, was acquitted at the Synod of Soissons (853) of illegally nullifying the acts of his predecessor (a charge brought by Lothair) and then met further disputes when he opposed the attempt of Lothair II, king of Lorraine, to divorce his wife, Teutberga. When Lothair II died in 869, Hincmar supported Charles in securing Lorraine, personally crowning him. The pope opposed this act, and in 876 Hincmar again differed with the papacy in the appointment of a papal legate for Germany and Gaul. Hincmar continued to argue with other prelates and political leaders until his death. He was the author of the *Life of St. Remigius.* He died while fleeing a Viking attack on Reims. See also REIMS.

**HISHAM** (691–743) The 10th Umayyad caliph of Damascus, reigning from 724 to 743 (the successor to Yzid II), the son of the caliph Abdul Malik. He consolidated his administration and permitted the advance of Islam into Europe, until the Muslims were defeated at Tours by Charles Martel in 732. From 727 to 733, the Khazars caused problems in the Caucasus but were defeated, and Hisham acquired Georgia. Revolts then erupted across the Umayyad caliphate, and he confronted rebels in Khorasan, Iraq, the Oxus region and in Maghrib. The unrest was a sign of the increasing Umayyad hold on the Islamic world. Bureaucratic deterioration and corruption added to the problems, although Hisham presided over a regime still strong enough to overcome such deficiencies but bequeathed to his nephew, al-Walid II (reigned 743–744), and his heirs a tottering empire. See also UMAYYAD CALIPHATE.

**HISHAM I** (d. 796) Spanish Umayyad emir of Córdoba from 788 to 796, the son of Abd al-Rahman I (ruled 756–

788). He inherited a sound government and reigned in peace, restricting military activities to an annual assault on the Kingdom of Asturias. These sorties ended in 795 when King Alfonso II (ruled 791–842) defeated his troops at the Battle of Lutos. Hisham was considered a learned, pious and charitable ruler. See also CÓRDOBA, EMIRATE OF.

**HISHAM II** (d. 1013?) Caliph of Córdoba from 976 to 1009 and again from 1010 to 1013. The son of al-Hakam II (961–976), he was 10 years old when he came to the throne. His mother, Subh, and her allies, including Ibn Abi Amir, protected him, even as Ibn Abi Amir became dictator of the caliphate, known as Almanzor. When Amir died, Hisham appointed his son, Abd al-Malik, to his father's post in 1002. A younger brother, Sanjul, inherited it on Malik's death. Hisham went so far as to name Sanjul caliph, an act that sparked an uprising and resulted in Hisham's abdication in 1009 in favor of Muhammad II. When Muhammad was assassinated in 1010, Hisham was restored and deposed three years later by Sulayman. The caliphate of Córdoba was severely damaged by his reign. See also CÓRDOBA, EMIRATE OF.

**HISHAM III** The last of the caliphs of Córdoba, whose reigned lasted from 1027 to 1031. An Umayyad, he was 54 when he came to the throne, succeeding the Hammadid caliph Yahya ibn Ali (ruled 1021–1023, 1025–1027). Ineffective as a ruler, Hisham was deposed by the nobles of Córdoba, who imprisoned him in the Great Mosque of the city and abolished the caliphate entirely. See also CÓRDOBA, EMIRATE OF.

**HISHAM IBN AL-KALBI** (d. c. 819) Arab historian and scholar, known for his extensive research into the history of Arabs before the rise of Islam. He was the author of several important studies, including the *Kitab al-Asnan (Book of Idols),* concerning the gods worshiped by the Arabs before the acceptance of the Prophet. He also wrote a genealogy and a study on the horse. See also ARABIA.

**HOCCLEVE, THOMAS** (d. 1426) English poet, a contemporary of Chaucer's, honoring him in his *De regimine principum,* or *The Regiment of Princes,* in which a portrait of Chaucer appears in the manuscript. His poetry never equaled Chaucer's but remains useful as a source for the social history of the period. See also CHAUCER, GEOFFREY.

**HOHENSTAUFEN** German noble house that became one of the foremost dynasties in the Holy Roman Empire, dominating the German throne and imperial politics from 1138 to 1254. The first of the Hohenstaufen (or Staufer) line was Count Frederick von Büren (d. 1105), who built the castle of Saufer in the Swabian Jura Mountains and became a loyal ally of Emperor Henry IV (ruled 1056–1106). As a reward he was made Frederick I, duke of Swabia, in 1079, marrying Henry's daughter Agnes. His sons, Frederick II of Swabia (1105–1147) and Conrad III (1138–1152), were named heirs to the emperor, Henry V (ruled 1106–1125), although Lothair II, duke of Saxony, became German king, reigning until 1137. In 1138 the Hohenstaufens achieved political ascendancy when Conrad was elected king (as Conrad III) and later crowned emperor. Subsequent Hohenstaufen rulers were frequently involved in conflicts with the papacy and other German houses, especially the Welf (Guelph) dynasty, and attempted to bring Italy into their sphere of control. They proved ultimately unsuccessful in their ambitions, and the line was ended on the death of Manfred, illegitimate son of Frederick II, in 1260 and the execution of Conradin in 1268, following the Battle of Tagliacozzo and his capture by Charles of Anjou. See also GERMANY; GUELPHS AND GHIBELLINES; HOLY ROMAN EMPIRE; INVESTITURE CONTROVERSY; LOMBARD LEAGUE; SALIAN DYNASTY; SWABIA; and individual rulers.

**HOHENZOLLERN** German noble house first established in the 11th century and deriving its name from its original home, Castle Zoloria (or Hohenzollern), situated in the Hohenzollern Mountains in Swabia. The first of the line was probably Burchard I, count of Zollern (d. 1061), the earliest member of the house of importance. A descendant, Frederick of Hohenzollern (d. c. 1200), became burgrave of Nuremberg in 1192. His two sons sired the major lines of the house, the Swabian and Franconian. Of the two, the Franconian line was more prestigious, members receiving the margravates of Ansbach and Bayreuth and in 1415 named to the electorate of Brandenburg. The Hohenzollerns went on to play a major role in the history of Prussia. See also GERMANY.

**HOLLAND** See NETHERLANDS, THE.

**HOLY GRAIL** The celebrated sacred object the search for which became a major theme in medieval legend and literature. More than the Holy Lance or the True Cross, the Holy Grail was a powerful symbol of veneration, mystery and spiritual perfection and came to be identified by Christians as the chalice from which Christ drank at the Last Supper. It also appeared, however, variously as a cup, dish or even a stone or cauldron into which would drip blood from a bleeding lance. The Grail legend began independently, but it was associated in time with ARTHURIAN LEGEND and with the story of the knight Percival.

The Grail legend was perhaps inspired by Celtic or classical mythology, although scholars have offered other views, including origins of both Christian and Oriental nature. In time, however, the original elements became fused with the tale of Joseph of Arimathea and the introduction of Christianity in the British Isles. A strong literary tradition inevitably developed, with the body of Grail romances evolving in the late 12th and early to mid-13th centuries. While most versions were in French or the Provençal dialect, there were accounts in German, English, Norwegian and Italian. It is generally agreed that the earliest Grail romance was conceived by Chrétien de Troyes in his *Perceval* or *Conte de Graal,* written around 1180. Other notable works on the theme were *Parzival* by Wolfram von Eschenbach; *Estoire dou Graal* by Robert de Boron; *L'Estoire del Saint Graal (Grand Saint Graal),* a 13th-century prose romance; and Malory's *Morte d'Arthur.* See also MYSTICISM and individual writers.

**HOLY ROMAN EMPIRE** Medieval political body that encompassed many regions in central Europe, ruled by the Frankish and later the German kings for 10 centuries after the coronation of Charlemagne by Pope Leo III (795–816) on Christmas Day in 800. The term Holy Roman Empire came into use in 1157 and the title Holy Roman Emperor (Sacrum Romanum Imperium) in 1254. The empire was called Roman because it claimed succession to imperial Rome and Holy because of its traditional claim to supremacy over Christendom.

Important in viewing the Holy Roman Empire is the fact that it was an evolving institution with conflicting realities and theories. Further, its universality was never recognized by the Byzantine Empire, and its position was undermined by the rise of the Western Christian states of England, France and Castile. There were theories and philosophical views about the empire, produced by popes, theologians and those politically astute, such as Arnold of Brescia and literary figures such as Dante and Petrarch.

While certainly Charlemagne recognized the value of his title in place of the simpler "King of the Franks," it has long been debated among scholars as to whether or not he was annoyed at the presumption of the pope to claim the right of investiture. Nevertheless, he strove to restore an order and unity of the West that had not been known since the days of imperial Rome. The Frankish Carolingian empire was splintered during the reigns of his successors, and the title lapsed in 919 with the ascent of the Saxon emperors. Otto I (962–973) brought together Germany and Italy, creating an empire based on feudal principles. The tradition was thus established that its rulers were to be chosen by the princes of Germany and, after 1356, by a set number of Electors. The full title of emperor was claimed by a candidate crowned by the pope, otherwise he was known as German king or king of the Romans, the latter titles often borne by imperial heirs to maintain the succession in the existing line, the election coming during the lifetime of the heir's father. In ideal circumstances, the German king was crowned at Aachen and then journeyed to Rome to be invested by the pope as emperor.

Crowning of Charlemagne

One of the inherent political problems facing the German kings was the fact that they ruled only their hereditary domains and held jurisdiction over the imperial cities such as Frankfurt and Augsburg. Everything else in the empire they controlled only to the degree that they could influence the Diet, the deliberative assembly of the Holy Roman Empire. Allies were found by creating useful vassals in ecclesiastical or lay princes, who could lend their support to the imperial cause. It also became expedient to break up the numerous duchies that dotted Germany, in order to divide political power.

The Holy Roman Empire also confronted a major difficulty in the papacy, for both the emperor and the pope claimed the dominant role in guiding the Christian world, the emperors concerning themselves with temporal affairs and the popes with spiritual matters. The inevitable conflict between them was complicated further by the positions of both men in Italy. When they failed to cooperate, hostilities arose, such as in the Investiture Controversy, settled by the Concordat of Worms.

Imperial ambitions in Italy proved difficult to maintain, as Frederick I Barbarossa (ruled 1152–1190) learned when his power was abrogated by the Lombard League supported by the papacy. Generally when an emperor invaded Italy, the pope caused opposition in Germany, requiring imperial retreat. If an emperor contented himself with remaining in Germany, his Italian holdings deteriorated. Frederick II (ruled 1215–1250), who was also king of Sicily, moved his sphere of influence to Italy. Triumphant while he lived, Frederick could not provide a stable maintenance of imperial control, and within years Hohenstaufen power was nonexistent because of the machinations of the popes and the princes of Europe.

An interregnum followed the demise of the Hohenstaufens (1254–1273), ending with the election of Rudolf I of Habsburg (1273–1291). The Habsburg dynasty competed with the Luxembourg and the Bavarian Wittelsbach dynasties until the accession of Albert II in 1438, when it came to possess firmly the crown of the empire. The Habsburgs were resilient and concentrated on expanding their own domains. The concept of the Holy Roman Empire endured until 1806, when it was dissolved.

**HOLYROOD** An abbey founded in 1128 by King David I in Edinburgh, Scotland, the final resting place of the Scottish kings. See also EDINBURGH.

**HOLY SEPULCHRE, KNIGHTS OF THE** See MILITARY ORDERS.

**HOLY WAR** See CRUSADES.

**HOMAGE** See FEUDALISM.

**HONORIUS I** (d. 683) Pope from 625 to 638, at the core of the major doctrinal controversy concerning the nature of Christ. Elected successor to Boniface V (619–625),

## Holy Roman Empire, 1250

KINGDOM OF DENMARK
Baltic Sea
North Sea
COUNTY OF HOLSTEIN
PRUSSIA
SLAVINIA
DUCHY OF POMERANIA
FRIESLAND
DUCHY OF SAXONY
MARCH OF BRANDENBURG
KINGDOM OF POLAND
BRABANT
MARCH OF LAUSITZ
LANDGRAVATE OF THURINGIA
DUCHY OF SILESIA
FLANDERS
DUCHY OF LOWER LORRAINE
MARCH OF MEISSEN
OPOL AND RATIBOR
HAINAULT
KINGDOM OF BOHEMIA
FRANCONIA
MARCH OF MORAVIA
DUCHY OF UPPER LORRAINE
DUCHY OF AUSTRIA
DUCHY OF SWABIA
KINGDOM OF FRANCE
DUCHY OF BAVARIA
COUNTY OF BURGUNDY
KINGDOM OF HUNGARY
DUCHY OF STYRIA
DUCHY OF CARINTHIA
KINGDOM OF BURGUNDY
PATRIARCHATE of ST. PETER
MARCH OF CARNIOLA
SAVOY
MARCH OF VERONA
Adriatic Sea
EMILIA
KINGDOM OF ITALY
ROMAGNA
PROVENCE
MARCH OF ANCONA
TUSCANY
DUCHY OF SPOLETO
KINGDOM OF SICILY
Mediterranean Sea
Corsica
PATRIMONY of ST. PETER
Boundary of Empire, 1250
Boundary of Kingdoms
Boundary of Duchy or March
0
150 km
0
150 mi

he lent immediate support to missionaries in England, promoted Anglo-Saxon conversions and called on the Celts to accept the Roman liturgical rite. His reign, however, was marred by the heretical doctrines of Monophysitism and Monothelitism. Replying in a letter in 634 to Sergius I, patriarch of Constantinople, on whether Christ had one or two natures, Honorius supported the Chalcedonian model, interpreting Christ's nature as indivisible. His use of the phrase "one will," however, brought attacks and condemnation at the Council of Constantinople in 681, a condemnation upheld by Pope Leo II (682–683). Honorius's contention was used in later centuries as an example countering the concept of papal infallibility.

**HONORIUS II** (d.1130) Pope from 1124 to 1130, born Lamberto Scanabecchi, representative of Pope Calixtus II (1119–1124) to Germany and instrumental in negotiating the Concordat of Worms (1122), ending the Investiture Controversy. Elected successor to Calixtus, he maintained amicable relations with the German king Lothair III (1125–1137), whom he supported in winning the throne in 1125, but he was forced to recognize Roger II of Sicily as duke of Apulia (1095–1154).

**HONORIUS III** (d.1227) Pope from 1216 to 1227, born Cencio Savelli, appointed to the post of papal treasurer in 1188. Successor to Innocent III (1198–1216), he encouraged a Crusade and church reform. He approved the Dominican, Franciscan and Carmelite orders in 1216, 1223 and 1226 respectively, giving special attention to their Tertiary Orders, and in 1226 instructed King Louis VIII of France (1223–1226) to launch a holy war against the Albigensians in France. He supported the claims of Henry III (1216–1272) to the English throne over those of Prince Louis of France in 1223, negotiated the release of King Waldemar II of Denmark (1202–1240) in 1225 and was a staunch defender of the church in Bohemia. Only in his dealings with Emperor Frederick II (1220–1250) did he encounter problems, crowning him in 1220 but only in return for a promise that the emperor would embark on a Crusade. Honorius's death ended the conflict for he had threatened to excommunicate Frederick II for not honoring his promise. Honorius was the author of a collection of decretals, the *Compilatio quinta* (the *Fifth Compilation*), as well as letters, sermons, an extension of the *Liber pontificalis* and a life of Gregory VII. According to legend he was an accomplished sorcerer. See also GRIMOIRES.

**HONORIUS IV** (1210–1287) Pope from 1285 to 1287, born Giacomo Savelli, the grand-nephew of Pope Honorius III (d. 1227) and the successor to Martin IV (1281–1285). He was in conflict with King Pedro III of Aragon (1276–1285) over control of Sicily, which had been lost to the papacy in 1282, following its conquest by Aragon during the war of the Sicilian Vespers. He was also a supporter of the mendicant orders.

**HORMISDAS, SAINT** Pope from 514 to 523, successor to Symmachus (498–514) and the pontiff who ended the Acacian Schism (484–519) separating the Eastern and Western Churches, caused by the excommunication of Acacius, patriarch of Constantinople, for heresy. Unable to resolve the conflict with Emperor Anastasius I (ruled 491–518), he finally negotiated a settlement with Justin I (ruled 518–527) and John of Cappadocia, patriarch of Constantinople. Not only was unity within the church achieved, but the pope on acceptance for the Tome of Leo I, the decisions of the Council of Chalcedon (451) and the increased authority of the Roman see. See also SCHISMS.

**HOSPITALERS** See MILITARY ORDERS.

**HOWEL THE GOOD** (d. 950) Also called Howel Dda, ruler of much of Wales but called in the Welsh tradition the king of Wales. Through marriage or succession he acquired control over much of the country, including Dyfed in the southwest, Gwynedd in the northwest and Powis in the northeast. The key to his success was his amity with the English kings, to whom he declared allegiance. He submitted in 918 to Edward the Elder and to the other Saxon kings, including Athelstan and Edred. According to tradition he was the codifier of Welsh law. See also WALES.

**HRABANUS MAURUS** See RABANUS MAURUS.

**HROSVIT** See ROSVITHA, SAINT.

**HUBERT, ARCHBISHOP OF CANTERBURY** See WALTER, HUBERT.

**HUBERT DE BURGH** (d. 1243) Chief justiciar in England during the reigns of John (1199–1216) and Henry III (1216–1272). Originally John's chamberlain, he was named justiciar in 1215, defeating an uprising of barons later that year. Following the death of the regent, William Marshal, earl of Pembroke, in 1219, he became the most important figure in Henry's reign until the boy declared himself of age in 1227. Named justiciar for life, he found his authority reduced by Henry, especially after the return of his rival, Peter des Roches, from crusade. In 1232 he was dismissed and imprisoned for treason, released in 1234 and reconciled with the king, although he was never reinstated to a position of prominence.

**HUGH CAPET** (c. 938–996) King of France from 987 to 996 and the first of the Capetian line. Few details of his life are available, but he was the son of Hugh the Great and received the name Capet from the cape that he wore. He succeeded to the title of duke of the Franks in 956, on the death of his father, emerging on the scene during the decline of the Carolingians. Throughout the reign of King Lothair (954–986) he amassed power, allying himself with Emperors Otto II (973–983) and Otto III (983–1002) and Adalbern, archbishop of Reims. Thus, when Lothair died in 986, Hugh had considerable influence. He chose to accept the heir, Louis V (986–987), presumably to avoid a civil war. In 987 Louis fell from a horse and died, and Hugh was elected king over the Carolingian claimant, Charles of Lorraine. Several years of intrigue followed, as Charles attempted his overthrow, and the country was troubled by rebellions, most notably one raised by Eudes

I, count of Blois. Hugh died of smallpox and was buried in the basilica of Saint-Denis. The dynasty he founded would last until 1328. See also CAPETIAN DYNASTY; FRANCE.

**HUGH OF CLUNY, SAINT** (1024–1109) Abbot, reformer and an influential ecclesiastic. He entered Cluny at the age of 14 and was made its abbot by 1049, becoming an adviser to popes and bringing Cluny to prestigious heights. Its acclaim furthered the cause of monasticism in the West. A supporter of Pope Gregory VII (1073–1085) and the Gregorian Reform, he was mediator during the Investiture Controversy between the pontiff and Emperor Henry IV (1056–1106), especially during the submission of Henry to the pope at Canossa in 1077. Hugh was instrumental in the condemnation of Berengar in 1063 and attended the Council of Clermont in 1095, which he had also organized, with Pope Urban II, who had called the First Crusade.

**HUGH OF LINCOLN, SAINT** (c. 1140–1200) Founder of the first Carthusian monastery in England (1175 or 1176), at the request of King Henry II (1154–1189). Named bishop of Lincoln in 1186, he opposed many of the policies of Henry II and Richard the Lion-Hearted (1189–1199) but retained their respect. Hugh died while returning from a trip to the Grand Chartreuse, near Grenoble, his first monastery. His tomb at Lincoln became a popular place of pilgrimage, and he earned the distinction of being the first Carthusian canonized. See also CARTHUSIANS.

**HUGH OF SAINT VICTOR** (c. 1096–1141) French theologian, mystic and scholar who had a vital influence (with Richard of Saint Victor) on the abbey of Saint Victor in Paris, guiding its formation into one of the foremost institutions known for mysticism in Christendom. The nephew of Archdeacon Reinhard of Halberstadt and a noble, he entered Saint Victor and in 1133 was appointed director of studies. A devoted adherent of Saint Augustine, he was called "Alter Augustinus" (the "Other Augustine"), combining Augustianian thought with the writings of Dionysius the Areopagite (see PSEUDO-DIONYSIUS), stressing three stages of the contemplative life, the *cogitatio, meditatio* and *contemplatio*. He was the author of many theological works, including *De sacramentis christianae fidei (The Sacraments of the Christian Faith)* and *Didascalicon*, a guide to knowledge, as well as studies on grammar and mathematics. See also MYSTICISM.

**HUGH THE GREAT** (d. 956) Count of Paris, duke of the Franks and father of Hugh Capet (987–996), first of the Capetian dynasty. Son of Robert, who had reigned briefly as a rival king in 922–923, Hugh was also the brother-in-law of King Raoul (ruled 926–936) and extended his control over Neustria, Burgundy, Blois, Anjou and Champagne. He was forced in 936 to accept as king Louis IV d'Outre-Mer (936–954), so named because of the years he had spent in England. Hugh married Eadheld, sister of King Athelstan of England, while attempting to bring Louis into his camp. His brother-in-law, Otto I, foiled his plans, and Hugh was condemned by a church assembly at Ingelheim in 946. He was reconciled with Louis in 950 and was again compelled to recognize a Carolingian king when Louis died in an accident and Lothair (954–986) was named his successor. He died in Dourdan. See also FRANCE.

**HUGO OF SAINT VICTOR** See HUGH OF SAINT VICTOR.

**HUMILIATI** A movement by lay penitents originating in Lombardy during the 12th century and attracting men and women to lives of austerity, mortification, poverty and care for those who were poor and ill, including lepers. Calling for reforms in the church, the Humiliati were often confused with the similar Waldensian, Cathar and Patarine brethren and thus suffered persecution by less-discerning ecclesiastical authorities. In 1179 they were forbidden by the Third Lateran Council from preaching, and in 1184 Pope Lucius III (1181–1185) excommunicated those members who had ignored the papal ban. Pope Innocent III (1198–1216) recognized the Humiliati in 1201, establishing three orders with canons and sisters, celibate laity and married laity. The movement was finally suppressed in 1571. See also HERESIES.

**HUNAYN** (808–873) A much-respected Arabic scholar and translator, whose full name was Hunayn ibn Ishag. He made Arabic translations of classical Greek texts, including those of Aristotle, Plato and Galen. Through his school of translators, Hunayn thus provided the Islamic world with many works, among them the writings of the Neoplatonists.

**HUNDRED YEARS' WAR** A major conflict between England and France from 1337 to 1453, with periods of intense military activity and political upheaval as well as sporadic calm. Although England achieved many victories in the field and in diplomatic negotiations, the war ended in the virtual expulsion of the English from the Continent, with only Calais remaining in their hands. France, having recovered from economic devastation and anarchy, emerged as a strong, centralized monarchy during the reign of Kings Charles VII (1422–1461) and Louis XI (1461–1483). The Hundred Years' War signaled the trend from feudalism to the awakenings of national consciousness and the transformation of medieval to modern warfare, especially the increased application of artillery.

The causes of the war were many, although it is generally agreed that the principal reason for the emergence of hostilities was the reluctance of the English kings, as dukes of Guienne, to pay homage to the French monarchy. The English feared the French kings and refused to acknowledge French sovereignty over their holdings on the Continent. Contributing causes were the assistance of Philip VI (1328–1350) of France to the Scots against England; the rivalry between England and France in Flanders; territorial disagreements between Philip and King Edward III (1327–1377) of England; and the claim of Edward to the French crown as a descendant of Philip IV the Fair (1285–1314).

The first phase of the war (1337–1360) began when Edward III declared himself king of France and was successful on land and at sea. With the support of the Flemish, under the aegis of Jacob van Artevelde, he won the Battle of Sluys (Sluis) in 1340, followed by a major triumph at Crécy (1346), the capture of Calais (1347) and the routing of the French at Poitiers (1356) in which King John II (1350–1364) was captured. The French were forced to accept the Treaty of Brétigny (1360), ceding Calais and parts of western and southwestern France to the English. The reign of King Charles V the Wise (1364–1380) brought a remarkable French recovery, sparked by the oppressive taxation of Edward the Black Prince of England and the skill of Bertrand de Guesclin, who recovered most of the lost territories, his campaign constituting the second period of the war (1369–1373).

A period of relative quiet followed, but it ended violently in 1415, with the renewal of hostilities by King Henry V of England (1413–1422), who destroyed the French at Agincourt (1415) and in 1419, as a result of internal French desputes between Armagnac and Burgundy, made an alliance with Philip the Good, duke of Burgundy. The Treaty of Troyes was signed the following year, by which Henry was recognized as regent for the mentally unsound Charles VI (1380–1422) and as heir of France. The dauphin Charles (VII), however, refused to accept the circumstances, and in 1422, at Charles's death, the fighting began anew. A dark era for the French ensued, for by 1429 the English and Burgundians controlled nearly all of France north of the Loire and were besieging the city of Orléans.

Essential support in troops led by Joan of Arc appeared in 1429, however, relieving Orléans and defeating the English at Patay. Charles was crowned at Reims. Victory was possible in 1435, with the signing of the Treaty of Arras, bringing the Burgundians to the French cause. The final phase of the war thus began. The French recaptured Paris (1436), Normandy (1449–1450) and Guienne except for Bordeaux (1449–1451). Bordeaux fell in 1453, leaving only Calais in English hands. Distracted and divided by the Wars of the Roses, the English could mount no efforts to reclaim their positions, and the war ended in a French victory. See also COEUR, JACQUES; ENGLAND; FRANCE; WARFARE.

**HUNGARY** Country of eastern Europe, lying in the Danubian plain to the south and west of the Carpathian Mountains. The territory emerged from parts of the Roman provinces of Pannonia and Dacia, although it is generally agreed that Hungary came into existence in the late ninth century during the region's occupation by the Magyars, who succeeded the Huns, Ostrogoths and Avars. A Finno-Ugric people who lived mainly on the Volga and Kama Rivers, the Magyars were on the Don River by the ninth century, as part of a confederation of tribes, driven west by the Petchenegs (c. 889). In 892 they dispatched a force to support the Carolingian emperor Arnulf in his dispute with the Moravians, sending back stories that the region of the Carpathian plain was hospitable. A large body of Magyars migrated across the Carpathians, settled their new land (c. 896) and, having quelled local peoples, annihilated the Moravians and occupied Pannonia led by their chief, Arpad, first of the Hungarian dynasty. The Magyars served as mercenaries but were known chiefly as feared marauders. This way of life was altered in 955, when they were defeated by Otto I (962–973) at the Battle of Lechfeld. Christianity was introduced, and the tribes began trade and diplomatic negiotiations with Bavaria and other neighbors. In 975 an important religious and political step was taken by Prince Geza, Arpad's great-grandson, when he accepted baptism into the Christian faith.

Saint Stephen I ruled (997–1038) effectively, receiving his crown and royal insignia on Christmas Day in the year 1000 from the pope, thereby bringing his kingdom into the Christian fold. His reign, however, was followed by unrest and strife. Ladislas I (ruled 1077–1095) consolidated Hungary politically and religiously, but the power of the crown rested almost entirely on the personal will of the current king. Thus, when the weak monarch Andrew II (ruled 1205–1235) was forced in 1222 by the nobles to issue the Golden Bull, which affirmed the rights of the common people and the privileges of the aristocracy, autocratic rule was reduced. Andrew was succeeded by Béla IV (ruled 1235–1270), who reigned during the virtual destruction of Hungary by the Mongols (1241–1242). He rebuilt, but in 1301, with the death of Andrew III (1290–1301), the Arpad line ended. In 1308 the first foreign king claimed Hungary's throne.

He was Charles Robert of Anjou (ruled 1308–1342), who with his son, Louis the Great (ruled 1342–1382), did much to bring Western culture, industry and general progress to Hungary. The court was notable, the population rose and the economy was strengthened. Louis's daughter Mary was crowned in 1352, and her husband, Sigismund of Luxembourg (1387–1437), ruled as her successor and consort until his death in 1437. He encouraged trade and the arts but was resented by the Hungarians because of his duties as German king, Bohemian king and emperor. His taxation, the radical Hussite doctrines he permitted and the fear of the approaching Ottoman Turks sparked rebellion. Sigismund marched against the Turks but was routed at Nicopolis in 1396, as Serbia, Bosnia, Wallachia and Moldavia fell.

At the death of Sigismund, his daughter's husband, Albert V of Austria (1437–1439), was accepted as king on the condition that he never become emperor. He died, however, in 1439, and another battle, at Varna in 1444, brought his son, Ladislas V (Ladislas Posthumus), to the throne under the guardianship of the celebrated general János Hunyadi. Ladislas died in 1457, and the nobles, wishing a Hungarian ruler, chose Hunyadi's son, Matthias Corvinus, as king. Matthias (ruled 1458–1490) offered Hungary a golden age, as he was a patron of the arts and possessed his capable "Black Army," which reestablished Hungarian control of Serbia, Bosnia, Wallachia, and Moldavia, opposing both Austria and Bohemia. In 1469 he captured Moravia, Lusatia and Silesia and in 1478 Styria and Lower Austria. Achieving these successes, he ignored the threat of the Ottoman Turks. His sudden death in 1490 thus put Hungary in danger. See also AVARS; BAVARIA; BOHEMIA; BOSNIA; BYZANTINE EMPIRE; HOLY ROMAN EMPIRE; KHAZARS; MONGOLS; OTTOMAN EMPIRE; PETCHENEGS; POLAND; SERBIA; and individual rulers.

**HUNNERIC** (d. 484) King of the Vandals from 477 to 484 and the successor to his father, Geiseric. Already advanced in age when he came to the throne, he departed from previous policies of aggressive expansion and military activity, curbing the ravaging of the Mediterranean by the Vandal fleet. He was intent rather on persecuting the orthodox Christian population of the kingdom, adhering to his own strict Arian beliefs. It was said of him that he preferred mutilation to execution, although thousands probably died during his reign. The Vandals confronted many enemies during his reign, including the Moors of the Atlas Mountains. Hunneric died while planning a campaign against them. His wife of 16 years was Eudocia, the daughter of Emperor Valentinian III, who had been taken hostage in the Vandal sack of Rome in 455. See also VANDALS.

**HUNNIADES, JOHN** See HUNYADI, JÁNOS.

**HUNYADI, JÁNOS** (c. 1407–1456) Hungarian general and hero, the most successful military figure opposing the Ottoman Turks in the 15th century. A Wallachian by descent, he was in the service of Emperor Sigismund (1410–1437), traveling to Italy and studying the arts of war with Francisco Sforza, the Milanese condottiere. Hunyadi defeated the Ottomans, receiving the governorship of the region of Severia, then the governorship of Transylvania, where he drove the Turks from the region. In 1443 he launched the "Long Campaign" against the Turks in the Balkans, capturing Sofia and disabling the Turkish presence in Bosnia, Serbia and Bulgaria. His triumph ended, however, in 1444, with the annihilation of the Hungarians at Varna, where he barely escaped.

Serving as governor of Hungary during the minority of King Ladislas V in 1446, he restored order and countered the Turks, being defeated at Kossovo. He saw his popularity wane but remained captain general of Hungary until 1456, when he won his greatest victory, the relief of the besieged city of Belgrade on July 22. Days later he died of plague.

**HUS, JAN** (c. 1373–1415) Bohemian religious reformer, whose teachings were a major influence on the events of the 15th century, foreshadowing the spirit of the Reformation and called heretical by the papacy. Hus was born in Husinec and studied at the University of Prague. Ordained in 1400 and attracted by the teachings of John Wycliffe, he earned a reputation as a preacher. He associated himself with Jerome of Prague and a reform movement that led to his being denounced in Rome in 1407 and forbidden to preach by Shinko von Hasenburg, the archbishop of Prague, in 1408, on instructions from Pope Innocent VII.

When King Wenceslas IV (1363–1419) ousted Germans from the University of Prague in 1409, Hus became the rector and instituted Wycliffe's doctrines, which challenged papal authority. The archbishop pronounced a bull ordering the destruction of all Wycliffe's materials in 1410, and Hus was excommunicated in 1411 and again formally in 1412. Wenceslas removed him from the university and Hus fled, taking that time to write his major work, *De ecclesia* (1413). In 1414 the Council of Constance demanded his appearance to answer charges of heresy, and Hus left Bohemia after Emperor Sigismund (1411–1437) promised safe conduct. The Dominicans incarcerated him, however, and he was condemned, despite the emperor's efforts. On July 6, 1415, he died at the stake, an act causing dramatic repercussions in Bohemia. The Hussites rose as a force for radical reform, and Hus became a symbol of Bohemian (later Czech) nationalism. See also BOHEMIA; HUSSITE WARS; TABORITES.

**AL-HUSAYN** (c. 629–680) Son of the fourth caliph Ali and thus the grandson of Muhammad by his daughter, Fatima. Al-Husayn (or al-Husain) was a great Islamic figure, holding with his brother, al-Hasan, the title of imam. Although he was considered a major candidate for the caliphate after the death of Mu'awiya in 680, it was the dead caliph's last wish that he be succeeded by his own son, Yazid. Yazid was not considered suitable, and a faction arose to support Husayn. While journeying to Kufa, he was murdered by Yazid's followers. Subsequently revered as a martyr by the Shiites of Persia, Husayn was remembered and mourned each year on the anniversary of his death. See also ISLAM.

**HUSSITE WARS** A series of conflicts fought from 1419 to 1436 in Bohemia and Moravia, caused by the hostilities between the nationalist Bohemians and the Catholic German inhabitants of the region, and later between the Hussites (supporters of Jan Hus), who had split into two camps, the Utraquists (moderates) and the Taborites (radicals). The Hussites, favoring the Bohemians, took up arms in 1419 to oppose the succession of Emperor Sigismund (1411–1437) to the throne of Bohemia, relying on their gifted general, Jan Zizka, and the leadership of Prokop (Procopius) the Great to defeat the imperial armies in 1420 and 1422 and to invade Silesia (1425–1426) and then Franconia (1429–1430). The Council of Basel (1431–1449) presented the Hussite delegates with the Compactata of Prague, offering them a return to the church. The Utraquists accepted, but the radical Taborites refused, thereby sparking another war. At the Battle of Lipany in 1434, the Taborites were routed. Two years later the Compactata was signed, Sigismund became king of Bohemia and the Hussite movement died. See also BOHEMIA; HUS, JAN.

**HYACINTH OF CRACOW, SAINT** (1185–1257) Christian missionary in Poland and Scandinavia, who was called the "Apostle of the North." He entered the Dominicans order in 1220, setting out for his native Poland as an evangelizer. He taught among the Slavs throughout much of eastern Europe and then went to Denmark, Norway and Sweden, possibly reaching the Black Sea in his later years. He was called Saint Iaccho or Jacek in Poland.

# I

**IAROSLAV** See YAROSLAV.

**IBN AL-ARABI** (1165–1240) His full name Muhyuddin ibn al-Arabi, one of the acclaimed mystics of Muslim Spain, who had was major influence on Islamic philosophy and thought. Born in Murcia, Spain, he spent years in Seville, departing in 1198 on a pilgrimage to Mecca. During his journey he traveled to Egypt and regions of the Islamic East and settled in Damascus around 1223. His principal work was a philosophical encyclopedia *Al-futuhal al-makkiya (The Meccan Revelations).* Among his other widely read works were *al-Isra'ila maqam al-Asra (Nocturnal Journey to the Place of God), Fusus al-hikam (The Bezels of Wisdom)* and the love poems, *Tarjuman al-ashwaq (The Interpreter of Desires).*

**IBN AL-ATHIR** (1160–1233) Arab historian considered the major Islamic historical writer of the 13th century, the son of an official in the government of the Zangids of Mosul. He lived there for a time before traveling to Baghdad later residing in both Aleppo and Damascus. His greatest work was *Kamil at-tawarikh (Historical Compendium),* a history of the Muslim world from the Creation. His scholarship was careful, and he was a major source for contemporary events, relying on both personal experience and the literary circle surrounding Saladin. Ibn al-Athir was also the author of the *History of the Atabegs of Mosul.* See also MOSUL.

**IBN BAJJAH** (c. 1095–c. 1138) Also called as Avempace, a Spanish-Arab Aristotelian philosopher, an important predecessor of Averroës, writing the unfinished *Tadbir al-mutawahhid,* or *Rule of the Solitary,* in which he discussed the union of the human soul with the divine. A scientist and physician, he also wrote a work on botany.

**IBN BATTUTA** (1304–1368) Known as Muhammad Ibn Abdullah Ibn Battuta, the foremost Arab traveler in the Middle Ages, whose exploits were recounted in the celebrated work *Rihlah.* Born in Tangier, Ibn Battuta embarked on his journeys in 1325, when he went to Egypt and Syria. Subsequently he traveled throughout virtually the entire Islamic world (except for Persia and Armenia) and beyond. After visiting the khan of the Golden Horde (c. 1323), he arrived in Delhi, spending nearly eight years in the service of the sultan Muhammad Tughlag. About 1342 he went to China, reaching the Maldive Islands, where he was named *qadi* (judge), as he had been at Delhi. In 1352 or 1353, he journeyed into the interior of West Africa, reaching the Empire of Mali and the city of Timbuktu. Account of his travels also included his years in India and described Indian culture and life at the sultan's court. See also CARPINI, GIOVANNI DE PIANO; POLO, MARCO.

**IBN EZRA, ABRAHAM BEN MEIR** (d. c. 1167) Jewish scholar, traveler and Neoplatonist. Born in Spain, he visited Rome, Mantua, Lucca, London and southern, France. Known originally for his considerable talent as a poet as well as for being an associate of the Jewish philosopher Judah Halevi, he won later fame as a biblical exegete. His commentaries on the Psalms, the books of Job and Daniel and the Pentateuch were widely disseminated during what has been called the golden age of Spanish Judaism. He died while returning to Spain. See also JEWS AND JUDAISM.

**IBN EZRA, MOSES** (c. 1060–c. 1138) One of the major Jewish poets of Spain, called Moses ben Jacob Ibn Ezra, in the family of the biblical exegete Abraham Ibn Ezra (d. c. 1167). The rejection by one of his older brothers for his marriage to a niece had a major effect on his life and his poetry. A brilliant poet in Hebrew, he was the first to write secular verse, his subjects love, nature and growing old, later writing penitential prayers for the holy days. His treatise on poetry, in Arabic, *Kitab al-muhadara wa al-mudhabarah (Conversations and Recollections),* was concerned with not only Jewish but Arabic and Castilian poetry as well. See also JEWS AND JUDAISM.

**IBN GABIROL** (c. 1021–1070) Poet and Neoplatonic philosopher, his full name Solomon ben Yehuda ibn Gabirol and also called, in the West, Avicebron. One of the major literary figures of the Jewish golden age in Moorish Spain, he won the patronage of an influential courtier, Yehutial ibn Hasan, becoming fluent in both Hebrew and Arabic literature and religious traditions. His celebrated rhymed verse was *Keter malkut (The Crown of the Kingdom).* His views as a confirmed Neoplatonist also affected Christian philosophy, respected by the Cabalists and later by Spinoza. His major philosophical work was the *Fountain of Life,* five treatises examining the purpose of existence. See also JEWS AND JUDAISM.

**IBN HANBAL, AHMAD** Ninth-century Islamic legalist who espoused the cause of traditionalism in the religious laws of Islam. This means that he argued that literal interpretation of the Koran and close adherence to the deeds of Muhammad were sufficient guidance, and he argued against more liberal interpretation of the Koran. An imam, he was a student of the teachings of Shafii, the founder of the Shafi school. Staunchly conservative, Ahmad was imprisoned by liberal caliphs such as al-Mamun and al-Mu'tasim, once in 833 for opposing the popular Mu'tazili doctrines. He found supporters, called Hanbalis, in Saudi Arabia.

**ALI IBN HAZM,** (994–1064) The most illustrious writer of Moorish Spain, who reportedly was the author of some 400 books on a wide variety of subjects, including history, poetry and religion. A vizier to the Umayyads of Spain, Abd er-Rahman V and Hisham III, Ibn Hazm went into retirement upon the collapse of the Spanish caliphate. His best-known book was the *al-Fast, fi-al-milal, w-al-Ahwa, w'al-Nihal (The Final Word on Creeds and Heresies).*

**IBN KHALDUN** (1332–1406) His full name Abu Zaid Abd al-Rahman ibn Muhammad ibn Khaldun, the celebrated Arab historian, responsible for the advancement of a crucial philosophy of history. Born in Tunis, he obtained a position at court and commenced a life of adventure, which led to travel, imprisonment and the favor of many princes. In 1375 he sought refuge in Algeria from political chaos, living with the Awlad 'Arif and composing his masterpiece, the *Muqaddimah,* a work in which he observed human history from the perspective of social transformation. He noted the elements of learning, historiography, economics, politics and culture held together by what he called *'asabiyah,* or social cohesion.

In Algeria he completed his masterwork and began the *Kitab al-'ibar (Book of Examples),* which would serve as a major source of information on the history of Muslim North Africa. He then went to Alexandria, serving the Mamluk ruler there and appointed chief judge, or *qadi,* of the Maliki rite of the Sunni Islamic faction. His family, finally allowed to leave Tunis, sailed to join him but died in a shipwreck. In his later years, ibn Khaldun met Tamerlane (Timur the Lame), discussing various topics with him.

**IBN KHALLIKHAN** (1211–1282) Arab historian and noted *qadi* (judge). Born in Irbil Iraq, studying in Damascus and Aleppo and serving as *qadi* in Egypt until 1261, he rose to the position of *qadi al-qudat* (chief judge) in Damascus. The author of the valuable biographical dictionary on important figures in Islamic history, the *Wafuyat al-'avan wa Anba' abna' al-Zaman (Obituaries of Famous Men and the Biographies of Famous Contemporaries),* he listed 865 celebrated Muslims, not including the Prophet Muhammad.

**IBN QUTAYBAH** (828–c. 899) Arab scholar and writer, his name is also written as Abu Muhammad 'Abd-Allah Ibn Muslim Ibn Qutaybah. He was born in al-Kufah (Iraq) and served as a *qadi* (judge) in Dinawar before becoming a teacher in Baghdad. Respected for his fluency in Arabic, he was the author of works on theology, literature and philosophy, including *Kitab adab al-katib (Secretary's Guide),* a compilation of Arabic vocabulary and usage; *Kitab ash-shir'wa ash-shu'ara' (Book of Poetry and Poets); Kitab al-Arab (Arab Book),* a defense of Arabic culture as opposed to that of Iran; and a study of history, *Kitab al-ma'arif (Book of Knowledge).*

**IBN RUSHUD** See AVERROËS OF CÓRDOBA.

**IBN SINA** See AVICENNA.

**IBN TIBBON** A Jewish family of the 12th and 13th centuries in southern France notable for its having produced translators of Arabic works on science, language and philosophy into Hebrew. Through their efforts Arabic and Greek culture were disseminated throughout Europe. Judah ben Saul ibn Tibbon was first of the line (c. 1120–1190), fleeing Spain to settle in Lunel, France, where he practiced medicine and translated texts on philosophy from the Arabic. His son, Samuel ben Judah ibn Tibbon (c. 1150–c. 1230), was a physician and traveler and translated Aristotelian works as well as a treatise by Moses Maimonides. His son, Moses ben Samuel ibn Tibbon (d. c. 1283), made similar translations, as well as commentaries on the Pentateuch, The Song of Songs, elements of the Talmud, commentaries on Aristotle by Averroës, works by Maimonides and a medical text written by Avicenna. Jacob ben Machir ibn Tibbon (c. 1236–c. 1312) earned distinction at the university at Montpellier as a doctor but was also a noted translator and astronomer. He translated Euclid's *Elements* and Ptolemy's *Almagest* as well as other works. His writings were known to Dante and Copernicus. See also JEWS AND JUDAISM.

**IBN TUMART** See ALMOHADS.

**IBN ZUHR** (c. 1090–1162) Called also Avenzoar, one of the major Islamic medical writers of the Middle Ages and a pioneer in experimental medicine. A teacher of Averroës, he had a lasting influence on Western medicine, especially treatment of disease and surgical procedures. See also MEDICINE.

**ICELAND** Island lying west of Norway and south of the Arctic Circle, discovered by the Irish before 800 but sparsely inhabited except for Irish monks who fled when the Norse arrived, about 850–870. The Norse were led by Ingólfur Arnarson, settling at Reykjavik, which became the island's capital in 874. The Icelanders, independent, restricted the number of chieftancies to 36 and later to 39, agreeing to meet once a year to enact laws and settle disputes. The Althing (parliamentary assembly) was thus established in 930, power being held equally by the participating groups. The lawspeaker, elected every three years, was master of proceedings at the Althing, and a supreme court was added in 1005 to ensure a greater degree of democratic procedure.

Christianity was introduced in Iceland and in 1000 was accepted by the Althing, but paganism was preserved in Icelandic literature. The church in Iceland and the nobles amassed considerable power in the 12th century, and civil war erupted in 1262. Norwegian influence increased as a result, culminating with the claim of sovereignty over the island by King Haakon IV of Norway from 1261 to 1264. The power of Althing waned in the late 13th century, and royal officials came to power. In 1380, Iceland, with Norway, was claimed by the Danish crown. See also SNORRI STURLUSON.

**ICELANDIC LITERATURE** A body of works in Iceland, written from the 9th to the 14th century chiefly by Norse poets, called skalds, and composed of the poetic and prose *Edda,* sagas and skaldic poetry. The *Edda* was the title given to two works: The first, the *Prose Edda* (or *Edda* of Snorri Sturluson), was intended as a guide to skaldic versecraft and also contained information on mythology; the *Poetic Edda* (or *Elder Edda*) contained more than 30 heroic lays, which, while incomplete, were compiled at a later time. Skalds adhered to strict rules of composition, reciting rather than reading their efforts. Such intricate and rigid rules had a stultifying effect on the quality of verses and in time brought about a decline, obvious in the second half of the 13th century, when Iceland also lost its independence. Medieval Icelandic literature had a distinct influence on subsequent Icelandic literary achievement. See also ICELAND.

**ICONOCLASTICISM** Also called the Iconoclastic Controversy or iconoclasm, a dispute concerning the veneration of icons within the Byzantine Empire from about 726 to 842, which arose because there was a tendency among the uneducated to worship the icons themselves. Translated as the "breakers of images," the iconoclasts referred to the biblical ban on graven images as their argument opposing icons, finding support from the Monophysites, Manichaeans and Paulicians and from Asia Minor, where the influence of Islam had increased. Icons, however, were extremely popular, especially in the seventh century.

In 726, Emperor Leo III the Isaurian (717–741) declared all images idolatrous, an act designed to allow him to add to the state's powers in ecclesiastical affairs and to remove an impediment to the conversion of Jews and Muslims.

The ruling brought about an upheaval, but Leo's son, Constantine V (ruled 741–775), continued his father's policies. Leo IV (ruled 775–780) and his wife, Irene, regent for Constantine VI, reversed the decision on iconoclasticism, summoning the Seventh General Council at Nicaea (787), where degrees of veneration were defined and icons restored.

In 814 the second Iconoclastic Controversy began in the reign of Leo V the Armenian (ruled 813–820), who decreed the removal of icons from churches and other buildings and sent monks to prison or into exile or executed them. His successor, Michael II (ruled 820–829), was less violent, but his son, Theophilus (ruled 829–842), reinstated violent persecutions once again. After his death his widow, Theodora, regent for Michael III, ordered an end to iconoclasticism and restored the icons, an event still celebrated in the Orthodox Eastern Church. The Iconoclastic Controversy increased the already strained relations between the Roman and Byzantine churches. See also ART AND ARCHITECTURE, BYZANTINE; BYZANTINE EMPIRE; CONSTANTINOPLE; SCHISMS.

**IDRISI** (c. 1100–1165) Arab geographer, traveler and poet, who was the author of the notable geographical work *The Book of Roger.* Named in full Abu Abd Allah Muhammad al-Idrisi, he was born in the Spanish quarter of Ceuta in Morocco, later studying at Córdoba. He traveled and then entered the service of King Roger II of Sicily (1130–1154) as a geographer and cartographer. At the request of Roger he composed *Nuzhat al-mushtaq fi khtiraq al-afaq (The Pleasure Excursion of One Who Is Eager to Travel the Regions of the World).* This great work, completed in 1154, contained much information on Sicily, the Mediterranean region and the Balkans but has long been criticized for its reliance on the work of earlier inaccurate geographers and a lack of scientific method, as well as the failure to include recent contributions such as those of al-Biruni.

**IDRISIDS** Islamic dynasty of North Africa, named for its founder Idris ibn Abd Allah. A descendant of Hasan, the son of Fatima and Ali (daughter and son-in-law of the prophet Muhammad), he fled the Abbasids and found refuge with the Berbers of northern Morocco in 788. He became their leader in 789, conquering Tlemcen and establishing a new capital at Fez. From the time of Idris II (d. 828), the line was divided between Fez and Tlemcen, where Idris's cousin, Muhammad ibn Sulayman, ruled. Further division came with Idris's son, who partitioned the kingdom among the principalities of Fez, Tangier, Basra, the Rif and other regions. In the 10th century the Idrisids became embroiled in the conflict between the Fatimids and Umayyads of Spain, causing their eventual collapse. See also FATIMID CALIPHATE.

**IGOR** (d. 945) Grand prince of Kiev, reigning from 912 to 945. The son of Rurik, prince of Novgorod, Igor succeeded his father but was considered greedy and rapacious according to the account in the *Russian Primary Chronicle* of the 12th century. He embarked on unsuccessful foreign ventures, beginning in 913–914, when he led an army into Transcaucasia and was defeated. In 941 and 944 he failed in an attempt over the Byzantines, losing most of his fleet to the ravages of Greek Fire and was forced to accept very unfavorable terms of peace. Winning sovereignty over the Slavic tribe of the Drevlyane (in the region of the Pripyat River), he demanded additional tribute, causing a revolt in which he was slain. See also RUSSIA.

**IGOR SVYATOSLAVICH** (d. 1202) Russian prince ruling the lands of Novgorod-Seversky and, from 1198 to 1202, Chernigovsky. He is best known for his campaign against the Cumans in 1185. After a long battle, his army was crushed, and he, along with three relatives, was captured. He escaped the following year and returned home to rule until his death. The campaign was immortalized as the "Lay of the Host of Igor," probably written in the 12th century and discovered in 1795. Presenting Igor as a great hero, the lay was the plot for Anton Borodin's opera *Prince Igor.* See also RUSSIA.

**IKSHIDIDS** Ruling dynasty in Egypt from 935 to 969, founded by Muhammad ibn Tughj al-Ikshid. A Turk from the region of Fergana, he was appointed governor of Egypt in 935 but in 937 was named *ikshid* (or *ikkshid*), meaning prince, by the Abbasid caliph. Successfully defending his position from threats by ambitious Abbasid officials, he awarded the title to his sons, Abu'l-Qasim Anujur and Ali, although true power rested in the hands of the vizier, Abu'l-Misk Kafur, a former slave from Ethiopia or the Sudan. The dynasty met its defeat in 969 at the hands of the Fatimids. See also EGYPT.

**ÎLE-DE-FRANCE** Region in northern France surrounding Paris, the traditional capital of the nation, called the cradle of the French monarchy and the territory from which France derived its name (originating in the 15th century). During the era of Merovingian rule, the term Francia designated the region between the Seine and the Rhine Rivers, receiving a more specific meaning from the Carolingians, who declared it the region bounded by the Seine, Aisne and Oise Rivers. The word *île* (island) was adopted because the region was surrounded by water. Hugh Capet, ruler of this county of Paris, became king in 987, and the crown added other domains, including parts of Brie and the Vexin, becoming a province in the 15th century. See also FRANCE.

**ILLUMINATED MANUSCRIPTS** See MANUSCRIPT ILLUMINATION.

**IMAM** See Glossary.

***IMITATION OF CHRIST*** See THOMAS À KEMPIS.

**INDULF** (d. 962) King of Scotland from 954 to 962. Little is known about his reign, which was noted for only one event: Edinburgh (Dun Eideann) was abandoned by the English, becoming a permanent Scottish possession. Indulf's successor was Dubh. See also SCOTLAND.

**INE** (d. after 726) King of Wessex from 688 to 726, one of the most powerful and ablest of the Anglo-Saxon kings before Alfred the Great. He encouraged the church, exercised dominion over neighboring lands and gave the notable code of laws that served as the basis for Alfred's later legal system. The son of Cenred, in 688 he became the successor to Caedwalla (c. 685–688), who retired. Ine compelled the people of Kent in 694 to pay a compensatory fee for burning Caedwalla's brother, Mul, and removed other rivals for the throne. The See of Sherborne was established in his reign, as was the complex and significant code of law for the West Saxons, preserved as an appendix to King Alfred's laws. In 726, following Caedwalla's example, Ine retired and went to Rome, where he is thought to have founded the first English school. See also WESSEX.

**INEZ DE CASTRO** See CASTRO, INÉS DE.

**INGI I HARALDSSON** (c. 1134–1161) King of Norway from 1136 to 1161, sharing power with his brothers, Sigurd III Mouth (1136–1161) and Eystein II (1142–1157). The son of King Harald IV Gilchrist (ruled 1130–1136), Ingi, called "the Hunchback," inherited the throne with Sigurd, later joined by Eystein. Ingi, the only legitimate heir, inherited the throne at age two and was supported by the Norwegian aristocracy and clergy. Injured as an infant, he was a hunchback, a condition that did not lessen his popularity, even among his thanes. In 1155, however, Sigurd and Eystein were allied against Ingi, and he had Sigurd killed. His soldiers slew Eystein in 1157. Sigurd's bastard son, Haakon II the Broad Shouldered (1161–1162), was proclaimed king by Sigurd's allies. Ingi died in battle in 1161. See also NORWAY.

**INGI BARDSSON** (c. 1185–1217) King of Norway from 1204–1217, named to the throne by the political faction of the Trendekag and the Church. He was the grandson of Sigurd III Mouth (1136–1161). A weak ruler, he was dominated by the powerful nobles of the kingdom. His successor was Haakon IV the Old (1217–1263). See also NORWAY.

**INGOLSTADT** City in Bavaria, situated on the Schutter and Danube Rivers, first mentioned in 806 as a holding of the crown, becoming a duchy in 1392. The first town charter was granted in 1250, and its university was established there in 1472. Many medieval structures remain, including the Cross Gate (14th century) and the Late Gothic Cathedral of Our Lady (1425–1500). See also BAVARIA; UNIVERSITIES.

**INNOCENT II** (d.1143) Pope from 1130 to 1143, born Gregorio Paparesch Dei Guidoni, and ambassador from Pope Calixtus II (1119–1124) to the Concordat of Worms (1122). Succeeding Honorius II (1124–1130), he faced a rival claimant, Anacletus II, and Innocent fled to France. Only with the support of Bernard of Clairvaux, the German king Lothair III (1125–1137) and King Henry I of England (1100–1135) was he able to claim his papal throne. Anacletus II, allied with King Roger II of Sicily, remained a threat until his death in 1138. Roger sponsored another antipope, Victor IV, who resigned after the intervention of Bernard. Innocent was captured by Roger, however, who forced him to acknowledge his claim to Sicily. Innocent upheld the condemnation of Peter Abelard at the Council of Sens in 1140.

**INNOCENT III** (c. 1160–1216) Pope from 1198 to 1216, considered one of the most powerful medieval popes. An ardent advocate of papal power, he strove to reform the church and involved himself in the conflicts between England and France. He also quarreled with Emperor Frederick II (1220–1250). Born Lothair of Segni, he succeeded Celestine III (1191–1198) and set about reducing the independence of the Italian aristocracy, reclaiming papal supremacy in the Papal States. He opposed the possession of Sicily by the Holy Roman Empire and issued the bull *Venerabilem* (1202), delineating papal authority in the election of the Holy Roman Emperors. He supported Frederick II in his quest for the throne, forced King Philip II Augustus of France (1180–1223) to be reconciled with his wife and compelled King John of England (1199–1216) to accept Stephen Langton as the archbishop of Canterbury, as well as the sovereignty of the papacy. A patron of the Franciscan and Dominican orders, he presided over the Fourth Lateran Council (1215) and called for a Crusade against the Albigensians and other heretical movements. The Fourth Crusade, ensuing from his call, resulted in the overthrow of the

Byzantine Empire in 1204. Innocent named Thomas Morasini, a Venetian, as Latin patriarch of Constantinople. He also attempted to strengthen the influence of the church in the Balkans.

**INNOCENT IV** (d. 1254) Pope from 1243 to 1254, whose reign was occupied principally by his bitter conflict with the Hohenstaufens, particularly Emperor Frederick II (1220–1250). Born Sinibaldo Fieschi, from Genoa, he served in various capacities until succeeding to the papal throne. An enemy of Frederick II, he was forced to flee Italy after convening the Council of Lyons in 1245. The council excommunicated Frederick, and Innocent was instrumental in the rise of Henry Raspe, the landgrave of Thuringia, as German anti-king in 1246. After Frederick's death in 1250, he opposed the other Hohenstaufens, Conrad IV (1250–1254) and Manfred, earning criticism by many because of the heavy taxation demanded to finance his wars. Innocent favored continuance of efforts to convert Muslims, sending an emissary to the Mongols as well.

**INNOCENT V** (c. 1224–1276) Pope from January to June 1276. Known as Pierre of Tarentaise, he was a Dominican and colleague of Albertus Magnus and Thomas Aquinas, and the first Dominican to become pope. Named French provincial of the order (c. 1264–1267 and 1269–1272), he became archbishop and then cardinal. During his brief tenure as pope he made efforts to unite the Roman and Greek churches. He was also the author of a well-known commentary on Lombard's *Sentences.*

**INNOCENT VI** (1282–1362) Pope from 1352 to 1362, born Étienne Aubert, and successor to Pope Clement VI (1342–1352). Two issues dominated his reign, the Curia and the condition of the Papal States. He reformed and reorganized the Curia at Avignon, using his representative, Cardinal Gil Albornoz, as vicar general of the Papal States to reestablish authority there. Innocent also called for a Crusade and entered into negotiations to unite the Roman and Greek churches.

**INNOCENT VII** (c. 1335–1406) Pope from 1404 to 1406, known as Gentile de'Migliorati while a teacher at Perugia and Padua. He succeeded Boniface IX (1389–1404) as pope, and his reign was plagued by the conflict wrought by the Great Schism causing the election of the antipope Benedict XIII (1394–1417). An attempt to halt the schism by summoning a council at Rome in 1404 came to nothing because of the opposition from the Roman populous.

**INNOCENT VIII** (1432–1492) Pope from 1484 to 1492, a member of a Roman senatorial family, born Giovanni Battista Cibò. Elected through the influence of Cardinal Giuliano della Rovere (later Pope Julius II, 1503–1513), Innocent acquired a reputation for immorality and corruption as pope. He sold offices and created new ones to sell to raise monies, his treasury depleted from wars with several Italian states. Of note was his bull, *Summis desiderantes* (1484), condemning witchcraft, which was then outlawed in Germany by papal inquisitors. After his call for a Crusade against the Turks failed, he negotiated with Sultan Bayezid II, receiving the sultan's brother as hostage to the Vatican.

**INQUISITION** A method employed in the extirpation of heresy by a special ecclesiastical tribunal. The Inquisition originated in the 13th century to stem the dissemination of heretical doctrines, particularly those of the Albigensians and Cathars. At the outset physical punishments were not condoned by the church, but in the Middle Ages the church turned to the secular authorities, who were more extreme. In 1232, Emperor Frederick II (1220–1250) issued an edict for the Holy Roman Empire against heretics, causing Pope Gregory IX (1227–1241) to appoint official papal inquisitors. The Dominican and Franciscan orders took up the posts, turning over recalcitrant heretics to the courts that were established, where the legal defenses of the accused were violated by torture. The bull *Ad extirpanda* (1252), of Pope Innocent IV (1243–1254), allowed for punishments ranging from fasting and pilgrimages for those who confessed quickly to confiscation of goods, imprisonment or execution by secular magistrates for others. Used in Germany, France and Italy, the Inquisition grew in popularity during the 13th century, declining in the following century.

The Spanish Inquisition, separate from the medieval Inquisition practiced elsewhere, remained a feared aspect of Spanish religious life until the 19th century. Approved by Pope Sixtus IV (1471–1484) in 1478, it was established by Ferdinand and Isabella (1479–1516) and remained centralized. Its original goal was to root out insincere converts among the Jews and Moors, the Marranos and Moriscos, but emerged as a broad and powerful means of regulating the practice of Catholicism. The grand inquisitor at its head was assisted by a council nominated by him and approved by the king. The first grand inquisitor was Tomás de Torquemada.

**INVESTITURE CONTROVERSY** A conflict between church and state concerning the claim of secular leaders to the right of investing abbots and bishops with their rings and staffs, receiving homage before the religious leader was consecrated. By the 11th century the papacy was eager to assert its own authority, and in 1059, Pope Nicholas II (1058–1061) attacked the custom. In 1075, Pope Gregory VII (1073–1085) issued a decree forbidding it.

The battle raged largely between the popes and the German kings, especially Emperors Henry IV (1056–1106) and Henry V (1106–1125), and involved broader political issues in time. In England, Saint Anselm enforced the decree of the Council of Rome (1099), excommunicating any participant in lay investiture and refusing in 1100 to pay homage to King Henry I of England (1100–1135). Solutions to the controversy came in the form of compromises. In England Henry received homage and the right to grant investiture but did not involve himself in ecclesiastical elections. In Germany, the Concordat of Worms (1122) brought a settlement generally acceptable to the popes and the German kings. See also GERMANY; HOLY ROMAN EMPIRE.

**IONA** Island in the Inner Hebrides, off the coast of Scotland, renowned as a center of learning and Celtic Christianity because of the monastery founded there about

563 by Saint Columba. The name of the island was derived, incorrectly, from the Gaelic *Ioua*. Probably a sacred place before Columba's arrival, Iona earned a reputation for holiness because of the presence of the saint and his followers. Converting the Picts, the monks eventually evangelized all of Scotland. In time Iona became a place of pilgrimage, despite the frequent savage attacks of the Norse from 985 until the late 10th century. The monastery was destroyed by Norse raiders, and many islanders were slain. Rebuilt, the institution became a Benedictine house in 1203. Many kings of Scotland and Norway were buried at Iona, which also served as a temporary burial place for the body of Saint Columba. See also CELTIC CHURCH; SCOTLAND.

**IPSWICH** City in Suffolk, England, that had a long history of trade and industry. Situated at the head of the Orwell Estuary, it was sacked by the Danes in the late 10th century but remained prosperous, owing to the manufacture of Ipswich ware and later the high-quality Thetford ware. Ipswich also profited from the export of East Anglia cloth. See also TRADE AND COMMERCE.

**IRELAND** Second largest British isle, situated to the west of Britain and invaded before the Christian era by Celtic tribes, who raided Roman posts in Britain and on the Continent. Among the captives brought back to Ireland was Saint Patrick (Patricius), who escaped and returned after ordination in 432 and worked for the conversion of the populace. At the start of the fifth century Druidism predominated, with a scattered Christian minority. In 431, Pope Celestine I (422–432) sent a Roman, Palladius, as bishop, and his heir was Patrick. The resulting church in Ireland became a powerful national institution, with its archepiscopal see at Armagh. The Irish church promoted learning and sent missionaries to Scotland, England and the Continent, among them Saint Columba and Saint Columbanus.

Ireland was divided into ancient kingdoms, the Pentarchy (Five Kingdoms) or the Five Fifths of Ireland: Ulster, Munster, Leinster, Connacht and Meath. The rulers of these kingdoms exercised limited control over their own chieftains and gave obedience to the high kings of Ireland, at Tara. The period from 500 to 800 was a golden age, when literary and artistic culture flourished. This was ended with the arrival of the Norse raiders in 795. By 850 the Danes had established themselves at Dublin, Limerick and Waterford, challenged by Brian Boru, who attacked and defeated them at the Battle of Clontarf in 1014. He was killed there, but the Viking raids were ended.

Brian Boru also instituted national cultural unification, culminating in 1166 with the rise of a national king, Rory O'Connor of Connacht, who ruled from Dublin. Some chieftains, such as Dermot MacMurrough of Leinster, refused to submit. He fled to England to seek the help of King Henry II (1154–1189), who had received from Pope Adrian IV (1154–1159) the right to extend English authority over Ireland, in the bull *Laudabiliter*. Henry supported Dermot, sending Richard de Clare, earl of Pembroke, called Strongbow, to Ireland. The campaign was successful, and in 1171 Henry sailed to Ireland to assert his supremacy.

Irish bronze plaque

He received homage and made feudal grants, thereby sparking Irish rebellion. English immigrants and Anglo-Saxon nobles claimed lands, especially around the Pale, the territory around Dublin. Gradually the Irish mounted a recovery, and in 1315 Irish leaders, joined by several English lords, invited Edward Bruce, brother of Robert the Bruce of Scotland, to become king. His invasion (1315–1318) failed, but soon afterward the local English families began feuding. English control was weakened, and an Irish parliament was called to deal with the crisis. In 1366 the Statutes of Kilkenny were issued, enforcing the separation of the English and Irish populations and outlawing Gaelic culture. Throughout the 15th century, most notably under the Lancastrian kings of England, Ireland was left on its own, the government ignoring the colonists and colonial possessions. Irish independence efforts increased, but the island endured famines and wars. With Tudor rule, England mounted a concentrated effort to bring the Irish under English control.

**IRELAND, JOHN** (c. 1435–c. 1500) Called also Johannes de Irlandia, a Scottish literary figure, diplomat, theologian and chaplain, who entered the service of King Louis XI of France (1461–1483) as a doctor of theology. He was dispatched on several diplomatic missions by Louis, returning to Scotland after the king's death in 1483. There he was private chaplain to King James III (1460–1488) and then James IV (1488–1513). For the latter he wrote, in 1490, the earliest work of original Scottish prose, the *Meroure of Wyssdome*, a treatise on the need for wisdom on the part of temporal rulers. See also SCOTLAND.

**IRENE** (c. 752–803) Byzantine empress and first woman to exercise imperial power over the Byzantine Empire, reigning as emperor (*basileus*, Greek for king) rather than empress (*basilissa*) from 797 to 802. She was the wife of Emperor Leo IV (775–780), becoming regent for her son Constantine VI (780–797) but serving as well as co-emperor. Irene convened the Second Council of Nicaea in 787, recognized by both the Roman and Greek churches as the Seventh Ecumenical Council, to restore veneration of icons in the empire. In 790, Irene was compelled to step down, returning two years later. A coup proving successful in 797 resulted in the arrest and blinding of Constantine, and for the next years Irene was, in fact, emperor. In 802, however, another conspiracy resulted in her fall and exile to the island of Lesbos, where she died. See also BYZANTINE EMPIRE.

**IRNERIUS** (c. 1055–c. 1130) Respected teacher and legal scholar at Bologna, probably a German and thought to have been in the service of Countess Matilda of Tuscany (d. 1115) and the Holy Roman Emperor Henry V (1106–1125). He was the first medieval scholar to make glosses of Roman legal texts, his most valuable work being an annotation of the *Corpus juris civilis* of Justinian I (527–565). Irnerius was instrumental in establishing Bologna as the leading legal center of the time. See also GLOSSATORS.

**ISAAC I COMNENUS** (c. 1005–1061) Byzantine emperor from 1057 to 1059, the first of the Comneni dynasty and successful in reviving the economic and military fortunes of the Eastern Empire. The son of the imperial officer Manuel Comnenus, he and his brother were raised by Emperor Basil II (976–1025), who gave them positions in the government and in the army. He was chosen to succeed the deposed Michael VI (1056–1057) in 1057 and concentrated on strengthening the defenses of the state. In 1059 he launched campaigns against the Hungarians and the Petchenegs. His need for additional funds, however, led him to confiscate church property, which alienated him from his former ally, the patriarch of Constantinople, Michael Cerularius. Isaac had Cerularius arrested and exiled in 1058. Declining health and general unrest compelled him to abdicate in December 1059 in favor of Constantine X Ducas (1059–1067). He retired to a monastery. See also BYZANTINE EMPIRE.

**ISAAC II ANGELUS** (c. 1155–1204) Byzantine emperor from 1185 to 1195 and from 1203 to 1204 (with his son, Alexius IV Angelus), whose second reign was concurrent with the devastating Fourth Crusade. Named as successor to his murdered cousin, Andronicus Comnenus, who died at the hands of a mob, Isaac was confronted by the Normans, who invaded Greece and ransacked Thessalonica. The Normans were defeated, but Isaac was unable to suppress a Bulgar revolt and had to recognize the Second Bulgarian Empire in 1187. Negotiating a treaty with Saladin to avoid involvement in the Third Crusade, he was compelled to deal with Frederick I Barbarossa (1152–1190), who invaded the empire on his way to the Holy Land. He signed the Treaty of Adrianople with Frederick in 1190. Alliances with the Hungarians and the defeats of the Serbs gave him hope of a resurgence of Byzantine influence in the Balkans, but in 1195 he was overthrown by his brother, Alexius III, who blinded him. After eight years of confinement in a dungeon, Isaac was rescued in August 1203, when the troops of the Fourth Crusade restored him to the throne with his son. Alexius was eventually assassinated by the Crusaders, and Isaac was deposed. He died a short time later. See also BYZANTINE EMPIRE; CRUSADES.

**ISABEAU OF BAVARIA** (1371–1435) Known also as Isabel, wife of Charles VI of France (1380–1422) and daughter of Stephen III, duke of Bavaria-Ingolstadt. Isabeau wed Charles in 1385, bearing him six children, including the dauphin, later Charles VII (1422–1461). Because of her husband's frequent bouts of insanity, she acted as regent, finding political allies in her brother-in-law, Louis duc d'Orléans, and after his murder by John the Fearless, duke of Burgundy, in 1407, in the Burgundian duke himself. Disagreements with her son led to her imprisonment and rescue by John in 1417. Three years later she accepted the Treaty of Troyes, disinheriting her son and marrying her daughter, Catherine, to Henry V of England (1413–1422). Her final years were disappointing, as she was deserted by John the Fearless, who took up Charles's cause. See also FRANCE.

**ISABELLA OF ANGOULÊME** (d. 1246) Wife of King John of England (1199–1216), already promised to Hugh of Lusignan when the marriage took place. This union gave King Philip II Augustus (1180–1223) the pretext he needed to seize Normandy. See also JOHN, KING OF ENGLAND.

**ISABELLA OF CASTILE** (1451–1504) Queen of Castile and Aragon and consort of Ferdinand II of Aragon, one of the celebrated monarchs of Spain, playing a major role in its unification. The daughter of King John II of Castile, she married Ferdinand in 1469 and succeeded to the throne of Castile in 1474 in place of her stepbrother, Henry IV (1454–1474). A civil war ensued over her royal claim with her niece Juana La Beltraneja that was not settled until 1479. That same year Ferdinand became king of Aragon, declaring Isabella his co-ruler, thus uniting Castile and Aragon. Known as the "Catholic Kings" from 1481, they were responsible for the final conquest of Granada (1482–1492), which ended with the expulsion of the Moors from Spain. A patron of the arts and literature as well as reform in the church, Isabella was a vitally important patron of Christopher Columbus. See also CASTILE.

**ISABELLA OF FRANCE** (1292–1358) Wife of King Edward II of England (1307–1327), mother of Edward III (1327–1377) and queen consort, who was infamous for her role in deposing her husband in 1327. The daughter of Philip IV the Fair of France (1285–1314), she married Edward in 1308, subsequently attempting to effect an accord between the king and his barons, especially in the presence of the royal favorite, Piers Gaveston. Unhappy with the influential Despensers, she left England in 1325, ostensibly to settle a dispute over the claims to Gascony. There she was joined by her son and a paramour, Roger Mortimer, earl of March. In 1326, with Mortimer and other exiled barons, Isabella invaded England, crushed the Despensers and deposed her husband the following year. She and Mortimer wielded great power until 1330, when her son, now king, arrested and executed Mortimer and sent Isabella into exile. She died as a member of the Poor Clares, an austere religious order. Her reputation earned her the nickname the "She-wolf of France." See also EDWARD II; EDWARD III.

**ISABELLA OF HAINAUT** (1170–1190) Queen consort of King Philip II Augustus (1180–1223) of France, marrying him in 1180 and bringing him as a dowry the province of Artois. This brought about a severe dispute among members of the House of Champagne. Isabella was the mother of Louis VIII (1223–1226). See also FRANCE.

**ISIDORE OF SEVILLE, SAINT** (c. 560–636) Archbishop of Seville, theologian and encyclopedist, considered the last of the Western Latin Fathers. He was the brother of Leander, evangelist to the Visigoths, converting them from Arianism. Isidore continued his brother's efforts after about 600, advising King Sisibut (ruled 612–621) and establishing councils to provide the Spanish church with theological and ecclesiastical unity. The Fourth Council of Toledo (633) called for unity between the church and state, toleration of Jews and uniformity in the liturgy.

An able scholar, Isidore was respected throughout Europe for works that included *Etymologiae,* an encyclopedic compilation of human and religious knowledge, also called *Orgines; De natura rerum (On the Nature of Things)*; linguistic treatises; theological works; hagiographies; and possibly the *Hispana collectio,* a compilation of canon law for the Spanish church.

**ISIDORUS OF MILETUS** The name given to two architects who flourished during the reign of Justinian I (527–565). One worked as one of the principal architects, with Anthemius of Tralles, in the construction of the Hagia Sophia from 532 to 537. Another was responsible for rebuilding the dome of the Hagia Sophia after its destruction in an earthquake in 553. See also HAGIA SOPHIA.

Saint Isidore of Seville

Mosque of al-Azhar, Egypt

**ISLAM** A major world religion and one of the most recent, appearing in the seventh century and taught by the prophet Muhammad. Deriving its name from the word for surrender (its adherents are called Muslims, those who surrendered themselves to God), Islam extended from Arabia throughout the Middle East, Africa and beyond. Within years of the death of the Prophet, the Islamic world had a real identity, beginning the conflict between Muslims and Christians that would rage for centuries. Islam, however, continued to evolve, encouraged by dynasties of Muslim rulers and the rise of diverse sects, while achieving literary, scientific and artistic heights that would influence the world. The reader is referred to the following entries, divided into Dynasties, Sects, Religious or Cultural Sites and Figures of Note:

Dynasties: See ABBASID CALIPHATE; AGHLABIDS; ALMOHADS; ALMORAVIDS; AYYUBIDS; BUYIDS; CÓRDOBA, EMIRATE OF; FATIMID CALIPHATE; GHAZNAVIDS; IDRISIDS; NASRID KINGDOM OF GRANADA; OTTOMAN EMPIRE; SAFFARID DYNASTY; SELJUK TURKS; TULUMIDS; ZENGIDS.

Sites: See ALHAMBRA; ARABIA; BAGHDAD; CAIRO; CÓRDOBA; DAMASCUS; GRANADA; AL-FUSTAT; JERUSALEM; MEDINA; SEVILLE.

## MAJOR DYNASTIES OF THE MEDIEVAL ISLAMIC WORLD

| NAME | DATES | LOCATION |
|---|---|---|
| Abbasid | 749–1258 | Ruled Islamic world |
| Aghlabids | 801–909 | Tunisia |
| Almohads | 1147–1269 | Maghrib (Iberian Peninsula) |
| Almoravids | 1086–1147 | Maghrib (Iberian Peninsula) |
| Ayyubids | 1169–1260 | Egypt, Syria and some parts of Arabian Peninsula |
| Buyids | 945–1055 | Persia (Iran) and Mesopotamia (Iraq) |
| Fatimids | 909–1171 | Egypt, Syria and Maghrib |
| Hafsids | 1228–1574 | Tunisia |
| Ghaznavids | 962–1186 | Persia (Iran) and Afghanistan |
| Idrisids | 789–926 | Morocco, North Africa |
| Ikhanids | 1256–1336 | Persia (Iran) and Mesopotamia (Iraq) |
| Mamluks | 1250–1517 | Egypt and Syria |
| Marinids | 1196–1464 | Morocco, North Africa |
| Muluk al-tawa'if ("party kings") | 11th century | Moorish Spain |
| Nasrid of Granada | 1230–1492 | Andalusian (Moorish) Spain |
| Ottoman Empire | 1281–1922 | Turkey, Levant, Egypt, North Africa and parts of the Mediterranean region |
| Rasulids | 1229–1454 | Yemen |
| Rustamids | 779–909 | Algeria |
| Saffarids | 867-late 15th century | Eastern Persia (Iran) |
| Samanids | 819–1005 | Parts of Persia (Iran) and Central Asia (Oxus Valley) |
| Seljuks, Great | 1037–1157 | Persia (Iran) and Mesopotamia (Iraq) |
| Seljuks of Iraq | 1105–1194 | Persia (Iran) and Mesopotamia (Iraq) |
| Seljuks of Rum | 1077–1307 | Anatolia (parts of Turkey) |
| Seljuks of Syria | 1078–1117 | Syria |
| Seville, Kingdom of (House of Bani Abbad) | 1023–1091 | Seville, Spain |
| Tahirids | 820–872 | Khorasan (Iraq) |
| Timurids | 1370–1506 | Parts of Persia (Iran) and Central Asia |
| Tulunids | 868–905 | Egypt and Syria |
| Umayyads | 661–750 | Ruled Islamic world |
| Umayyads of Spain | 756–1031 | Moorish Spain (Iberian Peninsula) |
| Zirids | 972–1167 | North Africa, independent of Fatimids |

Sects: See ASSASSINS, ORDER OF; DRUZES; ISMAILI SECT; SHIAH; SUFISM; SUNNI.

Figures or Related Topics: See ABBAS; ABD ALLAH IBN AL-ZUBAYR; AISHA; ALI; ART AND ARCHITECTURE, ISLAMIC; AL-ASH'ARI; AL-GHAZALI; IBN AL-ARABI; MEDICINE; SHAFII; WARFARE.

**ISLAMIC EMPIRE** See ABBASID CALIPHATE; ABU BAKR; ALI; ARABIA; BYZANTINE EMPIRE; CHARLES MARTEL; EGYPT; HASAN IBN SABBAH; AL-HUSAYN; MU'AWIYA; OSMAN; SYRIA; UMAR; UMAYYAD CALIPHATE.

**ISMAIL I** (d. 1325) Nasrid king of Granada from 1314 to 1325, the cousin of King Nasr (1309–1314), whom he overthrew in 1314. He was assassinated in 1325 by a court conspiracy, replacing him with his son, Muhammad IV (1325–1333). See also NASRID KINGDOM OF GRANADA.

**ISMAIL II** Nasrid king of Granada, ruling only from 1359 to 1360, coming to power by overthrowing his half brother, Muhammad V (1354–1359, 1362–1391). He was deposed the following year by his cousin, Muhammad VI (1360–1362). See also NASRID KINGDOM OF GRANADA.

**ISMAILI SECT** Also called Ismailiyah, a sect of the Shiite (Shiah) branch of Islam that played a role in Islamic medieval history through its proselytizing and its subjects, most notably the Fatimids and the Assassins. The Ismaili sect originated in the eighth century as a result of a dispute over succession in the Shiite imamate: whether the sixth imam, Ja'far al-Sadiq (d. 765), should be followed by his eldest son, Ismail, or by his younger son, Musa. Those who followed Musa were known as the Ithna Ashariyah, or "Twelvers" due to their belief that the line of descent ends with the twelfth imam, those who adhered to the belief in Ismail (the Ismailiyah) were called Sabiyah, or "Seveners." Members of the Ismaili sect believed in a dual interpretation of the Koran and declared a sharp distinction between the initiated Ismailis and ordinary Muslims. They

# CHRONOLOGY OF MEDIEVAL ISLAMIC HISTORY

| DATE | EVENT |
|---|---|
| 570 | Birth of Muhammad in Mecca. |
| 595 | Marriage of Muhammad to Khadija, a rich widow. |
| 608 | The Kaaba in Mecca is built. |
| 610 | Muhammad has his first revelation while in seclusion on Mount Hira; the angel Gabriel tells him that he is the Prophet. |
| 613 | Muhammad begins to preach publicly. |
| 622 | The Hegira (or Hejira) takes place from Mecca to Medina. |
| 630 | Muslims capture Mecca, making it the spiritual heart of Islam. |
| 632 | Muhammad dies in Medina, in the house of his wife A'isha. Abu Bakr, father of A'isha, becomes the first caliph of Islam. |
| 633 | Beginning of the Islamic empire as a war of conquest is launched against the Persian empire. |
| 634 | Abu Bakr dies, and Umar becomes caliph. |
| 642 | Destruction of the Persian Sassanid empire. |
| 644 | Assassination of Umar and accession of Uthman. |
| 650 | An official version of the Koran is adopted. |
| 656 | Death of Uthman and succession of Ali. |
| | Civil war erupts. |
| 661 | Ali is assassinated. |
| | Mu'awiya becomes caliph, establishing the Umayyad caliphate at Damascus. It will last until 750. |
| 669 | Islamic forces besiege Constantinople for the first time. |
| 670 | Qayrawan is established as the Islamic Africa. |
| 680 | Death of Mu'awiya and accession of his son Yazid. |
| 691 | The Dome of the Rock is constructed at Jerusalem by the caliph Abd al-Malik. |
| 696 | Arabic is designated the official administrative language of the Islamic empire. |
| 697 | Defeat of the Byzantines in Africa. |
| 711 | Advance of Islamic troops into the Iberian Peninsula from North Africa. |
| 712 | Islamic advance into India. |
| 717 | Umar II comes to the throne and initiates reforms. |
| 732 | Defeat of Islamic forces at the Battle of Tours by Charles Martel; highwater mark of the Islamic advance into western Europe. |
| 747 | Internal deterioration of the Umayyad caliphate as the caliphate is rocked by internal revolts, particularly the one led by the obscure Persian general Abu Muslim. Beginnings of the Abbasid overthrow of the caliphate. |
| 750 | End of the Umayyad caliphate brought by the Abbasids under Abbas. The Abbasid caliphate establishes a rule that will last until 1258. |
| 756 | Córdoba emerges as the chief city of Islamic Spain under the Emirate of Córdoba. |
| 762 | Mansur, brother of Abbas, founds Baghdad as his capital. |
| 766 | Baghdad is completed as the Abbasid capital. |
| 767 | Arab legalist Abu Hanifa dies in prison. |
| 785 | Construction of the Great Mosque of Córdoba is begun. |
| 786–809 | Reign of Harun al-Rashid. |
| 789 | The Idrisid dynasty of Morocco is established; it will last until 926. |
| 795 | Death of Malik ibn Anas, founder of the Maliki school of law. |
| 800 | The Aghlabids rise in Tunisia. They will survive until 909. |
| 809 | Death of Harun and eruption of civil war between his sons. |
| 813 | Al-Ma'mun, son of Harun, defeats his brother and ascends as caliph. |
| 813–833 | Reign of al-Ma'mun; it will include the flourishing of Hunayn, the translator, and Khwarizmi, the mathematician. |
| 815 | Death of Abu Nuwas the poet. |
| 827 | Islamic invasion of Sicily by the Aghlabids. |
| 830 | The "House of Wisdom" is founded at Baghdad by the caliph Ma'mun. |
| 833–842 | Reign of al-Mu'tasim. He will move the capital from Baghdad to Samarra in 836. |
| 868 | The Tulunids under Ibn Tulun take control of Egypt. They will last until 905. |
| 870 | Death of Bukhari, collector of the *Traditions.* |
| 892 | Return of the caliphate to Baghdad from Samarra under al-Mu'tadid. |
| 909 | Foundation of the Fatimid caliphate in Egypt. |
| 921 | Ibn Fadlan writes the earliest Islamic description of Russia. |
| 922 | The Sufi mystic Hallaj is executed. |
| 925 | Death of the famed physician Razi. |
| 929 | Foundation of the caliphate of Córdoba. |
| 932 | The Buyids emerge in Persia and Mesopotamia. They will come to control Baghdad and the caliphate. |

| DATE | EVENT |
|---|---|
| 965 | Death of al-Mutannabi, the panegyrist. |
| 970 | The mosque university of al-Azhar is built by the Fatimids in Cairo. |
| 986 | Subuktigan, sultan of Ghazni, invades India. |
| 1010 | *The Epic of Kings* is completed by the poet Firdawsi. |
| 1031 | Fall of Umayyads of Córdoba. |
| 1037 | Death of Avicenna (Ibn Sina). |
| 1055 | Fall of Baghdad to the Seljuk Turks. The Abbasid caliphs are retained as their puppets. |
| 1056 | Death of al-Biruni, author of works on astronomy, medicine and philosophy. |
| 1071 | The Seljuk Turks rout the Byzantines at the Battle of Manzikert, gaining control of Anatolia. |
| 1085 | Fall of Toledo to Christian forces. |
| 1087 | Timbuktu is built to serve as a center for trade and learning. |
| 1092 | Assassination of the powerful vizier to the Seljuks Nizam al-Mulk. |
| 1096 | Launching of the First Crusade to reclaim the holy places in the Middle East. |
| 1099 | Capture of Jerusalem by the Crusaders and establishment of the Crusader States. |
| 1111 | Death of al-Ghazali, theologian and mystic. |
| 1123 | Death of Omar Khayyam. |
| c. 1130 | Rise of the Almohads in Spain. |
| 1147–1149 | The Second Crusade; it fails. |
| 1165 | Death of Idrisi, traveler, geographer and author of *The Book of Roger.* |
| 1171 | Islamic general Saladin captures Egypt, bringing an end to the Fatimid caliphate and founding the Ayyubid dynasty. |
| 1176 | Sadadin captures Syria as part of his on-going jihad (holy war) against the Crusader States. |
| 1187 | Saladin captures Jerusalem after a crushing defeat of the Crusaders at the Battle of Hattin. |
| 1189–1192 | The Third Crusade; it ends in military failure, although a truce is achieved between Saladin and Richard the Lion-Hearted that allows Christians access to Jerusalem and the Holy Sepulchre. |
| 1198 | Death of Averroës (Ibn Rushd), influential philosopher and author of a commentary on Aristotle. |
| 1202–1204 | The Fourth Crusade results in the overthrow of the Byzantine Empire and the capture of Constantinople. |
| 1212 | The Moors are defeated at the Battle of Navas de Tolosa by King Alfonso VIII. |
| 1221 | Mongol armies pour into Persia after annihilating kingdom of Transoxiana and pillaging Samarkand. |
| 1222 | Mongols reach Russia. |
| 1228–1229 | The Sixth Crusade results in the occupation of Jerusalem by Emperor Frederick II through a treaty. |
| 1232 | The Nasrid Kingdom of Granada is founded. It will last until 1492. |
| 1236 | Córdoba is captured by the Christians. |
| 1244 | Jerusalem is overrun and captured by the Khwarizmians. |
| 1248–1254 | The Seventh Crusade is launched by King Louis IX of France. It fails. |
| 1250 | The Ayyubid dynasty, which has ruled Egypt since 1169, is ended by their Mamluk soldiery. The Mamluks will rule Egypt until 1517. |
| 1258 | Mongol armies under Hulagu Khan capture and sack Baghdad. Caliph Al-Muzta'sim is taken by them and kicked to death, bringing an end to the Abbasid caliphate. |
| 1260 | Defeat of the Mongols at Ain-Jalut by the Mamluks. |
| 1270 | The Eighth Crusade is again headed by King Louis IX. It is ended with his death in Egypt. |
| 1272 | The Ninth Crusade, led by Prince Edward (later Edward I) of England, ends the era of the Crusades. |
| 1273 | Death of Jalal al-Din Rumi, Persian mystic and poet. |
| 1281 | Foundation of the Ottoman Empire. It will last until 1922. |
| 1291 | The Mamluks capture Egypt and conquer the last Crusader state in the Middle East. |
| 1334 | Ibn Battuta travels to the Far East. |
| 1362–1391 | Muhammad V of Granada makes extensive additions to the Alhambra, including the Court of the Lions. |
| 1365 | The Ottoman Turks capture Adrianople in Thrace. They make the city their capital. |
| 1379 | Mongol conqueror Tamerlane (Timur the Lame) invades Persia. |
| c. 1390 | Death of Hafiz, Persian lyric poet. |
| 1393 | Armies under Tamerlane capture Baghdad. |
| 1396 | The Ottoman Turks repulse the Christian crusade of Nicopolis. |
| 1402 | Tamerlane destroys the Ottomans at the Battle of Ankyra, capturing the Ottoman sultan Bayezid I. The Ottoman Empire is thrown into disarray. |
| 1405 | Sudden death of Tamerlane. |
| 1406 | Death of Ibn Khaldun, Arab historian. |
| 1453 | Constantinople is captured by the Ottoman Turks. Fall of the Byzantine Empire. |
| 1492 | Fall of Granada to the Reconquista under Ferdinand and Isabella, end of Islamic presence in Spain as Muslim libraries are burned and the Moors and Jews are expelled. |

Elephant clock, from a treatise of al-Jazan

also claimed that Ismail's son, Muhammad at-Tamun, would return at the end of the world as the Mahdi, "the expected one." See also ASSASSINS, ORDER OF; DRUZES; FATIMID CALIPHATE.

**ISRAELI, ISAAC** (c. 855–c. 955) Jewish physician and theologian, known also as Isaac the Elder and, in the Arabic, as Abu Yaqub ibn Sulayman al-Israili. His writings had considerable influence and were translated from the Arabic into Latin and Hebrew. Born in Egypt, he became court physician in 904 to the last ruler of the Aghlabids, later entering into the service of the first of the Fatimids, the caliph al-Mahdi. He composed for him eight of his texts on medicine, in Arabic. Among his writings were *Kitab al hudud (The Book of Definitions); Sefer ha'ru'ah ve-ha-Nefesh (Treatise on Spirit and Soul);* and his medical works, which were translated by the monk Constantine into Latin in 1087. Israeli was considered an important figure in the development of Jewish Neoplatonic thought. See also MEDICINE.

**ITALY** In the Middle Ages Italy did not exist as one nation. The Italian peninsula was occupied by a collection of independent kingdoms, city-states and a section of the Holy Roman Empire, all anchored by the political and religious power of the papacy. The history of medieval Italy can be traced the division of the Roman Empire in 379 into the Eastern and Western Empires. Throughout the fifth century, the stability and power of the empire in the West deteriorated steadily. Rome had been abandoned politically by Emperor Constantine the Great (d. 337), who had built as his capital the new eastern city of Constantinople. The seat of government for the West was Ravenna, a safer location defensively than Rome, with both walls and swamps surrounding the city. The sack of Rome in 410 by the Visigoths under Alaric sent shock waves through the Roman world. Germanic incursions continued throughout the century. The Vandals pillaged the city in 455, and the final demise of the empire in the West was brought about in 476 with the deposition of Romulus Augustulus by the Heruli chieftain Odoacer.

By this time, central authority had collapsed on the Italian peninsula, replaced by the rule of the Germanic tribes, first under Odoacer (476–493) and then the Ostrogoths. The gifted and generally enlightened Ostrogothic king Theodoric (d. 526) overthrew Odoacer, though the Ostrogothic Kingdom only survived until 553. In that year, the armies of the Byzantine Empire, under Generals Belisarius and Narses, restored imperial authority. The government returned to Ravenna under an exarch.

In 568, a Germanic people, the LOMBARDS or Langobardi, descended on Italy. The papacy, particularly under Gregory I (r. 590–604), became the chief defender of Roman civilization and Rome itself, laying the foundation for the Papal States. By the middle of the eighth century the Lombards had virtually annihilated the exarchate of Ravenna and were threatening Rome, and with it the papacy. As the Lombards drove toward Rome, Pope Stephen II journeyed across the Alps and successfully petitioned King Pepin III to intervene in 754. With his intervention came the Donation of Pepin, establishing the Papal States. When the Lombards once more threatened, Pope Adrian II appealed to Charlemagne. The Franks stormed into Italy and Charlemagne destroyed the Lombard Kingdom, claiming for himself the iron crown of the Lombards. He also gave extensive gifts to the Holy See, permitting the popes to continue as the quasi-political leaders in central Italy through the States of the Church, a position they had gradually assumed in the absence of a single government. See also CHARLEMAGNE, INVESTITURE CONTROVERSY and PAPAL STATES.

## Islamic Empire, 750

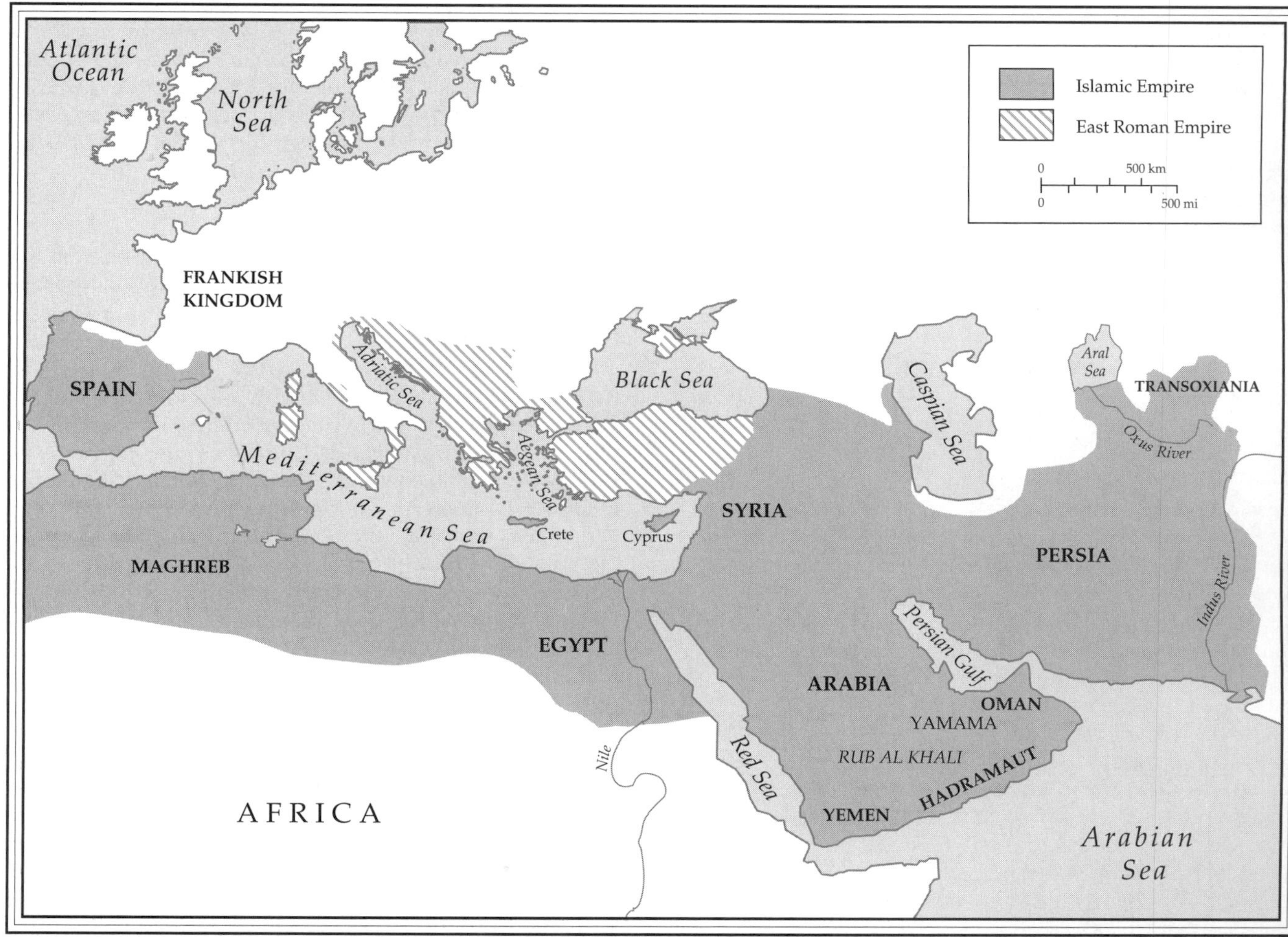


Charlemagne was crowned emperor of the West at Rome in 800 on Christmas Day by Pope Leo III, and over the next 200 years his successors would lay claim to the title of king of Italy. They would be opposed by the heirs of the powerful Frankish nobles and the ambitious Roman nobles—such as the Counts of Tusculum—who struggled to gain supremacy in Rome, most often at the expense of the papacy. The 9th and 10th centuries brought the darkest period in papal history as pontiffs were deposed, murdered and installed by scheming factions. To this chronic upheaval was added the arrival of the Saracens.

The Saracens, Muslim raiders from North Africa, captured Corsica in the early ninth century and thereafter constantly menaced southern Italy. In 846 they sailed up the Tiber and actually sacked St. Peter's Basilica, prompting Pope Leo IV to construct the famed Leonine Wall. In the 11th century, the Saracens conquered Sardinia and Sicily. The arrival of the Normans in the region put an end to their conquests.

In response to pleas from the pope for protection, the German king Otto I invaded Italy in 961. The following year he was crowned emperor, leading to the union of Italy and Germany and the start of the Holy Roman Empire. Otto sought to sustain the influence of the imperial crown through various ecclesiastical appointments in northern and central Italy. The highly secular bishops soon adopted a feudal style of administration, becoming supporters of the emperors from whom they received so much of their temporal influence. The cities over which they ruled, however, were increasingly resentful and eager to be free of the imperial yoke. The rights of investiture by the emperor became the heart of a long and bitter struggle between the papacy and the empire, whose main protagonists were Pope Gregory VII (d. 1085) and Emperor Henry IV (d. 1106).

The papacy was aided in its conflict with the empire by two main allies. The cities of Lombardy, hoping to secure their independence from imperial authority, formed themselves into the Lombard League and went to war with the popes against Emperor Frederick I Barbarossa. The Normans, meanwhile, had established themselves in southern Italy, defeating the Byzantines, the Saracens and the remnants of the Lombard duchies and by 1070 establishing a kingdom held in fief from the Holy See. With the Normans' help and especially the aid of the Lombard League, the popes were able to organize the defeat of

Frederick I in 1176 and negotiate the Peace of Vienna in 1177.

In 1194 Emperor Henry VI married Constance, heiress of the Norman house of the Kingdom of Sicily, leading to the renewal of the hostilities between the popes and emperors. By their union, Sicily and southern Italy passed to the Hohenstaufen dynasty, a development much feared by the popes, who rightly anticipated the danger. Henry's son, Frederick II, would be one of the most indomitable enemies of the Holy See, but after his death in 1250, the papacy found a formidable ally in Charles of Anjou, brother of King Louis IX of France. Supported enthusiastically by the popes, Charles exterminated the heirs of Frederick II and by 1268 the Hohenstaufens were extirpated. As a result, Charles was able to become king of Naples, thereby creating the Angevin house of Naples. This would survive only a few years in Sicily as the population of the island rose up in bloody revolt, the Sicilian Vespers, in 1282. The French were ejected from the island, replaced by the Spanish house of Aragon.

As imperial influence declined in the peninsula, France sought to fill the vacuum, sparking a new conflict between Pope Boniface VIII and King Philip IV the Fair. It ended in 1303 with Boniface's seizure by Philip's lieutenant Guillaume de Nogaret, with help from the Colonna family (devoted enemies of the pope), and the pope's imprisonment for several days; he died a short time later. In 1307, under the influence of King Philip, Pope Clement V moved the papal court to Avignon, marking a period that Petrarch called the Babylonian Captivity. During this time, the popes appointed French cardinals and represented French interests in such matters as the liquidation of the Knights Templar. In the popes' absence, the Papal States and especially Rome declined severely, to such a point that the popes appointed the redoubtable Cardinal Gil Albornoz to restore order; his efforts made possible the return of the papacy to Rome in 1377. The next year, Pope Urban VI's erratic rule led to the Great Schism, dividing the church until 1417. See also COLA DI RIENZO.

In the face of waning papal influence and the ill-fated attempts of Emperors Henry VII (1308–1313) and Louis the Bavarian (1314–1347) to restore imperial influence, there descended the *nubes tyrannorum,* the "age of the despots," with fierce rulers in each of the major cities, Milan (Sforza and Visconti), Perugia (Baglioni), Ravenna (Malatesta), Padua (Carrara), Mantua (Gonzaga) and Verona (Scaliger); smaller communities and cities relied upon the *podesta,* or hired local ruler. The 14th century also witnessed the end of the considerable economic prosperity of the previous years. The chief cause of this collapse was the wholesale loss of life brought by the Black Death, in particular throughout 1347 and 1348. The economic and social conditions of the peninsula were much altered by the pestilence. Economic stability was undermined by the loss of population, with prices and profits for the merchants plummeting calamitously. There was as well a pervasive sense of gloom and deep anxiety, both assisting the rise of the despots.

The most significant states during this period were Milan, Florence and Venice. In Milan, the Visconti, devoted Ghibellines, gained control when Gian Galeazzo (1351–1402) secured the ducal title in 1395. Under the Visconti, Milan became militarily aggressive and, through the ambitions of Gian Galeazzo, the city came close to forging a united state over much of northern Italy; it might very well have succeeded had the duke not died suddenly of the plague. See also GUELPHS AND GHIBELLINES.

Florence, with its tradition of republicanism, was in stark contrast to the other states ruled by despotism. The War of the Eight Saints (1375–1378) with the papacy, which had called into question the very nature of Florentine social and political institutions, heightened the awareness of the inhabitants of the republic to their own unique existence.

Venice, meanwhile, continued its republican government, with power in the hands of the oligarchical merchant class. Unlike Florence and Milan, however, Venice had been a major power in northern Italy for centuries, its durability rooted in the wide-ranging commercial interests in which it was involved throughout the Mediterranean. While increasingly alarmed by the advance of the Ottoman Turks, the Venetians came into the 15th century in a state of great prosperity, flush with their triumph in 1380 over the Genoese at Chioggia, and the proud possessors of a considerable mercantile empire along the Adriatic and Aegean.

The 15th century would witness the continuation of the princely domination of major cities, but new faces and events would trumpet the transitional period between Medieval and Renaissance Italy. This was evident in Florence, where in 1434, thanks to the total incompetence of the Florentine oligarchy, Cosimo de Medici the Elder assumed near total control over Florentine life. While republicanism would be maintained as a facade, the de Medici family wielded power while maintaining order. They also transformed Florence into the center of Italian humanism and the cradle of the Italian Renaissance.

The Papal States too underwent a process of centralization after the resolution of the Great Schism in 1417 with the Council of Constance, electing Pope Martin V, a member of the Colonna family, the first universally recognized pontiff since 1378. Under Martin and his successors, papal administration was once more solidly planted in Rome, the Papal States were in the control of the popes and the Holy See involved itself in the politics and culture of Italy. The most significant of these 15th century pontiffs—and the first to be termed a Renaissance pope—was Nicholas V (1447–1456). He was an enthusiastic patron of the arts and humanism, and he made a decisive intervention in 1453 at a moment when the other states of Italy seemed on the verge of a fratricidal war. Through his work, the Peace of Lodi was signed; the seizure of power in Milan by Francesco Sforza (1450) was recognized and a balance of power was formulated that precariously placed Milan and Florence against Venice and Naples, with the papacy between them. A tenuous peace lasted for the next forty years.

The political independence of the Italian states was threatened by France, Spain and Austria. Taking advantage of the quarreling among the states, King Charles VIII of France invaded in 1494, initiating a series of wars that ended in the mid-16th century with Italy largely under the control of Spain. During this period of wars Italian statesmen, including Machiavelli, believed that political unity was the only way to end foreign domination.

**IVALJO** (d. c. 1280) Ruler of the Second Bulgarian Empire from 1278 to 1279, believed to have been a swineherd who won renown and a following in 1277 for his defeat of the Tatar (Tartar) invaders. With the throne as his goal, he marched on Trnovo, killing Constantine Tich and taking the crown by marrying Constantine's widow, Maria. Unpopular as a ruler almost immediately, Ivaljo was replaced while away fighting the Tatars. The Byzantine-supported Ivan Asen III (1279) was his replacement. Ivaljo returned, defeated the Byzantines and Asen but was ousted once again in favor of George Tartar. Ivaljo fled but was later murdered. See also BULGARS, EMPIRE OF THE.

**IVAN I DANILOVICH, GRAND PRINCE OF MOSCOW** (d. 1341) Grand prince of Moscow from 1325 to 1341 and grand prince of Vladimir from 1328 to 1341, called Kalita, or "Moneybags," for his financial shrewdness. The son of Prince Daniel of Moscow, he succeeded him in 1325 and used diplomacy and shrewd financial acumen to increase his holdings. He allied himself with the Tatar Khan against Prince Alexander of Tver, claiming the title of grand prince in 1331, as well as the right to collect the tribute due the khan from the Russian principalities. Enhancing the power of Moscow, Ivan arranged the transfer of the seat of the Metropolitan of the Russian Orthodox Church there in 1326 and moved his own residence from Vladimir. See also RUSSIA.

**IVAN II, GRAND PRINCE OF MOSCOW** Called "the Red," the grand prince of Moscow from 1353 to 1359. See also MOSCOW, GRAND PRINCES OF.

**IVAN III VASILIEVICH, GRAND PRINCE OF MOSCOW** (1440–1505) Grand prince of Moscow and czar of Russia from 1462 to 1505, the architect of Muscovite expansion and centralization of the Russian state. Called "the Great," he was the son of Grand Prince Vasily II of Moscow, succeeding him after a difficult childhood. Ivan embarked on a series of campaigns to add to his holdings and to reduce the independence of Russian and neighboring princes. He defeated the Tatar Mongols in 1480, terminating his vassal status and the necessity for wars. From 1463 to 1485, expansion brought under his control Yaroslav, Rostov, Novgorod and Tver. His later years were spent at war against Poland and Lithuania, but he acquired only part of the Ukraine. He married Zoë (or Sophia), niece of the Byzantine emperor Constantine XI (1449–1453), thereby giving him the means to declare himself Roman Caesar (Czar) and empowering him in organizing his cautiously cultivated position as protector of the Greek Orthodox Church. In 1502 he chose Vasily III, and Zoë's his eldest son to succeed him, although Vasily never lived to rule. His grandson was Ivan IV (1530–1584), called "the Terrible." See also RUSSIA.

**IVAN ALEXANDER, KING OF THE BULGARS** (d. 1371) Ruler of the Second Bulgarian Empire from 1331 to 1371, the nephew of Michael Sisman. Ivan (or John) Alexander secured the throne probably by participating in the plot to overthrow Ivan Stephen in 1331, while serving as provincial governor. Named Czar in August or September 1331, he quickly made peace with the Serbs, using his newly strengthened relations to ready his troops for an attack on the Byzantine Empire, thus acquiring lands in the subsequent peace agreements. On his death in 1371, his successor was Ivan Sisman, a son by his second marriage to Theodora, a convert from Judaism. He had declared his other son, Ivan Stracimir, by his first marriage, no longer the heir but gave him much of the empire as compensation. See also BULGARS, EMPIRES OF THE.

**IVAN ASEN II, KING OF THE BULGARS** (d. 1241) Ruler of the Second Bulgarian Empire from 1218 to 1241 and heir to the throne on the death of Kalojan in 1207. He was superseded by Kalojan's nephew, Boril (1207–1218), because Ivan was only 11 at the time. In 1218, however, the nobles deposed and blinded Boril, bringing Ivan to power. He defeated Theodore, head of Thessalonica, in 1230, at Klokotnica, and an alliance with Nicaea against the Latin Empire of Constantinople was broken to prevent the Greeks from regaining Constantinople. A plague then caused the death of Ivan's wife, and his son convinced him to make peace in 1237. He died in 1241 and was succeeded by Koloman (1241–1246). See also BULGARIA.

**IVAN ASEN III, KING OF THE BULGARS** Bulgar ruler reigning briefly (1279), who was the son of Mico, a boyar (noble), and supported by the Byzantine Empire. With an army supplied by Constantinople, he tried unsuccessfully to win the Bulgarian throne from Ivaljo (1278–1279). In 1279, however, he returned with a large army and was accepted while Ivaljo was away on campaign. A Byzantine puppet king, he was defeated on Ivaljo's return and fled to Constantinople. See also BULGARIA.

**IVAN SISMAN, KING OF THE BULGARS** (d. 1393) Ruler of much of the Bulgarian Empire from 1371 to 1393, whose reign was ended during the Ottoman invasion of the Balkans. The son of Ivan Alexander (1331–1371) and his second wife, Theodora, Ivan Sisman was named heir to the throne but had to share power with his half brother, Ivan Stracimir (1360–1396). Stracimir attempted to conquer all of Bulgaria, draining the nation, and the Ottoman Turks advanced into the region around 1376. Ivan's sister was forced into a harem, and the country was declared a vassal. Attempts at breaking Ottoman control failed, and Ivan died as his country fell to the Turks. See also BULGARIA.

**IVAN STEPHEN, KING OF THE BULGARS** Ruler of the Bulgars from 1330 to 1331, the son of Michael Sisman (1323–1330) and his Serbian wife, Anna. In the complex dealings with the Byzantine Empire, Michael chose to disinherit Ivan and to imprison him after repudiating his marriage to Anna, in order to marry Theodora, sister of Andronicus III (1328–1341). In 1330, Michael was killed in battle against the Serbs, giving the Serbian king, Stefan Decanski (1321–1331), considerable power over the Bulgars. Ivan was installed on the throne, his reign lasting only a year. He was overthrown by Ivan Alexander (1331–1371), and the death of Stefan Decanski ended his hope of regaining the throne. See also BULGARIA.

**IVAN STRACIMIR, KING OF THE BULGARS** Ruler of much of Bulgaria, specifically the principality of Vidin, from 1360 to 1396. He was the son of Ivan Alexander (1331–1371) and his first wife, disinherited in favor of Ivan Sisman (c. 1360). As compensation he was granted Vidin, losing this region in 1365 to the Hungarians but recapturing it in 1370. When Ivan Sisman was named heir in 1371, Stracimir launched a campaign to conquer all of Bulgaria. Unsuccessful, it put a severe strain on the nation. Stracimir survived his brother's subjugation by the Ottoman Turks, supporting the Crusade for Nicopolis in 1396. One of those crushed by the defeat inflicted on the Crusaders by the Turks, he lost his principality. See also BULGARIA.

**IVO OF CHARTRES, SAINT** (c. 1040–1115) Bishop of Chartres and esteemed as the most learned canonist of his era. Prior of the Canons Regular of Saint Quentin, he was elected bishop of Chartres and approved by Pope Urban II (1088–1099) in 1090. Two years later he was imprisoned by King Philip I of France (1060–1108) for opposing the king's plans to divorce his wife to marry Countess Bertrade of Anjou. Public outrage forced his release, and the pope excommunicated the king. In 1104, attending the Council of Beaugency, Ivo proposed that the ban against Philip be lifted. Ivo wrote treatises including *Decretum* (17 books), *Panormia* (8 books) and *Collectio tripartita*, as well as a collection of letters and 24 sermons.

# J

**JACOBINS** The original name of the Dominican order of friars in France, derived from the first Dominican house there, founded on the Rue Saint Jacques in 1218. See also DOMINICANS.

**JACOBITES** The name designating members of the Syrian Monophysite Church, derived from the name of the reputed founder of the movement, Jacob Baradaeus (c. 500–578), bishop of Edessa. He traveled throughout the Middle and Near East as a missionary, ordaining priests and organizing what was to become the national church of Syria. The term Jacobite was not adopted until the Second Council of Nicaea in 787. Repressed by the laws of the Byzantine Empire, Jacobites welcomed the Arab invasions of the mid-seventh century, and many members of the group became Muslims. See also SYRIA.

**JACOB OF VORAGINE** (c. 1230–1298) Archbishop of Genoa and a noted hagiographer and historian. He joined the Dominican order in 1244 and wrote a chronicle on Genoa, where he served as episcopal head, titled the *Chronicon Genuense,* as well as sermons and the famous *Legenda aura* (the *Golden Legend),* a collection of saints' lives and articles on Christian festivals. Written between 1255 and 1266, the book was organized according to the church year and was very popular, known also as the *Lombardica historia.*

**JACOPONE DA TODI** (c. 1230–1306) Mystic and Franciscan poet, born Jacopo de Benedetti. A lawyer, Jacopone was drawn to an ascetic life in 1268, when, on the death of his wife, he discovered that she wore a hair shirt under her fine clothing. He became a Franciscan tertiary and then a brother about 1278. Later, as a member of the Spiritual Franciscans, he wrote poems satirizing Pope Boniface VIII (1294–1303) and was excommunicated and then imprisoned in 1298. Pope Benedict XI (1303–1304) released him in 1303, and he retired to a monastery at Collazone. Jacopone composed mystical works of great depth, including the *laudi spirituali,* in Latin and in Umbrian, and was once credited with having composed the *Stabat Mater.*

**JACQUERIE** A peasant revolt erupting north of Paris in May–June 1358, sparked by peasant outrage against the nobility. The defeat of the French at the Battle of Poitiers had a disastrous effect on the countryside in September 1356. Constituting the French lower class, called Jacques or Jacques Bonhomme by the nobles, the peasants and artisans were confronted by free companies of mercenaries who pillaged the region and demands by the nobles that they pay heavier taxes to rearm the country and to build castles around Paris. The uprising began on May 21, 1358, near Compiègne, eventually controlled by a rebel named Guillaume Cale, who joined the Parisian uprising led by Étienne Marcel. While castles were destroyed and nobles killed, the peasants were defeated at Meaux on June 9, and Cale was crushed by Carlos II of Navarre (1349–1387) on June 10. A massacre followed as retributions were mounted against the peasantry. See also HUNDRED YEARS' WAR.

**JACQUES DE VITRY** (c. 1170–1240) Bishop of Acre and later cardinal of Tusculum and an important source on the Fifth Crusade (1218–1221). Elected bishop in 1216, he took part in the Crusade and left a useful body of letters on the campaign. See also CRUSADES.

**JADWIGA** See WLADYSLAW II JAGIELLO AND JADWIGA.

**JAGIELLO DYNASTY** Monarchical family emerging in the 15th century as one of the most powerful in eastern Europe. The first of the line was Wladyslaw Jagiello, grand duke of Lithuania, who married Queen Jadwiga of Poland in 1386, becoming King Wladyslaw II Jagiello, king of Poland, thereby uniting Poland and Lithuania. The dynasty produced rulers of Poland and Lithuania from 1386 to 1572 and of Hungary (1440–1444, 1490–1526) and Bohemia (1471–1526).

**JALAL U'D-DIN RUMI** (1207–1273) Persian poet, mystic and celebrated Sufi poetic spokesman in the Persian tongue. Originally from Balkh in Afghanistan, he migrated with his family to Asia Minor (Konya, Turkey) to escape the Mongols. He was a teacher of theology and philosophy and espoused Sufism after meeting the influential dervish Shams ad-Din in 1244. Jalal u'd-Din wrote a great number of verses honoring Shams and an epic, *Masnavi-ye ma'navi (Spiritual Couplets).* See also SUFISM.

**JAMES I, KING OF ARAGON** (1208–1276) King of Aragon and count of Barcelona from 1213 to 1276, called "the Conqueror" and an important figure in the Reconquista, the reconquest of Spain from the Muslims. The son and successor of Pedro II of Aragon (1196–1213), James became king in 1213 but did not control the state until

1227, then embarking on a series of campaigns to extend Aragonese holdings and influence. Majorca and the Balearic Islands were taken from the Moors from 1229 to 1235, and Valencia fell in 1238. By the terms of the Treaty of Corbeil (1258) with King Louis IX of France (1226–1270), Catalonia was taken from the French, while Languedoc was lost to James. A patron of learning and a proponent of sound civil government, he established an assembly, the *corts* (in Castile, *cortes*), and compiled a maritime code. He also wrote a chronicle of his reign. See also ARAGON.

**JAMES II, KING OF ARAGON** (1264–1327) Ruler of Aragon from 1291 to 1327 and of Sicily from 1285 to 1295. The son of Pedro III of Aragon (1276–1285), he came to the throne on the death of his brother, Alfonso III (ruled 1285–1291), in 1291. He had received from his father the crown of Sicily in 1285 but chose to surrender his title in 1295 to the Angevins of Naples, in return for Corsica and Sardinia. He founded the University of Lérida in 1300. See also ARAGON.

**JAMES I, KING OF SCOTLAND** (1394–1437) Ruler of Scotland from 1406 to 1437, although controlling the state only from 1424. The son of King Robert III (1390–1406), he was sent to France in 1406 to avoid being murdered by conspirators at court, especially Robert Stewart, duke of Albany. He was captured on the way, however, and made a royal prisoner of the English, remaining there as Stewart became regent after Robert's death in 1406. Stewart's son, Murdac, regent until 1424 after his father, was also not anxious to ransom James. Finally released in 1424, James returned home, determined to break the power of the nobles. Many were arrested, some lost their lands and others, including Murdac, were executed. James won general acclaim for his efforts to the reform government. He was murdered, however, in 1437, by a group of nobles. His wife was Joan Beaufort, an Englishwoman. James was also the author of poems, including *The Kingis Quair (The King's Book).*

**JAMES II, KING OF SCOTLAND** (1430–1460) Ruler of Scotland from 1437 to 1460, the son of James I (1406–1437), who came to the throne on his father's assassination. He was young at the time and unable to take control. After his marriage to Mary of Gueldres (1449) he began to defy his nobles, crushing the Livingston family and breaking an alliance with the Douglases. He had William, earl of Douglas, charged with treason and murdered in 1452. Having securely established himself as ruler, he made improvements in the royal justice system, centralized the state and, after 1456, was strong enough to interfere in English affairs on the side of the Lancastrians during the Wars of the Roses. He was killed in battle at Roxburgh in 1460. See also SCOTLAND.

**JAMES III, KING OF SCOTLAND** (1452–1488) Ruler of Scotland from 1460 to 1488, a patron of the arts but unsuited to reign over a divisive realm. He succeeded James II (1437–1460) in 1460, but real power rested in the hands of his mother, Mary of Gueldres, James Kennedy, the bishop of Saint Andrews, and a faction of nobles. When he did assume control, James confronted rebellions and was forced to arrest his brothers in 1479 on charges of treason. One, Alexander, duke of Albany, escaped to England to appeal for support in restoring his former position. Edward IV of England (1461–1470; 1471–1483) defeated James in 1482, and in 1488 James was captured and killed by Scottish lords who preferred his son, the future James IV (1488–1513). See also SCOTLAND.

**JANISSARIES** See OTTOMAN EMPIRE.

**JEAN DE FRANCE, DUC DU BERRY** See BERRY, JEAN DE FRANCE, DUC DE.

**JEAN DE MEUN** (c. 1240–1350?) French poet noted for having written a continuation of the *Roman de la rose*, begun around 1240 by Guillaume de Lorris. See also ROMAN DE LA ROSE.

**JEAN LE BEL** See LE BEL, JEAN.

**JEANNE I** (c. 1273–1305) Queen of Navarre from 1274 to 1305 and queen of France from 1285. The daughter of King Henry I of Navarre (1270–1274), Jeanne (also Joan) married Philip, the future King Philip IV of France (1285–1314), in 1284, becoming his queen the following year. Philip then acquired Navarre, Brie and Champagne. Jeanne was the mother of three sons to become French kings: Louis X (1314–1316), Philip V (1316–1322) and Charles IV (1322–1328). See also NAVARRE, KINGDOM OF.

**JEANNE II** (d. 1349) Queen of Navarre from 1328 to 1349, the daughter of King Louis X (1314–1316) and granddaughter of Jeanne I. Removed from any possible consideration as heir to Louis by her uncle, Philip V (1316–1322), who succeeded to the French throne in 1316, she was given Navarre. Philip took Navarre and the counties of Brie and Champagne at the outset, but when Philip VI of Valois came to the throne in 1328, he ceded Navarre to Jeanne. She and her husband, Philip of Evreaux, were welcomed by the populace. Jeanne's son was King Carlos II of Navarre (1349–1387), and her line remained in control of Navarre until the mid-15th century. See also NAVARRE, KINGDOM OF.

**JENSON, NICHOLAS** (d. 1480) French publisher and printer, born in Sommevoire, near Troyes, and studying printing in Germany, probably at Mainz, under Johann Gutenberg. In 1470 he moved to Venice, where he established a shop, producing the first designs for printed roman typeface, subsequently used in Rome and Strasbourg and by many other printing houses during the next centuries. He published many books, most of them in classical Greek or Latin.

**JEROME OF PRAGUE** (c. 1365–1416) Philosopher, theologian and reformer, born in Prague and influenced by Jan Hus and John Wycliffe. Studying at the University of Prague, he collaborated with Hus and at Oxford adopted the views of Wycliffe. Returning to Prague in 1401, he was a leading advocate of Wycliffe, teaching at Paris (1405),

Heidelberg (1406) and Cologne (1406) but forced by local church authorities to leave each city. Agreeing with Hus again, Jerome led a march in Prague in 1412 in which the decree of the antipope John XXIII (1410–1415), allowing the sale of indulgences, was burned. He went to the Council of Constance three years later to defend Hus and was arrested, imprisoned and burned at the stake with Hus. See also BOHEMIA.

**JERUSALEM** City in central Palestine, one of the sacred places for Christians and Jews and the site of the Dome of the Rock revered by Muslims. During the Middle Ages Jerusalem was occupied by many invaders, being a major objective during the Crusades. Virtually destroyed in A.D. 70 by the Roman forces led by Titus, the city was underpopulated until the third century, when local inhabitants protested Hadrian's plans to build a pagan Roman city, Aelia Capitolina, on the site. Constantine (306–337), taking control of the Roman Empire, declared Jerusalem a holy place, and extensive building was undertaken, lasting until 614, when the city fell to the Persians.

Another era began in 637–638, when the Muslims entered the city. Believing that the prophet Muhammad had visited there, they respected Jerusalem and pursued a policy of toleration toward Christian and Jewish inhabitants. Only under the Fatimid caliph al-Hakim was there persecution (1010), and Christian shrines were destroyed. The Seljuk Turks, however, took Jerusalem in 1071, making pilgrimages to the city dangerous. This resulted in the First Crusade, during which, christian armies captured Jerusalem in 1099. The Latin Kingdom of Jerusalem was established soon afterward, ending until 1187, when Sal-

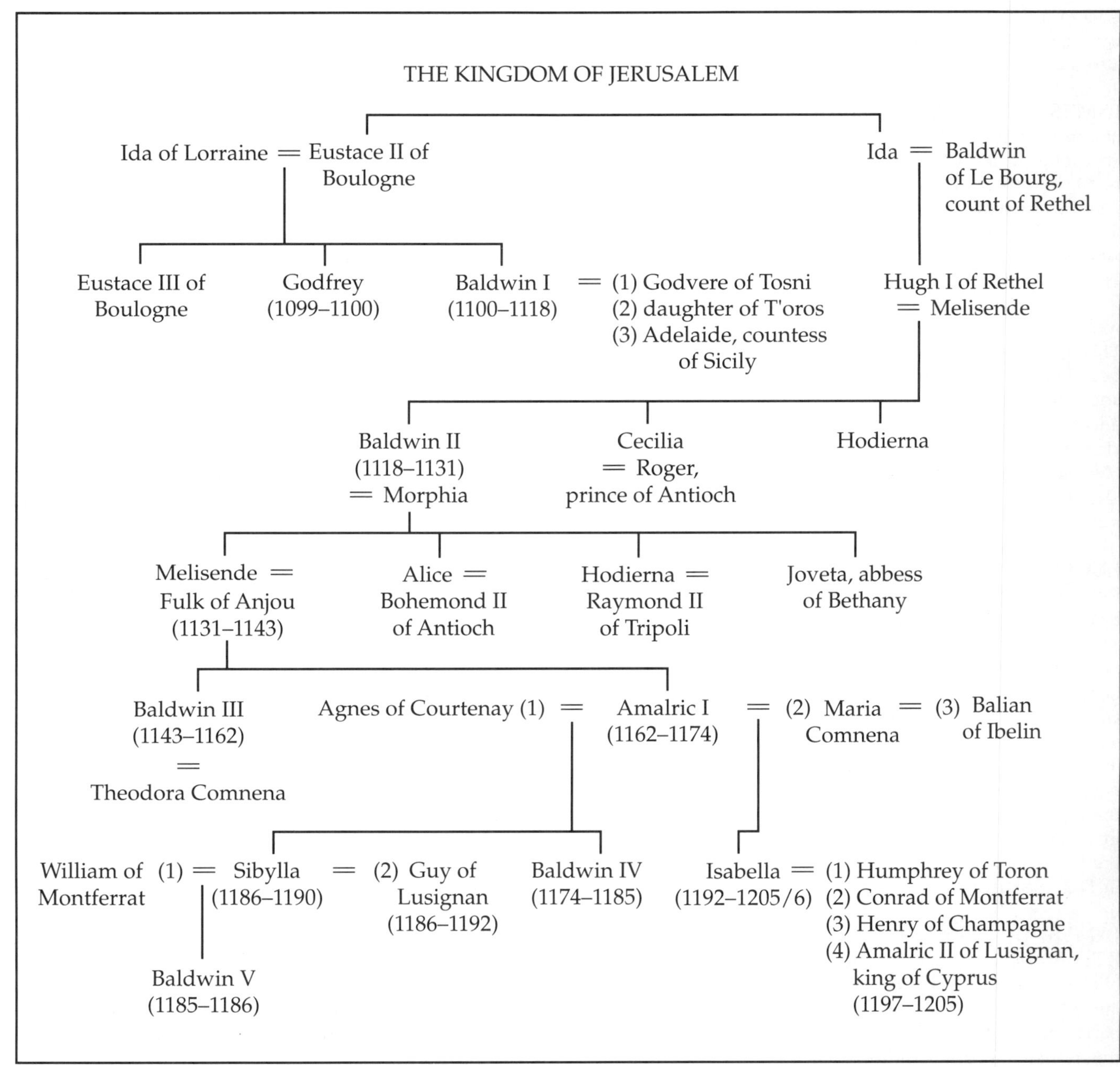

adin destroyed it and reinstated Islamic rule. Through diplomatic measures the city was regained by the Christians from 1229 to 1239 and from 1243 to 1244, the last period ending with Jerusalem's sacking by the Khwarizmian Turks in 1244. The Mamluks later established their sovereignty, which would continue until 1517 and the rise of the Ottoman Turks. See also CRUSADER STATES; CRUSADES; JERUSALEM, KINGDOM OF.

**JERUSALEM, KINGDOM OF** Also called the Latin Kingdom of Jerusalem, one of the most important Crusader States in Palestine, lasting from 1099 until 1291, although the city of Jerusalem was lost in 1187. The kingdom was established by the leaders of the First Crusade following the capture of Jerusalem in 1099 and was organized under the feudal system of government with the neighboring Crusader States (Edessa, Antioch and Tripoli) designated as vassals. These principalities held four major subfiefdoms or baronies: Krak, Galilee, Sidon and Jaffa, and Ascalon. While the kings of Jerusalem, with their holdings at Acre, Tyre and Jerusalem, held considerable prestige, the political reality was quite different, for the vassals exhibited independence, undermining royal authority that was debilitated further by the rise of the military orders in Palestine.

The first ruler of Jerusalem was the esteemed Godfrey de Bouillon (d. 1100), who refused the title of king, adopting instead the name protector of the Holy Sepulchre. Baldwin I, his brother, became king in 1100 (ruled until 1118). Muslim relatiation reduced the size and strength of the domain in 1144 with the capture of Edessa. In 1187 Saladin, leading his jihad (holy war) against the Crusaders, captured Jerusalem, forcing the move of the kingdom's capital to Acre.

Unable to stem the Muslim advance, especially of the Mamluks, the Christians watched as their lands were taken, ending in 1291 with the fall of Acre. Titular rule had been held by various princes, most notably Emperor Frederick II (1215–1250), but the ruling house of Lusignan, leaving Acre, moved to Cyprus, where it reigned until the 15th century. Of interest was Jerusalem's code of feudal law, the Assizes of Jerusalem, considered to have implemented the ideal feudal legal government. See also CRUSADES.

In Jerusalem, the Church of the Holy Sepulchre

**JEWS AND JUDAISM** A people and religion. The Diaspora, or dispersal of the Jews, resulted from the destruction of the Great Temple of Jerusalem in A.D. 70 by the Romans and gave rise the establishment of schools in Mesopotamia designed to maintain the religion and learning of the Jews. The teachers in these schools were rabbis; the spiritual leaders, the *geonim;* and the political leaders the *exilarchs.* Of major importance in this era was the compilation of the Jewish body of law, customs and historical commentaries called the Talmud, or "teaching."

During the Middle Ages the patterns of religious persecution against the Jews alternated with eras of tolerance, based on a number of varying circumstances. Pope Gregory I the Great (590–604) promoted Jewish conversion to Christianity but voiced opposition to persecutions. Throughout the time following the collapse of the Roman Empire, the Jews were persecuted by the Germanic converts to Christianity, most notably the Visigoths, who forbade the practice of Judaism. The economic conditions of the early Middle Ages allowed Jewish communities to thrive and to form international trading ventures, in which traveling merchants, called Radanites, set forth from southern France and journeyed to India and China, returning with spices and other goods.

By the 11th century Jewish settlements beyond Spain were found in much of northern and western Europe. After the Norman Conquest of England (1066), the Jews moved to the isles, but they were also found in Italy, the Balkans and the Byzantine Empire. The First Crusade, launched in 1095, sparked an extreme reaction against non-Christians, and massacres occurred in places such as the Rhineland. Subsequent pogroms took place elsewhere, and in 1240 the Talmud was condemned at Paris, accompanied by the circulation of spurious accounts of Jewish atrocities committed for their religion. In 1190, in York, the Jewish community chose mass suicide to prevent its massacre by its Christian neighbors. Papal legislation included decrees (at the Third Lateran Council of 1179) against Jews employing Christian servants or housing Christians. These sentiments made Jewish quarters called ghettos in many cities inevitable. At the Lateran Council of 1215, Pope Innocent III (1198–1216) freed Christians from their financial debts to Jews and demanded that Jews wear distinctive symbols of identification.

This release from payment of debt struck at the Jews, who were permitted finance and the administration of state financial systems as one of the few means of livelihood, paying excessive taxes and fees for each transaction. Problems arose with the establishment of banking houses and financial systems among Christians. Expulsions and pogroms were initiated freely against the Jews once the Christians had financial institutions of their own. The Jews were expelled from England in 1290, from France in 1306, 1322 and 1394, and from Spain beginning in 1492. The name

Ashkenazi applied to the Jews living in Europe outside Spain and Italy, and such Jews endured many hardships in Germany, migrating to Poland and Hungary, where they found relative peace. Here they remained for centuries, maintaining their religious and intellectual heritage.

The condition and development of the Sephardic (Spanish) Jews demands special attention, for here Jewish culture and achievement were particularly bright. When Spanish holdings fell to the Muslims, the Jews found their new masters more tolerant. Throughout the eighth century, then, Jews migrated into Moorish Spain, taking part in the government of the caliphate of Córdoba. Parallel with this was an intense revival of Hebrew studies and learning, the movement producing such figures as Maimonides and Judah Halevi. As the Reconquista began to drive the Moors from the peninsula, Spanish Jews found initial toleration from the Christians, and many continued to hold prestigious positions such as physician and banker. As was true elsewhere, the financiers and government officials, such as Abraham ben Samuel Abulafia, treasurer to King Pedro the Cruel of Castile (1350–1369), earned the enmity of the lower classes and jealous nobles.

The movement against Spanish Jewry was hastened by the continued holy wars and the fiery rhetoric of the Dominicans. Disputations between Jews and Christians were staged, the most famous of which took place between the Christian convert Pablo Christiani (d. c. 1267) and Rabbi Moses ben Nahman (d. 1270) in 1263 at Barcelona. Massacres, once infrequent, became more widespread, beginning in the late 14th century with a slaughter in Seville in 1391, which brought others throughout Spain. Jewish converts to Catholicism who were suspected of insincerity (Marranos) spurred renewed attempts, through the efforts of the Dominican Saint Vincent Ferrer (1350–1419) and through additional disputations, to make legitimate conversions. Nevertheless, the Marranos remained a problem and contributed to the rise of the Spanish Inquisition in 1478. In 1492, Ferdinand and Isabella took the step of expelling the Jews from Spain. Other expulsions followed in Sicily and Sardinia (1492), Navarre (1541), Portugal (1497) and the Kingdom of Naples (1541). Spanish Jewry was dispersed to the Low Countries, as well as to Italy, the Ottoman Empire and North Africa.

**JOAN, POPE** The name of a purely legendary female pontiff who supposedly reigned as John VIII after the pontificate of Victor III (1086–1087). She was, according to the legend, a scribe disguised as a man who achieved election but, being pregnant, delivered a child while in procession to the Lateran and was stoned to death. The legend first appeared in the writings of the Dominican chroniclers Jean de Mailly and Stephen of Bourbon, disseminated in time through the works of the 13th-century Polish Dominican Martin of Trappau. Widely accepted during the Middle Ages, the account is held to be false by scholars. An important fact countering the tale is that the gap between the death of Victor III (1087) and the accession of Urban II (1088–1099) was not as long as previously believed. The story probably evolved from memories of women dominating the papacy, especially the 10th-century figures of Theodora and her daughter, Marozia.

**JOAN OF ARC** (c. 1412–1431) The "Maid of Orléans," or La Pucelle, the most celebrated religious and political heroine in medieval French history, who rose from total obscurity to lead the armies of France to victory over the English at Orléans, thereby ensuring the crowning of Charles VII of France (1422–1461). The daughter of a peasant in Domrémy, Champagne, Joan experienced visions and heard the voices of the saints Michael, Margaret and Catherine telling her to save France. Unsuccessful at first (1428) in convincing Sir Robert de Beaudricourt, the officer commanding the army at Vaucouleurs that she was sincere, she cited fulfilled prophecies in 1429 to gain entrance at court. There, after recognizing the disguised dauphin, Charles VII, and winning the approval of the theologians at Poitiers, she was appointed to lead the Orléans relief force, where, clad in white armor, she spurred the French to victory. Joan inflicted what was to be a mortal wound to the English and Burgundian cause in the Hundred Years' War.

Charles was crowned at Reims on July 17, 1429, and more campaigns followed until Joan was captured by the Burgundians (allies of the English) near Compiègne and sold to the English. Brought before a tribunal headed by Pierre Cauchon, the bishop of Beauvais, at Rouen, on charges of witchcraft and heresy, she was condemned on May 30, 1431, and burned at the stake. Pope Calixtus III (1455–1458) ordered a posthumous examination of her trial and in 1456 declared her innocent. In time she was canonized (1920) and named the patron saint of France. See also HUNDRED YEARS' WAR.

**JOANNA I** (1326–1382) Queen of Naples from 1343 to 1382 and the countess of Provence, whose reign was turbulent because of her marriages and her choice of heirs. The successor to and granddaughter of King Robert, she had married Andrew, the brother of Louis I of Hungary (1342–1382). Bringing many Hungarians with him, Andrew thereby alienated the court and was assassinated, perhaps at Joanna's order, in 1345. Remarrying in 1347, this time to Louis of Taranto, she faced a Hungarian invasion, led by Louis of Hungary, to avenge Andrew's death. Seeking safety with the pope at Avignon, Joanna secured a declaration of innocence in return for selling Avignon to the papacy. Through the help of Pope Innocent VI (1243–1254) she returned to Naples in 1352, marrying James III, king of Majorca, after Louis's death in 1362. James died in 1375, and Joanna married Otto of Brunswick. She named Charles of Durazzo as heir but then chose Louis of Anjou, brother of Charles V, as king of France (1364–1380). Charles invaded Naples, captured Joanna in 1382 and imprisoned her. Once crowned as the king of Naples, Charles executed the queen. See also NAPLES, KINGDOM OF.

**JOANNA II** (1371–1435) Queen of Naples from 1414 to 1435, whose reign was one of war and intrigue. The sister of King Lancelot of Naples, Joanna succeeded him. She acquired a reputation for promiscuity. She married Jacques de Bourbon in 1415, and he executed Joanna's lover and thereby caused an uprising of the Neopolitan nobility. Louis III of Anjou then laid claim to the throne, and to prevent the Angevins from taking possession of

Naples, Joanna adopted Alfonso V the Magnanimous of Aragon (1416–1458) as heir but soon broke with him and was besieged in 1423 in Castel Caperano. Rescued, she renounced her adoption of Alfonso and named Louis heir. In 1434 Joanna named René of Anjou the heir. See also NAPLES, KINGDOM OF.

**JOÃO I OF AVIS, KING OF PORTUGAL** See JOHN I, KING OF PORTUGAL.

**JOHN, KING OF ENGLAND** (1167–1216) Ruler of England from 1199 to 1216 and one of the manifestly unpopular monarchs of English history, despite the fact that he was probably not as cruel as suggested by later scholars.

The son of Henry II (1154–1189) and Eleanor of Aquitaine, he was born in Oxford and became his father's favorite. Given the nickname Lackland because of the failure of proposed plans for a marriage for him that would have brought him territorial holdings, he was named earl of Gloucester and then lord of Ireland by 1177. After Richard the Lion-Hearted (his brother) became king in 1189, John was made count of Mortain and was later angered by Richard's choice of Arthur I, duke of Brittany, as royal heir. John was not meant to enter England in Richard's absence but did so while Richard was on crusade, alienating the chancellor, Stephen Longchamp. When Richard was held hostage in Germany, John allied himself with Philip II Augustus of France (1180–1223). Banished by Richard in 1199, he succeeded him as king of England, again negotiating with Philip.

War erupted with France, and John lost Normandy (1204) as well as Anjou, Maine and land in Poitou (1206). He attempted to mount a campaign to regain these lands by conducting a ruthless policy of taxation and seizure of estates in England. John then entered into a conflict with the papacy, following the death of Hubert Walter, the archbishop of Canterbury, in 1305, and was unable to place his own man in the see. Pope Innocent III (1198–1216), elevating Stephen Langton to archbishop in December, excommunicated John in 1209 when he refused to accept Langton. John had to recognize papal power in 1213 in order to be free of the interdicts and excommunication.

At peace with the pope, John went to war in France, signing a truce over the campaigns in 1212. Civil war broke out in England in May 1215, and John was forced to sign Magna Carta at Runnymede on June 19. This document stipulated the king's accountability to English law and the place of the nobles in the feudal system (see MAGNA CARTA). Finding his political position unacceptable, he appealed to the pope and then tried to oppose his barons. He died in Newark in October 1216, despised by elements of his baronial clans and berated by chroniclers of the time. See also ENGLAND.

**JOHN I, SAINT** (d. 526) Pope from 523 to 526, the first prelate to visit Constantinople, thus reuniting the Eastern and Western Churches. This reunion caused a rift between the papacy and Theodoric, king of the Ostrogoths (493–526), who asked John to revoke Emperor Justin's (518–527) edict against Arianism. Failing in his task, the pope was imprisoned by the Ostrogoth ruler, dying there, probably from starvation.

**JOHN II** (d. 535) Pope from 533 to 535, the first pope to change his name on election. He devoted most of his pontificate to controlling the heresy of Nestorianism. He excommunicated Nestorian monks in Constantinople at the request of Emperor Justinian I (527–565). He changed his name (Mercury) for two reasons: because it was the name of a pagan god and to honor Pope John I, martyred in 526.

**JOHN III** (d. 574) Pope from 561 to 574, reigning during the era of the Lombard invasions of Italy (568) and calling on the Byzantine general Narses for support. The Romans, believing Narses involved with the Lombard attack, rebelled and forced the pope to hide in the Catacombs until Narses' death in 573.

**JOHN IV** (d. 642) Pope from 640 to 642, of Dalmatian birth, succeeding Pope Severinus (640) and continuing papal condemnation of Monothelitism. He opposed the Celtic dating of Easter and defended the position of Honorius I (625–638) concerning the unity of Christ's will.

**JOHN V** (d. 686) Pope from 685 to 686, especially concerned for the poor. He had served as legate for Pope Agatho (678–681) to the Sixth Ecumenical Council at Constantinople (680–681).

**JOHN VI** (d.705) Pope from 701 to 705, of Greek birth. He convinced Duke Gisulfo of Benevento to withdraw from papal territory, gave protection to the Eastern bishop Theophylact and ordered the deposed Wilfrid of York restored to his see (704).

**JOHN VII** (d. 707) Pope from 705 to 707, of Greek birth, giving much effort to the restoration of Roman churches and maintaining amicable relations with the Lombards. Noted for his Marian devotions, he was involved with the Council of Trullo (692).

**JOHN VIII** (d.882) Pope from 872 to 882, successor to Pope Adrian II (867–872), who supported the missionary efforts of Saint Methodius among the Slavs. He also reinstated the condemned patriarch of Constantinople, Photius, thus resolving a point of difference between the Eastern and Western Churches. Intrigues in Rome and Saracen invasions in southern Italy beset his reign, and John was forced to excommunicate the future Pope Formosus (891–896) and his advocates in 876. In 882 he was assassinated by members of his entourage.

**JOHN IX** (d. 900) Pope from 898 to 900, a former Benedictine abbot, who was opposed in his election by the future Pope Sergius III (904–911), whom he excommunicated. John exonerated Pope Formosus (891–896), who in a bizarre trial, had been exhumed and tried by Pope Stephen VI (VII) (896–897). He also lent support to ensure the rights of the emperors in papal elections by confirming the

Constitutio Romana (also known as the Constitutions of Lothair, 824).

**JOHN X** (d. 929) Pope from 914 to 928, formerly archbishop of Ravenna, who devoted much of his reign to war with the Saracens in southern Italy. He joined an alliance with Emperor Constantine VII (913–959) and Berengar I of Italy against the Saracens and, in 915, with the support of the Roman senator Theophylact and the duke of Spoleto, defeated the Saracens at the Battle of the Garigliano River. His subsequent support of King Hugh of Italy outraged Marozia, the daughter of Theophylact, who imprisoned him and probably had him murdered one year after his deposition. John X also blessed the rule of the Order of Cluny and fostered improved relations with the Eastern Church.

**JOHN XI** (d. c. 936) Pope from 931 to 935, the son of Marozia, belonging to the Crescenti family and the daughter of Theophylact, and her lover, Pope Sergius III (904–911). Alberic II, Marozia's son by her first marriage, thus John's half brother, overthrew her in c. 933, and John was imprisoned, dying in custody.

**JOHN XII (c. 937–964)** Pope from 955 to 964, the illegitimate son of Alberic II of Spoleto, who dominated Roman politics, and elected pope at the age of 18. In 962 he crowned Otto I the Great Holy Roman Emperor (936–973) but became his enemy when John found that he was meant to be a vassal of the empire (as in the Privilegium Ottonianum and the Constitutions of Lothair of 824). Otto deposed John in November 963, putting Pope Leo VIII (963–965) in his place. In 964, however, John deposed Leo; then, while Otto was marching on Rome, John suffered a stroke and died.

**JOHN XIII** (d. 972) Pope from 965 to 972, called "the Good" because of his piety and learning. Emperor Otto I (936–973) had sponsored his election, which brought protests from Roman nobles. John was kidnapped by the nobles and rescued by Otto. Besides crowning Otto II (967, ruled 973–983) and his wife (972), John supported Cluniac reform.

**JOHN XIV** (d. 984) Pope from 983 to 984, owing his election to Emperor Otto II (973–983) and opposed by the noble Roman house of Crescenti, who supported the antipope Boniface VII (974, 984–985). John was taken prisoner by the Crescentii after Otto's death and murdered in Castel Sant'Angelo in 984.

**JOHN XV** (d.996) Pope from 985 to 996, owing his election to John Crescentius II, head of the powerful Roman family. His most important act was to establish the practice of solemn canonization. He tried to free the papacy from Crescenti domination by making an appeal to Emperor Otto III (983–1002) but died before imperial forces could arrive.

**JOHN XVI** (d. 1001) Antipope from 997 to 998, favored by Emperor Otto II (973–983) and his widow, Empress Theodora. Allied with Crescentius II, he was made antipope against Gregory V (996–999). Both John and Crescentius were captured by Otto III (983–1002). Crescentius was beheaded, and John was blinded, mutilated and banished to a monastery for his actions against Gregory V, the imperial choice. See also ANTIPOPE.

**JOHN XVII** (d. 1003) Pope from May 16, 1003, to November 6, 1003. He was elected by the Crescenti family, specifically Crescentius III, and his papacy was dominated by them. He authorized missions to Poland to convert the Slavic peoples.

**JOHN XVIII** (d. 1009) Pope from 1004 to 1009, owing his election to the Crescenti family but retaining some independence. He retired to a monastery, where he died.

**JOHN XIX** (d. 1032) Pope from 1024 to 1032, brother of and successor to Pope Benedict VIII (1012–1024). Although not of the clergy, he was elected pope through the efforts of his family the Tusculani. He crowned Conrad II (1024–1039) Holy Roman Emperor on Easter, 1027. Known for his rapacious habits, he offended the Roman populace.

**JOHN XX** There was no Pope John XX.

**JOHN XXI** (c. 1210–1277) Pope from 1276 to 1277, Peter of Spain was an esteemed teacher of medicine before his election and the author of medical treatises on the eye, as well as works on logic, theology and philosophy. Physician to Pope Gregory X (1271–1276), he was elected successor to Adrian V (1276) on September 8, 1276, after having served in other ecclesiastical positions. He was killed when the ceiling of the papal palace at Viterbo fell on him on May 20, 1277.

**JOHN XXII** (c. 1244–1334) Pope from 1316 to 1334, a scholar of canon law who rose through the ecclesiastical ranks and became pope as the candidate of Robert of Anjou. Residing at Avignon, he reorganized the Curia, improved papal finances and established new dioceses. He agreed with the Conventuals of the Franciscans in their desire to hold property, causing the Spirituals of the Order to ally with King Louis IV of Bavaria. Louis, who had been opposed by Pope John in his election, supported the Spiritual Franciscans, becoming embroiled in a conflict ending when Louis took Rome and placed a Franciscan on the papal throne as Nicholas V (antipope, 1328–1330). John excommunicated and imprisoned Nicholas, leading to a reconciliation with Louis. John also encouraged missionary work in Asia, codified church law and devoted his last years to debate on the Beatific Vision.

**JOHN XXIII** (d. 1419) Antipope from 1410 to 1415, whose reign was brought to an end at the Council of Constance, a body he had convened in 1414. Involved in the Council of Pisa, which tried to depose rival popes of the time, John was elected by Sigismund (king and the future emperor, 1433–1437). Faced with the decision of the council that he and the other two popes resign, John fled Constance but was arrested and imprisoned until 1419.

That year he was named cardinal of Tusculum, dying a short time later. See also CONSTANCE, COUNCIL OF; SCHISM, GREAT.

**JOHN I TZIMISCES, BYZANTINE EMPEROR** (925–976) Ruler from 969 to 976 and a statesman and general. A member of an Armenian noble family, he was related to the emperor Nicephorus II Phocas (963–969), with whom he fought as a soldier against the Muslims in Syria. Promoted in the Byzantine military, he entered into an affair with Empress Theophano and, with her complicity, murdered Nicephorus in 969. Although compelled to do penance for the act (Theophano was banished), he was crowned emperor and embarked on campaigns to fortify the empire's defenses. The Bulgars were defeated in 971, the year that John crushed Russia and Prince Svyatoslav. He then routed the Fatimids, seizing Antioch and Damascus in 974–975. John married Theodora, sister of Constantine VII Porphyrogenitus (913–959) to strengthen his domestic situation and then negotiated the marriage of his niece to the future Otto II (973–983), Holy Roman Emperor. He died of typhoid while on campaign. See also BYZANTINE EMPIRE.

**JOHN II COMNENUS, BYZANTINE EMPEROR** (1088–1143) Ruler from 1118 to 1143, son of and successor to Alexius I Comnenus (1081–1118), who came to power after surviving the intrigues of his sister, Anna Comnena. She hoped to prevent him from ascending the throne. He concentrated on recovering lost Byzantine territory and increased the finances of the empire. He also attempted to curtail Venetian trading privileges and failed in a subsequent war in 1122. As general he defeated the Pechenegs, regained Cilicia from the Kingdom of Lower Armenia and won the recognition of his suzerainty by the Crusader State of Antioch. The Turkish Danismends were defeated in 1135, but campaigns against the Turkish Atabegs of Syria were not as successful. See also BYZANTINE EMPIRE.

Emperor John II Comnenus

**JOHN V PALAEOLOGUS, BYZANTINE EMPEROR** (1332–1391) Byzantine emperor from 1341 to 1376 and from 1379 to 1391, whose reign saw conflict with the Ottoman Turks. The son of Andronicus III, John inherited the crown at the age of nine; he was forced to endure a regency and then a conflict between his mother, Anna of Savoy, and the minister John Cantacuzenus, who became emperor from 1347 to 1354, when John V recovered his throne. The Ottomans, however, were advancing, and John's pleas for Western support went unanswered. He was deposed in 1376 by his son, Andronicus IV, but was reinstalled with the support of the Turks in 1379. Attempts to improve Constantinople's defenses were rendered impossible because of the Ottoman threat to blind John's heir, the hostage Manuel II (1391–1425). See also BYZANTINE EMPIRE; JOHN VII PALAEOLOGUS.

**JOHN VI CANTACUZENUS, BYZANTINE EMPEROR** Byzantine emperor from 1347 to 1354, sharing power with John V Palaeologus (1341–1376; 1379–1391) after becoming his regent when Andronicus III Palaeologus (ruled 1328–1341) died. He was opposed by the young emperor's mother, Anna of Saxony, who imprisoned his supporters. Declaring himself emperor, he concentrated on consolidating his power and coming to an understanding with the Ottoman Turks, who supported him in defeating Anna and in his claim to his share of the throne. By agreement his term was meant to last only 10 years, and in an effort to remain on the throne in 1354 he crowned his son Matthew emperor, an act that drove John V Palaeologus into an alliance with the Venetians. John VI Cantacuzenus was forced to abdicate and retire to a monastery, where he wrote his memoirs. See also BYZANTINE EMPIRE.

**JOHN VII PALAEOLOGUS, BYZANTINE EMPEROR** (1360–c. 1410) Byzantine emperor for a brief period in 1390, the son of Andronicus IV Palaeologus, approached by the Turks who supported his claim to the throne by overthrowing his grandfather, John V Palaeologus. His uncle, Manuel II (1391–1425), recovered the city, and John VII was reduced to the role of regent while Manuel was visiting the West (1399–1402). See also BYZANTINE EMPIRE.

**JOHN VIII PALAEOLOGUS, BYZANTINE EMPEROR** (1390–1448) Byzantine emperor from 1425 to 1448, made co-emperor by his father, Manuel II Palaeologus (1391–1425), in 1421 and succeeding him to rule over a much-reduced domain. Confronted by a siege of Constantinople in 1422, led by Sultan Murad II (1362–1389), ruler of the Ottoman Turks, John spent much time trying to obtain support from the West. A trip to Italy in 1437 led to his attendance at the Council of Ferrara-Florence in 1439 and to the agreement uniting the Eastern and Western Churches. His subjects refused to accept unification, however, and any hope he had of saving Constantinople was dashed when the Crusader army was annihilated at Varna in 1444 and the Hungarians defeated in 1448. See also BYZANTINE EMPIRE; CONSTANTINOPLE.

**JOHN I, KING OF ARAGON** (1350–1395) Ruler from 1387 to 1395 and a noted patron of learning. Beset with a serious illness for most of his life, he left much of the administration of the government to his wife, Yolande, and to his advisers, much of his time devoted to the arts and hunting. He did recognize antipope Clement VII (1378–1394) of Avignon as the true pontiff and through Yolande pursued a policy of amity toward the French. See ARAGON.

**JOHN II, KING OF ARAGON** (c. 1398–1479) Ruler from 1458 to 1479, and king of Navarre from 1425 to 1479. He married Blanche of Navarre and became monarch there, succeeding his brother, Alfonso V, in Aragon in 1458, thus inheriting possessions in both Sicily and Sardinia. After Blanche's death in 1441, he married Juana Enríquez of Castile (1447) and faced a civil war led by his son, Carlo of Viana, in Navarre, ended only in 1461 by Carlos's sudden death. Catalan leaders then rebelled against him in 1462, and although the revolt was ended in 1472, it weakened the throne. John arranged the wedding of his son, Ferdinand II, to Isabella of Castile in 1469. See also ARAGON.

**JOHN I, KING OF DENMARK, NORWAY AND SWEDEN** (1455–1513) Late medieval ruler of Denmark and Norway (1482–1513) and Sweden (1497–1501), son of Christian I of Denmark and Norway (1448–1481). He was confronted by severe restrictions on monarchical powers and was opposed by Sten Sture the Elder, Swedish regent, who delayed his being crowned there. John ignored the restrictions placed on him, supported Danish merchants against the Hanseatic League and faced a peasant revolt in 1500. Sten Sture was restored as regent of Sweden, but John stayed secure in Denmark and Norway. He fought a war against Lübeck from 1510 to 1512, damaging Lübeck's economic base. See also HANSEATIC LEAGUE.

**JOHN II, KING OF FRANCE** (1319–1364) Ruler from 1350 to 1364, who reigned during the early part of the Hundred Years' War. The son of King Philip VI of Valois (1328–1350), he succeeded to the throne on August 22, 1350, and decided to maintain a truce with England while negotiating with his bitter enemy, Charles II the Bad of Navarre (1349–1387). Despite a peace in 1355 and the marriage of his daughter, Jeanne, to Charles, the differences between them were irreconcilable, culminating with Charles's capture and imprisonment in April 1356. King Edward III of England (1327–1377), unable to maintain the truce because of John's negotiations with Navarre, launched an invasion. His son, Edward, the Black Prince, annihilated the French at Poitiers (1356), taking John prisoner. Humiliating peace treaties were signed by John while in England but repudiated when he returned to France. The treaties of Bretigny and Calais (1360) secured his release to raise a ransom and to surrender to England large parts of southwestern France. In 1364, when one of the hostages who had taken his place in England escaped, John (called "the Good") felt honor bound to return to England himself, where he died. See also HUNDRED YEARS' WAR.

**JOHN I, KING OF LEÓN AND CASTILE** (1358–1390) Ruler from 1379 to 1390, the son of King Henry (Enrique) II (ruled 1369–1379), who attempted to unite Castile with Portugal, invading the country after the death of King Ferdinand in 1383. He was defeated at the decisive Battle of Aljubarrota in 1385, losing Portugal to John I. John of Gaunt, the duke of Lancaster, then launched an attack on León, but the Castilian king won the day, forcing John of Gaunt to make peace in 1388, with the payment of an indemnity and the marriage of John's daughter, Catherine, to the future Henry (Enrique) III of Castile.

**JOHN II, KING OF CASTILE** (1405–1454) Ruler from 1406 to 1454, the son of King Henry (Enrique) III (1390–1406). Regents, including his mother, Catherine of Lancaster, and his uncle, Don Fernando, ruled during the early years of his reign, but ultimately Alvaro de Luna won control, causing friction between the minister and the Castilian nobles, who threatend to wage war against the king. John was forced to rid himself of de Luna in 1453, and then only at the insistence of his wife, Isabella of Portugal, whom he had married in 1447. A monarch who was a patron of men of letters and learning, he died the following year.

**JOHN I, KING OF PORTUGAL** (1357–1433) Known as "the Great," ruling from 1385 to 1433. The illegitimate son of King Pedro of Portugal (1357–1367), he became a leader of the anti-Castilian party in the kingdom, joining with Nun'Alvarez Pereira in 1384 opposing Castilian hegemony over Portugal following the death of his half brother Ferdinand. He broke with the regency of Castile for Ferdinand's daughter, Beatrice, wife of John I of Castile. Elected king by the *cortes* of Coimbra, he defeated the army of John of Castile at the Battle of Aljubarrota (1385), thus assuring Portuguese independence. As protection against further Castilian ambitions, John allied himself with England in 1386, marrying Philippa, daughter of John of Gaunt. It was with his patronage that Portugal began its colonial and maritime expansion, a venture supported by one of his sons, Henry the Navigator. He also encouraged literary endeavors. See also PORTUGAL.

**JOHN I SVERKERSSON, KING OF SWEDEN** (d. 1222) Ruler from 1216 to 1222, a member of the Sverker dynasty. His successor was Eric XI Ericsson (1222–1229). See also SWEDEN.

**JOHN II, KING OF SWEDEN** See JOHN I, KING OF DENMARK, NORWAY AND SWEDEN.

**JOHN III DUCAS VATATZES, NICAEAN EMPEROR** (1193 –1254) Emperor of Nicaea from 1222 to 1254, a pivotal figure in the defeat of the Latin Empire at Constantinople and the reinstatement of the Byzantine Empire. A member of the Byzantine nobility, he wed the daughter of Theodore I Lascaris, the Nicaean emperor, and succeeded him, defeating Theodore's sons, Alexius and

Isaac, in 1223 and blinding them. By allying himself to the Bulgars he was able to defeat Theodore Ducas, despot of Epirus, in 1230, actually besieging Constantinople in 1235. The Bulgars turned on him but negotiated peace in 1237. With the death of the Bulgar ruler Ivan Asen II in 1241, John was able to acquire regions of Bulgaria. Epirus eventually became a vassal entity (1242), and he was successful in recovering Adrianople and Thessalonica (Salonica), thus isolating the Latin Empire. To advance his political cause he married Constance, daughter of Emperor Frederick II (1215–1250). He was very popular with his subjects because of his saintliness and for his efforts to improve the plight of his people. See also NICAEA, EMPIRE OF.

**JOHN IV LASCARIS, NICAEAN EMPEROR** (1250–1261?) Emperor of Nicaea from 1258 to 1261, a weak ruler dominated by his regents. The strongest of these was Michael Palaeologus, who became co-emperor, as Michael VIII, in December 1258. After Michael restored the Byzantine Empire in 1261, John was blinded and died in prison. See also NICAEA, EMPIRE OF.

**JOHN XI BECCHUS, PATRIARCH OF CONSTANTINOPLE** (c. 1235–1297) Patriarch of Constantinople from 1275 to 1282, who strove to unify the Eastern and Western Churches. He was originally opposed to the union and was imprisoned by Emperor Michael VIII Palaeologus (ruled 1259–1282) until he revised his views and supported Michael, organizing the Council of Lyons in 1274. The opposition to the Latin supremacy forced him to resign as patriarch, after having succeeded Arsenius (1261–1267), Germanos III (1267), and Joseph I (1268–1275). He resigned in 1279, was recalled by Michael to the post but stepped down again in 1282, with the accession of the anti-Latin Andronicus II Palaeologus (1282–1328). John was exiled for his beliefs, dying in Nicomedia. See also SCHISMS.

**JOHN I, SEBASTOCRATOR OF THESSALY** (d. c. 1298) Ruler of the Greek principality of Thessaly from 1271 to 1296, the illegitimate son of Michael II, despot of Epirus (d. 1271), who took control of Thessaly and was granted the title of sebastocrator (a title combining *sebastus* and *autorator,* signifying a position greater than that of caesar) by Emperor Michael VIII Palaeologus (1259–1882) who married his nephew Andronicus Tarchaneiotes to John's daughter. Unfortunately for Michael VIII, John soon displayed imperial ambitions and, with Andronicus's support, became a formidable foe of the Byzantine emperor.

**JOHN II, SEBASTOCRATOR OF THESSALY** (d. c. 1318) Ruler of Thessaly from 1303 to 1318, whose reign witnessed the end of the Greek state established by his grandfather, John I. Always in poor health, John allowed himself to be guided by Guy II de la Roche of Athens and then by Emperor Andronicus II Palaeologus (1282–1328), whose illegitimate daughter he married. The Thessalian state became dependent on the nearby Frankish duchy of Athens. After John's death, Thessaly was claimed by the empire, opposed by the already independent nobles of the region.

**JOHN CAPISTRAN, SAINT** (1386–1456) Noted Franciscan friar born Giovanni Capistrano, who studied law in Perugia and then during a war with the powerful Malatestas was imprisoned. There he had a vision of Saint Francis, which subsequently influenced him to join the Franciscan order on his release. Ordained in 1420 or 1426, he soon won recognition in Italy as a preacher but was charged and subsequently acquitted in 1429 with fellow Observant friars on charges of heresy concerning the poverty of Christ, an issue dividing the Franciscans. In 1451 Pope Nicholas V (1447–1455) sent him to Austria to convert the Hussites, and he later went on to Hungary to encourage opposition to the advance of the Ottoman Turks. With the celebrated general Hunyadi, John raised an army that defeated the Turks and saved the city of Belgrade in July 1456. He died of the plague later that same year.

**JOHN CLIMACHUS, SAINT** (c. 570–649) Also called John of the Ladder, a Byzantine ascetic and writer, a monk in the monastery of Saint Catherine of Sinai. John retired from monastic life to become a hermit in a nearby cell. He was subsequently chosen abbot around 639. A writer on the spiritual life, John wrote the *Climax,* or *Ladder of Paradise,* a guide to the attainment of Christian ideals of spiritual perfection. The book was written in 30 chapters for each step of the ladder, the final rungs representing divine union and the age of Christ at His baptism. See also MYSTICISM.

**JOHN DUNS SCOTUS** (c. 1266–1308) An important theologian and philosopher, called "Doctor Subtilis" ("Subtle Doctor"). Few details of his life have survived, but it is known that he was born in Scotland, probably at Maxton, near Roxburgh. Joining the Franciscan Order around 1280, he studied theology at Oxford with William de Ware. Later (c. 1302) he continued his studies at Paris and was chosen for the English Franciscan chair of theology in Paris. Because of a dispute between King Philip IV (1285–1314) and Pope Boniface VIII (1294–1303), John and other theologians who supported the papacy were exiled. Returning briefly, John went to Cologne in 1307, possibly to flee continued persecution, dying there the following year.

John Duns Scotus was extremely influential, responsible for a major school of thought (Scotist) that found wide acceptance during the Middle Ages. He believed that emphasis should be placed primarily on God's love and his will. All in nature depended entirely on that will and was supreme over the intellect, for the will commanded it and provided strength of purpose and direction from the grace of God. In this he departed radically from the teachings of Thomas Aquinas, who emphasized the primary role played by reason and the intellect. In agreement with Thomas, however, he believed that reason was not contradicted by revelation. Complex and subtle, as his own title reflected, Duns Scotus promoted the doctrine of the Immaculate Conception, the first theologian to do so.

**JOHN MALALAS** See MALALAS, JOHN.

**JOHN OF BEVERLY, SAINT** (d. 721) Bishop of York and a popular English saint during the Middle Ages. Born in Yorkshire and studying at Canterbury, he entered Whitby Abbey and was consecrated bishop of Hexham about 687 and bishop of York in 705. He was instrumental in the establishment of the Abbey of Inderawood, known later as Beverley. John retired there sometime around 717 or 720. After his death, he was venerated and thought to have been a miracle worker. King Henry V (1413–1422) credited him for the English victory at Agincourt, ordering that his feast day, May 7, be observed throughout England.

**JOHN OF BRIENNE** (c. 1148–1237) Count of Brienne, king and later regent of Jerusalem and Latin Emperor of Constantinople from 1231 to 1237. The son of Count Erard of Brienne and Agnes of Montbeliard, John won the favor of King Philip II Augustus of France (1180–1223), marrying Mary of Montferrat, the queen of Jerusalem. He was crowned in 1210 and on Mary's death became regent for their infant daughter and royal heir, Isabella. Two years later he married Princess Stephanie, the daughter of the Armenian king Leo II (1199–1219). Subsequently participating in the Fifth Crusade (1218–1221), he argued with the papal legate, Pelagius, left Egypt in 1220 but returned in July 1221, in time to be part of the crushing defeat of the Crusaders at Damietta. After Stephanie died in 1219, John wed Berengaria, daughter of Ferdinand III of Castile (1217–1252). He was invited in 1228 to Constantinople, as regent and co-emperor with the young Baldwin II (1228–1261), receiving the crown in 1231, devoting the next years defending the Latin Empire from Greek and Bulgar attacks. See also CONSTANTINOPLE, LATIN EMPIRE OF.

**JOHN OF DAMASCUS, SAINT** (c. 675–749) Syrian theologian, doctor of the church and an influential writer and thinker, called also Johannes Damascenus. The son of a caliphate official, he was compelled to relinquish civic participation because of his Christian faith about 719. He entered a monastery near Jerusalem to devote his life to prayer and writing and composed between 726 and 730 spirited defenses of the veneration of icons against Emperor Leo III (717–741) and the iconoclasts. A prolific writer, he was responsible for some 150 works on philosophy, theology and religious education, as well as sermons, hymns, hagiography, Christian morality and asceticism. His two major works were *Fount of Wisdom* and *Sacred Parallels*. Known to Peter Lombard and Thomas Aquinas, these works were respected throughout Christendom and provided John a place in the advancement of Christian theological concepts.

**JOHN OF GAUNT** (1340–1399) Duke of Lancaster from 1362 and a powerfully influential figure in medieval England, the virtual ruler during the last years of the reign of his father, King Edward III (1327–1377), and in the early years of King Richard II (1377–1399). Born in Ghent, John became duke of Lancaster in 1362 through his first marriage and owned massive Lancastrian estates in England and Wales. From 1367 to 1374 he fought in the Hundred Years' War with France and was opposed at court from 1372 to 1376 by his brother, Edward the Black Prince, especially after John largely held control of state affairs because of Edward's increasing senility. Overcoming opposition, he retained his position into the reign of his nephew, Richard II, in 1377. The Peasant Revolt (1381), which John ruthlessly repressed, brought him more animosity. Having married Constance of Castile in 1371, he pursued his claim to the throne of Castile from 1386 to 1388, embarking on a futile military venture. His daughter, Catherine, married the future Henry III of Castile and León (1390–1406). Returning to England in 1389, John resumed his role as mediator between the king and his hostile barons, dying in 1399. Henry Bolingbroke, John's son, became Henry IV (1399–1413). The name John of Gaunt was a corruption of John of Ghent; his character was later a role created by Shakespeare in *Richard II*. See also ENGLAND; LANCASTER, HOUSE OF.

**JOHN OF JANDUN** (c. 1286–1328) Noted philosopher at the University of Paris and an important interpreter of Averroism. Born in the Champagne region, John became a lecturer on Aristotle and the author of an influential commentary on the philosopher. He was an associate of Marsilius of Padua, author of the *Defensor pacis*. A defender of imperial policy against the Avignonese papacy, John, with Marsilius, was excommunicated in 1327, finding protection with Louis IV of Bavaria (1314–1347). See also AVERROISM.

**JOHN OF LANCASTER** See BEDFORD, JOHN, DUKE OF.

**JOHN OF LUXEMBOURG, KING OF BOHEMIA** (1296–1346) Ruler from 1310 to 1346, the son of Emperor Henry VII (1308–1313) and father of Emperor Charles IV (1346–1378). Made count of Luxembourg, he married Elizabeth, the daughter of King Wenceslas II, ruler of Bohemia, in 1310 and was crowned in 1311 at Prague. Widely respected as a soldier, John brought Upper Lusatia, Tirol and Silesia under domination of the throne but ignored the administration of the holdings. He was first a friend and then enemy of Louis the Bavarian in his quest to become emperor, and in 1346 he had Louis deposed to put forward a claim for his own son, Charles. Having fought against the Lithuanians, Hungarians and Russians, in 1346 he offered his sword to King Philip VI of France (1328–1350). According to tradition, he marched to the Battle of Crécy, where, despite his blindness, he ordered that he be led to the thick of the fray, where he was killed. See also BOHEMIA.

**JOHN OF MATHA, SAINT** (1160–1213) Founder of the Ordo Sanctisimae Trinitatis Redemptiones Captivorum (Order of the Most Holy Trinity for the Redemption of Captives), commonly called the Trinitarians. The order was established to free Christian captives in Muslim hands. Few facts are known about his life, as much that has been written about him was fabricated in the 15th and 16th centuries.

**JOHN OF NEPOMUK, SAINT** (c. 1340–1393) Also John of Pomuk, a martyred vicar-general of the Archdiocese of Prague. Appointed to his post in 1390, John supported the archbishop in his excommunication of a favored courtier of King Wenceslas IV of Bohemia (1363–1419) and was later instrumental in resisting the king's plans to establish a new see in the province of Prague. By royal command John was arrested and tortured and eventually drowned in a river to hide evidence that might make him worthy of martyrdom. A story, originating with an Austrian chronicler, Thomas Ebendorffer, in the 15th century, recounts that he was murdered after refusing to reveal the confession of Wenceslas's wife, Sophia. It is now generally accepted that this tale was false or that it referred to some other members of royalty. See also BOHEMIA.

**JOHN OF PARMA** (1209–1289) Minister-general of the Franciscan order who strove to restore it to traditional discipline and ascetic principles. Joining the order in 1233, he earned his reputation as a preacher and teacher and was elected minister-general in 1247. His teachings were associated with those of Joachim of Fiore, and John was charged and eventually acquitted of heresy. He resigned in 1257, retiring to a hermitage, where he spent his last years in penance and prayer, with the exception of a mission to Greece in 1289. He died traveling to Camerino. See also FRANCISCANS.

**JOHN OF PIANO-CARPINI** See CARPINI, GIOVANNI DE PIANO.

**JOHN OF PROCIDA** (c. 1210–1248) Italian Ghibelline who held a major role in organizing the war of the SICILIAN VESPERS in 1282.

**JOHN OF SALISBURY** (c. 1115–1180) Humanist, philosopher and bishop of Chartres who was an associate of Thomas à Becket. Studying at Paris with influential scholars, including Abelard, he moved on to Chartres and then served in the Papal Curia before returning to England, entering the service of Theobald, archishop of Canterbury, as secretary, holding the same position under Becket and supporting him in his conflict with King Henry II (1154–1189). He was thus exiled to Reims from 1163 to 1170 but was present in the cathedral at Canterbury when Becket was murdered, although he was not a witness. In 1176, with the support of King Louis VII of France (1137–1180), he became bishop of Chartres and emerged as an intellectual leader of the Renaissance, holding the distinction of being the first medieval author to write with familiarity on Aristotle's works on logic, the *Organon.* He also produced the *Pelicraticus,* a treatise on the political theory; the *Metalogicon,* advocating the study of logic and metaphysics, and the *Historia pontificalis,* an account of his years in Rome. He compiled a collection of Becket's correspondence in addition to his own letters.

**JOHN ORSINI** See EPIRUS, DESPOTATE OF.

**JOHN SCHOLASTICUS** (c. 503–577) Also John III Scholasticus or John of Antioch, the patriarch of Constantinople from 565 to 577, named by Emperor Justinian I (527–565) after a distinguished career. He was patriarch throughout most of Justin II's reign (565–578) and served as mediator between those espousing imperial religious orthodoxy and the heretical Monophysites. John is remembered for his compilation of Byzantine church canons, including the *Novellae* of Justinian, the supplementary legislation on church affairs, and the canons of the fourth-century theologian and legislator Basil of Cappadocia. He is not to be confused with John Climachus, sometimes called John Scholasticus.

**JOHN SCOTUS ERIGENA** (d. c. 877) Irish philosopher and scholar whose thinking was perhaps the most unique of his era. Granted the favor of the king of the West Franks, Charles the Bald (843–877), John was in charge of the palace school at Paris and was commissioned to translate the writings of Dionysius the Areopagite (see PSEUDO-DIONYSIUS) into Latin, as well as those of other officials of the Greek church. He disputed Gottschalk on predestination and Paschasius Radbertus on the Eucharist. The author of *De divisione naturare,* he wrote that nature was divided into four categories, beginning and ending in God. His treatise was condemned in 1210 and in 1225 for its pantheistic tendencies. It is believed that John may have gone to England at the invitation of King Alfred the Great (871–899), as he has been associated, perhaps erroneously, with the revival of learning at Alfred's court.

**JOHN THE FEARLESS, DUKE OF BURGUNDY** (1371–1419) Duke from 1404 to 1419, a major figure in the political upheavals gripping France in the early years of the 15th century, earning notoriety for his role in the murder in 1407 of the duke of Orléans. The son of Duke Philip the Bold and hence the second duke of the Valois line who were closely related to the royal family, John fought and was captured in the Crusade of Nicopolis (1396), earning his freedom by payment of a ransom to the Turks. In 1404 he inherited the duchy and entered into an intense conflict with Louis of Orléans, with whom he fought for control of the politically weak and mentally unstable King Charles VI of France (1380–1422). The quarrel with Louis and the Armagnac party was not ended on the death of Louis in 1407, as Bernard VII, count of Armagnac, won authority over the state in 1413, capturing Paris and executing his enemies. Negotiating with England (during the Hundred Years' War), while talking with the Armagnacs, John was lured to his death in a meeting with the dauphin Charles VII (1422–1461). On September 10, 1419, he was cut down by an ax on the Montereau Bridge, possibly by Charles' own hand. See BURGUNDY, DUCHY OF.

**JOINVILLE, JEAN** (c. 1224–1317) More precise, Jean, sire de Joinville, French historian and author of the important *Histoire de Saint-Louis.* Jean had accompanied King Louis IX (1226–1270) on the Seventh Crusade (1248–1254) to Egypt, and the king was captured during the campaign. Joinville, confined with Louis, became a close and trusted friend to the king. In 1254 both returned to France, where Jean, the seneschal of Champagne, spent time between his estates and the court. Believing another crusade hopeless, he did not join Louis on his fatal expedition in 1270 but was a major witness in the monarch's canonization in 1282. He saw the king exhumed in 1298 and began his biography at the request of Queen Jeanne of Champagne and Navarre, the wife of King Philip IV the Fair (1285–1314). It was presented in completed form to Louis X (1314–1316) in 1209. An objective work, the biography was a major source for the Seventh Crusade. Jean also wrote *Credo* in 1252, a summation of his beliefs. See also CRUSADES.

**JONGLEURS** Professional minstrels or entertainers in France from the 12th to the 14th century. Similar in their role to the troubadours *(trouveres),* the jongleurs were masters of amusement, able to perform music, acrobatics and juggling and to recite various forms of verse, as well as lays, fables and the chanson de geste. Associated with chivalry and court life, they roved about the countryside, performing in marketplaces on holidays, or before the nobility, and even in abbeys. Those jongleurs who were fortunate enough to find constant employment became minstrels and added their own compositions to their repertoires.

**JOSCELIN I OF COURTENAY** (d. 1131) Count of Edessa from 1118 to 1131, a trusted associate of Baldwin II of Le Bourge. He helped him gain the throne of the Kingdom of Jerusalem in 1118 after the death of Baldwin I and in return received from Baldwin the county of Edessa. See also CRUSADER STATES; CRUSADES; EDESSA.

**JOSCELIN II OF COURTENAY** (d. 1159) Count of Edessa from 1131 to 1144, the last of the counts (except for the titular count Joscelin III) with the fall of Edessa to the forces of Imad al-Din Zengi. The son of Joscelin I, he succeeded his father in 1131 but was thought not to be as competent, although he was a good soldier. In 1144 he was away from Edessa with the bulk of his army when the city was attacked and subsequently fell on December 26. In 1150 Joscelin was captured by Zengi's son, Nur al-Din, blinded and imprisoned until his death. See also CRUSADER STATES; CRUSADES; EDESSA.

**JOSEPH OF ARIMATHEA, SAINT** The "good and just man" recorded as having provided Christ with a proper burial following His crucifixion. Joseph was accorded a role in the literature of the Middle Ages, especially in the complex history of the Holy Grail. He was included in the Gospel of Peter (dating from the second century), and the Gospel of Nicodemus (dating from the fourth or fifth century) and appeared in medieval literature in Robert de Barron's romance, *Joseph d'Arimathie* (early 13th century), William of Malmesbury's *De antiquitate Glastoniensis ecclesiae* (12th century) and Thomas Malory's *Morte d'Arthur* (15th century). According to tradition, Joseph came to England bearing with him the Holy Grail, building the first church there at Glastonbury. See also HOLY GRAIL.

**JOUSTING** See TOURNAMENTS.

**JUANA LA BELTRANEJA** (1462–1530) Castilian princess who fought unsuccessfully to take the throne of Castile from her aunt, the future Isabella I (1474–1506). Possibly the daughter of King Henry (Enrique) IV of Castile, Juana was declared the illegitimate child of Queen Juana and the courtier Beltrán de la Cueva by the king, who acquiesced to the demands of his nobles and named as his heir his younger brother, Alfonso. After Alfonso died and Isabella proved a disappointment through her marriage to Ferdinand of Aragon in 1469, Henry declared Juana legitimate again. When he died in 1474, however, Isabella was made queen. Juana's supporters advanced her cause, betrothing her to King Alfonso V of Portugal, who marched on Isabella but was routed at Toro in 1476 and then failed to secure French support. Juana's marriage to Alfonso was never solemnized, and, refusing to wed a Castilian prince, she retired to a convent in Lisbon, claiming until her death her right to the throne.

**JUDAH BEN SAMUEL HE-HASID** (c. 1149–1217) Also called Hasid of Regensburg, a mystic and author of the *Sefer Hasidim* (Book of the Pietists). The son of another mystic, Samuel the Hasid, Judah founded an academy in Regensburg attracting the most notable Jewish mystics and intellectuals of the time, including Eleazar of Worms and Isaac ben Moses. The *Sefer Hasidim* was a compilation of the thoughts of his father and Eleazar and presented a clear portrait of the Jewish community and contemporary practice of religion while stressing the role of prayer and study of the Bible. See also JEWS AND JUDAISM.

**JUDAH HALEVI** (c. 1075–1141) Jewish physician, philosopher and poet, born in Spain and residing for many years in Granada and in other Muslim cities. Returning to Christian lands, he was a physician in Toledo until persecutions forced him go to Córdoba. Setting out on a journey to the Holy Land in 1140, he was welcomed by the Jewish communities in Cairo and Alexandria but died before reaching Jerusalem. He was the author of the *Sefer ha-Kuzari (Book of the Kazar),* arguing the superiority of religious truth when it is achieved through intuition rather than logic.

**JULIAN OF NORWICH** (c. 1342–after 1412) English mystic, author of the celebrated *Revelations of Divine Love.* Few details of her life have survived except the fact that she was an anchoress (a recluse) who spent her days in prayer and devotion. In May 1373, she experienced a series of visions concerning the Passion and the Holy Trinity. The *Revelations* were an account of what she had experienced and were written some 20 years later. Considered one of the most profound works in English religious literature, the *Revelations* examined the deepest mysteries of the Christian faith. See also MYSTICISM.

**JUSTIN I** (c. 450–527) Byzantine emperor from 518 to 527, born a peasant but achieving major influence by promoting the political rise of his nephew and adopted son, Justinian I (527–565). Born to an Illyrian family, he earned a position in Constantinople's palace guard and succeeded Anastasius in 518. Justin agreed with Christian orthodoxy and strove for the suppression of Monophysitism. His edict against Arianism (523) caused a breakdown in relations with Theodoric, king of the Ostrogoths (471–526) in Italy, who sent Pope John I (523–526) to plead for an easing of the decree. Justin agreed in part, but it was not enough to preserve Pope John from Theodoric's wrath. He chose Justinian to be his heir shortly before his death. See also BYZANTINE EMPIRE.

**JUSTIN II** (d. 578) Byzantine emperor from 565 to 578, the nephew of and successor to Justinian I (527–565), he proved incapable of maintaining the empire. Starting his reign with promise, Justin, in 571, began persecutions of the Monophysites but then launched a series of foreign policies that were disastrous. He lost Italy to the Lombards in 568, and his refusal to pay tribute to the Avars led to hostilities, culminating in the payment of yearly tribute to maintain peace. The Turks took part of Crimea in 576, and a Byzantine army sent to support Armenia against the Persians was defeated. The Persians then attacked and captured several imperial cities, events that triggered Justin's eventual madness, about 574. That same year he was induced to adopt General Tiberius I Constantine, who succeeded him in 578 after spending years in virtual control of the state. See also BYZANTINE EMPIRE.

**JUSTINIAN, CODE OF** In Latin the *Corpus juris civilis (Body of Civil Law)*, an extensive collection of laws and their interpretations made at the order of Emperor Justinian I (ruled 527–569). The Code of Justinian was actually a compilation in four books, consisting of the *Codex constitutionum*, the *Digesta (Pandectae)*, the *Institutiones* and *Novella constitutiones post codicem*. The *Codex constitutionum* was begun in 527 and promulgated in 529, amassing over 4,000 imperial enactments, dating from the time of Hadrian (ruled 117–138), arranged in chronological order. A revision was issued in 534 under the name *Codex repetitae praelectionis* (in 12 books). The *Digesta (Digest)*, compilations from 530 to 533, was assembled by a body of lawyers, directed by the jurist Tribonian. It brought together all of the writings of known and accepted jurists such as Gaius (second century) to create a textbook or manual for basic principles of law for law students. Finally, the *Novella constitutiones* was a collection of new ordinances, passed by Justinian between 534 and 565. One of the major sources for modern civil law, the Code of Justinian was written almost entirely in Latin, except for the *Novella constitutiones* which were written in Greek for the Eastern provinces and in Latin for the Western ones. See also JUSTINIAN I.

**JUSTINIAN I** (483–565) Byzantine emperor from 527 to 565, whose reign was influential in achieving a temporary return to imperial greatness. He has been called the "Last Roman" and the "First Byzantine Emperor." The nephew of Emperor Justin I (ruled 518–527), Justinian was experienced in government and public affairs. He became caesar in 525 and co-emperor in 527. His wife, Theodora, was granted the title of Augusta. On the death of Justin on August 1, 527, Justinian became sole emperor.

His chief goal was the reestablishment of the Roman Empire, the Western provinces of which had been lost to the Germanic kingdoms. Through his generals, Narses and especially Belisarius, Justinian recovered large parts of the West, including Dalmatia, Italy, a portion of southeastern Spain and North Africa, where the Vandal kingdom was destroyed. These military endeavors required vast sums, and the frontiers in the north and east, along the Danube River and opposite the Sassanid Persians, were constantly menaced. He used tribute, alliances and the skills of his lieutenants to prevent these regions from becoming major threats to imperial stability, all the while draining the treasury.

Justinian's lasting achievements were domestic, as he ordered the construction of the celebrated Hagia Sophia in Constantinople and other basilicas in the capital, Ravenna, and elsewhere. He established the codification of Roman law (see JUSTINIAN, CODE OF), which became the primary source for Roman law. He also advocated caesaro-papism, the supremacy of the emperor over the church, championing orthodoxy, persecuting Montanists, closing the ancient school at Athens in 529 and encouraging the conversion of pagans. In 552 he summoned the Second Council of Constantinople in an effort to reconcile the Monophysites and brought administrative reforms to the government by curbing abuses. His heavy taxation, however, led to the Nika Revolt of 532, an uprising that he ruthlessly suppressed, in large part owing to the influence of his wife, Theodora, who was a major adviser in imperial policy until her death in 548. Within a decade of his death, many of the lands regained by his empire were lost. See also BYZANTINE EMPIRE.

**JUSTINIAN II** (d. 711) Byzantine emperor from 685 to 695 and from 705 to 711, also known as "Rhinotmetus" because his nose was cut off when he was deposed and exiled. The son of and successor to Constantine IV (668–685), he launched a war against the Slavs from 688 to 689, taking territory in Macedonia and Thrace. Diplomatic deterioration with the Arabs, however, over the agreed-on joint sovereignty of Armenia, Cyprus and Georgia led to war in 691–691, in which the Byzantines were defeated and Armenia lost. Justinian exercised a ruthless policy in raising money, and his collectors went to extreme lengths to collect the needed funds. So intolerable did this campaign become that in 695 there was a revolt that caused Justinian's downfall and he was replaced by Leontius. As punishment his nose was cut off and he was exiled to Crimea. After spending some time with the Khazars, Justinian allied himself with the Bulgars in 705, recapturing Constantinople. His second reign proved harsher than his first, massacres and executions demonstrating his vengeance. In 711 a second revolt brought about Justinian's murder, as Philippicus took the city. See also BYZANTINE EMPIRE.

**JUSTUS OF CANTERBURY, SAINT** (d. 627) An important figure in the conversion of England and the archbishop of Canterbury. Sent to England in 601 by Pope Gregory I the Great (590–604) to assist archbishop Augustine of Canterbury, Justus was made bishop of Rochester in 604 and granted lands by King Aethelbert of Kent, who also ordered the construction of the Cathedral of Saint Andrew. A pagan reaction ensued after Aethelbert's death in 616, and Justus, with Mellitus, bishop of London, fled to Gaul, returning the following year when royal protection was reinstated. In 624 he was named archbishop of Canterbury, consecrating Paulinus for his missionary efforts in Northumbria. See also CANTERBURY.

**JUTES** A Germanic people who invaded Britain in the fifth century concurrent with the Angles and Saxons. It is generally accepted that their origins were in the region of Jutland, migrating to the British Isles and settling the Isle of Wight, Kent and Hampshire, according to Bede. Although elements of Jute culture and language were retained on Wight and especially Kent, Jute culture was absorbed ultimately by the Danes who appeared later. See also ANGLO-SAXONS; ENGLAND.

# K

**KABASILAS, NICHOLAS** (c. 1322–1390) Byzantine mystic, writer and theologian, most known for his extensive works *Commentary on the Divine Liturgy* and *Life in Christ*. The works were written in Greek and were important in preserving the highest forms of Byzantine religious thought. He is not to be confused with the other 14th-century Neilos Kabasilas, who became the archbishop of Thessalonica (c. 1355).

**AL-KADIR** (d. 1031) Also called al-Qadir, an Abbasid caliph from 991 to 1031. He became caliph on the abdication of his brother, al-Tai, in November 991. He was, by repute, learned, having studied science and law and having written a treatise on the fundamentals of the Islamic faith. His successor was al-Kaim. See also ABBASID CALIPHATE.

**AL-KAHIR** (d. 950) Abbasid caliph from 932 to 934, known also as al-Qahir, succeeding to the throne on the death of his brother, al-Muktadir, in the place of his nephew. The house of Muktadir was soon out of favor, and al-Muktadir's mother, a Greek or a Turk, was flogged to death. The mother of al-Kahir was a slave concubine. He was confronted by opposition from the army and several conspiracies and was finally toppled and replaced by al-Radi. Deposed and blinded, he was imprisoned for a number of years and then released. An outburst in a mosque brought about second imprisonment and eventual death. See also ABASSID CALIPHATE.

**AL-KAIM** (d. 1075) Abbasid caliph from 1031 to 1075, the son of the caliph al-Kaim who came to the throne on the death of his father. His reign was dominated by the Turkish general of the troops in Baghdad, Arslan al-Basasire, eventually calling on the Turkish chief Toghril-Beg to come to his aid. Toghril marched on Baghdad in 1058, defeating Basasiri and bringing his head to the caliph. Now dependent on Toghril, al-Kaim was forced to betroth his own daughter to the Turk, but Toghril died on the eve of his marriage. Al-Kaim died April 2, 1075, after being bled for an illness. The bandages came loose, causing severe loss of blood. Ibn al-Athir described al-Kaim as pious and charitable. See also ABASSID CALIPHATE.

**KAIROUAN** Also Qairouan, a city in Tunisia to the south of Tunis and an important holy site in Islam. Founded in 670 on the same land as a former Byzantine fortress, Kairouan was the base for the Muslim conquest of the Maghreb, the northwestern region of Africa. It later served as the capital of the first Aghlabid ruler and was important to the early Fatimids and the Zirids. The city declined in the 11th century as Tunis rose to prominence. Its most renowned structure was the Grand Mosque, dating from the time of the Aghlabids (ninth century).

***KALEVALA*** The Finnish national epic consisting of a compilation of old Finnish oral traditions, including ballads and songs extolling the deeds of the "sons of Kalevala." Meaning the Land of Heroes, *Kalevala* was a poetic name for Finland and described a country inhabited by mighty warriors. Chief among these was Väinäimöinen, a leader possessing supernatural powers, owing to his semidivine origins. Other characters, including Lemminkainen, Ilmarinen and Kullervo, peopled the land. The central themes of the epic were the creation of the world and the adventures of its heroes, culminating in the departure of Väinäimöinen from the land without his famous harplike instrument, the *kantele*, in favor of a new king. Väinäimöinen is believed to have represented the old paganism, which surrendered to Christianity. The *Kalevala* was collected by Elias Lönnrot and was published in two editions (1835 and 1849). See also FINLAND; PAGANISM.

**KALMAR UNION** The union of Scandinavia (Denmark, Sweden and Norway) formed in 1397, largely through the efforts of Queen Margaret (d. 1412) and possibly because of the dynastic ties between the countries. Following the accession of Margaret to the three thrones in Scandinavia, she attempted to ensure the union by having her sister's grandson, Eric of Pomerania, accepted as her successor, Norway acknowledging him in 1389, Sweden and Denmark in 1396. The following year, at Kalmar, two important documents were presented: the first providing for an act of homage to Eric and Margaret and the second calling for one monarch and one foreign policy, while ensuring that the individual countries could retain control over their domestic affairs.

Probably never ratified, the Kalmar Union had influence until 1523. Margaret was succeeded by Eric (VII, d. 1459), but he was removed by the Danes in 1438, by the Swedes in 1439 and by the Norwegians in 1442. His nephew, Christopher of Bavaria, was his replacement on the three thrones, but his death in 1448 brought a temporary dissolution of the union, which ended in 1450 with the rise of Christian I Oldenburg. The premise on which the Kalmar Union was based was Scandinavian opposition to German expansion, including that by the Hanseatic League.

**KALOJAN** Ruler of the Bulgars from 1197 to 1207, a brother of the two Bulgar leaders Peter and Asen. Sent to Constantinople about 1188 as a hostage following Byzantine recognition of Bulgar independence, he escaped and returned home. After the deaths of Peter and Asen he succeeded to the throne, proving competent. His attacks on Byzantine territory were halted by adroit Byzantine diplomacy, for the Byzantines convinced the Russians of Kiev to attack the Cumans, thereby depriving the Bulgars of important allies. The result was a treaty signed in 1201, returning Thrace to the empire. Kalojan later took Nis from the Serbs and then control of the Danube and Morava Rivers. Maintaining sound relations with the papacy, Kalojan was crowned king by a papal legate. See also BULGARIA.

**KARDAM** Ruler of the Bulgars from 777 to about 803. See also BULGARIA.

**KARL KNUTSSON** See CHARLES VIII KNUTSSON, KING OF SWEDEN.

**KARLSEFNI, THORFINN** See THORFINN KARLSEFNI.

**KAYKHUSRAW I** (d. 1211) Seljuk sultan of Rum from 1192 to 1196 and from 1204 to 1210, the youngest son of Qilij Arslan II (1156–1192). He was involved for years in conflicts with his brothers for the succession, able to secure protection for his father in 1190 and ruling in the capital from 1191 to 1196, when he was overthrown by his brother, Sulaiman II, and forced to flee to Constantinople. With Byzantine assistance he deposed Sulaiman and reigned until 1211, when he was killed in a battle against Theodore I Lascaris, emperor of Nicaea (1206–1222). See also SELJUK TURKS.

**KAYKHUSRAW II** (d. 1245) Seljuk sultan of Rum from 1236 to 1246, whose reign was noted for the loss of Seljuk independence to the Mongols, who reduced the sultanate to that of vassalage. Kaykhusraw died in 1245, and his realm was divided between his sons, Qilij Arslan III (1261–1267) and Kayqawus II (1247–1261). See also SELJUK TURKS.

**KAYKHUSRAW III** (d. 1283) Seljuk sultan of Rum from 1264 to 1276, who ruled as a vassal to the Mongols. Only 15 years old on his accession, he was beset by severe political difficulties because of the independence of the Turkish atabegs, or nobles. See also SELJUK TURKS.

**KAYQAWUS I** (d. 1219) Sultan of the Seljuks of Rum from 1210 to 1219, the son of and successor to Kaykhusraw II (1193–1211). He made peace with the Nicaean emperor Theodore I Lascaris (1206–1222) but was soon involved in a campaign of expansion. He conquered Sinope and defeated the Armenians, only to fail in his efforts to capture Aleppo, where he was defeated by the Ayyubids. See also SELJUK TURKS.

**KAYQAWUS II** Sultan of the Seljuks of Rum from 1247 to 1261, the son of Kaykhusraw II (1236–1246) and ruling the sultanate with his brother, Qilij Arslan III (1261–1267) on the death of their father (c. 1245). Kayqawus attempted negotiations with the Mamluks and the Byzantines and was driven from power, seeking safety in Constantinople. See also SELJUK TURKS.

**KAYQUAB I** (1237) Seljuk sultan of Rum from 1219 to 1237, one of the great rulers of the Rum sultanate, the brother of and successor to Kayqawus I. Kayquab embarked on a successful series of military ventures while proving himself an able administrator and encouraging economic growth in Asia Minor. He advanced into Seleucia and later won the submission of Lesser Armenia. Such acquisitions, however, brought him into conflict with the leader of Khwarazm, Jalal-ad-Din. Allied with the Ayyubid prince Ashraf, Kayquab defeated the Khwarazmian Shah at Erzincan in 1230, ending the presence of a strong buffer state between the Turks and the advancing nomads of Asia. Further, the Seljuk victory alarmed the Ayyubid prince, who made an alliance with 16 other princes from Iraq and Egypt, invading Anatolia under Malik al-Kamil. They were defeated by Seljuk military superiority, by the mountainous terrain and their own mistrust of one another. Kayquab died before the folly of his policies was demonstrated by the arrival of the Mongols. See also SELJUK TURKS.

**KAYQUAB II** One of the lesser-known Seljuk sultans of Rum, the son of Kaykhusraw II (d. 1245) who ruled the sultanate with his two brothers, Kayqawus II and Qilij Arslan IV, from 1249 to 1257. He was apparently sent to the Mongols to placate their Khan Batu, for he was seen by the friar, William of Rubriquis, probably dying on the way home. See also SELJUK TURKS.

**KAYQUAB III** (d. c. 1302) Seljuk sultan of Rum from about 1283 until his death. The nephew of Kaykhusraw III (1247–1276), he came to the throne on his uncle's demise but was soon challenged by a cousin, Masud II, who won the eastern half of the kingdom. Masud tried for many years to achieve total control, a conflict that continued into the next reign, that of the son of Kayquab. The Seljuk dynasty of Rum would not long survive him. See also SELJUK TURKS.

**KELLS, BOOK OF** A magnificent illuminated manuscript of the Gospels in Latin, so named for the monastery of Kells in county Meath, Ireland. It was produced 775–800 and is considered to be the finest extant example of Celtic art. There was an erroneous tradition suggesting that the Book of Kells was the possession of Saint Columba (d. 597), something now known to be impossible because of the verified age of the manuscript. It is preserved in the Library of Trinity College, Dublin. See also MANUSCRIPT ILLUMINATION.

**KEMPE, JOHN** (c. 1380–1454) Cardinal archbishop of Canterbury, chancellor of England and statesman in the reigns of Henry V and Henry VI. King Henry V (ruled 1413–1422) relied on him for diplomatic missions, and he was a member of the regent's council for King Henry VI (ruled 1422–1461), supporting Henry Beaufort, bishop of

Winchester, against the ambitions of Humphrey, duke of Gloucester. Named bishop of Rochester in 1419, he held the successive sees of Chichester (1421), London (1421), York (1425) and Canterbury (1452), becoming cardinal in 1439. Twice chancellor and an advocate of peace with France, Kempe supported the suppression of Jack Cade's Rebellion in 1450. See also CANTERBURY.

**KEMPE, MARGERY** (b. c. 1373; d. after 1439) English mystic and author of the *Book of Margery Kempe.* Born in Norfolk, the daughter of John Burnham, the mayor of Lynn, she married John Kempe and bore him 14 children. She and her husband embarked on a pilgrimage, starting at Canterbury, and, about 1413, traveled to the Holy Land, Rome, Germany and Spain. Considered difficult because of her extreme views on the pursuit of pleasure and her own austerity, she was charged with the Lollard heresy but acquitted. Her autobiography described her mystical experiences and her travels and was dictated to clerks about 1432–1436, because she was illiterate. See also MYSTICISM.

**KEMPIS, THOMAS À** See THOMAS À KEMPIS.

**KENILWORTH** Town in Warwickshire, England, noted for its castle, which was immortalized in Sir Walter Scott's 1821 novel *Kenilworth.* Constructed around 1120, the castle was granted to Simon de Montfort by King Henry III (1216–1272) and later belonged to John of Gaunt.

**KENNETH I McALPIN** (d. 858) Ruler of the Scots of Dál Riata and the Picts (c. 834–858) and the traditional founder of the Scottish kingdom. He strove to bring unity to his realm constantly threatened by the Britons, Vikings and the peoples of neighboring Lothian. To provide for a site for the national religion while preventing the plundering of Saint Columba's remains, he had the relics of the saint moved from Iona to Dunheld, thus establishing an ecclesiastical capital. Kenneth was succeeded by his brother, Donald. See also SCOTLAND.

**KENNETH II** (d. 995) King of Scotland from 971 to 995, the son of King Malcolm I, beset by incursions of the Danes into his realm. The Danes attacked Iona on Christmas Eve, 986, massacring the abbot and 15 clerics. According to tradition, Kenneth submitted to the English king Edgar, receiving in return the lands of Lothian, thereby establishing the first border between England and Scotland. Kenneth was assassinated by a group of vengeful Scottish nobles. See also SCOTLAND.

**KENNETH III** (d. 1005) Little-known king of the Scots, reigning from 997 to 1005. He was defeated and killed in battle against the son of Kenneth II, Malcolm II. See also SCOTLAND.

**KENT** Maritime territory in southeastern England, the region of the country closest to the European continent, reached by crossing the Strait of Dover. Kent, because of its geographical position, endured invasions by the Romans, Jutes and Saxons and eventually became part of the network of Saxon kingdoms in England, acquiring religious

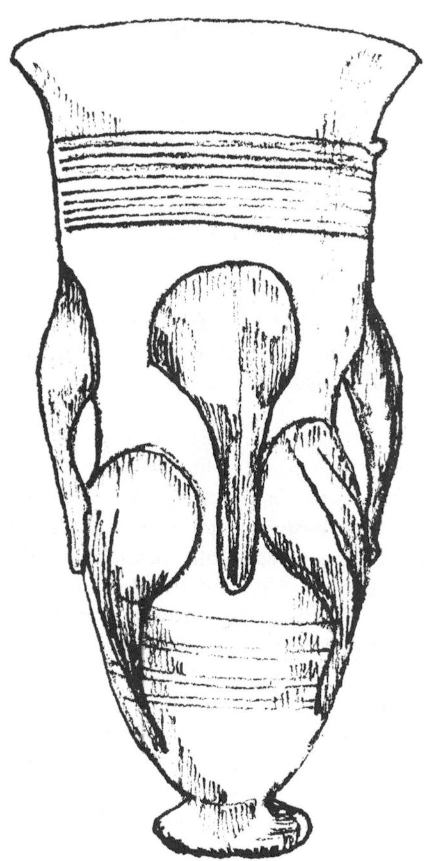

Kentish grave glass beaker

importance in the early seventh century with the arrival of Augustine of Canterbury and the subsequent acceptance of Christianity. Under Norman dominance, the Canterbury and Rochester cathedrals were rebuilt and many castles were constructed throughout the region. Following the murder of Thomas à Becket in 1170, Canterbury became a venerated place of pilgrimage, immortalized by Chaucer in his *Canterbury Tales.* Kent was rich in fruits, wheat, barley, oats, sheep and cattle. See also ENGLAND; KENT, KINGDOM OF.

**KENT, KINGDOM OF** Realm in Anglo-Saxon England of roughly the same area as the county of Kent, in southeastern England. The kingdom was founded, according to tradition, by the Anglo-Saxon adventurers Hengist and Horsa, sometime in the mid-fifth century, after they landed in England at the invitation of Vortigern, king of the Britons. Following the reign of Aesc, the son of Hengist, Kent declined in importance from about 512 until the time of King Aethelbert (560–616). During his reign Kent dominated the region south of the Humber River, and probably through the counsel of his wife, a Christian named Bertha, Aethelbert welcomed in 597 the missionary Saint Augustine (of Canterbury). He supported the missionary cause, and Canterbury subsequently emerged as the most important episcopal see in England. Aethelbert was a prominent figure of Kentish influence, although his grandson Egbert (ruled 664–673) wielded vast power in southern England. During the mid-eighth century, the kingdom fell under the domination of Mercia and in 825 was conquered by Egbert, king of Wessex. See also ENGLAND.

**KENTIGERN, SAINT** (d. c. 612) Bishop of Glasgow, called the Apostle to Scotland, also called Mungo. He is reported as having been of British royal descent, raised in Scotland in a monastic school on the Firth of Forth. A missionary, he established a Christian community around 550 and earned the patronage of the king of Strathclyde. In the pagan counterreaction he fled to Cumberland and Wales, where he founded the monastery of Saint Asaph. Returning to Scotland, he restored Christian practices in the region around Glasgow.

**KHAZARS** An association of Turkish and Iranian tribes that carved out a vast empire in the region north of the Black Sea, to the south of the Volga River. It is believed that the Khazars were originally a group of Turkestanis in the northern Caucasus, eventually becoming independent in the early seventh century and traditionally on amicable terms with the Byzantine Empire, supporting Emperor Heraclius I (ruled 610–641) in his war against the Persians. The Khazars also warred with the Arabs of the Islamic empire, and forced to move westward, they established their capital at Itil (Atil), at the mouth of the Volga. This city soon became important for commerce, and by the late eighth century the Khazars had extended their empire from the Black Sea to the Caspian Sea, north along the Volga in the east and the Dnieper in the west. Their client states included the eastern Slavs, the Magyars and the Volga Bulgars. Deriving most of their wealth from extensive trading, as well as from tribute, the Khazar nobles, called begs, wielded enough power to secure the marriage of several Byzantine emperors to Khazar women. The Russians of Kiev and the Petchenegs, however, were competitors, and Khazar power was shattered in 965 by the Kievan Russians. By 1030 they ceased to exercise any political or military authority. The Khazars had proven extremely valuable to the Byzantines, keeping watch on the Danubian frontier and preventing the advance of destabilizing Turkic tribes, while serving as loyal allies against Islam. It is noteworthy that the Khazar ruling class converted to Judaism sometime in the eighth century. See also BYZANTINE EMPIRE; RUSSIA.

**AL-KHWARIZMI** (c. 780–850) Islamic mathematician and astronomer who wrote several influential works on algebra and Hindu numerals. From his treatise on Hindu-Arabic numbers, preserved in Latin, is derived the name for algorithms (*Algoritmi de numero Indorum—Al-Khwarizmi Concerning the Hindu Reckoning*). He also drew up astronomical tables.

**KHWARIZMIAN TURKS** See KHWARIZMSHAHS.

**KHWARIZMSHAHS** Also, popularly, the Khwarizmians, a dynasty ruling the central Asian province of Khwarizm (Khwarazm). Originally the name was associated with the early, semilegendary Iranian kings, but by the late 12th century it was associated with a dynasty of Seljuk Turks. The Khwarizmshahs were founded by a former Seljuk slave who rose through the ranks to become a governor of Khwarizm. His grandson, Atsiz (1127–1156), conquered his nomadic neighbor and thus acquired Turkish mercenaries. Tekish (1172–1200), allied with the Abbasid caliph al-Nasir, destroyed the Seljuk Turks in 1194 and assumed the title of sultan as the protector of the caliphate. The ambitions of Tekish's son, Muhammad, caused a conflict with the caliph, and in 1217 he marched on Baghdad. The Khwarizmshahs advanced to the frontiers of India but were crushed by the Mongols. Muhammad was driven from power, and his son, Jalaluddin, tried in vain to recover dynastic supremacy. See also MONGOLS; SELJUK TURKS.

**KIEL** City in northern Germany, the capital of Schleswig-Holstein and a port on the Baltic Sea that was first recorded in the 10th century as Kyle. The Law of Lübeck was adopted there in 1242 to ensure its trading rights. In 1284 the city belonged to the Hanseatic League and was vital the trade in the region. See also HANSEATIC LEAGUE.

**KIEV** City in the Ukraine, situated on the Dnieper River, for a time the capital of medieval Russia, called "the mother of Russian cities." It probably originated as a Slavic trading deposit sometime early in the Christian era, supposedly founded by three brothers, Kii (Kiy), Shtchek and Khariv. It was dominated by the Khazars but was seized in 864 by Varangians from Novgorod and, in 882, became, under the leadership of Oleg (879–912), the chief city of the Varangian-Russian principality and the first major state in Russia. As the seat of the Christian church in the region, the city was called the Jerusalem of Russia, and its inhabitants were forced to convert to Christianity by Vladimir I (980–1015) in 988. The Kievan zenith was reached in the 12th century when its population and prominence in trade increased enormously. Decline soon set in, however, as a result of quarrels among the princes. In 1169 Kiev was sacked by a rival prince, and the Mongols virtually destroyed it in 1240. Other setbacks included the loss of its archepiscopal seat to Vladimir (1299), the tribute the city was compelled to pay to the Golden Horde (1240–1320) and its ruin by the Crimean khan in 1483. From 1320 Kiev was ruled by the Lithuanians. See also RUSSIA.

**KIEVAN RUS** See RUSSIA.

**KILIJ ARSLAN I** See QILIJ ARSLAN I.

**KILIJ ARSLAN II** See QILIJ ARSLAN II.

**KILIJ ARSLAN III** See QILIJ ARSLAN III.

**KILIJ ARSLAN IV** See QILIJ ARSLAN IV.

**KILKENNY, STATUTES OF** Decrees issued in 1366 by King Edward III (1327–1377) establishing the English presence in Ireland in the Pale, the territory surrounding Dublin. Kilkenny, a town in a county in southeastern Ireland, in the province of Leinster, was celebrated for its church of Saint Canice. The Statutes of Kilkenny included bans on marriage between the Irish and members of the Anglo-Saxon colony and restrictions on Gaelic culture and enforced the use of English as the primary language of the country. See also IRELAND.

**KIMCHI** Also Kimhi, a noted Jewish family that produced three important scholars: Joseph and his two sons, David and Moses. Born in Spain, Joseph (d. c. 1170) lived in Narbonne, France, where he was responsible for major contributions to Hebraic language studies including Hebrew translations of Arabic works by Spanish Jews. His son David, identified by his initials REDAK representing Rebbi David Kimchi, was better known as a Hebrew linguist and a biblical interpreter. He wrote two influential works, the *Sefer mikal* (*Book of Completeness*) on grammar and the *Sefer ha-shorashim* (*Book of the Roots*). Moses (d. c. 1190) was the older brother and David's teacher, writing *Mahalakh shevile ha-da'at* (*Journey on the Paths of Knowledge*), which was a widely read Hebrew grammar, translated into Latin in 1508. See also JEWS AND JUDAISM.

**AL-KINDI** (d. c. 870) His full name Abu Yusuf Ya'quib ibn Ishaq, called "Philosopher of the Arabs." Of noble birth, he lived in Baghdad, where he was encouraged by the patronage of the caliphs al-Mamun (d. 833) and al-Mutasim (d. 842). He attempted to unite Islamic teaching with the doctrines of Aristotle and Neoplatonism. The author of more than 270 works, al-Kindi had an interest in mathematics, astrology, weaponry and other fields.

**KNIGHTS AND KNIGHTHOOD** See ARTHURIAN LEGEND; CHANSON DE GESTE; CHIVALRY; CRUSADES; FEUDALISM; HOLY GRAIL; LOVE, COURTLY; MANORIAL SYSTEM; MILITARY ORDERS; TOURNAMENTS; WARFARE.

**KNUT** See CANUTE.

**KOLOMAN ASEN** (d. 1246) Ruler of the Bulgars from 1241 to 1246, the successor of Ivan (John) Asen II (1218–1241). Koloman was unable to maintain control over the Bulgar boyars, who vied with one another, and as a result the empire was unprepared for the Mongol invasion of 1242. Koloman was forced to submit and to pay tribute. His heir was his younger brother, Michael Asen. See also BULGARIA.

**KOLOMAN, KING OF HUNGARY** See COLOMAN.

**KOMNENI DYNASTY** See COMNENI DYNASTY.

**KÖNIGSBURG** Called since 1945 Kaliningrad, a city and port on the Baltic Sea, first established in 1255 as a fortress of the Teutonic Knights, becoming a town in 1286. Named for the Bohemian king Ottokar II ("King's Fortress"), the town joined the Hanseatic League in 1340, wielding considerable influence. During the second half of the 15th century, Königsburg was the residence of the grand master of the Teutonic Order. See also HANSEATIC LEAGUE.

**KONRAD I, DUKE OF MOZOVIA** (d. 1247) Polish duke who was noted for his repulsion of threats from the Lithuanians, Prussians and Jatvingians. He requested support from the Teutonic Knights (1225–1226), granting them the region of Chelmno as a buffer against the Prussians. See also POLAND.

**KONRAD VON MARBURG** See CONRAD OF MARBURG.

**KONRAD VON WÜRZBURG** (d. 1287) A poet of Middle High German, a man of humble origins who received noble patronage. Influenced by Gottfried von Strassburg, he composed narrative poems and epics; his best known work was *Der Trojanerkrieg*, an account of the Trojan War. He was considered one of the 12 masters of German medieval poetry by the Meistersingers, who drew on his works in their performances.

**KORNISAS** Early ruler of the Bulgars, from 739 to 756, coming to the throne during a period of political chaos. See also BULGARIA.

**KOSOVO, BATTLE OF (1)** Engagement fought in 1389 at Kosovo Polje (Field of the Blackbird) between the Ottoman Turks of Murad I (1362–1389) and the Serbs of Prince Lazar and resulting in a decisive defeat of the Serbian army. Lazar had organized a coalition of Serbs, Albanians, Wallachians and Bosnians, marching to confront the Turks at Kosovo in what is now Yugoslavia. The Ottoman sultan was murdered just before the battle by a Serbian who claimed to be deserting and then killed Murad. The new sultan, however, Bayezid I (1389–1403), the son of Murad, led his troops to triumph. The Serbs were crushed, and Lazar was captured and executed. Serbia was compelled to pay tribute. This battle was crucial in allowing the Ottoman Turks to encircle the Byzantine Empire. See also OTTOMAN EMPIRE.

**KOSOVO, BATTLE OF (2)** Engagement fought from October 17 to 20, 1448, between the troops of Murad II (1421–1451) and the Hungarian army led by János Hunyadi. The conflict marked the final defeat of the Christian Crusaders, who hoped to break the hold of the Ottoman Turks on the Balkans. In 1448 Hunyadi organized a Crusade to support the Albanians in their fight against the Turks. He joined the Albanians and marched to Kosovo, where they met the Turks, who proved triumphant. This battle was to herald the demise of the Byzantine Empire. See also OTTOMAN EMPIRE.

**KRAK DES CHEVALIERS** The strategically important castle erected in Syria by the Crusaders. The Krak des Chevaliers (Castle of the Knights) was also one of the most impressive examples of a medieval fortress. Founded in 1131 by the Knights of Saint John (or Knights Hospitalers) at Qal'at al-Hisn, Syria, the site was a former Muslim bastion, affording natural defenses and an excellent tactical position, able to accommodate some 2,000 troops. Occupied from 1142 until its capture in 1271, the fortress fell to the Mamluks under Baybars I (d. 1277). See also CASTLE; CRUSADES.

**KRAKOW** See CRACOW.

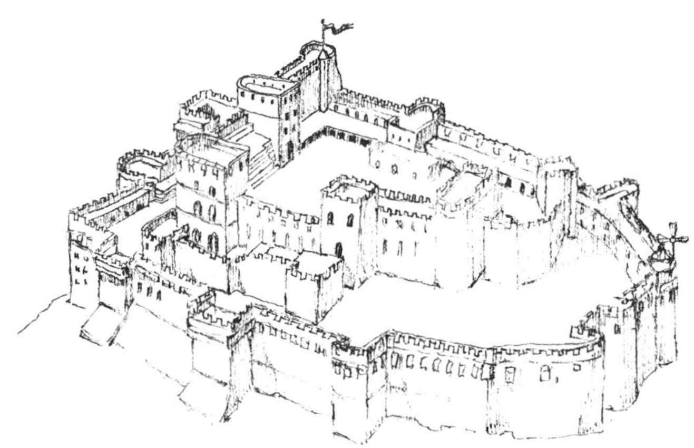

Krak des Chevaliers

**KREMLIN** The central fortress of Moscow but also the citadel in medieval Russian cities housing their administrative and religious buildings. From the Russian *kreml* (fortress), the kremlin was designed to serve as a strategic bastion within a city and was constructed with massive walls, towers and moats, encompassing cathedrals, palaces, government offices and considerable stores of food and munitions. Kremlins were constructed in important cities such as Novgorod, Astrakhan, Pskov, Rostov, Smolensk, Vladimir and Suzdal. The best known was in Moscow, built in 1156 in the historic core of the city. Originally of wood, it was reconstructed in brick in the 14th century and considerably altered. Triangular in shape, it had four gates and a secret exit leading to the Moscow River. Within, among other buildings, were the Uspenski and the Arkhangelski cathedrals. See also MOSCOW.

**KRUM** (d. 814) Ruler of the Bulgars from about 803 to 814, responsible for extending the Bulgarian state into southern Romania and eastern Hungary. A tribal chief of Pannonia, Krum claimed the throne and in 805 attacked and subjugated the Avars, who had already been defeated by Charlemagne and the Franks. From 807, the Bulgars were constantly at war against the Byzantine Empire; Krum's assaults were repulsed in 811 by Emperor Nicephorus I (802–811), with the destruction of the city of Pliska. Later that year, however, Krum destroyed a Byzantine army and killed the emperor. He then unsuccessfully besieged Constantinople, dying of a stroke during the attempt. He was responsible for issuing a set of legal codes in laying the foundation of the Bulgarian Empire. According to tradition, Krum fashioned the skull of Nicephorus into a goblet. See also BULGARIA.

**KUBLAI KHAN** (1215–1294) Called in both the East and the West the Great Khan, he was ruler of the Mongol empire from 1259 to 1294 and a celebrated historical figure. The grandson of Genghis Khan, Kublai Khan was instrumental in the consolidation of the Mongol empire and succeeded his brother Mangu (Mongke) in 1260. In 1279 he defeated the Sung dynasty of China, uniting all of China under his banner, and establishing the Yuan dynasty. He reconciled China to foreign occupation and moved the Mongol capital from Karakorum to Cambaluc (Peking). He was a patron of learning and the arts and tolerant of all religions, personally espousing a form of Lamaist Buddhism. A believer in Mongol supremacy, Kublai Khan attempted to conquer Japan but failed in this endeavor. His campaign against Japan was thwarted by the *kamikaze*, divine winds that wrecked his fleet, and by the fearless Japanese warriors. Marco Polo's accounts added to Kublai Khan's glory after his visit to his court in 1275. See also MONGOLS.

Kublai Khan, from *The Book of Marco Polo*

**KULIKOVO, BATTLE OF** See DIMITRY DONSKOI.

**KÜRENBERGER** Also Der von Kürenberg or the Knight of Kürenberg, a mid-12th-century minnesinger. One of the earliest of the German courtly love poets, Kürenberger was probably an Austrian noble, but few details of his life survived. Some scholars believe that he may have been the author of a lost epic on which the anonymous *Nibelüngenlied* was based.

**KURT** (d. c. 642) One of the early Bulgar rulers, called also Kovrat. He was a tribal chieftain who overthrew the Avars (c. 635) and united the seminomadic Bulgar clans, thus forging the Bulgar state. See also BULGARIA.

# L

**LADISLAS, KING OF NAPLES** (1377–1414) Ruler of Naples from 1386 to 1414, under whose reign the country was wrecked by war as he advanced his ambitions in Hungary, Dalmatia and Italy. The son of and successor to Charles III of Naples, Ladislas (Ladislao) was driven from his throne in 1387 by his rival of many years, Louis II of Anjou. He recovered Naples in 1399 but struggled with his Angevin foe through the Great Schism, supporting Pope Innocent VII (1404–1406) against Louis's antipope, Benedict XIII (1394–1417). Ladislas repeatedly occupied Rome, but in 1411 the antipope John XXIII (1410–1415), crowned Louis king of Naples. Ladislas responded by forging an alliance with the condottiere Muzio Attendolo Sforza and by making peace with Florence. To continue the family's territorial expansion he invaded Dalmatia and was crowned king of Hungary in 1403. In 1413 he sacked Rome and was on the verge of establishing his supremacy in central Italy when he died in Naples. See also NAPLES, KINGDOM OF.

**LADISLAS I, KING OF HUNGARY, SAINT** (1040–1095) Ruler of Hungary from 1077 to 1095; in Hungarian, László I. The son of King Béla I (1060–1063) and a Polish princess, Ladislas was born in exile and refused to oppose the accession of his cousin, Salomon. In 1073, however, he agreed to join his brother Géza in overthrowing Salomon, coming to power after Géza's death. An enlightened ruler, he established a legal code, constructed churches and introduced Catholicism into Croatia after its occupation in 1091. In the Investiture Controversy, Ladislas supported the pope but was reconciled with Emperor Henry IV (1056–1106). Beloved as an ideal of chivalric honor, he died while preparing to join the First Crusade. See also HUNGARY.

**LADISLAS II, KING OF HUNGARY** Claimant to the Hungarian throne from 1162 to 1163, an uncle of Stephen III (ruled 1161–1173). He disputed Stephen's right to the crown but failed in his efforts to take the throne. See also HUNGARY.

**LADISLAS III, KING OF HUNGARY** (d. 1205) Ruler from 1204 to 1205, the infant son of King Emeric (ruled 1196–1204), who was removed by Emeric's brother, Andrew II (1205–1235). Ladislas died the following year, and Andrew died soon thereafter. See also HUNGARY.

**LADISLAS IV, KING OF HUNGARY** (1262–1290) Called "the Cuman," reigning from 1272 to 1290. The son of Stephen V (1270–1272) and a Cuman princess, he succeeded his father in 1272, embarking on a reign beset by conflicts with his Cuman associations. Civil unrest and palace intrigues during his minority (until 1277) plagued him, and he supported the German king Rudolf I of Austria (1273–1291) in 1278 against Ottokar II of Bohemia (1253–1278), defeating Ottokar with a large army at the Battle of Dürnkrut. At home, however, he antagonized his nobles by taking a Cuman mistress and by encouraging Cuman culture. In 1282, to allay the fears of his Magyars, Ladislas made war on the Cumans but soon returned to Cuman ways. So widespread was the antagonism to this that in 1288 the pope ordered a crusade against Ladislas and civil war followed, ending with Ladislas's murder at the hands of his fellow Cumans. See also HUNGARY.

**LADISLAS V, KING OF HUNGARY** (1440–1457) Ruler of Hungary from 1444 and of Bohemia from 1453. The posthumous son of the German king Albert II (also king of Hungary and Bohemia, 1437–1439), he was crowned ruler of Hungary in 1440 at the request of his mother, Elizabeth, despite the election of Władysław III of Poland as king. Placed in the care of his cousin, the future Emperor Frederick III (1440–1493), following the death of Władysław in 1444, the child was made monarch of Hungary. Real power rested with Ulrich, count of Cilli, until he was dominated by János Hunyadi. Crowned king of Bohemia in 1453, Ladislas divided his time between Vienna and Prague but never exercised royal authority, the government remaining in the hands of his regents. He died in Prague as the result of either plague or poison. See also BOHEMIA; HUNGARY.

**LADISLAV, KING OF BOHEMIA** See LADISLAS V, KING OF HUNGARY.

**LAETUS, JULIUS POMPONIUS** (1428–1498) Called formerly Pomponio Giulio Leto, an Italian humanist and founder of the Academia Romana, a semisecret pagan society encouraging the study of all aspects of Roman culture. The enthusiasm of Laetus and the Roman Academy for pagan ritual caused Pope Paul II (1464–1471) to imprison him and to torture the academy's leaders on the grounds that they planned to depose the pope. The academy was revived by Pope Sixtus IV (1471–1484), a dedicated Latinist. Laetus was also a noted lecturer and writer.

**LA MARCHE, OLIVIER DE** (d. 1502) Burgundian poet and chronicler, born about 1425 and entering service to the House of Burgundy as a page to Philip the Good (1419–1467) and then becoming trusted secretary and representative of Charles the Bold (1467–1477). His work continued even after Charles's death in 1477, as he advised the heiress, Mary, and her husband, Archduke Maximilian. A partisan supporter of the Burgundian cause, La Marche wrote *Mémoires* (completed c. 1490), describing two periods, 1435–1467 and 1467–1488, and *L'etat de la maison du duc Charles de Bourgogne* (*The State of the House of Duke Charles of Burgundy*, 1474). La Marche has also been called a spokesman for the chivalric tradition. See also BURGUNDY, DUCHY OF.

**LAMBERT OF SPOLETO** (d. 898) Ruler of Italy (as Holy Roman Emperor) from 892 to 898, the son of Guy of Spoleto, crowned emperor with his father at Ravenna and then assuming sole power on Guy's death in 894. The following year Arnulf of Carinthia invaded Italy, capturing Rome in February 896. Crowned emperor by Pope Formosus (891–896), Arnulf marched on the deposed Lambert but fell ill and retreated to Germany. Lambert instructed Pope Stephen VI (VII) (896–897), successor to Boniface VI (896, who had succeeded Formosus), to exhume Formosus's body and to place the corpse on trial. The body was condemned, mutilated and thrown into the Tiber River. War erupted again in 898 with the arrival of Berengar, marquis of Friuli, in Lombardy. Lambert defeated him but died that same year, perhaps by assassination but more likely after a fall from his horse.

**LANCASTER, EDMUND, EARL OF** (1245–1296) Fourth son of King Henry III of England (1216–1272) and brother of King Edward I of England (1272–1307), the first of the Lancastrian line that would produce three kings of England. Known as "the Crouchback" (from "crossback," or crusader), he profited from the death of Simon de Montfort in 1265, receiving many of his estates, to which he added the earldom of Lancaster in 1267, a gift from his father, and a new title. His descendant, Henry Bolingbroke (later king Henry IV, 1399–1413), claimed that he was, in fact, his father's eldest son but had been ignored in his claim to the throne because he was a hunchback; that charge allowed Bolingbroke to take the throne in 1399. See also LANCASTER, HOUSE OF.

**LANCASTER, HENRY, DUKE OF** (d. 1361) English nobleman, trusted adviser to King Edward III (1327–1377) and grandfather of King Henry IV (1399–1413). He became the earl of Derby in 1337 and succeeded to the earldoms of Lancaster and Leicester in 1345. In recognition for his many achievements for England during the Hundred Years' War, he was elevated to the rank of duke of Lancaster in 1351. A brilliant soldier, he fought many campaigns against the French as Edward's chief captain in southern France from 1345 to 1347. He sacked Poitiers in 1346 and in 1349 was named to the post of vice-regent of Gascony and Poitou. Through his negotiations the Treaty of Bretigny was signed in 1360. His daughter, Maud, was his heir, and she died in 1362. Blanche of Lancaster, and thus her husband, John of Gaunt, inherited the Lancastrian title. John of Gaunt was the father of Henry IV. See also LANCASTER, HOUSE OF.

**LANCASTER, HOUSE OF** English noble family and a branch of the Plantagenet line, eventually producing three kings: Henry IV (1399–1413), Henry V (1413–1422) and Henry VI (1422–1461). The title of Lancaster was established in 1267 when King Henry III (1216–1272) bestowed it on his fourth son, Edmund, who was the first of the house. Through the marriage of his descendant, Blanche, the title belonged to John of Gaunt, fourth son of Edward III (1327–1377). His son was Henry Bolingbroke, who deposed Richard II in 1399 and reigned as Henry IV. The rivalry between the houses of Lancaster and York precipitated the Wars of the Roses. See also PLANTAGENET.

**LANCASTER, JOHN OF, DUKE OF BEDFORD** See BEDFORD, JOHN, DUKE OF.

**LANCASTER, JOHN OF GAUNT, DUKE OF** See JOHN OF GAUNT.

**LANCASTER, THOMAS, DUKE OF** (d. 1322) The strongest opponent to King Edward II of England (1307–1327) and the noble responsible for the banishment of Piers Gaveston and the Despensers. A grandson of Henry III of England (1216–1272), he inherited the domains of Lancaster, Leicester and Derby from his father, Edmund, and the earldoms of Lincoln and Salisbury from his wife, Alice, daughter of Henry de Lacy. Lancaster secured the removal of Gaveston in 1308 and in 1311, heading the conspiracy responsible for the murder of the royal favorite in 1312 on his own lands. He then opposed the Despensers but, after their exile in 1321, found himself in conflict with the king. Captured by royal troops, he was executed at Pontefract castle on March 22, 1322. See also ENGLAND; LANCASTER, HOUSE OF.

**LANCE OF LONGINUS** See LONGINUS; RELICS.

**LANDINI, FRANCESCO** (d. 1397) The most notable Italian composer of the 14th century. Born in Fiesole, he won fame in Florence, renowned for his memory of music and for his compositions and skill as an organist. Blind from his youth, as a result of smallpox, he nevertheless composed a large body of musical pieces, including madrigals and his own favorite, the *ballate*, an Italian song form based on the Italian *laude spirituale* and French musical forms. He also impressed his contemporaries with his knowledge of philosophy and astrology and won a laurel wreath in Venice in 1364 for his poetry.

**LANDO** Pope from 913 to 914, a Roman by birth who was elected through the influence of the House of Theophylact, which dominated his brief reign, of which little is known.

**LANFRANC** (c. 1005–1089) Archbishop of Canterbury, scholar, theologian and one of the intellectual giants of the 11th century. Born in Pavia, Italy, he was educated as a lawyer and journeyed to France, sometime around

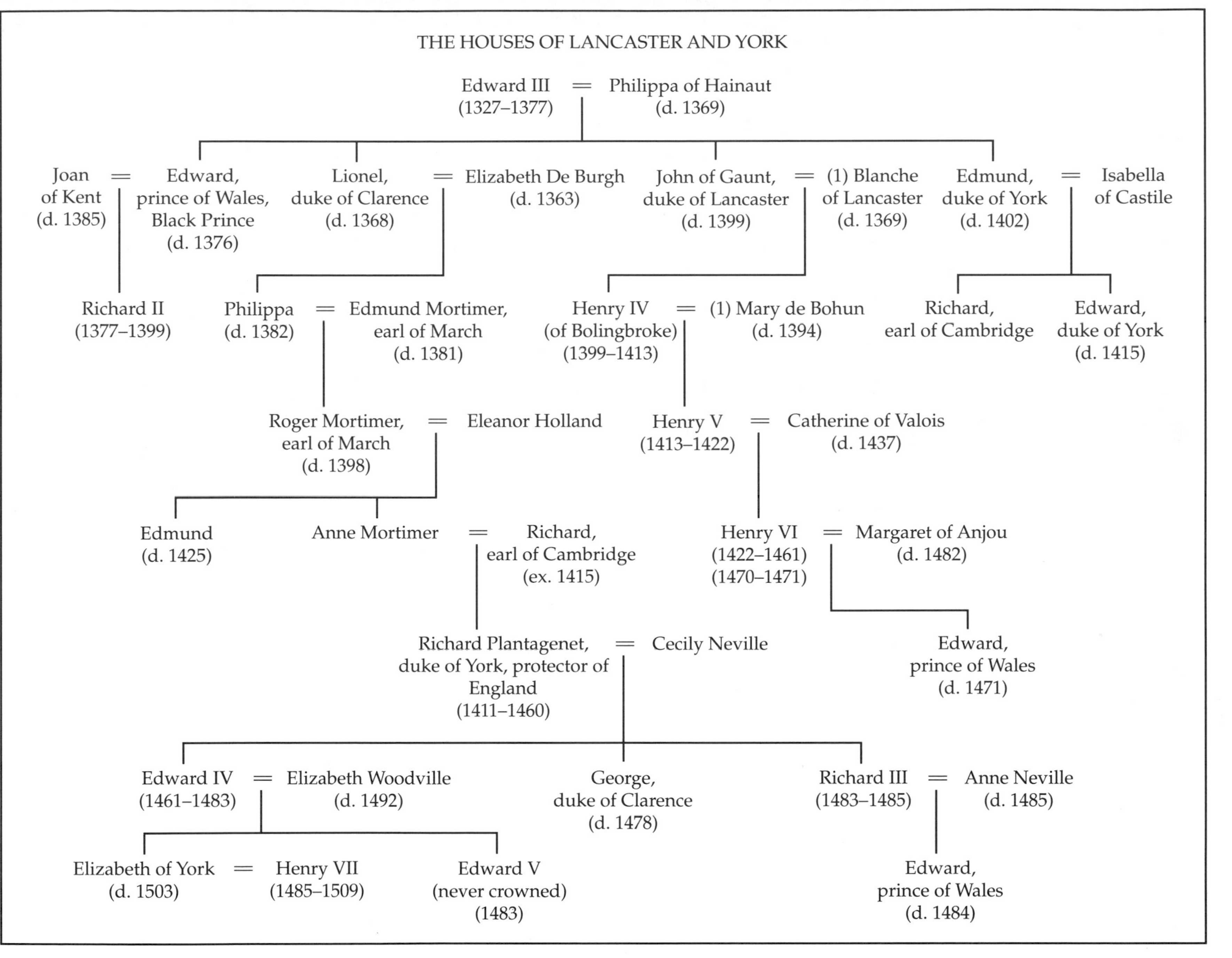
THE HOUSES OF LANCASTER AND YORK
Edward III (1327–1377) = Philippa of Hainaut (d. 1369)
Joan of Kent (d. 1385) = Edward, prince of Wales, Black Prince (d. 1376)
Lionel, duke of Clarence (d. 1368) = Elizabeth De Burgh (d. 1363)
John of Gaunt, duke of Lancaster (d. 1399) = (1) Blanche of Lancaster (d. 1369)
Edmund, duke of York (d. 1402) = Isabella of Castile
Richard II (1377–1399)
Philippa (d. 1382) = Edmund Mortimer, earl of March (d. 1381)
Henry IV (of Bolingbroke) (1399–1413) = (1) Mary de Bohun (d. 1394)
Richard, earl of Cambridge
Edward, duke of York (d. 1415)
Roger Mortimer, earl of March (d. 1398) = Eleanor Holland
Henry V (1413–1422) = Catherine of Valois (d. 1437)
Edmund (d. 1425)
Anne Mortimer = Richard, earl of Cambridge (ex. 1415)
Henry VI (1422–1461) (1470–1471) = Margaret of Anjou (d. 1482)
Richard Plantagenet, duke of York, protector of England (1411–1460) = Cecily Neville
Edward, prince of Wales (d. 1471)
Edward IV (1461–1483) = Elizabeth Woodville (d. 1492)
George, duke of Clarence (d. 1478)
Richard III (1483–1485) = Anne Neville (d. 1485)
Elizabeth of York (d. 1503) = Henry VII (1485–1509)
Edward V (never crowned) (1483)
Edward, prince of Wales (d. 1484)

1030 or 1035, teaching there and then entering a Benedictine monastery at Bec in Normandy, in 1042. Named prior in 1045, he taught and expounded on theological issues, including views opposing Berengar of Tours. He also quarreled with William of Normandy (king of England, 1066–1087) over his marriage to Matilda of Flanders but was later reconciled and, about 1063, was named abbot of Saint Stephen's in Caen. After the Norman Conquest he received the See of Canterbury in England, joining the king to reform the English church, while maintaining secular independence. Lanfranc's influence was instrumental to the succession of William II Rufus in 1087. See also CANTERBURY.

**LANGLAND, WILLIAM** (c. 1330–c. 1400) The presumed author of the Middle English alliterative poem *The Vision Concerning Piers Plowman,* a work ranked second in importance only to Chaucer's *Canterbury Tales.* Few details of Langland's life have survived beyond those reflected in his masterpiece. He was possibly born in Worcestershire, near the Welsh marches, and received a Benedictine education. It is believed that he lived in London (because of his familiarity with the city) and that he was married. This union prevented him from becoming a cleric, despite his having taken minor orders. Well versed in theology and in church doctrine, Langland was a vital literary figure of his time. See also VISION CONCERNING PIERS PLOWMAN, THE.

**LANGTON, STEPHEN** (d. 1228) Archbishop of Canterbury, theologian and scholar who played a major role in the political events leading to the signing of Magna Carta. English by birth, he went to Paris, where he was educated and was befriended by the future Pope Innocent III (1198–1216), who made him a cardinal in 1206 and a candidate for Canterbury's see, succeeding Hubert Walter (d. 1205). King John of England (1199–1216) opposed Langton, sparking a dispute that went on until 1213, ending with the lifting of the papal interdict and excommunication of John and the arrival of Langton in England. As archbishop he was sympathetic to the barons in their conflict against the Crown, probably convincing the nobles to stand on the coronation oath and charter of King Henry I (1100–1135), an important basis for Magna Carta. He also served as royal counselor at Runnymede in June 1215, his name appearing on Magna Carta, which was signed by King John. He later (1218–1219) lent his support to Henry III (1216–1272) and the regency, against the barons. Langton had the papal legate to England withdrawn so that Canterbury stood as the *legatus natus* of the pope in England. Langton was renowned for his commentary on the Peter Lombard's *Sentences* and for special constitutions he promulgated for the English church.

**LANGUEDOC** Province in southern France, situated along the Mediterranean Sea, its capital the city of Toulouse. Associated with the county of Toulouse before its incorporation into the domains of the crown, Languedoc was the heart of a unique culture, its name derived from its language (*langue d'oc*). Taken by the Visigoths in the fifth century, it was conquered in the sixth century by the Franks, and the region's ultimate cultural and political demise was brought about by its size, strategic location and the wide support of the region for the Albigensians. A French army invaded it in 1209, and the eastern part of Toulouse was annexed by the king. The remaining territories fell to the royal house in 1271. See also TOULOUSE.

**LAON** City in northern France, the capital of the department of Aisne and the chief city of the Carolingian kings. It was seized by Hugh Capet in 987, in preparation for his move to Paris. During the Hundred Years' War (1337–1453) Laon fell repeatedly to the English and the French, finally becoming a French possession. It was praised for its architecturally transitional cathedral of Notre Dame, completed in 1235. There are other medieval remains in Laon.

**LA SALE, ANTOINE DE** (d. c. 1464) French writer who had a role in the development of French fictional prose, having written *Le Petit Jehan de Saintré.* A tutor, soldier and administrator for the House of Anjou, La Sale served many of the dukes, including Louis II, with whom he went to Italy in campaigns against Ladislas of Naples. A traveler as well, he fought for the Portuguese against the Moors in 1415. In *Le Petit Jehan de Saintre* (c. 1456), La Sale extolled chivalry in a graceful literary style. His other works included *La Salle* (1415), a compilation of moral anecdotes, and *Lettre sur les tournois* (1459).

**LATERAN COUNCILS** Four church councils convened in the 12th and 13th centuries, so named because they met in the Lateran Palace in Rome. The First Lateran Council (ninth Ecumenical) was summoned by Pope Calixtus II (1119–1124) in 1123 to confirm the Concordat of Worms, bringing an end to the Investiture Controversy. The Second Lateran Council (10th Ecumenical) took place in 1139, summoned by Pope Innocent II (1130–1143) to condemn the antipope Anacletus II (1130–1138), as well as the followers of Arnold of Brescia. The Third Lateran Council (11th Ecumenical), convened by Pope Alexander III (1159–1181) in 1179, provided for the election of the pope by the College of Cardinals, with a necessary two-thirds majority. A treaty was also ratifed with Frederick I Barbarossa (1152–1190) and each bishopric was required to conduct a school for clerics. The Fourth Lateran Council (12th Ecumenical) was convened in 1215 by Pope Innocent III (1198–1216) and was one of the most important church assemblies prior to the Council of Trent. It provided for annual confession and communion of the faithful during the Easter season, defined the doctrine of Transubstantiation, condemned the teachings of the heretical Cathari and Waldenses, required Muslims and Jews to adopt specific attire, reminded bishops of their duties as teachers and forbade the establishment of new religious orders.

**LATIN EMPIRE** See CONSTANTINOPLE, LATIN EMPIRE OF.

**LATINI, BRUNETTO** (c. 1220–c. 1292) Florentine poet, statesman and scholar, who was a friend and teacher of Dante's. Latini was involved in the politics of Florence and was forced into exile in 1260, returning in 1266. He compiled an encyclopedia in French.

***LAUDABILITER*** See ADRIAN IV.

**LAUENBURG** Duchy situated in northern Germany along the Elbe River. It was established about 1181 when it came into the possession of the Ascanian dynasty, a line ruling there until the late 17th century. See also GERMANY.

**LAUSITZ** Territory in eastern Germany bounded by the Lusatian Mountains and the Oder River, called also Lusatia or Luzyce (Polish). Lausitz was composed of upper and lower regions, the former extending across northeastern Saxony, the latter comprising Lower Silesia and southern Brandenburg. First settled by the Slavic Wends (called Serbs), it was claimed by the Germans in 928 and was disputed by the Poles. In 1033 the Germans reconquered the region, dividing the land between Meissen and Brandenburg. Lausitz was attached to the crown lands of Bohemia by Emperor Charles IV (1368–1370). See also GERMANY.

**LAW** See ALFRED THE GREAT; ASSIZES OF JERUSALEM; BOLOGNA; BRACTON, HENDRY DE; BREVIARY OF ALARIC; CASIMIR III, KING OF POLAND; CHARLEMAGNE; CHARLES IV, EMPEROR; CHIVALRY; CLARENDON, CONSTITUTIONS OF; CONCILIAR MOVEMENT; CORTES; FEUDALISM; FREDERICK II, EMPEROR; GLANVILLE, RANULF DE; GLOSSATORS; GOLDEN BULL; GRATIAN; HENRY II, KING OF ENGLAND; INVESTITURE CONTROVERSY; IRNERIUS; JUSTINIAN I; JUSTINIAN, CODE OF; MAGNA CARTA; MAGNUS VII ERICSSON, KING OF NORWAY; PARLIAMENT; SALIC LAW; STATES GENERAL; THEODORIC; UNIVERSITIES.

**LAYAMON** (d. 1205) Early 13th-century Middle English poet who was the author of the important romance *Brut* as well as a priest in Worcestershire. *Brut* was a legendary history of Britain from the arrival of Aeneas's grandson, Brutus, to the final triumph of the Saxons in 689. Largely a translation of the *Roman de Brut* of Wace, this was the first English treatment of the "Matter of Britain" of ARTHURIAN LEGEND.

**LAZAR** (1329–1389) Prince of the Serbs from 1371 to 1389, a widely respected national hero of Serbia because of his ardent opposition to the advance of the Ottoman Turks into the Balkans. While successful against the Ottoman sultan Murad I (1362–1389) in 1386, he led his army to ultimate destruction in 1389 at the Battle of Kosovo. Captured by the Turks, Lazar was executed. See also SERBIA.

**LAZAR BRANKOVIC** Last ruler of the Serbs, reigning from 1456 to 1458, when the Ottoman Turks ended Serbia's vassal status. See also SERBIA.

**LE BEL, JEAN** (d. 1370) Belgian chronicler, canon, soldier and confidant of his patron, Jean de Beaumont. With Beaumont he visited England and Scotland in 1327 and for him wrote the account *Vrayes chroniques* on the reign of King Edward III (1327–1377). Le Bel's accuracy and methods of research, including the use of interviews, were very influential. Jean Froissart gave Le Bel much credit for the development of his own literary style.

**LECHFELD, BATTLE OF** An important engagement fought in 955 between Otto I (936–973), the German king, and the Magyars, on the Lech plain (Lechfeld) near Augsburg. A crushing defeat for the Magyars, the battle halted their attacks on Germany and provided Otto the Great with the means to overpower his rebellious magnates and to prepare the way for his crowning as emperor in 962. See also MAGYARS.

**LEGNANO, BATTLE OF** Engagement fought on May 29, 1176, between the forces of Emperor Frederick I Barbarossa (1152–1190) and those of the Lombard League. Part of Frederick's fifth campaign in Italy (1174–1177), Legnano took place near Milan in Lombardy. Frederick agreed to engage the superior army of the league, having only his heavy cavalry of knights and facing the infantry and horse of the enemy. His assault was beaten back by the pikes and crossbows of the infantry, and his knights were routed by the cavalry of the league. Frederick, whose long-term ambitions in Italy thus received a major setback, eventually made peace with the Lombard League (1183). See also LOMBARD LEAGUE.

**LEICESTER, SIMON, EARL OF** See MONTFORT, SIMON DE (2).

**LEIF ERICSSON** Celebrated 11th-century Norse explorer, the son of Eric the Red, who has often been called the first European to discover North America. Raised in Greenland, Leif went to Norway (c. 1000) and was converted to Christianity by King Olaf I (995–c. 999). Returning home, he is reported to have sailed off course, landing somewhere in North America, possibly Nova Scotia, in a region that he called Vinland. Many questions remain concerning Lief's life and discoveries, and he may not have led the first expedition to America. According to the *Saga of the Greenlanders (Groenlendinga saga)*, he learned of Vinland from Bjorni Herjulfsson, an Icelander who had been to the continent a decade earlier. Lief visited Vinland and perhaps Newfoundland and Labrador after 1000. See also VINLAND.

**LEIPZIG** City in Saxony, Germany, situated on the Pleisse River, first established as a German settlement in the early 10th century and known by the name of the fortified town Urbs Libzi. When it was chartered in 1174, the city rights of Magdeberg were granted as well, and Leipzig was advanced in its economic growth by its strategic location on the major trade routes of Germany and the favor granted by its rulers. Two annual markets (Easter and Michaelmas) were given the status of imperial fairs there. The University of Leipzig, founded in 1409, was established as a result of Czech ascendancy at the University of Prague. See also GERMANY.

**LEO II** (d. 683) Pope from 682 to 683, elected in December 681 but not confirmed by the Byzantine emperor,

Constantine IV (668–685), and thus was not consecrated until August 682. His chief act was to ratify the decision of the Council of Constantinople (680) condemning the heresy of Monothelitism.

**LEO III** (d. 816) Pope from 795 to 816, he was responsible for the decisive act of crowning Charlemagne Emperor of the West. The successor to Adrian I (772–795), Leo was confronted by fierce opposition from many Romans and was driven from the city in 799. He fled to Paderborn, where sanctuary was given him by Charlemagne. The Frankish ruler marched on Rome, restored Leo and cleared him of all charges. Then, on Christmas Day, 800, Leo crowned Charlemagne, setting the precedent for all Holy Roman Emperors being given their crowns by the popes, thus allying the papacy with the secular realms of western Europe. Leo also confirmed the accepted nature of the *filioque* (the concept holding that the Holy Spirit proceeded from both the Father and the Son) but asked that it not be read in the public liturgy for fear of offending the Eastern church.

**LEO IV** (d.855) Pope from 847 to 855, formerly a Benedictine monk, the successor to Sergius II (844–847). Threatened by Saracen attacks, Leo organized an alliance of city-states in Italy (849) that routed the invaders in a naval battle near Ostia. Refortifying Rome against future peril, he strengthened Civitavecchia, which was renamed Leopoli in his honor (854). A believer in obedience to papal authority, Leo punished Hincmar of Reims because the archbishop had excommunicated an imperial vassal without prior papal approval. He also permitted Hincmar's suffragen bishops to appeal directly to Rome.

**LEO V** (d.903) Pope from August to September 903, whose obscure pontificate was cut short by his murder. He was probably strangled by Christopher, a cardinal and antipope (903–904), who was later executed by Pope Sergius III (904–911) in 904.

**LEO VI** (d. 928) Pope from May to December 928, pontiff who reigned briefly owing his election to Marozia and the Roman family of the Crescentii. He was the successor to John X (914–928), who had been deposed and imprisoned.

**LEO VII** (d. 939) Pope from 936 to 939, probably a Benedictine, chosen by Duke Alberic II of Spoleto to succeed the imprisoned John XI (931–935/6). An advocate of reform in Germany, he gave his support to the emperors in bringing about changes there. Leo objected to the forced conversion of the Jews by Archbishop Frederick of Mainz but did not prohibit the expulsion of those Jews who did not accept Christianity.

**LEO VIII** (d. 965) Pope from 963 to 965, made pontiff through the influence of Emperor Otto I (962–973), who had just deposed John XII (955–964). On Otto's departure from Rome, however, John returned and organized the synod responsible for Leo's removal. On John's sudden death, Leo was ignored as a candidate, and Benedict V (964) was elected. Otto marched back into Italy, quelled all opposition and in June 964 reinstated Leo, who died the following year. According to some papal lists, Leo was an antipope, either during his entire pontificate or until his return in 964.

**LEO IX, SAINT** (1002–1054) Pope from 1049 to 1054, born Bruno of Egisheim, elected through the influence of Emperor Henry III (1039–1056) after serving as bishop of Toul. Of noble birth, Leo proved himself an able pontiff who strove to extend papal powers while bringing reform to the church. He expanded the role of the Roman Curia, sent out papal legates to the courts of Europe and presided over councils in France, Germany and elsewhere, elevating the papacy to the status of a temporal power. Hildebrand, the future Gregory VII (1073–1085), and Peter Damian supported him in these efforts. A military campaign against the Normans in Sicily resulted in his defeat and capture in 1053, and the remainder of his pontificate was marred by deteriorating relations with the Byzantine Empire. A schism with Constantinople began in the 1050s and was never healed.

**LEO I, BYZANTINE EMPEROR** (d. 474) Ruler from 457 to 474, a Thracian by birth, who emerged from obscurity to rule the Eastern Empire while the Roman Empire in the West was confronting its ultimate demise. He entered the service of Aspar, the *magister militum* (master of the soldiers), who chose him in 457 to succeed Anthenius, who was without heir. Leo soon tried to reduce Aspar's influence, as well as that of the Germans, by relying on a new army formed by levies recruited from the wild region of Isauria. By 461 he had broken the strength of Aspar and ensured his murder at the hands of palace eunuchs. He thus saved the East from the fate of Germanic rule that had befallen the West. In 468, Leo also launched a massive campaign against the Vandals of Africa and their king, Geiseric. The war was a total disaster, and Leo lost most of his fleet and a portion of the imperial treasury. See also BYZANTINE EMPIRE.

**LEO II, BYZANTINE EMPEROR** (d. 474) Ruler from February to November 474, the grandson of Emperor Leo I (457–474), the son of Leo's daughter, Aelia Ariadne, and her husband, the Isaurian general Zeno. Leo II died probably of severe illness, and Zeno was proclaimed his successor. See also BYZANTINE EMPIRE.

**LEO III, BYZANTINE EMPEROR** (d. 741) Ruler from 717 to 741, known as the Isaurian, winning fame for his active rule, his military campaigns and his introduction of iconoclastic policies. A Syrian by birth, he was an imperial attendant to Justinian II (685–695, 705–711), becoming a general under Anastasius II (713–715), joining in the revolt against Theodosius III (716–717) in protest over the deposition of Anastasius. Through negotiations, Leo was elevated to the throne on March 25, 717, and faced an immediate threat to Constantinople by the Arabs. He beat back a siege that lasted from 717 to 718, aided by the weapon Greek fire and by skill in dealing with the enemy. Leo then made war in Asia Minor and in 740 brought the region under Byzantine control again.

In 726, Leo promulgated the Ecloga, a revision of the Corpus Juris Civilis (Code of Justinian), issued by Justinian I (527–565). He also began to declaim against icons, proclaiming in 730 that the official rule of the empire was iconoclasm. Harsh measures were taken against those who did not remove and destroy sacred images, and when the papacy voiced opposition, Leo removed Sicily, Greece and Illyria from papal jurisdiction. His adherence to iconoclasm alienated the papacy, which caused a renewal of papal amity toward the Frankish kings. See also ICONOCLASTICISM.

**LEO IV, BYZANTINE EMPEROR** (749–780) Ruler from 775 to 780, called "the Khazar," the son of and successor to Constantine V (741–775). Leo appointed his own son, Constantine, as co-emperor, suppressing the resulting court intrigues surrounding his stepbrother, Nicephorus, who had been ignored in his claim. In addition to several campaigns against the Muslims (777–780), he was noted for his partial reversal of his father's iconoclastic policies, taking a moderate stance toward the adherents of icons. He changed this policy, adopting orthodox opposition to icons, in his later years. See also ICONOCLASTICISM.

**LEO V, BYZANTINE EMPEROR** (d. 820) Ruler from 813 to 820, called "the Armenian," a general in the service of the emperors Nicephorus I (802–811) and Michael I (811–813) and a participant in the campaign of 813 against the Bulgars. That same year he deposed Michael, made peace with the Bulgars and revived iconoclasticism, inaugurating more persecutions. He was assassinated by the supporters of Michael the Amorian, who succeeded him as emperor. See also BYZANTINE EMPIRE; ICONOCLASTICISM.

**LEO VI, BYZANTINE EMPEROR** (866–912) Ruler from 886 to 912, called Leo the Wise or Leo the Philosopher, the son of Emperor Basil I (867–886). Leo served as co-emperor with his father from 870 and was generally thought to be a weak ruler. His chief achievement was the completion of his father's legal work, the Basilica, legal reforms that became the code for the Byzantine Empire, thus bringing needed modernization to Justinian's Code (the Corpus Juris Civilis). See also BASIL I, BYZANTINE EMPEROR; BYZANTINE EMPIRE.

**LEÓN** Spanish kingdom in the northwestern part of the country, comprising the regions of modern León, Valladolid, Valencia, Salamanca, Zamora and Oviedo. Established by García I (ruled 910–914), the realm lost much of its territory to the Moors and to Navarre, and the region was compelled to recognize the suzerainty of the Moorish kingdom of Córdoba. It was twice united with Castile (under Ferdinand I, 1035–1065, and under Alfonso VI Urraca and Alfonso VII, 1072–1157), and a permanent union was effected in 1230 by Ferdinand III (1217–1252). Leónese institutions were maintained for a time, but by the end of the Middle Ages the territory had become inseparable, culturally as well as politically, from Castile.

**LEONARD** According to legend, a sixth-century hermit, patron of peasants, prisoners and the ill. According to an 11th-century biography, Leonard was a Frankish nobleman in the court of Clovis, who was converted to Christianity, retired to a cell at Noblac, near Limoges, and established a monastery.

**LEONARDO OF PISA** (c. 1170–c. 1240) One of the important mathematicians of the medieval world, formerly called Leonardo Fibonacci. Perhaps born in Pisa, he spent much of his childhood in North Africa, where his father led the community of Pisan commercial agents in Bugia, Algeria. Leonard was taught by an Arab master who instructed him in the use of Hindu-Arabic numerals. Few other details of his life are available beyond those mentioned in his works. He traveled to Greece, France, Syria and Egypt and wrote several important mathematical treatises: *Liber abaci (Book of the Abacus), Liber quadratorum (Book of Square Numbers)* and *Practica geometriae (Practice of Geometry).*

**LEONTIUS, BYZANTINE EMPEROR** Ruler from 695 to 698, the successor to Justinian II (685–695), who failed in preventing the fall of Byzantine Africa to the Arabs. In 697 the Muslims rode into Africa, capturing Carthage. A fleet was sent to recapture the region, but the Arabs returned in the spring of 698, driving out the Byzantines and causing the overthrow of Leontius, who was replaced by Tiberius III (698–705). See also BYZANTINE EMPIRE.

**LEONTIUS OF BYZANTIUM** (d. 543) Theologian who was the chief opponent of Monophysitism. A monk, he was a gifted theologian and participated in the debates of his era. An Origenist, he was an adherent of Chalcedonian Christology. Leontius's most important work was the *Libri III contra Nestorianos et Eutychianos (Three Books against the Nestorians and Eutychians),* in which he attacked the theories of Theodore of Mopsuestia.

**LEOPOLD III** (1075–1136) Margrave of Austria from 1095 to 1136 and a member of the Babenberg line who increased his power through political maneuvering. In 1106 he supported Emperor Henry IV's son, Henry (V, 1106–1125) in his rebellion against his father, receiving the hand of Henry V's sister, Agnes, and thus royal favor. Leopold strengthened Austria, contributed to the church and issued common laws for his subjects. See also BABENBERG, HOUSE OF.

**LEOPOLD V** (1154–1194) Duke of Austria from 1177 to 1194, son of Henry Jasomirgot. He participated in the Third Crusade, in which he quarreled with Richard the Lion-Hearted (1189–1199) at Acre. Leopold captured Richard while he was traveling in Austria in disguise, handing the English king to Emperor Henry VI (1190–1197) in return for a portion of the ransom paid for Richard's return. With the ransom money he built fortresses, established towns and issued a new coin, the Wiener pfennig. Leopold also brought the duchy of Styria into the control of the Babenbergs.

**LEOPOLD VI** (1176–1230) Duke of Austria from 1198 to 1230, called "the Glorious," an active ruler and the brother of Frederick I of Austria (1194–1198). A Crusader, he fought in Spain against the Moors and in France against the Albigensians, as well as in Egypt and Palestine. A patron of monastic institutions, he nevertheless tried to rid Austria of ecclesiastical control by creating an independent in Vienna. He also helped to negotiate the Treaty of San Germano (1230) between Pope Gregory IX (1227–1241) and Emperor Frederick II (1215–1250). He died soon thereafter. See also BABENBERG, HOUSE OF.

**LEO THE PHILOSOPHER** See LEO VI, BYZANTINE EMPEROR.

**LEOVA I** King of the Visigoths from 568 to 572, the duke of Narbonne chosen as successor to Athanagild (d. 568). Unacceptable to the Visigoths below the Pyrenees, however, because of his holdings in Gaul, he had to share power with his brother Leovigild. He died without an heir in 572, and Leovigild united the Visigoths.

**LEOVA II** (d. 603) King of the Visigoths from 601 to 603, the son of King Reccared. He was pious and a believer in orthodoxy and too young and inexperienced to survive among the Visigothic nobles. Leova's murder by Count Witterich inaugurated an era of civil strife. See also VISIGOTHS.

**LEOVIGILD** (d. 586) King of the Visigoths from 572 to 586, the brother of King Leova I, named co-ruler in 570 to appease the nobles of Visigothic Spain, who held him in high regard. On Leova's death in 572, he united the realm and strove until about 576 to oppose the Byzantine Empire, the Suevi and his own nobles. He established the royal seat at Toledo, issuing new currency, with the inscription LIVIGILDVS INCLITVS REX. In 580, however, a rebellion erupted as his son, Hermenegild, coverted from Arianism to Orthodox Christianity and entered into an alliance with the Suevi and Byzantines to overthrow Leovigild. Leovigild routed the Suevi, appeased the Byzantines monetarily and captured his son, executing him in April 585. Fighting against the Burgundians, Leovigild died a year to the day after the execution of his son. Another son, Reccared, succeeded to the throne. See also VISIGOTHS.

**LESZEK THE WHITE** (d. 1227) Piast duke of Poland, the last to hold the title senior duke in the system used to govern Poland at the time. He was assassinated by the scheming governor of Eastern Pomerania. See also POLAND.

**LEVI BEN GERSHOM** (1288–1344) Jewish philosopher, astronomer and biblical scholar, called also Gersonides, Ralbag and Leo Hebraeus. He was the author of many treatises on various subjects, including mathematics astronomy and philosophy, some of which were written for Philip of Vitry, bishop of Meaux. Other works included commentaries on the Bible, commentaries on Aristotle and Averroës and the *Sefer ha-keshet ha-yashar* (*The Book of the Straight Arrow*), a critical examination of the arguments of Aristotle. He also designed the "Jacob's Ladder," a measuring device used to determine angular distances between celestial bodies. See also ASTRONOMY.

**LEWES, BATTLE OF** See BARONS' WAR.

***LEX ROMANA VISIGOTHORUM*** See BREVIARY OF ALARIC.

***LIBER CENSUUM*** The register of the Roman church, which was an accounting of tithes owed the papacy by various dioceses, cities, monasteries and kingdoms. It contained as well a list of dependent monasteries and episcopal sees and was compiled by Cencio Savelli (the future Pope Honorius III, from 1216–1227), serving then as secretary to Clement III (pope, 1187–1191) and Celestine III (pope, 1191–1198).

***LIBER PONTIFICALIS*** *Book of the Popes*, a compilation of papal biographies from Saint Peter to the popes in the second half of the 15th century (c. 1464). Intended as a detailed study, the book was published in late editions with the biographies of additional popes. The author was probably a priest during the early sixth century, who wrote the first biographies, the portion thought to be least reliable. Other sections in the later editions were more accurate and provided a useful source for the study of the development of the papacy.

***LIBRI CAROLINI*** The Caroline Books (c. 790–792), which contained attacks on the Iconclastic Council of 754 and the Second Council of Nicaea in 787. Supposedly written for Charlemagne, they were probably compiled by an experienced theologian for the purpose of ridiculing the Byzantine empress Irene, thereby giving greater credibility to Charlemagne's assumption of the imperial title, an act opposed by the Byzantine Empire.

**LIÈGE** City in eastern Belgium, situated on the Meuse River, and the capital of the province of Liège. Traditionally thought to have been founded by Saint Lambert in the seventh century, it received the official distinction of becoming a town with the establishment of a bishopric in 721. Through the influence of Prince-Bishop Notker, around 1000, Liège had developed as center for learning and for commerce as well. Social upheavals took place there as the guilds and nobles vied for civil control. These quarrels culminated in the Male Saint Martin, during which the nobles were trapped in the Church of Saint Martin and burned to death. The following year full social equality was granted to the populace. Liège was sacked twice by Charles the Bold of Burgundy, in 1467 and 1468.

**LIMBOURG, THE BROTHERS OF** These three Dutch brothers, Pol, Herment and Jean, flourished as illuminators of the Late Gothic manuscripts in the early 15th century. The sons of the sculptor Arnold von Limbourg, they were apprenticed to a Parisian goldsmith in 1400, eventually entering the service of the duc du Berry (after 1404). Under his patronage they produced a magnificent book of hours for him. This celebrated work was *Très riches heures*, unfinished in 1416 but completed by Jean Colombe about 1485. One of the supreme examples of International Gothic style, the *Très riches heures* was remarkable in the detail of its illuminations, demonstrating sophistication, delicacy and elegance.

**LIMERICK** City in Ireland situated at the mouth of the Shannon Estuary, called in Irish Luimneach. A port and chief city of county Limerick, it was sacked in 812 by the Norse, who established a Viking kingdom of Limerick that survived until the end of the 10th century, when they were expelled by Brian Boru. The capital of the kings of North Munster, or Thomond, from 1106 to 1174, it was captured by the English and granted a charter in 1197 by Richard the Lion-Hearted (1189–1199). William de Burgh established an English town (early 13th century) defended by one of the strongest fortresses in Ireland.

**LIMOGES** City in south central France and the historical capital of the province of Limousin. The site of a Roman settlement, it was originally the chief city of the Gallic tribe of the Lemovices. Its inhabitants converted to Christianity by Saint Martial in the third century, Limoges became a pilgrimage city, especially for those on their way to the shrine of Santiago de Compostela. During the Hundred Years' War, Limoges was burned and its people massacred by Edward the Black Prince of England (1370).

**LINCOLN** City in eastern England, county seat of Lincolnshire and an important episcopal see, called Lindum during its Roman period. The residence of the Mercian kings, Lincoln fell to the Danes in the ninth century and remained under Danish influence in England until about 1157, when it was granted a charter by King Henry II (1154–1189). Having a large population and strong economy based on trade in wool and leather, Lincoln was also the see of Remigius (d. 1092). It is the site of Lincoln Cathedral, begun in the late 11th century, built of limestone and a fine example of Gothic architecture.

**LINDISFARNE** Island off the Northumberland coast, called Holy Island from the 11th century, the site of Lindisfarne Abbey, an important monastic community founded in 635 by Saint Aidan, who arrived there from Iona. The island became a missionary base, and following the Synod of Whitby (664) the Scots-Irish (and some English) monks left for Iona in protest over the decision to end the inclusion of Celtic traditions in the church. Lindisfarne was twice attacked and pillaged by the Vikings, forcing the monks to flee in 793 and 883. A bishopric until 995, the island was then transferred to the authority of Durham, but use of the monastery continued until the reign of Henry VIII. Esteemed church figures were educated at Lindisfarne, including Chad, Egbert, and Wilfrid of York. Saint Cuthbert's presence added to the island's prestige.

**LIPPI, FRA FILIPPO** (c. 1406–1469) Italian painter, orphaned in Florence while very young and joining the Carmelites at the age of eight, taking orders in 1421 at Santa Maria del Carmine in Florence. Masaccio influenced his early style, but in 1437 he painted a *Madonna*, departing from the early influence, and demonstrated his independence in the Barbadori altarpiece (begun in 1437). Appointed abbot of San Quirico, near Florence, in 1442, he produced a *Madonna Enthroned in the Saints, The Annunciation* and *The Coronation of the Virgin* over the next years. Some of his finest frescoes were those in the cathedral at Prato. A major event altered his life, however, when he met a nun, Lucrezia Buti, with whom he fled, eventually receiving papal permission to marry her, a union producing the early Renaissance painter Filippino Lippi. With Medici patronage, Lippi became the mentor of Botticelli. His other projects included the *Alessandri Altarpiece, Adoration of the Magi, Seven Saints* and unfinished frescoes in the cathedral of Spoleto.

Lindisfarne Gospels

**LISBON** Also Lisboa or Lissabon, the capital of Portugal, situated at the mouth of the Tagus River. Built on seven hills, Lisbon originated about 1200 B.C. when it was a Phoenician trading site, occupied subsequently by the Romans, Alani, Suebi and Visigoths. In the eighth century the town fell to the army of Islam sweeping into the Iberian Peninsula from Africa. Known by a variety of names under Moorish domination, the city fell in 1147 to the combined Crusader armies of Normans, English, Flemish and Portuguese led by King Alfonso Henriques (1139–1185). The court, however, was not moved to Lisbon (from Coimbra) until 1256. Burned by the Castilians in 1375, Lisbon was rebuilt by King Ferdinand I (1367–1383). Castilian forces were again repulsed in 1384. The University of Lisbon was founded in 1290 by King Dinis (1279–1325) but was moved during the 14th century to Coimbra. After the fall of Constantinople to the Turks in 1453, Lisbon welcomed Greek and Genoese traders, joined in the latter part of the 15th century by merchants from all over Europe. See also PORTUGAL.

**LITERATURE, ISLAMIC** See AVERROËS OF CÓRDOBA; AVICENNA; AL-HARIRI; HISHAM IBN AL-KALBI; IBN AL-ATHIR; IBN HAZM, ʿALI; IBN KHALDUN; IBN KHALLIKHAN; IBN ZUHR; AL-KHWARIZMI; OMAR KHAYYAM; THOUSAND AND ONE NIGHTS, THE.

**LITERATURE, MEDIEVAL** See ABBO OF SAINT GERMAIN-DES-PRÉS; ADAM DE LA BASSÉE; ADAM OF BREMEN; ADELARD OF BATH; AELRED OF RIEVAULX, SAINT; AIMION DE FLEURY; ALAIN OF LILLE; ALBERIC OF MONTE CASSINO; ALBERT OF AIX; ALCUIN; ALFRED THE GREAT; ALPERT OF METZ; ALPHANUS OF SALERNO; AMALRIC; AMBROISE; ANGLO-SAXON CHRONICLE; ANTHONY OF NOVGOROD; APPOLONIUS OF TYRE; ARI THORGILSSON; ARMAGH, BOOK OF; ARTHURIAN LEGEND; ASTROLOGY; ASTRONOMY; BARLAAM AND JOSAPHAT; BEDE, SAINT; BEOWULF; BERNERS, JULIANA; BOETHIUS; CANTAR DEL MIO CID; CARMINA BURANA; CHANSON DE GESTE; CHAUCER, GEOFFREY; CHESTER PLAYS; CHRONICLES; COMNENA, ANNA; DAFYDD AP GWILYM; DECAMERON; EINHARD; FROISSART, JEAN; FULCHER OF CHARTRES; GALLUS ANONYMOUS; GEOFFREY OF MONMOUTH; GEORGE HAMARTALOS; GESTA ROMANORUM; GILDAS, SAINT; GILLES LE MUISIT; GIRALDUS CAMBRENSIS; GREGORY OF TOURS, SAINT; GRIMOIRES; HARTMANN VON AUE; HIGDEN, RANULF; HILDEBERT OF LAVARDIN; ICELANDIC LITERATURE; IRELAND, JOHN; JOHN CLIMACHUS, SAINT; JOINVILLE, JEAN; KABASILUS, NICHOLAS; KALEVALA; KEMPE, MARGERY; LA MARCHE, OLIVIER DE; LE BEL, JEAN; LIBRI CAROLINI; LIUTPRAND OF CREMONA; LOPEZ DE AYALA, PEDRO; MABINOGION; MALALAS, JOHN; MALORY, SIR THOMAS; MARIANUS SCOTUS; MARSILIUS OF PADUA; MARTIANUS CAPELLA; MIDDLE ENGLISH; MIDDLE HIGH GERMAN; NITHARD; ORDERICUS VITALIS; PACHYMERES, GEORGE; PARIS, MATTHEW; PAUL THE DEACON; PEARL, THE; PETER LOMBARD; ROBIN HOOD; ROMAN DE LA ROSE; RUYSBROECK, JAN VAN; SAVONAROLA, GIRALAMO; SAXO GRAMMATICUS; THOMAS À KEMPIS; THOMAS AQUINAS, SAINT; TRISTAN AND ISOLDE; VILLANI, GIOVANNI; VINCENT OF BEAUVAIS; VISION OF PIERS PLOWMAN, THE; WALSINGHAM, THOMAS; WARFARE; WILLIAM OF MALMESBURY; WILLIAM OF OCKHAM; WILLIAM OF TYRE.

**LITHUANIA** Baltic country whose history differed considerably from that of its neighbors, Livonia and Estonia, for while they fell to the forces of the Livonian and Teutonic Knights in the 12th century, Lithuania was successful in maintaining its independence and in flourishing as a nation. A grand duchy from the 13th century, the home of

# CHRONOLOGY OF MEDIEVAL LITERARY HISTORY

The following is a general listing of literary events from the sixth century until 1485. Readers are encouraged to consult also the reference guide included under the entries LITERATURE, MEDIEVAL; and LITERATURE, ISLAMIC.

### 6TH CENTURY

| | |
|---|---|
| 524 | Boethius, *De consolatione philosophiae (The Consolation of Philosophy).* |
| 540 | Foundation of the monastery of Vivarium in Italy by Flavius Magnus Cassiodorus; he stresses the translation of Greek texts. |
| 542 | Gildas, *De excidio et conquestu Britanniae,* a history of early Britain. |
| 553 | Procopius, *Anecdota,* a history of Byzantine imperial family's history and gossip. |
| 575 | Alexander of Tralles, *De re medica,* on medicine. |

### 7TH CENTURY

| | |
|---|---|
| | George the Pisidian (mid-seventh century). |
| 629 | Appearance of the Koran. |
| c. 670 | Caedmon active in England. |
| c. 698 | Lindisfarne Gospels. |

### 8TH CENTURY

| | |
|---|---|
| 731 | Bede, *Historia ecclesiastica gentis anglorum (History of the English Church).* |

### 9TH CENTURY

| | |
|---|---|
| | Cynewulf active (early ninth century). |
| c. 800 | *Hildebrandslied.* |
| 804 | Death of Alcuin. |
| 849 | Death of Walafrid Strabo, Benedictine poet and theologian. |
| 868 | Death of Gottschalk, poet and theologian. |
| c. 892 | Start of the *Anglo-Saxon Chronicle.* |
| 893 | Asser, *The Life of Alfred the Great.* |

### 10TH CENTURY

| | |
|---|---|
| c. 985 | *Beowulf.* |
| 986 | Albucasis (Abul Kasim), *al-Tasrif,* a manual on surgical practice that becomes the standard work on the subject for centuries. |
| c. 991 | *Battle of Maldon* completed. |

## 11TH CENTURY

| | |
|---|---|
| 1010 | Firdawsi, *Shah-nama (The Book of Kings)*, presented to Mahmud of Ghazni. |
| 1028 | Avicenna, *Canon of Medicine*, an influential manual on medicine. |
| 1065 | Foundation of the university at Parma. |
| 1070 | Death of Ibn Gabirol. |

## 12TH CENTURY

| | |
|---|---|
| | Flourishing of minnesingers (12th–13th centuries). |
| 1100 | *Culhwch and Olwen.* |
| 1110 | Earliest known miracle play staged at Dunstable. |
| 1120 | William of Malmesbury, *Gesta regum Anglorum.* |
| 1123 | Death of Omar Khayyam, author of the *Rubaiyat.* |
| 1136 | Peter Abelard, *Historia calamitatum mearum (History of My Calamities).* |
| 1150 | Beginnings of the university at Paris. |
| | Estimated completion of *The Black Book of Carmarthen* in Wales. |
| | *Cantar del mio Cid.* |
| 1154 | Death of Geoffrey of Monmouth, author of *Historia rerum Britanniae.* |
| 1159 | John of Salisbury, *Policratus.* |
| c. 1164 | Chrétien de Troyes active, author of *Perceval.* |
| 1167 | Beginnings of Oxford University. |
| c. 1170 | Eilhart von Oberg, *Tristan und Isolde.* |
| 1174 | Wace, *Roman de Brut.* |
| 1176 | Beginnings of the Eisteddfod in Wales. |
| c. 1185–1222 | Saxo Grammaticus, *Gesta Danorum.* |
| 1190 | Death of Chrétien de Troyes. |
| | Blondel de Nesle active, troubadour of Richard I (late 12th century). |

## 13TH CENTURY

| | |
|---|---|
| | The *fabliau* flourishes (leading practitioners: Jehan Bodel, Rutebeuf, and Jean de Condé). |
| | *Carmina Burana.* |
| | *Book of Deer*, earliest extant document on Gaelic matters. |
| | Terminal period of the chansons de geste. |
| 1200 | Jehan Bodel, *Jeu de Saint Nicolas.* |
| | Layamon, *Brut.* |
| 1209 | Beginnings of Cambridge University. |
| 1210 | Death of Gottfried von Strassburg, author of another version of *Tristan und Isolde.* |
| c. 1220 | Death of Hartmann von Aue. |
| | Death of Wolfram von Eschenbach. |
| 1222 | The University of Padua is founded. |
| 1225 | Guillaume de Lorris, *Roman de la rose.* |
| c. 1230 | Death of Walther von der Vogelweide. |
| 1231 | Foundation of the medical school of Salerno. |
| 1236 | Death of Neidhart von Reuenthal. |
| 1240 | Foundation of *dolce stil nuovo* school of poetry by Guido Guinizelli. |
| c. 1245 | Gautier de Metz, *L'image du monde.* |
| 1247 | Beginnings of the university at Siena. |
| 1249 | Foundation of University College, Oxford. |
| c. 1250 | Death of Rudolf von Ems. |
| c. 1261 | Rutebeuf, *Miracle de Theophile.* |
| 1264 | Thomas Aquinas, *Summa contra Gentiles.* |
| | Roger Bacon, *De computo naturali.* |
| 1270 | Death of Tannhäuser. |
| 1273 | Thomas Aquinas, *Summa theologica.* |
| 1274 | Death of Thomas Aquinas. |
| c. 1275 | Joinville, *Grandes chronique de Saint-Denis.* |
| 1280 | Adam de la Halle, *Le jeu de Robin et Marian*, the first French pastoral play. |
| 1290 | Beginnings of the university at Lisbon. |

## 14TH CENTURY

| | |
|---|---|
| | *Havelock the Dane* (14th century), metrical romance. |
| | Chester plays. |
| 1300 | Death of Guido Cavalcanti. |
| 1300–1325 | *White Book of Rhydderch* in Wales (includes the *Mabinogion*). |
| 1315 | Death of Ramon Llull, author of *Libre de contemplacio Deu.* |
| 1321 | Death of Dante Alighieri in Ravenna. |

| | |
|---|---|
| 1330 | Juan Ruiz, *Libro de buen amor.* |
| 1343 | William of Ockham, *Dialogues.* |
| 1348 | Foundation of the university at Prague. |
| 1353 | Giovanni Boccaccio, the *Decameron.* |
| c. 1355 | Santob de Carrion de los Condes, *Proverbios morales.* |
| 1364 | Foundation of the university at Cracow. |
| | Death of Ranulf Higden, author of *Polychronicon.* |
| 1366 | Petrarch, *Canzoniere.* |
| 1370–1390 | *The Pearl,* alliterative West Midland poem. |
| c. 1372–1389 | William Langland, *The Vision of Piers Plowman.* |
| 1374 | Death of Petrarch. |
| c. 1375–1400 | *Sir Gawain and the Green Knight.* |
| 1375 | Guillaume Tirel, *Le viander de Taillevent,* a noted cook book, by Tirel, the cook to the French kings Philip VI and Charles V. |
| | Death of Boccaccio. |
| c. 1387 | Chaucer, *Canterbury Tales.* |
| 1388 | First English translation of the Bible made by John Purcey. |
| 1392 | Eustace Deschamps, *Art de dictier.* |
| c. 1393 | John Gower, *Confessio Amantis.* |
| **15TH CENTURY** | |
| | Meistersingers active (fl. 14th–16th century). |
| | Catalan poetry (fl. 15th century). |
| 1400 | Death of Geoffrey Chaucer. |
| 1407 | Death of Pedro Lopez de Ayala, *Rimado de Palacio.* |
| 1410 | Death of Jean Froissart, French chronicler. |
| 1424 | Thomas à Kempis, *The Imitation of Christ.* |
| 1425 | Alain Chartier, *La belle dame sans merci.* |
| 1426 | Death of Thomas Hoccleve, author of *De regimine principum.* |
| c. 1429–1430 | Death of Christine de Pisan. |
| c. 1430 | John Lydgate, *Falle of Princis.* |
| c. 1433 | Death of Alain Chartier. |
| 1444 | Juan de Mena, *El laberinto de fortuna.* |
| 1461 | François Villon, *Le grand testament.* |
| 1472 | Beginnings of the university at Munich. |
| 1474 | Death of Georges Chastellain, court historian in Burgundy. |
| 1475 | William Caxton, *The Recuyell of the Historyes of Troye,* the first book printed in English. |
| 1485 | Sir Thomas Malory, *Morte d'Arthur.* |

the Liths, Lithuania retained its pagan heritage, becoming a unified state to resist the advance of the Christian military orders into the Baltic region. Conversion by force or by missionary endeavor was opposed, but Grand Duke Mindaugas accepted baptism in 1251 joined by part of the population. He was recognized by Pope Innocent IV (1243–1254) in 1253 as king, and Western and Russian customs were welcomed into the region. His murder in 1263 brought a pagan counterreaction. Under the 14th-century grand dukes Gedimin and Olgerd, the Lithuanians acquired Belorussia and parts of the Ukraine and Great Russia, emerging as one of the largest states in Europe.

The menace of the knightly orders continued, however, leading to the alliance of the Lithuanians with the Poles through the marriage of Grand Duke Jagiello with Jadwiga, heiress of Poland. Lithuania reached its heights under the Jagiello dynasty. The eastward expansion of the Teutonic Knights was repelled in 1410 at Tannenberg (or Grunwald). The struggle with the knights continued throughout the 15th century, with the Peace of Torun (Thorn) in 1466 granting Pomerania to Lithuania. Increasingly the country absorbed Polish culture, with the priests introducing their traditions and the nobility of the two states intermarrying. As the danger of the Teutonic Knights decreased, a new and greater enemy appeared from the East, the expanding grand duchy of Moscow, under Ivan III (ruled 1462–1505). See also RUSSIA.

**LITTLE FLOWERS OF ST. FRANCIS** Also *Fioretti di San Francesco,* a collection of legends and tales about Saint Francis of Assisi and his companions, written in Tuscany about 1322, probably based on a Latin original. Derived from sources on the life of Saint Francis, such works as *Actus Beati Francisci et Sociorum ejus,* the work was an invaluable glimpse into the early years of the Franciscan order. See also FRANCIS OF ASSISI.

**LIUTBERT** (d. 701) King of the Lombards who reigned briefly, from 700 to 701, the son of King Cunibert. He was entrusted to the regency of Count Ansprand, who faced a rebellion of Lombard nobles, led by Regenbert and his son, Aribert. The child king was captured and, at the order of Aribert, strangled in his bath. See also LOMBARDS.

**LIUTPRAND** (d. 744) King of the Lombards, the most important of the Lombard rulers, reigning from 712 to 744, the son of King Ansprand. Energetic and ambitious, Liutprand used the outrage caused by the iconoclastic policies of Leo III the Isaurian (717–741) to begin a campaign against the Byzantines in Italy in 727. He crossed the Po River, taking Bologna, Ancona, Rimini and the region south of Ravenna (the Pentapolis). Planning to march on Rome, he was confronted by rebellious Lombard dukes of Benevento and Spoleto, who had made an alliance with Pope Gregory II (715–731). By making peace with the Byzantine exarch, Liutprand subdued the nobles and pacified all of Italy but left the Exarchate of Ravenna and the Romans as they were. Gregory appealed directly to Liutprand. In 738, another uprising by the duke of Spoleto marred the peace but was unsuccessful. The duke sought the shelter of the papacy and was given asylum by Pope Gregory III (731–741). Liutprand invaded Rome in 739 as a result. When papal appeals to Charles Martel (d. 741) were rejected, a settlement was made between Pope Zacharias (741–752) and the Lombards in 742. Liutprand introduced legal reforms in his kingdom, made his courts efficient and abolished the Lombard tradition of *guidrigild,* money given in compensation for injury or murder. See also LOMBARDS.

**LIUTPRAND OF CREMONA** (c. 922–c. 972) Italian chronicler and bishop of Cremona. He served Berengar II of Italy and was named bishop by Otto I (936–973) in 961, taking part in the synod that deposed Pope John XII (955–964). Sent to Constantinople in 968, Liutprand tried unsuccessfully to negotiate a marriage between Otto I's son, Otto II (973–983), and a Byzantine princess. He wrote several notable works: *Antapodosis (Revenge),* a history from 888 to 958; *Historia Ottonis (History of Otto);* and *Relatio de legatione Constantinopolitana (Account of a Mission to Constantinople).*

**LIVERY COMPANIES** The English guilds of London, chartered mainly in the reign of King Edward III (ruled 1327–1377). They were distinctive in ceremonies because of their costume or livery, especially their badges, attire that was visible at pageants and royal events. The livery companies were incorporated, owning private property and having monopolies over certain wares. They owned schools, including Saint Paul's and Merchant Taylor's. Political power came under Edward III when these guilds were granted the right to elect the Common Council of London, thus controlling the election of the mayor and other officials. See also GUILDS.

**LIVONIA** Region bordering the Baltic Sea in northern Europe, comprising modern Estonia and northern Latvia. The name Livonia was derived from the Livs, a Finnish people, falling in the 13th century to the Livonian Knights, a German military religious order also called the Brothers of the Sword or the Knights of the Sword. The knights reduced Livonia to a serfdom and forced the introduction of Christianity with the support of the Teutonic Knights and Bishop Albert of Riga. The Livonian cities of Riga, Tallinn and Tartu spearheaded the dissemination of Germanic culture and were members of the Hanseatic League.

**LIVONIAN KNIGHTS** See MILITARY ORDERS.

**LLANDAFF** Welsh cathedral city situated northwest of Cardiff in East Glamorgan. Llandaff (Welsh, Llandaf) was one of the four oldest bishoprics in Wales, reportedly established by Saint Teilo (according to the *Llyfr Teilo,* the *Book of Llandaff,* 12th century) in the sixth century. The cathedral was constructed in 1120, and soon afterward the diocese was placed under the control of Canterbury. The episcopal castle was destroyed about 1403 by the Welsh rebel Owen Glendower. See also WALES.

**LLEWELYN AP GRUFFYDD** (d. 1282) Prince of Gwynedd, the only Welsh leader to be recognized as the Prince of Wales. He tried unsuccessfully to free Wales from English domination. The grandson of Llewelyn ap Iorwerth (Llewelyn the Great), he divided power in Wales with his brother, Owain, from 1246 until 1255, when he siezed Owain's lands and set out to unite Wales. In 1258 he declared himself Prince of Wales, using the domestic conflicts of King Henry III of England (1216–1272) to demand the homage of Welsh princes. He allied himself with Simon de Montfort during the Barons' War but after Simon's death in 1265 made peace with Henry III, receiving recognition of his title in return for vassal status. The accession of King Edward I (1272–1307) ended amity between England and Wales, as Llewelyn refused to pay homage. Edward invaded Wales twice as a result, subjecting the Welsh in the first campaign (1276–1277) and killing Llewelyn in the second and ending Welsh independence.

**LLEWELYN THE GREAT** (d. 1240) Called also Llewelyn ap Iorweth, a Welsh prince and one of the celebrated figures of Welsh history. The grandson of the prince of Gwynedd, Owain Gwynedd, Llewelyn returned from exile to depose his uncle, David, in 1194. Over the next years he extended his political authority over most of Wales and in 1205 married Joan, the illegitimate daughter of King John (1199–1216). Continued ambitions, especially toward English holdings in southern Wales, aroused John's suspicions. The English king invaded Wales in 1211, but Llewelyn's recovery and subsequent alliance with the baronial opponents of John were contributing factors in the royal acceptance of Magna Carta in 1215. In 1218 the English acknowledged his position in Wales. He retired in 1238, turning over the affairs of state to his son and retiring to a monastery. See also WALES.

**LLULL RAMÓN** See LULL, RAMÓN.

**LOCHNER, STEPHEN** (d. 1451) Important Cologne painter in the Late Gothic style, considered Cologne's finest artistic representative. Lochner possibly studied with Robert Campin (the master of Flemalle), reflecting his influence as well as that of van Eyck. The latter presumably impressed Lochner during the German artist's visit to the Netherlands in the 1430s. Lochner earned a reputation as a brilliant painter of mystical subjects, without equal in late medieval Germany. Among his works were *Altar of the*

*Patron Saints* in Cologne cathedral, *Madonna of the Rose Bower* and *Presentation in the Temple.*

**LODI, PEACE OF** Important treaty signed at Lodi on April 9, 1454, between Milan and Venice, ending a war that had raged over the succession to the duchy of Milan. According to its terms, Venice recovered its territory in northern Italy, while Francesco Sforza was made ruler of Milan. The treaty augmented nearly 40 years of general peace between the major Italian states. It also led to the formation of an agreement not to wage war and the Lega Italica (Italian League) of the cities, providing mutual support. Recognized in 1455 by the pope, the league remained essentially intact until the French invasion of Italy in 1494.

**LOHENGRIN** The Swan Knight of medieval German lore, associated in part with the tradition of tales concerning the Grail (see HOLY GRAIL) and probably already old when recounted by Wolfram von Eschenbach in his *Parzival* (c. 1210). In von Eschenbach's epic, Lohengrin was the son of Parzival (Parsifal), who arrived to aid Elsa of Brabant in a boat drawn by a swan. Lohengrin and Elsa were wed, but she was forbidden to question his origins. When she broke her promise, Lohengrin returned to the Grail Castle. Other versions of the story were the Middle High German poem *Lohengrin* (c. 1275–1290) and the *Lorengel* (15th century), on which the 19th-century opera by Richard Wagner was based.

**LOLLARDY** The movement ascribed to by followers of John Wycliffe (d. 1384), although the term was also used to describe poor and uneducated adherents of the views of radical preachers or, less properly, anyone critical of the church. Lollards included in the intellectual circle around Wycliffe at Oxford included such men as Nicholas Hereford and Philip Repington. The name Lollard was probably derived from the Latin *lollium* (darnel) but may have come from the Old Dutch *lollen* (to sing), becoming a term for mumblers of prayers. Lollard teaching argued that the principal authority for faith was the Bible, each person possessing the right of interpretation. They attacked pilgrimages, clerical celibacy and other Roman traditions, holding that the morality of the priest determined the validity of his acts.

The Wycliffites were suppressed in 1382 by Archbishop William Courtenay, and aggressive persecutions, as well as the passing of *De haeretico comburendo* (1401), brought an effective end to the academic aspects of the movement. Henceforth the membership was more popular, finding support among the poor. It declined steadily, however, especially after the crushing of the unsuccessful revolt of Sir John Oldcastle in 1413. Lollardy was an influence on the Hussite movement.

**LOMBARD, PETER** See PETER LOMBARD.

**LOMBARD LEAGUE** Alliance of Lombard communes during the 12th and 13th centuries to oppose the expansion of imperial power in northern Italy. Formed on December 1, 1167, and supported enthusiastically by Pope Alexander III (1159–1181), the Lombard League strove to present a united political and military front against Emperor Frederick I Barbarossa (1152–1190), who was attempting to reduce the independence of Lombardy and to assert imperial authority over the region. Members included Venice, Mantua, Milan, Padua and Lodi. There were 16 original allies, which came to include 20 in time. The league was effective, as demonstrated in 1176, when Frederick was severely defeated at the Battle of Legnano. The Peace of Venice resulted (1177) and the Peace of Constance (1183), by which the Lombard communes retained many rights in return for their nominal fealty. Renewed in 1198 and 1208, the alliance was again useful, beginning in 1226, when unity was needed to act against Emperor Frederick II (1215–1290). With Frederick's death in 1250, the league ceased to have a vital function. See also GUELPHS AND GHIBELLINES.

**LOMBARDS** A Germanic people called in Latin the Langabardi, occupying much of northern Italy from 568 to 774. Their origins in northwestern Germany, the Lombards were members of a larger tribe called Suevi. Participating in the migrations of the fourth century, they moved into the region corresponding with modern Austria and to the north of the Danube River by the fifth century. There they fought with the Heruli and later the Gepidae (Gepids), whom they destroyed under the leadership of their king, Alboin, who supposedly had a drinking cup made from the skull of the slain Gepid ruler. It was Alboin who led his people across the Alps into Italy in 568, where they were virtually unopposed as they took the Po Valley and captured Pavia in 572. All of Italy might have fallen had Alboin not been murdered. Internal feuds ensued after the death of Alboin's son, Cleph (574), and the Lombards reverted to their traditional pattern of social organization, power resting in the hands of dukes. Important cities such as Rome, Ravenna and Naples thus remained in Byzantine hands, and a Byzantine-Frankish counterattack in the late sixth century convinced the Lombard dukes of the need for a king. Cleph's son, Authari (584–590), was placed on the throne in Pavia, the heart of Lombard rule.

During the reign of King Liutprand (ruled 712–744) the Lombards recovered their position in Italy and made major inroads into Byzantine possessions in the peninsula. The most celebrated of the Lombard kings, Liutprand quelled his restless nobles and made important advances in government and administration. The decline of the Lombards began with the invasion of Ravenna in 751 and the subsequent threat to Rome. Pope Stephen II (752–757) made an appeal to Pepin the Short, king of the Franks, who inflicted a defeat on the Lombards and granted extensive holdings to the papacy. When King Desiderius (757–774) renewed the advance on Rome in 772, Pope Adrian I (772–795) called on Charlemagne, who marched into Italy, defeated the Lombards, captured Desiderius and claimed his iron crown, ending forever the Lombard ascendancy.

**LONDON** The chief city of England, situated on the Thames River, important during the occupation by the Romans, when they established Londinium about A.D. 43 after subduing the surrounding region. London retained its place as the heart of Roman Britain until the early fifth century when the Roman legions were withdrawn, bringing to an end imperial occupation there. During the Anglo-Saxon invasions the city held less prominence, but in the late sixth century a recovery began. King Aethelbert of Kent (d. 616) founded Saint Paul's Cathedral, and the bishop, Mellitus, was installed there in 604. Occupied by the Danes from 871 to 872, London was reclaimed by Alfred the Great in 886.

During the reign of William the Conqueror (1066–1087) London emerged as the political and military heart of England. To control his strategic position and the nearby trading community, William constructed the white tower that would be called the Tower of London. A fire destroyed a large portion of the city, and the subsequent rebuilding (c. 1136) allowed for the use of stone and the opening of sewers to keep the paved streets cleaner. By 1180 London was the largest city in England and its effective capital; granted a charter by Richard the Lion-Hearted (1189–1199) in 1191, the city had a mayoral office the following year. Henry Fitzailwin was the first to hold that post. See also CADE, JACK; HANSEATIC LEAGUE; LIVERY COMPANIES; PEASANT REVOLT; TOWER OF LONDON; WARS OF THE ROSES; and individual kings.

**LONGINUS** According to tradition, the centurion present to oversee the Crucifixion of Christ, thence a legendary figure in Christian lore. He supposedly drove his spear into the side of Christ and was converted in that instant to become the first Roman Christian. Longinus left the legions to wander, bearing his spear, called the Lance in legend. This weapon emerged as a powerful relic, fading in importance for a time, its symbolism revitalized in the Middle Ages. The lance may have been taken by Joseph of Arimathea into England with the Holy Grail or might have been the Maurice or Mauritius Lance included in the Habsburg regalia (currently housed in the Hofburg, Vienna). Another lance was discovered miraculously by the Crusaders at Antioch in 1098, and with it they defeated the Islamic forces on June 28, 1098, at the Orontes, called the Battle of the Lance. Longinus was later incorporated into the legend of the Holy Grail. See also HOLY GRAIL; RELICS.

**LOPEZ DE AYALA, PEDRO** (1332–1407) Spanish poet, chronicler and satirist, called as "el Canciller," the chancellor, serving four Castilian kings: Pedro I the Cruel, Henry II, John I and Henry III. He was also ambassador to France (1379–1380) and chancellor (1398–1399). Lopez de Ayala wrote the *Cronicas* (completed 1393), which covered events in the years 1350–1390, and his *El rimado de palacio* (1385–1407) was an autobiographical and satirical view of the court and contemporary society. It was one of the last examples of the Spanish narrative verse form called *cuaderna via*. He also made translations of Livy, Boccaccio and Boethius.

**LORDS APPELLANT** See Glossary.

**LORENZO MONACO** (c. 1370–c. 1424) Italian painter who forged a synthesis of the Sienese and Florentine styles, a member of the Camaldolese Order, joining it in 1391. Living at Santa Maria degli Angeli in Florence, he produced paintings reflecting the influence of Agnolo Gaddi, eventually incorporating the International Gothic style. Some of his works included *Madonna and Child*, *Adoration of the Magi* and *Life of the Virgin*, which bore a marked naturalistic similarity to the work of Lorenzo Ghiberti.

**LORRAINE** See LOTHARINGIA.

**LOTHAIR, KING OF FRANCE** (941–986) Ruler from 954 to 986, the son of King Louis IV (936–954) and one of the Carolingian line. His reign was beset by feudal conflict and repeated but unsuccessful attempts to acquire Lorraine. He spent many years subject to the domination of Hugh the Great and then Bruno, archbishop of Cologne. See also FRANCE.

**LOTHAIR I, EMPEROR** (795–855) Frankish emperor from 840 to 855, the son of Louis I the Pious (814–840) and the grandson of Charlemagne (768–814). Crowned king of Bavaria on his father's accession as emperor in 814, he was named co-emperor in 817 with Louis. Living in Italy from 822, Lothair grew discontent with Louis's plans for the succession, which included Charles the Bald (843–877) in the intended division of the empire. Supported by his brothers, Lothair rebelled twice (830, 833) and was defeated. On Louis's death in 840, each surviving brother received a share of the empire, Lothair taking the eastern lands (see LOTHARINGIA). His subsequent attempts to become sole emperor were defeated at the Battle of Fontenoy in 841. In 843 he signed the Treaty of Verdun, taking the central domain that extended from the North Sea to Italy. While emperor, Lothair failed to unite the Franks, and on his retirement to a monastery in 855 his lands were partitioned between his sons, Lothair, Louis and Charles. See also HOLY ROMAN EMPIRE.

**LOTHAIR II, KING OF THE FRANKS** (c. 835–869) Also simply Lothair, a Frankish king, son of Lothair I (840–855) and ruler of Lotharingia. On his father's retirement in 855 (and subsequent death) the central kingdom was divided among his sons, with Lothair II receiving an area from the Alps to the North Sea, the region contained by the Meuse, Scheldt and Rhine Rivers. This was the Lotharii Regnum, or Lotharingia, modern Lorraine. Lothair also inherited territory around Lyon and Vienne from his brother Charles. Lothair had been forced to marry Theutberga, who was childless, and made an effort to divorce her so that he could marry Waldrada, his mistress, thus legitimizing his children by her. Pope Nicholas I (858–867) was firm in refusing to allow the divorce, and Lothair died without a legitimate heir. According to the Treaty of Mersen (870), Lotharingia was divided between Louis the German and Charles the Bald (843–877). See also HOLY ROMAN EMPIRE.

**LOTHAIR III, EMPEROR** (1075–1137) Also called Lothair II, German king (1125–1137) and Holy Roman Emperor (1133–1137). The son of Gebhard of Saxony, he was born a few days before the death of his father in battle. Reaching manhood, Lothair supported Henry (V, 1106–

1125) in the revolt against Emperor Henry IV (1056–1106) and was rewarded with the title of duke of Saxony in 1104. Six years later he married Richenza, heiress to the houses of Brunswick and Nordheim. In 1112, however, he quarreled with Henry V and was defeated by him in 1115. He recovered enough to be elected Henry's successor in 1125, and his election sparked hostilities between Saxony and the Hohenstaufens of Swabia. After his coronation as emperor in 1133, Lothair was granted as papal fief the lands of the late Matilda of Tuscany, thus preventing the Hohenstaufens from claiming them. Returning to Germany in 1134, he continued to campaign against the Hohenstaufens, finally making peace with them at Bamberg in 1135 and with the anti-king Conrad in that same year. Lothair also promoted the acceptance of Christianity beyond the Elbe River. See GERMANY; HOLY ROMAN EMPIRE.

**LOTHARINGIA** Also called Lotharingen, a region in northeastern France, a historically important border between France and Germany, and the name from which modern Lorraine is derived. Lotharingia's origins began with the Treaty of Verdun (843), which divided the vast Carolingian empire into three parts, the central portion or middle kingdom coming into possession of Lothair I, a son of Louis the Pious. The realm was further divided with Lothair's retirement in 855, and the northern part was inherited by Lothair II, called Lotharingia in his name. The region extended from the Netherlands into northwestern Germany and Alsace. When Lothair died (869) without an heir, the Treaty of Mersen was signed between Louis, king of the East Franks, and Charles the Bald, king of the West Franks, in 870, partitioning Lotharingia. Taken as part of the empire in 939, Otto divided it into the duchies of Upper Lorraine (in the south) and Lower Lorraine (in the north). Upper Lorraine remained in existence until the 18th century; Lower Lorraine was partitioned into numerous fiefs, including Hainaut, Cleves, Brabant, Bouillon and the bishopric of Liège.

**LOUIS, DUKE OF ORLÉANS** (d. 1407) Brother of Charles VI of France (ruled 1380–1422) who was prominent in the bitter court conflicts surrounding the mentally ill monarch. From about 1392, Louis strove to gain control of the state because of Charles's undeniable incompetence. He was opposed by Philip the Bold, duke of Burgundy (d. 1367), and then by Philip's son, John the Fearless (d. 1419). In 1407 John took the step of having Louis murdered, launching the endless conflicts between the Burgundians and Louis's faction, called the Armagnacs. See also FRANCE.

**LOUIS, GERMAN KING** (c. 804–876) Called "the German," ruler of the East Franks from 843 to 876, a son of Louis I the Pious (814–840), who received control of Bavaria from his father in 817 but participated in the revolts of his brother, Lothair I (840–855), changing sides when it proved expedient. After Louis's death in 840, he allied himself with his half brother, Charles the Bald, to defeat the imperialist plans of Lothair at Fontenoy in 841 and forced the Treaty of Verdun (843), separating France and Germany. Hostilities erupted later against Charles in 858–859, but the two kings agreed to partition Lotharingia in the Treaty of Mersen in 870. See also GERMANY.

**LOUIS, GERMAN KING** (d. 911) Called "the Child," ruler of the East Franks who reigned from 899 to 911, the son of Arnulf (881–899). Many duchies rose in Germany during his reign, including Saxony and Swabia, and he survived Magyar and Viking assaults. He was the last Carolingian ruler of Germany. See also GERMANY.

**LOUIS IV, EMPEROR** (d. 1347) Called "the Bavarian," German king from 1314 to 1347 and Holy Roman Emperor from 1328 to 1347, who strove to free the election of the emperors from papal influence. A member of the House of Wittelsbach, he was raised by his uncle, Albert I of Austria, and became duke of Bavaria in 1294; he was elected German king in 1314 to succeed Henry VII (1308–1313). Frederick the Fair of Hungary opposed him but was captured in 1322. Two years later he began his conflict with the papacy, and Pope John XXII (1316–1334) excommunicated him in 1324. Louis's court thus became a haven for such controversial figures as William of Ockham and Marsilius of Padua. Louis, who had come to believe that emperors should derive their rights from the people, was crowned in 1328 as emperor with the approval of the Romans. Ten years later he issued *Licet juris,* stating that the imperial title could be conferred by the Electors without the approval of the popes. Declared deposed by Pope Clement VI (1342–1352) in 1346, who elected Charles IV (1347–1378) in his place, Louis had begun to make his presence felt once again when he died in a hunting accident. See also HOLY ROMAN EMPIRE.

**LOUIS I, FRANKISH EMPEROR** (778–840) Called "the Pious," the son of Charlemagne, reigning as emperor from 814 to 840 and ruling during the collapse of the Carolingian empire. Named king of Aquitaine in 781, he became co-emperor in 813 and succeeded his father in 814. Louis then chose as his heir and co-emperor his son Lothair (840–855), hoping to satisfy his other sons, Pepin and Louis the German (843–876) by granting them their own holdings. This lasted only until 829 when he added Charles the Bald to the succession, Charles being born of a second marriage. Lothair and his brothers twice revolted, deposing Louis in 833. Restored in 835, he remained on the throne attempting to enforce a division of the empire between his sons, a partition making the empire's collapse inevitable. A patron of learning and an advocate of reform in the church, he supported the efforts of Benedict of Aniane.

**LOUIS II, FRANKISH EMPEROR** (d. 875) Emperor in Italy from 855 to 875, the son of Lothair I (818–855) and brother of Lothair II, appointed the king in Italy in 844 and crowned emperor in 850 by the pope, succeeding his father in 855. While successful against the Saracens in southern Italy, especially with the support of the Byzantine fleet, his power was reduced by the Lombard dukes, who acted independently. After the death of his brother Lothair, he claimed Lotharingia but was thwarted in this instance by the Treaty of Mersen (870) signed by his uncles, Louis the German and Charles the Bald, who would succeed him.

**LOUIS III, FRANKISH EMPEROR** (d. 928) Called "the Blind," emperor from 901 to 905 and ruler of Provence from 890, the son of Boso of Provence and Irmingard, daughter of Louis II, the emperor. Louis III, under the protection of Emperor Charles III the Fat, was made ruler of Provence and marched on Berengar of Friuli in Italy in 900, capturing Bologna, Piacenza and Pavia, where he was crowned king of the Lombards in February 901. Berengar recovered, however, defeating Louis in 902. An attempt to regain Italy ended with Louis's capture and his blinding by Berengar, who sent him back to Provence.

**LOUIS II, KING OF FRANCE** (d. 879) Called "the Stammerer," king of the West Franks (France) from 877 to 879, the son of Charles (I) the Bald (843–877), who named him king of Aquitaine in 867 and regent in 877 when Charles went to the aid of Pope John VIII (872–882). After Charles died that same year, Louis became king in France, refusing to assume the role of papal champion but deciding to adhere to the division of Lotharingia as agreed to by his father in 870, in the Treaty of Mersen. See also FRANCE.

**LOUIS III, KING OF FRANCE** (863–882) King of the West Franks (France) from 879 to 882, acclaimed for his triumph over the Normans in 881. The son of King Louis II the Stammerer (877–879), he shared in the succession in 879 with his brother, Carloman (co-regent, 882–884), receiving Neustria and Francia. He disputed with Louis the Younger, ruler of the East Franks, who was satisfied with the Treaty of Ribemont in 880, which allowed him a portion of Lotharingia. That same year Louis fought an indecisive engagement with the Normans but then routed them at Saucourt, Ponthieu, in 881. See also FRANCE.

**LOUIS IV, KING OF FRANCE** (921–954) Ruler from 936 to 954, called "d'Outremer" ("from Overseas"), the son of Charles III the Simple (898–922). Louis was brought as a child to England, in 923, by his mother, Eadgifu, daughter of the Anglo-Saxon king Edward the Elder, following the imprisonment of his father. He returned in 936 to succeed to the throne, and his reign was challenged by the nobleman Hugh the Great. Besieged in Laon, where he had moved from Paris, in 940, Louis seemed on the verge of defeat when he negotiated an end to the support given to Hugh the Great by Otto I (942) and brought Hugh to submission in 943. Captured in 945 by Hugh, Louis was later released and, with the support of Otto, secured the noble's excommunication in 948. See also FRANCE.

**LOUIS V, KING OF FRANCE** (967–987) Ruler from 986 to 987, called "le Faineant," "the Indolent" or "Do-Nothing," the last Carolingian king of France. The son of King Lothair (954–986), Louis was crowned in 879 but became sole ruler on Lothair's death. Always feeble, he died in a hunting accident. The Carolingian line ended with him because his uncle, Charles of Lower Lorraine never admired, was ignored in favor of Hugh Capet. See also FRANCE.

**LOUIS VI, KING OF FRANCE** (1081–1137) Ruler from 1108 to 1137, called "le Gros," "the Fat," a formidable ruler of a stable French monarchy. Succeeding his father, Philip I (1060–1108), in 1098, Louis reduced the power of the nobility and fostered amity with the church. At war with Henry I of England (1100–1135), Louis was engaged in campaigns from 1104 to 1113 and from 1116 to 1120, curtailing English expansion from Normandy. One of his last acts was to negotiate the marriage of his son, Louis (VII, 1137–1180), with Eleanor of Aquitaine. His brilliant adviser was Abbot Suger of Saint-Denis. See also FRANCE.

**LOUIS VII, KING OF FRANCE** (c. 1120–1180) Ruler from 1137 to 1180, designated heir to Louis VI (1108–1137) in 1131. He married Eleanor of Aquitaine, who advised him in his pursuit of consolidation of monarchical power, improvement of government administration and encouragement of the towns. From 1147 to 1149 he participated in the Second Crusade, an endeavor that led to the annulment of his marriage to Eleanor. She married Henry, count of Anjou, duke of Normandy and the future Henry II of England (1154–1189). France had thus lost Aquitaine and given the English a foothold in the southwestern part of the country. Louis failed to conquer Normandy in 1152 but was aided by Henry's struggle with Thomas à Becket and his own sons, whom Louis supported in their own revolt from 1173 to 1174. His son was Philip II Augustus (1180–1223). See also FRANCE.

**LOUIS VIII, KING OF FRANCE** (1187–1226) Ruler from 1223 to 1226, called "Coeur-de-Lion," "the Lion-Hearted," the son of Philip II Augustus (1180–1223) and married to Blanche of Castile, daughter of Alfonso VIII of Castile (1158–1214), in 1200. In 1216 he invaded England in response to the invitation of the English nobles, who promised him the throne for his support against King John (1199–1216). Defections and the defeat of his fleet in 1217 forced him to withdraw, making peace at Kingston and receiving a large covert payment in compensation. Succeeding to the throne in 1223, he strove to extend the royal holdings by adding Toulouse and Languedoc. Useful toward this end was his participation in the Albigensian Crusade in 1226. Through the creation of appanages, he secured the succession of his son, Louis IX. See also FRANCE.

**LOUIS IX, KING OF FRANCE (SAINT)** (1214–1270) Ruler from 1236 to 1270, revered as one of the most pious, peace-loving and chivalrous monarchs of France. The fourth son of Louis VIII (1223–1226) and Blanche of Castile, he became heir on the death of his older brothers. He was crowned at Reims and spent his minority (1226–1234) under the regency of his capable mother. She suppressed a rebellion of nobles, persecuted the Albigensians in southern France and, in Louis's name, compelled Raymond, count of Toulouse, to accept the Treaty of Paris (1229) by which Raymond's daughter married Louis's brother Alphonse, thereby ensuring the acquisition of Languedoc by the throne.

King Louis IX

After assuming control of the government in 1234, Louis married Margaret of Provence, to whom he was apparently devoted. The union produced 11 children but also aroused the jealousy of Blanche, who had chosen Margaret. In 1242 Louis defeated Hugh of Lusignan, who had the support of King Henry III of England (1216–1272), falling ill from a strain of malaria shortly thereafter. Two years later (1244) he decided to undertake a Crusade, and accompanied by loyal but generally unenthusiastic barons, Louis embarked on the Seventh Crusade (1248–1254), traveling to Egypt. He was defeated and captured at El Mansura (1250), gaining freedom after payment of a ransom. He remained in Palestine until 1254, concluding alliances and improving the position of Christian cities in Syria. He returned to France after the death of his mother, and his considerable prestige allowed him to make peace with England in 1258. Louis's efforts included curbing abuses in government and passing decrees in 1254 and 1256 to define the duties of royal agents. Private warfare was prohibited, taxes distributed more evenly, currency circulated and stabilized and the right of appeal to the crown made possible for all cases.

In 1270, Louis undertook the disastrous Eighth Crusade, landing at Tunis. He captured Carthage but then fell ill during an outbreak of plague. He entrusted France to his son Philip (III) and died on August 25, 1270. The construction of important Gothic buildings such as Sainte-Chapelle in Paris, was accomplished during his reign. Celebrated for his fairness and as the embodiment of Christian ideals, Louis was asked to mediate in disputes in other kingdoms, particularly between Henry III and his barons. A testament to his fairness was his treaty with England, notable for its generous terms, granted at a time when he might have driven the English from the Continent. See also CRUSADES; FRANCE; GOTHIC ART AND ARCHITECTURE; JOINVILLE, JEAN; VINCENT OF BEAUVAIS.

**LOUIS X, KING OF FRANCE** (1289–1316) Ruler from 1314 to 1316 in France and from 1305 to 1314 in Navarre. Called Louis le Hutin or "the Quarrelsome" or "Stubborn," he was the son of Philip IV the Fair (1285–1314) and Joan of Navarre, inheriting her throne in 1305. After Philip's death, he abdicated in favor of his brother Philip (the future Philip V of France) so that he could take the French crown. Despite purging a large number of his father's less popular advisers and ministers, he proved unequal to Philip IV. His son, John I, was born after Louis X's death, living but a few days. John was followed by Philip V (1316–1322). See also FRANCE.

**LOUIS XI, KING OF FRANCE** (1423–1483) Member of the House of Valois, reigning from 1461 to 1483 and continuing the efforts of his father, Charles VII (1422–1461). After an austere and reclusive childhood, Louis, as dauphin, engaged in conspiracies against his father and was essentially exiled to Dauphiné following the death of his wife, Margaret, daughter of James I of Scotland. In 1456, Charles advanced on Dauphiné, and Louis, fearing for his safety, fled to the Netherlands. He inherited the throne and set about consolidating royal power, confronting enemies such as Charles the Bold of Burgundy, over whom he ultimately triumphed. The League of Public Weal

King Louis X

was established in 1465 by Charles the Bold and his allies, and Louis surrendered to its demands, attempting in ensuing the years to wear down his foes, violating every agreement he had made. Francis of Brittany was forced to submit in 1468 in the Peace of Ancenis, and Charles, despite rare victories over the king, was finally destroyed in 1477 after Louis negotiated a treaty with King Edward IV of England (1461–1483) and became allied with the Swiss. With Charles removed, the crown seized part of his inheritance from Mary of Burgundy, taking Burgundy, Picardy, Franche-Comté and Artois. The duchy of Burgundy was claimed by France in the Treaty of Arras (1482), completing the subjugation of France. Louis, beset by enemies as a result, spent his days a self-incarcerated prisoner in the castle of Plessis-les-Tours. He was derisively called the "Spider King" for his many intrigues and was not recalled with admiration by chroniclers of the era. See also FRANCE.

**LOUIS I, KING OF HUNGARY** (1326–1382) Called "the Great," king of Hungary from 1342 to 1382 and of Poland from 1370 to 1382, the son of King Charles I (1308–1342). He spent much of his reign at war with Venice or Naples, beginning in 1346, when he was defeated by the Venetians and lost the port city of Zara. In a campaign against Naples the following year, Louis attacked the queen of Naples, Joanna I, in revenge for the death of her husband, his brother Andrew, in 1345. He occupied Naples in 1348 but was forced to withdraw because of plague in the city. Later Louis supported Charles of Durazzo in his war against Joanna. Two more conflicts with Venice occurred in 1357–1358 and about 1381, the former ended in the acquisition of Dalmatian towns and the latter in the acquisition of nearly all of Dalmatia. Crowned king of Poland in 1370, as heir to Casimir III, Louis was not allowed supreme influence in the state. Contrary to his plans, a daughter, Jadwiga, rather than his choice, Maria, was recognized by the Poles as their next queen. A patron of the arts and learning, Louis confirmed a modified Golden Bull in 1351 and encouraged sound government. He died having fought the Turks and having been recognized as overlord of Serbia, Wallachia, Bulgaria and Moldavia and influential as a force in Hungary's golden age. See also HUNGARY.

**LOUVAIN** City in Brabant (Belgium) and for many years the residence of the dukes of Brabant and an important trading center for cloth. Louvain's origins date from the ninth century, when a fortress was constructed near the Dyle (Dijle) River to afford protection against Norman raids. Beginning in the 11th century, the city was the home of the counts of Louvain, who later (c. 1190) were the dukes of Brabant. Important for its weaving, the city was plagued by internal strife as the workers fought and even massacred (in 1379) some of the nobles. The leadership in the cloth trade was eventually claimed by Brussels in the 15th century, and Louvain salvaged its prestige with the founding of its university in 1425, with the blessing of Pope Martin V.

**LOVE, COURTLY** The theme of extensive literature composed by court poets and troubadours from the 11th to the 13th century. Courtly love was an intense and idealized emotion existing outside the bonds of marriage in which the lover was the servant of the god of love (love being the source of virtue), worshiping his lady and serving her as he served his leige lord. Love of this kind found expression in a number of ways, from idealized passion to the respect given a lady by her knight. Marriage was not a consideration in courtly love. Couples united in marriage did so often as a result of a political alliance or familial arrangement. The theme of courtly love first appeared in the 11th century, in poetry and song by the troubadours of Aquitaine and especially Provence. An important patron of this literary conceit was Eleanor of Aquitaine. Her daughter, Marie of Champagne, encouraged Chrétien de Troyes to compose his *Lancelot*. Accepted throughout Europe, the ideal was richly expressed by such masters of verse as Gottfried von Strassburg, Petrarch and Dante. See also MINNESINGERS.

**LOWER SAXONY** See SAXONY.

**LÜBECK** Major port city in northern Germany, in Schleswig-Holstein, on the Trave and Wahenitz Rivers along the Baltic Sea. Its origins were Slavic; the Wendish settlement there was destroyed around 1138, and a new German city was established by Count Adolf II of Holstein in 1143. Ceded to the duke of Saxony, Henry the Lion, in 1158, Lübeck was rebuilt after a devastating fire in 1157. Its charter was an influence in other communities, and by 1226 Lübeck was a free imperial city, profiting from its location, the historical patronage of its lords and its development by local merchants. Lübeck was strategic to the advance of Germans and the Teutonic Knights into the regions of the eastern Baltic. Its mercantile interests led eventually to Lübeck's joining the political and commercial union of the Hanseatic League, with the city becoming its administrative center in 1358. The city survived the Black Death in 1350 and social strife in the early 15th century, caused by the uprising of the artisan guilds against the ruling council controlled by the merchants. By the 14th century, Lübeck was the second largest city in Germany and one of the wealthiest in Europe. See also HANSEATIC LEAGUE.

**LUCCA** City in Tuscany, Italy, northeast of Pisa, known during the Middle Ages for its velvets and especially for its banking ventures. Lucca was an ancient community of Ligurian and Etruscan origins and was a Roman colony until conquered by the Goths around 476. Dominated for a time by the Byzantines, in 568 it fell to the Lombards, who made it a capital for a Lombard duke. During the 9th and 10th centuries, Lucca was home to the powerful margraves of Tuscany, but the city warred with Pisa and Florence, losing its prominence in the region. Lucca maintained its prosperity, however, throughout the medieval period.

**LUCERNE** City in central Switzerland, capital of the Lucerne canton, situated on Lake Lucerne. Luzern in German, it began as a fishing village of the Benedictine monastery of Saint Leodegar, founded in the eighth century. Granted its charter about 1178, Lucerne grew in population and prosperity as a result of the opening of the Saint Gotthard Pass (c. 1230), which made trade possible over the Alps with Lombardy. In 1291 Rudolf IV of Habsburg purchased the monastery and the city, an act opposed by the local inhabitants who ultimately (1332) joined the Swiss Confederation. Complete independence was secured in 1386 with a Swiss triumph at the Battle of Sempach. See also SWITZERLAND.

**LUCIUS II** (d. 1145) Pope from 1144 to 1145, papal chamberlain to Pope Innocent II (1130–1143) and elected to succeed Celestine II (1143–1144). Making peace with Roger of Sicily, who had invaded papal territory, Lucius was confronted by a Roman revolt, organized by supporters of the late antipope Anacletus (1130–1138). He died as a result of injuries received while repressing the revolt.

**LUCIUS III** (c. 1110–1185) Pope from 1181–1185, a Cistercian monk made cardinal in 1141 and a trusted adviser to Alexander III (1159–1181), his predecessor. Despite strained relations with Emperor Frederick I Barbarossa (1152–1190), Lucius convinced him to participate in the Third Crusade and was granted his support at the Synod of Verona (1184) decreeing the extirpation of heretics. See also INQUISITION.

**LUCY, RICHARD DE** (d. 1179) Chief justiciar of England during the reign of King Henry II (1154–1189), in 1155 appointed to his post with Robert de Beaumont and holding the office alone after Beaumont died in 1168. De Lucy was an influence in every major decision made for the realm, including property law reforms and justice and the Constitutions of Clarendon (1164), of which he is thought to have been the principal author. Excommunicated twice by Thomas à Becket, he retired in 1179 to Lesnes Abbey to do penance for his role in the archbishop's murder in 1170. See also CLARENDON, CONSTITUTIONS OF.

**LULL, RAMÓN** (c. 1232–1315) Catalan philosopher, influential mystic and student of Arabic called the "Enlightened Doctor" (Doctor Illuminatus), a native of Majorca, also called Ramón Llull or Lullus. In the service of King James I of Aragon (1213–1276), Lull experienced mystical visions and joined the Third Order of Saint Francis, traveling in North Africa and Asia Minor to convert the Muslims. While living in Majorca, Lull acquired extensive knowledge of Arabic and Muslim philosophical traditions. His celebrated *Libre de contemplació en Déu (Book of the Contemplation of God)* presented first principles for establishing ultimate truths. A prolific writer, Lull produced poetry and works on mysticism and philosophy. He was condemned in 1376 for connecting faith and reason (as in his chief work, *Ars magna* [the great art]), a view that the church altered officially in later centuries. According to tradition, he was stoned to death by Muslims at Bougie in North Africa. Scholarly interest in Lull and his writings has been revived, especially the study of his works on mysticism. See also MYSTICISM.

**LUNA, ALVARO DE** (c. 1388–1453) Constable of Castile and poet, tutor to the young King John II of Castile (1406–1454) and governmental adviser when John came of age in 1419. Despite aristocratic opposition, Luna was appointed constable in 1423, driven from the court in 1427 and then promoted a crusade against the Moors in 1431, which was a failure. His ultimate destruction was arranged by John's wife, Isabel of Portugal, who demanded his trial for witchcraft and his execution at Valladolid. See also CASTILE.

**LUNA, PEDRO DE** See BENEDICT XIII.

**LUSATIA** See LAUSITZ.

**LUSIGNAN** Important French aristocratic family originating in Poitou that was active during the Crusades, producing rulers of Jerusalem, Cyprus and Armenia. The ancestral castle, in legend supposedly built by Melusine, a water sprite who married a mortal, was the residence of the Lusignan family. Guy de Lusignan was one of the most important members of the line, marrying Sibylla (Sibyl), sister of Baldwin IV of Jerusalem (1174–1185) and wearing the crown of the city in 1186 on the death of Baldwin V. Captured by Saladin in the following year, in the Battle of Hattin, Guy lost Jerusalem. He was released in 1188 and launched the siege of Acre, which fell in 1191, Lusignan having been joined by Richard the Lion-Hearted (1189–1199) and Philip II Augustus of France (1180–1223). Guy was unable to meet the challenge of Conrad of Montferrat for the throne of Jerusalem after Sibylla's death in 1190 but contented himself with the Kingdom of Cyprus, buying the island from Richard in 1192. Lusignan maintained control of Cyprus until 1145. A branch of the family reigned in Lesser Armenia from 1342 to 1375, and the house claimed the titles of Jerusalem and Armenia for many years, although both had been officially lost to Lusignan. See also JERUSALEM, KINGDOM OF.

**LUSIGNAN, GUY DE** See LUSIGNAN.

**LUXEMBOURG** Grand duchy situated between Belgium, Germany and France, emerging in the 10th century to become a county of the Holy Roman Empire under Conrad (d. 1086). Gradually losing territory to competing counties, Luxembourg, however, produced four emperors: Henry VII (ruled 1308–1313), Charles IV (ruled 1347–1378), Wenceslas (ruled 1378–1400) and Sigismund (1410–1437). Emperor Charles IV raised Luxembourg to a duchy in 1354. In 1443, Philip the Good of Burgundy (1419–1467) came into possession of the region, but it was returned to German hands in 1477, with the marriage of the heiress, Mary of Burgundy, to the Habsburg Maxmilian. While German language and culture were dominant for centuries, French custom gained ascendancy in Luxembourg, especially in the 15th century. See also HOLY ROMAN EMPIRE.

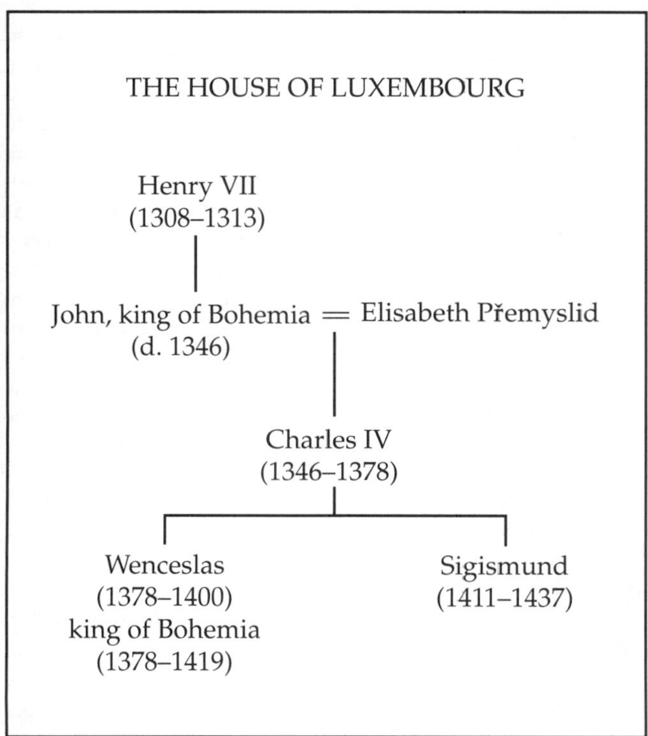


**LYDGATE, JOHN** (c. 1370–c. 1450) English poet, one of the most prolific writers of his time, a Benedictine of Bury Saint Edmunds, ordained in 1397. Lydgate was considered a peer of Chaucer and noted for his works *The Serpent of Division, The Troy Book, The Siege of Thebes, The Fall of Princes* and *The Temple of Glass.*

**LYONS** French city (French, Lyon) at the confluence of the Rhône and Saône Rivers and called the Cradle of Christianity in France. Founded in 43 B.C. as a Roman colony (Lugdunum), the city was important in Roman Gaul until its brutal devastation in the late second century by Emperor Septimius Severus in vengeance for the support that Lyons gave to a rival for the imperial throne. A Christian community was present from a relatively early time, and a bishopric was established there in the third century. Through Lyons, Christianity was introduced into France (Gaul), and its prelates exercised broad temporal power until about 1312, when the French crown annexed it, during the reign of King Philip I. Throughout the 15th century, the city grew in economic prosperity with the establishment of Italian banks and a thriving silk trade. Two ecumenical councils were held in Lyons, in 1245 and 1274. See also FRANCE.

**LYONS, COUNCILS OF** Two general councils of the church, convened in 1245 and 1274, numbered the 13th and 14th Ecumenical Councils.

The first Council of Lyons was an assembly convened by Pope Innocent IV (1243–1254) to deal with a variety of difficulties confronting the church, including the schism with the Byzantines, the deterioration of clergical morality and the invasion of Hungary by the Mongols. The major problem the council had to deal with, however, was the emperor Frederick II (1215–1250), who was at war with the Lombard cities and was deposed by the council, an act having no real or lasting significance.

The second Council of Lyons, summoned by Pope Gregory X (1271–1276), aimed at regulating the election of the pope, establishing moral reform and the union of the Eastern and Western Churches. It was attended by more than 500 bishops and church figures such as Albertus Magnus, Bonaventure and Peter of Tarentaise (the future Pope Innocent V). The council heard the delegates from the Byzantine emperor, Michael VIII Palaeologus (1259–1282) accept the supremacy of the pope and support all the articles of faith required by the Western Church. This success was short lived, however, as another rupture occurred in 1289 (see SCHISMS). Thomas Aquinas died while en route to the Council of Lyons.

# M

**MABINOGION** A collection of Welsh stories based on folklore and legends originating in the oral tradition but recorded between the 11th and 13th centuries in numerous manuscripts. The name Mabinogion (or Mabinogi) is meaningless, but because of an error by a scribe it became the generally accepted title for the mythological and heroic tales. The first four were the "Four Branches of the Mabinogi," and other sections included the *White Book of Rhydderch* and the *Red Book of Hergest*. Versions of these tales appear in Arthurian Legend.

**MACBETH** (d. 1057) King of Scotland from 1040 to 1057, an able and just claimant to the throne, unlike Shakespeare's villain. Probably a grandson of King Kenneth II (ruled 971–995), he was *moarmaer,* or chief, of Moray and had as rightful a claim to the throne as his cousin, King Duncan I (1034–1040), whom he killed in battle in 1040. Defending himself against his rebellious nobles, Macbeth also made a pilgrimage to Rome. In 1057, however, he was defeated and killed by Duncan's son, Malcolm (III, 1058–1093). Buried at Iona, Macbeth was included as a legitimate ruler of Scotland. See also SCOTLAND.

**MACEDONIAN DYNASTY** Ruling line of the Byzantine Empire from 867 to 1056, founded by Basil I (ruled 867–886) and ending with the second reign of Theodora (1055–1056).

**MACHAUT, GUILLAUME DE** (d. 1377) French poet and composer, in the service of John of Luxembourg, king of Bohemia (c. 1323). He received an appointment as the canon of Verdun, Arras and Reims by Pope John XXII (1316–1334) and was well respected by his contemporaries. When John died at Crécy in 1346, Machaut was besieged by patrons, including the future King Charles V (1364–1380). His compositions were largely secular, with some religious works, and included *chants royaux,* rondeaux, lays, ballades and motets, earning him a place as the foremost French musician of the 14th century and the leading composer of the noted *ars nova* style.

**MADRID** City in central Spain, in New Castile, situated on the Manzanares River. Madrid was established in the eighth century as a Moorish fortress, called Majrit in the Arabic, and part of the defenses of Toledo to the southwest. It fell to Castile in 1083, serving occasionally as the royal residence and the site, in 1329, of the first *cortes,* or parliament. Chosen as their residence by Ferdinand and Isabella (1474–1516) in 1477, Madrid became the capital of Spain in 1561.

**MAERLANT, JACOB VAN** (1225–c. 1300) Flemish poet and the earliest important figure in Dutch literature, probably in the service of the count of Holland and learned in French and Latin. The author of epic romances, van Maerlant also composed works on didacticism, relying on extensive Latin sources and providing appropriate reading. He wrote lyric, chivalric and didactic poetry as well.

**MAGDEBURG** City in east-central Germany on the Elbe River, originally a Slavic settlement, first mentioned in 805. In 968 it received an archepiscopal see with vast, fixed holdings, which included Meissen, Havelberg, Brandenburg, Merseburg and Zeitz-Naumburg. The archbishops of Magdeburg, ultimately princes of the Holy Roman Empire, wielded considerable influence in German colonies across the Elbe. Burned down in 1188, Magdeburg was rebuilt, and in the 13th century it was granted a charter known as the "Magdeburg Law" (Magdeburger Richt) establishing an autonomous municipal administration, a form of self-rule that was followed by towns throughout eastern Europe and Germany. The city was also a member of the Hanseatic League but was unable to overcome the domination of its archbishops until the 15th century. See also HANSEATIC LEAGUE.

**MAGGIOR CONSIGLIO** The Great Council or ruling body of Venice. See also VENICE.

**MAGHRIB** An extensive region in North Africa, bordered by the Sahara to the south and the Mediterranean Sea to the north and including Tunisia, parts of Libya, Algeria, Morocco and Moorish Spain (Andalusia). The name is also sometimes recorded as Maghreb, derived from the Arabic word for West.

**MAGIC** See ALCHEMY; ASTROLOGY; ASTRONOMY; BACON, ROGER; GOLEM; GRIMOIRES; HONORIUS III; MALLEUS MALEFICARUM; WITCHCRAFT.

**MAGNA CARTA** The Great Charter of English liberties, issued at Runnymede in 1215 by King John (1199–1216) at the insistence of his barons, by whom he was threatened with civil war. Reissued with some changes in 1216, 1217 and 1225, it originally was intended to ensure feudal rights and to guarantee that the king could not

Magdeburg Cathedral statue

encroach on the privileges of the barons. Previous kings, Henry I (1100–1135), Stephen (1135–1154) and Henry II (1154–1189) had each issued their own charters, but as these were granted by and not exacted from the monarchs, their value to the barons was limited. John, weakened politically by rival claimants and a lack of funds after his loss of Normandy in 1204 and his conflict with Pope Innocent III from 1208 to 1213, was demanding taxes from the church and the barons, thus bringing him into conflict with Stephen Langton, the archbishop of Canterbury, who also promoted the charter. The resulting Articles of the Barons led to the signing of Magna Carta at Runnymede.

In addition to the promise to safeguard baronial rights, Magna Carta ensured the freedom of the church, customs of towns and protection of communities and provided for institutional reforms in justice, later interpreted as the guarantee of trial by jury and habeas corpus. A council of 25 barons was formed to ensure the monarch's compliance. John later repudiated Magna Carta, claiming he was coerced, and was released from it with papal blessing, which caused another eruption of hostilities. Later reissues had significant omissions, and it soon became clear that continued revisions were impractical. Nevertheless, the Great Charter emerged as a symbol of constitutional supremacy, serving as the basis for other developments in the granting of liberties. See also ENGLAND.

**MAGNUS I OLAFSSON, KING OF NORWAY** (1024–1047) Called "the Good," ruler of Norway from 1035 to 1047 and of Denmark from 1042 to 1047. An illegitimate son of Olaf II (Saint Olaf, ruled 1015–1028), Magnus spent much of his youth in Russia, as his father had been exiled by King Canute II. In 1035 he entered Norway, where the nobles proclaimed him king rather than Canute's son, Hardecanute. As part of the agreement, Magnus inherited the Danish crown on Hardecanute's death in 1042. The Danes rebelled in favor of Sven Estridsson, and in 1045 Harold III Hardraade returned from Constantinople. Magnus, his nephew, was compelled to share the throne. See also DENMARK; NORWAY.

**MAGNUS II, KING OF NORWAY** Ruler from 1066 to 1069. See also NORWAY.

**MAGNUS III, KING OF NORWAY** (d. 1103) Called Bareleg, ruler from 1093 to 1103, the son of Olaf III (1066–1093) and a warrior, who ruled briefly with his cousin, Haakon, who died in 1094. He extended Norwegian domination over the Orkney and Hebrides Islands and for a time controlled the Isle of Man. While on campaign in Ireland, Magnus was killed near Ulster, according to tradition while hunting for food. See also NORWAY.

**MAGNUS IV SIGURDSSON, KING OF NORWAY** (d. 1139) Called "the Blind," joint co-ruler from 1130 to 1135, the son of King Sigurd I Jerusalemfarer (1125–1130), who had to rule with Harald IV Gilchrist (1130–1136). War ensued between them, and Magnus was placed in a monastery in 1135, having been captured, maimed and blinded. After Harald was killed the following year, Magnus was rescued in 1137 by Sigurd Slembi, who attempted unsuccessfully to restore him to the throne. Another attempt ended in 1139, when Magnus died in battle. See also NORWAY.

**MAGNUS V ERLINGSSON, KING OF NORWAY** (1156–1184) Ruler from 1162 to 1184, the son of Erling the Crooked, defeating the forces of King Haakon II the Broad-shouldered (1161–1162) and thus winning the throne. He was crowned in 1163, the first monarch to be so distinguished as the result of repeated negotiation with the church. His father was regent until his death in 1179. That same year Magnus was driven from Norway by Sverre, a rival claimant, returning in 1184 and dying in battle. See also NORWAY.

**MAGNUS VI HAAKONSSON, KING OF NORWAY** (1238–1280) Called in Norwegian Lagaboeter ("Lawmender"), ruler from 1263 to 1280, bringing major reforms to the legal system. The son of King Haakon IV (1217–1263), he made peace with Scotland by surrendering the Hebrides and improved relations with the church through the Concordat of Toensburg. His major achievements, however, were in legal reform. New national legal codes were introduced, replacing the traditional provincial ones, and a new municipal code was established for Bergen, followed by similar codes in other Norwegian cities. See also NORWAY.

**MAGNUS VII ERICSSON, KING OF NORWAY** (1316–1374) Also called Magnus II Ericsson in Sweden, ruler of Norway from 1319 to 1355 and of Sweden from 1319 to 1365. The son of Ingeborg, daughter of King Haakon V (1299–1319) and the Swedish duke Erik, Magnus was accepted as successor to Haakon V, coming of age in 1332. Eventually he earned the enmity of Swedish and Norwegian nobles, the Norwegians chiefly because of his absence from the country. Magnus was compelled to abdicate in 1355, to be succeeded by his son, Haakon VI (1355–1380). In Sweden his attempts to curtail the power of the church and the aristocracy met with harsh resistance and finally rebellion, and he fled the country in 1371. See also SWEDEN.

**MAGNUS BIRGERSSON, KING OF SWEDEN** (d. 1290) Called "Barnlock," ruler of Sweden from 1275 to 1290. See also SWEDEN.

**MAGNUS II ERICSSON** See MAGNUS VII ERICSSON, KING OF NORWAY.

**MAGYARS** Originally nomadic people of Hungary who spoke a Finno-Ugric language. In the fifth century they migrated from the Ural Mountains to the Caucasus, coming into contact with the local Turkic tribes. Driven west by the Pechenegs in the ninth century, the Magyars settled in Hungary and thence in Moravia and Germany. Superb horsemen and warriors, they were defeated in 955 at the Battle of Lechfeld by Otto I (936–973), thus ending their imperial ambitions. Christianized during the reign of their king Stephen I (ruled 1001–1038), the Magyars became identified with Hungarians. See also HUNGARY.

**AL-MAHDI (1)** Abbasid caliph from 775 to 785, the son of the caliph al-Mansur, who reversed his father's financial austerity. Utilizing the treasury, al-Mahdi improved communications, defenses and cities of the caliphate and was a generous patron of the arts. He did take harsh measures against a heretical party attempting to reintroduce traditional Persian religious practices, and he conducted a jihad (holy war) against the Byzantine Empire, with a successful campaign led by his son Harun al-Rashid. See also ABBASID CALIPHATE.

**AL-MAHDI (2)** The name adopted by Ubayd Allah (c. 910) after winning the support of the Berber tribes of North Africa. It was intended to provide him with additional religious and political influence beyond that which he possessed as an imam in the Islamic movement. See also FATIMID CALIPHATE.

**MAHMUD** Ruler of the Seljuk Turks of Iraq from 1118 to 1131. See also SELJUK TURKS.

**MAHMUD OF GHAZNI** See GHAZNAVIDS.

**MAID OF NORWAY** See MARGARET OF SCOTLAND, SAINT.

**MAID OF ORLÉANS** See JOAN OF ARC.

**MAIMONIDES, MOSES** (1135–1204) Jewish philosopher and medical writer who was a prominent figure in medieval Jewish intellectualism. Known to Jewish writers as Rambam, derived from some letters in the name of Rabbi Moses ben Maimon, he was born and educated in Córdoba. He and his family fled in 1148 when Córdoba was captured by the Almohads, settling in Fez, Morocco. In 1165 he left Fez and went to Palestine and then to al-Fustat, near Cairo. There he became the most distinguished member of the Jewish community, practicing medicine and serving as court physician to Saladin and his son, al-Afdal. A brilliant and prolific writer, Maimonides composed his first work at age 16, a treatise on the terminology of metaphysics and logic. Other major works included *Kitab al-Siraj* (1168), a commentary on Jewish law; *Mishneh Torah (Torah Reviewed), Moreh Nevukhim (Guide for the Perplexed,* completed in 1190), and other minor works, including letters, medical books and commentaries on Talmudic law. His writing had a profound influence on exponents of Christian thought, such as Thomas Aquinas and Albertus Magnus. See also JEWS AND JUDAISM.

**MAINE** Also Le Maine or The Maine, a province in northwestern France occupying the region of the present departments of Sarthe and Mayenne. The culture of Maine was influenced throughout its history by its neighbors, Normandy and Anjou. A county from the late ninth century, it was made a fief for a time to Normandy and then to Anjou after 1110. Sharing in Anjou's association with England at that time, Maine was taken by King Philip II Augustus (1180–1223) from King John of England (1199–1216) in 1205. Granted as an appanage to Charles of Anjou by King Louis IX (ruled 1226–1270), it became a royal domain in 1481.

**MAINZ** In French, Mayence, a city in western Germany on the Rhine River, the capital of the Rhineland palatinate. Of Celtic origins, Mainz became an important Roman military post, called Maguntiacum, emerging as the chief city of the Roman province of Germania Superior. Overrun in the fifth century by tribal migrations, it was sacked by successive waves of invaders, and a new town was erected in the sixth century, becoming prominent through the influence of Saint Boniface. A bishopric in 747, it became an archbishopric, whose prelates wielded power in the Holy Roman Empire, ranking as imperial Electors, holding territory on both sides of the Rhine and Main. Certain rights of self-rule were granted in 1118, and Mainz was declared a free city in 1244. Johann Gutenberg was born there about 1399. See also GERMANY.

**MAJORCA** See BALEARIC ISLANDS.

**MALACHY, SAINT** (1094–1148) Archbishop of Armagh, papal legate and an important figure in Irish history. Called in Gaelic Máel Máedoc Úa Morgair, he strove to introduce the reforms of Pope Gregory VII (1073–1085) and thus has been credited with bringing the Roman liturgy to Ireland. Throughout his life he confronted opposition by antipapal forces and eventually went to Rome seeking his pallium, the symbol of his office as archbishop, as he had been nominated in 1129 but had been unable to secure his see. In Rome he was made a papal legate in 1139, meeting Saint Bernard at Clairvaux at that time. He returned to England with a group of Cistercians, who founded a monastery in 1142. In 1148 he finally secured his see but died on his return from Rome, where he had received his pallium. Tradition holds that he died in the arms of Bernard. Malachy was the reputed author of a collection of prophecies (probably actually dating from the 16th century) giving a descriptive Latin motto for every pope from Celestine II (1143–1144) to the last pontiff, to be called Peter II. See also IRELAND.

**MALALAS, JOHN** (d. c. 578) Byzantine chronicler known to scholars as John Rhetor or John Scholasticus and perhaps identified as well with John III Scholasticus, who served as patriarch of Constantinople from 565 to 577. Malalas was the author of the *Chronographia* (in 18 volumes), although it is extant only to 563.

**MALATESTA** See RIMINI.

**MALCOLM I** (d. 954) King of Scotland from 942/943 to 954, whose reign was noted principally for his amicable relations with the Saxons of England. He died in combat, probably against his enemies in Moray. See also SCOTLAND.

**MALCOLM II** (d. 1034) King of Scotland from 1005 to 1034, during which time he produced major political advances for the Scottish kingdom. He invaded Lothian and successfully acquired it as a permanent possession. Soon afterward he gained control of the once independent territory of Strathclyde. In 1031, however, he faced an invasion by Canute the Great, the Danish king of England, and was forced temporarily to acknowledge Canute's superiority while remaining strong enough to ensure that the Scottish successor would be his grandson, Duncan. Malcolm was termed "King of Scotia," a title transferred from Ireland to Scotland. See also SCOTLAND.

**MALCOLM III** (c. 1031–1093) King of Scotland from 1057 to 1093, called Malcolm III Canmore, the son of King Duncan I, who was killed in battle and replaced by MACBETH (ruled 1040–1057). Malcolm spent many years during Macbeth's reign in exile, returning to defeat and kill him. Crowned in 1058, he did not forget the refuge allowed him by Edward the Confessor (1042–1066), providing asylum to the Anglo-Saxon prince Edgar Aetheling, following the Norman Conquest of England in 1066. In 1072 Malcolm acknowledged the lordship of William the Conqueror (1066–1087) but spent much time launching raids into northern England, and during one of these campaigns he was killed in battle with the troops of William II Rufus (1087–1100). Malcolm's wife was Margaret of Scotland. See also SCOTLAND.

**MALDON, BATTLE OF** An engagement fought between the East Saxons (people of Essex) and an army of marauding Danes in 991. The battle ended in total disaster for the English, who were not only driven from the field but lost their chief, Byrhtnoth, who was slain with most of his relatives. The Battle of Maldon was immortalized in an Old English poem. See also DANEGELD.

**AL-MALIK, ABD** (d. 705) Umayyad caliph from 685 to 705, the son of Marwan, and called the Father of Kings, as four of his sons became caliphs. During the rule of his sons Walid and Hashim, the Islamic empire reached its height. He relied militarily on two competent generals, Al-Hajjaj ibn Yusuf and Musa ibn Nusayr, extending and consolidating the conquests of the caliphate. He was also responsible for adopting Arabic as the official language of the state, with Arab coins replacing the Greek. Al-Malik constructed the Dome of the Rock in Jerusalem and introduced a regular postal service. See also UMAYYAD CALIPHATE.

**MALIK IBN ANAS** (c. 715–195) Influential Islamic theologian and jurist, the founder of one of the four Sunni schools of Islamic law, the *Maliki (Malikite).* He spent most of his life in Medina, earning a reputation for his independence of thought and his brilliance, and after the failure of a rebellion against a caliph he was flogged for espousing the view that devotion to the caliph was not necessary because such loyalty was compulsory. Despite this, the caliph Harun al-Rashid (786–809) paid him a visit while on a pilgrimage to Mecca. The Maliki School was popular, and remains so, in parts of Egypt, Sudan and in northern and western Africa. It stressed the role of community practice *(sunnah),* opinion and reason while reducing reliance upon the Hadith, the traditions of the Prophet's pronouncements.

Malik Shah mosque, Isfahan, Iraq

**MALIK SHAH I** (1055–1092) Sultan of the Seljuk Turks from 1072 to 1092 and one of the most formidable Turkish rulers, the son of Alp Arslan (1064–1072). Malik relied on the talents and advice of his vizier, Nizam al-Mulk, who supported him in overcoming early uprisings and in consolidating and expanding Seljuk dominance across the Middle East through diplomatic means. Syria and Palestine fell to his control, and limited suzerainty was established over Mecca and Medina. His final years were beset by a deteriorating relationship with Nizam and by the rise of the Assassins (who murdered the vizier in 1092). Malik Shah was a patron of the arts, and during his reign the calendar was reformed, splendid mosques were built at Isfahan and the poet Omar Khayyam flourished. See also SELJUK TURKS.

**MALIK SHAH II** Sultan of the Seljuk Turks (Great Seljuks) in 1104. He was the son and successor of Berk-Yarug. See also SELJUK TURKS.

**MALIK SHAH I, SULTAN OF RUM** (d. 1116) Ruler of the Seljuk Turks of Rum from about 1107 to 1116. He followed Qilij Arslan I (1092–1106) but could not maintain his position, being overthrown by his nephew, Masud I. See also SELJUK TURKS.

**MALIK SHAH II, SULTAN OF RUM** Ruler of the Seljuk Turks of Rum, reigning in 1142. See also SELJUK TURKS.

***MALLEUS MALEFICARUM*** The famous *Witches' Hammer* (or *Hammer of the Witches*), a treatise on all aspects of witchcraft that was considered the supreme source on witches for centuries after its original publication in 1486. The *Malleus maleficarum* was compiled by two Dominicans, Johann Sprenger, dean of the University of Cologne, and Henrich (Institoris) Kraemer (Krämer), a teacher of theology at the University of Salzburg and the Inquisitor of Tirol. They wrote the book at the request of Pope Innocent VIII (1484–1492), who had just issued the papal bull *Summus Desiderantes,* condemning the rise of witchcraft in Germany.

In lurid and elaborate detail the work described the characteristics of witches, their practices, habits, perversions and diabolical works, advocating torture and savage trials to rid the world of their evil. Published in some 28 editions between 1486 and 1600 and respected by both Protestants and Catholics of the time, the *Malleus maleficarum* gave major impetus to the hysteria against witchcraft that was to sweep across Europe in the next decades. See also WITCHCRAFT.

**MALLORCA** The Spanish name for Majorca.

**MALMESBURY** Benedictine abbey in Wiltshire, England, that was one of the religious centers of the country during the Middle Ages, founded about 635 by the Irish or Scottish monk Maildulf, whose pupil, Saint Aldhelm, served as its first abbot (c. 673), converting it from a hermitage to a monastery. Malmesbury was granted royal patronage by English kings, including Athelstan the Glorious (ruled 924–940), William the Conqueror (ruled 1066–1087), Richard II (reigned 1377–1399) and Henry V (ruled 1413–1422). The monastery was dissolved in 1539 by Henry VIII. William of Malmesbury, the 12th-century historian, was raised there.

**MALOMIR** Ruler of the Bulgars from 831 to 836, a son of King Omurtag. Malomir, also Malimir, came to the throne after his brother, Enravota, was executed for his practice of Christianity. He was replaced by General Presiam, although it is thought that he was Malomir using another name. The mysterious demise of the ruler, or the change of names, came during a war against the forces of the Byzantine Empire. See also BULGARIA; PRESIAM.

**MALORY, SIR THOMAS** (d. 1471) English writer and the author of *Le Morte d'Arthur,* the first prose account in English describing the origins and deeds of King Arthur and his Knights of the Round Table. There has been scholarly debate as to the identity of Malory and a number of possible candidates proposed. The *Morte d'Arthur* was first published and titled by William Caxton in 1485 and was reprinted in 1498 by Wynkym de Worde. See also ARTHURIAN LEGEND.

**MALTA** An island nation in the Mediterranean Sea to the south of Sicily, comprising five islands: Malta, Gozo, Comino, Comminotto and Filfla. Under Roman control from 218 B.C., the islands were granted to the Eastern Empire in 395 with the division of the Roman Empire. The succeeding years brought repeated invasions by the Vandals, Ostrogoths and Arabs. The Normans occupied it in 1091, followed by a number of feudal lords. In 1266, Charles of Anjou took control but lost it after the war of the Sicilian Vespers in 1282, whereupon Malta was claimed by Aragon. Finally, in 1530, Emperor Charles V granted it to the Order of the Hospital of St. John of Jerusalem.

Mamluks, from a Persian miniature

**MAMLUKS** The Arab word for slaves that came to be applied specifically to the slave troops forming the bulk of the armies of Islam from the ninth century and a ruling dynasty descended from these slaves. While the Mamluks were valued militarily by the Abbasids and Ghaznavids, they were most illustrious in Egypt, where they established a formidable dynasty of rulers. The Mamluks of Egypt began as slaves brought to the country by the Fatimid caliphs in the 10th century and later by the Ayyubid sultans. The danger inherent in slave levies, especially those trained in the military, was made obvious on the death of al-Silah Ayyub in 1249. In the resulting conflict over the succession, the Mamluks, led by their general, Aybak, killed the last Ayyubid ruler and took the throne, initiating an era of Mamluk ascendancy in Egypt and Syria that endured from 1250 to 1517 and was divided into two eras: the Bahri, from 1250 to 1382, and the Burji, from 1382 to 1517.

The Bahri period, also called the Turkish period, was the age in which the Mamluks achieved their greatest gains, reconstructing the Islamic Egyptian empire, crushing the last of the Crusader States and reviving the caliphate, which had been ended by the Mongols at Baghdad in 1258. The Mamluks sultans, especially Baybars I and al-Nasir Muhammad (1260–1277 and 1293–1340 respectively), promoted trade and commerce, built lavishly and were patrons of the arts and learning in Medina and Mecca. Egypt was once again established as the chief trading conduit between the West and the Orient in the 14th century.

Decline characterized the Burji period, also called the Circassian period because of the supremacy of Circassians in the government, a fact that probably contributed to the decay. The plague, industrial and agricultural losses from internal upheaval and a crushing tax system were problems faced in a briefly successful effort to restore Mamluk glory under Barsbay (ruled 1422–1438). As the Ottomans advanced into Syria, the outdated Mamluk war machine was incapable of resisting effectively. From 1517, Egypt was attached to the Ottoman Empire. See also EGYPT.

**AL-MAMUN** (786–833) Seventh Abbasid caliph, ruling from 813 to 833, the son of Harun al-Rashid (786–809). At Harun's death in 809 civil war erupted between al-Mamun and his brother, al-Amin, the successor who had attempted to strip him of his right to rule the eastern provinces of the caliphate. The war ended in 813 with al-Amin's death, although al-Mamun was not entirely secure until 819. A generous and liberal ruler, he was called Mamun the Great and encouraged scholars and artists, promoted translations of Greek writings on science and philosophy and erected two observatories, near Baghdad and Damascus. Of particular note was his House of Wisdom or Knowledge, near Baghdad. Scholarly pursuits conducted there included translations of texts in Persian, Sanskrit, Greek and Syrian, often made by Christians. The House of Knowledge or Wisdom (Bayt al-Hikmah) epitomized al-Mamun's open encouragement of outside influences to shape the caliphate culturally. Less successful was his determination to support the liberal movement of the Mu'tazilites, who believed in a rationalist interpretation of Islamic scripture. When al-Mamun died suddenly, the fundamentalist Muslims interpreted the event as a divine judgment. See also ABBASID CALIPHATE.

**MAMUN'S HOUSE OF WISDOM OR KNOWLEDGE** See AL-MAMUN.

**MANDEVILLE, SIR JOHN** Mid-14th-century (d. 1370?) writer once called the most peripatetic person in the world. His renown rested on his highly imaginative account of his journeys, called *The Voyage and Travels of Sir John Mandeville, Knight,* called also *Travels of Sir John Mandeville.* He claimed to have visited Constantinople, Palestine, Egypt, Africa, the Near East and Asia, as well as less-frequently traversed regions, such as the realm of Prester John, the Land of Darkness and the place of the Lost Tribes of Israel. Mandeville probably pieced together his book by borrowing from other writings and encyclopedias, enriching these accounts with his own fertile imagination. His work was extremely popular during the Middle Ages.

**MANDRAKE** European plant species *(Mandragora)* that has long been reputed to possess magical or hypnotic properties. Shaped in human form, the plant was the subject of many tales and legends and was associated with the practice of both medicine and witchcraft. During the Middle Ages the root plant was popular as a painkiller, largely because of its narcotic properties. See also MEDICINE; WITCHCRAFT.

**MANFRED** (1232–1266) King of Sicily from 1258 to 1266, the illegitimate son of Emperor Frederick II (1215–1250), serving as regent in Sicily after 1250 for his brother, Conrad IV (1250–1254) and his nephew, Conradin. In 1254 he was compelled to return Sicily to the papacy, retaining only Taranto, but soon his Hohenstaufen lineage brought him to rebellion. He wrested Sicily and southern Italy from the popes, assuming leadership of the Ghibelline cause and, in 1258, had himself crowned at Palermo. Pope Urban IV (1261–1264) invested Charles of Anjou as ruler of Sicily, and in February 1266 Manfred was crushed and slain at Benevento. Dante placed him in *Purgatory* in his *Divine Comedy*.

**MANIACES, GEORGE** (d. 1043) Byzantine general who was triumphant over the Arabs in Sicily and won victories in Asia Minor, despite the deteriorating resources of the Byzantine Empire. Ordered removed by Emperor Constantine IX (ruled 1042–1055), Maniaces allowed his loyal troops to proclaim him emperor, for which he ultimately lost his life. See also BYZANTINE EMPIRE.

**MANNYNG, ROBERT** Fourteenth-century Gilbertine canon, probably Sir Robert de Brunne, notable for two poems, *Handlyng Synne* and the *Story of England. Handlyng Synne* was completed in 1307 and was probably an adaptation of a 13th-century work by William of Waddington, the *Manuel des péchés (Handbook of Sins).* The poem was 13,000 lines long and intended to prepare the lay person for confession. The work is a valuable source for the social customs of the time. The *Story of England,* in two parts, gives an account of English history from Noah to the death of King Edward I in 1307.

**MANORIAL SYSTEM** Also manorialism or the seigeurial system, the social and economic structure in Europe that flourished from the 11th to the 15th century. The manorial system was essentially one of mutual interdependence, as it provided the serf, or villein, with a livelihood while giving the lord or seigneur the means for engaging in politics or war should he need to call on him for service. There are scholarly theories concerning the rise of the manor, thought to have originated in either the Roman villa of the late empire or the free village communities of the Germans that had developed prior to their contact with Roman custom. The evolution of the manor was hastened by the increasing political disorder in the Frankish lands during the collapse of the Carolingian empire and the rule of the weak Merovingian kings. The remaining peasants worked the land of a nobleman or an ecclesiastical prelate and thus were connected to the estates.

The serf gave labor and payment of various rents in money or kind. Generally during the summer months and at harvest time the serfs worked for five days each week on the demesne, the private lands retained by the lord for his own use, and was responsible for additional labor, called boon work, when it was demanded. Each serf had his own plot of ground as well, but these were scattered around the fields in use to ensure cooperation, joint responsibility and community labor. The serfs gave service and fixed dues and were bound to the soil, remaining so even when the manor changed ownership. The serfs were not slaves, however, and there were several classifications within their ranks. The free tenants held generally superior positions, giving specific services to the lord that were less menial than those of other serfs. They held the right to sell their lands and could leave the estate if they chose. Most of the manor's labor force, however, was composed of lesser serfs, called cotters or cottars, who owned barely a hut and were inferior in rank.

The lord held additional rights, controlling the local market and trade and receiving tolls and charges for the use of his mills, wine press and oxen. Foresting, hunting and fishing were under his domain, and additional monies were collected through the usual heriot, or tribute, from the death of a serf or the desired marriage of a villein or a villein's daughter to someone outside the manor.

Manors differed greatly in size, but for the most part each was a virtually self-contained economic unit, pastoral or agricultural, with various types of land. There were the lord's garden, paddocks and fields, which were maintained by the tenants and lesser serfs, and plots divided among the serfs, tenants, villagers and freeholders. The demesne lands were often near the house, in a square of several hundred acres or divided among the tenant lands. The serfs worked the extensive fields using a system known as three-course crop rotation. In earlier periods the two-course system was adopted, but this proved wasteful. The three-course system was thus employed, in which a winter crop was sown in the fall (wheat or rye) and a summer crop sown in the spring (oats, peas, barley, etc.) while the third field was left fallow and used for pasturage of draft animals, thus fertilizing the land. The fields were then rotated to prevent soil exhaustion; each field was subdivided into approximately one-acre strips, each serf holding a certain number of strips, receiving only what was grown on his designated land.

Factors contributing to the decline of the manorial system were varied. Massive depopulation caused by plague, especially from 1347 to 1349, devastated entire manors, reducing the agriculture to primitive conditions. Peasant revolts took place in reaction to the lord's refusal to accept the need for greater liberality toward his serfs. The two most outstanding uprisings were the Jacquerie in 1358 in France and the Peasant Revolt of 1381 in England. An important step was made with recognition by the nobles that their manors could be exploited for profit rather than managed to eke out mere subsistence. They found it more profitable to convert services into money and to hire workers. The increase in the circulation of money from the 14th century brought the replacement of payment by labor with monetary payment. Furthermore, towns increased in size owing to the demographic changes through depopulation, and the market for wool convinced many lords to convert their fields to pasture, thereby releasing serfs from service and allowing them to enter the towns and cities. The demise of the manorial system was thus the evolution of serfs as well as lords, moving from dependent workers to free men utilizing their skills in various markets.

**AL-MANSUR** (d. 775) Second caliph of the Abassids (754–775), called Abu Ja'far Abd Allah ibn Muhammad al-Mansur, the brother of Abu'l-Abbas as-Saffah and considered the true founder of the caliphate. A descendant of Abbas, uncle of the Prophet, al-Mansur supported the overthrow of the declining Umayyed caliphate and the rise of his brother as the first Abassid caliph. When as-Saffah died in 754, al-Mansur supressed a number of army revolts and liquidated many influential members of the Abbasid cause who had outlived their usefulness to him, chief among these Abu Muslim. The Abbasids crushed the Alids in 762–763, and al-Mansur maintained the claim to his throne. In 762 he ordered construction to begin on his new capital, Baghdad, providing a suitable venue from which to administer the caliphate, and he introduced Persian traditions and practices into government. Al-Mansur was harsh but was also a patron of poets. His death occurred while he was making a pilgrimage to Mecca. See also ABBASID CALIPHATE.

**MANTEGNA, ANDREA** (1431–1506) Italian painter whose work was influenced largely by Donatello and whose skills included sculpture and engraving. Born near Vicenza, he was apprenticed to Francesco Squarcione near Padua and learned methods for achieving perspective and foreshortening in a manner that would be emulated for centuries. Of particular note were his ceiling decorations, especially those in the Camera degli sposi in the Gonzaga ducal palace at Mantua. Giovanni Bellini, his brother-in-law, was influenced by his style as was Albrecht Dürer. Mantegna pursued an interest in humanism and in the revival of classicism. Among his most notable works were *The Agony in the Garden* (1450), *St. Sebastian* (c. 1459), *The Death of the Virgin* (c. 1465), *The Triumph of Caesar* (begun c. 1486), *Madonna della Vittoria* (1495) and *Parnassus* (1497). See also PAINTING, MEDIEVAL.

**MANTUA** A city (Italian Mantova) in Lombardy, northern Italy, surrounded on three sides by lakes formed by the Mincio River. Of Etruscan origin, Mantua was colonized by the Romans (c. 220 B.C.) and came into the hands of various rulers before emerging as a fief of Boniface of Canossa, Marquis of Tuscany, in the 11th century. The status of free commune was earned in 1115 after the death of Matilda of Tuscany. A member of the Lombard League in the 12th century, Mantua was governed from 1276–1328 by the Bonacoli family, who were driven from power by the Gonzagas, who provided the city with security and prestige. See also ITALY.

**MANUEL, DESPOT OF EPIRUS** Ruler from 1230 to about 1240. See also EPIRUS.

**MANUEL I COMNENUS, BYZANTINE EMPEROR** (c. 1122–1180) Ruler from 1143 to 1180, the son of and successor to Emperor John II Comnenus (d. 1143), who attempted to restore Byzantine influence. He encouraged the settlement of Greeks, Venetians and other foreigners at court and achieved diplomatic and military success. He recaptured Corfu from the Normans (1149), received recognition of Byzantine supremacy by the Crusader States of Antioch and Jerusalem (1159) and annexed Croatia, Dalmatia and Bosnia in 1167. He was not successful in his dealings with the Holy Roman Emperors, however, for Emperor Frederick I Barbarossa (1152–1190) proved implacable, and Manuel allied himself with Pope Alexander III (1159–1181) against him. Byzantine influence ended in Italy in 1156, when a combined force of Venetians, Sicilians and Normans allied against him at Brindisi. He was also confronted by the threat of the Seljuk Turks and was

Manuel I Comnenus

blamed for the failure of the Second Crusade (1147–1149) because of his refusal to anger the Turks. Later the Byzantine army was crushed by the Turks at Myriocephalon in 1176, discouraging completely Manuel's ambitions in Asia Minor. See also BYZANTINE EMPIRE.

**MANUEL II PALAEOLOGUS, BYZANTINE EMPEROR** (1350–1425) Ruler from 1391 to 1425, the son of John V Palaeologus (d. 1391), crowned co-emperor as his brother, Andronicus IV, attempted to overthrow John. Manuel was confronted by two more coups, the second attempted by John VII, Andronicus's son. He also had to stem the advance of the Ottoman Turks, who had surrounded the Byzantine Empire, and to that end he sought support from the West. A peace treaty was signed with the Turks in 1403 (which endured until 1421), principally because of the annihilation of a Christian Crusader army at Nicopolis in 1396. Byzantium probably would have been destroyed by the Turks, but Tamerlane (Timur the Lame) was victorious over the Turks in 1402. Manuel visited Rome, Milan, London and Paris but was denied military support from these cities. A patron of the arts, Manuel was a poet and the author of theological treatises. See also BYZANTINE EMPIRE.

**MANUSCRIPT ILLUMINATION** The illustration of folios, codices, a books made of parchment or vellum with miniature paintings and drawings. Those manuscripts represent some of the most brilliant artwork produced between the eras of the early Middle Ages and the 15th century. Early illuminated manuscripts of a Christian nature were found in the late Roman Empire, particularly in the Eastern provinces that were to become part of the Byzantine Empire. These manuscripts, with their traditional use of rich color and gold, influenced subsequent artists in the West, with Ireland and Northumbria providing the finest illuminators. Often they were monks who produced such works as the Books of Lindisfarne, Kells and Durrow (seventh and eighth centuries). These volumes were notable for their marginal celtic designs that consisted of interlacing patterns, counterpointed with mythical and actual animal motifs. There was wide use of large initial letters, decorated with foliage, human figures and scenery.

The succeeding Carolingian era produced books reflective of both the Byzantine and Celtic tradition, writing and illuminating manuscripts in monasteries such as Regensburg, Paris, Reims and Winchester. These reached a peak during the Romanesque period at Reichenau in Switzerland, which was known for its extraordinary productions. After 1200 there was a trend toward the art of miniatures in books, such as the Bible or the Book of Hours. The *Très riches heures de duc de Berry* (c. 1400), produced by Pol of Limbourg and his brother, was probably the most acclaimed of these volumes at the time. The illumination of manuscripts ended with the invention of printing. See also GOTHIC ART AND ARCHITECTURE; ROMANESQUE ART AND ARCHITECTURE; and individual monasteries.

Illuminated manuscript

**MANUTIUS, ALDUS** (1449–1515) Venetian printer and scholar, a member of the Mannusci or Manuzio family, whose name is associated with the Aldine Press, which he established around 1494 or 1495 with the goal of producing inexpensive editions of Greek and Latin classics. Born in Bassiano, Italy, he studied in Rome and Ferrara before settling in Venice in 1490. There he gathered Greek scholars and exiles, and relying on the vast resources of the city, he published editions of Aristotle, Aristophanes, Demosthenes, Euripides, Virgil, Sophocles and Herodotus. His typecutter, Francesco Griffo, designed the first italic typeface, which was used in 1501 in the Aldine publication of Virgil. The symbol of the Aldine Press was a dolphin and an anchor.

**MANZIKERT, BATTLE OF** Engagement fought in August 1071 between the Seljuk Turks led by Alp Arslan (1064–1072) and the Byzantine army of Emperor Romanus IV Diogenes (1067–1071), ending in a major defeat for the Byzantines. Early that year Romanus had launched a campaign against the Armenian Turks, advancing into the region around Lake Van and capturing the fortress of Manzikert (the modern Malazgirt, Turkey). Alp Arslan marched with his army against the Byzantines, sweeping aside the covering forces of General Basilacius, who retreated to the south without informing Emperor Romanus, presumably as part of a plot against him. Alp Arslan compelled Romanus to do battle, and during the night the Turkish mercenaries of the Byzantines deserted. During the battle, Romanus saw his chief lieutenant, Andronicus Ducas, retreat from the field with half of the army. Outnumbered and surrounded as a result of the defections, Romanus was captured and his forces crushed. The consequences of this Turkish victory were enormous, because the intrigues over the imperial succession in Byzantium gave the Seljuks opportunity to overrun most of Anatolia, severely damaging the Byzantine Empire. See also BYZANTINE EMPIRE; SELJUK TURKS.

**MARBURG, CONRAD OF** See CONRAD OF MARBURG.

**MARCEL, ÉTIENNE** (d. 1358) Provost of merchants in Paris and popular French leader who achieved prominence in 1355 by proposing that taxes requested from the States General (the Estates General) by King John II (1350–1364), to continue the war with England, be placed under the control of the assembly. The crushing defeat of the French at Poitiers the following year (including the capture of John II) added strength to his position, and he led the assembly into compelling the dauphin (the future King Charles V) to make major political concessions. The dauphin was bound to agree to grant the council the right to levy and spend taxes and to authorize military levies (the Grande Ordonnance, 1357). Marcel intimidated Charles by having two of his marshals murdered, but he soon lost favor by entering into an alliance with Charles the Bad of Navarre and by supporting the peasant revolt of the Jacquerie. The dauphin fled Paris in 1358, and Marcel began to prepare the city against a siege, but he had lost the support of the States General and was assassinated in July, unable to obtain popular rural support or English aid. See also JACQUERIE.

**MARCH, AUZIÀS** (1397–1459) Catalan poet of the late Middle Ages, who was a major influence on contemporary and later poets of Castile and Catalonia. His verse dealt with the anguish he endured because of his weakness of the flesh and was expressed in images reflecting the conflict between idealism and sensuality. His style was subtle and uncompromising and of a morbid and essentially modern expressionism.

**MARCHE** Also La Marche, a province in central France, comprising the modern departments of Creusse and parts of Haute-Vienne and Indre. Part of Limousin for a long time, Marche became a county in the 10th century, serving as a buffer for the duchy of Aquitaine. In 1199 it belonged to the House of Lusignan and was under its control until 1308, when it became a crown territory. A branch of the Bourbons held Marche from 1342 to 1435, followed by the Armagnacs from 1435 to 1477.

**MARCHES, THE** Region in central Italy situated on the Adriatic Sea and comprising the provinces of Ancona, Piceno, Ascoli, Macerata and Pesaro Urbino. Following the collapse of Roman imperial administration in the West, the region was effectively divided between the Lombards in the south and the Byzantines in the north. The popes received the Marches as part of the Donation of Pepin (756), but in the 10th century the emperors granted fiefs in the region (such as Ancona and Camerino) to serve as border marches, hence the name. Conflict began in the 12th–13th centuries as the popes pressed their claim to the Marches, opposed by the local noble houses, the Malatesta of Rimini and the Montefeltro of Urbino. The papacy acquired the region in the 16th century. See also PAPAL STATES.

**MARGARET, MAID OF NORWAY** (d. 1290) Queen of Scotland from 1283 to 1290, although still a child at the time of her accession. The daughter of King Eric II of Norway (1280–1299) and Margaret (d. 1293), daughter of King Alexander III of Scotland (1249–1286). In 1286, on Alexander's death, Margaret was chosen queen of the Scots by the Scottish lords. A marriage was negotiated by King Edward I (1272–1307) for Margaret and his son, the future Edward II (1307–1327). When Margaret died, however, on the way to Scotland from Norway, civil war erupted, and Edward pressed his claim to the throne of Scotland. See also SCOTLAND.

**MARGARET MAULTASCH** (1318–1369) Duchess of Carinthia and countess of Tyrol, nicknamed Maultasch, or pocket mouth, and called the Ugly Duchess, according to legend a woman of considerable power and propensity for evil. Her reign was long and beset by conflict. She divorced her husband, John, to prevent his brother, Charles (the future Emperor Charles IV), and the Habsburgs from acquiring Tyrol and then married Louis, margrave of Brandenburg, son of Emperor Louis IV of Bavaria (1314–1347). The papacy disagreed with these arrangements, and she was under increasing pressure to retire, following the deposition of Emperor Louis in 1346 and the death of her husband in 1361 and that of her son in 1363. Margaret surrendered Tyrol to Rudolf of Habsburg in 1363, leaving for a convent in Vienna.

**MARGARET OF ANJOU** (1430–1482) Queen consort of Henry VI of England (1422–1461) and one of the central figures in the Wars of the Roses (1455–1485). The daughter of René I of Anjou, she married Henry VI in 1445, emerging as the leader of the royal party and guiding the state herself because of her husband's mental weaknesses. Her opposition to Richard, duke of York, became so bitter that hostilities erupted in 1455, in which Lancastrians were defeated at Saint Albans. Richard administered the government until 1456, when Margaret removed him. Henry was captured in 1460 at Northampton, and Margaret put forth her son Edward's claim to the throne and refused to accept the compromise that named Richard the royal heir. Richard was killed at Wakefield in December 1460, but his son, Edward, took the crown as Edward IV (1461–1483), routing the Lancastrians at Towton in March 1461.

Margaret fled to Scotland and then to France, and from there she negotiated with her former enemy Richard Neville, duke of Warwick (called the King Maker), to overthrow Edward. The plot was initially successful, but Edward retaliated in 1471, and Margaret's faction was crushed at Tewkesbury. Her son was killed and Henry captured and later slain. Imprisoned for a time, Margaret was ransomed by King Louis XI (1461–1483) in 1475, to die penniless in France. See also WARS OF THE ROSES.

**MARGARET OF CARINTHIA** See MARGARET MAULTASCH.

**MARGARET OF DENMARK, NORWAY AND SWEDEN** (1353–1412) One of the most remarkable Scandinavian rulers, responsible for initiating the Kalmar Union (1397). The daughter of King Waldemar IV Atterdag (1340–1375), she was married to King Haakon VI of Norway (1355–1380) at the age of six and began to influence royal government in 1370. In 1375 she had her son Olaf named king of Denmark when he was five. In 1380 Haakon died, and Margaret retained control of both Norway and Denmark as regent for Olaf, becoming queen in 1387 on the death of Olaf. She claimed Sweden a short time later, and her Swedish rival, Albert of Mecklenburg, was defeated in 1389, thus allowing her to be crowned queen of Scandinavia. Adopting as her heir Eric of Pomerania in 1397, Margaret persuaded the governing bodies of the three countries to accept his coronation at Kalmar. Eric was merely a puppet, however, as actual power remained in her hands until her death. Margaret won concessions from the Hanseatic League and reduced the ambitions of the German princes of Holstein. See also KALMAR UNION.

**MARGARET OF PROVENCE** (1221–1295) Queen consort of King Louis IX of France (1226–1270), the daughter of Ramon Berenguer IV of Provence. She wed Louis in 1234. Blanche of Castile had arranged the marriage, which was a true love match. Margaret accompanied Louis on the Seventh Crusade (1248–1254), distinguishing herself at Damietta in 1250 by restoring the morale of the Christian troops after their defeat at al-Mansurah, a rout that included the capture of her husband. See also BLANCHE OF CASTILE.

**MARGARET OF SCOTLAND, SAINT** (c. 1045–1093) Scottish saint and queen consort of King Malcolm III Canmore (reigned 1058–1093) and the daughter of King Edward Aetheling. She was raised at the Hungarian court, to which her father was exiled. Returning to England in 1057, she fled to Scotland in 1066 with her brother, Edgar Aetheling, after the Saxon defeat at the Battle of Hastings. Despite a tendency toward an austere life, she married Malcolm III (c. 1070) but was influential in introducing religious reforms, including conformity with Gregorian Reform, as well as anglicizing the court. Her efforts in ecclesiastical matters and her restoration of monasteries led to her canonization in 1250. See also SCOTLAND.

**MARGRAVATE** See Glossary.

**MARIANUS SCOTUS** (1028–c. 1082) Irish monk and chronicler called originally Moel-Brigte (Irish for "Servant of Brigit"). He joined a Benedictine order in 1052 but was banished from Ireland in 1056 for breaking monastic rules, going to join an Irish monastery at Cologne in 1058, where he was ordained a year later. His last years were spent as a recluse in a monastery in Mainz, where he wrote the valuable *Chronicon,* or *Chronicle,* written in Latin, which was an account of the history of the world from the Creation until the year 1082. The *Chronicle* was popular and presented a useful picture of the Irish monastic movement in Germany.

**MARIE DE FRANCE** Earliest known French poetess, active in the late 12th century as the author of lays, romantic verse narratives and fables drawn from Aesop. It is generally believed that she was born in France but wrote in England, where her works reflected an interest in contemporary affairs.

**MARIENBURG** Town in East Prussia, called in Polish Malbork, established in 1236 by the Teutonic Knights as part of their consolidation of territory in eastern Europe. In 1309 it was designated as the seat of the Grand Master of the Order and was administrative center for the knights. It was sold to Poland in 1457. Marienburg Castle, restored in the 19th century, is a superb example of German medieval architecture. See also TEUTONIC KNIGHTS.

**MARINUS I** (d. 884) Pope from 882 to 884, a Tuscan by birth who served twice as a papal emissary to Constantinople, the second time representing Pope John VIII (872–882), who had named him bishop of Caere (Cerveteri, Italy). He was elected pope following John's assassination and spent much of his pontificate attempting to reconcile with Photius, the condemned patriarch of Constantinople.

**MARINUS II** (d. 946) Pope from 942 to 946, a priest in Rome who was elected to the papacy by Alberic II of Spoleto. Alberic dominated Marinus's pontificate, which encouraged church reform.

**MARMOUSETS** The ministers of King Charles V of France (ruled 1364–1380), translated as "little fellows," a reference to their humble origins. The most prominent Marmouset was Olivier Clisson. These ministers served Charles VI (1380–1422) as well, from 1388 to 1392, when the control of the state became a point of dissension between the Orléanists and the Burgundians. Owing to the mental instability of the king, it was necessary for more competent men to act as advisers. See also FRANCE.

**MARRAKESH** Also Marrakech, a city in southern Morocco, founded in 1062 by Yusuf ibn Tashfin and serving as the capital of the Almoravids until 1147. Subsequent rulers included the Almohad and Marinid dynasties. The city was dominated by a 220-foot minaret of the Koutoubia Mosque, completed about 1195. See also ALMORAVIDS.

**MARSEILLES** In French, Marseille, a port city on the Mediterranean Sea in southern France, probably the oldest of the major French cities, founded around 600 B.C. by the Greeks. Called by the Romans Massilia, the city was annexed by Rome in 49 B.C. and respected as a place of Greek learning. Captured by the Goths in 481, Marseilles underwent subsequent invasions, epidemics and depopulation. Revitalization began in the 10th century under the aegis of the counts of Provence, who promoted building programs that were further necessitated by the embarkation of the Crusader armies from the port. The counts also permitted considerable independence to Marseilles, which purchased the right of self-government early in the 13th century. Charles of Anjou forced the people of the city to acknowledge his domination in 1252. In 1423 the city was sacked by Alfonso V of Aragon (1416–1458), then claimed by the crown with Provence as well in 1481. Marseilles was administered separately from the rest of Provence. See also PROVENCE.

**MARSHAL, WILLIAM** See PEMBROKE, WILLIAM MARSHAL, EARL OF.

**MARSILIUS OF PADUA** (d. 1342 or 1343) Italian political scholar and author of the controversial treatise *Defensor pacis (Defender of the Peace).* Born in Padua, he was educated at the University of Paris and then spent time in northern Italy and Avignon. He probably practiced medicine in Paris from 1320, writing *Defensor pacis* between 1320 and 1324, most likely with the collaboration of John of Jandun. The contents of the treatise sparked a major controversy, and Marsilius fled to the court of the recently excommunicated Louis IV of Bavaria. He was excommunicated as a heretic by Pope John XXII (1316–1334) the following year. Marsilius accompanied Louis on his Italian expedition (1327–1329), supporting the removal of John XXII in favor of Nicholas V (an antipope), and held the post of imperial vicar. He spent the remaining years of his life at court in Munich.

*Defensor pacis* was one of the most influential and original works of the Middle Ages, based on Aristotle's work and presenting political theory that foreshadowed not only the Reformation but many concepts of modern democracy. Marsilius called the state, not the church, the unifying factor in society, believing the church must be held separate from the state and subordinate to it. The treatise also supported the concept that the state received its power from the people. Marsilius also believed that the church should derive its authority in ecclesiastical and moral matters from a general council, composed of clerics and laymen. In essence, these concepts ran counter to the established thinking of the time, actually contrary to the tenets on which medieval society was based. His commentaries brought about his condemnation by the church but won admiration from future reformers and political thinkers.

**MARTEL, CHARLES** See CHARLES MARTEL.

**MARTIANUS CAPELLA** Fifth-century Latin writer. A pagan, Martianus wrote a long allegory, *The Marriage of Mercury and Philology,* an introduction to the seven liberal arts. The work was both popular and influential throughout the Middle Ages.

**MARTIN I** (d. 655) Pope from 649 to 653, elected successor to Pope Theodore I (642–649) without the approval of the Byzantine emperor Constans II (641–668). Martin, attempting to settle the controversy concerning the heresy of Monothelitism, convened a Lateran Council in 649, condemning that heresy as well as the *Typos,* the order of the emperor forbidding discussion of the matter. In 653 Constans ordered Martin's arrest, bringing him to Constantinople, where the pope was humiliated (654) and then deposed and banished to the Crimea (654). He died in Cherson, Crimea, in 655 and was ranked as the last papal martyr.

**MARTIN II** See MARINUS I.

**MARTIN III** See MARINUS II.

**MARTIN IV** (c. 1220–1285) Pope from 1281 to 1285, originally Simon de Brie, a nobleman and trusted adviser to King Louis IX of France (1226–1270), also chancellor and Keeper of the Great Seal in 1260. Elected as successor to Nicholas III (1277–1280), Martin owed his position to Charles of Anjou, whom he restored to the Kingdom of Naples and whose policies he espoused. Pope Martin thus agreed with Charles that the only way to bring about a permanent reunion with the Eastern Church was to conquer Byzantium. Martin excommunicated Emperor Michael VIII Palaeologus (1259–1282) in 1282, thereby ending any hope of reunion through negotiation. Following the Aragonese victory in war of the Sicilian Vespers (1282), he attempted to support Charles, eventually turning his attention to the defeat of Aragon. He died without having accomplished that end.

**MARTIN V** (1368–1431) Pope from 1417 to 1431, born Oddo Colonna, elected by the Council of Constance to end the Great Schism of 1378–1417. Through diplomacy, military action and sheer force of will, Martin restored the Western Church and the papacy. Rejecting conciliarism, he declared the Holy See to be the final authority. The Curia was reorganized, and control over the Papal States was strengthened. His task was made easier after the defeat of the papal vicar and soldier Braccio de Montone in 1424. Martin also summoned the Council of Pavia in 1423 but opposed it and finally secured its dissolution. In matters of European affairs, he attempted to organize crusades against the Hussites and to act as mediator in the Hundred Years' War. His pontificate was opposed by the antipopes Benedict XIII (1394–1417) and Clement VIII (1423–1429). The Council of Basel was summoned by Martin just before his death.

**MARTIN I, KING OF ARAGON** (d. 1410) Ruler of Aragon from 1395 to 1410, called "the Humane." Martin and his son, Martin the Younger, king of Sicily, attempted to pacify unrest in their Aragonese possessions in Sicily and Sardinia. In 1408 Martin the Younger defeated the viscount of Narbonne in his attempts to take Sardinia but died the following year. His father was thus deprived of an heir and died in 1410 without appointing a successor. Martin was the last male heir of the house of Barcelona (1137–1410). After a two-year interregnum the Castilian Trastámara family succeeded to the Aragonese throne. See also ARAGON.

**MARTINI, SIMONE** (c. 1284–1344) Italian painter of Siena, an early master of the Gothic style probably studying with Duccio di Buoninsegna. His earliest documented work was the large fresco the *Maesta* (1315) in the Sala del Mappamondo of the Palazzo Publico in Siena. In 1317 in Naples he worked on the altarpiece *St. Louis Crowning His Brother, King Robert of Anjou* and painted a Madonna polytych two years later. Of particular note was his 1328 portrait of Guidoriccio da Fogliano (general of Siena), an equestrian work that established a stylistic precedent for the Renaissance. Settling in Avignon (1340), Martini became a friend of Petrarch and was attached to the papal court.

**MARWAN I** (c. 623–685) Fourth Umayyad caliph for the brief period 684–685, a secretary to the caliph Uthman (reigned 644–656) who was severely wounded while attempting to defend Uthman from assassination. During the rule of the caliph Mu'awiya (ruled 661–680) he held the post of governor of Medina and the Hijaz but was viewed with suspicion for being ambitious. He fled to Syria during the rule of Yazid I and was acclaimed caliph on Yazid's death in 683. Marwan's major efforts were to strengthen the unity of the Umayyad government and to regain lost territories, most notably Egypt. See also UMAYYAD CALIPHATE.

**MARWAN II** (d. 750) The last of the Umayyad caliphs, reigning from 744 to 750, the son of an Umayyad governor and a Kurdish slave girl, coming to power in 744 after claiming victory in a civil war following the death of Yazid III. After the resignation of Ibrahim (744) Marwan was proclaimed caliph at Damascus.

His reign was beset by rebellions and disorders as the Umayyad empire collapsed. Finally, in 750, at the Battle of Zab, he was defeated by the Abbasids and fled toward Egypt. Marwan was captured and executed, the last of the Umayyad dynasty, which had ruled from 661. See also UMAYYAD CALIPHATE.

**MARY OF BURGUNDY** (1456–1482) Heiress of Burgundy and daughter of Duke Charles the Bold (1467–1477), gaining control of Burgundian lands in 1477 after the death of her father in battle. She was confronted by an immediate threat in King Louis XI of France (1461–1483), who seized Burgundy and Picardy. To check his next ambitions, Mary issued the Grand Privilege restoring the rights and autonomy of the provinces of Holland, Brabant and Hainaut. In response to Louis's demands that she marry the future Charles VIII of France (1483–1498), Mary married instead Archduke Maximilian (later Maximilian I), thus gaving the Habsburgs control of the Netherlands. See also BURGUNDY, DUCHY OF.

**MASACCIO, TOMMASO** (1401–1428) Florentine painter and one of the early masters of the Italian Renaissance, born Tommaso di Giovanni di Simone Guidi, given the name Masaccio ("Slovenly Tom") because of his appearance. His style was influenced by Giotto, Brunelleschi and Donatello, and he became expert in the art of perspective and in his naturalistic treatment of figures and landscapes. His genius was evident in his fresco of the Trinity (1425–1427) for the Santa Maria Novella in Florence and the frescoes for the Brancacci Chapel of Santa Maria del Carmine, Florence. He was a forerunner of Michelangelo, but his career was cut short by his early death.

**MASOLINO DA PANICALE** (c. 1383–c. 1447) Italian painter born Tommaso di Cristoforo Fini. Trained in Florence, probably with Lorenzo Ghiberti, he perhaps worked on the baptistery doors there (1403–1407). A colleague of Masaccio's, he began work on the *Virgin and Child with St. Anne,* dated at about 1423. Collaborating on other works for a time, he went to Hungary in 1427, returning to Florence to complete work in the Brancacci Chapel in the Church of Santa Maria del Carmine in Florence (1425–1427), abandoning it again in 1428. On the death of Masaccio, Masolino reverted to his own decorative style in the International Gothic tradition.

**MAS'UD I** (d. 1156) Sultan of the Seljuks of Rum from 1117 to 1157, the son of Qilij Arslan I. Unable to oppose the accession of his uncle, Malik Shah I (1107–1117), after the death of his father in 1107, he was held a hostage at times at the court of the Danismends. By marrying a Danismend princess in 1116, he obtained support in overthrowing Malik Shah. In 1125, however, he was toppled by his brother, Arap, long a prisoner of the Great Seljuks. Mas'ud fled to Constantinople, where he was allowed to mount another campaign to win his throne. Supported again by his father-in-law, he defeated Arap (who went into exile in Constantinople). Subsequent relations with the Byzantines were sound, to such a degree that the empire gave little support to the Second Crusade (1147–1149). Mas'ud thus was free to defeat Emperor Conrad III (1137–1152) at Dorylaeum in 1147 and King Louis VII of France (1137–1380) in 1148. On his death in 1156, the sultanate of Rum was strong and influential. Mas'ud was succeeded by Qilij Arslan II (1156–1193). See also SELJUK TURKS.

**MAS'UD II** (d. c. 1298) Seljuk sultan of Rum (1276–1283) who shared the sultanate with his cousin, Kayqubad III, ruling over the eastern provinces. His reign was dedicated chiefly to attempts to acquire Kayqubad's territory, an effort continued by his son, Mas'ud III. See also SELJUK TURKS.

**MAS'UD III** (d. 1308) Son of Mas'ud II who contended with the sultan Kayqubad III for control of the sultanate of Rum. The conflict raged even after the death of Kayqubad in 1302, levied against his heir, but ended in 1308 with Mas'ud's assassination. See also SELJUK TURKS.

**MATILDA** (1102–1167) Also called Maud, the daughter of King Henry I of England (1100–1135) and mother of King Henry II (1154–1189). She married Emperor Henry V (1106–1125) in 1114 but was widowed in 1125. Three years later she was convinced to marry Geoffrey Plantagenet of Anjou. Designated as the successor by Henry I after his death in 1135, Matilda was opposed by Stephen of Blois, a cousin. Invading England in 1139, she captured Stephen in 1141 but soon lost ground because of her political arrogance and endless demands for money. Stephen was released and resumed the throne, and Matilda retired to Normandy, to see her son crowned in 1154. See also ENGLAND.

**MATILDA, COUNTESS OF TUSCANY** (1046–1115) A major ally of Pope Gregory VII (1073–1085) in his struggle with Emperor Henry IV (1056–1106) over the Investiture Controversy, continuing her support of the papacy after Gregory's death in 1085. Her castle at Canossa was the scene in 1077 of Henry's humiliation and plea for papal absolution. Matilda joined the opposition to Henry after his excommunication in 1080, sending part of her treasury to Rome to finance the papal endeavors. Marrying Welf V, duke of Bavaria, in 1089, Matilda emerged as the leader of the Guelph (Welf) cause, encouraging Henry's son, Conrad, to rebel against him. Matilda, who had made the papacy heir to her domains, made peace with Henry V (1106–1125) in 1110, giving him her lands instead. On her death, these territories, called Matildine, were the source of still another controversy between pope and emperor.

**MATTHEW OF AQUASPARTA** (d. 1302) Franciscan philosopher and theologian, born in Umbria, Italy. He joined the Franciscans, studying at Todi and at Paris under Saint Bonaventure. Lector of the Sacred Palace in Rome in

1281, he became minister general of the Franciscans in 1287 and cardinal in 1288. He wrote sermons, biblical commentaries and a treatise on the *Sentences of Peter Lombard* and was a defender of the Augustinian tradition.

**MATTHEW PARIS** See PARIS, MATTHEW.

**MATTHIAS I CORVINUS** (1443–1490) King of Hungary from 1458 to 1490, responsible for a number of social and political reforms and for bringing Hungary into the Renaissance. A son of the celebrated Hungarian hero János Hunyadi (d. 1455), he was elected ruler by the Diet in 1458 but soon faced war as pretenders challenged him, especially Emperor Frederick II (1215–1250), with whom he was engaged in conflict for many years. By 1464 he was secure enough to be crowned and five years later inherited the crown of Bohemia through his wife, the daughter of George of Podiebrad. Matthias reigned there until 1478, when he surrendered the throne to the Jagiello claimant from Poland, adding large territories to Hungary in the meantime, including Moravia, Silesia, Carinthia, Styria and Vienna, the last chosen as his capital after driving out Frederick in 1485. His military success was made possible by his powerful standing force, the Black Army, commanded by "Black" John Haugwitz.

Within Hungary Matthias encouraged industry and major reforms in government and finance. The arts and learning were promoted, and the University of Budapest was founded in 1475. His library was thought by many contemporary scholars to be the largest and most impressive ever assembled, and many Italian writers journeyed to his court to study and copy his books. Matthias died suddenly at Vienna on April 6, 1490, while attempting to settle the question of succession. Hungary's position as the major power in central Europe did not long survive his death. See also HUNGARY.

**MAUREGATUS** Ruler of Asturias from 783 to 788, successor to Silo (ruled 774–783). Mauregatus was a little-known king who maintained peace with the Moors.

**MAURICE** (d. 602) Byzantine emperor from 582 to 602, born in Cappadocia and entering the imperial government as a notary and eventually distinguishing himself as a general. Marrying Constantine, daughter of Emperor Tiberius II (578–582), he was crowned just before Tiberius's death. He embarked on military campaigns and introduced significant administrative reforms immediately. After supporting Khosrow II (Chosroes II) in his attempt to claim the Persian throne, peace was signed with Persia. He next turned to the Avars and Slavs who had settled in the Balkans, and in Italy and Africa he instituted new provincial systems, called exarchates, controlled by military governors and designed to halt the advance of the Lombards in Italy and the Berbers in Africa. His increase in taxation, however, prompted an uprising in 602, in which Maurice was killed and replaced by Phocas. See also BYZANTINE EMPIRE.

**MAXIMILIAN** (1459–1519) German king and Holy Roman Emperor from 1493 to 1519, who raised the Habsburgs to prominence in Europe. The son of Emperor Frederick III (1440–1493), he was elected king of the Romans in 1486, receiving from his father the bulk of imperial authority and duties. German king after the death of his father in 1493, Maximilian was never crowned emperor but claimed the title in 1508. Through marriages he obtained extensive territories for the Habsburgs. From Mary of Burgundy (1471) he acquired the Low Countries, but his unions with Anne of Brittany (by proxy) in 1490 and the niece of Ludovico Sforza in 1493 brought him into war with France. Campaigns in Italy were failures and taxed his financial resources, and he was never able to overcome the Ottoman Turks, although he stabilized the Danube region. Maximilian introduced constitutional reforms in the empire and at his death held Austria, the Netherlands, Bohemia, Hungary and the Spanish empire. His reign saw the transition of the Holy Roman Empire from the Middle Ages to the modern era, and as patron of humanism and German art he was called the Last of the Knights. See also HOLY ROMAN EMPIRE.

**MAXIMUS THE CONFESSOR** (c. 580–662) Byzantine theologian and writer, serving Emperor Heraclius (610–41) until becoming a monk (c. 614) at the monastery of Chrysopolis. Fleeing to Africa in 626 during the Persian invasion, Maximus opposed the heresy of Monothelitism at African synods and at the Lateran Council in 649. With Pope Martin I (649–655), he was arrested and exiled to Thrace in 653, by Emperor Constans II (641–668). Recalled in 661, he remained adamant against the heresy, thereby being punished with the loss of his tongue and right hand. He was banished to the Caucasus, where he died. Maximus wrote many works (about 90) on theology, mysticism and doctrine, including *Ambigua* on Gregory of Nazianzus and *Opuscula theologica et polemica (Short Theological and Polemical Treatises).*

**MAZARIN BIBLE** Also called the Gutenburg, or 42-line, Bible, probably the first book printed by Gutenburg from movable type at Mainz, about 1456. A magnificent work with folio pages of two columns having 42 lines each, it was printed in Gothic typeface and illuminated. The name was derived from the place of the Bible's discovery, in the library of the French cardinal Mazarin (d. 1661). See also GUTENBURG, JOHANN.

**MECKLENBURG** German territory situated on the Baltic Sea, originally populated by Germans. In the seventh century the Wends and Slavic Obodrites occupied the town, which was reclaimed by the German duke of Saxony, Henry the Lion, in 1160, with a native prince, the son of the defeated Obodrite ruler, named as vassal to Henry. Thus the Mecklenburg dynasty was founded, its members becoming dukes and princes of the empire in 1348, ordered by the German king Charles IV. In 1358 the counts of Schwerin were added. Christianity was introduced in the late 12th century, as well as German colonization and culture. A university was founded at Rostock in 1419. See also GERMANY.

**MEDICI, COSIMO DE'** See MEDICI, HOUSE OF.

**MEDICI, HOUSE OF** Italian family dominating Florence from the 15th century until 1737, producing notable figures in Italian political history as well as influential patrons of Renaissance arts and learning. The house emerged from obscurity in early-13th-century Florence, amassing great wealth as bankers and merchants. Allying themselves with the lower classes against the guild merchants and artisans allowed the Medici to exert nearly total control of the Florentine state throughout the 15th century, despite the outward adherence of the city to its democratic constitution. The Medici were exiled from 1494 to 1512 and again from 1527 to 1530, but in each instance they returned and reestablished their supremacy, although never holding any official position. Important members of the Medici were Giovanni di Bicci de Medici (d. 1429) ancestor of both the junior and senior lines of the family, whose efforts brought the Medicis to political prominence; Cosimo de Medici (1389–1464), son of Giovanni di Bicci, who was the first member of the family to rule Florence, exerting as little pressure as possible on the city while also a patron of the arts and learning; Lorenzo de' Medici, Cosimo's grandson, called "il Magnifico," who attained preeminence in the Renaissance for political and cultural patronage. The Medici also produced four popes: Leo X, Clement VII, Pius IV and Leo XI, as well as two queens of France, Catherine de' Medici and Marie de' Medici. See also FLORENCE.

**MEDICI, LORENZO DE'** See MEDICI, HOUSE OF.

**MEDICINE** The healing art, the study of which declined in the ancient world from the time of Galen (130–201) to the era contemporaneous with the fall of Rome in the fifth century. Nevertheless, while the study of medical arts underwent a long period of inactivity, in the East it was pursued in the writings of Oribasius (325–403) and in the work of Arab scholars.

It was thought that the church did much to hinder medical progress in the early Middle Ages, for disease was viewed as retribution for sin, curable by penance and prayer. While this view was certainly prevalent at the time, the church also provided much-needed care, and, more important, the monasteries were responsible for the preservation and transcription of Greek medical texts. Outside the monasteries, in the West, medical practice and study were pursued within the Jewish communities.

In the East, medical teachings in classical texts were translated into the Arabic by scholars with the patronage of Islamic leaders. These writers were not uniquely Arab, for they included Jews, Christians and Muslims from many regions in the Islamic world, from Persia to Spain. Many prominent figures in medicine arose, including Al Rhazes (c. 860–932), a Persian; Avicenna (980–1037), called the Prince of Physicians; and Averroës (1126–1198), a philosopher. Jewish physicians and translators contributed to the dissemination of texts to the Western world, and the medical school at Córdoba, associated with those in Cairo and Baghdad, was a respected institution. The practice of surgery in Córdoba was enhanced by the brilliant physician Abulcasis (Abu al-Qasim), and excellent commentaries were written by the Jewish practitioner and philosopher Maimonides, who was the personal physician to Saladin.

The practice of the classical tradition in medicine was encouraged with the establishment of the first organized school of medicine in Europe in the 10th century at Salerno. Soon after its founding other institutions were established at Montpellier, Paris, Bologna and Padua. Scholars flocked to Salerno to study, among them Constantine the African. In 1221, Emperor Frederick II (1215–1250) decreed that no medicine could be practiced until the physician had been approved by the teachers at Salerno. Around 1200, however, Salerno was surpassed by Montpellier as new techniques and innovations were added. Among the medical pioneers of the 13th and 14th centuries were Roger Bacon, Albertus Magnus, Guy de Chauliac, and Mondino de'Luzzi of Bologna, who wrote the *Anothania* (1316), the first work to deal exclusively with the study of anatomy. The period of the Renaissance, with its emphasis on discovery and anatomical accuracy in its art, encouraged the continued revival of classical learning and exploration in medical fields.

**MEDINA** City located in the Hijaz region of Saudi Arabia (see ARABIA), considered one of the two most holy places in Islam, with Mecca, some 250 miles to the south. Medina was probably established around 135 at an oasis and was called Yathrib before the rise of Islam. The city became historically important as the place to which Muhammad fled in 622 from Mecca, during the Hegira. Renamed Medina (Arabic, al-Madinah from al-Madinah al-Mudawwarah for the "Most Glorious City"), it became prominent in the developing Islamic state, serving as the residence of the first three caliphs. In 661 it was replaced by Damascus as the administrative heart of the Islamic empire, governed locally by its emirs. An important place of pilgrimage, Medina is the site of the tomb of the Prophet in the Prophet's Mosque.

**MEHMET I** (d. 1421) Sultan of the Ottomans from 1402 to 1413, ruling alone after 1413. Following the defeat of the Ottomans at Ankara in 1402, Timur the Lame (Tamerlane) divided the territory of the Ottoman sultanate between the sons of the vanquished Bayazid I (1389–1403). Mehmet was granted Amasya, while his other brothers, Isa and Suleyman, were granted their shares. The next years were spent attempting to reunify the Ottoman domain. Isa was defeated in 1404–1405, and Suleyman in 1410. Another brother, Musa, who had defeated Suleyman, was vanquished in 1413, with Byzantine support. Mehmet consolidated his kingdom, dominating Asia Minor and retaining a strong presence in the Balkans, including the reduction of Wallachia in 1416 and campaigns into Albania and Hungary. See also OTTOMAN EMPIRE.

**MEHMET II** (1432–1481) Sultan from 1444 to 1446 and from 1451 to 1481, earning the name Fatih, or "the Conqueror." He is considered the ruler responsible for establishing the Ottoman Empire, while introducing major reforms in the government. Born at Adrianople (Edirne), the fourth son of Sultan Murad II (1421–1444; 1446–1451), he ascended the throne in 1446 when his father abdicated. A large allied Christian army crossed the Danube River in

Mehmet II, from Topkapi Saray Museum

September 1444, and Murad took command, winning a victory at Varna on November 10. Murad was forced to retain control until his death in 1451, whereupon Mehmet ruled again. He punished certain elements that had opposed his rule and then set out to besiege Constantinople. His preparations were extensive and meticulous, including the building of a fleet of galleys and the forging of massive cannons. The siege lasted from April 6 until May 29, 1453, ending with the fall of the ancient city. He allowed his troops to sack Constantinople but then rode through the gates to the Hagia Sophia, which he declared a mosque thereby ushering in a new era of Ottoman supremacy in Constantinople (modern Istanbul), now its capital.

For the remainder of his reign he extended his conquests, marching across Asia Minor, the Balkans and into Hungary, Wallachia, Moldavia and the Crimean region. With victory came consolidation and extensive reorganization of the Ottoman government. Mehmet encouraged tolerance, restoring the Christian patriarchate and establishing religious offices for his Jewish and Armenian subjects. Constantinople was rebuilt and repopulated, and foreign merchants were urged to return. Mehmet was also a patron of arts and letters, and Italian and Greek scholars were invited to his court. Learning was encouraged. The laws were also codified into two major codes, the basis for all Ottoman law. He died on May 3, 1481, near Maltepe, reportedly from complications from gout, although he was possibly poisoned. See also OTTOMAN EMPIRE.

**MEINRAD** See EINSIEDELN, ABBEY OF.

**MEISSEN** City on the Elbe River in Saxony, originally a Slavic community called Misni and then a German settlement, established in 929 by Henry I. In 965 Meissen became the seat of the margravate of Meissen, claimed in the late 11th century by the Wettin dynasty, later Electors of Saxony. See also GERMANY.

**MEISTERSINGERS** German poets and musicians from the 14th to the 16th century who were members of artist and trade guilds. The Meistersingers (German for "master singers") claimed to be the successors to the minnesingers, founded supposedly by Heinrich of Meissen (or Frauenlob) as heirs to the 12 old masters. Organized into guildlike groups, called *Singschülen* (song schools), they existed to perpetuate their craft, principally by holding song competitions, usually in churches. Compositions, however, had to adhere to specific rules *(Tablatus)* concerning subject matter, meter and language, so that originality or spontaneity was not encouraged. Rather, the formal model of earlier poets was followed so assiduously that there was a decline in the art in time. Changes were made in the early 16th century when new musical forms and subjects were permitted, a practice initiated by Hans Tolz of Worms. Hans Sachs was the most notable Meistersinger, but the field itself was never widely approved by professional musicians, humanists or much of the population. See also MINNESINGERS.

**MEMLING, HANS** (d. 1494) Flemish painter and an acclaimed member of the Bruges school in his era, possibly a student of Roger van der Weyden. Born in Seligenstadt near Frankfurt, he settled at Bruges and was possibly influenced by Dirk Bouts and the van Eycks. The Medicis of Florence and officials of the Hanseatic League were his patrons. Especially proficient in his work on altarpieces and portraits, Memling used a style that was quite harmonious, which he never altered, making the dating of his works difficult. Among his works were the *Portinary Triptych* (c. 1470), triptych with *The Virgin and Child with Saints and Donors* (c. 1475), *Adoration of the Magi* (1479) and his last major commission, the *Passion Triptych* (1491).

**MENANDER PROTECTOR** Sixth-century Byzantine historian who wrote a valuable history continuing a work begun by Agathias. Written at the request of Emperor Maurice (ruled 582–602), the work began where Agathias's ended, in 558. It thus covered the advance of the Kotrigur Huns into Thrace in 558 and the negotiations with the Avars concerning Sirmium in 582. While extant only in fragments, it has served as a useful source on sixth-century events.

**MENDICANT ORDERS** Religious begging orders, those organizations forbidden to own property and thus having to work or beg for food. They came into being in the 12th century as part of the reaction against the corruption and materialism of the church, and members renounced all worldly possessions and supported themselves through charity or labor, in imitation of Christ's attitude toward poverty. The Franciscans and Dominicans were the earliest mendicants, although there were also later orders, such as the Carmelites and the Augustinians, which were approved by Alexander IV in 1256. Generally active in towns, they were opposed by local prelates and other clergy because of their popularity and the privileges permitted them, including the right to hear confession and to preach. The orders were also permitted other exemptions from episcopal authority. The term *friar* came to be used for such men, instead of monks, from the Latin *frater*, meaning brother, which suggested their bond with the laity.

**MERCEDARIANS** Spanish religious order founded by Saint Peter Nolasco about 1220. The name was derived from the Order of Our Lady of Mercy (Orden de Nuestra Señora de la Merced). The Mercedarians cared for the ill and were especially active in rescuing Christians who had been taken prisoner by the Muslims. If necessary, the Mercedarians offered themselves as replacements or hostages.

**MERCIA, KINGDOM OF** One of the realms of Anglo-Saxon England that eventually encompassed the lands from the Welsh border to the North Sea, from the Humber to the Thames and East Anglia, essentially the Midlands. It was the dominant political entity in England from the mid-seventh to the ninth century, probably established by the Angles, who moved into the region around 500. During the reign of King Penda (d. 654) it achieved independence from Northumbria, extending political control over East Anglia and Wessex. Further advances were made by Aethelbald (ruled 716–757), but true prominence was achieved by Offa (ruled 757–796), who reigned over a Mercian kingdom encompassing nearly all of England. He accepted the fealty of Essex, East Anglia and, for a time, Kent. Only Northumbria escaped his grasp, and even Charlemagne, with whom he was in communication, considered him an equal. Offa constructed a massive dike (Offa's Dike), which was intended to serve as a defensive barrier against Wales. After his death, however, decline set in, as Mercia lost influence concurrent with the rise of Wessex. The Danes began their attacks in the ninth century, and part of the region was included in the Danelaw (886). In the early 10th century, the Danish-held territory was reconquered by Edward the Elder, who placed Mercia under the governorship of ealdormen loyal to the Saxons. See also ENGLAND.

**MEROVINGIAN ART AND ARCHITECTURE** An artistic period in Frankish lands from the fifth to the seventh century and named for the Merovingian kings. An influential art form, the Merovingian style was characterized by a blend of Germanic and Roman classical traditions. Little of it has survived, however. The artists' talents lay particularly in metalworking and in manuscripts. Metalwork included jewelry and religious articles, most found in burial sites. Manuscripts contained exceptionally intricate lettering and animal motifs. Among the finest of their extant manuscripts was the Gellone Sacramentary (eighth century). Merovingian art, while limited in scope and duration, had a lingering influence on European artistic development, especially in the succeeding Carolingian period.

**MEROVINGIAN DYNASTY** Ruling line of the Franks from 481 to 751, founded by Clovis (481–511), who claimed descent from Merovis, the legendary chief of the Salian Franks. The Merovingian line was plagued by political instability, arising principally from the Frankish custom of dividing the kingdom among all male heirs. Thus were established the smaller kingdoms of Austrasia, Neustria, Burgundy, Paris, Orléans and Aquitaine. Civil wars were common. The last strong Merovingian king was Dagobert I (ruled 630–633). After him the Merovingians were called the "lazy kings," leaving government affairs to be administered by the mayors of the palace. In 751 Pepin the Short received papal approval to depose Childeric III, the last of the Merovingian dynasts. See also FRANCE; Genealogical Table.

**MERSEN, TREATY OF** Agreement of 870 between Charles II the Bald (843–877) of the West Franks (France) and Louis the German (843–876) of the East Franks (Germany), dividing the kingdom of Lotharingia (Lorraine) between them. The treaty thus deprived the rightful heir, Lothair II (855–869), of his inheritance and altered the tripartite division of the Carolingian empire created by the Treaty of Verdun in 843.

Merovingian castle

**MERTON, WALTER DE** (d. 1277) English bishop and founder of Merton College, Oxford. He established the House of Scholars at Malden, Surrey, having received a charter in 1264. Merton College was transferred to Oxford, and its administration was a model for other colleges established there. See also OXFORD.

**METHODIUS** See CYRIL AND METHODIUS, SAINTS.

**METOCHITES, GEORGE** (d. c. 1328) Byzantine theologian and writer who encouraged the union of the Eastern and Western Churches, the representative of Emperor Michael VIII Palaeologus (1259–1282) to Rome and Pope Gregory X (1271–1276). He had a hand in writing the decree of unification at the Council of Lyons in 1274. In 1282, however, Emperor Andronicus II Palaeologus (1282–1328) reversed imperial policy (with broad popular and religious support), and Metochites was arrested and banished to Nicomedia. Metochites wrote the valuable *Historia dogmatica,* an examination of the schism between the Latin and Greek churches. See also SCHISMS.

**METOCHITES, THEODORE** (d. 1332) Byzantine minister, the son of George Metochites, who earned the favor of Emperor Andronicus II Palaeologus (1282–1328), despite his father's exile. Theodore directed peace negotiations with the Serbs in order to ask their help in defending the Byzantine Empire from the advancing Ottoman Turks. He became "Grand Logothete" as a result, a chancellor, and from 1321 until the fall of Andronicus in 1328 virtually administered the state. In the reign of Andronicus III his wealth was dissipated, and he was banished to Chora monastery, where he retired in 1331. A prolific writer, Metochites produced works on physics, astronomy, philosophy, history, rhetoric and poetry. See also BYZANTINE EMPIRE.

**METZ** City in northeastern France, in Upper Lorraine, at the confluence of the Moselle and Seille Rivers, the major city of the Gallic tribe of the Mediomatrici. Metz was for many years a forward post of the Roman Empire along the Rhine River, and Christianity was introduced there in the third century. The city was attacked by the Huns in 451, and the Franks assumed control in the early sixth century. Metz received both a bishopric and designation as the capital of Austrasia. With the division of the Carolingian empire in 843, with the Treaty of Verdun, it was granted to Lothair, who made it part of his kingdom (see LOTHARINGIA). The bishops of Metz ruled extensive territory as a fief of the Holy Roman Empire, but in the 13th century the city was free, growing prosperous enough for Emperor Charles IV (1346–1378) to issue his Golden Bull there in 1356. Many medieval buildings remain, including the Gothic cathedral of Saint-Ètienne and the Porte des Allemands (Gate of the Germans). See also HOLY ROMAN EMPIRE.

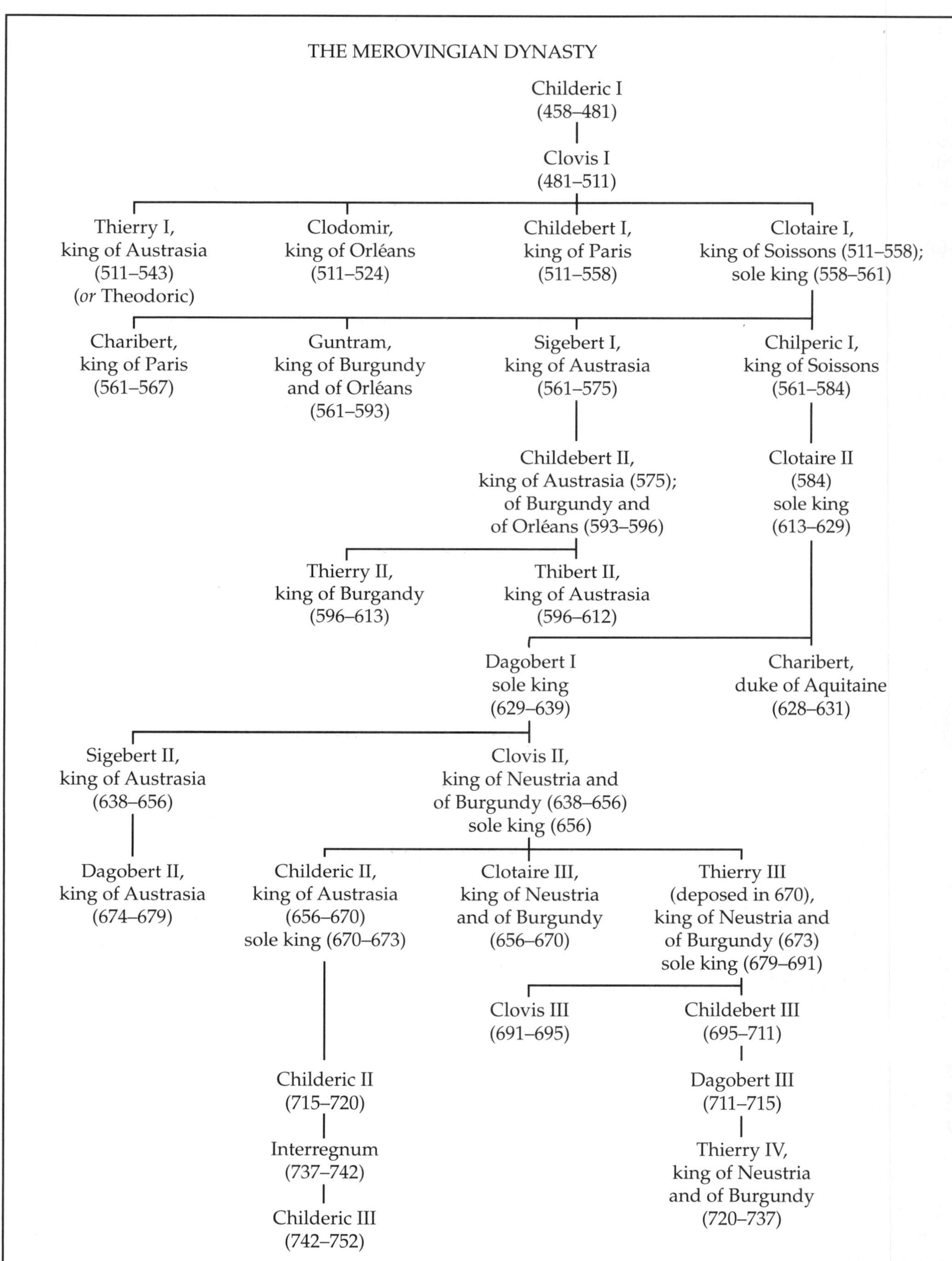
THE MEROVINGIAN DYNASTY
Childeric I
(458–481)
Clovis I
(481–511)
Thierry I,
king of Austrasia
(511–543)
(*or* Theodoric)
Clodomir,
king of Orléans
(511–524)
Childebert I,
king of Paris
(511–558)
Clotaire I,
king of Soissons (511–558);
sole king (558–561)
Charibert,
king of Paris
(561–567)
Guntram,
king of Burgundy
and of Orléans
(561–593)
Sigebert I,
king of Austrasia
(561–575)
Chilperic I,
king of Soissons
(561–584)
Childebert II,
king of Austrasia (575);
of Burgundy and
of Orléans (593–596)
Clotaire II
(584)
sole king
(613–629)
Thierry II,
king of Burgandy
(596–613)
Thibert II,
king of Austrasia
(596–612)
Dagobert I
sole king
(629–639)
Charibert,
duke of Aquitaine
(628–631)
Sigebert II,
king of Austrasia
(638–656)
Clovis II,
king of Neustria and
of Burgundy (638–656)
sole king (656)
Dagobert II,
king of Austrasia
(674–679)
Childeric II,
king of Austrasia
(656–670)
sole king (670–673)
Clotaire III,
king of Neustria
and of Burgundy
(656–670)
Thierry III
(deposed in 670),
king of Neustria and
of Burgundy (673)
sole king (679–691)
Clovis III
(691–695)
Childebert III
(695–711)
Childeric II
(715–720)
Dagobert III
(711–715)
Interregnum
(737–742)
Thierry IV,
king of Neustria
and of Burgundy
(720–737)
Childeric III
(742–752)

**MICHAEL I RANGABE, BYZANTINE EMPEROR** Ruler from 811 to 813, the son-in-law of Emperor Nicephorus I (802–811), who succeeded him after the death of the heir, Stauracius. He opposed the iconoclasts and recognized the title of emperor assumed by Charlemagne, in thanks for which he was given Venice and other land grants in the Adriatic region. His support of the use of icons brought about an uprising in Constantinople, delaying his response to the advancing Bulgars led by Krum in 812. In 813 he was severely defeated by the Bulgars near Adrianople, in part because of the desertion of his troops led by Leo the Armenian, who deposed Michael and took the crown. Michael retired to a monastery. See also BYZANTINE EMPIRE.

**MICHAEL II, BYZANTINE EMPEROR** (d. 829) Ruler from 820 to 829, founder of the Amorian dynasty and a Phrygian by birth. Long a friend of Leo (V) the Armenian (813–820), Michael fell out of favor in 820 and was sentenced to death by being hurled into a furnace. Before the execution could take place, however, Leo was murdered, and Michael was raised to the throne. During his reign he had to suppress a bitter rebellion, leaving the empire financially drained. The result was the loss of Crete to the Arabs (c. 826) and severe raids in Sicily by the Saracens. Michael II's approach to the controversy surrounding iconoclasticism was one of moderation. See also BYZANTINE EMPIRE.

**MICHAEL III, BYZANTINE EMPEROR** (838–867) Ruler from 842 to 867, called "the Amorian" or "Phrygian," also "the Drunkard." Recorded by Byzantine chroniclers as cruel and dissolute, Michael nonetheless achieved victories for the empire. The son of Emperor Theophilus (829–842), he became emperor while still a child, his mother, Theodora, acting as regent. In March 856, however, he broke the power of Theodora with the support of his uncle, Bardas, later sending her to a convent. Michael tolerated the iconoclasts but also permitted the use of icons. His deposition of Ignatius, patriarch of Constantinople, in favor of Photius led to a break with Rome. Throughout his reign the Byzantines were victorious against the Slavs and Arabs, although in 860 he had to return to Constantinople to defend it against the Russians. Influenced by his chamberlain, Basil the Macedonian, Michael participated in the murder of Bardas but was assassinated in turn by Basil, who claimed the throne. See also BYZANTINE EMPIRE.

**MICHAEL IV, BYZANTINE EMPEROR** (d. 1041) Ruler from 1034 to 1041, owing his crown to his brother, John the Orphanotrophus, a eunuch and highly respected member of the court of Romanus III, who brought Michael to the palace. Empress Zoë fell in love with Michael, marrying him after the death of her husband in 1034. Although suffering from epilepsy, he was gifted ruler, negotiating a peace treaty with the Fatimid caliphate (c. 1037) and suppressing a Bulgar revolt. Just before his death he retired to a monastery in Constantinople. See also BYZANTINE EMPIRE.

**MICHAEL V, BYZANTINE EMPEROR** (d. 1042) Ruler from 1041 to 1042, the nephew of Michael IV (1034–1041) who was adopted by Empress Zoë and succeeded his uncle. He then exiled Zoë, causing a revolt that resulted in his blinding and incarceration in a monastery. See also BYZANTINE EMPIRE.

**MICHAEL VI, BYZANTINE EMPEROR** Ruler from 1056 to 1057, the successor to Theodora who was confronted by a military coup in favor of Isaac I Comnenus (1057–1059). Michael was overthrown after the defeat of his supporters. See also BYZANTINE EMPIRE.

**MICHAEL VII DUCAS, BYZANTINE EMPEROR** (1059–1078) Ruler from 1071 to 1078, the son of Emperor Constantine X Ducas, succeeding to the throne as a child, his mother serving as regent until her marriage to Romanus IV Diogenes, who was crowned co-emperor. Romanus ruled only until 1071, when he was defeated and captured at Manzikert by the Seljuk Turks. Proclaimed sole emperor, Michael saw the Turks advance across Asia Minor as revolts erupted in the empire. He abdicated on March 31, 1078, retiring to a monastery, where he died later that same year.

**MICHAEL VIII PALAEOLOGUS, BYZANTINE EMPEROR** (1224–1282) Ruler from 1259 to 1282, who reestablished the empire and founded the Palaeologi dynasty that would endure until 1453, when Constantinople fell to the Turks. Born in Nicaea, he was named regent for John, son of Emperor Theodore II Lascaris (1254–1258), in 1258, and the following year he blinded the heir and was crowned emperor of Nicaea. In 1261 he recaptured Constantinople from the Venetians and Latins and was proclaimed emperor. The problems of a ruined economy, the threat of the Turks and the attempt of Baldwin II of Courtenay, the last Latin emperor, to reclaim the throne were all ably confronted by Michael. He made peace with the papacy and the Council of Lyons (1274), where a union of Greek and Latin churches was proposed. He needed papal support to act against Charles of Anjou. Charles's proclamation of Martin IV as pope in 1281 ended the alliance, but Michael had enlisted other allies, such as the Hohenstaufens in Italy and Pedro III of Aragon (1276–1285). This resulted in the war of the Sicilian Vespers (1282), which dealt a serious blow to Charles's Italian position and saved Constantinople from invasion. The Turks, however, took advantage of the situation and were able to conquer most of Asia Minor. Michael managed to restore the empire to greatness and to ensure its continuance for two centuries. See also BYZANTINE EMPIRE.

**MICHAEL I, DESPOT OF EPIRUS** See EPIRUS, DESPOTATE OF.

**MICHAEL II, DESPOT OF EPIRUS** See EPIRUS, DESPOTATE OF.

**MICHAEL ASEN** (d. 1257) Half brother of and successor to Kaloman I, ruling the Bulgars from 1246 to 1257. His reign was dominated by war against the Nicaeans, who took Thrace and Macedonia as far as the Varder River but were defeated after the death of Emperor John III Ducas Vatatzes (1222–1254). Michael was assassinated in 1257 by his cousin, Koloman II, who replaced him. See also BULGARIA.

**MICHAEL CERULARIUS** (d. 1058) Patriarch of Constantinople, a favorite of Emperor Constantine IX Monomachus (1042–1055). Excommunicated for his stance against Rome by the papal legate, Cardinal Humbert, in 1054, Michael attacked papal supremacy and issued a manifesto declaring Byzantium's ecclesiastical independence. These actions made the schism within the church unavoidable, while strengthening the absolute position of the church in Byzantine imperial spheres. He was removed in 1058 and exiled by Emperor Isaac I Comnenus (1057–1059).

**MICHAEL SISMAN** (d. 1330) Ruler of the Bulgars from 1322 to 1330, the son of Sisman of Vidin, who reunited the Bulgar kingdom, divided since the late 13th century. His war with the Byzantines led to negotiations and to his marriage to Theodora, sister of Andronicus (III) Palaeologus (1259–1282), who became emperor in 1328 with Michael's support. An alliance between Sisman and Constantinople did not provide Byzantine troops at the Battle of Velbuzd (July 1330), and Michael confronted Stephen Decanski and the Serbs alone. He was slain in the battle, and the Bulgars fell to Serbian domination. See also BULGARIA.

**MICHELOZZO DI BARTOLOMMEO** (1396–1472) Italian sculptor and artist working with the patronage of Cosimo de Medici. Born in Florence, Michelozzo was an assistant to Lorenzo Ghiberti and later shared a workshop with Donatello, designing a number of tombs in collaboration with him, including one for the antipope John XXII in Florence. In 1446 he succeeded Brunelleschi as the architect for the cathedral in Florence, and for the Medicis he designed several villas and palaces, his masterpiece the Palazzo Medici-Riccardi, constructed from 1444 to 1459.

**MIDDLE ENGLISH** The language spoken and written in England from around 1100 to 1500. It was transitional in the evolution of the Anglo-Saxon language to modern English.

**MIDDLE HIGH GERMAN** The language spoken and written from the late 11th century until the mid-14th century, evolving from Old High German and in use in Austria, Switzerland and parts of Germany. Middle High German was the language employed by well-known poets such as Wolfram von Eschenbach, Hartmann von Aue, Gottfried von Strassburg and Walther von der Vogelweide. See also GERMANY.

**MIESZKO I** (d. 992) Piast duke or prince of Poland, ruling from 963 to 992, considered the founder of Christian Poland and the man largely responsible for its transformation. Anxious to resist the advance of the Germans, Mieszko made an alliance with Bohemia's Duke Boleslav II in 966, accepting baptism to avoid enforced conversion to Christianity. The next years witnessed the addition of territories to the Polish empire, including the conquest of the coastal regions of the Baltic, Silesia and Little Poland. Before his death, he avoided having the Polish church placed under German ecclesiastical authority by acknowledging the supremacy of the papacy.

**MIESZKO II LAMBERT** (990–1034) King of Poland from 1025 to 1034, a son of Boleslav I the Brave. He succeeded his father to the throne but lost Polish territories to the Bohemians and the Holy Roman Empire. German advances and internal unrest forced Mieszko to recognize German supremacy in 1033. His death in 1034 precipitated five years of chaos. See also POLAND.

**MIESZKO III** (c. 1126–1202) Prince of Great Poland from 1173 and, for a time, grand duke of Poland. Called "the Old," he reigned as grand duke, from Cracow, from 1173 to 1177 and from 1194 to 1202, during time of considerable upheaval in Poland. See also POLAND.

**MILAN** City in the northern part of Italy, in Lombardy, that emerged as the chief member of the Lombard League. Originally a Celtic site, it was taken by the Romans and was called Mediolanum. In time it became the administrative heart of the Western Empire and vital to the acceptance of Christianity. Twice destroyed by Germanic invasions (c. 450 and 539), Milan declined as it could not defend itself against the Magyars. Trade flourished, however, in part because of the Crusades, and the city became a free commune in the 12th century. Milan stood against Frederick I Barbarossa (1152–1290) as he advanced into Italy, and he sacked the city in 1162. The Milanese rebuilt, led the Lombard League and opposed Frederick and his grandson, Frderick II (1215–1250). The Peace of Constance in 1183 forced the emperor to recognize Milan's autonomy, but Milan was torn by the Guelph and Ghibelline factions until 1277, when the Visconti family took control of the city. Galeazzo Visconti was granted title duke of Milan by the Holy Roman Emperor. Francesco Sforza married the daughter of the last Visconti, inaugurating a new era of Sforza rule in 1447. In 1499, a French army occupied the city. The Duomo of Milan, begun in 1386, is considered an outstanding example of Italian Gothic ecclesiastical architecture.

**MILICZ, JOHN** (d. 1374) Also called Milicz of Kremsier, head of the chancery of Emperor Charles IV (1346–1378) before becoming a religious reformer. Ordained about 1350, he was enthused by the spirit of reform in 1363, resigning his position in imperial service and giving up all worldly possessions to preach at Prague calling for a return to spiritual idealism. His views brought his arrest and imprisonment by the Inquisition in 1367, but in 1373 he was absolved by Pope Gregory XI (1370–1378) and was invited to preach before the College of Cardinals. While in prison, Milicz composed his *Libellus de Antichristo (Booklet on the Antichrist)*, calling for reform in the church. See also BOHEMIA; HUS, JAN.

**MILITARY ORDERS** Knightly, religious, monastic and often political organizations that were formed during the Middle Ages, often as a result of the crusading movement or an offshoot of the efforts against the Moors in Spain. The chivalric orders, most notably the Teutonic Knights and the Knights Templars, came to exercise enormous political influence and acquired prestige and wealth, which aroused the jealousy of others and even their patrons throughout Europe. The following were the major Military Orders:

*Teutonic Knights* See the entry TEUTONIC KNIGHTS.

*Templars* See the entry TEMPLARS.

*Knights Hospitalers* Also called the Knights of Saint John of Jerusalem (or Knights of Saint John or Order of the Hospital of Saint John of Jerusalem), established about 1070 in Jerusalem as a hospital to care for pilgrims in the Holy Land, financed by merchants of Amalfi. Gradually a military function was added, as the charter allowed for defense of the hospitals, Jerusalem or the order itself. By 1126 there was a constable of the order, indicating the growing military power of the knights. They subsequently participated with the Templars in virtually all the major military endeavors in the Holy Land, growing in wealth and prestige, adding subsidiary branches and preceptories throughout Europe.

A knight of the Hospitalers

Following the loss of Jerusalem to Saladin, in 1187, the knights moved to Acre, remaining there until 1291, when the region fell to the Mamluks. The knights sailed to Cyprus and in 1309 conquered Rhodes, profiting enormously owing to the extirpation of the Knights Templars by King Philip IV the Fair of France (1285–1314). Called during this period the Knights of Rhodes, the order dominated much of the Mediterranean, driving Muslim pirates from the sea, while they embarked on piracy of their own. Following the capture of Constantinople in 1453, Rhodes became the last outpost of Christianity in the East. After refusing to pay tribute to the Ottoman Turks, the knights were besieged in 1480 by a massive Turkish fleet. With the guidance of Pierre d'Aubusson they resisted for three months, finally triumphant with the arrival of relief ships. Rhodes fell to the Turks of Suleiman the Magnificent in 1522. In 1530, Emperor Charles V settled the order at Malta, which became their permanent home.

*Hospitalers of Saint Thomas of Canterbury* An order established at Acre, following the siege and capture of the city in 1189–1191, by a chaplain of the Dean of Saint Paul's in England, using funds provided by Richard the Lion-Hearted for the care of wounded Englishmen. It adhered to the Cistercian rule, with headquarters in London and others in Sicily, Greece, Cyprus and Naples. Never large, the order declined after the death of its master and of nine knights at Acre in 1291. The last known knight was Richard de Tickhill. The symbol of the order was a red cross on a white ground, the cross decorated with a scallop shell, the traditional symbol of pilgrims.

*Knights of Saint Lazarus* An organization in Jerusalem whose origins were an Armenian leper hospital, under Greek aegis. The knights held a very limited military role and were concerned chiefly with hospital care. In time the knights were called the Leper Brothers of Jerusalem.

*Knights of Calatrava* A Spanish order originating in the mid-12th century when an abbot, Ramón Sierra, with a group of monks from Fitero and soldiers from Navarre, occupied the fortress of Calatrava, which had been abandoned by the Knights Templars. After the abbot's death in 1164 and the return of the monks to Fitero, the knights remained, receiving papal recognition as an order that year. They eventually wielded considerable influence in Castile and by 1476 were under the more lenient control of the Crown.

*Knights of Santiago* One of the most unusual orders, allowing its members to marry and to own personal possessions, contrary to regular medieval monastic concepts. The knightly group was established about 1158 in Spain (Castile) to counteract the Moors, receiving papal approval in 1175 and adhering to the Augustinian rule. Designed as a largely military force, the order made extensive incursions against the Moors, in time becoming more prosperous and acquiring property in England, France, Italy, Palestine and even Hungary. An illustrious constable of the order was Alvaro de Luna (master from 1445 to 1453), who won the Battle of Higuera in 1431.

*Knights of the Sword* See the entry LIVONIAN KNIGHTS.

*Knights of Aviz* A Portuguese order called originally the Knights of Evora, adhering to Benedictine rule. They later fell under the jurisdiction of the Order of Calatrava, receiving the town of Aviz in 1211 from the Crown, changing the name to that of their new city. In 1218 the order's possessions were increased as the Knights of Calatrava ceded their holdings in Portugal, although the Knights of Aviz remained nominally a part of the Calatravan order.

*Knights of Our Lady of Montjoie* A major Spanish order founded about 1176 in the Holy Land by a former knight of Santiago, Count Rodrigo. These knights were granted recognition by the pope in 1180 and adhered to the Cistercian rule. The order held land in Aragon, Castile and Ascalon and made its headquarters just outside Jerusalem at Montjoie.

*Knights of Saint Julian* A body of knights first recognized by the pope in 1183, having received land from Ferdinand II of León (1157–1188). In 1187 the order placed itself under the Knights of Calatrava, and was renamed the Knights of Alcantara.

*Knights of Saint George of Alfama* A minor order in Aragon founded about 1200 adhering to the Augustinian rule. It was absorbed by the Knights of Our Lady of Montesa in 1400.

*Knights of Our Lady of Montesa* A Spanish order in Aragon, established about 1326 to replace the order of the Knights Templars, which had been dissolved earlier in the century. The order later (c. 1400) absorbed the Knights of Saint George of Alfama.

*Knights of Christ* A Portuguese order established in 1318 by King Dinis of Portugal (1279–1325) to serve as a replacement for the Templars who had been dissolved, and to ensure that the Knights Hospitalers did not gain supremacy. The order was strengthened by having Prince Henry the Navigator as its master, and its members participated in voyages and expeditions, coming to control Madeira, the Canaries and the Azores and exploring the western coast of Africa. Vasco da Gama was a Knight of Christ.

*Order of Saint James of Altopascio* One of the oldest of the orders, established probably in the 10th century. Formed at a hospital at Altopascio, the order aimed to aid pilgrims journeying to Italy or to the Shrine of Santiago del Compostela. It later established hospitals in France, England and elsewhere. The order was administered in 1585 by the Knights of Saint Stephen of Tuscany. It was also called the Order of the Tau, derived from its symbol, the tau cross.

*Livonian Knights* Also called the Knights of the Sword or the Brethren of the Sword, a German military and religious order established about 1202 by Albrecht von Buxhovden, bishop of Riga, to defend the German colony in Livonia and to Christianize Livonia and the Baltic region. Despite setbacks, the knights had control of Livonia by 1226, but in 1236 they were ambushed and routed at the Battle of Siauliai by the Lithuanians, losing half their number. The survivors formed a union with the Teutonic Knights (1237–1239), retaining, however, a high degree of autonomy. Their association with the Teutonic order endured until the 16th century.

*Knights of Saint John of Jerusalem* See Knights Hospitalers above.

*Leper Brothers of Jerusalem* See Knights of Saint Lazarus above.

*Knights of Evora* See Knights of Aviz above.

*Knights of Alcantara* See Knights of Saint Julian above.

*Order of the Tau* See Order of Saint James of Altopascio above.

*Brethren of the Sword* See the entry LIVONIAN KNIGHTS.

See also CHIVALRY; CRUSADES; FEUDALISM; MERCEDARIANS; TOURNAMENTS; WARFARE.

**MINIMS** The Ordo Fratrum Minimorum, the religious group established in 1435 by Saint Francis of Paola. Drawing much inspiration from Francis of Assisi, the Minims primarily practiced humility or virtue, believing themselves the least important and most humble of all religious communities. The members wore black and took a special vow of abstinence from all fish, meat and cheese, as well as other dairy products.

**MINNESINGERS** German poet musicians who flourished during the 12th and 13th centuries, their name derived from their songs, which dealt with courtly love, *Minne,* although the term *Minnesang* has come to mean not only love songs but also those that treat religious or secular material. The minnesingers evolved as a result of the popularity of the theme of courtly love, which originated in Provence or possibly northern France. In form, their early compositions were based on Provençal models, and in time the theme of courtly love as presented by the troubadours was increasingly influential. Among the best-known minnesingers were Heinrich von Morungen, Walther von der Vogelweide, Neidhart von Reuenthal and Heinrich von Meissen (Frauenlob). See also MEISTERSINGERS.

**MOHAMMED I** See MEHMET I.

**MOHAMMED II** See MEHMET II.

**MOLAY, JACQUES DE** (1243–1314) Last grand master of the Knights Templars, who died with his order which was dissolved in part because its wealth and power aroused the jealousy of King Philip IV the Fair of France (1285–1314). Joining the Templars in 1265, Molay fought in Syria and Cyprus and was elected grand master in 1298. Summoned to France in 1306 by Pope Clement V (1305–1314) to discuss the union of the Knights Templars with the Knights Hospitalers, he opposed the proposal and faced charges of heresy and misconduct. The guiding hand behind the accusations was that of Philip IV, who wished to break the order and to possess its extensive holdings. The king arrested all Knights Templars in France on October 13, 1307, and within days Molay had been tortured to make him confess to heresy (but not to sodomy, another charge). A retraction from Molay and many of his fellow knights was followed by an appeal to Pope Clement, who was dominated by Philip. The order was suppressed, and Molay was condemned by a commission in 1314, with other leading members of the Templars, who were sentenced to life imprisonment. He was sentenced to death and burned at the stake. See also MILITARY ORDERS; TEMPLARS.

**MOLDAVIA** Province and later a principality situated on the Lower Danube River to the west of the Dniester River, once part of the Roman province of Dacia and thus both Latinized and subject to invasion. The domination of the Cumans in the region was superseded by the Mongols in the 13th century, allowing the eventual independence of Moldavia in 1359, during the rule of Prince Bogdan. The principality included Bessarabia and defended itself from incursions by Hungary and Poland. Prince Stephen the Great (ruled 1457–1504) brought Moldavia to its zenith, after defeating an Ottoman army. After his death in 1504, however, the Turks compelled the principality to pay tribute, asserting Ottoman dominance in the region that would endure for nearly three centuries.

**MONASTICISM** See ABBO; ADAMNAN, SAINT; AELRED OF RIEVAULX, SAINT; AGNELLUS OF PISA; AIDAN, SAINT; ANTHONY OF KIEV, SAINT; ANTHONY OF NOVGOROD; AUGUSTINIAN CANONS; AUGUSTINIAN HERMITS; BEC; BEGHARDS; BEGUINES; BENEDICT, RULE OF; BENEDICT BISCOP, SAINT; BENEDICTINES; BENEDICT OF ANIANE, SAINT; BENEDICT OF NURSIA, SAINT; BERNARD OF CLAIRVAUX; BERNARD OF CLUNY; BONAVENTURE, SAINT; BRENDAN, SAINT; BRIGIT OF SWEDEN, SAINT; BRIGIT OF IRELAND, SAINT; BRUNO, SAINT; CARMELITES; CARTHUSIANS; CISTERCIANS; CLUNY; COLUMBA, SAINT; COLUMBANUS, SAINT; COMMON LIFE, BRETHREN OF THE; DOMINIC, SAINT; DOMINICANS; DUNSTAN, SAINT; EKKEHARD; ELIAS OF CORTONA; FRANCISCANS; FRANCIS OF ASSISI, SAINT; FRANCIS OF PAOLA, SAINT; FULDA; GALL, SAINT; GODFREY OF SAINT VICTOR; GOTTHARD, SAINT; GREGORIAN REFORM; GREGORY I; GROOTE, GERHARD; HADRIAN THE AFRICAN; HAYMO OF FAVERSHAM; HIGDEN, RANULF; HUGH OF SAINT VICTOR; JACOBINS; JACOPONE DA TODI; JOHN CAPISTRAN, SAINT; JOHN OF MATHA, SAINT; JOHN OF PARMA; LAMBERT VON HERSFELD; LINDISFARNE; LITTLE FLOWERS OF ST. FRANCIS; MALMESBURY; MARIANUS SCOTUS; MENDICANT ORDERS; MONTE CASSINO; MONT-SAINT-MICHEL; ODO OF CLUNY; PETER THE VENERABLE; RATRAMNUS OF CORBIE; STEPHEN HARDING; THEODORE OF STUDIOS; WALAFRID STRABO; WALSINGHAM, THOMAS.

**MONGOLS** (also Tatars; Tartars) An Asiatic people who emerged from their nomadic journeying to build one of the largest empires in world history, reaching from the Pacific Ocean to beyond the Black Sea, from Canton to the lands along the Tigris and Euphrates Rivers. The conquests by the Mongols in China, the Near East, Russia and eastern Europe had the most far reaching ramifications as dynasties were liquidated, entire countries overrun and once-thriving cities torched or razed. Nevertheless, the Mongol empire was well administered, and, at its peak it was said that a virgin carrying a sack of gold could walk in its provinces without fear of attack.

The union of the Mongol clans was accomplished by Temujin, the son of Yesugai, who in 1206 at the *kurultai* of the Mongols, the tribal assembly, claimed the title of Genghis Khan. From 1206 to 1227, he led massive campaigns of conquest (see GENGHIS KHAN), from which evolved an empire. After a regency of two years under the aegis of his youngest son, Tolui, Genghis's third son, Ogodai became khan, ruling from 1229 to 1241. He launched Mongol campaigns against the countries of Europe under the command of Batu and Subotai. Russia was attacked in 1237, Kiev was destroyed in 1240 and in the following year a combined German and Polish army was crushed at Liegnitz. Hungary was invaded and the Danube crossed, but Ogadai's death in 1241 halted these incursions. The troops retreated early in 1242, never to return.

Mongol heavy cavalry

The reign of Mangu (1251–1259) witnessed the renewal of campaigns of Mongol expansion. Kublai Khan, Mangu's brother, marched against the Sung of southern China, while another brother, Hulagu, led an army to the west. In 1258 Baghdad was sacked, thus ending the Abbasid caliphate, and the Assassins in Persia were broken as a power when their fortress at Alamut was captured. Mangu died in 1259, and Hulagu withdrew, leaving a small force behind. This army was defeated by the Mamluks at the Battle of Ain-Jalut, the first major defeat of the Mongols.

Mangu's death brought an end to the unified Mongol empire, for several splinter states emerged as hordes or khanates. In China the Yuan dynasty founded by Kublai Khan (ruled 1260–1294) extended Mongol supremacy over all of China, with vassals established in Korea, Tibet, southeast Asia and southern China. That dynasty endured until about 1368, when the last Yuan emperor, Tokon-Temür, fell to the advancing armies of the Ming dynasty.

Kublai Khan was not recognized as the Great Khan by the Mongols of the Golden Horde created by Batu following Batu's retreat from Hungary. The Golden Horde, so named after the tent of the khan, dominated Russia's principalities. It was eventually rent by internal disputes and weakened by Russian victories, most notably that of the brilliant strategist Dimitry Donskoi, the grand duke of Vladimir and Moscow. In 1378, Toqtamish, khan of the White Horde, massed in western Siberia, launched his armies against the Golden Horde, overcoming the khan Mamai. Combining the two, Toqtamish subjugated the Russians again, sacked Moscow in 1382 and then made the error of opposing Tamerlane (Timur the Lame), whose own Mongol empire was vast. Tamerlane, angered at incursions into his region, routed Toqtamish's armies in 1391 and 1395.

Tatar (Mongol)

Toqtamish was overthrown three years later by a rival. The Horde began to disintegrate in the 15th century, as smaller khanates (Kazan and Crimea) declared their independence and allied themselves with the Russians. This lasted until the early 16th century, when Sarai, the capital, was sacked by the khan of Crimea.

The Mongol empire and its successor states were characterized by an inability to translate swift conquests, military prowess and legal flexibility in the form of the Yasa (Mongolian legal code) into enduring and stable governments. With each new territorial acquisition, however, they altered the cultural composition of vast regions by allowing peoples of many races and beliefs to flourish. The Yuan dynasty of China encouraged Chinese cultural traits, and the khans of the Golden Horde accepted Islam. Kublai Khan's reign was peaceful and prosperous, and the conversion of the Russian Mongols brought about a golden age in civilization, softening the original Mongolian ferocity. The Mongol instinct for migratory living and their superior military skills were not adaptive to settled existence, and internal squabbles arose, making them vulnerable. The fact that the Mongols posed one of the greatest dangers in the world was made evident by the campaigns of Tamerlane and the subsequent Moghuls, descendants of Genghis Khan. See also AIN-JALUT, BATTLE OF; ASSASSINS, ORDER OF; BAGHDAD; BAYBARS; GOLDEN HORDE; KUBLAI KHAN; POLO, MARCO; RUSSIA; TAMERLANE; TRADE AND COMMERCE; WILLIAM OF RUBRUQUIS.

**MONOPHYSITISM** Christian heresy of the fifth and sixth centuries, which held that there was but one nature in the person of Christ (a divine one), which was in opposition to the orthodox doctrine established at the Council of Chalcedon in 451, declaring that Christ possessed a double nature, both divine and human. In part a reaction to Nestorianism, Monophysitism appeared in the works of Apollonarius of Laodicea (d. c. 390), Cyril of Alexandria (d. 444) and especially those of the monk Eutyches (d. 454), who was condemned by a Constantinople synod in 448.

The heresy developed with radical views (such as those of Julian, bishop of Halicarnassus, d. c. 518) to moderate or nearly orthodox views, such as those held by Severus, patriarch of Constantinople. Official condemnation did not dim the popularity of Monophysitism in the Byzantine Empire, becoming entrenched among the Copts of Egypt, Syria and Armenia. Attempts were made to bring about a reconciliation, most notably by the emperors Zeno (ruled 474–491) and Justinian I (ruled 527–565), but all efforts failed, causing a break that proved irreconcilable. See also HERESIES; MONOTHELITISM.

**MONOTHELITISM** Christian heresy of the seventh century that advanced the doctrine that Christ possessed two natures but a single will. Monothelitism began as an attempt to return to the orthodox faith the followers of the heretical movement of Monophysitism (which held that Christ had but one nature, a divine nature), so as to present a more unified, religious and political front against the Persian and later Islamic threats. The view held by the orthodox elements of the Byzantine Empire was upheld by Emperor Heraclius (ruled 610–641), who met with the leaders of the Monophysites, declaring that Christ possessed two natures but a single will. This was supported by Sergius, the patriarch of Constantinople, and was to a large degree approved by Pope Honorius I (625–638), who took the unfortunate step of writing of Christ's one will, a view condemned by his successors. A breach was caused with the Eastern Church, which had accepted that concept. Several councils condemned the heresy, culminating with the Council of Constantinople in 680, declaring that Christ had two wills, divine and human. See also HERESIES.

**MONTE CASSINO** Well-known monastery situated on a hill lying equidistant between Rome and Naples, and the principal house of the Benedictine order. Monte Cassino was founded about 529 by Saint Benedict of Nursia, after he left Subiaco. It was destroyed several times: by the Lombards (c. 581), by the Saracens (883), and by an earthquake (1349). Throughout the Middle Ages Monte Cassino was one of the great institutions for Christian learning, reaching the peak of recognition in the 11th century under the aegis of the abbots Desiderius and Oderisius. See also BENEDICTINES.

**MONTE CORVINO, GIOVANNI DA** (1247–1328) Franciscan missionary and the first archbishop of Peking. Working as a missionary in Armenia and Persia (c. 1280), in 1289 he was sent by Pope Nicholas IV (1288–1292) as an emissary to the ilkhan of Persia at Tabruz, journeying, from there into India. By 1294 he had reached Peking and in 1307 was named archbishop of the city and patriarch of the Orient. Successful as a prelate, he was nonetheless opposed by the Nestorians and had to deal with difficulties encountered by bishops sent to support him.

**MONTENEGRO** A mountainous and heavily forested region in southwestern Yugoslavia, bordered by the Adriatic Sea once a semiindependent principality called Zeta. It was contained within the larger Serbian empire and incorporated in the 12th century. The region retained its autonomy even after the crushing defeat of the Serbs at Kossovo in 1389 and provided a haven for Serbian refugees. Its coast was lost to the Venetians, but Turkish conquest, the real and lasting threat, was resisted for centuries. See also SERBIA.

**MONTFORT, SIMON DE (1)** (d. 1218) French nobleman and leader of the crusade against the Albigensian heretics in southern France, and a participant in the Fourth Crusade to the Holy Land (1202–1204). De Montfort participated in military engagements at Zara and in Syria, returning to France to become a general in the Crusade declared by Pope Innocent III (1198–1216). Beginning in 1209, he waged a savage war against the Albigensian heretics in the south of France, assuming the governorship over Béziers and Carcassonne and later calling himself the count of Toulouse after winning the Battle of Muret (1213). Raymond VI of Toulouse, the defeated count, refused to accept de Montfort's title, occupying Toulouse in 1217 and enduring a siege. The following year de Montfort was killed outside the city walls. He was the father of Simon de Montfort, who led the English barons in their war with Henry III (1216–1272). See also ALBIGENSIAN MOVEMENT.

**MONTFORT, SIMON DE (2)** (c. 1208–1265) Earl of Leicester and the leader of the baronial faction in its struggle with King Henry III of England (1216–1272). The son of Simon de Montfort, the leader of the Albigensian crusade, he was born and educated in France but journeyed to England in 1229 hoping to restore the family title of Leicester. With the support of his cousin, Ranulf, earl of Chester, Simon became a favorite of Henry III, claiming his title and marrying the king's sister, Eleanor, in 1238. He met baronial opposition to his marriage and was forced to leave England. Reconciled with Eleanor's brother, Richard, earl of Cornwall, Simon went on crusade with him from 1240 to 1242 and fought with distinction. He returned to France and regained Henry's trust.

Appointed in 1248 to quell unrest in Gascony, Simon took such ruthless measures that he was recalled and faced charges brought against him, of which he was acquitted. Returning to Gascony, he resumed his campaign with such zealous ferocity that Henry ended his term of office as regent. The breach was thus established, and Simon, influenced by Robert Grosseteste, joined the baronial opposition to the king. The barons forced Henry to accept the Provisions of Oxford in June 1258, but Simon's own intractable nature caused disunity again, and in 1261 he was forced to leave England. Henry then annulled the provisions, prompting a baronial uprising led by Simon in April 1263. He was eventually triumphant at Lewes on May 14, 1264, capturing the king and his son, Edward. Simon was virtual ruler of England, but support for him declined soon. Thus, when Edward escaped in May 1265, the prince was able to take advantage of Simon's isolation, which led to his eventual destruction. On August 4, 1265, he was trapped at Evesham and killed by Edward's forces. Simon was remembered as one of the formidable figures of his day, responsible for summoning the Great Parliament of 1265, an assembly of representatives from English towns and shires. See also BARONS' WAR; ENGLAND; HENRY III, KING OF ENGLAND.

**MONTPELLIER** City in southern France, capital of the Herault department, near the Mediterranean Sea, originally a fief of the counts of Toulouse (after the fifth century) and becoming a trading city known for its wines, brandies and the import of spices. Granted its charter in 1141, Montpellier had several notable schools, including one for the study of medicine and law and a university. Its charter was confirmed by Pope Nicholas IV (1288–1292) in 1289. In the 13th century the city was claimed by the kings of Majorca, from whom King Philip VI of France (1285–1314) bought it in 1349. See also TOULOUSE.

**MONT-SAINT-MICHEL** Benedictine monastery and fortress situated on a rocky islet off the Normandy coast near the town of Saint Malo and connected to the mainland by a causeway accessible only at low tide. Originally an oratory founded by Saint Aubert, bishop of Avranches, in 708, according to tradition at the behest of Saint Michael the Archangel, the monastery was built in 966, with a fortress and walls added later. Called La Merveille, it had structures facing the sea (built 1203–1208) that were some of the finest Gothic buildings ever erected. Attacked repeatedly during the Hundred Years' War, Mont-Saint-Michel was never captured.

**MOORS** Nomadic peoples of North Africa and also the Islamic inhabitants of Andalusia in Spain. The term Moor is derived from the Latin *Mauri,* from the Roman province of Mauretania. Accepting Islam, the populations of Algeria and Morocco joined the invasion of the Iberian Peninsula in 711 and ultimately in the destruction of the Visigoths there. Over the next centuries they established several kingdoms until driven out by the Reconquista launched by the Christians. Driven back to Africa, the Moors had nevertheless made many contributions to medieval culture in art, architecture, learning, science and medicine. See also ALHAMBRA; ALMOHADS; ALMORAVIDS; ANDALUSIA; ART AND ARCHITECTURE, ISLAMIC; BALEARIC ISLANDS; CORDOBA; CORDOBA, EMIRATE OF; GRANADA; NASRID KINGDOM; RECONQUISTA; SEVILLE; SEVILLE, KINGDOM OF; and individual rulers.

**MORAVIA** Region in central Europe, east of Bohemia, with which it was to be associated for much of its history. Moravia was first occupied by the Celts, followed by the Germans and then the Moravians, a branch of the West Slavs. Avar domination was established in the sixth century, allowing for the establishment of an independent Moravian state. Under the rule of their princes, especially

Rotislav (ruled 846–870) and Svatopluk (ruled 870–894), the Moravians molded an empire that came to include Bohemia, Silesia, southern Poland and western Hungary. Christianity was introduced during the reign of Rotislav, when Methodius was sent to the region. In the early 10th century Moravia fell to the Magyars but was later controlled by the kingdom of Bohemia. The region was ultimately ruled by the Habsburg dynasts (1526). See also BOHEMIA.

***MORTE D'ARTHUR, LE*** See MALORY, SIR THOMAS.

**MORTIMER** Anglo-Norman family whose lands lay on the Welsh border and who wielded great influence in the 13th and 14th centuries. Eventually they held the titles of the earls of March and Ulster and even laid claim to the English throne in the 15th century. Actively involved in the war with the Welsh, Roger Mortimer (d. 1282) defeated Simon de Montfort in 1265. Of particular note was Roger Mortimer, first earl of March (d. 1330), who was an opponent of the Despensers in the reign of Edward II (1307–1327). Escaping to France, he became the paramour of Queen Isabella, invading England with her and compelling king Edward to abdicate in 1326. Roger was virtual ruler of England until Edward III (1327–1377) had him arrested, tried and executed. Another Roger, the fourth earl of March and second earl of Ulster (1374–1398), was proclaimed heir presumptive in 1385 to Richard II (1377–1399) but died in Ireland. His son, Edmund, fifth earl of March and third earl of Ulster (1391–1425), was also named heir to Richard but did not succeed to the throne because of Richard's deposition in 1399 by Henry V (1413–1422) and was in his service during a period of the Hundred Years' War. His death brought an end to the male line, but a nephew, Richard of York, acquired the family titles, granting them to his son Edward (IV, 1461–1483). See also YORK, HOUSE OF.

**MOSCHUS, JOHN** (d. 619) Byzantine monk and spiritual writer, traveling extensively in Egypt, Antioch, Mount Sinai, Cyprus and the Jordan before settling in Rome. There he compiled a collection of anecdotes concerning monastic life, the *Pratum spirituale (The Spiritual Meadow)*, which was popular in the Middle Ages.

**MOSCOW** City in central Russia, situated on the Moskva River, established (according to tradition) in 1147 by the prince of Suzdal, Yuri Dolgoruki, who held a great feast on April 4 to honor his ally, the prince of Novgorod-Seversk. There was certainly a settlement there prior to that date, but this event was the first written mention of the site. Fortified to resist attacks over the next years, Moscow's fortress of the Kremlin was built about 1156. Threats were made by adjacent states, and the Mongols sacked and burned Moscow twice in the 13th century. In each case the city was rebuilt, eventually attaining power over the adjoining Russian lands and challenging the Golden Horde of the Mongols. Designated as the seat of the principality of Vladimir-Suzdal during the reign of Ivan I (1328–1341), the city increased in commercial importance, and the grand dukes of Vladimir became the grand dukes of Moscow or Muscovy. Although the Tatars burned the city in 1382, Moscow was restored swiftly. During the reign of Ivan III the Great (ruled 1462–1505), Moscow was the acknowledged capital of Russia. See also MOSCOW, GRAND PRINCES OF; RUSSIA.

**MOSCOW, GRAND PRINCES OF** Line of rulers controlling the principality of Moscow (Muscovy), members of the Rurik dynasty, the princes responsible for bringing Moscow to political supremacy in Russia. It was during the rule of Daniel, son of Alexander Nevsky (ruler of Novgorod), that Moscow became a principality (c. 1280–1303), adding to its prestige in 1326 with the arrival of the metropolitan of the Russian church. Despite political conflicts with their neighbor, Tver, the Moscow princes in 1328 secured from the khan of the Golden Horde the title of grand prince of Vladimir, with the right to collect tribute for the khan from other princes, an important political privilege. The princes henceforth strove to purchase or acquire territories, the completion of Russian unification achieved during the reign of Ivan III (ruled 1462–1505). See also RUSSIA.

**MOSQUE** See ART AND ARCHITECTURE, ISLAMIC.

**MOSUL** City in northern Iraq, on the Tigris River, opposite the ruins of Nineveh, called in Arabic al-Mawsil. The city was established on earlier settlements, emerging in the eighth century to become a major city and trading center for northern Mesopotamia. Ruled from the 10th to the 11th century by local dynasties, Mosul profited from its location on the major caravan routes of the region. Irreparable harm was done, however, in 1256, with the advance of the Mongols, who destroyed both the city's economy and government. Recovery came only under the Ottoman Empire.

**MOZARAB** Spanish Christians living under Moorish rule in Spain, and who adopted the Arabic language and many aspects of Arabic culture while maintaining their Christian faith. Large cities such as Córdoba, Toledo and Seville allowed these people to prosper, and they were governed by their own officials and subject to Visigothic law. Mozarabic art and architecture were a fusion of Christian subject matter and Islamic decorative style. The Mozarabic liturgy was based on the Latin liturgy of Spain that had flowered under the Visigoths in the sixth and seventh centuries. It included the Mozarabic chant, preserved in manuscripts dating from the 8th to 11th century but unclear because of the lack of a musical staff. Influences on the chant included the Gallican Rite, the Ambrosian Rite, the Eastern Church and the Gothic style. The word Mozarab was derived from the Arabic *musta'rib* (arabicized).

**MU'AWIYA I** (d. 680) Caliph from 661 to 680 and the first of the Umayyad dynasty, which ruled the Islamic empire from 661 to 750. Mu'awiya ibn Abi Sufyan was born to a wealthy family that did not support Muhammad and opposed him after he went to Medina. He was converted only after the fall of Mecca but, as part of the Prophet's conciliatory policy, became a scribe in Muhammad's service and was sent to Syria with the advancing Islamic armies. There he became governor of Damascus (640), appointed by the caliph Umar, proving himself a gifted administrator. Syria was consolidated as a Muslim territory, and the forces of the Byzantines were defeated on land and at sea.

After his kinsman, Uthman, was assassinated in 656, and succeeded as caliph by Ali, Mu'awiya refused to acknowledge him, believing that he had been involved in the murder. The new caliph was attacked by Mu'awiya, who took Egypt and then watched as Ali was murdered in 661. Now caliph Mu'awiya embarked on a long reign that resulted in changes in the administrative nature of the empire. He conducted the jihad, the holy war, to expand his territories with a well-trained and fiercely loyal army that he employed against the Byzantines, while the non-Syrian forces, especially the fanatical Bedouins, were launched across North Africa. Mu'awiya transferred the capital of the caliphate to Damascus. He also promoted religious toleration within his domain, retaining the especially useful Christians in the government. Centralization of authority and improvements in the bureaucracy allowed him to consolidate his gains and to strengthen the regime. Mu'awiya is considered one of the most important figures in the early history of Islam, although his many reforms brought condemnation from elements of both the Sunni and Shiite sects of Islam for having deviated from tradition. See also ISLAM.

**MU'AWIYA II** (d. 683) Umayyad caliph ruling briefly in 683. He was the son of Yazid I and the grandson of Mu'awiya I. See also UMAYYAD CALIPHATE.

**MUHAMMAD I, EMIR OF CÓRDOBA** (d. 886) Umayyad emir of Córdoba, ruling from 852 to 886, whose reign was troubled by Mozarab unrest (Christians under Muslim control) and the *muwalladun* (children of converts to Islam). These uprisings were supported by King Ordoño I of Asturias (850–866), but Muhammad quelled them in 854. In an effort to alleviate Christian discontent he launched an invasion of Asturias, only to have his forces routed in 878 by King Alfonso III (866–910), forcing Muhammad to seek a truce and, of note, to submit to the will of the Asturian king. Meanwhile, he was forced to turn his attention to the *muwalladun*, especially the powerful family of the Banu Qasi in the north. To the south was the equally dangerous Umar ibn Hafsun. Muhammad died with these crises unresolved. See also CÓRDOBA, EMIRATE OF.

**MUHAMMAD II, CALIPH OF CÓRDOBA** (d. 1010) Caliph from 1009 to 1010, one of the last rulers of Córdoba, who succeeded Hisham II (976–1009; 1010–1013), who abdicated. Unable to restore order, Muhammad was defeated by an allied force of Berbers and Castilians in November 1009, and Córdoba was plundered. His restoration of Hisham as caliph was to no avail, and Muhammad fled to Barcelona. With the support of Count Ramon Borrell I (992–1018), he returned to Córdoba in June 1010. Two weeks later he was assassinated. See also CÓRDOBA, EMIRATE OF.

**MUHAMMAD III, CALIPH OF CÓRDOBA** Caliph from 1024 to 1025, a member of the Umayyads and one of the last rulers of Córdoba. See also CÓRDOBA, EMIRATE OF.

**MUHAMMAD I, KING OF GRANADA** (d. 1273) Nasrid ruler of Granada from 1232 to 1273, compelled to acknowledge the suzerainty of Alfonso X, king of Castile (1252–1284). In 1264, he made an unsuccessful attempt to revolt against Castilian domination. The uprising having failed, Muhammad had to give yearly tribute to Castile, although the terms of peace were never fully honored. He also began construction on the fortress of the Alhambra. Muhammed was called Ibn al-Ahmar. See also NASRID KINGDOM OF GRANADA.

**MUHAMMAD II, KING OF GRANADA** (d. 1302) Nasrid ruler of Granada from 1273 to 1302, his reign witness to the invasion of Spain by the Marinids, with whom he was first allied (1275). This union did not last, and Muhammad made peace with Castile and joined in the capture of the key ports of Tarifa and Algeciras, which made further invasion of Spain from Morocco extremely difficult. Differences with King Sancho IV (1284–1295) led to an eventual breach between the states and a return to Muhammad's alliance with the Marinids. See also NASRID KINGDOM OF GRANADA.

**MUHAMMAD III, KING OF GRANADA** Nasrid monarch from 1302 to 1309, the son of and successor to Muhammad II (1273–1302), whose policies for strengthening the kingdom led to his downfall. In 1306 he seized the Moroccan port of Centa to prevent the ambitions of both the Marinids in Africa and the Castilians to approach his domain. A blockade resulted, initiated by the Marinids, while in Granada he met unrest. In 1309 he was overthrown by his brother, Abn-I-Juyush Nasr (ruled 1309–1314). See also NASRID KINGDOM OF GRANADA.

**MUHAMMAD IV, KING OF GRANADA** Nasrid ruler from 1325 to 1333, coming to the throne after the assassination of his father. Controlled for many years by the conspirators, in reponse to the advance of Alfonso XI of Castile (1312–1350) against the Moors in Spain, Muhammad enlisted the support of the Marinids of Morocco. They captured Gibraltar in 1333 but soon aroused the antagonism of Granadan nobles who blamed Muhammad for their return. Muhammad was murdered and replaced by his brother, Yusuf I (1333–1354). See also NASRID KINGDOM OF GRANADA.

**MUHAMMAD V, KING OF GRANADA** (d. 1391) Ruler of the Nasrid kingdom of Granada from 1354 to 1359 and from 1362 to 1391. The son of Yusuf I (ruled 1333–1354), Muhammad inherited the throne when his father was assassinated. In turn, he was deposed by his half brother, Ismail II (1359–1360), who was removed by his cousin, Muhammad VI (1360–1362). Two years later, supported by Pedro the Cruel of Castile (1350–1369), Muhammad V regained his throne. He was grateful to Pedro and remained a close ally of Castile as a result. See also NASRID KINGDOM OF GRANADA.

**MUHAMMAD VI, KING OF GRANADA** A usurper who reigned from 1360 to 1362, after deposing his cousin, Ismail II (ruled 1359–1360), eventually overthrown by the returning Muhammad V (1354–1359; 1362–1391). Fleeing to Pedro the Cruel of Castile, Muhammad V's ally, he was run through with a lance by the Spanish king. His followers were also killed. See also NASRID KINGDOM OF GRANADA.

**MUHAMMAD VII, KING OF GRANADA** (d. 1408) Ruler of the Nasrid kingdom of Granada from 1392 to 1408, succeeding his father, Yusuf II (ruled 1391–1392), and embarking on a campaign against Castile and its king, Henry III (1390–1406). Although thwarted in his invasion of Murcia, Muhammad continued the war, responding to Castilian attacks in 1407. His death brought his brother, Yusuf III (ruled 1408–1417), to the throne, who sought an end to the hostilities. See also NASRID KINGDOM OF GRANADA.

**MUHAMMAD VIII, KING OF GRANADA** (d. 1429) Nasrid king from 1417 to 1419 and from 1427 to 1429, succeeding his father, Yusuf III (ruled 1408–1417), but overthrown in 1419 by Muhammad IX (1419–1427; 1429–1445; 1447–1453). He returned in 1427 and drove the usurper into exile. Supported by African allies, however, Muhammad IX returned and was victorious, putting Muhammad VIII to death. See also NASRID KINGDOM OF GRANADA.

**MUHAMMAD IX, KING OF GRANADA** (d. 1453) Nasrid ruler of Granada, who survived repeated attempts to overthrow him, reigning three times: 1419–1427, 1429–1445 and 1447–1453. He came to power by deposing Muhammad VIII (1417–1419; 1427–1429) but was in turn driven from Granada. Two years later he gained the throne again and executed his rival. The Castilians then supported Yusuf IV (1430–1432) in his claim to the throne, and years of fighting ensued until Yusuf died in 1432. A truce between the factions was signed in 1439. In 1445, however, a nephew, Muhammad X the Lame, usurped the throne. Muhammad IX regained the throne in 1447, accepting as his co-ruler his cousin Muhammad XI. See also NASRID KINGDOM OF GRANADA.

**MUHAMMAD X, KING OF GRANADA** Nasrid ruler from 1445 to 1447, called "the Lame." He overthrew his uncle, Muhammad IX, but was unable to remain in power. In 1447, Muhammad IX returned to depose him. See also NASRID KINGDOM OF GRANADA.

**MUHAMMAD XI, KING OF GRANADA** Ruler from 1448 to 1454, sharing the throne with his cousin, Muhammad IX (1419–1427; 1429–1445; 1447–1453). On the death of Muhammad IX, however, his power was reduced and he was deposed the following year by Sad (1454–1464). See also NASRID KINGDOM OF GRANADA.

**MUHAMMAD XII, KING OF GRANADA** (d. 1527?) Last Nasrid ruler of Granada, reigning from 1482 to 1492, called Abu Abd Allah by the Moors and Boabdil by the Christians. He attempted to overthrow his father, Abu-l-Hasan Ali (1464–1485) but was defeated and captured by the Castilians, pledging fealty to Ferdinand and Isabella (1474–1516) in order to win his freedom. A second attempt to claim the throne brought him to Castile as his uncle, Muhammad ibn Sad (el Zagal) removed Abu-l-Hasan and controlled Granada from 1485 to 1487 as Muhammad XIII. Ferdinand and Isabella, meanwhile, began the final conquest of the Moors and Granada. El Zagal retired to Morocco, and on January 1–2, 1492, the Alhambra fell to the Christian troops. Muhammad XII surrendered Granada, accepting a territorial possession from the Castilians and then retiring to Morocco. See also NASRID KINGDOM OF GRANADA; RECONQUISTA.

**MUHAMMAD XIII, KING OF GRANADA** Disputed ruler of Granada from 1485 to 1487, the brother of King Abul Hasan and uncle of King Muhammad XII, called Muhammad ibn Sad and el Zagal. He deposed his brother, assuming control of Granada as Muhammad XII fought to take the throne. Ferdinand and Isabella launched the campaign to rid Spain of the Moors, taking advantage of the civil strife. When the fortress of Baza fell, Muhammad XIII negotiated his departure. He was offered a lordship under Castilian supremacy but retired to Morocco. See also NASRID KINGDOM OF GRANADA.

**MUHAMMAD I, OTTOMAN SULTAN** See MEHMET I.

**MUHAMMAD II, OTTOMAN SULTAN** See MEHMET II.

**MUHAMMAD IBN TUMART** See ALMOHADS.

**MUHAMMAD AL-MAHDI** (d. c. 887) Twelfth and last imam, or Muslim leader, venerated by the Shiite sect of the Twelvers. Traditional holds that he still lives and will reappear in the future to save the world.

**MUHAMMAD TAPAR** (d. 1118) Sultan of the Seljuks, the first of the Seljuk dynasty ruling in Iraq, reigning from 1105 to 1118. His successor was his son, Mahmud. See also SELJUK TURKS.

**AL-MUHTADI** Abbasid caliph, ruling from 869 to 870. His reign was ended with his murder at the hands of the Turks. See also ABBASID CALIPHATE.

**AL-MUKAMMAS, DAVID** (d. c. 937) Called in full Dawud ibn Marwan al-Muqammas or David Ha-Bavli, a Jewish medieval philosopher and the first to mention Aristotle in his writings. Born in Raqqah, modern Syria, he was a convert to Christianity but left the faith after becoming disillusioned with Christian doctrine. Recognized as a Jewish philosopher, he wrote several polemics against Christianity as well as treatises and commentaries on the Bible. See also JEWS AND JUDAISM.

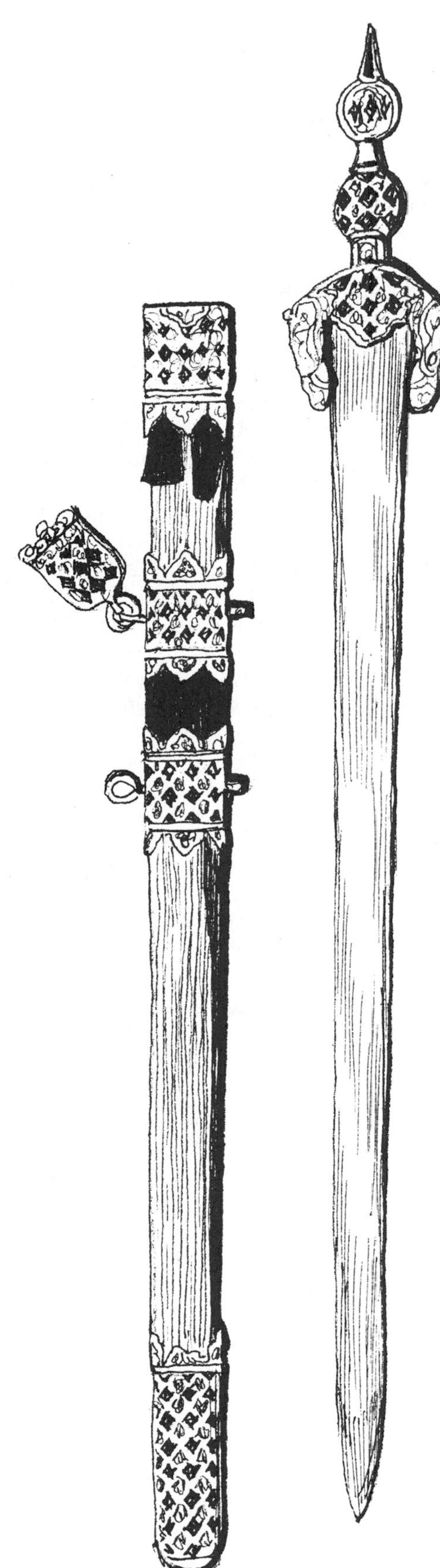

Sword of Muhammad XII

**AL-MUKTADI** (d. 1094) Abbasid caliph (also called al-Mugtadi), reigning from 1075 to 1094. See also ABBASID CALIPHATE.

**AL-MUKTAFI (1)** (d. 907) Abbasid caliph who reigned from 902 to 907 and whose reign was noted for two events: the loss of Tunisia to the Fatimids, and the rising of the Tigris River (904), which caused damage to the city of Baghdad. See also ABBASID CALIPHATE.

**AL-MUKTAFI (2)** (1096–1160) Abbasid caliph from 1135 to 1160, whose reign was noted for an attempt to restore the prestige of the caliphate while reducing the power of the Seljuk Turks. Capitalizing on the internal disorder within the Turkish realm, al-Muktafi proved temporarily successful and was widely recognized in the provinces. He was said to be concerned with the affairs of state, religion and learning. See also ABBASID CALIPHATE.

**MUMIN, ABDUL** (1094–1163) First of the ALMOHADS.

**AL-MUNDHIR** (d. 888) Umayyad emir of Córdoba from 886 to 888, concerned chiefly with the suppression of the revolt of Ibn Hafsun. He died suddenly while besieging Babastro and may have been poisoned by his brother and successor, Abd Allah (888–912). See also CORDOBA, EMIRATE OF.

**MUNICH** In German, München, a city in Bavaria, situated on the Isar River, near the Bavarian Alps, its origins a Benedictine monastery, located at Tegernsee, founded about 750. The name of the city means "Home of the Monks." Henry the Lion is considered to have been its founder. As duke of Bavaria he gave his blessing for the monks to establish a market in 1157, granting a charter in the following year, and Munich emerged as a fortified marketplace. Under the rule of the House of Wittelsbach, Munich became the capital of Bavaria in 1255. Its university was established in 1472. See also BAVARIA.

**MUNSTER** Called in Old Irish Muma, a province in southwestern Ireland comprising the counties of Clare, Kerry, Cork, Limerick, Waterford and Tipperary. One of the "Fifths" or ancient kingdoms of the country, Munster was dominated by the Érainn clan in the south, although from about 400 the effective rulers were the people of Eoganacht, who tried unsuccessfully to break the power of the high kings of Leinster. They lost Waterford and Limerick in the 10th century to the Vikings. Munster was politically controlled by the feudal families of Fitzgerald, the earls of Desmond and Butler and the earls of Ormonde, following the Anglo-Norman invasion. See also IRELAND.

**MÜNSTER** City in northwestern Germany in North Rhine–Westphalia, established as a bishopric in 804 by the missionary Liudger (Ludger, sent by Charlemagne). It was called Mimigernaford, or "Ford over the Aa" until 1068, when it was given its present name. Granted its charter in 1137, it became an imperial city in the 13th century and a prominent member of the Hanseatic League in the 14th century. See also GERMANY.

**AL-MUNTASIR** (d. 862) Abbasid caliph from 861 to 862. See also ABBASID CALIPHATE.

**AL-MUQTADIR** (d. 932) Abbasid caliph from 907 to 932. See also ABBASID CALIPHATE.

**MURAD I** (d. 1389) Sultan of the Ottomans from 1359 to 1389, who was responsible for the extension of Ottoman power from the Balkans and Anatolia, while establishing important offices in the imperial government. In 1362 he advanced into Thrace and captured Adrianople, which became his capital. His troops defeated a coalition of Serbs and Bulgars, reducing Bulgaria, parts of Serbia and ultimately the Byzantine region to Ottoman vassalage. Sofia fell in 1385, and his threat to the west hastened the creation of another coalition, this time between the Serbs and the Bosnians. At Kosovo the Turks destroyed the allies, marking a new era of Ottoman supremacy. Murad did not live to see it, however, for he was assassinated just before the battle by a Serb, posing as a deserter. See also OTTOMAN EMPIRE.

**MURAD II** (c. 1403/1404–1451) Ottoman sultan from 1421 to 1444 and 1446 to 1451, a formidable general and ruler, whose reign witnessed the consolidation of Ottoman power. His early years on the throne were spent overcoming rivals, reasserting control over the Turks in western Anatolia and forcing the Byzantines once again to accept vassal status and to pay tribute. In 1430 he captured Salonika as part of his campaign to extend Ottoman rule in the Balkans. A coalition of Serbs, Hungarians, Poles and Albanians then met and defeated his forces in 1441 and 1444, bringing about a peace in June 1444. Murad's abdication in favor of his son, Muhammad II (1444–1446, 1451–1481), was cut short by the outbreak of new hostilities that year. In November 1444, Murad defeated a Christian army at Varna and returned to the sultanate two years later. In 1448 he routed the Hungarians at the Second Battle of Kosovo. Murad II died in 1451, having brought the Ottoman Empire to the verge of conquering Byzantium. See also OTTOMAN EMPIRE.

**MURCIA** Independent Moorish kingdom in southeastern Spain, its major city Muric (in Arabic, Mursiyah), conquered by the Moors in the eighth century. The kingdom was established independently in 1063 by Abd al-Rahman ben Tabir, following the decline of the caliphate of Córdoba. Abd al-Rahman took the title of minister *(hachite)* to preserve the appearance of Umayyad unity. Murcia fell under the influence of the Almoravids and then the Almohads. After a brief reassertion of independence in 1144, the kingdom became a vassal of Castile in 1243, annexed in 1266.

**MURET, BATTLE OF** See ALBIGENSIAN MOVEMENT MONTFORT, SIMON DE (1).

**MUSA** (d. 1413) Ottoman Sultan from 1411 to 1413. The son of Sultan Bayazid I (1389–1402), Musa was granted a share of the Ottoman territory on the death of his father but was soon involved in a war with his brother Suleyman. In 1410 he overthrew Suleyman, precipitating a crisis in the sultanate as he massacred his brother's followers. Two years later his brother Muhammad I defeated him and henceforth ruled alone. See also OTTOMAN EMPIRE.

**MUSIC** See ADAM DE LA HALLE; ALBA; DUNSTABLE, JOHN; GOLIARDS; JONGLEURS; LANDINI, FRANCESCO; MACHAUT, GUILLAUME DE; MEISTERSINGER; MINNESINGER; TROUBADOURS.

**MUSLIM ART AND ARCHITECTURE** See ART AND ARCHITECTURE, ISLAMIC.

**MUSLIM IBN AL-HAJJAJ** (c. 817–875) Noted Arab scholar and traveler, an authority on the Hadith (an account of the sayings and deeds of the Prophet). He was author of the *Sahih (The Genuine)*, a collection of some 300,000 traditions concerning the Prophet. They were compiled during his travels in Arabia, Syria, Iraq and Egypt.

**MUSSATO, ALBERTINO** (1261–1329) Italian poet and historian, a knight and a member of the Council of Padua, serving as ambassador to Pope Boniface VIII (1294–1303) (1302) and as part of the embassy to Emperor Henry VII (1308–1313) (1311). Eventually crowned as a poet (c. 1314), he was exiled in 1325 after quarreling with the ruler of Padua, Marsilio da Carrara. His Latin poems, styled after Seneca, included the tragedy *Ecerinis*, making his poetry a forerunner to that of the Renaissance and its humanistic viewpoint. His historical writings, such as *Historia Augusta*, an account of Henry VII's deeds in Italy, remain an important historical source for the 14th century.

**AL-MUSTADI** (d. 1180) Abbasid caliph from 1170 to 1180. See also ABBASID CALIPHATE.

**AL-MUSTAIN** (d. 867) Abbasid caliph from 861 to 866, when he abdicated in favor of al-Mu'tazz. See also ABBASID CALIPHATE.

**AL-MUSTAKFI** (d. 949) Abbasid caliph from 944 to 946, forced to abdicate in favor of his cousin, al-Muti, and dying four years later in a prison. See also ABBASID CALIPHATE.

**AL-MUSTANJID** (d. 1170) Abbasid caliph from 1160 to 1170, noted for his justice and clemency. See also ABBASID CALIPHATE.

**AL-MUSTANSIR (1)** (d. 1242) Abbasid caliph from 1226 to 1242. See also ABBASID CALIPHATE.

**AL-MUSTANSIR (2)** (d. 1094) Eighth Fatimid caliph in Egypt, ruling from 1036 to 1094, having one of the longest reigns despite proving generally incompetent. He left the affairs of state to his father's former vizier, to his mother and finally to his Armenian general, Badr al-Jamali. The last was invited into Egypt in 1073 when al-Mustansir confronted internal uprisings. Al-Jamali arrived with an army and massacred many in the government and suppressed the various factions in Egypt. Al-Jamali assumed nearly total control of the caliphate, and al-Mustansir was forced to marry al-Jamali's daughter and allow him to live in great opulence. Elsewhere, however, Fatimid control in Syria and in North Africa deteriorated. See also FATIMID CALIPHATE.

**AL-MUSTARSHID** (d. 1134) Abbasid caliph from 1118 to 1134. See also ABBASID CALIPHATE.

**AL-MUSTASIM** (1212–1258) Last caliph of the Abbasids, ruling from 1242 to 1258, when the Mongol invasion under the command of Hulagu destroyed the dynasty. An Abbasid army was routed near Baghdad, and the caliph was counseled to negotiate. The most important jurists and advisers were captured, as well as al-Mustasim, and Baghdad sacked. Of no further use to the Mongols, the caliph was trampled to death, bringing an end to a royal line that had ruled since the eighth century. See also ABBASID CALIPHATE.

**AL-MUSTAZHIR** (d. 1118) Abbasid caliph from 1094 to 1118. He was described by Ibn al-Athir as gentle and generous. See also ABBASID CALIPHATE.

**AL-MU'TADID** (d. 902) Abbasid caliph from 892 to 902, an active ruler who instituted government reforms and was considered courageous. He was not noted for mercy, burying one general alive because he had displeased him. See also ABBASID CALIPHATE.

**AL-MU'TAMID** (d. 892) Abbasid caliph from 870 to 892, one of the earliest of the caliphs to fall under the power of a political figure at court, in this case his brother, al-Muwaffag. Al-Mu'tamid died suddenly, under mysterious circumstances, and it was rumored that he had been poisoned or suffocated. See also ABBASID CALIPHATE.

**AL-MUTANABBI** (915–965) His full name Abu'l-Tayyib Ahmad ibn al-Husayn al-Mutanabbi, an influential Arab poet and one of the most respected in Islam. Briefly the leader of a heretical faction in Syria, he was given the name al-Mutanabbi, the "Would-Be Prophet." After two years in prison for his revolutionary activities, he began writing and seeking patrons for his work. Several princes did become patrons, only to meet with an erratic relationship. His death came at the hands of thieves who killed him while he was traveling to Iraq to seek another prince who would support him. Al-Mutanabbi composed panegyrics and satires. His verse was ornately rhetorical and was an enduring influence on Arabic poetry.

**AL-MU'TASIM** (d. 842) Abbasid caliph from 833 to 842, the successor to the caliph al-Mamun and notable for introducing Turkish mercenaries into the forces of the caliphate. This decision had a major influence in Abbasid history, for the Turks came to dominate the caliphate. He also launched a successful campaign against the Byzantine Empire, destroying the fortresses of Ancyra and Amorium (838). See also ABBASID CALIPHATE.

**AL-MU'TAWAKKIL** (d. 861) Abbasid caliph from 847 to 861, who pursued a policy of intense religious orthodoxy, persecuting both non-Islamic populations and any he believed did not adhere to strict Muslim doctrine. He engaged in warfare with the Byzantine Empire and was eventually murdered by the Turkish mercenaries in his forces, probably with the blessing of his son. See also ABBASID CALIPHATE.

**MU'TAZILITES** Also al-Mu'tazila, "Those Who Withdraw," a school of Islamic theologians at Basra and Baghdad during the 8th to 10th centuries. The school was the first important institution of its kind in Islam, applying rational methods from Greek philosophy to reach understanding of Muslim doctrine. It taught that there was absolute unity in God, that the Koran was created and not of the essence of God and that humans were responsible for their own actions. The Abbasid caliph al-Mamun declared the dogma of the created Koran a state doctrine in 827, a view that was officially abolished in 849 by the caliph al-Mu'tawakkil.

**AL-MU'TAZZ** (d. 869) Abbasid caliph from 866 to 869, influenced by the Turks at court and forced to abdicate in 869. A few days later, after being mistreated, he was allowed to drink melted snow and died. See also ABBASID CALIPHATE.

**AL-MUTI** (d. 975) Abbasid caliph from 946 to 974, whose long reign was ended when he lost his ability to speak and suffered paralysis. He abdicated in favor of his son, al-Tai, dying the following year. See also ABBASID CALIPHATE.

**AL-MUTTAQI** (d. 968) Also al-Muttaki, Abbasid caliph from 940 to 944, blinded and forced to abdicate in favor of his son, al-Mustakfi. He spent his last years in exile on a small island near Baghdad. See also ABBASID CALIPHATE.

**MYRIOCEPHALON, BATTLE OF** Engagement fought in September 1176 between the Seljuk Turks led by Qilij Arslan II (1156–1193) and the Byzantine forces of Emperor Manuel I Commenus (1143–1180). It took place in the mountains of Phrygia, near the destroyed fortress of Myriocephalon. Determined to reassert Byzantine dominance in Anatolia, Manuel advanced on and fought the Turks, whom he found waiting for battle near the pass of Tzibritze. Disregarding the advice of his seasoned generals, Manuel launched his troops and was severely defeated. See also BYZANTINE EMPIRE.

**MYSTICISM** See ALBIGENSIAN MOVEMENT; BERNARD OF CLAIRVAUX; BOGOMIL; BONAVENTURE, SAINT; CATHARI; CATHERINE OF SIENA, SAINT; ECKHART, MEISTER; FRANCIS OF ASSISI, SAINT; GERTRUDE THE GREAT; GOTTESFREUNDE; SAINT; HILDEGARD OF BINGEN, SAINT; HILTON, WALTER; HOLY GRAIL; HUGH OF SAINT VICTOR; JULIAN OF NORWICH; PILGRIMAGES; RELICS; RICHARD OF SAINT VICTOR; ROLLE DE HAMPOLE, RICHARD; RUYSBROECK, JAN VAN; SUSA, HENRY; TAULER, JOHANNES; THOMAS À KEMPIS; THOMAS AQUINAS.

# N

**NANCY** City in eastern France, the capital of the department of Meurthe-et-Moselle, situated in the province of Lorraine on the Meurthe River. Nancy was originally (11th century) a small community surrounding a castle. Strengthened by the construction of extensive walls in the 12th century, it was made the residence and political capital of the dukes of Lorraine. A city noted for commerce and culture, Nancy was also the site of the defeat and death of Charles the Bold of Burgundy in 1477 at the hands of the Swiss.

**NANNI DI BANCO** (c. 1385–1421) Italian sculptor of Florence, the son of Antonio di Banco; his work was transitional in the change from Gothic to Renaissance style. His first major work was the statue *Isaiah* (c. 1408), a Gothic piece on the west side of the cathedral of Florence. Banco's last work of consequence was the *Assumption of the Virgin Mary* (begun c. 1414) over the Porta della Mandorla of the cathedral of Florence. It was completed by Luca della Robbia. See also FLORENCE.

**NAPLES** City in southern Italy, the capital of Campania, originally a Greek colony (mentioned as Parthenope and Neapolis). The city fell to the Romans in the fourth century B.C. and in the sixth century was dominated by the Byzantines and the Ostrogoths, becoming an independent duchy in the eighth century, until Roger II claimed it for the Kingdom of Sicily in 1139. During that period Naples joined in the efforts of the maritime provinces of Pisa, Genoa and Venice to drive the Saracens from Italy in 1087. After the war of the Sicilian Vespers in 1282, Naples emerged as the capital of the Kingdom of Naples (see NAPLES, KINGDOM OF). Its university was founded in 1224.

**NAPLES, KINGDOM OF** State encompassing the region of southern Italy with its capital at Naples, conquered by the Normans led by Robert Guiscard and ruled by his successors (11th–12th centuries). Naples became part of the Kingdom of Sicily, later controlled by the Hohenstaufens. With the extinction of that line Naples was controlled by Charles of Anjou in 1266, when he responded to a request from the pope to assume power rather than risk a claimant who might oppose the papacy. Charles transferred its capital from Palermo to Naples, but the harshness of his rule combined with heavy taxation brought about the war of the Sicilian Vespers (1282), resulting in the expulsion of the Angevins from Sicily, the Angevin possessions on the mainland becoming known as the Kingdom of Naples. Throughout the 14th and 15th centuries the kingdom endured constant warfare among the Angevin dynasts and between the Neapolitan Angevins and the Aragonese kings of Sicily. In 1442, Naples fell to Alfonso V of Aragon (1416–1458), and in 1443 the pope invested him as king. After Alfonso's death in 1458, the kingdom was controlled by a branch of the Aragonese dynasty, the Angevin claim passing to Charles VIII of France (ruled 1483–1498), who held it briefly in 1495. See also SICILY.

**NARBONNE** City in southern France near the Mediterranean Sea, in the department of Aude, first established as the earliest (118 B.C.) Roman colony in Transalpine Gaul and emerging as the capital of Gallia Narbonensis and as an archepiscopal see in the early fifth century. Captured by the Visigoths in 413, Narbonne was their major city. In 719, however, it fell to the Saracens, who lost it in 759 to the Franks. Prospering as a result of extensive trade throughout much of the Middle Ages, the city also had a large Jewish population. Their expulsion in the late 13th century, combined with the process of silting in its harbor, caused its irrevocable decline both as a port and city. See also FRANCE.

**NARSES** See BELISARIUS; JUSTINIAN I.

**AL-NASIR** Abbasid caliph from 1180 to 1225. See also ABBASID CALIPHATE.

**NASR** Nasrid ruler of Granada from 1309 to 1314, who came to power by overthrowing his brother, Muhammad III (ruled 1302–1309). In turn, he was toppled by his cousin, Ismail I. See also NASRID KINGDOM OF GRANADA.

**NASRID KINGDOM OF GRANADA** Last Moorish dynasty in Spain, ruling in Granada from 1238 to 1492, coming to power after the crushing defeat of the Almohads at the Battle of Las Navas de Tolosa in 1212 and the subsequent deterioration of Almohad power. Muhammad I was its first ruler, dying in 1273. His relations with Castile were generally sound, although he was forced to recognize Castilian supremacy and tried unsuccessfully to break with that Christian kingdom. He also initiated the Nasrid custom of accepting Muslim refugees from the peninsula and began construction of the remarkable monument to Nasrid art and architecture, the fortress of the Alhambra. Dynastically weak and threatened by the ambitions of both the

Castilians and the Marinids of Fez, the Nasrids were unable to increase their influence. Under Yusuf I (ruled 1333–1354) the alliance of Nasrids with the Marinids proved catastrophic as they were defeated by King Alfonso XI of Castile (1312–1350) in 1340. Torn by internal conflict throughout the 15th century, the kingdom was finally ended in 1492 with the conquest of Granada by Ferdinand and Isabella (1474–1516). The last ruler was Muhammad XII (reigned 1482–1492), called also Abu Abd Allah, or Boabdil. See also GRANADA.

**NASSAU** Region (county) in Germany, situated in western Hesse, north of the Rhine River. Its name was derived from the small town of Nassau on the Lahn River, where the count of Laurenburg built his castle, establishing local ascendancy of his family. The dynasty split into two major lines, established by the grandsons of Walram I (d. 1198), who was the first to assume the title of count: Walram II, in the south, founded the Walramian branch; his younger brother, Otto, began the Ottonian line, which came to possess extensive holdings in the Netherlands.

**NAUMBERG** City in east-central Germany on the Saale River, founded around 1000 by the margraves of Meissen, who gave it to the bishop of Zeit in 1028. Its German Gothic cathedral (13th–14th centuries) noted for its magnificent sculpture, lent fame to the city. See also GOTHIC ART AND ARCHITECTURE.

**NAVARRE, KINGDOM OF** Small state in northern Spain, bordered by France and situated between the western Pyrenees and the Ebro River, occupying the modern province of Navarre. Until the second half of the 12th century the Kingdom of Pamplona, it was dominated by Muslim control in 711, but the Basques in the region were able to maintain some independence (see BASQUES). About 798, Iñigo Arista (c. 810–851) was successful in establishing himself as the ruler, the royal title being assumed during the time of García Iñiquez (c. 860–880). The Basque kingdom expanded swiftly, reaching its zenith under Sancho III Garcés, who ruled over most of Christian Spain from 1000 to 1035. On his death the kingdom was ruled by his son García III Sánchez (1035–1054), but in 1076 Aragon seized control, holding it until its recapture by Garcia IV the Restorer in 1134 (ruled until 1150). The crown was held through marriage by the counts of Champagne (1234), the kings of France (1305) and the counts of Evreux (1349), thereby falling to French domination. In 1512, Ferdinand II of Aragon (1479–1516) occupied the Spanish portion of Navarre, the French lands belonging to the crown during the 16th century. Navarre was important because of its strategic mountain passes through the Pyrenees into Spain. The road traveled by pilgrims going to the shrine of Santiago de Compostela lay in Navarre. See also individual rulers.

**NAVIES, MEDIEVAL** See SHIPS.

**NECKHAM, ALEXANDER** (1157–1217) Scientist and teacher at Oxford, the author of the textbook *De utensilibus*, which mentioned the use of the compass to aid in navigation, and *De naturis rerum*, a collection of scientific information popular with his contemporaries. Neckham served as abbot of the Augustinian community at Circencester, Gloucestershire.

**NESTORIANISM** Christian heresy that became widespread throughout the East, identified with the followers of Nestorius, the fifth-century patriarch of Constantinople. Nestorians believed that there were two separate persons in Christ, one divine, one human, unified in a voluntary manner, a creed differing from Christian orthodoxy, which declared that Christ was a single person, both God and man. Nestorian teaching thus raised objection to the title of the Virgin Mary as the Mother of God. Opposition to Nestorian doctrine was led by Cyril of Alexandria, and the heretical teachings were condemned at the councils of Ephesus and Chalcedon (431 and 451 respectively).

Nestorius found a following among the Eastern bishops, who refused to accept his condemnation and gradually formed an independent church. This Nestorian (or Persian) Church was at Nisibus and conducted missionary work throughout Iraq, Egypt, India and China. Under the Muslims Nestorianism fared well and was accepted as a religion. The Mongols, however, oppressed it, as did Tamerlane (Timur the Lame). Many members of the faith were massacred by his forces. Survivors were found in Mesopotamia, chiefly in Kurdistan, near the Tigris River. Their descendants came to establish the Assyrian Church. See also HERESIES.

**NETHERLANDS, THE** Called in the Dutch Nederland or Nederlanden, a region in northwestern Europe, on the North Sea and bordered by Belgium and Germany. Part of the Low Countries, the Netherlands fell to the Franks in the fifth century, remaining under their domination until the eighth century. After the partitioning of the Carolingian empire, it was incorporated into the Kingdom of Lotharingia (Lorraine), eventually becoming a border between Germany and Capetian France (as part of the duchy of Lorraine). From the 12th century, the people of the Netherlands profited from their location on the trade routes of northern Europe. Political control effectively lay in the hands of the counts of Holland, although a period of intense civil and political disorder was ended ultimately by the ascendancy of the dukes of Burgundy, who claimed the region in the 15th century. After 1482 the Netherlands was under the control of the House of Habsburg.

**NETTER, THOMAS** (d. 1430) Carmelite theologian of Essex, England, confessor to Henry V (1413–1422) and spiritual adviser to Henry VI (1422–1461). Called "Doctor Praestantissimus," the "Excellent Doctor," he served as representative to the Council of Pisa (1409), the Council of Constance (1414–1418) and to Poland (1419). His major work was a treatise refuting the doctrines of John Wycliffe and the Hussites. See also CARMELITES.

**NEUSTRIA** Western Frankish kingdom of the Merovingian era that survived from the sixth to the eighth century. Neustria (or New Land) was held to be distinct from the adjacent region, the eastern Frankish realm of Austrasia.

Often called Francia by contemporary writers, it comprised largely the regions of modern France west of the Meuse River and north of the Loire River, with its capital at Soissons and cities such as Tours, Paris and Orléans falling under its jurisdiction. The rivalry between Neustria and Austrasia was at times heated, especially during the seventh century. Conflicts were ended with the victory of the Austrasian mayor of the palace Pepin of Héristal, over the Neustrians at the Battle of Tertry in 687. Austrasia was dominant thereafter. See also FRANCE.

**NEVILLE** English baronial family, closely related to the York and Lancaster families, that became prominent in the political life of the kingdom, rising to power in the 12th century and eventually controlling northern England with the Percy family. Its two most illustrious members were Ralph Neville (d. 1425), first earl of Westmoreland, and Richard Neville (d. 1471), earl of Warwick, called the "King Maker" for his successful restoration of Edward VI as king in 1470. See also WARS OF THE ROSES.

**NEVSKY, ALEXANDER** (d. 1220–1263) Illustrious grand prince of Vladimir and prince of Novgorod, who became a Russian national hero for his defeat of the Teutonic Knights. The son of Grand Prince Yaroslav II of Vladimir, Alexander was elected prince of Novgorod in 1236, defeating in 1240 the Swedes who had invaded the region to punish Novgorod for its incursions. Two years later he achieved his greatest success by destroying the German knights in the Battle on the Ice, fought on Lakes Peipus (Chud) and Pskov. His victories in the West were not equaled in the East, where Alexander foresaw the futility of opposing the Mongol empire. After the death of his father in 1246, Alexander was appointed prince of Kiev, while his brother was named grand prince of Vladimir by the Great Khan. In 1452 he replaced Andrew as grand prince, appointing his own son, Vasily, as the prince of Novgorod. As a vassal of the Mongols, Alexander assisted them in their census and in establishing their supremacy in northern Russia. He built extensively, constructed fortifications and enacted laws. His death, however, signaled civil unrest among the people and rival princes. See also RUSSIA.

**NIBELUNGENLIED** Middle High German epic composed about 1200 by an anonymous Austrian poet, probably from the Danube region. The "Song of the Nibelungen" concerns the Burgundian princess Kriemhild; her henchman, Hagen; the heroic Sigfried; and the powerful Brunhild. Sigfried, who has acquired the hoard of the Nibelungen, aids Kriemhild's brother, King Gunther, in winning the hand of Brunhild and thus acquires Kriemhild as his own wife. Brunhild discovers that Sigfried had duped her and Hagen, on her behalf, murders Sigfried and buries his treasure in the Rhine. Plotting to avenge Sigfried, Kriemhild weds Etzel (Attila the Hun) and slaughter ensues, from which Etzel and a few others emerge. The *Nibelungenlied* was one of the most influential of the German epics, providing a source for many variations, among them Richard Wagner's operatic trilogy *Der Ring das Nibelungen.*

**NICAEA, EMPIRE OF** The strongest and most enduring of the independent Greek states, established in 1204 by Theodore I Lascaris (1206–1222), following the overthrow of the Byzantine Empire by the forces of the Fourth Crusade. With the fall of Constantinople, the son-in-law of Emperor Alexius III (1195–1203), Theodore, fled to Nicaea with his followers, where he founded a splinter principality only some 40 miles southeast of the old capital. In 1208 Theodore was crowned the Nicaean emperor, spending the remainder of his reign (1208–1222) consolidating his position and advancing into western Asia Minor. His successor, John III Ducas Vatatzes (ruled 1222–1254), defeated the despot of Epirus, Theodore Angelus, in 1230. Finally the Nicaean general, Michael (VIII) Palaeologus (1261–1282), took the crown and, in 1261, recaptured Constantinople, reorganizing the Byzantine Empire and founding its last imperial dynasty. See also BYZANTINE EMPIRE; CONSTANTINOPLE, LATIN EMPIRE OF.

**NICCOLI, NICCOLÒ DE** (c. 1364–1437) Italian humanist from Florence whose extensive wealth allowed him to compile a massive collection of classical manuscripts and works of art. His Greek and Latin classical works were the basis of the Laurentian Library of Florence. See also FLORENCE.

**NICEPHORUS, SAINT** (d. 829) Patriarch of Constantinople (806–815), a theologian and historian, and an ardent supporter of the use of icons, being deposed in 815 for his stand by the iconoclast synod in Constantinople. Exiled to a monastery near Chalcedon, he composed his principal work, the *Apologeticus major* (817). Nicephorus also wrote two very popular histories: *Breviarium Nicephori* (*Nicephorus's Short History*) on Byzantine history from 601 to 796, and *Chronological Tables,* including religious and civil offices until 829. See also ICONOCLASTICISM.

**NICEPHORUS I, BYZANTINE EMPEROR** (d. 811) Ruler from 802 to 811, financial minister to Empress Irene and declared emperor after her deposition in 802. His reign included a conflict with the Abbasid caliph Harun al-Rashid (786–809) after the emperor refused to continue paying tributoe to Baghdad. Harun's armies invaded Asia Minor and Nicephorus was forced to submit. He had a dispute with Charlemagne (768–814) as well, over regions of the Dalmatian coast, Venice and Istria, a matter settled by treaty (signed eventually by Michael I Rangabe, 811–813), granting the Byzantines territorial control in return for their recognition of Charlemagne's title. Nicephorus also launched several campaigns against the Bulgars during the years 807–809 and again in 811. In the last effort he was trapped and captured by the Bulgar ruler, Krum, who annihilated his army, beheaded the emperor and made use of his skull as a drinking cup. See also BYZANTINE EMPIRE.

**NICEPHORUS II PHOCAS, BYZANTINE EMPEROR** (c. 913–969) Ruler from 963 to 969, a Cappadocian nobleman who commanded the eastern Byzantine armies and conducted successful campaigns against the Arabs during the reign of Romanus II (959–963), capturing Crete in 960–961. In 963 he wed the emperor's widow,

Theophano, usurping the throne. He then embarked on wars against the Muslims and extended imperial territory into Cilicia and Syria. Opposition to his marriage by the church led to legislation against the clergy, while his oppressive taxation made him unpopular. A plot, probably devised by Theophano and led by her lover, John (I) Tzimisces (969–976), brought about Nicephorus's murder in December 969. He was replaced by John. See also BYZANTINE EMPIRE.

**NICEPHORUS III BOTANEIATES, BYZANTINE EMPEROR** (d. after 1081) Ruler from 1078 to 1081, originally the chief of a theme (administrative unit) in Anatolia, coming to the throne following the deposition of Emperor Michael VII Ducas (1071–1078). He entered Constantinople with his troops and the support of the Seljuk Turks, who thus extended their influence over much of Asia Minor. Confronted by rival claimants, Nicephorus abdicated in April 1081, retiring to a monastery in Constantinople. He was succeeded by Alexius I Comnenus. See also BYZANTINE EMPIRE.

**NICEPHORUS I** Despot of Epirus from 1271 to 1296. See also EPIRUS, DESPOTATE OF.

**NICEPHORUS II** (d. 1358) Last despot of Epirus, reigning from 1335 to 1340, during the regency of Anna Palaeologina. In 1340 the despotate was conquered by Emperor Andronicus III Palaeologus, and Nicephorus was unsuccessful in his attempts to regain his title, dying in 1358 while fighting the Albanians. See also EPIRUS, DESPOTATE OF.

**NICEPHORUS CALLISTUS** (c. 1256–c. 1335) Byzantine historian, a priest in the Hagia Sophia and later a teacher of rhetoric and theology. In his later years he became a monk and wrote the *Ecclesiasticue historiae* (*Church History*). Its 18 volumes included events from the origins of Christianity until the death of Phocas in 610. There was also a five-volume appendix to the work, summarizing additional history to the death of Leo VI the Wise (912). His work was a major source for the study of early of Christianity, its heresies and controversies and for the study of Byzantine culture and legends. He also wrote commentaries and a treatise on the Byzantine cycles of worship.

**NICETAS ACOMINATOS** See NICETAS CHONIATES.

**NICETAS CHONIATES** (d. 1213) Also called Nicetas Acominatos, a Byzantine scholar who was governor of Philippopolis at the time of the Third Crusade (1189–1192) and present at Constantinople when it fell to the army of the Fourth Crusade in 1204. He fled to Nicaea, where he remained, writing until his death. Chief among his works was, in Greek, a *Treasury of Orthodoxy*, written between 1201 and 1210, a history of Byzantium from 1180 to 1206. See also BYZANTINE EMPIRE.

**NICHOLAS I, SAINT** (d. 867) Pope from 858 to 867, called "the Great," a strong advocate of papal supremacy, contesting Carolingian influence in ecclesiastical affairs. He also engaged in several major controversies. A Roman noble by birth, he was successor to Pope Benedict III (855–858) and in 863 heard the appeal of Ignatius, patriarch of Constantinople, who had been deposed in 858 by Emperor Michael III and replaced by Photius. He excommunicated Photius, thus precipitating the Photian Schism, a breach between the Eastern and Western Church. He ordered also that suffragen bishops have the right to make appeals to the pope against their metropolitans, restoring Bishop Rothad II of Soissons, who had been removed by Hincmar of Reims. Finally he entered into a dispute with King Lothair II of Lorraine (855–869), who hoped to divorce his wife, Theutberga, on a false charge of incest. Nicholas refused to grant the divorce, deposing the archbishops of Trier and Cologne who had permitted the king to proceed with a new marriage.

**NICHOLAS II** (c. 1010–1061) Pope from 1058 to 1061, born Gerard and serving as the bishop of Florence (from 1045) until his election as successor to Pope Stephen IX (X, 1057–1058). A supporter of papal reform, he was chosen as a rival to the antipope Benedict X (1058–1059), who was removed in 1059. Nicholas played an important role in laying the groundwork for the extensive Gregorian Reform of the church, summoning the Lateran Council of 1059, at which he issued the papal bull on the procedure for elections. His countermanding of imperial influence in the election of popes caused controversy in Germany.

**NICHOLAS III** (c. 1220–1280) Pope from 1277 to 1280, a Roman member of the Orsini family, elected as successor to Pope John XXI (1276–1277) and responsible for reorganization of the papal states and the Curia. Having served as protector of the Franciscans during the papacy of Pope Urban IV (1261–1264), he was familiar with the order and attempted to resolve its internal disputes concerning the vow of poverty. See also FRANCISCANS.

**NICHOLAS IV** (1227–1292) Pope from 1288 to 1292, born Girolamo Masci, the first Franciscan to become pope, having served as head of the order and as cardinal. The successor to Pope Honorius IV (1285–1287), he attempted to end the bitter conflict over Sicily by strongly encouraging the Aragonese to give it to the House of Anjou. He brought peace in 1291 between France and Aragon, but his hopes to mount a Crusade were unfulfilled. In an effort to enlist the support of the Mongols, in 1289 Nicholas sent missionaries to the court of Kublai Khan, thus establishing the first mission in China. Franciscans were also sent to Africa and the Near East. The political supremacy of the Colonna family emerged during his reign. See also MONTE CORVINO, GIOVANNI DA.

**NICHOLAS V** (1397–1455) Pope from 1447 to 1455, considered a Renaissance pope and viewed as the finest pontiff in his era. Born Tommaso Parentucelli, he rose through the ranks of the church and became papal legate to the Diet of Frankfurt and a cardinal in 1446. The following year he succeeded Eugene IV (1431–1437). He ended the schism in the church with diplomatic skill and gained the submission of the antipope Felix V and the Council of Basel (1449). In celebration, 1450 was proclaimed a jubilee year. A short time later Nicholas reformed and stabilized the Papal States and restored many churches, including Saint Peter's. He founded the Vatican Library and was patron to artists, scholars and humanists. In 1452, Emperor Frederick III (1440–1493) was crowned by Nicholas, the last coronation to be held in Rome. The fall of Constantinople in the following year probably hastened his death, as he mourned the lack of Christian enthusiasm for mounting a Crusade.

**NICHOLAS OF CUSA** (1401–1464) German theologian, humanist, mystic and philsopher, who was ordained in 1430 and held the title doctor of canon law. He participated in the Council of Basel (1431–1438), working to bring about a reconciliation with the Hussites. He initially favored but later denounced conciliarism (see CONCILIAR MOVEMENT) and was frustrated by the failure to unite with the Greek church. In 1437 he was sent by Pope Eugene IV (1431–1447) to Constantinople to discuss reunification with the Byzantine church. He was named cardinal and granted other honors as reward for this service. He also was appointed vicar-general to Pope Pius II (1458–1464), bringing reforms to Rome. Considered an ideal man of the Renaissance, Nicholas was learned in mathematics, science, art and philosophy, writing *De concordantia catholica* (1433, *On Catholic Concordance*); *De docta ignorantia* (1440, *On Learned Ignorance*) and four dialogues on wisdom and the human soul (1450), as well as a synthesis of Aristotelian and Platonist thought on God.

**NICHOLAS OF HEREFORD** (d. c. 1420) A follower of John Wycliffe and fellow of Queen's College, Oxford (c. 1374). Condemned and excommunicated in 1382 for his religious views, he escaped and fled first to Rome and then to his English home, where he resumed his activities, again facing imprisonment. By 1391 he had recanted and was appointed an inquisitor against the Lollard heresy. That same year named the chancellor of Hereford cathedral, he resigned and became a Carthusian monk in 1417. He probably collaborated with John Purvey in translating the Bible into English. See also LOLLARDY.

**NICHOLAS OF LYRA** (c. 1270–1349) Franciscan scholar considered one of the notable biblical experts during the Middle Ages. He joined the Franciscan order about 1300, becoming regent master of the University of Paris (c. 1309). Appointed the head of the order in 1319, he founded the College of Burgundy (Paris, c. 1325). He spoke Hebrew but not Greek and attempted to find literal understanding of texts; his major work was the 50-volume *Postillae perpetuae in universam S. Scripturam* (*Commentary Notes to the Universal Holy Scripture*). The first printed work of its kind, the *Postillae* was popular. See also FRANCISCANS.

**NICHOLAS ORESME** See ORESME, NICHOLAS.

**NICHOLAS ORSINI** (d. 1323) Despot of Epirus from 1318 to 1323, murdering his uncle, Thomas (ruled 1296–1318), to gain the throne. He also married his uncle's widow, Anna. See also EPIRUS, DESPOTATE OF.

**NICHOLAS VON FLÜE, SAINT** (1417–1487) Swiss hermit and ascetic called also Brother Klaus. A noted scholar and judge, he relinquished his wife and 10 children to become a hermit in the Ranft Valley (Switzerland). With his wife's permission he left home and earned a reputation for sanctity and was instrumental in settling local disputes.

**NICOPOLIS, BATTLE OF** Engagement fought on September 25, 1396, between the Ottoman Turks and a Christian Crusader army commanded by King Sigismund of Hungary (1411–1437), ending in the crushing defeat of the Crusaders. Sigismund had gathered the army in response to the call of Pope Boniface IX (1389–1404) to oppose the Ottoman advance into the Balkans. Support came from France, England, Germany and Burgundy, and knights such as Duke John the Fearless of Burgundy and Jean Boucicaut joined the cause. Uniting at Buda, the Christians confronted Sultan Bayazid I (1389–1403), who had just laid siege to Constantinople. The knights moved into the Danube Valley and took Vidin, besieging Nicopolis. Bayazid marched in support and met the attack of the overconfident Christians, especially the French, who refused to heed Sigismund's warnings. These knights were lured into Ottoman ranks and shattered as Sigismund's Hungarians were driven off, weakened by desertions from the ranks of Transylvanians and Wallachians. A general slaughter ensued with only a small force escaping. A few important figures were ransomed. The loss to the Christians permitted renewed pressure by the Ottomans on Constantinople and Central Europe. See also OTTOMAN EMPIRE.

**NIELS** (1063–1134) King of Denmark from 1104 to 1134. See also DENMARK.

**NIJMEGEN** In German, Nimwegen, a city in the eastern Netherlands, in the Gelderland province, on the Waal River. It began as a Roman settlement of Noviomagus and thus was the oldest town in the Netherlands. A Carolingian residence, the city was granted its charter in 1184, becoming an imperial city in 1230. It later joined the Hanseatic League.

**NIKA REVOLT** A major insurgence in Constantinople in 532, ultimately strengthening the hand of Justinian I (527–565) but the bloodiest episode of his reign. The origins of the Nika ("Victory") Revolt were found in the two charioteering factions, the Greens and the Blues, who competed against each other in both racing and in the political arena. Politically powerful because they had the ear of the emperor and represented public opinion, the Blues belonged to the orthodox senatorial class and the Greens the mercantile segment of society. A riot that had been suppressed by the urban police led to the Nika Revolt, during which the leaders of the two factions were freed and a march began on the palace. Empress Theodora confronted the mob, saved her husband and thus freed the hands of generals Belisarius and Narses, who herded the rioters into the Hippodrome and slaughtered them there. Perhaps 30,000 died, as well as the leaders of the Blue and Green factions. See also BYZANTINE EMPIRE.

**NIKOPOL** See NICOPOLIS, BATTLE OF.

**NIMWEGEN** See NIJMEGEN.

**NINTH CRUSADE** This military effort in the Holy Land, the final crusade, was undertaken from 1271 to 1272, led by Prince Edward (later King Edward I of England). The crusade failed, and was the last, feeble effort to stave off the imminent collapse of the Crusader States.

**NITHARD** (d. 844) Frankish historian, the son of Charlemagne's daughter Bertha and the celebrated poet Angilbert. Raised at court, he became an adviser and soldier in the service of Charles the Bald (843–877) (son of the emperor Louis I), fighting in the Battle of Fontenoy in 841. Later appointed lay abbot of Saint Riquier (843), he died in battle against Pepin II of Aquitaine. He wrote the *Historiarum libri IV* (*History*, 4 volumes), including the struggles of the sons of Louis (840–843) and the Strasbourg Oath of 842. The work was invaluable as an account of contemporary Frankish history.

**NIZAM AL-MULK** (c. 1018–1092) Iranian vizier for the Seljuk Turk sultan Alp Arslan from 1063 to 1092, a distinguished statesman and administrator. Born in Tus, Khorasan, the son of an official in the Ghaznavid government, he entered Ghaznavid service but then was employed by the Seljuk Turk prince Alp Arslan (1063–1073), becoming the administrative chief of Khorasan in 1059. When, in 1063, Alp became sultan, Nizam al-Mulk was appointed his vizier. He served Alp from 1063 to 1072/1073 and then held even greater influence with Malik Shah from 1072/1073 until his assassination. He introduced Persian traditions and social customs to the sultanate and advanced the cause of the Sunni sect, founding colleges, establishing public works and giving generously to the poor and to members of the Sufi orders. His championing of the Sunni cause brought him enemies among the Shiites, most notably, the Ismailite Order of the Assassins. He was murdered by them on October 14, 1092, and his death signaled the disintegration of the Seljuk empire. He was the author of *Seyasat-nameh (The Book of Government*, or the *Rules for Kings)*, written just before his death for Malik Shah. See also SELJUK TURKS.

**NIZARI ISMAILIS** See ISMAILI SECT.

**NOGARET, GUILLAUME DE** (d. 1313) Adviser and magistrate to King Philip IV the Fair of France (1285–1314), an ardent supporter of monarchical supremacy. Distinguishing himself as a member of the royal council, he was given the task in 1303 of dealing with Pope Boniface VIII (1294–1303), who refused to allow Philip to tax the French clergy. He seized the pope at Anagni on September 7, 1303, which allowed papal enemies, particularly the Colonna family, to brutalize the pontiff; this in turn roused the people and compelled Nogaret to rescue Boniface. Excommunicated by Pope Benedict XI (1303–1304), despite his supposed sincerity, Nogaret was protected by Philip while attempting on his king's behalf to destroy the Knights Templars. He died before he could undertake a pilgrimage to the Holy Land, a requirement for absolution by Pope Clement V (1305–1314). See also BONIFACE VIII.

**NORBERT OF XANTEN, SAINT** (c. 1080–1134) Archbishop of Magdeburg and founder of the Premonstratensian Canons, or Norbertines, also called the "White Canons." He led a worldly life until 1115, when he was converted to a life of austerity. Trained by the abbot Cuno, he attempted to make reforms in Xanten, the town of his birth, but met with clerical opposition. He then had papal approval to preach throughout northern France and with the assistance of Bartholomew, bishop of Laon, founded the Order of the Premonstratensians in 1120, receiving recognition of the order in 1126. In 1132–1133, Norbert journeyed to Rome with Emperor Lothair II (1125–1137), where he supported Innocent II (1130–1143) against the antipope Anacletus. He was appointed archbishop of Magdeburg in 1126.

**NORDGAU** Region in medieval Germany lying to the north of Bavaria, east of Franconia and west of Bohemia. See also GERMANY.

**NORFOLK** Maritime county in eastern England on the North Sea, its traditional capital at Norwich. Long inhabited by various tribes, Norfolk was settled by the Iceni people in the third century B.C., later to be ruled by Queen Boadicea, who led them against the Romans. Following the Roman occupation, Norfolk was invaded by the Frisians and Anglo-Saxons, eventually becoming part of the Kingdom of East Anglia. Subject to Danish attack from the mid-ninth century, it was attached by treaty to the Danelaw, emerging by the time of Domesday Book (1086) as one of the most populous regions in England. Its economy was based on agriculture, cattle, poultry and fishing. See also ENGLAND.

**NORFOLK, EARLS AND DUKES OF** English title, one of the most illustrious in the country, originating about 1067 when William the Conqueror granted it to Ralph the Staller, although Hugh Bigod (d. 1177) was the first earl of Norfolk. He supported Stephen (1135–1154) in 1135 and Henry II (1154–1189) in 1153 but was stripped of the title and his lands after an unsuccessful 1173 rebellion against Henry. Another major familial figure was Thomas Mowbray, the first duke of Norfolk (d. 1399). He was the son of John, the fourth Lord Mowbray, receiving the title earl of Nottingham in 1383. A member of the Lords Appellant, he partly dominated the reign of King Richard II (1377–1399) (most notably from 1387 to 1389). After Richard recovered control, Mowbray still held royal favor until he came into conflict with Henry (IV) Bolingbroke (1399–1413) and was banished. He died in Venice. From 1483 the rank of duke of Norfolk belonged to the Howards.

**NORMAN CONQUEST** See ENGLAND; HASTINGS, BATTLE OF; NORMANS; WILLIAM I, KING OF ENGLAND.

**NORMANDY** Region in northern France, situated on the English Channel, its capital at Rouen. Attached to the Merovingian kingdom of Neustria, it was granted in 911 by the Treaty of Saint Clair-sur-Epte by King Charles III the Simple of France (893–923) to the Norse leader, Rollo, as a fief from the Frankish king. This grant was intended to end the Norse raids on France, and the name was derived from the Norsemen (Normans), who took possession of the region. They adopted Christianity and French customs but retained their military goals and increased their territories and independence. In 1066, Duke William II (King of England, 1066–1087) conquered England, thus uniting England with Normandy. It was taken by France in 1204, under King Philip II Augustus (1180–1223), then returned to English control early in the Hundred Years' War. By the terms of the Treaty of Brétigny (1360) England ceded Normandy to France in return for Guienne, but in 1415 the region was claimed by English troops after the Battle of Agincourt. It was permanently restored to France in 1450, following the Battle of Formigny. See also HUNDRED YEARS' WAR; NORMANS.

**NORMANS** Viking invaders who settled in Normandy, France, from 820, their descendants later conquering England, Italy and Sicily and producing some of the illustrious soldiers of the period. The Norsemen began launching their raids on the Seine in the ninth century, establishing themselves at the mouth of the Seine and other rivers in northern France. Charles III the Simple (893–923), king of France, granted in 911 the region around Rouen to the Norse chieftain Rollo. Quickly colonizing the region, the Norse accepted Christianity and adopted French customs while maintaining their military prowess. The Normans invaded England in 1066 led by Duke William II (king of England, 1066–1087), defeating the English at the Battle of Hastings. While the Norman dukes remained in control of Normandy, the Normans in England accepted English customs but established Norman feudalism and the French language and customs on their new territory. Other Normans served as mercenaries in Italy against the Saracens and established small Norman principalities dominating indigenous population. The greatest of these Norman adventurers was Tancred of Hauteville, who seized Apulia in 1042. By 1071 the Normans had taken most of southern Italy from the Byzantines, Saracens and the papacy. Led by Robert Guiscard, a son of Tancred, the Normans supported the pope against Emperor Henry IV (1056–1106), and Robert's brother, Roger I, conquered Sicily. Roger II was crowned king of Sicily in 1130, thereby uniting Norman possessions. As in England, the Normans in Italy proved culturally tolerant and receptive to assimilation. The states that they established were enlightened and modern.

**NORSEMEN** See VIKINGS.

**NORTHAMPTON, ASSIZE OF** A decree issued by the English king Henry II (1154–1189) as a result of the council held at Northampton in 1176, the text of which was preserved in two works by the historian Roger of Hovedon. Based on the clauses put forth at Clarendon in 1166, the Assize of Northampton included codes on land law and criminal law and provided for six circuits of itinerant justices who were to visit the countryside. See also CLARENDON, CONSTITUTIONS OF.

**NORTHMEN** See VIKINGS.

**NORTHUMBERLAND, EARLS AND DUKES OF** See PERCY.

**NORTHUMBRIA** Anglo-Saxon kingdom situated in northern England, north of the Humber River, comprising originally the domains of Deira and Bernicia, a unified kingdom during the reign of the Bernician ruler Aethelfrith (593–616). His successor was the Deiran claimant Edwin, whose supporters killed Aethelfrith. Edwin introduced Christianity and extended Northumbrian influence into Wales and beyond the Humber. After Edwin was killed by Penda of Mercia (632), the kingdom was able to retain its independence, its kings generally coming from the Bernician royalty. From the ninth century the region faced threats from the Danes and other Norsemen who settled there after the fall of York to the Danes in 866. Norsemen from the Irish Sea conquered the western part of the kingdom and to the north, the new Kingdom of Scotland, extended the borders to the Tweed River. In the 10th century the rulers of Wessex won mastery over Northumbria, which eventually became an earldom within England. A culturally vital region in Anglo-Saxon England, especially during its golden age from the seventh to the eighth century, Northumbria had such an influence that King Oswy (ruled 641–670) was able to achieve the triumph of Roman Christianity over the Celtic church at the Synod of Whitby in 664. See also ENGLAND.

**NORWAY** Kingdom in western Scandinavia that was first united about 872 under the leadership of Harald Fairhair (c. 860–c. 930), through his victory over other petty kings and claimants. His triumph, coming during the age of the Viking invasions of western Europe, had an effect on the movements of Viking raiders and travelers, for those who had left the country because of a growth in population were joined by defeated chieftains, who brought with them their skill in battle. Harald, meanwhile, ruled until 930, leaving an inheritance bitterly contested. His son, Eric I Bloodaxe (c. 940–945), was driven from power by King Haakon I, who reigned from 945 to 960. Olaf II (Saint Olaf, ruled 1016–1030) was responsible for the final conversion of the Norwegians. He was slain in 1030 by rebels allied with the Danes. After the reign of Canute the Great (1030–1035) and Svein (1028–1035), Olaf's son, Magnus I the Good (1035–1047), came to the throne, sharing power with his uncle Harald III Hardraade, who ruled alone from 1047 until his death in battle in 1066. Harald was the last Norwegian king to claim sovereignty over England.

Despite constant civil war over the succession during the 12th century, a lasting peace was achieved under Haakon IV the Old, whose long rule (1217–1263) brought Norway an age of greatness. Royal authority was reestablished, learning promoted and Norwegian supremacy asserted

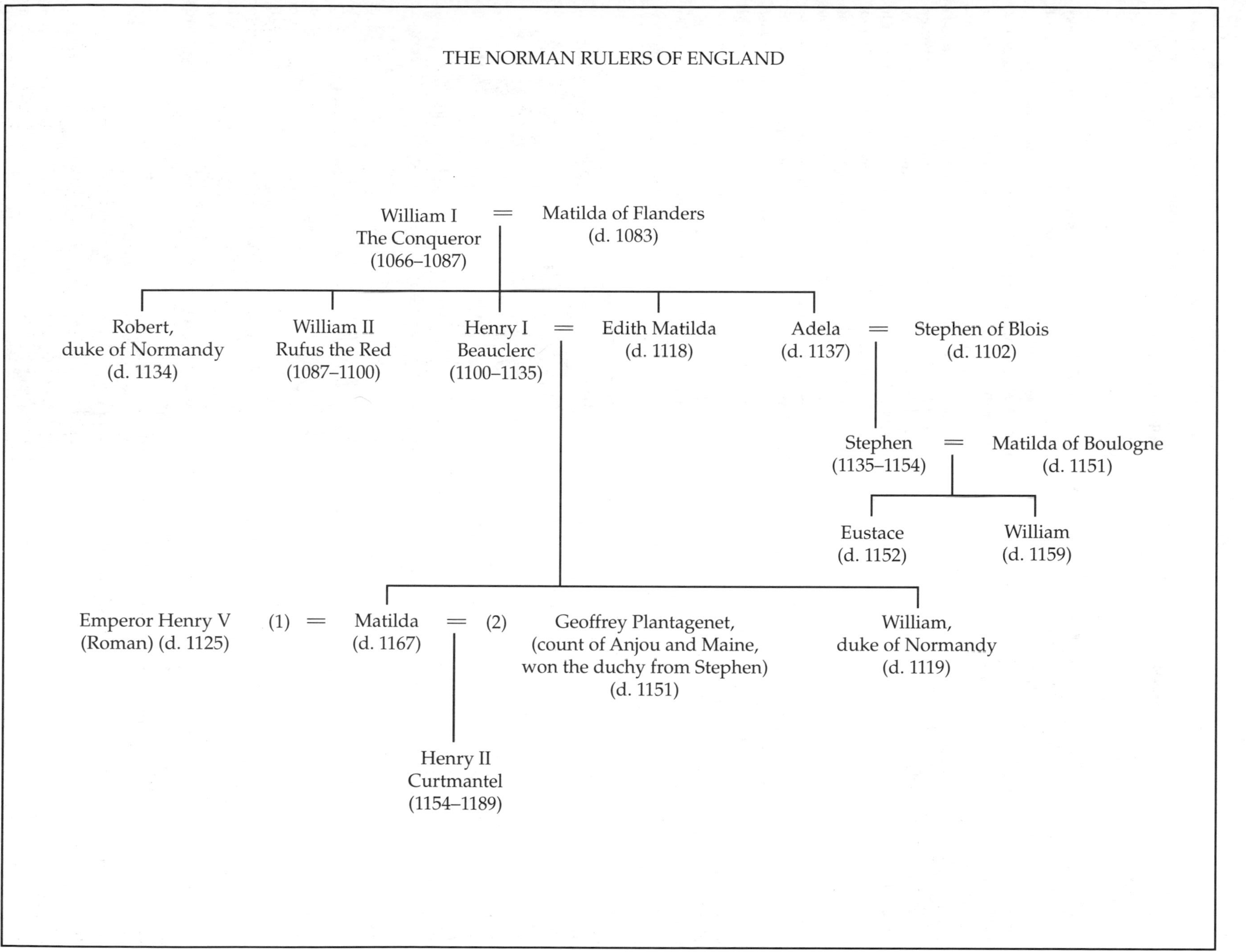
THE NORMAN RULERS OF ENGLAND
William I The Conqueror (1066–1087)
=
Matilda of Flanders (d. 1083)
Robert, duke of Normandy (d. 1134)
William II Rufus the Red (1087–1100)
Henry I Beauclerc (1100–1135)
=
Edith Matilda (d. 1118)
Adela (d. 1137)
=
Stephen of Blois (d. 1102)
Stephen (1135–1154)
=
Matilda of Boulogne (d. 1151)
Eustace (d. 1152)
William (d. 1159)
Emperor Henry V (Roman) (d. 1125)
(1) =
Matilda (d. 1167)
= (2)
Geoffrey Plantagenet, (count of Anjou and Maine, won the duchy from Stephen) (d. 1151)
William, duke of Normandy (d. 1119)
Henry II Curtmantel (1154–1189)

Norwegian ship design

over Iceland, Greenland and the Shetland, Orkney and Faeroe islands. Overseas trade was encouraged, and in 1217 a commercial treaty was signed with King Henry III of England (1216–1272). Before the end of Haakon's reign, however, agents of the Hanseatic League established themselves at Bergen (c. 1250). The Black Death struck in 1349, bringing severe depopulation, especially in the agricultural and dairy farming regions, allowing a massive influx of Swedes into the country. The political stage was thus set for the union of Norway, Denmark and Sweden in 1397 during the reign of Queen Margaret (1397–1412), under the Union of Kalmar (or Kalmar Union), a unity that endured until 1814. See also DENMARK and individual rulers.

**NORWICH** Cathedral city in Norfolk, England, founded by the Saxons and called Northwic. Sacked by the Danes in 1004, Norwich emerged as one of the most prosperous market towns in England, having been granted a charter in 1158 (and again in 1194). Norwich wealth was later due to the Flemish wool trade, especially after 1336, when King Edward III (1327–1377) persuaded Flemish weavers to settle there. A cathedral and a Benedictine monastery were established in the second half of the 11th century, the cathedral having a surviving Norman apse and nave. See also NORFOLK.

**NOTRE DAME DE PARIS** The cathedral of Paris, situated on the Île de la Cité and one of the most celebrated Gothic cathedrals in the world. It was conceived by Maurice de Sully, bishop of Paris, and the cathedral's foundation was laid by Pope Alexander III (1159–1181) in 1163 on the site of an earlier Roman temple and two churches. It was completed about 1230, although the spires in the original design were never added to its twin towers. Of particular note are the flying buttresses of the apse and the cathedral's magnificent 13th-century rose windows. See also CATHEDRAL.

**NOTTINGHAM** County town of Nottinghamshire, situated on the Trent River. An Anglo-Saxon site from the sixth century, Nottingham was part of the Danelaw in the ninth century and was granted its charter in 1155. In 1449 King Henry VI (1422–1461) confirmed its right to have a market and granted it the privilege of autonomy within the county. The legendary figure of Robin Hood was associated with Nottingham and Nottinghamshire.

**NOVGOROD** City in northwestern Russia on the Volkhov River, near Lake Ilmen, thought to be one of the oldest settlements in Russia, first mentioned in chronicles dating from 859. According to tradition, it was here that Rurik established the Russian state in 862. In 882, Oleg, prince of Novgorod and successor to Rurik, captured Kiev, moving his capital there. Christianity was forced on the inhabitants of Novgorod in 989 by Prince Vladimir, while a charter was granted in 1019 by Prince Yaroslav I the Wise of Kiev. Independence from Kiev was won around 1150, although sporadic struggles with the princes of Suzdal lasted throughout the 12th century. The supremacy of the Mongols was also accepted in the mid-13th century, and the city was spared destruction because of the local marshes, the dangers there convincing the Mongols not to attack. Novgorod's most glorious era followed—the reign of Alexander Nevsky, prince of Vladimir (d. 1263), who defeated the Swedes in 1240 and the Teutonic Knights at the Battle on the Ice (Lake Peipus) in 1242.

From the 14th century Novgorod's major threat lay in Moscow, which sought to reduce the city to vassal status.

Cathedral of Notre Dame de Paris

The city asked the Lithuanians for aid but was defeated in 1471 at the hands of Ivan III the Great (1462–1505), who won recognition for Muscovite suzerainty in 1478. In 1570, Ivan the Terrible annihilated most of Novgorod's inhabitants, deporting the survivors. Novgorod long relied on its economic wealth and its position as a trading center for eastern Europe. A close tie with the Hanseatic League was maintained, and the city's fur trade was immensely prosperous. See also RUSSIA.

**NUR AL-DIN MOHAMMAD** (d. 1174) Nur al-Din Abu al-Qasim Mahmud ibn Imad ed-Din Zangi, the ruler of Syria and the son of the first of the Zengid line, Zangi. The successor to his father in 1146 as atabeg (ruler) of Halab, Nur al-Din gave his oath of loyalty to the Abbasid caliphs but then forged an extensive empire. A believer that a jihad, or holy war, was needed to rout the Crusaders, he also desired Islamic unity. His armies conquered Damascus and Edessa, and from 1169 to 1171 he annexed Egypt. By the time he died, Syria, Egypt, parts of Iraq and Anatolia were under his control, which was a boon for his successor, Saladin. Nur al-Din was honored for his piety and his use of captured treasure to build mosques, hospitals and schools. See also SALADIN.

**NUREMBERG** In German, Nürnberg, a city in northern Bavaria, considered second only to Munich, established about 1040 as a castle erected by the German emperor Henry III (1039–1356), duke of Bavaria. A community called Noremberg was first mentioned in 1050, as artisans and merchants built around the castle. Destroyed early in the 12th century by fire, the community rebuilt and, in 1219, was granted its first charter as an imperial city. A council was formed (or first mentioned) in 1256, as Nuremberg emerged as a prosperous trading city of the region, with ties to virtually every major economic site in Europe. In 1356, the Golden Bull of Emperor Charles IV (1346–1378) was proclaimed there at the first Imperial Diet. The imperial crown jewels were moved to Nuremberg's Church of the Holy Ghost in 1424. See also GERMANY; HOLY ROMAN EMPIRE.

# O

**OATH** See FEUDALISM.

**OATH OF STRASBOURG** See STRASBOURG OATH.

**OCCLEVE, THOMAS** See HOCCLEVE, THOMAS.

**OCHRIDA** Town in Macedonia, modern southeastern Yugoslavia. It lies on the northeastern shore of Lake Ohrid. Called Ohrid in Serbo-Croatian, it is also spelled Okhrida, and was known in ancient times as Lychnidus. Under Roman domination the town prospered because of trade. In the 10th century it was the political and cultural capital of the Bulgars, eventually coming under Byzantine control. Many churches were built there, including the cathedral of Saint Sophia, founded in the ninth century, and Saint Clement's, dating from 1295. See also BULGARS.

**OCKHAM, WILLIAM OF** See WILLIAM OF OCKHAM.

**ODILO, SAINT** (d. 1049) Fifth abbot of Cluny, who was influential in the Cluniac order. Joining the monastery in 991, he became abbot in 994. Strengthening the order, Odilo was respected by popes and emperors, promoted the Truce of God and was successful in establishing it throughout southern France and Italy. See also CLUNY.

**ODOACER** (d. 493) Also called Odovacar, the first tribal leader who became king of Italy and who earned lasting recognition for his deposition of Emperor Romulus Augustus in 476, an event precipitating the fall of the Roman Empire in the West. A German warrior of the Sciri (or Rugian) tribe, Odoacer joined the Roman army in 470, which was by then dominated by German contingents. By 475 he was in a powerful position with the troops and the following year overthrew the general Orestes, who administered the Western Empire in the name of the emperor Romulus Augustus. Orestes was executed at Placentia, and the emperor was deposed. Odoacer accepted the suzerainty of the eastern emperor Zeno, in return receiving the title of patrician, which he used in claiming the rule of Italy. He resisted the return of a Western emperor, including Zeno's candidate, Julius Nepos. His ambitions caused Zeno to allow the advance of the Ostrogothic king Theodoric (471–526) to attack him. Theodoric invaded Italy in 489, and by 493 Odoacer was trapped at Ravenna, where he was invited to a banquet and murdered there on March 5.

**ODO OF BAYEUX** (c. 1036–1097) Bishop of Bayeux and half brother of William the Conqueror (king of England, 1066–1087), the son of Herluin of Conteville and Arlette, the former mistress of Robert I, of Normandy. Named bishop in 1049, despite his notoriously dissolute way of life, Odo took part in the Battle of Hastings in 1066, wielding a massive club, as it was forbidden for a member of the clergy to carry a metal weapon intended to draw blood. He was granted the earldom of Kent in 1067 as a reward but was imprisoned in 1082 for illegally raising troops. Released in 1087 by William II Rufus (1087–1100), Odo supported a rival, Robert Curthose, duke of Normandy, in an unsuccessful rebellion. He died while en route to the First Crusade. Odo is believed to have been responsible for commissioning the Bayeux Tapestry. See also WILLIAM I, KING OF ENGLAND.

**ODO OF CLUNY** (879–942) Second abbot of Cluny and a prominent figure in the establishment of Cluniac Reform. Born in Tours and raised in the family of William, duke of Aquitaine, Odo joined the monastery at Baume in 909, becoming abbot in 927 and supporting promotion of the order. Pope John XI (931–936) authorized him to reform the monastic institutions of France and Italy, and in 936 he served as arbitor between Alberic II (d. 954) and Hugh, king of Italy. See also CLUNY.

**ODO OF PARIS** (d. 898) Count of Paris and king of the West Franks (France) from 888 to 898, also called Eudes, the son of Robert the Strong (d. 866). He distinguished himself by his brilliant defense of Paris against the Vikings (885–886) and on the deposition of Charles the Fat in 888 was elected king by the French nobles, who then proved unreliable during his reign. In 893 a group of aristocrats had the Carolingian claimant, Charles III the Simple (893–923), consecrated king, causing a civil war. While Charles eventually acknowledged Odo's rights, Odo instructed his brother to support Charles after his death. Even after his victory in 886, Viking harassment continued against the kingdom during his reign. See also FRANCE.

**ODORIC OF PORDENONE** (c. 1286–1331) Franciscan friar and missionary who was a renowned medieval traveler. Sent to Asia, he journeyed through Asia Minor, Persia and India and on to Java, Sumatra and China. He spent years in China, living in Peking, and returned home through Tibet and northern Persia. His account, dictated to another friar, was the basis for the 14th-century English work *The Voyage and Travels of Sir John Mandeville, Knight.* See also MANDEVILLE, SIR JOHN.

**OFFA** (d. 796) One of the illustrious Anglo-Saxon kings who reigned in Mercia from 757 to 796 and was overlord of most of England. Offa claimed the Mercian throne by winning the civil war that followed the murder of his cousin, King Aethelbald (d. 757). Once secure, he extended his influence and power through marriage and by force over adjacent kingdoms, including Northumbria, Sussex, Wessex and Kent. He struck new coins bearing his name and title, constructed a massive dike on the western frontier bordering Wales (see OFFA'S DYKE) and claimed the title Rex Anglorum. A symbol of his might was his relationship with Charlemagne, with whom he concluded a trade treaty, and Pope Adrian I (772–795), who designated the archepiscopal see of Lichfield to limit the power of Canterbury. His code of laws was respected by Alfred the Great (871–899). See also MERCIA, KINGDOM OF.

**OFFA'S DYKE** Also Offa's Dike, the great earthwork erected by order of King Offa of Mercia to protect his western frontier from the Welsh. A reflection of his military strength, the dike was a major achievement of his long reign. See also OFFA.

**OLAF, PRINCE OF NORWAY** (d. 1115) Ruler from 1103 to 1115, a son of Magnus III Bareleg. Olaf was a child on his accession, and government was controlled by his brothers, Eystein and Sigurd Jerusalemfarer. He is not always listed as an actual king of Norway but as prince. See also NORWAY.

King Offa of Mercia

**OLAF I, KING OF DENMARK** (d. 1095) Ruler of the Danes from 1086 to 1095. See also DENMARK.

**OLAF I TRYGGVASON, KING OF NORWAY** (c. 964–1000) Ruler of Norway from 995 to 1000, the grandson of King Harald I Fairhair (c. 900–940), who according to legend fled Norway with his mother to the prince of Kiev, Saint Vladimir. He later joined the Viking invasion of England in 991 and in 994, with the Danish king Sven Forkbeard (985–1014). He returned to Norway in 995, receiving the crown on the death of Haakon the Great (970–995), whose final years had been beset by rebellions. Olaf's reign was noted for the royal policy toward conversion, as Olaf, who had been confirmed in 994, promoted the acceptance of Christianity throughout his domain. With his patronage, Christianity was introduced to Iceland, Greenland and the Orkney Islands, although the religion was not wholly accepted in large parts of the kingdom. Olaf died in battle against Swein of Denmark and his allies (c. 1000). See also NORWAY.

**OLAF II HARALDSSON, KING OF NORWAY** (c. 995–1030) Later called Saint Olaf, ruling from 1015 to 1028 and completing the task of Christian conversion, becoming Norway's patron saint. A descendant of King Harald I Fairhair (c. 900–940), Olaf was born a pagan, participating in Viking raids and fighting against the English from 1009 to 1011, eventually going to Spain and to France. In 1013 he was baptized at Rouen. Returning home two years later, Olaf claimed the throne, embarking on campaigns to reduce Danish and Swedish influence. His royal policy was aimed at extending the influence of Christianity and was very successful. His efforts to unify the country met with aristocratic opposition, and eventually the nobles rebelled in favor of Canute the Great of England and Denmark (1014–1035), driving Olaf from the throne in 1028. He went to Russia, returning in 1030, but failed to regain the throne, dying in the famous Battle of Stiklestad (1030). Canonized a year later, Olaf and his deeds acquired immense popularity throughout Scandinavia. See also NORWAY.

**OLAF III HARALDSSON, KING OF NORWAY** (d. 1093) Ruler from 1066 to 1093, known as Kyrri, "the Peaceful" or "Quiet," a son of Harald III Hardraade (1047–1066), succeeding him on the old king's death at Stamford Bridge, where an unsuccessful invasion of England was ended. Making peace with King Harald Godwinson and the Saxons, Olaf returned home, ruling with his brother Magnus II (1066–1069) until the latter's death in 1069. A year earlier, Olaf signed a treaty with the Danes that would endure for 25 years. He also strove to strengthen the church in Norway, founding towns and churches, including Bergen. See also NORWAY.

**OLAF IV, KING OF NORWAY AND DENMARK** (1370–1387) Ruler of the Danes from 1376 to 1387 and king of the Norwegians from 1380 to 1387. The son of King Haakon VI of Norway (1355–1380) and Margaret, daughter of King Waldemar IV Atterdag of Denmark (1340–1375), he was only five when his grandfather died and his mother secured his elevation to the Danish throne. In 1380 Haakon died as well, allowing Margaret to press for the unification of the kingdoms. Olaf spent his remaining years, his mother acting as regent, in what was to become known as the Kalmar Union of 1397 after the unification of Denmark, Norway and Sweden. See also KALMAR UNION; MARGARET OF DENMARK, NORWAY AND SWEDEN.

**OLAF HARALDSON** See OLAF II HARALDSSON, KING OF NORWAY.

**OLDCASTLE, SIR JOHN** (c. 1378–1417) English knight and the most celebrated member of the Lollard movement, who won considerable glory as a soldier, campaigning against the Scots and Welsh. During the Welsh war he became a friend of the Prince of Wales, the future Henry V (1413–1422). Through marriage (1408) Sir John held the title Lord Cobham and the following year entered the House of Lords. A Lollard, deeply committed to his beliefs, he was indicted in 1413, imprisoned and convicted of heresy. King Henry V tried to save him, granting a stay of execution, but Oldcastle escaped, was captured again in 1417 and executed in London on December 14. See also LOLLARDY.

**OLDENBURG** German state in Lower Saxony, in northwestern Germany, bordered by the North Sea. A line of counts came to prominence there in the 12th century, culminating in the 1448 accession of Count Christian of Oldenburg to the Danish throne. In 1450 he became ruler of Norway and in 1457 that of the Swedes. Oldenburg was then ceded to his brother Gerhard. The Oldenburg line survived in Denmark until 1863. See also CHRISTIAN I OLDENBURG.

**OLD MAN OF THE MOUNTAIN** See ASSASSINS, ORDER OF.

**OLEG** (d. c. 912) Viking warrior who became the first grand prince of Kiev and founder of the Russian state, a Viking or Varangian kinsman of Rurik. Oleg became ruler of Novgorod about 879, seizing Kiev in 882 and making his capital there. He then extended his power over the Slavic and Finnish tribes, attacking Constantinople (c. 905). While unsuccessful in his campaign, he did force the Byzantines to sue for peace, which led to a useful trading agreement that was the basis for subsequent economic ties between Kiev and Constantinople. See also KIEV.

**OLGA OF KIEV** (d. 969) Regent of the grand principality of Kiev from 945 to 964, the wife of Prince Igor, avenging the assassination of her husband in 945 by boiling the murderers and massacring hundreds of their followers. As her son, Svyatoslav, was too young to rule, she became regent and encouraged the conversion of the Russian people. Baptized about 957 at Constantinople, Olga was the first saint of the Russian Orthodox Church. See also RUSSIA.

**OLGERD** (d. 1377) Grand duke of Lithuania from 1345 to 1377, also called Algirdas or Algierd, originally prince of Krevo, becoming grand duke in 1345. He made Lithuania one of the strongest states in his era, defending the country from the Teutonic Knights and launching an assault on the Mongol-held territories in Russia and the Ukraine. Wars with Poland gave him part of Volhynia, while his assaults against the Tatars (1362–1363) resulted in his capture of Kiev. He died while conducting a campaign against the Tatars. See also LITHUANIA.

**OLOF I** Early king of Sweden, ruling about 850. See also SWEDEN.

**OLOF II SKÖTKONUNG** (d. 1022) King of the Swedes from 944 to 1022, the son of King Eric the Victorious (d. 944). A Christian, he promoted the conversion of his country but was forced to rely on missionaries because of opposition by his nobles. He also opposed Norwegian nationalism, fighting with Norway (c. 1000) but later making peace with Olaf II Haraldsson. See also SWEDEN.

**OMAR (1)** See UMAR (1).

**OMAR (2)** See UMAR (2).

**OMAR KHAYYAM** (d. c. 1132) Persian mathematician, astronomer and poet, best known for his *Rubaiyat (Quatrains)* and called Khayyam, "the Tentmaker." He was born in Nishapur, Persia, the son, probably, of a tentmaker, and received an excellent education as he had won recognition for a treatise he had written on algebra. With the patronage of the Sultan Jalal ad-Din Malik Shah, he was commissioned to reform the calendar with astronomical observations. Later he helped construct an observatory at Isfahan. Admired for his poetry, Omar possibly did not compose verse, as his contemporaries, who held him in high regard, did not mention that aspect of his work. The quatrains produced under his name were translated by the Victorian poet, Edward Fitzgerald. Omar was clearly one of the great intellects of medieval Persia, mastering mathematics, philosophy, history, astronomy and law. A false account stated that he attended the same school as Hasan ibn Sabbah (see ASSASSINS, ORDER OF) and the vizier Nizam al-Mulk.

**OMAYYAD CALIPHATE** See UMAYYAD CALIPHATE.

**OMURTAG** (d. 831) Ruler of the Bulgars from 814 to 831, the son of Krum. Ascending the throne, he concluded a peace with the Byzantine Empire that would endure until 846 (with a brief war in 836). With peace established on one border, he launched a campaign against the Slavs, taking Belgrade and Sirminium. He rebuilt the city of Pliska and founded the capital of Preslav. An opponent of Christianity, he persecuted its adherents but was unable to eradicate it. See also BULGARIA.

**ORCAGNA, ANDREA** (d. c. 1368) Italian painter and sculptor, a prominent Florentine of his age, born Andrea di Cione, the son of a goldsmith. His style, rejecting the innovations of Giotto, was a return to the Gothic, and the only painting definitely attributed to him is the *Redeemer* altarpiece in the Strozzi Chapel of Santa

Maria Novella, in Florence, dated at 1354–1357. It is possible that he painted the frescoes in the nave of Santa Croce in Florence (c. 1350). His most notable sculptural achievement was the tabernacle of Orsanmichele (1359). In 1358 he became an architect at Orvieto. The di Cione family included his three younger brothers: Nardo, Matteo, and Jacopo. His name, Orcagna, was Florentine jargon for archangel. See also FLORENCE.

**ORCHAN** (d. 1360) Ruler of the Ottomans from 1324 to 1360, the son of Osman I (1288–1324) and one of the architects of Turkish expansion into the Balkans. Called also Orkhan or Orhan, he succeeded his father and launched campaigns against Turkomen and the Byzantine Empire, capturing Bursa (1326), Nicaea (1331) and Nicomedia (1337). As a result of an alliance with the Byzantine claimant, John VI Cantacuzenus (1347–1355), in 1346, Ottoman troops crossed into the Balkans. Once there, Orchan laid plans for future conquests, capturing Gallipoli in 1354, establishing a permanent gateway into Europe. See also OTTOMAN EMPIRE.

**ORDERICUS VITALIS** (d. c. 1142) Benedictine monk at Saint Evroul in Normandy who wrote the *Historia ecclesiastica,* which began as a history of his own monastery and became a chronological history of the church from the birth of Christ to the year 1141. Noted for its extensive use of source material, including William of Poitiers and Fulcher of Chartres, the *Historia* was also a valuable source for the study of English, French and Norman society from 1082 to 1141.

**ORDERS, MILITARY** See MILITARY ORDERS.

**ORDOÑO I, KING OF ASTURIAS** (d. 866) Ruler from 850 to 866. See also LEÓN.

**ORDOÑO II, KING OF LEÓN** (d. 925) Ruler from 910 to 925, the son of King Alfonso III of Asturias (866–910), who shared in the division of the kingdom on his father's death with his brothers García and Fruela II, receiving Galicia. When García died in 914, Ordoño claimed León, building a palace and cathedral there, marking the establishment of the Kingdom of León. See also LEÓN.

**ORDOÑO III, KING OF LEÓN** (d. 956) Ruler from 951 to 956, the son of Ramiro II (930–951), whose accession was challenged by his half brother, Sancho I (956–966). He defeated Sancho and then won a victory at San Esteban de Gormaz in 955. See also LEÓN.

**ORDOÑO IV, KING OF LEÓN** (d. 962) Called "the Bad," he reigned from 958 to 960, the son of Alfonso IV. The replacement for his half brother, Sancho I, who had been deposed, Ordoño was overthrown in 960 by Sancho, who returned with an army supported by Córdoba. Ordoño died in Córdoba while planning a recovery of the throne. See also LEÓN.

**ORESME, NICHOLAS** (c. 1320–1382) French philosopher, bishop of Lisieux and a contribution toward the foundation of modern mathematics and science. Consecrated bishop of Lisieux in 1378, he was former chaplain to King Charles V of France (1364–1380), commissioned by him about 1375 to translate Aristotle. His own writings, in French and in Latin, treated such subjects as economics, natural science, mathematics, politics and theology, including *De moneta (On Coinage),* dated at about 1360 and an early scientific examination of money. His studies of moving bodies, with Jean Buridan, anticipated later developments by da Vinci and Copernicus. His work in analytical geometry foreshadowed the theories of Galileo and René Descartes.

**ORLÉANS** City in north-central France on the Loire River, the capital of the department of Loiret, called during the Roman occupation Aurelianum. In the sixth century it emerged as the capital of a Frankish kingdom, united in the seventh century with Neustria. Recognized for its intellectual circle in Charlemagne's era, it became a Capetian royal domain, in the 10th and 11th centuries a city second only to Paris. Orléans won lasting recognition during the Hundred Years' War when, from 1428 to 1429, it was besieged by the English. Its threatened collapse meant the conquest of France. The city was rescued by Joan of Arc, who captured several English forts, broke the siege and turned the course of the war. See also HUNDRED YEARS' WAR; JOAN OF ARC.

**ORLÉANS, DUKE OF** Title (in French, duc d'Orléans) originating in 1344 when King Philip VI (1328–1350) gave it to his younger son, Philip. On his death in 1375, without an heir, the title reverted to the crown. A new line began in 1392, when King Charles VI (1380–1422) granted the title to his brother, Louis (1372–1407). His murder by Duke John the Fearless of Burgundy precipitated civil war between the Burgundians and the Armagnacs. Louis's son, Charles (1391–1465), was captured at Agincourt (1415), spending the years 1415–1440 as an English prisoner. A brilliant poet whose court attracted a celebrated literary circle, Charles was fluent in French and English. His son, the last of the line, became King Louis XII (1498–1515). See also FRANCE.

**ORSINI, HOUSE OF** An old and prominent Roman family whose origins lay in Ursus de Baro, in the late 10th century. The House of Orsini became a major proponent of

Orléans, from the *Grandes chroniques de France*

the Guelph party, participating in a conflict with Ghibelline sympathizers, the Colonna family, plunging Rome into frequent anarchy. Orsinis served as cardinals, and two were elected pope in the Middle Ages: Celestine III (1191–1198) and Nicholas III (1277–1280). A third would be elected as Benedict XIII (1724–1730). See also GUELPHS AND GHIBELLINES.

**ORTHODOX EASTERN CHURCH** See ART AND ARCHITECTURE, BYZANTINE; BASEL, COUNCIL OF; CONSTANTINOPLE; CONSTANTINOPLE, LATIN EMPIRE OF; COPTIC CHURCH; FERRARA-FLORENCE, COUNCIL OF; HAGIA SOPHIA; HESYCHASM; ICONOCLASTICISM; MONOPHYSITISM; MONOTHELETISM; NESTORIANISM; NICEPHORUS, SAINT; NICEPHORUS CALLISTUS; PACHYMERES, GEORGE; PALAMAS, GREGORY, SAINT; PHOTIUS; ROME; RUSSIA; SCHISMS.

**OSLO** The major city of Norway, situated at the head of the Oslo Fjord on the southeastern coast. It was founded around 1050 by King Harald III Hardraade, emerging as the country's capital in the 14th century. From that time it fell under the influence of the Hanseatic League. See also NORWAY.

**OSMAN** (d. 656) Also Uthman and Othman, the third caliph after the death of the prophet Muhammad, ruling from 644 to 656. A member of the Umayyad clan, Osman became a convert to Islam about 620, the first follower from the Meccan upper class. Married to a daughter of the Prophet some years earlier, he was chosen caliph and pursued the policies of his predecessors, including those of conquest. He was responsible for the capture of Cyprus. He also attempted to reform the government, thereby increasing its centralization. His family's profit caused an uprising among the army, including the one in 656 that resulted in Osman's death at Medina. Standardization of the texts of the Koran is attributable to his efforts.

**OSMAN I** (1258–1326) Considered the founder of the Ottoman Turkish state, which derived its name from his (Uthman or Othman). A member of the Gazis, the Turkish fighters for Islam, he was a vassal of the Seljuk Turks, becoming an emir, or prince, in northwestern Anatolia. Concurrent with the disintegration of Seljuk power, Turkomen principalities emerged in Anatolia, of which Osman was a ruler. He consolidated his position thwarting the Byzantines, fighting them on occasion, and also confronted Turkish aggression. Bursa, however, fell either just before or just after his death, a major event, as it made possible the military and political advances of his son, Orchan (1324–1360). See also OTTOMAN EMPIRE.

**OSRED** (d. 716) King of Northumbria from 705 to 716, viewed by Saint Boniface as a terrible king. The son of King Aldfrith (686–705), he came to the throne at the age of eight, spending his next years alienating the church and his nobles. He was assassinated in 716. See also NORTHUMBRIA.

**OSTROGOTHS** Also called the East Goths, one of the two major branches of that tribal group, who with the Visigoths played a part in the great migrations of the fifth century and in the events following the collapse of the Roman Empire after 476 in the West. Their origins lay in an extensive region that extended from the Don to the Dneister along the Black Sea, and they retained their independence until about 370, when they were subjugated by the Huns. As a result of the breakdown of Hunnish power (c. 453) the Ostrogoths moved west, settling in Pannonia, as federated allies *(foederati)* of the Roman Empire. Coming perilously close to Constantinople in 487, the Ostrogoths and their king, Theodoric (471–526), were convinced by Emperor Zeno to invade Italy, destroying the Germanic ruler there, Odoacer.

Theodoric successfully invaded in 493, thereby assuring Ostrogothic ascendancy in Italy, where he ruled at Ravenna. Recognized as an imperial representative by the Roman Senate, Theodoric ruled tolerantly and did not persecute orthodox Christians, although the Ostrogoths were Arians. At the close of his reign some atrocities took place and social strains developed. Emperor Justinian I of Constantinople (527–565) saw an opportunity and sent his general Belisarius to Italy, where he conquered the Ostrogoths and dispersed the tribes. See also BELISARIUS and individual rulers.

**OSWALD** (d. 641) King of Northumbria from 633 to 641, the son of King Aethelfrith (d. 616) who was prevented by his uncle Edwin from claiming the throne and fled to Scotland in 616. Converted to Christianity by the monks of Iona, he returned to Northumbria after Edwin's death in 633, defeating the British king Caedwalla, according to tradition with the encouragement of a wooden cross erected on the battlefield. Oswald spent his reign encouraging the conversion of his people and extending his domain south of the Humber River. On December 5, 641, however, he was defeated by the pagan Penda of Mercia (632–654) and killed. Throughout the Middle Ages Oswald was venerated as a martyr. See also NORTHUMBRIA.

**OSWY** (d. 670) King of Northumbria from 655 to 670, the son of King Aethelfrith (d. 616) and brother of King Oswald, who was killed in battle by Penda of Mercia in 641. Oswy was a vassal to Penda, controlling only Bernicia from 641 to 655. Penda then invaded Oswy's lands and was defeated at the Battle of Winwaed, losing his life at Oswy's hands. Reuniting Northumbria, Oswy confronted a Mercian revolt in 657. His support of the Roman liturgy at the Synod of Whitby in 664 was critical to the ultimate decline of the Celtic church. See also NORTHUMBRIA.

**OTHMAN** See OSMAN.

**OTTO I** (912–973) Called "the Great," German king from 936 and emperor from 962, consolidating the holdings of the imperial ruling house. The son of King Henry I the Fowler (919–936), he became king on the death of his father in 936, confronting rebellious nobles such as Duke Eberhard of Franconia (whom he defeated in 939) and his younger brother, Henry, whom he twice fought, in 939 and 941. After involving himself in the political affairs of the French from 940 to 950, he invaded Italy in 951, ostensi-

Otto I the Great

bly answering the appeal of Adelaide, widow of King Hugh of Italy, who was in conflict with Berengar II. Otto defeated Berengar, claimed the Iron Crown of the Lombards and married Adelaide. Returning home, he was forced to deal with the uprising of Conrad the Red, which was not sustained because of the growing Magyar threat. Their incursions were ended in 955 at the Battle of Lechfeld. Germanic influence was extended beyond the Oder River, strengthening Otto's position, and Christianizing the region was assured through his establishment of dioceses at Magdeburg, Brandenburg and in Denmark. Otto later marched into Italy to assist Pope John XII (955–964) and was crowned emperor in 962, establishing the creation of the Holy Roman Empire, thereby granting Otto some leverage in church affairs. When the pope opposed him in other matters, Otto had him deposed and replaced by Leo VIII (963–965) in December 963. In 972 he married his son Otto (II, 973–983) to a Byzantine princess, Theophano. His reign also saw the growth of economic prosperity for the German towns. See also GERMANY; HOLY ROMAN EMPIRE.

**OTTO II** (855–983) German king from 961 and Holy Roman Emperor from 973, the son of Emperor Otto I (936–973) and Adelaide. Named co-regent in 967, he married Theophano, a Byzantine princess, in 972 and became sole ruler in 973. His early years were spent suppressing revolts in Lorraine and Bavaria, which ended in 978–979 with the submission of Bavaria, Bohemia and Poland. In 980 he marched into Italy to secure his position there, although he was severely defeated by the Saracens in 982. Otto died the following year while attacking the rebellious Venetians. See also HOLY ROMAN EMPIRE.

**OTTO III** (980–1002) German king from 983 and emperor from 996, the son of Otto II (973–983) and Theophano, a Byzantine princess. Crowned while young, he was at the mercy of Henry I the Quarrelsome, former duke of Bavaria, but in 984 Theophano became regent (she served as regent until her death in 991). In 996, Otto crossed the Alps, invaded Italy and installed Bruno of Carinthia as Pope Gregory V (996–999). In turn he was crowned emperor by the pontiff, who was later driven from the papal throne by the Crescenti family, precipitating Otto's return to Italy in 997. Rome fell, Crescentius was executed and Gregory reinstated. Otto chose to remain in Rome, making it the heart of his imperial administration in 998. His tutor, Gerbert of Aurillac, was made Pope Sylvester II (999–1003) at Otto's behest, and his involvement in political affairs angered the Romans, who rebelled in 1001. Otto died while awaiting reinforcements to quell the rebellion. See HOLY ROMAN EMPIRE.

**OTTO IV** (d. 1218) German king from 1208 to 1215 and emperor from 1209 to 1215, called Otto of Brunswick, the son of Henry the Lion and thus a member of the Welf dynasty. His mother was Matilda, daughter of King Henry II of England (1154–1189). A candidate to succeed Emperor Henry VI (1190–1197), Otto lost the succession to Philip of Swabia, who received recognition by Pope Innocent III in 1208. Later that year, however, Philip was assassinated, and Otto elected in November and crowned emperor in Rome the following year, on October 4. Having won papal support by promising to restrain his ambitions in Sicily,

Otto III

Otto invaded the region and was excommunicated. He had conquered southern Italy by late 1210. An imperial claimant, Frederick II (1215–1250), was elevated by a number of German princes and soon won control of parts of southern Germany and made an alliance with France. Otto invaded France but was defeated at the Battle of Bouvines on July 27, 1214, suffering a mortal political blow, which also inflicted severe damage on his ally, John of England. In 1215, Otto was deposed, dying in relative obscurity three years later. See also HOLY ROMAN EMPIRE.

**OTTOKAR I PRZEMYSL** (c. 1155–1230) First ruler of Bohemia from 1198, and the architect of the strong Bohemian state that was to develop in succeeding years. Originally named duke of Bohemia by Emperor Henry VI (1190–1197) and confirmed in 1192, Ottokar recovered from a coup the following year, obtaining the title of king from Emperor Philip of Swabia. Another important concession granted by Frederick II of Germany (1215–1250) was the recognition of the hereditary nature of the Bohemian crown. See also BOHEMIA.

**OTTOKAR II PRZEMYSL** (1230–1278) Ruler from 1253 to 1278, who was for a time the most powerful figure in the Holy Roman Empire. The second son of King Wenceslas I, Ottokar was duke of Austria from 1251 until his succession. One of his first act was to launch a crusade against the Slavs of East Prussia (1254), thereby supporting the Teutonic Knights and thus having the great castle at Königsburg named for him. By various means he then acquired Styria, Carinthia, Carniola and Istria, earning the enmity of Holy Roman princes. In 1273 the Electors chose Rudolf of Habsburg as German king, and he convened the Diet of Regensburg (1274) divesting Ottokar of his rights to Austria, Carinthia and Styria. An invasion of Ottokar's domain followed, and the king surrendered all his holdings except Bohemia and Moravia. In 1278 he made an effort to regain the lands but died at the Battle of Marchfeld (Dürnkrut) in August. See also BOHEMIA.

**OTTOMAN EMPIRE** The ultimately massive Islamic state established by the Ottoman Turks, the most enduring of the Muslim empires, surviving from the 14th to the 20th century. Ottoman rule was centralized in Anatolia, also called Turkey, and from there the Turks designed the destruction of the moribund Byzantine Empire and the conquest of the Balkans, Egypt, Hungary, Iraq, parts of Russia, Arabia and North Africa. The Ottomans originated as members of a Turkic tribe, who fought for Islam against the Byzantines and Mongols, deriving their name from Osman (Othman) I (d. 1326), chief of the Osmanli Turks.

Following the destruction of the Seljuks in 1293 by the Mongols, Osman established himself as the prince of Bithynia (in northwestern Anatolia), an independent territory emerging as the principal opponent of the Byzantines, using the continued deterioration of the Eastern Empire's

## Expansion of the Ottoman Empire, 1355-1453

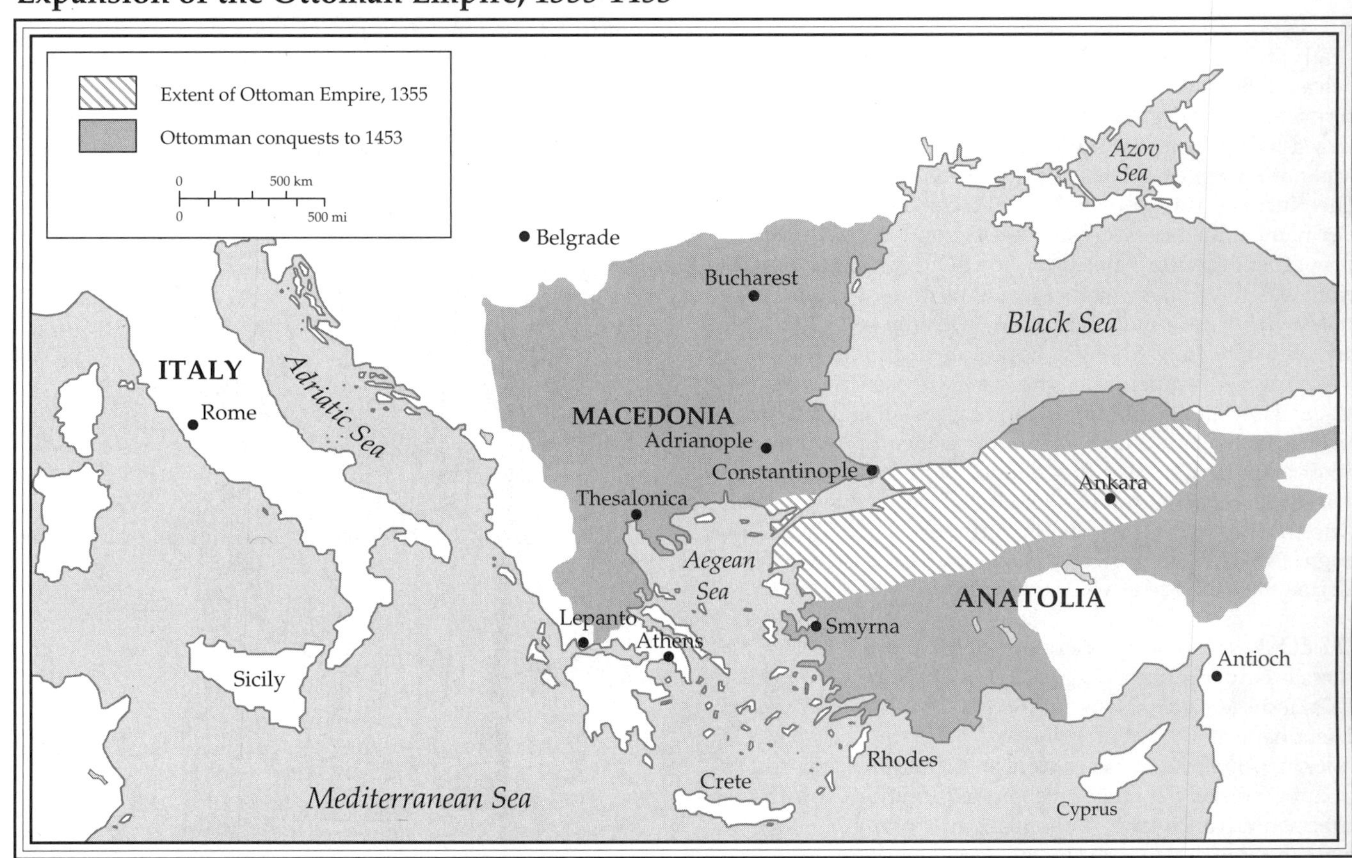

Sultan Mehmet II

defenses to expand. This process began under Osman and was a major policy followed by his successors, Orchan (Orkhan, ruled 1324–1360) and Murad I (ruled 1360–1389). Towns in northwestern Anatolia fell, a vital acquisition being Bursa in 1324. As allies of the Byzantine emperor John VI Cantacuzenus (1347–1354), the Ottomans twice crossed into Europe. Under Murad I (1362–1389) the Turks swept into Thrace and captured Adrianople in 1362, which became their new capital. Murad forced the Byzantines to accept his suzerainty and marched north, capturing Macedonia before annihilating a force of Balkan allies at the Battle of Kosovo in 1389.

Bayazid I (ruled 1389–1402) first turned his attention to the Turkish tribes in Anatolia and annexed parts of eastern Anatolia before returning to the Balkans to quell rebellions among his vassals (1390–1393), culminating in the Ottoman victory at Nicopolis in 1396, which provided Bayazid with enormous prestige and influence and the title of sultan. His campaigns in Anatolia began anew about 1397, but his successes attracted concern from Tamerlane (Timur the Lame), whose Mongol empire was the largest then in existence. At the Battle of Ankara, in 1402, the Ottomans were routed and Bayazid captured. The defeat of the Turks and the resulting conflict over the succession curtailed the Ottoman advance into the Balkans and spared Constantinople for half a century. The recovery began under Sultan Mehmet I (ruled 1413–1420) and Sultan Murad II (ruled 1421–1451). Bayazid's empire was restored in the Balkans and Asia Minor once more reduced. Murad also launched a war against Venice (1423–1430) and was remarkable for his determination to levy units that were not Turkish to counteract the influence of the Turkish magnates. The bulk of these troops were Christian slaves, converts to Islam, forming the extraordinary Janissary corps that would play a major role in Ottoman military ventures and court politics well into the 19th century. The fear of renewed Turkish advance give rise to another crusade, a final Christian effort that was thwarted at the Battle of Varna on November 10, 1444. By the time of Murad's death in 1451, the Ottomans were in nearly total control of the Balkans, with the exception of Belgrade and Constantinople.

In the reign of Sultan Mehmet II (ruled 1451–1481), further expansion was undertaken. From April 6 to May 29, 1453, Constantinople was besieged, falling ultimately to Turkish armies. Serbia was annexed, another war fought against Venice (1463–1479) and, in 1463, Bosnia occupied. His many achievements made possible the sweeping victories of the Ottomans in the Near East and Central Europe under Bayazid II (ruled 1481–1512), Selim I (ruled 1512–1520) and the great Suleiman the Magnificent (ruled 1520–1566). See also ART AND ARCHITECTURE, ISLAMIC; BOSNIA; BULGARIA; BYZANTINE EMPIRE; EGYPT; HUNGARY; MAMLUKS; SELJUK TURKS; SERBIA; SYRIA; WARFARE.

**OTTONIAN ART AND ARCHITECTURE** Art produced in the German empire during the period of the Ottonian or Saxon emperors and their immediate Salic successors, roughly from 950 to 1050. It was found in most of the lands of the empire (except for Italy) and was shaped by Christian, Carolingian and even Byzantine art and architecture, the last a result of the marriage in 972 of Otto II (973–983) with the Byzantine princess Theophano. Sculpture was a major artistic form, especially freestanding statues. While stone was rare and most of the early artistic specimens reliquaries, there were important pieces, including the Gero Crucifix, made before 986. Ivory reliefs were also produced, their subjects becoming associated with book illumination. This field, reaching its height at the school of Reichenau, was one of the particular Ottonian achievements leading directly to the employment of the Romanesque style and influencing illumination in countries such as England. Painting continued on murals, the finest considered to be at the Church of Saint George at Aberzell and San Vincenzo at Galliano (which reflect the effects of the Byzantine stylistic tradition). Architecturally the Ottonian era was marked by its conservatism, most efforts going into the continued expansion or enhancement of existing Carolingian edifices. See also ROMANESQUE ART AND ARCHITECTURE.

**OTTO OF FREISING** (d. 1158) Bishop of Freising from 1138 and a chronicler of his age. A Cistercian, Otto joined the Second Crusade with his half brother, Conrad III (1147–1148), and, as a relative of both Conrad and Frederick (the uncle of Barbarossa), he influenced imperial policy to some extent. He is widely considered the greatest medieval historical writer. His chronicle of world history (written 1143–1146), *Chronica sive historia de duabus civitati-*

*bus,* presented a modified view of Saint Augustine's conception of the conflict between the City of God and the world. He also wrote *Gesta Friderici* (1156–1158), including the activities of Frederick and the House of Hohenstaufen.

**OUTREMER** A term meaning "over the sea," used to describe the Crusader kingdoms established in the Middle East in the 12th and 13th centuries. See also CRUSADER STATES.

**OWEN GLENDOWER** (c. 1354–c. 1416) Also Owain ap Gruffyd and Owain Glyn Dwr, a Welsh national hero who fought to end English domination of the country. A descendant of a Welsh princely family, Owen studied in London and served for a time in the army of King Richard II (1377–1399) against Henry Bolingbroke (the future Henry IV, 1399–1413). Returning home about 1400, he began a feud with Reynold, Lord Grey of Ruthin, which led to a major uprising in Wales. By 1404 most of the country was under his rule, but his efforts to establish a Welsh parliament failed as he was defeated by Prince Henry (the future Henry V, 1413–1422). His cause was finally defeated as Owen's allies, including the French, could not arrive in time to save it. Owen was driven into the hills, spending his last years waging an ultimately futile guerrilla war. See also WALES.

**OXFORD** Town situated between the Upper Thames (called the Isis at Oxford), and the Cherwell Rivers, first mentioned in 912 in the *Anglo-Saxon Chronicle* and called Oxnaford. The first Norman governor appointed over the town was Robert d'Oilly, who built Oxford Castle and the region's first bridges, the Folly, Hythe and Magdalen. Oxford's principal institution was its university, established in the mid-12th century, perhaps because English students were refused entry to the University of Paris in 1167. Oxford University derived much of its early organization from Paris, originally having faculties for law, theology, medicine and the arts and divided into two sections: north, for Scottish scholars, and south, for scholars from England, Wales, Ireland and the Continent. After 1274 there was only one student body. The various colleges came into existence as boardinghouses for needy students, emerging into the noted institutions of later years: Balliol (1263), Merton (1264), Saint Edmund Hall (1269), Exeter (1314), Oriel (1326), Queen's (1340), New (1379), Lincoln

Oxford Castle

(1427), All Soul's (1437) and Magdalen (1458). Among the luminaries associated with Oxford were Robert Grosseteste, Roger Bacon, John Duns Scotus, William of Ockham and John Wycliffe.

**OXFORD, PROVISIONS OF** Reforms forced on King Henry III of England (1216–1272) by the barons in 1258, coming about as a result of the king's need for funds. He summoned Parliament (the Mad or Easter Parliament) in spring, 1258. In return for funds, the barons demanded reforms be undertaken by a commission. The subsequent report, issued around June 10, was largely written by Simon de Montfort and, known as the Provisions of Oxford, was regarded as the first written constitution in England. Among its clauses were the creation of a 15-member baronial council, appointment of the justiciar, the required meeting of Parliament and the control over sheriffs and local administration. Papal bulls (in 1261 and 1262) annulled the provisions, leading to the Barons' War. The provisions were annulled finally in 1266 with the Dictum of Kenilworth. See also BARONS' WAR.

# P

**PACHYMERES, GEORGE** (d. c. 1310) Byzantine scholar and historian and an opponent of the union of the Eastern and Western Churches, ordained and serving as a teacher at the academy of Hagia Sophia in Constantinople. His principal work was a chronicle of the reigns of the two Palaeologi emperors, Michael VIII and Andronicus II, in the second half of the 13th century. His chronicle, a continuation of the writings of George Acropolites, was a major source for the era. He also wrote a compendium of Aristotelian philosophy, rhetorical exercises and a handbook on mathematics, astronomy, music and geometry.

**PADUA** City in northeastern Italy, west of Venice in Venetia, called in Italian Padova. The city had legendary origins, supposedly founded by Antenor, a Trojan hero. Mentioned first with the date 302 B.C. by Livy, it was called Patavicum throughout the Roman era, surviving the early Middle Ages to become prosperous and a major commune in northern Italy from the 11th to the 13th century. Long a free city, except for a period during the rule of Ezzelino da Romana (d. 1259), Padua was then ruled by the Carrara family in 1318 and under Venetian domination in 1405. Celebrated for its encouragement of the arts, the city claimed works by DONATELLO, Mantegna (see MANTEGNA, ANDREA) and Gattamelatta. Of particular note was its university, established in 1222, the oldest in Italy, except for Bologna's. The city's intellectual circles drew many humanistic scholars. It established the first hall for the study of anatomy in Europe. See also ANTHONY OF PADUA, SAINT.

**PAGAN** King of the Bulgars from 767 until 770, reigning during a time of Bulgar political unrest. See also BULGARIA.

Hammer of Thor, object of pagan worship

**PAGANISM** Worship often of a pantheon of gods, the practice of rituals not associated with Christian or Muslim monotheistic belief. See ARIANISM; BOHEMIA; BONIFACE, ARCHBISHOP OF MAINZ; BULGARIA; CLOVIS I; DENMARK; DRANG NACH OSTEN; ENGLAND; FRANKS; GERMANY; IRELAND; LITHUANIA; LIVONIA; LOMBARDS; NORWAY; OSTROGOTHS; POLAND; RUSSIA; SAXONS; SCOTLAND; SERBIA; SLAVS; SWEDEN; VANDALS; VIKINGS, VISIGOTHS.

**PAINTING** See ALBERTI, LEON BATTISTA; ANGELICO, FRA; ANTONELLO DA MESSINA; ART AND ARCHITECTURE, BYZANTINE; ART AND ARCHITECTURE, ISLAMIC; BALDOVINETTI, ALISSO; BELLINI, GIOVANNI; BELLINI, JACOPO; BOTTICELLI, ALESSANDRO; BOUTS, DIRK; CAMPIN, ROBERT; CASTAGNO, ANDREA DEL; CIMABUE; COSSA, FRANCESCO; DADDI, BERNARDO; DOMENICO VENEZIANO; DUCCIO DI BUONINSEGNA; EYCK, HUBERT VAN; EYCK, JAN VAN; FOUQUET, JEAN; GADDI, AGNOLO; GADDI, TADDEO; GENTILE DA FABRIANO; GHIRLANDAIO, DOMENICO; GIOTTO; GOTHIC ART AND ARCHITECTURE; LIMBURG, THE BROTHERS OF; LIPPI, FRA FILIPPO; LOCHNER, STEPHEN; LORENZO MONACO, MANTEGNA, ANDREA; MANUSCRIPT ILLUMINATION; MARTINI, SIMONE; MASACCIO, TOMMASO; MASOLINO DA PANICALE; OTTONIAN ART AND ARCHITECTURE; PIERO DELLA FRANCESCA; PISANELLO; POLLAIUOLO, ANTONIO DEL; ROMANESQUE ART AND ARCHITECTURE; SQUARCIONE, FRANCESCO; WEYDEN, ROGER VAN DER.

**PALAEOLOGI DYNASTY** Byzantine noble family that first rose to prominence in the 11th century but came to establish the last dynasty of Byzantine emperors, which included Michael VIII Palaeologus (1259–1282), Andronicus II (1282–1328), Andronicus III (1328–1341), John V (1341–1391), Andronicus IV (1376–1379), John VII (1390), Manuel II (1391–1425), John VIII (1425–1448) and the last ruler of the Byzantine Empire, Constantine XI (1449–1453). See also BYZANTINE EMPIRE.

**PALAMAS, GREGORY, SAINT** (c. 1296–1359) Byzantine monk, theologian, and influential spokesman for the mystical sect of Hesychasm. A native of Constantinople, Palamas joined the monastic community of Mount Athos about 1316, mastering Hesychast techniques of prayer and meditation and studying the writings of the church fathers. He fled to Thessalonica in the wake of the Turkish threat and was ordained in 1326. In 1331 he retired to a mountain near Beroea and conducted debates with theologians of the Greek and Latin churches involving Hesychasm. Condemned for his views, he was excommunicated in 1344 but

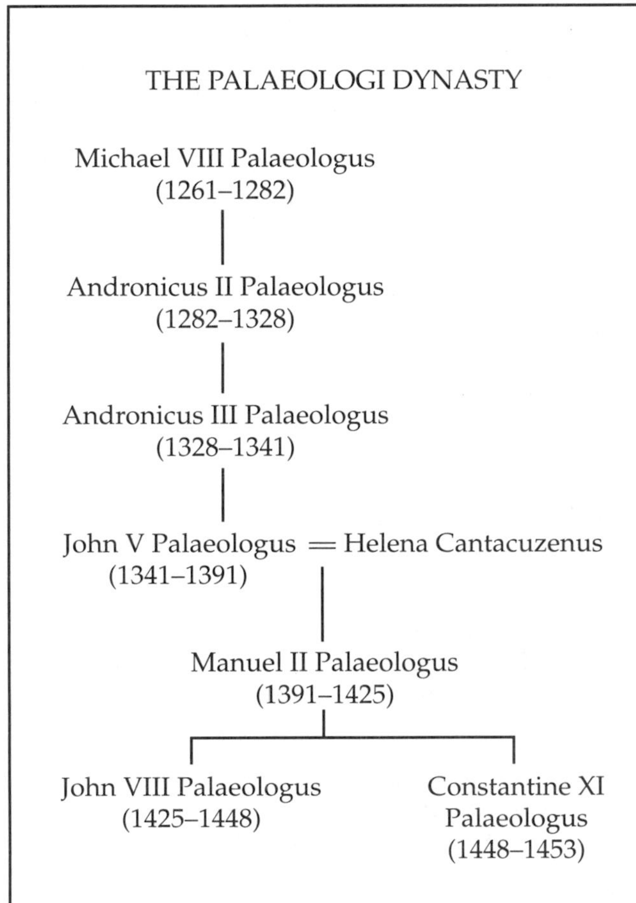


reinstated under Emperor John VI Cantacuzenus (1347–1354), who usurped the throne. That year he was named bishop of Thessalonica, and in 1351 the Blackerna Synod accepted his teachings. Palamas was canonized and given the titles of doctor and father of the church in 1369. See also HESYCHASM.

**PALATINATE** Called in German Pfalz, two regions of Germany unrelated geographically but associated historically. The Palatinate consisted of the Rhenish (or Lower) Palatinate (German, Reinpfalz or Niederpfalz) and the Upper Palatinate (German, Oberpfalz), deriving its name from the original Roman title Count Palatine. The Wittelsbach dynasty took control of the Rhenish Palatinate in 1214, eventually claiming the Upper Palatinate. In 1356 the rank of Elector was granted to the senior line of the Wittelsbach family, with the Rhenish Palatinate becoming known as the Electoral Palatinate (German, Kurpfalz).

**PALE,** The Region around Dublin ruled by the English. A similar region existed around Calais until 1558. See also IRELAND.

**PALERMO** A major city and port in Sicily, notable for its mix of cultures, which included the Byzantine, Arab and Norman. Palermo was probably founded by the Phoenicians, coming under Carthaginian domination in the fifth century B.C. and controlled by the Romans in 254 B.C. Of limited importance in the Roman era, Palermo was conquered by the Vandals in 440 and was subsequently occupied by the forces of Odoacer (d. 493) and Theodoric (471–526). Through the campaigns of Belisarius, Byzantium introduced imperial administration again, from 535 to 831, when the Muslims captured the city. Palermo benefited economically as a result, being vital to Arab trade routes in the Mediterranean. The city's golden age began in 1072 when the Normans, under Roger I and Robert Guiscard, established the Norman Kingdom of Sicily (1130). Byzantine, Latin and Arabic cultures all thrived in the city, producing art and architecture of enduring beauty. In 1194 the Normans were replaced by the German Hohenstaufens, an event marked by the crowning of Emperor Henry VI (1190–1197) as king of Sicily. Emperor Frederick II (1215–1250) made Sicily the focus of his ambitions, but his deportation of Arabs brought about cultural and economic deficiencies. Palermo supported the imperial cause, however, and was punished by Charles of Anjou, who destroyed the last of the Hohenstaufens in 1266. The city's response to Angevin harshness was the war of the Sicilian Vespers of 1282, followed by an invitation to the Aragonese to assume authority. In 1412 a union between Aragon and Sicily ushered in a new period that endured beyond the Middle Ages. See also SICILY.

**PALESTINE** See CRUSADER STATES; CRUSADES; JERUSALEM; JEWS AND JUDAISM; MAMLUKS; OTTOMAN EMPIRE; OUTREMER; SELJUK TURKS.

**PAPACY** See ALBIGENSIAN MOVEMENT; ALBORNOZ, GIL ÁLVAREZ CARRILO DE; ALEXANDER III; AVIGNON; BABYLONIAN CAPTIVITY; BONIFACE VIII; CANOSSA; CATHARI; CHARLEMAGNE; CLERMONT, COUNCIL OF; CLUNY; CONCILIAR MOVEMENT; CRUSADES; DONATION OF CONSTANTINE; DONATION OF PEPIN; FEUDALISM; FERRARA-FLORENCE, COUNCIL OF; FREDERICK I, EMPEROR; FREDERICK II, EMPEROR; GRATIAN; GREGORIAN REFORM; GREGORY I; GREGORY VII; GUELPHS AND GHIBELLINES; HENRY IV, KING OF GERMANY; HENRY V, KING OF GERMANY; HERESIES; INNOCENT III; INQUISITION; INVESTIGATURE CONTROVERSY; LATERAN COUNCILS; LIBER PONTIFICALIS; LOMBARD LEAGUE; LOMBARDS; MARTIN V; MATILDA, COUNTESS OF TUSCANY; NICHOLAS I; NORMANS; PAPAL STATES; PISA, COUNCIL OF; PRAGMATIC SANCTION OF BOURGES; ROME; SCHISM, GREAT SCHISMS; URBAN II; WORMS, CONCORDAT OF; see also individual popes and related topics in glossary.

**PAPAL STATES** The territory under the temporal authority of the papacy, also called the Pontifical States, consisting (with variations) of the regions of Umbria, Latium, the Marches and parts of Emilia-Romagna. According to tradition, the Papal States originated in the fourth century with the Patrimonium Petri, or Patrimony of Saint Peter, which was an endowment of extensive lands around Rome. Real authority came in the fifth century with the decline of the Roman Empire in the West, when the popes gave the inhabitants of the region their protection. Confronted by the Lombard threat in the eighth century, Frankish support was sought, leading to the Donation of Pepin, in 756, which provided the papacy with additional lands, equal to the old Byzantine Exarchate of Ravenna and the Pentapolis (a territory along the Adriatic coast, consisting of Rimini, Fano, Pesaro, Senigallia and Ancona).

As was true of virtually every feudal possession, the Papal States endured the rise of independent vassals, especially in the ninth and 10th centuries, and the bequest of Countess Matilda of Tuscany to the Holy See of her lands, in 1115, touched off a long conflict with the Holy Roman Emperors that deepened during the Investiture Controversy. As the temporal strength of the popes diminished, the regions, most notably Romagna, energetically resisted all papal authority, a situation that worsened when the papacy moved its residence to Avignon in the 14th century. The BABYLONIAN CAPTIVITY and the Great Schism, which continued into the 15th century, brought chaos to the Papal States. An important step was taken, however, by Cardinal Albornoz, who campaigned repeatedly in the 1350s to reinstate papal authority. After the return of the papacy to Rome, the primary concern was Rome itself and the wealthy regions to the northwest. Reclamation of papal power and influence would come with the Renaissance popes, especially Julius II (reigned 1503–1513). See also DONATION OF CONSTANTINE; DONATION OF PEPIN; ROME; and individual popes.

**PARIS** French city situated on the Seine River. It began as a town of the Gallic tribe of the Parisii and became the capital city of the kingdom of France. Paris, called Lutetia, was first mentioned by Julius Caesar in his commentaries on his Gallic campaigns. Conquered by the Romans in 52 B.C., it endured German invasions in the third century, and Saint Genevieve defended the city from the Huns in the fifth century, thereby being named the patron saint of France at that time. The city's status as a royal residence began in 508 when Clovis, king of the Franks, made it his capital, and it was maintained as such in the 6th to the 10th century by the Merovingian and Carolingian dynasties. With the accession in 987 of Hugh Capet, count of Paris, as king of France, Paris was designated the French capital and permanent residence of its monarchs. By the 12th century Paris had taken on a building pattern, with the government situated on the Île de la Cité, the commercial center on the Right Bank and the city's cultural and academic institutions on the Left Bank.

Substantial building was accomplished under King Philip II Augustus (ruled 1180–1223); schools, churches and abbeys were founded and a wall around the city constructed. The Louvre, a fortress outside the city wall on the Right Bank, was also built. The University of Paris was assured self-government in 1200 and granted a charter in 1215 by Pope Innocent III (1198–1216). The school was celebrated throughout Europe (see UNIVERSITIES) and was the venue for some of the most intense and important academic, philosophical and theological debates of the Middle Ages and attracted the most influential intellects of the time.

Problems began in the 14th century during the Hundred Years' War, difficulties reflecting the rebellious and independent nature of the Parisians. In 1356 the merchant's provost, Étienne Marcel, took advantage of the French defeat at Poitiers to reduce royal power. After his murder, the dauphin Charles (V, 1364–1380) reestablished royal authority, moving the residence of the king to the Louvre and building new ramparts around the Right Bank, the fortresses within these walls including the formidable prison of Bastille. The war with England brought pestilence and economic decline. Paris fell to the English in 1420, and King Henry VI of England (1422–1461) was crowned the king of France at Notre Dame in 1431. In 1436 the French recaptured the city, an major step toward their triumph in the Hundred Years' War. See also FRANCE.

**PARIS, MATTHEW** (d. 1259) Benedictine monk and chronicler whose works served as a major source on the events of the 13th century, especially the years 1235–1239. A Benedictine at Saint Albans from 1217, he wrote the *Chronica majora,* a history from the Creation to the year 1259. Part of it was drawn from Roger of Wendover's *Flores historiarum,* although the later portions were clearly Paris's own work.

**PARLIAMENT** Legislative assembly of England that came to consist of the Crown, the House of Lords and the House of Commons. Parliament had its origins in two earlier bodies, the Magnus Concilium (Great Council) and the Curia Regis (King's Court), the former including the important religious and secular figures, and the latter a group of advisers summoned by the king. During the Norman regime it was a gathering of the king's feudal tenants but nevertheless was similar in many regards to the Anglo-Saxon Witan. In time only those vassals actually summoned attended, the meeting of the Curia Regis gaining political force as the Concilium Regis in Parliamento, the "King's Council in Parliament."

Joint meetings of the Curia Regis and the Magnus Concilium were held to discuss matters that the king judged to be important, adjournment possible only on completion of specified tasks, although it was often the right of the Curia members to finish the business at hand after the departure of the Magnus Concilium, as these magnates wielded much more influence. Rarely did King Edward I (ruled 1272–1307) summon knights from shires and burgesses from the towns. The Model Parliament was held in 1295, when it drew both commoners and temporal and spiritual lords to the assembly.

Until the 14th century the function of Parliament was largely judicial, but its development was hastened by the gradual control its assumed over finances and taxation. Transfer of taxation rights was made by the Crown to Parliament in 1340, as a result of the need of the kings to finance the Hundred Years' War with France. It thus became possible for Parliament to exert influence on the king. In return for finances, the ruler had to agree to hear petitions. This supported Parliament in its taking of an active role in legislation. The practice of having the lords convene in one chamber and the knights and burgesses in another was probably the result of commoners being uncomfortable in the presence of their superiors. Clearly, however, the House of Lords was much stronger politically, the Lancastrian kings drawing their principal advisers from their ranks. The Tudors supplemented their authority in the Commons by appointing privy councillors to fill seats in that chamber, often making Parliament an instrument of the royal will. See also ENGLAND.

**PARMA** City in north-central Italy, in the Emilia Romagna region, situated on the Parma River. Originally a Roman colony, Parma was destroyed by the Ostrogoths during the reign of King Theodoric (471–526) but was rebuilt, receiving a bishopric once again in the ninth century (the original see having been founded in the fourth century). It became a free commune in the 12th century. Involvement in the conflict between the popes and the Holy Roman Emperors subjected Parma to various rulers. It was annexed to the Papal States in the 16th century.

***PARSIVAL*** See WOLFRAM VON ESCHENBACH.

**PASCHAL I** (d. 824) Pope from 817 to 824, a Roman by birth and an abbot when elected. Generally unpopular, he confronted a revival of iconoclastic policies in the Byzantine Empire under Leo V the Armenian (813–820), which he opposed unsuccessfully. He was also attempting to maintain amicable relations with the Frankish emperors, exerting his own independence while Emperor Louis I the Pious (814–840) forced major reforms on the church. Paschal, accused of complicity in the murder of two Frankish officials in the Curia, had to swear an oath of purgation to clear his name. He was responsible for the construction of several buildings in Rome, including Santa Maria in Domnica and Santa Prassede.

**PASCHAL II** (d. 1118) Pope from 1099 to 1118, serving as cardinal and as papal legate to Spain for his predecessor, Pope Urban II (1088–1099). Paschal confronted the Investiture Controversy, which was renewed, and a conflict with Emperor Henry VI (1056–1106) and then his son, Henry V (1106–1125) whom the pope had originally supported against his father. Although the question of investiture had been solved in England and in France by 1106–1107, negotiations with the emperor proved fruitless. At the Council of Rome (1102) the pontiff excommunicated Henry IV and supported the revolt of Henry V. The new emperor proved as determined on the subject, and Paschal opposed him at the synods of Guastalla (1106) and Troyes (1109), confirming his condemnation at Benevento in 1108 and at the Lateran in 1110. A meeting between the pope and Henry at Sutri was thwarted early in 1111 by the German bishops. Paschal was seized and forced to consent to Henry's demand, crowning him on April 13, 1111. The treaty signed by Paschal under duress was voided the following year by the Lateran Council, and other synods excommunicated Henry by 1116. In 1117 the imperial army marched on Rome, driving Paschal into exile in Benevento. He died the next year with the crisis unresolved. See also INVESTITURE CONTROVERSY.

**PASCHASIUS RADBERTUS, SAINT** (c. 785–c. 860) Benedictine abbot and theologian, of the Benedictine monastery at Corbie, where he studied with Adalherd and his brother, Wala. In 822 he accompanied Adalherd into Saxony, where he established the Westphalian community of Corvey. Elected abbot of the foundation, he attended the councils of Paris (847) and Quercy (845) and then retired to study and to write. His life of Adalhard and his commentaries, poems and letters were important, but his critical work was the treatise *De corpore et sanguine Domini, On the Body and Blood of Christ,* written in 831 and revised in 834. The monograph emerged as the major source for a doctrinal study of the Eucharist. It was criticised by Ratramnus (c. 800), who wrote his own treatise.

**PATARINES** Also Patarelli, a Milanese religious party that called for reform and was composed of tradesmen and peasants. The name probably derived from the name for the poor quarter of Milan, the *pataria.* The group opposed lay investiture, papal corruption and simony. Although they did not exist much past 1075, the Patarines gave the spirit and name to subsequent reform movements that were condemned by the church as heretical. See also HERESIES.

**PATRIMONIUM PETRI** See PAPAL STATES.

**PAUL I, SAINT** (d. 767) Pope from 757 to 767, the brother of his predecessor, Stephen II (III) (752–757), who spent much of his pontificate in conflict with the Lombard king Desiderius (757–774) and the Byzantine emperor Constantine V (741–775). He allied himself with Pepin III the Short (751–768) against Desiderius when the Lombards threatened the Papal States and opposed Byzantine iconoclastic policies in Constantinople.

**PAUL II** (1417–1471) Pope from 1464 to 1471, born in Venice, made a cardinal in 1440 and the governor of Campania in 1456. Paul earned the enmity of the humanists by purging the Roman Academy in 1468 and by putting one of its members under torture. He also condemned the Pragmatic Sanction of Bourges (1438), issued by King Charles VII of France (1422–1461), and excommunicated George of Podiebrad, king of Bohemia (1458–1471) for his refusal to curb the Utraquist national church of Bohemia. To punish George, Paul supported Mattias Corvinus of Hungary in his campaign against Bohemia, crowning him king in 1469. He also tried unsuccessfully to mount a Crusade against the Turks.

**PAUL BRANOVIC** Ruler of the Serbs from 917 to 920. See also SERBIA.

**PAULINUS, SAINT** (d. 644) First prelate of York and a Christian missionary in Anglo-Saxon England who was crucial to the conversion of Northumbria. Sent from Rome in 601 to assist Augustine on behalf of Pope Gregory I (590–604), Paulinus became bishop of Kent in 625, serving as escort to the Kentish princess Aethelburga when she married Edwin, king of Northumbria (d. 632). In 627 Edwin was converted and baptized, bringing his chiefs with him and ensuring Paulinus's appointment as bishop of York. Five years later, when Edwin was slain in battle against the pagan Caedwalla and Penda, Paulinus and Ethelburga were forced to return to Kent, where he served as prelate of Rochester. See also YORK.

**PAUL THE DEACON** (c. 725–c. 799) Lombard historian, also called Paulus Diaconus, a noble from Friuli, serving King Desiderius (757–774) and counselor and tutor to his daughter, Adelberga. A Benedictine of Saint Peter at Civate (entering c. 774), he and his brother were implicated in a plot against the Franks, and his brother was sent to France as a prisoner. In 782 Paul went to Charlemagne to ask for his brother's release, which was obtained with the promise that Paul join the court at Aachen. After spending a number of years there, he moved to Monte Cassino, where he wrote his principal work, *Historia Langobardum*, the *History of the Lombards*, comprising Lombard history from 568 to 744, employing both written and oral sources. Paul also wrote a *Historia Romana*, a continuation of the *Breviarum* of Eutropius, as well as a commentary on the rule of Saint Benedict. He was also called Paulus Levita and has been referred to as the father of Italian History. See also LOMBARDS.

**PAULUS DIACONUS** See PAUL THE DEACON.

**PAVIA** City in Lombardy (northern Italy) on the Ticino River near its confluence with the Po. An old Roman site, Pavia was sacked by Attila the Hun in 452 and again in 476 by Odoacer (d. 493). Under Lombard domination in the sixth century it became an important city, surviving the collapse of the Lombards at the hands of Charlemagne in 774. It was the chief city of the Carolingians in Italy, becoming a free commune in the 12th century. In 1359 control was claimed by the Visconti family. Gian Galeazzo II Visconti established the University of Pavia in 1361, associated with the law school dating from the ninth century. Notable remains include the Church of San Michele, the cathedral in which the Lombard kings were crowned, San Pietro in Ciel d'Oro (12th century) and San Teodoro (12th century). See also LOMBARDS.

**PEACE OF GOD** A widespread movement in Europe, beginning in the 10th century, arising from a need to end the violence of the times and to make travel safer for pilgrims and merchants. It was first officially declared perhaps in 989 in Charroux, calling for the preservation of peasant rights, safety for traders and the sanctity of the churches. In the early 11th century an additional peace effort was made with the Truce of God, which produced armistices in blood feuds and prohibited fighting from Wednesday night until Monday morning. Bands of militia helped enforce the truce while prelates threatened spiritual punishments for oath breakers. Never particularly effective, especially because of the participation of nobility in warfare, the Peace and Truce of God found new life during the Crusades, when Pope Urban II at Clermont (1095) called for a march to the Holy Land. Most of the serious offenders went on crusade. See also CHIVALRY; CLERMONT, COUNCIL OF; CRUSADES; FEUDALISM.

**"PEARL, THE"** Celebrated 14th-century allegorical poem composed by an anonymous Middle English poet. It is generally considered to have been written as an elegy for the poet's daughter, and its main theme is the acceptance of God's will in times of adversity.

**PEASANT REVOLT** A popular uprising in 1381 in England. The causes of the rebellion were harsh economic conditions endured by the lower classes; the Statute of Laborers (1351), which fixed maximum wages for labor; and the 1381 imposition of the hated poll tax. Erupting in May, the revolt was organized by Wat Tyler, who led the rebels in a march on London, entering the city on June 13, where they instigated a massacre, bringing King Richard II (1377–1399) into a compromise meeting. Although he promised to abolish serfdom and make land available, the chancellor, archbishop Simon of Sudbury, and the treasurer, Sir Robert of Hales, both unpopular, were beheaded. Tyler was murdered immediately thereafter, and the rebels dispersed in London. Elsewhere, the uprising in East Anglia was crushed later that month, ending a short-lived revolt. See also ENGLAND.

**PECKHAM, JOHN** (c. 1225–1292) Archbishop of Canterbury from 1279 and a vigorous defender of papal supremacy. Born in Sussex, he joined the Franciscan order about 1250, studying at Oxford and Paris, and was profoundly influenced by Saint Bonaventure. In 1279 he was named successor to Robert Kilwardly at Canterbury, overcoming King Edward I's (1272–1307) choice, Robert Burnell, bishop of Bath. Peckham encouraged clerical reform and an end to religious abuses. He also wrote scientific works and hymns. See also CANTERBURY.

**PEDRO I, KING OF ARAGON** (1068–1104) Ruler from 1094 to 1104, who pursued an aggressive policy against the Moors, receiving from Pope Paschal II (1099–1118) a crusading indulgence for his campaigns of reconquest. In 1096 he defeated the Moors at Alcoraz and in 1100 recovered Barbastro. See also RECONQUISTA.

**PEDRO II, KING OF ARAGON** Ruler from 1196 to 1213, who fought in the Battle of Las Navas de Tolosa (1212) and took part in the crushing defeat of the Almohads. The following year he became unavoidably embroiled in the Albigensian Crusade, marching to support his vassals in southern France against Simon de Montfort. He and his allies were annihilated on September 12, 1213, near Muret, and the king was killed. Chroniclers declared that Pedro was a good Catholic who was defending his vassals and not supporting the Albigensians. He had been crowned in Rome in 1204 by Pope Innocent III (1198–1216), declaring his kingdom a feudal holding of the papacy.

**PEDRO III, KING OF ARAGON** (1239–1285) Ruler from 1276 to 1285, the son of King James I (1213–1276), called "the Great" because of his height and his conquests, which inaugurated an era of Aragonese expansion. A supporter of the Reconquista, he wed Constance, daughter of the Hohenstaufen claimant Manfred, in 1262 and thus was drawn into the conflict over Sicily. Pedro supported Sicilian rebels in their fight against Charles of Anjou, which culminated in the war of the Sicilian Vespers of 1282. He sailed to Sicily, claimed the throne and began years of conflict with Pope Martin IV (1281–1285). The pope excommunicated him and granted the crown of Sicily to the son of the king of France, promoting the campaign of Philip III (1270–1285) which end unsuccessfully. At the time of Peter's death, the Aragonese position in Sicily was secured. See also ARAGON; SICILY.

**PEDRO IV, KING OF ARAGON** (1319–1387) Ruler from 1336 to 1387, noted chiefly for his recovery of the Balaeric Islands in 1343 and for reducing the powers and privileges of the Aragonese nobility. In 1348 he crushed those nobles who attempted to challenge his policy. In foreign affairs he conducted a war against Pedro I of Castile (Pedro the Cruel, 1350–1369) from 1356 to 1366, as a French ally and on behalf of the Castilian claimant, Henry of Trastámara. This effort nearly ruined the Aragonese economy, so that Pedro was forced to maintain a neutral stance in the Hundred Years' War. See also ARAGON.

**PEDRO I, KING OF LEÓN-CASTILE** (1334–1369) Ruler from 1350 to 1369, called "the Cruel" because of his harsh nature and deviousness, which contributed to his overthrow at the hands of his half brother and successor, Henry II of Trastámara (1369–1379). The son of King Alfonso XI (1312–1350), Pedro found rivals among his half brothers and was forced to murder two of the them in 1358. The chief challenge to his throne came from Henry, who allied himself with Aragon and the French, defeating Pedro in 1366. Pedro, having obtained the support of Edward the Black Prince, returned the following year, smashing Henry on April 13, 1367, at Nájera, capturing Henry's French ally, Bertrand de Guesclin. In 1369, another effort was made to defeat Pedro, who was routed at Montiel. Pedro met with Henry on March 23, 1369, and was murdered by Henry. His daughter, Constance, married John of Gaunt.

**PEDRO I, KING OF PORTUGAL** (1320–1367) Monarch from 1357 to 1367, called Pedro the Severe or the Justiciar and remembered for his desperate love of a lady at the court, Inés de Castro, despite his own marriage to a Castilian noblewoman. The murder of Inés in 1355, with the complicity of Peter's father, King Alfonso IV (1325–1357), caused a brief rebellion. Alfonso forced his son to pardon the assassins, but after gaining the throne he cut out the murderers' hearts. See also CASTRO, INÉS DE.

**PEGOLOTTI, FRANCESCO** Fourteenth-century trader and writer from Florence. His *Practica della mercatura* (*Practice of Marketing*), organized about 1335–1343, was a valuable glimpse into the conditions of travel and mercantile business in that era. Pegolotti was a noted traveler and an agent of the House of Bardi, in which capacity he journeyed to Belgium, England, Cyprus and Armenia. See also BARDI, HOUSE OF.

**PELAGIUS I** (d. 561) Pope from 556 to 561, an architect of papal power who earned greater esteem for his efforts prior to his election as successor to Pope Vigilius (537–555). He served three popes, persuaded the Ostrogothic king Totila not to massacre the Romans, and settled differences with Emperor Justinian I (527–565) concerning the Nestorians. Elected pope on April 16, 556 Pelagius rebuilt Rome and established the temporal authority of the papacy. He proved generally competent, despite the threat of Germanic attack, the superior position of the Eastern emperor and the widespread chaos and destruction of the time.

**PELAGIUS II** (d. 590) Pope from 579 to 590, the pontiff during the Lombard invasion of Italy, a Goth by descent. He appealed to Emperor Tiberius II (578–582) for support and then appealed to the Franks, an act with serious historical consequences. Pelagius instigated the conversion of the Visigoths in Spain, and peace with the Lombards was negotiated in 585, with the mediation of the Byzantine exarch of Ravenna. Pelagius also inaugurated a building program in Rome that had endured a plague following a ruinous flood.

**PELAYO** (d. c. 737) Semilegendary figure in the Christian kingdom of Asturias, first mentioned in the ninth century in the *Chronicle of Albelda*. Probably a Visigothic nobleman, he was exiled by King Witiza (ruled 702–710), journeying to Asturias and fomenting a revolt there against its Moorish overlords. Few details of his life are available, but he was supposedly associated with Roderic, the last Visigothic king. Pelayo certainly won a battle against the Moors and established the kingdom that was to become Asturias (c. 722). His original realm was consolidated by his son-in-law, Alfonso I (ruled 739–757).

**PEMBROKE, RICHARD DE CLARE, EARL OF** (d. 1176) Anglo-Norman nobleman, also called Richard "Strongbow," the son of Gilbert de Clare, succeeding his father in 1148. About 1168 he met Dermot MacMurrough, the king of Leinster, who had been driven from his Irish throne and was seeking English support. Pembroke agreed, obtain permission from King Henry II (1154–1189) in 1170 to invade Ireland. Arriving on August 23, near Waterford, Pembroke quickly won Dublin, thereby implementing the English conquest of Ireland. Acknowledging Henry's sovereignty, Pembroke was awarded the right to rule Ireland, although his powers were limited. See also IRELAND.

**PEMBROKE, WILLIAM MARSHAL, EARL OF** (d. 1219) English nobleman who was influential in the late 12th and early 13th centuries, the son of John FitzGilbert, the marshal. Pembroke distinguished himself as guardian of Prince Henry (d. 1183) and then as a loyal soldier fighting for Henry II in France. Powerful during Richard the Lion-Heart's (1189–1199) time on crusade and captivity in Germany (1190–1194), Pembroke opposed Richard's regent, William Longchamp, and attempted to prevent Prince John (1199–1216) from taking the throne. He was adviser to John and was designated regent to John's heir, Henry III (1216–1272). In his name he defeated the allied English barons and a French army that had invaded the kingdom in 1217, negotiating a peace treaty with the future Louis VIII (1223–1226) of France. Through marriage to the heiress of Richard de Clare, earl of Pembroke, he owned vast holdings in England, Ireland, Normandy and Wales and was later confirmed as earl of Pembroke.

**PENDA** (d. 654) King of Mercia from 632 to 654, one of the illustrious Mercian kings who extended his control over much of the region south of the Humber River. He secured his throne through his 632 invasion of Northumbria, where he defeated and killed King Edwin. Soon afterward, however, his triumph was offset by the return of the Northumbrian ascendancy, which continued until 642. In that year Penda crushed and killed King Oswald, making possible the rapid expansion of Mercian power. By 654 Penda was powerful enough to make war king OSWIU of Northumbria but fell at the Battle of Winwaed. See also MERCIA, KINGDOM OF.

**PEPIN I, KING OF AQUITAINE** (d. 838) Ruler from 817 to 838, the son of Emperor Louis I and a descendant of Charlemagne (768–814), who participated in revolts against his father in 830 and 833. Later he helped restore Louis to power. His son Pepin II (d. c. 864) eventually lost the throne of Aquitaine to Charles the Bald.

**PEPIN, KING OF ITALY** (d. 810) Second son of Charlemagne (768–814) and ruler of Italy from 781. Granted his crown by his father, Pepin was an active king, conducting campaigns in Bavaria, against the Avars and in the region around Venice. His death preempted Charlemagne's plans for him to inherit Italy and Bavaria. See also CHARLEMAGNE.

**PEPIN OF HÉRISTAL** (d. 714) Also Pepin II or Pepin the Young, mayor of the palace and the virtual ruler of the Franks from 687 to 714. Mayor of the palace in Austrasia from 679, Pepin was a staunch defender of Austrasian rights over Neustria, defeating the Neustrians under Thierry III in 687. Pepin chose to maintain the fiction of Merovingian rule, retaining Thierry and then installing three successive "lazy" kings, Clovis III, Childebert III and Dagobert III, at the same time uniting the Franks. He also conducted wars against the Frisians and Bavarians, encouraging the acceptance of Christianity in Bavaria. His son was Charles Martel (714–741). See also FRANCE.

THE HOUSE OF PEPIN (THE PEPINIDS)

Pepin of Landen (d. 640)
- daughter
  - Pepin of Héristal (d. 714)
    - Charles Martel (d. 741)
      - Pepin the Short (751–768)
        - Charlemagne (768–814)
        - Carloman
      - Grifo
      - Carloman
- Grimaud
  - Childebert

**PEPIN OF LANDEN** (d. 640) Also Pepin I, mayor of the palace in Austrasia, who is considered the first of the Carolingian dynasts. Pepin was invaluable in the service of King Clotaire II, supporting his conquest of Austrasia in 613, which he governed as mayor of the palace for King Dagobert I. He married the daughter of Arnulf, bishop of Metz, from which union arose the Carolingian line.

**PEPIN THE SHORT** (d. 768) Also Pepin III, king of the Franks from 751, father of Charlemagne. A son of Charles Martel (714–741), Pepin inherited divided rule of the Franks with his brother, Carloman, wielding power as mayor of the palace in Neustria, Burgundy and Provence. Carloman received Austrasia, Alamannia and Thuringia. A third brother, Grifo, was not considered, rebelled and died in 753. Pepin and his brother decided to retain the weak Merovingians on the throne, crowning Childeric III in 743, but Carloman's retirement to a monastery in 747 altered future policy. Now sole mayor, Pepin sought and received papal approval to end nominal Merovingian rule, deposing Childeric in 751 and obtaining his anointing at Soissons by Archbishop Boniface. Additional papal support came in 754, when Pope Stephen II (752–757), seeking his assistance against the Lombards, anointed Pepin and his sons king and heirs. In return, Pepin twice defended Rome from the Lombard threat (754, 756), wresting from the Lombards control of Ravenna and other regions. His grant of these territories to the pope, called the Donation of Pepin, was the foundation of the Papal States. Subsequent pleas were met with less enthusiasm, as Pepin faced unrest at home. He was also threatened by the Moors, whom he drove back across the Pyrenees. He died at Saint-Denis. See also FRANCE.

**PERCY** Powerful English family that emerged as the major landholder in Northumbria and the chief guardians of the Scottish border. Their origins in the 11th century as vassals of William the Conqueror (1066–1087), the Percys settled in Northumbria under the aegis of Henry de Percy (d. 1314). The family, holding title of earls of Northumbria from 1377 to 1537 (and again later), was repeatedly implicated in rebellions during the 14th and 15th centuries. Henry Percy, first earl of Northumberland, received the title from King Richard II (1189–1199) but was banished in 1398 and threw his support behind Henry Bolingbroke (Henry IV, 1399–1413) the following year. In 1403 he rebelled against Henry, fled to France and died in 1408 at Branham Moor. His son, Sir Henry Percy, called Hotspur because of his military exploits, fought against the Scots and was for a time a partisan of Henry IV. In 1403 he initiated a major uprising and was killed at the Battle of Shrewsbury. His uncle, Thomas Percy, earl of Worcester, was captured at Shrewsbury and executed. Hotspur was a major character in Shakespeare's play *Henry IV*. See also BORDER, THE.

**PEREIRA, NUN ÁLVAREZ** (1360–1431) Portuguese national hero who was called "the Great Constable." A general of and adviser to King John I of Portugal (1385–1433), Pereira was largely responsible for the triumph at Aljubarrota in 1385, which enabled John to claim his throne. Pereira's daughter married a natural son of the king, from which union originated the House of Braganza. See also PORTUGAL.

**PERRERS, ALICE** (d. 1400) Mistress of King Edward III (1327–1377) of England during his final years, a competant woman but grasping and in royal favor from 1369 until her banishment by Parliament. Edward died alone the next year. See also EDWARD III.

**PERSIA** See SASSANIDS.

**PERUZZI, HOUSE OF** One of the important Florentine banking families, emerging from Florence's popular party to become proponents of the Guelph League (papal supporters) against the Ghibelline forces (imperial adherents). Their banking endeavors began in the second half of the 13th century, bringing them second only to the Bardi in prestige and influence. Like the Bardi (and in concert with them) the Peruzzi were ruined by excessive loans to princes. Massive loans were granted to King Edward III (1327–1377) of England to finance his wars in France and Scotland. Repayment came in wool, money or assigned taxes. By 1340, however, the grants of funds had virtually liquidated the Bardi and Peruzzi banks, and they went bankrupt in 1343 and 1344; Bonifazio, the head of the Peruzzi family, died from grief. The king refused to repay his debt, and other recipients of loans, most notably the king of Naples, also defaulted. The financial decline of the Peruzzi family caused severe economic upheaval in Florence and thus an economic depression in Europe. See also BANKING.

**PESELLINO, IL** (1422–1457) Florentine painter whose name at birth was Francesco di Stefano, the grandson of the painter Giuliano 'I Pesello (d. 1446), as well as his pupil and assistant. Il Pesellino was also an associate of Filippo Lippi. He was best known for his *cassone* paintings, which were decorative panels on chests, in a style employing romantic and tapestrylike designs.

**PETCHENEGS** A nomadic Turkic people also called the Pechenegs, Buseni and, to the Byzantines, the Patzinaks (Patzinakoi). Their origins in the region lying between the Volga and the Yack (Ural) Rivers, the Petchenegs were driven from there in the late ninth century by the Khazars moving into Russia. In their turn they forced the Hungarians out. They invaded Thrace repeatedly in the 10th and 11th centuries, emerging as a serious threat to the Byzantine Empire, especially after the Byzantines extended their control into Bulgaria. The crisis came in 1090–1091, when the Petchenegs stormed the walls of Constantinople, only to be defeated by Emperor Alexius I Comnenus (1081–1118), supported by the Cumans. Thirty years of peace followed, but in 1122 the Petchenegs recrossed the Danube River, sweeping into Thrace and Macedonia. Emperor John II Comnenus (1118–1143) crushed them so completely that they ceased to pose any threat. Numbers of Petcheneg survivors were absorbed by the empire, and Petcheneg troops were pressed into the Byzantine forces.

**PETER I, KING OF ARAGON** See PEDRO I, KING OF ARAGON.

**PETER II, KING OF ARAGON** See PEDRO II, KING OF ARAGON.

**PETER III, KING OF ARAGON** See PEDRO III, KING OF ARAGON.

**PETER IV, KING OF ARAGON** See PEDRO IV, KING OF ARAGON.

**PETER I, KING OF THE BULGARS** (d. 969) Ruler of Bulgaria from 927 to 969, the son of Symeon I (893–927), whose reign was largely peaceful, negotiating a treaty in 927 with Constantinople that lasted until 965. Despite several unsuccessful uprisings among the people, Bulgaria prospered in trade until 965, when the new Byzantine emperor, Nicephorus II Phocas (963–969), refused to pay the agreed tribute and initiated hostilities. The Russians of Kiev, allies of the Byzantines, attacked Bulgaria in 967. Peter became ill, retired to a monastery and was succeeded by his son, Boris II. See also BULGARIA.

**PETER II, KING OF THE BULGARS** (d. 1197) King reigning briefly in Bulgaria, from 1196 to 1197. See also BULGARIA.

**PETER I, KING OF LEÓN-CASTILE** See PEDRO I, KING OF LEÓN-CASTILE.

**PETER I, KING OF PORTUGAL** See PEDRO I, KING OF PORTUGAL.

**PETER CASTELNAU** See ALBIGENSIAN MOVEMENT.

**PETER DAMIEN, SAINT** (1007–1072) Doctor of the church and important reformer, joining the Benedictine order at Fonte Avellana in 1035. Named cardinal of Ostia in 1057, Peter became widely known and respected for his tireless efforts in opposing corruption, simony, concubinage and other clerical abuses. He was a vigorous opponent of the antipopes and served as a diplomat to Germany and France for the papacy. The author of sermons and letters, he also wrote treatises and attacks on corruption, including *Liber gratissimus*, opposing the legitimacy of simoniac ordinations, and the well-known *Liber gomorrhianus*, an attack on clerical marriage.

**PETER DE BRUYES** (d. c. 1140) Priest and heretic, condemned for his views on the Mass, infant baptisms and the veneration of the Cross. His followers, called the

Petrobrusians, increased despite opposition. Peter, however, was killed by a monk who was enraged by his custom of burning crosses. Peter was thrown into the flames at Saint-Gilles. Abelard and Peter the Venerable wrote of him. See also HERESIES.

**PETER DES ROCHES** (d. 1238) Bishop of Winchester from 1205 to 1238, diplomat and royal adviser who began his career in Richard the Lion-Hearted's (1189–1199) court in France, becoming a favorite of King John (1199–1216), Richard's successor. He served as John's chief justiciar (1214) and as counselor. He was also tutor to young King Henry III (1216–1272) until 1227, crowning him in 1216. Defeated politically in 1223–1224 by Hubert de Burgh, Peter went on Crusade with Frederick II (1228–1229) and returned to England to bring about de Burgh's downfall in 1231. Peter des Roches was dismissed in turn by Henry in 1234.

**PETER GOJNIKOVIC** King of the Serbs from 892 to 917. See also SERBIA.

**PETER LOMBARD** (c. 1095–1160) The illustrious bishop of Paris and author of the *Sentences (Sententiarium libri IV),* which became the standard theological text of the Middle Ages. Called the "Master of the Sentences," or Petrus Lombardus, he studied in Bologna, Reims and Paris, eventually teaching at the cathedral school of Notre Dame. In 1159 he was appointed bishop of Paris, having been present at the Council of Reims (1148), where he had opposed the teachings of Gilbert de la Porrée. He was also author of *Commentaries* on the Pauline epistles and the Psalms, as well as sermons and letters, but his most important work was the *Sentences,* composed about 1148–1150/51.

A collection of the teachings of the church fathers, the *Sentences* contained scriptural traditions and important theological opinions of learned masters, divided into four books: on God and the Trinity; on the Creation and sin, as well as angels, demons and the Fall; on the Incarnation; and on the sacraments and the Four Last Things—death, judgment, heaven and hell. The *Sentences* gave rise to many commentaries, including one by Thomas Aquinas, and it served as an official textbook in the universities. The Fourth Lateran Council in 1215, in considering attacks made on it by other theologians, maintained that the *Sentences* was not contrary to orthodox views. See also THOMAS AQUINAS, SAINT.

**PETER MARTYR, SAINT** (1205–1252) Inquisitor and later patron of Inquisitors, also called Peter of Verona (after his birthplace), but not to be confused with the 16th-century reformer Peter Martyr. The son of Cathari parents, Peter, whose parents were of the Cathari sect, entered the Dominican order in 1221. He received appointment as the Inquisitor of the northern regions of Italy by Pope Gregory IX (1227–1241), and his efforts were successful among some of the Cathari, although he made enemies as well. Peter was assassinated by the Cathari while journeying to Milan. According to tradition, he wrote on the ground as he died: "Credo in Deum." See also INQUISITION.

**PETER NOLASCO** See MERCEDARIANS.

**PETER OF BLOIS** (d. c. 1212) Humorist, poet, author and tutor to the future King William II of Sicily. He was widely known for his letters, his own and those written under the name of other illustrious people. He also wrote treatises on theology, history and politics.

**PETER OF COURTENAY** Latin emperor of Constantinople in 1217, married to Yolande, sister of the Latin emperor Baldwin I (1204–1205) and Henry of Flanders (1206–1216), which union allowed him to inherit the throne on Henry's death in 1216. He was crowned by the pope in Rome before setting out for Constantinople, but in the mountains of Albania he was captured by Theodore I Lascaris (1206–1222), emperor of Nicaea. Peter died in prison some years later, and Yolande became regent in Constantinople. See also CONSTANTINOPLE, LATIN EMPIRE OF.

**PETER OF TARANTAISE** See INNOCENT V.

**PETER THE HERMIT** (d. 1115) French preacher who devoted much of his time calling for the First Crusade, and a leader of the Peasants' Crusade in 1096. He was not among the major group when the Turks attacked them and thus survived. He had gone to Constantinople to ask for support from the Byzantine Empire. Joining the Crusader army led by Godfrey de Bouillon, he attempted to flee during the siege of Antioch (1098) but was caught. The following year he entered Jerusalem with the victorious Crusaders. Returning to Europe, Peter helped establish an Augustinian monastery at Neufmoutier in Belgium. See also CRUSADES.

**PETER THE VENERABLE** (c. 1092–1156) Abbot of Cluny from 1122, honored by his contemporaries for his saintliness and gentleness and thus called Venerable. While less illustrious than his friend, Bernard of Clairvaux, Peter brought many reforms to the order. He had joined Cluny at the age of 17 and had become prior in 1120 and abbot two years later. Effecting changes in financial and educational matters in the order, Peter traveled to England, Rome and Spain but found time for prayer, study and meditation. He was the first to have a translation made of the Muslim Koran, to assist in conversions, writing treatises opposing Judaism and Peter de Bruyes, as well as sermons and poems. He also gave refuge to Peter Abelard after his condemnation by the church at the Council of Sens in 1140. See also CLUNY.

**PETER URSEOLO, KING OF HUNGARY** (1011–1058) Ruler from 1038 to 1041 and from 1044 to 1046. The son of a Venetian doge and the sister of King Stephen I (d. 1038), Peter ascended the throne on the death of his uncle. His policy of accepting foreign elements at court offended the Hungarian nobility, contributing to his overthrow and the crowning of Samuel Aba as his replacement. Peter obtained the support Emperor Henry III (1039–1056), who crushed Samuel, restored Peter and exacted an oath of fealty from him in return. In 1046 Peter was again deposed, this time by a pagan rebellion. See also HUNGARY.

**PETRARCH** (1304–1374) Italian poet and humanist, one of the major literary figures in the transition from the style of the Middle Ages to that of the Renaissance. Born in Arezzo, named Francesco Petrarca, he was the son of a Florentine notary. Petrarch's father had been exiled from Florence by the Black faction of the Guelph party, and in 1311 the family moved to Provence. Petrarch studied at Montpellier and Bologna, returning to Avignon in 1326. He took minor orders in 1330 but fathered two illegitimate children, Giovanni (b. 1337) and Francesca (b. 1343). In 1353 he moved to Provence and then flourished with the patronage of rulers in Milan, Venice and Padua after returning to Italy.

A brilliant poet, Petrarch was surpassed in Italian literature only by Dante and is often considered the first of the humanists, his work reflecting his classical learning. He had completed a text of Livy during his twenties and strove to uncover classical manuscripts and to improve his knowledge of Latin, having Latinized his name as well. These efforts earned him the title "Father of Humanism," and, despite acclaim for his poetry, he was proudest of his Latin verse, biographies and letters. His earliest surviving poems date from the time of his mother's death, in 1318 or 1319, although these were revised later. In 1341 in Rome he accepted the crown of the poet laureate, preferring Rome to Paris because it gave him an opportunity to promote the revival of classical tradition in poetry. He counted among his many famous friends Boccaccio, who presented him in 1366 with a translation of Homer's poems in Latin. Spending the years 1362–1367 in Venice, Petrarch concentrated on a number of projects. He returned to Padua in 1367, dividing his time there with trips to Argua, where he died in July 1374, supposedly found the morning of July 18, his head resting on a manuscript of Virgil.

Petrarch was the author of a vast body of works. His Latin works include *Epistolae metrical* (1350, 1357, 1363); *Africa* (begun 1338 or 1339), on Scipio Africanus and the Second Punic War; *De viris illustribus* (begun in 1338–1339 and revised in 1341–1343); *Secretum meum* (1342–1343), a treatise on dialogues between Petrarch and Saint Augustine in the presence of Truth; *De vita solitaria* (1346, with an addition in 1371); *De otio religioso* (1347, revised 1357); *Familiarum rerum libri XXIV* (organized between 1351 and 1366), letters to his friends and celebrated classical authors; *Senilium rerum libri* (after 1361–1374), more letters; *De remedius utriusque fortunae* (published 1366); and *De sui ipsius et multorum ignorantia* (1367), a defense of humanism.

His Italian works include *Canzoniere* (first edition 1340, second 1373), also *Rime in vita di Laura* and *Rime in morte die Laura,* his song book, recounting his love for Laura, whom he adored chastely; and *Trionfi* (begun in 1351 and revised between 1356 and 1374), a poetic account of the human soul evolving toward fulfillment in God.

**PEUERBACH, GEORG** (1423–1461) Austrian mathematician and astronomer, educated in Vienna and Italy, and court astrologer for King Ladislas V of Hungary. He later held the chair of astronomy and mathematics at Vienna, writing the *Theoricae novae planetarum,* an elementary treatise on planetary astronomy. Peuerbach completed six chapters of *Epitome of the Almagest* just before his death, the work completed by a student, Regiomontanus. See also ASTRONOMY.

**PHILIP I, KING OF FRANCE** (1052–1108) Ruler from 1060 to 1108, the son of King Henry I (1031–1060), crowned in 1059 but succeeding to the throne the following year on the death of his father. An active king who was devious in his behavior toward his nobles, Philip's major efforts concerned Normandy. He gave his support to Robert II Curthose against King William I the Conqueror (1066–1087), his father, and William II (1087–1100), his brother, hoping to reduce the Norman threat. Philip later attempted to divorce his wife, Bertha, to marry Bertrada, the wife of Fulk IV of Rechin, but his high-handed methods brought excommunication from the pope, a situation resolved only in 1104. His final years were spent with his son, Louis VI (1108–1137), in control of the government, as Philip had become so obese he was unfit to rule. See also FRANCE.

**PHILIP II AUGUSTUS, KING OF FRANCE** (1165–1223) One of the illustrious rulers of medieval France, reigning from 1180 to 1223, doubling the size of the royal domain and responsible for the destruction of the Angevin dynasty in England. The son of King Louis VII (1137–1180) and Adela of Champagne, he was made co-ruler with his increasingly ill father in 1179 to ensure a smooth transition

Philip I and Bertrada of France

of power. He confronted a challenge in the House of Champagne, including Henry I, count of Champagne, and Thibaut V, count of Blois and Chartres, defeating their plans by negotiating an agreement with King Henry II of England (1154–1189) in June 1180. Crowned sole king on September 18, 1180, Philip dealt successfully with a rebellion by the count of Flanders and the House of Champagne, signing the Peace of Boues in July 1185 and the Treaty of Gisors in May 1186. He was thus free to turn his attention to the English.

Philip had participated in the Third Crusade with Richard the Lion-Hearted (1189–1199) and had taken part in the siege of Acre. He made illness a pretext for his return to France in 1191, and Richard was taken captive by Leopold V, duke of Austria, receiving his freedom in 1194, whereupon he declared war on Philip, defeating the French in a series of engagements from 1194 to 1198. Richard died, however, in April 1199, leaving King John to confront Philip. The French king took from John the territories of Evreaux, Maine, Touraine, Anjou, Brittany and Normandy, and then he defeated John's ally, Otto IV of Germany (1208–1215), at Bouvines in July 1214. Additional territories were acquired as Philip took Artois, Vermandois and Valois, supporting the Albigensian Crusade in southern France, which made possible the eventual annexation of Toulouse. His victory at Bouvines not only dealt the English a crushing blow but made France the major power in Europe.

Domestically Philip attempted to strengthen royal powers while reducing feudal power, granting rights and privileges to towns and merchants and supporting them against the nobles. A new government official emerged, the *bailli*, who was responsible for local officers, the execution of justice and the collection of royal revenues. His royal advisory council was designed to broaden his political reach while lessening the influence of his aristocracy. Such policies proved so effective that serfdom had practically disappeared by the end of his reign, and France prospered. Philip also fortified Paris and constructed cathedrals. His relations with the church in France were excellent, a reflection of his awareness of the usefulness of the French clergy as allies against the nobles. See also FRANCE.

**PHILIP III, KING OF FRANCE** (1245–1285) Called "the Bold," ruler from 1270 to 1285 and the successor to Saint Louis IX (1226–1270), the second son of the saint (his brother Louis dying in 1260). He accompanied his father on crusade in 1270, succeeding to the throne while in Africa, and maintaining most of his predecessor's governmental structures. Philip acquired the county of Toulouse (1271) and negotiated the betrothal of the heiress of Navarre, Joan, to his son while he administered Navarre as regent. This led to a union of the crowns of France and Navarre. In foreign matters he was less fortunate, embarking on a campaign against Aragon in 1285 that proved wasteful and cost him his life as a result of a fever. See also FRANCE.

**PHILIP IV, KING OF FRANCE** (1268–1314) Called "the Fair," an illustrious Capetian monarch reigning from 1285 to 1314. His effort to centralize government and his raising of vast revenues, as well as his summoning of the first States General (Estates General), were somewhat overshadowed by his other characteristics and by his humiliation of Pope Boniface VIII (1294–1303). The successor to Philip III (1270–1285), he promoted centralized government and waged a protracted war with England over Gascony (1294–1303) and another one in Flanders (1302–1305). His quarrel with the papacy began in 1296 as a result of Philip's attempt to continue an emergency tax on the clergy. Boniface capitulated the following year when the king forbade the export of precious metals, thereby depriving the pontiff of important revenues. The conflict was renewed in 1301 with the arrest of Bishop Saissett on charges of inciting rebellion. Philip summoned the States General, and the pope issued the bull *Unam sanctam* (1302). The king then siezed Boniface at Anagni in 1303, whose humiliation allowed Philip extensive control over the church in France, including the election of POPE CLEMENT V (reigned 1305–1314), who transferred the papacy to Avignon (see BABYLONIAN CAPTIVITY). Efforts to obtain funds included debasement of the coinage and the cruel expulsion of the Jews and Lombard bankers, whose wealth Philip confiscated. He was particularly harsh in his merciless treatment of the Knights Templars, suppressing the order on charges of heresy in order to legitimize his seizure of their vast properties and money. These measures financed his wars, which nevertheless ended in his ceding of Guienne to Edward I and the defeat of the French at the Battle of the Spurs (Courtrai, 1302) against the Flemish. He was the father of Louis X (1314–1316). See also FRANCE.

**PHILIP V, KING OF FRANCE** (1293–1322) Called "the Tall," the second son of Philip IV the Fair, reigning from 1316 to 1322. On the death of his brother, King Louis X, in 1316, Philip became regent for the as yet unborn child of the king and the infant daughter, Joan. He consolidated his position, making peace with Joan's supporters, and named as heir his brother Charles (the future Charles IV, 1322–1328) after his own son died. Philip's principal achievement was the institution of reforms in government. He suppressed anti-Semitic outbreaks but confiscated Jewish property. See also FRANCE.

**PHILIP VI, KING OF FRANCE** (1293–1350) First ruler of the Valois dynasty, reigning from 1328 to 1350, the son of Charles of Valois and cousin to the last three Capetian kings, Louis X (1314–1316), Philip V (1316–1322) and Charles IV (1322–1328). He was the only acceptable claimant to the throne on the death of Charles IV in 1328, as the king's daughter was forbidden by Salic law to inherit the crown. Another claimant was Edward III of England (1327–1377), Charles's nephew, but Philip was crowned in May 1328. One of his first actions was to support the count of Flanders in suppressing a revolt by the Flemish, winning the Battle of Cassel. The major event during his reign, however, was the outbreak of the Hundred Years' War in 1337, in which hostilities were at first limited. In 1340, however, the French were defeated at sea at Sluys and, in 1346, were crushed at Crécy. A truce was signed in 1347 that was still in force at the time of his death. See also FRANCE; HUNDRED YEARS' WAR.

**PHILIP OF SWABIA** (1178–1208) Hohenstaufen claimant to the German crown who fought a civil war with Otto of Brunswick. The youngest son of Frederick I Barbarossa (1152–1190), he was the brother of Emperor Henry VI (1190–1197) and brother-in-law of the Byzantine emperor, Alexius IV Angelus (1203–1204). After Henry's death in 1197, the German princes, unwilling to elect the two-year-old heir, Frederick II (1215–1250), chose Philip in March 1198. An opposition party elected Otto of Brunswick, crowning him at Aachen. The resulting civil war continued until a former ally of Otto, Adolf, archbishop of Cologne, defected and crowned Philip at Aachen in 1205. By 1208 Philip had the approval of Pope Innocent III (1198–1216) and was planning to end the war forcibly when he was assassinated by Otto von Wittelsbach, an irate vassal. See HOLY ROMAN EMPIRE.

**PHILIPPA OF HAINAUT** (d. 1369) Queen consort of King Edward III of England (ruled 1327–1377), marrying Edward in 1327, shortly after his accession. She was popular and much respected, accompanying the king on his campaign into Scotland (1333) and Flanders (1338–1340). According to tradition, she pleaded for the lives of six burghers of Calais, whom Edward had threatened with execution. She was the patron of the chronicler Jean Froissart. See also EDWARD III.

**PHILIPPICUS** Byzantine emperor from 711 to 713, the son of a nobleman and of Armenian extraction. He was exiled by Emperor Tiberius II (ruled 698–705) but was recalled by Justinian II (685–695, 705–711) in 711. Sent to Crimea to suppress a revolt, he joined it instead, sailing to Constantinople to put Justinian to death. His brief reign was noted for the assault on Constantinople by the Bulgars (712) and the successes of the Arabs on the imperial frontier (712–713). Philippicus was overthrown on June 3, 713, blinded and replaced by his secretary, Anastasius II. See also BYZANTINE EMPIRE.

**PHILIP THE BOLD** (1342–1404) Duke of Burgundy from 1364, the son of King John II the Good (1350–1364) and brother of King Charles V (1364–1380), from whom he received confirmation of his duchy. Through marriage in 1369 to Margaret of Flanders, he inherited in 1384 the extensive possessions of Flanders, Rethel, Nevers, Artois, parts of Champagne and the Franche-Comté. He eventually held a role in the French government during the minority of his nephew, Charles VI (1380–1422), first as regent and later as virtual ruler of the country during Charles's bouts of mental instability. Because of his power and his diversion of money from the treasury, a conflict was precipitated with Louis, duc d'Orléans, Charles's brother. Philip died in debt, having financed his son John's crusade against the Ottoman Turks in 1396. He was also a collector of manuscripts and illuminated books and a patron of the arts. See BURGUNDY, DUCHY OF.

Philip the Bold

**PHILIP THE GOOD** (1396–1467) Duke of Burgundy and count of Flanders from 1419, considered the architect of the Burgundian state during the 15th century. The son of Duke John the Fearless (1404–1419), he inherited the duchy on his father's murder, an act for which he blamed the dauphin Charles (VII, 1422–1461). A supporter of England during a part of the Hundred Years' War, Philip sponsored the Treaty of Troyes (1420) recognizing King Henry VI (1422–1461) as the ruler of France. His loyalties altered, however, and he signed the Treaty of Arras in 1435 with King Charles VII, which gave him extensive privileges. Through marriage, war and diplomacy, Philip came to own Holland, Zeeland, Brabant, Namur, Friesland, Luxembourg, Liège and Hainaut. His court reflected his patronage of music, art and literature, and he also founded the Order of the Golden Fleece (Toison d'Or). See also BURGUNDY, DUCHY OF.

**PHILOSOPHY, ISLAMIC** See AVERROËS OF CÓRDOBA; AVICENNA; ISLAM; AL-KINDI; MALIK IBN ANAS; RAZI; SHIAH; SUFISM;SUNNI.

**PHILOSOPHY, MEDIEVAL** See ABELARD, PETER; ANSELM OF CANTERBURY; AVERROËS OF CÓRDOBA; AVERROISM; AVICENNA; BACON, ROGER; BERNARD OF CLAIRVAUX; BOETHIUS; BONAVENTURE, SAINT; CHARTRES; ECKHART, MEISTER; AL-GHAZALI; GILBERT DE LA PORRÉE; GROSSETESTE, ROBERT; HUGH OF SAINT VICTOR; IBN GABIROL; JOHN DUNS SCOTUS; JOHN OF JANDUN; JOHN OF SALISBURY; JOHN SCOTUS ERIGENA; MAIMONIDES, MOSES; MAXIMUS THE CONFESSOR; NICHOLAS OF CUSA; PSEUDO-DIONYSIUS; SCHOLASTICISM; SIGER OF BRABANT; THOMAS AQUINAS; UNIVERSITIES; WILLIAM OF AUVERGNE; WILLIAM OF OCKHAM.

**PHOCAS** Byzantine emperor from 602 to 610, a soldier of Thracian descent who was chosen to replace the deposed Emperor Maurice (582–602), who, with his son, was executed. Despite praise from Pope Gregory I (590–604), the emperor was unpopular in the empire, persecuting Jews and adherents of the Monophysyte heresy and responsible for a reign of terror in the capital, directed mainly against the aristocracy. His fate was sealed with the advance of the Persians into Asia Minor. The exarch of Carthage in 610 sent his son Heraclius to Constantinople, and Phocas was executed, Heraclius replacing him. See also BYZANTINE EMPIRE.

**PHOTIUS** (c. 820–895) Patriarch of Constantinople from 858 to 867 and from 877 to 886, whose staunch support of Byzantine religious tradition caused a controversy with the papacy. A noble of Constantinople, he was appointed imperial secretary and then patriarch, replacing Ignatius, who had been deposed by Emperor Michael III (842–867). Pope Nicholas I (858–867) at first appeared to agree to the change but then backed Nicholas in 863, deposing Photius and his supporters. The Byzantines, annoyed by this, ignored the papal order until 867, at which time Photius denounced the presence of Latin missionaries in Bulgaria and opposed the *Filioque* clause of the Creed. A Council at Constantinople then declared the pope excommunicated and deposed.

The murder of Michael in that year, however, and his replacement by Basil I (867–886) brought about the reinstatement of Ignatius. Basil, on amicable terms with the pope, fostered Eastern bishops in Bulgaria (870), drawing censure from the papacy. On Ignatius's death in 877, Photius was reinstated as patriarch, having already been recognized in his appointment by Basil as tutor to his sons. In 886, Leo VI became emperor (886–912), and Photius was removed, probably excommunicated as well. He may have retired and died in a convent in Armenia. An esteemed theologian and scholar, he left a vast body of works, including treatises on doctrine, theology and philosophy and homilies and letters. His best-known work was *Myriobiblion,* a synopsis of about 280 books. A *Treatise on the Holy Ghost* remained a major source for the study of Byzantine dogma, and his name became synonymous with the opponents of unification of the churches.

**PIAST DYNASTY** First dynasty of Polish dukes and kings, originating with Duke Mieszko I (963–992), who was instrumental in Christianizing and unifying the country. The line ended in 1370 on the death of Casimir III the Great, when Louis I of Hungary took the crown. See also Poland and individual rulers.

**PICTS** An indigenous tribe of Scotland during and after the Roman occupation of Britain, derived from the Latin *picti* (painted), probably in reference to the body tattoos customary among them. The Picts were first mentioned by Roman historians in the late third century. Their assaults on Roman territory became fiercer in the fourth century, and by the sixth century the Picts had established a kingdom that extended across most of Scotland, north of the Firths of Forth and Clyde and west to the coast opposite Ireland. A unified kingdom was forged in the eighteenth century, and there followed increased communication with the Irish on the west coast. The unification of Scotland occurred under Kenneth I McAlpin (ruled until 858), about 843. Christianity was introduced to the Picts in the sixth century. See also SCOTLAND.

**PIEDMONT** Region in northwestern Italy, called in Italian the Piemonte, with its capital at Turin. Bounded by the Alps and lying in the Po Valley, the Piedmont was strategically important because of the passes connecting it to the countries beyond Italy. During Lombard domination it was divided into marches, those of Ivrea and Torino (Turin). In the 11th century these two marquisates belonged to the House of Savoy, which emerged in the 15th century as the major power in the region. See also SAVOY.

**PIERO DELLA FRANCESCA** (d. 1492) Also Piero dei Franceschi, a painter and mathematician from Umbria, the son of a shoemaker. He was an assistant to Domenico Veneziano (c. 1439) and his later work reflected the influence also of Masaccio and Alberti. He was noted for his mastery of atmosphere and light in his paintings. Among his most celebrated works were the *Baptism of Christ* (c. 1445), the *Flagellation of Christ* (c. 1457) and the *Legend of the True Cross* (c. 1451–1464). Interested also in mathematics, he wrote several treatises, including one in Italian on geometry.

**PIERS PLOWMAN** See VISION CONCERNING PIERS PLOWMAN, THE.

**PILGRIMAGES** Journeys to shrines and holy places, associated with both Christianity and Islam and popular during the Middle Ages. The earliest Christian pilgrimages probably took place in the second century, including visits to Jerusalem and Rome, although Constantine's mother, Helena, visited Jerusalem in 326, and Saint Jerome went to the Holy Land in the fourth century. Popular Christian shrines were found in Jerusalem and Bethlehem, and perils arose for Christian pilgrims concurrent with the threat by the Seljuk Turks, a factor contributing to the call for a Crusade to liberate Jerusalem. There were also many pilgrimage sites in Europe. Rome and Santiago de Compostela were popular, as well as the tombs of saints, including those of Thomas à Becket at Canterbury, Saint Francis at Assisi, Saint Martin at Tours and Saint Boniface at Fulda.

The typical pilgrim embarked on his trip with a priest's blessing and with distinguishable clothing, often adorned with the scallop shell, the symbol of the pilgrim. Pilgrimages were often acts of devotion, penances or atonement, and pilgrims wore badges identifying their journey. Christian pilgrimages were frequent, but the Muslims undertook even more frequent journeys to Mecca and Medina, an act reflecting their faith and honor, a custom that endures to this day. See also CHAUCER, GEOFFREY; RELICS; and individual sites.

**PIPE ROLLS** See ROLLS, PIPE.

**PISA** City in central Italy, in Tuscany, on the Arno River, near the Tyrrhenian Sea, which was a Roman colony, occupied later by the Lombards and emerging as a major city during the 10th century. The city conducted commerce and overseas trade in agriculture, and the Pisan fleet was effective in defending the coast against Saracen raiders and in the capture of Sardinia and the attack of Palermo. The Crusades brought commercial expansion in Palestine and Syria, leading to the acquisition of Corsica and Sardinia. Pisa, however, clashed with another maritime power, Genoa, and Pisan naval supremacy was ended in 1284, with its crushing defeat by Genoa at the Battle of Meloria. While an increase in industry took place in the 12th and 13th centuries, political and other disasters struck in the 14th century, most notably the Black Death (1348), which took the lives of at least one-half of the inhabitants. By 1406 Pisa was under Florentine domination.

**PISA, COUNCIL OF** Council of the church convened in 1409 with the aim of ending the Great Schism, which had divided the papacy into rival camps at Rome and Avignon. Organized by cardinals from both factions, the council was well attended and included delegates from most of the major courts in Europe. The result of the council was decisive in deposing the two popes, Benedict XIII (1394–1417) and Gregory XII (1406–1415), electing in their stead Alexander V (1409–1410). The two deposed pontiffs, however, refused to accept the council's decision, thus prolonging the schism. See also CONSTANCE, COUNCIL OF; SCHISM, GREAT.

**PISAN, CHRISTINE DE** (1364–1429/1431) Italian-born French poet considered one of the first professional women writers, respected for both her character and her virtue. She composed lyric poems on romance and chivalry; her most well known work is *The City of Women.*

**PISANELLO** (c. 1395–1455) Called Antonio Pisano or, incorrectly, Vittore Pisanello, an Italian painter and designer of medals. He studied with Stefan de Zevio (of Verona) and then painted frescoes in the palace of the doge in Venice (c. 1415–1422) and in Saint John Lateran at Rome (after 1427) with Gentile da Fabriano. Pisanello was noted for his drawings of animals, especially horses, and also produced some of the most beautiful medals in his time. Among his finest medals were those of Emperor John VIII Palaeologus (1438), Lionello d'Este (1444), Sigismondo Pandolfo Malatesta (1445) and Alfonso V of Aragon (1448). His drawings were preserved in the Vallardi Codex (now at the Louvre).

**PISANO, ANDREA** (c. 1290–c. 1348) Also called Andrea da Pontedera, an Italian sculptor influential in the arts in Florence during the 14th century. He succeeded Giotto as the chief architect of the bell tower of the cathedral in 1337. He added two stories of paneled reliefs to Giotto's work. In 1329 Pisano was commissioned to produce a pair of bronze doors for the south portal of the baptistery, which he completed in 1336. These doors held 20 quatrefoil panels depicting scenes from the life of Saint John the Baptist and reliefs of eight Virtues. Pisano influenced Ghiberti's own doors. His son, Nino Pisano (d. c. 1368), was noted for his having completed his father's projects on the cathedral at Orvieto. See also FLORENCE.

**PISANO, NICOLA AND GIOVANNI** Father and son, both sculptors of the 13th and 14th centuries who left an enduring influence on Italian Renaissance sculpture. Nicola (Niccolo) Pisano (c. 1220–c. 1283) was born in Apulia and trained there or in Lombardy, moving to Pisa about 1250. His first known work was the hexagonal pulpit in the baptistery of the cathedral of Pisa (c. 1260), decorated with magnificent reliefs. An octagonal pulpit for the Siena cathedral reflected the influence of the French Gothic style. His last major work was the fountain at Perugia, in which effort he was assisted by his son.

Pisano's pulpit in the Pisa cathedral

Giovanni Pisano (c. 1250–c. 1314) was born in Pisa and studied with his father, becoming his assistant. After 1284–1285 he settled in Siena, where he designed the facade of the cathedral, a High Gothic building honoring the Virgin Mary. Called the most notable Italian sculptor of his time, he combined Gothic and classical elements and made a major impression on succeeding artists of the trecento. Among his other works were the pulpits for the church of San Andrea at Pistoia (1301) and the Pisa cathedral (1302–1310), the *Madonna della Cintola* (c. 1312) in the Prato cathedral, and his last major commission, the tomb of Margaret of Brabant, the wife of Emperor Henry VII.

**PIUS II** Pope from 1458 to 1464, born Aenea Silvia Piccolomino near Siena, a poet, humanist, historian and statesman. Studying with Filelfo at Florence, he acquired a fine education and became involved in church affairs, attending the Council of Basel in 1432. In 1442 he was summoned to Vienna by Emperor Frederick III (1440–1493), who, impressed with his poetic skill, crowned him poet laureate and employed him from 1442 to 1455. After renouncing his support of the antipope Felix V (1439–1449) and abandoning a materialistic life, Pius won the support of Pope Eugene IV (1431–1437), was ordained and given prelate rank, including the cardinalate in 1456. He was elected pope in 1456. His most notable effort as pontiff was to effect a crusade against the Ottoman Turks, who had captured Constantinople in 1453. He wrote an autobiography, a history of the Council of Basel and letters. Humanists during his pontificate were encouraged, although he demanded more Christian behavior than other patrons, such as Pope Nicholas V (1447–1455).

**PLAGUE OF 542** See PLAGUE.

**PLAGUE** An infectious and widespread outbreak of disease, generally carried by fleas that infected other animals, particularly rats. Plague, called in the 14th century the Black Death, struck several times during the Middle Ages, annihilating vast populations and having the most severe consequences for the social, political and economic life of the times. The disease as it was spread across the Middle East and Europe was of two strains, bubonic and pneumonic. Bubonic plague was indicated by a swelling in the lymph nodes (buboes), and pneumonic plague affected the lungs. A third type, the most deadly, was septicimic plague, in which the bloodstream was invaded, causing death before one of the other two strains could manifest itself. The agent of the disease was the bacillus now called *Pasteurella pestis*.

Early pandemics occurred in the sixth century, ending a period of freedom from plague since 450. Severe depopulation rendered parts of Constantinople and Antioch devoid of life, and Damascus, once a thriving city, was nearly deserted when it fell to the Arabs. The Umayyad caliphs, whose capital was at Damascus, fled the city during the summer plague season, going to desert dwellings, their armies leaving for camps in the mountains. Epidemics struck like waves, bearing down on both the Islamic and Western worlds. A terrible plague in Ireland, called the Children's Plague (second half of the seventh century), annihilated, as the name implies, segments of the population lacking immune defenses, the young. The plague disappeared from the West by 750.

Its return was so terrible that it was simply called the Black Death. Arising in Central Asia, it struck in Constantinople in 1348, spreading to Italy, France and England (1348–1349) before its outbreak in Germany, Poland and Scandinavia in 1350. Deaths associated with plague were astronomical as the regions of Europe affected lost two-thirds to three-fourths of their populations. Estimates have been made that 25 million people, or one-quarter of Europe's population, died during the Black Death.

Reactions to the epidemic varied to casting blame on the Jews to the creation of fanatic religious groups that attempted to perform penance for sins for which they thought humanity was being punished. Chief among these groups were the Flagellants, who performed acts of self-mortification. Of greater importance were the enduring social ramifications of severe depopulation. Attempts to reinstate the institution of feudalism were thwarted by a serf class that was now independent, leading to uprisings such as the Peasant Revolt in England and the Jacquerie in France. The essentially agrarian society was forced to adapt to a markedly reduced labor force, and the departure of laborers took place as the people went to the cities in search of work and food. See also DANCE OF DEATH; DECAMERON; FEUDALISM; GUILDS; MANORIAL SYSTEM; TRADE AND COMMERCE.

**PLANTAGENET** Ruling dynasty of England from the reign of King Henry II (1154–1189) until either the abdication of King Richard II in 1399 or the death of King Richard III in 1485. The name Plantagenet was used by Henry II and his sons, Richard I the Lion-Hearted and John (also called the Angevin kings), but was also applied more specifically to Edward I (1272–1307) and Edward II (1307–1327).

**PLANTAGENET, GEOFFREY** (d. 1151) Count of Anjou from 1129 to 1151, the first of the Plantagenet dynasty of England. The son of Fulk of Anjou, Geoffrey married Matilda, daughter of King Henry I of England (1100–1135), and in her name conquered Normandy in 1144. In 1147 he went on crusade with King Louis VII of France (1137–1180). His son became King Henry II of England in 1154 (ruled until 1189). The name Plantagenet was derived from Geoffrey's habit of wearing a sprig of broom in his helmet. Another tradition holds that he planted broom to provide additional cover while hunting. See also PLANTAGENET.

**PLATINA, BARTOLOMEO** (1421–1481) Italian humanist and Vatican librarian, called Platina for his birthplace near Cremona. He settled in Florence and flourished with the patronage of the Medicis. A member of the Roman Academy with Pomponius Leto, Platina was imprisoned and tortured after the academy's suppression by Pope Paul II in 1468. After his release he was appointed Vatican librarian (1475–1481) by Pope Sixtus IV (1471–1484) and wrote a biographical study of the popes.

**PLETHO, GEORGIUS GEMISTUS** (c. 1355–1450) Greek philosopher and influential humanist, who studied at Constantinople and at the Ottoman court in Adrianople. He founded a school of esoteric religious study in Misra and supported the revival of Neoplatonism, persuading Cosimo de Medici to establish the Platonic Academy of Florence, which was to have an influential role in Renaissance learning and thought. Respected by the Byzantine emperors, Pletho was adviser in 1428 to John VIII Palaeologus (ruled 1425–1448) and member of the Byzantine delegation to the Council of Ferrara-Florence (1438–1445), which hoped to unite the Latin and Greek churches. His name meant "full" in Greek (synonymous with Gemistus) and was similar to "Plato," given him in respect for the philosopher of whom Pletho was called the reincarnation.

**POETRY, ISLAMIC** See ABU AL-ATAHIYA; ABU'L-'ALA AL-MA'ARRI; ABU NUWAS; ABU SAID IBN ABI KHAIR; ABU TAMMAM; FERID EL-DIN ATTAR; FIRDAWSI; HAFIZ; AL-HAMADANI; AL-HARIRI; JALALU'D-DIN RUMI; AL-MUTANABBI.

**POETRY, MEDIEVAL** See AGNIS OF CORVEY; ALVAREZ DE VILLASANDINO, ALFONSO; AMADIS OF GAUL; ANGILBERT; ARNAUT, DANIEL; ARTHURIAN LEGEND; ASGRIMSSON, EYSTEIN; BARBOUR, JOHN; BEOWULF; BERNERS, JULIANA; BLONDEL; BOCCACCIO, GIOVANNI; BODEL, JEHAN; BRAGI BODDASON THE OLD;

BYLINI; CAEDMON; CANTAR DE MIO CID; CARMINA BURANA; CAVALCANTI, GUIDO; CHANSON DE GESTE; CHARTIER, ALAIN; CHASTELLAIN, GEORGES; CHAUCER, GEOFFREY; CHRÉTIAN DE TROYES; CINO DA PISTOIA; CYNEWULF; DANTE ALIGHIERI; DECAMERON; DESCHAMPS, EUSTACE; DOLCE STIL NUOVO; EGILL SKALLAGRIMSSON; EILHART VON OBERGE; EISTEDDFOD; FROISSART, JEAN; GAUTIER DE METZ; GEORGE OF PISIDIA; GILLES LE MUISET; GOTTFRIED VON STRASSBURG; GOWER, JOHN; GUILLAUME DE LORRIS; HEINRICH VON MEISSEN; HELIAND; HILARIUS; HILDEBRANDSLIED; JACOPONE DA TODI; JEAN DE MEUN; JONGLEURS; KONRAD VON WÜRZBURG; LA MARCHE, OLIVIER DE; LANGLAND, WILLIAM; LANGUEDOC; LA SALE, ANTOINE DE; LATINI, BRUNETTO; LYDGATE, JOHN; MACHAUT, GUILLAUME DE; MAERLANT, JACOB VAN; MEISTERSINGERS; MINNESINGERS; MUSSATO, ALBERTINO; NIEBELUNGENLIED; PEARL, THE; PETER OF BLOIS; ROMAN DE LA ROSE; RUDOLF OF EMS; SNORRI STURLUSON; SORDELLO; VENANTIUS FORTUNATUS; VILLON, FRANÇOIS; VISION CONCERNING PIERS PLOWMAN, THE; WACE; WALAFRID STRABO; WOLFRAM VON ESCHENBACH.

**POITIERS** City in west-central France, the historical capital of Poitou, the name derived from the local Gallic tribe, the Pictavi (or Pictones). An episcopal see from the fourth century, its first bishop was the esteemed Hilary of Poitiers (d. c. 367). Occupied for a time by the Visigoths and a residence of their kings, the city fell to the Franks in 507. In 732 Charles Martel won a victory there against the Arabs, thus saving Europe (also called the Battle of Tours). Part of the dowry of Eleanor of Aquitaine, Poitiers belonged to the English in 1152 and was attached to the French crown only to be lost to England again in 1356, after the Battle of Poitiers. Joan of Arc was interrogated in the city in 1429. See also POITOU.

**POITIERS, BATTLE OF** (1356) See HUNDRED YEARS' WAR.

**POITOU** Province in western France on its Atlantic coast, occupying the region of the modern departments of Vienne, Deux-Sèvres and Vendée; its traditional capital is Poitiers. Originally occupied by the Gallic Pictavi (or Pictones), Poitou was attached to the Roman province of Gallia Aquitania. Occupied by the Visigoths for a time, it was conquered by the Franks in 507. The counts of Poitou took the title of dukes of Aquitaine in the 10th century, and the province belonged to England in 1152, having been a portion of the dowry of Eleanor of Aquitaine. King Philip II Augustus of France (1180–1223) recovered it in the early 13th century, but another conflict over Poitou erupted during the Hundred Years' War between France and England. In the treaties of Brétigny and Calais (1360) Poitou was ceded to the English, only to be reclaimed by du Guesclin (c. 1370) for France. See also POITIERS.

**POLAND** Country in east-central Europe, situated between the Baltic Sea to the north and the Carpathian Mountains to the south. The origins of the Polish state date from the late 10th century with the rise of the first identified monarch of Poland, Mieszko I of the Piast dynasty (d. 992). Aware of the Bohemian threat to his country, Mieszko swore allegiance to Otto I of Germany (936–973), accepted Christianity and placed Poland under papal protection. His son, Boleslav I the Brave (ruled 992–1025), was the first titular Polish king, but on his death the influence of the Holy Roman Emperor reduced kingly royal status to that of duke. The death of Boleslav III the Wry-Mouthed in 1138 brought on political decline as Poland was divided among his sons. A seniority system was established with the "senior" ruling from Cracow, Pomerania and important central provinces. Confronted with threats by the Prussians, Lithuanians and Mongols, the Poles invited the Teutonic Knights into Poland in 1226. The Teutonic Knights established their own state as a result.

A revival in Poland began in the 14th century, and the reign of Casimir III the Great (1333–1370) witnessed a resurgence of royal power and governmental reforms. His successor was his nephew, Louis I of Hungary (ruled 1370–1382), but his death brought an interregnum, ended by the marriage of the Polish queen Jadwiga to Jagiello, grand duke of Lithuania, who ruled as Władysław II Jagiello (1386–1434). This alliance between Poland and Lithuania forged a massive state in eastern Europe, able to crush the Teutonic Knights at the Battle of Tannenberg (Grünwald) in 1410. In the reign of Casimir IV (ruled 1447–1492) the Teutonic Knights signed the Peace of Torun (Thorn) in 1466, ceding Pomerania and West Prussia, holding East Prussia as a Polish fief. See also LITHUANIA.

**POLE** See SUFFOLK, EARLS AND DUKES OF.

**POLLAIUOLO, ANTONIO DEL** (1432–1498) Italian painter, sculptor, goldsmith and engraver, as well as a student of anatomy, influencing Renaissance art. He studied dissection to further his awareness of the human form, and his skill was evident in his engravings and drawings, especially in his masterpiece, *Battle of the Nude Men* (c. 1470), and in *Martyrdom of Saint Sebastian* (1475). With his brother Piero (d. 1496) he had a respected workshop in Florence. He and his brother cast the bronze tombs of Popes Sixtus IV (1471–1484) and Innocent VIII (1484–1492) in Saint Peter's, their most important commissions. See also FLORENCE.

**POLO, MARCO** (c. 1254–1324) Renowned traveler of the Middle Ages, whose experiences were recorded in the work originally called *Il milione* (*The Million*), which was the chief source on the East during the Renaissance. The Polo family had a trading house in Venice, and Marco's father, Niccolo, and his uncle, Maffeo, chose in 1260 to liquidate their holdings in Constantinople, setting out for the East. They reached the court of Kublai Khan and returned to Venice in 1269, inspiring Marco in his travels. When the Polos journeyed to the East again in 1271, with the blessing of their friend Pope Gregory X (1271–1276), two friars accompanied Marco and his father and uncle during the journey home. Four years of travel brought the three men to Persia, Afghanistan, Kashmir, along the Silk Route, and into China, where they presented letters from the pope to Kublai Khan in 1274 or 1275 at his summer residence at Shang-tu, near Peking.

Kublai Khai apparently respected Marco Polo, sending him on imperial missions and instructing him in Mongol customs. Marco visited southwestern China and Burma. In 1292, however, the traders received permission to return home. This journey took them by sea to Vietnam, the Malay Peninsula, Sumatra, Ceylon and the Gulf of Hormuz. By land they probably journeyed to Khorasan, Tabriz, Trebizond and Constantinople. From there they returned to Venice in 1295. A short time later, Marco was captured in a brief naval engagement against Genoa. While imprisoned he met a convict, a Pisan writer named Rustichello (Rusticano), to whom he dictated his account, *Il Milione*. After his release, Marco returned to Venice, married into a respected Venetian family and died stating that he had recounted only half of what he had seen. His account, called also *Travels of Marco Polo,* was extremely popular in its time and fueled the imagination of his contemporaries and succeeding generations. See also KUBLAI KHAN and MONGOLS.

**POLO FAMILY** See POLO, MARCO.

**POMERANIA** Region in northern Germany bordered by the Baltic Sea, situated between the Oder and Vistula Rivers, occupied by the Slavs by the fifth century A.D. Pomerania (German, Pommern; Polish, Pomorze) was conquered by the Polish ruler Mieszko I, and about 1000 Boleslaw I the Brave established an episcopal see at Kodobrzeg, while a local ducal dynasty emerged in the 11th century. Polish domination was recognized in the early 12th century, but parts of western and central Pomerania were lost to the advancing Germans. Under control of the German king this western region came under the jurisdiction of the archbishop of Magdeburg, remaining a duchy of the Holy Roman Empire until the 17th century. East Pomerania, called Pomerelia (including Danzig), was annexed by Poland in 1295 and then ceded to the Teutonic Knights, who ruled it from 1308 to 1466, when it was reclaimed by the Poles.

**POPES** See PAPAL STATES; see also Appendix for list of popes.

**PORTUGAL** Country on the Iberian Peninsula corresponding largely to the ancient Roman province of Lusitania and overrun in the fifth century by the Germanic Suebi and Visigoths. It was dominated in the early eighth century by the Moors; a Christian reconquest was initiated in the 11th century. Ferdinand I of Castile (1035–1065) captured Coimbra in 1064, and his son Alfonso VI (1072–1109) named Henry of Burgundy count of Coimbra after he responded to the Castilian call for French assistance against the Muslims. Through Henry's marriage to Alfonso's illegitimate daughter, a dynasty was established that would endure until 1385. Henry's son called himself Alfonso I, king of Portugal (1139–1185), and employed foreign crusaders in the conquest of Lisbon in 1147.

During the next centuries, Portuguese expansion reduced Moorish power and the kingdom consolidated in 1249 with the conquest of the Algarve. There was, however, continued warfare with the Spanish kingdoms, especially during the reign of Ferdinand I (ruled 1367–1383). Two other important kings were Alfonso III (ruled 1248–

Ship design from a Portuguese vase

1279) and Dinis (reigned 1279–1325). Ferdinand was also noted for his alliance with John of Gaunt against the Castilians, a common front established with the Treaty of Windsor in 1386. The crown of Portugal would have been claimed by the Castilians had Nun Álvarez Pereira not defeated them at Aljubarrota in 1385. A new dynasty, the House of Aviz, came to the throne, beginning with John I (ruled 1385–1433). His son was Prince Henry the Navigator, who laid the foundation for the Portuguese empire overseas. See also RECONQUISTA and individual rulers.

**PRAGMATIC SANCTION OF BOURGES** Pronouncement issued on July 7, 1438, by King Charles VII of France (1422–1461) and the French clergy (under royal direction) asserting the supremacy of a general council over the papacy. The rights of the French church were established (see GALLICANISM), with the Crown having control over ecclesiastical appointments, validity of papal bulls in the kingdom and appeals to the Holy See. The Pragmatic Sanction was revoked in 1461 by Louis XI (1461–1483) but could be revived by the French kings when they found it expedient. See also CHARLES VII, KING OF FRANCE.

**PRAGUE** Capital of Bohemia, situated on the Vltava River, dating from the eighth century as a city, having a castle erected on the river during the ninth century. Prague was first mentioned in 928, and in 975 the plans were made for an episcopal see. Ideally situated for trade, the community prospered and underwent considerable development during the Przemyslid (Premyslid) dynasty of Bohemia, which ruled from Prague until 1306, granting the city its charter in 1232. Prague's golden age came during the reign of Emperor Charles IV (1346–1378) of the Luxembourg dynasty. With his patronage the city became became one of the most beautiful in Europe. He founded the Charles University (University of Prague) in 1348, promoting extensive building and bridgeworks and raising the bishopric to an archepiscopal see. The city's problems during the 15th century included the reform movement of the Hussites and subsequent social upheaval. See also BOHEMIA.

**PRAGUE, COMPACTATA OF** See BOHEMIA; HUS, JAN; HUSSITE WARS.

**PRAGUERIE** A revolt early in 1440 on the part of a number of princes and other nobles against King Charles VII of France (1422–1461), deriving its name from uprisings occurring in Prague. The cause of the rebellion was the sweeping reform decreed by the king (1439), which forbade the raising or maintenance of armies. Placing the dauphin Louis (XI, 1461–1483) at their head, Charles I, duc de Bourbon, and Jean II, duc d'Alençon, gathered troops and supporters but were defeated by Constable de Richemont, signing a peace treaty in July at Cusset.

**PRESIAM** (d. 852) King of the Bulgars from 836 to 852, a mysterious figure who succeeded Malimir in the midst of war against the Byzantine Empire. He may have been Malomir taking a second name, or he may have been a general who took the throne. Presiam conducted an unsuccessful war with Serbia (c. 850) and was succeeded by Boris. See also BULGARIA.

**PRESTER JOHN** Legendary Christian king of the East who was immortalized in chronicles written during the Middle Ages. The tale of Prester John first emerged during the Crusades, when word was spread of a Nestorian king-priest who had marched to join in the capture of Jerusalem from Islamic hands. His exploits were first recorded by Otto of Freising in his *Chronicon* (1145), and subsequent mention was made of his purported grandson (or son) King David of India. Alberic de Trois-Fontaines in the 13th century recorded that in 1165 Prester John sent a letter to several European princes, including Frederick I Barbarossa and Manuel I Comnenus. The letter was fiction, but in 1177 Pope Alexander III wrote a message to the "King of the Indies, the most holy priest," the ultimate response to which is unknown. Expeditions in the 13th and 14th centuries searched for the kingdom of Prester John, thus inadvertently establishing contacts with the Mongol empire. One of the Prester John legends held that the Nestorian king-priest was to be found in Abyssinia, that country being confused with India. See also MONGOLS.

**PROCOPIUS OF CAESAREA** (d. c. 562) Byzantine historian who was considered the finest Greek historian since Polybius. Born in Caesarea, he served as secretary to General Belisarius of the Byzantine Empire, accompanying him on his Persian campaigns as well as his military actions against the Vandals and Ostrogoths. As witness to these military ventures, Procopius wrote the *History of the Wars,* a major work giving an account of the reign of Justinian I (527–565). He also wrote *Buildings,* in which Justinian's construction efforts were praised, including the erection of the Hagia Sophia. In marked contrast, Procopius's *Secret History,* a critical and uncompromising work, revealed unflatteringly accurate details about the emperor, his court and its notorious practices. It was not intended for publication. See also JUSTINIAN I.

**PROVENCE** Province in southeastern France, comprising the departments of Bouches-du-Rhône, Vaucluse, Basses-Alpes, Alpes-Maritimes and Var, bordered by the Mediterranean Sea, the Alps and the Rhône River. Always distinct from the rest of France, Provence was colonized by Greeks and then Romans (forming Gallia Transalpina) in the second century B.C. Wealthy and civilized, it was in strong contrast to other, more primitive territories. In the fifth century the region was invaded by Visigoths, Ostrogoths and Burgundians, finally claimed by the Franks. In 879 Provence was made part of a kingdom by the count of Arles. In 933 it was joined with part of Burgundy to become the Kingdom of Arles. By the 13th century the dynasty no longer existed, and the region was held by Aragon until it passed to the Angevins of Naples, who willed the province to the king of France in 1481.

Culturally and linguistically Provence reflected an amalgam of Greek, Latin and Arabic influences. Provençal cities flourished, especially in the 12th century, and trade was conducted with Palestine and beyond. The Provençal language resembled Latin and was written and sung by the troubadours of the province. The dialect emerged as the literary medium for southern France and the means by which poetry was disseminated throughout Europe. See also TROUBADOURS.

**PROVISIONS OF OXFORD** See OXFORD, PROVISIONS OF.

**PRUSSIA** Region along the Baltic Sea, situated between the Vistula and Memel Rivers, inhabited by members of the Baltic group of Indo-Europeans related to the Latvians and Lithuanians. Ardent pagans, they resisted Christianity, martyring the revered Saint Adalbert of Prague about 997. At the invitation of the Polish duke of Mazovia, the Teutonic Knights swept into Prussia after 1230, conquering and converting the survivors. The knights held the region until 1466, introducing German culture and their peasants to work the land. By the terms of the Treaty of Torum (Thorn) in 1466, the knights ceded the lands east of the Vistula to the Polish crown, retaining East Prussia as a fief. See also TEUTONIC KNIGHTS.

**PRVOSLAV** King of the Serbs from 891 to 892. See also SERBIA.

**PRZEMYSLID DYNASTY** See OTTOKAR I PRZEMYSL; OTTOKAR II PRZEMYSL.

**PSELLUS, MICHAEL** (1018–1078) Byzantine theologian, historian and philosopher who brought about a revival of Byzantine classical learning. As secretary to Emperor Michael V (ruled 1041–1042) and Constantine IX (ruled 1042–1054) he promoted the study of Platonic philosophy and classical learning, becoming a professor of philosophy at the newly established University of Constantinople in 1045. Holding the post for nine years, he fell from favor and retired to a monastery in 1054, recalled to serve again in the government until 1072. He wrote many letters, treatises and poems, the best known a "Commentary on Plato's Teaching on the Origin of the Soul" and the *Chronographia* of events from 967 to 1078.

**PSEUDO-DIONYSIUS** (fl. 500) Called also Dionysius the Areopagite, he was probably a Syrian monk and mystical theologian attempting to arrive at a synthesis between Christian and Neoplatonic thought. He stressed the need for an intimate union between God and the soul, achieved by denying the intellect and the senses. His view that the Creation was an expression of God and must eventually return to its source was of particular interest to the Scholastic philosophers of the time. His writings included the *Celestial Hierarchy*, on the nine orders of angels; *Ecclesiastical Hierarchy*, on the sacraments and the three ways of the spiritual life; *Mystical Theology*, on the ascent of the soul to God; and *Divine Names*, on the attributes and being of God. See also SCHOLASTICISM.

# Q

*QADI* See Glossary.

**QUADRIVIUM** See Glossary.

**QUATTROCENTO** Italian word for "four hundred," used to describe the cultural, artistic and literary events of the 15th century in Italy. It is generally accepted that the quattrocento was a time of great prosperity and richness, leading to the thought and artistic expression of the High Renaissance. Traditionally this period began in 1401, with a competition for the design of the baptistery doors in Florence and ended with the election of Pope Julius II in 1503.

**QILIJ ARSLAN I** (d. 1107) Seljuk sultan of Rum from 1092 to 1107, who restored Rum. The son of Sulaiman Shah I, Qilij spent years in captivity at the hands of the ruler of the Seljuk Empire, Malikshah. Escaping in 1092, on Malikshah's death, he returned to Anatolia where he reforged the Rum state, which had been dominated from 1086 by the Greater Seljuk Empire. Waging war on the Danishmends (a Turkish dynasty that had established itself in north-central Anatolia), he was interrupted by the armies of the First Crusade. In 1096 Walter the Penniless and the People's Crusade were routed near Nicaea. The following year, however, the Turks were beaten at Dorylaeum, a defeat that allowed a Byzantine resurgence in Asia Minor. Qilij was prevented from fulfilling his ambitions against the Seljuk Empire, and years of war with the Crusaders followed, culminating with Qilij's success in acquiring the sultanate. He then extended his position to the east, capturing Malatya in 1106 and Mosul in 1107. He died in battle, by drowning, near Mosul. See also SELJUK TURKS.

**QILIJ ARSLAN II** (d. 1192) Seljuk sultan of Rum from 1156 to 1192, the son of Masud I, who defeated his brother Shahanshah in battle, thereby securing his throne. The Byzantine emperor Manuel I Comnenus (1143–1180) defeated him, forcing Qilij to sue for peace. He then turned his attention to the Danishmends, crushing them in central Anatolia and eliminating their dynasty in 1175. The defeat of the Danishmends, allies of the Byzantines, won Qilij acclaim. In another war with the Byzantine Empire, the Seljuks routed the Byzantines at Myriocephalon. Qilij abdicated in 1188, but his sons feuded for the throne, and he had to live protected by one of them, Kaykhusraw I (1192–1210), until his death. See also SELJUK TURKS.

**QILIJ ARSLAN III** Seljuk sultan of Rum in 1204, the son of Sulaiman II, who was overthrown within a year by his uncle, Kaykhrusraw I. See also SELJUK TURKS.

**QILIJ ARSLAN IV** (d. 1264?) Seljuk sultan of Rum from 1246 to 1264, a son of Kaykhusraw II, dividing the rule with his brother, Kayqawus II, on the death of their father (1245). When Kayqawus was deposed in 1259, Qilij ruled over a united Rum, a vassal to the Mongols. He was controlled by the *pervane* Muin ed-Din Sulaiman, his chief minister, who had him murdered about 1264. See also SELJUK TURKS.

# R

**RABANUS MAURUS** (d. 856) Benedictine theologian, abbot of Fulda and archbishop of Mainz. Ordained a priest in 814 and appointed abbot of Fulda in 822, he strove to increase the value of the monastery both materially and spiritually, welcoming students such as Walafrid Strabo. After retiring in 842, he became the archbishop of Mainz and began efforts to encourage Christianity in Germany. He wrote a manual for clerics on the sacraments, *De clericorum institutione,* as well as commentaries on the Scriptures, poetry and attacks on the teachings of Paschasius Radbertus.

**RADEGUNDA, SAINT** (518–587) The wife of the Merovingian king Clotaire I, who became one of the first Merovingian saints. She was the daughter of a Thuringian prince, captured in 529 by the Franks, and, as an act of charity and piety, married Clotaire, who subsequently complained that he had married "a nun." After the king murdered her brother, Radegunda fled the court (c. 550) and persuaded Medard, bishop of Noyon, to make her a deaconess. She founded a convent outside Poitiers, which adopted the rule of Caesarius of Arles. Her final years were spent there.

**AL-RADI** Abbasid caliph from 934 to 940, considered a gifted poet. He was the last of the caliphs to have his poetry compiled in a collection. See also ABBASID CALIPHATE.

**RAGUSA** Port city on the coast of Dalmatia in Yugoslavia, also called Dubrovnik, Ragusa its Italian name. Established in the seventh century by Roman refugees fleeing Slavic attacks on Epidaurus, the city was ruled by the Byzantines in the 9th through 12th centuries. From 1205 to 1358 it was forced to accept Venetian supremacy but retained considerable independence as a republic, relying on its coastal position to expand its extensive trade throughout the Balkans and with the Byzantine Empire. The city remained largely autonomous even after Venice acquired Dalmatia in 1420. See also DALMATIA.

**RAIS, GILLES DE** (1404–1440) Marshal of France and a soldier who was notorious as a satanist and murderer of children. Serving as an honor guard of Joan of Arc, Rais was made a marshal by King Charles VII (1422–1461), attending the ruler's coronation at Reims in 1429. After Joan's death he retired to his estate in Brittany, where he squandered his vast fortune, becoming a patron of the arts and an alchemist. Charged in 1440 with having abducted more than 100 children for satanic rites, he confessed under duress and was found guilty by an ecclesiastical court at Nantes and executed. His name was later associated with Bluebeard. See also WITCHCRAFT.

**RAMIRO I, KING OF ARAGON** (d. 1063) First ruler of Aragon, from 1035 to 1069, an illegitimate son of King Sancho III of Navarre (1004–1035), receiving from him the right to govern Aragon. On Sancho's death, Ramiro held the rank of king. He took lands belonging to his brother, conquered some Moorish territories and forced other Moorish kings to recognize his dominion. See also ARAGON.

**RAMIRO II, KING OF ARAGON** (d. 1157) Called "the Monk," ruling from 1134 to 1137. A son of Sancho V Ramírez (1063–1094), he became the bishop of Barbastro but was elected to succeed Alfonso I (1104–1134), his brother, as king. During a revolt by Aragonese nobles, Ramiro was supported by RAMON BERENGUER IV (1131–1162), count of Barcelona, rewarding him with the hand of his daughter, Petronilla. A short time later he abdicated, making possible the union of Aragon and Barcelona. He retired to a priory and died years later. See also ARAGON.

**RAMIRO I, KING OF ASTURIAS** (d. 850) Ruler from 842 to 850, who repulsed a large raiding fleet of Vikings at Dijon.

**RAMIRO II, KING OF LEÓN** (d. 951) Ruler from 930 to 951, who pursued an aggressive policy against the caliphate of Córdoba. He succeeded his brother, Alfonso IV (925–930), after Alfonso abdicated, but his brother returned from a cloister to claim the throne again. Ramiro captured him, blinding him and other relatives to avoid rivalry. He was a bitter enemy of Abd al-Rahman III of Córdoba (912–961), defeating a Muslim force near Osma in 933 and routing the caliph in 939. The Kingdom of León entered a period of political turmoil on his death.

**RAMIRO III, KING OF LEÓN** (d. 984) Successor to the poisoned King Sancho I (956–966), ruling from 966 to 984. The son of Sancho, Ramiro came to the throne at the age of five, and for many years his aunt Elvira acted as regent. He was eventually overthrown by a revolt of nobles favoring Vermudo II (984–999). Ramiro fled to Astorga, where he died.

**RAMON BERENGUER I** Count of Barcelona from 1035 to 1076, responsible for a program of construction. Ramon promulgated the earliest *Usatges of Barcelona,* the basis for Catalan legal development. See also BARCELONA; CATALONIA.

**RAMON BERENGUER II** Count of Barcelona from 1076 to 1082, dividing power with his brother, Berenguer Ramon II (1076–1096). In 1082, however, he was assassinated by his brother, who ruled alone until 1096. See also BARCELONA;CATALONIA.

**RAMON BERENGUER III** Count of Barcelona from 1096 to 1131, responsible for introducing a policy of overseas and continental territorial expansion. He consolidated Catalan interests beyond the Pyrenees in Provence and launched an invasion of the islands of Majorca and Ibiza in 1114. The following year the islands were evacuated, and the Almoravids claimed them after the death of the Majorcan king. Catalan interests in maritime commercial expansion had increased. See also BARCELONA; CATALONIA.

**RAMON BERENGUER IV** Count of Barcelona from 1131 to 1162, a son of Ramon Berenguer III (1096–1131), receiving as his inheritance Barcelona, Vich, Besalú, Gerona and Cerdagne, while his brother ruled the country of Provence, thereby ending the possible union of Provence and Catalonia. Ramon supported King Ramiro II of Aragon (1134–1137) in a dispute with the Aragonese nobles and was rewarded with the hand of Ramiro's daughter, Petronilla. In 1137 the birth of their son, Alfonso II (1162–1196), united Catalonia and Aragon. An ally of Alfonso VII of Castile (1126–1157), Ramon fought the Moors, taking part in the siege of Almería in 1147 and moving on to capture Tortosa Lérida, Fraga and Mequinenza. In 1151 he signed a treaty at Tudillén, renewing the partition of Navarre and designating the share of the territory captured from the Muslims. See also BARCELONA; CATALONIA.

**RAON OF PENAFORTE** (c. 1175–1275) Dominican friar and canonist, the confessor of Pope Gregory IX (1227–1241). He was the author of the *Summa de casibus poenitentiae (Concerning the Cases of Penance),* a manual on canon law for confessors. He collected the pontifical decretals issued in 1234, called the *Decretals of Gregory IX.* Returning to his native Spain in 1236, Raon was elected general of the Dominican order and drew up a reformed constitution before retiring in 1240. He then attempted conversions of Muslims and Jews, organizing a school of Arabic and Hebrew studies, and suggested to Thomas Aquinas that he write his *Summa contra gentiles,* a work intended for theologians dealing with those who were not Christians. See also DOMINICANS.

**RAOUL** (d. 936) Duke of Burgundy and king of France from 926 to 936, the son-in-law of King Robert I. He supported Robert in 922 in the uprising causing the overthrow of Charles III the Simple, inheriting the throne when Robert died in battle and crowned at Soissons. Much of his reign was spent disputing the claims of Charles III and dealing with threats by the Normans. Henry I the Fowler (919–936) of Germany seized Lorraine, and Raoul was also imperiled by restless nobles. His problems were somewhat lessened with Charles's death in 929, but he fell ill and died just having won recognition of his title. See also FRANCE.

**RASHI** (1040–1105) Jewish biblical scholar respected as a commentator, whose name was derived from the initials for Rabbi Solomon ben Isaac (Rabbi Shlomo Yitzhaqi). Born in Troyes, he studied in Worms and Mayence and was appointed rabbi of Troyes. There he was acknowledged as a Jewish spokesman, drawing to the city other rabbis, thus making it highly esteemed for its encouragement of rabbinical learning in western Europe. His commentaries on the Bible were to have lasting influence on successive Jewish and Christian scholars. See also JEWS AND JUDAISM.

**AL-RASHID** Abbasid caliph from 1134 to 1135. See also ABBASID CALIPHATE.

**RATCHIS** King of the Lombards from 744 to 749, originally a duke of Friuli and then a successor to Hildebrand, elected by the Great Council of the Lombards. He was personally pious and mild. However, in 749 he attacked Perugia, but a visit from Pope Zachary (741–752) convinced him to end his campaign and to abdicate, retiring to a monastery. He tried unsuccessfully to reclaim his throne from Desiderius at a later time (c. 756). See also LOMBARDS.

**RATRAMNUS OF CORBIE** (d. 868) Monk and theologian of the Benedictine monastery of Corbie whose writings on predestination and the Eucharist involved him in the major theological controversies of the times. *De praedestinatione* defended the views of Saint Augustine of Hippo on the subject, opposing those of Archbishop Hincmar of Reims. His *Contra Graceorum opposita (Against Greek Opposition)* was an attack on the Eastern Church. His best-known work dealt with the Eucharist: *De corpore et sanguine Domina (On the Body and Blood of Our Lord),* in which he disagreed with the thinking of Paschasius Radbertus and argued for symbolic interpretation. That work was condemned at the Synod of Vercelli in 1050 and was confused there as being the creation of John Scotus Erigena. Ratramnus may have influenced later Protestant reformers.

**RAVENNA** City in northern Italy, on the Po River near the Adriatic, for centuries the major urban center in the area. Tradition holds that Ravenna was an Etruscan site, later part of Gallia Cisalpina in the Roman era, important economically and strategically. Its situation made it vital to trade and a headquarters of the imperial fleet guarding the Mediterranean. Emperor Honorius sought refuge in Ravenna in 402 as the Western Roman Empire declined, believing that the region's mosquito-ridden marshes would protect him from a Gothic assault. Until 476 Ravenna served as the Roman capital, and during the reign of Odoacer (ruled 476–493) and the Ostrogoths, beginning with Theodoric (ruled 493–526), it was the capital of the peninsula.

In 540 the Byzantines captured Ravenna, making it their chief city on the peninsula. It served from 584 until 751 as the exarchate (see EXARCHATE). The Byzantine decline in

Church of San Vitale in Ravenna

Italy permitted the Lombards to seize the city in 751, and three years later Pepin III, king of the Franks, expelled the Lombards and deeded the city to the papacy (see DONATION OF PEPIN). Political power was then held by the archbishop of Ravenna, who ruled there until 1278, after which true authority was vested in the House of Da Polenta. Decline brought about by Venetian maritime supremacy resulted in Venice taking Ravenna in 1441. The city remained important because of its Roman and Byzantine antiquities and its architectural splendors, including the Church of Saint John the Evangelist (fifth century), the mausoleum of Theodoric and the churches of San Vitale, Sant' Appolinare Nuovo, and Sant' Appolinare in Classe. See also ART AND ARCHITECTURE, BYZANTINE.

**RAVENNA, EXARCHATE OF** See EXARCHATE; RAVENNA.

**RAYMOND, COUNTS OF TOULOUSE** Noblemen influential during the Crusades and in France, including Raymond IV (d. 1105), count of Saint-Gilles and marquis of Provence from 1066 and count of Toulouse from about 1093, one of the leaders of the First Crusade (1096–1099). Independent, Raymond refused the crown of Jerusalem and accepted no territorial gains. After the capture of Antioch he was the true leader of the expedition, taking part in the capture of Jerusalem in 1099. He was killed during the siege of Tripoli, which later became a county ruled by his descendants (see RAYMOND I, COUNT OF TRIPOLI).

Archbishop Theodore's sarcophagus in Ravenna

Raymond VI (d. 1222) refused to initiate harsh measures against the Albigensians and faced condemnation by Pope Innocent III (1198–1216), forcing him to send the legate Peter de Castlenan, who was murdered in 1208. This resulted in the crusade against the ALBIGENSIAN MOVEMENT and the attack by Simon de Montfort, who defeated Raymond and his allies at the Battle of Muret (1213). The Fourth Lateran Council (1215) stripped Raymond of his title, but he recovered his territories before dying. His son, Raymond VII (d. 1249), supported the family's efforts, making a truce in 1223, but he was excommunicated three years later and his lands declared forfeit because of his refusal to purge the Cathari sect. Compelled to sign the Treaty of Meaux in 1229, he surrendered part of his holdings to France, thereby allowing the Inquisition into Languedoc. The proposed marriage of his daughter Joan to Alphonse, brother of Louis IX (Saint Louis) of France (1226–1270), resulted in the cession of much of his land to the French crown. Raymond rebelled in 1242 but was defeated and forced to sign the Treaty of Lorris (1243), confirming French control and authority over Toulouse. See also TOULOUSE.

**RAYMOND I, COUNT OF TRIPOLI** (d. 1187) Count from 1152 to 1187, a descendant of Raymond IV, count of Toulouse, and an able statesman and soldier. He served as regent for the rulers of the Latin Empire of Jerusalem, Baldwin IV (1174–1177) and Baldwin V (1183–1185). After Baldwin V's death he was opposed to the accession of Baldwin's mother, Sibyl, and her husband, Guy of Lusignan. Thus, when Saladin launched another war on the kingdom, Raymond made a separate truce with him. A reconciliation between Guy and Raymond took place, and they participated in the disastrous Battle of Hattin (July 1187). Wounded and fortunate to avoid capture, he retired to Tripoli, where he died a short time later. See also CRUSADES.

**RAYMOND-BERENGUER** See RAMON BERENGUER.

**RAYMOND OF SAINT-GILLES** See RAYMOND, COUNTS OF TOULOUSE.

**AL-RAZI** (d. 923 or 935) In full, Abu Bakr Muhammad ibn Zakariya, a philosopher, alchemist, scientist and the respected physician in the Islamic world of his era. Born in Persia, he served as chief physician in a hospital there and then moved to Baghdad, where he received enough patronage to write extensively on medicine and philosophy. He was a Platonist but disagreed with the interpretations of Avicenna and Averroës. He was also undoubtedly familiar with the writings of Democritus (in Arabic translation). Other than short medical treatises, al-Razi was known for two works: *Kitab al-Mansuri* (translated by Gerard of Cremona) and *Kitab al-hawi, The Comprehensive Book,* which had a lasting influence on the study of medicine in universities. Razi considered himself the Islamic counterpart of Socrates and Hippocrates. See also MEDICINE.

**RECARRED I** (d. 601) King of the Visigoths from 568 to 601, the son and successor of Leovigild. He spent the years 586–588 converting the Visigoths from Arianism to orthodox Christianity. Forced to suppress several uprisings, he succeeded ultimately and thus removed a powerful barrier separating the Visigoths from their subjects. The strength of the church soon became formidable, and the usually tolerant Reccared persecuted lingering Arians and Jews. See also VISIGOTHS.

**RECARRED II** (d. 621) King of the Visigoths ruling briefly from 620 to 621. The son of King Sisibut, he survived his father by less than a year. See also VISIGOTHS.

**RECCESWINTH,** (d. 672) King of the Visigoths whose long reign (649–672) was a time of peace. He was greatly loved and was a supporter of the church. Throughout his reign, however, royal power declined, and the nobles reclaimed their independence, while the clergy became more demanding. Recceswinth died without heir and was succeeded by Wamba. See also VISIGOTHS.

**RECONQUISTA** The reconquest of Spain from the Moors, a campaign conducted by the Christian kingdoms. It began about 718 with the Battle of Covadonga, which marked the opposition of the Asturians to the Moorish advance. Realistically, however, it was not until the 11th century that the Christian realms were in a position to exploit the increasing disorder among the Muslim communities, responding to an appeal of the times to mount crusades against Islam. In 1064 King Ferdinand I (1033–1065) captured Coimbra, a triumph followed by the fall of Toledo in 1085. Subsequent campaigns led to the formation of the kingdom of Portugal and the Christian victory at Las Navas de Tolosa in 1212. Seville and Córdoba fell to Christian armies, so that by the end of the 13th century only the Moorish kingdom of Granada remained. The Reconquista was ended in 1492 when Ferdinand and Isabella took Granada. See also INQUISITION; JEWS AND JUDAISM; and individual kingdoms and rulers.

**REGENSBURG** Also Ratisbon, a city in Bavaria on the Danube River, originally Celtic, becoming a Roman legionary camp called Castra Regina (founded A.D. 179). From 530 the city was the capital of the dukes of Bavaria, receiving an episcopal see in 739. For a time Regensburg was the Carolingian capital and became a free imperial city after 1245, enjoying prosperity as the major trading city in southern Germany. Of note architecturally were the patrician houses (12th–14th centuries), the *Steinerne Brücke* (Stone Bridge, 12th century) and the Cathedral of Saint Peter (1275–1524), the most important Gothic church in Bavaria.

**REGIOMONTANUS** See ASTRONOMY.

**REIMS** Also Rheims, a city in northeastern France, northeast of Paris in the department of Marne, traditionally the site of the coronation of the French kings. Once belonging to the Gallic Remi tribe, the region was conquered by the Romans, and later Reims was economically prosperous as a trade center. Clovis I was crowned at Reims, and in remembrance of the occasion the archbishop of the city was granted the right to crown the king in the 12th century; the most famous of these monarchs is Charles VII (1422–1461), who was crowned with Joan of Arc at his side. The cathedral, a superb example of Gothic architecture, was begun by Robert de Coucy in 1211. See also CATHEDRAL; HUNDRED YEARS' WAR.

Window from Reims Cathedral

**RELICS** Mortal remains of a saint or sacred objects once in contact with their body. Christian relics during the Middle Ages were popular and thought to be instrumental to miraculous acts. Early relics included the bones of Saint Polycarp (second century), which were said to be "more valuable than precious stones" by the *Martyrium Polycarpi*, an account of Polycarp's martyrdom. The cult of relics spread swiftly in both the Eastern and Western Churches, although the veneration of icons in the Eastern Orthodox Church lessened the importance of relics there. The Second Council of Nicaea (787) condemned those who denied the value of relics, and the Council of Constantinople (1084) approved the veneration of such objects. In the West the number of relics increased significantly during the Crusades, as objects from the Holy Land were brought to Europe, many of which were of dubious authenticity. Powerful relics of Christian significance included the Holy Grail, the Lance of Longinus, the True Cross and relics associated with Santiago de Compostela, as well as the Holy House of Loreto.

**REMIGIUS, SAINT** (c. 438–c. 533) Also Remi, called the Apostle of the Franks, important for his having baptized King Clovis I in 496, thereby bringing the Franks into the Christian fold. The son of the count of Laon, Aemilianus Remigius became archbishop of Reims at the age of 22, establishing the sees of Laon, Tournai, Cambrai, Arras and Terouanne and, according to tradition, conferring on Clovis the "royal touch" (the belief in the ability of the king to lay his hands on a subject and heal scrofula, called the "King's Evil").

**REMIGIUS OF AUXERRE** (c. 841–c. 908) Philosopher and author of treatises on philosophy and theology, a pupil of Heiric at the monastic school of Saint Germain at Auxerre. Remigius was well known during the Middle Ages for his commentary on Martianus Capella and on Boethius's *Consolation of Philosophy*, as well as his commentaries on certain books of the Bible, including the Psalms.

**RENÉ OF ANJOU** (1409–1480) Duke of Anjou and titular king of Naples from 1435 to 1442, called "the Good," the second son of Louis II, duc d'Anjou. He became by marriage the duke of Lorraine and by adoption successor to Joanna II, queen of Naples (d. 1435). A prisoner from 1431 to 1437 of Philip the Good, the duke of Burgundy (1419–1467), he was able to sail to Naples in 1438 to defend his claim against Alfonso V of Aragon (1416–1458), joining his wife, Isabella of Lorraine, who had been in charge of the defenses of the city in his absence. That same year, however, he was defeated by Alfonso, retiring to Angers and later to Tarasson, where he inherited Provence. He was a distinguished patron of poetry and the arts, promoting medieval Provençal culture while demonstrating abilities as a poet and possibly as a painter. His daughter, Margaret of Anjou, was married in 1445 to King Henry VI of England (1422–1461). See also NAPLES, KINGDOM OF.

**RHASIS** See AL-RAZI.

**RHAZES** See AL-RAZI.

**RHEIMS** See REIMS.

**RHODES** Island in the Aegean Sea, southwest of Asia Minor, an ancient place known to the Romans. It became part of the Byzantine Empire in 395, remaining an imperial possession until 1204, with the exception of periods of Arab control (653–658 and 717–718). The Byzantines lost Rhodes as a result of the Fourth Crusade (1204), which toppled the empire and brought the island under the rule of various lords, including the emperor of Nicaea. Throughout the Crusades it was a vital supply depot, falling in 1309 to the Knights Hospitalers, whose fortifications made it impregnable. The knights repulsed the assaults of the Ottoman Turks for many years but surrendered and evacuated Rhodes in 1522 threatened by the forces of Suleiman I the Magnificent. See also CRUSADES.

**RICHARD, EARL OF CORNWALL** (1209–1272) English magnate and titular king of the Romans. The second son of King John I (1199–1216) and brother of King Henry III (1216–1272), whom he frequently opposed, he embarked in 1236 on crusade, commanding an English force that fortified Ascalon. Returning home, he served as an adviser to his brother and as regent during Henry's trip to Gascony (1253–1254). During this period Richard declined the offer of the crown of Sicily but was willing to advance the imperial cause. He secured his election as king of Rome and was crowned at Aachen in May 1257. Through more bribery he then won recognition from parts of the Rhineland, although never ruling the entire region and journeying back to England in 1259. Following the repudiation of the Provisions of Oxford, Richard supported his brother against the barons (1263–1264) and was captured at Lewes in 1264 and imprisoned until the fall of Simon de Montfort at Evesham in 1265. See also HOLY ROMAN EMPIRE.

**RICHARD I** (1157–1199) King of England called Richard Coeur de Lion, Richard the Lion-Hearted, an illustrious ruler (1189–1199) but more distinguished as a knight and soldier. He spent less than a year in England during his reign of a decade. The son of King Henry II (1154–1189) and Eleanor of Aquitaine, he adored his mother while resenting the attention given his brother John by his father. Made the duke of Aquitaine at the age of 11, he later held the titles of duke of Normandy and count of Anjou as king. He joined his brothers in a rebellion in 1173–1174 but was defeated by Henry and pardoned. His attention was then devoted to curbing baronial discontent, receiving support from his father when his brothers, Henry and Geoffrey, support a Gascon revolt.

Richard became heir to the throne on the death of Henry (d. 1183) but refused to yield Aquitaine to John. The dispute led him to make an alliance with King Philip II Augustus of France (1180–1223), paying homage to the French crown for the English-held territory in France. King Henry was forced to recognize Richard as his successor and died in 1189, a broken man. Richard, on becoming king, broke with Philip, whom he recognized as a formidable rival. His major interest, however, lay not in the governing of England but in a Crusade to the Holy Land. Both Philip and Richard delayed their personal feud by taking the Cross in 1190. Richard's role in the Third Crusade (1189–1192) demonstrated his martial prowess as he played a pivotal role in the capture of Acre in 1191 and in the Battle of Arsuf against Saladin. Unable to capture Jerusalem, he made a truce with Saladin that allowed pilgrims to visit holy places in peace and the Crusaders to maintain Acre as their city. Richard, however, was suspected of complicity in the death of Conrad of Montferrat and was on poor terms with his fellow Christians.

Philip II Augustus, pleading illness, sailed home to France, and Richard feared for his Angevin possessions there. On his return to England, however, he was captured by Duke Leopold of Austria, whom he had humiliated in the Holy Land, remaining imprisoned in Vienna's Durnstein Castle until 1192, when he was handed over to Emperor Henry VI (1190–1197). A massive ransom paid to the emperor insured Richard's release in February 1194. Once home, he was crowned again to strengthen his position, embarking on campaign in Normandy from which he never returned. While besieging a castle in Limoges he was wounded and died on April 6, 1199. He is thought to have been homosexual, and his marriage to Berengaria of Navarre was a formality, producing no heirs. At his death

England was ruled by John Lackland (1199–1216), his brother. See also CHATEAU GAILLARD; CRUSADES; ENGLAND.

**RICHARD II** (1367–1400) King of England, the son of the Black Prince, Edward. He ruled from 1377 until his deposition favoring Henry IV in 1399. Grandson of Edward III (1327–1377), he succeeded him at the age of 10, and John of Gaunt and other nobles served as regents. During the regency social conditions in England deteriorated, leading to the Peasant Revolt of 1381. During the uprising Richard met with the rebels and pacified them with promises. Married in 1382 to Anne of Bohemia, he took up the reins of government the following year, creating factions at court. A baronial opposition, led by Thomas of Woodstock, was formed, joined by Richard Fitzalan, earl of Arundel, and Thomas de Beauchamp, earl of Warwick. John of Gaunt, the duke of Lancaster, sought to shield the king, but his departure for Spain in 1386 gave the Lords Appellant their chance to strike.

Richard's chancellor, Michael de la Pole, was deposed (1386), and the Parliament in 1388 outlawed some of the king's closest friends. He submitted but managed to save his government as John of Gaunt returned in 1389. By 1397 Richard was powerful enough to execute the earl of Arundel, murder Gloucester and banish Warwick. He then took advantage of a dispute between two of the Appellants, Gaunt's son, Henry Bolingbroke, and Thomas Mowbray, duke of Norfolk, to exile them both in 1398. The next year, on John of Gaunt's death, he confiscated what should have been Bolingbroke's extensive Lancastrian inheritance. Richard then went to Ireland, discovering that Henry had invaded England. Having no support from his nobles, he abdicated in September 1399, relinquishing the crown to Bolingbroke, who became Henry IV 1399–1413. Richard was imprisoned at Pontefract Castle, dying there in February 1400, probably of starvation and not by murder, as Shakespeare wrote in his *Richard II*. Although Richard's reign was politically disastrous, it was an outstanding one from a literary viewpoint, producing men of letters such as Chaucer and John Gower. See also ENGLAND.

**RICHARD III** (1452–1485) King of England, the last Yorkist ruler of England (1483–1485), whose defeat and death at the Battle of Bosworth Field ended the Wars of the Roses. The youngest son of Richard, duke of York, and brother of King Edward IV (ruled 1461–1483), he played a prominent role in Edward's victories and probably was accomplice to the murder of King Henry VI in May 1461. Rewarded for his part, he was named lieutenant of northern England and, on the death of Edward, became protector of the realm for Edward's son, Edward V (1483). Through the destruction of the Woodvilles, led by Edward IV's widow, Elizabeth, Richard was able to take the crown. He was endorsed by an assembly of lords and commoners on June 25, supplanting the 12-year-old heir.

In August, Edward V and his younger brother, Richard, disappeared in the Tower of London, and the story circulated that they had been murdered. Soon afterward Henry Tudor, a Lancastrian who was widely supported by the English, invaded England. Richard gathered an army but was betrayed during the battle at Bosworth Field (August 22, 1485) and died. A potentially capable ruler, Richard was villified by historians and literary figures of the Tudor period, notably Shakespeare and Saint Thomas More. See also WARS OF THE ROSES.

**RICHARD OF SAINT VICTOR** (d. 1173) Influential Scottish mystic and theologian, studying with Hugh of Saint Victor and becoming prior in 1162. He was known for his mystical works, although he also wrote exegetical and theological pieces. Chief among his writing was *De Trinitate*, in six volumes, reflecting his philosophical views. He considered empiricism necessary for the proof of God's existence, maintaining that speculative reasoning could lead to understanding essentials of Trinitarian doctrine. He influenced Saint Bonaventure. See also MYSTICISM.

**RICHEMONT, ARTHUR, COMTE DE** (1393–1458) Also Constable de Richemont, the constable of France who organized the French army and made it the fighting force that defeated the English in the Hundred Years' War. Captured in 1415, he was imprisoned by the English until 1420, after which he fought briefly for the English and married Margaret of Burgundy in 1423. A quarrel with the English regent, John, duke of Bedford, led him to return to the French. He was made constable in 1425 and fought beside Joan of Arc (1429) at Orléans, arranged the Treaty of Arras (1435) and reconciled Burgundy with the French king. He also captured Paris in 1436. Through reform and organization, Richemont led France to final victory, participating in the Battle of Formigny (1450) and the campaigns that restored Normandy and Guinne to France. In 1457 he became duke of Brittany. See also BRITTANY.

**RIENZO, COLA DI** (1313–1354) Tribune of the Romans, a popular leader and humanist, the son of a Roman shopkeeper. He lived in Anagni until 1333, returning to Rome, where he became a papal notary and was sent to Pope Clement VI (1342–1352) in Avignon to seek the pope's return to Rome. Three years later, in Rome, he assumed with wide public support dictatorial powers, styling himself the Tribune of the Sacred Roman Republic. His dream was to create a unified Italian state having Rome as its capital, but his pretensions brought opposition from the Roman nobles, whom he ruthlessly suppressed. Pope Clement denounced him, and he was forced to resign in December 1347. In 1354, however, he made a remarkable political recovery, receiving the favor of the new pope, Innocent VI (1352–1362). A triumphant return to Rome took place on August 1, with Rienzo holding the additional title of senator. His rule in the city proved harsh, and he was murdered by a mob in October of that same year. See also ROME.

**RIGA** City of Latvia, situated at the mouth of the western Dvina River on the Gulf of Riga. The site of an old settlement of the Livs, the city was first mentioned in 1201 as an episcopal see, becoming an archbishopric in 1253. It was the city from which the Livonian Knights conquered the Baltic coast. In 1282 it joined the Hanseatic League, becoming economically vital in the region. See also MILITARY ORDERS; TEUTONIC KNIGHTS.

**RIMINI** Port city on the Adriatic Sea in north-central Italy, in the region of Emilia-Romagna. Called Ariminium by the Romans, it was situated at the junction of the Aemilian and Flaminian Ways. Under the Byzantines the city belonged to the Pentapolis, falling to the Goths but recaptured and then claimed by the Lombards and the Franks. It was included in the Donation of Pepin (754) and was administered by nobles as representatives of the popes. By the 12th century it was an independent commune, and in 1238 Malatesta da Verucchio was made *podestà* (mayor), although the Malatesta family did not assert true power until 1295, controlling the city until 1509, when Rimini joined the Papal States. See also PAPAL STATES.

**ROBBIA, LUCA DELLA** (d. 1482) Florentine sculptor whose work was vital to his family's profitable workshop, which produced terra-cotta sculpture. Della Robbia discovered the technique of applying pottery glazes to terra-cotta, producing polychrome enameled pieces, in which he excelled. His skill in marble was remarkable, and he was called Donatello's equal in the medium. His most important effort in marble was the *cantoria,* or singing gallery, originally placed over the door of the north sacristy of the cathedral in Florence. Among his projects in terra-cotta were the roof of Michelozzo's Chapel of the Crucifix in San Miniato al Monte, Florence, and an altarpiece in the Palazzo Vescovile at Pescio.

**ROBERT I, DUKE OF NORMANDY** (d. 1035) Called Robert the Magnificent or Robert the Devil, who opposed his brother, Richard III, in his claim to the duchy on the death of their father in 1026–1027. Richard III died a few years later, and Robert became duke. He died at Nicaea while returning from a pilgrimage to Jerusalem. His son was William I the Conqueror (king of England, 1066–1087). Robert's name became confused with the legendary figure Robert the Devil, the son of a duke of Normandy born supposedly in answer to prayers to the Devil, the tale found in the 12th-century *Robert le Diable* and in other 14th-century poems. See also NORMANDY.

**ROBERT II, DUKE OF NORMANDY** (d. 1124) Called Curthose, the eldest son of William I the Conqueror (1066–1087), who succeeded his father in Normandy but then took part in two rebellions against William (1077–1078, 1082–1083) and was exiled to Italy until William's death in 1087. Incompetent as a ruler, he was at odds with his brother, William II Rufus (1087–1100), before joining the First Crusade, fighting at Dorylaeum (1097), Jerusalem (1099) and Ascalon (1099). On the succession of King Henry I (1100–1135), Robert invaded England, was defeated and in turn was attacked by the English forces. Captured at the Battle of Tinchebrai (1106), he spent the remainder of his life as a prisoner. See also NORMANDY.

**ROBERT I, KING OF FRANCE** (d. 923) Ruler of the Franks in 922–923, the younger son of Robert the Strong of Neustria, brother of King Eudes (ruled 888–898). He acquired extensive power and territory as a Frankish lord, defeating the Normans at Chartres in 911. Despite his oath of fealty to Charles III the Simple (893–923), he led a revolt by the Neustrian nobles in 919 and was crowned at Reims in 922. The following year, at Soissons, he died in battle with Charles. See also FRANCE.

Robert II, duke of Normandy

**ROBERT II, KING OF FRANCE** (d. 1031) Called "The Pious," the successor to his father, Hugh Capet, reigning from 996 to 1031, noted for his vigorous efforts to acquire the duchy of Burgundy, launching his campaign in 1002 and subduing the region only in 1015. Although he supported monastic reform, his relations with the papacy deteriorated as a result of his marriage in 996 to Bertha, the widow of Eudes (Odo) I of Blois, a union considered incestuous by the church. Pope Gregory V (996–999) excommunicated him, but matters were eased by the accession of Pope Sylvester II (999–1003), who had once served as Robert's tutor. See also FRANCE.

**ROBERT I, KING OF SCOTLAND** (1274–1329) Called "the Bruce," a national hero of Scotland, reigning from 1306 to 1329, who delivered Scotland from English rule. He was the grandson of Robert de Bruce (d. 1295), who claimed the Scottish throne in 1290, losing his claim to John de Balliol through the influence of England's Edward I (1272–1307). For a time Robert was a supporter of William Wallace, reconciling with Edward I until 1306, when the murder of John Comyn the Red took place, a rival for the throne as a relative of de Balliol. Robert was crowned at Scone on March 25, 1306, but in that same year he was defeated at Methven and Dalry by the English and forced to seek refuge on a small island off the Irish coast.

Returning to Scotland in 1307, he began attracting supporters while taking advantage of the political ineptitude of Edward's incompetent son, Edward II (1307–1327). In 1314 he forced the decision at the Battle of Bannockburn, crushing the superior English force. This triumph was followed by the capture of Berwick (1318), and finally, in 1328, the Treaty of Northampton was signed, affirming English recognition of Robert's rank as king. As monarch he acted to bring order to Scotland, forming a centralized and generally efficient government. Many legends concern him and his era, the best known the account of his time as a fugitive. In flight and in despair, he regained hope by observing a spider doggedly weaving a web. The Bruce's body lies in Dunfermline Abbey, but his heart was taken by Sir James Douglas when he made a pilgrimage to the Holy Land. The heart was supposedly returned to Melrose Abbey when Douglas died in 1330. See also SCOTLAND.

**ROBERT II, KING OF SCOTLAND** (d. 1390) Ruler from 1371 to 1390, the first of the House of Stuart (Stewart), the grandson of Robert I the Bruce (1306–1329) and heir to King David II by 1326, when he served as regent to the exiled monarch. Robert served in this capacity with John Randolph, third earl of Moray, from 1334 to 1335 and alone from 1338 to 1341 and from 1346 to 1357. On David's death in 1371 he was crowned king, but the government was already in the hands of his son, the future Robert III, and thereafter in the hands of Robert, earl of Fife. During his reign the English were defeated (1388) after an invasion. See also SCOTLAND.

**ROBERT III, KING OF SCOTLAND** (d. 1406) Ruler from 1390, the son of King Robert II, born John Stuart. Made earl of Carrick in 1368 by King David II, he assumed virtual control of the government in his father's reign, from 1384 to 1388. A horse kicked him, however, in 1388, causing a physical disability that reduced his effectiveness and led to the ascendancy of his brother, Robert, earl of Fife (made duke of Albany in 1398). Succeeding Robert II, he changed his name to avoid any association with the memory of John de Balliol. The king's brother was the true power, imprisoning a rival, Robert's son, David, who died in prison in 1402. See also SCOTLAND.

**ROBERT II CURTHOSE** See ROBERT II, DUKE OF NORMANDY.

**ROBERT GUISCARD** (c. 1015–1085) Norman conqueror of Sicily, also Robert de Hauteville but called Guiscard ("wily"). The son of Tancred de Hauteville, a Norman noble, he was preceded to Sicily by his brothers, William "Iron-Arm," Drogo and Humphrey, arriving about 1047. Robert was sent to Calabria to attack the Byzantine territory, defeating a combined Byzantine and Lombard force at Civitate in 1053. Four years later he succeeded Humphrey as count of Apulia, spending the next years consolidating his power and using the strained relations between the papacy and the Byzantines to advantage. He sent his brother Roger to capture Sicily, Bari (1071) and Salerno (1076), making his capital in southern Italy. Increasingly ambitious, Robert sailed against the Byzantine Empire, capturing Corfu and defeating Emperor Alexius I (1081–1118) and his Venetian allies in 1084. That same year he was asked by the pope to support him against the German king Henry IV (1056–1106). Robert expelled Henry's supporters, marched on Rome and escorted the pope to Salerno in the summer of 1084. Returning to his campaign in the East, he died of fever at Cephalonia. See also NORMANS; SICILY.

**ROBERT OF COURTENAY** (d. 1228) Ruler of the Latin Empire of Constantinople from 1219 to 1228, the son of Peter of Courtenay and Yolande. He became emperor after his older brother, Philip of Namur, renounced the crown. He proved incompetent, losing most of the Eastern territories to the Nicaean emperor John III Vatatzes (1222–1254). Confronted by an uprising of his barons, Robert fled and died while journeying to the pope, abandoning a realm that had been reduced to the boundaries of Constantinople alone. See also CONSTANTINOPLE, LATIN EMPIRE OF.

**ROBERT OF GENEVA** See CLEMENT VII.

**ROBERT OF MELUN** (d. 1167) English Scholastic philosopher, the successor to Peter Abelard at the school of Mount Saint Geneviève. Going to Melun in 1142 to direct the school there, he participated in the Synod of Reims in 1148, which condemned Gilbert de la Porrée. Returning to England, he was appointed bishop of Hereford in 1163. The author of theological treatises, he advanced a doctrine concerning the Trinity that was close to that of Abelard, assigning the quality of power to the Father, wisdom to the Son and goodness to the Holy Spirit. See also SCHOLASTICISM.

**ROBERT THE DEVIL** See ROBERT I, DUKE OF NORMANDY.

**ROBERT THE STRONG** (d. 866) Neustrian count and first of the Capetian dynasty, which would come to rule France. A nobleman in the service of King Charles II the Bald (843–877), he distinguished himself in campaigns against the Normans, defeating them in 865 only to die in a skirmish with them in 866. His sons, Eudes and Robert (I), became kings of the Franks. See also FRANCE.

**ROBIN HOOD** Legendary outlaw of England, the hero of English ballads from the 14th century and many later accounts. Most often Robin was presented as a figure who killed or punished figures of authority, most notably the sheriff of Nottingham and rich members of the clergy, lending his support to the poor and to women. There have been repeated efforts to trace the source of the legend, as well as attempts to prove his historical authenticity. Some scholars have suggested that he was a supporter of Simon de Montfort, but the name was often applied to a forest robber. The legends of Robin Hood reflected the social discontent and turbulence as well as the resentment of government and unjust laws, not the least of which was the ban on hunting rights for the ordinary man.

**ROCH, SAINT** (c. 1295–1378) Also Rocco and Rock, a saint and healer of plague victims, supposedly born at Montpellier. He was recorded as traveling through Italy when he came upon the town of Aquapendente, curing many of the town's plague victims and then performing the same miracle in Modena, Parma and Mantua. His name was invoked against the plague, most notably in 1414 during the Council of Constance, and his relics were moved to Venice in 1485. See also PLAGUE.

**ROCHESTER** City in Kent, on the Medway River in England, noted in Roman times as being on the road from the Channel to London. In 604 the city was made an episcopal see, founded by Saint Augustine of Canterbury, and the oldest and smallest suffragan see of Canterbury. Its cathedral was damaged in the seventh century by the Danes and Mercians. A castle was erected during the reign of William I the Conqueror (1066–1087) and extensive privileges were granted by King Henry III (1216–1272) in 1227. A new cathedral was begun by Bishop Gundulf (bishop from 1077 to 1108) and was consecrated in 1130; its nave is one of the finest and oldest examples of Norman architecture in England. See also KENT.

**RODERIC** See RORY O'CONNOR.

**RODERIC, KING OF THE VISIGOTHS** (d. c. 713) Last Visigothic ruler in Spain, whose reign (710–711) was ended by the Muslim invasion of the Iberian Peninsula. Elected king by the Visigothic nobles, he was faced with rebellions of the Basques and the Franks. While campaigning against these elements, he was invaded by General Tariq-ibn Ziyad and a Moorish force and defeated by them in 711, probably dying at the hands of one of his own soldiers or by drowning. He may have survived until 713 and was the subject of Spanish legends that referred to him as Don Rodrigo or "the last of the Goths." See also VISIGOTHS.

**RODOALD** (d. 653) King of the Lombards for barely six months, from 652 to 653, succeeding his father Rothari. He was killed by an outraged husband. See also LOMBARDS.

**RODRIGO DÍAZ DE VIVAR** (c. 1043–1099) Called El Cid (Lord), the most illustrious knight and soldier in Spanish history and a national hero. A native of Vivar, Rodrigo Díaz was the son of a minor nobleman of Castile and was raised in the court of Ferdinand I (1033–1065). On the accession of Sancho II in 1065, he was appointed commander of the royal troops and assisted the king in his campaigns (1067–1072) of expansion against his brother, Alfonso VI (1065–1109), who had been made king of León on the death of their father. Childless, Sancho was killed while besieging Zamora in 1072, leaving Alfonso as his heir. Alfonso won the support of Rodrigo and retained him, but Rodrigo's influence waned as he conducted feuds and humiliated important members of the court, especially Count García Ordoñez. After serving the king of Seville (1079) in a defense of the realm against an attack by Granada, supported by Ordoñez, Rodrigo launched in 1081 a campaign against Toledo, which was controlled by Alfonso. The king then exiled him, and, unable to bring about a reconciliation, Rodrigo offered his services to the Moorish kingdom of Zaragoza. On behalf of that city's ruler he defeated a Muslim army in 1082 and a Christian force led by King Sancho Ramirez of Aragon in 1084. Having amassed a considerable fortune, while increasing his formidable military reputation, he was in a position to begin a campaign for the control of Valencia.

Rodrigo gained increasing control over Valencia and its ruler, al-Qadir, who became his tributary in 1192. When al-Qadir was assassinated by the *qadi* Ibn Jahhaf, Rodrigo laid siege to the city, defeating an Almoravid attempt to break it in 1093. Ibn Jahhaf surrendered in May 1094, believing Rodrigo's peace overture. He was burned alive, and the city was placed under Rodrigo's control, held nominally for Alfonso VI. Rodrigo died there on July 10, 1099. The realities of his life and achievements were altered by the tales of his heroism, accounts that obscured his political ambitions and reflected a shining example of knighthood in Castile. See also CANTAR DE MIO CID.

**ROGER I, COUNT OF SICILY** (1031–1101) Youngest son of Tancred de Hauteville and a brother of Robert Guiscard, count from 1072. He journeyed to Italy in 1057 to join Robert on his campaigns in Calabria and then was given the task of conquering Sicily, relying on the formidable assistance of his brother to complete the conquest in 1091. In 1072 he had captured Palermo and shown a reluctance to remain merely Robert's lieutenant. He was thus invested with the titles of count of Sicily and Calabria and, in 1085, succeeded his brother as the ruler of southern Italy. Control of the church in Sicily was assured in 1098 when Pope Urban II (1088–1099) appointed him papal legate. A largely tolerant leader, Roger centralized his administration and laid the groundwork for the success of his son, Roger II. See also SICILY.

**ROGER II, KING OF SICILY** (1095–1154) Norman ruler of southern Italy and the creator of the Norman kingdom of Sicily, receiving his crown in 1130. The son of Roger I, he was only nine when he inherited the county of Sicily from his brother, Simon, in 1105. Assuming control of his affairs in 1112, he soon extended his authority throughout the southern part of the peninsula. Calabria fell in 1122, followed by Apulia in 1127. The following year Pope Honorius II invested him as the duke of Apulia, Calabria and Sicily. In 1130 he gave his support to the antipope Anacletus II (1130–1138) and was crowned king, forcing Innocent II (1130–1143) to confirm him in that office in 1138. With his navy, largely composed of Greek ships, he captured Corfu and even sailed up the Bosporus to fire arrows at the palace of the Byzantine emperors. Despite often stormy relations with the pope, the Byzantines, the Venetians and the German kings, Roger was able to pacify his vassals, centralize his government, enact new laws and promote the arts, literature and science, drawing to his court at Palermo a brilliant intellectual circle. An enlightened and tolerant king, Roger brought Norman influence to its height. See also NORMANS; SICILY.

**ROGER I GUISCARD** See ROGER I, COUNT OF SICILY.

**ROBERT II GUISCARD** See ROGER II, KING OF SICILY.

**ROGER BACON** See BACON, ROGER.

**ROGER OF LORIA** (d. 1304) Also called Roger of Lauria, a Sicilian admiral who fought for the Aragonese rulers Pedro III (1276–1285) and James II (1291–1327) in their struggle with the Angevins (House of Anjou) for control of Sicily. He was responsible for several Aragonese victories.

**ROGER OF WENDOVER** (d. 1236) English Benedictine monk of Saint Albans who was the author of the *Flores historiarum,* a chronology from the Creation to the year 1235. The work was the primary source for details on the reign of King Henry III (1216–1272).

**ROLAND** French hero immortalized in the 11th-century epic *La Chanson de Roland.* He was actually the prefect of the Breton march in the service of Charlemagne (768–814), killed in 778 when the rear guard of Charlemagne's army was ambushed by the Basques in the Pyrenees while returning from Spain. Trapped at Roncesvalles, he died with the flower of Frankish chivalry, his achievements recorded in a chronicle attributed to Turpin, archbishop of Reims. Legend changed the Basque enemy to Saracens, increasing the danger of the circumstances and importance of the hero and the engagement. *La Chanson de Roland,* some 4,000 lines long, was ascribed to the Norman *trouvere* Theroulde or Turoldus. The simple but affecting poetry made it one of the most popular epics in medieval literature, and Roland appeared in other versions of the chansons de geste. His sword was called Durandal (or Durindana), supposedly once the possession of the Trojan hero Hector. See also CHANSON DE GESTE.

**ROLLE DE HAMPOLE, RICHARD** (d. 1349) English hermit, mystic and author, studying at Oxford and Paris before becoming a hermit on the estate of his friend John Dalton of Pickering in 1326. He wandered extensively, often meeting opposition because of his preaching and attacks on the vices of the time, while also winning supporters and eventually serving as the spiritual guide to a convent of Cistercian nuns. Rolle wrote devotional poetry and a commentrary the Psalter, made translations of the Bible and also wrote the *Meditation on the Passions,* a treatise on Christ's suffering. He wrote in Latin and in English. See also MYSTICISM.

**ROLLE, RICHARD** See ROLLE DE HAMPOLE, RICHARD.

**ROLLO** (c. 860–c. 922) Chief of the Norse raiders who signed the Treaty of Saint-Clair-sur-Epte in 911 with King Charles III of France (893–923), granting them in fief the region that came to be the duchy of Normandy. While officially it was a fiefdom, Rollo maintained virtual autonomy there. He accepted Christianity, and William I the Conqueror was his direct descendant. See also NORMANDY; NORMANS.

**ROLLS, PIPE** The records of accounts received maintained by the English Exchequer, extant from 1156, although there is an isolated roll from 1130. Officially referred to as the "Great Rolls of the Exchequer," these were a major source for information on the financial history of England in the Middle Ages, deriving their name from the resemblance the sheepskin rolls bore to pipe stacks. Among the information preserved were accounts of the sheriffs, feudal dues and royal incomes. See also EXCHEQUER.

**ROMAGNA** Region in north-central Italy on the Adriatic Sea, now in Emilia-Romagna, under Byzantine control from 540 to 751 and part of the Exarchate of Ravenna before coming under the influence of the Franks. It was included in the Donation of Pepin (754), confirmed by Charlemagne in 774, but retained limited papal authority because of local rulers and the rise of free commerce. Cesare Borgia was named duke of Romagna by Pope Alexander VI (1492–1503) in 1501, but his fall allowed the region to become incorporated into the Papal States by Julius II. See also PAPAL STATES.

***ROMAN DE LA ROSE*** Popular Old French poem of 22,000 lines written in two parts. The first section was by Guillaume de Lorris, composed between 1225 and 1240, and the second was written by Jean de Meun, in 1275–1280. Guillaume's offering was a subtle allegory on the psychology of love, whereas Jean's reflects a satirical tone. Jean's account reflects the bourgeois spirit; Gillaume's epitomized the traditional concept of courtly love. The *Roman de la rose* is the tale of a youth who dreams of a rose, symbolizing a maiden, enclosed in a garden. Wounded by the arrows of Amor, he strives to reach the rose, confronting setbacks and achieving victories, encountering personifications of vice and virtue along the way. A conclusion to the first part was lacking, allowing Jean de Meun to present a vast amount of information and opinions on many and diverse topics, including the hypocrisy of friars, women, nature, literature, science and mythology. Extremely popular, the poem was translated into Middle English, with a portion by Chaucer. The work was a major influence on Chaucer's writings.

**ROMAN EMPIRE** See BYZANTINE EMPIRE; HOLY ROMAN EMPIRE.

**ROMANESQUE ART AND ARCHITECTURE** The artistic style prevalent in Europe and flourishing from the 11th to the 13th centuries until superseded by the Gothic. Its name was derived from an artistic revival fostered by the monasteries, beginning in the 10th century with the building of churches and abbeys. It was therefore most often associated with architectural achievements, although it extended to other art forms and was often a fusion of Roman, Byzantine, Eastern, Celtic, Lombard and Teutonic stylistic elements.

### *Art*

Romanesque art encompassed all the visual arts in addition to metalwork, bronze casting and embroidery (see BAYEUX TAPESTRY). Sculptural decorations for Romanesque buildings abounded, with magnificent examples produced by such artists as Nicholas Pisano and Benedetto Antelami. Among the greatest sculptural works were the bronze *Christ's Column,* traditionally cast by Saint Bernward in Hildesheim; the *Pentecost* at Vezelay; and the *Last Judgment* at Autun. Mural painting flourished during the monastic movement, as did manuscript illumination, an art that was itself a direct product of the European monasteries. See also MANUSCRIPT ILLUMINATION.

### *Architecture*

As has been noted, the monastic revival of the 10th century provided the spirit and impetus for the magnificent structures that were to be created during the Romanesque period. Early Romanesque churches took the basic form of the Christian basilica, which evolved after 1050, to the Gothic, with its greater complexity. Romanesque architecture relied on masonry vaulting, but unlike ancient Roman construction, the vaults were not made of brick but of blocks of stone. The typical Romanesque church featured round arches, thick walls and columns, barrel vaults and small windows.

The sheer weight of the barrel vault of the nave necessitated the dimensions of the windows; the problem of connecting the vaults, supports and abutments was solved by the implementation of stone skeletons, called groin vaults, supported by strong upright shafts. Characteristically, Romanesque churches lacked much light because of the limits placed on the window size. Interior decoration consisted largely of sculpture and relief in stone. There were many variations in Romanesque architecture found throughout Europe; however, there were certain general characteristics, found everywhere: arched windows, barrel vaults and massive walls. See also ART AND ARCHITECTURE, BYZANTINE; CATHEDRAL; GOTHIC ART AND ARCHITECTURE.

**ROMANUS** (d. 897) Pope from August to November 897, successor to the murdered Stephen VI (896–897), who had died because of the indignities he had inflicted on the corpse of Pope Formosus (891–896). Romanus ordered Formosus's body retrieved from the Tiber and invalidated the acts of his predecessor. Official nullification did not come for many years, for Romanus was deposed and died a short time later.

**ROMANUS I LECAPENUS** (d. 948) Byzantine emperor from 920 to 944, dividing power with Constantine VII (ruled 913–919, 944–959), his regent, and, in 919, arranging the marriage of the young ruler to his daughter, Helena. In September 920 he became caesar and then coemperor in December of that year. As emperor he proved to be an able statesman, issuing laws to protect peasant and military land holdings from absorption into the estates of magnates. Romanus was deposed by his own sons, who feared that on his death they would be excluded from ruling. He was exiled to the island of Prote, where he died in 948 as a monk. Ironically, Constantine took advantage of the political vacuum to arrest Romanus's sons in 945, sending them into exile. See also BYZANTINE EMPIRE.

**ROMANUS II** (d. 963) Byzantine emperor from 959 to 963, the son of Constantine VII (919–959), who left the government in the hands of the eunuch Joseph Bringas while influenced by his wife, Theophano, who may have encouraged him to poison his father. His reign was notable for the capture of Crete in 961, a feat accomplished by his general, Nicephorus II Phocas, who succeeded him with the support of Theophano. See also BYZANTINE EMPIRE.

**ROMANUS III ARGYRUS** (d. 1034) Byzantine emperor from 1028 to 1034, coming to the throne through his marriage to the empress Zoë. He was 60 when made emperor and was reputedly handsome and cultivated. He failed to maintain taxes on the wealthy and strained the treasury by aiding earthquake victims and plague survivors, as well as supporting his ambitious building projects. Poor relations with Zoë led to his death in his bath and the rise of the empress's lover, Michael IV. In 1032, Edessa had fallen to the gifted general of Romanus, Georges Maniaces. See also BYZANTINE EMPIRE.

**ROMANUS IV DIOGENES** (d. 1072) Byzantine emperor from 1067 to 1071, best remembered for the crushing defeat of his army at Manzikert in August 1071. A Cappadocian noble, he married the widow of Constantine X Ducas, having fought against the Petchenegs. Confronted by the Seljuk Turks, he launched several campaigns and was successful in 1068 and 1069. In 1071, he was routed and captured by Alp Arslan. On his release he found himself deposed by Michael VII Ducas and was blinded with hot irons, dying in the summer of 1072 as a result of his injuries. See also BYZANTINE EMPIRE; MANZIKERT, BATTLE OF; SELJUK TURKS.

**ROME** The most important city in Italy, situated on the Tiber River, called the Eternal City, and for centuries the capital of the Roman Empire. Its decline was evident in 410 when the Ostrogoths led by Alaric sacked Rome. Additional humiliations occurred in 455 at the hands of Geiseric and the Vandals, an omen presaging the doom of the empire in the West. In 476 Romulus Augustulus was deposed by the Germanic chief Odoacer, and Rome entered the Middle Ages as a city of limited importance. Ravenna was the political capital of Italy, and Rome's monuments fell into decay or were used for restoration of other building, as the Romans endured wars between the Goths and Byzantines during the sixth century.

A revival and increasing prosperity were concurrent with the rise of the papacy. The popes became the primary political defenders of Rome, nominally under Byzantine domination but transferring their loyalties to the Franks in the eighth century in opposition to the iconoclastic policies of Emperor Leo III the Isaurian (ruled 717–741). On Christmas Day in 800, Pope Leo III (795–816) crowned Charlemagne Roman emperor, thereby binding the papacy to the Holy Roman Empire and its Carolingian rulers. Considerable upheaval occurred as the Carolingian empire disintegrated, and the popes fell victim to the power of local noble houses, a condition that endured until the 11th century. A peace was established with the Roman nobles, and the papacy found money to finance reforms. With changes in administration a certain order was restored, facilitating an economic revival in the city. Rome suffered, nevertheless, from the conflict between Pope Gregory VII (1073–1086) and the Holy Empire and the occupation of the city by the Normans in 1084.

In 1143 a communal revolution occurred in Rome, leading to the establishment of a commune in which the Roman Senate was revived. The preacher Arnold of Brescia, a forceful influence, was with the commune surviving attack by the pope and emperors to receive papal approval in 1188. A notable pope during this period was Innocent III (1198–1216), as Rome was beset by quarrels between Innocent's family and the Orsinis. The latter part of the 13th century witnessed additional conflicts among other powerful Roman houses, such as the Colonna, Orsini, Conti and Caetani. Confronting such strife, as well as antipapal sentiment, in 1309 Pope Clement V (1305–1314), under French domination, moved the papal residence to Avignon, leaving Rome to its own factionalism. The city declined economically again, as the financial industries involving the papacy were gone. The Romans supported the populist tribune Cola di Rienzo in 1347 but later killed him in a riot. The Black Death (1348) reduced the population further. Cardinal Albornoz, the papal legate, restored some order, but even after the popes returned to Rome in 1377 the city was little improved, its revitalization hampered by the attention given the Great Schism (1378–1417). It was said that wolves stalked the streets around Saint Peter's at night.

A major change in fortune came with the election in 1417 of Martin V (1417–1431), a Roman of the Colonna family. The first of the Renaissance pontiffs, Martin strove to transform Rome into a papal state, extending control of the Holy See over the Roman commune and the papal state. During the papacy of his successors, Nicholas V (1447–1455), Pius II (1458–1464) and Sixtus IV (1471–1484), Rome became a true Renaissance city, the popes giving patronage to scholars and artists. Through their efforts Rome was a magnet for Renaissance culture by the end of the 15th century. See also PAPAL STATES.

**RONCEVAUX, BATTLE OF** See ROLAND.

**RORY O'CONNOR** (d. 1198) Also called Roderic or Ruadri (in the Irish), king of Connacht and the high king of Ireland. He succeeded his father, Turloch, as ruler in 1156 and became high king in 1166. His decision to attack Dermot MacMurrough, king of Leinster, necessitated an appeal for help from the English, and in 1170 the Anglo-Norman Richard de Clare, earl of Pembroke, called "Strongbow," invaded at Waterford. Rory besieged and captured Dublin in 1171 but was later defeated. By the agreement signed in 1175 with the English, Rory accepted vassal status for Connacht from King Henry II of England (1154–1189), relinquishing his title of high king. He retired to a monastery in 1191. See also IRELAND.

**ROSAMOND** (c. 1140–c. 1176) Mistress of King Henry II of England (1154–1189), called as "Fair Rosamond," the daughter of Walter de Clifford and probably Henry's paramour for some time. She received acknowledgment from him about 1174, after his imprisonment of Eleanor of Aquitaine. She was the subject of many legends, including one recording that she was murdered by Eleanor. See also HENRY II, KING OF ENGLAND.

**ROSAMOND, QUEEN OF THE LOMBARDS** (d. after 572) Wife of the Lombard king Alboin, the daughter of Cunimund, king of the Gepidae. Rosamond was bound to wed Alboin after he beheaded her father. In 572 he forced her to drink from a cup fashioned from her father's skull. She then had Alboin murdered and fled with her accomplices. She supposedly attempted to poison her Lombard lover, Helmichis, but he drank only half the contents, forcing her to drink the remainder. See also LOMBARDS.

**ROSCELLINUS OF COMPIÈGNE** (c. 1050–c. 1125) Also called Roscelin, a theologian and the theorist behind the philosophical concept of nominalism. He probably came from Compiègne, studying at Soissons and Reims and teaching for a time; his most distinguished pupil was Peter Abelard. The chief sources on his theories were his opponents, Anselm, Abelard and John of Salisbury. If not the founder of nominalism, the doctrine stating that universals were merely verbal expressions, he was its first great defender. He retracted his beliefs concerning the Trinity after his theory—that the Trinity was composed of three separate persons in God—was condemned at the Council of Soissons (1092). See also SCHOLASTICISM.

**ROSES, WARS OF THE** See WARS OF THE ROSES.

**ROSKILDE** City in eastern Zeeland, Denmark, situated on the Roskilde Fjord. Its name was derived from its legendary founder, Hroar, and the nearby springs, *kilde*. From the early 11th century until 1416 the city was the residence of the Danish kings, remaining the capital until 1443. A bishopric was established in the second half of the 11th century, having great prestige and a cathedral of combined Romanesque and Gothic styles that was begun about 1170 by Absalon. Numerous Danish kings were buried in the cathedral. See also DENMARK.

**ROSVITHA, SAINT** (d. c. 1000) Also Roswitha and Hrosvit, a German poetess and Benedictine nun. Of noble Saxon birth, she entered the Benedictine convent of Gandersheim at a young age. Her writings included two chronicles, eight poems and six comedies. The chronicles were on the achievements of Otto the Great (left incomplete) and a history of Gandersheim Abbey from its founding until 919. Her comedies were plays on Christian themes presented in comedy form, based upon the works of the

Roman dramatist Terence but intended to denounce and correct the morality prevalent in classical times. Rosvitha's poems were on St. Agnes, St. Basil and the Blessed Virgin Mary. Forgotten for a long period, her works were rediscovered around 1500 by the German humanist Conradus Celtis at Ratisbon and published soon after.

**ROTHARI** (d. 652) King of the Lombards, one of the prominent Lombard rulers, reigning from 636 and completing the conquest of northern Italy. Originally the duke of Brescia, Rothari succeeded Ariwald as king, subduing the Ligurian coast and capturing the city of Genoa in 641. He was also known for his efforts in framing the Lombard code of laws, publishing in 643 a code called the *Edictum Rotharis,* which contained civil and criminal laws of Germanic tradition. There were extensive lists of laws against armed violence, requirements of a warrior to his lord and rules governing inheritance. In effect, the volume preserved glimpses into both Lombard law and society. Rothari was the last of the practicing Arian kings of the Lombards. See also LOMBARDS.

**ROUEN** City in Normandy on the Seine River, in the Seine-Maritime department. An ancient settlement, Rouen was called by the Romans Rotomagus, becoming Christian in the third century through the efforts of Saint Mallon. An archepiscopal see in the fifth century, Rouen was captured by the Normans in 841 and 876 and held by the English following the Norman Conquest (1066). The French took possession of the city in 1204, and it remained in French hands with the exception of the years 1418–1449, during the Hundred Years' War. Joan of Arc was imprisoned and executed there in 1431, on the Place du Vieux Marché. After its recapture, Rouen became a magnet for cultural pursuits and learning. The cathedral of Rouen, reflecting a variety of architectural styles, has survived as one of the finest Gothic edifices in France, with its two unique towers, the left one dating from the 12th century, the right from the 15th century. Other medieval structures also remain there. See also HUNDRED YEARS' WAR.

**ROUND TABLE** See ARTHURIAN LEGEND.

**ROUVRAY, BATTLE OF** See HERRINGS, BATTLE OF THE.

***RUBAIYAT*** See OMAR KHAYYAM.

**RUBRUQUIS, WILLIAM OF** See WILLIAM OF RUBRUQUIS.

**RUDOLF I** (1218–1291) A son of Albert IV, count of Habsburg, Rudolf inherited extensive territories about 1239, including parts of Upper Alsace, Breisgau and the Aargau, and strove to increase his lands and prestige. His election as German king in 1273 ended the Great Interregnum, when there was neither a Holy Roman Emperor nor a designated successor to that title (German king). He was crowned at Aachen and won papal approval from Gregory X (1271–1276), agreeing to surrender all claims to Sicily or the Papal States. Rudolf issued the Diet of Regensburg (1274), which divested Ottokar, king of Bohemia, of his acquired possessions, Austria, Styria and Carinthia. He then invaded and defeated Ottokar in 1276, forcing the Bohemian ruler to relinquish everything but Bohemia and Moravia. When, two years later, Ottokar attempted to regain his lost lands, Rudolf defeated and killed him at the Battle of Marchfeld (Dürnkrut) in August. He then laid the groundwork for future Habsburg greatness by granting territories to his sons Albert and Rudolf. He failed in his efforts to have Albert elected as king of the Romans or Germany, the Electors refusing to make the crown a hereditary possession of the Habsburgs. See also HOLY ROMAN EMPIRE.

**RUDOLF OF EMS** (d. c. 1250) Popular and prolific Middle High German poet, whose castle, near Lake Constance at Hohenems, survives. He was the author of five epic poems; the most notable in the opinion of scholars is *Der guote Gerhart (Gerhard the Good).* His other works include *Barlaam und Josephat* (a version of the Buddha legend) and three historical epics, *Alexander, Wilehalm von Orlens* and *Weltchronik.* Rudolf was influenced by the writers Gottfried von Strassburg and Hartmann von Aue.

**RUDOLF OF SWABIA** (d. 1080) German anti-king to King Henry IV (1056–1106), also called Rudolf of Rheinfelden, originally a supporter of Henry. After his excommunication in 1076, he became an opponent of Henry's and was elected king at Mainz on 1077. After two conflicts with Henry, in 1078 and 1080, Rudolf was finally recognized by Pope Gregory VII (1073–1085), only to die from wounds received at the Battle of Elster River in October 1080. See also HOLY ROMAN EMPIRE.

**RUM, SELJUKS OF** See SELJUK TURKS.

**RUPERT III OF THE PALATINATE** (1352–1410) German king from 1400 to 1410 and a member of the House of Wittelsbach, called also Rupert III, Elector Palatine of the Rhine (from 1398). He was elected king following the deposition of King Wenceslas. Crowned at Cologne (Köln) in January 1401, he was handicapped throughout most of his reign by limited recognition and authority. Pope Boniface IX (1389–1404) gave him his approval finally in 1403, and Rupert spent much time suppressing the supporters of Wenceslas, his own enthusiastic support coming chiefly from the Rhineland. See also HOLY ROMAN EMPIRE.

**RURIK** (d. c. 879) A leader of the Vikings (Varangians), considered the traditional founder, with his two brothers, of the first Russian principality at Novgorod in 862. His son Igor was successor to Rurik's kinsman, Oleg, as ruler of the principality of Kiev and thus ensured the survival of the Rurikid dynasty. Much of what is known about Rurik comes from the semilegendary accounts of the period or from the *Russian Primary Chronicle,* considered by some as unreliable in its presentation of details concerning Rurik's rise to power. See also RUSSIA.

**RURIKID DYNASTY** The line of Russian princes that ruled regions in Russia from about 862 until the dynasty's extinction in 1596. See also KIEV; MOSCOW, GRAND PRINCES OF; NOVGOROD; RUSSIA; VLADIMIR.

**RUSSIA** A vast region extending eastward from Europe possessing a complex history, with a population influenced by Eastern and Western culture. Such was the evolution of the Russian state that by the end of the 15th century, Ivan III (ruled 1462–1505) was able to make claim to the succession of the Byzantine or Eastern Roman Empire.

Migratory peoples and invaders were attracted to the steppes of southern Russia from an early time; among the many groups coming into the region were the Scythians, Sarmatians, Avars, Khazars, Bulgars, Goths, Huns and Magyars. By the ninth century the East Slavs occupied much of the western region, subject for a time to the Khazars of the south. The foundation of the first Russian state, and hence the introduction of Russia into history, is generally considered the work of Rurik (d. c. 879), chief of a group of Varangian (Viking) traders. He established himself at Novgorod (862), the first of the Rurikid dynasty. Under Olaf, the Varangians took Kiev, establishing the Kievan state that dominated the Russian political scene until the mid-12th century.

The Kievans destroyed the Khazar empire, extended their influence into the Caucasus and, under Vladimir I (970–1015), developed ties with the Byzantine Empire. These associations helped bring the influence of the Eastern Orthodox Church into the country, with all of its religious and cultural significance. Kiev began to decline as a state after 1154, when it broke apart into several principalities under Rurikid domination. Cuman invasions were severe, worsened by the almost incessant warfare between the principalities. In 1169, Kiev was sacked by the prince of Suzdal, bringing the Kievan era of dominance to a close.

The successor state to Kiev was Vladimir, to the northeast, but the principal historical events in the 13th century were the invasions of Russia by the Mongols. Their first invasion occurred in 1223, returning from 1237 to 1240, during which time they subjugated the Russians, establishing the empire of the Golden Horde. Tribute was exacted from the Russian princes, and damage caused by the Mongols was severe, including the destruction of Kiev in 1240. From Mongol domination a state emerged uniting Russia and establishing an empire, the grand duchy of Moscow. Because of its strategic location and prosperity from trade, Moscow rose to political prominence. David, son of Alexander Nevsky, became the first to hold the title of prince of Moscow, his son Ivan I (d. 1341) the first grand prince. Ivan was largely successful in aggrandizing Moscow, but efforts to break the Tatar yoke were not fulfilled until 1480, in the reign of Ivan III (1462–1505). He conquered Novgorod, repulsed the Lithuanians and expelled the Hanseatic League, thereby preparing the way for the reign of his grandson, Ivan IV, called "the Terrible." See also ART AND ARCHITECTURE, BYZANTINE; AVARS; BULGARIA; BYZANTINE EMPIRE; CUMANS; GOLDEN HORDE; HANSEATIC LEAGUE; KHAZARS; KREMLIN; LITHUANIA; MONGOLS; MOSCOW; MOSCOW, GRAND PRINCES OF; NOVGOROD; POLAND; RURIKID DYNASTY; SLAVS; TRADE AND COMMERCE; VIKINGS.

**RUYSBROECK, JAN VAN** (1293–1381) Flemish mystic and a respected mystical writer of the Middle Ages. Born at Ruysbroek, he was ordained a priest about 1318. Retiring in 1343, he founded the Augustinian abbey at Groenendael, near Brussels, becoming prior in 1350. Here he wrote all but the first of his works, the *Vanden Rike der Ghelievan (Kingdom of the Lovers of God).* His other works included treatises in Flemish: *The Adornment of the Spiritual Marriage, The Mirror of Eternal Salvation* and *The Seven Steps of the Ladder of Spiritual Love.* His most important work was *The Spiritual Espousals,* a guide for the soul that presented a view of the Trinitarian system but remained within the boundaries established by church authorities. Ruysbroeck was influenced by Meister Eckhart and Pseudo-Dionysius and in turn influenced Johann Tauler, Gerhard Groote and the Brethren of the Common Life. See also MYSTICISM.

# S

**SAADI** See SA'DI.

**SA'ADIA BEN JOSEPH** (882–942) Jewish biblical scholar, polemicist and philosopher, born in Egypt, eventually traveling to Babylonia via Palestine. There he emerged as a brilliant and forceful defender of the oral tradition and the traditional Jewish calendar, departing from the scholar Aaron ben Meir, who proposed changes. He wrote a defense of the Rabbanite calendar in his *Kitab at-tamyiz (Book of Discernment)*. Appointed director in 928 of the esteemed Jewish academy at Sura (Baghdad), he strove to systematize Talmudic law, but a dispute in 932 with the exilarch, the leader of the Jews in Babylon, led to his removal in 935. He then went into seclusion and wrote his illustrious work *The Book of Beliefs and Opinions,* in which he attempted to explore the cohesion of reason and revelation. Reconciled with the exilarch in 937, he returned to his post at the academy. Sa'adia also made many translations and commentaries on the Bible, his translation of the Old Testament becoming the standard accepted by Arabic-speaking Jews.

**SABIN** King of the Bulgars from 764 to 766. See also BULGARIA.

**SABINIAN** (d. 606) Pope from 604 to 606, papal legate to Constantinople on behalf of Gregory the Great (590–604) before succeeding him. Considered a cautious pontiff, he was forced to deal with a famine and the constant threat by the Lombards.

**SAD** Nasrid king of Granada from 1454 to 1464 and the grandson of King Yusuf II (1391–1392). His reign was remembered principally for the Castilian invasion launched against him by King Henry IV (1454–1474) in 1455. The war, largely a series of raids that included the capture of Gibraltar by the Christians, ended in a truce in 1463. See also NASRID KINGDOM OF GRANADA.

**SA'DI** (c. 1213–1292) Also Mushariff-ud-Din, an acclaimed Persian poet and author who produced two masterpieces, *Bustan (The Orchard)* and *Gulistan (The Rose Garden)*. Born in Shiraz, Persia, Sa'di studied at Baghdad but took to a life of wandering after the Mongol invasion, traveling to Syria, Egypt, North Africa, Anatolia and possibly India and Central Asia. He returned to Shiraz and spent the remainder of his life there. *Bustan* (1257) was written entirely in verse and consisted of stories describing and recommending the virtues of the traditional Islamic life (justice, modesty and contentment). *Gulistan,* chiefly prose, contained stories and anecdotes sprinkled with short poems, aphorisms, moral considerations and humorous reflections. Sa'di also composed odes.

**AL-SAFFAH** Abbasid caliph from 750 to 754. See also ABBASID CALIPHATE.

**SAFFARID DYNASTY** Persian (Iranian) royal line that held much of eastern Iran from about 867 to 908, the first of which was Yaqub ibn Layth, called *al-saffar* (the coppersmith). He was an official in the service of caliphs who seized his native territory of Seistan and then launched a campaign of expansion into northeastern India. The Saffarids reached the pinnacle of power in 873, with the acquisition of Khorasan, but three years later Yaqub was defeated by the army of the caliph al-Mu'tamid while advancing on Baghdad. The decline of the Saffarids began soon afterward, although they retained control of Seistan for a long period.

**SAINT ALBANS** Cathedral city in Hertfordshire, England, that derived its name from a Roman convert to Christianity who was martyred nearby in 304. Saint Alban was the earliest martyr in England; his bones were supposedly found by King Offa of Mercia, who erected a Benedictine monastery on the spot. The town evolved around the monastery, and in 1213 Stephen Langton read the first draft of Magna Carta to a gathering of clerics and nobles in its abbey. In the aftermath of the Battle of Poitiers (1356), King John of France (1350–1364) was kept there, and in 1455 and 1461 two battles during the Wars of the Roses were fought on the site. See also WARS OF THE ROSES.

**SAINT-DENIS** See GOTHIC ART AND ARCHITECTURE.

**SAINTE-CHAPELLE** See GOTHIC ART AND ARCHITECTURE.

**SAINT-GALL** See GALL, SAINT.

**SAINT GERMAIN-DES-PRÉS** Historic abbey and church in Paris, founded about 513 by Childebert I. The present Romanesque church dates from the 11th century. See also Paris.

**SAINT JAMES OF COMPOSTELA, ORDER OF** See MILITARY ORDERS.

**SAINT MARK'S** An outstanding cathedral in Venice originally built as a Romanesque church, consecrated 832, to house the relics of Saint Mark. The first structure burned in 976 as a result of a revolt against doge Pietro Candiano IV. Restoration was undertaken by doge Domenico Cantarini, the work being completed by 1071. The new Saint Mark's was constructed with the advice of architects from Constantinople and thus reflected extensive Byzantine influence. Its design was a Greek cross with a dome centered over it and over each arm of the cross. Each dome was decorated with mosaics on a gold ground. Over the gallery at the main entrance rear the Four Horses of Saint Mark's cast in gilded bronze. These were brought to Venice after the looting of Constantinople during the Fourth Crusade (1202–1204) and were installed in the mid-13th century. They may have been originally designed for Nero's triumphal arch, later decorating the hippodrome in Constantinople. Additional works of art, sculpture and mosaics, and modifications and alterations of a later date made Saint Mark's one of the most beautiful buildings in Europe. See also ART AND ARCHITECTURE, BYZANTINE; VENICE.

**SAINT-MICHEL, MONT** See MONT SAINT-MICHEL.

**SALADIN** (1137/38–1193) Sultan of Egypt and Syria, brilliant and esteemed Islamic general, poet and the formidable opponent of the Crusaders in the Holy Land. Salah ad-Din, Yusuf ibn Ayyub, was born in Mesopotamia to a Kurdish family, the son of Najm ad-Din Ayyub. He was also a nephew of Asad ad-Din Shirkuh, a commander in the army of Nur ed-Din, son of and successor as emir to Imad ad-Din Zangi, under whom Saladin's father served. He grew up in Baalbek and Damascus, embarking on his career by joining his uncle in the service of Nur ed-Din, participating in several campaigns into Egypt to prevent its conquest by the Crusaders.

Following the death of Shirkuh, Saladin, in 1169, was named vizier of Egypt and general of the Syrian troops there, solidifying his position by removing the troublesome vizier Shawar. In 1171 he took the decisive step of abolishing the Fatimid caliphate in Egypt, according to tradition ordering a return to Sunni practice by calling the faithful to prayer while the last Shiite Fatimid caliph lay dying. While maintaining the fiction of an allegiance to Nur ed-Din, Saladin was master of Egypt, with all its resources, bearing the title of *malik* (king), and was called sultan. Upon Nur ed-Din's death, he embarked on a long campaign (1174–1186) to unite all Islam under his banner. He brought Syria, Palestine, Egypt and Mesopotamia under his sway, extending his influence into Yemen and as far as Tunisia, while adding to his reputation as a general and an enlightened ruler.

His ultimate goal was his campaign against the Crusader States in Palestine, a jihad, or holy war, that he would lead. Saladin launched his war in 1187, destroying a Crusader army at the Battle of Hattin on July 4, 1187. In October of that year he completed a brilliantly conceived series of maneuvers by capturing Jerusalem, which had been in Christian hands since 1099. Although he failed to subdue Tyre, a powerful port fortress, he dealt a crushing blow to the Latin cause in Palestine. Acre, Beirut, Caesarea, Jaffa, Ascalon and Jerusalem were all in Muslim control. The Third Crusade (1189–1192) followed, led by Richard the Lion-Hearted (1189–1199), Philip II Augustus of France (1180–1223) and Frederick I Barbarossa (1152–1190). Saladin's continued military prowess, with the exception of the Battle of Arsuf, prevented the Christians from recovering Jerusalem and resulted in a truce with Richard that allowed the Muslims to retain the holy city while permitting pilgrims to visit Christian sites unharmed. Saladin retired to Damascus after the departure of Richard, dying on March 4, 1193. His extensive empire was bequeathed to the Ayyubid dynasty, which he had established, a legacy that his successors would be unable to maintain.

Saladin's lasting fame was preserved by the Islamic world, in which he was hailed as the greatest foe of the Christians during the era of the Crusades, and by the West, where he was remembered for his chivalry, justice and generosity. A gifted poet, Saladin was also a patron of learning and literature. See also ASSASSINS, ORDER OF; AYYUBIDS; CRUSADER STATES; CRUSADES; EGYPT; HATTIN, BATTLE OF.

**SALAMANCA** City in western Spain in the region of León, an ancient settlement dating from the Roman era. A bishopric in the seventh century, the city was captured by the Moors early in the eighth century and not reclaimed by the Christians until 1087. After a period of revitalization by the Christian populace, Salamanca became important in the kingdom of León, and Ferdinand II (1157–1188) held a *cortes* (parliament) there in 1188. Around 1230 the University of Salamanca was founded by Alfonso IX (1188–1230) and eventually became renowned in Europe, making Arabic science and philosophy available to the Western world through the works of Arabic and Jewish scholars.

**SALERNO** Port in the southern Italian region of Campania, the principality of the province of Salerno, founded (197 B.C.) as a Roman colony called Salernum, possibly on the site of an Etruscan settlement. Attached to the Lombard duchy of Benevento (c. 646), it became the capital of an independent Lombard principality in the ninth century. Roger Guiscard and his Normans conquered Salerno in 1076, and it became his capital. In 1419 the city was dominated by the Colonna and later the Orsini families, finally becoming part of the kingdom of Naples. An important offshoot of the cosmopolitan society found there was the city's ninth-century rise to fame for the study of medicine. Salerno's school of medicine, flourishing in the 11th and 12th centuries, received the sanction of Frederick II in 1221 and has been called the first university in Europe, claiming students from Asia, Africa and the West. See also MEDICINE.

**SALIAN DYNASTY** Ruling line of the Holy Roman Empire, dating from 1024 to 1125, so named after the election of the Salian Frank Conrad of Swabia as the German king Conrad II (ruled 1024–1039). Also called the Franconian dynasty, its members included Henry III (ruled

1039–1056), Henry IV (ruled 1056–1106) and Henry V (ruled 1106–1125). The dynasty ended after the death of Henry V, who left no male heir. See also GERMANY; HOLY ROMAN EMPIRE.

**SALIC LAW** Lex Salica, the legal code of the Salian Franks, issued about 507–511 at the order of Clovis, first of the Merovingian dynasty. Reissued twice by Charlemagne and his Carolingian descendants and translated into Old High German, the Salic Law was essentially a penal code, listing crimes and offenses, as well as appropriate fines and punishments. Among its enactments in civil law was the important declaration that daughters were barred from inheriting lands. This custom was maintained by the Valois dynasty of France. Salic Law was issued in Latin, but Roman law had little influence on it.

**SALIMBENE** (1221–c. 1290) Italian Franciscan monk and historian, a native of Parma who entered the Franciscan order in 1238. He spent many years traveling to monasteries and encountering influential men there, including Fra Giovani da Carpini. Salimbene was the author of a practical chronology *(Cronica),* an account of the years 1168–1288.

**SALISBURY** Cathedral city in Wiltshire, England, officially called New Sarum, built on the site of Old Sarum, which became a bishopric when the see was transferred from Sherborne in 1075. Around 1220 the see was moved to New Sarum, which was later to become Salisbury, the town evolving around the cathedral and granted a charter in 1227. During the later Middle Ages Salisbury was economically prosperous, as its trade in cloth and wool flourished. Its Gothic cathedral, erected between 1220 and 1258, had both a tower and spire, the highest in England at 404 feet, both in the Decorative style.

**SALONIKA** Also Salonica, Thessalonica and Thessalonika, a port city in northeastern Greece on the western side of the Chalcydice Peninsula. Found in 315 B.C., it served as the capital of the Roman province of Macedonia from 148 and in the fourth century was the chief city of the prefecture of Illyricum. Salonika prospered economically during the eras of the Eastern, and later Byzantine, Empires and was noted in the eighth century as a bastion for defenders of the veneration of icons (see ICONOCLASTICISM. It was, however, susceptible to attacks by the Avars, Slavs, Bulgars, Normans and finally the Ottoman Turks. The Turkish threat resulted in the surrender of Salonika to the Venetians in 1423. Seven years later it fell victim to a slaughter by the Turkish forces of Murad II. See also BYZANTINE EMPIRE.

**SALUTATI, COLUCCIO** (1331–1406) Florentine statesman and influential humanist, serving as chancellor of Todi (1367) and Lucca (1371) and in the Papal Curia at Viterbo. He eventually assumed the chancellorship of Florence in 1375, holding that post for 30 years. An avid politician and humanist, Salutati promoted Renaissance arts and learning in Florence, arranging for the copying of Cicero's *Epistolae ad familiares* and making his massive library (over 800 volumes) available to scholars. He was also instrumental in bringing Manuel Chrysoloras to Florence in 1396. See also FLORENCE.

**SALZBURG** City and province in west-central Austria, originally Celtic, called in the Roman era Iuvavum. By the late seventh century Saint Rupert had founded the Benedictine abbey of Saint Peter and the Nonnberg convent there, and an episcopal see was established in 739 by Saint Boniface, becoming an archbishopric in 798. Its charter granted in 996, the city was protected by the fortress of Höhensalzburg, erected in 1077. In 1278 its archbishops were recognized as princes of the Holy Roman Empire.

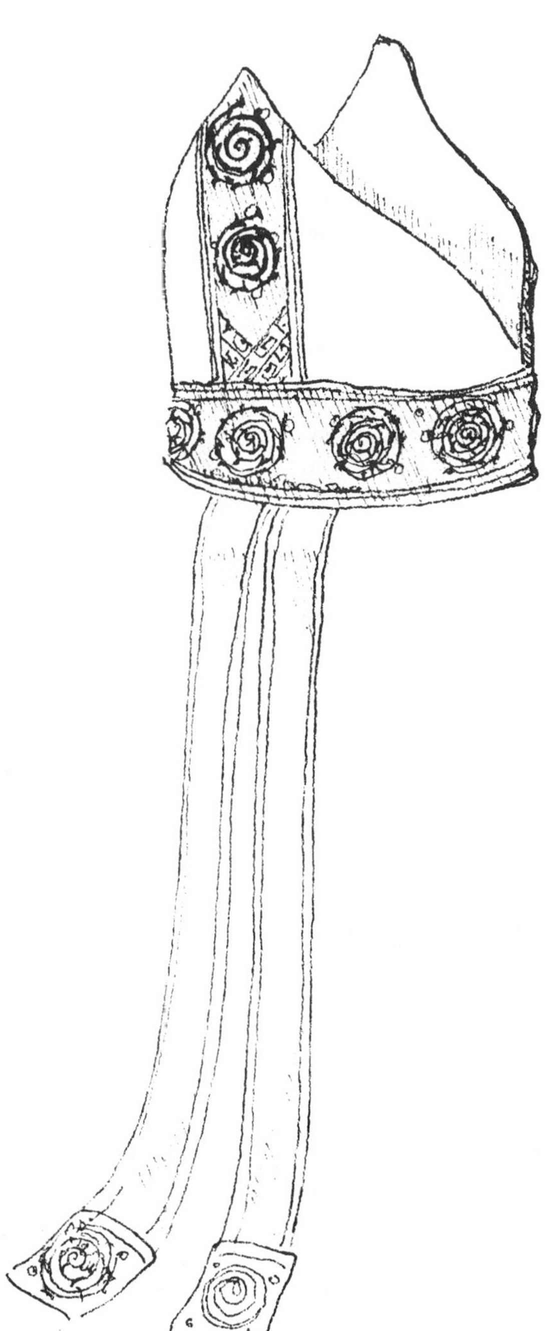

Salzburg miter

**SAMARKAND** See MONGOLS; TAMERLANE; TRADE AND COMMERCE.

**SAMO** (d. c. 660) Ruler of a large territory extending from Bohemia and Moravia into Austria from about 624. He was originally a Frankish merchant sent to the Slavs of Bohemia by King Dagobert I of the Franks to arrange an alliance against the Avars and was made king by the Slavs. See also BOHEMIA.

**SAMUEL** (d. 1014) King of the Bulgars from about 980 until his death, the son of Count Nicholas of Macedonia, who, with his brothers, led an uprising that led to control of Macedonia (c. 976), later murdering his brothers and taking their lands. Samuel then extended his power into Serbia and directed his regime from Ochrida, reviving the Bulgarian patriarchate. Emperor Basil II attacked him in 986 but was defeated, and Samuel then proceeded to use the Byzantine civil war to advantage. He conquered Thessaly, Epirus and Dyrrhachium as well as parts of Albania. From 1001, Basil, now politically recovered, launched a relentless war of attrition, culminating in his crushing defeat of the Bulgars in 1014. Basil then blinded all 14,000 Bulgar prisoners, sparing one eye of every 100th man so they could lead their piteous comrades back to their king. Samuel, beholding his blind warriors, died of a stroke. See also BULGARIA.

**SANCHO I RAMÍREZ, KING OF ARAGON** (1043–1094) Ruler of Aragon from 1063, succeeding in uniting his crown with that of Navarre (Pamplona) in 1076, following the assassination of Sancho IV (1054–1076). See also ARAGON; NAVARRE, KINGDOM OF.

**SANCHO I, KING OF LEÓN** (d. 966) Called "the Fat," ruling from 956 to 966, half brother of Ordoño III (951–956). He was deposed shortly after commencing a war with the Moors replaced by Ramiro III (966–984). Sancho sought the support of the caliph Abd al-Rahman III (912–961) and regained his throne in 960, having lost much of his obesity by means of a diet prescribed by the Jewish physician Hasday ibn Shaprut. He died by poisoning.

**SANCHO II, KING OF CASTILE** (d. 1072) Ruler from 1065 to 1072, the oldest son of Ferdinand I (1035–1065) and brother of Alfonso VI of León (1065–1109) and García of Galicia (1065–1072). On the death of Ferdinand, the sons inherited portions of the kingdom, with Sancho receiving Castile. He soon drove García out of Galicia (1071) and Alfonso from León (1072) but was assassinated. The assassin was probably in the employ of his sister, Urraca, possibly with the complicity of Alfonso. Rodrigo Díaz de Vivar (El Cid) was his military adviser.

**SANCHO III, KING OF CASTILE** (d. 1158) Son of King Alfonso VII (1126–1157), dividing his inheritance with his brother, Ferdinand II (1157–1188), and given Castile, which he ruled for only a year. Sancho showed governmental promise but died, leaving a son, Alfonso VIII (1158–1214), only two years old. Disorder and conflict followed his death. See also CASTILE.

**SANCHO IV, KING OF CASTILE AND LEÓN** (1257–1295) Ruler of Castile and León from 1284, the second son of Alfonso X (1252–1284). Sancho was designated as heir on the death of his older brother, but his claim was disputed by his nephews. He confronted several threats during his reign, including French invasions and assaults by the Muslim Marinids of Morocco, as well as civil unrest because of his usurpation. An attack by the Marinids was repulsed in 1290, and in 1291 he entered into a brief alliance with Muhammad II of Granada (1273–1302), which resulted in the capture of the port of Tarifa. Sancho was generally described as energetic and cunning and a patron of scholars.

**SANCHO I GARCÉS, KING OF NAVARRE** (d. c. 926) Ruler from 905, energetically pursuing expansion, acquiring territories beyond the Ebro River. In 924, however, his capital of Pampolona was sacked by the caliph Abd al-Rahman III (912–961), ending his years of political activity. See also NAVARRE, KINGDOM OF.

**SANCHO II GARCÉS, KING OF NAVARRE** (d. 994) Ruler of Navarre from 970 to 994, the son of García I Sánchez, succeeding him as king. He was forced to recognize the supremacy of the dictator of Córdoba, Almanzor, giving him his daughter in marriage. See also NAVARRE, KINGDOM OF.

**SANCHO III GARCÉS, KING OF NAVARRE** (c. 992–1035) Called "the Great," ruling from 1000 to 1035 and eventually extending control over all the Christian kingdoms of Spain. Inheriting Navarre and Aragon, he conquered the Moors and then through diplomatic means and marriage acquired control of Castile and León, occupying the latter in 1034 and striking coins with the word *imperator* stamped on them. He had brought Navarre to its political zenith, but his death in 1035 ended the brief unity of Spain, as his possessions were divided among his sons. He also managed to open Spain to European influence, supporting Cluniac reform and pilgrimages to Santiago de Compostela. See also NAVARRE, KINGDOM OF.

**SANCHO IV GARCÉS, KING OF NAVARRE** (d. 1076) Ruler from 1054 to 1076, succeeding his father, García III (1035–1054), when the king died in the Battle of Atapuerca (1054) at the hands of the Castilians. He was forced to surrender territory to Castile but disputed the claim of King Sancho II of Castile to Zaragoza. He was assassinated in 1076. See also NAVARRE, KINGDOM OF.

**SANCHO V, KING OF NAVARRE** See SANCHO I, RAḾIREZ KING OF ARAGON.

**SANCHO VI, KING OF NAVARRE** (d. 1194) Called "the Wise," reigning from 1150. The son of García IV Ramírez, he avoided the proposed partitioning of Navarre in 1151 between Castile and Aragon by acknowledging the supremacy of Alfonso VII of Castile (1126–1157).

On the succession of Alfonso VIII (1158–1214), Sancho took towns on the Castilian frontier for his own domain. See also NAVARRE, KINGDOM OF.

**SANCHO VII, KING OF NAVARRE** (1154–1234) Called "the Strong," ruling from 1194 to 1234, an adventurous ruler with a dashing manner who maintained amity with the Moors and outraged the Christians by his association with the Muslim dynasty of the Almohads. Nevertheless he participated with Castile in the decisive Battle of Las Navas de Tolosa in 1212, which broke Almohad power. His death brought an end to Spanish rule of Navarre, which was taken by Thibault I (1234–1253) the son of the count of Champagne, who had married his sister, Blanche. See also NAVARRE, KINGDOM OF.

**SANCHO I, KING OF PORTUGAL** (d. 1211) Son of Alfonso I Henriques (conqueror of Portugal and its first king), who ruled from 1185 to 1211. Sancho strove to organize the kingdom, establishing new towns and building castles and frontier fortresses. He also repopulated regions that had been devastated by war and unrest. For this he was called "the Settler." See also PORTUGAL.

**SANCHO II, KING OF PORTUGAL** (c. 1209–1248) Ruler from 1223 to 1248, succeeding his father, Alfonso II (1211–1223), while still in his minority. On gaining full control of the state, he launched an extensive campaign to reconquer Portugal, proving to be an able soldier. He was unable, however, to deal with his nobles and clergy, who accused him of excessive interference in their affairs. Pope Innocent III indicted Sancho at the Council of Lyons (1245), and he was deposed in 1248, retiring to Toledo, where he died. His throne was claimed by his brother, Alfonso III (1248–1279). See also PORTUGAL.

**SANCTUARY, RIGHT OF** The custom in Christian Europe that permitted a criminal or fugitive from justice to take refuge safely in a church. Sanctuary originated from the Roman law that allowed a bishop to intercede on behalf of a criminal, granting him safety. Varying by country, the custom in German lands allowed the church to surrender the prisoner with the guarantee that no harm would come to him. In England, however, the custom was more elaborate. The criminal could not be removed but was allowed the oath of abjuration, made before the coroner, followed by safe conduct to a seaport and from there exile. If this act was not performed by the criminal within 40 days, secular officials could starve him into submission. Limited sanctuary was also given to those who had committed a violent act, so as to ensure compensation to the victim or his family. The royal charter also allowed a secular or royal sanctuary, which recognized the right of an individual to flee to a designated site; there were 22 such places in England. These were regulated by a local lord who exacted an oath of fealty from the fugitive, giving him a place of refuge for the rest of his life.

**SANJAR** (d. 1157) Seljuk ruler of Khorasan from about 1096 to 1157 and the head of the ruling house of the Seljuk Turks from 1117 to 1118. He met defeat in 1141 near Samarkand at the hands of a confederacy of tribes from Central Asia, a loss the news of which reached the West and added to the legendary exploits of PRESTER JOHN. See also SELJUK TURKS.

**SANTIAGO DE COMPOSTELA** City in Galicia in northwestern Spain that was one of the most popular Christian shrines in the ninth century, following Jerusalem and Rome. According to tradition, the tomb of Saint James was discovered there through supernatural means (c. 813), thus becoming an inspiration for the Christians of Spain. An earthen church was built over the tomb by Alfonso II of Asturias (791–842), replaced with one of stone during the reign of Alfonso III (866–910). The town grew around the church, becoming a pilgrimage site. In 997, however, the Moors destroyed the town (sparing the tomb), and the region remained in Christian hands. Finally, in 1078, King Alfonso VI of León-Castile (1065–1109) began construction of its celebrated cathedral, consecrated in 1128. This magnificent Romanesque structure was later transformed by baroque and plateresque additions. See also CATHEDRAL; PILGRIMAGES.

**SAN VITALE** See ART AND ARCHITECTURE, BYZANTINE; RAVENNA.

**SARACENS** The name used in the Middle Ages by Christian writers to describe Arabs, or, more generally, Muslims. As a term it was applied originally to the ancient Arab inhabitants of northwestern Arabia, coming into use to describe the bulk of Arab peoples and then, after the establishment of the caliphate, its Muslim subjects. During the Crusades the term was applied primarily to the Seljuk Turks. See also CRUSADES.

**SARAGOSSA** See ZARAGOZA.

**SARDINIA** Called Sardegna in Italian, a large island in the western Mediterranean sea, separated from Corsica by the Strait of Bonifacio. Conquered by Rome in 238 B.C., Sardinia fell to the Vandals around 477 but was restored to imperial Byzantine rule in the sixth century. Arab attacks began in the eighth century and included the sack and occupation of Cagliari, its capital, in 711. Raids continued until 1016, by which time the maritime provinces of Genoa and Pisa were competing for supremacy over the island. Long subject to papal influence, Sardinia was claimed by the Kingdom of Aragon, and Alfonso IV (1327–1336), with papal support, defeated the Pisans in 1326 and, taking Cagliari, established Spanish supremacy that would last until 1713. See also ARAGON.

**SASSANIDS** Also called the Sassanians, the ruling dynasty of Persia and bitter enemy of the Roman and then the Byzantine Empire from 224 to about 651. The last native rulers of Persia, they derived their name from Sasan, an ancestor of the line's founder, the great Ardashir I. He overthrew the Parthian empire and established a vigorous regime that challenged Rome for supremacy in the East. A peace was signed between Emperor Theodosius I and the Persian ruler Shapur III (ruled 383–388), remaining in effect between 387 and 502, with only two minor violations. After that, however, hostilities were renewed and included the conquest of Syria by the Persians, as well as Palestine and Egypt. The regions were recaptured by Emperor Heraclius in 622–628. The Sassanids did not survive much longer, as they were inundated by the tide of Islam, their last king, Yazdagird III, ruling from 632 to 651. See also BYZANTINE EMPIRE.

**SAVA, SAINT** (c. 1176–1236) Also Sabas, the third son of the Serbian ruler Stephen Nemanja and the recognized patron of Serbia. In 1191 he traveled to Mount Athos, where he became a monk, joined in 1196 by his father, who had abdicated. Together they founded the monastery of Khilandar (Hilandar), the institution for Serbian religious study. Sava opposed his brother's policy of relations with the Western Church, supporting the church in Constantinople. The patriarch of Nicaea consecrated him the first archbishop of the Serbian church, establishing in 1219 the independent Church of the Serbs, which tended to espouse Eastern doctrine. He strove to establish churches, to improve learning and to encourage Serbian literature, writing a chronicle of his father's reign. See also SERBIA.

**SAVONAROLA, GIROLAMO** (1452–1498) Italian religious reformer, born in Ferrara and entering the Dominican order in 1474. Moving to the priory of San Marcos in Florence in 1482, he became a popular preacher and attacked the corruption of the clergy and the immorality of the Florentines. As prior in 1491, he continued to speak out against the Medicis, who ruled there, and following their overthrow in 1494 he became the head of a democratic republic, guided by theocratic principles. The nature of his severe rule led to a summons from Pope Alexander VI (1492–1503) in 1495, but Savonarola refused to go to Rome, which resulted in a papal ban on his sermons. Two years later he was excommunicated. Disregarding the sentence, he proposed that a general council be convened to depose the pope. A Franciscan, Fra Domenico de Pescia, ultimately challenged one of Savonarola's followers to an ordeal by fire to test spiritual faith, but the ordeal never took place, as the populace turned on Savonarola. He was arrested and tortured, tried and executed as a heretic. Some revere Savonarola as a martyr and saint, whereas others view him as a fanatic. See also FLORENCE.

**SAVOY** Called in French Savoie and in Italian Savoia, an Alpine region in eastern France, bordered by Italy and Switzerland. The region had strategic Alpine passes including the Great and Little Saint Bernard, and was originally a settlement of the Celtic tribe of Allobroges. Conquered by Rome, it became part of the province of Gallia Narbonensis, belonging to Burgundy in the fifth century and later attached to the kingdoms of Burgundy and Arles. The House of Savoy arose in the 11th century, founded by Humbert I the Whitehanded, count of Savoy, who held the region as a vassal of the Holy Roman Empire. Subsequent Savoyard history was tied to the fortunes of the counts, later dukes, of Savoy. See also SAVOY, HOUSE OF.

**SAVOY, HOUSE OF** Powerful noble family that ruled the region of Savoy from the 11th century, coming to wield extensive political influence and owning holdings on both sides of the Alps. The line was founded by Humbert I the Whitehanded (d. c. 1047), who was a count and controlled the region between Lake Geneva and the Rhône River. Through war and marriage the counts extended Savoyard territory into Lower Valois, Geneva, Vaud, Bresse, Nice and most of Piedmont. Among the most prominent counts were Amadeus VI the Green Count (d. 1383), Amadeus VII the Red Count (d. 1391) and Amadeus VIII (d. 1440), who became duke in 1416. See also GENEALOGY.

**SAXO GRAMMATICUS** Late-12th-century Danish historian, the author of the first major work of Danish history, written in fluent and ornate Latin, hence the name Grammaticus. He was from Zeeland, most likely a notary clerk, in the service of Archbishop Absalon of Lund, possibly a priest. His *Gesta Danorum,* written at the behest of Absalon, was contained in 16 books, covering the history of the Danes from the time of the legendary King Dan to the conquest of Pomerania by Canute VI in 1185. The first nine books combined lays, sagas and accounts of the oral tradition, as well as myths, to examine 60 legendary kings, making mention of gods and heroes. The last seven books, dealing with the historical eras, provided accounts of contemporary events. See also DENMARK.

**SAXON DYNASTY** Powerful ruling line of German kings that lasted from 919 to 1024, founded by Henry I the Fowler, duke of Saxony, who was elected king in 919. His son, Otto I the Great, ruled from 936 to 973, was crowned emperor in 962 and was victor at the decisive Battle of Lechfeld in 955. The other members of the dynasty were Otto II (ruled 973–983), Otto III (983–1002) and Henry II (ruled 1002–1024), who died without an heir and was succeeded by Conrad II (1024–1039), the first of the Salian dynasty. See also GERMANY; HOLY ROMAN EMPIRE.

**SAXONS** A Germanic people first mentioned in the second century as inhabiting the region of modern Schleswig along the Baltic Sea. As the Roman Empire in the West declined in the early fifth century, the Saxons took part in the migratory advance of other tribes, raiding in the North Sea against the Franks and into Britain against the Romans and Celtic populations. They eventually moved across North Germany, along the coast of Gaul (France) and into France. Their sorties into Britain led to the establishment of settlements in the sixth century and eventually to the rise of the Anglo-Saxon kingdoms in Britain (see ANGLO-SAXONS). Those Saxons remaining on the Continent (Old Saxons) came into direct conflict with the Franks. The Merovingians were only partially successful in suppressing them, Frankish victory being achieved in Charlemagne's reign (d. 814), when he launched a three-decade war of conquest and conversion that brought the downfall of the Saxons. They were compelled to accept Christianity and were assimilated into the Frankish empire. See also CHARLEMAGNE.

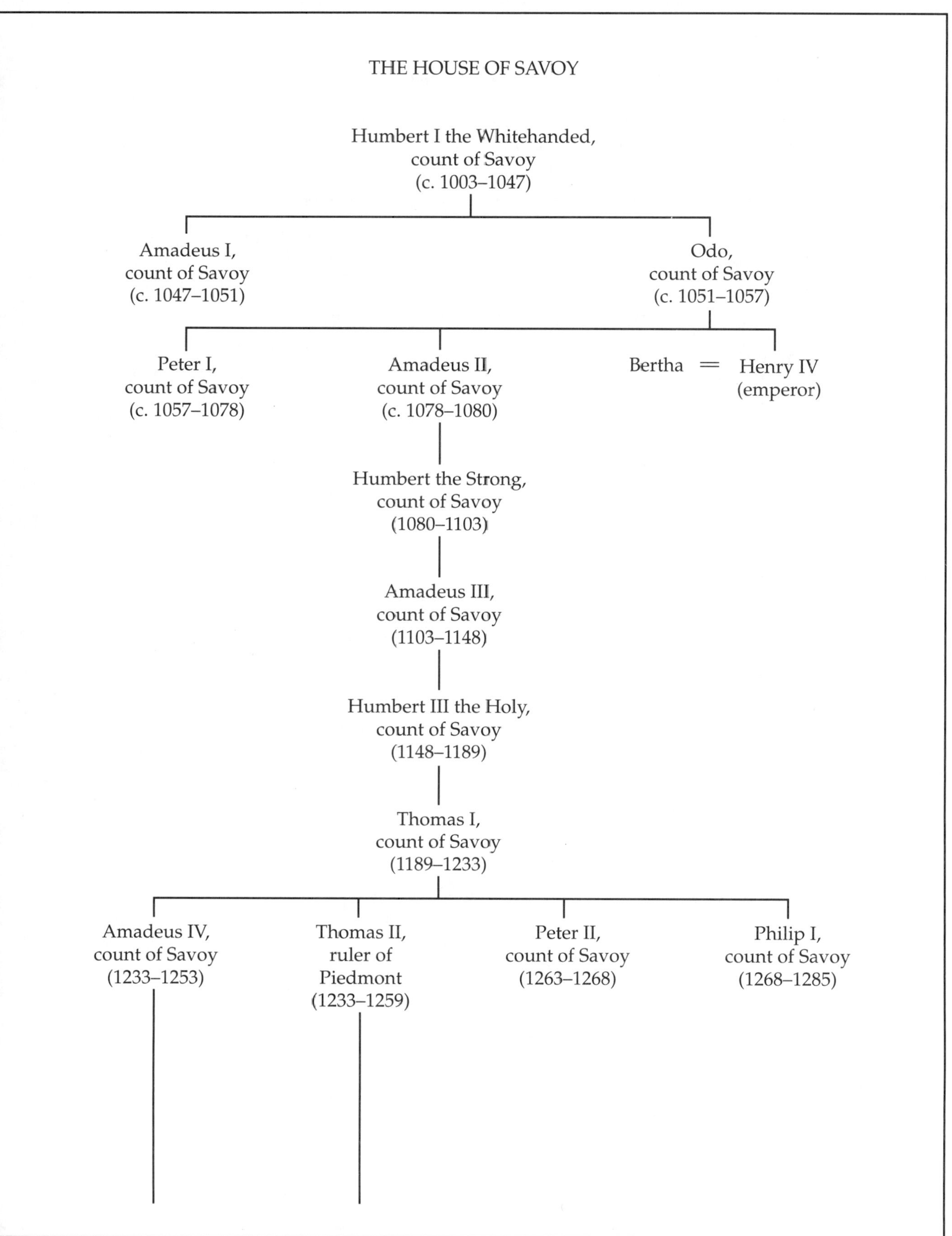
THE HOUSE OF SAVOY
Humbert I the Whitehanded, count of Savoy (c. 1003–1047)
Amadeus I, count of Savoy (c. 1047–1051)
Odo, count of Savoy (c. 1051–1057)
Peter I, count of Savoy (c. 1057–1078)
Amadeus II, count of Savoy (c. 1078–1080)
Bertha = Henry IV (emperor)
Humbert the Strong, count of Savoy (1080–1103)
Amadeus III, count of Savoy (1103–1148)
Humbert III the Holy, count of Savoy (1148–1189)
Thomas I, count of Savoy (1189–1233)
Amadeus IV, count of Savoy (1233–1253)
Thomas II, ruler of Piedmont (1233–1259)
Peter II, count of Savoy (1263–1268)
Philip I, count of Savoy (1268–1285)

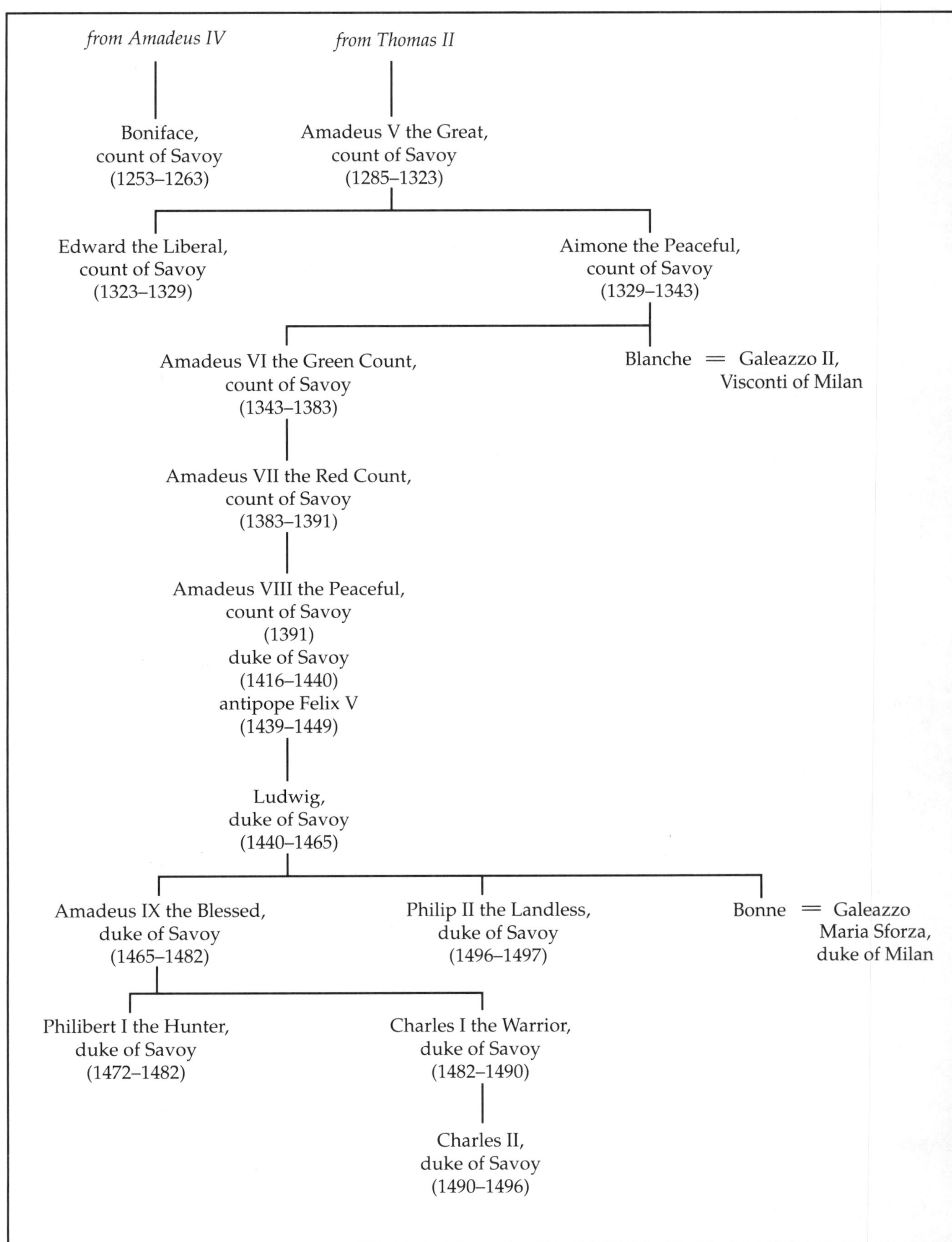
from Amadeus IV
from Thomas II
Boniface, count of Savoy (1253–1263)
Amadeus V the Great, count of Savoy (1285–1323)
Edward the Liberal, count of Savoy (1323–1329)
Aimone the Peaceful, count of Savoy (1329–1343)
Amadeus VI the Green Count, count of Savoy (1343–1383)
Blanche = Galeazzo II, Visconti of Milan
Amadeus VII the Red Count, count of Savoy (1383–1391)
Amadeus VIII the Peaceful, count of Savoy (1391) duke of Savoy (1416–1440) antipope Felix V (1439–1449)
Ludwig, duke of Savoy (1440–1465)
Amadeus IX the Blessed, duke of Savoy (1465–1482)
Philip II the Landless, duke of Savoy (1496–1497)
Bonne = Galeazzo Maria Sforza, duke of Milan
Philibert I the Hunter, duke of Savoy (1472–1482)
Charles I the Warrior, duke of Savoy (1482–1490)
Charles II, duke of Savoy (1490–1496)

**SAXONY** Known in German as Sachsen, a region in Germany comprising virtually all of the territory between the Elbe and the Rhine Rivers, its name derived from the Saxons, the original inhabitants who were conquered by Charlemagne (768–814), who introduced Christianity to the tribe. Saxony was attached in 843 to the German or East Frankish kingdom by the terms of the Treaty of Verdun under Louis the German. One of his counts, Liudolf, was named duke of the East Saxons, thereby establishing the powerful Liudolf dynasty of Saxon dukes. In 919, Duke Henry of Saxony was elected German king, founding the Saxon or Ottonian dynasty of rulers that endured until 1024. The ducal title, however, was given in 961 to the Billung family, which held it until 1106, whereupon it was transferred to the Bavarian duke Welf. The duchy was controlled in 1137 or 1139 by Henry the Lion, who lost it in 1180 when he was outlawed by Frederick I Barbarossa (1152–1190).

Saxony was partitioned in 1180 into small fiefs, its ducal title held by Bernard of Anhalt, son of Albert the Bear of Brandenburg, first of the Ascanian line of Saxon dukes. His territories included Lauenberg, Anhalt and the land around Wittenberg. These were ruled by separate branches of the family after 1260. The duke of Saxony was recognized as an imperial Elector, a dispute between the branches of the house being settled in 1356 in favor of the dukes of Saxe-Wittenberg. Their dominions, called Electoral Saxony, were situated along the Middle Elbe and lay outside the original duchy, in eastern Germany, on lands taken from the Slavs. In 1423 the margrave of Meissen, Frederick the Warlike, was granted Saxony by Emperor Sigismund (1410–1437). The Wettin lands were partitioned in 1485 between two brothers; one founded the Ernestine line (from Ernest) in Electoral Saxony and Thuringia, the other the Albertine line (from Albert) in the Meissen territories. These included Dresden and Leipzig, with the ducal title. See also GERMANY; HOLY ROMAN EMPIRE.

**SCALA, DELLA** Ruling family of Verona from 1259 to 1387, the first of whom was Mastino I della Scala (d. 1277), who held the offices of podesta and captain of the people. He was a leader of the Ghibellines but was killed, probably as a result of a Guelph plot. Cangrande I (d. 1329) brought the della Scala to the height of their power, conquering Vicenza (1312–1314), Padua (1317–1318) and Feltre, and was imperial vicar of Mantua in 1327. His successor was Mastino II (d. 1351), who attempted continued expansion. Provoking a Florentine-Venetian coalition, he lost all the family territories except Verona and Vicenza. The della Scala declined immediately thereafter, and in 1387 Verona was annexed by the Visconti. See also VERONA.

**SCALLOP** See PILGRIMAGES.

**SCANDINAVIA** See DENMARK; ICELAND; NORWAY; SWEDEN; VIKINGS; and individual rulers.

**SCHILTBERGER, JOHANN** (c. 1380–c. 1440) Bavarian nobleman and traveler who was the author of *Reisebuch (Travel Book)*, an invaluable source for later medieval topography and history. Also called Hans Schiltberger, he participated in the crusade of King Sigismund of Hungary (1411–1437) against the Ottoman Turks, was captured in 1396 at Nicopolis and enslaved. In 1402 he fell into the hands of the Mongols of Tamerlane (Timur the Lame) after the crushing Turkish defeat at Ankara. He was then encouraged in his travels by Tamerlane, journeying to Armenia, Siberia, Georgia, parts of Russia and Samarkand. Finally escaping, Schiltberger returned home to Bavaria (1427) by way of Constantinople and central Europe. His book was an account of his experiences and was the first German work on geography.

**SCHISM, GREAT** Also called the Great Western Schism or the Western Schism, the division of the Christian church in the West from 1378 to 1417. The schism began after the death of Pope Gregory XI (1370–1378) in 1378, the pontiff who had ended the Babylonian Captivity, whereby the papacy had been in residence at Avignon. The subsequent election to name a successor was convened under severe pressure from the Roman mobs to choose an Italian, to keep the French from papal power. Urban VI (1378–1389), an Italian, was elected, but the cardinals were enraged by his arrogance and by his deliberate alienation of the French prelates. They declared the election invalid on the grounds of coercion, supporting instead Robert of Geneva, the antipope Clement VII (1378–1394), who established himself at Avignon.

Western Europe was effectively divided into two camps over the matter; England, the Holy Roman Empire, Aragon, Scandinavia, Hungary and major regions of Italy supported Urban. Clement was supported by France, Scotland, Castile, Sicily and Savoy. In Rome Urban was succeeded by Boniface IX (1389–1404), Innocent VII (1404–1406) and Gregory XII (1406–1415), while Clement was followed by Pedro de Luna, the antipope Benedict XIII (1394–1417). Such was the degree of separation that both refused to summon a general council to resolve the schism. Theologians such as Pierre d'Ailly and John Gerson supported the idea of conciliarism and promoted the Council of Pisa in 1409, convened by the cardinals. The council succeeded only in electing a third pope, Alexander V (1409–1410). His successor, antipope John XXIII (1410–1415), was convinced by Emperor Sigismund to convene the Council of Constance (1414–1418). This assembly brought a successful end to the schism by accepting the resignation of Gregory XII, by deposing John and Benedict and by electing Martin V (1417–1431) as the sole pope. See also AVIGNON; BABYLONIAN CAPTIVITY; CONCILIAR MOVEMENT; CONSTANCE, COUNCIL OF.

**SCHISMS** The willful and conscious separation of groups from the unity of the church. Schism differs from heresy in that it is not based on doctrine and is a sin against charity, whereas heresy is contrary to faith and is a sin against truth in the eyes of the church. There is no loss of orders for clerics within a schism, so that a bishop may still ordain and a priest may celebrate the sacraments.

There have been a number of schisms in the history of the Christian church, among them Novationism and Donatism, but the most notable and enduring were those dividing the Eastern and Western Churches. An early

## The Great Schism, 1390

indication of the difficulties that beset these two elements of the church was the Acacian Schism from 482 to 519, the term derived from the name of the patriarch of Constantinople, Acacius. The difference began as a result of Emperor Zeno's efforts to reunite the Monophysites with orthodox Christianity. While accepted in the East, the reunion effort was not supported by Rome, with a resulting schism that continued until the reign of Justin.

The most severe of the schisms, and the one that caused the virtually irrevocable breach between the churches, came finally in 1054, although pressure had been building for some time. In an effort to redress the traditional animosity between the papacy in Rome and the ecclesiastical institution in Constantinople, a delegation was sent from the West. Unfortunately, both sides proved totally intransigent, especially the Frankish clergy and the patriarch of Constantinople, Michael Cerularius. Negotiations broke down quickly, and both factions excommunicated each other. Such was the degree of resentment over the next centuries that the Schism of 1054 could not be healed. The efforts of Emperor Constantine XI to reunite the churches, thereby securing support from the West against the Ottoman Turks in 1452, were opposed by the people of Constantinople, thereby dooming the city and the Byzantine Empire. See also BYZANTINE EMPIRE; CONSTANTINOPLE.

**SCHOLASTICISM** The term used to describe broadly the philosophical and theological thought of medieval

Christian Europe as practiced in schools and universities or by philosophers and theologians. First applied pejoratively in the 16th century, Scholasticism can be defined as the attainment of a deeper understanding of Christian doctrine and the existence of God through reason, analogy and careful analysis of faith. While thought by later, more sophisticated philosophers to have been intellectually uniform, Scholasticism was, in fact, both varied and rich in its expression and in the gifted individuals who contributed to it.

Scholasticism had its origins in the writings of Saint Augustine of Hippo and the other church fathers, as well as the Roman authors Boethius and Cassiodorus. The latter was instrumental in establishing the studies that included the seven liberal arts and thus helped give shape to the thought of the Carolingian renaissance. Saint Augustine was crucial to Scholastic thinking, with his emphasis on dialectic and especially with his work *De praedestinatione sanctorum.* His maxim *ergo intellige ut credos, crede ut intelligas*—"Understand in order to believe, believe in order to understand"—was adhered to by John Scotus Erigena, who was the force behind the ninth-century revival of learning. Erigena was one of the first philosophers to introduce speculative thought to the philosophy of the time, making a distinction between the Holy Scripture and reason, which adds to human understanding of doctrinal authority.

The 10th century saw the development of monastic schools, until by the 11th century there were the respected cathedral schools and their Scholastics (or schoolmen) who were examining many questions. One of the most important was the controversy between the realists and nominalists over the nature of universal concepts (the fundamental ideas about things). Realists held that basic forms had reality in and of themselves; the nominalists adhered to the view that forms were mere abstractions from specific examples. Another dispute arose between those who used dialectic for theological examination and those who did not. Esteemed Scholastics of this period were Anselm of Canterbury, Anselm of León, Lanfranc, Alger of Liège, Hugh of Saint Victor, William of Champeaux, Gilbert de la Porrée, Peter Lombard and Peter Abelard. The schools of Chartres and Saint Victor were also influential institutions for Scholastic thought.

A process of enormous value to Scholasticism was the dissemination of Aristotle's writings and ideas throughout Europe, largely through translations of Arab texts. Translated in the 12th century from the Greek and Arabic, the treatises of Aristotle were fully appreciated only in the 13th century. This period brought Scholasticism to its height, as it produced the brilliant synthesis of Aristotelian rationalism with Christian thought. This was accomplished by finding a harmony between the Latin Averroists (who read Averroës and the Arab commentaries and thus pursued purely Aristotelian doctrines) and the Augustinians (who accepted only those Aristotelian views not in conflict with the premises of Saint Augustine). The synthesis was foreshadowed by the writings of Albertus Magnus and was actually accomplished by Saint Thomas Aquinas, whose system was one of the outstanding medieval intellectual endeavors, presented in what is called the crown of Scholastic theology, his *Summa theologicae.*

Thomas's rationalism was opposed by several Franciscan theologians who stressed Augustinian concepts in opposition to Dominican Aristotelianism. The most vociferous opponent was John Duns Scotus, who was joined by Saint Bonaventure and later by William of Ockham, who drew on Scotus. William concentrated his argument against Thomas Aquinas in nominalism, holding that reason was deficient in resolving questions of theology. His work was a factor in bringing about the decline of Scholasticism, which lost its influence with the rise of humanism and the study of natural science in the Renaissance.

**SCHONGAUER, MARTIN** (d. 1491) German engraver and painter, also called Schön Martin (or Martin Schön), born and raised in Colmar and taking up permanent residence in Breisach in 1488. He was a prolific painter according to contemporary accounts, although few examples have survived. His reputation was based on his unrivaled ability as an engraver, being outstanding at that time. He brought a technical maturity to his work and imbued his art with new textures and contrasts not thought of by the goldsmiths who had previously dominated engraving. Among his finest engravings were *Temptation of St. Anthony, Passion of Christ, Madonna in a Courtyard,* and *St. Sebastian.* As a painter he was influenced by Rogier van der Weyden; his most important work was the *Madonna in the Rose Garden.*

**SCIENCE** See ADELARD OF BATH; ALBERTUS MAGNUS, SAINT; ALCHEMY; ASTRONOMY; BACON, ROGER; GERARD OF CREMONA; MAIMONIDES, MOSES; MEDICINE; ORESME, NICHOLAS; AL-RAZI; THOMAS AQUINAS, SAINT.

**SCOT, MICHAEL** (d. c. 1235) Scottish astronomer, astrologer and mathematician, also reputed to be a powerful wizard. He visited Oxford in 1230 and introduced the study of Aristotle there, having made translations of Aristotelian texts and commentaries by Averroës. The author as well of treatises on astronomy and astrology, he was in the brilliant circle at Emperor Frederick II's (1215–1250) court in Sicily. Scot was mentioned as a magician by Dante in the *Inferno.* See also ASTROLOGY; ASTRONOMY.

**SCOTLAND** Country situated to the north of England, known for its rugged terrain and its people for their warlike independent spirit and self-determination. Scotland was traditionally separated from England by the region called the Border, a strip of territory notorious for its grim history. Scotland was divided geographically into three regions: the Highlands, Central Lowlands and Southern Uplands. Settled by the Picts and Celts (or Gaels), it was never conquered by Rome, but Christianity was introduced by Saint Ninian early in the fifth century and furthered by Saint Columba, who arrived there in 563. His monastery at Iona became an influential Christian institution that encouraged the gradual conversion of the Scots to the doctrine of the Celtic church. Celtic Christianity came into conflict with Roman doctrine accepted in the south in time, a dispute that ended with the Synod of Whitby in 664 that demanded acceptance of Roman doctrine. This decision

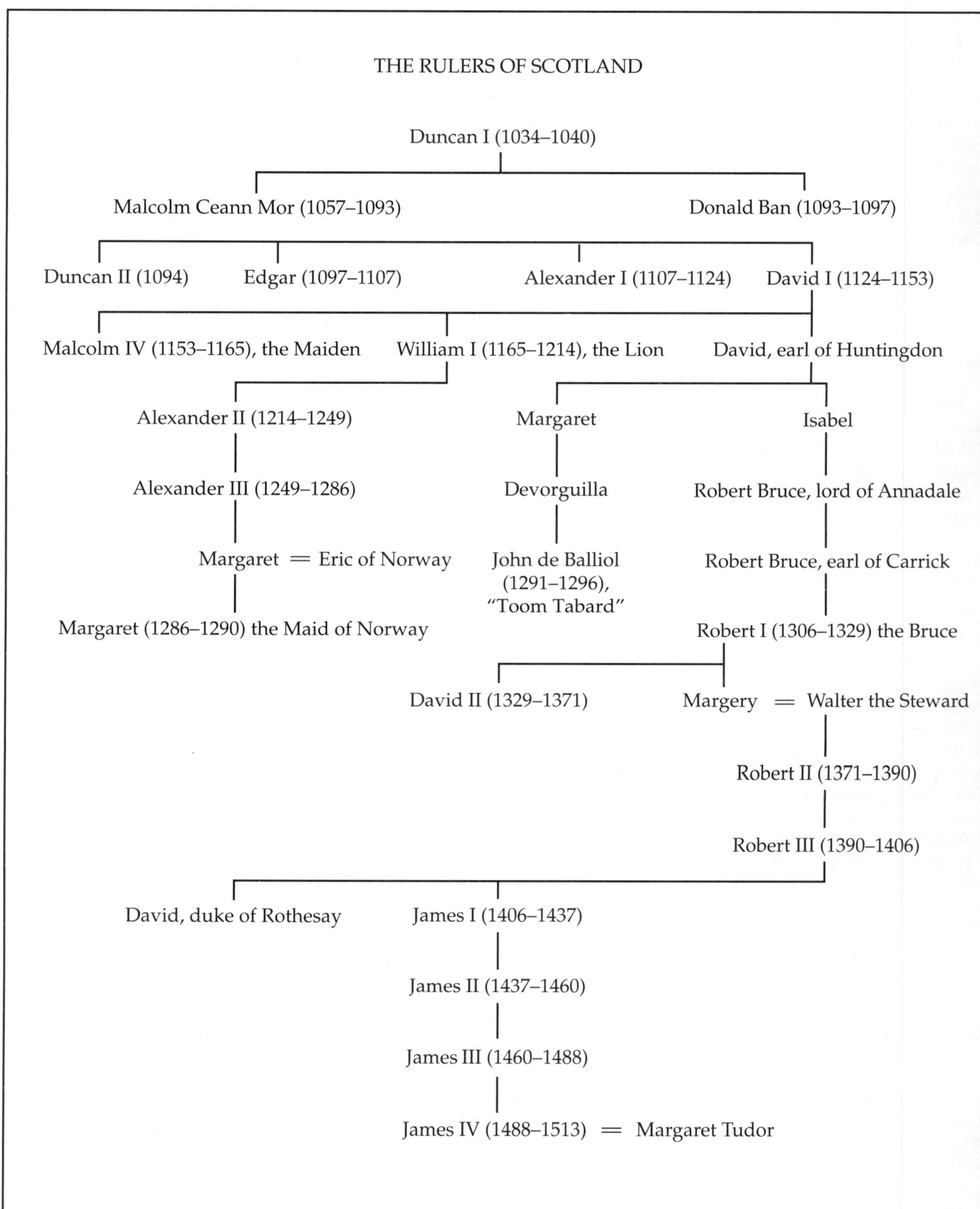
THE RULERS OF SCOTLAND
Duncan I (1034–1040)
Malcolm Ceann Mor (1057–1093)
Donald Ban (1093–1097)
Duncan II (1094)
Edgar (1097–1107)
Alexander I (1107–1124)
David I (1124–1153)
Malcolm IV (1153–1165), the Maiden
William I (1165–1214), the Lion
David, earl of Huntingdon
Alexander II (1214–1249)
Margaret
Isabel
Alexander III (1249–1286)
Devorguilla
Robert Bruce, lord of Annadale
Margaret = Eric of Norway
John de Balliol (1291–1296), "Toom Tabard"
Robert Bruce, earl of Carrick
Margaret (1286–1290) the Maid of Norway
Robert I (1306–1329) the Bruce
David II (1329–1371)
Margery = Walter the Steward
Robert II (1371–1390)
Robert III (1390–1406)
David, duke of Rothesay
James I (1406–1437)
James II (1437–1460)
James III (1460–1488)
James IV (1488–1513) = Margaret Tudor

brought Scotland to acceptance of universal European Christian practice.

Scotland emerged as four culturally unique kingdoms, the Picts in the north, the Celts from Ireland, the Britons (Britains) from Strathclyde, and Northumbria, settled by the Angles. Union came only in 844, when the Picts and Celts were united by King Kenneth McAlpin. Succeeding kings strove to secure Lothian from the English and to control Strathclyde. King Malcolm II (ruled 1005–1034) accomplished most of this, but his grandson, Duncan I (ruled 1034–1040), was deposed by Macbeth of Moray, who reigned until 1057, until murdered by Malcolm III. The reign of Malcolm (1058–1093) witnessed the introduction of English practices. While these were opposed in the Highlands, the feudal system and the spread of monasticism encouraged the economy of Scotland, establishing the era from 1153 to 1286 as its golden age.

Conflict began with the accession of Margaret, called the Maid of Norway, in 1286, after the death of Alexander III (1249–1286). The plans for Margaret to marry the son of Edward I of England (1272–1307) were aborted by her death in 1290, bringing civil strife and a disputed question of inheritance. Edward was asked to mediate, choosing John de Balliol, who acknowledged English supremacy. An effort by John to free himself, including an alliance with France, was crushed by Edward. Scottish resistance continued, however, culminating in the rise of Robert the Bruce, crowned Robert I. In 1314 he routed the English led by King Edward II (1307–1327) and in 1328 signed the Treaty of Northampton, winning recognition from England. War continued, however, draining the economy, reducing royal authority and thereby giving increasing power to the clans. Their ability to defy the king made possible the collapse of Scotland into civil war after the murder of King James I in 1437. See also ENGLAND.

**SCOTUS, JOHN DUNS** See JOHN DUNS SCOTUS.

**SCROPE, RICHARD LE** (c. 1350–1405) Chancellor of Cambridge (1378), bishop of Coventry and Lichfield (1386) and archbishop of York from 1398, who took part in a rebellion against King Henry IV (1399–1413) in 1405. Initially agreeing with the abdication of King Richard II (1377–1399) in 1399, Scrope became disenchanted and joined the earl of Northumberland in his uprising, leading an army of discontented citizens against the king. The earl of Westmoreland tricked him into disbanding his forces, and le Scrope was condemned to death and executed for treason. The irregularity of the proceedings, and le Scrope's own piety, made his execution appear a martyrdom to some. Miracles were soon claimed at his tomb.

**SCULPTURE** See ART AND ARCHITECTURE, BYZANTINE; ART AND ARCHITECTURE, ISLAMIC; GOTHIC ART AND ARCHITECTURE; OTTONIAN ART AND ARCHITECTURE; ROMANESQUE ART AND ARCHITECTURE.

**SELJUK TURKS** Also Seljuqs, a Turkic family of nomadic origin establishing several dynasties in Asia, with minor lines in Iraq, Syria and Anatolia (Rum). The name was derived from the early chieftain, Seljuk, although the

Seljuk Turk

Great Seljuk dynasty was founded by Toghril-Beg (d. 1053). He conquered Khorasan in 1037 and then extended his influence westward, capturing Baghdad in 1055. He dominated the Abbasid caliphate as a result, claiming the title sultan. Waging war on the Byzantines, he invaded Cappadocia and Phrygia. Alp Arslan, his successor (ruled 1063–1072), founded the sultanate of Rum, overrunning Armenia and Asia Minor and destroying a Byzantine army at Manzikert in 1071. Jerusalem fell to him the following year, followed by Antioch in 1085. Ardent Muslims, the Seljuks posed a major threat to the Byzantine Empire and made Christian pilgrimages to the Holy Land both dangerous and difficult. Their threat thus provided a potent emotional pretext for mounting of the First Crusade in 1096–1099.

Alp Arslan and his son and successor, Malik Shah, were supported significantly by the vizier and statesman Nizam al-Mulk, with Seljuk influence reaching its peak under his gifted administration. His murder in 1092 by the Assassins was a major cause of subsequent Seljuk decline. The reign of Sanjar (1117–1157) witnessed the end of the Great Seljuks and the deterioration of the Seljuks in Rum and in Iraq. The Mongol invasions of the 13th century brought an end to hope for a Seljuk recovery. The sultanate of Rum survived until the early 14th century. See also BYZANTINE EMPIRE; CRUSADES; MANZIKERT, BATTLE OF; MONGOLS; NICAEA, EMPIRE OF; OTTOMAN EMPIRE; SYRIA; and individual rulers.

**SERBIA** The land of the Serbs, a Slavic people who migrated into the region south of the Danube and Sava Rivers in the late sixth and early seventh centuries. Initially organized into loose clans, the Serbs achieved a certain degree of unity in the eighth century, led by the Slavic leader Vlastimir, who, influenced by the Byzantine and

Carolingian models, founded the first Serbian state, known as Rascia. The Serbs of Ras (from which the name Rascia was derived) extended their control over other Slavic tribes, which were henceforth called Serbs.

Byzantine power was such that the Serbs were forced to acknowledge Byzantine suzerainty, although for a time Rascia was conquered (924) by the Bulgars. The Byzantines dominated, however, until the end of the 11th century, when Rascia came under the sovereignty of the rival state of Zeta (Montenegro) in the south. The Byzantines returned in the 12th century. A change came in 1167 when the Serbian leader Stephen Nemanja was recognized by Constantinople as grand zupan (chief) of Serbia. He strove to consolidate his political position while making his land virtually independent of the Byzantine Empire. His son, Stephen the First-Crowned (ruled 1196–c. 1228), had his coronation conducted by papal legates in 1217, but his illustrious brother, Sava, introduced Byzantine church practices, convincing Stephen to remove papal influence. Sava also helped to eradicate the last traces of the heretic Bogomils.

The next century and a half witnessed the rise of Serbian power and prosperity. Commercial activity was considerable, with the expansion of trade extending to Byzantium, Venice and elsewhere and with the Bulgars, allowing for extensive Serbian territorial advances. As the Serbian kings required the support of the feudal lords of the kingdom, the power of the nobility grew. The most dominant Serbian king was Stephen Dusan, who reigned from 1331 to 1355. He acquired Macedonia, Albania, Thessaly and Epirus, made the Serbian church independent and was declared emperor of of the Serbs and Romans (or czar of the Serbs and Greeks). His reign was the zenith of Serbian influence and prestige. After his death internal disputes weakened the Serbs, who were defeated by the Ottoman Turks in 1371, thereby losing Macedonia. The Ottoman advances culminated in 1389 with the destruction of the Serbian army at Kosovo. Turkish suzerainty was accepted, a Serbian principality remaining in existence until the 15th century, when the country was annexed outright by the Ottomans. See also BULGARIA; BYZANTINE EMPIRE; HUNGARY; and individual rulers.

**SERBIAN EMPIRE** See SERBIA; STEPHEN DUSAN, KING OF SERBIA.

**SERF** See MANORIAL SYSTEM.

**SERGIUS I** (d. 701) Pope from 687 to 701, born in Palermo of Syrian descent and elected irregularly, having a bribed with gold the exarch of Ravenna to ensure his succession as pope. Despite such dubious beginnings he proved energetic, consecrating Saint Willibrord as bishop of the Frisians in 695 and introducing the liturgical chant of the Agnus Dei to the Mass. Sergius also rejected several of the decrees of the Council of Trullo (692) that would have made Constantinople Rome's ecclesiastical equal and would have tolerated clerical marriages.

**SERGIUS II** (d. 847) Pope from 844 to 847, a nobleman elected successor to Gregory IV (827–844), an event that so enflamed the Roman populace that they elected an antipope, John (844). Sergius imprisoned John in a monastery and was consecrated without the approval of Emperor Lothair I (840–855). After a Frankish army threatened Rome, he settled the dispute by affirming imperial supremacy. Because of his severe gout, Sergius left most of the papal administration to his brother, Bishop Benedict of Albano, who was in charge as well of the extensive building program in Rome, including the enlargement of Saint John Lateran. During his reign, Rome was attacked by the Saracens (846), and the basilicas of Saint Peter and Saint Paul were pillaged.

**SERGIUS III** (d. 911) Pope from 904 to 911, a Roman noble who was elected in 898 but driven from Rome after failing to seize the papacy from his rival, John IX (898–900). He returned in 904 with the support of Duke Alberic I of Spoleto, deposing and strangling Pope Leo V (903–904) and the antipope Christopher (903–904). He invalidated the decrees of Pope Formosus (891–896), considering John IX, Benedict IV (900–903) and Leo V to have been antipopes. A close ally of the nobleman Theophylact, he allowed him to administer the papacy. With Theophylact's daughter, Marozia, Sergius probably fathered a son, the future John XI (931–935/6).

**SERGIUS IV** (d. 1012) Pope from 1009 to 1012, born Peter Buccaporci, hence the name he gave to himself, Bucca Porci, or Pig's Snout. Despite his aid to the poor, Sergius spent his pontificate almost powerless, true authority resting in the hands of the Crescentii.

**SERGIUS I, PATRIARCH OF CONSTANTINOPLE** (d. 638) Patriarch from 610 to 638 and one of the influential Monothelites. He donated the church treasury to Emperor Heraclius to finance his wars with the Avars and the Persians, serving as regent during the campaigns (622–628). He was best known, however, for his efforts to reconcile heretical Monophysitism with the decrees of the Council of Chalcedon (451). Toward this end he formulated the doctrines of Monothelitism, which stated that Christ had two natures but one will. No faction was satisfied, and he was condemned by both sides and his concept attacked by the Romans as well. The Third Council of Constantinople (681) rejected his ideas completely. See also MONOPHYSITISM; MONOTHELITISM.

**SERGIUS OF RADONEZH** (1314–1392) Russian monk and spiritualist, the founder of the Monastery of the Trinity. A native of Rostov, he became a monk in 1337 and founded a chapel retreat in the forest of Radonezh, which about 1354 became the monastery that was to play a crucial role in the religious and cultural recovery of Russia after the Mongol invasions. Revered for his humility and sanctity, he established more than 70 monasteries and was a powerful voice in calling for Russian resistance to the Mongols, which culminated in the Mongol defeat at Kulikovo in 1380.

**SEVAR** King of the Bulgars from 724 to 739. See also BULGARIA.

**SEVERINUS** (d. 640) Pope from May to August 640, although elected in 638 as successor to Honorius I (625–638). He sent his legates to Constantinople to secure the confirmation of Emperor Heraclius (610–641), but the emperor demanded that Severinus accept the *Ecthesis,* Heraclius's decree on Monothelitism. When Severinus refused, his consecration was delayed. Two years passed before his legates were granted imperial permission, whereupon Severinus affirmed Christian orthodoxy, thereby creating tension between Rome and Constantinople. See also MONOTHELITISM.

**SEVERUS OF ANTIOCH** (c. 465–538) Patriarch of Antioch, monk and a prominent Monophysist. Born in Asia Minor, he studied at Alexandria and Berytus and became a monk, earning the favor of Emperor Anastasius (ruled 491–518) in Constantinople and becoming the patriarch of Antioch in 512. He held this post until the reign of Justin in 518, when he was deposed and forced to flee to Egypt. Excommunicated by a synod at Constantinople in 536, he again took refuge in Egypt. Severus was the author of a treatise on Christ's nature, as well as 125 homilies and some 400 letters. See also MONOPHYSITISM.

**SEVILLE** In Spanish, Sevilla, a city in southwestern Spain, the chief city of Andalusia and Muslim capital there. Situated on the Guadalquivir Estuary, Seville was an ancient site, belonging to the Carthaginians, the Romans and then the Vandals, who made it their chief city in the fifth century. After a period of occupation by the Visigoths, the city surrendered to the Muslims in 711, an act encouraged by the Jewish inhabitants who had been persecuted. A traditional source of discontent during the period of the Córdoban caliphate, Seville was conquered by Abd al-Rahman III around 918 but with the end of the Spanish caliphate, the Abbadid dynasty made the city its capital from 1023 to 1091. The Abbadids were replaced by the Almoravids and the Almohads, who continued the process of making Seville the cultural center for western Europe with buildings and mosques. Despite its frequent political upheaval, Seville was a beautiful city, with magnificent walls, thriving markets, increasing population and a strong economy. It was also noted for its lavish gardens.

Its Moorish cultural tradition ended in 1248 when the city fell to King Ferdinand III (1217–1252) of León-Castile and the Reconquista. The Repartimiento followed, the departure of the Muslims from Seville and its repopulation by Christians. King Alfonso X of León-Castile (1252–1284) resided in Seville, promoting learning in the Arabic and Latin schools and introducing Gothic architecture in his building programs. After an economic decline in the 14th century, the city recovered late in the reign of Alfonso XI (ruled 1312–1350), who supported its trade in olive oil. Seville attained its greatest prosperity in the 16th century as the city from which Spanish exploration and conquest were designed.

**SEVILLE, KINGDOM OF** Name given to the Abbadid dynasty of Muslim rulers of Seville, which ruled from 1023 to 1091. The Abbadids were founded by the *qadi* (judge) Abu al-Qasim Muhammad ibn Abbad in 1023, when he declared Seville free and independent of the declining caliphate of Córdoba. His son, al-Mu'tadid, reigned from 1042 to 1069, adding numerous small territories to the kingdom, while earning a reputation both as a poet and a merciless killer. The most notorious incident concerning him involved his suffocation of several Berber chiefs in a steam bath, thereby enabling him to seize their lands. His successor was also a poet, al-Mu'tamid (ruled 1069–1091). He captured Córdoba and strove to make Seville a culturally important city of the Islamic world. Confronted by a growing Christian menace, he turned to the Almoravids for aid but was besieged by them. Seville fell in 1091, and the dynasty was ended.

**SFORZA, HOUSE OF** Powerful ruling line of Milan from 1450 to 1535, the first prominent member of which was Muzio Attendola (1369–1424), who was a distinguished condottiere and father of Francesco I Sforza (1401–1466). Francesco, probably the preeminent condottiere of the age, married Bianca Maria, daughter of Duke Filippo Maria Visconti of Milan. After the duke's death, he had the support of the Medicis to disband the brief republic of Milan and have himself proclaimed duke in 1450. He ruled as an enlightened despot until his death. Galeazzo Maria Sforza (1444–1476) ruled after Francesco as a patron of the arts but his political cruelties led to his assassination. His son, Gian Galeazzo Sforza (1468–1494), survived as duke only until 1480, when his paternal uncle, Ludovico Sforza (1451–1508), known as Il Moro ("the Moor"), because of his complexion, usurped control of the duchy. He proved a brilliant Renaissance prince, though was later defeated by King Louis XII of France (1498–1515) in 1499. He died in a French prison. See also MILAN.

**SHAFI'I** (767–820) Islamic theologian and jurist, the founder of the Sunni school of Islamic Law, the Shafi'iyah. About 787 he journeyed to Medina to study law at the residence of the distinguished Malik ibn Anas, going then to Yemen. He was jailed for a time in Baghdad (c. 803) and then studied the teachings of the schools at Hanafi and Medina. His extensive ideas on the nature of Muslim law were compiled in his book, the *Risalah,* written in Cairo during his last years. His school, the Shafi'iyah, called for the acceptance of Hadith (the traditions based on the sayings and life of the Prophet) as the basis of law, while using reason to answer questions not revealed in the Koran or Hadith. He was considered one of the fathers of Islamic law.

**SHIAH** Also Shiism, one of the two principal branches of Islam, with the Sunni (which constituted the majority of believers). The Shiites began as political supporters of the son-in-law of the Prophet, Ali, who was married to Fatima and served as fourth caliph. On his murder in 661, however, the *shi'at Ali* (the party of Ali) refused to accept the accession of Mu'awiya, supporting Ali's son, Husayn, and inviting him to become caliph. Husayn was killed in 680, and the Shiah vowed vengeance, encouraging the revolution that ended in the establishment of the Abbasid caliphate in 750, although their true hope, that the Alids (House of Ali) would come to power, was never realized.

The Shiites revered their imams (religious leaders) as descendants of Ali through Husayn, some granted virtually divine honors, most held sinless, infallible and the proper interpreters of the Koran. Doctrinal differences ensued between the Sunni and Shiites, leading to persecutions and severe factional disputes. See also ISMAILI SECT; SUNNI.

**SHIPS** Vessels used in medieval maritime advances that culminated in the rapid territorial acquisitions of the 16th century. Following the collapse of the Roman Empire in the West, the foremost maritime power in the Mediterranean was the Byzantine Empire. This supremacy was severely shaken in the late fifth century by Vandals raiding from Africa and by the Muslims in the seventh century. Relying on ancient maritime practices, the Byzantines were challenged to overcome their rivals, succeeding in the eighth century in defeating their competitors. The Byzantine navy was composed of swift and generally efficient galleys, carrying two banks of oars, two masts and two lateen sails (sails angled rather than square so as to receive the wind on both sides). Larger warships carried revolving turrets with war engines; their chief and most deadly weapon was (from c. 670) Greek fire. Constantinople's power thus endured through the excellence of its maritime forces, although a crushing blow came after 1070 and the Battle of Manzikert, when the Seljuk Turks overran Asia Minor, depriving the Byzantines of revenues and their major Anatolian naval base at Cibyrrhaeots.

Arab shipbuilding and the rise of maritime states in Italy, particularly Venice, Pisa and Genoa, encouraged new rivalry in the Mediterranean. The Italians, joined by the Norman kingdom of Sicily, became the Christian naval power in the Mediterranean, playing a major role in the Crusades. They kept the Muslim fleets at bay, supplied the Crusader armies and earned large profits by transporting the Crusaders to the Holy Land, or to Constantinople, as they did in the Fourth Crusade. Naval warfare was conducted by galleys, but changes began to take place in general ship construction in the 13th century. The rudder was introduced, adding to maneuverability, and improvements in the use of sails eventually led to the disappearance of oars on merchant ships, thereby allowing greater cargo space. Larger ships and the compass opened the seas to further navigation. By the 15th century voyages of exploration were under way, especially the Portuguese encouraged by Prince Henry the Navigator.

Voyages of exploration, of course, had been undertaken by the Vikings centuries before, earning these Norse adventurers a reputation for remarkable seamanship. Knowledge of Viking ships is extensive because of the archaeological remains available that allow the study of their construction, from the Nydam ship (from the early migratory period) to the magnificent vessels of Gokstad and Oseberg. These ships carried the Vikings through the northern waters, allowing them to reach Greenland, Iceland, even Russia as well as the coasts of North Africa and Italy. While the Norsemen developed far-ranging mercantile interests, the sight of their shallow-keeled vessels for centuries was synonymous with dread of the Viking raider. See also TRADE AND COMMERCE.

**SHREWSBURY, BATTLE OF** See HENRY IV, KING OF ENGLAND; PERCY.

**SICARD** (1160–1215) Italian historian and canonist, bishop of Cremona, papal legate to Germany. Sicard wrote *Chronicon,* a history of the world to 1201, later revised to include the years until 1213. His work served as the principal source on the crusade of Frederick I Barbarossa (1152–1190). Sicard was also responsible for a collection of canons and a treatise on liturgical practices.

**SICILIAN VESPERS** The 1282 rebellion of Sicily against the rule of King Charles I (Charles of Anjou), the French king of Naples and Sicily. Its name was derived from the fact that violence erupted in a church outside Palermo at vespers on March 30. The cause was Charles's decision to transfer his royal residence from Palermo to Naples, thus leaving Sicily in the hands of arrogant and despised French officials. Although the uprising occurred prematurely with the killing of some French soldiers, it had been organized with the help of John of Procida, an agent of King Pedro III of Aragon (1276–1283), Charles's rival for the Neopolitan throne. As word spread of the riot at the church, a general massacre of the French ensued, with 2,000 men, women and children dying in the city. All Sicily joined the revolt, and in August Aragonese troops landed, initiating the war of the Sicilian Vespers. This conflict was fought between Anjou, supported by the papacy and its Guelph faction and by France, and the Aragonese, supported by the Ghibellines. The Treaty of Anagni (1295) allowed King James II of Aragon (1291–1327) to make peace with Anjou, renouncing Sicily, although his brother, Frederick III, became king of Sicily (1355–1377), securing his crown by the Peace of Caltabellotta in 1302. See also SICILY.

**SICILY** Island in the Mediterranean Sea, separated from Italy by the Strait of Messina, its traditional chief city Palermo. Settled in ancient times, Sicily was occupied by the Phoenicians, Carthaginians, Greeks and Romans. When the Roman Empire of the West collapsed, Sicily was subject to attacks by the Vandals and Ostrogoths, claimed finally by Constantinople as an imperial territory under the illustrious General Belisarius in 535. The Byzantines held the island until 826, when Arab raiders began assaults there. The Arabs took Sicily by 901, establishing two dynasties, the Aghlabids and the Fatimids. The period of Muslim occupation was a bright one, with agricultural, scientific and cultural development, especially under the Fatimids, whose emirs governed Sicily from Palermo.

By the 11th century, however, Arab mastery was in decline, and Norman adventurers led by Roger I (son of Tancred de Hauteville and brother of Robert Guiscard) captured Palermo in 1072 and completed his subjugation of Sicily by 1091. Under Roger II, king of Sicily (ruled 1130–1154), the Norman kingdom was brought to its greatest glory, with his court at Palermo drawing men of letters and intellect. A dynastic change took placed with the marriage of Constance, aunt of William II of Sicily, to Emperor Henry IV (1056–1106). After the death of Tancred of Lecce (1194), her son, Frederick II, inherited the Sicilian

Crowned eagle of King William I of Sicily

crown. The kingdom, which included southern Italy and Naples, thus was claimed by the Hohenstaufens and achieved an even loftier reputation for culture encouraged by Emperor Frederick II (ruled 1197–1250). His successors struggled against the pope and his agent, Charles of Anjou, unsuccessfully, and the last Hohenstaufen claimant, Conradin, was executed in Naples in 1268. Sicily was taken by Charles, whose French rule was harsh and unpopular. In 1282 the Sicilian Vespers erupted, a rebellion ending Charles's rule of the island, with the Crown of Aragon taking control.

The Sicilian parliament called on the Aragonese for support. Despite discontent with their choice, the Sicilians witnessed continued Spanish expansion. Peter IV of Anjou acquired the island in 1377, rule being granted to viceroys in 1409. In 1442 the Kingdom of the Two Sicilies was established, uniting Naples and Sicily, following the conquest of Alfonso V the Magnanimous of Aragon (1416–1458). The two realms were divided a short time later but were then reunified by Ferdinand of Spain in 1504. The grandeur of Sicily declined as a result of the inefficiency, corruption and cruelty of the Spanish. See also NAPLES, KINGDOM OF.

**SIENA** City in central Italy, in Tuscany, originally Etruscan and called Sena Julia by the Romans, a site that disappeared and was replaced by the surviving city after the invasions of the fourth and fifth centuries. The Lombards then came into control. The local government of counts and bishops was replaced in the 12th century by a free commune. Economic and territorial rivalry with Florence led to the rise of Siena as the Tuscan stronghold of the Ghibellines (the imperial faction) against the Florentine Guelphs, defeating the Florentines in 1260, affirming Sienese political ascendancy. Soon afterward, however, the Ghibelline caused declined as the imperialists were crushed at Tagliacozzo in 1268. Papal pressure on the city's finances also increased. The Ghibelline nobility lost its power to the Guelphs, who were a major force in the city after 1277, and the economic condition of the city deteriorated further in the 14th century as the Sienese lacked real industries and could not compete with Florence. Famines and wars led to the severe outbreak of the Black Death in 1348, which annihilated about half the population. Nevertheless, Siena flourished culturally; its university was founded in the 13th century, and its school of art attracted such men as Duccio di Buoninsegna, Simone Martini and Pietro and Ambrogio Lorenzetti.

**SIGEBERT, KING OF WESSEX** Ruler from 756 to 757, deposed by the West Saxons after barely a year on the throne. His successor was Cynewulf. See also WESSEX.

**SIGEBERT I, KING OF AUSTRASIA** (d. 575) Frankish king of Austrasia from 561, noted for the vicious civil war that he fought against his brother Chilperic. The son of Clotaire I, he shared in the inheritance with his brothers, receiving Austrasia. In 567 he wed Brunhilde, daughter of the Visigothic king Athanagild, while Brunhilde's sister, Galswintha, married Chilperic. Relations between the brothers were never cordial, erupting into bitter strife when Chilperic murdered Galswintha to marry his mistress, Fredegunde. Sigebert triumphed, conquering Neustria and driving Chilperic into refuge at Tournai. As Sigebert was about to be crowned at Vitry, he was assassinated by men hired by Fredegunde. See also AUSTRASIA; NEUSTRIA.

**SIGEBERT II, KING OF AUSTRASIA** (d. 656) Frankish ruler of Austrasia from 634 to 656, one of the "lazy kings" of the Merovingian dynasty. His reign was controlled by several mayors of the palace, including Pepin the Old (d. 639) and his son Grimoald. See also FRANCE.

**SIGEBERT OF GEMBLOUX** (d. 1112) Monk and chronicler, teaching at the School of Saint Vincent at Metz until 1070, when he returned to the Benedictine monastery at Gembloux and wrote polemics in defense of the position of King Henry IV (1056–1106) against Pope Gregory VII (1073–1085) in the Investiture Controversy. He also wrote a treatise in favor of imperial investiture (1103) opposing the views of Pope Paschal II and a chronicle including the years 381–1111, which was a valuable source of information for historians of the Middle Ages. Sigebert was also author of a history of the early abbots of Gembloux, *De viris*

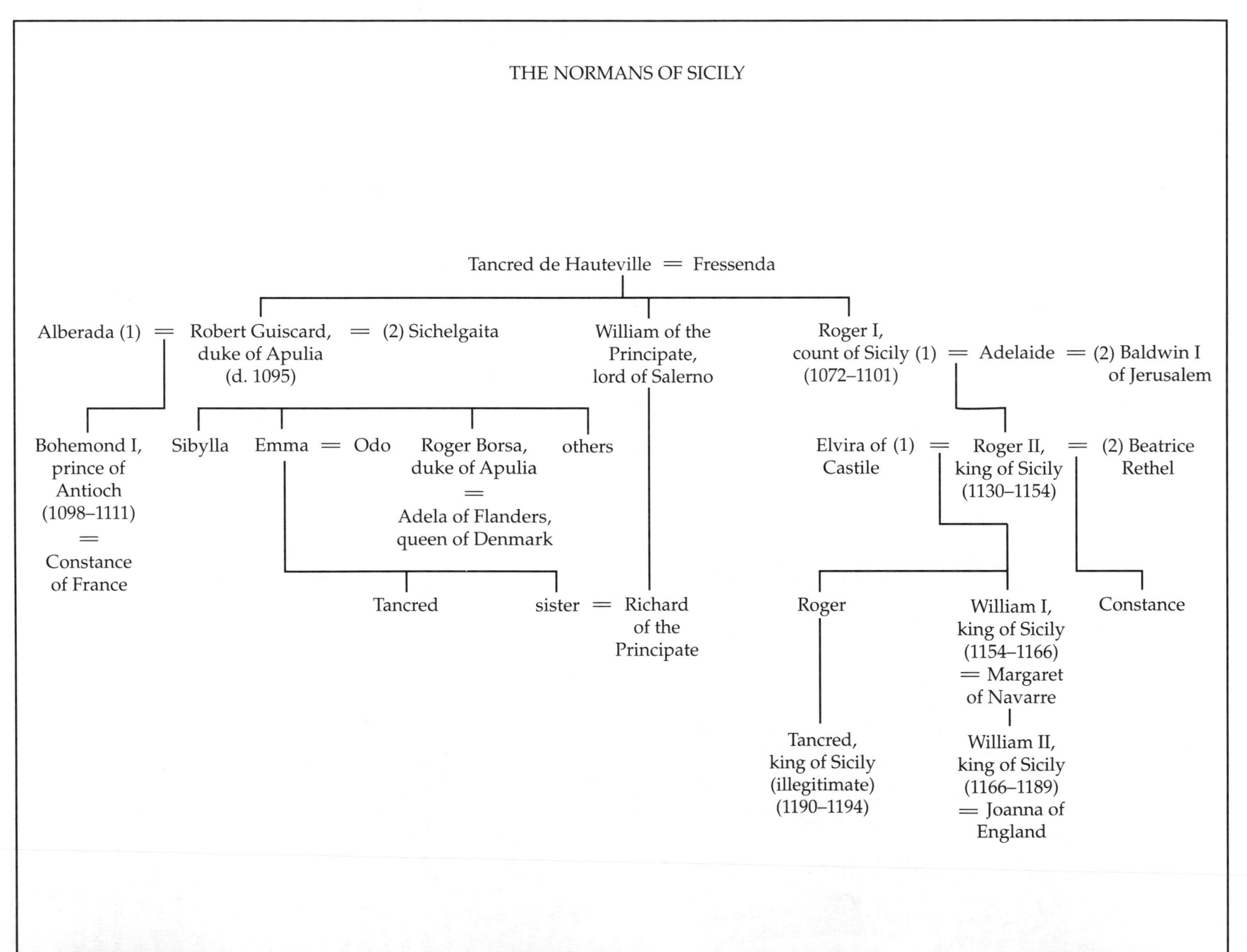
THE NORMANS OF SICILY
Tancred de Hauteville = Fressenda
Alberada (1) = Robert Guiscard, duke of Apulia (d. 1095) = (2) Sichelgaita
William of the Principate, lord of Salerno
Roger I, count of Sicily (1072–1101) (1) = Adelaide = (2) Baldwin I of Jerusalem
Bohemond I, prince of Antioch (1098–1111) = Constance of France
Sibylla
Emma = Odo
Roger Borsa, duke of Apulia = Adela of Flanders, queen of Denmark
others
Elvira of Castile (1) = Roger II, king of Sicily (1130–1154) = (2) Beatrice Rethel
Tancred
sister = Richard of the Principate
Roger
William I, king of Sicily (1154–1166) = Margaret of Navarre
Constance
Tancred, king of Sicily (illegitimate) (1190–1194)
William II, king of Sicily (1166–1189) = Joanna of England

*illustribus,* a collection of biographies on ecclesiastical historians and several hagiographic works.

**SIGER OF BRABANT** (c. 1235–1282) Professor at the University of Paris and an influential spokesman for the Averroist philosophy. A native of Brabant, he served as canon at the cathedral of Liège before teaching at Paris, starting around 1266. He and several colleagues lectured on an interpretation of Aristotle that combined Aristotelianism with the theories of Avicenna and Averroës. He disputed Saint Bonaventure on the nature of his teachings and was attacked by both Bonaventure and Thomas Aquinas. In 1270, Stephen (Ètienne) Tempier, the bishop of Paris, condemned Siger for heresy, and in 1277 he was summoned before Simon Duval, the Grand Inquisitor of France. He and his followers fled to Italy, probably appealing to the Papal Curia. At Orvieto he was stabbed to death by his secretary, who suffered bouts of insanity. Siger was the author of many works, most of them only recently discovered. Among his writings were *Impossibilia, De anima intellectiva* and commentaries on the works of Aristotle. See also AVERROISM.

**SIGISMUND, EMPEROR** (1368–1437) Holy Roman Emperor from 1433, king of Hungary from 1387, German king from 1411 and king of Bohemia from 1419. A son of Emperor Charles IV (1346–1378), Sigismund married Mary of Hungary and in so doing secured the Hungarian throne, although he spent years defending himself from the threat of the ruling house of Naples. In 1396 he led a Crusader army against the Ottoman Turks in the Balkans but was defeated at Nicopolis, losing virtually his entire force and barely escaping capture. Returning home, he tried to take Bohemia from his politically weakened half brother, Wenceslas IV (1363–1419), imprisoning him in 1402 but releasing him in the next year because of troubles in Hungary. Sigismund was elected successor to Rupert but was not sole ruler until his rival, Jobst, died in 1411.

As German king he fought against the Venetians (1412–1413) and was responsible for the summoning of the Council of Constance (1414–1418), which ended the Great Schism in the Western Church. He probably had a role in the seizure and burning of Jan Hus in 1415, who had been invited to the council. Succeeding to the Bohemian throne in 1419, he was unable to hold his coronation for some time, because of the bitter conflict with the Hussites, against whom he was largely unsuccessful. He agreed to the Compactata of Prague and was finally accepted as the Bohemian king in Prague in 1436. Three years earlier he had been crowned emperor. He was considered an estimably chivalric figure. See also BOHEMIA; HOLY ROMAN EMPIRE; HUNGARY.

**SIGISMUND, KING OF BOHEMIA** See SIGISMUND, EMPEROR.

**SIGISMUND, KING OF HUNGARY** See SIGISMUND, EMPEROR.

**SIGURD I** (c. 1090–1130) King of Norway from 1103 to 1130, whose name, Jerusalemfarer, was derived from his visit to Jerusalem, marking him as the first Scandinavian monarch to undertake a Crusade. A natural son of King Magnus III Bareleg (1093–1103), he came to the throne in 1103 but had to divide power with his brothers, Eystein and Olaf Magnusson (1103–1125). Olaf died in 1115 and Eystein in 1122, leaving Sigurd as sole king. His reign was distinguished by the strengthening of the church in Norway, through tithes and construction. His journey to Palestine began in 1107 when he set out with 60 ships, visiting first England, Spain and Sicily and fighting Moorish pirates off the Balearic Islands. He was received cordially by Baldwin I, king of Jerusalem (1100–1118), assisting the Franks in the capture of Sidon. After returning to Constantinople, Sigurd gave his fleet to Emperor Alexius I (1081–1118), returning home by land. See also NORWAY.

**SIGURD II** (d. 1139) King of Norway from 1136 to 1139, claiming the throne after murdering Harald IV Gilchrist (1130–1136). Before he could consolidate his position, however, two other claimants were proclaimed, and Sigurd was unable to achieve a decisive victory. In 1139 he was captured in battle and tortured to death. See also INGI I HARALDSSON; NORWAY; SIGURD III.

**SIGURD III** (d. 1161) King of Norway from 1136 to 1161, called "the Mouth" because of the ugliness of that facial feature. He shared power with Ingi Hunchback (from 1136) and Eystein II (from 1142). In 1155 he joined in a plot with Eystein to remove Ingi, but the king heard of the conspiracy and convened the royal council to help him. Sigurd denied the charge but was cut down by Ingi's supporters. It was recorded that so many weapons were hurled at Sigurd's shield that it seemed like a snowstorm. See also NORWAY.

**SILESIA** Called in German Schlesien, in Czech Slezko and in Polish Slask, a region in eastern Europe situated in the area east of the Upper Oder River. Settled by the Slavs around 500, it became the territory of several Slavic tribes by the ninth century but then was the cause of disputes between the Poles and the Czech dynasty of the Przemyslids. In the late 10th century Silesia was seized by Mieszko I (960–992), prince of Poland, with consolidation coming under King Boleslav I, the Brave (992–1025). A bishopric was established in 1000, while in 1063 Silesia was divided into the principalities of Upper and Lower Silesia. Germanic immigration was long promoted, and Germanicization of the area was an inevitable result. In 1335 the region was attached to the kingdom of Bohemia, its German cultural tendencies leading to its union with the cause of Emperor Sigismund against the Bohemian Hussites during the Hussite Wars (1425–1435).

Broken into principalities, Silesia was ruled for a time by Hungary (1469–1490), returned to Bohemia and finally acquired by the Habsburgs in 1526. See also BOHEMIA; POLAND.

**SILO** A lesser king of Asturias, reigning from 774 to 783.

**SILVERIUS, SAINT** (d. 537) Pope from 536 to 537, the son of Pope Hormisdas (514–523) (born before Hormisdas entered the priesthood), serving as a subdeacon before his election as successor to Agapitus I (535–536). He angered Empress Theodora, wife of Emperor Justinian I (527–565), by refusing to support Monophysitism or to restore the patriarch of Constantinople Anthimus, who had been condemned by Agapitus. Theodora probably arranged his deposition, his degredation to the rank of monk and his eventual banishment to Palmaria (near Naples), where he died under cruel circumstances (probably starvation). He was revered as a martyr.

**SIMEON, KING OF THE BULGARS** See SYMEON.

**SIMEON METAPHRASTES** (d. c. 984) Noted Byzantine biographer, also called Logothetes. He was an official of the Byzantine government and then became a monk. He was the author of *Menologion,* a 10-volume collection of the lives of the saints, arranged according to the Orthodox liturgical calendar. His name was derived from his "verse translation" (Greek *metaphrasis*) of earlier collections, which he revised to suit contemporary style. His *Menologion* was so much read that earlier manuscripts were forgotten and even lost, causing the absence of source texts on the subject. He was also the author of a chronicle and devotional literature.

**SIMEON THE PROUD** Grand Duke of Moscow from 1341–1353. See MOSCOW; GRAND PRINCES OF.

**SIMON OF SUDBURY** See PEASANT REVOLT.

**SIMONY** See GLOSSARY.

**SIMPLICIUS** (d. 483) Pope from 468 to 483, a native of Tivoli, the successor to Hilary (461–468) and the pontiff during the fall of the Roman Empire in the West (476) at the hands of the German general Odoacer. Simplicius strove to improve the ecclesiastical organization in Rome and erected several churches, most notably San Stefano Rotondo.

**SISIBUT** (d. 820) King of the Visigoths from 812 to 820, a monarch of considerable learning, reportedly skilled in grammar and rhetoric and writer of the lost *Chronicle of the Kings of the Goths.* He opposed the Byzantine Empire for acquisition of territories on the Spanish coast of Andalusia and later crossed the Strait of Gibraltar to seize additional lands from the exarch of Africa. By the terms of his treaty with Emperor Heraclius he was able to retain the conquered regions. Sisibut also supported the Spanish church, listening to his bishops and instigating persecutions of the Jews. He was succeeded by his son, Reccared II. See also VISIGOTHS.

**SISINAND** (d. 636) King of the Visigoths, a weak ruler, reigning from 631 to 636. Originally governor of the province of Septimania, he rose in revolt in 631 against King Swinthila, obtaining the support of King Dagobert I and taking the throne. Given Swinthila by the Visigothic nobles, Sisinand spared the monarch, sending him to a monastery. His reign was notable for the power of the church in Spain, as Sisinand adhered to the will of his bishops. See also VISIGOTHS.

**SISINNIUS** (d. 708) Pope from January 15 to February 4, 708, a Syrian whose brief pontificate was overshadowed by the Lombard threat in Italy.

**SIXTUS IV** (1414–1484) Pope from 1471 to 1484, born Francesco della Rovere, former minister general of the Franciscans, succeeding Pope Paul II (1464–1471). A patron of the arts and a builder, Sixtus erected the Sistine Chapel in 1475, commissioned artists such as Botticelli and was concerned with the restoration of churches. He was also deeply involved in aggrandizing the Papal States and his own family's fortunes. Conspiring to destroy the Medicis in Florence, he commenced a two-year war (1478–1480) and then compelled Venice to attack Ferrara, later placing an interdict on the Venetians (1483) when they continued to advance against the Papal States. A supporter of the unpopular idea of crusades against the Turks, he failed to find enthusiasm for such a venture. Relations with France were also strained during his pontificate because of King Louis XI's (1461–1483) firm adherence to the Pragmatic Sanction of Bourges. Sixtus IV gave permission for the Spanish Inquisition, trying in vain to curb its excesses (1482) and giving refuge to many Jews exiled from Spain.

**SKALDS AND SKALDIC POETRY** See ICELANDIC LITERATURE.

**SKALLAGRIMSSON, EGILL** See EGILL SKALLAGRIMSSON.

**SLAVS** The largest ethnic and linguistic group belonging to the Indo-European language family in Europe, found principally in eastern and southwestern European regions. The Slavs were divided into three groups: the Western Slavs, comprising Poles, Slovaks, Wends and Czechs, in addition to small groups in western Germany; the Southern Slavs, comprising Serbs, Bulgars, Macedonians, Slovenes and Croats; and the Eastern Slavs, including Great Russians, White Russians (Bylorussians) and Ukrainians. Aside from their pagan traditions, the Slavs were separated further from one another by their adherence to the two major religious bodies of Christendom, the Orthodox Eastern Church and the Western Roman Church. Slavic migrations from the Lower Vistula and Lower Oder began in the fifth century, continuing into the sixth century. They headed westward, penetrating into the region between the Oder and the Elbe Rivers and into Bohemia, Hungary and the Balkans and north along the Upper Dneiper River. In these varied Slavic regions the communities and states evolved uniquely, the Western Slavs becoming European and the Eastern Slavs remaining generally free of European influence. See also BOHEMIA; BULGARIA; HUNGARY; LITHUANIA; POLAND; PRUSSIA, RUSSIA.

**SMILETZ** (d. 1300) King of the Bulgars from 1292 to 1300, installed through Tatar (Tartar) influences. Originally a boyar, Smiletz succeeded George I Tatar (1280–1292), who was forced to flee to the Byzantines. Smiletz maintained amicable relations with Constantinople. On his death there followed a brief interregnum as his widow and then George's son-in-law, Caka, tried unsuccessfully to usurp power. See also BULGARIA.

**SMOLENSK** City in western Russia, situated on the Dneiper River. First mentioned in 882, it held a strategic position on the trade routes from Moscow and the West, becoming vital to commerce in the region. Sacked during the Mongol invasion (1237–1240), the city was rebuilt and later captured by the Lithuanians, initiating centuries of strife between Lithuania and Russia. Smolensk fell to the Russians in 1370, was recaptured by the Lithuanians in 1408 and was reclaimed by the Russians in 1514. See also RUSSIA.

**SNORRI STURLUSON** (1178–1241) Icelandic poet and historian, author of the *Prose Edda* (c. 1220), *Heimskringla* (c. 1220) and probably the *Egils Saga*. A descendant of the illustrious skaldic poet Egill Skallagrimsson, he was raised in the household of the powerful Icelandic chieftain Jon Loptsson, from whom he learned history and the oral tradition. He settled in Reykjaholt (Reykholt) in 1206, serving as chief or "law speaker" of the Icelandic high court from 1215 to 1218 and from 1222 to 1232. Becoming active in politics, he supported King Haakon IV of Norway (1217–1263) but fell from favor and was killed at Haakon's command by his son-in-law, Gissur Thorvaldsson. The most celebrated of the saga writers, Snorri was especially honored for his *Prose Edda* (see ICELANDIC LITERATURE) and for his handbook on poetry, in which he elaborated on an outline of Old Norse mythology. In his *Heimskringla,* he recounted the story of the kings of Norway from their legendary origins in Odin to Magnus V Erlingsson (ruled 1162–1184). See also ICELAND.

**SOFIA** City in central-western Bulgaria, situated at the foot of the Balkan Mountains. Originally settled by the Thracian tribe of the Serdi and conquered by the Romans about 29 B.C., it was renamed Serdica (Sardica). Called in the early second century Ulpia Serdica, it emerged as the principal outpost of the Romans in the province of Inner Dacia. Sacked by the Huns in 447, Sofia was rebuilt by Justinian I in the sixth century. The name was adopted after the restoration of the Church of Saint Sofia. In 809 it fell to the Bulgarians and was incorporated into Bulgar lands, reverting to the Byzantines in the 11th and 12th centuries and then returning to Bulgaria in the Second Bulgarian Empire. The Ottoman Turks captured Sofia in 1382. See also BULGARIA.

**SOISSONS** City in northern France, in the department of Aisne on the Aisne River, the name derived from the Gallic tribe of the Suessiones. An important Roman city, it later received a bishopric in the third century and was revered as the site of martyrdom for Saint Crispin and Saint Crispinian (c. 285). In 486 Clovis and the Franks defeated Syagrius and claimed Soissons, which served as the capital of Neustria under the Merovingian dynasts, including Childeric III, who was deposed in 752 by Pepin the Short. The counts of Soissons held the city during the Capetian era (987–1328), and its charter dates from 1131. The Council of Soissons (1121) condemned some of the views of Abelard, forcing him to burn his work, *De unitate et trinitate divina.* During the Hundred Years' War (1337–1453), Soissons suffered severely. Notable structures were the Gothic cathedral of Saint-Gervais et Saint Protais (12th–13th century) and the abbeys of Saint Jean-des-Vignes, founded in the 11th century, and Saint Médard (sixth century).

**SOLOMON** King of Hungary from 1063 to 1074, most of his reign spent in conflict with his cousins, Géza (I) and Ladislas. The son of King Andrew I (ruled 1047–1061), Solomon was named heir, but a resulting dispute with Andrew's brother, Béla (I), led to Solomon's flight to his brother-in-law, Emperor Henry IV (1056–1106). After the death of King Béla in 1063, Solomon returned as monarch, while Béla's sons were granted princely holdings. Civil war soon erupted, and in 1074 Solomon was defeated, returning to Henry IV. See also HUNGARY.

**SOLOMON BEN ADRET** (1235–1310) Rabbinical leader in Spain, called Rashba, the initials for Rabbi Sholomo Ben Adret, a respected Talmudic scholar. He wrote a response to questions on the subject as well as commentaries. He was also involved in a dispute with the supporters of Moses Maimonides, issuing a decree in 1305 that threatened the excommunication of any Jew under the age of 30 who studied philosophy or science, with the exception of medical students.

**SOMERSET, EDMUND BEAUFORT, SECOND DUKE OF** (d. 1495) English noble and statesman who played a leading role in the events leading to the Wars of the Roses (1455–1485). He exercised considerable power in the government of King Henry VI (1422–1461), dividing authority with William de la Pole, duke of Suffolk, during the 1430s. In 1447 he replaced Richard, duke of York, as captain general in France. In command of the war with France, his incompetence ensured the loss of all of England's French holdings by 1453, with the exception of Calais, and the end of the Hundred Years' War. Imprisoned in 1453, following the mental decline of the king, he was restored as chief minister in the following year, defeating the plans of Richard of York. A leader of the Lancastrian faction at the start of the war, he was killed in May 1455 at the first Battle of Saint Albans. See also WARS OF THE ROSES.

**SONG OF ROLAND** See ROLAND.

**SORBON, ROBERT DE** (1201–1274) French theologian of Paris, the confessor to King Louis IX (1226–1270). Sorbon was the founder of the first endowed college at the University of Paris (c. 1257), giving his name to the Sorbonne. See also UNIVERSITIES.

**SORDELLO** (c. 1200–c. 1269) Also Sordello di Gioto after his birthplace, an Italian poet and the most distinguished troubadour in Italy. A composer of Provençal poetry, he composed a didactic poem of 1,325 lines called

*L'Ensenhamen d'onor,* as well as satires and love songs. In 1224 he abducted the wife of his patron, Richard de Bonifacio, at her brother's behest, fleeing Italy and traveling as a troubadour in Spain and France. He later served Ramon Berenguer IV of Barcelona and at the court of Charles of Anjou. Sordello was immortalized in a reference to him by Dante.

**SOREL, AGNES** (c. 1422–1450) Mistress of King Charles VII of France (1422–1461) after 1444, celebrated for her beauty and intelligence. She had a beneficial influence on the king and his policies and was portrayed by the painter Jean Fouquet as a Madonna. The story that Agnes was poisoned is probably untrue and was rumored by enemies of Jacques Coeur.

**SPAIN** The term *Spain* is a modern one and during the Middle Ages had no political or geographical meaning until after the union of the Kingdoms of Aragon and Castile in the late 15th century. Prior to that time it was a group of independent kingdoms.

The medieval era of Spanish history effectively began with the disintegration of Roman authority in the Iberian Peninsula in the wake of the invasions by the Vandals, Alans and Suebi. These peoples were displaced by the Visigoths, starting in 415. The Visigoths established a kingdom that stretched across old Roman Spain (Hispania) and into southern Gaul. Their holdings in Gaul were lost to the Franks in 507 through the Battle of Chalons. Unlike their predecessors, the Visigoths were able to bring about religious and cultural unity under King Reccared (r. 586–601), through his conversion to orthodox Christianity, thereby ending the long-standing Visigoth adherence to Arian Christianity, which had been a facet of their lives since their initial conversion under St. Uphilas in the fourth century.

The Visigothic kingdom was destroyed starting in 711 with the onslaught of the Arab armies into Spain. The Islamic invaders poured into the peninsula from Africa, having been summoned by the political enemies of the last Visigothic king, Roderick (r. 710–711). The Arab forces were initially under the authority of the caliphate, but this changed in 756 when the Umayyad prince Abd al-Rahman founded the independent emirate of Córdoba. The emirate was transformed into a caliphate in 929 through the efforts of Abd al-Rahman III. The caliphate dominated much of Spain, driving the Christian populations into the north. Under the leadership of the caliphs, Moorish Spain emerged as the center of a brilliant culture, with such notable cities as Córdoba, Granada and Seville.

The earliest Christian kingdoms were born as the heirs to the moribund Visigothic dynasty in the north of Spain where the Moors were unable to extend their suzerainty. The seeds of the reconquest of Spain would be planted in Asturias, where Pelayo (r. c. 718–737) was elected king. From this beginning, other Christian states sprouted in the 10th century—Leon (to which Asturias was joined), Castile, Aragon and Navarre. While the Christian realms would vie for positions of advantage, including the forging of alliances with various Moorish kingdoms, they were all united in their effort to eject the Moors from the peninsula, the holy war called the Reconquista.

The Reconquista initially had largely political aspirations, but it eventually assumed a deeply religious connotation and fervor due to the influence exercised by the Christian church over much of Spanish life. Monasticism flourished, as did the religious orders that found fertile ground for new members (most notably in the 13th century with the flowering of the Franciscans and Dominicans). Especially important were pilgrimages by the faithful to sites of religious devotion, the greatest being Santiago de Compostela. The Spanish church was also remarkable for its preservation of the Mozarabic rite, the liturgical form less commonly called the Visigothic or Old Spanish rite and which was replaced gradually by the Roman rite.

The imposition of the Roman rite in the late 11th century was indicative of the change in atmosphere and attitude accompanying the Reconquista. Where previously the line between Moorish and Christian Spain had been vague and the two populations intermingling and generally tolerant of each other, the Christian (and to a degree the Moorish) states moved to a harder line of intolerance and polarization. The capture of Toledo under Alfonso VI of Castile in 1085 is considered a decisive turning point in the history of medieval Spain, for the Mozarabic inhabitants (those Christians living under Islamic rule) failed to secure freedom of worship for their Muslim counterparts. The faith became a more critical element in the crusading effort, furthered by the increase in papal power. The popes had already taken the leading place in calling for the First Crusade—declared by Pope Urban II in 1085 at Clermont—and the Holy See would expend much effort over the next several hundreds of years in urging further military adventures to the Holy Land and to repel the Islamic threat. The popes would thus encourage the Spanish kings in their endeavors; Pope Eugenius III, for example, in 1148 gave formal recognition of Spain as a theater of operations for the crusading movement, with all of its attendant spiritual benefits. Perhaps the foremost example of the crusading zeal in the 12th century was the formation of the Military Orders, such as the Orders of Alcantara, Calatrava and Santiago. These chivalric groups would amass much prestige and financial influence, while providing the Christian kingdoms with badly needed troops.

Owing to internal political and dynastic strife, the caliphate collapsed and broke apart into a series of smaller realms (the *taifa,* or party kingdoms, which gave cash payments and political homage to the Christians), in the 11th century. In the 11th and 12th centuries the Almohads and Almoravids invaded from Africa. These dynasties were gradually reduced by internal bickering and the advance of the Christian armies. The Islamic culture of Moorish Spain would survive in a severely reduced condition in Granada from 1232 to 1492, when Granada's fall to the forces of Ferdinand and Isabella marked the end of the Reconquista.

Despite chronic differences and martial squabbling, the Christian kingdoms made much progress in the 13th century against the Moors. Zaragoza fell in 1118 to the troops of Alfonso I of Aragon and, despite the efforts of the Almohads to mount a counter to the Christian attack, the stage was set for the crushing triumph of Alfonso VIII of Castile (r. 1158–1214) in 1212 at the Battle of Navas de Tolosa, won with the crucial help of the Military Orders. In the ensuing years, the Christian tide would sweep over Seville, Cordoba, Valencia and the Balearic Islands.

The victories helped propel Aragon and Castile into international affairs. Aragon was to cast its policy on the aggrandizement of its position in the Mediterranean. James I transformed Aragon into a powerful Mediterranean kingdom with the conquest of Valencia and the Balearic islands. Aragon's ambitions toward Sicily (exemplified by the War of the Sicilian Vespers beginning in 1282) brought it into conflict with both France and the popes.

In the 14th century, the House of Trastamara came to power in Castile with the death of King Pedro (Peter) the Cruel in 1369. The Trastamaran line would become involved in the events of southern France and in 1412, one of the line, Ferdinand I became king of Aragon. The final political unification of Spain was brought about by the marriage in 1469 of two members of the Trastamaran line: Ferdinand II, son of Juan (John) II of Aragon and Isabella I, daughter of Juan (John) II of Castile. The union of the kingdoms of Castile and Aragon marked the beginning of the terminal period of the Reconquista. Having brought their two realms together, their Catholic majesties, as they would be called, completed the eradication of the Moorish domains—on January 2, 1492, Granada fell. That same year, Christopher Columbus landed in the New World.

Spain during the Middle Ages presented a cultural amalgam of Christian, Muslim, and Jewish traditions, ended by the Reconquista and the triumph of Christianity throughout the peninsula. Along the way, Spain made lasting contributions to the scientific, medical, intellectual and philosophical life of the West. Jewish scholars included Moses Maimonides (d. 1204) and the brilliant translators who made important translations of Arab texts and were fluent in Hebrew, Latin and Arabic. From Cordoba came the highly influential philosophical writings of Averroës, who would be the source of much contention within the Scholastic Movement in the 13th century at the University of Paris. Christian translators—most notably those of the Toledan school under Gerard of Cremona (d. 1187)—made many of the translation of Arab texts that widened scientific knowledge across Christendom. Spanish translations of Arab texts also reintroduced into the West the long lost writings of Aristotle and facilitated the scholarly refutation of Islamic teachings by Christian missionaries and theologians.

As mentioned, the Reconquista brought the most unfortunate consequences for Spanish cultural life. The Islamic population came under mounting oppression and were forced to convert to the faith of their new overlords. Persecutions also descended upon the Jews, as they had in the Holy Land during the Crusades there. Royal protection proved insufficient to prevent the regular waves of anti-Semitism throughout Spain as thousands of Jews were put to death. Severe disabilities and mistreatment only grew worse for both the Jews and the Muslims with the foundation of the Inquisition in the late 15th century. Strict religious orthodoxy was enforced, leading to the expulsion of the Jews from Spain in 1492. Those Muslims refusing to convert were expelled, but even converted Moors were looked upon with suspicion by the state and the Inquisition.

Under Ferdinand and Isabella the Spanish kingdom was given greater centralization. The *Cortes,* the assembly of nobility, clergy and townspeople that predated the Parliament of England as a political institution, declined in the frequency of its meetings and in its power to moderate the authoritarian tendencies of the monarchy, as absolutist tendencies were exemplified by the power of the *Consejo Real,* the Royal Council. The absolutism of the royal house would grant the Kings of Spain total control over the wealth and empire that would be established in the 16th century and which would make Spain an international power. See also ARAGON; CASTILLE; CORTES; and MOORS.

**SPANISH INQUISITION** See INQUISITION.

**SPOLETO** Town in the Italian region of Umbria, situated to the north of Rome. A Roman colony from 241 B.C., it lay on the Via Flaminia and became an important episcopal see in the fourth century. About 570, Spoleto was the capital of a major Lombard duchy that extended across Umbria and the Abruzzi into the Marches. Its preeminence endured until the eighth century, after which it lost much of its independence; it was destroyed in 1155 by Frederick I Barbarossa (1152–1190). The supreme authority of the Holy Roman Empire ended early in the 13th century, and it was claimed by the papacy. The cathedral of Spoleto (12th century) boasted a superb fresco, the *Coronation of the Virgin,* by Filippo Lippi. See also LOMBARDS.

**SPURS, BATTLE OF THE** Also called the Battle of the Golden Spurs and the Battle of Courtrai, an engagement fought on July 11, 1302, between an army of French cavalry supported by Flemish noblemen and a force of largely untrained Flemish militia, led by a small group of knights. The Flemish militia, largely composed of pikemen, chose to take up their position near marshy terrain divided by canals and bridges, rendering any direct assault by the French quite difficult. After the crossbowmen and the small numbers of French infantrymen failed to provoke the Flemish, the French knights charged forward and were repulsed. Unable to maneuver, the horsemen were cut down and massacred, ending French ambitions in Flanders. The name Spurs derived from the plundering of spurs from the fallen knights by the victorious Flemish. See also WARFARE.

**SQUARCIONE, FRANCESCO** (d. 1468) Painter of Padua generally considered to have been the founder of the Paduan school of art. He attracted a vast number of students, including Mantegna, Marco Zoppo, Carlo Crivelli and Giorgio Schiavone. An excellent example of his style was a cycle of frescoes depicting scenes from the life of Saint Francis, applied to the exterior of San Francesco in Padua. See also PADUA.

**STAINED GLASS** The name given in general to windows made of colored glass, and a major decorative device in medieval art and architecture, especially during the 12th and 13th centuries. Glaziers utilized glass colored with metallic oxides while in the melting pot, thereby producing clear, transparent glass (known as colored pot metal). With this, flashed glass (glass fused with a thin film of colored glass) and white glass were used. Outlining in a broader picture was achieved by applying a brownish paint *guisaille* of powdered glass and iron oxide and then fusing it with the glass surface. Red-hot iron was then used to form desired shapes, which were fitted into lead strips with channels. The strips of lead were soldered at connecting points, strengthened by being placed in a bracing framework of iron.

The use of stained glass evolved slowly in western Europe, finding application in windows during the architectural periods of the Carolingian and Romanesque. Such windows were small, but the Romanesque and especially the Gothic styles brought a change. Henceforth emphasis was placed on extensive use of windows and openness, allowing stained glass to become a major art form in church decoration. See also CATHEDRALS; GOTHIC ART AND ARCHITECTURE; ROMANESQUE ART AND ARCHITECTURE.

**STAMFORD BRIDGE, BATTLE OF** See HARALD III SIGURDSSON, KING OF NORWAY; HAROLD II GODWINSON, KING OF ENGLAND; HASTINGS, BATTLE OF.

**STANISLAUS, SAINT** (1030–1079) Bishop of Cracow from 1072 and a patron saint of Poland, also called Stanislaw. A noble, he received his education at Gniezno and probably at Paris and was named bishop. Coming into conflict with King Boleslav II the Bold (1058–1079), he reproached him for his behavior and apparently joined the opposition to the king. Arrested in 1079 on charges of treason, he was sentenced to death, but the knights refused to dismember him, forcing the king to perform the deed himself. Much mystery surrounded his death, as Polish historians extol him as a saintly prelate murdered by a vicious ruler after Stanislaus had excommunicated him, while others viewed him as a meddlesome bishop who was justly executed for participating in a treasonous plot. See also POLAND.

**STATES GENERAL** Also Estates General (French, Etats-Generaux), the French representative body composed of the three estates or orders of the kingdom: the clergy, nobility and people. The States General originated in the reign of King Philip IV the Fair (ruled 1285–1314), who summoned the three estates in 1302 for their support in his conflict with Pope Boniface VIII (1294–1303). Realistically, however, the early meetings of the assembly were little more than sessions of the Curia Regis, the Royal Council, its political power arising only during the Hundred Years' War (1337–1453) with England, when the monarchy needed the support of all elements of French society. Given an opportunity to consolidate and improve its position, the States General took control of the taxes that it had approved (1355), and then, guided by the third estate (the people) and the populist figure Ètienne Marcel, it declared the right to vote new taxes, demanding the removal of certain ministers and calling for a greater role in the government. The Jacquerie, with the assassination of Marcel, aborted the ambitions of the States General. By the end of the war its privileges had been curbed greatly, its primary role that of granting taxes requested by the king. See also PARLIAMENT.

**STAURACIUS** (d. 811) Byzantine emperor for a brief period in 811, the son of Emperor Nicephorus I, sharing in his father's defeat at the hands of the Bulgars in July 811, in which Nicephorus was slain and he was badly wounded. Retreating to Adrianople with a few Byzantine survivors, he was proclaimed emperor but his power was limited, being assumed by Michael I Rangabe in Constantinople in October of that year. Stauracius abdicated, retired to a monastery and died a short time later. See also BYZANTINE EMPIRE.

**STENKIL** (d. c. 1066) King of Sweden from 1060 to 1066 and the founder of a new dynasty of kings named after him. He was an ardent advocate of Christianity, promoting missionary work, although he recognized the political power of the remaining pagan establishment and thus did not permit the destruction of a pagan temple at Uppsala. See also SWEDEN.

**STEPHEN II** (d. 752) Roman priest elected successor to Pope Zachary (741–752) but dying two days later of a stroke. As he was not consecrated, his name was omitted from the *Liber pontificalis,* causing confusion in the succession of later popes of that name.

**STEPHEN II (III)** (d. 757) Pope from 752 to 757, responsible for the establishment of the Papal States. Confronted with the Lombard threat, he took the important step of crossing the Alps in 754 to confer with the Frankish king Pepin III the Short (751–768). He crowned Pepin at Saint-Denis, and the Franks in gratitude marched into Italy, defeating the Lombards and returning to France. In 756 another appeal was sent, and Pepin once more came to Stephen's defense. This time, however, he granted the Donation of Pepin, which guaranteed the papacy's right to territory in central Italy and Rome, the foundation for the Papal States and the temporal power of the papacy. Stephen thus freed the papacy of dependence on Byzantium, a decision with lasting historical ramifications.

**STEPHEN III (IV)** (d. 772) Pope from 768 to 772, a native of Sicily and a Benedictine priest when elected. His pontificate was noted for the problems it encountered from King Desiderius (757–774) and the Lombards, who were attempting to arrange an alliance with the Franks, an action opposed by Stephen. The union was accepted in 771 and thereby led to the murder of members of the Frankish party in Rome.

**STEPHEN IV (V)** (d. 817) Pope from 816 to 817, a member of the Roman nobility, responsible for initiating the tradition of papal consecration of the emperor by anointing Emperor Louis I the Pious (814–840) at Reims on October 18, 816. This act ensured the alliance between the papacy and the Frankish empire, establishing the tradition of papal authority in the consecration of emperors.

**STEPHEN V (VI)** (d. 891) Pope from 885 to 891, ruling during the political disintegration of the Carolingian empire. A noble of Rome, he succeeded Adrian III (884–885) but did not receive the approval of Emperor Charles III the Fat (881–888), who was deposed in 887 by Arnulf, king of the East Franks. Stephen also faced severe disorder in Italy, as there were Saracen threats, famine, feuds between the Italian nobles and a contest for political control in Italy. He secured the exile of the patriarch of Constantinople, Photius (886), and opposed successfully the use of the Slavic liturgy in Moravia, which had been approved by Pope John VIII (872–882).

**STEPHEN VI (VII)** (d. 897) Pope from 896 to 897, responsible for one of the most lurid episodes in papal history. A Roman and bishop of Anagni, he was elected successor to Boniface III (896) at a time when the papacy was subject to the bitter political conflict for supremacy in Italy. A supporter of Lambert of Spoleto and the Spoletan faction, which despised Pope Formosus (891–896) for his consecration of Arnulf as Holy Roman Emperor (896–899) rather than of Guy of Spoleto, Stephen summoned the "Cadaver Synod" in 897. At these proceedings he ordered the exhumed and rotting corpse of Pope Formosus to be dressed in robes, seated and then tried for various offenses. Condemned, the body was mutilated, dragged through Rome and thrown into the Tiber. Soon afterward, a revolt took place in Rome, and Stephen was imprisoned and strangled.

**STEPHEN VII (VIII)** (d. 931) Pope from 928 to 931, a Roman who owed his election to the powerful Marozia, head of the house of Theophylact. Stephen was generally powerless politically, although he did support Cluniac Reform.

**STEPHEN VIII (IX)** (d. 942) Pope from 939 to 942, whose pontificate was dominated by Alberic II of Spoleto, who controlled Rome. Stephen encouraged Cluniac Reform.

**STEPHEN IX (X)** (d. 1058) Pope from 1057 to 1058, an initiator of Gregorian Reform, born Frederick of Lorraine, brother of Godfrey, duke of Lorraine. He was an adviser to his cousin, Pope Leo IX (1049–1054), serving as legate to Constantinople and then retiring to Monte Cassino until 1057, when he was appointed cardinal by Pope Victor II (1055–1057), whom he succeeded. His pontificate was noted for its efforts at reform, as he summoned a Roman synod to condemn simony and other abuses and promoted the work of reformers such as Hildebrand (the future Gregory VII), Humbert of Silva Candida and Peter Damian.

**STEPHEN, KING OF ENGLAND** (c. 1097–1154) Ruler from 1135 to 1154, the grandson of William I the Conqueror (1066–1087) by his daughter, Adela, and son of Stephen, count of Blois and Chartres. Raised by King Henry I (ruled 1100–1135), he became a powerful English noble with holdings in Normandy and Boulogne. Stephen agreed to support Matilda, Henry's daughter, as successor to the throne but then claimed the crown, supported by nobles in England and by Normans. He arrived in England soon after Henry's death but lost his initial gains through lack of leadership and the harshness of his Flemish mercenary troops. Matilda invaded England in 1139, achieved victories and captured Stephen in 1141. Releasing him in return for her ally, Robert, earl of Gloucester, Matilda lost popular support because of her arrogance. In 1148 she retreated from England, leaving Stephen in control. His remaining years were spent in political impotency. After the death of his son, Eustace, in August 1153, he accepted Henry of Anjou, Matilda's son, as his heir. See also ENGLAND.

**STEPHEN I, KING OF HUNGARY, SAINT** (977–1038) Called Saint Stephen, Hungary's first king, ruling from 997 to 1038, the son of the Magyar chief Géza, succeeding him and initiating a vast program of Christianization. Stephen suppressed a pagan uprising, sending missionaries throughout the country and converting by force the Black (or pagan) Hungarians. He eventually relied on the church as a powerful political institution and in 1000 received his crown from Pope Sylvester II (999–1003), a treasure that subsequently came to symbolize Hungarian nationalism. In introducing government to his people, Stephen relied on the German model, promoting agricultural activity, creating an army and establishing laws to safeguard property and rights. See also HUNGARY.

**STEPHEN II, KING OF HUNGARY** Ruler from 1116 to 1131. The successor to King Colman I (1095–1116), he lost control of Dalmatia for a decade to the Venetians. See also HUNGARY.

**STEPHEN III, KING OF HUNGARY** (d. 1173) Ruler from 1161 to 1173, whose reign witnessed the advance of the Byzantines and Venetians in the Balkans. Stephen was quite young at his accession, paralyzing Hungarian politics for a time. On his death, Béla III (ruled 1173–1196) came to the throne. See also HUNGARY.

**STEPHEN IV, KING OF HUNGARY** Ruler from 1163 to 1165, an uncle of King Stephen III. See also HUNGARY.

**STEPHEN V, KING OF HUNGARY** (d. 1272) Ruler from 1270 to 1272, whose brief reign was beset by considerable upheaval. He was unable to keep the nobles in check and could not match the foreign monarchs aligned against him. Stephen fought with King Ottokar II Przemysl of Bohemia and died suddenly after the Bohemians kidnapped his son for the purposes of blackmail. See also HUNGARY.

**STEPHEN DRAGUTIN, KING OF SERBIA** Ruler of the Serbs from 1276 to 1282, succeeded by Stephen Uros II Milutin. See also SERBIA.

**STEPHEN DUSAN, KING OF SERBIA** (1308–1355) The most illustrious ruler in Serbian history, reigning from 1331 to 1355. The son of Stephen Uros III Decanski (ruled 1321–1331), he spent years (1314–1320) in Constantinople, where his father had been exiled. He was reconciled with his grandfather, Stephen Uros II Milutin (ruled 1285–1321), and returned to Serbia, crowned co-ruler on his father's succession and governing Serbia's maritime territories. In 1330, however, having campaigned against the Bosnians and Bulgarians, Stephen began a conflict with his father and deposed him. After cementing relations with the Bulgarians, he launched a campaign in 1334 against the Byzantines, claiming Albania, Macedonia, Epirus and Thessaly. In 1345 he bore the title "Emperor of the Serbs and Greeks," convening the Diets of 1349 and 1354 to issue a new code of law for Serbia. He also raised Serbian bishops to the rank of patriarch. Amicable relations were maintained with the papacy, and he hoped, in vain, to become the designated leader of a crusade against the Ottoman Turks in the Balkans. Stephen died suddenly, and his son, Stephen Uros (ruled 1355–1371) was unable to hold together the empire created by "Dusan the Mighty." See also SERBIA.

**STEPHEN HARDING** (d. 1134) English monastic reformer and abbot of Citeaux who wrote the "Charter of Love," the Cistercian constitution. He studied at the order's monasteries in England, France and Italy and then settled at Molesme, leading a life of strict austerity. In 1098, however, he departed with other members of the community, going to Citeaux, where they pursued a still more rigorous monastic regime. He was appointed subprior, then prior and finally abbot in 1109. The monastery was about to fail because of poverty and its demanding rule when Saint Bernard (of Clairvaux) arrived with other followers, initiating a revival and requiring the eventual foundation of other communities. It was for this purpose that Stephen wrote the regulations, which served as a guide for the system of visitation and the general chapters. See also CISTERCIANS.

**STEPHEN LAZAREVIC** See SERBIA.

**STEPHEN NEMANJA** (d. 1200) Serbian leader from about 1167 to 1196, when he fought against the Byzantine Empire and won in 1190 through a peace treaty the recognition of Serbian independence. In 1167 he was made grand zupan of Rascia, a title granting chieftain status, although he was a Byzantine vassal. He soon rebelled, made an alliance with the Venetians but was defeated in 1172. Granted a pardon by the Byzantines, Stephen remained obedient to Emperor Manuel I Comnenus (1143–1180) until the ruler's death in 1180, whereupon he joined the Bulgars in an invasion of the empire, defining Serbian national interests and uniting previously divided Serbian territories under his banner. Emperor Isaac II Angelus recovered Byzantine supremacy in the region, defeating Stephen at Morava in 1090, but he agreed to allow the Serbs to retain their conquered territories and allowed Stephen to marry his niece, Eudocia, to his second son. Stephen abdicated in 1196 to become a monk and was succeeded by Stephen the First-Crowned. His third son was Sava, the patron saint of Serbia. See also SAVA, SAINT; SERBIA.

**STEPHEN OF MURET** See GRANDMONT, ORDER OF.

**STEPHEN THE FIRST-CROWNED, KING OF SERBIA** Ruler of the Serbs from 1196 to about 1228, the son of and successor to Stephen Nemanja, and a brother of Serbia's patron saint, Sava. He entered into a dispute with Sava on the religious disposition of the kingdom, advocating the Western Church, Sava preferring the Eastern doctrine, and the question remains as to whether Stephen was crowned by legates of the pope or by Sava, then archbishop of Serbia. Stephen was succeeded by Stephen Radaslav, about whom little is known. See also SERBIA.

**STEPHEN UROS I, KING OF SERBIA** Ruler of the Serbs from 1242 to 1276. See also SERBIA.

**STEPHEN UROS II, KING OF SERBIA** Successor to Stephen Dragutin (ruled 1276–1282), also called Stephen Uros II Milutin, or Milutin, reigning from 1282 to 1321. He invaded Macedonia in 1282 and in 1308, making an alliance against the Byzantines with Charles of Valois. In time, however, Stephen became an ally of Emperor Andronicus II Palaeologus of Constantinople. See also SERBIA.

**STEPHEN UROS III, KING OF SERBIA** Also Stephen Decanski, ruling from 1321 to 1331, successor to Stephen Uros II, overthrowing his father, blinding him and sending him to Constantinople. He ruled an increasingly powerful Serbian state, forcing the Byzantines into an alliance with the Bulgars. On July 28, 1330, Stephen destroyed the Bulgars at Velbuzd, killing the Bulgar leader Michael Sisman. While his triumph laid the foundation for Serbian greatness, Stephen was overthrown by his nobles, who replaced him with his son, Stephen Dusan.

**STEPHEN UROS IV, KING OF SERBIA** The successor to Stephen Dusan, ruling from 1355 to 1371. See also SERBIA.

**STEPHEN VLADISLAV, KING OF SERBIA** Ruler from about 1233 to 1242, usurping the throne by deposing his brother, Stephen Radaslav (ruled c. 1228–1233). Stephen was married to the daughter of the Bulgar king Asen II. See also SERBIA.

**STOCKHOLM** City in Sweden, situated on Lake Malaren (Mälaren) on the Baltic Sea and the chief city of the country. According to tradition, probably correct, and as recorded by Eric's chronicle, Stockholm was founded by Birger Jarl, the first mention of this made in 1252. Its rapid economic rise owing to the treaty signed by Birger Jarl with the traders and merchants of Lübeck (c. 1250) gave them extensive privileges in Sweden and brought Stockholm into the mercantile sphere of the Hanseatic League. See also SWEDEN.

**STRASBOURG** Also Strasburg or Strassburg, a city in eastern France, in the Alsace region, the capital of the modern department of Bas-Rhin. Originally a Celtic settlement, it served as a Roman garrison called Strateburgum, from which the present name is derived. It had a bishopric by the fourth century. The Huns sacked the city in the fifth century, and it was later captured by the Franks. In 842 the city was the site of the STRASBOURG OATH. While the bishops there wielded considerable power, they drew opposition from the citizenry, culminating in the designation of Strasbourg as a free imperial city. It was here that German literature flowered during the Middle Ages, the writer Gottfried von Strassburg one of the city's illustrious men. Gutenberg may have invented the printing press in Strasbourg.

**STRASBOURG OATH** The pledge taken in 842 by Charles II the Bald, king of the West Franks, and Louis I the German, king of the East Franks, called in French the Serment de Strasbourg. The oath confirmed their alliance against their brother, Lothair I. Charles made his pledge in Old French, and Louis made his in Old German, thus defining the division of the Carolingian empire as French and German spheres respectively. A surviving text of the oath is the oldest written document in Old French.

**STRONGBOW** See PEMBROKE, RICHARD DE CLARE, EARL OF.

**STURLUSSON, SNORRI** See SNORRI STURLUSON.

**STUDIUM GENERALE** See Glossary.

**STYRIA** Called in German Steiermark, a province in southeasten and central Austria, divided into Lower and Upper Styria, originally attached to the Celtic kingdom of Noricum and then to the Roman Empire. Styria was conquered by migrating Germanic tribes, settled by the Avars in the sixth century and the Slavs in the seventh. A territory of Bavaria in the eighth century, it was later incorporated into the Frankish empire and, in 1180, became the duchy of Styria (or Steiermark). From 1192 to 1246 it belonged to the Babenbergs of Austria and was ceded nearly intact to the Habsburgs in 1276, designated a crown land in 1282.

**SUBIACO** Town situated 40 miles to the east of Rome, in Italy, renowned during the Middle Ages as the place to which Saint Benedict of Nursia retired about 494 as a hermit. Benedict founded 12 monasteries in the region before leaving for Monte Cassino, and Subiaco was the cradle of the Benedictine order. A church there built in honor of Saint Scholastica, the sister of Benedict (981), was destroyed in an earthquake in 1282. It was rebuilt in the Gothic style. The German monks Arnold Pannartz and Conrad Schweinheim established the first Italian printing press in Subiaco in 1464. The site was also associated with the legends of Saint Francis of Assisi. See also BENEDICTINES; BENEDICT OF NURSIA, SAINT.

**SUBINFEUDATION** See FEUDALISM.

**SUFFOLK, EARLS AND DUKES OF** An English title first granted in 1337 by King Edward III (1327–1377) and held throughout the 15th century by the de la Pole family. The first de la Pole to receive the title was Michael, first earl of Suffolk (d. 1389), a trusted adviser of King Richard II (1377–1399) and his chancellor. His grandson was William de la Pole, fourth earl and first duke of Suffolk (1396–1450), who held extensive power under King Henry VI (1422–1461), arranging his marriage and holding the rank of general in the closing years of the Hundred Years' War. Charged with treason by his enemies for his role in the final English defeat in that war, he was banished by Henry in order to save his life, but in 1450 he was murdered despite this precaution. His son, John de la Pole, second duke of Suffolk (1442–1491), married the sister of Edward IV.

**SUFISM** A mystical Islamic philosophy arising in the late 10th and early 11th centuries, becoming immensely popular in Persia. It began as a counterreaction on the part of Muslim ascetics to what they perceived to be a worldly attitude adopted by many in the Islamic world. Sufis adhered to a belief in a personal union with God. Their most respected theologian was al-Ghazali, who attempted to advance a union of Sufism with Sunni theology, while retaining Sufi religious orthodoxy. A radical view was advocated by Ibn al-Arabi, a Spanish mystic who argued that the Sufi saint was superior to the Prophet because a saint received knowledge directly from God, whereas the Prophet was given knowledge by an angel. This conflict was resolved in Sufi thought through the concept of spiritual states. Sufism found rich expression in symbolic Persian poetry in the works of such writers as Ferid el-Din Attar, Jami, Hafiz and Omar Khayyam. See also ISLAM.

**SUGER** (c. 1081–1151) Abbot of Saint-Denis in Paris, royal adviser and instrumental in the introduction of the Gothic architectural style to western Europe. Of humble origin, he studied at Saint-Denis with the future King Louis

Abbot Suger's chalice

VI (1108–1037), becoming a monk and in 1106 secretary to the abbot. By 1118 he was in the service of Louis VI, sent to the court of Pope Gelasius II (1118–1119) and later to the court of Pope Calixtus II (1119–1124). In 1122 he returned to France and was appointed abbot of Saint-Denis, striving from 1127 to 1137 to bring reform and reorganization to the monastic administration, about which he wrote in *Liber de rebus in administratione sua gestis.* As chancellor to Louis VI and Louis VII (1137–1180), Suger advised against the latter's participation in the Second Crusade but acted as regent during the king's absence, improving taxation methods and suppressing a revolt of the nobles. On the return of Louis in 1149, Suger was called "Father of the Country." In addition to his many political and religious achievements, he was equally respected for his efforts in restoring the church at Saint-Denis, the first building to reflect the principles of Gothic architecture. See also GOTHIC ART AND ARCHITECTURE.

**SULAIMAN SHAH** Ruler of the Seljuks of Iraq from 1159 to 1161. See also SELJUK TURKS.

**SULAIMAN SHAH I** Ruler of the Seljuks of Rum from 1077 to 1086. See also SELJUK TURKS.

**SULAIMAN SHAH II** Ruler of the Seljuks of Rum from 1196 to 1203. See also SELJUK TURKS.

**SULAYMAN (1)** (d. 717) Umayyad ruler, reigning from 715 to 717. During his rule another attack on Constantinople was defeated, and Muslim forces crossed the Pyrenees into southern France. See also UMAYYAD CALIPHATE.

**SULAYMAN (2)** Caliph of Córdoba in 1009 and again from 1013 to 1016, a grandson of Abd al-Rahman III, installed at Córdoba by the Berbers allied with the Castilians, who overthrew Muhammad II and plundered the city. Soon afterward, however, Muhammad returned supported by Count Ramon Borrell I of Barcelona, defeating the Berbers and entering Córdoba in triumph. In 1013 Sulayman was reinstated with Berber support, reigning until his execution by Ali ibn Hammud. See also CÓRDOBA, EMIRATE OF.

**SULEIMAN** (d. 1410) Ottoman ruler from 1402 to 1410, sharing power with his brothers and in conflict with them. The son of Bayazid I (d. 1402), he inherited a portion of the Ottoman territories but was overthrown in 1410 by his brother, Musa, who proceeded to massacre Suleiman's followers. See also OTTOMAN EMPIRE.

**SUMMA THEOLOGICA** See THOMAS AQUINAS, SAINT.

**SUNNI** Or Sunnites, those Muslims adhering to the *sunnah (sunna),* the traditions concerning the life, sayings and deeds of the Prophet. These traditions were the basis for Islamic social and legal practices and, after their organization by the scholar Shafi'i (767–820), became second only to the Koran in legal importance. Sunni Muslims were the majority in the Islamic world and predominated in Arabia, Asia Minor and Africa. They belonged to no sects and held the power of Allah above all others. Sunni rulers often persecuted unorthodox Muslims who adhered to the Shiah. See also ABBASID CALIPHATE; ASSASSINS, ORDER OF; CÓRDOBA, EMIRATE OF; FATIMID CALIPHATE, SUFISM; UMAYYAD CALIPHATE.

**SUSA, HENRY** (c. 1295–1366) Also Henry Suso, celebrated German mystic, born Heinrich von Berg in Swabia (probably at Constance), who joined the Dominican order and became a student of Meister Eckhart from about 1324 to 1328. In defense of his teacher he wrote *Little Book of Truth* (1327) and in 1328 composed what has been considered his masterpiece, the *Little Book of Eternal Wisdom,* which became the most widely read religious work until the appearance of Thomas à Kempis's *Imitation of Christ.* Susa was honored as a spiritual leader, especially among the Dominicans and the Friends of God *(Gottesfreunde).* See also MYSTICISM.

**SUSSEX, KINGDOM OF** Realm in Anglo-Saxon England, situated on the English Channel and comprising roughly the region of the county of Sussex. According to tradition, the kingdom was founded by the Saxons under Aelle (Aella), who landed there in 477 and defeated the indigenous Britons. Bede mentioned that Aelle ruled as king over the lands south of the Humber, but few details of the period have survived. The historical records begin in the late seventh century, when Bishop Wilfrid of York spent the years 681–686 converting the people. The kingdom survived but fell to the control of Offa of Mercia (ruled 757–796), which established a period of Mercian supremacy until Sussex was claimed by King Egbert of Wessex in 825. Subsequently an earldom, Sussex was witness to the invasion of William I the Conqueror in 1066.

**SUTTON HOO** Site near Woodbridge, Suffolk, England, in which an early grave was discovered in 1939, a possible cenotaph of an Anglo-Saxon king containing a burial ship, fully equipped, for the afterlife. The Sutton Hoo find was of considerable value in revealing details of Anglo-Saxon wealth and culture, as well as the foreign contacts of the local monarchs. Although no body was found in the ship, the site contained gold-mounted weapons, armor, buttons, a purse lid with seven ornamented plaques, a silverware dish (with the stamp of the Byzantine emperor Anastasius I, 399–401), silver cups, bowls, spoons and a Near Eastern bronze bowl. The date of the ship has been placed in the early seventh century (probably in the first quarter), owing to Frankish coins also found there. The beauty and richness of the remains indicate a high level of culture for the Anglo-Saxon rulers, while the site of this burial ship, rare in England, has led to some speculation that there may have been an unsuspected Swedish origin or connection for the ruling line of East Anglia.

**SVATOPLUK, PRINCE OF MORAVIA** See MORAVIA.

**SVEIN** King of Norway from 1028 to 1035, the son of Canute the Great, owing his throne to his father, who sent

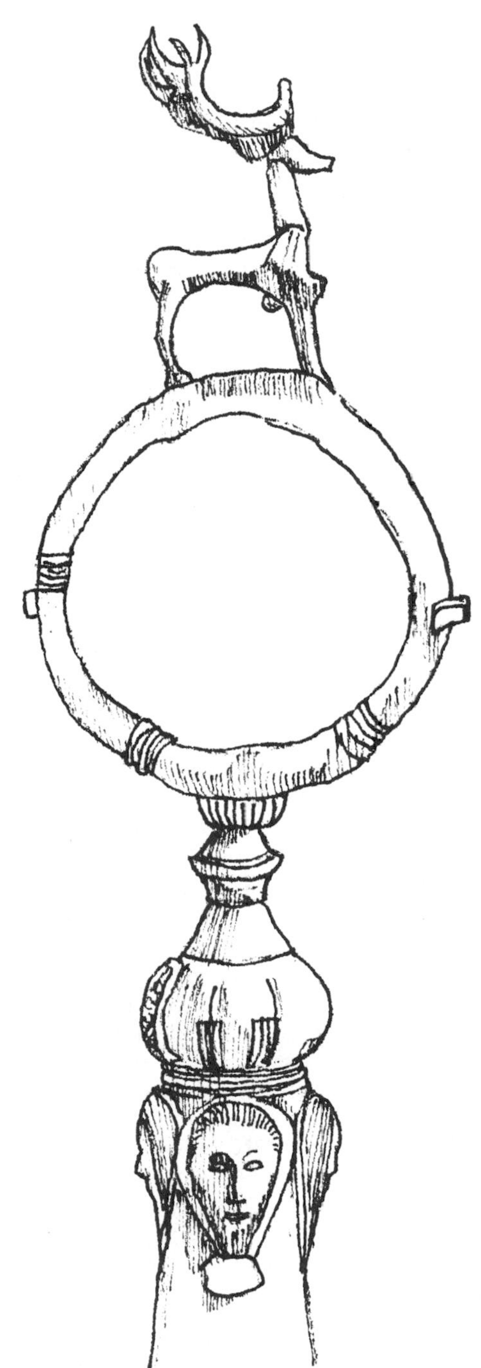

Sutton Hoo ceremonial scepter

him to reign over the country with his mother, Aegilfu. His time in power was difficult for the Norwegians, for he was both arbitrary and demanding. In 1035 he was driven from Norway with his mother by supporters of Magnus I the Good, son of King Olaf II (ruled 1015–1030), who had died in 1030 defending the throne. See also NORWAY.

**SVEN I FORKBEARD** (d. 1014) King of Denmark from 985 to 1014, the son of King Harald Bluetooth (c. 935–985) and father of Canute II (1018–1035) the Great, king of Denmark and England. Sven attacked Norway shortly after his accession but was defeated by King Haakon the Great. He then sailed with the Norwegian prince Olaf (I) Tryggvason in 994 to England, accepting from King Aethelred II the Unready a large payment to cease such raids. Soon after this, Sven's relations with Olaf, now king, deteriorated, and about 1000 Sven allied himself with the Swedes and Eric, earl of Lade, defeating Olaf and becoming the virtual master of Norway. He strengthened the North Sea empire and raided England between 1003 and 1004, returning once again in 1013, crushing all opposition, driving Aethelred into exile and winning recognition of his supremacy. Sven died the following year, but his empire endured until 1042. See also DANEGELD; DENMARK.

**SVEN II ESTRIDSON** (d. 1074) King of Denmark from 1047 to 1074, the founder of the Estrith dynasty of Danish kings, the son of a Danish chief, Ulf, and Estrid, sister of King Canute II the Great, fleeing to Sweden after the murder of his father in 1027 at Canute's order. On the accession, by agreement, of Magnus I Olafsson, king of Norway, as the Danish monarch in 1042, Sven was appointed viceroy. Proclaimed king in 1043 by the Danish magnates, who preferred him to Magnus, Sven was confronted by war with his Norwegian rival and then with the Norwegian successor, Harald III Sigurdsson (ruled 1045–1066). Years of conflict ended only in 1064, with joint recognition of each other's right to reign, a peace brought about by Harald's need to prepare for his invasion of England. Sven's power was increased with Harald's death in 1066, and he then launched an assault on England in 1069 that ended with a favorable treaty with William I the Conqueror (1066–1087). Sven also helped to establish the independence of the Danish church from English ecclesiastical authority and that of the archbishop of Bremen. See also DENMARK.

**SVERKER THE ELDER** (d. 1155) King of Sweden from c. 1135 to 1156, a nobleman from East Gotland (Gothland) who assured his claim to the throne by marrying the widow of a former king. A firm adherent of Christianity, he established monasteries and lived in a Cistercian monastery at Alvastra that he had built. He was killed there. See also SWEDEN.

**SVERKER II CHARLESSON** (d. 1218) King of Sweden from 1196 to 1208, also called Sverker the Younger, the son of King Charles VII Sverkersson (c. 1160–1167). He adhered to a concilatory policy with respect to the church in Denmark but failed to strengthen his position politically. In 1208 he was driven into exile by Eric (X) Canutesson, returning 10 years later to reclaim the throne and dying in battle. See also SWEDEN.

**SVERRE** (d. 1202) King of Norway from 1177 to 1202, although he was not crowned until 1184. Sverre was raised in the Faeroe Islands and studied with Bishop Hroi, who ordained him. His mother, Gunhild, arrived in his 24th year to tell him that he was the son of King Sigurd III the Mouth (d. 1155). Believing he had a better claim to the throne than Magnus V (1162–1184), he set out for Norway and became leader of the Birchlegs political faction in

1177. Proclaimed king that same year, he achieved his first victory over Magnus in 1179. On the death of Magnus in 1184, at the hands of Sverre's troops, Sverre was sole ruler. Even though he had been ordained a priest, he was a firm believer in the supremacy of the Crown over the church and strove to curb the powers of the archbishop of Trondheim. His eventual excommunication led to a war with the episcopacy called the Crosier War. The unrest caused by this conflict continued even after Sverre's death. He was the author of "Speech against the Bishops," an argument for secular authority over the church. See also NORWAY.

**SVYATOSLAV** (d. 972) Grand prince of Kiev from 845 to 972, who was responsible for bringing Kievan Russia to its glory. The son of Grand Prince Igor and Saint Olga, he spent most of his reign in wars of expansion, leaving the domestic affairs of state to his mother until her death in 969. He crushed the empire of the Khazars (c. 963–965), defeated the Ossetians and Circassians in the northern Caucasus and fought both the Balkan and Volga Bulgars, the Balkan group at the request of the Byzantines. They, in turn, became alarmed by his ambitions in the Danube region and in 971 campaigned against him. Svyatoslav was killed the following year in an ambush by the Petchenegs. See also KIEV.

**SWABIA** Called in German Schwaben, a region in southwestern Germany comprising southwestern Bavaria, southern Württemberg, Hohenzollern and southern Baden, including the Swabian and Jura Mountains and the Black Forest. The name Swabia was derived from the Germanic people called Suebi (Sueves), who occupied the region in the third century, with the Alemanni, and it was called Alemannia until the 11th century. Conquered by the Franks around 500, the region was governed by the Frankish Lex Alemannorum. Christianity was introduced in the seventh century, and conversions took place encouraged by the Celtic missionaries there.

Eventually under the ecclesiastical jurisdiction of Mainz, Swabia erected the abbeys of Saint Gall and Reichenau and included the episcopal sees of Augsburg, Basel and Constance in its domain. One of the five duchies of the early kingdom of the East Franks (Germany), it was given to Frederick I Hohenstaufen in 1079 and became a possession of that dynasty until the extinction of the Hohenstaufen male line in 1268. Owned for a time by the son of the German king Rudolf of Habsburg, Rudolf II of Austria, on the death of his son (1313) the ducal title expired. Swabian cities found it politically and militarily useful to form leagues, the first of which was a union of 22 cities established in 1321, including Ulm and Augsburg. It was defeated in 1372 by a counterleague of Swabian knights, reorganized in 1376 (with 14 cities), but was again defeated in 1388. The most formidable and successful Swabian League was created in 1488 and included 26 members, playing a leading role in German affairs until the 16th century. See also GERMANY; HOLY ROMAN EMPIRE.

**SWEDEN** Kingdom in eastern Scandinavia, bordered by Norway, Denmark and Finland and the Baltic Sea to the south. Most of the Swedes were descendants of Germanic tribes that settled in the region, probably in the Neolithic period. The first identifiable state in Sweden was the kingdom of the Svear in the Mälaren region, around Uppsala. Its inhabitants extended their control southward, giving their name to the entire country and establishing communities along the Baltic that involved them in the Viking raids. They were known in Russia as Varangians. Christianity was introduced in 829 by Saint Ansgar, but it was only in the reign of King Olaf Skötkonung that the crown accepted the rite of baptism and actual steps were taken to reduce pagan influence. King Eric IX (ruled c. 1155–1160) led a crusade into Finland but was killed in 1160, becoming the patron saint of Sweden. Eric XI Ericsson (ruled 1234–1250) was the last ruler of the dynasty of Saint Eric, true power resting in the hands of his brother-in-law, Birger Jarl. Jarl's son, Waldemar (Valdemar), became king in 1250, founding the Falkung dynasty. Continued political difficulties culminated in the Kalmar Union, in which all of Scandinavia was united. In 1448, however, the Swedish magnates elected Karl Knutson, who reigned as Charles VIII until 1470. His nephew, Sten Sture the Elder, became regent, initiating a series of regencies enduring until the 16th century.

**SWINTHILA** (d. after 631) King of the Visigoths from 620 to 621, known as the "Father of the Poor" for his care of the Gothic freeholders, especially in the face of opposition by the Visigothic nobility. Swinthila was a count and respected general who was chosen successor to Reccared (d. 620), owing to his reputation as a soldier. He was never supported by the nobles or the church, and his overthrow was inevitable, coming in 631 at the hands of Sisinand, governor in Septimania. Swinthila was allowed to retire to a monastery. His chief military achievement was the capture of the last Byzantine stronghold in Spain in 623. See also VISIGOTHS.

**SWISS CONFEDERATION** See SWITZERLAND.

**SWITZERLAND** Country situated between France, Germany, Austria and Italy, dominated by the Alps and a number of large lakes, including Geneva, Constance, Neuchâtel, Zurich and Lucerne. The region of Switzerland was called Helvetia for a long time, chiefly because of the powerful Helvetii, a Celtic people who settled there. They were subdued in 58 B.C. by Julius Caesar, marking the beginning of Roman occupation, which lasted until the fourth and fifth centuries, when Germans, particularly the Alemanni and Burgundians, overran the region. The Franks encroached in the sixth and seventh centuries, and Carolingian rule began in the eighth. Henceforth the region was associated with the Holy Roman Empire, but the decline of imperial authority allowed several large feudal families to exert their influence. Among these were the Zähringers and the Habsburgs in the east and the House of Savoy in the west. It was resistance to the Habsburgs, however, that led to the formation of the Swiss independent state. The towns, seeing that the Habsburgs intended to consolidate their holdings, resisted the loss of their privileges, and a movement began in Schwyz, Uri and

Unterwalden to oppose the family. Using the Great Interregnum in the Holy Roman Empire (1250–1273) to strengthen their alliance, the people signed a treaty in August 1291, the perpetual alliance called the Swiss Confederation.

A crucial test of the Swiss Confederation came in 1315 when the forces of Uri, Schwyz and Unterwalden defeated a larger Habsburg army at the Battle of Morgarten. Other Swiss communities soon joined, such as Bern, Zurich and Lucerne, and virtual independence was won from the Habsburg through victories at Sempach (1386) and Näfels (1388). Having achieved self-determination, the Swiss used their military prowess to campaign against the Habsburgs, the House of Savoy, Milan, King Francis I of France and Burgundy, their prestige reaching a climax with triumphs over Charles the Bold of Burgundy and in the Italian wars. Swiss mercenaries were highly prized, but the Swiss defeat at Marignano in 1515 resulted in a policy of political neutrality.

**SYAGRIUS** (d. c. 486) Gallo-Roman general who ruled a district of Roman Gaul around Soissons (Suessiones) from 463 to 486, in the name of the Roman emperors of the West, who were toppled in 476. He was probably the son of the patrician Aegistius, taking that title for himself, although the Franks called him king of the Romans. His territory was invaded in 486 by the Franks led by Clovis, who defeated him and sent him fleeing to Alaric, king of the Visigoths. Alaric handed Syagrius over to Clovis, who executed him. See also FRANCE.

**SYLVESTER II** (c. 945–1003) Pope from 999 to 1003, whose reputation as one of the most learned figures of the age was earned before his election to the Holy See. Born Gerbert of Aurillac, in Auvergne, he was educated at the Benedictine monastery of Aurillac and later at Vic in Spain. Teaching at Reims, he won notice as a mathematician. Emperor Otto I (962–973), impressed, engaged him as a tutor for his son. Otto II (973–983) appointed him abbot of Babbio, and on the advice of Emperor Otto III (996–1002) he was elected pope in 999. As Sylvester II he was active in attempting to curb simony and clerical marriages and strengthened the church in Poland and Hungary, sending the crown of Hungary to King Stephen I in 1000. Sylvester was the first of the French to be elected pope. He was a scholar as well as a statesman and promoted learning, utilizing Arabic numerals and dialectical method in reasoning. He was esteemed for his knowledge of astronomy, Latin, mathematics and science, much of which was purportedly acquired through the use of magic.

**SYLVESTER III** (d. c. 1063) Pope during 1045, considered by some scholars to have been an antipope. He was bishop of Sabina at the time of his election, replacing the deposed Pope Benedict IX (1032–1044; 1045; 1047–1048) in January. In April Benedict returned, ousted Sylvester and sold the papacy to Gregory VI (1045–1046). Sylvester resigned but apparently reclaimed the throne. He was deposed by the Synod of Sutri (December 1046). See ANTIPOPES.

**SYLVESTER IV** Antipope from 1105 to 1111, elected during the Investiture Controversy against Pope Paschal II (1099–1118). He had little influence.

**SYMEON** (d. 927) King of the Bulgars from 893 to 927, much of his reign spent at war with the Byzantine Empire. He was nonetheless a patron of culture, his court attracting a brilliant intellectual circle. Symeon built churches and palaces, supported artisans and encouraged monasteries, especially in his new capital at Preslav. His contest with the Byzantines, however, defined his reign, lasting for many years. From 894 to 897 he fought not only the Byzantines but their Magyar allies, first defeating the Magyars with the support of the Petchenegs, then routing the Byzantine army in 897. In the peace that followed he received tribute. Another war began in 913, but the resulting peace was repudiated at Constantinople, so hostilities continued until 927. Symeon sacked Thrace and Greece, crushed another Byzantine force in 917 but failed to take Constantinople. He died of a stroke on the way there with his troops. See also BULGARIA.

**SYMMACHUS, SAINT** (d. 514) Pope from 498 to 514, a Christian convert from Sardinia, successor to Anastasius II (496–498). He was chosen as a counterforce to the Byzantine faction in Rome and his rival, Laurentius. A schism developed that was ended by the Ostrogothic king Theodoric (493–526), who confirmed Symmachus. The Laurentian forces, however, accused Symmachus of simony, of causing irregularities in the calendar and of fornication, forcing Theodoric to summon a council in 501, which freed him of all charges. Laurentius was recalled and Symmachus restricted to Saint Peter's for a number of years, but in 506–507 Theodoric subdued the Laurentian forces. Symmachus was embroiled in the complex Acacian Schism (484–519) between Rome and Constantinople, expelled the Manichaeans and burned their books. He also confirmed the primatial rites of Arles over the Gallican and Spanish churches and gave aid to the poor.

**SYRIA** An extensive region lying between Lebanon, Turkey, Iraq and Jordan with an ancient historical background, including its occupation by Rome. In time the region was controlled by the Eastern Empire, caught in the conflict between the Byzantines and the Sassanid Persians. Syria was first invaded in 633, becoming a Muslim territory in 640. The period of the Umayyad caliphate in Syria (661–750) was one of considerable prosperity and prestige. Damascus, its capital, was the seat of the caliphs and the political heart of the Islamic world. The Syrians administered the caliphate, and the Hellenic culture, so pervasive in the region, left its stamp on Umayyad institutions. Christian and Jewish communities, while excluded from the rights of Muslims, were granted a high degree of tolerance and religious freedom. They were also permitted the right to maintain their own customs and laws, although required to make payment of a poll tax.

The fall of the Umayyads and the rise of the Abbasids, who moved their capital to Baghdad, adopting an Eastern orientation, brought changes. The arrival of the Seljuk

Turks and the creation of a Syrian Seljuk state brought additional fragmentation, as the Syrian Seljuk line was divided into two branches, at Damascus and Aleppo. Additional problems were introduced by the Crusaders, who arrived in the First Crusade (1096–1099), receiving support from the local Christians. The Crusaders established themselves along the Syrian coast and in parts of the interior, promoting trade between Syria and the merchants of Pisa, Genoa and other maritime states. Conflict raged as the Crusaders and Muslims vied for supremacy, the forces of Islam proving ultimately victorious. The last Christian fortress in the region, at Acre, fell in 1291.

The growing Egyptian influence in Syria, so clear under Saladin (d. 1193) and his Ayyubid dynasty, led to domination by the Mamluks, who exiled the last of the Christians and brought Syria into their extensive empire. Druze and Shiite rebellions were crushed by the Mamluks, and in 1401 both Damascus and Aleppo were sacked by Tamerlane, who sent all captured artisans to his capital at Samarkand. Economic deterioration continued throughout the 15th century, so that in 1516–1517 the already weakened region was subdued easily by the Ottoman Turks. See also CRUSADER STATES; CRUSADES; ISLAM; UMAYYAD CALIPHATE.

# T

**AL-TABARI** (839–923) Called fully Abu Ja'far Muhammad ibn Jarir Tabari, an esteemed historian and commentator on the Koran. Born in Tabaristan, Iran, he studied in Syria, Iraq and Egypt, settling in Baghdad, where he became the the first important Muslim historian. He wrote the influential *History of Prophets and Kings (Tarikh al-rasul wa al-muluk)* but also made lasting contributions through his commentaries on the Koran and his condensation of earlier historical and exegetical writings by Islamic scholars.

**TABORITES** The radical element among the Hussites, opposed to the more moderate Utraquists, deriving their name from that of their fortress south of Prague and from the biblical Mount Tabor. The Taborites adhered to the belief that the Bible was the principal source of faith and received the Eucharist under both species, bread and wine, while denying the Real Presence and rejecting many rites. Under the leadership of Jan Zizka they were a feared and dangerous military force, triumphing in the Hussite Wars but earning such widespread hatred that, refusing to accept the Compactata of Prague (1434), they were defeated by the Utraquists and Catholics at the Battle of Lipany. The fortress of Tabor itself was not captured until 1452. See also BOHEMIA; HUSSITE WARS.

**TAHIRIDS** Islamic dynasty of Khorasan that endured from 821 to 872, founded by Tahir ibn al-Husayn. A former Persian slave of the caliph al-Mamun, he became a trusted general of the caliphate, receiving as a reward territory in northeastern Persia. The Tahirids gave nominal loyalty to the caliphs but exercised independence in their own affairs, expansion reaching the Indian frontiers and into Transoxiana. See also ABBASID CALIPHATE.

**AL-TAI** Abbasid caliph from 974 to 991. See also ABBASID CALIPHATE.

**TALIESIN** Semilegendary Welsh poet, considered a distinguished bard of sixth-century Wales. The *Book of Taliesin,* written about seven centuries later, contained his verses, 12 of which were determined by scholars to be authentic. He was mentioned in the *Historia Britonum* by Nennius as composing poetry during the period of war with the Northumbrians and their king, Ida (547–559).

**TAMERLANE** (1336–1405) More accurately Timur (also Timur Leng, Timur Lank or Timur the Lame), one of the great conquerors in world history. His brief empire extended from the Euphrates to the Jaxartes and Indus Rivers. His renown was derived as much from his cruelty as from his cultural achievements. Born near Samarkand, he was of Turkic descent but was not apparently of Mongol blood, although he later claimed to be a descendant of Genghis Khan. He emerged as the leader of a small force of nomadic warriors, successful in acquiring lands around Samarkand until all Transoxiana was under his control (c. 1370). He then embarked on a series of campaigns against India (including the capture of Delhi), Persia, southern Russia, Syria and Anatolia. His troops caused desolation and suffering and brought political upheaval in their wake. The Golden Horde was routed in Russia, a defeat that had lasting ramifications for Russian history. In 1402, he also crushed the Ottoman Turks at the Battle of Angora (Ankara), capturing Sultan Bayazid I, thereby delaying the fall of Constantinople for nearly half a century.

Returning to Transoxiana in 1404, Tamerlane celebrated his triumph and made plans for a massive campaign against China. He died on his way to the East, however, of a fever. His empire did not long survive him in the West, enduring for a century in Central Asia. While he rarely spent much time at Samarkand, Tamerlane attempted to make it the most beautiful city in Asia. Captured artisans from Syria and from other regions were brought to the city to transform its architecture and decorative details. The emperor also encouraged learning, the arts and sciences, as a patron of scholars. A dynastic successor to Tamerlane founded the Moghul dynasty in India. Tamerlane's name was derived from injuries he had received, probably while on a sheep-raiding expedition, damage leaving him unable to bend his right knee or lift his right arm. See also MONGOLS.

**TAMMAM, ABU** See ABU TAMMAM.

**TANCRED** (d. 1112) Norman Crusader and a leader of the First Crusade (1096–1099). A nobleman of Taranto, Tancred joined his uncle Bohemond of Taranto on crusade, playing a role in the capture of Tarsus and Jerusalem, fighting in several battles and proving instrumental in the acquisition of Antioch. After the fall of Jerusalem in 1099, Tancred was named prince of Galilee, serving as regent for the principality of Antioch for Bohemond from 1101 to 1103, and after 1108, and was regent of Edessa from 1104 to 1108. As the most powerful of the Crusader knights in Syria, he refused to give homage to Emperor Alexius I and was engaged in conflicts with both the Byzantines and the Seljuk Turks. See also CRUSADER STATES; CRUSADES.

**TANCRED OF LECCE** (d. 1194) King of Sicily from 1190 to 1194, an illegitimate son of Duke Roger of Apulia, exiled for participation in several failed coups against his uncle, William I of Sicily. Eventually returning, he became a trusted lieutenant of William II, commanding Sicilian attacks on Alexandria and Constantinople. In 1189, after the death of William II, Tancred obtained the support of the papacy and the people to acquire the throne for himself and was crowned in 1190. His reign was troubled by the arrival of the English king Richard I the Lion-Hearted (1189–1199) and King Philip II Augustus (1180–1223) of France on their way to the Third Crusade. Richard's presence caused unrest and he sacked Messina. Tancred was then faced with an attempt by Emperor Henry VI to claim Sicily through his wife, Constance, daughter of Roger II of Sicily. Tancred died just before Henry launched another campaign. See also SICILY.

**TANNENBERG, BATTLE OF** See TEUTONIC KNIGHTS.

**TANNHÄUSER** (d. c. 1270) Well-known minnesinger, respected as a lyric poet and noted as a world traveler. He probably took part in the Crusade of 1228–1229 and had the patronage of many nobles. Few other details of his life survive, although he was immortalized in legend. Among his works were dances, love songs and six surviving lyric lays *(leiche).*

**TARANTO** Seaport in southern Italy, major city of Taranto province in the region of Apulia, called by the Romans Tarentum. From the 6th to the 10th century the city changed hands repeatedly, from the Goths to the Byzantines, to the Lombards, then reverting to the Byzantines. Destroyed by Saracens in 927, Taranto was rebuilt in 967 by the Byzantine emperor Nicephorus II. In 1063 it fell to the Normans under Robert Guiscard and later became part of the Kingdom of Naples. During the Crusades, Taranto was a crucial point of departure for Crusader armies. See also NAPLES, KINGDOM OF.

**TATARS** See MONGOLS.

**TAULER, JOHANNES** (c. 1300–1361) German mystic and Dominican who was also one of the Rhineland mystics including Henry Susa and Meister Eckhart. After joining the Order of Preachers at Strasbourg in 1315, he was influenced by Susa and Ekhart, and during his time at Basel (1338–1343) he developed a close association with the *Gottesfreunde,* the "Friends of God." A preacher of some note, he was also lauded for his care of the victims of the Black Death in 1348. Two letters and several of his sermons, reportedly genuine, have survived, although a number of other, dubious works have been attributed to him. His mystical teachings were based on Thomist doctrines, and they were far more practical than those of Ekhart. Martin Luther valued Tauler's sermons. See also MYSTICISM.

**TEIA** (d. 553) King of the Ostrogoths from 552 to 553, the last Ostrogothic king in Italy. Formerly a general in King Totila's army, he was designated his successor when Totila died in the war with the Byzantines led by the general Narses. Faced with a difficult strategic position, Teia retreated to Pavia and tried in vain to continue the war. Eventually cornered in Campania, near Naples, he fought a two-day battle with the Byzantines and was killed leading his troops into the final fray. See also OSTROGOTHS.

**TELERIG** King of the Bulgars from about 770 to 777, reigning during a period of political turmoil. See also BULGARIA.

**TELETZ** King of the Bulgars from 762 to 764. See also BULGARIA.

**TELL, WILLIAM** Legendary Swiss hero whose actual existence has been debated. Supposedly a peasant from Bürglen who lived during the late 13th or early 14th century, he refused to pay homage to Gessler, the Austrian governor of Altdorf, and as punishment was forced to shoot an apple from the head of his small son. Arrested, nevertheless, for threatening Gessler, he was taken by boat to the governor's castle on Lake Lucerne but escaped on the way during a storm. He later was reported to have killed Gessler in an ambush, which was one of the signals for the rebellion of the Swiss against Austrian rule. See also SWITZERLAND.

**TEMPLARS** Also called the Knights Templars, the Poor Knights of Christ or Knights of the Temple of Solomon, one of the militarily important chivalric orders of the Middle Ages. The Templars were formed at the time of the

Imprisonment of the Templars

Crusades, with the purpose of protecting the pilgrims who were traveling to the Holy Land, first banding together in late 1119 or early 1120, under the French knight Hugh de Payens. The name of the organization was derived from the quarters given them in Jerusalem by King Baldwin II, a part of the royal palace supposedly near the site of Solomon's temple.

Starting with a small group, the Templars increased in number and in celebrity, distinguishing themselves through courageous actions and adopting the rule of the Augustinian Canons, taking vows of chastity and poverty. With a rise in their membership and reputation, they emerged as a formidable military force, winning fame for their dashing exploits and for their protection of pilgrims. They held Acre until 1291, when it fell to the Mamluks, retiring to Cyprus. The knights, however, had amassed vast wealth through gifts of land and money throughout Europe and took the unfortunate step of adopting strict codes of secrecy to avoid intrusions into their activities. Having aroused the fear and jealousy of King Philip IV the Fair of France (1285–1314), the Templars were accused of heresy and assorted crimes, including devil worship (an idol called Baphomet) and sodomy. Using his influence, Philip had Pope Clement V (1305–1314) suppress the order in 1312, its grand master, Jacques de Molay, burned at the stake. Its members were distinguished by their white capes, adorned with an eight-pointed red cross. See also MILITARY ORDERS.

**TEMPLE, KNIGHTS OF THE** See TEMPLARS.

**TERVEL** King of the Bulgars from 701 to 718, responsible for diplomatic triumphs that brought his people to political prominence. In 705 he supported the exiled Justinian II in reclaiming the throne of the Byzantine Empire, and in 717–718 he sent vital Bulgar troops to bolster the Byzantine forces enduring a siege of Constantinople by the Arabs, helping to overcome the Muslim threat. See also BULGARIA.

**TEUTONIC KNIGHTS** Also called the German Order, in Latin the Ordo Domus Sanctae Mariae Teutonicorum, the German Order of the Hospital of Saint Mary, one of the prominent and victorious military orders in Europe that dominated Prussia and the Baltic coast. The Teutonic Order was founded during the Crusades in 1190, at Acre, as a charitable organization, associated with a German hospital and financed by the merchants of Lübeck and Bremen. Composed of knights, priests and lay brothers, it devoted its earliest attentions to the conflict with the Saracens in Syria and the Holy Land, receiving approval as a military religious force in 1199 from Pope Innocent III (1198–1216). Under grand master Hermann von Salza (held office from 1210 to 1239) the knights transferred their activities to eastern Europe, where they hoped to encourage the acceptance of Christianity.

The order supported King Andrew II of Hungary against the Cumans but were expelled in 1225, accepting an invitation from the Polish duke Conrad of Mazovia to campaign in Prussia, to relieve the threat posed by the indigenous pagan population. With utter ruthlessness the knights crushed the Prussians, enforcing Christianization and ultimately establishing control over the region, not sparing the native populations. German immigration was promoted, and the order, despite giving one third of its gains to the church, forged a formidable state, with fortresses, trading rights and vassals recruited from Germany and the Polish nobility, as well as extensive land grants. An important step was taken in 1263 when the pope granted permission for the knights to participate in trade and commerce. By 1309, based at Marienburg in Prussia, they were masters of a feudal regime that extended from the Baltic coasts of Estonia and Livonia to Pomerania.

The ambitions of the Teutonic Knights were enhanced by the Livonian Knights, a branch of the order in Livonia and Estonia. Their expansion aroused the hatred of the Poles and Lithuanians, and their presence contributed to the union of Poland with Lithuania in 1386. Teutonic hostility toward Lithuania continued, despite the nation's conversion to Christianity, and a war resulting in the crushing defeat of the knights in 1410 took place at the Battle of Tannenberg (Grünwald), in which the armed might of the order was shattered. Territorial and political losses by the Poles ensued throughout the 15th century, culminating in a war that lasted from 1454 to 1466, ending with the Treaty of Thorn (Torun). By its terms the knights retained only East Prussia, accepting that region as a vassal to Poland. Polish members were admitted to the order, and its headquarters was transferred to Königsburg. See also CRUSADES; LITHUANIA; LIVONIA; MARIENBURG; MILITARY ORDERS; NEVSKY, ALEXANDER; POLAND.

**TEWKESBURY, BATTLE OF** See WARS OF THE ROSES.

**THE HAGUE** See HAGUE, THE.

**THEMES** In Greek, *thema,* the term for large military districts in the Byzantine Empire during the seventh century, originally intended as a bulwark against Islamic invasions in Anatolia but later extended across the entire empire. Emperor Heraclius (ruled 610–641) established the themes, placing military units under the auspices of governors *(strategoi),* settling permanent troops for stability, a work force and a citizen army. The deterioration of the themes hastened the decline of the empire. See also BYZANTINE EMPIRE.

**THEODAHAT** (d. 536) King of the Ostrogoths from 535 to 536, whose usurpation of power and assassination of his queen, Amalasuntha, led to the Byzantine invasion of the Italian peninsula. The son of the sister of Theodoric the Great, Theodahat was corrupt, despite his Platonic philosophical tendencies. He was chosen by Amalasuntha to join her on the throne of the Ostrogoths after the death of her son. He deposed her, imprisoned her on an island in Lake Bolsena (near Orvieto) and then had her strangled in May 535. Justinian used this act as a pretext for assaulting the peninsula, sending General Belisarius to campaign against Theodahat. The Ostrogoths, meeting in the Pontine Marshes, deposed him, and he fled to Ravenna.

Before he reached safety, however, he was killed by a Goth assassin. See also OSTROGOTHS.

**THEODELINDA** (d. 628) Queen of the Lombards who encouraged promotion of orthodox Christianity against the heresy of Arianism among her people. The daughter of Garibald, duke of Bavaria, she married the Lombard king Authari (d. 590), who died soon after their marriage. Allowed to choose her next husband, she selected Agilulf, duke of Turin, who was baptized as an orthodox Christian. She continued to promote the faith, requiring the baptism of her son, Adaloald, and, with Agilulf, building the basilica of Monza, in which the Iron Crown of the Lombards was later preserved. Pope Gregory the Great (590–604) was her friend and supporter. See also LOMBARDS.

**THEODORA** (d. 548) Byzantine empress and wife of Emperor Justinian I (ruled 527–565). Of humble birth, she was the daughter of the bear keeper for the hippodrome in Constantinople. An actress at an early age, she supposedly bore an illegitimate child, left the city and returned as a wool spinner. She met the young Justinian, won his affection and became his mistress. Raised to the rank of patrician, she married him in 525 and was crowned empress in 527. Her intelligence and political astuteness assured her a major role in Justinian's administration, and she welcomed foreign envoys, conducted correspondence with distant rulers and advised the emperor on all matters. Through her astuteness Justinian was encouraged to retain his throne during the Nika Revolt in 532, and because of her adherence to Monophysitism she encouraged its practice on behalf of the sect. That she was a guiding political force was borne out by the marked decrease in notable legislative enactments after her death from cancer. She was characterized by the historian Procopius in his *Secret History* as a wanton, evil woman, a view not shared by most scholars. See also BYZANTINE EMPIRE; JUSTINIAN I.

**THEODORE I** (d. 649) Pope from 642 to 649, whose pontificate was noted for its confrontations with the adherents of Monothelitism. He was also reportedly generous to the poor.

**THEODORE II** (d. 897) Pope in 897 for 20 days, whose chief act was to validate the acts of the posthumously humiliated Pope Formosus (891–896), granting the mutilated corpse of the pontiff a decent burial after the "Cadaver Synod."

**THEODORE I LASCARIS** (d. 1222) Byzantine emperor from 1204 to 1222, although this title was held in exile because of the fall of Constantinople to the armies of the Fourth Crusade in 1204. A son-in-law of the Byzantine emperor Alexius III, Theodore played a role in the defense of Constantinople, escaping from the capital and establishing a Byzantine state in Nicaea, called the Empire of Nicaea. Assuming the title of emperor in 1208, he defeated his rival, David Comnenus of Trebizond, and the Seljuk Turks. In 1214, after a conflict with Henry, the Latin emperor of Constantinople, Theodore signed a treaty defining the borders of the Latin Empire and Nicaea, eventually marrying Maria, daughter of the Latin empress Yolande (c. 1216). He negotiated a trade agreement with the Venetians at Constantinople in 1219. See also BYZANTINE EMPIRE.

**THEODORE II LASCARIS** (1222–1258) Byzantine emperor at Nicaea from 1254 to 1258, the son of Emperor John III Vatatzes and grandson of Theodore I Lascaris, crowned co-emperor before his father's death. He proved generally competent, renewing Nicaea's alliance with the Seljuk Turks of Rum (1254) and defeating the Bulgars in 1255–1256 after their invasion of Macedonia and Thrace. See also BYZANTINE EMPIRE.

**THEODORE OF STUDIOS** (759–826) Also Theodore of Studium and Theodore Studites, saint, abbot, one of the most influential figures in Byzantine monasticism and monastic reformer who opposed iconoclasm. His uncle, Saint Plato, abbot of Saccudium, trained him as a monk (c. 780), and he replaced him in 794, when Plato resigned in his favor. After opposing the adulterous marriage of Emperor Constantine VI (780–797), he was exiled to Thessalonica, being recalled in 797 after Constantine's deposition by his mother, Irene. Two years later Theodore moved his monastery from Saccudium, where it was subject to Arab attacks, to Studios in Constantinople, where it became the religious heart of the empire. Theodore was exiled again from 809 to 811 by Emperor Nicephorus I (802–811) and from 815 to 820 by Emperor Leo V (813–820), because of his opposition to iconoclasm. He practiced religious austerity and wrote nearly 600 letters, as well as three polemics and a number of sermons.

**THEODORE OF TARSUS, SAINT** (c. 602–690) Archbishop of Canterbury, consecrated in 667, responsible for the establishment of Canterbury as a see with extensive metropolitan powers. A Greek, Theodore studied at Tarsus and Athens, eventually going to Rome, where he received his appointment to Canterbury. Consecrated by Pope Vitalian (657–672), he was accompanied to England by Benedict Biscop and Hadrian to ensure that his Greek background did not give rise to the expression of unorthodox views on his part. In 672 he summoned the Synod of Hertford for the entire English church and presided at the Synod of Hatfield in 680, where a declaration of orthodoxy was made. He promoted learning and brought reforms to the church in England, dividing dioceses and preparing for the parochial system. See also CANTERBURY.

**THEODORE SVETOSLAV** (d. 1322) King of the Bulgars from 1300 to 1322, son of George I Terter, who came to power after the incompetent reigns of the widows of Smiletz and Caka. Theodore concentrated on rebuilding the weakened Bulgar state, suppressing the boyars and seizing part of Thrace from the Byzantines. The peace treaty signed with Constantinople honored his conquests and probably led to his marriage to Theodora, granddaughter of Emperor Andronicus II (c. 1308). He also improved trade with Genoa and Venice. See also BULGARIA.

**THEODORIC** (c. 454–526) King of the Ostrogoths, called "the Great" and referred to in the *Nibelungenlied* as Dietrich of Bern, the illustrious ruler of the Ostrogoths. He reigned from 471 to 526 and distinguished himself as a learned, generally enlightened figure in the early Middle Ages. The son of an Ostrogothic chieftain, he became chief in 471, having been raised in Constantinople, as his people were a federated state of the Byzantine or Eastern Empire. In 489 he was commissioned by Emperor Zeno to march on Italy against Odoacer, who had deposed the last Roman emperor of the West in 476. Odoacer was defeated and slain in 493 at Ravenna, and the Ostrogoths established their supremacy on the Italian peninsula, an empire that would, in time, include Sicily and regions along the Adriatic.

An admirer of Rome, Theodoric conducted affairs concerning the Roman subjects of his empire with tolerance, maintaining Rome's institutions. He appointed Roman officials to his court in Ravenna, bringing there notable scholars such as Boethius and Cassiodorus, while reserving crucial military posts for the Ostrogoths. Although espousing Arianism, he maintained cordial relations with adherents of orthodox Christianity until the reign of Justinian and the movement against Arianism in the Eastern Empire. His counterreaction to this clouded his final years, especially his execution of Boethius. Plans for sterner measures were prevented by his death. The conflict over the succession in the Ostrogothic kingdom made possible General Belisarius's campaigns in Italy. The tomb of Theodoric in Ravenna is one of the city's finest monuments. See also OSTROGOTHS.

Theodoric, king of the Ostrogoths

**THEODOSIUS III** (d. after 717) Byzantine emperor from 715 to 717, successor to Anastasius II. Formerly a tax collector, he was chosen emperor by the forces fomenting a rebellion and, despite trying to flee the honor, was installed in late 715. Called the "reluctant emperor," he reigned barely two years, to be followed by Leo III. See also BYZANTINE EMPIRE.

**THEODULF** (d. 750–821) Bishop of Orléans, also noted poet, theologian and a member of the brilliant court of Charlemagne at Aachen. A Goth from Spain, he served as abbot of Fleury and was consecrated bishop of Orléans before 798 through Charlemagne's influence. In 818 he was deposed and banished to Angers after being accused of conspiring against Louis the Pious. Theodulf's theological works included *De Spiritus Sancto,* writings on the Holy Spirit, and a treatise on baptism. His poems, considered to be some of the finest of the age, included *Carmina,* of great historical interest. His hymn *Gloria, laud et honor* served as the Palm Sunday processional for the Western Church.

**THEOPHILUS** (d. 842) Byzantine emperor from 829 to 842, whose reign witnessed the last period of iconoclasm and constant warfare with the Muslims. The son of Emperor Michael II, he was crowned co-emperor in 820, ruling alone in 829. Despite his admiration for the caliph Harun al-Rashid, Theophilus warred against the caliphate, losing Palermo, Sicily, to the Muslims in 831 after being defeated by al-Mu'tasim. He tried in vain to stem the tide of Islam into Asia Minor and endured another rout in 838, during which Mu'tasim captured Ancyra (Ankara) and the important fortress of Amorium. A recovery was achieved in 841, and the caliph was convinced to sign a treaty. In Constantinople, Theophilus promoted a cultural revival, including revitalization of its university, appointing Leo the Mathematician as its rector. With the influence of his tutor, John Philoponus, whom he appointed patriarch of Constantinople, the emperor initiated another persecution of those supporting the use of icons, taking advantage of iconoclasm as a means of weakening the monastic system of the Eastern Church. See also BYZANTINE EMPIRE; ICONOCLASTICISM.

**THEOPHYLACT** (d. c. 926) Roman consul, senator and nobleman, a member of the House of Tusculani, wielding much influence in Rome and over the papacy. He controlled the city and dominated the pope, joined in this by his wife, Theodora. Their daughter, Marozia, was a mistress of Pope Sergius III (904–911) and the mother of Pope John XI (931–935/6) and Alberic II, who ruled in Rome for many years.

**THEOPHYLACT OF OCHRIDA** (d. c. 1109) Byzantine exegete, theologian and a major figure in bringing Byzantine culture to the Balkans. A pupil of Michael Psellus, he served as tutor to Constantine (VII) Porphyrogenitus, son of Michael III, and was appointed archbishop of Ochrida about 1078. He wrote many letters on the political state of affairs among the Bulgars as well as a series of commentaries on parts of the Old Testament and all of the New Testament, except for the Book of Revelation. Defending the Bulgars from the harsh policies of imperial tax collectors, Theophylact insisted on a practical morality. He maintained a conciliatory stance in the division between the Eastern and Western Churches.

**THEUDIGISEL** (d. 549) King of the Visigoths from 548 to 549, considered by his contemporaries the most valiant warrior of the Visigoths, winning fame for his defeat of the Franks at Zaragoza in 542. Elected successor to Theudis, he soon disappointed the nobles because of his debauchery and cruelty. He was murdered at dinner one night. See also VISIGOTHS.

**THEUDIS** (d. 548) King of the Visigoths from 531 to 548, originally an Ostrogoth, serving as regent for Amalric (ruled 522–531) during his minority and elected to succeed him. Theudis repelled the Frankish attacks against him and reclaimed part of the lands beyond the Pyrenees that had been lost, specifically Septimania, including the cities of Narbonne and Carcassonne. In 544, however, he feared Byzantine advances by Justinian and ordered an assault on Byzantine Africa. His army was annihilated in an advance against the city of Centa (Septa). Four years later he was assassinated at Seville, never having recovered his former military reputation. See also VISIGOTHS.

**THIBAULT I** (1201–1253) King of Navarre from 1234 to 1253, also Thibault IV of Champagne and count of Champagne and Brie. The son of Thibault III and Blanche of Navarre, he spent several years at the court of Philip II Augustus of France (1180–1223) but turned against his son, Louis VIII (1223–1226) during the siege of Avignon against the Albigensians (1226). Becoming the king of Navarre, he spent his time between Champagne and Navarre, and from 1239 to 1240 he led a crusade that led to the capture of Ascalon from the Muslims. Thibault was also a renowned aristocratic *trouvere,* or poet musician, composing 60 lyrics, mostly love songs and debates in verse, as well as *pastourelles* (love songs between a knight and a shepherdess) and several religious poems. See also NAVARRE, KINGDOM OF.

**THIBAULT II** (d. 1270) King of Navarre from 1253 to 1270, the son of Thibault I (1234–1253), who participated in the Eighth Crusade (1270) with King Louis IX of France (Saint Louis, 1226–1270), accompanying the French monarch to Tunis. Thibault died shortly after his return to Sicily. See also NAVARRE, KINGDOM OF.

**THIERRY II** (d. 613) King of Burgundy from 596 to 613, a son of King Childebert II, who received Burgundy as his inheritance, with Orléans as his capital. His rivals were his older brother, Thibert, king of Austrasia, and Clotaire II, son of King Chilperic. Thierry defeated Clotaire in 1104 near Ètampes and, in 610, entered into war with Thibert, being forced to yield his possession, Alsace. Two years later he made an alliance with Clotaire, defeating Thibert, who was stripped of his crown and forced into monastic seclusion. Thibert was murdered, but Thierry came into conflict with Clotaire once again. He died of dysentery at Metz.

**THIERRY III** (d. after 687) King of Neustria and Burgundy from 670 to 687, although he was replaced for a time by the mayor of the palace, Ebroin. One of the "lazy kings" of the Merovingian line, Thierry was perhaps mentally retarded and thus dominated by Ebroin. He fled in 687 after the victory of Pepin of Héristal over the Neustrians at Tertry. See also NEUSTRIA.

**THIERRY IV** (d. 737) King of Neustria and Burgundy, one of the last "lazy kings" of the Merovingian line, ruling from 720 to 737, although actual power was held by the mayor of the palace, Charles Martel. A probable son of Thierry III, he was installed after being brought out of the monastery of Chelles in order to maintain the fictional power of the Merovingian line. See also NEUSTRIA.

**THIERRY OF CHARTRES** (c. 1100–c. 1151) Also Thierry the Breton, a theologian, teacher and Scholastic philosopher. He was the younger brother of Bernard of Chartres who attended the Council of Soissons (1121) that denounced Peter Abelard. Teaching then at Paris, Thierry included among his students John of Salisbury. He became chancellor of Chartres in 1141, taking part in the Synod of Reims in 1148, condemning GILBERT DE LA PORRÉE. After taking part in the Diet of Frankfort (1149), he retired to a monastery. An ardent Platonist, he wrote the *Heptakuchon,* a work on the seven liberal arts, a commentary on Boethius's *De Trinitate* and a commentary on Cicero's *De inventione.* See also CHARTRES.

**THOMAS, DESPOT OF EPIRUS** (d. 1318) Despot from 1296 to 1318, the last member of the Angeli dynasty in Epirus. His nephew, Nicholas Orsini of Cephalonia, murdered him. See also EPIRUS, DESPOTATE OF.

**THOMAS À BECKET, SAINT** (1118–1170) Archbishop of Canterbury, chancellor of England and martyr. A Norman by birth, he was born in the Cheapside quarter of London, receiving an education in Merton Priory and at Paris, where he studied with Robert of Melun. About 1141, after three years of service as a clerk for the sheriffs, he became a member of the household of archbishop Theobald of Canterbury. He was sent to study canon law at Bologna and Auxerre and in 1154 was appointed archdeacon of Canterbury. Having proved his worth to Theobald, he was appointed by King Henry II of England (1154–1189) as chancellor in 1155.

As chancellor Thomas applied his brilliance in reducing baronial opposition, initiating royal policy (often detrimental to the church), and became confidant of Henry, his companion and friend. Thomas reveled in the hunt and the brilliance of life at court. The degree of trust between the king and Thomas was made evident when Henry appointed him archbishop of Canterbury to succeed Theobald (d. 1161). Thomas displayed considerable reluctance in accepting the post, but he was consecrated in 1162.

Becket soon adopted a life of austerity and intense religiosity, upholding the rights of the church, the papacy and the instrumentation of canon law. He resigned his position as chancellor because he found himself at odds with his king. He opposed a tax proposal, excommunicated a baron and then found himself opposed to Henry on issues in the Constitutions of Clarendon (1164) that granted the Crown wide powers over the church. He also refused to accept Henry's contention that "criminous clerks" (clerics charged with crimes) should be tried in secular courts. Sharp reprisals by the king included the demand that Becket settle the finances of which he had charge as chancellor. The king summoned a council at Northampton, condemning Becket, who escaped to France, supposedly in disguise, thus beginning a period of exile (1164–1170).

Under the protection of King Louis VII of France (1137–1180), Becket appealed to Pope Alexander III (1159–1181) and retreated to the Cistercian abbey at Pontigny, moving to Sens in 1166 when Henry threatened to expel all Cistercians from England. A half-hearted reconciliation came in 1170, and Becket returned to England in November. His excommunication of English bishops who did not declare allegiance to the pope, and the popular support of the people for Becket, enraged Henry, who is reputed to have asked: "Will no one here rid me of this meddlesome priest?" Four knights, William de Tracy, Reginald Fitz-Urse, Richard le Breton and Hugh de Morville, rode to Canterbury and on December 29, 1170, entered the cathedral and murdered the archbishop. Becket's violent end brought outrage from the populace, and miracles were reported to have taken place at the cathedral and his tomb soon after his burial. Canterbury became a revered place of pilgrimage, and Becket was canonized by Alexander III on February 21, 1173. On July 12, 1174, King Henry II performed a public penance at Canterbury for his complicity in the murderous act. See also ENGLAND.

**THOMAS À KEMPIS** (c. 1380–1471) Born Thomas Hemerken, an ascetic, writer and probably author of the *Imitation of Christ*. He was born at Kempen, near Cologne, studying at Deventer in the school of the Brethren of the Common Life and influenced by Florentius Radewyns. In 1399 he entered the monastery of Agnietenberg, a house of the Canons Regular, taking vows in 1406 or 1408. He remained there for the rest of his life, preaching, copying manuscripts, writing and giving advice on spiritual matters. In addition to *Imitation* he composed sermons, devotional works and hagiographies. His major work, *Imitatio Christi* in Latin, was a guide to the achievement of spiritual perfection. Divided into four parts, the book was first circulated in 1418. It was traditionally ascribed to À Kempis, although other possible authors were thought to have included Jean Gerson and Pope Innocent III. See also MYSTICISM.

**THOMAS AQUINAS, SAINT** (1224/1225–1274) Dominican philosopher and theologian distinguished for being one of the powerful intellects of the Middle Ages and in church history. He was called the Angelic Doctor and Doctor Communis, writing two major works, the *Summa contra Gentiles* and the *Summa theologica*. Born in Roccasecca, Italy, the son of Count Landulf of Aquino, he entered the Benedictine school at Monte Cassino, his parents hoping that he would become abbot in order to enhance the family's reputation. About 1240, while studying in Naples, he was drawn to the Dominican order, an ambition opposed by his parents, who abducted him and held him captive for more than a year. He was finally liberated and allowed to join the order in April 1244. He entered the convent of Saint Joseph and studied with Albertus Magnus, accompanying him to Cologne, where the order had established a new *studium generale*. There he was introduced to the writings of Aristotle and the precepts of Aristotelian rationalism and the primacy of intelligence.

Returning to Paris in 1252, he earned the title master of theology in 1256, and three years later he was sent to Italy, receiving appointment as lecturer to the Papal Curia. Teaching in various Dominican institutions, he was recalled to Paris in 1269, where he respectfully disputed the writings of Siger of Brabant, regarding the works of Averroës and the resulting precepts of Averroism. He also helped establish the Dominican school at the University of Naples and began work on his *Summa theologica*. Thomas fell ill in 1274 on the way to the Second Council of Lyons, having been summoned by Pope Gregory X (1271–1276). He died at the Cistercian abbey of Fossanuova on March 7.

The apparent simplicity of his life did not diminish the prodigious intellectual contributions for which he was responsible. Called the "Dumb Ox" in school because he was slow and heavy (so heavy, in fact, that a half moon was cut into the refectory table to accommodate his girth), he possessed an intellect that was far from dull. He wrote a vast body of treatises, some of which were condemned in 1277 and 1284. The Franciscans also forbade the study of his writings. He was canonized in 1323 and named a doctor of the church in 1567.

He adhered to the belief that science and theology could not contradict each other, as truth was indivisible. He drew a sharp distinction between reason and faith. The universe was, he wrote, an expression of God's will and the manifestation of God's intelligence. He attempted to reconcile Aristotelian thought with Christian belief, thereby finding a harmony of reason and faith and arriving at a synthesis of Aristotelianism and Augustinian doctrine. This effort resulted in the *Summa theologica*, the supreme document of Scholasticism. Written from 1265/1266 to 1273, and although incomplete, it was his chief work of dogma. Other religious treatises included *Summa contra Gentiles* (c. 1258–1264, *Against the Gentiles* [or nonbelievers in Christian doctrine]); *De potentia Dei* (1259–1268, *On the Power of God*); *De spiritualibus creaturis* (n.d., *On Spiritual Creatures*); *De malo* (n.d., *On Evil*); and *De anima* (n.d., *On the Soul*). His philosophical treatises included *De ente et essentia* (before 1256, *On Being and Essence*); *Contra impugnantes Dei cultum et religionem* (1256, an apologia written in defense of religious orders); and *De unitate intellectus contra Averroistas* (1270, an attack on Averroism and Siger of Brabant). He also wrote commentaries on Aristotle and the Bible, as well as hymns, composed for Pope Urban IV (1261–1264) for the newly created Feast of Corpus Christi. These included the masterpiece *Pange lingua gloriosi* (1264). See also DOMINICANS; SCHOLASTICISM.

**THOMAS OF CELANO** (d. 1260) The earliest biographer of Saint Francis of Assisi, a Franciscan who wrote two lives of the saint, one in 1228, two years after Francis's death, at the behest of Pope Gregory IX (1227–1241), and a second in 1246–1247, at the request of the General of the order. In 1250–1253 he wrote the *Tractatis de miraculis S. Francisci* and in 1255 composed the *Legend of St. Clare.* His elegant prose was applauded, but the accuracy of his biographies has been questioned. Thomas was the reputed author of the *Dies irae (Days of* Wrath). See also FRANCIS OF ASSISI, SAINT.

**THORFINN KARLSEFNI** (fl. 1002–1010) Icelandic chief who made the first attempt to colonize North America. It is generally agreed that about 1004–1005 he and more than 100 others spent the winter on the northeastern coast of North America, probably south of the Gulf of Saint Lawrence. See also VINLAND.

***THOUSAND AND ONE NIGHTS, THE*** Also called the *Arabian Nights,* a collection of tales, romances, fables, anecdotes and adventures, first mentioned in the ninth century. Most of the names are Arabic, but the framework is Indian and the major characters Iranian. This supports the theory that the stories were compiled by several authors, a view subscribed to because of the obvious variety of the tales, their geographical origin and their settings, which include India, Turkey, Egypt, Iran and Iraq. Despite uncertainties about the origin of the work, the characters, such as Ali Baba, Aladdin and Sinbad, were popularized in the folklore of the East and West. The tales are meant to have been told by the imaginative Sheherazade (Scherezade), who avoids death at her husband's hands by a agreeing to recount a story each night for 1,001 nights, thereby sparing her life.

**THRASAMUND** (d. 523) King of the Vandals from 496 to 523 over a declining Vandal state. The successor to his brother, Gunthamund (ruled 484–496), he reversed the royal policy of tolerance toward Catholic (or orthodox) Christians, persecuting them and deporting 200 bishops to Sardinia. He confronted incursions by the Moors of North Africa, supposedly dying after learning that a force of Vandals had been defeated at their hands. See also VANDALS.

**THURINGIA** Historical region in central Germany, called in German Thüringen, derived from the Germanic tribe of the Thuringians, who first appeared in the mid-fourth century. They were conquered by the Huns in the fifth century, recovering to establish a kingdom in the Harz Mountains along the Danube, enduring a defeat by the Franks in 531 and marked territorial reduction under the Frankish dukes. The Thuringians were Christianized by Boniface, and the duchy was divided into countships in the eighth century. With the extinction of the Saxon line in 1024, control of the region was taken by the Ludowing family, through the efforts of Louis the Bearded. His grandson was appointed landgrave of Thuringia in 1130 by King Lothair III. The landgraves, with their seat at Wartburg, were princes of the Holy Roman Empire, but after the death of the landgrave Henry Raspe in 1247 there was a long contest for the succession, ending in 1263 with the victory of Henry III, margrave of Meissen, of the House of Wettin. The division of Wettin lands in 1485 left most of Thuringia in the hands of the family's Ernestine branch. See also GERMANY.

**TIBERIUS I CONSTANTINE** (d. 582) Byzantine emperor from 578 to 582, a native of Thrace who had distinguished himself in the service of Emperor Justin II against the Avars and had become considerably influential in the state. About 574 Empress Sophia and Tiberius took control of the government, as Justin was increasingly mentally unstable. They convinced the emperor to adopt Tiberius, naming him co-emperor (December 574) and crowning him emperor before his own death in 578. His reign was war torn, as he battled against the Persians, Avars and Slavs. He maintained a military balance with the Persians but in 582 lost Sirmium to the Avars and was unable to prevent the Slavic invasion of Thrace, Illyricum and parts of Greece. Just before his death he named as his successor Maurice. Tiberius is sometimes listed as Tiberius II Constantine. See also BYZANTINE EMPIRE.

**TIBERIUS II** (d. 705) Byzantine emperor from 698 to 705, originally called Apsimer. He was a general in the service of Emperor Leontius (ruled 695–698) who was proclaimed emperor when the Byzantine fleet rebelled after an unsuccessful attempt to recapture the Exarchate of Ravenna. He ordered Leontius sent to a monastery after having his nose cut off. In 705, however, Tiberius was overthrown by Justinian II, who had been exiled by Leontius. Captured after the fall of his regime, he was publicly humiliated and executed. See also BYZANTINE EMPIRE.

**TIMURIDS** See TAMERLANE.

**TIMUR** See TAMERLANE.

**TOGHRIL-BEG** (d. 1063) Leader of the Seljuk Turks and founder of a dynasty that came to rule Iraq, Syria, Iran and Asia Minor. A grandson of the chief of the Oguz tribe, Seljuk (or Seljug), Toghril and his brother, Chagtri, entered the service of the prince of Bukhara in 1023 but were soon defeated by Mahmud of Ghazna and fled to Khwarizm. Later moving into Khorasan, they conquered Merv and Nishapur and, in 1040, routed Mas'ud, son of Mahmud. While his brother was the master of Khorasan, Toghril embarked on campaigns to extend his influence and control, taking Rayy, Hamadan and Isfahan. He then raided Anatolia and subdued the regions around Baghdad. In 1055 he entered Baghdad and took control of the Abbasid caliphate. He promised to overthrow the Fatimids but was unable to fulfill his pledge because of a massive revolt by Arab, Buyid and Turkic forces. Baghdad was lost in 1058 but recaptured in 1060, at which time Toghril was restored to power. See also SELJUK TURKS.

**TOLEDO** City in central Spain and a cultural center for the Christian population of the peninsula. Noted for its workmanship in steel, it was known especially for its swords. A colony under the Romans, Toledo fell to the Visigoths and was as a residence for the Visigothic court from the sixth century. Captured by the Moors in 712, it was the capital of an emirate (after 1031 an independent kingdom) and the site of a large community of Mozarabs. In 1085 King Alfonso VI of Castile (1065–1109) conquered Toledo, making it his chief royal city, but it was eventually superseded by Valladolid in the 15th century. Arab, Jewish and Christian cultures thrived in Toledo, giving rise to the establishment of institutions such as the Escuela de Traductores, the School of Translators, founded by Alfonso X the Wise (ruled 1253–1284).

**TORQUEMADA, TOMÁS DE** (1420–1498) Infamous Dominican and confessor to Ferdinand and Isabella (1474–1516), who was responsible for the establishment of the Spanish Inquisition. A nephew of the Spanish cardinal Juan de Torquemada, and of Jewish descent, he received appointment in 1483 as the Grand Inquisitor for Castile and León and later that year for the Crown of Aragon. Tribunals of inquisition were established in Seville, Córdoba, Zaragoza and elsewhere, and he wrote 28 articles to guide his agents in uncovering heresy, the practice of witchcraft, and other sins, employing torture as a useful means by which to extract confessions and evidence. Torquemada was also a major influence in persuading Ferdinand and Isabella to expel the Jews from Spain in 1492. Probably as many as 2,000 people were tortured and then burned during his years as Grand Inquisitor. See also INQUISITION.

**TORUN, PEACE OF** See TEUTONIC KNIGHTS.

**TOSTIG** (d. 1066) Earl of Northumbria (1055–1066), son of Earl Godwin of Wessex and brother of King Harold II Godwinson of England, who became his mortal enemy. Although he supported Harold in subduing the Welsh in 1062, hatred arose between them in 1065 when Harold accepted Morcar as Tostig's replacement as earl after Tostig was ousted by the Northumbrians for his harsh rule. He went to Flanders and in the following year (1066) joined Harald II of Norway in his invasion of England. On September 15, 1066, Tostig and Harald were defeated and killed at Stamford Bridge by Harold. See also ENGLAND.

**TOTILA** (d. 552) King of the Ostrogoths from 541 to 552, also called Baduila, recovering central and southern Italy after their conquest by the Byzantines in 540. Elected by the Goth nobles in late 541, Totila undertook a campaign of reconsolidation in 543, capturing Naples in 543 and Rome in 546 after a three-month siege. The Byzantines sent General Belisarius back to Italy, regaining Rome but losing it to the Goths after Belisarius was recalled in 549. Totila then restored ascendancy of the Goths in Italy and Sicily. In 552 the Byzantines led by General Narses routed the Ostrogoths in Umbria, and Totila sustained mortal wounds during the battle. See also OSTROGOTHS.

**TOULOUSE** City in southern France, in the modern department of Haute-Garonne in Languedoc, and a center of commerce for the region. The court of the counts of Toulouse was the heart of southern French culture during the Middle Ages. From 419 to 507 the city was the capital of the Visigoths, falling in 508 to Clovis and the Franks and becoming attached to the Merovingian kingdom. Attacked unsuccessfully by the Saracens in 721, it was the seat of the county of Toulouse in 778, and the counts (claiming the title dukes of Aquitaine in the 10th century) emerged as prestigious nobles and patrons of the troubadour poets and men of letters. They took a tolerant stance toward Jews but earned the enmity of the crown by evincing a sympathetic attitude toward the Albigensians, resisting the Albigensian Crusade in the early 14th century, a resistance that cost them their position and power. The countship ended in 1249, and Toulouse was ceded to Alphonse, brother of King Louis IX (1226–1270). In 1271 it was added to the royal domain. To combat heresy, rampant in the city, many religious houses were founded, as well as a university, established in 1229 at the end of the crusade. See ALBIGENSIAN MOVEMENT.

**TOURNAMENTS** Also called a tourney, an organized series of encounters or military exercises designed to display skill, courage and martial prowess in an exhibit of knightly chivalry. Tournaments, arising late in the medieval era, were one of the most romantic and well-known aspects of knightly activity. Originating in France during the 11th century, they were supposedly the idea of the nobleman Geoffroi de Preully, becoming popular in the 12th century throughout western Europe for their recreational characteristics and the opportunities afforded landless knights who otherwise earned their keep by kidnapping and ransoming prisoners. Early tourneys were often bloody and violent, bringing together as they did numbers of heavily armed fighters who often posed a possible threat to social order. The violence prompted criticism from the church. Becoming more structured, the mock battles evolved to pageantry by the end of the 15th century.

The first tourneys were generally composed of the *melée,* a mock battle between two forces of armed horsemen. Here injuries could be quite severe, but the *melée* was enjoyed enough by the combatants, so that it endured even after the rise of the joust. This was a trial of skill between two mounted knights, usually carrying lances. Each charged the other, aiming to unhorse his opponent, the charges continuing until a victor was determined. Inevitably a system or set of rules was established called the Statutum Armorum (Statute of Arms), dating from about 1292. Its terms set down such regulations as requiring only squires to be allowed to assist their fallen knights, and demanding that no pointed swords or other weapons, including clubs or daggers, be used on the field. By the 14th century lances were made less dangerous by the use of crown-shaped heads, the end result of an earlier process to blunt the lance heads. At the same time, armorers began making suits of armor that were heavier and less flexible, compared with the equivalent worn in war, a development adding to the pageantry associated with tournaments during the close of the Middle Ages and later. See also WARFARE.

**TOURS, BATTLE OF** See CHARLES MARTEL.

**TOWER OF LONDON** Fortress and royal residence in London, England, situated on the north bank of the Thames River. The tower was begun late in 1066 by William I the Conqueror (1066–1087), immediately following his coronation at Christmas. His goal was to provide a fort for protection of the merchant community and nearby posts for the city. The central keep, the White Tower, was begun in 1078 with additional fortifications added during the 12th and 13th centuries. It served as a royal residence until the 17th century and was also strategic to the defense of the city as well as a prison. See also LONDON.

**TOWTON, BATTLE OF** See WARS OF THE ROSES.

**TRADE AND COMMERCE** Two vital activities in the Middle Ages, the practice of which created an era of sustained growth that endured for 300 years, thereby transforming the economy of Europe. It is generally accepted that medieval European trade was conducted in two major geographical regions: the Mediterranean and the Baltic regions of northern Europe, with the two spheres meeting at market fairs throughout Europe.

The economic life of the Roman Empire, based on agriculture, deteriorated in the third century A.D. As civil strife and political upheaval increased the crisis in the fourth and fifth centuries, the economy was in severe decline as western Europe broke apart into smaller kingdoms. Peasants continued to exist at a subsistence level, and the upper classes suffered from a shortage of luxury goods, a situation that continued until the 9th and early 10th centuries.

The revival of trade in the West was brought about by a number of influences. By the close of the 10th century the dangers presented by the Magyars, Vikings and Saracen raiders had lessened, ending much of the turmoil that had marked the end of the early Middle Ages. While trade had fallen severely, it had not completely ceased. There was always trade in luxury items with the markets of the East (the Byzantine and Islamic mercantile centers), including spices, salt, slaves, grains, timber and leather. Further, the royalty and nobility of Europe, now entrenched, began to demand luxury goods and precious items to provide themselves commodities befitting their rank or to present to others. Increased populations, a result of the relative tranquillity of the social, economic and political environment, allowed towns to rise, industry to form and new trade routes to be explored.

Of great importance was the development of the Italian cities as maritime commercial powers in the Mediterranean. Initially, trade was in the hands of the Greeks, Syrians and Jews called Radanites. By the late 10th century, however, the men of such cities as Pisa, Genoa and especially Venice were beginning to advance commerce. These men won control of Byzantine trade slowly, acquiring as well naval supremacy in the western Mediterranean as the Byzantine fleet declined and as their squadrons mounted offensives against the Muslims. In the years prior to the Crusades, these maritime cities were endeavoring to increase their presence in the eastern Mediterranean, a process that gained impetus during the Crusades. Venice, forging for itself a remarkable mercantile empire, added greatly to its wealth and influence by its support and encouragement the Fourth Crusade (1202–1204) in which Constantinople was captured and the Byzantine Empire overthrown.

While supplying and transporting the Crusader armies and trading with the Crusader States of the Holy Land and the ports of the Levant, the merchants sought and brought back to Europe the luxury items that fired the imagination: spices, perfumes, rugs, silks, mirrors, gems and a variety of exotic foodstuffs. They sold, in return, agricultural goods (most notably in North Africa), linens, grain, alum, iron and copper. The Genoese dealt largely in bulk commodities, the grains from the Black Sea region where they had colonies, but they also plied a luxury trade as caravans from the Orient arrived frequently at their far-flung outposts. The Venetians coveted the Eastern trade as well, and after Genoa superseded Pisa in naval strength, conflict between these cities was inevitable. War erupted in the mid-13th century, and the Venetians were the ultimate victor. They thus monopolized trade with the Orient. The Genoese shifted their interests to the markets of the western Mediterranean, France and Spain, thereby expanding lucrative trade, while Venice was to suffer a severe loss when the trade routes to the East were disrupted by the Ottoman Turks and new routes to India were opened by the Portuguese.

Northern Italy was rivaled in its trade by northern Europe, particularly the Low Countries, and the cities of the North Sea and the Baltic. Merchants transported their goods over the Alps, up the Rhine, Oder, Weser and Elbe Rivers, merging trade of the Mediterranean with that of northern Europe. Chief among the Flemish cities were Bruges and Ghent, Bruges eventually being superseded in commerce by Antwerp. Trade was facilitated by the establishment of market fairs and encouraged merchants to embark on active regional enterprise. Along the Baltic, cities such as Lübeck traded in commodities including wine, fish (herring especially), tin, textiles, leather and, most important, salt. The Germans expanded trade eastward into Prussia, recently reconquered and colonized by the Teutonic Knights, and established posts in England, Flanders and elsewhere. Uniting to strengthen and to organized their efforts, they formed the HANSEATIC LEAGUE.

Progress in trade was a major impetus to the rise of towns, different from the manorial villages in that they were not predominantly agricultural, their citizens engaged in activities such as manufacturing, buying, selling and trading. Such communities were composed of free men, eventually organized into merchant and artisanal guilds and who demanded a voice in the manner in which their lives were administered by government.

From the 10th to the 14th century there was economic expansion, but a series of crises struck causing disruption and constriction. The plague, which first struck Europe in 1348, called the Black Death, brought severe depopulation in its wake, thus affecting trade and commerce. This was exacerbated by the political upheaval of the Hundred Years' War (1337–1450), an acute problem in the Low Countries and France. After 1350 parts of Europe went into a decline, not as serious as that which followed Rome's collapse, but one that continued until the start of the 16th century. See also ALEXANDRIA; BANKING; BRUGES; BYZANTINE EMPIRE; CONSTANTINOPLE; CRUSADES; ENGLAND; FAIRS; FLANDERS; FLORENCE; FRANCE; GENOA; GERMANY; GHENT; GUILDS; LÜBECK; MILAN; NORMANS; PISA; RAVENNA; SHIPS; VENICE; VIKINGS.

**TREBIZOND, EMPIRE OF** One of the Greek splinter states arising after the fall of Constantinople to the forces of the Fourth Crusade in 1204 and the establishment of the Latin Empire of Constantinople. The Trebizond Empire lasted from 1204 to 1461, its capital a city in northeastern Anatolia (Turkey), situated on the Black Sea near the Pontic Mountains, called in ancient times Trapezus. Under Roman rule the city was prosperous but was sacked by the Goths in 257, rebuilt and was important to the commercial renewal of the Byzantine Empire of Justinian I (ruled 527–565), although major prosperity came after 1204. Founded by David and Alexius Comnenus, grandsons of Emperor Andronicus I Comnenus, the empire flourished during the period of the Latin Empire (1204–1261) and retained its independence after the restoration of the Byzantine Empire in 1261. Despite periods of vassalage to the Seljuk Turks and Mongols, Trebizond avoided outright conquest because of its isolation and the awkward terrain surrounding it. Its commercial success was due to its position on the trade routes to the Middle East and Russia, and its commodities including products such as cloth, black wine, silver and iron. The enduring Komnene Dynasty of Trebizond was finally ended in 1461 by the Ottoman Turks, who established their rule, removing the last vestige of Hellenic civilization in the East. See also BYZANTINE EMPIRE.

**TRÈVES** See TRIER.

**TRIER** Trèves in French, a city in the Rhineland-Palatinate on the Moselle River, founded as a Roman colony and called (c. 15 B.C.) Augusta Trevorum by Emperor Augustus. A flourishing community owing to trade and its administrative role in its province, it became an imperial capital of the Western Empire after the reorganization of the empire by Diocletian in the late third century but fell to the Franks in the fifth century. A bishopric was installed in the fourth century, elevated to archbishopric status in 815. The archbishops of Trier came to wield vast power and to rule extensive territory on both sides of the Rhine as princes and Electors of the Holy Roman Empire.

**TRINITARIANS** See JOHN OF MATHA, SAINT.

**TRIPOLI** See CRUSADER STATES.

**TRISTAN AND ISOLDE** A universally popular romance, probably Irish in origin, concerning two star-crossed lovers. Tristan to whose care she has been entrusted, drinks a love potion with Isolde, originally intended for King Mark of Cornwall, whom Isolde is to marry. The consuming passion for each other leads to their death. Versions of the tale were composed by Gottfried von Strassburg (c. 1210) and Sir Thomas Malory. Variations in their names included Tristram and Isolt, Yseult or Iseult.

**TRONDHEIM** Port city on the central coast of Norway on the Trondheim Fjord. Once called Nidaros, it was the political and religious heart of the kingdom from its founding in 997 until 1537 and the Reformation, when its present name came into use. King Olaf I built a church and residence there, the city becoming a place of pilgrimage because of the tales arising from the remarkable state of preservation of the corpse of King Olaf II (Saint Olaf), who died in 1030 in the Battle of Stiklestad. A bishop's see in 1029, Trondheim became an archbishopric in 1152 and prospered until the 14th century when the Hanseatic League acquired control of regional trade and designated Bergen as its chief port. See also NORWAY.

**TROUBADOURS** Lyric poets of southern France (Provence), northern Spain and northern Italy. They flourished from the 11th to the late 13th century, composing their verse in the Provençal dialect. The word *troubadour* was derived from the Occitan *trobar*, meaning to invent or find, and songs and lays composed by troubadours had a lasting influence on medieval poetry. The major topic was courtly love, but many other themes were introduced. See LOVE, COURTLY. Rules for composition were set down in the *Leys d'amors* (1340), with compositional form varying from the *pastorela* (the love of a knight for a shepherdess), the *debat* (a debate between two poets on love), five or six stanzas of the *conso* and the *alba* or song of dawn. The acclaimed troubadours of the time were Bertrand de Born, Gaucelm Faidit and Peire Vidal.

Poets of France, whose songs were composed in the *langue d'oïl*, were called *trouvire*, and they flourished during the 12th and 13th centuries, differing from their Provençal counterparts by writing on satirical themes or on life's pleasures (as Colin Muset), rather than love. Among the best-known *trouvires* were Adam de la Halle, Thibaut dė Champagne, Rutebeuf and the citizen poets of Champagne.

**TROYES** City in northeastern France on the Seine River, the traditional capital of Champagne, the site of a courageous stand against Attila the Hun in the fifth century by Saint Loup, its bishop. Troyes, however, was important until the 14th century as the site of two annual fairs, the most active in western Europe. The troy weight was established at these fairs as an international standard. The Treaty of Troyes (signed May 21, 1420) produced a truce in the Hundred Years' War and stipulated that Henry V of England was to marry Catherine, daughter of Charles VI of France (1380–1422), thereby designating Henry as heir to the French crown. See also FAIRS.

**TRUCE OF GOD** An agreement appearing about 1027 as an addition to the PEACE OF GOD, proclaimed to protect pilgrims and travelers and to abolish violence. Specifically, the oath provided truce periods, banned fighting from

Wednesday night to Monday morning and imposed spiritual penalties on those who broke that pledge.

**TRUE CROSS** Christian relic traditionally believed to be the wood on which Christ was crucified and supposedly found by Saint Helena, mother of Constantine the Great, during her pilgrimage to the Holy Land about 326. Subsequent stories concerning the relic embellished details of its history and mystical attributes. The Byzantine emperor Heraclius launched a campaign against the Persians to reclaim the cross from 622 to 628, and its reputation was such that its safekeeping was motivation for the Fourth Crusade against Constantinople in 1204. See also RELICS.

**TUDOR DYNASTY** Ruling house in England from 1485 to 1603, originating in a Welsh family whose fortune was established by Owen Tudor (d. 1461), in the service of King Henry V of England (1413–1422). Owen married Henry's widow, Catherine of Valois, a union that produced five children, including three sons. A supporter of his stepson, Henry VI (1422–1461), Owen was executed by the Yorkists after the Battle of Mortimer's Cross. His eldest son, Edmund, became earl of Richmond and married Margaret Beaufort. Their son, Henry Tudor, led an invasion of England in 1485, defeated King Richard III (1483–1485) at Bosworth Field in August 1485, thus ending the Wars of the Roses. Claiming the throne by inheritance, Henry founded a royal dynasty that would eventually include Henry VIII and Elizabeth I. See also ENGLAND.

**TULGA** (d. after 641) King of the Visigoths from 640 to 641, the son of King Chinthila, who had him crowned as successor before his death. Tulga was dominated entirely by the church and was dethroned in a conspiracy by nobles, jealous of the clergy in the government. He retired to a monastery. See also VISIGOTHS.

**TULUNIDS** Local ruling dynasty of Egypt and Syria, lasting from 868 to 905, founded by Ahmad ibn Tulun, a Turk sent in 868 to be vice governor of Egypt. He consolidated his position and took control of the treasuries of Egypt and Syria, which allowed him to act independently of the Abbasid caliphs, although they were his superiors. His reign, from 868 to 884, was responsible for advances in the provinces and a major building program, including the construction of the mosque of Ibn Tulun. The succeeding Tulunids were ineffective, and the line ended in 905. See also EGYPT.

**TURKS** See BYZANTINE EMPIRE; CRUSADES; OTTOMAN TURKS; SELJUK TURKS.

**TUSCANY** See CANOSSA; FLORENCE; GUELPHS AND GHIBELLINES; LOMBARDS; MATILDA, COUNTESS OF TUSCANY; MEDICI, HOUSE OF; PISA; SIENA.

**TVER, PRINCES OF** The rulers of the principality of Tver, a city northwest of Moscow, in modern Kalinin. Rival of Moscow, the principality was founded in 1246 by Prince Yaroslav Yaroslavich (brother of Alexander Nevsky), and his descendants were in conflict with Moscow from the 14th through the 15th century. Prince Michael I in 1305 was made grand prince of Vladimir by the khan of the Golden Horde but was killed in 1318 by the khan after refusing to accept the degradation of being replaced by Yuri (Yury) of Moscow. The title was restored in 1322 to Prince Dimitry, but he was put to death in 1326 for murdering Yuri. Dimitry's brother, Alexander, lost the title after rebelling against the Mongols in 1327. The princes of Tver never again held their former rank of grand prince. Subsequently Tver opposed Moscow, allying itself with Lithuania and Poland. In 1485, however, Ivan III of Moscow annexed Tver, forcing the last prince, Michael III, into exile. See also RUSSIA.

**TYLER, WAT** (d. 1391) A leader of the Peasant Revolt of 1381. Probably a military veteran, he became captain of the rebels of Kent on June 7, leading them to success, including the capture of Canterbury, London Bridge and the Tower of London. Wat (Walter) was promised concessions by King Richard II (1377–1399), but his troops refused to disband, and on June 15 he met with the king, making radical demands. Fighting ensued and Tyler was stabbed. Carried by his supporters to Saint Bartholomew's Hospital, he was arrested later that day and beheaded by order of the lord mayor of London, his death delivering a mortal blow to the rebellion. See also PEASANT REVOLT.

# U

**ULRICH** (d. 973) Bishop of Augsburg from 923, a supporter of the reforms of Emperor Otto I (936–973), appointed to his see by Henry I the Fowler (919–936). Ulrich was also responsible for fortifying Augsburg, thus enabling the city to survive the Magyar siege in 955. Shortly thereafter the Magyars were defeated at the Battle of Lechfeld by Otto. His resultant privileges included Ulrich's right to coin money. He was the first person to be formally canonized by the pope, John XV, the pronouncement coming at St. John Lateran, signed in January 993.

**UMAR (1)** (c. 586–644) Second caliph, successor to Abu Bakr, reigning from 634 to 644 and the man largely responsible for the sweeping campaigns conducted by the Muslims in the forging of the Islamic empire. Umar was converted to Islam by 618, serving later as one of the chief supporters of Abu Bakr before and after his rise as caliph. Named successor in 634, he proved to be a gifted leader and cemented Arab unity as his armies drove across adjacent lands. He decreed that Arabs might not own land in any conquered region so as to preserve centralization of Arab power. The resulting tent cities became major communities in Syria, Iraq and Egypt, including al-Fustat (the town of tents). He gave solidity to Islamic administrative and legal practice, and his reign witnessed the conquest of the lands lying between Egypt and Khorasan. In 644 Umar was assassinated by a Persian slave in the mosque at Medina. See also ARABIA.

**UMAR (2)** (682/683–720) Umayyad caliph from 717 to 720 a descendant of the caliph UMAR (1) and educated at Medina. Appointed governor of the Hejaz (Saudi Arabia) in 706, he was named caliph in 717 at the request of his predecessor, Sulayman. Esteemed and revered as a pious and deeply religious ruler, Umar strengthened the caliphate, reforming the tax system and encouraging conversions to Islam. No major military campaigns were initiated in his reign, and the siege of Constantinople, begun by Sulayman, was ended. See also UMAYYAD CALIPHATE.

**UMAYYAD CALIPHATE** Also called the Omayyad caliphate, the first major Islamic dynasty, surviving from 661 to 750 and responsible for extending the limits of Islam into Europe and beyond the Indus River to the east. The line is also called the Arab Kingdom, defeated ultimately by the Abbasids, who initiated a deliberate propaganda effort to discredit them. The Umayyads began as a merchant family in Mecca, its patriarch Abu Sufyan, whose son was Mu'awiya. Initially resistant to Islam, the family eventually became followers of the Prophet (c. 627) and held important posts in Islamic government. Mu'awiya served as governor during the civil war of 656–661, following the murder of Uthman in 656. He strove for a resolution to civil strife and then embarked on a campaign against Ali, the fourth caliph and the son-in-law of the Prophet. Defeating Ali, in 661 he declared himself the first caliph of the Umayyad line, which was to have Sufyanid members dominating from 661 to 684. At that time Mu'awiya (reigned 661–680) established his capital at Damascus, thereby inaugurating Syrian ascendancy in the military. The caliphate, however, was organized on traditional Arab tribal lines, its political power resting in Arab hands while administration was conducted by Syrians or Persians within the provinces. This led to accusations of secularism, offset by aggressive, imperialist expansion.

The successors to the Prophet, the caliphs who guided Islam from 632 to 661 had launched extensive conquests, capturing Syria, Iraq, Persia, Egypt and parts of North Africa. The Umayyads conducted expansion with the Syrian troops at their disposal, and controlling the provinces and suppressing internal dissent, especially among the old Arab tribes. Islamic rule was extended east into Khorasan and into northwestern India, while preliminary steps were taken to conquer North Africa. A fleet was sent against Constantinople and the Byzantine Empire (669–678), adding prestige to a regime with the propaganda potential of a war against the Infidel (nonbelievers).

A change of dynasty took place in 684, with the rise of Marwan I, who founded the second ruling branch of the Umayyads, which was in place until 750, called the Marwanids. The vitality of this new line was clear in the reign of Abdul Malik (ruled 685–705) and his son, al-Walid I (ruled 705–715). Through them the caliphate reached the pinnacle of power, partly owing to the generals al-Hajjaj ibn Yusuf and Musa ibn Nusays. Umayyad armies marched beyond the Oxus to Samarkand and into the Sind region of India in the East. In the West the Islamic armies swept into Spain, destroying the Visigoth kingdom there. Domestically a major shift was made in the government, with Arabs replacing the Persian and Greek officials of the state and Arabic was declared the language of the empire.

From the reign of Sulayman (715–717) the caliphate was confronted by severe problems. An Umayyad army was defeated in 717 by Emperor Leo III the Isaurian, and the caliph Umar (II) (ruled 717–720) was forced to find a solution to the growing financial and social crises caused by

Umayyad ware, 10th-century Granada

expansion and conversions among the conquered populations. The state did not encourage wholesale conversion, preferring to have a wider tax base, as Muslims were exempt from taxation. New converts, known as *mawali,* were required to pay a poll tax *(jizyah)* and gradually met severe discrimination by the socially superior Arabs. Even with these handicaps the converts were numerous, as the average Muslim, even a *mawali,* was better off financially than a non-Muslim, although most non-Islamic populations had greater freedom under Muslim rule than that of the Byzantines. Umar encountered increasing distress among the *mawali* and as a solution placed all Muslims on an equal footing, in regard to taxation. While this eased the social problems, it added to the financial ones. At the same time, peasants were migrating into the cities, where the tax collectors had a more difficult time identifying them.

Hisham's reign (724–743) was one of gradual decline. In France, Islamic expansion was halted at Tours (Poitiers) in 732, and challenges in the provinces were increased by threats from the Turks in Central Asia and the Berbers in North Africa. The Islamic empire was still essentially stable, but the financial crisis remained, cutting off revenues to the central government and isolating the provinces, many of which were beset by rebellions. These revolts stemmed from several conditions. The Shiites opposed the Sunni doctrines of the Umayyads, the *mawali* strove for a greater social and political voice in the Arab-dominated government and members of the Abbasid line were conspiring to bring down the caliphate. Through subtle diplomacy and alliances and by taking advantage of the problems plaguing the Umayyads, the Abbasids were ultimately successful, bringing the war into Syria. In 750, at the Battle of Zab (or the Zab), they defeated the last Umayyad caliph, Marwan II. Surviving members of the dynasty were massacred. One survivor, Abd al-Rahman, fled to Spain, where he founded the Umayyad dynasty of Córdoba. The end of this first caliphate, succeeded by the Abbasids, was the finale as well to the concept of an Islamic empire and Arab supremacy. Henceforth Islam was to be universal, with governments maintained by agents who owed their allegiance to the caliphs. Westward expansion was replaced by eastern consolidation. See also CÓRDOBA, EMIRATE OF; DAMASCUS; ISLAM; SYRIA; and individual figures or rulers.

***UNAM SANCTAM*** See BONIFACE VIII.

**UNIVERSITIES** Institutions of learning established during the Middle Ages, eventually vital to shaping the social, political, educational and intellectual life of the West. Most arose from the cathedral schools, known as *studia generalia,* or *studium generale,* schools serving a diocese, attracting scholars from other dioceses and then from other countries. It was the presence of foreign students that distinguished the *studia* from the original cathedral school.

The term *university* (*universitas*) was used generally to apply to the guilds or even communes, and the earliest universities were actual guilds or societies erected within a *studium* to provide protection for foreign faculty and students. Such organizations were called "nations" in time, having no academic authority at the onset by participating in the institution. In the 12th century this process began, gaining impetus from the favored positions held by specific scholars. In Paris, for example, students were eager to study with Abelard, Hugh of Saint Victor and others, flocking to the city and causing the creation of new *studia* when those in existence could no longer support their students. Early universities did not win respect from authority, and as the instructors strove to control their particular academic subjects, conflicts were inevitable, often taking the form of riots. Schools were closed and students went elsewhere, with a new university often the result. Such events gave rise to several universities, including Oxford, which came into existence when English scholars fled France in 1167. The school masters arose in this early period with wide authority, soon challenged by new influences. Chief among these were the friars, the clerical orders who came to Paris in the 13th century, bringing with them their views on Aristotle. Meanwhile, at Bologna, students won for themselves remarkable control over their institution, dominating the choice of subject matter and exacting promises of loyalty and obedience from their faculty. These student universities, however, could not survive without recognition by higher authority, both temporal and spiritual.

Frederick I Barbarossa (1152–1190), in 1158, granted certain rights to the scholars of Bologna, protecting them from illegal arrest and permitting them trial by their peers. They could also conduct strikes (*cessatio*) in protest against assorted grievances. Papal and imperial patronage was instrumental in placing Paris and Bologna on sure academic and institutional footing. Paris became noted for its instruction in theology and Bologna for its law courses, but both universities set the standard for schools of higher learning and were vital to the intellectual and political life of their cities or countries. Thus, the theologians of Paris were influential in disputes regarding the Great Western Schism, and the scholars of the University of Prague had a hand in disseminating the Hussite doctrine within the broader Bohemian reform movement.

Within the cathedral schools the power lay with the chancellors, held in the university system by the rector, who was answerable to the faculty or, as in Italy, to the students themselves. Universities were essentially places for professional training, as a degree provided a license to teach or to move on to a higher academic level. While the university might be distinguished for a particular academic field of study, larger institutions usually had four specific types of scholarship: arts, theology, medicine and law. The average doctorate required 16 years of study, thus mobility and flexibility became essential, especially after competition between universities became intense. Foreign students continued to congregate under the heading of "nations." At Bologna, by the end of the 12th century, there were four such "nations" present, the Lombards, Romans, Tuscans and Ultramontanes (a union of English, German and French students).

Traditionally, Latin was the language of learning. Students studied the seven liberal arts with greater emphasis placed on the trivium (grammar, rhetoric and logic) than on the quadrivium (arithmetic, astronomy, music and geometry). The *Sentences* by Peter Lombard was the accepted text for the study of theology, with additional material provided by the writings of the church fathers and biblical commentaries. The *Digest* and the *Decretum* of Gratian were the texts for the study of civil and canon law. See also ASTRONOMY; AVIGNON; BENEDICTINES; BOLOGNA; DOMINICANS; FRANCISCANS; LONDON; MEDICINE; OXFORD; PARIS; PETER LOMBARD; SALERNO; SCHOLASTICISM; SORBONNE.

**UNTERWALDEN** Canton in central Switzerland that was ruled after 1173 by the Habsburg counts in the name of the German king. The canton played a leading role in the movement for Swiss independence by joining with Uri and Schwyz to form the Everlasting League in 1291. These cantons were the nucleus of the Swiss League. See also SWITZERLAND.

**UPPSALA** City in east-central Sweden to the north of Stockholm, originally a pagan site, Ostra Aros, becoming a Christian episcopal see in 1130 and an archepiscopal see in 1270. Replaced as a power politically by Stockholm, Uppsala remained the metropolitan see for the religious affairs of the nation, having the largest cathedral in Sweden, consecrated in 1435. The University of Uppsala, founded in 1477, was the oldest in the kingdom and emerged as one of the distinguished institutions of learning in Europe. See also SWEDEN.

**URBAN II** (c. 1035–1099) Pope from 1088 to 1099, best known for having called of the First Crusade (1095–1099). Born Odo of Lagery, he entered Cluny around 1070 and was appointed cardinal in 1078 by Pope Gregory VII (1073–1085), who sent him as papal legate to France and Germany. He presided over a synod at Quadlingburg in Saxony (1085) that condemned the antipope Clement III (1080; 1084–1100). Elected successor to Victor III (1086–1087), Urban continued the Gregorian Reform, issuing 16 canons against simony and lay investiture at the Council of Melfi (1089). In Rome he expelled Clement with the support of Matilda of Tuscany but was forced to flee Rome in 1090 when Clement returned with the German king Henry IV's (1056–1106) forces. He went into exile but in 1093 returned to Rome, crowning Henry's son, Conrad, king of Italy.

In 1095 Urban summoned two councils, at Piacenza and Clermont. The Council of Clermont proclaimed the Truce of God and called for a crusade to liberate the Holy Land from the Muslims, a response to an appeal from Emperor Alexius I Comnenus (1081–1118). This plea was to have a major influence on the crusading movement, with all its ramifications. See also CRUSADES.

**URBAN III** (d. 1187) Pope from 1185 to 1187, born Umberto Crivelli to a noble family of Milan, succeeding Pope Lucius III (1181–1185). His pontificate was dominated by his conflict with Emperor Frederick I Barbarossa (1152–1190) arising from the pope's opposition to the marriage of Frederick's son, Henry, to Constance. She was the Norman heiress to Sicily, and the union advanced the Hohenstaufen dynasty in southern Italy. Another dispute over the consecration of the archbishop of Trier moved Frederick to order Henry to invade the Papal States. After Frederick convened the Diet of Gelnhausen (1186), where imperial support was secured from German bishops, Urban ordered the emperor to Verona. Unable to convince the city's inhabitants to allow Frederick's excommunication, Urban went to Venice, dying en route.

**URBAN IV** (c. 1200–1264) Pope from 1261 to 1264, born Jacques Pantaléon, a professor of canon law in Paris before becoming a bishop. He was then appointed patriarch of Jerusalem, eventually succeeding Alexander IV (1054–1061). Urban helped curtail the Ghibelline cause in Italy and the ambitions of the Hohenstaufen claimant, Manfred, by offering in 1263 the crown of Sicily to the brother of King Louis IX (Saint Louis) (1226–1270), Charles of Anjou. Urban ordered the celebration of the Feast of Corpus Christi throughout the church in 1264.

**URBAN V** (1310–1370) Pope from 1362 to 1370, born Guillaume de Grimoard, from Languedoc, a Benedictine who taught canon law at Avignon. After serving as abbot in his order's monasteries, he succeeded Pope Innocent VI (1352–1362) at Avignon. Considered pious and austere, he strove to reform the Curia and returned the papal court to Rome in 1367. He encouraged restoration of churches and received Emperor John V Palaeologus of Constantinople (1354–1391) in 1369, hoping to unite the Eastern and Western Churches. Under pressure from the French cardinals, in 1370 he returned to Avignon, despite the pleas of the Romans and of Saint Bridget of Sweden.

**URBAN VI** (c. 1320–1389) Pope from 1378 to 1389, whose election and subsequent actions gave rise to the Great Western Schism. Born Bartolomeo Prignano, he succeeded Gregory XI (1370–1378) in an election designed to appease the Romans, who wanted an Italian pontiff and feared a French pope might return to Avignon. Although devout and efficient, Urban lost support and alienated the French prelates by appointing only Italians to his papal offices. The French prelates declared the election null and chose Robert of Geneva as antipope Clement VII (1378–1394). This schism would plague the church from 1378 to 1417. Urban was perhaps murdered, and Clement took up residence at Avignon.

**USURY** See Glossary.

**UTRAQUISTS** See also BOHEMIA; HUS, JAN; HUSSITE WARS.

# V

**VACLAV** See WENCESLAS.

**VALDEMAR** See WALDEMAR.

**VALENCIA** Capital city of the Valencia region in eastern Spain on the Mediterranean Sea, a thriving Roman colony that fell to the Visigoths in 413 and to the Moors in 714. After the decline of the caliphate of Córdoba, Valencia was established as an independent emirate in 1021. The celebrated Spanish hero, El Cid (Rodrigo Díaz de Vivar), fought for the kingdom from 1089 to 1094, controlling it until his death in 1099. It was recovered from the Moors in 1102. In 1238, Valencia was incorporated into the Aragonese kingdom by King James I (1213–1276). The city, however, retained considerable autonomy and continued to prosper. Its cultural importance was maintained after 1479 by its association with Castile ruled by Ferdinand and Isabella (1474–1516).

**VALENTINE** (d. 827) Pope for a brief period in 827, revered for his piety although pontiff for barely 40 days.

**VALLA, LORENZO** (1407–1457) Italian philosopher and humanist whose contributions influenced Renaissance thought. A native of Rome and ordained in 1431, he became secretary to King Alfonso V of Aragon and Naples (1416–1458), for whom he wrote his *Declamatio,* proving the spuriousness of the Donation of Constantine (1440) and attacking the temporal powers of the papacy. In 1447 he served as a scriptor and apostolic secretary in Rome, defended by King Alfonso and Pope Nicholas V (1447–1455) against charges of heresy because of his views. The first exponent of historical criticism, Valla was audacious, thought shocking by his contemporaries for advancing his view that the Scholastic approach was confusing to the study of Aristotelian thought. He denied the apostolic origin of the Apostle's Creed and criticized monastic vows. Among his works were *De elegantiis linguae Latinae* (1442) on Humanist Latin; *Callatio Novi Testamenti* (1444), a critical comparison of the Greek and Vulgate New Testaments; and *Dialecticae disputationes contra Aristotelicos* (printed in 1499), which was a critique of Scholasticism.

**VALLADOLID** City in northwestern Spain, the capital of Valladolid province, called by the Moors Belad Ulid, falling into Christian hands in the 10th century. The city became prominent during the rule of Castile by Count Pedro Ansurez in the 11th century. Such was its influence that Valladolid replaced Toledo as the royal residence. King Alfonso VIII (1158–1214) incorporated it into crown lands and Isabella and Ferdinand (1474–1516) were married there in 1469. Valladolid University was founded in 1346, the oldest in Spain. Decline came to the city in the 16th century when the Habsburg King Philip II moved Spain's capital to Madrid.

**VALOIS DYNASTY** Ruling dynasty of France from 1328 to 1589, during the passage of the country from the strictures of the Middle Ages and into modern history. Founded by Charles of Valois, third son of King Philip III the Bold (ruled 1270–1285), the brother of Philip IV the Fair (ruled 1270–1285), the house arose in the historical region of Valois acquired by the French crown under Philip II Augustus (1180–1223) in 1214. Charles's descendant, Philip of Valois, succeeded the Capetians in 1328 as Philip VI of Valois, ruling until 1350. The early kings were concerned principally with surviving the Hundred Years' War (1337–1453), during which the crown suffered severe political setbacks but recovered under Charles VII (ruled 1422–1461), winning the war and restoring its political power. Through consolidation and the reduction of feudal nobility's influence, the Valois kings were able to establish royal absolutism, especially under Louis XI (ruled 1461–1483). See also FRANCE and Genealogy.

**VANDALS** An ancient Germanic people largely responsible for the decline of the regional power held by the Western Roman Empire, moving westward in the early fifth century as a result of the advancing Huns. Invading and devastating Gaul in 406, they migrated into the Iberian Peninsula (409) and settled there, dividing into smaller tribal groups, including the Asding and Siling Vandals. The Asding (Asdingi) were the most powerful people in the region, especially in the reigns of King Gunderic and his brother and successor, the powerful Geiseric (Gaiseric), who ruled from 428 to 477. He invaded Africa in 429 and by 439 had established an independent Vandal kingdom following his capture of Carthage. The Vandals became a formidable threat force in the West, the Vandal fleet dominating much of the Mediterranean. Zealous Arians, the Vandals persecuted their orthodox Catholic subjects and exiled their bishops. Decline began after the death of Geiseric, culminating in 533 with the invasion of North Africa by the Byzantines led by general Belisarius, who destroyed them in one campaign. The Vandals ceased to be a major threat. Their sack of Rome in 455 probably led

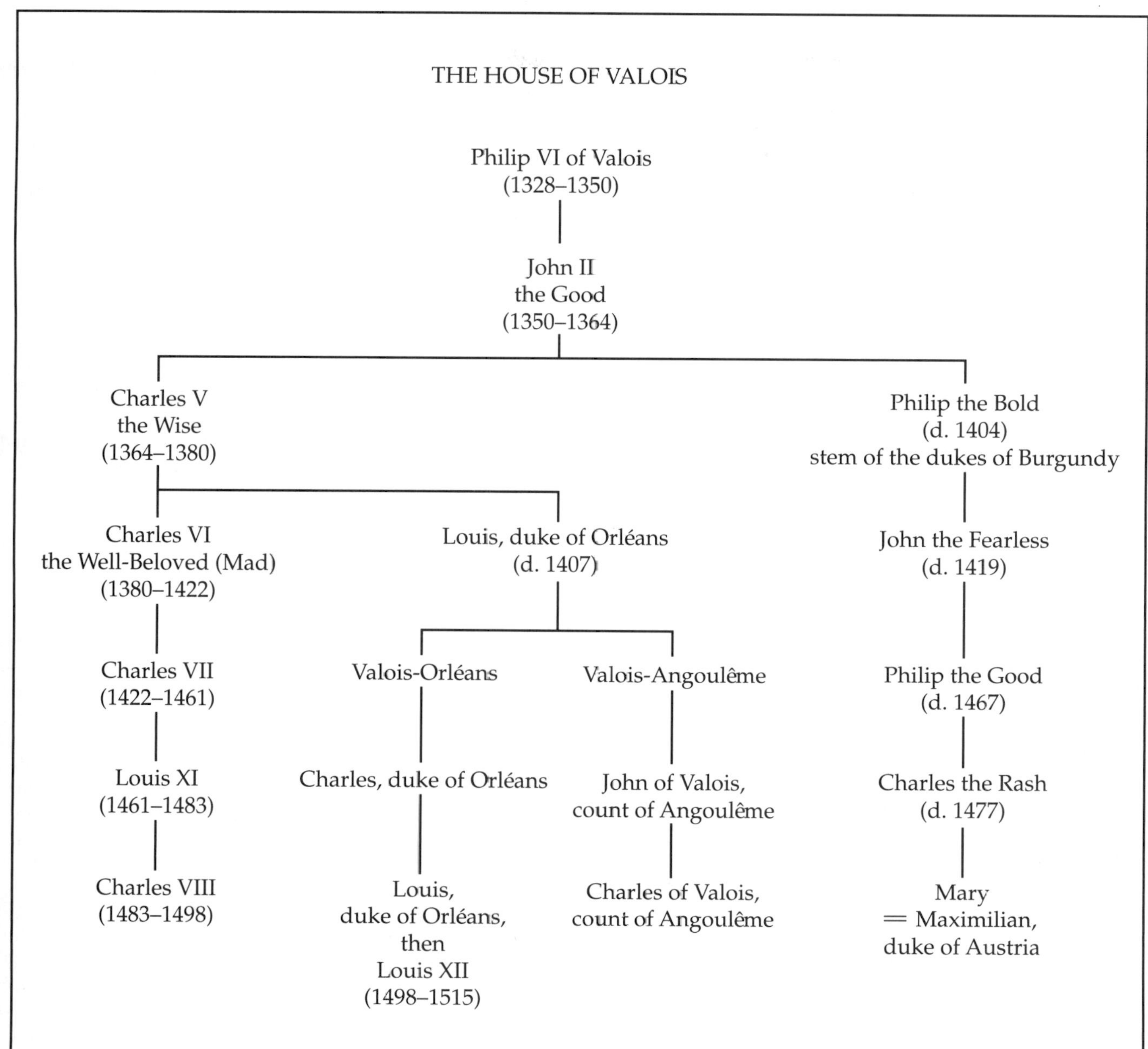


to their name becoming synonymous with willful destruction and desecration. See also BELISARIUS; CARTHAGE; and individual kings.

**VAN EYCK, HUBERT** See EYCK, HUBERT VAN.

**VAN EYCK, JAN** See EYCK, JAN VAN.

**VARANGIANS** Scandinavian warriors who penetrated into Russia in the ninth century. Always subject of an intense scholarly debate, they supposedly were in the command of Rurik, who in 862 established himself at Novgorod, an act traditionally held to be the founding of the Russian state. The Varangians launched raids throughout the Volga region and into Byzantine territories, serving also as mercenaries for the Byzantine emperors as the Varangian Guard. See also VIKINGS.

**VASCONIA** See GASCONY.

**VASILY I** (1371–1425) Also Vasily I Dimitrievich (or Dmitriyevich), grand prince of Moscow from 1389 to 1425, striving to free his land from Tatar control while at the same time extending his holdings. The eldest son of Grand Prince Dimitry Donskoi (d. 1389), he was successful in winning from his father's Mongol overlords the right of his father to hold the title prince of Vladimir. He remained hostage by the khan until 1386, escaping during the advance of the khanate against Tamerlane. Nevertheless, in 1388, he led a force against Tamerlane on behalf of the khan. In 1389 he succeeded his father, embarking on a campaign of aggrandizement for Moscow. He won control of the Volga region, settled a dispute with the Lithuanians and continued until 1417 to fight with Novgorod. Taking advantage of the political upheaval caused by Tamerlane among the Tatars, Vasily won his virtual independence from them until 1408, when the new khan laid siege to Moscow. Thereafter Vasily recognized Tatar suzerainty and continued to pay them tribute. See also MOSCOW, GRAND PRINCES OF.

**VASILY II** (1415–1462) Also called Vasily II the Blind, grand prince of Moscow, succeeding Vasily I in 1425 and meeting serious rivals in his uncle Yury and his cousins. A conflict ensued in which Vasily ultimately triumphed but only after being deposed twice (1434 and 1446–1447). He was blinded in 1446. Final peace was achieved in 1452, and thereafter Vasily began to consolidate Moscow's holdings. He made peace with the Lithuanians in 1449, allowing him to expand his control over neighboring principalities. At the same time he strove to reduce Tatar control, defeating a force in 1451 and becoming the overlord of a vassal Tatar group in the southeast in 1453. While still under the nominal suzerainty of the Tatars, Moscow grew in size, power and influence. See also MOSCOW, GRAND PRINCES OF.

**VENANTIUS FORTUNATUS** (c. 540–c. 600) Also Venantius Honorius Clementianus Fortunatus, the last Gallic Latin poet, whose works were transitional in his employment of both ancient and medieval styles of composition. He was educated at Ravenna and later served Queen Radegunde as secretary in her convent at Poitiers (c. 567). Impressed with her saintliness, he became a priest and was appointed bishop of Poitiers about 600. Venantius produced 11 books of poems, a life of Saint Martin of Tours in metered verse and in prose, *Lives* of 11 other Gallic saints, including the *Vita Radegundis,* and an elegy, *De excidio Thuringiae.* His six poems on the Cross included two hymns of exceptional quality: *Vexilla regis* and *Pange lingua gloriosi.*

**VENETIA** Region in northeastern Italy lying between the Alps, the Po River and the Adriatic Sea, with its capital at Venice. Severely damaged during the era of tribal migrations, the region eventually became (by the 10th century) a group of free communes. Chief among these was Venice, which came to dominate the region. From the 14th and 15th centuries the region was absorbed by the Republic of Venice, sharing in its subsequent history. Other cities in Venetia include Padua and Verona. See also VENICE.

**VENICE** City in northern Italy, the capital of the region of Venetia, built on 118 islets in a lagoon on the Gulf of Venice. Once a haven for refugees from war, it rose to became a major mercantile power in the Mediterranean. Venice was established in the final years of the Roman Empire in the East, when the Hun and Ostrogoth invasions in the fifth century drove the inhabitants of other cities, Padua, Verona and especially Aquileia, to seek the safety of the lagoon. Overcoming many natural challenges and joined by other migrant groups, the Venetians laid the groundwork for a city unique in Europe, water borne and water bound.

Originally under Byzantine jurisdiction, specifically the exarch of Ravenna, Venice moved toward independence, and the republican city-state was ruled by the first of its doges as early as 697. Paulutius Anafestus was doge, although some called him a Byzantine governor. The doges already controlled the city, however, in the early ninth century, as its independence was confirmed in a treaty of 810 between Emperor Nicephorus I and Charlemagne, although there was never a formal break between Venice and Constantinople. With the Byzantine influence removed, the city government was maintained by the merchant aristocracy, who conducted affairs guided by a republican constitution. The doges held formidable power from the 9th to the 11th century, but their efforts to force their political will on the Venetians or to make the post hereditary were defeated by the powerful families of the republic. From the 11th century the office of doge declined in authority, its chief activity limited to command of the navy and matters concerning public safety. A major contribution to this development was the organization of councils or committees for administrative and legislative affairs. Chief among these was the Maggior Consiglio (Great Council), composed of nobles. The Council of Ten also administered the security details for Venice, and the Senate, the body governing decisions on finance, war and trade, controlled these matters on behalf of the republic. The Venetians, while concerned with trade, maintained close watch on their government. The aristocracy was a close-knit and powerful class, and the Great Council restricted its membership to families whose names were listed in the Golden Book (Libro d'Oro). There was only one exception to this rule in 1380, and the nobility did not open its ranks until the 17th century. Conspiracies against the republic were taken seriously, especially after the investigation of Baiamonte Tiepolo, which prompted the formation of the Council of Ten. Supported by the doge, who was a member, and aided by the information made available by spies, torturers, assassins, ordinary citizens and, after 1519, three Inquisitors, the council maintained political calm in the city, a situation markedly different from that in other Italian cities and a factor in Venice's economic success.

Having contributed to the defeat of the Arab pirates, Venice became a formidable maritime power around 1000, defeating Dalmatian pirates and allied with the Byzantines against the Norman lords of southern Italy and Sicily. The Crusades allowed Venice to open new ports and avail itself of new eastern Mediterranean trading rights. Under the aegis of the doge Enrico Dandolo, Venice secured contracts for the transportation of the Crusader armies. When the Crusaders were unable to finance this matter, the doge asked them instead to capture the Hungarian dependency of Zara, land at Constantinople and overthrow the Byzantine Empire in 1204. The Venetians received plunder taken from the conquered lands and came to dominate much of Greece and the Aegean. In its primacy as a commercial state, Venice was in a position to defend its holdings and to embark on war with its rivals. From 1253 to 1381 it fought with Genoa, the conflict ending in the War of Chioggia (1378–1381), in which the Genoese navy, and hence its trading capacity, was destroyed. As a result, Venice ruled the Mediterranean as the "Queen of the

Seas." During the 15th century the city captured Cyprus, Crete, Venetia and most of Dalmatia. Venetian ships sailed to the Levant, Egypt, Constantinople and up to Flanders, trading gold and silver for the treasures of the East: silks, spices, and other luxuries. Its ambitious program in the Italian peninsula, while diverting attention from its Mediterranean empire, provided the Venetians with revenue from taxes and strategic holdings, creating envy among its neighbors. The 15th century ended as Venice faced the advance of the Ottoman Turks in the Balkans and into the Mediterranean. The Portuguese were also discovering (1498) new trade routes to India. See also AMALFI; BYZANTINE EMPIRE; CANDIA; CONSTANTINOPLE; CONSTANTINOPLE, LATIN EMPIRE OF; CRETE; CRUSADES; CYPRUS; DALMATIA; GENOA; HUNGARY; POLO, MARCO; OTTOMAN EMPIRE; PISA; SHIPS; TRADE AND COMMERCE; VENETIA; and individual doges.

**VERDUN, TREATY OF** (843) The partition of the Frankish empire among the three sons of Emperor Louis I the Pious (814–840). According to its terms, Louis the German received the eastern portion (Germany), Charles II the Bald the western (France), and Lothair I, confirmed in his imperial title, much of Italy and parts of Belgium, the Netherlands, Switzerland, France and Germany, a strip of extensive holdings that would form Lotharingia. The treaty was the first step toward the fragmentation of the Frankish Carolingian realm.

**VERMUDO I, KING OF ASTURIAS** Ruler from 788 to 791, who abdicated to be succeeded by his cousin, Alfonso II (791–842).

**VERMUDO II, KING OF LEÓN** (d. 999) Son of Ordoño III (951–956), who came to the throne in 984 as the result of an uprising of Galician nobles, who deposed Ramiro III (966–984). He was succeeded by his son, Alfonso V (999–1028).

**VERMUDO III, KING OF LEÓN** Ruler from 1028 to 1037, succeeding to the throne in his minority, a fact used to advantage by the ambitious Sancho III Garcés, el Mayor (1000–1035), king of Navarre. In his attempt to build a Spanish empire, Sancho occupied León in 1034, forcing Vermudo to flee to Galicia. The following year Sancho died, and Vermudo returned to León.

**VERONA** City in Venetia, northern Italy, situated on the Adige River, a Roman colony occupied by the Ostrogoths by 489. King Theodoric built a castle there, later a Lombard residence. Conquered by Charlemagne in 774, Verona was the residence of Pepin, his son. A free commune in the 11th century, the city led a group of towns that joined the Lombard League in its conflicts with the Hohenstaufen emperors. It endured the conflict between the Guelphs and Ghibellines, coming under the control of Ezzelino da Romano in 1226 and remaining so until 1256. In 1260, Mastino I Della Scala became podesta, or chief magistrate, and the Della Scala emerged as lords of the city in 1277. During this period the romance between Romeo and Juliet supposedly took place. Verona fell to Milan in 1387 and to the Venetians in 1405, who held it for the next centuries, with the exception of a period of occupation by Maxmilian I (1509–1517). See also GUELPHS AND GHIBELLINES.

**VESPERS, SICILIAN** See SICILIAN VESPERS.

**VICTOR II** (c. 1018–1057) Pope from 1055 to 1057, a supporter of church reform, born Gebhard of Dollnstein-Hirschberg to a noble family. He served as adviser to Emperor Henry III (1039–1056) who secured his election as successor to Pope Leo IX (1049–1054) in 1054. Consecrated in 1055, he convened several synods and councils (Florence, 1055; Lyons, 1055; and Toulouse, 1056) to combat the practice of simony and to promote reform. After Henry's death in 1056, Victor was guardian to Henry IV (1056–1106) and chief counselor to the regent, Agnes.

**VICTOR III** (c. 1025–1087) Pope from 1086 to 1087, born Dauferi in Benevento, joining the Benedictines at Monte Cassino, where he took the name Desiderius. Abbot of Monte Cassino in 1058, he was made a prelate by Pope Nicholas II (1058–1061) in 1059 and was elected pope in 1085 but refused to accept the office until compelled to the following year. He was forced to leave Rome by the supporters of Emperor Henry IV (1056–1106), who had named the antipope Clement III (1080; 1084–1100) in 1084. Victor spent most of his remaining years at Monte Cassino as imperial factions limited his time in Rome. He died at Monte Cassino, having condemned lay investiture and excommunicating Clement.

**VIGILIUS** (d. 555) Pope from 537 to 555, a Roman noble who traveled to Constantinople with Pope Agapitus I (535–536) in his attempt to convince Emperor Justinian I (527–565) not to reconquer Italy. Although he failed in his mission, Vigilius earned the patronage of Empress Theodora. Thus, when Silverius (536–537), Agapatius's successor, was deposed by Belisarius in December 536, Vigilius replaced him. His pontificate was dominated by the "Three Chapters Controversy" resulting after the condemnation in 544 of three authors and their writings or chapters that had been opposed by the Monophysites, whom Justinian had attempted to placate. Vigilius refused to join in the censure and was dealt with harshly by Justinian. His subsequent vacillation only widened the schism that ensued in the opposition between Eastern and Western doctrine, lasting for some 150 years. See also SCHISMS.

**VIKINGS** Scandinavian sailors and warriors who conducted raiding expeditions and campaigns of expansion during the 9th to the 11th centuries. Adventurous and warlike, the Vikings from Norway, Denmark and Sweden sailed and fought throughout the medieval world, from England, Ireland, France and the Baltic to Russia, Spain, Italy and Africa. The first of the great voyagers, they settled in Ireland and journeyed to North America, the last of the invaders and the first European explorers. The term Viking was probably derived from the Old Norse word *Vikingr*, probably meaning "sea man," once used to describe pirates of the Scandinavian coast. In Europe they were the Danes,

Viking brooch

and in France Normans. Swedish Vikings penetrated into Russia and later came into contact with Slavs, Arabs and Byzantines and were called Varangians or Rus by these people.

The causes for the rise of Viking activities in the early ninth century were varied. Scandinavian population growth was a major influence, and there were defeated chieftains who discovered that they could make a living as raiders. The defenseless regions of Europe offered opportunities for swift and easy plunder, and commerce was made possible, especially under the Varangians in Russia and beyond. Whatever the specific reasons, the military skill of the Vikings and their remarkable shipbuilding capabilities made them perfectly suited for raiding ventures.

The earliest recorded Viking attack of note took place in 793 at the monastery of Lindisfarne on Holy Island. This assault, probably conducted by Norwegians, was followed by raids on Iona and then by actual conquest of the Hebrides, Shetland and Orkney Islands. The Norwegians also embarked on campaigns in Ireland in the ninth century, establishing themselves over much of the country until their defeat by Brian Boru at the Battle of Clontarf in 1014. Remaining Viking possessions in Ireland survived until the Anglo-Norman invasion of the late 12th century. Norman sorties in France were resisted for many years owing to the strength of the Frankish Carolingian empire, but with its disintegration, the northern coast became susceptible to their raids. Liège, Aachen, Hamburg and Cologne were attacked, and in 845 Paris was besieged. Further attacks came on the Iberian Peninsula, the African coast and in Italy, where Pisa was burned in 860. The Vikings (or Normans) were mollified in 911, by King Charles III granting Rollo and his Norsemen territories that were to constitute the duchy of Normandy. These Normans were to conquer England and southern Italy, thereby altering the map of Europe. England itself was subject to repeated onslaughts prior to the Norman Conquest of 1066. The earlier raids, conducted by the Danes, began in 835, with a massive invasion following. Much of the island was brought under their control until the Danish advance was halted by Alfred the Great. Negotiations led to the establishment of a Viking region in England, the Danelaw. In the 11th century the Danes returned and the English were defeated, the kingship taken by Canute the Great and held by the Danes until 1042. The Varangians, meanwhile, entered Russia, where, according to tradition, they established the Russian states of Kiev and Novgorod, thereby ensuring their supremacy. Varangian traders also conducted commercial activities along the Black and Caspian Seas, traveling to Constantinople, where many become members of an imperial guard for the Byzantine emperors. Viking adventurers eventually sailed to Iceland, Greenland and North America.

The Viking Age came to an end in the 11th century. Scandinavian monarchies striving to centralize their kingdoms curtailed widespread overseas adventurism, especially on the part of the nobility, replacing such activities with trade. Conversions were also important, as Christianity had a civilizing effect as compared with warlike pagan activity. Germanic paganism, however, was preserved in Old Norse Literature. See also DANEGELD; DANELAW; ERIC THE RED; ICELANDIC LITERATURE; THORFINN KARLSEFNI; VINLAND; and individual countries and rulers.

**VILLANI, GIOVANNI** (c. 1275–1348) Italian chronicler of Florence, associated with the banking house of the Peruzzi, in which he became partner in 1300. He journeyed to Rome, France, Switzerland and Flanders on its behalf, but in 1308 he left the Peruzzi and became prominent in Florence, named the head of a guild on three occasions. In 1345 he was involved in the bankruptcy of the House of Bardi and three years later died of the plague. Villani wrote an ambitious *Cronica,* intended to record in 12 books world history from the Tower of Babel until his own era. A monument to Italian prose, the *Cronica* embraced a broad European historical view and was instrumental in the acceptance of Tuscan as the standard language of Italy. See also FLORENCE.

**VILLEHARDOUIN, HOUSE OF** French noble family that participated in the Fourth Crusade and wielded considerable influence in the Latin Empire of Constantinople. Geoffroi de Villehardouin (d. 1213) was marshal of Champagne and a leader of the Fourth Crusade (1202–1204) and was granted a rich fief in Thrace. His exploits were recorded in his *De la conqueste de Constantinople,* considered a masterpiece of early French historical writing. His nephew, Geoffroi I de Villehardouin (d. 1218), ruled the principality of Achaia as a fief to the Latin Empire, his sons, Geoffroi II (d. 1246) and Guillaume (d. 1278), succeeding him. Guillaume fought against Emperor Michael VIII Palaeologus (1259–1282) and the restored Byzantine Empire.

**VILLON, FRANÇOIS** (b. 1431; d. after 1463) French lyric poet acclaimed for his composition and wit. A native of Paris who studied at the university, he was associated with criminal gangs and was imprisoned for robbery and murder and sentenced to hang in 1463. His popularity was such, however, that he received a commutation of his sentence to 10 years in exile, during which time he probably died. His major works were *Le lais* or *Le petit testament* (1456) and *Le grand testament* (1461), written in the form of bequests to his family, associates and even his enemies. He also composed ballades, chansons and rondeaux, such as the celebrated *Ballade des dames du temps d'antan jadis,* "The Ladies of Yesteryear," with the refrain: "But where are the snows of yester-year?" "Où sont les neiges d'antan?"

**VINCENT OF BEAUVAIS** (c. 1190–1264) French encyclopedist, author of the work *Speculum major* (*Great Mirror*). He joined the Dominican order about 1220 and as a priest and theologian earned the favor of King Louis IX (1226–1270), receiving an appointment to the royal court about 1250, where he wrote the treatise *De eruditione filiorum nobilium* (1260–1261, *On the Education of Noble Sons*). His celebrated effort *Speculum major* was composed between 1247 and 1259 and was an esteemed encyclopedia of the Middle Ages. It originally consisted of three parts; a fourth was added in the 14th century by an anonymous author, with the title *Speculum morales (Mirror of Morals).* Vincent's ambition was to provide documentation of world history to the time of Louis IX, with a compendium on law, economics, scientific knowledge, alchemy, astronomy, and other subjects. He also compiled a glossary of 3,000 words, giving credit to classical and contemporary authors. He relied on the work of 450 authors and 2,000 other sources, producing a magnum opus of 80 books in 9,885 chapters.

**VINICH** King of the Bulgars from 756 to 762. See also BULGARIA.

**VINLAND** The name given by the Vikings to the region of North America discovered by Leif Ericsson in the 11th century. The settlement was later sought by Thorfinn Karlsefni.

**VISCONTI** See VISCONTI, HOUSE OF.

**VISCONTI, FILIPPO MARIA** See VISCONTI, HOUSE OF.

**VISCONTI, GIAN GALEAZZO** See VISCONTI, HOUSE OF.

**VISCONTI, HOUSE OF** A powerful Ghibelline family that ruled Milan and northern Italy in the 14th and 15th centuries. They first came to prominence during the 11th century when they acquired the hereditary office of viscount of Milan, their name derived from that title. A major step was taken in 1262 when Ottone Visconti was appointed archbishop of Milan by Pope Urban IV (1261–1264), who used the support of that see to defeat his rival Della Torre in 1277. He bequeathed his power to his nephew, Matteo I, and the house to acquire the ranks of imperial vicar and lord (signore) of Milan. Gian Galeazzo Visconti (d. 1402) brought the house to the pinnacle of power, when he bought the title of hereditary duke from Emperor Wenceslas in 1395, defeating Emperor Rupert in his attempt to restore imperial authority in Italy in 1401. He then launched an ambitious expansionist campaign of diplomacy and war. Centralizing the government, he consolidated Visconti influence, became a patron of the arts and allied himself with the French crown by marrying Isabella, a daughter of King John II (1350–1364). Giovanni Maria (d. 1412) came to power when Gian died of plague; he was a cruel and dissolute ruler who was later assassi-

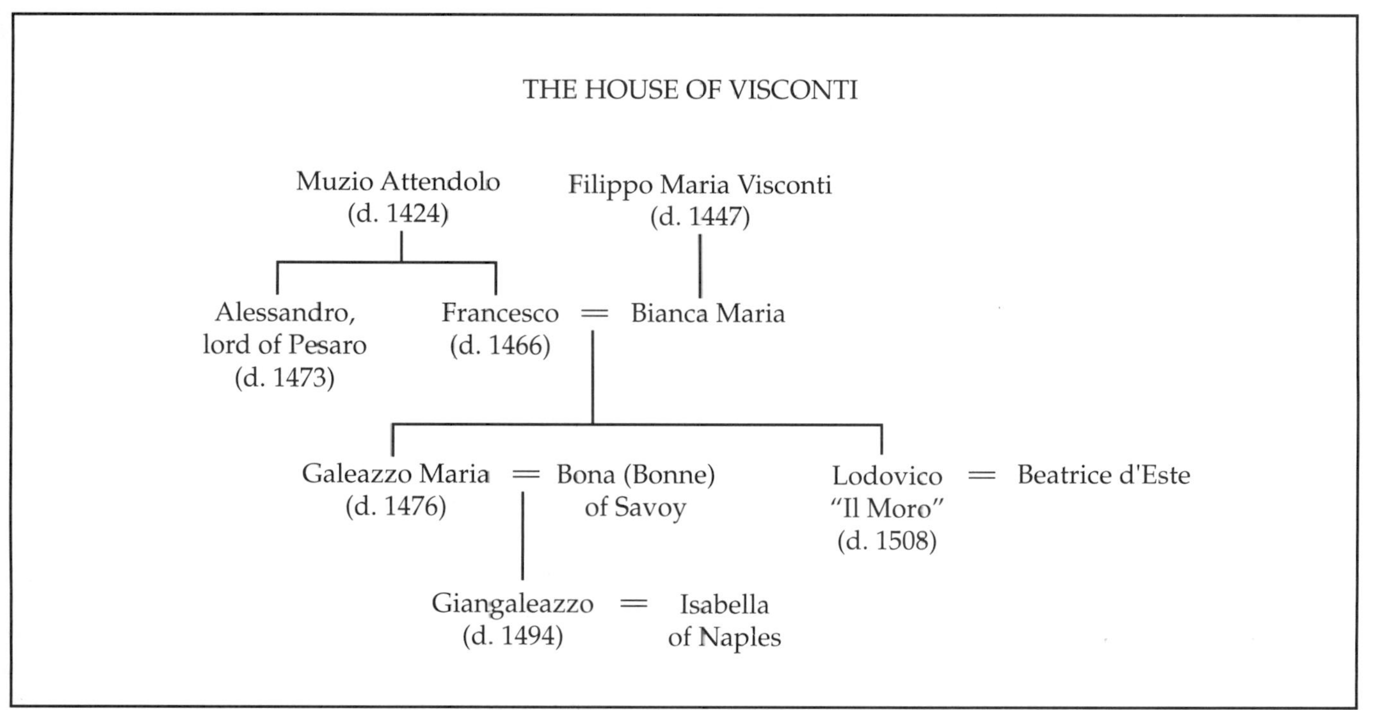

nated. His rule was inherited by his brother, Filippo Maria (1392–1447), who strove to restore the duchy to its former glory, warred on Florence and Venice and then died, thus allowing the formation of the short-lived Ambrosian Republic (1447–1450). Francesco Sforza, Filippo's son-in-law, restored the duchy ruling as the husband of the sole Visconti heiress, Bianca Maria. See also MILAN; SFORZA, HOUSE OF.

**VISIGOTHS** A powerful German people also called the West Goths, one of the two major divisions of the Goths, separating from the Ostrogoths in the fourth century and penetrating into the Danubian regions of the Eastern Roman Empire. They were converted to the Arian faith by the missionary Ulfilas. As pressure from the Huns increased in the East, the Visigoths surged into Roman territory and were drawn into a war with the empire. They fought and destroyed Emperor Valens at Adrianople in 378, and their king, Alaric I, led them westward. In 410 the Visigoths sacked Rome, moving into southern Gaul and the northern Iberian Peninsula in 412. From there they migrated north to the Loire and south into the Iberian Peninsula, with Visigoth power reaching its height under Euric. Alaric II, however, in 507, was routed by the Franks, and the Visigoths were largely forced beyond the Pyrenees. The Visigoth kingdom of Spain survived until 711, the Goths accepting orthodox Christianity and eventually assimilated into the local Iberian and Roman populations. Political unrest and anarchy characterized the later years of the kingdom, although the church was a major influence for good. The last king of the Visigoths was Roderic, who was defeated by the Moors in 711. See also OSTROGOTHS.

***VISION CONCERNING PIERS PLOWMAN, THE*** A major Middle English alliterative poem, dated at the 14th century and attributed to William Langland. Called simply *Piers Plowman,* it is an allegory, reflecting simple but powerful imagery. It recounts the dreams of a poet who sees a "fair field full of folk" lying between the Tower of Truth and the Dale of Death that is peopled with many characters. An interpretation of what he sees is given by Lady Holychurch and other allegorical figures who are brought into the account. A seemingly unsophisticated character, Piers Plowman (or Piers the Plowman) offers to help them find Truth if they will assist him in ploughing his half acre. The poem attacks, among other things, failings by the clergy, describes a spiritual journey and praises dedicated Christians. Other contemporaneous topics are also considered. See also LANGLAND, WILLIAM.

**VITALIAN** (d. 672) Pope from 657 to 672, dealing with the problems caused by the Monothelite heresy. He avoided condemning the *Typos* (the decree of Emperor Constans II [641–668] in 648 forbidding discussion of the Monothelite question) and thus secured his acceptance by the emperor. Vitalian played an important part in the evangelization of the Anglo-Saxons, and in 668 he consecrated Saint Theodore of Tarsus as archbishop of Canterbury.

**VITERBO** City northwest of Rome in Latium, central Italy. Granted to the papacy by Matilda of Tuscany in the 11th century, it was provided with an episcopal see in 1193 but became a pawn in the conflicts between the popes and the Holy Roman emperors, reverting to the papacy in 1396. Its principal value was as a residency for the popes, especially after 1257, although the city declined in importance when the papacy was moved to Avignon in 1309.

**VIVARINI** Influential family of Venetian painters. Antonio Vivarini (d. c. 1480) was the founder of the family workshop in Murano, collaborating with his brother-in-law, Giovanni d'Alemagna, from 1444. They lived in Padua from 1447 to 1450, working with Andrea Mantegna on a series of frescoes for the Ovetari Chapel. His brother, Bartolomeo (d. c. 1499), was his pupil, later reflecting the influence of Francesco Squarcione and Andrea Mantegna. Antonio's son, Alvise (d. c. 1505), worked in southern Italy, producing altarpieces at Barletta (1483) and Naples (1485). He produced paintings for the doge's palace in Venice with Giovanni Bellini (1488).

**VLADIMIR** City in western Russia, northeast of Moscow, founded in 1108 by Vladimir II Monomakh, eventually becoming the capital of the grand duchy of Vladimir-Suzdal, one of the major Russian principalities after the fall of the Kievan state. It derived its wealth from trade along the Klyazma River. After Vladimir was destroyed by the Mongols in 1238, the grand dukes of Moscow emerged as Russia's most influential princes. Vladimir, however, was rebuilt. Acquired by the Muscovites in 1364, Vladimir was again stormed by the Tatars in the 15th century, thereafter declining in importance. Notable buildings included the Uspenski and Demetrius cathedrals (12th century) and the Golden Gate (erected 1164). Vladimir-Suzdal architecture fused Romanesque and Byzantine styles, and its school of mural and icon painting flourished during the 12th and 13th centuries. See also RUSSIA.

**VLADIMIR, KING OF THE BULGARS** Ruler from 889 to 893, the son of Boris, inheriting the throne when his father abdicated and retired to a monastery. He reversed the royal policy of supporting Christianity in Bulgaria, destroying churches, including the Pliska basilica. Boris left his monastery in 893, overthrew Vladimir and replaced him with another son, Symeon. On being deposed he was blinded. See also BULGARIA.

**VLADIMIR I, SAINT, GRAND PRINCE OF KIEV** (d. 1015) First Christian ruler of Russia. He was the son of Prince Svyatoslav of Kiev, driven into exile in Scandinavia following the death of his father by his brother Yaropolk, who attempted to attach Novgorod to Kiev. Returning with help from his Norse relatives, Vladimir defeated his brother and consolidated Kiev and Novgorod. An avowed pagan at one time, he accepted Christianity about 987 as part of an agreement with the Byzantine Empire, accepting in marriage Anne, sister of Emperor Basil II. He then forcibly converted his subjects and embraced the Byzantine rite in the Old Slavonic language, a decision that discouraged the rise of the Roman Rite in the

East and determined the character of Russian religious practices for the next centuries. Vladimir's achievements were recorded in the Kiev Cycle. See also KIEV; RUSSIA.

**VLADIMIR II MONOMAKH, GRAND PRINCE OF KIEV** (1053–1125) Ruler from 1113 to 1125, a warrior who conducted campaigns against many enemies, including members of his own family. Becoming prince of Chernigov in 1078, he remained there until 1094 and subdued his cousins in Volhynia from 1084 to 1086 and in 1113, following the death of a cousin, Svyatopolk II (ruled 1093–1113), was named successor to the Kievan throne by the city council. He proved able, supposedly taking part in 80 campaigns, most often against the Polovtsy, who menaced Kiev from the southeast. Vladimir composed a testament for his sons, the earliest written lay in Russian literary history. See also KIEV; RUSSIA.

**VLADISLAV** King of Hungary from 1440 to 1444. See also HUNGARY.

**VOLHYNIA** Also Volynia and in Polish, Wolyn, a region in northwestern Urkraine and a Russian principality from the 10th to the 14th century. A neighbor of Galicia, Volhynia benefited from the decline of the Kievan state in the 12th century. Prince Roman of Volhynia (d. 1205) united Galicia with his lands and established a powerful state that he defended from many who threatened it, including the Poles, Hungarians and Lithuanians. His son, Daniel, ruled from 1225 to 1264, returning the principality (including Galicia) to its regional prominence. Trade was promoted and a building program instituted, but the onslaught of the Mongols in 1260 brought some destruction. Early in the 14th century, with the death of Daniel's son, Leo, in 1301, the principality was annexed by Lithuania. Galicia was taken by the Poles. See also LITHUANIA; RUSSIA.

**VRATISLAV** Prince of Bohemia from 1061 to 1092, becoming king in 1085, named by Emperor Henry IV. See also BOHEMIA.

**WACE** (c. 1100–1183) Anglo-Norman poet, the author of two verse chronicles, the *Roman de Brut* and the *Roman de Rou.* A native of Jersey, Wace held the patronage of King Henry II (1154–1189) of England, probably composing the *Rou* for him (1160–1174) and the *Brut,* which added the theme of the Knights of the Round Table to the story of King Arthur, for Henry's queen, Eleanor of Aquitaine (1155). The *Rou* was a history of Norman dukes from Rollo to Robert II Curthose. The *Brut* was a romantic version of the *Historia regum Britanniae,* an account of English history from its founding by Brutus the Trojan. See also ENGLAND.

**WALAFRID STRABO** (c. 808–849) Benedictine abbot, poet and theologian, born in Swabia and educated at Reichenau and later at Fulda, where he was influenced by Rabanus Maurus. He became abbot of Reichenau but was forced to flee to Speyer, probably in 839, for supporting Lothair I against Charles the Bald. He returned in 842. His poetry marked him as a successor to Alcuin, but Walafrid was known chiefly for his theological works. Among these were *De exordis et incrementis quarundam in observationibus ecclesiasticus rerum* (841, *Book on the Origins and Development of Certain Matters in Church Practice*). His poetry included *Visio Wettini* (c. 826, *The Vision of Wettin), De cultura hortorum (The Art of Gardening)* and the panegyric *Versus de imagine Tetrici (Verse on the Statue of Theodoric).* He also wrote hagiographical works and a revision of Einhard's *Life of Charlemagne.*

**WALDEMAR, KING OF SWEDEN** Ruler from 1270 to 1275. See also SWEDEN.

**WALDEMAR I, KING OF DENMARK** (1131–1182) Ruler from 1157 to 1182, who consolidated the holdings of the Waldemar dynasty and improved the political position of Denmark with respect to the Holy Roman Empire. The son of Canute Lavard, he claimed the throne and initiated a number of campaigns against the Wends (Slavs), largely defeating them by 1169. While he accepted the supremacy of the Holy Roman Emperor, Frederick I Barbarossa, with his foster brother Absalon, he chose about 1165 to recognize Pope Alexander III instead of Frederick's antipope Victor IV (V). In 1181, however, Waldemar improved relations with Frederick, forging an alliance with him through the marriage of his daughter to one of Frederick's sons. See also DENMARK.

**WALDEMAR II, KING OF DENMARK** (1170–1241) Son of King Waldemar I (1157–1182), reigning from 1202 to 1240 after holding the title duke of Schleswig (from 1188) and conquering Holstein and Hamburg. Succeeding his father, he acquired lands in northern Germany through his support of the future Emperor Frederick II (1215–1250). He next campaigned in the eastern Baltic region, fighting in Estonia in 1219 with the support of the Knights of the Sword. Captured in 1223 by Count Heinrich of Schwerin, he was held hostage until 1225 because his vassals refused to arrange his release. Forced to surrender many of his Baltic acquisitions, offering his sons as hostages and paying a ransom, Waldemar was freed and ordered a counterattack. He was defeated in 1227, able to retain his possessions in Estonia only. He introduced reforms in Denmark, reorganizing the Danish army and legal system. See also DENMARK.

**WALDEMAR IV ATTERDAG, KING OF DENMARK** (1321–1375) Ruler from 1340 to 1375, the son of King Christopher II (1319–1326, 1330–1332), educated at the court of the Holy Roman Emperor Louis IV the Bavarian (1314–1347), whose support he received in 1338 to launch an offensive to claim the Danish throne. Fighting the Holstein counts, who controlled the country, he secured the crown and spent the next years consolidating his position through taxation and a marriage to the sister of Duke Waldemar of Schleswig. He fought with King Charles IV of Bohemia (the future Holy Roman Emperor, 1346–1378) on behalf of his ally, the margave Louis of Brandenburg, in 1349–1350. Returning home, he suppressed a rebellion by the magnates of Jutland, supported by the Holstein counts. He also reclaimed territory from Sweden (1360) and captured Gotland (1361), acts that so alarmed the Baltic powers controlling trade that he was attacked by a coalition of the Hanseatic League, Sweden, Holstein and Mecklenburg. Defeated by them in 1368, he was forced to accept in 1370 the Treaty of Stralsund, giving the Hanseatic League privileges. His daughter was Margaret, who married Haakon VI of Norway (1355–1380) in 1363. See also DENMARK.

**WALDENSES** Also Waldensians or Vaudois, the name given to the followers of Peter Waldo of Lyons (d. 1217). Waldo accepted conversion in Lyons, where he was a wealthy merchant, and adopted a mendicant's life, preaching and distributing his wealth to the poor. Early settlements of his followers appeared on the French side of the Alps, with the Waldenses attacking the clergy for worldliness, bringing censure on the sect. The Waldensians believed in the superiority of spirit over matter, which led them to condemn sacraments and veneration of saints and relics, which in turn led to further condemnation of the sect. They failed in 1179 to win recognition from the Third Lateran Council and were banned in 1184 by Pope Lucius III (1181–1185) at the Council of Verona. They then organized themselves into a separate body with their own clergy, and their numbers increased, especially in Provence, where Waldo made a translation of the New Testament. In 1209 a crusade was organized by Pope Innocent III (1198–1216) to crush them. The Waldenses were accepted by many in Germany, Spain, Lombardy and Piedmont, but persecution and doctrinal differences reduced their numbers. In Bohemia the Waldenses were absorbed by the Hussites and in the 16th century established ties with other dissenters of the Reformation.

**WALES** A mountainous country in the British Isles, called in Welsh Cymru and deeply rooted in Celtic culture. Medieval Wales produced several notable princes, but the Welsh, because of linguistic, geographical and political reasons, never united and were thus vulnerable to English influence. Welsh poetry, music and learning flourished, making the region unique.

The influence of Roman occupation on Wales was slight, although Christianity was accepted and monastic communities and bishoprics were in existence by the fourth century. The traditional patron saint of Wales is Saint David, credited with having completed the conversion of the nation. Anglo-Saxon migrations into England had only a small effect, but as the kingdoms of the heptarchy emerged, the border wars became fierce. King Offa of Mercia (d. 796) supposedly built his formidable dike (see OFFA'S DYKE) to delineate clearly the boundary between Mercia and Wales. Welsh efforts toward unity were only partially successful, as the king of Gwynedd, Rhodri Mawr, the Great (d. 878), extended his influence over Powys and the former domain of Seisyldwig. His sons submitted to Alfred the Great (871–899), achieving English ascendancy in Wales. Howel the Good (d. 950) accepted the position of underking to Wessex but was nevertheless nominal ruler of Gwynedd, Powys and his own kingdom of Deheubarth. Much changed, however, with the Norman Conquest of England in 1066.

William I the Conqueror (1066–1087) established what was called the Welsh March, lands along the English border controlled by earldoms. Norman lords utilized these holdings to protect English territory from Welsh attack and to serve as launching points for invasion. Opposition to English advances was fierce, producing such Welsh leaders as Gruffydd ap Cynan (d. 1137) and his son, Owain Fawr of Gwynedd (d. 1170), who fought King Henry II (1154–1189) in his efforts to extend English control. By the late 12th century there were spheres of control for the Welsh and English, the three major Welsh kingdoms, including Gwynedd, Powys and Deheubarth, the rulers of which were often called princes.

Gwynedd was the most stable of these realms, overcoming the dynastic conflicts inevitable in succession, through the effort of Llewelyn ap Iorwith, the Great (d. 1240) and Llewelyn ap Gruffydd (d. 1282). Gruffydd took the title Prince of Wales in 1258 and entered into war with King Edward I of England (1272–1307). Coming to terms, Wales was again involved in hostilities by 1282, a campaign that developed into a full-scale war for independence. The movement was thwarted by Gruffydd's death and collapsed the following year. Edward consolidated English power in Wales but as a conciliatory gesture designated the eldest son of the king as the Princes of Wales in 1301. In the early 15th century Owen Glendower (d. c. 1416) raised a large force in rebellion that was not suppressed until about 1409. Rather than weaken English rule, however, the unrest hastened the acceptance of English law in Wales. This process ended with the Act of Union in 1536, in which all Welsh laws at variance with those of England were abolished. See also ENGLAND.

**AL-WALID (1)** (d. 715) Umayyad caliph from 705 to 715, whose reign was one of continued Islamic expansion, especially under the aegis of his general, Musa ibn Nusayr, who, with his lieutenant Tarik (Tariq), conquered Spain in 711. Tarik destroyed the Visigoth kingdom. Al-Walid was considered kinder than his father, Abd al-Malik, and encouraged literature and the arts. He also promoted the construction of schools, hospitals, orphanages and mosques. The latter included mosques in Medina and Mecca. He claimed the Basilica of Saint John the Baptist in Damascus, remodeling the interior and adding minarets to transform it into an Islamic place of worship.

**AL-WALID (2)** (d. 744) Umayyad caliph from 743 to 744, a libertine caliph of the Umayyads who proved unfit to rule. A musician and patron of poets, he supposedly had a bath constructed that poured wine instead of water so that he could drink while bathing. See also UMAYYAD CALIPHATE.

**WALLACE, SIR WILLIAM** (d. 1305) One of the illustrious Scottish national heroes who fought against King Edward I of England (1272–1307). The son of Sir Malcolm Wallace, he burned Lanark and killed an English sheriff in May 1297, emerging as the Scottish resistance leader. In September 1297, Wallace defeated an English force under John de Warenne, earl of Surrey, later capturing Sterling Castle and launching raids into northern England (Northumberland and Cumberland). Knighted on his return to Scotland, he became the guardian of the realm in the name of John de Balliol until Edward invaded Scotland in March 1298 and defeated him at the Battle of Falkirk on July 22. Wallace was unable to restore his reputation and resigned his guardianship to be replaced by Robert the Bruce and Sir John Comyn. Eventually captured by the English in 1305, he was executed in London as a traitor, despite the fact that he had never sworn allegiance to Edward. The primary source on his life is the poem attributed to Blind Harry (Henry the Minstrel). See also SCOTLAND.

**WALSINGHAM, THOMAS** (d. c. 1422) English Benedictine monk and a chronicler of the Abbey of Saint Albans, whose work is a major source on the reign of Richard II (1377–1399), Henry IV (1399–1413) and Henry V (1413–1422). He was the author of the *Historia Anglicana,* which was a continuation of the *Chronica majora* of Matthew Paris, an account of the years 1272–1422. He also wrote an abridged version of the *Chronicon angliae,* from 1328 to 1388. See also PARIS, MATTHEW.

**WALTER, HUBERT** (d. 1205) English statesman and archbishop of Canterbury who was nephew and a chaplain of Ranulf de Glanville, then dean of York in 1186 and bishop of Salisbury. He accompanied King Richard the Lion-Hearted (1189–1199) on the Third Crusade (1189–1192), visiting the imprisoned monarch at Durnstein Castle on his return to England and helping to raise the ransom for the king's release. In 1193 he was appointed archbishop and justiciar for Richard while the king was away from England. Virtual ruler during this period, he was forced to introduce heavy taxation to finance the king's campaigns and encountered difficulties with the monks of Christ Church, Canterbury, who had the support of Pope Innocent III (1198–1216). He resigned in 1198 but resumed his duties to serve King John (1199–1216). Walter was sent in 1201 and 1203 on missions to Philip II Augustus of France (1180–1223). He died on his way to Boxley to mediate a dispute between the monks of Rochester and their bishop. See also CANTERBURY.

**WALTER THE PENNILESS** (d. 1097) French knight, called Walter Sansavoir (the Penniless). With Peter the Hermit he helped to organize the Peasant's Crusade (1096). See also CRUSADES.

**WALTHER VON DER VOGELWEIDE** (d. c. 1230) Distinguished lyric poet of the Middle Ages in Germany, who won the patronage of many nobles, including Leopold V of Austria, Leopold VI of Austria and Philip of Swabia. He was consistantly disappointed in their treatment of him, which he thought ungrateful. He was, however, granted a fief from Frederick II of Germany (1215–1250), probably in the see of Würzburg. The subjects of his poems included political, moral and religious themes, but love predominated in his work, and he devised original treatments on the theme of courtly love. See also MINNESINGERS.

**WAMBA** (d. after 680) The last of the powerful Visigoth Kings, reigning from 672 to 680, chosen successor to Recceswinth (d. 672) and forced to accept the crown at swordspoint. His first days of rule were troubled by the Basques, who remained incalcitraut. He confronted rebellions in Septimania beyond the Pyrenees, and the general he sent to quell the revolt, Duke Paulus, joined the rebels, forcing Wamba to launch a major campaign to suppress them. Having restored order, he strove to restore royal authority and to enact legal reforms. Wamba fell ill in 680 and was replaced by Count Erwig. Eventually restored to health, he was convinced to retire to a monastery, where he died some years later. After Wamba's reign the Visigoth kingship declined. His reign was chronicled by his biographer, Bishop Julian of Toledo. See also VISIGOTHS.

**WARBECK, PERKIN** (d. 1499) English imposter and pretender to the throne of Henry VII (ruled 1485–1509). Born in Tournai, he was persuaded by Yorkist adherents to impersonate Richard, duke of York, who had been presumed murdered with his brother, King Edward V, in 1483 in the Tower of London. He journeyed to Ireland in 1491 to ask for Irish support and then returned to the Continent, where he won brief support from Maxmilian I of Austria (1493–1519) and King James IV of Scotland. After fruitless invasions of England (1495 and 1496) Warbeck finally landed at Cornwall in 1497 and was captured by Henry's forces. Admitting his complicity in the plot, he was hanged on November 23, 1499. See also HENRY VII, KING OF ENGLAND.

**WARFARE** Military practice and method that underwent a gradual process of change during the Middle Ages, necessitated by the Crusades, Viking raids and the incessant military campaigns of the early Middle Ages. The eventual use of artillery in the later Middle Ages rendered impractical the traditional fortresses and mounted, heavily armored knights. Warfare became a rudimentary science, integrating cavalry, infantry and artillery by the late 15th century.

### *Warfare*

As the Roman Empire in the West was being overrun by Germanic peoples, in the East a military system was arising that would permit the Byzantines to survive the onslaughts of Persians, Saracens, Bulgars and others. The basis for Byzantine tactics on the battlefield was the expert use of cavalry, a development forced on them by the annihilation of the Roman Army in 378 at Adrianople by the Goths. Mounted archers and lancers, as well as heavy cavalry, disciplined and schooled in mobility, feinting and combined in operations with infantry, enabled the Byzantines to triumph in Italy, Africa and Anatolia. The weakening of the empire diminished the strength of the armed forces, and after the Battle of Manzikert (1071) and the loss of much of Asia Minor to the Seljuk and later Ottoman Turks, those major regions of recruitment were lost. The Byzantines quickly declined as a military power, falling prey to other forces, notably those of the Fourth Crusade (1202–1204), and finally to the Ottoman Turks, who captured Constantinople in 1453.

The great threat of the Byzantine military was the weapon called Greek fire. A highly flammable substance consisting of uncertain ingredients, Greek fire was supposedly discovered by Callinicus of Heliopolis during the reign of Constantine IV (668–685) and probably contained elements of sulfur and lime, which reacted with water to produce enormous heat. Especially valuable in burning enemy ships, the use of Greek fire was instrumental in discouraging the invasion of Constantinople in 673.

While the Byzantine Empire opposed a number of enemies, its defeat came at the hands of Islam, which used levied armies, led by the dynastic nobility and mercenaries

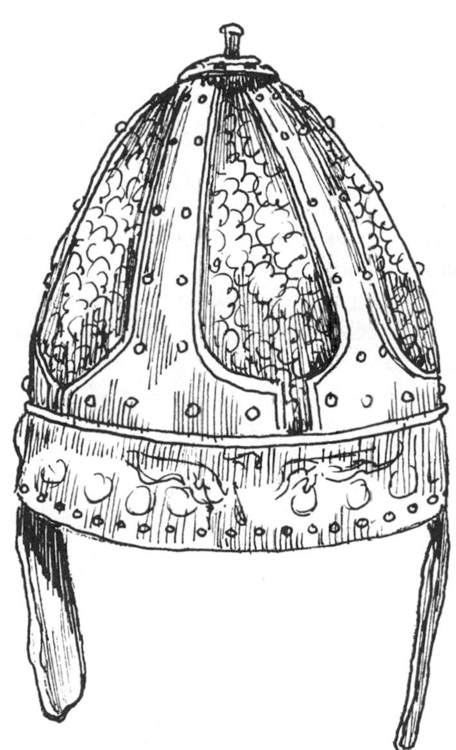

Sprangenheim helmet

composed of Turks, Berbers, or slave armies called Mamluks. Early Islamic campaigns placed a premium on infantry, especially in the seventh century. Infantry continued to play a dominant role until the ninth century, with the rise of Turkish troops or slave armies in Iran and Iraq. The Seljuk Turks, from the 11th century, conducted their campaigns with armies of light cavalry, trained in the use of the bow. The use of such troops relegated infantry to a supporting role and was effective in the Crusader wars in the Levant. The Mamluks of Egypt continued to employ major formations of cavalry until the 16th century but were eventually overcome by the Ottoman Turks.

The Ottomans initially utilized cavalry, as had the Seljuk Turks, but they gradually came to appreciate the use of infantry, as Ottoman armies became larger and more uniform and disciplined. Infantry regiments were divided into groups such as archers, spearmen, and the like, with the addition of the highly trained units called Janissaries. The implementation of the Janissary Corps meant the reliance, once again, on infantry, which in turn facilitated the use of muskets by footsoldiers in the 16th century. Ottoman forces were also distinguished by the use of field artillery, positioned in the field before the infantry, heavy or siege guns being particularly deadly in the siege of Constantinople (1453). The Mamluks, the last major opponents of Ottoman expansion, failed to apply the use of firearms until it was too late. Their mistrust of such weapons placed them at a severe disadvantage.

In the West, meanwhile, crucial to the military defeat of the Western Roman Empire by the Germanic peoples was the demise of the legion, a formation that had been the backbone of the Roman army. The Germanic and Scandinavian armies that swept into western Europe from the 4th to the 10th century were, with one notable exception, heavily dependent on cavalry. The Romans had been destroyed at Adrianople by Goth horsemen, proving with apparent decisiveness the supremacy of the mounted arm of the military. The great exception to this were the Frankish warriors. The Franks arrived on foot, without armor, wielding swords, spears, shields and their distinctive throwing axes. What allowed them to achieve victories against their enemies was probably a combination of ineptitude on the part of their foes, Frankish strength and, probably, the ability of Frankish leaders to instill a certain amount of discipline into their forces. The latter was no doubt true of Clovis (d. 511) and Charles Martel (d. 741), who also recognized that in order to compete with the Saracens they would need cavalry. Charlemagne (d. 814) strove to improve the Frankish-Carolingian military machine, rallying support to feed his troops, utilizing Lombard heavy cavalry and demanding greater discipline.

Gradually, Frankish reliance on infantry as a military mainstay changed. The reasons for this were the emergence of the feudal system, the introduction of the stirrup (a Muslim innovation) in the early eighth century and the pressing need to defeat the Vikings, who began raiding Europe in the late eighth century. The Franks learned quickly that the infantry could not provide adequate protection for coastal regions nor could it react swiftly enough. The solution was mounted troops, a situation associating military need with feudal society, a system dominated by mounted, armored knights.

Feudal adoption of cavalry inaugurated a mounted war effort that was to endure for centuries. The final demise of an army largely dominated by infantry came in 1066 at the Battle of Hastings, when the Normans led by William the Conqueror defeated Harold II's Saxon force of foot soldiers. In the feudal system the beneficed knight became attached to the upper class, escaping the traditional military service to his lord by paying a set amount of money. Mercenaries, hardened soldiers not subject to feudal allegiance or the rules of knighthood, were always available for hire, their professional skills essential in an age dominated by constant warfare and ruthless use of force. Such troops were of increasing demand in the 14th and 15th centuries, and units composed of Burgundians, Genoese, English and Swiss were available. Feudalism varied from region to region in Europe. In Italy, where the communes held political control, the cities provided their own armies by passing ordinances requiring service from their citizens. These military groups, especially those of the Lombard League, were surprisingly efficient and capable, defeating, for example, the troops of Emperor Frederick I Barbarossa (1125–1190) at the Battle of Legnano in 1176. During the late Middle Ages, Italy also produced the condottiere, exceptional military figures, who commanded the city forces in their frequent conflicts with one another.

Strategic and tactical considerations during the Middle Ages were often primitive. Armies lacked proper communications and logistical support to carry out extensive or complicated maneuvers. Chronicles recount the terrible effect of moving armies over a region, and the Jacquerie uprising in France (1358) was caused in part by the depredation of roaming soldiers. Battles were generally pitched with two sides engaging in bloody, tactically limited and essentially mounted campaigns. Infantry support consisted of crossbowmen, although large numbers of ragged, poorly trained serfs also fought, their losses held in little regard by their noble commanders.

The revival of infantry began with the recognition by the Crusaders that infantry had a role to play in campaigns against the Muslims, a trend that had begun to some degree in Europe. An army trained in varied methods was much more deadly than one reliant solely on cavalry. This was true especially when territory was to be claimed and occupied. In 1302, at the Battle of the Spurs (Courtrai), an army of Flemish militia defeated a force of French knights by choosing its position across a bog and then slaughtering the knights, who lacked any tactical sense of the danger before them. The proof of combined warfare was given at the Battle of Crécy in 1346. There King Edward III's (1327–1377) trained, well-paid English army used the six-foot longbow to mow down row after row of French knights, who were severly hampered by heavy armor. Mobile infantry, armed with halberds, spears and missiles (crossbows, longbows and later muskets) thus earned a permanent place in battle. It took the imagination of military strategists and continued progress in the manufacture of artillery and weapons to make them supreme once again.

Prior to the proliferation of gunpowder weaponry, the best long-distance battlefield instrument was the cumbersome crossbow, which was superseded by the fast and lightweight longbow. Cannons slowly came into use, usually after inflicting a severe loss on an enemy previously unwilling to adopt new technology or to accept that older tactics were now impractical. The Hundred Years' War was an excellent testing ground for new strategic and tactical ideas. At Orléans (1428–1429) both sides used artillery, but at the Battle of Patay (1429) the French triumphed by refusing to allow the English to dress their usual defensive lines. Charles VII of France (ruled 1422–1461) revolutionized the raising of armies by levying and paying for his own force. As a professional army, it was largely responsible for the capture of English-held territories in France and for French victories at Formigny (1450) and Castellon (1453). At Formigny, the French guns decimated the English longbows, stripping the English of their prized tactical edge.

Finally, a glimpse of future warfare was provided by the Bohemian general Jan Zizka (d. 1424). A soldier and supporter of the Hussites, he integrated cavalry, infantry and artillery into a battlefield unit, thereby combining defensive strength with offensive prowess and shock ability. His system was invincible against the Germans and Hungarians and was in use after his death. Its demise was brought about by internal divisiveness, but Zizka's vision would be restored by Gustavus Adolphus in the 17th century.

### *Armor*

Armor underwent continual development during the Middle Ages, increasing in weight and bulk until it was rendered virtually unnecessary by the increased use of firearms. The use of armor in the West originated with Roman troops and then the Byzantines, most notably the cataphract (armored horsemen). Byzantine cavalry wore chain-mail shirts, a conical helmet with a colored tuft of horsehair and a small, round shield. Roman armor and equipment, such as the *lorica* (segmented body armor) and the *thorax* (an iron cuirass), were adopted with variations by the Germanic tribes and others. This style of armor became more effective and more common as adjustments were made to meet specific needs and with improvement in metallurgy.

The mail shirt was extended to the knees of a rider, and the helmet, devoid of the tuft of hair, was fashioned with a nose guard. Round shields were dropped in favor of

Armor from the 15th century

kite-shaped ones, made of wood with a leather covering. Excellent examples of mailed soldiers from the 11th century are found in the Bayeux Tapestry, depicting the Norman Conquest of England in 1066. The trend was now toward greater weight and overall protection, the armor shirt being shortened and replaced by mailed breeches. Under the armor it was fashionable and practical to wear coats of heavy felt or leather to prevent bruising. Helmets were larger and heavier, covering the head and neck with slits to permit breathing and frontal vision.

By the 13th century, armorers had begun using plate armor, iron plates used at first under chain mail to protect the legs and shoulders, where blows were likely to fall. Soon the plates were used outside the chain mail and were distributed over a wider area. Chain was replaced when a combination of weaponry rendered the chain mail incapable of protecting the wearer completely, especially in the joints. Plate armor suits were developed in the 14th century, making the knights quite impervious to launched weapons. There were drawbacks, however, as the helmets were heavy and cumbersome and sometimes made breathing difficult. The weight of the suit required a heavy, and hence less swift, mount. The horses were slowed further when armor was used to protect them as well. This tactical consideration grew out of a tendency to strike the mount in combat in order to unhorse the knight, the weight of his arms preventing him from rising. During the Crusades, a defeat could mean total annihilation, for a body of knights could not ride fast enough to avoid death or capture. In Europe it was often customary to deal a death blow to an unhorsed enemy with the Knife of Mercy (inserted into one of the helmet slits), when ransom for the captive was not asked.

As the Hundred Years' War proved, heavy, immobile armor was both obsolete on the battlefield and no longer capable of protecting its wearer. Firearms, artillery and even long-range missiles could bring down or kill outright an encumbered rider. Thus, by the end of the 15th century, with the last, vain efforts of armorers to create heavily protective suits, plate armor had assumed a largely ceremonial purpose, useful only in events associated with pageantry or in tournaments. Some armor was worn still, but the efforts of most practical soldiers were devoted to reacquiring mobility, a necessity in the face of ever-changing conditions in war. See also BYZANTINE EMPIRE; CASTLE; CHIVALRY; CRUSADES; FEUDALISM; HUNDRED YEARS' WAR; MAMLUKS; MANZIKERT, BATTLE OF; MILITARY ORDERS; MONGOLS; OTTOMAN EMPIRE; SALADIN; SELJUK TURKS; SHIPS; VIKINGS; WARS OF THE ROSES.

**WARS OF THE ROSES** The dynastic contest waged from 1455 to 1485 for the English throne between the houses of Lancaster and York, the name derived from the badges worn by the two sides: the red rose of Lancaster and the white rose of York. The origins of the war were the claim of descent by both houses to being the sons of King Edward III (1327–1377), and the efforts of the two lines to acquire political ascendancy during the weak regime of King Henry VI (1422–1461). Lancastrians had held the crown since the deposition of Richard II in 1399 and the accession of Henry of Bolinbroke (IV, ruled 1399–1413), but their control over the country declined during the minority of Henry VI, who was dominated by his queen, Margaret of Anjou, and her supporters, William de la Pole, duke of Suffolk, and Edmund Beaufort, duke of Somerset. Their policies proved ineffectual, allowing the English position against France to deteriorate in the Hundred Years' War and English nobles to act with virtual independence, their armies roaming the countryside. Margaret and her faction were opposed by the Yorkists led by Richard, duke of York, supported by Richard Neville, earl of Warwick, who used his influence to install York as protector of the realm in 1453, when Henry lapsed into insanity. The king recovered in 1455, reinstalling Margaret's faction, a situation resisted by York. Hostilities ensued, and the first battle of the war took place at Saint Albans May 27, 1455. The Yorkists were triumphant, and a period of truce endured until 1459.

The Yorkists claimed victory after an indecisive battle at Blore Heath (September 23, 1459) but suffered a sound defeat at Ludford Bridge (October 12, 1459). In July of the following year the Lancastrians were routed from Northampton. The Yorkists captured Henry and arranged a compromise, whereby York was named heir to the throne on Henry's death, an agreement disinheriting Prince Edward. Margaret, bitterly opposed this plan, raised an army and surprised and killed York at Wakefield in December 1460. She then defeated Warwick at the Second Battle of Saint Albans (February 17, 1461). York's son, Edward, meanwhile, overcame a Lancastrian army at Mortimer's Cross (February 2), marching on London, where he was proclaimed king on March 4. Joining Warwick, Edward opposed Margaret, bringing her forces to their knees at Towton. In the longest, largest and bloodiest engagement of the war, the Yorkists emerged triumphant.

With the Lancastrians in disarray, and Margaret exiled to France, Edward and the Yorkists consolidated their political position until strife surfaced between the king and Warwick over the royal marriage and foreign policy. Warwick, called "the Kingmaker," conspired against the king with Edward's brother, George, duke of Clarence. They were ultimately defeated, fleeing to France. Warwick there reconciled himself with Margaret and returned to England, deposing Edward and restoring Henry. Edward sailed to the Continent, allied himself with the Burgundians, and mounted a campaign to regain his throne. Edward returned to England and on April 14, 1471, routed Warwick at Barnet. Margaret and her supporters were then destroyed at Tewkesbury (May 4), and Warwick and Prince Edward were killed. Henry was murdered in the Tower of London, leaving Edward secure on the throne until his death in 1483.

Edward was succeeded by his young son, Edward V. The child was controlled by his uncle Richard of Gloucester, who usurped the throne. Edward and his brother, Richard of York, disappeared in the tower and were never seen again. Richard III was challenged unsuccessfully by Henry Stafford, duke of Buckingham in 1483, subsequently alienating his Yorkist supporters, who gave their allegiance to the Welshman Henry Tudor, the Lancastrian claimant. Henry landed in England and defeated Richard at the Battle of Bosworth Field on August 22, 1485. His coronation as Henry VII (1485–1509) and his marriage to Elizabeth of York thus united the houses of York and Lancaster. The conflict had resulted in the termination of feudalism in England, as the nobles were decimated, leaving no institution capable of resisting the rise of Tudor absolutism in the reigns of Henry and his successor, Henry VIII. See also ENGLAND.

**WARTBURG** Castle near Eisenack in Thuringia renowned in German history and legend. Originally constructed around 1070 or 1080, Wartburg was rebuilt by Herman I of Thuringia (d. 1217), who made it his residence. The court there welcomed poets and musicians, including Wolfram von Eschenbach and Walther von der Vogelweide.

**WARWICK, RICHARD BEAUCHAMP, EARL OF** (1382–1439) English nobleman and soldier who became one of the largest landholders in England through marriage. In the service of King Henry IV (1399–1413), he fought at the Battle of Shrewsbury (1403) against Henry Percy "Hotspur" and later supported the suppression of the rebellious Owen Glendower in Wales. A member of the King's Council in 1410, he was appointed captain of Calais in 1414, as a lieutenant of King Henry V (1413–1422) in Normandy and Picardy (1417–1422). Appointed tutor to the young king, Henry VI (1422–1461), from 1428 to 1436, he attended the trial of Joan of Arc and defeated the French at Beauvais in 1431. In 1437 he was appointed governor in France, dying at his post. Distinguished as a chivalric knight, Warwick made a pilgrimage to the Holy Land in 1408–1410.

**WARWICK, RICHARD NEVILLE, EARL OF** (1428–1471) A powerful English nobleman and baronial figure in the Wars of the Roses, called since the 16th century "the Kingmaker." The son of Richard Neville, earl of Salisbury, he became earl of Warwick in 1449 through his marriage to the daughter of Richard Beauchamp. Warwick joined Richard, duke of York, against the Lancastrians and was instrumental in the Yorkist victory at Saint Albans in 1455. Appointed captain of Calais, he returned to England in 1460, captured King Henry VI (1422–1461) at Northampton, but strove to have the weak ruler retained as king. Defeated by the Lancastrians in 1461, Warwick joined the dead Richard's son, Edward, in his effort to win the crown. In March 1461, the two allies crushed the Lancastrians at Towton, and Warwick was an influence in the early years of Edward IV's reign (1461–1483). Gradually Edward asserted himself. In 1469, when Warwick seized the king, he was driven out with his ally, George, duke of Clarence, and forced into exile in the following year. Reconciled in France with his former enemy, Margaret of Anjou, Warwick returned to England, deposed Edward and restored Henry (1470–1471) to the throne. His political supremacy was short lived, however, as Edward landed in northern England in March 1471, defeating and killing Warwick at the Battle of Barnet. See also WARS OF THE ROSES.

**AL-WATHIQ** (d. 847) Abbasid caliph from 842 to 847. See also ABBASID CALIPHATE.

**WELF, HOUSE OF** See GUELPHS AND GHIBELLINES.

**WENCESLAS** (1361–1419) German king from 1378 to 1400 and king of Bohemia from 1363 to 1419, as Wenceslas IV.

**WENCESLAS, DUKE OF BOHEMIA** (c. 907–929) Patron saint of Bohemia, immortalized in the carol, ruler of the country from 924 or 925 until his murder. He was raised as a Christian by his grandmother, Saint Ludmilla, but she was murdered by his mother, Drahomira, a pagan. After the death of his father (c. 920) Drahomira became his regent, estranging the people by her harsh government. Pious and anxious to spread the Christian faith, Wenceslas, once empowered, promoted missionary efforts in Bohemia by Germans. He submitted to the German king, Henry the Fowler (919–936), in 929 when met with invasion. He was then killed by his brother, Boleslav, the leader of a group of antagonistic nobles. His feast was celebrated in 985, and his image appeared on Bohemian coins from 1000, the crown of Wenceslas symbolizing Bohemian (or Czech) independence. His relics at the Church of Saint Vitus in Prague drew pilgrims throughout the Middle Ages. See also BOHEMIA.

**WENCESLAS I, KING OF BOHEMIA** (d. 1253) Son of Ottokar I Przemysl, he ruled from 1230. Confronted in 1241 by a Mongol invasion, Wenceslas avoided the destruction of his country but could not save Moravia. To improve Bohemia economically he encouraged the settlement of German merchants and colonists and profited by their influence. One of his principal efforts during his reign was control of Austria. When Frederick II, the last Babenberg duke, died in 1246, Wenceslas negotiated the marriage of his son with the duke's niece. This alliance failed because of his son's death, and it was not until 1251 that he succeeded in forcing the Austrians to recognize another son, Ottokar II Przemysl, as their duke. See also BOHEMIA.

**WENCESLAS II, KING OF BOHEMIA** (1271–1305) Ruler of Bohemia from 1278 and king of Poland from 1300, succeeding his father, Ottokar II Przemysl, in Bohemia. He spent the years 1278–1283 at the court of his cousin, Otto IV of Brandenburg, who acted as his regent. Returning to Bohemia, he found political power in the hands of his mother's lover (and future husband), Zavis of Falkenstein. Wenceslas arrested him in 1289 and executed him the following year. He then suppressed dissident nobles and took control of his country, accepting the duchy of Cracow and becoming the Polish monarch. Declining the Hungarian crown for himself, he attempted to claim it on behalf of his son, Wenceslas III, in 1301. Albert I of Germany attempted unsuccessfully in 1304 to compel him to relinquish Poland and Hungary. See also BOHEMIA.

**WENCESLAS III, KING OF BOHEMIA** (1289–1306) Son of Wenceslas II, ruler of Hungary from 1301 to 1304, claimant to the Polish crown and briefly monarch in Bohemia from 1305 to 1306. Installed in Hungary through his father's efforts, he was forced to withdraw and renounce his rights to Hungary and Austria. Succeeding his father, he was an incompetent ruler and died at the hands of an assassin while preparing to invade Poland. His death brought an end to the Przemyslid line, a dynasty that had ruled Bohemia for almost 400 years. Henry (1307–1310) and John of Luxembourg, his brother-in-law, succeeded him. See also BOHEMIA.

**WENCESLAS IV, KING OF BOHEMIA** See WENCESLAS.

**WENDS** A Slavic tribe in Germany, east of the Elbe River. See also SLAVS.

**WESSEX** An Anglo-Saxon kingdom of England, comprising the region south of Mercia, whose kings eventually ruled the entire region. Wessex was supposedly founded by Cerdic and Cynric, who landed at Hampshire in 494 or 495. Details for this period are few, but the two established themselves in central Wessex. Ceawlin (ruled 560–592) extended the territory. In the seventh century, however, the power of Mercia was great, and Wessex lost lands to Mercia. Christianity was adopted under Cynegils (ruled 611–642), and Wessex expanded westward, encroaching on the Britons. A notable king of this period was Ine (ruled 688–726), who advanced a code of laws for the West Saxons.

The enduring ascendancy of the Mercians was ended finally with Egbert (ruled 802–839), who broke Mercian domination and conquered Surrey, Sussex, Kent, Devon and Cornwall, thereby achieving mastery over England south of the Humber. Wessex then mounted a resistance to the Danish threat. The Great Army of the Danes was victorious against most of the Anglo-Saxon realms but encountered major opposition in the West Saxons led by Aethelred (ruled 865–871) and especially Alfred the Great (reigned 871–899). Alfred compelled the Danes to accept baptism and to live within set boundaries (see DANELAW), in the northeast of England. The reconquest of the Danelaw, completed in 927 by Alfred's grandson, Athelstan (924–939), established the monarchs of the West Saxons, originally Wessex, as kings of England. See also ENGLAND.

**WESTMINSTER, STATUTES OF** Three legislative enactments made by King Edward I of England (1272–1307) in parliaments held at Westminster in 1275, 1285 and 1290. Including a variety of clauses, these clarified or altered certain aspects of criminal and civil law. Westminster I (1275) written in Old French, was issued at the first of the general parliaments, and constituted a code of law. Westminster II (1285) included a clause which altered practices in English landholding, restraining the alienation of land, known as *De donis conditionalibus* (concerning conditional gifts). Westminster III (1290) dealt with land tenure, forbidding subinfeudation to curtail practices limiting the lords in receipt of their dues.

**WESTMINSTER ABBEY** Originally a Benedictine monastery in London and a superb example of Gothic architecture. It was the site for the coronation of every English monarch since William the Conqueror (1066–1087), with the exceptions of Edward V and Edward VIII, and many monarchs and other illustrious men and women were also buried there. According to legend, Sebert, the first Christian king of the East Saxons, founded the first church on the site in the early seventh century. It was called Thorney but later referred to as the west munster or monastery. Under Saint Dunstan's direction extensive remodeling took place about 960. A new church was erected by Edward the Confessor (consecrated 1065), but this was replaced, beginning in 1245, by Henry III (1216–1272), who began construction of the present church in the Gothic style, cruciform in plan, reflecting the French influence of the architect Henry of Reims. Other architects included Henry of Gloucester and Henry Yevele in subsequent years, the nave being rebuilt, commencing in 1376 under Yevele's guidance. The English Gothic style, however, predominates in the abbey. See also GOTHIC ART and ARCHITECTURE.

**WESTMORELAND, RALPH NEVILLE, EARL OF** (c. 1364–1425) English nobleman who married the half sister of Henry IV (1399–1413), lending his support to the king against Richard II (1377–1399) and then suppressing the Percy revolts in 1403 and 1405. His daughter, Cicely, was the mother of Edward IV (1461–1483) and Richard III (1483–1485), and his grandson was Richard Neville, earl of Warwick.

**WESTPHALIA** Called in German Westfalen, a region in northwestern Germany, dominated by the Saxon tribe who settled there. The region's peoples resisted the advance of the Franks led by Charlemagne (768–814) in the late eighth century, managing to retain their separate identity for the next few centuries. From the 12th century, however, the old tribal distinctions among the Saxons dissolved, and the region west of the Weser in Saxony was called Westphalia. In 1180 it was converted into a duchy granted to the archbishops of Cologne, although realistically its boundaries were limited to the region around Cologne. Most of Westphalia was controlled by various ecclesiastical princes, including the bishops of Münster, Osnabruck, Paderborn and Minden, as well as the counts of Waldeck, Schaumberg, Lippe, Ravensberg and Mark and the imperial city of Dortmund, and the abbey of Essen. Westphalian towns prospered as members of the Hanseatic League. See also COLOGNE; GERMANY.

**WETTIN** German dynasty deriving its name from a castle near Halle, Germany. Early members of the line participated in the *Drang nach Osten*, the "Drive to the East," the Germanic advance into the Slavic regions. By the end of the 11th century, the Wettins held, as well as their countship, the margravate of Meissen. From this position they became landgraves of Thuringia in 1264 and Electors of Saxony in 1423. From 1485 the Wettin line was divided into two branches, the Ernestine and the Albertine. See also SAXONY.

**WEYDEN, ROGIER VAN DER** (1399/1400–1464) Flemish painter called also Roger de la Pasture, successor to Jan van Eyck as chief painter of the Flemish school. A

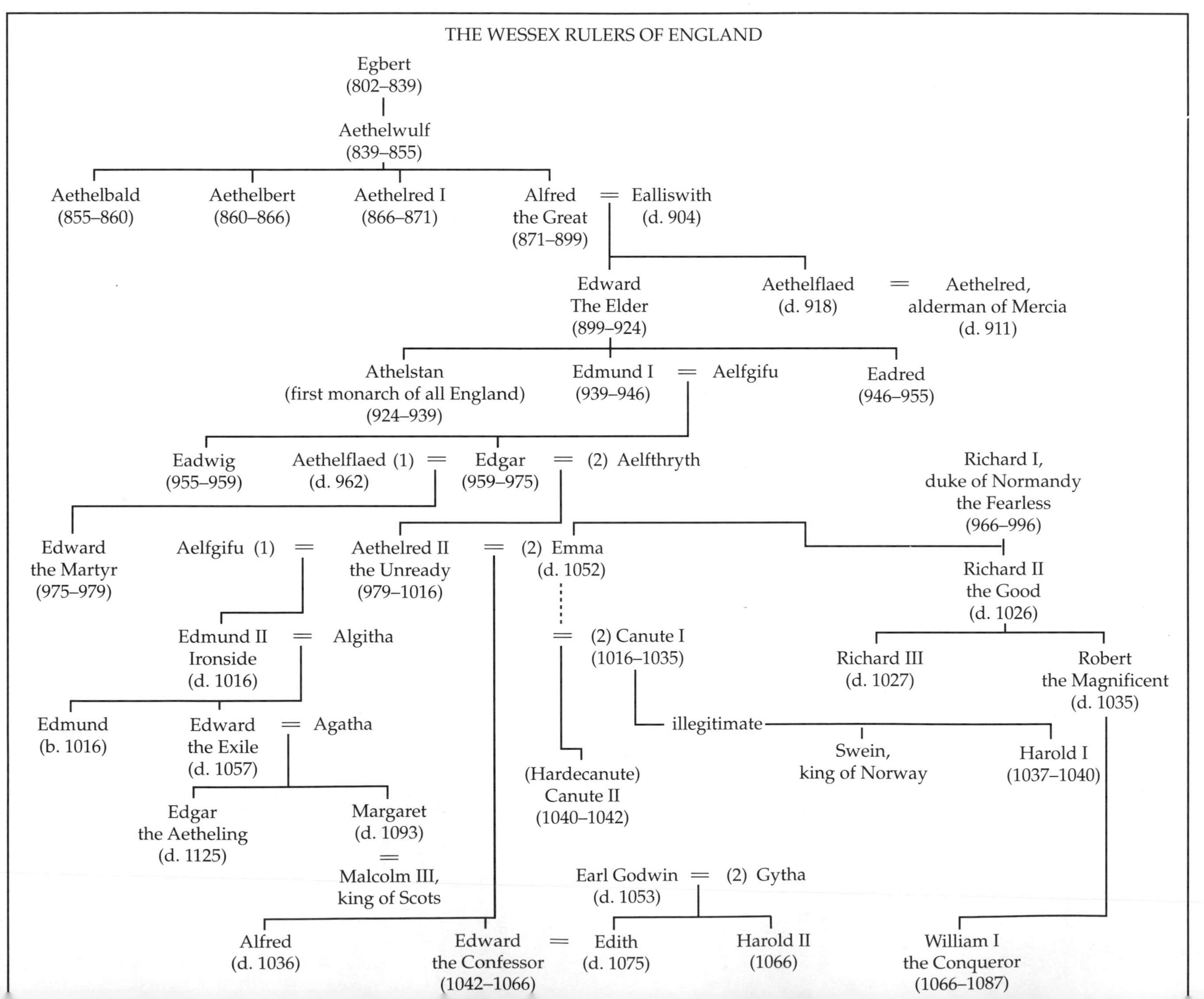

THE WESSEX RULERS OF ENGLAND
Egbert (802–839)
Aethelwulf (839–855)
Aethelbald (855–860)
Aethelbert (860–866)
Aethelred I (866–871)
Alfred the Great (871–899)
=
Ealliswith (d. 904)
Edward The Elder (899–924)
Aethelflaed (d. 918)
=
Aethelred, alderman of Mercia (d. 911)
Athelstan (first monarch of all England) (924–939)
Edmund I (939–946)
=
Aelfgifu
Eadred (946–955)
Eadwig (955–959)
Aethelflaed (1) (d. 962)
=
Edgar (959–975)
=
(2) Aelfthryth
Richard I, duke of Normandy the Fearless (966–996)
Edward the Martyr (975–979)
Aelfgifu (1)
=
Aethelred II the Unready (979–1016)
=
(2) Emma (d. 1052)
Richard II the Good (d. 1026)
Edmund II Ironside (d. 1016)
=
Algitha
=
(2) Canute I (1016–1035)
Richard III (d. 1027)
Robert the Magnificent (d. 1035)
Edmund (b. 1016)
Edward the Exile (d. 1057)
=
Agatha
illegitimate
Swein, king of Norway
Harold I (1037–1040)
(Hardecanute) Canute II (1040–1042)
Edgar the Aetheling (d. 1125)
Margaret (d. 1093)
=
Malcolm III, king of Scots
Earl Godwin (d. 1053)
=
(2) Gytha
Alfred (d. 1036)
Edward the Confessor (1042–1066)
=
Edith (d. 1075)
Harold II (1066)
William I the Conqueror (1066–1087)

student of Robert Campin, Weyden settled in Brussels around 1435, becoming the civic painter with wide patronage. Religious themes dominated his work, but he also produced portraits, resembling van Eyck's in clarity but demonstrating unique dramatic power and severity. Attracting students from Italy, van der Weyden became the leading northern painter of the 15th century. Among his works were *Annunciation* (influenced by Campin), *The Justice of Emperor Trajan* and *Count Herkinbald* (1439–1441), *Last Judgment* (1440s), *St. Columba* (his final work) and the *Descent from the Cross* (second half of the 1430s), his celebrated masterpiece.

**WHITBY** Port town in North Yorkshire, England. The Abbey of Whitby (founded 656 or 657) was the residence of Caedmon, the first poet in the English language, who died there in 680. Some parts of the abbey remain. Having survived the Danish onslaughts of the 9th and 10th centuries, the town became prosperous as a fishing port. The important Synod of Whitby was held here in 663/664. See also WHITBY, SYNOD OF.

**WHITBY, SYNOD OF** Ecclesiastical gathering held at Whitby in 663/664, where it was decided that the date of Easter should be accepted according to the Roman calendar, thereby ending the association between the English church and the Irish or Celtic church. The Irish custom was supported by Saints Colman and Chad, whereas the use of the Roman liturgical calendar was supported by Saint Wilfrid. King Oswy settled the issue by accepting Saint Wilfrid's view, and had cited Saint Peter as the ultimate authority in his argument. Bede is the primary source for the synod.

**WHITTINGTON, RICHARD** (d. 1423) English merchant and lord mayor of London, believed to be the son of a knight of Gloucester, serving as mayor three times (1397–1399, 1406–1407, and 1419–1420). He was distinguished by his wealth, making loans to King Henry IV (ruled 1399–1413) and Henry V (ruled 1413–1422). He was also the subject of a popular legend.

**WILFRID** (634–709) Bishop of York who introduced the Benedictine rule to England and was responsible for the acceptance of Roman practice rather than that of the Celtic church at the Synod of Whitby in 663/664. The son of a Northumbrian noble, he was educated at Lindisfarne and Canterbury, journeying to Rome in 654 with Benedict Biscop. Returning to England, he was appointed Abbot of Ripon and later Bishop of York after his participation in the Synod of Whitby. A dispute with Theodore of Canterbury led to his seeking support from Rome. He was imprisoned on his return to England, retiring to Sussex and then restored to his see after a reconciliation with Theodore. He resigned and accepted the See of Hexham, spending his later years at Ripon. While traveling to Rome he stopped to preach in Frisia among the Saxons. See also YORK.

**WILLIAM I, KING OF ENGLAND** (c. 1028–1087) the Norman conqueror of England, ruling from 1066 to 1087, introducing Norman government and institutions and one of the illustrious kings of England, he is known as "the Conqueror." The natural son of Robert I, duke of Normandy, he became the effective master of the Norman duchy in 1042, suppressing rebellious barons and demonstrating great military skill. While visiting England in 1051, he was probably named by Edward the Confessor as heir to the English throne. In 1064 he apparently bolstered that claim by releasing Harold Godwinson, who had been shipwrecked on the French coast and had been compelled to support William's rights to the English throne. On the death of Edward in early January 1066, however, Harold took the crown, thereby giving William his pretext for invading England. He defeated Harold at the Battle of Hastings on October 14, 1066, then proceeding to London, where he was crowned.

William erected castles in order to make more thorough his subjugation of England. He replaced native bishops with foreign prelates and introduced separate ecclesiastical courts. His goal was to encourage Norman feudalism, its premise being that obedience and loyalty to the king took precedent over fealty to a subordinate lord. A demonstration of that policy was made in 1085–1086, with the survey of England, the Domesday Book, a detailed accounting of its citizenry that made manifest the Norman belief that the entire country was subject to the king.

After 1072 William attended to his Continental possessions, especially Normandy. Leaving English administration to Lanfranc, the archbishop of Canterbury, he dealt with Robert II "Curthose," his son, who succeeded him in Normandy. William (II) Rufus became the heir (1087–1100). A man of considerable personal power and stature, William fulfilled his ambitions and died as the first feudal lord in Europe. See also ENGLAND.

**WILLIAM II, KING OF ENGLAND** (c. 1056–1100) A stern son of William I the Conqueror (1066–1087). Ruling from 1087 to 1100 and called Rufus, the Red, because of his ruddy complexion, he succeeded his father only in England. Normandy was inherited by his older brother, Robert II "Curthose," as demanded by feudal custom. He wished, however, to claim Normandy as well, as did his English barons. He confronted two baronial uprisings but suppressed the second one in 1095 and reigned in peace thereafter. A war (1089–1096) was initiated against Robert in Normandy, and William was victorious. In 1096, when Robert departed for the Crusades, he was forced to mortgage Normandy to William, who added the Maine to his territories. Thought a demanding, grim and brutal monarch, William campaigned in Scotland in 1091 and subjugated Wales in 1097. Having reduced King Malcolm III of Scotland (1058–1093) to vassal status in 1091, William defeated and killed him in 1093. Attempting to dominate the church in England, he encountered resistance from Anselm of Canterbury and drove the prelate into exile in 1097. He was himself killed during a hunt in Hampshire, by an arrow drawn by Walter Tirel, Lord Poix, who may have been in the pay of William's brother, Henry I, who then claimed the throne. See also ENGLAND.

**WILLIAM I, KING OF SCOTLAND** (1143–1214) Called "the Lion," ruler of the Scots from 1165 to 1214,

Death of King William II Rufus

successful in winning Scottish independence from England. The brother and successor of King Malcolm IV (1153–1165), William was the son of Henry, earl of Northumberland, inheriting that title in 1152. Forced to surrender the earldom to Henry II of England (1154–1189) in 1157, William ascended the throne and then joined the revolt of Henry's sons (1173) hoping to regain his lands. Captured near Alnwick, Northumbria, he was released in 1174 after recognizing English overlordship. He was unable to win Scotland's release as a vassal state until 1189, when he paid King Richard the Lion-Hearted (1189–1199) a vast sum. Scottish independence was supported by Pope Celestine II's (1143–1144) decree that its church was answerable only to Rome. William's relations with King John (1199–1216) were poor. See also SCOTLAND.

**WILLIAM I, KING OF SICILY** (1120–1166) Norman ruler of Sicily from 1154, called "the Bad," the son of King Roger II, appointed co-ruler in 1151 and succeeding to the throne on his father's death. His reign was violent as he sought to strengthen royal authority, thereby causing uprisings and rebellions. The barons tried to ally themselves with Emperor Frederick I Barbarossa (1152–1190) and Emperor Manuel I Comnenus (1143–1180), but William survived, routing the Byzantines at Brindisi (1155) and signing the Concordat of Benevento in 1156 with Pope Adrian IV (1154–1159), in which the papacy recognized his rule over Norman territory in Italy. He was plagued by conflicts later but managed to retain his throne and to name his son as heir. He was a patron of science and letters, welcoming scholars to his court, including the Muslim al-Idrisi. See also SICILY.

**WILLIAM II, KING OF SICILY** (1154–1189) Ruler from 1166 to 1189, the last Norman king of Sicily, called "the Good," in contrast to his father, William I (1154–66) the Bad, whom he succeeded. The first five years of his reign were conducted under the regency of his mother, Margaret of Navarre, but William took up the reins of government in 1171, maintaining amicable relations with Byzantium until Emperor Manuel I Comnenus (1143–1180) refused him the hand of Princess Maria. William then turned to Emperor Frederick I Barbarossa (1152–1190), arranging the marriage of his aunt, Constance, with Frederick's son, Henry (VI). William married Joan, daughter of King Henry II of England (1154–1189). Eager to inflict harm on the Byzantines, he embarked on an expedition to Macedonia in 1185, capturing Thessalonica but defeated within sight of Constantinople. He died abruptly while planning his role in the Third Crusade. See also SICILY.

**WILLIAM OF AUVERGNE** (c. 1180–1249) Also called William of Paris, a French philosopher and theologian, professor at the university and then bishop of Paris in 1228. He protected the mendicant orders and was a respected member of the court of King Louis IX (1226–1270). His major work was the massive encyclopedia of philosophy and theology, *Magisterium divinale* (*Divine Teaching*), compiled between 1223 and 1240, in seven parts. He included much Aristotelian material derived from the commentaries of Avicenna and Avicebron.

**WILLIAM OF AUXERRE** (d. 1231) French Scholastic theologian and philosopher, a student of Richard of Saint Victor, who taught at Paris and was at one time the archdeacon of Beauvais. The author of the *Summa aurea,* William was one of the first philosophers to utilize recently discovered writings by Aristotle in his work. In 1231 he was appointed by Pope Gregory IX (1227–1241) as a member of a commission to examine and amend the physical treatises of Aristotle, as the study of these had been forbidden by the University of Paris in 1210.

**WILLIAM OF CONCHES** (d. c. 1160) Philosopher, member of the school of Chartres and a student of Bernard of Chartres, teaching there and at Paris. He was tutor to the future King Henry II of England (1154–1189). Among his works were two treatises on natural philosophy: *Philosophia mundi* and *Dragmaticon,* as well as glosses on Plato and Macrobius.

**WILLIAM OF MALMESBURY** (c. 1080–c. 1143) English historian and monk at the Benedictine monastery of Malmesbury and the most distinguished English historian of his time. His two major works included the secular and ecclesiastical history of England: *Gesta regum Anglorum* (1120) and *Gesta pontificum Anglorum* (1125). He also wrote an abridged version of the *De ecclesiasticis officiis* of Amalarius of Metz, as well as theological and biographical works.

**WILLIAM OF MOERBEKE** (d. 1286) Flemish Dominican philosopher and a leading translator of Aristotle into Latin. Studying at Paris and Cologne, he was probably an associate of Albertus Magnus and later of Thomas Aquinas, making translations of Aristotle at his request.

William was appointed chaplain and confessor to Pope Clement IV (1265–1268) and Gregory X (1271–1276), a participant in the Second Council of Lyons (1274) and appointed archbishop of Corinth in 1278.

**WILLIAM OF NEWBURGH** (1136–c. 1200) English chronicler and a member of the Augustinian priory at Newburgh. He was best known for his *Historia rerum Anglicarum,* a history of England from the Norman Conquest in 1066 to the year 1198. Written between 1196 and 1198, at the request of the abbot of Rievaulx, his history is of considerable value as a source on the events in England during this period. He is also credited with the first mention of an imaginary creature similar to the vampire.

**WILLIAM OF OCKHAM** (d. 1349) Distinguished Nominalist philosopher of the 14th century, called Doctor Invincibilis, controversial for his dispute with the papacy. Born in Ockham, Surrey, England, he joined the Franciscan order at an early age and studied at Oxford, lecturing on Peter Lombard's *Sentences* and raising opposition from the faculty and chancellor John Lutterell. He left the institution as a result without his master's degree. Following the completion of his *Commentaries* on the *Sentences,* he was called to Avignon to defend on his writings (1324), meeting denunciation by Lutterell and six other theologians. He was never condemned, however. While at Avignon he became involved in the Franciscan controversy concerning vows of poverty, supporting the Spiritual Franciscans (who advocated strict poverty), opposing Pope John XXII (1316–1334) and eventually fleeing to Emperor Louis IV the Bavarian (1314–1347), who had been excommunicated in 1324. Under his protection he continued writing, taking steps to reconcile himself with the church before his death in Munich, which occurred while he was probably still at odds with the papacy.

An adherent of nominalism, William denied the concept of universals, arguing that reality exists solely in individual things and that knowledge is acquired by intuition, not abstraction, denying the proof of the existence of God. He rejected Thomas Aquinas's position that there was harmony between faith and reason, and his celebrated principle, "Ockham's razor," stated that beings should not multiply without necessity. Among his works, were treatises on logic, sermons and commentaries confuting the papacy. He believed in the separation of church and secular matters, thereby influencing the subsequent controversy on conciliarism. See also SCHOLASTICISM.

**WILLIAM OF RUBRUQUIS** (d. c. 1295) Also called William of Ruysbroeck, a Franciscan traveler to the Mongol empire, sent in 1253 by King Louis XI of France (1226–1270), Saint Louis, to seek the Mongol khan. He set out from Constantinople in early May 1253, reaching the camp of Batu Khan, Mongol ruler of the Volga region, and there received permission to go on to the court of the Great Khan. Traveling north of the Caspian and Aral Seas, he reached Karakorum, remaining there until May 1254, when he began his long journey home. Arriving at Tripoli in August 1255, he learned of the departure of King Louis to France and composed a narrative for him on his adventures. It is a work noted for its remarkably informed observations. Roger Bacon, his contemporary, referred to William frequently in his *Opus majus.* See also MONGOLS.

**WILLIAM OF SAINT-THIERRY** (c. 1085–1148) Scholastic philosopher, theologian and mystic. Of noble lineage, he was born at Liège and studied under Anselm of Laon. He entered a monastery at Reims in 1113, becoming the abbot in 1119 of the monastery of Saint-Thierry. He remained abbot at the request of his friend, Bernard of Clairvaux, despite his preference for a life devoted to contemplation. In 1135, however, he resigned and became a Cistercian at Signy in the Ardennes. His writings, largely in defense of Christian orthodoxy, were noted for his familiarity with Greek and Latin, the writings of the church fathers and the Bible. He quarreled with the dissenting views of Abelard, attacking him in his *Disputatio adversus Petrum Abaelardum.* He also wrote commentaries and treatises. See also ABELARD, PETER; BERNARD OF CLAIRVAUX.

**WILLIAM OF SCOTLAND** See WILLIAM I, KING OF SCOTLAND.

**WILLIAM OF TYRE** (d. c. 1187) Noted chronicler and archbishop of Tyre. Born in Syria to a French or Italian family of merchants, he studied in Paris and Bologna, where he mastered Greek, Latin and Arabic, returning to Palestine in 1160 and becoming archbishop of Tyre in 1167. He was sent on missions to Constantinople and Rome and in 1170 was appointed tutor to Baldwin (IV), son of King Amalric of Jerusalem, and granted appointment as chancellor of the kingdom in 1174. William participated in the Third Lateran Council of 1179, where he was named to a diplomatic mission to Constantinople by Pope Alexander III (1159–1181). Failing to receive appointment as patriarch of Jerusalem in 1180, he retired to Rome in 1183. He wrote the still extant *Historia rerum in partibus transmarinis gestarum (History of the Deeds Across the Sea),* written between 1169 and 1173 recounting the history of Palestine from 614 to 1184. His history of the Arab East, *Historia de principibus orientalibus,* is lost.

**WILLIAM OF WAYNFLETE** (c. 1395–1486) Bishop of Winchester from 1447 and founder of Magdalen College at Oxford. Dedicated to Saint Mary Magdalen, it was established to promote theological and philosophical study and reestablished in 1457 as Magdalen College from the original hall. In 1450 William negotiated with Jack Cade during his rebellion and was appointed chancellor by King Henry VI (1422–1461) in 1456, resigning in 1460. He was pardoned by King Edward IV (1461–1483) for his continued support of King Henry. See also OXFORD.

**WILLIAM OF WYKEHAM** (1324–1404) Bishop of Winchester from 1367 and a statesman. Entering royal service around 1349, he was appointed keeper of the Privy Seal in 1364 and chancellor in 1367, being forced out of office for his incompetence during the war against the French. In 1376 he was accused of malversation, through the instigation of John of Gaunt, and was declared innocent by King Richard II (1377–1399) in 1377. He served as chancellor once again from 1389 to 1391, but his name endures as founder of New College, Oxford (1379) and Winchester College (1394).

**WILLIAM THE BAD** See WILLIAM I, KING OF SICILY.

**WILLIAM THE GOOD** See WILLIAM II, KING OF SICILY.

**WISBY** City in Gotland, southeastern Sweden, called in Swedish Visby. Its prosperity increased as a result of German and other trade in the 12th century. The city was an early member of the Hanseatic League and was respected throughout Europe in the 13th century. The Swedes conquered the region in 1280, and the Danes claimed it about 1361–1362. Wisby was restored to membership in the Hanseatic League in 1370 but had declined in economic importance. See also SWEDEN.

**WITAN** The Anglo-Saxon council in England, an assembly of nobles and ecclesiastical figures summoned at by order of its kings. The witan supported the king by consenting to new laws, accepting various land grants and providing military assistance in war or in the suppression of rebellion. It differed from subsequent Anglo-Norman councils in that its members were not bound to the crown by feudal obedience. When meeting in formal session the council was called as the witenagemot.

**WITCHCRAFT** The ancient practice of magic, both for good and evil, differing, according to some scholars, from sorcery in that witches (or male witches, called by witch hunters warlocks) possess inherent powers, whereas sorcerors or wizards derive their strength from spells or incantations. Throughout the Middle Ages, however, such subtle delineation was not made, and witchcraft was synonymous with evil magic, practiced to cause harm or injury and associated with worship of the devil. The precise intent of witchcraft was altered to meet changing requirements.

Witchcraft's principal opponent was, naturally, the Christian church. Adhering to the biblical maxim "Thou shall not permit a witch to live," the church traditionally attacked witches as diabolical and evil, considering their magic to be an illusion created by the devil. As early as Charlemagne's (768–814) rule the Frankish secular leaders, in conjunction with the clergy, passed laws condemning the practice of magic as evil. Nevertheless, a skeptical view of witchcraft was found within the church, approaching popular beliefs with a surprising degree of patience, seeing these as remnants of papan practices. Further, white magic, that connected with good, had many associations with Christian symbolism, as opposed to the satanic symbols of black magic.

Changes in church and society's outlooks were made manifest around the 12th century. The Crusades and contact with the Islamic world brought with it the study of alchemy and astrology, creating new interest in magic in learned circles of the Christian world. The elements of natural magic, invocations, and extensive theological speculation on demons become sources for discussion and question. Fear thus increased concerning dangerous sorcerers, who invoked spirits and devils in their practice. An important element in the resulting vigorous and often ruthless campaign launched by the church was the widespread anxiety that had been caused by the rise of heretical groups such as the Cathars. The courts of inquisition, established in the 13th century, pursued witches under the broader heading of heretics, punishing them for assorted crimes.

By the early 15th century it was the view of the Inquisition that witches and warlocks were guilty of idolatry, satanism and heresy. An example of the political usefulness of such accusations was clear in the suppression of the Templars in the early 14th century and in the ruin of individuals such as Gilles de Rais by scheming and jealous rivals. The process of witch hunting fostered the writing of pseudoscientific manuals or guides on witchcraft. Chief among these was the *Malleus maleficarum (Hammer of the Witches),* written by Henrich Kraemer and Johann Sprenger. This work became the accepted encyclopedia for seeking, identifying and destroying witches. It was respected for nearly 300 years and did much to personify the witch, thereby initiating the bloody, hysterical witch-hunts of the 16th and 17th centuries in Europe.

**WITELO** (d. c. 1275) Polish philosopher and scientist. Born in Silesia, he studied at Padua and was the author of the influential *Perspectiva* (c. 1274). This work presented the first analysis of space perception and included theories of light, doctrine on human thought and action, and metaphysical teaching based on Neoplatonism. It was derived in large part from the writings of the Arabic scholar Alhazen. Parts of the *Perspectiva* contained ideas similar to the concepts of Robert Grosseteste and Roger Bacon.

**WITIGES** King of the Ostrogoths from 536 to 540, responsible for the Ostrogoths' effort to retain their territories in Lombardy, Tuscany and elsewhere. Elected as successor to the deposed Theodahad, Witiger was incompetent and no match for the Byzantine general Belisarius, and he lost Rome while at his wedding to Matasuntha, the granddaughter of Theodoric, in Ravenna. In early 537 he launched a campaign against Rome that was broken off in 538 as Belisarius subdued the Goths in the Italian peninsula. By 540, however, Witiges held only Ravenna, agreeing to abdicate as the Goths offered the crown to Belisarius. Upon Belisarius's return to Constantinople, Witiges and his queen, with the treasure of Theodoric, were taken. The facts concerning Witiges's final years are unknown. See also OSTROGOTHS.

**WITIZA** A lesser king of the Visigoths who reigned from 701 to 710, in a period of Visigoth decline. See also VISIGOTHS.

**WITOWT** (1350–1430) Grand duke of Lithuania who brought about an ascendancy in his country's political power and consolidated its territorial possessions. After many years of conflict with the Poles, Witowt was able to negotiate a peace with his cousin, Władysław II Jagiello (1386–1434), and in 1392 was recognized as grand duke by agreeing to recognize Władysław's position as his

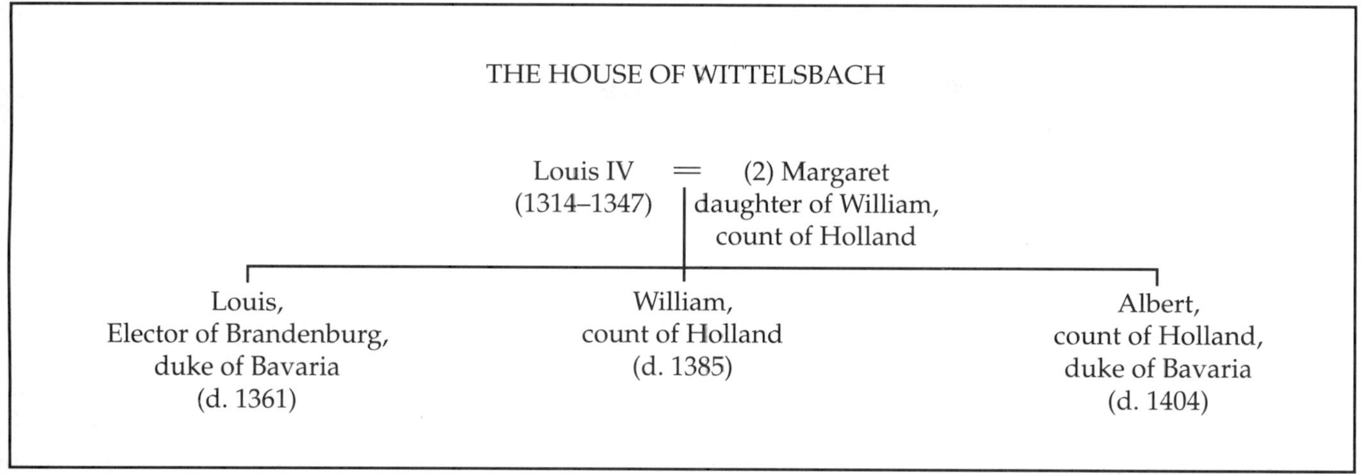


overlord. After suppressing rebellions against his authority within Lithuania, he put aside his fear of the TEUTONIC KNIGHTS and entered into an alliance with them against the Tatars to the east. His defeat in 1399 by the Tatars brought him into an alliance with the Poles, culminating in the unification of Poland and Lithuania in 1401. In 1409 he launched an allied assault on the Teutonic Knights, breaking them at the Battle of Tannenburg (Grünwald) on July 15, 1410. Witowt died before his coronation as king of Lithuania. He was also called Vytautas the Great. See also LITHUANIA.

**WITTELSBACH** Bavarian dynasty that was granted the duchy of Bavaria in 1180 and the Rhenish Palatinate in 1214. The line consisted of two branches after the reign Emperor Louis IV of Wittelsbach in 1329. See also PALATINATE.

**WITTERICH, KING OF THE VISIGOTHS** (d. 610) a weak ruler from 603–610, who was assassinated at a feast. See VISIGOTHS.

**WŁADYSŁAW I HERMAN** King of Poland from 1079 to 1102, succeeding his brother, Boleslav II the Bald, who had been forced into exile. Władysław married Judith, the sister of the German king Henry IV, thereby supporting the imperial cause in the question of the Polish kingship. He eventually relinquished all claim to the throne, although his younger son, Boleslav III the Wry-Mouthed, reigned from 1102 to 1138. See also POLAND.

**WŁADYSŁAW I THE SHORT** (c. 1260–1333) Prince of Great Poland from 1296 and king of Poland from 1320, the son of Casimir I of Kujawy, succeeding to the small principality in 1275. Elected prince by the nobles of Great Poland, he lost their loyalty to King Wenceslas II of Bohemia, who was crowned ruler of Poland in 1300. Władysław thereafter sought to retain his claim to the Polish throne. With the support of Pope Boniface VIII (1294–1303), he launched a war against Wenceslas, a conflict complicated by the ambitions of the Teutonic Knights. Władysław was given his crown in 1320 at Cracow, defeated the knights in 1331 and united the Polish principalities into a single kingdom. Ties with Hungary and Lithuania were forged by marriage. See also POLAND.

**WŁADYSŁAW II JAGIELLO AND JADWIGA** King and queen of Poland, whose marriage made possible the unification of Poland and Lithuania, thereby establishing a dominant European monarchy. Jagiello (1351–1434) was grand duke of Lithuania from 1377 to 1401, but his claim was challenged after his father's death by his cousin, Vytautas, the matter being settled ultimately in Władysław's favor. His political situation improved in 1385 when he was adopted by the Polish queen dowager Elizabeth. He accepted Christianity and was wed to the crown princess, Jadwiga (c. 1373–1399), the daughter of Louis I of Hungary, who had reigned from 1370 to 1382 over the Poles. Jagiello thus became king of Poland in 1386, taking the name Władysław II Jagiello.

He reigned with Jadwiga until her death and then alone, controlling a vast realm that included Lithuania and Kiev and in time Red Ruthenia and Moldavia. He appointed Vytautas governor of Lithuania, and then, as part of a treaty in 1401, he was made duke, becoming grand duke in 1413. With these titles and rank, Vytautas was a powerful ally in conflicts with the Mongols and the Teutonic Knights. Vytautas was defeated, however, at the hands of the Mongols in 1399, driving him into the Polish camp and convincing him of the need to concentrate on the threat made by the knights. The Teutonic order declared war on Władysław in 1409 and was destroyed at the Battle of Tannenberg (Grünwald) in 1410. The subsequent Treaty of Torun in 1411 secured territorial concessions from the knights, who retained only Pomerania. To allay charges that he showed favoritism toward the Hussites, Władysław issued the Edict of Wielun in 1424 to purge Hussite tendencies and suppressed a Hussite rebellion among his noble as part of his campaign. See also POLAND.

**WŁADYSŁAW III, OF VARNA** (1424–1444) King of Poland from 1434 to 1444, the son of Władysław II Jagiello, known for his important campaign against the Ottoman Turks in the Balkans. He succeeded his father, but real power in the state lay with his chief adviser, the magnate Zbigniew Olesnicky, bishop of Cracow. Władysław was crowned king of Hungary in 1440, his coronation sparking a war despite the support given him by the Hungarian soldier János Hunyadi. Peace was arranged by Pope Eugene IV (1431–1447) so that Władysław would be free to lead a crusade against the Turks. He was defeated at the Battle of Varna in 1444 and died in the engagement. See also POLAND.

**WŁADYSŁAW THE EXILE** Ruler of Poland from 1138 to 1146, also called Władysław II, the first of those called seniors in the system used determine the succession to the throne of Poland after the reign of Boleslav III (1107–1138). He was driven from power by his brother, Boleslav IV, the Curly (1146–1173), fleeing to Germany. See also POLAND.

**WOLFRAM VON ESCHENBACH** (c. 1170–c. 1220) A distinguished German poet of the Middle Ages, author of the epic *Parzival*. A Bavarian knight, he was of the lesser nobility and relied on the patronage of Franconian lords. He was probably familiar with the court of the Landgrave of Thuringia, Hermann I, meeting there the noted lyric poet Walther von der Vogelweide. Wolfram's surviving works include eight lyric poems, chiefly *Tagelieder* (Dawn Songs), fragments of an epic, *Titurel*, the unfinished epic *Willehalm* (on William of Toulouse), and *Parzival*. *Parzival* was written between 1200 and 1210, an epic poem of 25,000 lines and written in 16 books. It recounts the tale of Percival (Parzival), King Arthur, and the Holy Grail, introducing the Grail theme into German literature, and was based in part on earlier romances, especially the work of Chrétien de Troyes, *Perceval ou le conte du Graal*. A powerful allegory, the work demonstrated the spiritual growth of Percival as he takes up his quest, as well as that of all humanity. Wolfram's work was influential to later poets, and he was ranked for his literary achievement with Gottfried von Strassburg and Hartmann von Aue among the Middle High German poets.

**WOODVILLE, ELIZABETH** (1437–1492) Wife of King Edward IV (1461–1483) of England and mother of Edward V (1483), whose marriage to Edward in May 1464 brought her vilification by the Yorkists. She was of Lancastrian descent and not of royal blood, and her previous union had left her a widow with two sons. Opposed by Richard Neville, earl of Warwick, she led a major faction at court by the time her husband died in 1483, but her continued unpopularity allowed Richard, duke of Gloucester (King Richard III, ruled 1483–1485), to crush her and her supporters, thus taking the throne from Edward V.

For some reason not altogether certain, Elizabeth gave Richard control of her sons, who disappeared a short time later in the Tower of London. Her daughter married Henry VII (1485–1509), although her own final years were endured in disgrace in a convent because of her complicity in treasonable activities. See also WARS OF THE ROSES.

**WORMS, CONCORDAT OF** Agreement reached in 1122 between Pope Calixtus II (1119–1124) and Emperor Henry V (1106–1125) that ended the Investiture Controversy. By the terms of the Concordat abbots and bishops were to be elected by the clergy, with the emperor having the privilege of deciding contested elections. The chosen candidate was then invested by the emperor with his *regalia*, or privileges, paying homage to the crown. Investiture was then made by his church superiors, who granted him his *spiritualia*, or ecclesiastical powers. The German king ceased the practice of investiture regarding the spiritual rights of church officials within the Holy Roman Empire. See also INVESTITURE CONTROVERSY.

**WYCLIFFE, JOHN** (c. 1330–1384) English reformer, theologian and philosopher whose works and writings foreshadowed the thought of the Reformation. Born in Yorkshire, he was educated at Oxford, becoming regent of Balliol College in 1360, resigning in 1361 to serve as vicar of Fillingham. By 1372 he held a doctorate in divinity after continuing his studies, and in 1374 he was appointed rector of Lutterworth by King Edward III (1327–1377), granted protection by John of Gaunt. He was responsible for the first translation of the Bible into English and has been called the "Morning Star of the Reformation." His views, perpetuated by the Lollards and Hussites, had an enduring influence in Bohemia, as he attacked the medieval church, calling for the clergy to practice poverty and questioning the doctrine of transubstantiation. He maintained that the scriptural position of the pope was weak and that a person's only lord was Christ.

Pope Gregory XI (1370–1378) in 1377 issued a bull against acceptance of Wycliffe's arguments, and in 1382 his works were condemned by a London synod. Although he died unharmed, the Council of Constance (1414–1418) ordered his writings burned and his remains removed from holy ground. Among his works were *De potestate papae* (c. 1379), on the papacy; *De Eucharista*, on the Eucharist; and *De dominio divino* and *De civili dominice*, in which he argued that lordship was based on grace, a virtue lacking in the church. His concept that personal lordship was possible through grace may have been used to justify the Peasant Rebellion of 1381, an uprising in which Wycliffe apparently had no part. See also HUS, JAN; HUSSITE WARS; LOLLARDY.

**WYNTOUN, ANDREW OF** (d. c. 1423) Canon of Saint Andrew's, Scotland, and a chronicler, the author of the *Orygynale Cronykil*, a valuable source for the 14th and 15th centuries and an excellent example of Middle Scots composition. The chronicle made the first mention of Macbeth meeting the prophetic sisters, an event found in Shakespeare's play *Macbeth*. See also SCOTLAND.

# X

**XYSTUS** See SIXTUS IV.

# Y

**YAROSLAV** (980–1054) Called "the Wise," grand prince of Kiev from 1019 to 1054, responsible for extending Russian influence in the region along the Baltic Sea and for strengthening the Kievan state. He came to power with the support of Novgorod, defeating the Petchenegs in their efforts of expansion. His primary achievements, however, were cultural and religious. Trade was promoted, laws codified, churches and monasteries founded and Greek religious texts translated into the Slavic during his reign. Yaroslav also fortified the city with the construction of the Golden Gate. See also KIEV.

**YAZID I** (d. 683) Second Umayyad caliph (680–683), succeeding his father Mu'awiya. He was general in charge of the troops besieging Constantinople but was opposed by many as heir because of his dissolute practices. He thus met with uprisings and was notable for his suppression of the revolt of Husayn, the grandson of the Prophet. Yazid nevertheless proved a generally able caliph, bringing reform to the empire's financial system, improving agricultural practices and strengthening governmental administration. See also UMAYYAD CALIPHATE.

**YAZID II** (d. 724) Umayyad caliph from 720 to 724, followed by Hisham. See also UMAYYAD CALIPHATE.

**YAZID III** (d. 744) Umayyad caliph in 744. See also UMAYYAD CALIPHATE.

**YEMEN** See ARABIA.

**YOLANDE** (d. 1214) Regent for the Latin Empire of Constantinople from 1217, the sister of Baldwin I (1204–1205) and Henry of Flanders (1205–1216), the first two Latin emperors, and wed to Peter of Courtenay, who thus became heir to the throne in 1217. After setting out from France, however, he was captured by Theodore I Lascaris of Nicaea (1206–1222), spending his remaining years a prisoner. Yolande became regent, controlling the state until her death, the crown then belonging to her son, Robert. See also CONSTANTINOPLE, LATIN EMPIRE OF.

**YORK** City and county borough in Yorkshire, England, called by the Romans Eboracum, where Constantine the Great (306–337) was proclaimed emperor. A see was established in York in 314, but the Saxons destroyed the Christian community there. It was restored in the seventh century with the consecration of Paulinus as bishop in 625 and was elevated to an archbishopric in 735. York was thus the primary ecclesiastical power in northern England, second only to Canterbury in importance. The chief city of the kingdom of Northumbria, York fell to the Danes in 867 but was eventually taken by the West Saxons. Its position in Norman England began with William I the Conqueror (1066–1087) who found York critical to his establishment of Norman supremacy. York then grew prosperous because of extensive trade there, and it was granted its charter by King Henry II (1154–1189). See also NORTHUMBRIA.

**YORK, HOUSE OF** Royal house of England founded with the naming of Edmund of Langley as duke of York in 1385. A later branch of the Plantagenet dynasty, the house produced three kings, Edward IV (1461–1483), Edward V (1483) and Richard III (1483–1485). The Yorkists vied with the House of Lancaster during the Wars of the Roses and were defeated ultimately by the army of Henry Tudor. The houses of York and Lancaster were united with the marriage of Henry (VII) Tudor (1485–1509) and Elizabeth, daughter of the Yorkist king Edward IV. See also WARS OF THE ROSES.

**YUSUF I** (d. 1354) Nasrid king of Granada from 1333 to 1354, succeeded by his son, Muhammad V (1354–1359; 1362–1391). See also NASRID KINGDOM OF GRANADA.

**YUSUF II** (d. 1392) Nasrid king of Granada, briefly reigning from 1391 to 1392. See also NASRID KINGDOM OF GRANADA.

**YUSUF III** (d. 1417) Nasrid king of Granada from 1408 to 1417, who took part in the political affairs of Morocco and whose reign was threatened by Portuguese expansion into North Africa. See also NASRID KINGDOM OF GRANADA.

**YUSUF IV** (d. 1433) Nasrid claimant to the throne of Granada who reigned briefly from 1430 to 1432, a grandson of Muhammad VI (1360–1362), who challenged the claim to the throne of Muhammad IX (1419–1427; 1429–1445; 1447–1453). With the help of Castile, he acquired control of western Granada and the city itself in January 1432. Several months later he was assassinated. See also NASRID KINGDOM OF GRANADA.

**YUSUF V** Claimant to the throne of the Nasrid kingdom of Granada, who ruled briefly in 1445, 1450 and again from 1462 to 1463. See also NASRID KINGDOM OF GRANADA.

# Z

**ZACHARIAS** See ZACHARY.

**ZACHARY** (d. 752) Pope from 741 to 752, born a Greek and successor to Gregory III (731–741). His pontificate involved coming to terms with the Lombards, Byzantines and the Franks. He used his personal influence with the Lombard king Liutprand (712–744) to prevent the conquest of the Exarchate of Ravenna, thereby ensuring amicable ties with the Byzantines, despite his opposition to iconoclasm, especially Emperor Constantine V (ruled 741–755). Dealings with the Franks were cordial, and Zachary confirmed the deposition of the last Merovingian king, Childeric III, in 750, while instructing the Frankish church to anoint Pepin III the Short (751–768) as king. So began the alliance between the Carolingian dynasts and the papacy. Zachary also supported Boniface, Apostle of Germany, in his missionary efforts and reforms. He held two synods in Rome, in 743 and 745, and made a Greek translation of the *Dialogues* of Saint Gregory the Great.

**AL-ZAHIR** Abbasid caliph from 1225 to 1226. See also ABBASID CALIPHATE.

**ZÄHRINGEN** German dynasty holding extensive fiefs in western Switzerland, Swabia and later in Baden. The family derived its name from the ancestral keep of Zähringen, near Freiburg in Breisgau; it was granted possession of a ducal title, despite the lack of a formal duchy. The original line ended in 1218 with the death of Duke Berthold V, his domains claimed by related families, such as the Habsburgs, but an offshoot of the line remained in Baden.

**ZARA** Port city on the Adriatic Sea, called Zadar in Serbo-Croation. It was established in ancient times by the Liburnians, later belonging to Rome. It became the chief city in Dalmatia for the Byzantine Empire and was forced to defend itself against the advancing Venetians, falling to them in 1000. It was later conquered by Hungary and attacked during the Fourth Crusade and sacked in 1202. That act earned papal condemnation. In 1409 Zara was sold outright to Venice, enduring poor administration under the Venetians but standing as their bulwark on the Adriatic against the Ottoman Turks. See also DALMATIA.

**ZARAGOZA** City in Zaragoza province, in northeastern Spain, on the Ebro River. An early Christian site, Zaragoza had a bishopric in the third century, falling to the Germanic Suebi in the early fifth century and then dominated by the Visigoths and later the Moors, about 714. The Moors survived a siege by Charlemagne in 778, thanks to his Saxon conflicts. From 1110 to 1118 Zaragoza belonged to the Almoravids, until it was captured by King Alfonso I of Aragon (1104–1134). On the site of the first mosque constructed in Spain was a Romanesque church, the very few remains of which were used in the Gothic cathedral de La Seo (or Cathedral del Salvador), which was begun in the 12th century. The University of Zaragoza was founded in 1474.

**ZENGIDS** Also Zangids, the Turkish dynasty that controlled Syria and northern Iraq from 1127 to 1222, founded by Imad ed-Din Zengi (1084–1146). He became atabeg, or governor, of Mosul in 1127, through the support he gave to the Seljuk sultan Mahmud II against the Abbasid caliph al-Mustarsid, appointed in charge of defeating the Crusaders in Palestine. Confronted by both Christian and Muslim enemies, he acted vigorously and captured Edessa in 1144. Two years later he was assassinated. Zengi's extensive territories were divided among his sons, the strongest being Nur al-Din Mahmud, who reigned from 1146 to 1174. He conquered Damascus in 1154 and subjugated Egypt in 1168. The Zengids, however, lost control of Syria to Saladin and the Ayyubids. Their rule in Mosul came to an end in 1222, when Nasr ed-Din, the last Zengid, was succeeded by the former slave Badr ed-Din Lulu, who was as regent and then atabeg.

**ZENGI, IMAD ED-DIN** See ZENGIDS.

**ZENO** Byzantine or Eastern Roman emperor from 474 to 491, called formerly Tarasicodissa, commander of the Isaurian troops of Emperor Leo I (457–474), who prevented German ascendancy in the Eastern Empire. Now called Zeno, he wed Leo's daughter, Ariadne (c. 466), and in 474 his seven-year-old son became successor to Leo as Leo II. Appointed co-emperor, he came to the throne when Leo II died, before the end of the year. He was soon deposed to allow his brother-in-law, Basiliscus, to take the throne. He proved so incompetent that Zeno was returned to power in 476. He endured many rebellions, including one by the Ostrogoths led by Theodoric. He appointed Theodoric to replace Odoacer in Italy, thereby ensuring the departure of the Ostrogoths from regions of the Eastern Empire. See also BYZANTINE EMPIRE.

**ZIRIDS** Muslim Berber dynasty that ruled in North Africa from 972 to 1125, called also the Banu Zirir, allies of the Fatimids. Their leader, Yusuf Buluggin I ibn Ziri, became governor when the Fatimids established their capital in Cairo in 972. In 1048 the Zirids seemed strong enough to refute their allegiance to the Fatimids, but the resultant war destroyed much of their territory. The last of the Zirids in Africa fell to the Almohads in 1152.

**ZIZKA, JAN** (d. 1424) Bohemian national hero, general and follower of Jan Hus, who had one remaining eye but distinguished himself as a mercenary, fighting for the Poles at the Battle of Tannenberg (Grünwald) in 1410 against the Teutonic Knights. Returning home, he joined the Hussite sect and became leader of the Taborite faction against Sigismund, the German king and ruler of Bohemia (1411–1437). His disciplined, even fanatical, forces proved superior to any troops sent against them, routing Sigismund's army near Prague in 1420. Zizka lost his remaining eye after the battle but remained in command of the Taborite armies until his death from plague. His methods of warfare were both sound and tactically innovative, combining horse, infantry and cannon into a unified body acting in concert, a revolutionary concept foreshadowing military tactics adopted in the 17th century. See also HUSSITE WARS.

**ZOË** (d. 1050) Byzantine empress from 1028 to 1050, the daughter of Constantine VIII (1025–1028) and wife of Romanus III (1028–1034), Michael IV (1034–1041) and Constantine IX (1042–1055). In 1042 she ruled with her sister, Theodora, but their mutual hatred compelled Zoë to embark on her marriage to Constantine IX Monomachus. Her earlier marriages had failed because of her jealous nature, but she allowed her now considerably younger husband to pursue his own pleasure. Her corrupt rule is believed to have weakened the Byzantine Empire.

**ZONARAS, JOHANNES** (d. after 1160) Twelfth-century Byzantine historian, who held positions in Constantinople and then retired to the island of Niandro, where he led a monastic life. He was the author of a universal history in 18 volumes, of great value in providing details on the 11th century. He also wrote a commentary on Greek canon law, a hymn to the Blessed Virgin and a commentary on the poems of Saint Gregory of Nazianzus. Zonaras's writings preserved the first 21 books of Dio Cassius's history.

**ZURICH** City in northern Switzerland, the capital of the Zurich canton, situated on the Limmat River and Lake Zurich. Originally a Roman settlement, it was resettled by the Alamanni and then by the Franks, becoming a royal residence of the Carolingians in the ninth century. Growing in stature after 1000, because of its strategic position to increase commerce, Zurich became a free imperial city in 1218, joining the Swiss Confederation in 1351. It later bought its freedom from the German emperor, writing a city constitution that ensured the social and political balance between its guilds, artisans and nobles. See also SWITZERLAND.

# APPENDIX 1: RULERS OF MEDIEVAL EUROPE

## WESTERN EUROPE

### DENMARK

*Gorm Dynasty*
Gorm, king of Jutland (c. 940–935)
Harald Bluetooth (935–985)
Sven Forkbeard (985–1014)
Canute the Great (1014–1035)
Hardacanute (1035–1042)
Magnus I (king of Norway, 1042–1047)

*Estrith (Estrid) Dynasty*
Sven Estridson (1047–1074)
Harald Hen (1074–1080)
Canute II (IV) (1080–1086)
Olaf (1086–1095)
Eric I Ejegod (1095–1103)
Niels (1104–1134)
Eric II Emune (1134–1137)
Magnus the Strong }
Eric III the Lame } Civil War (1138–1156)
Canute III (V) Lavard }
Waldemar I (1157–1182)
Canute IV (VI) (1182–1202)
Waldenmar II Sejr (1202–1241)

Eric IV Plovpennig (1241–1250) }
Abel (1250–1252) } Civil War
Christopher I (1252–1259) }
Eric V Glipping (1259–1286)
Eric VI Menved (1286–1319)
Christopher II (1319–1332)

*Holstein Counts*
Waldemar IV Atterdag (1340–1375)
Olaf, son of Margaret and Haakon (1375–1380)
Margaret of Norway (1380–1412)
Eric VII of Pomerania (1412–1439)
Christopher of Bavaria (1440–1448)

*Oldenburg Dynasty*
Christian I Oldenburg (1448–1481)
John I (1481–1513)

### ENGLAND

*Wessex*
Cerdic (519–534)
Cynric (534–560)
Ceawlin (560–592)
Ceola (592–597)
Ceolwulf (597–611)
Cynegils (611–642)
Cenwealh (642–672)
Aescwine (673–676)
Centwine (676–686)
Ceadwalla (686–688)
Ine (688–726)
Aethelheard (726–740)
Cuthred (740–756)
Sigebert (756–757)
Cynewulf (757–786)
Brihtric (786–802)
Egbert (802–839)
Aethelwulf (839–858)
Aethelbald (858–860)
Aethelbert (860–866)
Aethelred (866–871)
Alfred (871–899)

*Northumbria*
Aethelfrith (593–616)
Edwin (616–633)
Oswald (633–641)
Oswy (641–670)
Ecgfrith (670–685)
Aldfrith (685–705)
Osred (705–716)
Coenred (716–718)
Osric (718–729)
Ceolwulf (729–737)

*Saxons*
Edward the Elder (899–924)
Athelstan the Glorious (924–940)
Edmund I (940–946)
Edred (946–955)
Edwy the Fair (955–959)
Edgar the Peaceful (959–975)

Edward the Martyr (975–978)
Aethelred the Unready (978–1016)
Edmund II Ironside (1016)
Canute the Great (1016–1035)
Harold I Harefoot (1035–1040)
Hardacanute (1040–1042)
Edward the Confessor (1042–1066)
Harold II (1066)

***Norman Dynasty***
William I (1066–1087)
William II (1087–1100)
Henry I (1100–1135)
Stephen (1135–1154)

***Angevin Dynasty***
Henry II (1154–1189)
Richard I the Lion-Hearted (1189–1199)
John (1199–1216)

***Plantagenet Dynasty***
Henry III (1216–1272)
Edward I (1272–1307)
Edward II (1307–1327)
Edward III (1327–1377)
Richard II (1377–1399)

***Lancastrian Dynasty***
Henry IV (1399–1413)
Henry V (1413–1422)
Henry VI (1422–1471)

***Yorkist Dynasty***
Edward IV (1461–1483)
Richard III (1483–1485)

***Tudor Dynasty***
Henry VII (1485–1509)

## FRANCE

***Merovingian Dynasty***
Childeric I (458–481)
Clovis (481–511)
Clotaire (511–558, 558–561)
- Thierry I, king of Austrasia (511–543)
- Clodomir I, king of Orléans (511–524)
- Childebert I, king of Paris (511–558)

Various (561–613)
- Charibert, king of Paris (561–567)
- Guntram, king of Burgundy and Orléans (561–592)
- Sigebert I, king of Austrasia (561–575)
- Chilperic I, king of Soissons (561–584)
- Childebert II, king of Austrasia (575) king of Burgundy and Orléans (593–596)
- Thierry II, king of Burgundy (596–613)
- Thibert II, king of Austrasia

Clotaire (584), sole king (613–629)
- Charibert, duke of Burgundy (628–631)

Dagobert (629–639)
Clovis II, king of Neustria and Burgundy (638–656), king of France (656)
- Sigebert II, king of Austrasia (634–659)
- Dagobert, king of Austrasia (674–679)

Childeric II, king of Austrasia (656–670), king of France (670–673)
- Clotaire III, king of Neustria and Burgundy (656–670) Thierry III, king of Neustria and Burgundy (673), king of France (679–691)

Clovis III (691–695)
Childebert III (695–711)
Dagobert III (711–715)
Chilperic (715–720)
- Thierry IV, king of Neustria and Burgundy (720–737)

Interregnum (737–742)
Childeric III (742–752)

***Pepinid Dynasty***
Pepin of Landen (d. 640)
Pepin of Héristal (d. 714)
Charles Martel (d. 741)
Pepin the Short, head of state (751–768)

***Carolingian Dynasty***
Charlemagne (768–814)
Louis I the Pious (814–840)
- Charles, king of Aquitaine (d. 811)
- Pepin, king of Italy (d. 810)
- Bernard, son of Pepin (810–818)

Charles the Bald (840–877)
- Lothair, emperor of Italy and Lorraine (840–855)
- Pepin, king of Aquitaine (d. 838)
- Louis, king of Bavaria and Germany (840–876)

Louis II the Stammerer (877–879)
Louis III (879–882)
Carloman (879–884)
Charles the Simple (893–923)
Charles the Fat, emperor of Germany (876), king of France (884–887)
Louis IV (936–954)
Lothaire (954–986)
Louis V (986–987)

***Capetian Dynasty***
Hugh Capet (987–996)
Robert the Pious (996–1031)
Henry I (1031–1060)
Philip I (1060–1108)
Louis VI the Fat (1108–1137)
Louis VII the Young (1137–1180)
Philip II Augustus (1180–1223)
Louis VIII the Lion (1223–1226)
Louis IX (Saint Louis) (1226–1270)
Philip III the Bold (1270–1285)
Philip IV the Fair (1285–1314)
Louis X (1314–1316)
Philip V the Long (1316–1322)
Charles IV the Fair (1322–1328)

***Valois Dynasty***
Philip VI of Valois (1328–1350)
John II the Good (1350–1364)
Charles V the Wise (1364–1380)
Charles VI the Well-Beloved (or the Mad) (1380–1422)
Charles VII (1422–1461)

Louis XI (1461–1483)
Charles VIII (1483–1498)
Louis XII (1498–1515)

## GERMANIC KINGDOMS

*Vandals*
Geiseric (427–477)
Hunneric (477–484)
Gunthamund (484–496)
Thrasamund (496–523)
Hilderic (523–530)
Gelamir (530–534)

*Ostrogoths*
Theodoric (493–526)
Athalric (526–534)
Theodahat (534–536)
Witiges (536–540)
Hildibad (540–541)
Eraric (541)
Totila (541–552)
Teia (552–553)

*Visigoths*
Euric (466–483)
Alaric II (483–506)
Theodoric and Amalric (506–522)
Amalric (522–531)
Theudis (531–548)
Theudigisel (548–549)
Agila (549–554)
Athanagild (554–567)
Leova I (567–572)
Leovigild (570–586)
Reccared I (586–601)
Leova II (601–603)
Witterich (603–610)
Gundimar (610–612)
Sisibut (612–620)
Reccared II (620–621)
Swinthila (620–631)
Sisinand (631–636)
Chinthila (636–640)
Tulga (640–641)
Chindaswinth (641–652)
Recceswinth (652–672)
Wamba (672–680)
Erwig (680–687)
Egica (687–701)
Witiza (701–710)
Roderic (710–711)

*Lombard Kings of Italy*

| *House of Alboin* | *Others* |
|---|---|
| Alboin (568–572) | |
| Clepho (572–573) | |
| Autheri (583–590) | |
| Agilulf (590–615) | |
| Adaloald (615–625) | |
| Arioald (625–636) | Rothari (636–652) |
| Aribert (653–662) | Rodoald (652–653) |
| Godebert (662) | |
| Grimoald (662–700) | |
| Berthardi (672–688) | |
| Cunibert (688–700) | |
| Luitbert (700–701) | |
| Aribert (701–711) | |
| | Ansprand (712) |
| | Liutprand (712–743) |
| | Hildebrand (743–744) |
| | Ratchis (744–749) |
| | Aistulf (749–756) |
| | Desiderius (756–774) |

## HOLY ROMAN EMPIRE

*Saxon Dynasty*
Henry I (919–936)
Otto I (936–973)
Otto II (973–983)
Otto III (983–1002)
Henry II (1002–1024)

*Salien or Franconian Dynasty*
Conrad II (1024–1039)
Henry III (1039–1056)
Henry IV (1056–1106)
Henry V (1106–1125)
Lothair, duke of Saxony (1125–1137)

*Hohenstaufen Dynasty*
Conrad III (1138–1152)
Frederick I (1152–1190)
Henry VI (1190–1196)
Philip of Swabia (1197–1208)
Otto IV (Anti-king, 1198; deposed 1215)
Frederick II (1215–1250)
Conrad IV (1250–1254)
William, count of Holland (Anti-king) (1247–1256)
Conradin (1252–1268)

Interregnum (1254–1273)

Rudolf I (1273–1291)
Adolf of Nassau (1292–1298)
Albert I (1298–1308)
Henry VII (1308–1313)
Louis IV (1314–1346)
Charles IV (1346–1378)
Wenceslas (1378–1410)
Rupert (1400–1410)
Sigismund (1410–1437)

*Habsburg Dynasty*
Albert II (1438–1439)
Frederick III (1440–1493)
Maxmilian I (1493–1519)

## NORWAY

*Yngling Dynasty*
Harald I Fairhair (872–930)
Eric Blood-Axe (930–934)
Haakon I the Good (934–961)
Harald II Graypelt (961–970)

Jarl Haakon of Lade (970–995)
Olaf I Trygvason (995–1000)
Jarls Eric and Svein (1000–1016)
Saint Olaf II (1015–1030)
Canute the Great and Svein (1028–1035)
Magnus I the Good (1035–1047)
Harald III Hardraade (1042–1066)
Magnus II (1066–1069)
Olaf III Kyrri the Peaceful (1066–1093)
Magnus III Bareleg (1093–1103)
Olaf IV (1103–1116)
Eystein I (1103–1122)
Sigurd I Jerusalemfarer (1103–1130)
Magnus IV the Blind (1130–1135)
Harald IV Gilchrist (1130–1136)
Sigurd II Slembe (1136–1139)
Ingi Hunchback (1136–1161)
Sigurd III Mouth (1136–1155)
Eystein II (1142–1157)
Haakon II the Broadshouldered (1157–1162)
Magnus V Erlingsson (1162–1184)
Sverre (1177–1202)
Haakon III (1202–1204)
Ingi Bardson (1204–1217)
Haakon IV the Old (1217–1263)
Magnus VI Lawmender (1263–1280)
Eric II Priesthater (1280–1299)
Haakon V (1299–1319)

***Folkung Dynasty***
Magnus VII (1319–1355)
Haakon VI (1350–1380)
Olaf V (1380–1387)
Margaret (1388–1405)
Erik of Pomerania (1389–1442)
Christopher of Bavaria (1442–1448)
Karl Knutsson and Christian of Oldenburg, rival claimants (1448–1450)
Christian I (1450–1481)

Interregnum (1481–1483)

Hans (1483–1513)

## SCOTLAND

***McAlpin and Dunkeld-Canmore Dynasties***
Kenneth I McAlpin (843–858)
Donald I (858–862)
Constantine I (862–877)
Aed (877–888)
Eochaid w/ Giric (878–889)
Donald II (889–900)
Constantine II (900–943)
Malcolm I (943–954)
Indulf (954–962)
Dubh (962–966)
Culen )966–971)
Kenneth II (971–995)
Constantine III (995–997)
Kenneth III (997–1005)
Giric (997–1005)
Malcolm II (1005–1034)
Duncan I (1034–1040)
Macbeth (1040–1058)
Malcolm III (1058–1093)
Donald III ban (1093–1097)
Duncan II (1094)
Edgar (1097–1107)
Alexander I (1107–1124)
David I (1124–1153)
Malcolm IV (1153–1165)
William (1165–1214)
Alexander II (1214–1249)
Alexander III (1249–1286)
Margaret, Maid of Norway (1286–1290)

***Balliol, Bruce and Stuart Dynasties***
John Balliol (Toom Tabard) (1291–1296)
Robert I the Bruce (1306–1329)
David II (1329–1371)
Robert II (1371–1390)
Robert III Stuart (1390–1406)
James I (1406–1437)
James II (1437–1460)
James III (1460–1488)
James IV (1488–1513)

## CHRISTIAN SPAIN

***Aragón***
Aznar I Galindo (c. 809–839)
Galindo I Aznarez (c. 844–867)
Aznar II Galindo (867–893)
Galindo II Aznarez (893–922)
Sancho II Garcés (970–994)
García II Sanchez (994–1000)
Sancho III Garcés el Mayor (1000–1035)
Ramiro I (1035–1063)
Sancho I Ramírez (1063–1094)
Pedro I (1094–1104)
Alfonso I (1104–1134)
Ramíro II (1134–1137)
Alfonso II (1162–1196)
Pedro II (1196–1213)
James I (1213–1276)
Pedro III (1276–1285)
Alfonso III (1285–1291)
James II (1291–1327)
Alfonso IV (1327–1336)
Pedro IV (1336–1387)
John I (1387–1395)
Martin I (1395–1410)
Ferdinand I (1412–1416)
Alfonso V (1416–1458)
John II (1458–1479)
Ferdinand II (1479–1516)

***Asturias-León-Castile***
Pelayo (718–737)
Fafila (737–739)
Alfonso I (739–757)
Fruela I (757–768)
Aurelius (768–774)
Silo (774–783)

Mauregatus (783–788)
Vermudo I (788–791)
Alfonso II (791–842)
Ramíro I (842–850)
Ordoño I (850–866)
Alfonso III (866–910)
Fruela II (910–925)
Alfonso IV (925–930)
Ramíro II (930–951)
Ordoño III (951–956)
Sancho I (956–966)
Ramíro III (966–984)
Vermudo II (984–999)
Alfonso V (999–1028)
Vermudo III (1028–1037)
Ferdinand I (1035–1065)
Castile-Sancho II (1065–1072)
León-Alfonso VI (1065–1109)
Galicia-García (1065–1072)
Raymond of Burgundy (1109–1126)
Alfonso VII (1126–1157)

| *Castile* | *León* |
|---|---|
| Sancho III (1157–1158) | Ferdinand II (1157–1188) |
| Alfonso VIII (1158–1214) | Alfonso IX (1188–1230) |

Henry I (1214–1217)
Ferdinand III (1217–1252)
Alfonso X (1252–1284)
Sancho IV (1284–1295)
Ferdinand IV (1295–1312)
Alfonso XI (1312–1350)
Pedro the Cruel (1350–1369)
Henry II (1369–1379)
John I (1379–1390)
Henry III (1390–1406)
John II (1406–1454)
Henry IV (1454–1474)
Isabella (1474–1504)

***Navarre***
Inigo Arista (c. 810–851)
García Iniquez (851–870)
Fortun Garcés (870–905)
Sancho I Garcés (905–926)
García I Sanchéz (926–970)
Sancho II Garcés (970–994)
García II Sanchéz (994–1000)
Sancho III Garcés el Mayor (1000–1035)
García III Sanchez (1035–1054)
Sancho IV Garcés (1054–1076)
García IV Ramírez (1134–1150)
Sancho VI (1150–1194)
Sancho VII (1194–1234)
Thibault I (1234–1253)
Thibault II (1253–1270)
Henry I (1270–1274)
Jeanne I (1274–1305)
Louis X (1314–1316)
Philip V (1316–1322)
Charles X (IV) (1322–1328)
Jeanne II (1328–1349)
Carlos II (1349–1387)
Carlos III (1387–1425)
Blanche (1425–1441)
Leonor (1479)
Francisco (1479–1483)

***Catalonia***
Ramon Berenguer I (1035–1076)
Ramon Berenguer II (1076–1082)
Berenguer Ramon II (1076–1097)
Ramon Berenguer III (1097–1131)
Ramon Bergenuer IV (1131–1162)

***Portugal***
Henry of Burgundy (1093–1128)
Alfonso I Henriques (1128–1185)
Sancho I (1185–1211)
Alfonso II (1211–1223)
Sancho II (1223–1248)
Alfonso III (1248–1279)
Dinis (1279–1325)
Alfonso IV (1325–1357)
Pedro (1357–1367)
Ferdinand (1367–1383)
John I of Avis (1385–1433)
Duarte (1433–1438)
Alfonso V (1438–1481)
John II (1481–1495)
Manuel (1495–1521)

## SWEDEN

Aun
Egil
Ottar
Adils
Osten
Yngvar
Anund
Ingjald
} Early rulers (c. 500–650)

Eric (c. 800)
Anund and Bjorn (c. 825)
Olof (c. 850)
Ring (c. 930)
Eric and Edmund (c. 935)
Emund Ericsson (c. 970)
Eric the Victorious (c. 980–995)
Olof (995–1022)
Anund (1022–1056)
Edmund (1056–1060)

***Stenkil Dynasty***
Stenkil (c. 1060–1066)
Halsten and Inge the Elder (c. 1080–1111)
Philip and Inge the Elder (c. 1111–1122)

***Sverker and Eric Dynasties***
Sverker the Elder (1131–1155)
Eric IX (c. 1155–1160)
Charles VII Sverkersson (1161–1167)
Canute Ericsson (1167–1196)
Sverker II Charlesson (1196–1208)
Eric X Canutesson (1208–1216)

John I Sverkersson (1216–1292)
Eric XI Ericsson (1222–1229)
Canute II the Tall (1229–1234)
Eric II Ericsson (1234–1250)

***Folkung Dynasty***
Birger Jarl (regent, 1250–1266)
Valdemar (1250–1275)
Magnus Barnlock (1275–1290)
Birger (1290–1318, regent 1298)
Magnus II Ericsson (regent, 1319–1332, 1319–1363)
Eric XII Magnusson (1357–1359)
Hagon Magnusson (1362–1365)
Albert of Mecklenburg (1364–1389)
Margaret of Denmark (regent, 1389–1412)
Eric XIII of Pomerania (regent, 1396–1400, 1396–1439)
Engelbrekt (regent, 1435–1436)
Karl Knutsson (regent, 1436–1440)
Christopher of Bavaria (1440–1448)
Karl (Charles VIII) Knutsson (1448–1457, 1465, 1467–1470)
Christian I of Oldenburg (1457–1464)
Sten Sture the Elder (regent, 1470–1497, 1501–1503)
John II (1497–1501)

## POPES

Leo I (440–461)
Hilary (461–468)
Simplicius (468–483)
Felix II (483–492)
Gelasius I (492–496)
Anastasius II (496–498)
Symmachus (498–514)
Hormisdas (514–523)
John I (523–526)
Felix III (526–530)
Boniface II (530–532)
John II (533–535)
Agapitus I (535–536)
Silverius (536–537)
Vigilius (537–555)
Pelagius I (556–561)
John III (561–574)
Benedict I (575–579)
Pelagius II (579–590)
Gregory I the Great (590–604)
Sabinianus (604–606)
Boniface III (607)
Boniface IV (608–615)
Deusdedit (615–618)
Boniface V (619–625)
Honorius I (625–638)
Severinus (640)
John IV (640–642)
Theodore I (642–649)
Martin I (649–655)
Eugene I (654–657)
Vitalian (657–672)
Adeodatus II (672–676)
Donus (676–678)
Agatho (678–681)
Leo II (682–683)
Benedict II (684–685)
John V (685–686)
Conon (686–687)
Sergius I (687–701)
John VI (701–705)
John VII (705–707)
Sisinnius (708)
Constantine (708–715)
Gregory II (715–731)
Zachary (741–752)
Stephen II (III) (752–757)
Paul I (757–767)
Stephen III (IV) (768–772)
Adrian I (772–795)
Leo III (795–816)
Stephen IV (V) (816–817)
Paschal I (817–824)
Eugene II (824–827)
Valentine (827)
Gregory IV (827–844)
Sergius II (844–847)
Leo IV (847–855)
Benedict III (855–858)
Nicholas I the Great (858–867)
Adrian II (867–872)
John VIII (872–882)
Marinus I (882–884)
Adrian III (884–885)
Stephen V (VI) (885–891)
Formosus (891–896)
Boniface VI (896)
Stephen VI (VII) (896–897)
Romanus (897)
Theodore II (897)
John IX (898–900)
Benedict IV (900–903)
Leo V (903)
Sergius III (904–911)
Anastasius III (911–913)
Landus (913–914)
John X (914–928)
Leo VI (928)
Stephen VII (VIII) (928–931)
John XI (931–935)
Leo VII (936–939)
Stephen VIII (IX) (939–942)
Marinus II (942–946)
Agapitus II (946–955)
John XII (955–964)
Leo VIII (963–965)
Benedict V (964–966)
John XIII (965–972)
Benedict VI (973–974)
Benedict VII (974–983)
John XIV (983–984)
John XV (985–996)
Gregory V (996–999)
Sylvester II (999–1003)
John XVII (1003)

John XVIII (1004–1009)
Sergius IV (1009–1012)
Benedict VIII (1012–1024)
John XIX (1024–1032)
Benedict IX (1032–1044)
Sylvester III (1045)
Benedict IX (second reign, 1045)
Gregory VI (1045–1046)
Clement II (1046–1047)
Benedict IX (third reign, 1047–1048)
Damasus II (1048–1049)
Leo IX (1049–1054 or 1055)
Victor II (1054/1055–1057)
Stephen IX (X) (1057–1058 or 1059)
Nicholas II (1058/1059–1061)
Alexander II (1061–1073)
Gregory VII (1073–1086)
Victor III (1086–1087)
Urban II (1088–1099)
Paschal II (1099–1118)
Gelasius II (1118–1119)
Calixtus II (1119–1124)
Honorius II (1124–1130)
Innocent II (1130–1143)
Celestine II (1143–1144)
Lucius II (1144–1145)
Eugene III (1145–1153)
Anastasius IV (1153–1154)
Adrian IV (1154–1159)
Alexander III (1159–1181)
Lucius III (1181–1185)
Urban III (1185–1187)
Gregory VIII (1187)
Clement III (1187–1191)
Celestine III (1191–1198)
Innocent III (1198–1216)
Honorius III (1216–1227)
Greogry IX (1227–1241)
Celestine IV (1241–1243)
Innocent IV (1243–1254)
Alexander IV (1254–1261)
Urban IV (1261–1264)
Clement IV (1265–1268)
Gregory X (1271–1276)
Innocent V (1276)
Adrian V (1276)
John XXI (1276–1277)
Nicholas III (1277–1280)
Martin IV (1281–1285)
Honorius IV (1285–1287)
Nicholas IV (1288–1293)
Celestine V (1293–1294)
Boniface VIII (1294–1303)
Benedict XI (1303–1304)
Clement V (1305–1314)
John XXII (1316–1334)
Benedict XII (1334–1342)
Clement VI (1342–1352)
Innocent VI (1352–1362)
Urban V (1362–1370)
Gregory XI (1370–1378)
Urban VI (1378–1389)
Boniface IX (1389–1404)
Innocent VII (1404–1406)
Gregory XII (1406–1415)
Martin V (1417–1431)
Eugene IV (1431–1447)
Nicholas V (1447–1455)
Calixtus III (1455–1458)
Pius II (1458–1464)
Paul II (1464–1471)
Sixtus IV (1471–1484)
Innocent VIII (1484–1492)
Alexander VI (1492–1503)

## EASTERN EUROPE

### BULGARIA

*First Bulgarian Empire*
Asparukh (680–701)
Tervel (701–718)
Unknown (718–724)
Sevar (724–739)
Kornisos (739–756)
Vinech (756–762)
Teletz (762–764)
Sabin (764–766)
Umar, Toktu (766)
Pagan (767-c. 770)
Telerig (c. 770–777)
Kardam (777-c. 803)
Krum (c. 803–814)
Dukum, Dicevq (814)
Omurtag (814–831)
Malomir (831–836)
Presiam (possibly Malomir) (836–852)
Boris I Michael (852–889)
Vladimir (889–893)
Symeon (893–927)
Peter (927–969)
Boris II (969–972)

*Macedonian Empire*
Samuel (976–1014)
Gabriel Radomir (1014–1015)
John Vladislav (1015–1018)

*Second Bulgarian Empire*
Asen I (1187–1196)
Peter (1196–1197)
Kalojan (1197–1207)
Boril (1207–1218)
Ivan Asen II (1218–1241)
Koloman Asen (1241–1246)
Michael Asen (1246–1256)
Constantine Tich (1257–1277)
Ivaljo (1278–1279)
Ivan Asen III (1279–1280)
George I Terter (1280–1292)
Smiletz (1292–1298)

Interregnum (c. 1298–1300)

Caka (1300)
Theodore Svetoslav (1300–1322)
George II Terter (1322–1323)
Michael Sisman (1323–1330)
Ivan Stephen (1330–1331)
Ivan Alexander (1331–1371)
Ivan Sisman (1371–1393)
in Vidin: Ivan Stracimir (1365–1396)

## BYZANTINE EMPIRE

Constantine I (324–337)
Constantius (337–361)
Julian (361–363)
Jovian (363–364)
Valens (364–378)
Theodosius I (379–395)
Arcadius (395–408)
Theodosius II (408–450)
Marcian (450–457)
Leo I (457–474)
Leo II (474)
Zeno (474–475)
Basiliscus (475–476)
Zeno (476–491)
Anastasius I (491–518)
Justin I (518–527)
Justinian I (527–565)
Justin II (565–578)
Tiberius I Constantine (578–582)
Maurice (582–602)
Phocas (602–610)
Heraclius (610–641)
Constantine III and Heraclonas (641)
Heraclonas (641)
Constans II (641–668)
Constantine IV (668–685)
Justinian II (685–695)
Leontius (695–698)
Tiberius II (698–705)
Justinian II (705–711)
Philippicus (711–713)
Anastasius II (713–715)
Theodosius III (715–717)
Leo III (717–741)
Constantine V (741–775)
Leo IV (775–780)
Constantine VI (780–797)
Irene (797–802)
Nicephorus (802–811)
Stauracius (811)
Michael I Rangabe (811–813)
Leo V (813–820)
Michael II (820–829)
Theophilus (829–842)
Michael III (842–867)
Basil (867–886)
Leo VI (886–912)
Alexander (912–913)
Constantine VII (913–959)
Romanus I Lecapenus (920–944)
Romanus II (959–963)
Nicephorus II Phocas (963–969)
John I Tzimisces (969–976)
Basil II (976–1025)
Constantine VIII (1025–1028)
Romanus III Argyrus (1028–1034)
Michael IV (1034–1041)
Michael V (1041–1042)
Zoë and Theodora (1042)
Constantine Monomachus (1042–1055)
Theodora (1055–1056)
Michael VI (1056–1057)
Isaac I Comnenus (1057–1059)
Constantine X Ducas (1059–1067)
Romanus IV Diogenes (1067–1071)
Michael VII Ducas (1071–1078)
Nicephorus III Botaneiates (1078–1081)
Alexius I Comnenus (1081–1118)
John II Comnenus (1118–1143)
Manuel I Comnenus (1143–1180)
Alexius II Comnenus (1180–1183)
Andronicus I Comnenus (1183–1185)
Isaac II Angelus (1185–1195)
Alexius III Angelus (1195–1203)
Isaac II Angelus and Alexius IV Angelus (1203–1204)
Alexius V Mourtzouphlos (Ducas) (1204)
Theodore I Lascaris (1204–1222)
John III Ducas Vatatzes (1222–1254)
Theodore II Lascaris (1254–1258)
John IV Lascaris (1258–1261)
Michael VIII Palaeologus (1259–1282)
Andronicus II Palaeologus (1282–1328)
Andronicus III Palaeologus (1328–1341)
John V Palaeologus (1341–1391)
John VI Cantacuzenus (1347–1354)
Andronicus IV Palaeologus (1376–1379)
John VII Palaeologus (1390)
Manuel II Palaeologus (1391–1425)
John VIII Palaeologus (1425–1448)
Constantine XI Palaeologus (1449–1453)

## LATIN EMPIRE OF CONSTANTINOPLE

Baldwin I of Flanders (1204–1205)
Henry of Flanders (1206–1216)
Peter of Courtenay (1217)
Yolande (1217–1219)
Robert of Courtenay (1221–1228)
Baldwin II (1228–1261)
John of Brienne (1231–1237)

## DESPOTATE OF EPIRUS

Michael I (1204–c. 1215)
Theodore (c. 1215–1224)
Theodore (1224–1230)
Manuel (1230–c. 1240)
John (1240–1244)
Demetrius (1244–1246)

*Despots of Epirus*
Michael II (c. 1237–1271)
Nicephorus I (1271–1296)
Thomas (1296–1318)
Nicholas Orsini (1318–1323)
John Orsini (1323–1355)
Nicephorus II (1335–1340)

*Sebastocrators of Thessaly*
John I (1271–1296)
Constantine (1296–1303)
John II (1303–1318)

## HUNGARY

*Arpad Dynasty*
Géza (972–997), Christianized Magyars
Saint Stephen I (997–1038)
Peter Urseolo (1038–1046)
Andrew I (1047–1061)
Béla I (1061–1063)
Solomon (1063–1074)
Géza I (1074–1077)
Saint Ladislas I (1077–1095)
Coloman I (1095–1114)
Stephen II (1114–1131)
Béla II (1131–1141)
Géza II (1141–1162)
Stephen III (1162–1172)
Béla III (1172–1196)
Emeric I (1196–1204)
Ladislas III (1204–1205)
Andrew II (1205–1235)
Béla IV (1235–1270)
Stephen V (1270–1272)
Ladislas IV (1272–1290)
Andrew III (1290–1301)

Interregnum (1301–1308)

Charles I (1308–1342)
Louis (1342–1382)
Mary of Anjou (1382–1385)
Charles II (1385–1386)
Sigismund (1387–1437)
Albert of Habsburg (1437–1439)
Vladislav I (1440–1444)
Ladislav V (1444–1457)
Matthias Corvinus (1458–1490)

## POLAND

Prince Svatopluk of Great Moravia (870–894)
Hungarian Magyars (896–907)
Boleslav I of Bohemia (d. 972)
Boleslav II (c. 973–999)

*Polanie (Piast) Dynasty*
Piast
Siemowit (Ziemowit)
Leszek (Lestko)
Siemomysl (Ziemomysl)
Mieszko I (963–992)
Boleslav I the Brave (992–1025)
Mieszko II Lambert (1025–1034)

Interregnum (1034–1039)

Casimir I the Restorer (1039–1058)
Boleslav II the Bold (1058–1079, exiled in 1079)
Władysław I Herman 1079–1102)
Zbigniev (1102–1106)
Boleslav III the Wry-Mouthed (1106–1138)

*Seniors*
Władysław II the Exile (1138–1146)
Boleslav IV the Curly (c. 1146–1173)

*Silesian Piasts*
Mieszko III the Old (1173–1177)
Casimir II the Just (1177–1194)
Leszik the White (d. 1227)

Konrad of Mazovia

Vaclav II, king of Bohemia (1289–1292)
Przemysl II, duke of Greater Poland (1295–1296)
Vaclav II of Bohemia (Wenceslas) (1300–1305)

*Piasts*
Władysław I the Short (1314–1333)
Casimir III the Great (1333–1370)
Louis I of Hungary (1370–1382)

*Jagiello Dynasty*
Jadwiga and Władysław II Jagiello (1382–1399)
Jagiello (sole ruler) (1399–1434)
Władysław III (1434–1444)

Interregnum (1444–1447)

Casimir IV Jagiellonczyk (1447–1492)

## RUSSIA

*Rurik Dynasty*
Rurik (862–879)
Oleg (879–912)
Igor (913–945)
Olga (945–969)
Svatyslav (962–972)
Yaropolk (973–980)
Vladimir the Saint (980–1015)
Sviatopolk (1015–1019)
Yaroslav the Wise (1036–1054)
Vladimir Monomakh (1113–1125)

*Grand Princes of Moscow*
Ivan I Kalita (1328–1341)
Simeon the Proud (1341–1353)
Ivan II the Red (1353–1359)
Dimitry II (1359–1362)
Dimitry III Donskoi (1362–1389)
Vasily Dimitrievitch I (1389–1425)
Vasily Dimitrievitch II (1425–1462)

Ivan III the Great (1462–1505)
Vasily Ivanovitch III (1505–1533)

## SERBIA

John Vlastimir (mid-ninth century)
Mutimir (c. 891)
Proslav (891–892)
Peter Gojnikovic (892–917)
Paul Branovic (917–920)
Zacharias Prvoslavljevic (920–c. 924)
Caslav Klonimirovic (927–after 950)

*Zeta*
John Vladimir (late 10th century)
Stephen Voislav (c. 1040–c. 1052)
Michael (c. 1052–c. 1081)
Constantine Bodin (c. 1081–c. 1101)

*Rascia*
Vukan (c. 1083–1114)
Various rulers (c. 1114–1167)
Stephen Nemanja (c. 1167–1196)
Stephen the First Crowned (1196–c. 1228)
Stephen Radoslav (c. 1228–1233)
Stephen Vladislav (c. 1233–1242)
Stephen Uros I (1242–1276)
Stephen Dragutin (1276–1282)
Stephen Uros II Milutin (1282–1321)
Stephen Uros III Decanski (1321–1331)
Stephen Dusan (czar, 1331–1355)
Stephen Uros (czar, 1355–1371)
Vukasin (king, 1366–1371)
Lazar (prince, 1371–1389)
Stephen Lazarevic (1389–1427)
George Brankovic (1427–1456)
Lazar Brankovic (1456–1458)

# APPENDIX 2: DYNASTIES OF MEDIEVAL ISLAM

Muhammad (c. 570–632)
Caliphs (632–661)
Umayyad caliphate (661–750)
Abbasid caliphate (750–1258)

*Spain*
Umayyads of Spain (756–1031)
Kingdom of Seville (1023–1091)
Reys de Teija (1031–1086)
Almoravids (1086–1147)
Almohads (1147–1250)
Nasrid Kingdom of Granada (1230–1492)

*Africa*
Rustamids of Tahir (779–909)
Idrisids of Fez (789–926)
Aghlabids of Kairwan (c. 801–909)
Zirids (972–1167; independent of Fatimids, 1041)
Kalbites of Sicily (c. 972–1040)

*Egypt*
Tulunids (868–905)
Ikshidids (935–969)
Fatimids (969–1171)
Ayyubids (1169–1250)
Mamluks (1250–1517)
- Bahri Mamluks (1250–1382)
- Burji Mamluks (1382–1517)

*The East*
Umayyads (661–750)
Abbasids (750–1258)
Tahirids (820–872)
Saffarids (867–15th century)
Samanids (819–1005)
Ghaznavids (962–1186)
Buyids (945–1055)
Seljuks
- Great Seljuks (1037–1057)
- Seljuks of Iraq (1105–1194)
- Seljuks of Syria (1078–1117)
- Seljuks of Rum (1077–1307)

Ottoman Empire (1288–1922)

# APPENDIX 3: RULERS OF MEDIEVAL ISLAM

### THE FIRST CALIPHS

Abu Bakr (623–624)
'Umar ibn 'Abd al-Khattab (634–644)
'Uthman ibn 'Affan (644–656)
'Ali ibn Abi Talib (656–661)

### THE UMAYYAD CALIPHATE

Mu'awiya ibn Abi Sufyan I (661–680)
Yazid I (680–683)
Mu'awiya II (683–684)
Marwan I (684–685)
'Abd al-Malik (685–705)
al-Walid (705–715)
Sulayman (715–717)
'Umar ibn 'Abd al-'Aziz (717–720)
Yazid II (720–724)
Hisham (724–743)
al-Walid (743–744)
Yazid III (744)
Ibrahim (744)
Marwan II (744–750)

### THE ABBASID CALIPHATE

Abu'l-'Abbas al-Saffah (749–754)
al-Mansur (754–775)
al-Mahdi (775–785)
Harun al-Rashid (786–809)
al-Amin (809–813)
al-Ma'mun (813–833)
al-Mu'tasim (833–842)
al-Wathiq (842–847)
al-Mutawakkil (847–861)
al-Muntasir (861–862)
al-Musta'in (862–866)
al-Mu'tazz (866–869)
al-Muhtadi (869–870)
al-Mu'tamid (870–892)
al-Mu'tadid (892–902)
al-Muktafi (902–908)
al-Muqtadir (908–932)
al-Qahir (932–934)
al-Radi (934–940)
al-Muttaqi (940–944)
al-Mustakfi (944–946)
al-Muti' (946–974)
al-Ta'i' (974–991)
al-Qadir (991–1031)
al-Qa'im (1031–1075)
al-Muqtadi (1075–1094)
al-Mustazhir (1094–1118)
al-Mustarshid (1118–1135)
al-Rashid (1135–1136)
al-Muqtafi (1136–1160)
al-Mustanjid (1160–1170)
al-Mustadi (1170–1180)
al-Nasir (1180–1225)
al-Zahir (1225–1226)
al-Mustansir (1226–1242)
al-Muzta'sim (1242–1258)

### THE TWELVE IMAMS

Ali (d. 661)
al-Hasan (d. 669)
al-Husayn (d. 680)
Ali Zayn al'Abidin (d. 714)
Muhammad al-Baqir (d. 731)
Ja'far al-Sadiq (d. 765)
Musa al-Kazim (d. 799)
Ali al-Rida (d. 818)
Muhammad al-Jawad (d. 835)
Ali al-Hadi (d. 868)
Hasan al-Askari (d. 874)
Muhammad al-Muntazar (d. c. 873)

### THE SEVEN IMAMS

al-Hasan (d. 669)
al-Husayn (d. 680)
Ali Zayn al-Abidin (d. 714)
Muhammad al-Baqir (d. 731)
Ja'far al-Sadiq (d. 765)
Isma'il (d. 760)
Muhammad al-Mahdi

### THE FATIMID CALIPHATE

al-Mahdi (909–934)
al-Qa'im (934–945)
al-Mansur (945–952)
al-Muizz (952–975)
al-Aziz (975–996)
al-Hakim (996–1021)
al-Zahir (1021–1036)
al-Mustansir (1036–1094)
al-Mustali (1094–1101)

al-Amir (1101–1130)
al-Hafiz (1130–1149)
al-Zafir (1149–1154)
al-Faiz (1154–1160)
al-Adid (1160–1171)

## HOUSE OF ZENGI (1127–1222)

Imad el-Din Zengi, atabeg of Mosul
Saif el-Din Gahzi I, atabeg of Mosul
Nur el-Din Mahmud, atabeg, king of Syria
Nasr el-Din
Qutb el-Din Mawdud, atabeg of Mosul
Izz el-Din Ghazi II, atabeg of Mosul
Imad el-Din Zengi, atabeg of Sanjar

## AGHLABID DYNASTY

Ibrahim ibn al-Aghlab (800–812)
Abd Allah I (812–817)
Ziyadat Allah I (817–838)
Abu Zikal (838–841)
Muhammad I (841–856)
Ahmad (856–863)
Ziyadat Allah II (863–864)
Muhammad II (864–875)
Ibrahim II (875–902)
Abd Allah II (902–903)
Ziyadat Allah III (903–909)

## SELJUK DYNASTIES

***Great Suljuks***
Duqaq
Seljuk
Mikhail
Toghril-Beg (1040–1063)
Alp Arslan (1063–1072)
Malik Shah (1072–1092)
Berk Yaruq (1093–1104)
Malik Shah II (1104–1105)
Muhammad Tapar (1105–1117)
Sanjar (1117–1157)

***Seljuks of Iraq***
Muhammad Tapar (1105–1118)
Mahmud (1118–1131)
Da'ud (1131–1132)
Toghril I (1132–1135)
Mas'ud (1135–1152)
Malik Shah (1152–1153)
Muhammad (1153–1159)
Sulaiman Shah (1159–1161)
Arslan Shah (1161–1177)
Toghril II (1177–1194)

***Seljuks of Syria***
Tutush (1078–1094)
Ridwan (1095–1113)
Duqaq (1098–1113)
Alp Arslan (1113–1114)
Sultan Shah (1114–1117)

***Seljuks of Anatolia***
Sulaiman I Shah (1077–1186)
Qilij Arslan I (1092–1107?)
Malik Shah (1107?–1116)
Mas'ud I (1116–1156)
Qilij Arslan II (1156–1192)
Malik II Shah (1192)
Kaykhusraw I (1192–1196)
Sulaiman Shah II (1196–1203)
Qilij Arslan III (1203–1204)
Kaykhusraw I (1204–1210)
Kayquwas I (1210–1219)
Kayquah I (1219–1236)
Kaykhusraw II (1236–1246)
Kayquwas II (1246–1259)
Qilij Arslan IV (1248–1264)
Kayquah II (1249–1257)
Kaykhusraw III (1264–1283)
Mas'ud II (1283–1298)
Kayquah III (1298–1301?, or 1284–1307)
Mas'ud II (1303–1308)
Mas'ud III (1307–1308)

## OTTOMAN EMPIRE

Osman (1288–1326)
Orchan (1326–1362)
Murad I (1362–1389)
Bayazid I (1389–1402)
Mehmet I (1402–1421; sole ruler from 1413)
Suleiman (1402–1410)
Musa (1411–1413)
Murad II (1421–1451)
Mehmet II the Conqueror (1451–1481)
Bayazid II (1481–1512)

## MAMLUK DYNASTIES

***Bahri Mamluks***
Aybak (c. 1250–1260)
Baybars (1260–1277)
Qalawun (1279–1290)
al-Ashraf (1290–1293)
al-Nasir (1293–1340)
Various (1340–1382)

*Umayyads of Spain*
Hisham caliph of Damascus (724–743)
Mu'awiya
Abd al-Rahman I (756–788)
Hisham I (788–796)
al-Hakam I (796–822)
Abd al-Rahman II (822–852)
Muhammad I (852–886)
al-Mundhir (886–888)
Abd-Allah (888–912)
Abd al-Rahman III (912–961)
al-Hakam II (961–976)
Hisham II (976–1009, 1010–1013)
Muhammad II (1009–1010)
Sulayman (1009, 1013–1016)
Abd al-Rahman IV (1018)

Abd al-Rahman V (1023–1024)
Muhammad III (1024–1025)
Hisham III (1027–1031)

***Other Usurpers***
Ali ibn Hammud (1016–1018)
al-Qasim (1018–1021)
Yahya ibn Ali (1021–1023, 1025–1027)

***Nasrid Kingdom of Granada***
Muhammad I (1232–1273)
Muhammad II (1272–1302)
Muhammad III (1302–1309)
Nasr (1309–1314)
Ismail (1341–1325)
Muhammad IV (1325–1333)
Yusuf I (1333–1354)
Muhammad V (1354–1359, 1362–1391)
Ismail II (1359–1360)
Muhammad VI (1360–1362)
Yusuf II (1391–1392)
Muhammad VII (1392–1408)
Yusuf III (1408–1417)
Muhammad VIII (1417–1418, 1427–1429)
Muhammad IX (1419–1427, 1429–1445, 1447–1453)
Yusuf IV (1430–1432)
Yusuf V (1445, 1450, 1462–1463)
Muhammad X (1445–1447)
Muhammad XI (1448–1454)
Sad (1454–1464)
Abu Hasan Ali (1464–1485)
Muhammad XII (Boabdil) (1482–1492)
Muhammad XIII (1485–1487)

# GLOSSARY OF MEDIEVAL TERMS

**Abbot** the head of an abbey or monastic community.

**Albigensianism** the name used for the sect of Catharism in southern France. The term derives from the city of Albi, the earliest of the movement's bishoprics. The Albigensians were ruthlessly extirpated in a crusade beginning in 1209.

**Antipope** a person elected or named pope in opposition to the current pontiff. The antipope is not recognized by the Holy See and is not ranked among the popes.

**Appanage** a parcel of territory set aside to provide for the needs of a younger brother of the king. The appanage came into being in the 13th century.

**Arianism** the Christian heresy named after the heresiarch Arius (c. 250–c. 336). Arians denied the true divinity of Jesus Christ. The heresy was popular among many of the Germanic tribes, particularly the Goths and Vandals, but was condemned at the Council of Constantinople in 381.

**Avignon papacy** the name given to the period during which the popes resided at Avignon, from 1309 to 1378. Also called the Babylonian Captivity.

**Ballade** a type of composition that flourished especially in French lyric poetry during the 14th and 15th centuries. It was characterized by three stanzas and a shorter final stanza; they had the same rhythmic scheme. Its earliest practitioner in polyphonic form was the 14th-century composer Guillaume Machaut.

**Ban** (1) variously, the right of a ruler to administer power or authority, including pain and punishment; the church's issuing of a sentence of excommunication; and a sentence of outlawry. (2) see **Banate.**

**Banate** a territory or district governed by a ban in the regions under the control of the Hungarian kingdom.

**Barbarian** a Greek term used to describe all peoples who were not Greek. Adopted by the Romans, it was used by them in referring to the peoples beyond the Roman Empire. Considered a pejorative term, it is not commonly used by scholars today.

**Baron** a feudal lord holding rights and title from a lord or king. The baron was one of the lowest ranks of the feudal nobility.

**Bogomil** a sect of Manichaean heretics (followers of Manichaean doctrine concerning the dual nature of humanity) found in Bulgaria but later spreading throughout the Balkans after the 10th century. Oppressed, they managed to survive until the 14th century and the Ottoman conquest of the region.

**Boyar** a member of the landed aristocracy in parts of eastern Europe, particularly Bulgaria (10th century) and Russia (12th century and later).

**Bull** from the Latin *bulla* ("seal"), a formal pronouncement by the pope, more formal than an encyclical.

**Caesaropapism** a political system that grants to a secular ruler total control over the church within his or her realm. Such authority extends even in matters of doctrine.

**Caliph** the title used by the successors (or self-declared successors) of Muhammad, claiming the authority to rule over Islam.

**Canton** the name used to describe the individual or constituent members of the Swiss Confederation.

**Catepan** the name used for the governor of a theme (province) in the Byzantine Empire. Used only until the 11th century.

**Catharism** a term derived from the Greek word *katharos,* for "pure"; it was used to refer to a heretical movement inspired by Bogomilism. The Cathars were found in parts of western Europe in the 12th and 13th centuries.

**Ceorl** a member of the social strata of Anglo-Saxon England. The ceorl was ranked above the slave and below the thane (thegn).

**Chanson** French term for the art song of the Middle Ages and Renaissance. It developed in a monophonic form in the 12th century, subsequently evolving through composition into accompanied form and then vocal ensemble.

**Charruage** a type of tax imposed on peasants by a lord for the use of his plows.

**Charter** a grant of rights and privileges that is given by a ruler to a group, individual, community or nation.

**Commune** the name used for municipal corporations that were formed in northern Italy starting in the 11th century.

**Conciliarism** the doctrine that argued that the general council possessed supreme authority in the church, even over the pope.

**Condottiere** (plural, condottieri) Italian term meaning the captain of a military force or unit of mercenary soldiers whom he has hired and pays. The condottiere was frequently engaged to fight for towns and cities in northern Italy during the later period of the Middle Ages when mercenaries were in great demand. The captain negotiated directly with a city, but his loyalty was contingent on being financially satisfied, and allegiances were always available to the highest bidder. Among the most notable condottieri were Sir John Hawkwood, the Attendolos and Colleoni.

**Constable** a powerful figure in the royal governments in France and England. The constable originated from the count *(comes)* of the late Roman Empire and was in charge of the stable under the Merovingian and Carolingian dynasties, but constables could also lead troops into battle. From this role, the constable came to assume greater military authority, so that by the 14th century he was the supreme commander of all French troops. In England, the constable was also a military commander, sharing duties with the marshal. Constables were also found in villages throughout the kingdom with the duty of keeping order.

**Crusade** a war or series of wars launched with the aim of reclaiming lost holy places or of attaining some religious victory. The most notable crusades of the Middle Ages were waged to recover the Holy Land from Muslim occupation (11th–14th centuries). Other crusades were the Reconquista of Spain, the crusades of the Teutonic Knights and other military orders into eastern Europe and the jihad (or holy war) of Saladin to destroy the Christian Crusader States in the Holy Land.

**Dauphin** the title created in 1350 and given to the heir to the French throne after the future Charles V purchased the province of Dauphiné.

**Demesne** the land owned directly by a lord in the feudal system. It was differentiated from the land still owned by the ruler but given to vassals.

**Despot** the title given in the 12th century to the son-in-law of the Byzantine emperor and hence the heir presumptive. It was later borne by all sons of the emperor and by some imperial governors.

***Destrier*** the name given to the warhorse ridden into battle by knights.

***Deus Volt!*** "God wills it!"—the cry adopted by the members of the First Crusade as they embarked to liberate the Holy Land from the control of Islam.

**Dialectic** one of the three liberal arts that was included in the trivium. It trained the student in the use of logic and reasoning and was an element in the rise of Scholasticism.

**Diocese** initially a term used for a province in the late Roman Empire. It came to mean a territory under the ecclesiastical control of a bishop. The bishops were themselves answerable to the larger authority of the metropolitan or archbishop in control of an archdiocese.

**Doge** the name of the Byzantine official who was chief magistrate of Venice from 697. In 726 the Venetians won the right to elect their own doge. After 1032 the broad powers of the doge were curtailed.

**Ducat** a type of cold coin first struck in Venice in 1284.

**Duke** a title derived from the Roman title *dux* and given to a very powerful member of the aristocracy. In France the duke was just below the royal prince; in England the noble title was reserved for members of the royal family until the time of Richard II (1377–1399).

**Dulcimer** a stringed instrument similar to the harp and the psaltery; it was first introduced into Spain by the Arabs in the 12th century.

**Earl** a noble in England originating from the time of Canute the Great (1016–1035) from the name *jarl,* or chieftain. The earl wielded considerable power in the kingdom, and the title was retained by the Normans.

**Elector** the title borne by certain princes of the Holy Roman Empire that gave them the right to choose or elect the emperor. The Electors in 1356 were declared the margrave of Brandenburg, the duke of Saxony, the king of Bohemia, the count Palatine of the Rhine, and the archbishops of Cologne, Trier and Mainz.

**Emir** originally a tribal leader in Arabia and later used as a title of a governor of a province during the period of the Umayyad and Abbasid caliphates.

***Estradiots*** Greek or Albanian mercenaries who were hired by the Venetians during the 15th century.

**Exarch** the governor of a province in the Eastern or Byzantine Empire.

***Exercitia Spiritualia*** spiritual exercises used by a contemplative to advance in the spiritual life.

**Fabliaux** (singular, fabliau) humorous tales in French verse that gently satirized women, peasants and burghers; they were popular in the 12th and 13th centuries.

**Falconry** the art and sport of training falcons to hunt small birds and animals. Falconry was quite popular among the nobility. Emperor Frederick II authored a book on the subject.

***Familia regis*** the king's bodyguard, guard or retinue. It was customarily composed of trusted knights.

**Faquin** a dummy used by youths practicing with the lance; the word is of Italian origin.

**Fealty, oath of** a feudal oath of allegiance, service and devotion taken by a vassal to a liege lord.

**Fief** the feudal term for a lordship or position granted to a vassal by a lord in return for military service.

**Fleur-de-lis** a heraldic device of the lily flower, first used probably in the reign of King Louis VI (1108–1137). It eventually became associated directly with the French royal arms.

**Florin** a gold coin first issued in Florence in 1252; it enjoyed wide distribution in the trading centers of Europe.

**Fossors** members of a lesser clergy who in the early church served as gravediggers (Latin, *fodere*—to dig or *fosse* L. ditch). In the late fourth century and early fifth, they emerged as a powerful corporation with control over the management of catacombs and tomb decoration.

**Fouage** a type of tax that was levied annually on every household.

**Franc** a French gold coin first minted in 1360 by King John the Good to pay his ransom to the English.

**Franchise** a special status enjoyed by certain lords or ecclesiastical personages exempting them from royal jurisdiction. It was given only to highly favored individuals.

**Free Cities** the cities in Germany that vanquished their overlord in the 13th and 14th centuries and thence were independent.

**Ghibelline** the name used by the supporters of the imperial cause in Italy during the period when the Holy Roman Emperors were in conflict with the papacy. The name was derived from Weibelungen (Waiblingen), an estate or castle of the Hohenstaufens in Swabia. They were opposed by the **Guelphs.**

**German** the name originally used by the Romans to describe the inhabitants of Germania, those peoples beyond the Rhine River and hence the boundary of the Roman Empire. It was in use until the eighth century when *deutsche* came into the vernacular to distinguish Germans from the Romans of the Carolingian empire.

**Ghetto** the section of a European city its name derived from the quarter in Venice that was customarily set aside for the Jews. The first of the ghettos were established in the fourth century after large elements of the Jewish population departed Palestine for Europe in the Great Diaspora. The Jews were required to live in the ghettos in order to limit their contact with other, predominantly Christian populations.

**Gonfalon** a type of battle standard used by the towns of northern Italy in the late medieval period; it was carried by the gonfalonier.

**Grandee** members of the highest class of nobles in Castile from about the 13th century.

**Grand Inquisitor** the title of the official in charge of the Court of Inquisition. It was also used by the head of the Spanish Inquisition.

**Grand Master** the chief of a knightly military order. Two of the best-known grand masters were Hermann von Salza of the Teutonic Knights and Jacques de Molay of the Knights Templars.

**Greek fire** the weapon of the Byzantines composed of sulfur, lime and other highly flammable but unidentified ingredients that had the extraordinary property of igniting on contact with water. It helped save Constantinople from attack by the Arabs in 673. The substance was supposedly invented by Callinicus in 673.

**Guelph** the name used in Italy to identify the sociopolitical party that supported the papacy in its conflict with the Holy Roman Empire. It was derived from the Welf family. The opponents of the Guelphs in Italy were the **Ghibellines.**

**Guild** initially a society or group of merchants who had secured a monopoly on trading rights in its town. Specific types of guilds were eventually formed, such as craft guilds.

**Hegira** from the Arabia *hijra* (departure), the flight of Muhammad from Mecca in 622 to Yathrib (Medina). The dating of the Muslim calendar traditionally begins with this event, the abbreviation A.H. used in the West to denote that the years of the calendar are after the Hegira.

**Heresy** a theological or doctrinal belief in opposition to traditional or orthodox teaching and doctrine. There were a number of heresies within the church during the Middle Ages (e.g., Catharism, Albigensianism, Arianism, Monophysitism).

**Hussite** the name given the followers of the Bohemian religious reformer Jan Hus during the early 15th century. They eventually split into two major factions, the Utraquists and the more radical Taborites.

**Iconoclasm** the movement in the Byzantine Empire that opposed the veneration of icons (from *iconoclast*—"image breakers"). The Iconoclastic Controversy lasted from about 725 to 842, during which time icons were forbidden within the churches of the empire.

**Imam** an Islamic leader of prayer on Fridays at the mosque. He is also much respected and revered. The term *imam* is also used as a synonym by the Shiites to denote the descendants of Ali.

**Inquisition** a court established to investigate heresies and to root them out. The first of the medieval inquisitions was established about 1233 when the pope commissioned the Dominicans to investigate the rise of Albigensianism in southern France. It soon spread to other countries and employed torture to extract confessions, although executions were rare. The most notorious courts of Inquisition were found in Spain, where the Spanish Inquisition, established in 1478, first was headed by Tomás de Torquemada and was so relatively free of scrutiny by the church.

**Investiture** a feudal act by which a lord transferred a fief to a vassal, receiving an oath of fealty and then investing the vassal with some symbol of the transaction and the transfer of land. Lay investiture was a source of major conflict between the papacy and secular rulers, particularly between the pope and the Holy Roman Emperor.

**Jihad** a term, from the Arabic, for holy war.

**Joust** a mock battle taking place during tournaments. It was composed of two horsemen charging each other with leveled lances, the object being to unhorse one's opponent. The joust often preceded the *melée* in tournaments held in the later Middle Ages.

**Justiciar** the name given to an English legal official who acted in the royal name or in the absence of the king. The justiciar was not a member of the royal household and had a position superior to all officers of the household. In the name of the king, the justiciar presided over the bench at Westminster, advised the king on legal matters and often made important decisions on judicial matters. During the reign of King Henry II (1154–1189), the justiciar was a major figure in the development of English law, although the office declined in prominence in the early 13th century and ceased to exist entirely after 1261.

**Knight** a member of the feudal order. The rank evolved over the centuries from an attendant to the lord to a formal social rank, an individual who was not of the nobility but who possessed military rank, privileges and the essential accoutrements of sword, armor and horse. The knight was created (or dubbed) by his lord after attaining proper age and position through training, experience and merit.

**Kontore** a kind of warehouse, storage facility or depot used by a German merchant while conducting business abroad. The *kontore* served as the extension of the merchant.

**Koran** the sacred text of Islam, meaning in Arabic "reading." Muslims consider the Koran to have been given to Muhammad in a series of revelations from God. The text of the Koran was formally established in 651–52 (A.H. 30 on the Islamic calendar) under the caliph Uthman according to the 114 chapters (or *suras*) organized by

Zaid ibn Thabit, secretary to the Prophet. To ensure doctrinal purity, all variant copies of the Koran were ordered burned.

**Landgrave** a rank signifying a count *(Graf)* of a province *(Land)* rather than a county. The rank of landgrave was superior to that of count.

**Liege lord** a lord in the feudal system to whom allegiance and obedience were given. The liege received the oath of fealty. The term *liege* also referred to the vassal or underling in the feudal system who gave fealty to a liege lord.

**Lollard** the supporter of the reform movement established by John Wycliffe, which argued that clerics should adhere to strict poverty, that the Bible was the means by which an individual might reach true faith and that the sacraments were false. The Lollards may have had an influence on the later Reformation.

**Lords Appellant** the leaders of the baronial opposition party that was formed in opposition to the government of King Richard II (1377–1399) of England. The party began about 1389 and was led by the nobles Thomas of Woodstock, duke of Gloucester; Richard Fitzalan, Earl of Arundel; and Thomas de Beauchamp, earl of Warwick. Henry Bolingbroke, the future King Henry IV, also joined their ranks. The Lords Appellant were powerful in England during the later years of the reign of King Richard.

**Manorialism** the European social and economic system of the Middle Ages. Within the system, the peasant received and worked lands from his lord (seigneur) and held it in return for fixed duties in kind, money and service.

**March** a frontier or wild border region. Because conditions in such regions were often unsettled or potentially violent, the march was frequently entrusted to a reliable vice-regent.

**Margravate** also margraviate, a province under the authority of a count. It was located in a march, and the margrave was similar to the landgrave except that the margrave was required to defend the holding from potentially hostile elements from both within and outside its borders.

**Mayor of the palace** the name given the majordomos of the palaces of the Frankish kingdom during the later years of the Merovingian dynasty. The mayors exercised nearly total control of the king and state.

**Metropolitan** the title held by an Eastern prelate responsible for a province. In the Western Church the metropolitan was an archbishop.

**Monophysitism** a heresy claiming that Christ possessed only one nature (a divine one) and not two. It was accepted by the Syrian and Coptic churches in the fifth century, thereby removing them from the theological and much of the ecclesiastical control of Constantinople.

**Nominalism** a philosophical view in which the reality of universal concepts is denied. The foremost exponent of nominalism was William of Ockham, who asserted that the universe was not based in reality at all but in the human mind.

**Oblate** (from the Latin *oblatus*—offered) a term used in the Middle Ages to denote children who were placed in a monastery by their parents in order to become members of the monastic community.

**Pale** the name given for a territory under English control in France and Ireland. The English Pale in France was around Calais, surviving until 1558. The Pale in Ireland was around Dublin.

**Palfrey** a woman's saddle horse. It was derived from the medieval Latin *palafredus* and denoted an extra post horse.

**Parlement** an assembly for discussion and debate that emerged in France as the primary court of law for the kingdom until the 15th century, when parlements were established for provinces.

**Parliamentary abbot** an abbot expected and required to attend meetings of Parliament. The practice began in the 14th century. Previously, all prelates (bishops and abbots) were required to attend the court only when summoned. Most parliamentary abbots were of the Benedictine order.

**Patriarch** the title given to certain prelates of great power: initially the bishops of Antioch, Rome and Alexandria, and later the bishops of Constantinople and Jerusalem.

**Pentapolis** the term for the imperial province in Italy that had belonged to the Byzantines but was taken by the Lombards in 752 and subsequently given to the papacy in 756 by King Pepin III as part of his donation to the pope. The Pentapolis was variously described as being composed of the coastal bishoprics of Ancona, Rimini, Pesaro, Fano and Senigallia.

***Qadi*** an Islamic judge who renders decisions based on the Shari'ah, the Muslim code of laws. The *qadi* generally hears only cases involving religion, although his authority theoretically extends to matters both spiritual and legal.

**Quadrivium** one of the segments of the liberal arts taught during the Middle Ages: arithmetic, geometry, music and astronomy.

**Rationalism** the philosophical theory stressing the application of reason to attain knowledge.

**Renaissance** (from the French, "rebirth") the term used to describe a new flowering of intellectual and cultural achievements. The Carolingian renaissance, supported by Charlemagne and exemplified by Alcuin, Peter of Pisa and Paul the Deacon and disseminated chiefly at Aachen, was a revival of learning stimulating the monastic institutions of the time. The term is most often applied to the Renaissance in Italy lasting from the 14th to the 16th century, marking the transition from the medieval to the modern era.

**Rondeau** (pl. *rondeaux*) a type of fixed composition in French lyric poetry popular in the 14th and 15th centuries. It was characterized by four stanzas and its earliest composer in polyphonic form was Adam de la Halle; other composers included Guillaume de Machaut, Gilles Binchois, and Guillaume Dufay.

**Saracen** the name used initially by the Romans for nomads who roamed the Arabian and Syrian deserts; it was used later by Crusaders and Europeans to refer to Arabs and Muslims in general.

**Schism** a break within the church that creates a willful and deliberate separation. However, a priest in schism is permitted to say Mass, and bishops in schism may ordain.

**See** the seat or the residence of a bishop or prelate. It is derived from the Latin *sedes* (seat) and may also imply the throne *(cathedra).*

**Seigneur** the name designating a feudal lord or lord of the feudal manor.

**Serf** a term for a peasant laborer within the feudal and manorial system. The serf was, in theory, compelled to serve a lord and to provide service at the lord's will in return for protection and the right to work the land. Unlike a slave, the serf supposedly had certain rights, although these rights were altered from era to era and varied sharply according to regional custom.

**Sheriff** the royal official or magistrate (reeve) of a shire or a county who was charged with managing royal interests, maintaining order and executing the royal will.

**Shiite** a member of the Muslim sect that split from the rest of Islam adhering to the concept that Ali and his successors were the divinely appointed caliphs. The Shiite disagreement with the Islamic majority (Sunni) was often severe during the Middle Ages, and harsh measures were taken against them by the Sunni and other dissenting Shiite groups such as the Order of Assassins.

**Simony** the illegal practice of selling spiritual favors to the laity by the clergy. Named after Simon Magus, simony became widespread during the Middle Ages and was vigorously opposed by the church, especially by the Third Lateran Council (1179) and Thomas Aquinas.

**Strategus** the title of a military commander in the Byzantine Empire.

***Studium generale*** the term used from the mid-14th century for what was to become the university. The *studium generale* specialized in teaching one or more of the higher faculties (e.g., theology, medicine, law) and sought to attract students from all over the Christian world.

**Sultan** the ruler of an Islamic country, a title used to designate the head of the Ottoman state.

***Summa*** a treatise that purports to be a complete study of a subject. The best known of all *summae* was the *Summa theologica* of Thomas Aquinas.

**Sunni** the majority party of Islam, found throughout Arabia, Africa and Turkey.

**Taborites** a member of the ultraradical Bohemian religious movement that split from the Hussite movement. They took their name from Mount Tabor, near Prague. The Utraquists were an opposing party.

***Taifa*** the name used for the numerous splinter kingdoms that arose in Moorish Spain after the demise of the caliphate of Córdoba in 1031 (from the Arabic *tawa'if*—petty kingdom or faction). Among the petty kingdoms were Seville, Badajoz, Toledo, Córdoba, Zaragoza, Valencia and Granada.

**Theme** the territorial or provincial designation used in the Byzantine Empire after the reign of Heraclius (610–641). The themes were expected to raise troops for the empire.

**Tilting** the event in tournaments during which a rider used a lance to thrust at rings hung from poles. Tilting in this form rather than at an opponent was evidence of the decline of the tournament as a purely martial event and its movement toward pageantry or chivalric display. The term *tilting* is also used in a general sense to denote a joust between two riders armed with lances or simply a thrust with a lance.

**Tonsure** the traditional shaving of part or all of the head of monks and clerics. It was required from the sixth century as a symbol of one's admission to the clergy.

**Tourney** another term for tournament.

**Trivium** one of the segments of the liberal arts taught during the Middle Ages. It included grammar, logic and rhetoric.

**Usury** the charging or extracting of exorbitant interest on a loan. The practice was forbidden to Christians by the church. Jews were allowed to charge interest, as sanctioned by the Fourth Lateran Council (1179). The charging of interest, however, contributed greatly to the vicious characterization of Jews as undesirable elements in society, adding to the anti-Semitism rampant during the Middle Ages.

**Utraquists** members of the Hussite reform movement in Bohemia who took their name from the Latin term referring to the belief that the laity should be allowed to receive communion under both bread and wine *(sub utraque specie).* They were condemned by the Council of Constance in 1415 and the Council of Basel in 1432. Within the Hussite movement they were opposed to the more radical Taborites.

**Vassal** a feudal term denoting someone who holds land by feudal tenure and is obliged in return to give military or other service.

**Vizier** (Arabic, *wazir-porter*) a high-ranking ministerial official in an Islamic government, customarily the chief counselor to the ruler. One of the best known of all viziers was Nizam al-Mulk.

**Vrelay** also *vrelai,* a type of composition in French lyric poetry. It appeared in various forms in the literature of the late Middle Ages and early Renaissance in various localities, including Italy and Spain. The *vrelay* developed slowly, probably not originating in France. Notable composers included Jacob de Senleches, Jean Vaillant, Guillaume de Machaut and Antoine Busnois.

# SUGGESTED READING LIST

The following is a suggested reading list drawn from the literally thousands of sources consulted in the preparation of this volume. The works cited here have been chosen with the general reader in mind. They are generally readily available, are in English or English translation and are not overly specialized. Readers are encouraged to consult these excellent works in preparation for more advanced materials and sources.

The list is divided broadly by region, and within each region there is a separate listing of books on art and architecture. In the western Europe section, there is also a separate listing of books on the Crusades.

## EASTERN EUROPE AND BYZANTIUM


Auty, R., and Obolensky, D., eds. *An Introduction to Russian History*. Cambridge: Cambridge University Press, 1976.

Blum, J. *Lord and Peasant in Russia*. Princeton, N.J.: Princeton University Press, 1961.

Bury, J. B. *A History of the Eastern Roman Empire from the Fall of Irene to the Accession of Basil I*. New York: Russell & Russell, 1965.

Chirovsky, N. *A History of the Russian Empire*. London: Peter Owen, 1973.

Cross, S. H., and Sherbowitz-Wetzor, O. P., eds. *The Russian Primary Chronicle*, Cambridge: Medieval Academy of America, 1953.

Davies, N. *God's Playground: A History of Poland*, vol. 1. New York: Columbia University Press, 1984.

Dmytryshyn, B. *Medieval Russia*. Hinsdale, Ill.: Dryden Press 1972.

Dvornik, F. *The Slavs in European History*. East Brunswick, N.J.: Rutgers University Press, 1962.

Gimbutas, M. *The Slavs*. London: Thames & Hudson, 1971.

Haussig, H. W. *A History of Byzantine Civilization*. Trans. J. M. Hussey. New York: Praeger, 1971.

Jenkins, R. *Byzantium: The Imperial Centuries 610–1071*. New York: Random House, 1966.

Karger, M. *Novgorod the Great*. Moscow: Progress Publishers, 1973.

Kochan, L., and Abraham, R. *The Making of Modern Russia*. London: Weidenfeld & Nicholson, 1969.

Macdermott, M. *A History of Bulgaria*. London: Allen & Unwin, 1962.

Mango, C. A. *Byzantium: The Empire of New Rome*. London: Weidenfeld & Nicholson, 1980.

Meyendorff, J. *Byzantium and the Rise of Russia*. Cambridge: Cambridge University Press, 1981.

Mirsky, D. S. *Russia: A Social History*. London: Cresset Press, 1931.

Ostrogorsky, G. *History of the Byzantine State*. Trans. J. M. Hussey. East Brunswick, N.J.: Rutgers University Press, 1957.

Pamlenyi, E. *A History of Hungary*. Trans. L. Boros, et al. London: Collet's, 1975.

Petravich, M. B. *History of Serbia*. 2 vols. New York: Harcourt, Brace & Jovanovich, 1976.

Portal, R. *The Slavs*. London: Weidenfeld & Nicholson, 1969.

Pribechevich, S. *Macedonia: Its People and History*. University Park: Pennsylvania State University Press, 1983.

Rice, T. *The Byzantines*. London: Thames & Hudson, 1969.

Runciman, J. C. S. *Byzantine Civilization*. New York: St. Martin's Press, 1966.

Sinor, D. *A History of Hungary*. London: Allen & Unwin, 1959.

Urban, W. *The Baltic Crusade*. De Kalb: North Illinois University Press, 1975.

Vernadsky, G. *A History of Russia*. New Haven: Yale University Press, 1944.

———. *Kievan Russia*. New Haven: Yale University Press, 1959.

———. *The Origins of Russia*. Westport, Conn.: Greenwood Press, 1975.

Vlasto, A. P. *The Entry of the Slavs into Christendom: an Introduction to the Medieval History of the Slavs*. Cambridge: Cambridge University Press, 1970.

Vryonis, S. *Byzantium: Its Internal History and Relations with the Muslim World*. London: Variorum, 1971.

Yanagi, M., et al. *Byzantium*. Trans. N. Fry. London: Cassel, 1978.

Zamoyski, A. *The Polish Way*. London: John Murray, 1987.


### *Art and Architecture*


Amiranshvili, S. *Medieval Georgian Enamels of Russia*. New York: Abrams, 1964.

Bartebev, I. *North Russian Architecture*. Moscow: Progress Publishers, 1972.

Beckwith, J. *The Art of Constantinople: An Introduction to Byzantine Art (330–1453)*. New York: Phaidon, 1968.

———. *Early Christian and Byzantine Art*. Harmondsworth, England: Penguin, 1979.

Demus, O. *Byzantine Mosaic Decoration*. London: Paul, Trench, and Tubner, 1948.

Grabar, A. *Byzantine Painting*. Geneva: Skira, 1953.

Hamilton, G. *The Art and Architecture of Russia*. Harmondsworth, England: Penguin, 1983.

Kitzinger, E. *Byzantine Art in the Making*. Cambridge, Mass.: Harvard University Press, 1977.

Krautheimer, R. *Early Christian and Byzantine Architecture*. Harmondsworth, England: Penguin, 1965.

Mango, C. *Byzantine Architecture*. London: Faber and Faber, 1986.

Mathews, T. J. *Byzantine Churches of Istanbul: A Photographic Survey*. University Park: University of Pennsylvania Press, 1976.

Rice, D. T. *The Art of Byzantium*. New York: Abrams, 1959.

———. *Byzantine Art*. Harmondsworth, England: Penguin, 1968.

## ISLAM AND THE EAST

Ashtor, E. L. *A Social and Economic History of the Near East in the Middle Ages*. London: Colier's, 1976.

Brent, Peter. *The Mongol Empire*. London: Weidenfeld & Nicholson, 1976.

Cahen, C. *Pre-Ottoman Turkey*. London: Sidgwick & Jackson, 1968.

Chambers, J. *The Devil's Horsemen*. London: Weidenfeld & Nicholson, 1979.

Crone, P. *Meccan Trade and the Rise of Islam*. Princeton, N.J.: Princeton University Press, 1987.

Esposito, J. L. *Islam and Politics*. Syracuse: Syracuse University Press, 1984.

Gibson, M. *Genghis Khan and the Mongols*. London: Wayland, 1973.

al-Hassan, A., and Hill, D. R. *Islamic Technology: An Illustrated History*. Cambridge: Cambridge University Press, 1986.

Hayes, J. R. *The Genius of Arab Civilization*. London: Phaidon, 1978.

Hitti, P. K. *History of the Arabs*. New York: St. Martin's Press, 1964.

Holt, P. M. *The Age of the Crusades: The Near East from the Eleventh Century to 1517*. New York: Longman, 1986.

Humble, R. *Marco Polo*. London: Weidenfeld & Nicholson, 1975.

Irwin, R. *The Middle East in the Middle Ages: The Early Mamluk Sultanate, 1250–1382*. London: Croone Helm, 1986.

Phillips, E. D. *The Mongols*. London: Thames & Hudson, 1969.

Rice, T. T. *The Seljuks in Asia Minor*. London: Thames & Hudson, 1961.

Rogers, M. *The Spread of Islam*. Oxford: Elsevier-Phaidon, 1976.

Salibi, K. *A History of Arabia*. Delmar, N.Y.: Caravan Books, 1980.

Saunders, J. J. *A History of Medieval Islam*. London: Routledge & Kegan Paul, 1965.

———. *The History of the Mongol Conquests*. London: Routledge & Keegan Paul, 1971.

Von Gunebaum, G. E. *Medieval Islam*. Chicago: University of Chicago Press, 1966.

### *Art and Architecture*

Arnold, T. *Painting in Islam*. New York: Dover, 1965.

Aslanapa, T. W. *Turkish Art and Architecture*. London: Faber & Faber, 1971.

Atil, E. *Art of the Arab World*. Washington, D.C.: Smithsonian, 1975.

———. *Renaissance of Islam: Art of the Mamluks*. Washington, D.C.: Smithsonian, 1981.

———, ed., *Turkish Art*. Washington, D.C.: Smithsonian, 1980.

Creswell, K. A. C. *Early Muslim Architecture*. 2 vols. Oxford: Clarendon, 1979.

———. *The Muslim Architecture of Egypt*. Vol. 2. Oxford: Clarendon, 1959.

Ettinghausen, R. *Treasures of Asia: Arab Painting*. Lausanne: Skira, 1962.

Ettinghausen, R., and Grabar, O. *The Art and Architecture of Islam: 650–1250*. Harmondsworth, England: Penguin Books, 1987.

Grabar, O. *The Formation of Islamic Art*. New Haven: Yale University Press, 1973.

Grube, E. J. *Islamic Pottery*. London: Faber & Faber, 1976.

Grunebaum, G. von. *Classical Islam: A History, 600–1258*. Chicago: Aldine, 1970.

Hoag, J. *Islamic Architecture*. Milan: Electa/Editrice Milan, 1975.

Ipsiroglu, M. S. *Painting and Culture of the Mongols*. Trans. E. D. Phillips. London: Thames & Hudson, 1967.

Kuhnel, E. *Islamic Art and Architecture*. London: Bell, 1966.

Rice, D. T. *Islamic Art*. London: Thames & Hudson, 1975.

## WESTERN EUROPE

Almgren, B. *The Viking*. Gothenburg: AB Nordbook, 1975.

Anderson, W. F. *Castles of Europe from Charlemagne to the Renaissance*. London: Hutchinson, 1970.

Atkinson, Ian. *The Viking Ships*. Cambridge: Cambridge University Press, 1986.

Baker, D., ed. *Medieval Women*. Oxford: Blackwell, 1978.

Baker, T. *The Normans*. London: Cassell, 1966.

Barraclough, G. *The Medieval Papacy*. London: Thames & Hudson, 1968.

———. *The Origins of Modern Germany*. Oxford: Blackwell, 1988.

Barrow, G. *The Anglo-Norman Era in Scottish History*. Oxford: Blackwell, 1980.

Bautier, R. *The Economic Development of Medieval Europe*. London: Thames & Hudson, 1971.

Bede. *A History of the English Church and People*. Trans. L. Sherley-Price. Harmondsworth, England: Penguin, 1970.

Beeler, J. H. *Warfare in England 1066–1189*. Ithaca, N.Y.: Cornell University Press, 1966.

Blair, Claude. *European Armour c. 1066 to c. 1700*. London: Batsford, 1958.

Bloch, M. *Feudal Society*. Trans. L. Manyon. Chicago: University of Chicago Press, 1963.

Braunfels, W. *Monasteries of Western Europe*. London: Thames & Hudson, 1972.

Brondsted, J. *The Vikings*. Trans. K. Skov. Harmondsworth, England: Penguin, 1986.

Brooke, C. *The Twelfth Century Renaissance*. London: Thames & Hudson, 1969.

Brown, R. A. *The Normans*. Woodbridge, England: The Boydell Press, 1984.

Brown, P. *Society and the Holy in Late Antiquity*. Berkeley: University of California Press, 1971.
Bullough, D. A. *The Age of Charlemagne*. London: G. P. Putnam's Sons, 1965.
Bunson, M. *The Angelic Doctor: The Life and Times of Thomas Aquinas*. Indiana: OSV, 1994.
Burns, R. *Islam under the Crusaders: Colonial Revival in the 13th century Kingdom of Valencia*. Princeton, N.J.: Princeton University Press, 1973.
*Cambridge Medieval History*. 8 vols. Cambridge: Cambridge University Press, 1911–36.
Campbell, J., ed. *The Anglo-Saxons*. Oxford: Phaidon Books, 1982.
Cassady, R. F. *The Norman Achievement*. London: Sidgwick & Jackson, 1986.
Chadwick, H. *The Early Church*. Harmondsworth, England: Penguin, 1967.
Copleston, F. C. *Aquinas*. Harmondsworth, England: Penguin Books, 1955.
Curtius, E. R. *European Literature and the Latin Middle Ages*. Princeton, N.J.: Princeton University Press, 1973.
Davis, R. H. C. *The Normans and Their Myth*. London: Thames & Hudson, 1976.
Diuglas, D. C. *The Norman Achievement 1050–1100*. London: Eyre & Spottiswood, 1969.
Dronke, P., ed. *A History of Twelfth Century Philosophy*. Cambridge: Cambridge University Press, 1988.
Duby, G., ed. *A History of Private Life*. Vol. 2. *Revelations of the Medieval World*. Trans. A. Goldhammer. Cambridge, Mass.: Harvard University Press, 1988.
———. *The Early Growth of the European Economy: Warriors and Peasants from the Seventh to the Twelfth Century*. Trans. H. B. Clark. Ithaca, N.Y.: Cornell University Press, 1974.
Evans, J., ed. *The Flowering of the Middle Ages*. London: Thames & Hudson, 1966.
Fichtenau, H. *The Carolingian Empire*. Trans. P. Muntz. Toronto: University of Toronto Press, 1978.
Fuhrmann, H. *Germany in the High Middle Ages c. 1050–1200*. Cambridge: Cambridge University Press, 1987.
Gilson, E. *A History of Christian Philosophy in the Middle Ages*. New York: Random House, 1955.
Graham-Campbell, J. *The Viking World*. London: Frances Lincoln/Weidenfeld & Nicholson, 1980.
Green, C. *Sutton Hoo*. New York: Barnes and Noble, 1963.
Hallam, E. M. *Capetian France 987–1328*. London: Longman, 1980.
Halphen, L. *Charlemagne and the Carolingian Empire*. Trans. G. de Nie. New York: North Holland, 1977.
Hay, D. *The Italian Renaissance in Its Historical Background*. Cambridge: Cambridge University Press, 1977.
Hilgarth, J. *The Spanish Kingdoms 1250–1516*. 2 vols. Oxford: Oxford University Press, 1978.
Hinde, T. *The Domesday Book*. London: Hutchinson, 1985.
Hodges, R. *Dark Age Economics: The Origins of Towns and Trade, A.D. 600–1000*. New York: St. Martin's Press, 1969.
Holt, P. M. *The Age of the Crusades*. London: Longman, 1986.
Hyde, J. *Society and Politics in Medieval Italy: The Evolution of the Civil Life 1000–1350*. London: Macmillan, 1973.
James, E. *The Origins of France*. New York: St. Martin's Press, 1982.
Jones, A. H. M. *The Later Roman Empire 284–602: A Social, Economic, and Administrative Survey*. 3 vols. Oxford: Oxford University Press, 1964.
Kidson, P. *The Medieval World*. London: Hamlyn, 1967.
Knowles, M. D. *Christian Monasticism*. London: Weidenfeld & Nicholson, 1969.
Latourette, K. *History of the Expansion of Christianity: Thousand Years of Uncertainty 500–1500 A.D.* New York: Harper & Row, 1938.
Lawrence, C. H. *Medieval Monasticism*. London: Longman, 1984.
Leaf, W., and Purcell, S. *Heraldic Symbols*. London: Victoria and Albert Museum, 1986.
Leff, G. *Medieval Thought*. London: Merlin Press, 1980.
Lindberg, D. C., ed. *Science in the Middle Ages*. Chicago: University of Chicago Press, 1978.
Lindsay, J. *The Normans and Their World*, London: Hart-Davis, MacGibbon Ltd., 1974.
Lomax, D. *The Reconquest of Spain*. London: Longman, 1978.
Macdonald, J. *Great Battlefields of the World*. London: Michael Joseph, 1984.
Matthew, D. *Atlas of Medieval Europe*. New York: Facts On File, 1987.
Moss, H. St. L. B. *The Birth of the Middle Ages 395–814*. Oxford: Oxford University Press, 1935.
Munz, P. *Frederick Barbarossa: A Study in Medieval Politics*. Ithaca, N.Y.: Cornell University Press, 1969.
Murray, A. *Reason and Society in the Middle Ages*. Oxford: Oxford University Press, 1978.
Oman, G. W. C. *A History of the Art of War in the Middle Ages*. London: Methuen & Co., 1924.
Platt, C. *The English Medieval Town*. London: Secker & Warburg, 1976.
Poole, A. L. *From Domesday Book to Magna Carta*. Oxford: Oxford University Press, 1951.
Postan, M., ed. *The Agrarian Life of the Medieval West*. Cambridge: Cambridge University Press, 1966.
Raby, F. J. E. *A History of Secular Latin Poetry in the Middle Ages*. Oxford: Oxford University Press, 1957.
Riche, P. *Daily Life in the World of Charlemagne*. Trans. J. McNamara. Philadelphia: University of Pennsylvania Press, 1978.
Riley-Smith, J. *The Crusades: A Short History*. London: Athlone Press, 1987.
Roderick, A., ed. *Wales: A History*. London: Michael Joseph, 1986.
Shrewsbury, J. *A History of the Bubonic Plague*. Cambridge: Cambridge University Press, 1970.
Smith, D. *A History of Sicily*. 2 vols. London: Chatto & Windus, 1968.
Southern, R. W. *Western Society and the Church in the Middle Ages*. Harmondsworth, England: Penguin, 1970.
Stenton, F. M. *Anglo-Saxon England*. Oxford: Oxford University Press, 1971.
———, ed. *The Bayeux Tapestry*, London: Phaidon, 1957.
Strayer, J. R. *On the Medieval Origins of the Modern State*. Princeton, N.J.: Princeton University Press, 1970.
Temple, E. *Anglo-Saxon Manuscripts*. London: Harvey Miller, 1976.

Thompson, E. *The Goths in Spain.* Oxford: Oxford University Press, 1969.
Ullmann, W. *A Short History of the Papacy in the Middle Ages.* London: Methuen, 1974.
———. *The Growth of Papal Government in the Middle Ages.* London: Methuen, 1955.
Van Cleve, T. C. *The Emperor Frederick II of Hohenstaufen.* Oxford: Clarendon, 1972.
Waley, D. P. *The Italian City Republics.* London: Longman, 1978.
Wallace-Hadrill, J. *The Barbarian West 400–1000.* New York: Harper & Row, 1962.
Warner, P. *Sieges of the Middle Ages.* London: G. Bell and Sons, 1968.
White, L., Jr. *Medieval Technology and Social Change.* Oxford: Clarendon, 1962.
Wilson, D. *The Viking and Their Origins.* London: Thames & Hudson, 1980.
———, ed. *The Northern World: The History and Heritage of Northern Europe AD 400–1100.* New York: Abrams, 1980.

### Art and Architecture

Anderson, W. *Castles of Europe.* London: Paul Elek, 1970.
———. *The Rise of the Gothic.* London: Hutchinson, 1985.
Arnold, B. *A Concise History of Irish Art.* London: Thames & Hudson, 1977.
Branner, R. *Chartres Cathedral.* New York: Norton, 1969.
———. *Gothic Architecture.* New York: Braziller, 1961.
Conant, K. J. *Carolingian and Romanesque Architecture 800–1200.* Harmondsworth, England: Penguin, 1959.
De Hamel, C. *A History of Illuminated Manuscripts.* Oxford: Phaidon, 1986.
Dodwell, C. R. *Painting in Europe: 800–1200.* Harmondsworth, England: Penguin, 1971.
Finlay, I. *Celtic Art: An Introduction.* London: Faber & Faber, 1973.
Focillon, H. *The Art of the West in the Middle Ages.* 2 vols. London: Phaidon, 1963.
Frankl, P. *Gothic Architecture.* Harmondsworth, England: Penguin, 1963.
Goldshmidt, A. *German Illumination.* New York: Hacker, 1970.
Grodecki, L. *Stained Glass.* Ithaca, N.Y.: Cornell University Press, 1977.
Harvey, J. H. *The Master Builders: Architecture in the Middle Ages.* London: Thames & Hudson, 1971.
Henry, F. *Irish Art in the Early Christian Period.* Ithaca, N.Y.: Cornell University Press, 1965.
Hinks, R. *Carolingian Art.* Ann Arbor: University of Michigan Press, 1966.
Holmqvist, W. *Germanic Art during the First Millennium.* Stockholm: Kungl. Vitterhets, 1955.
Hubert, J. *The Carolingian Renaissance.* New York: Braziller, 1970.
Jackson, D. *The Story of Writing.* London: Barrie & Jenkins, 1981.
Jantzen, H. *High Gothic: The Classic Cathedrals of Chartres, Rheims, and Amiens.* New York: Pantheon, 1962.
Kitzinger, E. *Early Medieval Art.* Bloomington: Indiana University Press, 1940.
Kuback, H. E. *Romanesque Architecture.* New York: Abrams, 1975.
Laszlo, G. *The Art of the Migratory Period.* London: Allen Lane, 1974.
Martindale, A. *Gothic Art.* London: Thames & Hudson, 1967.
———. *The Rise of the Artist in the Middle Ages and Early Renaissance.* New York: McGraw-Hill, 1972.
Morey, C. R. *Medieval Art.* New York: Norton, 1970.
Pope-Hennessy, J. *Italian Gothic Sculpture.* London: Phaidon, 1972.
Robb, D. M. *The Art of the Illuminated Manuscript.* London: Thomas Yoseloff, 1973.
Schapiro, M. *Romanesque Art.* New York: Braziller, 1977.
Simpson, W. D. *Castles in England and Wales.* London: Batsford, 1969.
Stoddard, W. S. *Art and Architecture in Medieval France.* New York: Harper & Row, 1972.
Swaan, W. *The Gothic Cathedral.* London: Paul Elek, 1969.
White, J. *Art and Architecture in Italy 1250–1400.* Harmondsworth, England: Penguin, 1966.
Zarnecki, G. *Romanesque Art.* New York: Universe Books, 1972.

### The Crusades

Boase, T. S. R. *Kingdoms and Strongholds of the Crusades.* London: Thames & Hudson, 1971.
Christiansen, E. *The Northern Crusades: The Baltic and the Catholic Frontier, 1100–1525.* London: Macmillan, 1980.
Queller, D. E. *The Fourth Crusade.* Leicester, England: Leicester University Press, 1978.
Richard, J. *The Latin Kingdom of Jerusalem.* 2 Vols. Oxford: North Holland Publishing, 1979.
Riley-Smith, J. *The Crusades: A Short History.* London: Athlone Press, 1987.
———. *The First Crusade and the Idea of Crusading.* London: Athlone Press, 1986.
Runciman, J. C. S. *A History of the Crusades.* 3 vols. Cambridge: Cambridge University Press, 1951–54.
Setton, K. M. ed. *A History of the Crusades.* 4 vols. Madison: University of Wisconsin Press, 1969–77.
Seward, D. *The Monks of War: The Military Religious Orders.* London: Eyre Methuen, 1972.
Urban, W. *The Baltic Crusade.* De Kalb: Northern Illinois University Press, 1975.

# INDEX

This index is designed to be used in conjunction with the many cross-references within the A-to-Z entries. The main A-to-Z entries are indicated by **boldface** page references. The general subjects are subdivided by the A-to-Z entries. *Italicized* page references indicate illustrations; *t* following the page locator indicates tables; *m* indicates maps; *c* indicates chronology; and *g* glossary items.

## N



## O



## P

## Q



## R

## U



## V



## W



## X



## Y



## Z